Professional
C# 2008

MW01014560

(Continued)

Part IV: Data

Part V: Presentation

Part VI: Communication

Part VII: Appendices

Professional
C# 2008

Professional
C# 2008

Christian Nagel

Bill Evjen

Jay Glynn

Morgan Skinner

Karli Watson

WILEY

Wiley Publishing, Inc.

Professional C# 2008

Published by
Wiley Publishing, Inc.
10475 Crosspoint Boulevard
Indianapolis, IN 46256
www.wiley.com

ISBN: 978-0-470-19137-8

Manufactured in the United States of America

10 9 8 7 6 5 4 3 2

Library of Congress Cataloging-in-Publication Data is available from the publisher.

To my brother George – moving strong from basketball to coding (they're practically the same thing, aren't they?).
Congrats and keep moving forward in C# land!
—Bill Evjen

for Donna
—Karli Watson

To my parents, Joan and Donald Skinner, for their ever present love, support, and encouragement.
The world was made a sweeter place by their being in it and their memory will be cherished forever.
Thanks Mum & Dad — you were brilliant.

"Love is as strong as death.
Many waters cannot quench love,
neither can the floods drown it." (Song of Songs 8: 6 -7)
—Morgan Skinner

About the Authors

Christian Nagel of thinktecture is a software architect and developer who offers training and consulting on how to design and develop Microsoft .NET solutions. He looks back on more than 20 years of software development experience. Christian started his computing career with PDP 11 and VAX/VMS platforms, covering a variety of languages and platforms. Since the year 2000, when .NET was just a technology preview, he has been working with various .NET technologies to build numerous .NET solutions. With his profound knowledge of Microsoft technologies, he has written numerous .NET books, and is certified as a Microsoft Certified Trainer and Professional Developer for ASP.NET. Christian speaks at international conferences such as TechEd and Tech Days, and supports .NET user groups with INETA Europe. You can contact Christian via his Web sites, www.christiannagel.com and www.thinktecture.com.

Bill Evjen, Microsoft MVP is an active proponent of .NET Technologies and community-based learning initiatives for .NET. He has been actively involved with .NET since the first bits were released in 2000. In the same year, Bill founded the St. Louis .NET User Group (www.stlnet.org), one of the world's first such groups. Bill is also the founder and former executive director of the International .NET Association (www.ineta.org), which represents more than 450,000 members worldwide.

Based in St. Louis, Missouri, Bill is an acclaimed author (more than 15 books to date) and speaker on ASP.NET and SML Web services. In addition to writing and speaking at conferences such as DevConnections, VSLive, and TechEd, Bill works closely with Microsoft as a Microsoft regional director. Bill is the technical architect for Lipper (www.lipperweb.com), a wholly owned subsidiary of Reuters, the international news and financial services company. He graduated from Western Washington University in Bellingham, Washington with a Russian language degree. When he isn't tinkering on the computer, he can usually be found at his summer house in Toivakka, Finland. You can reach Bill at evjen@yahoo.cpm.

Morgan Skinner began his computing career at a young age on the Sinclair ZX80 at school, where he was underwhelmed by some code a teacher had written and so began programming in assembly language. Since then he's used all sorts of languages and platforms, including VAX Macro Assembler, Pascal, Modula2, Smalltalk, X86 assembly language, PowerBuilder, C/C++, VB, and currently C# (of course). He's been programming in .NET since the PDC release in 2000, and liked it so much he joined Microsoft in 2001. He now works in premier support for developers and spends most of his time assisting customers with C#. You can reach Morgan at www.morganskinner.com.

Jay Glynn started writing software nearly 20 years ago, writing applications for the PICK operating system using PICK basic. Since then, he has created software using Paradox PAL and Object PAL, Delphi, VBA, Visual Basic, C, C++, Java, and of course, C#. He is currently a project coordinator and architect for a large financial services company in Nashville, Tennessee, working on software for the TabletPC platform. You can contact Jay at jlsglynn@hotmail.com.

Karli Watson is a freelance author and a technical consultant of 3form Ltd (www.3form.net) and Boost .net, and an associate technologist at Content Master (www.contentmaster.com). He started out with the intention of becoming a world-famous nanotechnologist, so perhaps one day you might recognize his name as he receives a Nobel Prize. For now, though, Karli's main academic interest is the .NET Framework, and all the boxes of tricks it contains. A snowboarding enthusiast, Karli also loves cooking, spends far too much time playing Anarchy Online and EVE, and wishes he had a cat. As yet, nobody has seen fit to publish Karli's first novel, but the rejection letters make an attractive pile. If he ever puts anything up there, you can visit Karli online at http://www.karliwatson.com.

Credits

Acquisitions Editor
Katie Mohr

Development Editors
Ami Frank Sullivan
Lori Cerreto

Technical Editors
Michael Erickson
Doug Holland

Production Editor
Daniel Scribner

Copy Editor
Kim Cofer
Nancy Rapaport

Editorial Manager
Mary Beth Wakefield

Production Manager
Tim Tate

Vice President and Executive Group Publisher
Richard Swadley

Vice President and Executive Publisher
Joseph B. Wikert

Project Coordinator, Cover
Lynsey Stanford

Proofreaders
Word One:
Edward Moyer
Jen Larsen
Amy Rasmussen
Corina Copp
Scott Klemp
Joshua Chase

Indexer
Ron Strauss

Acknowledgments

Bill Evjen:

The .NET Framework 3.5 release came quickly for us writers and it wouldn't have been possible to produce this book as fast as they came out if it weren't for the dedication of the teams built for it. Tremendous thanks to Katie Mohr for being more than patient with me in getting this and some other .NET 3.5 books out the door. Also, big thanks go out to Ami Sullivan for getting at me and helping me be *somewhat* on schedule. Other big thanks go to all the editors of the book including Lori Cerreto, Daniel Scribner, and the copyeditors.

Finally, to the ones that paid the biggest price for this writing session — my wife, Tuija, and the three kids: Sofia, Henri, and Kalle. Thanks for all you do!

Karli Watson:

Thanks to all at Wiley for helping me through this project and reigning in my strange British stylings, to assorted clients for giving me the time to write, and to Donna for keeping me sane and coping with my temperamental back. Thanks also to friends and family for being patient with my deadline-laden lifestyle.

Contents

Contents

Contents

Contents

Contents

Contents

Contents

Contents

Contents

Contents

Contents

Contents

Contents

Contents

Contents

Contents

Contents

Contents

Contents

Contents

Contents

Contents

Contents

Contents

Contents

Contents

Introduction

If we were to describe the C# language and its associated environment, the .NET Framework, as the most important new technology for developers for many years, we would not be exaggerating. .NET is designed to provide a new environment within which you can develop almost any application to run on Windows, whereas C# is a new programming language that has been designed specifically to work with .NET. Using C# you can, for example, write a dynamic Web page, an XML Web service, a component of a distributed application, a database access component, a classic Windows desktop application, or even a new smart client application that allows for online/offline capabilities. This book covers the .NET Framework 3.5. If you are coding using version 1.0, 1.1, 2.0, or even 3.0, there may be sections of the book that will not work for you. We try to notify you of items that are new to the .NET Framework 3.5 specifically.

Don't be fooled by the .NET label. The NET bit in the name is there to emphasize Microsoft's belief that distributed applications, in which the processing is distributed between client and server, are the way forward, but C# is not just a language for writing Internet or network-aware applications. It provides a means for you to code up almost any type of software or component that you might need to write for the Windows platform. Between them, C# and .NET are set both to revolutionize the way that you write programs, and to make programming on Windows much easier than it has ever been.

That's quite a substantial claim, and it needs to be justified. After all, we all know how quickly computer technology changes. Every year Microsoft brings out new software, programming tools, or versions of Windows, with the claim that these will be hugely beneficial to developers. So what's different about .NET and C#?

The Significance of .NET and C#

In order to understand the significance of .NET, it is useful to remind ourselves of the nature of many of the Windows technologies that have appeared in the past 10 years or so. Although they may look quite different on the surface, all of the Windows operating systems from Windows 3.1 (introduced in 1992) through Windows Server 2008 have the same familiar Windows API at their core. As we've progressed through new versions of Windows, huge numbers of new functions have been added to the API, but this has been a process of evolving and extending the API rather than replacing it.

The same can be said for many of the technologies and frameworks that we've used to develop software for Windows. For example, *COM* (*Component Object Model*) originated as *OLE* (*Object Linking and Embedding*). At the time, it was, to a large extent, simply a means by which different types of Office documents could be linked, so that, for example, you could place a small Excel spreadsheet in your Word document. From that it evolved into COM, *DCOM* (*Distributed COM*), and eventually *COM+* — a sophisticated technology that formed the basis of the way almost all components communicated, as well as implementing transactions, messaging services, and object pooling.

Microsoft chose this evolutionary approach to software for the obvious reason that it is concerned about backward compatibility. Over the years, a huge base of third-party software has been written for Windows, and Windows wouldn't have enjoyed the success it has had if every time Microsoft introduced a new technology it broke the existing code base!

Although backward compatibility has been a crucial feature of Windows technologies and one of the strengths of the Windows platform, it does have a big disadvantage. Every time some technology evolves and adds new features, it ends up a bit more complicated than it was before.

It was clear that something had to change. Microsoft couldn't go on forever extending the same development tools and languages, always making them more and more complex in order to satisfy the conflicting demands of keeping up with the newest hardware and maintaining backward compatibility with what was around when Windows first became popular in the early 1990s. There comes a point where you have to start with a clean slate if you want a simple yet sophisticated set of languages, environments, and developer tools, which makes it easy for developers to write state-of-the-art software.

This fresh start is what C# and .NET are all about. Roughly speaking, .NET is a framework — an API — for programming on the Windows platform. Along with the .NET Framework, C# is a language that has been designed from scratch to work with .NET, as well as to take advantage of all the progress in developer environments and in our understanding of object-oriented programming principles that have taken place over the past 20 years.

Before we continue, we should make it clear that backward compatibility has not been lost in the process. Existing programs will continue to work, and .NET was designed with the ability to work with existing software. Presently, communication between software components on Windows almost entirely takes place using COM. Taking account of this, .NET does have the ability to provide wrappers around existing COM components so that .NET components can talk to them.

It is true that you don't need to learn C# in order to write code for .NET. Microsoft has extended C++, provided another new language called J#, and made substantial changes to Visual Basic to turn it into the more powerful language Visual Basic .NET, in order to allow code written in either of these languages to target the .NET environment. These other languages, however, are hampered by the legacy of having evolved over the years rather than having been written from the start with today's technology in mind.

This book will equip you to program in C#, while at the same time provide the necessary background in how the .NET architecture works. We not only cover the fundamentals of the C# language but also go on to give examples of applications that use a variety of related technologies, including database access, dynamic Web pages, advanced graphics, and directory access. The only requirement is that you be familiar with at least one other high-level language used on Windows — either C++, Visual Basic, or J++.

Advantages of .NET

We've talked in general terms about how great .NET is, but we haven't said much about how it helps to make your life as a developer easier. In this section, we discuss some of the improved features of .NET in brief.

❑ **Object-oriented programming** — Both the .NET Framework and C# are entirely based on object-oriented principles right from the start.

❑ **Good design** — A base class library, which is designed from the ground up in a highly intuitive way.

❑ **Language independence** — With .NET, all of the languages — Visual Basic .NET, C#, J#, and managed C++ — compile to a common *Intermediate Language*. This means that languages are interoperable in a way that has not been seen before.

❑ **Better support for dynamic Web pages** — Though ASP offered a lot of flexibility, it was also inefficient because of its use of interpreted scripting languages, and the lack of object-oriented design often resulted in messy ASP code. .NET offers an integrated support for Web pages, using a new technology — ASP.NET. With ASP.NET, code in your pages is compiled, and may be written in a .NET-aware high-level language such as C# or Visual Basic 2008.

❑ **Efficient data access** — A set of .NET components, collectively known as ADO.NET, provides efficient access to relational databases and a variety of data sources. Components are also available to allow access to the file system, and to directories. In particular, XML support is built into .NET, allowing you to manipulate data, which may be imported from or exported to non-Windows platforms.

❑ **Code sharing** — .NET has completely revamped the way that code is shared between applications, introducing the concept of the *assembly*, which replaces the traditional DLL. Assemblies have formal facilities for versioning, and different versions of assemblies can exist side by side.

❑ **Improved security** — Each assembly can also contain built-in security information that can indicate precisely who or what category of user or process is allowed to call which methods on which classes. This gives you a very fine degree of control over how the assemblies that you deploy can be used.

❑ **Zero-impact installation** — There are two types of assemblies: shared and private. Shared assemblies are common libraries available to all software, whereas private assemblies are intended only for use with particular software. A private assembly is entirely self-contained, so the process of installing it is simple. There are no registry entries; the appropriate files are simply placed in the appropriate folder in the file system.

❑ **Support for Web services** — .NET has fully integrated support for developing Web services as easily as you'd develop any other type of application.

❑ **Visual Studio 2008** — .NET comes with a developer environment, Visual Studio 2008, which can cope equally well with C++, C#, and Visual Basic 2008, as well as with ASP.NET code. Visual Studio 2008 integrates all the best features of the respective language-specific environments of Visual Studio .NET 2002/2003/2005 and Visual Studio 6.

❑ C# — C# is a new object-oriented language intended for use with .NET.

We look more closely at the benefits of the .NET architecture in Chapter 1, ".NET Architecture."

Looking at What's New in the .NET Framework 3.5

The first version of the .NET Framework (1.0) was released in 2002 to much enthusiasm. The .NET Framework 2.0 was introduced in 2005 and was considered a major release of the Framework. The .NET Framework 3.5, though not as big a release as the 2.0 release, is still considered a rather major release of the product with many outstanding new features.

With each release of the Framework, Microsoft has always tried to ensure that there were minimal breaking changes to code developed. Thus far, Microsoft has been very successful at this goal.

> Make sure that you create a staging server to completely test the upgrading of your applications to the .NET Framework 3.5 as opposed to just upgrading a live application.

The following section details some of the changes that are new to C# 2008, the .NET Framework 3.5, as well as new additions to Visual Studio 2008 — the development environment for the .NET Framework 3.5.

Implicitly Typed Variables

Using C# 2008, you can now declare a variable and allow the compiler to determine the type of the item implicitly. You will find that LINQ uses this capability to work with the queries that are created. To work with this new capability, you use the var keyword:

```
var x = 5;
```

When you use this statement, the compiler will actually use the value of 5 to figure out the type that this needs to be. That means, in this case, that the statement will actually be as you would expect:

```
int x = 5;
```

Automatically Implemented Properties

A common task of declaring your properties just got easier with C# 2008. Prior to this release, you would declare your properties as such:

```
private int _myItem;

public int MyItem
{
    get {
        return myItem
    }

    set {
        myItem = value;
    }
}
```

Now you can let the compiler do the work for you on your behalf. Instead of constantly putting the preceding structure in your code over and over again, you are now able to use the shortcut of automatic implemented properties:

```
public int MyProperty { get; set; }
```

Using this syntax will produce the same results as the lengthy example. The compiler will perform the operation of converting this short form to the proper format on your behalf, making your code simpler to read and work with and allowing you to code your solutions faster than before.

Object and Collection Initializers

C# 2008 now allows you to assign values to an object's properties at the moment the property is initialized. For instance, suppose you have the following object in your code:

```
public class MyStructure
{
        public int MyProperty1 { get; set; }
        public int MyProperty2 { get; set; }
}
```

Using C# 2008, you can instantiate the MyStructure object as follows:

```
MyStructure myStructure = new MyStructure() { MyProperty1 = 5,
    MyProperty2 = 10 };
```

This same capability allows you to declare many items of a collection at once:

```
List<int> myInts = new List<int>() { 5, 10, 15, 20, 25 };
```

In this case, all the numbers are added to the myInts object as if you used the Add() method.

Built-In ASP.NET AJAX Support

Although you could build ASP.NET AJAX web pages using the .NET Framework 2.0, this required additional installs. You will find that ASP.NET AJAX support is now built into ASP.NET 3.5 and Visual Studio 2008.

Now, every page that you build using ASP.NET with the .NET Framework 3.5 is Ajax-enabled (you can see all the Ajax configuration in the `Web.config` file). You will also find some new server controls within the ASP.NET toolbox of controls that allow you to add Ajax capabilities to your Web sites. See Chapter 39 for more information on ASP.NET AJAX.

.NET Language Integrated Query Framework (LINQ)

One of the coolest features and most anticipated of the bunch, LINQ offers you the ability to easily access underlying data. Microsoft has provided LINQ as a lightweight façade that provides a strongly typed interface to the underlying data stores. LINQ provides the means for developers to stay within the coding environment that they are used to and access the underlying data as objects that work with the IDE, IntelliSense, and even debugging.

Using LINQ, you can query against objects, data sets, the SQL Server database, XML, and more. The nice thing is that regardless of the underlying data source, getting at the data is done in the same manner because LINQ provides a structured way to query the data.

An example of getting at a pseudo XML document and grabbing all the customer names within the XML file is presented here:

```
XDocument xdoc = XDocument.Load(@"C:\Customers.xml");

var query = from people in xdoc.Descendants("CustomerName")
            select people.Value;

Console.WriteLine("{0} Customers Found", query.Count());
Console.WriteLine();

foreach (var item in query)
{
    Console.WriteLine(item);
}
```

Chapters 11, 27, and 29 all cover various aspects of LINQ.

Multi-Targeting within Visual Studio

In many cases, .NET developers are now working with multiple .NET applications that are targeted at either of the .NET Frameworks of 2.0, 3.0, or now 3.5. It would be silly to have to continue to have multiple versions of Visual Studio on your development computer in order to work with multiple versions of the .NET Framework.

For this reason, you will find that the latest version of Visual Studio 2008 now supports the ability to target the version of the framework that you are interested in working with. Now when creating a new application, you are giving the option of creating an application that targets either the .NET Framework 2.0, 3.0, or 3.5.

Supporting the Latest Application Types

It wasn't that long ago that the .NET Framework 3.0 was released and with it came some dramatic new capabilities. Included in that version was the ability to build a new application type using the Windows Presentation Foundation (WPF) as well as applications and libraries based on the Windows Communication Foundation (WCF), and the Windows Workflow Foundation (WF).

With the release of Visual Studio 2008, you will find that you are now able to build these applications — they are all now available as project types with new controls and Visual Studio wizards and capabilities.

Where C# Fits In

In one sense, C# can be seen as being the same thing to programming languages as .NET is to the Windows environment. Just as Microsoft has been adding more and more features to Windows and the Windows API over the past decade, Visual Basic 2008 and C++ have undergone expansion. Although Visual Basic and C++ have ended up as hugely powerful languages as a result of this, both languages also suffer from problems due to the legacies from how they have evolved.

In the case of Visual Basic 6 and earlier versions, the main strength of the language was the fact that it was simple to understand and made many programming tasks easy, largely hiding the details of the Windows API and the COM component infrastructure from the developer. The downside to this was that Visual Basic was never truly object oriented, so that large applications quickly became disorganized and hard to maintain. As well, because Visual Basic's syntax was inherited from early versions of BASIC (which, in turn, was designed to be intuitively simple for beginning programmers to understand, rather than to write large commercial applications), it didn't really lend itself to well-structured or object-oriented programs.

C++, on the other hand, has its roots in the ANSI C++ language definition. It isn't completely ANSI-compliant for the simple reason that Microsoft first wrote its C++ compiler before the ANSI definition had become official, but it comes close. Unfortunately, this has led to two problems. First, ANSI C++ has its roots in a decade-old state of technology, and this shows up in a lack of support for modern concepts (such as Unicode strings and generating XML documentation) and for some archaic syntax structures designed for the compilers of yesteryear (such as the separation of declaration from definition of member functions). Second, Microsoft has been simultaneously trying to evolve C++ into a language that is designed for high-performance tasks on Windows, and in order to achieve that, it has been forced to add a huge number of Microsoft-specific keywords as well as various libraries to the language. The result is that on Windows, the language has become a complete mess. Just ask C++ developers how many definitions for a string they can think of: `char*`, `LPSTR`, `string`, `CString` (MFC version), `CString` (WTL version), `wchar_t*`, `OLECHAR*`, and so on.

Now enter .NET — a completely new environment that is going to involve new extensions to both languages. Microsoft has gotten around this by adding yet more Microsoft-specific keywords to C++, and by completely revamping Visual Basic into Visual Basic .NET into Visual Basic 2008, a language that retains some of the basic VB syntax but that is so different in design that it can be considered, for all practical purposes, a new language.

It's in this context that Microsoft has decided to give developers an alternative — a language designed specifically for .NET, and designed with a clean slate. C# is the result. Officially, Microsoft describes C# as a "simple, modern, object-oriented, and type-safe programming language derived from C and C++." Most independent observers would probably change that to "derived from C, C++, and Java." Such descriptions are technically accurate but do little to convey the beauty or elegance of the language. Syntactically, C# is very similar to both C++ and Java, to such an extent that many keywords are the same, and C# also shares the same block structure with braces ({}) to mark blocks of code, and semicolons to separate statements. The first impression of a piece of C# code is that it looks quite like C++ or Java code. Beyond that initial similarity, however, C# is a lot easier to learn than C++, and of comparable difficulty to Java. Its design is more in tune with modern developer tools than both of those other languages, and it has been designed to provide, simultaneously, the ease of use of Visual Basic and the high-performance, low-level memory access of C++, if required. Some of the features of C# are:

❑   Full support for classes and object-oriented programming, including both interface and implementation inheritance, virtual functions, and operator overloading.

❑   A consistent and well-defined set of basic types.

❑   Built-in support for automatic generation of XML documentation.

- ❑ Automatic cleanup of dynamically allocated memory.

- ❑ The facility to mark classes or methods with user-defined attributes. This can be useful for documentation and can have some effects on compilation (for example, marking methods to be compiled only in debug builds).

- ❑ Full access to the .NET base class library, as well as easy access to the Windows API (if you really need it, which won't be all that often).

- ❑ Pointers and direct memory access are available if required, but the language has been designed in such a way that you can work without them in almost all cases.

- ❑ Support for properties and events in the style of Visual Basic.

- ❑ Just by changing the compiler options, you can compile either to an executable or to a library of .NET components that can be called up by other code in the same way as ActiveX controls (COM components).

- ❑ C# can be used to write ASP.NET dynamic Web pages and XML Web services.

Most of these statements, it should be pointed out, do also apply to Visual Basic 2008 and Managed C++. The fact that C# is designed from the start to work with .NET, however, means that its support for the features of .NET is both more complete, and offered within the context of a more suitable syntax than for those other languages. Though the C# language itself is very similar to Java, there are some improvements; in particular, Java is not designed to work with the .NET environment.

Before we leave the subject, we should point out a couple of limitations of C#. The one area the language is not designed for is time-critical or extremely high-performance code — the kind where you really are worried about whether a loop takes 1,000 or 1,050 machine cycles to run through, and you need to clean up your resources the millisecond they are no longer needed. C++ is likely to continue to reign supreme among low-level languages in this area. C# lacks certain key facilities needed for extremely high-performance apps, including the ability to specify inline functions and destructors that are guaranteed to run at particular points in the code. However, the proportions of applications that fall into this category are very low.

What You Need to Write and Run C# Code

The .NET Framework 3.5 will run on Windows XP, 2003, Vista, and the latest Windows Server 2008. In order to write code using .NET, you will need to install the .NET 3.5 SDK.

Also, unless you are intending to write your C# code using a text editor or some other third-party developer environment, you will almost certainly also want Visual Studio 2008. The full SDK isn't needed to run managed code, but the .NET runtime is needed. You may find you need to distribute the .NET runtime with your code for the benefit of those clients who do not have it already installed.

What This Book Covers

This book starts by reviewing the overall architecture of .NET in Chapter 1 in order to give you the background you need to be able to write managed code. After that the book is divided into a number of sections that cover both the C# language and its application in a variety of areas.

Part I: The C# Language

This section gives a good grounding in the C# language itself. This section doesn't presume knowledge of any particular language, although it does assume you are an experienced programmer. You start by looking at C#'s basic syntax and data types, and then explore the object-oriented features of C# before moving on to look at more advanced C# programming topics.

Part II: Visual Studio

This section looks at the main IDE utilized by C# developers world-wide: Visual Studio 2005. The two chapters in this section look at the best way to use the tool to build applications based upon either the .NET Framework 2.0 or 3.0. In addition to this, this section also focuses on the deployment of your projects.

Part III: Base Class Libraries

In this section, you look at the principles of programming in the .NET environment. In particular, you look at security, threading localization, transactions, how to build Windows services, and how to generate your own libraries as assemblies.

Part IV: Data

Here, you look at accessing databases with ADO.NET and LINQ, and at interacting with directories and files. This part also extensively covers support in .NET for XML and on the Windows operating system side, and the .NET features of SQL Server 2008. Within the large space of LINQ, particular focus is put on LINQ to SQL and LINQ to XML.

Part V: Presentation

This section focuses on building classic Windows applications, which are called Windows Forms in .NET. Windows Forms are the thick-client version of applications, and using .NET to build these types of applications is a quick and easy way of accomplishing this task. In addition to looking at Windows Forms, you take a look at GDI+, which is the technology you will use for building applications that include advanced graphics. This section also covers writing components that will run on Web sites, serving up Web pages. This covers the tremendous number of new features that ASP.NET 3.5 provides. Finally, this section also shows how to build applications based upon the Windows Presentation Foundation and VSTO.

Part VI: Communication

This section is all about communication. It covers Web services for platform-independent communication, .NET Remoting for communication between .NET clients and servers, Enterprise Services for the services in the background, and DCOM communication. With Message Queuing asynchronous, disconnected communication is shown. This section also looks at utilizing the Windows Communication Foundation and the Windows Workflow Foundation.

Part VII: Appendices (Online)

This section includes three appendices focused on how to build applications that take into account the new features and barriers found in Windows Vista. Also, this section looks at the upcoming ADO.NET Entities technology and how to use this new technology in your C# applications. You can find these three appendices online at www.wrox.com. See "Source Code and Appendices" later in this introduction for instructions.

Conventions

We have used a number of different styles of text and layout in the book to help differentiate between the different kinds of information. Here are examples of the styles we use and an explanation of what they mean.

Bullets appear indented, with each new bullet marked as follows:

❏ *Important Words* are in italics.

❏ Keys that you press on the keyboard take the form Ctrl + Enter.

Code appears in a number of different ways. If it's a word that we're talking about in the text — for example, when discussing the `if...else` loop — it's in `this font`. If it's a block of code that you can type in as a program and run, it appears like this:

```
public static void Main()
{
    AFunc(1,2,"abc");
}


        // If we haven't reached the end, return true, otherwise
        // set the position to invalid, and return false.
        pos++;
        if (pos < 4)
            return true;
        else {
            pos = -1;
            return false;
        }
```

Advice, hints, and background information come in an italicized, indented font like this.

> **Important pieces of information come in boxes like this.**

We demonstrate the syntactical usage of methods, properties (and so on) using the following format:

```
Regsvcs BookDistributor.dll [COM+AppName] [TypeLibrary.tbl]
```

Here, italicized parts indicate object references, variables, or parameter values to be inserted; the square braces indicate optional parameters.

Source Code and Appendices

As you work through the examples in this book, you may choose either to type in all the code manually or to use the source code files that accompany the book. All of the source code used in this book is available for downloading at www.wrox.com. Once at the site, simply locate the book's title (either by using the Search box or by using one of the title lists) and click the Download Code link on the book's detail page to obtain all the source code for the book.

Because many books have similar titles, you may find it easiest to search by ISBN; this book's ISBN is 978-0-470-19137-8.

Once you download the code, just decompress it with your favorite compression tool. Alternatively, you can go to the main Wrox code download page at www.wrox.com/dynamic/books/download.aspx to see the code available for this book and all other Wrox books.

Errata

We make every effort to ensure that there are no errors in the text or in the code. However, no one is perfect, and mistakes do occur. If you find an error in one of our books, such as a spelling mistake or faulty piece of code, we would be very grateful for your feedback. By sending in errata you may save another reader hours of frustration, and at the same time you will be helping us provide even higher-quality information.

To find the errata page for this book, go to www.wrox.com and locate the title using the Search box or one of the title lists. Then, on the book details page, click the Book Errata link. On this page, you can view all errata that have been submitted for this book and posted by Wrox editors. A complete book list, including links to each book's errata, is also available at www.wrox.com/misc-pages/booklist.shtml.

If you don't spot "your" error already on the Book Errata page, go to www.wrox.com/contact/techsupport.shtml and complete the form there to send us the error you have found. We'll check the information and, if appropriate, post a message to the book's errata page and fix the problem in subsequent editions of the book.

p2p.wrox.com

For author and peer discussion, join the P2P forums at p2p.wrox.com. The forums are a Web-based-system for you to post messages relating to Wrox books and related technologies and interact with other readers and technology users. The forums offer a subscription feature to email you topics of interest of your choosing when new posts are made to the forums. Wrox authors, editors, other industry experts, and your fellow readers are present on these forums.

At http://p2p.wrox.com you will find a number of different forums that will help you not only as you read this book but also as you develop your own applications. To join the forums, just follow these steps:

1. Go to p2p.wrox.com and click the Register link.
2. Read the terms of use and click Agree.
3. Supply the required information to join as well as any optional information you wish to provide and click Submit.

You will receive an email with information describing how to verify your account and complete the joining process.

> You can read messages in the forums without joining P2P, but you must join in order to post your own messages.

Once you join, you can post new messages and respond to other users' posts. You can read messages at any time on the Web. If you would like to have new messages from a particular forum emailed to you, click the Subscribe to this Forum icon by the forum name in the forum listing.

For more information about how to use the Wrox P2P, be sure to read the P2P FAQs for answers to questions about how the forum software works as well as many common questions specific to P2P and Wrox books. To read the FAQs, click the FAQ link on any P2P page.

Professional
C# 2008

Part I
The C# Language

.NET Architecture

1

Throughout this book, we emphasize that the C# language must be considered in parallel with the .NET Framework, rather than viewed in isolation. The C# compiler specifically targets .NET, which means that all code written in C# will always run within the .NET Framework. This has two important consequences for the C# language:

1. The architecture and methodologies of C# reflect the underlying methodologies of .NET.

2. In many cases, specific language features of C# actually depend on features of .NET, or of the .NET base classes.

Because of this dependence, it is important to gain some understanding of the architecture and methodology of .NET before you begin C# programming. That is the purpose of this chapter. The following is an outline of what this chapter covers:

❑ This chapter begins by explaining what happens when all code (including C#) that targets .NET is compiled and run.

❑ Once you have this broad overview, you take a more detailed look at the *Microsoft Intermediate Language* (MSIL or simply IL); the assembly language that all compiled code ends up in on .NET. In particular, you see how IL, in partnership with the *Common Type System* (CTS) and *Common Language Specification* (CLS), works to give you interoperability between languages that target .NET. This chapter also discusses where common languages (including Visual Basic and C++) fit into .NET.

❑ Next, you move on to examine some of the other features of .NET, including assemblies, namespaces, and the .NET base classes.

❑ The chapter finishes with a brief look at the kinds of applications you can create as a C# developer.

The Relationship of C# to .NET

C# is a relatively new programming language and is significant in two respects:

❑ It is specifically designed and targeted for use with Microsoft's .NET Framework (a feature-rich platform for the development, deployment, and execution of distributed applications).

❑ It is a language based on the modern object-oriented design methodology, and, when designing it, Microsoft learned from the experience of all the other similar languages that have been around since object-oriented principles came to prominence some 20 years ago.

One important thing to make clear is that C# is a language in its own right. Although it is designed to generate code that targets the .NET environment, it is not itself part of .NET. Some features are supported by .NET but not by C#, and you might be surprised to learn that some features of the C# language are not supported by .NET (for example, some instances of operator overloading)!

However, because the C# language is intended for use with .NET, it is important for you to have an understanding of this Framework if you want to develop applications in C# effectively. Therefore, this chapter takes some time to peek underneath the surface of .NET. Let's get started.

The Common Language Runtime

Central to the .NET Framework is its runtime execution environment, known as the *Common Language Runtime* (CLR) or the *.NET runtime*. Code running under the control of the CLR is often termed *managed code*.

However, before it can be executed by the CLR, any source code that you develop (in C# or some other language) needs to be compiled. Compilation occurs in two steps in .NET:

1. Compilation of source code to IL.
2. Compilation of IL to platform-specific code by the CLR.

This two-stage compilation process is very important, because the existence of the IL (managed code) is the key to providing many of the benefits of .NET.

Microsoft Intermediate Language shares with Java byte code the idea that it is a low-level language with a simple syntax (based on numeric codes rather than text), which can be very quickly translated into native machine code. Having this well-defined universal syntax for code has significant advantages: platform independence, performance improvement, and language interoperability.

Platform Independence

First, platform independence means that the same file containing byte code instructions can be placed on any platform; at runtime, the final stage of compilation can then be easily accomplished so that the code will run on that particular platform. In other words, by compiling to IL you obtain platform independence for .NET, in much the same way as compiling to Java byte code gives Java platform independence.

Note that the platform independence of .NET is only theoretical at present because, at the time of writing, a complete implementation of .NET is available only for Windows. However, a partial implementation is available (see, for example, the Mono project, an effort to create an open source implementation of .NET, at www.go-mono.com).

Performance Improvement

Although we previously made comparisons with Java, IL is actually a bit more ambitious than Java byte code. IL is always *Just-in-Time* compiled (known as JIT compilation), whereas Java byte code was often interpreted. One of the disadvantages of Java was that, on execution, the process of translating from Java byte code to native executable resulted in a loss of performance (with the exception of more recent cases, where Java is JIT compiled on certain platforms).

Instead of compiling the entire application in one go (which could lead to a slow startup time), the JIT compiler simply compiles each portion of code as it is called (just in time). When code has been compiled once, the resultant native executable is stored until the application exits so that it does not need to be recompiled the next time that portion of code is run. Microsoft argues that this process is more efficient than compiling the entire application code at the start, because of the likelihood that large portions of any application code will not actually be executed in any given run. Using the JIT compiler, such code will never be compiled.

This explains why we can expect that execution of managed IL code will be almost as fast as executing native machine code. What it does not explain is why Microsoft expects that we will get a performance *improvement*. The reason given for this is that, because the final stage of compilation takes place at runtime, the JIT compiler will know exactly what processor type the program will run on. This means that it can optimize the final executable code to take advantage of any features or particular machine code instructions offered by that particular processor.

Traditional compilers will optimize the code, but they can only perform optimizations that are independent of the particular processor that the code will run on. This is because traditional compilers compile to native executable before the software is shipped. This means that the compiler does not know what type of processor the code will run on beyond basic generalities, such as that it will be an x86-compatible processor or an Alpha processor. The older Visual Studio 6, for example, optimizes for a generic Pentium machine, so the code that it generates cannot take advantage of hardware features of Pentium III processors. However, the JIT compiler can do all the optimizations that Visual Studio 6 can, and in addition, it will optimize for the particular processor that the code is running on.

Language Interoperability

The use of IL not only enables platform independence; it also facilitates *language interoperability*. Simply put, you can compile to IL from one language, and this compiled code should then be interoperable with code that has been compiled to IL from another language.

You are probably now wondering which languages aside from C# are interoperable with .NET; the following sections briefly discuss how some of the other common languages fit into .NET.

Visual Basic 2008

Visual Basic .NET 2002 underwent a complete revamp from Visual Basic 6 to bring it up to date with the first version of the .NET Framework. The Visual Basic language itself had dramatically evolved from VB6, and this meant that VB6 was not a suitable language for running .NET programs. For example, VB6 is heavily integrated into Component Object Model (COM) and works by exposing only event handlers as source code to the developer — most of the background code is not available as source code. Not only that; it does not support implementation inheritance, and the standard data types that Visual Basic 6 uses are incompatible with .NET.

Visual Basic 6 was upgraded to Visual Basic .NET in 2002, and the changes that were made to the language are so extensive you might as well regard Visual Basic as a new language. Existing Visual Basic 6 code does not compile to the present Visual Basic 2008 code (or to Visual Basic .NET 2002, 2003, and 2005 for that matter). Converting a Visual Basic 6 program to Visual Basic 2008 requires extensive changes to the code. However, Visual Studio 2008 (the upgrade of Visual Studio for use with .NET) can do most of the changes for you. If you attempt to read a Visual Basic 6 project into Visual Studio 2008, it will upgrade the project for you, which means that it will rewrite the Visual Basic 6 source code into Visual Basic 2008 source code. Although this means that the work involved for you is heavily cut down, you will need to check through the new Visual Basic 2008 code to make sure that the project still works as intended because the conversion might not be perfect.

One side effect of this language upgrade is that it is no longer possible to compile Visual Basic 2008 to native executable code. Visual Basic 2008 compiles only to IL, just as C# does. If you need to continue coding in Visual Basic 6, you can do so, but the executable code produced will completely ignore the .NET Framework, and you will need to keep Visual Studio 6 installed if you want to continue to work in this developer environment.

Visual C++ 2008

Visual C++ 6 already had a large number of Microsoft-specific extensions on Windows. With Visual C++ .NET, extensions have been added to support the .NET Framework. This means that existing C++ source code will continue to compile to native executable code without modification. It also means, however, that it will run independently of the .NET runtime. If you want your C++ code to run within the .NET Framework, you can simply add the following line to the beginning of your code:

```
#using <mscorlib.dll>
```

You can also pass the flag /clr to the compiler, which then assumes that you want to compile to managed code, and will hence emit IL instead of native machine code. The interesting thing about C++ is that when you compile to managed code, the compiler can emit IL that contains an embedded native executable. This means that you can mix managed types and unmanaged types in your C++ code. Thus the managed C++ code

```
class MyClass
{
```

defines a plain C++ class, whereas the code

```
ref class MyClass
{
```

gives you a managed class, just as if you had written the class in C# or Visual Basic 2008. The advantage of using managed C++ over C# code is that you can call unmanaged C++ classes from managed C++ code without having to resort to COM interop.

The compiler raises an error if you attempt to use features that are not supported by .NET on managed types (for example, templates or multiple inheritances of classes). You will also find that you will need to use nonstandard C++ features when using managed classes.

Because of the freedom that C++ allows in terms of low-level pointer manipulation and so on, the C++ compiler is not able to generate code that will pass the CLR's memory type-safety tests. If it is important that your code be recognized by the CLR as memory type-safe, you will need to write your source code in some other language (such as C# or Visual Basic 2008).

COM and COM+

Technically speaking, COM and COM+ are not technologies targeted at .NET, because components based on them cannot be compiled into IL (although it is possible to do so to some degree using managed C++, if the original COM component was written in C++). However, COM+ remains an important tool, because its features are not duplicated in .NET. Also, COM components will still work — and .NET incorporates COM interoperability features that make it possible for managed code to call up COM components and vice versa (this is discussed in Chapter 24, "Interoperability"). In general, however, you will probably find it more convenient for most purposes to code new components as .NET components, so that you can take advantage of the .NET base classes as well as the other benefits of running as managed code.

A Closer Look at Intermediate Language

From what you learned in the previous section, Microsoft Intermediate Language obviously plays a fundamental role in the .NET Framework. As C# developers, we now understand that our C# code will be compiled into IL before it is executed (indeed, the C# compiler compiles *only* to managed code). It makes sense, then, to now take a closer look at the main characteristics of IL, because any language that targets .NET will logically need to support the main characteristics of IL, too.

Here are the important features of IL:

❑   Object orientation and use of interfaces

❑   Strong distinction between value and reference types

❑   Strong data typing

❑   Error handling using exceptions

❑   Use of attributes

The following sections explore each of these characteristics.

Support for Object Orientation and Interfaces

The language independence of .NET does have some practical limitations. IL is inevitably going to implement some particular programming methodology, which means that languages targeting it need to be compatible with that methodology. The particular route that Microsoft has chosen to follow for IL is that of classic object-oriented programming, with single implementation inheritance of classes.

> *If you are unfamiliar with the concepts of object orientation, refer to Appendix B, "C#, Visual Basic, C++/CLI," for more information.*

In addition to classic object-oriented programming, IL also brings in the idea of interfaces, which saw their first implementation under Windows with COM. Interfaces built using .NET produce interfaces that are not the same as COM interfaces. They do not need to support any of the COM infrastructure (for example, they are not derived from IUnknown, and they do not have associated globally unique identifiers, more commonly know as GUIDs). However, they do share with COM interfaces the idea that they provide a contract, and classes that implement a given interface must provide implementations of the methods and properties specified by that interface.

You have now seen that working with .NET means compiling to IL, and that in turn means that you will need to use traditional object-oriented methodologies. However, that alone is not sufficient to give you language interoperability. After all, C++ and Java both use the same object-oriented paradigms, but they are still not regarded as interoperable. We need to look a little more closely at the concept of language interoperability.

To start with, we need to consider exactly what we mean by language interoperability. After all, COM allowed components written in different languages to work together in the sense of calling each other's methods. What was inadequate about that? COM, by virtue of being a binary standard, did allow components to instantiate other components and call methods or properties against them, without worrying about the language in which the respective components were written. To achieve this, however, each object had to be instantiated through the COM runtime, and accessed through an interface. Depending on the threading models of the relative components, there may have been large performance losses associated with marshaling data between apartments or running components or both on different threads. In the extreme case of components hosted as an executable rather than DLL files, separate processes would need to be created to run them. The emphasis was very much that components could talk to each other but only via the COM runtime. In no way with COM did components written in different languages directly communicate with each other, or instantiate instances of each other — it was always done with COM as an intermediary. Not only that, but the COM architecture did not permit implementation inheritance, which meant that it lost many of the advantages of object-oriented programming.

An associated problem was that, when debugging, you would still need to debug components written in different languages independently. It was not possible to step between languages in the debugger. Therefore, what we *really* mean by language interoperability is that classes written in one language should be able to talk directly to classes written in another language. In particular:

- ❑ A class written in one language can inherit from a class written in another language.
- ❑ The class can contain an instance of another class, no matter what the languages of the two classes are.
- ❑ An object can directly call methods against another object written in another language.
- ❑ Objects (or references to objects) can be passed around between methods.
- ❑ When calling methods between languages you can step between the method calls in the debugger, even when this means stepping between source code written in different languages.

This is all quite an ambitious aim, but amazingly, .NET and IL have achieved it. In the case of stepping between methods in the debugger, this facility is really offered by the Visual Studio integrated development environment (IDE) rather than by the CLR itself.

Distinct Value and Reference Types

As with any programming language, IL provides a number of predefined primitive data types. One characteristic of IL, however, is that it makes a strong distinction between value and reference types. *Value types* are those for which a variable directly stores its data, whereas *reference types* are those for which a variable simply stores the address at which the corresponding data can be found.

In C++ terms, using reference types can be considered to be similar to accessing a variable through a pointer, whereas for Visual Basic, the best analogy for reference types are objects, which in Visual Basic 6 are always accessed through references. IL also lays down specifications about data storage: instances of reference types are always stored in an area of memory known as the *managed heap*, whereas value types are normally stored on the *stack* (although if value types are declared as fields within reference types, they will be stored inline on the heap). Chapter 2, "C# Basics," discusses the stack and the heap and how they work.

Strong Data Typing

One very important aspect of IL is that it is based on exceptionally *strong data typing*. That means that all variables are clearly marked as being of a particular, specific data type (there is no room in IL, for example, for the Variant data type recognized by Visual Basic and scripting languages). In particular, IL does not normally permit any operations that result in ambiguous data types.

For instance, Visual Basic 6 developers are used to being able to pass variables around without worrying too much about their types, because Visual Basic 6 automatically performs type conversion. C++ developers are used to routinely casting pointers between different types. Being able to perform this kind of operation can be great for performance, but it breaks type safety. Hence, it is permitted only under certain circumstances in some of the languages that compile to managed code. Indeed, pointers (as opposed to references) are permitted only in marked blocks of code in C#, and not at all in Visual Basic (although they are allowed in managed C++). Using pointers in your code causes it to fail the memory type-safety checks performed by the CLR.

You should note that some languages compatible with .NET, such as Visual Basic 2008, still allow some laxity in typing, but that is possible only because the compilers behind the scenes ensure that the type safety is enforced in the emitted IL.

Although enforcing type safety might initially appear to hurt performance, in many cases the benefits gained from the services provided by .NET that rely on type safety far outweigh this performance loss. Such services include:

- ❑ Language interoperability
- ❑ Garbage collection
- ❑ Security
- ❑ Application domains

The following sections take a closer look at why strong data typing is particularly important for these features of .NET.

The Importance of Strong Data Typing for Language Interoperability

If a class is to derive from or contains instances of other classes, it needs to know about all the data types used by the other classes. This is why strong data typing is so important. Indeed, it is the absence of any agreed-on system for specifying this information in the past that has always been the real barrier to inheritance and interoperability across languages. This kind of information is simply not present in a standard executable file or DLL.

Suppose that one of the methods of a Visual Basic 2008 class is defined to return an `Integer` — one of the standard data types available in Visual Basic 2008. C# simply does not have any data type of that name. Clearly, you will be able to derive from the class, use this method, and use the return type from C# code, only if the compiler knows how to map Visual Basic 2008's `Integer` type to some known type that is defined in C#. So, how is this problem circumvented in .NET?

Common Type System

This data type problem is solved in .NET using the *Common Type System* (CTS). The CTS defines the predefined data types that are available in IL, so that all languages that target the .NET Framework will produce compiled code that is ultimately based on these types.

For the previous example, Visual Basic 2008's `Integer` is actually a 32-bit signed integer, which maps exactly to the IL type known as `Int32`. This will therefore be the data type specified in the IL code. Because the C# compiler is aware of this type, there is no problem. At source code level, C# refers to `Int32` with the keyword `int`, so the compiler will simply treat the Visual Basic 2008 method as if it returned an `int`.

The CTS does not specify merely primitive data types but a rich hierarchy of types, which includes well-defined points in the hierarchy at which code is permitted to define its own types. The hierarchical structure of the CTS reflects the single-inheritance object-oriented methodology of IL, and resembles Figure 1-1.

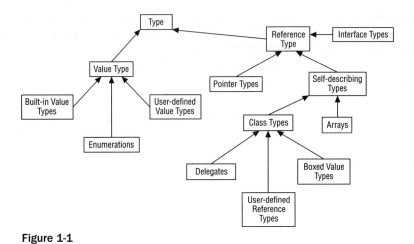

Figure 1-1

The following table explains the types shown in Figure 1-1.

Type	Meaning
Type	Base class that represents any type.
Value Type	Base class that represents any value type.
Reference Types	Any data types that are accessed through a reference and stored on the heap.
Built-in Value Types	Includes most of the standard primitive types, which represent numbers, Boolean values, or characters.
Enumerations	Sets of enumerated values.
User-defined Value Types	Types that have been defined in source code and are stored as value types. In C# terms, this means any struct.
Interface Types	Interfaces.
Pointer Types	Pointers.
Self-describing Types	Data types that provide information about themselves for the benefit of the garbage collector (see the next section).
Arrays	Any type that contains an array of objects.
Class Types	Types that are self-describing but are not arrays.
Delegates	Types that are designed to hold references to methods.
User-defined Reference Types	Types that have been defined in source code and are stored as reference types. In C# terms, this means any class.
Boxed Value Types	A value type that is temporarily wrapped in a reference so that it can be stored on the heap.

We will not list all of the built-in value types here, because they are covered in detail in Chapter 3, "Objects and Types." In C#, each predefined type recognized by the compiler maps onto one of the IL built-in types. The same is true in Visual Basic 2008.

Common Language Specification

The *Common Language Specification* (CLS) works with the CTS to ensure language interoperability. The CLS is a set of minimum standards that all compilers targeting .NET must support. Because IL is a very rich language, writers of most compilers will prefer to restrict the capabilities of a given compiler to support only a subset of the facilities offered by IL and the CTS. That is fine, as long as the compiler supports everything that is defined in the CLS.

> *It is perfectly acceptable to write non-CLS-compliant code. However, if you do, the compiled IL code is not guaranteed to be fully language interoperable.*

For example, take case sensitivity. IL is case sensitive. Developers who work with case-sensitive languages regularly take advantage of the flexibility that this case sensitivity gives them when selecting variable names. Visual Basic 2008, however, is not case sensitive. The CLS works around this by indicating that CLS-compliant code should not expose any two names that differ only in their case. Therefore, Visual Basic 2008 code can work with CLS-compliant code.

This example shows that the CLS works in two ways. First, it means that individual compilers do not have to be powerful enough to support the full features of .NET — this should encourage the development of compilers for other programming languages that target .NET. Second, it provides a guarantee that, if you restrict your classes to exposing only CLS-compliant features, then code written in any other compliant language can use your classes.

The beauty of this idea is that the restriction to using CLS-compliant features applies only to public and protected members of classes and public classes. Within the private implementations of your classes, you can write whatever non-CLS code you want, because code in other assemblies (units of managed code; see later in this chapter) cannot access this part of your code anyway.

We will not go into the details of the CLS specifications here. In general, the CLS will not affect your C# code very much because there are very few non-CLS-compliant features of C# anyway.

Garbage Collection

The *garbage collector* is .NET's answer to memory management and in particular to the question of what to do about reclaiming memory that running applications ask for. Up until now, two techniques have been used on the Windows platform for de-allocating memory that processes have dynamically requested from the system:

❑   Make the application code do it all manually.

❑   Make objects maintain reference counts.

Having the application code responsible for deallocating memory is the technique used by lower-level, high-performance languages such as C++. It is efficient, and it has the advantage that (in general) resources are never occupied for longer than necessary. The big disadvantage, however, is the frequency of bugs. Code that requests memory also should explicitly inform the system when it no longer requires that memory. However, it is easy to overlook this, resulting in memory leaks.

Although modern developer environments do provide tools to assist in detecting memory leaks, they remain difficult bugs to track down. That's because they have no effect until so much memory has been leaked that Windows refuses to grant any more to the process. By this point, the entire computer may have appreciably slowed down due to the memory demands being made on it.

Maintaining reference counts is favored in COM. The idea is that each COM component maintains a count of how many clients are currently maintaining references to it. When this count falls to zero, the component can destroy itself and free up associated memory and resources. The problem with this is that it still relies on the good behavior of clients to notify the component that they have finished with it. It takes only one client not to do so, and the object sits in memory. In some ways, this is a potentially more serious problem than a simple C++-style memory leak because the COM object may exist in its own process, which means that it will never be removed by the system. (At least with C++ memory leaks, the system can reclaim all memory when the process terminates.)

The .NET runtime relies on the garbage collector instead. The purpose of this program is to clean up memory. The idea is that all dynamically requested memory is allocated on the heap (that is true for all languages, although in the case of .NET, the CLR maintains its own managed heap for .NET applications to use). Every so often, when .NET detects that the managed heap for a given process is becoming full and therefore needs tidying up, it calls the garbage collector. The garbage collector runs through variables currently in scope in your code, examining references to objects stored on the heap to identify which ones are accessible from your code — that is, which objects have references that refer to them. Any objects that are not referred to are deemed to be no longer accessible from your code and can therefore be removed. Java uses a system of garbage collection similar to this.

Garbage collection works in .NET because IL has been designed to facilitate the process. The principle requires that you cannot get references to existing objects other than by copying existing references and that IL be type safe. In this context, what we mean is that if any reference to an object exists, then there is sufficient information in the reference to exactly determine the type of the object.

It would not be possible to use the garbage collection mechanism with a language such as unmanaged C++, for example, because C++ allows pointers to be freely cast between types.

One important aspect of garbage collection is that it is not deterministic. In other words, you cannot guarantee when the garbage collector will be called; it will be called when the CLR decides that it is needed, though it is also possible to override this process and call up the garbage collector in your code.

Security

.NET can really excel in terms of complementing the security mechanisms provided by Windows because it can offer code-based security, whereas Windows really offers only role-based security.

Role-based security is based on the identity of the account under which the process is running (that is, who owns and is running the process). *Code-based security*, by contrast, is based on what the code actually does and on how much the code is trusted. Thanks to the strong type safety of IL, the CLR is able to inspect code before running it to determine required security permissions. .NET also offers a mechanism by which code can indicate in advance what security permissions it will require to run.

The importance of code-based security is that it reduces the risks associated with running code of dubious origin (such as code that you have downloaded from the Internet). For example, even if code is running under the administrator account, it is possible to use code-based security to indicate that that code should still not be permitted to perform certain types of operations that the administrator account would normally be allowed to do, such as read or write to environment variables, read or write to the registry, or access the .NET reflection features.

Security issues are covered in more depth in Chapter 20, "Security."

Application Domains

Application domains are an important innovation in .NET and are designed to ease the overhead involved when running applications that need to be isolated from each other but that also need to be able to communicate with each other. The classic example of this is a Web server application, which may be simultaneously responding to a number of browser requests. It will, therefore, probably have a number of instances of the component responsible for servicing those requests running simultaneously.

In pre-.NET days, the choice would be between allowing those instances to share a process (with the resultant risk of a problem in one running instance bringing the whole Web site down) or isolating those instances in separate processes (with the associated performance overhead).

Up until now, the only means of isolating code has been through processes. When you start a new application, it runs within the context of a process. Windows isolates processes from each other through address spaces. The idea is that each process has available 4GB of virtual memory in which to store its data and executable code (4GB is for 32-bit systems; 64-bit systems use more memory). Windows imposes an extra level of indirection by which this virtual memory maps into a particular area of actual physical memory or disk space. Each process gets a different mapping, with no overlap between the actual physical memories that the blocks of virtual address space map to (see Figure 1-2).

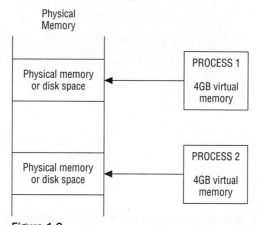

Figure 1-2

In general, any process is able to access memory only by specifying an address in virtual memory — processes do not have direct access to physical memory. Hence, it is simply impossible for one process to access the memory allocated to another process. This provides an excellent guarantee that any badly behaved code will not be able to damage anything outside of its own address space. (Note that on Windows 95/98, these safeguards are not quite as thorough as they are on Windows NT/2000/ XP/2003/Vista, so the theoretical possibility exists of applications crashing Windows by writing to inappropriate memory.)

Processes do not just serve as a way to isolate instances of running code from each other. On Windows NT/2000/XP/2003/Vista systems, they also form the unit to which security privileges and permissions are assigned. Each process has its own security token, which indicates to Windows precisely what operations that process is permitted to do.

Although processes are great for security reasons, their big disadvantage is in the area of performance. Often, a number of processes will actually be working together, and therefore need to communicate with each other. The obvious example of this is where a process calls up a COM component, which is an executable and therefore is required to run in its own process. The same thing happens in COM when surrogates are used. Because processes cannot share any memory, a complex marshaling process must be used to copy data between the processes. This results in a very significant performance hit. If you need components to work together and do not want that performance hit, you must use DLL-based components and have everything running in the same address space — with the associated risk that a badly behaved component will bring everything else down.

Application domains are designed as a way of separating components without resulting in the performance problems associated with passing data between processes. The idea is that any one process is divided into a number of application domains. Each application domain roughly corresponds to a single application, and each thread of execution will be running in a particular application domain (see Figure 1-3).

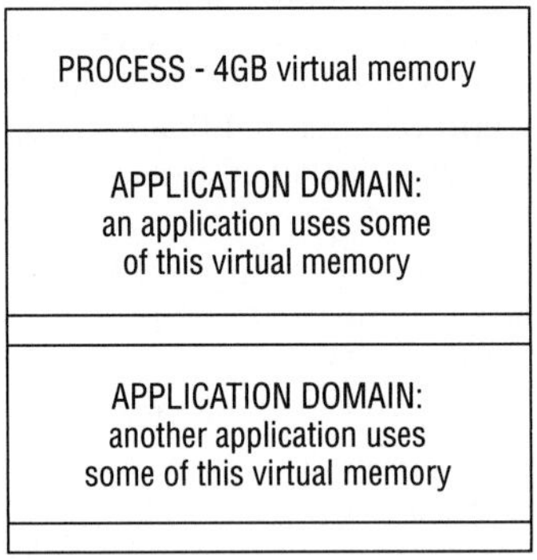

```
┌──────────────────────────────────────┐
│  PROCESS - 4GB virtual memory         │
│                                        │
│  ┌──────────────────────────────────┐ │
│  │  APPLICATION DOMAIN:             │ │
│  │  an application uses some        │ │
│  │  of this virtual memory          │ │
│  └──────────────────────────────────┘ │
│                                        │
│  ┌──────────────────────────────────┐ │
│  │  APPLICATION DOMAIN:             │ │
│  │  another application uses        │ │
│  │  some of this virtual memory     │ │
│  └──────────────────────────────────┘ │
│                                        │
└──────────────────────────────────────┘
```

Figure 1-3

If different executables are running in the same process space, then they are clearly able to easily share data, because, theoretically, they can directly see each other's data. However, although this is possible in principle, the CLR makes sure that this does not happen in practice by inspecting the code for each running application to ensure that the code cannot stray outside of its own data areas. This looks, at first, like an almost impossible task to pull off — after all, how can you tell what the program is going to do without actually running it?

In fact, it is usually possible to do this because of the strong type safety of the IL. In most cases, unless code is using unsafe features such as pointers, the data types it is using will ensure that memory is not accessed inappropriately. For example, .NET array types perform bounds checking to ensure that no out-of-bounds array operations are permitted. If a running application does need to communicate or share data with other applications running in different application domains, it must do so by calling on .NET's remoting services.

Code that has been verified to check that it cannot access data outside its application domain (other than through the explicit remoting mechanism) is said to be *memory type safe*. Such code can safely be run alongside other type-safe code in different application domains within the same process.

Error Handling with Exceptions

The .NET Framework is designed to facilitate handling of error conditions using the same mechanism, based on exceptions, that is employed by Java and C++. C++ developers should note that because of IL's stronger typing system, there is no performance penalty associated with the use of exceptions with IL in the way that there is in C++. Also, the `finally` block, which has long been on many C++ developers' wish lists, is supported by .NET and by C#.

Exceptions are covered in detail in Chapter 14, "Errors and Exceptions." Briefly, the idea is that certain areas of code are designated as exception handler routines, with each one able to deal with a particular error condition (for example, a file not being found, or being denied permission to perform some operation). These conditions can be defined as narrowly or as widely as you want. The exception architecture ensures that when an error condition occurs, execution can immediately jump to the exception handler routine that is most specifically geared to handle the exception condition in question.

The architecture of exception handling also provides a convenient means to pass an object containing precise details of the exception condition to an exception handling routine. This object might include an appropriate message for the user and details of exactly where in the code the exception was detected.

Most exception-handling architecture, including the control of program flow when an exception occurs, is handled by the high-level languages (C#, Visual Basic 2008, C++), and is not supported by any special IL commands. C#, for example, handles exceptions using `try{}`, `catch{}`, and `finally{}` blocks of code. (For more details, see Chapter 14.)

What .NET does do, however, is provide the infrastructure to allow compilers that target .NET to support exception handling. In particular, it provides a set of .NET classes that can represent the exceptions, and the language interoperability to allow the thrown exception objects to be interpreted by the exception-handling code, regardless of what language the exception-handling code is written in. This language independence is absent from both the C++ and Java implementations of exception handling, although it is present to a limited extent in the COM mechanism for handling errors, which involves returning error codes from methods and passing error objects around. The fact that exceptions are handled consistently in different languages is a crucial aspect of facilitating multi-language development.

Use of Attributes

Attributes are familiar to developers who use C++ to write COM components (through their use in Microsoft's COM Interface Definition Language [IDL]). The initial idea of an attribute was that it provided extra information concerning some item in the program that could be used by the compiler.

Attributes are supported in .NET — and hence now by C++, C#, and Visual Basic 2008. What is, however, particularly innovative about attributes in .NET is that you can define your own custom attributes in your source code. These user-defined attributes will be placed with the metadata for the corresponding data types or methods. This can be useful for documentation purposes, in which they can be used in conjunction with reflection technology to perform programming tasks based on attributes. In addition, in common with the .NET philosophy of language independence, attributes can be defined in source code in one language and read by code that is written in another language.

Attributes are covered in Chapter 13, "Reflection."

Assemblies

An *assembly* is the logical unit that contains compiled code targeted at the .NET Framework. Assemblies are not covered in detail in this chapter because they are covered thoroughly in Chapter 17, "Assemblies," but we summarize the main points here.

An assembly is completely self-describing and is a logical rather than a physical unit, which means that it can be stored across more than one file (indeed, dynamic assemblies are stored in memory, not on file at all). If an assembly is stored in more than one file, there will be one main file that contains the entry point and describes the other files in the assembly.

Note that the same assembly structure is used for both executable code and library code. The only real difference is that an executable assembly contains a main program entry point, whereas a library assembly does not.

An important characteristic of assemblies is that they contain metadata that describes the types and methods defined in the corresponding code. An assembly, however, also contains assembly metadata that describes the assembly itself. This assembly metadata, contained in an area known as the *manifest*, allows checks to be made on the version of the assembly, and on its integrity.

> `ildasm`, *a Windows-based utility, can be used to inspect the contents of an assembly, including the manifest and metadata.* `ildasm` *is discussed in Chapter 17, "Assemblies."*

The fact that an assembly contains program metadata means that applications or other assemblies that call up code in a given assembly do not need to refer to the registry, or to any other data source, to find out how to use that assembly. This is a significant break from the old COM way of doing things, in which the GUIDs of the components and interfaces had to be obtained from the registry, and in some cases, the details of the methods and properties exposed would need to be read from a type library.

Having data spread out in up to three different locations meant there was the obvious risk of something getting out of synchronization, which would prevent other software from being able to use the component successfully. With assemblies, there is no risk of this happening, because all the metadata is stored with the program executable instructions. Note that even though assemblies are stored across several files, there are still no problems with data going out of synchronization. This is because the file that contains the assembly entry point also stores details of, and a hash of, the contents of the other files, which means that if one of the files gets replaced, or in any way tampered with, this will almost certainly be detected and the assembly will refuse to load.

Assemblies come in two types: *private* and *shared* assemblies.

Private Assemblies

Private assemblies are the simplest type. They normally ship with software and are intended to be used only with that software. The usual scenario in which you will ship private assemblies is when you are supplying an application in the form of an executable and a number of libraries, where the libraries contain code that should be used only with that application.

The system guarantees that private assemblies will not be used by other software because an application may load only private assemblies that are located in the same folder that the main executable is loaded in, or in a subfolder of it.

Because you would normally expect that commercial software would always be installed in its own directory, there is no risk of one software package overwriting, modifying, or accidentally loading private assemblies intended for another package. And, because private assemblies can be used only by the software package that they are intended for, you have much more control over what software uses them. There is, therefore, less need to take security precautions because there is no risk, for example, of some other commercial software overwriting one of your assemblies with some new version of it (apart from software that is designed specifically to perform malicious damage). There are also no problems with name collisions. If classes in your private assembly happen to have the same name as classes in someone else's private assembly, that does not matter, because any given application will be able to see only the one set of private assemblies.

Because a private assembly is entirely self-contained, the process of deploying it is simple. You simply place the appropriate file(s) in the appropriate folder in the file system (no registry entries need to be made). This process is known as *zero impact (xcopy) installation*.

Shared Assemblies

Shared assemblies are intended to be common libraries that any other application can use. Because any other software can access a shared assembly, more precautions need to be taken against the following risks:

❑ Name collisions, where another company's shared assembly implements types that have the same names as those in your shared assembly. Because client code can theoretically have access to both assemblies simultaneously, this could be a serious problem.

❑ The risk of an assembly being overwritten by a different version of the same assembly — the new version being incompatible with some existing client code.

The solution to these problems is placing shared assemblies in a special directory subtree in the file system, known as the *global assembly cache* (GAC). Unlike with private assemblies, this cannot be done by simply copying the assembly into the appropriate folder — it needs to be specifically installed into the cache. This process can be performed by a number of .NET utilities and requires certain checks on the assembly, as well as the set up of a small folder hierarchy within the assembly cache that is used to ensure assembly integrity.

To prevent name collisions, shared assemblies are given a name based on private key cryptography (private assemblies are simply given the same name as their main file name). This name is known as a *strong name*; it is guaranteed to be unique and must be quoted by applications that reference a shared assembly.

Problems associated with the risk of overwriting an assembly are addressed by specifying version information in the assembly manifest and by allowing side-by-side installations.

Reflection

Because assemblies store metadata, including details of all the types and members of these types that are defined in the assembly, it is possible to access this metadata programmatically. Full details of this are given in Chapter 13, "Reflection." This technique, known as *reflection*, raises interesting possibilities, because it means that managed code can actually examine other managed code, and can even examine itself, to determine information about that code. This is most commonly used to obtain the details of attributes, although you can also use reflection, among other purposes, as an indirect way of instantiating classes or calling methods, given the names of those classes or methods as strings. In this way, you could select classes to instantiate methods to call at runtime, rather than at compile time, based on user input (dynamic binding).

.NET Framework Classes

Perhaps one of the biggest benefits of writing managed code, at least from a developer's point of view, is that you get to use the .NET *base class library*.

The .NET base classes are a massive collection of managed code classes that allow you to do almost any of the tasks that were previously available through the Windows API. These classes follow the same object model that IL uses, based on single inheritance. This means that you can either instantiate objects of whichever .NET base class is appropriate or derive your own classes from them.

The great thing about the .NET base classes is that they have been designed to be very intuitive and easy to use. For example, to start a thread, you call the `Start()` method of the `Thread` class. To disable a `TextBox`, you set the `Enabled` property of a `TextBox` object to `false`. This approach — though familiar to Visual Basic and Java developers, whose respective libraries are just as easy to use — will be a welcome relief to C++ developers, who for years have had to cope with such API functions as `GetDIBits()`, `RegisterWndClassEx()`, and `IsEqualIID()`, as well as a whole plethora of functions that required Windows handles to be passed around.

However, C++ developers always had easy access to the entire Windows API, unlike Visual Basic 6 and Java developers who were more restricted in terms of the basic operating system functionality that they have access to from their respective languages. What is new about the .NET base classes is that they combine the ease of use that was typical of the Visual Basic and Java libraries with the relatively comprehensive coverage of the Windows API functions. Many features of Windows still are not available through the base classes, and for those you will need to call into the API functions, but in general, these are now confined to the more exotic features. For everyday use, you will probably find the base classes adequate. Moreover, if you do need to call into an API function, .NET offers a so-called *platform-invoke* that ensures data types are correctly converted, so the task is no harder than calling the function directly from C++ code would have been — regardless of whether you are coding in C#, C++, or Visual Basic 2008.

> *WinCV, a Windows-based utility, can be used to browse the classes, structs, interfaces, and enums in the base class library. WinCV is discussed in Chapter 15, "Visual Studio 2008."*

Although Chapter 3 is nominally dedicated to the subject of base classes, once we have completed our coverage of the syntax of the C# language, most of the rest of this book shows you how to use various classes within the .NET base class library for the .NET Framework 3.5. That is how comprehensive base classes are. As a rough guide, the areas covered by the .NET 3.5 base classes include:

- ❏ Core features provided by IL (including the primitive data types in the CTS discussed in Chapter 3, "Objects and Types")

- ❏ Windows GUI support and controls (see Chapters 31, "Windows Forms," and 34, "Windows Presentation Foundation")

- ❏ Web Forms (ASP.NET, discussed in Chapters 37, "ASP.NET Pages" and 38, "ASP.NET Development")

- ❏ Data access (ADO.NET; see Chapters 26, "Data Access," 30, ".NET Programming with SQL Server," 27 and 29, "LINQ to SQL" and "LINQ to XML" and 28, "Manipulating XML")

- ❏ Directory access (see Chapter 46, "Directory Services")

- ❏ File system and registry access (see Chapter 25, "Manipulating Files and the Registry")

- ❏ Networking and Web browsing (see Chapter 41, "Accessing the Internet")

- ❏ .NET attributes and reflection (see Chapter 13, "Reflection")

- ❏ Access to aspects of the Windows OS (environment variables and so on; see Chapter 20, "Security")

- ❏ COM interoperability (see Chapters 44, "Enterprise Services" and 24, "Interoperability")

Incidentally, according to Microsoft sources, a large proportion of the .NET base classes have actually been written in C#!

Namespaces

Namespaces are the way that .NET avoids name clashes between classes. They are designed to prevent situations in which you define a class to represent a customer, name your class `Customer`, and then someone else does the same thing (a likely scenario — the proportion of businesses that have customers seems to be quite high).

A namespace is no more than a grouping of data types, but it has the effect that the names of all data types within a namespace are automatically prefixed with the name of the namespace. It is also possible to nest namespaces within each other. For example, most of the general-purpose .NET base classes are in a namespace called `System`. The base class `Array` is in this namespace, so its full name is `System.Array`.

.NET requires all types to be defined in a namespace; for example, you could place your `Customer` class in a namespace called `YourCompanyName`. This class would have the full name `YourCompanyName .Customer`.

> *If a namespace is not explicitly supplied, the type will be added to a nameless global namespace.*

Microsoft recommends that for most purposes you supply at least two nested namespace names: the first one represents the name of your company, and the second one represents the name of the technology or software package of which the class is a member, such as `YourCompanyName.SalesServices.Customer`.

This protects, in most situations, the classes in your application from possible name clashes with classes written by other organizations.

Chapter 2, "C# Basics," looks more closely at namespaces.

Creating .NET Applications Using C#

C# can also be used to create console applications: text-only applications that run in a DOS window. You will probably use console applications when unit testing class libraries, and for creating UNIX or Linux daemon processes. More often, however, you will use C# to create applications that use many of the technologies associated with .NET. This section gives you an overview of the different types of applications that you can write in C#.

Creating ASP.NET Applications

Active Server Pages (ASP) is a Microsoft technology for creating Web pages with dynamic content. An ASP page is basically an HTML file with embedded chunks of server-side VBScript or JavaScript. When a client browser requests an ASP page, the Web server delivers the HTML portions of the page, processing the server-side scripts as it comes to them. Often these scripts query a database for data and mark up that data in HTML. ASP is an easy way for clients to build browser-based applications.

However, ASP is not without its shortcomings. First, ASP pages sometimes render slowly because the server-side code is interpreted instead of compiled. Second, ASP files can be difficult to maintain because they are unstructured; the server-side ASP code and plain HTML are all jumbled up together. Third, ASP sometimes makes development difficult because there is little support for error handling and type-checking. Specifically, if you are using VBScript and want to implement error handling in your pages, you must use the On Error Resume Next statement, and follow every component call with a check to Err.Number to make sure that the call has gone well.

ASP.NET is a complete revision of ASP that fixes many of its problems. It does not replace ASP; rather, ASP.NET pages can live side by side on the same server with legacy ASP applications. Of course, you can also program ASP.NET with C#!

The following section explores the key features of ASP.NET. For more details, refer to Chapters 37, "ASP. NET Pages," 38, "ASP.NET Development," and 39, "ASP.NET AJAX."

Features of ASP.NET

First, and perhaps most important, ASP.NET pages are *structured*. That is, each page is effectively a class that inherits from the .NET System.Web.UI.Page *class* and can override a set of methods that are evoked during the Page object's lifetime. (You can think of these events as page-specific cousins of the OnApplication_Start and OnSession_Start events that went in the global.asa files of plain old ASP.) Because you can factor a page's functionality into event handlers with explicit meanings, ASP.NET pages are easier to understand.

Another nice thing about ASP.NET pages is that you can create them in Visual Studio 2008, the same environment in which you create the business logic and data access components that those ASP.NET pages use. A Visual Studio 2008 project, or *solution*, contains all of the files associated with an application. Moreover, you can debug your classic ASP pages in the editor as well; in the old days of Visual InterDev, it was often a vexing challenge to configure InterDev and the project's Web server to turn debugging on.

For maximum clarity, the ASP.NET code-behind feature lets you take the structured approach even further. ASP.NET allows you to isolate the server-side functionality of a page to a class, compile that class into a DLL, and place that DLL into a directory below the HTML portion. A code-behind directive at the top of the page associates the file with its DLL. When a browser requests the page, the Web server fires the events in the class in the page's code-behind DLL.

Last, but not least, ASP.NET is remarkable for its increased performance. Whereas classic ASP pages are interpreted with each page request, the Web server caches ASP.NET pages after compilation. This means that subsequent requests of an ASP.NET page execute more quickly than the first.

ASP.NET also makes it easy to write pages that cause forms to be displayed by the browser, which you might use in an intranet environment. The traditional wisdom is that form-based applications offer a richer user interface but are harder to maintain because they run on so many different machines. For this reason, people have relied on form-based applications when rich user interfaces were a necessity and extensive support could be provided to the users.

Web Forms

To make Web page construction even easier, Visual Studio 2008 supplies *Web Forms*. They allow you to build ASP.NET pages graphically in the same way that Visual Basic 6 or C++ Builder windows are created; in other words, by dragging controls from a toolbox onto a form, then flipping over to the code aspect of that form and writing event handlers for the controls. When you use C# to create a Web Form, you are creating a C# class that inherits from the Page base class and an ASP.NET page that designates that class as its code behind. Of course, you do not have to use C# to create a Web Form; you can use Visual Basic 2008 or another .NET-compliant language just as well.

In the past, the difficulty of Web development discouraged some teams from attempting it. To succeed in Web development, you needed to know so many different technologies, such as VBScript, ASP, DHTML, JavaScript, and so on. By applying the Form concepts to Web pages, Web Forms have made Web development considerably easier.

Web Server Controls

The controls used to populate a Web Form are not controls in the same sense as ActiveX controls. Rather, they are XML tags in the ASP.NET namespace that the Web browser dynamically transforms into HTML and client-side script when a page is requested. Amazingly, the Web server is able to render the same server-side control in different ways, producing a transformation appropriate to the requestor's particular Web browser. This means that it is now easy to write fairly sophisticated user interfaces for Web pages, without worrying about how to ensure that your page will run on any of the available browsers — because Web Forms will take care of that for you.

You can use C# or Visual Basic 2008 to expand the Web Form toolbox. Creating a new server-side control is simply a matter of implementing .NET's `System.Web.UI.WebControls.WebControl` class.

XML Web Services

Today, HTML pages account for most of the traffic on the World Wide Web. With XML, however, computers have a device-independent format to use for communicating with each other on the Web. In the future, computers may use the Web and XML to communicate information rather than dedicated lines and proprietary formats such as *Electronic Data Interchange* (EDI). XML Web services are designed for a service-oriented Web, in which remote computers provide each other with dynamic information that can be analyzed and reformatted, before final presentation to a user. An XML Web service is an easy way for a computer to expose information to other computers on the Web in the form of XML.

In technical terms, an XML Web service on .NET is an ASP.NET page that returns XML instead of HTML to requesting clients. Such pages have a `code-behind` DLL containing a class that derives from the `WebService` class. The Visual Studio 2008 IDE provides an engine that facilitates Web service development.

An organization might choose to use XML Web services for two main reasons. The first reason is that they rely on HTTP; XML Web services can use existing networks (HTTP) as a medium for conveying information. The other is that because XML Web services use XML, the data format is self-describing, nonproprietary, and platform-independent.

Creating Windows Forms

Although C# and .NET are particularly suited to Web development, they still offer splendid support for so-called *fat-client* or *thick-client* apps — applications that must be installed on the end user's machine where most of the processing takes place. This support is from *Windows Forms*.

A Windows Form is the .NET answer to a Visual Basic 6 Form. To design a graphical window interface, you just drag controls from a toolbox onto a Windows Form. To determine the window's behavior, you write event-handling routines for the form's controls. A Windows Form project compiles to an executable that must be installed alongside the .NET runtime on the end user's computer. Like other .NET project types, Windows Form projects are supported by both Visual Basic 2008 and C#. Chapter 31, "Windows Forms," examines Windows Forms more closely.

Using the Windows Presentation Foundation (WPF)

One of the newest technologies to hit the block is the *Windows Presentation Foundation* (WPF). WPF makes use of XAML in building applications. XAML stands for Extensible Application Markup Language. This new way of creating applications within a Microsoft environment is something that was introduced in 2006 and is part of the .NET Framework 3.0 and 3.5. This means that to run any WPF application, you need to make sure that the .NET Framework 3.0 or 3.5 is installed on the client machine. WPF applications are available for Windows Vista, Windows XP, Windows Server 2003, and Windows Server 2008 (the only operating systems that allow for the installation of the .NET Framework 3.0 or 3.5).

XAML is the XML declaration that is used to create a form that represents all the visual aspects and behaviors of the WPF application. Though it is possible to work with a WPF application programmatically, WPF is a step in the direction of declarative programming, which the industry is moving to. Declarative programming means that instead of creating objects through programming in a compiled language such as C#, VB, or Java, you declare everything through XML-type programming. Chapter 34, "Windows Presentation Foundation" details how to build these new types of applications using XAML and C#.

Windows Controls

Although Web Forms and Windows Forms are developed in much the same way, you use different kinds of controls to populate them. Web Forms use Web server controls, and Windows Forms use *Windows Controls*.

A Windows Control is a lot like an ActiveX control. After a Windows Control is implemented, it compiles to a DLL that must be installed on the client's machine. In fact, the .NET SDK provides a utility that creates a wrapper for ActiveX controls, so that they can be placed on Windows Forms. As is the case with Web Controls, Windows Control creation involves deriving from a particular class, `System.Windows .Forms.Control`.

Windows Services

A Windows Service (originally called an NT Service) is a program designed to run in the background in Windows NT/2000/XP/2003/Vista (but not Windows 9x). Services are useful when you want a program to be running continuously and ready to respond to events without having been explicitly started by the user. A good example is the World Wide Web Service on Web servers, which listens for Web requests from clients.

It is very easy to write services in C#. .NET Framework base classes are available in the `System .ServiceProcess` namespace that handles many of the boilerplate tasks associated with services. In addition, Visual Studio .NET allows you to create a C# Windows Service project, which uses C# source code for a basic Windows Service. Chapter 23, "Windows Services," explores how to write C# Windows Services.

Windows Communication Foundation (WCF)

Looking at how you move data and services from one point to another using Microsoft-based technologies, you will find that there are a lot of choices at your disposal. For instance, you can use ASP.NET Web services, .NET Remoting, Enterprise Services, and MSMQ for starters. What technology should you use? Well, it really comes down to what you are trying to achieve, because each technology is better used in a particular situation.

With that in mind, Microsoft brought all of these technologies together, and with the release of the .NET Framework 3.0 as well as its inclusion in the .NET Framework 3.5, you now have a single way to move data — the *Windows Communication Foundation* (WCF). WCF provides you with the ability to build your service one time and then expose this service in a multitude of ways (under different protocols even) by just making changes within a configuration file. You will find that WCF is a powerful new way of connecting disparate systems. Chapter 42, "Windows Communication Foundation," covers this in detail.

The Role of C# in the .NET Enterprise Architecture

C# requires the presence of the .NET runtime, and it will probably be a few years before most clients — particularly most home computers — have .NET installed. In the meantime, installing a C# application is likely to mean also installing the .NET redistributable components. Because of that, it is likely that we will see many C# applications first in the enterprise environment. Indeed, C# arguably presents an outstanding opportunity for organizations that are interested in building robust, *n*-tiered client-server applications.

When combined with ADO.NET, C# has the ability to access quickly and generically data stores such as SQL Server and Oracle databases. The returned datasets can easily be manipulated using the ADO.NET object model or LINQ, and automatically render as XML for transport across an office intranet.

Once a database schema has been established for a new project, C# presents an excellent medium for implementing a layer of data access objects, each of which could provide insertion, updates, and deletion access to a different database table.

Because it's the first component-based C language, C# is a great language for implementing a business object tier, too. It encapsulates the messy plumbing for intercomponent communication, leaving developers free to focus on gluing their data access objects together in methods that accurately enforce their organizations' business rules. Moreover, with attributes, C# business objects can be outfitted for method-level security checks, object pooling, and JIT activation supplied by COM+ Services. Furthermore, .NET ships with utility programs that allow your new .NET business objects to interface with legacy COM components.

To create an enterprise application with C#, you create a Class Library project for the data access objects and another for the business objects. While developing, you can use Console projects to test the methods on your classes. Fans of extreme programming can build Console projects that can be executed automatically from batch files to unit test that working code has not been broken.

On a related note, C# and .NET will probably influence the way you physically package your reusable classes. In the past, many developers crammed a multitude of classes into a single physical component because this arrangement made deployment a lot easier; if there was a versioning problem, you knew just where to look. Because deploying .NET enterprise components involves simply copying files into directories, developers can now package their classes into more logical, discrete components without encountering "DLL Hell."

Last, but not least, ASP.NET pages coded in C# constitute an excellent medium for user interfaces. Because ASP.NET pages compile, they execute quickly. Because they can be debugged in the Visual Studio 2008 IDE, they are robust. Because they support full-scale language features such as early binding, inheritance, and modularization, ASP.NET pages coded in C# are tidy and easily maintained.

Seasoned developers acquire a healthy skepticism about strongly hyped new technologies and languages and are reluctant to use new platforms simply because they are urged to. If you are an enterprise developer in an IT department, though, or if you provide application services across the World Wide Web, let us assure you that C# and .NET offer at least four solid benefits, even if some of the more exotic features like XML Web services and server-side controls don't pan out:

❑ Component conflicts will become infrequent and deployment is easier because different versions of the same component can run side by side on the same machine without conflicting.

❑ Your ASP.NET code will not look like spaghetti code.

❑ You can leverage a lot of the functionality in the .NET base classes.

❑ For applications requiring a Windows Forms user interface, C# makes it very easy to write this kind of application.

Windows Forms have, to some extent, been downplayed due to the advent of Web Forms and Internet-based applications. However, if you or your colleagues lack expertise in JavaScript, ASP, or related technologies, Windows Forms are still a viable option for creating a user interface with speed and ease. Just remember to factor your code so that the user interface logic is separate from the business logic and the data access code. Doing so will allow you to migrate your application to the browser at some point in the future if you need to. In addition, it is likely that Windows Forms will remain the dominant user interface for applications for use in homes and small businesses for a long time to come. In addition to this, the new smart client features of Windows Forms (the ability to easily work in an online/offline mode) will bring a new round of exciting applications.

Summary

This chapter has covered a lot of ground, briefly reviewing important aspects of the .NET Framework and C#'s relationship to it. It started by discussing how all languages that target .NET are compiled into Microsoft Intermediate Language (IL) before this is compiled and executed by the Common Language Runtime (CLR). This chapter also discussed the roles of the following features of .NET in the compilation and execution process:

❑ Assemblies and .NET base classes

❑ COM components

❑ JIT compilation

❑ Application domains

❑ Garbage collection

Figure 1-4 provides an overview of how these features come into play during compilation and execution.

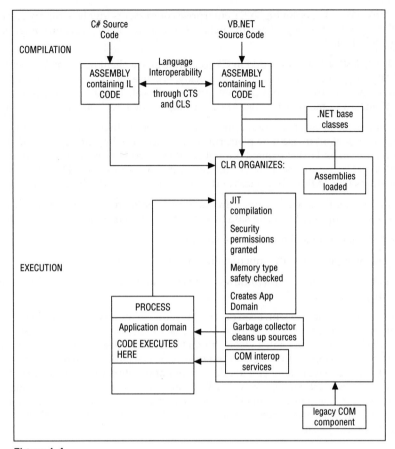

Figure 1-4

You learned about the characteristics of IL, particularly its strong data typing and object orientation, and how these characteristics influence the languages that target .NET, including C#. You also learned how the strongly typed nature of IL enables language interoperability, as well as CLR services such as garbage collection and security. There was also a focus on the Common Language Specification (CLS) and the Common Type System (CTS) to help deal with language interoperability.

Finally, you learned how C# could be used as the basis for applications that are built on several .NET technologies, including ASP.NET.

Chapter 2 discusses how to write code in C#.

2

C# Basics

Now that you understand more about what C# can do, you will want to learn how to use it. This chapter gives you a good start in that direction by providing you with a basic knowledge of the fundamentals of C# programming, which is built on in subsequent chapters. The main topics covered are:

- ❑ Declaring variables

- ❑ Initialization and scope of variables

- ❑ Predefined C# data types

- ❑ Dictating the flow of execution within a C# program using loops and conditional statements

- ❑ Enumerations

- ❑ Namespaces

- ❑ The `Main()` method

- ❑ Basic command-line C# compiler options

- ❑ Using `System.Console` to perform console I/O

- ❑ Using comments and documentation features

- ❑ Preprocessor directives

- ❑ Guidelines and conventions for good programming in C#

By the end of this chapter, you will know enough C# to write simple programs, though without using inheritance or other object-oriented features, which are covered in later chapters.

Before We Start

As already mentioned, C# is an object-oriented language. Throughout this chapter and later chapters, we assume that you have a good grasp of the concepts behind object-oriented (OO) programming. In other words, we expect that you understand what we mean by *classes*, *objects*, *interfaces*, and *inheritance*. If you have programmed in C++ or Java before, you should have a pretty good grounding in object-oriented programming (OOP). However, if you do not have a background in OOP, you may find it helpful to familiarize yourself with OOP basics before continuing.

In this chapter, we make many comparisons among C#, C++, Java, and Visual Basic 6 as we walk through the basics of C#. If you are an experienced developer in these programs, you might prefer to read a comparison between C# and your selected language before reading this chapter. If so, we have made introductions to C# from the point of view of each of these languages available in Appendix B.

Your First C# Program

Let's start by compiling and running the simplest possible C# program — a simple class consisting of a console application that writes a message to the screen.

> *Later chapters present a number of code samples. The most common technique for writing C# programs is to use Visual Studio 2008 to generate a basic project and add your own code to it. However, because the aim of these early chapters is to teach the C# language, we are going to keep things simple and avoid relying on Visual Studio 2008 until Chapter 15, "Visual Studio 2008." Instead, we will present the code as simple files that you can type in using any text editor and compile from the command line.*

The Code

Type the following into a text editor (such as Notepad), and save it with a `.cs` extension (for example, `First.cs`). The `Main()` method is shown here:

```
using System;

namespace Wrox.ProCSharp.Basics
{
    class MyFirstCSharpClass
    {
        static void Main()
        {
            Console.WriteLine("This isn't at all like Java!");
            Console.ReadLine();
            return;
        }
    }
}
```

Compiling and Running the Program

You can compile this program by simply running the C# command-line compiler (`csc.exe`) against the source file, like this:

```
csc First.cs
```

If you want to compile code from the command line using the `csc` command, you should be aware that the .NET command-line tools, including `csc`, are available only if certain environment variables have been set up. Depending on how you installed .NET (and Visual Studio 2008), this may or may not be the case on your machine.

If you do not have the environment variables set up, you have the following two options. The first is to run the batch file `%Microsoft Visual Studio 2008%\Common7\Tools\vsvars32.bat` *from the command prompt before running* csc, *where* `%Microsoft Visual Studio 2008` *is the folder to which Visual Studio 2008 has been installed. The second, and easier, way is to use the Visual Studio 2008 command prompt instead of the usual command prompt window. You will find the Visual Studio 2008 command prompt in the Start Menu, under Programs, Microsoft Visual Studio 2008, Microsoft Visual Studio Tools. It is simply a command prompt window that automatically runs* `vsvars32.bat` *when it opens.*

Compiling the code produces an executable file named `First.exe`, which you can run from the command line or from Windows Explorer like any other executable. Give it a try:

csc First.cs

```
Microsoft (R) Visual C# Compiler version 9.00.20404
for Microsoft (R) .NET Framework version 3.5
Copyright (C) Microsoft Corporation. All rights reserved.
```

First.exe

```
This isn't at all like Java!
```

Well, maybe that message isn't quite true! This program has some fairly fundamental similarities to Java, although there are one or two points (such as the capitalized `Main()` function) to catch the unwary Java or C++ developer. Let's look more closely at what's going on in the code.

A Closer Look

First, a few general comments about C# syntax. In C#, as in other C-style languages, most statements end in a semicolon (;) and can continue over multiple lines without needing a continuation character (such as the underscore in Visual Basic). Statements can be joined into blocks using curly braces ({}). Single-line comments begin with two forward slash characters (//), and multiline comments begin with a slash and an asterisk (/*) and end with the same combination reversed (*/). In these aspects, C# is identical to C++ and Java but different from Visual Basic. It is the semicolons and curly braces that give C# code such a different visual appearance from Visual Basic code. If your background is predominantly Visual Basic, take extra care to remember the semicolon at the end of every statement. Omitting this is usually the biggest single cause of compilation errors among developers new to C-style languages. Another thing to remember is that C# is case sensitive. That means that variables named `myVar` and `MyVar` are two different variables.

The first few lines in the previous code example have to do with *namespaces* (mentioned later in this chapter), which are a way to group together associated classes. This concept will be familiar to Java and C++ developers but may be new to Visual Basic 6 developers. C# namespaces are basically the same as C++ namespaces or, equivalently, Java packages, but there is no comparable concept in Visual Basic 6. The `namespace` keyword declares the namespace your class should be associated with. All code within the braces that follow it is regarded as being within that namespace. The `using` statement specifies a namespace that the compiler should look at to find any classes that are referenced in your code but that aren't defined in the current namespace. This serves the same purpose as the `import` statement in Java and the `using namespace` statement in C++.

```
using System;

namespace Wrox.ProCSharp.Basics
{
```

The reason for the presence of the `using` statement in the `First.cs` file is that you are going to use a library class, `System.Console`. The `using System` statement allows you to refer to this class simply as `Console` (and similarly for any other classes in the `System` namespace). The standard `System` namespace is where the most commonly used .NET types reside. It is important to realize that everything you do in C# depends on the .NET base classes. In this case, you are using the `Console` class within the `System` namespace in order to write to the console window. C# has no built-in keywords of its own for input or output; it is completely reliant on the .NET classes.

> *Because almost every C# program uses classes in the System namespace, we will assume that a* `using System;` *statement is present in the file for all code snippets in this chapter.*

Next, you declare a class called `MyFirstClass`. However, because it has been placed in a namespace called `Wrox.ProCSharp.Basics`, the fully qualified name of this class is `Wrox.ProCSharp.Basics.MyFirstCSharpClass`:

```
class MyFirstCSharpClass
{
```

As in Java, all C# code must be contained within a class. Classes in C# are similar to classes in Java and C++, and very roughly comparable to class modules in Visual Basic 6. The class declaration consists of the `class` keyword, followed by the class name and a pair of curly braces. All code associated with the class should be placed between these braces.

Next, you declare a method called `Main()`. Every C# executable (such as console applications, Windows applications, and Windows services) must have an entry point — the `Main()` method (note the capital `M`):

```
static void Main()
{
```

The method is called when the program is started, like the `main()` function in C++ or Java, or `Sub Main()` in a Visual Basic 6 module. This method must return either nothing (`void`) or an integer (`int`). A C# method corresponds to a method in C++ and Java (sometimes referred to in C++ as a member function). It also corresponds to either a Visual Basic `Function` or a Visual Basic `Sub`, depending on whether the method returns anything (unlike Visual Basic, C# makes no conceptual distinction between functions and subroutines).

Note the format of method definitions in C#:

```
[modifiers] return_type MethodName([parameters])
{
    // Method body. NB. This code block is pseudo-code.
}
```

Here, the first square brackets represent certain optional keywords. Modifiers are used to specify certain features of the method you are defining, such as where the method can be called from. In this case, you have two modifiers: `public` and `static`. The `public` modifier means that the method can be accessed from anywhere, so it can be called from outside your class. This is the same meaning as `public` in C++ and Java, and `Public` in Visual Basic. The `static` modifier indicates that the method does not operate on a specific instance of your class and therefore is called without first instantiating the class. This is important because you are creating an executable rather than a class library. Once again, this has the same meaning as the `static` keyword in C++ and Java, though in this case there is no Visual Basic equivalent (the `Static` keyword in Visual Basic has a different meaning). You set the return type to `void`, and in the example, you don't include any parameters.

Finally, we come to the code statements themselves:

```
Console.WriteLine("This isn't at all like Java!");
Console.ReadLine();
return;
```

In this case, you simply call the `WriteLine()` method of the `System.Console` class to write a line of text to the console window. `WriteLine()` is a `static` method, so you don't need to instantiate a `Console` object before calling it.

`Console.ReadLine()` reads user input. Adding this line forces the application to wait for the carriage return key to be pressed before the application exits, and, in the case of Visual Studio 2008, the console window disappears.

You then call `return` to exit from the method (also, because this is the `Main()` method, you exit the program as well.). You specified `void` in your method header, so you don't return any values. The `return` statement is equivalent to `return` in C++ and Java, and `Exit Sub` or `Exit Function` in Visual Basic.

Now that you have had a taste of basic C# syntax, you are ready for more detail. Because it is virtually impossible to write any nontrivial program without *variables*, we will start by looking at variables in C#.

Variables

You declare variables in C# using the following syntax:

```
datatype identifier;
```

For example:

```
int i;
```

This statement declares an `int` named `i`. The compiler won't actually let you use this variable in an expression until you have initialized it with a value.

Once it has been declared, you can assign a value to the variable using the assignment operator, =:

```
i = 10;
```

You can also declare the variable and initialize its value at the same time:

```
int i = 10;
```

This syntax is identical to C++ and Java syntax but very different from Visual Basic syntax for declaring variables. If you are coming from Visual Basic 6, you should also be aware that C# doesn't distinguish between objects and simple types, so there is no need for anything like the `Set` keyword, even if you want your variable to refer to an object. The C# syntax for declaring variables is the same no matter what the data type of the variable.

If you declare and initialize more than one variable in a single statement, all of the variables will be of the same data type:

```
int x = 10, y =20;    // x and y are both ints
```

To declare variables of different types, you need to use separate statements. You cannot assign different data types within a multiple variable declaration:

```
int x = 10;
bool y = true;           // Creates a variable that stores true or false
int x = 10, bool y = true;   // This won't compile!
```

Notice the `//` and the text after it in the preceding examples. These are comments. The `//` character sequence tells the compiler to ignore the text that follows on this line because it is for a human to better understand the program and not part of the program itself. We further explain comments in code later in this chapter.

Initialization of Variables

Variable initialization demonstrates an example of C#'s emphasis on safety. Briefly, the C# compiler requires that any variable be initialized with some starting value before you refer to that variable in an operation. Most modern compilers will flag violations of this as a warning, but the ever-vigilant C#

compiler treats such violations as errors. This prevents you from unintentionally retrieving junk values from memory that is left over from other programs.

C# has two methods for ensuring that variables are initialized before use:

❑ Variables that are fields in a class or struct, if not initialized explicitly, are by default zeroed out when they are created (classes and structs are discussed later).

❑ Variables that are local to a method must be explicitly initialized in your code prior to any statements in which their values are used. In this case, the initialization doesn't have to happen when the variable is declared, but the compiler will check all possible paths through the method and will flag an error if it detects any possibility of the value of a local variable being used before it is initialized.

C#'s approach contrasts with C++'s approach, in which the compiler leaves it up to the programmer to make sure that variables are initialized before use, and with Visual Basic's approach, in which all variables are zeroed out automatically.

For example, you can't do the following in C#:

```
public static int Main()
{
    int d;
    Console.WriteLine(d);    // Can't do this! Need to initialize d before use
    return 0;
}
```

Notice that this code snippet demonstrates defining `Main()` so that it returns an `int` instead of `void`.

When you attempt to compile these lines, you will receive this error message:

```
Use of unassigned local variable 'd'
```

Consider the following statement:

```
Something objSomething;
```

In C++, this line would create an instance of the `Something` class on the stack. In C#, this same line of code would create only a *reference* for a `Something` object, but this reference would not yet actually refer to any object. Any attempt to call a method or property against this variable would result in an error.

Instantiating a reference object in C# requires use of the `new` keyword. You create a reference as shown in the previous example and then point the reference at an object allocated on the heap using the `new` keyword:

```
objSomething = new Something();    // This creates a Something on the heap
```

Type Inference

Type inference makes use of the `var` keyword. The syntax for declaring the variable changes somewhat. The compiler "infers" what the type of the variable is by what the variable is initialized to. For example,

```
int someNumber = 0;
```

becomes

```
var someNumber = 0;
```

Even though `someNumber` is never declared as being an `int`, the compiler figures this out and `someNumber` is an `int` for as long as it is in scope. Once compiled, the two preceding statements are equal.

Here is a short program to demonstrate:

```
using System;

namespace Wrox.ProCSharp.Basics
{
  class Program
  {
    static void Main(string[] args)
    {
      var name = "Bugs Bunny";
      var age = 25;
      var isRabbit = true;

      Type nameType = name.GetType();
      Type ageType = age.GetType();
      Type isRabbitType = isRabbit.GetType();

      Console.WriteLine("name is type " + nameType.ToString());
      Console.WriteLine("age is type " + ageType.ToString());
      Console.WriteLine("isRabbit is type " + isRabbitType.ToString());
    }
  }
}
```

The output from this program is:

```
name is type System.String
age is type System.Int32
isRabbit is type System.Bool
```

There are a few rules that you need to follow. The variable must be initialized. Otherwise, the compiler doesn't have anything to infer the type from. The initializer cannot be null, and the initializer must be an expression. You can't set the initializer to an object unless you create a new object in the initializer. We examine this more closely in the discussion of anonymous types in Chapter 3, "Objects and Types."

Once the variable has been declared and the type inferred, the variable's type cannot be changed. This is unlike the Variant type used in Visual Basic. Once established, the variable's type follows all of the strong typing rules that any other variable type must follow.

Variable Scope

The *scope* of a variable is the region of code from which the variable can be accessed. In general, the scope is determined by the following rules:

❑   A *field* (also known as a member variable) of a class is in scope for as long as its containing class is in scope (this is the same as for C++, Java, and VB).

❑   A *local variable* is in scope until a closing brace indicates the end of the block statement or method in which it was declared.

❑   A local variable that is declared in a `for`, `while`, or similar statement is in scope in the body of that loop. (C++ developers will recognize that this is the same behavior as the ANSI standard for C++. Early versions of the Microsoft C++ compiler did not comply with this standard but scoped such variables to remain in scope after the loop terminated.)

Scope Clashes for Local Variables

It's common in a large program to use the same variable name for different variables in different parts of the program. This is fine as long as the variables are scoped to completely different parts of the program so that there is no possibility for ambiguity. However, bear in mind that local variables with the same name can't be declared twice in the same scope. For example, you can't do this:

```
int x = 20;
// some more code
int x = 30;
```

Consider the following code sample:

```
using System;

namespace Wrox.ProCSharp.Basics
{
    public class ScopeTest
    {
        public static int Main()
        {
            for (int i = 0; i < 10; i++)
            {
                Console.WriteLine(i);
            }   // i goes out of scope here

            // We can declare a variable named i again, because
            // there's no other variable with that name in scope

            for (int i = 9; i >= 0; i--)
            {
                Console.WriteLine(i);
            }   // i goes out of scope here.
            return 0;
        }
    }
}
```

This code simply prints out the numbers from 0 to 9, and then back again from 9 to 0, using two `for` loops. The important thing to note is that you declare the variable i twice in this code, within the same method. You can do this because i is declared in two separate loops, so each i variable is local to its own loop.

Here's another example:

```
public static int Main()
{
    int j = 20;
    for (int i = 0; i < 10; i++)
    {
        int j = 30;    // Can't do this - j is still in scope
        Console.WriteLine(j + i);
    }
    return 0;
}
```

If you try to compile this, you'll get an error:

```
ScopeTest.cs(12,14): error CS0136: A local variable named 'j' cannot be declared in
this scope because it would give a different meaning to 'j', which is already used
in a 'parent or current' scope to denote something else.
```

This occurs because the variable j, which is defined before the start of the for loop, is still in scope within the for loop, and won't go out of scope until the Main() method has finished executing. Although the second j (the illegal one) is in the loop's scope, that scope is nested within the Main() method's scope. The compiler has no way to distinguish between these two variables, so it won't allow the second one to be declared. This, again, is different from C++, where variable hiding is permitted.

Scope Clashes for Fields and Local Variables

In certain circumstances, however, you can distinguish between two identifiers with the same name (although not the same fully qualified name) and the same scope, and in this case the compiler will allow you to declare the second variable. The reason is that C# makes a fundamental distinction between variables that are declared at the type level (fields) and variables that are declared within methods (local variables).

Consider the following code snippet:

```csharp
using System;

namespace Wrox.ProCSharp.Basics
{
    class ScopeTest2
    {
        static int j = 20;

        public static void Main()
        {
            int j = 30;
            Console.WriteLine(j);
            return;
        }
    }
}
```

This code will compile, even though you have two variables named j in scope within the Main() method: the j that was defined at the class level, and doesn't go out of scope until the class is destroyed (when the Main() method terminates, and the program ends); and the j defined in Main(). In this case, the new variable named j that you declare in the Main() method *hides* the class-level variable with the same name, so when you run this code, the number 30 will be displayed.

However, what if you want to refer to the class-level variable? You can actually refer to fields of a class or struct from outside the object, using the syntax object.fieldname. In the previous example, you are accessing a static field (you look at what this means in the next section) from a static method, so you can't use an instance of the class; you just use the name of the class itself:

```csharp
...
public static void Main()
{
    int j = 30;
    Console.WriteLine(j);
    Console.WriteLine(ScopeTest2.j);
}
...
```

If you were accessing an instance field (a field that belongs to a specific instance of the class), you would need to use the `this` keyword instead. This keyword performs the same role as `this` in C++ and Java, and `Me` in Visual Basic.

Constants

As the name implies, a constant is a variable whose value cannot be changed throughout its lifetime. Prefixing a variable with the `const` keyword when it is declared and initialized designates that variable as a constant:

```
const int a = 100;    // This value cannot be changed.
```

Constants will be familiar to Visual Basic and C++ developers. C++ developers should, however, note that C# does not permit all the subtleties of C++ constants. In C++, not only could variables be declared as constant, but depending on the declaration, you could have constant pointers, variable pointers to constants, constant methods (that don't change the contents of the containing object), constant parameters to methods, and so on. These subtleties have been discarded in C#, and all you can do is declare local variables and fields to be constant.

Constants have the following characteristics:

❑   They must be initialized when they are declared, and once a value has been assigned, it can never be overwritten.

❑   The value of a constant must be computable at compile time. Therefore, you can't initialize a constant with a value taken from a variable. If you need to do this, you will need to use a read-only field (this is explained in Chapter 3, "Objects and Types").

❑   Constants are always implicitly static. However, notice that you don't have to (and, in fact, are not permitted to) include the `static` modifier in the constant declaration.

At least three advantages exist to using constants in your programs:

❑   Constants make your programs easier to read by replacing magic numbers and strings with readable names whose values are easy to understand.

❑   Constants make your programs easier to modify. For example, assume that you have a `SalesTax` constant in one of your C# programs, and that constant is assigned a value of 6 percent. If the sales tax rate changes at a later point in time, you can modify the behavior of all tax calculations simply by assigning a new value to the constant; you don't have to hunt throughout your code for the value `.06` and change each one, hoping that you will find all of them.

❑   Constants help to prevent mistakes in your programs. If you attempt to assign another value to a constant somewhere in your program other than at the point where the constant is declared, the compiler will flag the error.

Predefined Data Types

Now that you have seen how to declare variables and constants, let's take a closer look at the data types available in C#. As you will see, C# is much stricter about the types available and their definitions than some other languages are.

Value Types and Reference Types

Before examining the data types in C#, it is important to understand that C# distinguishes between two categories of data type:

❑   Value types

❑   Reference types

The next few sections look in detail at the syntax for value and reference types. Conceptually, the difference is that a *value type* stores its value directly, whereas a *reference type* stores a reference to the value. Value types in C# are basically the same as simple types (integer, float, but not pointers or references) in Visual Basic or C++. Reference types are the same as reference types in Visual Basic and are similar to types accessed through pointers in C++.

These types are stored in different places in memory; value types are stored in an area known as the *stack*, and reference types are stored in an area known as the *managed heap*. It is important to be aware of whether a type is a value type or a reference type because of the different effect each assignment has. For example, int is a value type, which means that the following statement will result in two locations in memory storing the value 20:

```
// i and j are both of type int
i = 20;
j = i;
```

However, consider the following code. For this code, assume that you have defined a class called Vector. Assume that Vector is a reference type and has an int member variable called Value:

```
Vector x, y;
x = new Vector();
x.Value = 30;    // Value is a field defined in Vector class
y = x;
Console.WriteLine(y.Value);
y.Value = 50;
Console.WriteLine(x.Value);
```

The crucial point to understand is that after executing this code, there is only one Vector object around. x and y both point to the memory location that contains this object. Because x and y are variables of a reference type, declaring each variable simply reserves a reference—it doesn't instantiate an object of the given type. This is the same as declaring a pointer in C++ or an object reference in Visual Basic. In neither case is an object actually created. In order to create an object, you have to use the new keyword, as shown. Because x and y refer to the same object, changes made to x will affect y and vice versa. Hence the code will display 30 then 50.

> *C++ developers should note that this syntax is like a reference, not a pointer. We use the . notation, not ->, to access object members. Syntactically, C# references look more like C++ reference variables. However, behind the superficial syntax, the real similarity is with C++ pointers.*

If a variable is a reference, it is possible to indicate that it does not refer to any object by setting its value to null:

```
y = null;
```

This is the same as setting a reference to null in Java, a pointer to NULL in C++, or an object reference in Visual Basic to Nothing. If a reference is set to null, then clearly it is not possible to call any nonstatic member functions or fields against it; doing so would cause an exception to be thrown at runtime.

In languages like C++, the developer can choose whether a given value is to be accessed directly or via a pointer. Visual Basic is more restrictive, taking the view that COM objects are reference types and simple types are always value types. C# is similar to Visual Basic in this regard: whether a variable is a value or reference is determined solely by its data type, so int, for example, is always a value type. It is not possible to declare an int variable as a reference (although in Chapter 6, "Operators and Casts," which covers *boxing*, you see it is possible to wrap value types in references of type object).

In C#, basic data types like bool and long are value types. This means that if you declare a bool variable and assign it the value of another bool variable, you will have two separate bool values in memory. Later, if you change the value of the original bool variable, the value of the second bool variable does not change. These types are copied by value.

In contrast, most of the more complex C# data types, including classes that you yourself declare, are reference types. They are allocated upon the heap, have lifetimes that can span multiple function calls, and can be accessed through one or several aliases. The Common Language Runtime (CLR) implements an elaborate algorithm to track which reference variables are still reachable and which have been orphaned. Periodically, the CLR will destroy orphaned objects and return the memory that they once occupied back to the operating system. This is done by the garbage collector.

C# has been designed this way because high performance is best served by keeping primitive types (like int and bool) as value types and larger types that contain many fields (as is usually the case with classes) as reference types. If you want to define your own type as a value type, you should declare it as a struct.

CTS Types

As mentioned in Chapter 1, ".NET Architecture," the basic predefined types recognized by C# are not intrinsic to the language but are part of the .NET Framework. For example, when you declare an int in C#, what you are actually declaring is an instance of a .NET struct, System.Int32. This may sound like a small point, but it has a profound significance: it means that you are able to treat all the primitive data types syntactically as if they were classes that supported certain methods. For example, to convert an int i to a string, you can write:

```
string s = i.ToString();
```

It should be emphasized that, behind this syntactical convenience, the types really are stored as primitive types, so there is absolutely no performance cost associated with the idea that the primitive types are notionally represented by .NET structs.

The following sections review the types that are recognized as built-in types in C#. Each type is listed, along with its definition and the name of the corresponding .NET type (CTS type). C# has 15 predefined types, 13 value types, and 2 (string and object) reference types.

Predefined Value Types

The built-in value types represent primitives, such as integer and floating-point numbers, character, and Boolean types.

Integer Types

C# supports eight predefined integer types, shown in the following table.

Name	CTS Type	Description	Range (min:max)
sbyte	System.SByte	8-bit signed integer	-128:127 (-2^7:2^7-1)
short	System.Int16	16-bit signed integer	-32,768:32,767 (-2^{15}:2^{15}-1)
int	System.Int32	32-bit signed integer	-2,147,483,648:2,147,483,647 (-2^{31}:2^{31}-1)
long	System.Int64	64-bit signed integer	-9,223,372,036,854,775,808: 9,223,372,036,854,775,807 (-2^{63}:2^{63}-1)
byte	System.Byte	8-bit unsigned integer	0:255 (0:2^8-1)
ushort	System.UInt16	16-bit unsigned integer	0:65,535 (0:2^{16}-1)
uint	System.UInt32	32-bit unsigned integer	0:4,294,967,295 (0:2^{32}-1)
ulong	System.UInt64	64-bit unsigned integer	0:18,446,744,073,709,551,615 (0:2^{64}-1)

Future versions of Windows will target 64-bit processors, which can move bits into and out of memory in larger chunks to achieve faster processing times. Consequently, C# supports a rich palette of signed and unsigned integer types ranging in size from 8 to 64 bits.

Many of these type names will be new to programmers experienced in Visual Basic. C++ and Java developers should be careful; some C# types have the same names as C++ and Java types but have different definitions. For example, in C#, an int is always a 32-bit signed integer. In C++ an int is a signed integer, but the number of bits is platform-dependent (32 bits on Windows). In C#, all data types have been defined in a platform-independent manner to allow for the possible future porting of C# and .NET to other platforms.

A byte is the standard 8-bit type for values in the range 0 to 255 inclusive. Be aware that, in keeping with its emphasis on type safety, C# regards the byte type and the char type as completely distinct, and any programmatic conversions between the two must be explicitly requested. Also be aware that unlike the other types in the integer family, a byte type is by default unsigned. Its signed version bears the special name sbyte.

With .NET, a short is no longer quite so short; it is now 16 bits long. The int type is 32 bits long. The long type reserves 64 bits for values. All integer-type variables can be assigned values in decimal or in hex notation. The latter require the 0x prefix:

```
long x = 0x12ab;
```

If there is any ambiguity about whether an integer is int, uint, long, or ulong, it will default to an int. To specify which of the other integer types the value should take, you can append one of the following characters to the number:

```
uint ui = 1234U;
long l = 1234L;
ulong ul = 1234UL;
```

You can also use lowercase u and l, although the latter could be confused with the integer 1 (one).

Floating-Point Types

Although C# provides a plethora of integer data types, it supports floating-point types as well. They will be familiar to C and C++ programmers.

Name	CTS Type	Description	Significant Figures	Range (approximate)
float	System.Single	32-bit single-precision floating point	7	$\pm 1.5 \times 10^{-45}$ to $\pm 3.4 \times 10^{38}$
double	System.Double	64-bit double-precision floating point	15/16	$\pm 5.0 \times 10^{-324}$ to $\pm 1.7 \times 10^{308}$

The float data type is for smaller floating-point values, for which less precision is required. The double data type is bulkier than the float data type but offers twice the precision (15 digits).

If you hard-code a non-integer number (such as 12.3) in your code, the compiler will normally assume that you want the number interpreted as a double. If you want to specify that the value is a float, you append the character F (or f) to it:

```
float f = 12.3F;
```

The Decimal Type

The decimal type represents higher-precision floating-point numbers, as shown in the following table.

Name	CTS Type	Description	Significant Figures	Range (approximate)
decimal	System.Decimal	128-bit high-precision decimal notation	28	$\pm 1.0 \times 10^{-28}$ to $\pm 7.9 \times 10^{28}$

One of the great things about the CTS and C# is the provision of a dedicated decimal type for financial calculations. How you use the 28 digits that the decimal type provides is up to you. In other words, you can track smaller dollar amounts with greater accuracy for cents or larger dollar amounts with more rounding in the fractional area. Bear in mind, however, that decimal is not implemented under the hood as a primitive type, so using decimal will have a performance effect on your calculations.

To specify that your number is a decimal type rather than a double, float, or an integer, you can append the M (or m) character to the value, as shown in the following example:

```
decimal d = 12.30M;
```

The Boolean Type

The C# bool type is used to contain Boolean values of either true or false.

Name	CTS Type	Description	Significant Figures	Range (approximate)
bool	System.Boolean	Represents true or false	NA	true false

You cannot implicitly convert `bool` values to and from integer values. If a variable (or a function return type) is declared as a `bool`, you can only use values of `true` and `false`. You will get an error if you try to use zero for `false` and a non-zero value for `true`, as is possible to do in C++.

The Character Type

For storing the value of a single character, C# supports the `char` data type.

Name	CTS Type	Values
char	System.Char	Represents a single 16-bit (Unicode) character

Although this data type has a superficial resemblance to the `char` type provided by C and C++, there is a significant difference. A C++ `char` represents an 8-bit character, whereas a C# `char` contains 16 bits. This is part of the reason that implicit conversions between the `char` type and the 8-bit `byte` type are not permitted.

Although 8 bits may be enough to encode every character in the English language and the digits 0–9, they aren't enough to encode every character in more expansive symbol systems (such as Chinese). In a gesture toward universality, the computer industry is moving away from the 8-bit character set and toward the 16-bit Unicode scheme, of which the ASCII encoding is a subset.

Literals of type `char` are signified by being enclosed in single quotation marks, for example `'A'`. If you try to enclose a character in double quotation marks, the compiler will treat this as a string and throw an error.

As well as representing `chars` as character literals, you can represent them with four-digit hex Unicode values (for example `'\u0041'`), as integer values with a cast (for example, `(char)65`), or as hexadecimal values (`'\x0041'`). You can also represent them with an escape sequence, as shown in the following table.

Escape Sequence	Character
\'	Single quotation mark
\"	Double quotation mark
\\	Backslash
\0	Null
\a	Alert
\b	Backspace
\f	Form feed
\n	Newline
\r	Carriage return
\t	Tab character
\v	Vertical tab

C++ developers should note that because C# has a native string type, you don't need to represent strings as arrays of `chars`.

Predefined Reference Types

C# supports two predefined reference types, object and string, described in the following table.

Name	CTS Type	Description
object	System.Object	The root type. All other types in the CTS are derived (including value types) from object.
string	System.String	Unicode character string.

The object Type

Many programming languages and class hierarchies provide a root type, from which all other objects in the hierarchy are derived. C# and .NET are no exception. In C#, the object type is the ultimate parent type from which all other intrinsic and user-defined types are derived. This is a key feature of C# that distinguishes it from both Visual Basic 6.0 and C++, although its behavior here is very similar to Java. All types implicitly derive ultimately from the System.Object class. This means that you can use the object type for two purposes:

❑ You can use an object reference to bind to an object of any particular subtype. For example, in Chapter 6, "Operators and Casts," you will see how you can use the object type to box a value object on the stack to move it to the heap. object references are also useful in reflection, when code must manipulate objects whose specific types are unknown. This is similar to the role played by a void pointer in C++ or by a Variant data type in VB.

❑ The object type implements a number of basic, general-purpose methods, which include Equals(), GetHashCode(), GetType(), and ToString(). Responsible user-defined classes may need to provide replacement implementations of some of these methods using an object-oriented technique known as *overriding*, which is discussed in Chapter 4, "Inheritance." When you override ToString(), for example, you equip your class with a method for intelligently providing a string representation of itself. If you don't provide your own implementations for these methods in your classes, the compiler will pick up the implementations in object, which may or may not be correct or sensible in the context of your classes.

We examine the object type in more detail in subsequent chapters.

The string Type

Veterans of C and C++ probably have battle scars from wrestling with C-style strings. A C or C++ string is nothing more than an array of characters, so the client programmer has to do a lot of work just to copy one string to another or to concatenate two strings. In fact, for a generation of C++ programmers, implementing a string class that wraps up the messy details of these operations was a rite of passage requiring many hours of teeth gnashing and head scratching. Visual Basic programmers have a somewhat easier life, with a string type, and Java people have it even better, with a String class that is in many ways very similar to a C# string.

C# recognizes the string keyword, which under the hood is translated to the .NET class, System.String. With it, operations like string concatenation and string copying are a snap:

```
string str1 = "Hello ";
string str2 = "World";
string str3 = str1 + str2; // string concatenation
```

Despite this style of assignment, `string` is a reference type. Behind the scenes, a `string` object is allocated on the heap, not the stack, and when you assign one string variable to another string, you get two references to the same string in memory. However, with `string` there are some differences from the usual behavior for reference types. For example, should you make changes to one of these strings, this will create an entirely new `string` object, leaving the other string unchanged. Consider the following code:

```
using System;

class StringExample
{
    public static int Main()
    {
        string s1 = "a string";
        string s2 = s1;
        Console.WriteLine("s1 is " + s1);
        Console.WriteLine("s2 is " + s2);
        s1 = "another string";
        Console.WriteLine("s1 is now " + s1);
        Console.WriteLine("s2 is now " + s2);
        return 0;
    }
}
```

The output from this is:

```
s1 is a string
s2 is a string
s1 is now another string
s2 is now a string
```

Changing the value of `s1` had no effect on `s2`, contrary to what you'd expect with a reference type! What's happening here is that when `s1` is initialized with the value a `string`, a new string object is allocated on the heap. When `s2` is initialized, the reference points to this same object, so `s2` also has the value a `string`. However, when you now change the value of `s1`, instead of replacing the original value, a new object will be allocated on the heap for the new value. The `s2` variable will still point to the original object, so its value is unchanged. Under the hood, this happens as a result of operator overloading, a topic that is explored in Chapter 6, "Operators and Casts." In general, the `string` class has been implemented so that its semantics follow what you would normally intuitively expect for a string.

String literals are enclosed in double quotation marks (`"..."`); if you attempt to enclose a string in single quotation marks, the compiler will take the value as a `char`, and throw an error. C# strings can contain the same Unicode and hexadecimal escape sequences as `char`s. Because these escape sequences start with a backslash, you can't use this character unescaped in a string. Instead, you need to escape it with two backslashes (`\\`):

```
string filepath = "C:\\ProCSharp\\First.cs";
```

Even if you are confident that you can remember to do this all the time, typing all of those double backslashes can prove annoying. Fortunately, C# gives you an alternative. You can prefix a string literal with the at character (`@`) and all the characters in it will be treated at face value; they won't be interpreted as escape sequences:

```
string filepath = @"C:\ProCSharp\First.cs";
```

This even allows you to include line breaks in your string literals:

```
string jabberwocky = @"'Twas brillig and the slithy toves
Did gyre and gimble in the wabe.";
```

Then the value of jabberwocky would be this:

```
'Twas brillig and the slithy toves
Did gyre and gimble in the wabe.
```

Flow Control

This section looks at the real nuts and bolts of the language: the statements that allow you to control the *flow* of your program rather than executing every line of code in the order it appears in the program.

Conditional Statements

Conditional statements allow you to branch your code depending on whether certain conditions are met or on the value of an expression. C# has two constructs for branching code — the if statement, which allows you to test whether a specific condition is met, and the switch statement, which allows you to compare an expression with a number of different values.

The if Statement

For conditional branching, C# inherits the C and C++ if...else construct. The syntax should be fairly intuitive for anyone who has done any programming with a procedural language:

```
if (condition)
    statement(s)
else
    statement(s)
```

If more than one statement is to be executed as part of either condition, these statements will need to be joined together into a block using curly braces ({...}). (This also applies to other C# constructs where statements can be joined into a block, such as the for and while loops):

```
bool isZero;
if (i == 0)
{
    isZero = true;
    Console.WriteLine("i is Zero");
}
else
{
    isZero = false;
    Console.WriteLine("i is Non-zero");
}
```

The syntax here is similar to C++ and Java but once again different from Visual Basic. Visual Basic developers should note that C# does not have any statement corresponding to Visual Basic's EndIf. Instead, the rule is that each clause of an if contains just one statement. If you need more than one statement, as in the preceding example, you should enclose the statements in braces, which will cause the whole group of statements to be treated as a single block statement.

If you want to, you can use an if statement without a final else statement. You can also combine else if clauses to test for multiple conditions:

```
using System;

namespace Wrox.ProCSharp.Basics
{
    class MainEntryPoint
```

```
    {
        static void Main(string[] args)
        {
            Console.WriteLine("Type in a string");
            string input;
            input = Console.ReadLine();
            if (input == "")
            {
                Console.WriteLine("You typed in an empty string.");
            }
            else if (input.Length < 5)
            {
                Console.WriteLine("The string had less than 5 characters.");
            }
            else if (input.Length < 10)
            {
                Console.WriteLine("The string had at least 5 but less than 10
                    Characters.");
            }
            Console.WriteLine("The string was " + input);
        }
    }
}
```

There is no limit to how many `else if`s you can add to an `if` clause.

You'll notice that the previous example declares a string variable called `input`, gets the user to enter text at the command line, feeds this into `input`, and then tests the length of this string variable. The code also shows how easy string manipulation can be in C#. To find the length of `input`, for example, use `input.Length`.

One point to note about `if` is that you don't need to use the braces if there's only one statement in the conditional branch:

```
if (i == 0) Let's add some brackets here.
    Console.WriteLine("i is Zero");        // This will only execute if i == 0
Console.WriteLine("i can be anything");    // Will execute whatever the
                                           // value of i
```

However, for consistency, many programmers prefer to use curly braces whenever they use an `if` statement.

The `if` statements presented also illustrate some of the C# operators that compare values. Note in particular that, like C++ and Java, C# uses == to compare variables for equality. Do not use = for this purpose. A single = is used to assign values.

In C#, the expression in the `if` clause must evaluate to a Boolean. C++ programmers should be particularly aware of this; in C#, unlike in C++, it is not possible to test an integer (returned from a function, say) directly. In C#, you have to convert the integer that is returned to a Boolean `true` or `false`, for example, by comparing the value with zero or with `null`:

```
if (DoSomething() != 0)
{
    // Non-zero value returned
}
else
{
    // Returned zero
}
```

This restriction is there in order to prevent some common types of runtime bugs that occur in C++. In particular, in C++ it was common to mistype = when == was intended, resulting in unintentional assignments. In C# this will normally result in a compile-time error, because unless you are working with bool values, = will not return a bool.

The switch Statement

The switch...case statement is good for selecting one branch of execution from a set of mutually exclusive ones. It will be familiar to C++ and Java programmers and is similar to the Select Case statement in Visual Basic.

It takes the form of a switch argument followed by a series of case clauses. When the expression in the switch argument evaluates to one of the values beside a case clause, the code immediately following the case clause executes. This is one example where you don't need to use curly braces to join statements into blocks; instead, you mark the end of the code for each case using the break statement. You can also include a default case in the switch statement, which will execute if the expression evaluates to none of the other cases. The following switch statement tests the value of the integerA variable:

```
switch (integerA)
{
    case 1:
        Console.WriteLine("integerA =1");
        break;
    case 2:
        Console.WriteLine("integerA =2");
        break;
    case 3:
        Console.WriteLine("integerA =3");
        break;
    default:
        Console.WriteLine("integerA is not 1,2, or 3");
        break;
}
```

Note that the case values must be constant expressions; variables are not permitted.

Though the switch...case statement should be familiar to C and C++ programmers, C#'s switch... case is a bit safer than its C++ equivalent. Specifically, it prohibits fall-through conditions in almost all cases. This means that if a case clause is fired early on in the block, later clauses cannot be fired unless you use a goto statement to mark that you want them fired, too. The compiler enforces this restriction by flagging every case clause that is not equipped with a break statement as an error similar to this:

```
Control cannot fall through from one case label ('case 2:') to another
```

Although it is true that fall-through behavior is desirable in a limited number of situations, in the vast majority of cases, it is unintended and results in a logical error that's hard to spot. Isn't it better to code for the norm rather than for the exception?

By getting creative with goto statements, however, you can duplicate fall-through functionality in your switch...cases. But, if you find yourself really wanting to, you probably should reconsider your approach. The following code illustrates both how to use goto to simulate fall-through, and how messy the resultant code can get:

```
// assume country and language are of type string
switch(country)
{
    case "America":
        CallAmericanOnlyMethod();
```

```
            goto case "Britain";
        case "France":
            language = "French";
            break;
        case "Britain":
            language = "English";
            break;
    }
```

There is one exception to the no-fall-through rule, however, in that you can fall through from one case to the next if that case is empty. This allows you to treat two or more cases in an identical way (without the need for `goto` statements):

```
switch(country)
{
    case "au":
    case "uk":
    case "us":
        language = "English";
        break;
    case "at":
    case "de":
        language = "German";
        break;
}
```

One intriguing point about the `switch` statement in C# is that the order of the cases doesn't matter — you can even put the `default` case first! As a result, no two cases can be the same. This includes different constants that have the same value, so you can't, for example, do this:

```
// assume country is of type string
const string england = "uk";
const string britain = "uk";
switch(country)
{
    case england:
    case britain:      // This will cause a compilation error.
        language = "English";
        break;
}
```

The previous code also shows another way in which the `switch` statement is different in C# compared to C++: In C#, you are allowed to use a string as the variable being tested.

Loops

C# provides four different loops (`for`, `while`, `do...while`, and `foreach`) that allow you to execute a block of code repeatedly until a certain condition is met. The `for`, `while`, and `do...while` loops are essentially identical to those encountered in C++.

The for Loop

C# `for` loops provide a mechanism for iterating through a loop where you test whether a particular condition holds before you perform another iteration. The syntax is

```
for (initializer; condition; iterator)
    statement(s)
```

where

- ❏ The initializer is the expression evaluated before the first loop is executed (usually initializing a local variable as a loop counter).

- ❏ The condition is the expression checked before each new iteration of the loop (this must evaluate to `true` for another iteration to be performed).

- ❏ The iterator is an expression evaluated after each iteration (usually incrementing the loop counter).

The iterations end when the condition evaluates to `false`.

The `for` loop is a so-called pretest loop because the loop condition is evaluated before the loop statements are executed, and so the contents of the loop won't be executed at all if the loop condition is `false`.

The `for` loop is excellent for repeating a statement or a block of statements for a predetermined number of times. The following example is typical of the use of a `for` loop. The following code will write out all the integers from 0 to 99:

```
for (int i = 0; i < 100; i=i+1)    // This is equivalent to
                                   // For i = 0 To 99 in VB.
{
    Console.WriteLine(i);
}
```

Here, you declare an `int` called `i` and initialize it to zero. This will be used as the loop counter. You then immediately test whether it is less than 100. Because this condition evaluates to `true`, you execute the code in the loop, displaying the value 0. You then increment the counter by one, and walk through the process again. Looping ends when `i` reaches 100.

Actually, the way the preceding loop is written isn't quite how you would normally write it. C# has a shorthand for adding 1 to a variable, so instead of `i = i + 1`, you can simply write `i++`:

```
for (int i = 0; i < 100; i++)
{
    // etc.
    }
```

C# `for` loop syntax is far more powerful than the Visual Basic `For...Next` loop because the iterator can be any statement. In Visual Basic, all you can do is add or subtract some number from the loop control variable. In C# you can do anything; for example, you can multiply the loop control variable by 2.

You can also make use of type inference for the iteration variable `i` in the preceding example. Using type inference the loop construct would be:

```
for (var i = 0; i < 100; i++)
...
```

It's not unusual to nest `for` loops so that an inner loop executes once completely for each iteration of an outer loop. This scheme is typically employed to loop through every element in a rectangular multidimensional array. The outermost loop loops through every row, and the inner loop loops through every column in a particular row. The following code displays rows of numbers. It also uses another `Console` method, `Console.Write()`, which does the same as `Console.WriteLine()` but doesn't send a carriage return to the output.

```
using System;

namespace Wrox.ProCSharp.Basics
{
    class MainEntryPoint
    {
        static void Main(string[] args)
        {
            // This loop iterates through rows...
            for (int i = 0; i < 100; i+=10)
            {
                // This loop iterates through columns...
                for (int j = i; j < i + 10; j++)
                {
                    Console.Write("   " + j);
                }
                Console.WriteLine();
            }
        }
    }
}
```

Although j is an integer, it will be automatically converted to a string so that the concatenation can take place. C++ developers will note that this is far easier than string handling ever was in C++; for Visual Basic developers this is familiar ground.

C and C++ programmers should take note of one particular feature of the preceding example. The counter variable in the innermost loop is effectively redeclared with each successive iteration of the outer loop. This syntax is legal not only in C# but in C++ as well.

The preceding sample results in this output:

csc NumberTable.cs

```
Microsoft (R) Visual C# Compiler version 9.00.20404
for Microsoft (R) .NET Framework version 3.5
Copyright (C) Microsoft Corporation. All rights reserved.

    0   1   2   3   4   5   6   7   8   9
   10  11  12  13  14  15  16  17  18  19
   20  21  22  23  24  25  26  27  28  29
   30  31  32  33  34  35  36  37  38  39
   40  41  42  43  44  45  46  47  48  49
   50  51  52  53  54  55  56  57  58  59
   60  61  62  63  64  65  66  67  68  69
   70  71  72  73  74  75  76  77  78  79
   80  81  82  83  84  85  86  87  88  89
   90  91  92  93  94  95  96  97  98  99
```

Although it is technically possible to evaluate something other than a counter variable in a for loop's test condition, it is certainly not typical. It is also possible to omit one (or even all) of the expressions in the for loop. In such situations, however, you should consider using the while loop.

The while Loop

The while loop is identical to the while loop in C++ and Java, and the While...Wend loop in Visual Basic. Like the for loop, while is a pretest loop. The syntax is similar, but while loops take only one expression:

```
while(condition)
    statement(s);
```

Unlike the for loop, the while loop is most often used to repeat a statement or a block of statements for a number of times that is not known before the loop begins. Usually, a statement inside the while loop's body will set a Boolean flag to false on a certain iteration, triggering the end of the loop, as in the following example:

```
bool condition = false;
while (!condition)
{
    // This loop spins until the condition is true.
    DoSomeWork();
    condition = CheckCondition();   // assume CheckCondition() returns a bool
}
```

All of C#'s looping mechanisms, including the while loop, can forgo the curly braces that follow them if they intend to repeat just a single statement and not a block of statements. Again, many programmers consider it good practice to use braces all of the time.

The do . . . while Loop

The do...while loop is the post-test version of the while loop. It does the same thing with the same syntax as do...while in C++ and Java, and the same thing as Loop...While in Visual Basic. This means that the loop's test condition is evaluated after the body of the loop has been executed. Consequently, do...while loops are useful for situations in which a block of statements must be executed at least one time, as in this example:

```
bool condition;
do
{
    // This loop will at least execute once, even if Condition is false.
    MustBeCalledAtLeastOnce();
    condition = CheckCondition();
} while (condition);
```

The foreach Loop

The foreach loop is the final C# looping mechanism that we discuss. Whereas the other looping mechanisms were present in the earliest versions of C and C++, the foreach statement is a new addition (borrowed from Visual Basic), and a very welcome one at that.

The foreach loop allows you to iterate through each item in a collection. For now, we won't worry about exactly what a collection is (it is explained fully in Chapter 10, "Collections"); we will just say that it is an object that contains other objects. Technically, to count as a collection, it must support an interface called IEnumerable. Examples of collections include C# arrays, the collection classes in the System .Collection namespaces, and user-defined collection classes. You can get an idea of the syntax of foreach from the following code, if you assume that arrayOfInts is (unsurprisingly) an array of ints:

```
foreach (int temp in arrayOfInts)
{
    Console.WriteLine(temp);
}
```

Here, foreach steps through the array one element at a time. With each element, it places the value of the element in the int variable called temp and then performs an iteration of the loop.

Here is another situation where type inference can be used. The foreach loop would become:

```
foreach (var temp in arrayOfInts)
...
```

temp would be inferred to int because that is what the collection item type is.

An important point to note with foreach is that you can't change the value of the item in the collection (temp in the preceding code), so code such as the following will not compile:

```
foreach (int temp in arrayOfInts)
{
    temp++;
    Console.WriteLine(temp);
}
```

If you need to iterate through the items in a collection and change their values, you will need to use a for loop instead.

Jump Statements

C# provides a number of statements that allow you to jump immediately to another line in the program. The first of these is, of course, the notorious goto statement.

The goto Statement

The goto statement allows you to jump directly to another specified line in the program, indicated by a *label* (this is just an identifier followed by a colon):

```
goto Label1;
    Console.WriteLine("This won't be executed");
Label1:
    Console.WriteLine("Continuing execution from here");
```

A couple of restrictions are involved with goto. You can't jump into a block of code such as a for loop, you can't jump out of a class, and you can't exit a finally block after try...catch blocks (Chapter 14, "Errors and Exceptions," looks at exception handling with try...catch...finally).

The reputation of the goto statement probably precedes it, and in most circumstances, its use is sternly frowned upon. In general, it certainly doesn't conform to good object-oriented programming practice. However, there is one place where it is quite handy: jumping between cases in a switch statement, particularly because C#'s switch is so strict on fall-through. You saw the syntax for this earlier in this chapter.

The break Statement

You have already met the break statement briefly — when you used it to exit from a case in a switch statement. In fact, break can also be used to exit from for, foreach, while, or do...while loops. Control will switch to the statement immediately after the end of the loop.

If the statement occurs in a nested loop, control will switch to the end of the innermost loop. If the break occurs outside of a switch statement or a loop, a compile-time error will occur.

The continue Statement

The continue statement is similar to break, and must also be used within a for, foreach, while, or do...while loop. However, it exits only from the current iteration of the loop, meaning that execution will restart at the beginning of the next iteration of the loop, rather than outside the loop altogether.

The return Statement

The `return` statement is used to exit a method of a class, returning control to the caller of the method. If the method has a return type, `return` must return a value of this type; otherwise if the method returns `void`, you should use `return` without an expression.

Enumerations

An *enumeration* is a user-defined integer type. When you declare an enumeration, you specify a set of acceptable values that instances of that enumeration can contain. Not only that, but you can give the values user-friendly names. If, somewhere in your code, you attempt to assign a value that is not in the acceptable set of values to an instance of that enumeration, the compiler will flag an error. This concept may be new to Visual Basic programmers. C++ does support enumerations (or enums), but C# enumerations are far more powerful than their C++ counterparts.

Creating an enumeration can save you a lot of time and headaches in the long run. At least three benefits exist to using enumerations instead of plain integers:

❑ As mentioned, enumerations make your code easier to maintain by helping to ensure that your variables are assigned only legitimate, anticipated values.

❑ Enumerations make your code clearer by allowing you to refer to integer values by descriptive names rather than by obscure "magic" numbers.

❑ Enumerations make your code easier to type, too. When you go to assign a value to an instance of an enumerated type, the Visual Studio .NET IDE will, through IntelliSense, pop up a list box of acceptable values in order to save you some keystrokes and to remind you of what the possible options are.

You can define an enumeration as follows:

```
public enum TimeOfDay
{
    Morning = 0,
    Afternoon = 1,
    Evening = 2
}
```

In this case, you use an integer value to represent each period of the day in the enumeration. You can now access these values as members of the enumeration. For example, `TimeOfDay.Morning` will return the value `0`. You will typically use this enumeration to pass an appropriate value into a method and iterate through the possible values in a `switch` statement:

```
class EnumExample
{
    public static int Main()
    {
        WriteGreeting(TimeOfDay.Morning);
        return 0;
    }

    static void WriteGreeting(TimeOfDay timeOfDay)
    {
        switch(timeOfDay)
        {
            case TimeOfDay.Morning:
                Console.WriteLine("Good morning!");
```

```
            break;
        case TimeOfDay.Afternoon:
            Console.WriteLine("Good afternoon!");
            break;
        case TimeOfDay.Evening:
            Console.WriteLine("Good evening!");
            break;
        default:
            Console.WriteLine("Hello!");
            break;
    }
  }
}
```

The real power of enums in C# is that behind the scenes they are instantiated as structs derived from the base class, `System.Enum`. This means it is possible to call methods against them to perform some useful tasks. Note that because of the way the .NET Framework is implemented there is no performance loss associated with treating the enums syntactically as structs. In practice, once your code is compiled, enums will exist as primitive types, just like `int` and `float`.

You can retrieve the string representation of an enum as in the following example, using the earlier `TimeOfDay` enum:

```
TimeOfDay time = TimeOfDay.Afternoon;
Console.WriteLine(time.ToString());
```

This will return the string `Afternoon`.

Alternatively, you can obtain an enum value from a string:

```
TimeOfDay time2 = (TimeOfDay) Enum.Parse(typeof(TimeOfDay), "afternoon", true);
Console.WriteLine((int)time2);
```

This code snippet illustrates both obtaining an enum value from a string and converting to an integer. To convert from a string, you need to use the static `Enum.Parse()` method, which, as shown, takes three parameters. The first is the type of enum you want to consider. The syntax is the keyword `typeof` followed by the name of the enum class in brackets. (Chapter 6, "Operators and Casts," explores the `typeof` operator in more detail.) The second parameter is the string to be converted, and the third parameter is a `bool` indicating whether you should ignore case when doing the conversion. Finally, note that `Enum.Parse()` actually returns an object reference — you need to explicitly convert this to the required enum type (this is an example of an unboxing operation). For the preceding code, this returns the value 1 as an object, corresponding to the enum value of `TimeOfDay.Afternoon`. On converting explicitly to an `int`, this produces the value 1 again.

Other methods on `System.Enum` do things such as return the number of values in an enum definition or list the names of the values. Full details are in the MSDN documentation.

Arrays

We won't say too much about arrays in this chapter because arrays are covered in detail in Chapter 5, "Arrays." However, we'll give you just enough syntax here that you can code one-dimensional arrays. Arrays in C# are declared by fixing a set of square brackets to the end of the variable type of the individual elements (note that all the elements in an array must be of the same data type).

A note to Visual Basic users: arrays in C# use square brackets, not parentheses. C++ users will be familiar with the square brackets but should carefully check the code presented here because C# syntax for actually declaring array variables is not the same as C++ syntax.

For example, whereas `int` represents a single integer, `int[]` represents an array of integers:

```
int[] integers;
```

To initialize the array with specific dimensions, you can use the `new` keyword, giving the size in the square brackets after the type name:

```
// Create a new array of 32 ints.
int[] integers = new int[32];
```

All arrays are reference types and follow reference semantics. Hence, in this code, even though the individual elements are primitive value types, the `integers` array is a reference type. So if you later write

```
int [] copy = integers;
```

this will simply assign the variable `copy` to refer to the same array — it won't create a new array.

To access an individual element within the array, you use the usual syntax, placing the index of the element in square brackets after the name of the array. All C# arrays use zero-based indexing, so you can reference the first variable with the index zero:

```
integers[0] = 35;
```

Similarly, you reference the 32 element value with an index value of 31:

```
integers[31] = 432;
```

C#'s array syntax is flexible. In fact, C# allows you to declare arrays without initializing them so that the array can be dynamically sized later in the program. With this technique, you are basically creating a `null` reference and later pointing that reference at a dynamically allocated stretch of memory locations requested with the `new` keyword:

```
int[] integers;
integers = new int[32];
```

You can find out how many elements are in any array by using this syntax:

```
int numElements = integers.Length;     // integers is any reference to an array.
```

Namespaces

As you have seen, namespaces provide a way of organizing related classes and other types. Unlike a file or a component, a namespace is a logical, rather than a physical, grouping. When you define a class in a C# file, you can include it within a namespace definition. Later, when you define another class that performs related work in another file, you can include it within the same namespace, creating a logical grouping that gives an indication to other developers using the classes how they are related and used:

```
namespace CustomerPhoneBookApp
{
    using System;

    public struct Subscriber
    {
        // Code for struct here...
    }
}
```

Placing a type in a namespace effectively gives that type a long name, consisting of the type's namespace as a series of names separated with periods (.), terminating with the name of the class. In the preceding example, the full name of the Subscriber struct is CustomerPhoneBookApp.Subscriber. This allows distinct classes with the same short name to be used within the same program without ambiguity. This full name is often called the fully qualified name.

You can also nest namespaces within other namespaces, creating a hierarchical structure for your types:

```
namespace Wrox
{
    namespace ProCSharp
    {
        namespace Basics
        {
            class NamespaceExample
            {
                // Code for the class here...
            }
        }
    }
}
```

Each namespace name is composed of the names of the namespaces it resides within, separated with periods, starting with the outermost namespace and ending with its own short name. So the full name for the ProCSharp namespace is Wrox.ProCSharp, and the full name of NamespaceExample class is Wrox.ProCSharp.Basics.NamespaceExample.

You can use this syntax to organize the namespaces in your namespace definitions too, so the previous code could also be written as follows:

```
namespace Wrox.ProCSharp.Basics
{
    class NamespaceExample
    {
        // Code for the class here...
    }
}
```

Note that you are not permitted to declare a multipart namespace nested within another namespace.

Namespaces are not related to assemblies. It is perfectly acceptable to have different namespaces in the same assembly or to define types in the same namespace in different assemblies.

The using Directive

Obviously, namespaces can grow rather long and tiresome to type, and the ability to indicate a particular class with such specificity may not always be necessary. Fortunately, as noted at the beginning of the chapter, C# allows you to abbreviate a class's full name. To do this, list the class's namespace at the top of the file, prefixed with the using keyword. Throughout the rest of the file, you can refer to the types in the namespace simply by their type names:

```
using System;
using Wrox.ProCSharp;
```

As remarked earlier, virtually all C# source code will have the statement using System; simply because so many useful classes supplied by Microsoft are contained in the System namespace.

If two namespaces referenced by `using` statements contain a type of the same name, you will need to use the full (or at least a longer) form of the name to ensure that the compiler knows which type is to be accessed. For example, say classes called `NamespaceExample` exist in both the `Wrox.ProCSharp` `.Basics` and `Wrox.ProCSharp.OOP` namespaces. If you then create a class called `Test` in the `Wrox.ProCSharp` namespace, and instantiate one of the `NamespaceExample` classes in this class, you need to specify which of these two classes you're talking about:

```
using Wrox.ProCSharp;

class Test
{
    public static int Main()
    {
        Basics.NamespaceExample nSEx = new Basics.NamespaceExample();
     // do something with the nSEx variable.
        return 0;
    }
}
```

Because `using` *statements occur at the top of C# files, in the same place that C and C++ list* `#include` *statements, it's easy for programmers moving from C++ to C# to confuse namespaces with C++-style header files. Don't make this mistake. The* `using` *statement does no physical linking between files, and C# has no equivalent to C++ header files.*

Your organization will probably want to spend some time developing a namespace schema so that its developers can quickly locate functionality that they need and so that the names of the organization's homegrown classes won't conflict with those in off-the-shelf class libraries. Guidelines on establishing your own namespace scheme along with other naming recommendations are discussed later in this chapter.

Namespace Aliases

Another use of the `using` keyword is to assign aliases to classes and namespaces. If you have a very long namespace name that you want to refer to several times in your code but don't want to include in a simple `using` statement (for example, to avoid type name conflicts), you can assign an alias to the namespace. The syntax for this is:

```
using alias = NamespaceName;
```

The following example (a modified version of the previous example) assigns the alias `Introduction` to the `Wrox.ProCSharp.Basics` namespace and uses this to instantiate a `NamespaceExample` object, which is defined in this namespace. Notice the use of the namespace alias qualifier (`::`). This forces the search to start with the `Introduction` namespace alias. If a class called `Introduction` had been introduced in the same scope, a conflict would happen. The `::` operator allows the alias to be referenced even if the conflict exists. The `NamespaceExample` class has one method, `GetNamespace()`, which uses the `GetType()` method exposed by every class to access a `Type` object representing the class's type. You use this object to return a name of the class's namespace:

```
using System;
using Introduction =  Wrox.ProCSharp.Basics;
class Test
{
    public static int Main()
    {
        Introduction::NamespaceExample NSEx =
            new Introduction::NamespaceExample();
```

```
            Console.WriteLine(NSEx.GetNamespace());
            return 0;
        }
    }

namespace Wrox.ProCSharp.Basics
{
    class NamespaceExample
    {
        public string GetNamespace()
        {
            return this.GetType().Namespace;
        }
    }
}
```

The Main() Method

As you saw at the start of this chapter, C# programs start execution at a method named `Main()`. This must be a static method of a class (or struct), and must have a return type of either `int` or `void`.

Although it is common to specify the `public` modifier explicitly, because by definition the method must be called from outside the program, it doesn't actually matter what accessibility level you assign to the entry-point method — it will run even if you mark the method as `private`.

Multiple Main() Methods

When a C# console or Windows application is compiled, by default the compiler looks for exactly one `Main()` method in any class matching the signature that was just described and makes that class method the entry point for the program. If there is more than one `Main()` method, the compiler will return an error message. For example, consider the following code called `MainExample.cs`:

```
using System;

namespace Wrox.ProCSharp.Basics
{
    class Client
    {
        public static int Main()
        {
            MathExample.Main();
            return 0;
        }
    }

    class MathExample
    {
        static int Add(int x, int y)
        {
            return x + y;
        }

        public static int Main()
```

(continued)

(continued)

```
        {
            int i = Add(5,10);
            Console.WriteLine(i);
            return 0;
        }
    }
}
```

This contains two classes, both of which have a `Main()` method. If you try to compile this code in the usual way, you will get the following errors:

csc MainExample.cs

```
Microsoft (R) Visual C# Compiler version 9.00.20404
for Microsoft (R) .NET Framework version 3.5
Copyright (C) Microsoft Corporation. All rights reserved.

MainExample.cs(7,23): error CS0017: Program 'MainExample.exe' has more than
one entry point defined: 'Wrox.ProCSharp.Basics.Client.Main()'
MainExample.cs(21,23): error CS0017: Program 'MainExample.exe' has more than
one entry point defined: 'Wrox.ProCSharp.Basics.MathExample.Main()'
```

However, you can explicitly tell the compiler which of these methods to use as the entry point for the program by using the `/main` switch, together with the full name (including namespace) of the class to which the `Main()` method belongs:

```
csc MainExample.cs /main:Wrox.ProCSharp.Basics.MathExample
```

Passing Arguments to Main()

The examples so far have shown only the `Main()` method without any parameters. However, when the program is invoked, you can get the CLR to pass any command-line arguments to the program by including a parameter. This parameter is a string array, traditionally called `args` (although C# will accept any name). The program can use this array to access any options passed through the command line when the program is started.

The following sample, `ArgsExample.cs`, loops through the string array passed in to the `Main()` method and writes the value of each option to the console window:

```
using System;

namespace Wrox.ProCSharp.Basics
{
    class ArgsExample
    {
        public static int Main(string[] args)
        {
            for (int i = 0; i < args.Length; i++)
            {
                Console.WriteLine(args[i]);
            }
            return 0;
        }
    }
}
```

You can compile this as usual using the command line. When you run the compiled executable, you can pass in arguments after the name of the program, for example:

ArgsExample /a /b /c

```
/a
/b
/c
```

More on Compiling C# Files

You have seen how to compile console applications using `csc.exe`, but what about other types of applications? What if you want to reference a class library? The full set of compilation options for the C# compiler is of course detailed in the MSDN documentation, but we list here the most important options.

To answer the first question, you can specify what type of file you want to create using the `/target` switch, often abbreviated to `/t`. This can be one of those shown in the following table.

Option	Output
/t:exe	A console application (the default)
/t:library	A class library with a manifest
/t:module	A component without a manifest
/t:winexe	A Windows application (without a console window)

If you want a nonexecutable file (such as a DLL) to be loadable by the .NET runtime, you must compile it as a library. If you compile a C# file as a module, no assembly will be created. Although modules cannot be loaded by the runtime, they can be compiled into another manifest using the `/addmodule` switch.

Another option we need to mention is `/out`. This allows you to specify the name of the output file produced by the compiler. If the `/out` option isn't specified, the compiler will base the name of the output file on the name of the input C# file, adding an extension according to the target type (for example, `exe` for a Windows or console application or `dll` for a class library). Note that the `/out` and `/t`, or `/target`, options must precede the name of the file you want to compile.

If you want to reference types in assemblies that aren't referenced by default, you can use the `/reference` or `/r` switch, together with the path and file name of the assembly. The following example demonstrates how you can compile a class library and then reference that library in another assembly. It consists of two files:

❑   The class library

❑   A console application, which will call a class in the library

The first file is called `MathLibrary.cs` and contains the code for your DLL. To keep things simple, it contains just one (public) class, `MathLib`, with a single method that adds two `int`s:

```
namespace Wrox.ProCSharp.Basics
{
    public class MathLib
    {
        public int Add(int x, int y)
```

(continued)

(continued)

```
        {
            return x + y;
        }
    }
}
```

You can compile this C# file into a .NET DLL using the following command:

```
csc /t:library MathLibrary.cs
```

The console application, `MathClient.cs`, will simply instantiate this object and call its `Add()` method, displaying the result in the console window:

```
using System;

namespace Wrox.ProCSharp.Basics
{
    class Client
    {
        public static void Main()
        {
            MathLib mathObj = new MathLib();
            Console.WriteLine(mathObj.Add(7,8));
        }
    }
}
```

You can compile this code using the `/r` switch to point at or reference the newly compiled DLL:

```
csc MathClient.cs /r:MathLibrary.dll
```

You can then run it as normal just by entering `MathClient` at the command prompt. This displays the number 15 — the result of your addition.

Console I/O

By this point, you should have a basic familiarity with C#'s data types, as well as some knowledge of how the thread-of-control moves through a program that manipulates those data types. In this chapter, you have also used several of the `Console` class's static methods used for reading and writing data. Because these methods are so useful when writing basic C# programs, this section quickly reviews them in more detail.

To read a line of text from the console window, you use the `Console.ReadLine()` method. This will read an input stream (terminated when the user presses the `Return` key) from the console window and return the input string. There are also two corresponding methods for writing to the console, which you have already used extensively:

❑   `Console.Write()`—Writes the specified value to the console window.

❑   `Console.WriteLine()`—This does the same, but adds a newline character at the end of the output.

Various forms (overloads) of these methods exist for all of the predefined types (including `object`), so in most cases you don't have to convert values to strings before you display them.

For example, the following code lets the user input a line of text and displays that text:

```
string s = Console.ReadLine();
Console.WriteLine(s);
```

`Console.WriteLine()` also allows you to display formatted output in a way comparable to C's `printf()` function. To use `WriteLine()` in this way, you pass in a number of parameters. The first is a string containing markers in curly braces where the subsequent parameters will be inserted into the text. Each marker contains a zero-based index for the number of the parameter in the following list. For example, `{0}` represents the first parameter in the list. Consider the following code:

```
int i = 10;
int j = 20;
Console.WriteLine("{0} plus {1} equals {2}", i, j, i + j);
```

This code displays:

```
10 plus 20 equals 30
```

You can also specify a width for the value, and justify the text within that width, using positive values for right-justification and negative values for left-justification. To do this, use the format `{n,w}`, where n is the parameter index and w is the width value:

```
int i = 940;
int j = 73;
Console.WriteLine(" {0,4}\n+{1,4}\n ---- \n {2,4}", i, j, i + j);
```

The result of this is:

```
  940
+  73
 ----
 1013
```

Finally, you can also add a format string, together with an optional precision value. It is not possible to give a complete list of potential format strings because, as you will see in Chapter 8, "Strings and Regular Expressions," you can define your own format strings. However, the main ones in use for the predefined types are shown in the following table.

String	Description
C	Local currency format.
D	Decimal format. Converts an integer to base 10, and pads with leading zeros if a precision specifier is given.
E	Scientific (exponential) format. The precision specifier sets the number of decimal places (6 by default). The case of the format string (e or E) determines the case of the exponential symbol.
F	Fixed-point format; the precision specifier controls the number of decimal places. Zero is acceptable.
G	General format. Uses E or F formatting, depending on which is more compact.
N	Number format. Formats the number with commas as thousands separators, for example 32,767.44.
P	Percent format.
X	Hexadecimal format. The precision specifier can be used to pad with leading zeros.

Note that the format strings are normally case insensitive, except for e/E.

If you want to use a format string, you should place it immediately after the marker that gives the parameter number and field width, and separate it with a colon. For example, to format a decimal value as currency for the computer's locale, with precision to two decimal places, you would use C2:

```
decimal i = 940.23m;
decimal j = 73.7m;
Console.WriteLine(" {0,9:C2}\n+{1,9:C2}\n ---------\n {2,9:C2}", i, j, i + j);
```

The output of this in U.S. currency is:

```
      $940.23
 +     $73.70
      ---------
    $1,013.93
```

As a final trick, you can also use placeholder characters instead of these format strings to map out formatting. For example:

```
double d = 0.234;
Console.WriteLine("{0:#.00}", d);
```

This displays as .23, because the # symbol is ignored if there is no character in that place, and zeros will either be replaced by the character in that position if there is one or be printed as a zero.

Using Comments

The next topic — adding comments to your code — looks very simple on the surface but can be complex.

Internal Comments within the Source Files

As noted earlier in this chapter, C# uses the traditional C-type single-line (// ...) and multiline (/* ... */) comments:

```
// This is a single-line comment
/* This comment
    spans multiple lines. */
```

Everything in a single-line comment, from the // to the end of the line, will be ignored by the compiler, and everything from an opening /* to the next */ in a multiline comment combination will be ignored. Obviously, you can't include the combination */ in any multiline comments, because this will be treated as the end of the comment.

It is actually possible to put multiline comments within a line of code:

```
Console.WriteLine(/* Here's a comment! */ "This will compile.");
```

Use inline comments with care because they can make code hard to read. However, they can be useful when debugging if, say, you temporarily want to try running the code with a different value somewhere:

```
DoSomething(Width, /*Height*/ 100);
```

Comment characters included in string literals are, of course, treated like normal characters:

```
string s = "/* This is just a normal string .*/";
```

XML Documentation

In addition to the C-type comments, illustrated in the preceding section, C# has a very neat feature that we want to highlight: the ability to produce documentation in XML format automatically from special comments. These comments are single-line comments but begin with three slashes (///) instead of the usual two. Within these comments, you can place XML tags containing documentation of the types and type members in your code.

The tags in the following table are recognized by the compiler.

Tag	Description
`<c>`	Marks up text within a line as code, for example `<c>int i = 10;</c>`.
`<code>`	Marks multiple lines as code.
`<example>`	Marks up a code example.
`<exception>`	Documents an exception class. (Syntax is verified by the compiler.)
`<include>`	Includes comments from another documentation file. (Syntax is verified by the compiler.)
`<list>`	Inserts a list into the documentation.
`<param>`	Marks up a method parameter. (Syntax is verified by the compiler.)
`<paramref>`	Indicates that a word is a method parameter. (Syntax is verified by the compiler.)
`<permission>`	Documents access to a member. (Syntax is verified by the compiler.)
`<remarks>`	Adds a description for a member.
`<returns>`	Documents the return value for a method.
`<see>`	Provides a cross-reference to another parameter. (Syntax is verified by the compiler.)
`<seealso>`	Provides a "see also" section in a description. (Syntax is verified by the compiler.)
`<summary>`	Provides a short summary of a type or member.
`<value>`	Describes a property.

To see how this works, add some XML comments to the `MathLibrary.cs` file from the "More on Compiling C# Files" section, and call it `Math.cs`. You will add a `<summary>` element for the class and for its `Add()` method, and also a `<returns>` element and two `<param>` elements for the `Add()` method:

```
// Math.cs
namespace Wrox.ProCSharp.Basics
{

    ///<summary>
    ///    Wrox.ProCSharp.Basics.Math class.
    ///    Provides a method to add two integers.
    ///</summary>
    public class Math
```

(continued)

61

(continued)

```
    {
        ///<summary>
        ///    The Add method allows us to add two integers.
        ///</summary>
        ///<returns>Result of the addition (int)</returns>
        ///<param name="x">First number to add</param>
        ///<param name="y">Second number to add</param>
        public int Add(int x, int y)
        {
            return x + y;
        }
    }
}
```

The C# compiler can extract the XML elements from the special comments and use them to generate an XML file. To get the compiler to generate the XML documentation for an assembly, you specify the /doc option when you compile, together with the name of the file you want to be created:

```
csc /t:library /doc:Math.xml Math.cs
```

The compiler will throw an error if the XML comments do not result in a well-formed XML document.

This will generate an XML file named Math.xml, which looks like this:

```
<?xml version="1.0"?>
<doc>
    <assembly>
        <name>Math</name>
    </assembly>
    <members>
        <member name="T:Wrox.ProCSharp.Basics.Math">
            <summary>
                Wrox.ProCSharp.Basics.Math class.
                Provides a method to add two integers.
            </summary>
        </member>
        <member name=
                "M:Wrox.ProCSharp.Basics.Math.Add(System.Int32,System.Int32)">
            <summary>
                The Add method allows us to add two integers.
            </summary>
            <returns>Result of the addition (int)</returns>
            <param name="x">First number to add</param>
            <param name="y">Second number to add</param>
        </member>
    </members>
</doc>
```

Notice how the compiler has actually done some work for you; it has created an <assembly> element and also added a <member> element for each type or member of a type in the file. Each <member> element has a name attribute with the full name of the member as its value, prefixed by a letter that indicates whether this is a type (T:), field (F:), or member (M:).

The C# Preprocessor Directives

Besides the usual keywords, most of which you have now encountered, C# also includes a number of commands that are known as *preprocessor directives*. These commands never actually get translated to any commands in your executable code, but instead they affect aspects of the compilation process. For example, you can use preprocessor directives to prevent the compiler from compiling certain portions of your code. You might do this if you are planning to release two versions of the code — a basic version and an enterprise version that will have more features. You could use preprocessor directives to prevent the compiler from compiling code related to the additional features when you are compiling the basic version of the software. Another scenario is that you might have written bits of code that are intended to provide you with debugging information. You probably don't want those portions of code compiled when you actually ship the software.

The preprocessor directives are all distinguished by beginning with the # symbol.

> *C++ developers will recognize the preprocessor directives as something that plays an important part in C and C++. However, there aren't as many preprocessor directives in C#, and they are not used as often. C# provides other mechanisms, such as custom attributes, that achieve some of the same effects as C++ directives. Also, note that C# doesn't actually have a separate preprocessor in the way that C++ does. The so-called preprocessor directives are actually handled by the compiler. Nevertheless, C# retains the name preprocessor directive because these commands give the impression of a preprocessor.*

The next sections briefly cover the purposes of the preprocessor directives.

#define and #undef

#define is used like this:

```
#define DEBUG
```

What this does is tell the compiler that a symbol with the given name (in this case DEBUG) exists. It is a little bit like declaring a variable, except that this variable doesn't really have a value — it just exists. And this symbol isn't part of your actual code; it exists only for the benefit of the compiler, while the compiler is compiling the code, and has no meaning within the C# code itself.

#undef does the opposite, and removes the definition of a symbol:

```
#undef DEBUG
```

If the symbol doesn't exist in the first place, then #undef has no effect. Similarly, #define has no effect if a symbol already exists.

You need to place any #define and #undef directives at the beginning of the C# source file, before any code that declares any objects to be compiled.

#define isn't much use on its own, but when combined with other preprocessor directives, especially #if, it becomes very powerful.

> *Incidentally, you might notice some changes from the usual C# syntax. Preprocessor directives are not terminated by semicolons and normally constitute the only command on a line. That's because for the preprocessor directives, C# abandons its usual practice of requiring commands to be separated by semi-colons. If it sees a preprocessor directive, it assumes that the next command is on the next line.*

#if, #elif, #else, and #endif

These directives inform the compiler whether to compile a block of code. Consider this method:

```
int DoSomeWork(double x)
{
    // do something
#if DEBUG
    Console.WriteLine("x is " + x);
#endif
}
```

This code will compile as normal, except for the Console.WriteLine() method call that is contained inside the #if clause. This line will be executed only if the symbol DEBUG has been defined by a previous #define directive. When the compiler finds the #if directive, it checks to see if the symbol concerned exists and compiles the code inside the #if clause only if the symbol does exist. Otherwise, the compiler simply ignores all the code until it reaches the matching #endif directive. Typical practice is to define the symbol DEBUG while you are debugging and have various bits of debugging-related code inside #if clauses. Then, when you are close to shipping, you simply comment out the #define directive, and all the debugging code miraculously disappears, the size of the executable file gets smaller, and your end users don't get confused by being shown debugging information. (Obviously, you would do more testing to make sure your code still works without DEBUG defined.) This technique is very common in C and C++ programming and is known as *conditional compilation*.

The #elif (=else if) and #else directives can be used in #if blocks and have intuitively obvious meanings. It is also possible to nest #if blocks:

```
#define ENTERPRISE
#define W2K

// further on in the file

#if ENTERPRISE
    // do something
    #if W2K
        // some code that is only relevant to enterprise
        // edition running on W2K
    #endif
#elif PROFESSIONAL
    // do something else
#else
    // code for the leaner version
#endif
```

Note that, unlike the situation in C++, using #if is not the only way to compile code conditionally. C# provides an alternative mechanism through the Conditional *attribute, which is explored in Chapter 13, "Reflection."*

#if and #elif support a limited range of logical operators too, using the operators !, ==, !=, and ||. A symbol is considered to be true if it exists and false if it doesn't. For example:

```
#if W2K && (ENTERPRISE==false)    // if W2K is defined but ENTERPRISE isn't
```

#warning and #error

Two other very useful preprocessor directives are #warning and #error. These will respectively cause a warning or an error to be raised when the compiler encounters them. If the compiler sees a #warning directive, it will display whatever text appears after the #warning to the user, after which compilation continues. If it encounters a #error directive, it will display the subsequent text to the user as if it were a compilation error message and then immediately abandon the compilation, so no IL code will be generated.

You can use these directives as checks that you haven't done anything silly with your #define statements; you can also use the #warning statements to remind yourself to do something:

```
#if DEBUG && RELEASE
    #error "You've defined DEBUG and RELEASE simultaneously!"
#endif

#warning "Don't forget to remove this line before the boss tests the code!"
    Console.WriteLine("*I hate this job.*");
```

#region and #endregion

The #region and #endregion directives are used to indicate that a certain block of code is to be treated as a single block with a given name, like this:

```
#region Member Field Declarations
    int x;
    double d;
    Currency balance;
#endregion
```

This doesn't look that useful by itself; it doesn't affect the compilation process in any way. However, the real advantage is that these directives are recognized by some editors, including the Visual Studio .NET editor. These editors can use these directives to lay out your code better on the screen. You will see how this works in Chapter 15, "Visual Studio 2008."

#line

The #line directive can be used to alter the file name and line number information that is output by the compiler in warnings and error messages. You probably won't want to use this directive that often. It's most useful when you are coding in conjunction with some other package that alters the code you are typing in before sending it to the compiler. In this situation, line numbers, or perhaps the file names reported by the compiler, won't match up to the line numbers in the files or the file names you are editing. The #line directive can be used to restore the match. You can also use the syntax #line default to restore the line to the default line numbering:

```
#line 164 "Core.cs"    // We happen to know this is line 164 in the file
                       // Core.cs, before the intermediate
                       // package mangles it.

// later on

#line default          // restores default line numbering
```

#pragma

The `#pragma` directive can either suppress or restore specific compiler warnings. Unlike command-line options, the `#pragma` directive can be implemented on a class or method level, allowing a fine-grained control of what warnings are suppressed and when. The following example disables the "field not used" warning and then restores it after the `MyClass` class compiles:

```
#pragma warning disable 169
public class MyClass
{
   int neverUsedField;
}
#pragma warning restore 169
```

C# Programming Guidelines

The final section of this chapter supplies the guidelines you need to bear in mind when writing C# programs.

Rules for Identifiers

This section examines the rules governing what names you can use for variables, classes, methods, and so on. Note that the rules presented in this section are not merely guidelines: they are enforced by the C# compiler.

Identifiers are the names you give to variables, to user-defined types such as classes and structs, and to members of these types. Identifiers are case sensitive, so, for example, variables named `interestRate` and `InterestRate` would be recognized as different variables. Following are a few rules determining what identifiers you can use in C#:

❑ They must begin with a letter or underscore, although they can contain numeric characters.

❑ You can't use C# keywords as identifiers.

The following table lists the C# reserved keywords.

abstract	event	New	struct
as	explicit	Null	switch
base	extern	Object	this
bool	false	Operator	throw
break	finally	Out	true
byte	fixed	Override	try
case	float	Params	typeof
catch	for	Private	uint
char	foreach	Protected	ulong
checked	goto	Public	unchecked
class	if	Readonly	unsafe

const	implicit	Ref	ushort
continue	in	Return	using
decimal	int	Sbyte	virtual
default	interface	Sealed	volatile
delegate	internal	Short	void
do	is	Sizeof	while
double	lock	Stackalloc	
else	long	Static	
enum	namespace	String	

If you do need to use one of these words as an identifier (for example, if you are accessing a class written in a different language), you can prefix the identifier with the @ symbol to indicate to the compiler that what follows is to be treated as an identifier, not as a C# keyword (so abstract is not a valid identifier, but @abstract is).

Finally, identifiers can also contain Unicode characters, specified using the syntax \uXXXX, where XXXX is the four-digit hex code for the Unicode character. The following are some examples of valid identifiers:

❑ Name

❑ Überfluß

❑ _Identifier

❑ \u005fIdentifier

The last two items in this list are identical and interchangeable (because 005f is the Unicode code for the underscore character), so obviously these identifiers couldn't both be declared in the same scope. Note that although syntactically you are allowed to use the underscore character in identifiers, this isn't recommended in most situations. That's because it doesn't follow the guidelines for naming variables that Microsoft has written to ensure that developers use the same conventions, making it easier to read each other's code.

Usage Conventions

In any development language, there usually arise certain traditional programming styles. The styles are not part of the language itself but are conventions concerning, for example, how variables are named or how certain classes, methods, or functions are used. If most developers using that language follow the same conventions, it makes it easier for different developers to understand each other's code — which in turn generally helps program maintainability. For example, a common (though not universal) convention in Visual Basic 6 was that variables that represent strings have names beginning with lowercase s or lowercase str, as in the Visual Basic 6 statements Dim sResult As String or Dim strMessage As String. Conventions do, however, depend on the language and the environment. For example, C++ developers programming on the Windows platform have traditionally used the prefixes psz or lpsz to indicate strings—char *pszResult; char *lpszMessage;—but on Unix machines it's more common not to use any such prefixes: char *Result; char *Message;.

You'll notice from the sample code in this book that the convention in C# is to name variables without prefixes: `string Result; string Message;`.

> *The convention by which variable names are prefixed with letters that represent the data type is known as Hungarian notation. It means that other developers reading the code can immediately tell from the variable name what data type the variable represents. Hungarian notation is widely regarded as redundant in these days of smart editors and IntelliSense.*

Whereas, with many languages, usage conventions simply evolved as the language was used, with C# and the whole of the .NET Framework, Microsoft has written very comprehensive usage guidelines, which are detailed in the .NET/C# MSDN documentation. This should mean that, right from the start, .NET programs will have a high degree of interoperability in terms of developers being able to understand code. The guidelines have also been developed with the benefit of some 20 years' hindsight in object-oriented programming, and as a result have been carefully thought out and appear to have been well received in the developer community, to judge by the relevant newsgroups. Hence the guidelines are well worth following.

It should be noted, however, that the guidelines are not the same as language specifications. You should try to follow the guidelines when you can. Nevertheless, you won't run into problems if you do have a good reason for not doing so — for example, you won't get a compilation error because you don't follow these guidelines. The general rule is that if you don't follow the usage guidelines you must have a convincing reason. Departing from the guidelines should be a positive decision rather than simply not bothering. Also, if you compare the guidelines with the samples in the remainder of this book, you'll notice that in numerous examples we have chosen not to follow the conventions. That's usually because the conventions are designed for much larger programs than our samples, and although they are great if you are writing a complete software package, they are not really so suitable for small 20-line standalone programs. In many cases, following the conventions would have made our samples harder, rather than easier, to follow.

The full guidelines for good programming style are quite extensive. This section is confined to describing some of the more important guidelines, as well as the ones most likely to surprise you. If you want to make absolutely certain that your code follows the usage guidelines completely, you will need to refer to the MSDN documentation.

Naming Conventions

One important aspect to making your programs understandable is how you choose to name your items — and that includes naming variables, methods, classes, enumerations, and namespaces.

It is intuitively obvious that your names should reflect the purpose of the item and should not clash with other names. The general philosophy in the .NET Framework is also that the name of a variable should reflect the purpose of that variable instance and not the data type. For example, `height` is a good name for a variable, whereas `integerValue` isn't. However, you will probably feel that that principle is an ideal that is hard to achieve. Particularly when you are dealing with controls, in most cases, you'll probably be happier sticking with variable names like `confirmationDialog` and `chooseEmployeeListBox`, which do indicate the data type in the name.

The following sections look at some of the things you need to think about when choosing names.

Casing of Names

In many cases you should use *Pascal casing* for names. Pascal casing means that the first letter of each word in a name is capitalized: `EmployeeSalary`, `ConfirmationDialog`, `PlainTextEncoding`. You will notice that essentially all of the names of namespaces, classes, and members in the base classes follow Pascal casing. In particular, the convention of joining words using the underscore character is discouraged. So, you should try not to use names like `employee_salary`. It has also been common in other languages to use all capitals for names of constants. This is not advised in C# because such names are harder to read—the convention is to use Pascal casing throughout:

```
const int MaximumLength;
```

The only other casing scheme that you are advised to use is *camel casing*. Camel casing is similar to Pascal casing, except that the first letter of the first word in the name is not capitalized: employeeSalary, confirmationDialog, plainTextEncoding. Following are three situations in which you are advised to use camel casing:

❑ For names of all private member fields in types:

```
public int subscriberId;
```

Note, however, that often it is conventional to prefix names of member fields with an underscore:

```
public int _subscriberId;
```

❑ For names of all parameters passed to methods:

```
public void RecordSale(string salesmanName, int quantity);
```

❑ To distinguish items that would otherwise have the same name. A common example is when a property wraps around a field:

```
private string employeeName;


public string EmployeeName
{
   get
   {
      return employeeName;

   }


}
```

If you are doing this, you should always use camel casing for the private member and Pascal casing for the public or protected member, so that other classes that use your code see only names in Pascal case (except for parameter names).

You should also be wary about case sensitivity. C# is case sensitive, so it is syntactically correct for names in C# to differ only by the case, as in the previous examples. However, you should bear in mind that your assemblies might at some point be called from Visual Basic .NET applications — and *Visual Basic .NET is not case sensitive*. Hence, if you do use names that differ only by case, it is important to do so only in situations in which both names will never be seen outside your assembly. (The previous example qualifies as okay because camel case is used with the name that is attached to a private variable.) Otherwise, you may prevent other code written in Visual Basic .NET from being able to use your assembly correctly.

Name Styles

You should be consistent about your style of names. For example, if one of the methods in a class is called ShowConfirmationDialog(), then you should not give another method a name like ShowDialogWarning() or WarningDialogShow(). The other method should be called ShowWarningDialog().

Namespace Names

Namespace names are particularly important to design carefully to avoid risk of ending up with the same name for one of your namespaces as someone else uses. Remember, namespace names are the *only* way that .NET distinguishes names of objects in shared assemblies. So, if you use the same namespace name for your software package as another package, and both packages get installed on the same computer, there are going to be problems. Because of this, it's almost always a good idea to create a top-level namespace with the name of your company and then nest successive namespaces that narrow down the technology, group, or department you are working in or the name of the package your classes are intended for. Microsoft recommends namespace names that begin with <CompanyName> .<TechnologyName> as in these two examples:

```
WeaponsOfDestructionCorp.RayGunControllers
WeaponsOfDestructionCorp.Viruses
```

Names and Keywords

It is important that the names do not clash with any keywords. In fact, if you attempt to name an item in your code with a word that happens to be a C# keyword, you'll almost certainly get a syntax error because the compiler will assume that the name refers to a statement. However, because of the possibility that your classes will be accessed by code written in other languages, it is also important that you don't use names that are keywords in other .NET languages. Generally speaking, C++ keywords are similar to C# keywords, so confusion with C++ is unlikely, and those commonly encountered keywords that are unique to Visual C++ tend to start with two underscore characters. Like C#, C++ keywords are spelled in lowercase, so if you hold to the convention of naming your public classes and members with Pascal-style names, they will always have at least one uppercase letter in their names, and there will be no risk of clashes with C++ keywords. However, you are more likely to have problems with Visual Basic .NET, which has many more keywords than C# does, and being non-case-sensitive means that you cannot rely on Pascal-style names for your classes and methods.

The following table lists the keywords and standard function calls in Visual Basic .NET, which you should avoid, if possible, in whatever case combination, for your public C# classes.

Abs	Do	Loc	RGB
Add	Double	Local	Right
AddHandler	Each	Lock	RmDir
AddressOf	Else	LOF	Rnd
Alias	ElseIf	Log	RTrim
And	Empty	Long	SaveSettings
Ansi	End	Loop	Second
AppActivate	Enum	LTrim	Seek
Append	EOF	Me	Select
As	Erase	Mid	SetAttr
Asc	Err	Minute	SetException
Assembly	Error	MIRR	Shared
Atan	Event	MkDir	Shell

Auto	Exit	Module	Short
Beep	Exp	Month	Sign
Binary	Explicit	MustInherit	Sin
BitAnd	ExternalSource	MustOverride	Single
BitNot	False	MyBase	SLN
BitOr	FileAttr	MyClass	Space
BitXor	FileCopy	Namespace	Spc
Boolean	FileDateTime	New	Split
ByRef	FileLen	Next	Sqrt
Byte	Filter	Not	Static
ByVal	Finally	Nothing	Step
Call	Fix	NotInheritable	Stop
Case	For	NotOverridable	Str
Catch	Format	Now	StrComp
CBool	FreeFile	NPer	StrConv
CByte	Friend	NPV	Strict
CDate	Function	Null	String
CDbl	FV	Object	Structure
CDec	Get	Oct	Sub
ChDir	GetAllSettings	Off	Switch
ChDrive	GetAttr	On	SYD
Choose	GetException	Open	SyncLock
Chr	GetObject	Option	Tab
CInt	GetSetting	Optional	Tan
Class	GetType	Or	Text
Clear	GoTo	Overloads	Then
CLng	Handles	Overridable	Throw
Close	Hex	Overrides	TimeOfDay
Collection	Hour	ParamArray	Timer
Command	If	Pmt	TimeSerial
Compare	Iif	PPmt	TimeValue
Const	Implements	Preserve	To

Cos	Imports	Print	Today
CreateObject	In	Private	Trim
CShort	Inherits	Property	Try
CSng	Input	Public	TypeName
CStr	InStr	Put	TypeOf
CurDir	Int	PV	UBound
Date	Integer	QBColor	UCase
DateAdd	Interface	Raise	Unicode
DateDiff	Ipmt	RaiseEvent	Unlock
DatePart	IRR	Randomize	Until
DateSerial	Is	Rate	Val
DateValue	IsArray	Read	Weekday
Day	IsDate	ReadOnly	While
DDB	IsDbNull	ReDim	Width
Decimal	IsNumeric	Remove	With
Declare	Item	RemoveHandler	WithEvents
Default	Kill	Rename	Write
Delegate	Lcase	Replace	WriteOnly
DeleteSetting	Left	Reset	Xor
Dim	Lib	Resume	Year
Dir	Line	Return	

Use of Properties and Methods

One area that can cause confusion in a class is whether a particular quantity should be represented by a property or a method. The rules here are not hard and fast, but in general, you ought to use a property if something really should look and feel like a variable. (If you're not sure what a property is, see Chapter 3, "Objects and Types.") This means, among other things, that:

❑ Client code should be able to read its value. Write-only properties are not recommended, so, for example, use a SetPassword() method, not a write-only Password property.

❑ Reading the value should not take too long. The fact that something is a property usually suggests that reading it will be relatively quick.

❑ Reading the value should not have any observable and unexpected side effect. Further, setting the value of a property should not have any side effect that is not directly related to the property. Setting the width of a dialog box has the obvious effect of changing the appearance of the dialog box on the screen. That's fine, because that's obviously related to the property in question.

❑ It should be possible to set properties in any order. In particular, it is not good practice when setting a property to throw an exception because another related property has not yet been set. For example, if in order to use a class that accesses a database, you need to set `ConnectionString`, `UserName`, and `Password`, then the author of the class should make sure the class is implemented so that the user really can set them in any order.

❑ Successive reads of a property should give the same result. If the value of a property is likely to change unpredictably, you should code it up as a method instead. `Speed`, in a class that monitors the motion of an automobile, is not a good candidate for a property. Use a `GetSpeed()` method here; but, `Weight` and `EngineSize` are good candidates for properties because they will not change for a given object.

If the item you are coding satisfies all of the preceding criteria, it is probably a good candidate for a property. Otherwise, you should use a method.

Use of Fields

The guidelines are pretty simple here. Fields should almost always be private, except that in some cases it may be acceptable for constant or read-only fields to be public. The reason is that if you make a field public, you may hinder your ability to extend or modify the class in the future.

The previous guidelines should give you a foundation of good practices, and you should also use them in conjunction with good object-oriented programming style.

A final helpful note to keep in mind is that Microsoft has been fairly careful about being consistent and has followed its own guidelines when writing the .NET base classes. So a very good way to get an intuitive feel for the conventions to follow when writing .NET code is to simply look at the base classes — see how classes, members, and namespaces are named, and how the class hierarchy works. Consistency between the base classes and your classes will help in readability and maintainability.

Summary

This chapter examined some of the basic syntax of C#, covering the areas needed to write simple C# programs. We covered a lot of ground, but much of it will be instantly recognizable to developers who are familiar with any C-style language (or even JavaScript).

You have seen that although C# syntax is similar to C++ and Java syntax, there are many minor differences. You have also seen that in many areas this syntax is combined with facilities to write code very quickly, for example high-quality string handling facilities. C# also has a strongly defined type system, based on a distinction between value and reference types. Chapters 3 and 4 cover the C# object-oriented programming features.

3

Objects and Types

So far, you've been introduced to some of the building blocks of the C# language, including variables, data types, and program flow statements, and you have seen a few very short complete programs containing little more than the `Main()` method. What you haven't really seen yet is how to put all of these together to form a longer, complete program. The key to this lies in working with classes — the subject of this chapter. In particular, this chapter covers:

❑   The differences between classes and structs

❑   Class members

❑   Passing values by value and by reference

❑   Method overloading

❑   Constructors and static constructors

❑   Read-only fields

❑   Partial classes

❑   Static classes

❑   The `Object` class, from which all other types are derived

Note that we cover inheritance and features related to inheritance in Chapter 4, "Inheritance."

> *This chapter introduces the basic syntax associated with classes. However, we assume that you are already familiar with the underlying principles of using classes — for example, that you know what a constructor or a property is. This chapter is largely confined to applying those principles in C# code.*

In this chapter, we introduce and explain those concepts that are not necessarily supported by most object-oriented languages. For example, although object constructors are a widely used concept that you should be familiar with, static constructors are something new to C#, so this chapter explains how static constructors work.

Classes and Structs

Classes and structs are essentially templates from which you can create objects. Each object contains data and has methods to manipulate and access that data. The class defines what data and functionality each particular object (called an *instance*) of that class can contain. For example, if you have a class that represents a customer, it might define fields such as CustomerID, FirstName, LastName, and Address, which you will use to hold information about a particular customer. It might also define functionality that acts upon the data stored in these fields. You can then instantiate an object of this class to represent one specific customer, set the field values for that instance, and use its functionality.

```
class PhoneCustomer
{
    public const string DayOfSendingBill = "Monday";
    public int CustomerID;
    public string FirstName;
    public string LastName;
}
```

Structs differ from classes in the way that they are stored in memory and accessed (classes are reference types stored in the heap; structs are value types stored on the stack), and in some of their features (for example, structs don't support inheritance). You will tend to use structs for smaller data types for performance reasons. In terms of syntax, however, structs look very similar to classes; the main difference is that you use the keyword struct instead of class to declare them. For example, if you wanted all PhoneCustomer instances to be allocated on the stack instead of the managed heap, you could write:

```
struct PhoneCustomerStruct
{
    public const string DayOfSendingBill = "Monday";
    public int CustomerID;
    public string FirstName;
    public string LastName;
}
```

For both classes and structs, you use the keyword new to declare an instance. This keyword creates the object and initializes it; in the following example, the default behavior is to zero out its fields:

```
PhoneCustomer myCustomer = new PhoneCustomer();          // works for a class
PhoneCustomerStruct myCustomer2 = new PhoneCustomerStruct();// works for a struct
```

In most cases, you'll use classes much more often than structs. Therefore, we discuss classes first and then the differences between classes and structs and the specific reasons why you might choose to use a struct instead of a class. Unless otherwise stated, however, you can assume that code presented for a class will work equally well for a struct.

Class Members

The data and functions within a class are known as the class's *members*. Microsoft's official terminology distinguishes between data members and function members. In addition to these members, classes can contain nested types (such as other classes). All members of a class can be declared as public (in which case they are directly accessible from outside the class) or as private (in which case they are visible only to other code within the class), just as in Visual Basic, C++, and Java. C# also has variants on this theme, such as protected (which indicates a member is visible only to the class in question and to any derived classes). Chapter 4 provides a comprehensive list of the different accessibilities.

Data Members

Data members are those members that contain the data for the class — fields, constants, and events. Data members can be either static (associated with the class as a whole) or instance (each instance of the class has its own copy of the data). As usual for object-oriented languages, a class member is always an instance member unless it is explicitly declared as static.

Fields are any variables associated with the class. You have already seen fields in use in the PhoneCustomer class in the previous example.

Once you have instantiated a PhoneCustomer object, you can then access these fields using the Object.FieldName syntax, as shown in this example:

```
PhoneCustomer Customer1 = new PhoneCustomer();
Customer1.FirstName = "Simon";
```

Constants can be associated with classes in the same way as variables. You declare a constant using the const keyword. Once again, if it is declared as public, it will be accessible from outside the class.

```
class PhoneCustomer
{
    public const string DayOfSendingBill = "Monday";
    public int CustomerID;
    public string FirstName;
    public string LastName;
}
```

Events are class members that allow an object to notify a caller whenever something noteworthy happens, such as a field or property of the class changing, or some form of user interaction occurring. The client can have code, known as an event handler, that reacts to the event. Chapter 7, "Delegates and Events," looks at events in detail.

Function Members

Function members are those members that provide some functionality for manipulating the data in the class. They include methods, properties, constructors, finalizers, operators, and indexers.

Methods are functions that are associated with a particular class. They can be either instance methods, which work on a particular instance of a class, or static methods, which provide more generic functionality that doesn't require you to instantiate a class (like the Console.WriteLine() method). Methods are discussed in the next section.

Properties are sets of functions that can be accessed from the client in a similar way to the public fields of the class. C# provides a specific syntax for implementing read and write properties on your classes, so you don't have to jury-rig methods whose names have the words Get or Set embedded in them. Because there's a dedicated syntax for properties that is distinct from that for normal functions, the illusion of objects as actual things is strengthened for client code.

Constructors are special functions that are called automatically when an object is instantiated. They must have the same name as the class to which they belong and cannot have a return type. Constructors are useful for initializing the values of fields.

Finalizers are similar to constructors but are called when the CLR detects that an object is no longer needed. They have the same name as the class, preceded by a tilde (~). C++ programmers should note that finalizers are used much less frequently in C# than their nearest C++ equivalent, destructors, because the CLR handles garbage collection automatically. Also, it is impossible to predict precisely when a finalizer will be called. Finalizers are discussed in Chapter 12, "Memory Management and Pointers."

Operators, at their simplest, are actions like + or –. When you add two integers, you are, strictly speaking, using the + operator for integers. However, C# also allows you to specify how existing operators will work with your own classes (*operator overloading*). Chapter 6, "Operators and Casts," looks at operators in detail.

Indexers allow your objects to be indexed in the same way as an array or collection. This topic is also covered in Chapter 6.

Methods

In Visual Basic, C, and C++, you could define global functions that were not associated with a particular class. This is not the case in C#. As noted earlier, in C# every function must be associated with a class or struct.

Note that official C# terminology does in fact make a distinction between functions and methods. In C# terminology, the term "function member" includes not only methods, but also other nondata members of a class or struct. This includes indexers, operators, constructors, destructors, and also — perhaps somewhat surprisingly — properties. These are contrasted with data members: fields, constants, and events.

Declaring Methods

The syntax for defining a method in C# is just what you'd expect from a C-style language and is virtually identical to the syntax in C++ and Java. The main syntactical difference from C++ is that, in C#, each method is separately declared as public or private. It is not possible to use `public:` blocks to group several method definitions. Also, all C# methods are declared and defined in the class definition. There is no facility in C# to separate the method implementation as there is in C++.

In C#, the definition of a method consists of any method modifiers (such as the method's accessibility), the type of the return value, followed by the name of the method, followed by a list of input arguments enclosed in parentheses, followed by the body of the method enclosed in curly braces:

```
[modifiers] return_type MethodName([parameters])
{
    // Method body
}
```

Each parameter consists of the name of the type of the parameter, and the name by which it can be referenced in the body of the method. Also, if the method returns a value, a return statement must be used with the return value to indicate each exit point. For example:

```
public bool IsSquare(Rectangle rect)
{
    return (rect.Height == rect.Width);
}
```

This code uses one of the .NET base classes, `System.Drawing.Rectangle`, which represents a rectangle.

If the method doesn't return anything, you specify a return type of void because you can't omit the return type altogether, and if it takes no arguments, you still need to include an empty set of parentheses after the method name (as with the `Main()` method). In this case, including a return statement is optional — the method returns automatically when the closing curly brace is reached. You should note that a method can contain as many return statements as required:

```
public bool IsPositive(int value)
{
    if (value < 0)
        return false;
    return true;
}
```

Invoking Methods

The syntax for invoking a method is exactly the same in C# as it is in C++ and Java. And, the only difference between C# and Visual Basic is that round brackets must always be used when invoking the method in C# — this is actually simpler than the Visual Basic 6 set of rules whereby brackets were sometimes necessary and at other times not allowed.

The following example, MathTest, illustrates the syntax for definition and instantiation of classes, and definition and invocation of methods. Besides the class that contains the Main() method, it defines a class named MathTest, which contains a couple of methods and a field.

```
using System;

namespace Wrox.ProCSharp.MathTestSample
{
    class MainEntryPoint
    {
        static void Main()
        {
            // Try calling some static functions.
            Console.WriteLine("Pi is " + MathTest.GetPi());
            int x = MathTest.GetSquareOf(5);
            Console.WriteLine("Square of 5 is " + x);

            // Instantiate at MathTest object
            MathTest math = new MathTest();    // this is C#'s way of
                                               // instantiating a reference type

            // Call non-static methods
            math.value = 30;
            Console.WriteLine(
                "Value field of math variable contains " + math.value);
            Console.WriteLine("Square of 30 is " + math.GetSquare());
        }
    }

    // Define a class named MathTest on which we will call a method
    class MathTest
    {
        public int value;

        public int GetSquare()
        {
            return value*value;
        }

        public static int GetSquareOf(int x)
        {
            return x*x;
        }

        public static double GetPi()
        {
            return 3.14159;
        }
    }
}
```

Running the `MathTest` example produces these results:

csc MathTest.cs

```
Microsoft (R) Visual C# Compiler version 9.00.20404
for Microsoft (R) .NET Framework version 3.5
Copyright (C) Microsoft Corporation. All rights reserved.

MathTest.exe
Pi is 3.14159
Square of 5 is 25
Value field of math variable contains 30
Square of 30 is 900
```

As you can see from the code, the `MathTest` class contains a field that contains a number, as well as a method to find the square of this number. It also contains two static methods, one to return the value of pi and one to find the square of the number passed in as a parameter.

Some features of this class are not really good examples of C# program design. For example, `GetPi()` would usually be implemented as a `const` field, but following good design here would mean using some concepts that we have not yet introduced.

Most of the syntax in the preceding example should be familiar to C++ and Java developers. If your background is in Visual Basic, just think of the `MathTest` class as being like a Visual Basic class module that implements fields and methods. There are a couple of points to watch out for though, whatever your language.

Passing Parameters to Methods

In general, parameters can be passed into methods by reference or by value. When a variable is passed by reference, the called method gets the actual variable — so any changes made to the variable inside the method persist when the method exits. But, when a variable is passed by value, the called method gets an identical copy of the variable — which means any changes made are lost when the method exits. For complex data types, passing by reference is more efficient because of the large amount of data that must be copied when passing by value.

In C#, all parameters are passed by value unless you specifically say otherwise. This is the same behavior as in C++ but the opposite of Visual Basic. However, you need to be careful in understanding the implications of this for reference types. Because reference type variables hold only a reference to an object, it is this reference that will be copied, not the object itself. Hence, changes made to the underlying object will persist. Value type variables, in contrast, hold the actual data, so a copy of the data itself will be passed into the method. An `int`, for instance, is passed by value to a method, and any changes that the method makes to the value of that `int` do not change the value of the original `int` object. Conversely, if an array or any other reference type, such as a class, is passed into a method, and the method uses the reference to change a value in that array, the new value is reflected in the original array object.

Here is an example, `ParameterTest.cs`, that demonstrates this:

```
using System;

namespace Wrox.ProCSharp.ParameterTestSample
{
    class ParameterTest
    {
        static void SomeFunction(int[] ints, int i)
        {
            ints[0] = 100;
            i = 100;
        }

        public static int Main()
```

```
        {
            int i = 0;
            int[] ints = { 0, 1, 2, 4, 8 };
            // Display the original values.
            Console.WriteLine("i = " + i);
            Console.WriteLine("ints[0] = " + ints[0]);
            Console.WriteLine("Calling SomeFunction...");

            // After this method returns, ints will be changed,
            // but i will not.
            SomeFunction(ints, i);
            Console.WriteLine("i = " + i);
            Console.WriteLine("ints[0] = " + ints[0]);
            return 0;
        }
    }
}
```

The output of this is:

csc ParameterTest.cs

```
Microsoft (R) Visual C# Compiler version 9.00.20404
for Microsoft (R) .NET Framework version 3.5
Copyright (C) Microsoft Corporation. All rights reserved.

ParameterTest.exe
i = 0
ints[0] = 0
Calling SomeFunction...
i = 0
ints[0] = 100
```

Notice how the value of i remains unchanged, but the value changed in ints is also changed in the original array.

The behavior of strings is different again. This is because strings are immutable (if you alter a string's value, you create an entirely new string), so strings don't display the typical reference-type behavior. Any changes made to a string within a method call won't affect the original string. This point is discussed in more detail in Chapter 8, "Strings and Regular Expressions."

ref Parameters

As mentioned, passing variables by value is the default, but you can force value parameters to be passed by reference. To do so, use the ref keyword. If a parameter is passed to a method, and if the input argument for that method is prefixed with the ref keyword, any changes that the method makes to the variable will affect the value of the original object:

```
static void SomeFunction(int[] ints, ref int i)
{
    ints[0] = 100;
    i = 100;      // The change to i will persist after SomeFunction() exits.
}
```

You will also need to add the ref keyword when you invoke the method:

```
SomeFunction(ints, ref i);
```

Adding the `ref` keyword in C# serves the same purpose as using the `&` syntax in C++ to specify passing by reference. However, C# makes the behavior more explicit (thus hopefully preventing bugs) by requiring the use of the `ref` keyword when invoking the method.

Finally, it is also important to understand that C# continues to apply initialization requirements to parameters passed to methods. Any variable must be initialized before it is passed into a method, whether it is passed in by value or by reference.

out Parameters

In C-style languages, it is common for functions to be able to output more than one value from a single routine. This is accomplished using output parameters, by assigning the output values to variables that have been passed to the method by reference. Often, the starting values of the variables that are passed by reference are unimportant. Those values will be overwritten by the function, which may never even look at any previous value.

It would be convenient if you could use the same convention in C#. However, C# requires that variables be initialized with a starting value before they are referenced. Although you could initialize your input variables with meaningless values before passing them into a function that will fill them with real, meaningful ones, this practice seems at best needless and at worst confusing. However, there is a way to short-circuit the C# compiler's insistence on initial values for input arguments.

You do this with the `out` keyword. When a method's input argument is prefixed with `out`, that method can be passed a variable that has not been initialized. The variable is passed by reference, so any changes that the method makes to the variable will persist when control returns from the called method. Again, you also need to use the `out` keyword when you call the method, as well as when you define it:

```
static void SomeFunction(out int i)
{
    i = 100;
}

public static int Main()
{
    int i; // note how i is declared but not initialized.
    SomeFunction(out i);
    Console.WriteLine(i);
    return 0;
}
```

The `out` keyword is an example of something new in C# that has no analogy in either Visual Basic or C++ and that has been introduced to make C# more secure against bugs. If an `out` parameter isn't assigned a value within the body of the function, the method won't compile.

Method Overloading

C# supports method overloading — several versions of the method that have different signatures (that is, the same name, but a different number of parameters and or different parameter data types). However, C# does not support default parameters in the way that, say, C++ or Visual Basic does. In order to overload methods, you simply declare the methods with the same name but different numbers or types of parameters:

```
class ResultDisplayer
{
    void DisplayResult(string result)
    {
        // implementation
    }
```

```
        void DisplayResult(int result)
        {
            // implementation
        }
    }
```

Because C# does not support optional parameters, you will need to use method overloading to achieve the same effect:

```
    class MyClass
    {
        int DoSomething(int x)     // want 2nd parameter with default value 10
        {
            DoSomething(x, 10);
        }

        int DoSomething(int x, int y)
        {
            // implementation
        }
    }
```

As in any language, method overloading carries with it the potential for subtle runtime bugs if the wrong overload is called. Chapter 4 discusses how to code defensively against these problems. For now, you should know that C# does place some minimum differences on the parameters of overloaded methods:

❑   It is not sufficient for two methods to differ only in their return type.

❑   It is not sufficient for two methods to differ only by virtue of a parameter having been declared as ref or out.

Properties

Properties are unusual in that they represent an idea that C# has taken from Visual Basic, not from C++ and Java. The idea of a property is that it is a method or pair of methods that are dressed to look like a field as far as any client code is concerned. A good example of this is the Height property of a Windows Form. Suppose that you have the following code:

```
    // mainForm is of type System.Windows.Forms
    mainForm.Height = 400;
```

On executing this code, the height of the window will be set to 400, and you will see the window resize on the screen. Syntactically, this code looks like you're setting a field, but in fact you are calling a property accessor that contains code to resize the form.

To define a property in C#, you use the following syntax:

```
    public string SomeProperty
    {
        get
        {
            return "This is the property value.";
        }
        set
        {
            // do whatever needs to be done to set the property.
        }
    }
```

The `get` accessor takes no parameters and must return the same type as the declared property. You should not specify any explicit parameters for the `set` accessor either, but the compiler assumes it takes one parameter, which is of the same type again, and which is referred to as `value`. As an example, the following code contains a property called `ForeName`, which sets a field called `foreName` and applies a length limit:

```
private string foreName;

public string ForeName
{
   get
   {
      return foreName;
   }
   set
   {
      if (value.Length > 20)
         // code here to take error recovery action
         // (eg. throw an exception)
      else
         foreName = value;
   }
}
```

Note the naming convention used here. You take advantage of C#'s case sensitivity by using the same name, Pascal-cased for the public property, and camel-cased for the equivalent private field if there is one. Some developers prefer to use field names that are prefixed by an underscore: `_foreName`; this provides an extremely convenient way of identifying fields.

Visual Basic 6 programmers should remember that C# does not distinguish between Visual Basic 6 `Set` and Visual Basic 6 `Let`: In C#, the write accessor is always identified with the keyword `set`.

Read-Only and Write-Only Properties

It is possible to create a read-only property by simply omitting the `set` accessor from the property definition. Thus, to make `ForeName` read-only in the previous example:

```
private string foreName;

public string ForeName
{
   get
   {
      return foreName;
   }
}
```

It is similarly possible to create a write-only property by omitting the `get` accessor. However, this is regarded as poor programming practice because it could be confusing to authors of client code. In general, it is recommended that if you are tempted to do this, you should use a method instead.

Access Modifiers for Properties

C# does allow the `set` and `get` accessors to have differing access modifiers. This would allow a property to have a public `get` and a private or protected `set`. This can help control how or when a property can be set. In the following code example, notice that the `set` has a private access modifier and the `get` does not have any. In this case, the `get` takes on the access level of the property. One of the accessors must follow the access level of the property. A compile error will be generated if the `get` accessor has the `protected` access level associated with it because that would make both accessors have a different access level from the property.

```
public string Name
{
  get
  {
    return _name;
  }
  private set
  {
    _name = value;
  }
}
```

Auto-Implemented Properties

If there isn't going to be any logic in the properties `set` and `get`, then auto-implemented properties can be used. Auto-implemented properties implement the backing member variable automatically. The code for the previous example would look like this:

```
public string ForeName  {get; set;}
```

The declaration `private string foreName;` is not needed. The compiler will create this automatically.

By using auto-implemented properties, validation of the property cannot be done at the property set. So in the previous example we could not have checked to see if it is less than 20 characters. Also both accessors must be present. So an attempt to make a property read-only would cause an error:

```
public string ForeName  {get;}
```

However, the access level of each accessor can be different. So the following is acceptable:

```
public string ForeName  {get; private set;}
```

A Note About Inlining

Some developers may worry that the previous sections have presented a number of situations in which standard C# coding practices have led to very small functions — for example, accessing a field via a property instead of directly. Is this going to hurt performance because of the overhead of the extra function call? The answer is that there is no need to worry about performance loss from these kinds of programming methodologies in C#. Recall that C# code is compiled to IL, then JIT compiled at runtime to native executable code. The JIT compiler is designed to generate highly optimized code and will ruthlessly inline code as appropriate (in other words, it replaces function calls with inline code). A method or property whose implementation simply calls another method or returns a field will almost certainly be inlined. Note, however, that the decision of where to inline is made entirely by the CLR. There is no way for you to control which methods are inlined by using, for example, some keyword similar to the `inline` keyword of C++.

Constructors

The syntax for declaring basic constructors in C# is the same as in Java and C++. You declare a method that has the same name as the containing class and that does not have any return type:

```
public class MyClass
{
    public MyClass()
    {
    }
    // rest of class definition
```

As in C++ and Java, it's not necessary to provide a constructor for your class. We haven't supplied one for any of the examples so far in this book. In general, if you don't supply any constructor, the compiler will just make up a default one for you behind the scenes. It will be a very basic constructor that just initializes all the member fields by zeroing them out (null reference for reference types, zero for numeric data types, and false for bools). Often, that will be adequate; if not, you'll need to write your own constructor.

> For C++ programmers: Because primitive fields in C# are by default initialized by being zeroed out, whereas primitive fields in C++ are by default uninitialized, you may find that you don't need to write constructors in C# as often as you would in C++.

Constructors follow the same rules for overloading as other methods (that is, you can provide as many overloads to the constructor as you want, provided they are clearly different in signature):

```
public MyClass()    // zero-parameter constructor
{
    // construction code
}
public MyClass(int number)    // another overload
{
    // construction code
}
```

Note, however, that if you supply any constructors that take parameters, the compiler will not automatically supply a default one. This is done only if you have not defined any constructors at all. In the following example, because a one-parameter constructor is defined, the compiler assumes that this is the only constructor you want to be available, so it will not implicitly supply any others:

```
public class MyNumber
{
    private int number;
    public MyNumber(int number)
    {
        this.number = number;
    }
}
```

This code also illustrates typical use of the this keyword to distinguish member fields from parameters of the same name. If you now try instantiating a MyNumber object using a no-parameter constructor, you will get a compilation error:

```
MyNumber numb = new MyNumber();    // causes compilation error
```

We should mention that it is possible to define constructors as private or protected, so that they are invisible to code in unrelated classes too:

```
public class MyNumber
{
    private int number;
    private MyNumber(int number)    // another overload
    {
        this.number = number;
    }
}
```

This example hasn't actually defined any public or even any protected constructors for MyNumber. This would actually make it impossible for MyNumber to be instantiated by outside code using the new operator (though you might write a public static property or method in MyNumber that can instantiate the class). This is useful in two situations:

❑   If your class serves only as a container for some static members or properties and therefore should never be instantiated

❑   If you want the class to only ever be instantiated by calling some static member function (this is the so-called class factory approach to object instantiation)

Static Constructors

One novel feature of C# is that it is also possible to write a static no-parameter constructor for a class. Such a constructor will be executed only once, as opposed to the constructors written so far, which are instance constructors that are executed whenever an object of that class is created. There is no equivalent to the static constructor in C++ or Visual Basic 6.

```
class MyClass
{
    static MyClass()
    {
        // initialization code
    }
    // rest of class definition
}
```

One reason for writing a static constructor is if your class has some static fields or properties that need to be initialized from an external source before the class is first used.

The .NET runtime makes no guarantees about when a static constructor will be executed, so you should not place any code in it that relies on it being executed at a particular time (for example, when an assembly is loaded). Nor is it possible to predict in what order static constructors of different classes will execute. However, what is guaranteed is that the static constructor will run at most once, and that it will be invoked before your code makes any reference to the class. In C#, the static constructor usually seems to be executed immediately before the first call to any member of the class.

Notice that the static constructor does not have any access modifiers. It's never called by any other C# code, but always by the .NET runtime when the class is loaded, so any access modifier like public or private would be meaningless. For this same reason, the static constructor can never take any parameters, and there can be only one static constructor for a class. It should also be obvious that a static constructor can access only static members, not instance members, of the class.

Note that it is possible to have a static constructor and a zero-parameter instance constructor defined in the same class. Although the parameter lists are identical, there is no conflict. That's because the static constructor is executed when the class is loaded, but the instance constructor is executed whenever an instance is created — so there won't be any confusion about which constructor gets executed when.

Note that if you have more than one class that has a static constructor, the static constructor that will be executed first is undefined. This means that you should not put any code in a static constructor that depends on other static constructors having been or not having been executed. However, if any static fields have been given default values, these will be allocated before the static constructor is called.

The next example illustrates the use of a static constructor and is based on the idea of a program that has user preferences (which are presumably stored in some configuration file). To keep things simple, we'll assume just one user preference — a quantity called `BackColor`, which might represent the background color to be used in an application. And because we don't want to get into the details of writing code to read data from an external source here, we'll make the assumption that the preference is to have a background color of red on weekdays and green on weekends. All the program will do is display the preference in a console window — but this is enough to see a static constructor at work.

```
namespace Wrox.ProCSharp.StaticConstructorSample
{
    public class UserPreferences
    {
        public static readonly Color BackColor;

        static UserPreferences()
        {
            DateTime now = DateTime.Now;
            if (now.DayOfWeek == DayOfWeek.Saturday
                || now.DayOfWeek == DayOfWeek.Sunday)
                BackColor = Color.Green;
            else
                BackColor = Color.Red;
        }

        private UserPreferences()
        {
        }
    }
}
```

This code shows how the color preference is stored in a static variable, which is initialized in the static constructor. This field is declared as read-only, which means that its value can only be set in a constructor. You learn about read-only fields in more detail later in this chapter. The code uses a few helpful structs that Microsoft has supplied as part of the Framework class library, `System.DateTime` and `System.Drawing.Color`. `DateTime` implements both a static property, `Now`, which returns the current time, and an instance property, `DayOfWeek`, which works out what day of the week a date-time represents. `Color` (which is discussed in Chapter 33, "Graphics with GDI+") is used to store colors. It implements various static properties, such as `Red` and `Green` as used in this example, which return commonly used colors. In order to use `Color`, you need to reference the `System.Drawing.dll` assembly when compiling, and you must add a `using` statement for the `System.Drawing` namespace:

```
using System;
using System.Drawing;
```

You test the static constructor with this code:

```
class MainEntryPoint
{
    static void Main(string[] args)
    {
        Console.WriteLine("User-preferences: BackColor is: " +
                          UserPreferences.BackColor.ToString());
    }
}
```

Compiling and running this code results in this output:

StaticConstructor.exe

```
User-preferences: BackColor is: Color [Red]
```

Of course if the code is executed during the weekend, your color preference would be Green.

Calling Constructors from Other Constructors

You may sometimes find yourself in the situation where you have several constructors in a class, perhaps to accommodate some optional parameters, for which the constructors have some code in common. For example, consider this:

```
class Car
{
    private string description;
    private uint nWheels;
    public Car(string description, uint nWheels)
    {
        this.description = description;
        this.nWheels = nWheels;
    }

    public Car(string description)
    {
        this.description = description;
        this.nWheels = 4;
    }
    // etc.
```

Both constructors initialize the same fields. It would clearly be neater to place all the code in one place, and C# has a special syntax, known as a constructor initializer, to allow this:

```
class Car
{
    private string description;
    private uint nWheels;

    public Car(string description, uint nWheels)
    {
        this.description = description;
        this.nWheels = nWheels;
    }

    public Car(string description) : this(description, 4)
    {
    }
    // etc
```

In this context, the `this` keyword simply causes the constructor with the nearest matching parameters to be called. Note that any constructor initializer is executed before the body of the constructor. Say that the following code is run:

```
Car myCar = new Car("Proton Persona");
```

In this example, the two-parameter constructor executes before any code in the body of the one-parameter constructor (though in this particular case, because there is no code in the body of the one-parameter constructor, it makes no difference).

A C# constructor initializer may contain either one call to another constructor in the same class (using the syntax just presented) or one call to a constructor in the immediate base class (using the same syntax, but using the keyword `base` instead of `this`). It is not possible to put more than one call in the initializer.

The syntax for constructor initializers in C# is similar to that for constructor initialization lists in C++, but C++ developers should beware: Behind the similarity in syntax, C# initializers follow very different rules for what can be placed in them. Whereas you can use a C++ initialization list to indicate initial values of any member variables or to call a base constructor, the only thing you can put in a C# initializer is one call to one other constructor. This forces C# classes to follow a strict sequence for how they get constructed, whereas C++ allows some leniency. This issue is studied more in Chapter 4, where you see that the sequence enforced by C# arguably amounts to no more than good programming practice anyway.

readonly Fields

The concept of a constant as a variable that contains a value that cannot be changed is something that C# shares with most programming languages. However, constants don't necessarily meet all requirements. On occasion, you may have some variable whose value shouldn't be changed, but where the value is not known until runtime. C# provides another type of variable that is useful in this scenario: the `readonly` field.

The `readonly` keyword gives a bit more flexibility than `const`, allowing for situations in which you might want a field to be constant but also need to carry out some calculations to determine its initial value. The rule is that you can assign values to a `readonly` field inside a constructor, but not anywhere else. It's also possible for a `readonly` field to be an instance rather than a static field, having a different value for each instance of a class. This means that, unlike a `const` field, if you want a `readonly` field to be static, you have to declare it as such.

Suppose that you have an MDI program that edits documents, and, for licensing reasons, you want to restrict the number of documents that can be opened simultaneously. Now assume that you are selling different versions of the software, and it's possible that customers can upgrade their licenses to open more documents simultaneously. Clearly this means you can't hard-code the maximum number in the source code. You'd probably need a field to represent this maximum number. This field will have to be read in — perhaps from a registry key or some other file storage — each time the program is launched. So your code might look something like this:

```
public class DocumentEditor
{
    public static readonly uint MaxDocuments;

    static DocumentEditor()
    {
        MaxDocuments = DoSomethingToFindOutMaxNumber();
    }
```

In this case, the field is static, because the maximum number of documents needs to be stored only once per running instance of the program. This is why it is initialized in the static constructor. If you had an instance `readonly` field, you would initialize it in the instance constructor(s). For example, presumably each document you edit has a creation date, which you wouldn't want to allow the user to change (because that would be rewriting the past!). Note that the field is also public — you don't normally need to make `readonly` fields private, because by definition they cannot be modified externally (the same principle also applies to constants).

As noted earlier, date is represented by the class `System.DateTime`. The following code uses a `System.DateTime` constructor that takes three parameters (the year, month, and day of the month — you can find details of this and other `DateTime` constructors in the MSDN documentation):

```
public class Document
{
    public readonly DateTime CreationDate;

    public Document()
    {
        // Read in creation date from file. Assume result is 1 Jan 2002
        // but in general this can be different for different instances
        // of the class
        CreationDate = new DateTime(2002, 1, 1);
    }
}
```

`CreationDate` and `MaxDocuments` in the previous code snippet are treated like any other field, except that because they are read-only, they cannot be assigned outside the constructors:

```
void SomeMethod()
{
    MaxDocuments = 10;      // compilation error here. MaxDocuments is readonly
}
```

It's also worth noting that you don't have to assign a value to a `readonly` field in a constructor. If you don't do so, it will be left with the default value for its particular data type or whatever value you initialized it to at its declaration. That applies to both static and instance `readonly` fields.

Anonymous Types

Chapter 2 discussed the `var` keyword in reference to implicitly typed variables. When used with the `new` keyword, anonymous types can be created. An anonymous type is simply a nameless class that inherits from `object`. The definition of the class is inferred from the initializer, just like in implicitly typed variables.

If you needed an object that contained a person's first, middle, and last name the declaration would look like this:

```
var captain = new {FirstName = "James", MiddleName = "T", LastName = "Kirk"};
```

This would produce an object with `FirstName`, `MiddleName`, and `LastName` properties. If you were to create another object that looked like this:

```
var doctor = new {FirstName = "Leonard", MiddleName = "", LastName = "McCoy"};
```

The types of `captain` and `doctor` are the same. You could set `captain = doctor`, for example.

If the values that are being set come from another object, then the initializer can be abbreviated. If you already have a class that contains the properties `FirstName`, `MiddleName`, and `LastName` and you have an instance of that class with the instance name `person`, then the `captain` object could be initialized like this:

```
var captain = new (person.FirstName, person.MidleName, person.LastName};
```

The property names from the `person` object would be projected to the new object named `captain`. So the object named `captain` would have the `FirstName`, `MiddleName`, and `LastName` properties.

The actual type name of these new objects is unknown. The compiler "makes up" a name for the type, but only the compiler will ever be able to make use of it. So you can't and shouldn't plan on using any type reflection on the new objects because you will not get consistent results.

Structs

So far, you have seen how classes offer a great way of encapsulating objects in your program. You have also seen how they are stored on the heap in a way that gives you much more flexibility in data lifetime, but with a slight cost in performance. This performance cost is small thanks to the optimizations of managed heaps. However, in some situations all you really need is a small data structure. In this case, a class provides more functionality than you need, and for performance reasons you will probably prefer to use a struct. Look at this example:

```
class Dimensions
{
    public double Length;
    public double Width;
}
```

This code defines a class called `Dimensions`, which simply stores the length and width of some item. Perhaps you're writing a furniture-arranging program to let people experiment with rearranging their furniture on the computer, and you want to store the dimensions of each item of furniture. It looks like you're breaking the rules of good program design by making the fields public, but the point is that you don't really need all the facilities of a class for this. All you have is two numbers, which you'll find convenient to treat as a pair rather than individually. There is no need for a lot of methods, or for you to be able to inherit from the class, and you certainly don't want to have the .NET runtime go to the trouble of bringing in the heap with all the performance implications, just to store two `doubles`.

As mentioned earlier in this chapter, the only thing you need to change in the code to define a type as a struct instead of a class is to replace the keyword `class` with `struct`:

```
struct Dimensions
{
    public double Length;
    public double Width;
}
```

Defining functions for structs is also exactly the same as defining them for classes. The following code demonstrates a constructor and a property for a struct:

```
struct Dimensions
{
    public double Length;
    public double Width;

    Dimensions(double length, double width)
```

```
    {
        Length=length;
        Width=width;
    }

    public double Diagonal
    {
        get
        {
            return Math.Sqrt(Length*Length + Width*Width);
        }
    }
}
```

In many ways, you can think of structs in C# as being like scaled-down classes. They are basically the same as classes but designed more for cases where you simply want to group some data together. They differ from classes in the following ways:

❑　Structs are value types, not reference types. This means they are stored either in the stack or in-line (if they are part of another object that is stored on the heap) and have the same lifetime restrictions as the simple data types.

❑　Structs do not support inheritance.

❑　There are some differences in the way constructors work for structs. In particular, the compiler always supplies a default no-parameter constructor, which you are not permitted to replace.

❑　With a struct, you can specify how the fields are to be laid out in memory (this is examined in Chapter 13, "Reflection," which covers attributes).

Because structs are really intended to group data items together, you'll sometimes find that most or all of their fields are declared as public. This is, strictly speaking, contrary to the guidelines for writing .NET code — according to Microsoft, fields (other than const fields) should always be private and wrapped by public properties. However, for simple structs, many developers would nevertheless consider public fields to be acceptable programming practice.

> *C++ developers beware — structs in C# are very different from classes in their implementation. This is unlike C++, in which classes and structs are virtually the same thing.*

The following sections look at some of these differences between structs and classes in more detail.

Structs Are Value Types

Although structs are value types, you can often treat them syntactically in the same way as classes. For example, with the definition of the Dimensions class in the previous section, you could write:

```
Dimensions point = new Dimensions();
point.Length = 3;
point.Width = 6;
```

Note that because structs are value types, the new operator does not work in the same way as it does for classes and other reference types. Instead of allocating memory on the heap, the new operator simply calls the appropriate constructor, according to the parameters passed to it, initializing all fields. Indeed, for structs it is perfectly legal to write:

```
Dimensions point;
point.Length = 3;
point.Width = 6;
```

If `Dimensions` was a class, this would produce a compilation error, because `point` would contain an uninitialized reference — an address that points nowhere, so you could not start setting values to its fields. For a struct, however, the variable declaration actually allocates space on the stack for the entire struct, so it's ready to assign values to. Note, however, that the following code would cause a compilation error, with the compiler complaining that you are using an uninitialized variable:

```
Dimensions point;
Double D = point.Length;
```

Structs follow the same rules as any other data type — everything must be initialized before use. A struct is considered fully initialized either when the `new` operator has been called against it, or when values have been individually assigned to all its fields. And of course, a struct defined as a member field of a class is initialized by being zeroed-out automatically when the containing object is initialized.

The fact that structs are value types will affect performance, though depending on how you use your struct, this can be good or bad. On the positive side, allocating memory for structs is very fast because this takes place inline or on the stack. The same goes for removing structs when they go out of scope. On the negative side, whenever you pass a struct as a parameter or assign a struct to another struct (as in `A=B`, where `A` and `B` are structs), the full contents of the struct are copied, whereas for a class only the reference is copied. This will result in a performance loss that depends on the size of the struct, emphasizing the fact that structs are really intended for small data structures. Note, however, that when passing a struct as a parameter to a method, you can avoid this performance loss by passing it as a `ref` parameter — in this case, only the address in memory of the struct will be passed in, which is just as fast as passing in a class. If you do this, though, be aware that it means the called method can in principle change the value of the struct.

Structs and Inheritance

Structs are not designed for inheritance. This means that it is not possible to inherit from a struct. The only exception to this is that structs, in common with every other type in C#, derive ultimately from the class `System.Object`. Hence, structs also have access to the methods of `System.Object`, and it is even possible to override them in structs — an obvious example would be overriding the `ToString()` method. The actual inheritance chain for structs is that each struct derives from a class, `System .ValueType`, which in turn derives from `System.Object`. `ValueType` does not add any new members to `Object`, but provides implementations of some of them that are more suitable for structs. Note that you cannot supply a different base class for a struct: every struct is derived from `ValueType`.

Constructors for Structs

You can define constructors for structs in exactly the same way that you can for classes, except that you are not permitted to define a constructor that takes no parameters. This may seem nonsensical, and the reason is buried in the implementation of the .NET runtime. Some rare circumstances exist in which the .NET runtime would not be able to call a custom zero-parameter constructor that you have supplied. Microsoft has therefore taken the easy way out and banned zero-parameter constructors for structs in C#.

That said, the default constructor, which initializes all fields to zero values, is always present implicitly, even if you supply other constructors that take parameters. It's also impossible to circumvent the default constructor by supplying initial values for fields. The following code will cause a compile-time error:

```
struct Dimensions
{
    public double Length = 1;      // error. Initial values not allowed
    public double Width = 2;       // error. Initial values not allowed
}
```

Of course, if `Dimensions` had been declared as a class, this code would have compiled without any problems.

Incidentally, you can supply a `Close()` or `Dispose()` method for a struct in the same way you do for a class.

Partial Classes

The `partial` keyword allows the class, struct, or interface to span across multiple files. Typically, a class will reside entirely in a single file. However, in situations where multiple developers need access to the same class, or more likely in the situation where a code generator of some type is generating part of a class, then having the class in multiple files can be beneficial.

The way that the `partial` keyword is used is to simply place `partial` before `class`, `struct`, or `interface`. In the following example the class `TheBigClass` resides in two separate source files, `BigClassPart1.cs` and `BigClassPart2.cs`:

```
//BigClassPart1.cs
partial class TheBigClass
{
  public void MethodOne()
  {
  }
}

//BigClassPart2.cs
partial class TheBigClass
{
  public void MethodTwo()
  {
  }
}
```

When the project that these two source files are part of is compiled, a single type called `TheBigClass` will be created with two methods, `MethodOne()` and `MethodTwo()`.

If any of the following keywords are used in describing the class, the same must apply to all partials of the same type:

- ❑ `public`
- ❑ `private`
- ❑ `protected`
- ❑ `internal`
- ❑ `abstract`
- ❑ `sealed`
- ❑ `new`
- ❑ generic constraints

Nested partials are allowed as long as the `partial` keyword precedes the `class` keyword in the nested type. Attributes, XML comments, interfaces, generic-type parameter attributes, and members will be combined when the partial types are compiled into the type. Given the two source files:

```
//BigClassPart1.cs
[CustomAttribute]
partial class TheBigClass : TheBigBaseClass, IBigClass
{
   public void MethodOne()
   {
   }
}

//BigClassPart2.cs
[AnotherAttribute]
partial class TheBigClass : IOtherBigClass
{
   public void MethodTwo()
   {
   }
}
```

After the compile, the equivalent source file would be:

```
[CustomAttribute]
[AnotherAttribute]
partial class TheBigClass : TheBigBaseClass, IBigClass, IOtherBigClass
{
   public void MethodOne()
   {
   }

   public void MethodTwo()
   {
   }
}
```

Static Classes

Earlier, this chapter discussed static constructors and how they allowed the initialization of static member variables. If a class contains nothing but static methods and properties, the class itself can become static. A static class is functionally the same as creating a class with a private static constructor. An instance of the class can never be created. By using the `static` keyword, the compiler can help by checking that instance members are never accidentally added to the class. If they are, a compile error happens. This can help guarantee that an instance is never created. The syntax for a static class looks like this:

```
static class StaticUtilities
{
   public static void HelperMethod()
   {
   }
}
```

An object of type `StaticUtilities` is not needed to call the `HelperMethod()`. The type name is used to make the call:

```
StaticUtilities.HelperMethod();
```

The Object Class

As indicated earlier, all .NET classes are ultimately derived from `System.Object`. In fact, if you don't specify a base class when you define a class, the compiler will automatically assume that it derives from `Object`. Because inheritance has not been used in this chapter, every class you have seen here is actually derived from `System.Object`. (As noted earlier, for structs this derivation is indirect: A struct is always derived from `System.ValueType`, which in turn derives from `System.Object`.)

The practical significance of this is that, besides the methods and properties and so on that you define, you also have access to a number of public and protected member methods that have been defined for the `Object` class. These methods are available in all other classes that you define.

System.Object Methods

For the time being, we simply summarize the purpose of each method in the following list, and then, in the next section, we provide more detail about the `ToString()` method in particular.

❑ `ToString()` — This is intended as a fairly basic, quick-and-easy string representation; use it when you just want a quick idea of the contents of an object, perhaps for debugging purposes. It provides very little choice of how to format the data: For example, dates can in principle be expressed in a huge variety of different formats, but `DateTime.ToString()` does not offer you any choice in this regard. If you need a more sophisticated string representation that, for example, takes account of your formatting preferences or of the culture (the locale), then you should implement the `IFormattable` interface (see Chapter 8, "Strings and Regular Expressions").

❑ `GetHashCode()` — This is used if objects are placed in a data structure known as a map (also known as a hash table or dictionary). It is used by classes that manipulate these structures in order to determine where to place an object in the structure. If you intend your class to be used as a key for a dictionary, you will need to override `GetHashCode()`. Some fairly strict requirements exist for how you implement your overload, and you learn about those when you examine dictionaries in Chapter 10, "Collections."

❑ `Equals()` (both versions) and `ReferenceEquals()` — As you'll gather by the existence of three different methods aimed at comparing the equality of objects, the .NET Framework has quite a sophisticated scheme for measuring equality. Subtle differences exist between how these three methods, along with the comparison operator, `==`, are intended to be used. Not only that, but restrictions also exist on how you should override the virtual, one-parameter version of `Equals()` if you choose to do so, because certain base classes in the `System.Collections` namespace call the method and expect it to behave in certain ways. You explore the use of these methods in Chapter 6, "Operators and Casts," when you examine operators.

❑ `Finalize()` — This method is covered in Chapter 12, "Memory Management and Pointers." It is intended as the nearest that C# has to C++-style destructors and is called when a reference object is garbage collected to clean up resources. The `Object` implementation of `Finalize()` actually does nothing and is ignored by the garbage collector. You will normally override `Finalize()` if an object owns references to unmanaged resources that need to be removed when the object is deleted. The garbage collector cannot do this directly because it only knows about managed resources, so it relies on any finalizers that you supply.

❑   `GetType()` — This method returns an instance of a class derived from `System.Type`. This object can provide an extensive range of information about the class of which your object is a member, including base type, methods, properties, and so on. `System.Type` also provides the entry point into .NET's reflection technology. Chapter 13, "Reflection," examines this topic.

❑   `MemberwiseClone()` — This is the only member of `System.Object` that isn't examined in detail anywhere in the book. There is no need to because it is fairly simple in concept. It simply makes a copy of the object and returns a reference (or in the case of a value type, a boxed reference) to the copy. Note that the copy made is a shallow copy — this means that it copies all the value types in the class. If the class contains any embedded references, then only the references will be copied, not the objects referred to. This method is protected and so cannot be called to copy external objects. It is also not virtual, so you cannot override its implementation.

The ToString() Method

You've already encountered `ToString()` in Chapter 2, "C# Basics." It provides the most convenient way to get a quick string representation of an object.

For example:

```
int i = -50;
string str = i.ToString();  // returns "-50"
```

Here's another example:

```
enum Colors {Red, Orange, Yellow};
// later on in code...
Colors favoriteColor = Colors.Orange;
string str = favoriteColor.ToString();     // returns "Orange"
```

`Object.ToString()` is actually declared as virtual, and all these examples are taking advantage of the fact that its implementation in the C# predefined data types has been overridden for us in order to return correct string representations of those types. You might not think that the `Colors` enum counts as a predefined data type. It actually gets implemented as a struct derived from `System.Enum`, and `System.Enum` has a rather clever override of `ToString()` that deals with all the enums you define.

If you don't override `ToString()` in classes that you define, your classes will simply inherit the `System.Object` implementation — which displays the name of the class. If you want `ToString()` to return a string that contains information about the value of objects of your class, you will need to override it. To illustrate this, the following example, `Money`, defines a very simple class, also called `Money`, which represents U.S. currency amounts. `Money` simply acts as a wrapper for the decimal class but supplies a `ToString()` method. Note that this method must be declared as `override` because it is replacing (overriding) the `ToString()` method supplied by `Object`. Chapter 4 discusses overriding in more detail. The complete code for this example is as follows. Note that it also illustrates use of properties to wrap fields:

```
using System;

namespace Wrox.ProCSharp.OOCSharp
{
    class MainEntryPoint
    {
        static void Main(string[] args)
        {
            Money cash1 = new Money();
            cash1.Amount = 40M;
```

```
                Console.WriteLine("cash1.ToString() returns: " + cash1.ToString());
                Console.ReadLine();
            }
    }
    class Money
    {
        private decimal amount;

        public decimal Amount
        {
            get
            {
                return amount;
            }
            set
            {
                amount = value;
            }
        }
        public override string ToString()
        {
            return "$" + Amount.ToString();
        }
    }

}
```

This example is here just to illustrate syntactical features of C#. C# already has a predefined type to represent currency amounts, decimal, so in real life, you wouldn't write a class to duplicate this functionality unless you wanted to add various other methods to it. And in many cases, due to formatting requirements, you'd probably use the String.Format() method (which is covered in Chapter 8) rather than ToString() to display a currency string.

In the Main() method, you first instantiate a Money object. The ToString() method is then called, which actually executes the override version of the method. Running this code gives the following results:

```
StringRepresentations
cash1.ToString() returns: $40
```

Extension Methods

There are many ways to extend a class. If you have the source for the class, then inheritance, which is covered in Chapter 4, is a great way to add functionality to your objects. What if the source code isn't available? Extension methods can help by allowing you to change a class without requiring the source code for the class.

Extension methods are static methods that can appear to be part of a class without actually being in the source code for the class. Let's say that the Money class from the previous example needs to have a method AddToAmount(decimal amountToAdd). However, for whatever reason the original source for the assembly cannot be changed directly. All that you have to do is create a static class and add the AddToAmount method as a static method. Here is what the code would look like:

```
namespace Chapter3.Extensions
{
    public static class MoneyExtension
```

(continued)

(continued)

```
    {
      public static void AddToAmount(this Money money, decimal amountToAdd)
      {
        money.Amount += amountToAdd;
      }
    }
  }
```

Notice the parameters for the AddToAmount method. For an extension method, the first parameter is the type that is being extended preceded by the this keyword. This is what tells the compiler that this method is part of the Money type. In this example Money is the type that is being extended. In the extension method you have access to all the public methods and properties of the type being extended.

In the main program the AddToAmount method appears just as another method. The first parameter doesn't appear, and you do not have to do anything with it. To use the new method, you make the call just like any other method:

```
    cash1.AddToAmount(10M);
```

Even though the extension method is static, you use standard instance method syntax. Notice that we called AddToAmount using the cash1 instance variable and not using the type name.

If the extension method has the same name as a method in the class, the extension method will never be called. Any instance methods already in the class take precedence.

Summary

This chapter examined C# syntax for declaring and manipulating objects. You have seen how to declare static and instance fields, properties, methods, and constructors. You have also seen that C# adds some new features not present in the OOP model of some other languages — for example, static constructors provide a means of initializing static fields, whereas structs allow you to define types that do not require the use of the managed heap, which could lead to performance gains. You have also seen how all types in C# derive ultimately from the type System.Object, which means that all types start with a basic set of useful methods, including ToString().

We mentioned inheritance a few times throughout this chapter. We examine implementation and interface inheritance in C# in Chapter 4.

Inheritance

4

Chapter 3, "Objects and Types," examined how to use individual classes in C#. The focus in that chapter was how to define methods, constructors, properties, and other members of a single class (or a single struct). Although you did learn that all classes are ultimately derived from the class `System.Object`, you did not see how to create a hierarchy of inherited classes. Inheritance is the subject of this chapter. In this chapter, you will see how C# and the .NET Framework handle inheritance. Topics covered include:

❑ Types of inheritance

❑ Implementing inheritance

❑ Access modifiers

❑ Interfaces

Types of Inheritance

Let's start off by reviewing exactly what C# does and does not support as far as inheritance is concerned.

Implementation versus Interface Inheritance

In object-oriented programming, there are two distinct types of inheritance — implementation inheritance and interface inheritance:

❑ **Implementation inheritance** means that a type derives from a base type, taking all the base type's member fields and functions. With implementation inheritance, a derived type adopts the base type's implementation of each function, unless it is indicated in the definition of the derived type that a function implementation is to be overridden. This type of inheritance is most useful when you need to add functionality to an existing type, or when a number of related types share a significant amount of common functionality. A good example of this comes in the Windows Forms classes, which are discussed in Chapter 31, "Windows Forms." Specific examples are the base class `System.Windows.Forms.Control`, which provides a very sophisticated implementation of a generic Windows control, and numerous other classes such as `System.Windows.Forms.TextBox` and `System.Windows.Forms.ListBox` that are derived from `Control` and that override functions or provide new functions to implement specific types of control.

❑ **Interface inheritance** means that a type inherits only the signatures of the functions and does not inherit any implementations. This type of inheritance is most useful when you want to specify that a type makes certain features available. For example, certain types can indicate that they provide a resource cleanup method called `Dispose()` by deriving from an interface, `System.IDisposable` (see Chapter 12, "Memory Management and Pointers"). Because the way that one type cleans up resources is likely to be very different from the way that another type cleans up resources, there is no point in defining any common implementation, so interface inheritance is appropriate here. Interface inheritance is often regarded as providing a contract: By deriving from an interface, a type is guaranteed to provide certain functionality to clients.

Traditionally, languages such as C++ have been very strong on implementation inheritance. Indeed, implementation inheritance has been at the core of the C++ programming model. Although Visual Basic 6 did not support any implementation inheritance of classes, it did support interface inheritance thanks to its underlying COM foundations.

C# supports both implementation and interface inheritance. Both are baked into the framework and the language from the ground up, thereby allowing you to decide which to use based on the architecture of the application.

Multiple Inheritance

Some languages such as C++ support what is known as *multiple inheritance*, in which a class derives from more than one other class. The benefits of using multiple inheritance are debatable: On one hand, there is no doubt that it is possible to use multiple inheritance to write extremely sophisticated, yet compact, code, as demonstrated by the C++ ATL library. On the other hand, code that uses multiple implementation inheritance is often difficult to understand and debug (a point that is equally well demonstrated by the C++ ATL library). As mentioned, making it easy to write robust code was one of the crucial design goals behind the development of C#. Accordingly, C# does not support multiple implementation inheritance. It does, however, allow types to be derived from multiple interfaces — multiple interface inheritance. This means that a C# class can be derived from one other class, and any number of interfaces. Indeed, we can be more precise: Thanks to the presence of `System.Object` as a common base type, every C# class (except for `Object`) has exactly one base class, and may additionally have any number of base interfaces.

Structs and Classes

Chapter 3 distinguishes between structs (value types) and classes (reference types). One restriction of using a struct is that structs do not support inheritance, beyond the fact that every struct is automatically derived from `System.ValueType`. In fact, we should be more careful. It's true that it is not possible to code a type hierarchy of structs; however, it is possible for structs to implement interfaces. In other words, structs don't really support implementation inheritance, but they do support interface inheritance. We can summarize the situation for any types that you define as follows:

❑ **Structs** are always derived from `System.ValueType`. They can also be derived from any number of interfaces.

❑ **Classes** are always derived from one other class of your choosing. They can also be derived from any number of interfaces.

Implementation Inheritance

If you want to declare that a class derives from another class, use the following syntax:

```
class MyDerivedClass : MyBaseClass
{
    // functions and data members here
}
```

This syntax is very similar to C++ and Java syntax. However, C++ programmers, who will be used to the concepts of public and private inheritance, should note that C# does not support private inheritance, hence the absence of a public or private qualifier on the base class name. Supporting private inheritance would have complicated the language for very little gain. In practice, private inheritance is used extremely rarely in C++ anyway.

If a class (or a struct) also derives from interfaces, the list of base class and interfaces is separated by commas:

```
public class MyDerivedClass : MyBaseClass, IInterface1, IInterface2
{
      // etc.
}
```

For a struct, the syntax is as follows:

```
public struct MyDerivedStruct : IInterface1, IInterface2
{
      // etc.
}
```

If you do not specify a base class in a class definition, the C# compiler will assume that System.Object is the base class. Hence, the following two pieces of code yield the same result:

```
class MyClass : Object  // derives from System.Object
{
    // etc.
}
```

and

```
class MyClass   // derives from System.Object
{
    // etc.
}
```

For the sake of simplicity, the second form is more common.

Because C# supports the object keyword, which serves as a pseudonym for the System.Object class, you can also write:

```
class MyClass : object   // derives from System.Object
{
    // etc.
}
```

If you want to reference the Object class, use the object keyword, which is recognized by intelligent editors such as Visual Studio .NET and thus facilitates editing your code.

Virtual Methods

By declaring a base class function as `virtual`, you allow the function to be overridden in any derived classes:

```
class MyBaseClass
{
    public virtual string VirtualMethod()
    {
        return "This method is virtual and defined in MyBaseClass";
    }
}
```

It is also permitted to declare a property as `virtual`. For a virtual or overridden property, the syntax is the same as for a nonvirtual property, with the exception of the keyword `virtual`, which is added to the definition. The syntax looks like this:

```
public virtual string ForeName
{
    get { return fName; }
    set { fName = value; }
}
private string foreName;
```

For simplicity, the following discussion focuses mainly on methods, but it applies equally well to properties.

The concepts behind virtual functions in C# are identical to standard OOP concepts. You can override a virtual function in a derived class, and when the method is called, the appropriate method for the type of object is invoked. In C#, functions are not virtual by default but (aside from constructors) can be explicitly declared as `virtual`. This follows the C++ methodology: for performance reasons, functions are not virtual unless indicated. In Java, by contrast, all functions are virtual. C# does differ from C++ syntax, though, because it requires you to declare when a derived class's function overrides another function, using the `override` keyword:

```
class MyDerivedClass : MyBaseClass
{
    public override string VirtualMethod()
    {
        return "This method is an override defined in MyDerivedClass.";
    }
}
```

This syntax for method overriding removes potential runtime bugs that can easily occur in C++, when a method signature in a derived class unintentionally differs slightly from the base version, resulting in the method failing to override the base version. In C#, this is picked up as a compile-time error because the compiler would see a function marked as `override` but no base method for it to override.

Neither member fields nor static functions can be declared as virtual. The concept simply wouldn't make sense for any class member other than an instance function member.

Hiding Methods

If a method with the same signature is declared in both base and derived classes, but the methods are not declared as `virtual` and `override`, respectively, then the derived class version is said to *hide* the base class version.

In most cases, you would want to override methods rather than hide them; by hiding them you risk calling the wrong method for a given class instance. However, as shown in the following example,

C# syntax is designed to ensure that the developer is warned at compile time about this potential problem, thus making it safer to hide methods if that is your intention. This also has versioning benefits for developers of class libraries.

Suppose that you have a class called `HisBaseClass`:

```
class HisBaseClass
{
    // various members
}
```

At some point in the future you write a derived class that adds some functionality to `HisBaseClass`. In particular, you add a method called `MyGroovyMethod()`, which is not present in the base class:

```
class MyDerivedClass: HisBaseClass
{
    public int MyGroovyMethod()
    {
        // some groovy implementation
        return 0;
    }
}
```

One year later, you decide to extend the functionality of the base class. By coincidence, you add a method that is also called `MyGroovyMethod()` and that has the same name and signature as yours, but probably doesn't do the same thing. When you compile your code using the new version of the base class, you have a potential clash because your program won't know which method to call. It's all perfectly legal in C#, but because your `MyGroovyMethod()` is not intended to be related in any way to the base class `MyGroovyMethod()`, the result is that running this code does not yield the result you want. Fortunately, C# has been designed to cope very well with these types of conflicts.

In these situations, C# generates a compilation warning that reminds you to use the new keyword to declare that you intend to hide a method, like this:

```
class MyDerivedClass : HisBaseClass
{
    public new int MyGroovyMethod()
    {
        // some groovy implementation
        return 0;
    }
}
```

However, because your version of `MyGroovyMethod()` is not declared as `new`, the compiler will pick up on the fact that it's hiding a base class method without being instructed to do so and will generate a warning (this applies whether or not you declared `MyGroovyMethod()` as `virtual`). If you want, you can rename your version of the method. This is the recommended course of action because it will eliminate future confusion. However, if you decide not to rename your method for whatever reason (for example, if you've published your software as a library for other companies, so you can't change the names of methods), all your existing client code will still run correctly, picking up your version of `MyGroovyMethod()`. That's because any existing code that accesses this method must be doing so through a reference to `MyDerivedClass` (or a further derived class).

Your existing code cannot access this method through a reference to `HisBaseClass`; it would generate a compilation error when compiled against the earlier version of `HisBaseClass`. The problem can happen in only client code you have yet to write. C# arranges things so that you get a warning that a potential problem might occur in future code — you will need to pay attention to this warning and take care not to attempt to call your version of `MyGroovyMethod()` through any reference to `HisBaseClass` in any future code you add. However, all your existing code will still work fine. It may be a subtle point, but it's quite an impressive example of how C# is able to cope with different versions of classes.

Calling Base Versions of Functions

C# has a special syntax for calling base versions of a method from a derived class: `base.<MethodName>()`. For example, if you want a method in a derived class to return 90 percent of the value returned by the base class method, you can use the following syntax:

```
class CustomerAccount
{
    public virtual decimal CalculatePrice()
    {
        // implementation
        return 0.0M;
    }
}
class GoldAccount : CustomerAccount
{
    public override decimal CalculatePrice()
    {
        return base.CalculatePrice() * 0.9M;
    }
}
```

Java uses a similar syntax, with the exception that Java uses the keyword `super` rather than `base`. C++ has no similar keyword but instead requires specification of the class name (`CustomerAccount::CalculatePrice()`). Any equivalent to `base` in C++ would have been ambiguous because C++ supports multiple inheritance.

Note that you can use the `base.<MethodName>()` syntax to call any method in the base class — you don't have to call it from inside an override of the same method.

Abstract Classes and Functions

C# allows both classes and functions to be declared as abstract. An abstract class cannot be instantiated, whereas an abstract function does not have an implementation, and must be overridden in any non-abstract derived class. Obviously, an abstract function is automatically virtual (although you don't need to supply the `virtual` keyword; doing so results in a syntax error). If any class contains any abstract functions, that class is also abstract and must be declared as such:

```
abstract class Building
{
    public abstract decimal CalculateHeatingCost();   // abstract method
}
```

C++ developers will notice some syntactical differences in C# here. C# does not support the =0 syntax to declare abstract functions. In C#, this syntax would be misleading because =<value> is allowed in member fields in class declarations to supply initial values:

```
abstract class Building
{
    private bool damaged = false;    // field
    public abstract decimal CalculateHeatingCost();   // abstract method
}
```

C++ developers should also note the slightly different terminology: In C++, abstract functions are often described as pure virtual; in the C# world, the only correct term to use is abstract.

Sealed Classes and Methods

C# allows classes and methods to be declared as `sealed`. In the case of a class, this means that you can't inherit from that class. In the case of a method, this means that you can't override that method.

```
sealed class FinalClass
{
    // etc
}
class DerivedClass : FinalClass        // wrong. Will give compilation error
{
    // etc
}
```

Java developers will recognize `sealed` *as the C# equivalent of Java's* `final`.

The most likely situation in which you'll mark a class or method as `sealed` will be if the class or method is internal to the operation of the library, class, or other classes that you are writing, so that you ensure that any attempt to override some of its functionality will lead to instability in the code. You might also mark a class or method as `sealed` for commercial reasons, in order to prevent a third party from extending your classes in a manner that is contrary to the licensing agreements. In general, however, you should be careful about marking a class or member as `sealed` because by doing so you are severely restricting how it can be used. Even if you don't think it would be useful to inherit from a class or override a particular member of it, it's still possible that at some point in the future someone will encounter a situation you hadn't anticipated in which it is useful to do so. The .NET base class library frequently uses sealed classes in order to make these classes inaccessible to third-party developers who might want to derive their own classes from them. For example, `string` is a sealed class.

Declaring a method as `sealed` serves a similar purpose as for a class:

```
class MyClass
{
    public sealed override void FinalMethod()
    {
        // etc.
    }
}
class DerivedClass : MyClass
{
    public override void FinalMethod()        // wrong. Will give compilation error
    {
    }
}
```

In order to use the `sealed` keyword on a method or property, it must have first been overridden from a base class. If you do not want a method or property in a base class overridden, then don't mark it as virtual.

Constructors of Derived Classes

Chapter 3 discusses how constructors can be applied to individual classes. An interesting question arises as to what happens when you start defining your own constructors for classes that are part of a hierarchy, inherited from other classes that may also have custom constructors.

Assume that you have not defined any explicit constructors for any of your classes. This means that the compiler supplies default zeroing-out constructors for all your classes. There is actually quite a lot going on under the hood when that happens, but the compiler is able to arrange it so that things work out nicely throughout the class hierarchy and every field in every class gets initialized to whatever its default value is. When you add a constructor of your own, however, you are effectively taking control of construction. This has implications right down through the hierarchy of derived classes, and you have to make sure that you don't inadvertently do anything to prevent construction through the hierarchy from taking place smoothly.

You might be wondering why there is any special problem with derived classes. The reason is that when you create an instance of a derived class, there is actually more than one constructor at work. The constructor of the class you instantiate isn't by itself sufficient to initialize the class — the constructors of the base classes must also be called. That's why we've been talking about construction through the hierarchy.

To see why base class constructors must be called, you're going to develop an example based on a cell phone company called MortimerPhones. The example contains an abstract base class, `GenericCustomer`, which represents any customer. There is also a (non-abstract) class, `Nevermore60Customer`, that represents any customer on a particular rate called the `Nevermore60` rate. All customers have a name, represented by a private field. Under the `Nevermore60` rate, the first few minutes of the customer's call time are charged at a higher rate, necessitating the need for the field `highCostMinutesUsed`, which details how many of these higher-cost minutes each customer has used up. The class definitions look like this:

```
abstract class GenericCustomer
{
    private string name;
    // lots of other methods etc.
}
class Nevermore60Customer : GenericCustomer
{
    private uint highCostMinutesUsed;
    // other methods etc.
}
```

We won't worry about what other methods might be implemented in these classes, because we are concentrating solely on the construction process here. And if you download the sample code for this chapter, you'll find that the class definitions include only the constructors.

Take a look at what happens when you use the `new` operator to instantiate a `Nevermore60Customer`:

```
GenericCustomer customer = new Nevermore60Customer();
```

Clearly, both of the member fields `name` and `highCostMinutesUsed` must be initialized when `customer` is instantiated. If you don't supply constructors of your own, but rely simply on the default constructors, then you'd expect `name` to be initialized to the `null` reference, and `highCostMinutesUsed` initialized to zero. Let's look in a bit more detail at how this actually happens.

The `highCostMinutesUsed` field presents no problem: the default `Nevermore60Customer` constructor supplied by the compiler will initialize this field to zero.

What about name? Looking at the class definitions, it's clear that the `Nevermore60Customer` constructor can't initialize this value. This field is declared as private, which means that derived classes don't have access to it. So, the default `Nevermore60Customer` constructor simply won't know that this field exists. The only code items that have that knowledge are other members of `GenericCustomer`. This means that if name is going to be initialized, that'll have to be done by some constructor in `GenericCustomer`. No matter how big your class hierarchy is, this same reasoning applies right down to the ultimate base class, `System.Object`.

Now that you have an understanding of the issues involved, you can look at what actually happens whenever a derived class is instantiated. Assuming that default constructors are used throughout, the compiler first grabs the constructor of the class it is trying to instantiate, in this case `Nevermore60Customer`. The first thing that the default `Nevermore60Customer` constructor does is attempt to run the default constructor for the immediate base class, `GenericCustomer`. The `GenericCustomer` constructor attempts to run the constructor for its immediate base class, `System.Object`. `System.Object` doesn't have any base classes, so its constructor just executes and returns control to the `GenericCustomer` constructor. That constructor now executes, initializing `name` to `null`, before returning control to the `Nevermore60Customer` constructor. That constructor in turn executes, initializing `highCostMinutesUsed` to zero, and exits. At this point, the `Nevermore60Customer` instance has been successfully constructed and initialized.

The net result of all this is that the constructors are called in order of `System.Object` first, then progressing down the hierarchy until the compiler reaches the class being instantiated. Notice also that in this process, each constructor handles initialization of the fields in its own class. That's how it should normally work, and when you start adding your own constructors you should try to stick to that principle.

Notice the order in which this happens. It's always the base class constructors that get called first. This means that there are no problems with a constructor for a derived class invoking any base class methods, properties, and any other members that it has access to, because it can be confident that the base class has already been constructed and its fields initialized. It also means that if the derived class doesn't like the way that the base class has been initialized, it can change the initial values of the data, provided that it has access to do so. However, good programming practice almost invariably means you'll try to prevent that situation from occurring if you can, and you will trust the base class constructor to deal with its own fields.

Now that you know how the process of construction works, you can start fiddling with it by adding your own constructors.

Adding a Constructor in a Hierarchy

We'll take the easiest case first and see what happens if you simply replace the default constructor somewhere in the hierarchy with another constructor that takes no parameters. Suppose that you decide that you want everyone's name to be initially set to the string `"<no name>"` instead of to the `null` reference. You'd modify the code in `GenericCustomer` like this:

```
public abstract class GenericCustomer
{
    private string name;
    public GenericCustomer()
        : base()  // We could omit this line without affecting the compiled code.
    {
        name = "<no name>";
    }
}
```

Adding this code will work fine. `Nevermore60Customer` still has its default constructor, so the sequence of events described earlier will proceed as before, except that the compiler will use the custom `GenericCustomer` constructor instead of generating a default one, so the `name` field will always be initialized to `"<no name>"` as required.

Notice that in your constructor you've added a call to the base class constructor before the `GenericCustomer` constructor is executed, using a syntax similar to that used earlier when we discussed how to get different overloads of constructors to call each other. The only difference is that this time you use the `base` keyword instead of `this` to indicate that it's a constructor to the `base` class rather than a constructor to the current class you want to call. There are no parameters in the brackets after the `base` keyword — that's important because it means you are not passing any parameters to the base constructor, so the compiler will have to look for a parameterless constructor to call. The result of all this is that the compiler will inject code to call the `System.Object` constructor, just as would happen by default anyway.

In fact, you can omit that line of code and write the following (as was done for most of the constructors so far in this chapter):

```
public GenericCustomer()
{
    name = "<no name>";
}
```

If the compiler doesn't see any reference to another constructor before the opening curly brace, it assumes that you intended to call the base class constructor; this fits in with the way that default constructors work.

The base and this keywords are the only keywords allowed in the line that calls another constructor. Anything else causes a compilation error. Also note that only one other constructor can be specified.

So far, this code works fine. One way to mess up the progression through the hierarchy of constructors, however, is to declare a constructor as private:

```
private GenericCustomer()
{
    name = "<no name>";
}
```

If you try this, you'll find you get an interesting compilation error, which could really throw you if you don't understand how construction down a hierarchy works:

```
'Wrox.ProCSharp.GenericCustomer()' is inaccessible due to its protection level
```

The interesting thing is that the error occurs not in the GenericCustomer class, but in the derived class, Nevermore60Customer. What's happened is that the compiler has tried to generate a default constructor for Nevermore60Customer but has not been able to because the default constructor is supposed to invoke the no-parameter GenericCustomer constructor. By declaring that constructor as private, you've made it inaccessible to the derived class. A similar error occurs if you supply a constructor to GenericCustomer, which takes parameters, but at the same time you fail to supply a no-parameter constructor. In this case, the compiler will not generate a default constructor for GenericCustomer, so when it tries to generate the default constructors for any derived class, it will again find that it can't because a no-parameter base class constructor is not available. A workaround would be to add your own constructors to the derived classes, even if you don't actually need to do anything in these constructors, so that the compiler doesn't try to generate any default constructors for them.

Now that you have all the theoretical background you need, you're ready to move on to an example of how you can neatly add constructors to a hierarchy of classes. In the next section, you start adding constructors that take parameters to the MortimerPhones example.

Adding Constructors with Parameters to a Hierarchy

You're going to start with a one-parameter constructor for GenericCustomer, which specifies that customers can be instantiated only when they supply their names:

```
abstract class GenericCustomer
{
    private string name;
    public GenericCustomer(string name)
    {
        this.name = name;
    }
```

So far, so good. However, as mentioned previously, this will cause a compilation error when the compiler tries to create a default constructor for any derived classes because the default compiler-generated constructors for `Nevermore60Customer` will try to call a no-parameter `GenericCustomer` constructor, and `GenericCustomer` does not possess such a constructor. Therefore, you'll need to supply your own constructors to the derived classes to avoid a compilation error:

```
class Nevermore60Customer : GenericCustomer
{
    private uint highCostMinutesUsed;
    public Nevermore60Customer(string name)
        :    base(name)
    {
    }
}
```

Now instantiation of `Nevermore60Customer` objects can occur only when a string containing the customer's name is supplied, which is what you want anyway. The interesting thing is what the `Nevermore60Customer` constructor does with this string. Remember that it can't initialize the `name` field itself because it has no access to private fields in its base class. Instead, it passes the name through to the base class for the `GenericCustomer` constructor to handle. It does this by specifying that the base class constructor to be executed first is the one that takes the name as a parameter. Other than that, it doesn't take any action of its own.

Next, you're going to investigate what happens if you have different overloads of the constructor as well as a class hierarchy to deal with. To this end, assume that Nevermore60 customers may have been referred to MortimerPhones by a friend as part of one of those sign-up-a-friend-and-get-a-discount offers. This means that when you construct a `Nevermore60Customer`, you may need to pass in the referrer's name as well. In real life, the constructor would have to do something complicated with the name, such as process the discount, but here you'll just store the referrer's name in another field.

The `Nevermore60Customer` definition will now look like this:

```
class Nevermore60Customer : GenericCustomer
{
    public Nevermore60Customer(string name, string referrerName)
        : base(name)
    {
        this.referrerName = referrerName;
    }

    private string referrerName;
    private uint highCostMinutesUsed;
```

The constructor takes the name and passes it to the `GenericCustomer` constructor for processing. `referrerName` is the variable that is your responsibility here, so the constructor deals with that parameter in its main body.

However, not all `Nevermore60Customers` will have a referrer, so you still need a constructor that doesn't require this parameter (or a constructor that gives you a default value for it). In fact, you will specify that if there is no referrer, then the `referrerName` field should be set to `"<None>"`, using the following one-parameter constructor:

```
public Nevermore60Customer(string name)
    : this(name, "<None>")
{
}
```

You now have all your constructors set up correctly. It's instructive to examine the chain of events that now occurs when you execute a line like this:

```
GenericCustomer customer = new Nevermore60Customer("Arabel Jones");
```

The compiler sees that it needs a one-parameter constructor that takes one string, so the constructor it will identify is the last one that you've defined:

```
public Nevermore60Customer(string Name)
   : this(Name, "<None>")
```

When you instantiate `customer`, this constructor will be called. It immediately transfers control to the corresponding `Nevermore60Customer` two-parameter constructor, passing it the values `"ArabelJones"`, and `"<None>"`. Looking at the code for this constructor, you see that it in turn immediately passes control to the one-parameter `GenericCustomer` constructor, giving it the string `"ArabelJones"`, and in turn that constructor passes control to the `System.Object` default constructor. Only now do the constructors execute. First, the `System.Object` constructor executes. Next comes the `GenericCustomer` constructor, which initializes the `name` field. Then the `Nevermore60Customer` two-parameter constructor gets control back, and sorts out initializing the `referrerName` to `"<None>"`. Finally, the `Nevermore60Customer` one-parameter constructor gets to execute; this constructor doesn't do anything else.

As you can see, this is a very neat and well-designed process. Each constructor handles initialization of the variables that are obviously its responsibility, and, in the process, your class is correctly instantiated and prepared for use. If you follow the same principles when you write your own constructors for your classes, you should find that even the most complex classes get initialized smoothly and without any problems.

Modifiers

You have already encountered quite a number of so-called modifiers — keywords that can be applied to a type or to a member. Modifiers can indicate the visibility of a method, such as `public` or `private`, or the nature of an item, such as whether a method is `virtual` or `abstract`. C# has a number of modifiers, and at this point it's worth taking a minute to provide the complete list.

Visibility Modifiers

Visibility modifiers indicate which other code items can view an item.

Modifier	Applies To	Description
public	Any types or members	The item is visible to any other code.
protected	Any member of a type, also any nested type	The item is visible only to any derived type.
internal	Any member of a type, also any nested type	The item is visible only within its containing assembly.
private	Any types or members	The item is visible only inside the type to which it belongs.
protected internal	Any member of a type, also any nested type	The item is visible to any code within its containing assembly and also to any code inside a derived type.

Note that type definitions can be internal or public, depending on whether you want the type to be visible outside its containing assembly.

```
public class MyClass
{
    // etc.
```

You cannot define types as protected, private, or protected internal because these visibility levels would be meaningless for a type contained in a namespace. Hence these visibilities can be applied only to members. However, you can define nested types (that is, types contained within other types) with these visibilities because in this case the type also has the status of a member. Hence, the following code is correct:

```
public class OuterClass
{
    protected class InnerClass
    {
            // etc.
    }
    // etc.
}
```

If you have a nested type, the inner type is always able to see all members of the outer type. Therefore, with the preceding code, any code inside InnerClass always has access to all members of OuterClass, even where those members are private.

Other Modifiers

The modifiers in the following table can be applied to members of types and have various uses. A few of these modifiers also make sense when applied to types.

Modifier	Applies To	Description
new	Function members	The member hides an inherited member with the same signature.
static	All members	The member does not operate on a specific instance of the class.
virtual	Classes and function members only	The member can be overridden by a derived class.
abstract	Function members only	A virtual member that defines the signature of the member, but doesn't provide an implementation.
override	Function members only	The member overrides an inherited virtual or abstract member.
sealed	Classes, methods, and properties	For classes, the class cannot be inherited from. For properties and methods, the member overrides an inherited virtual member, but cannot be overridden by any members in any derived classes. Must be used in conjunction with override.
extern	Static [DllImport] methods only	The member is implemented externally, in a different language.

Of these, `internal` and `protected internal` are the ones that are new to C# and the .NET Framework. `internal` acts in much the same way as `public`, but access is confined to other code in the same assembly — that is, code that is being compiled at the same time in the same program. You can use `internal` to ensure that all the other classes that you are writing have access to a particular member, while at the same time hiding it from other code written by other organizations. `protected internal` combines protected and internal, but in an OR sense, not an AND sense. A protected internal member can be seen by any code in the same assembly. It can also be seen by any derived classes, even those in other assemblies.

Interfaces

As mentioned earlier, by deriving from an interface, a class is declaring that it implements certain functions. Because not all object-oriented languages support interfaces, this section examines C#'s implementation of interfaces in detail.

> *Developers familiar with COM should be aware that, although, conceptually, C# interfaces are similar to COM interfaces, they are not the same thing. The underlying architecture is different. For example, C# interfaces are not derived from* IUnknown. *A C# interface provides a contract stated in terms of .NET functions. Unlike a COM interface, a C# interface does not represent any kind of binary standard.*

This section illustrates interfaces by presenting the complete definition of one of the interfaces that has been predefined by Microsoft, `System.IDisposable`. `IDisposable` contains one method, `Dispose()`, which is intended to be implemented by classes to clean up code:

```
public interface IDisposable
{
    void Dispose();
}
```

This code shows that declaring an interface works syntactically in pretty much the same way as declaring an abstract class. You should be aware, however, that it is not permitted to supply implementations of any of the members of an interface. In general, an interface can only contain declarations of methods, properties, indexers, and events.

You can never instantiate an interface; it contains only the signatures of its members. An interface has neither constructors (how can you construct something that you can't instantiate?) nor fields (because that would imply some internal implementation). An interface definition is also not allowed to contain operator overloads, although that's not because there is any problem in principle with declaring them — there isn't; it is because interfaces are usually intended to be public contracts, and having operator overloads would cause some incompatibility problems with other .NET languages, such as Visual Basic .NET, which do not support operator overloading.

It is also not permitted to declare modifiers on the members in an interface definition. Interface members are always implicitly `public`, and cannot be declared as `virtual` or `static`. That's up to implementing classes to decide. It is therefore fine for implementing classes to declare access modifiers, as is done in the example in this section.

Take for example `IDisposable`. If a class wants to declare publicly that it implements the `Dispose()` method, it must implement `IDisposable` — which in C# terms means that the class derives from `IDisposable`.

```
class SomeClass : IDisposable
{
    // This class MUST contain an implementation of the
    // IDisposable.Dispose() method, otherwise
    // you get a compilation error.
```

```
    public void Dispose()
    {
        // implementation of Dispose() method
    }
    // rest of class
}
```

In this example, if `SomeClass` derives from `IDisposable` but doesn't contain a `Dispose()` implementation with the exact same signature as defined in `IDisposable`, you get a compilation error because the class would be breaking its agreed-on contract to implement `IDisposable`. Of course, there's no problem for the compiler about a class having a `Dispose()` method but not deriving from `IDisposable`. The problem, then, would be that other code would have no way of recognizing that `SomeClass` has agreed to support the `IDisposable` features.

> `IDisposable` *is a relatively simple interface because it defines only one method. Most interfaces will contain more members.*

Another good example of an interface is provided by the `foreach` loop in C#. In principle, the `foreach` loop works internally by querying the object to find out whether it implements an interface called `System.Collections.IEnumerable`. If it does, the C# compiler will inject IL code, which uses the methods on this interface to iterate through the members of the collection. If it doesn't, `foreach` will raise an exception. The `IEnumerable` interface is examined in more detail in Chapter 10, "Collections." It's worth pointing out that both `IEnumerable` and `IDisposable` are somewhat special interfaces to the extent that they are actually recognized by the C# compiler, which takes account of these interfaces in the code that it generates. Obviously, any interfaces that you define yourself won't be so privileged!

Defining and Implementing Interfaces

This section illustrates how to define and use interfaces through developing a short program that follows the interface inheritance paradigm. The example is based on bank accounts. Assume that you are writing code that will ultimately allow computerized transfers between bank accounts. And assume for this example that there are many companies that may implement bank accounts, but they have all mutually agreed that any classes that represent bank accounts will implement an interface, `IBankAccount`, which exposes methods to deposit or withdraw money, and a property to return the balance. It is this interface that will allow outside code to recognize the various bank account classes implemented by different bank accounts. Although the aim is to allow the bank accounts to talk to each other to allow transfers of funds between accounts, we won't introduce that feature just yet.

To keep things simple, you will keep all the code for the example in the same source file. Of course, if something like the example were used in real life, you could surmise that the different bank account classes would not only be compiled to different assemblies, but would also be hosted on different machines owned by the different banks. That's all much too complicated for our purposes here. However, to maintain some attempt at realism, you will define different namespaces for the different companies.

To begin, you need to define the `IBankAccount` interface:

```
namespace Wrox.ProCSharp
{
    public interface IBankAccount
    {
        void PayIn(decimal amount);
        bool Withdraw(decimal amount);
        decimal Balance
```

(continued)

(continued)

```
        {
            get;
        }
    }
}
```

Notice the name of the interface, `IBankAccount`. It's a convention that an interface name traditionally starts with the letter I, so that you know that it's an interface.

> *Chapter 2, "C# Basics," pointed out that, in most cases, .NET usage guidelines discourage the so-called Hungarian notation in which names are preceded by a letter that indicates the type of object being defined. Interfaces are one of the few exceptions in which Hungarian notation is recommended.*

The idea is that you can now write classes that represent bank accounts. These classes don't have to be related to each other in any way; they can be completely different classes. They will, however, all declare that they represent bank accounts by the mere fact that they implement the `IBankAccount` interface.

Let's start off with the first class, a saver account run by the Royal Bank of Venus:

```
namespace Wrox.ProCSharp.VenusBank
{
    public class SaverAccount : IBankAccount
    {
        private decimal balance;
        public void PayIn(decimal amount)
        {
            balance += amount;
        }
        public bool Withdraw(decimal amount)
        {
            if (balance >= amount)
            {
                balance -= amount;
                return true;
            }
            Console.WriteLine("Withdrawal attempt failed.");
            return false;
        }
        public decimal Balance
        {
            get
            {
                return balance;
            }
        }
        public override string ToString()
        {
            return String.Format("Venus Bank Saver: Balance = {0,6:C}", balance);
        }
    }
}
```

It should be pretty obvious what the implementation of this class does. You maintain a private field, `balance`, and adjust this amount when money is deposited or withdrawn. You display an error message if an attempt to withdraw money fails because there is insufficient money in the account. Notice also that, because we want to keep the code as simple as possible, you are not implementing extra properties, such as the account holder's name! In real life that would be pretty essential information, but for this example it's unnecessarily complicated.

The only really interesting line in this code is the class declaration:

```
public class SaverAccount : IBankAccount
```

You've declared that SaverAccount is derived from one interface, IBankAccount, and you have not explicitly indicated any other base classes (which of course means that SaverAccount is derived directly from System.Object). By the way, derivation from interfaces acts completely independently from derivation from classes.

Being derived from IBankAccount means that SaverAccount gets all the members of IBankAccount. But because an interface doesn't actually implement any of its methods, SaverAccount must provide its own implementations of all of them. If any implementations are missing, you can rest assured that the compiler will complain. Recall also that the interface just indicates the presence of its members. It's up to the class to decide if it wants any of them to be virtual or abstract (though abstract functions are of course only allowed if the class itself is abstract). For this particular example, you don't have any reason to make any of the interface functions virtual.

To illustrate how different classes can implement the same interface, assume that the Planetary Bank of Jupiter also implements a class to represent one of its bank accounts — a Gold Account:

```
namespace Wrox.ProCSharp.JupiterBank
{
    public class GoldAccount : IBankAccount
    {
        // etc
    }
}
```

We won't present details of the GoldAccount class here; in the sample code, it's basically identical to the implementation of SaverAccount. We stress that GoldAccount has no connection with SaverAccount, other than that both happen to implement the same interface.

Now that you have your classes, you can test them out. You first need a couple of using statements:

```
using System;
using Wrox.ProCSharp;
using Wrox.ProCSharp.VenusBank;
using Wrox.ProCSharp.JupiterBank;
```

Now you need a Main() method:

```
namespace Wrox.ProCSharp
{
    class MainEntryPoint
    {
        static void Main()
        {
            IBankAccount venusAccount = new SaverAccount();
            IBankAccount jupiterAccount = new GoldAccount();
            venusAccount.PayIn(200);
            venusAccount.Withdraw(100);
            Console.WriteLine(venusAccount.ToString());
            jupiterAccount.PayIn(500);
```

(continued)

(continued)

```
            jupiterAccount.Withdraw(600);
            jupiterAccount.Withdraw(100);
            Console.WriteLine(jupiterAccount.ToString());
        }
    }
}
```

This code (which if you download the sample, you can find in the file BankAccounts.cs) produces this output:

```
C:> BankAccounts
Venus Bank Saver: Balance = £100.00
Withdrawal attempt failed.
Jupiter Bank Saver: Balance = £400.00
```

The main point to notice about this code is the way that you have declared both your reference variables as IBankAccount references. This means that they can point to any instance of any class that implements this interface. However, it also means that you can call only methods that are part of this interface through these references — if you want to call any methods implemented by a class that are not part of the interface, you need to cast the reference to the appropriate type. In the example code, you were able to call ToString() (not implemented by IBankAccount) without any explicit cast, purely because ToString() is a System.Object method, so the C# compiler knows that it will be supported by any class (put differently, the cast from any interface to System.Object is implicit). Chapter 6, "Operators and Casts," covers the syntax for how to perform casts.

Interface references can in all respects be treated like class references — but the power of an interface reference is that it can refer to any class that implements that interface. For example, this allows you to form arrays of interfaces, where each element of the array is a different class:

```
IBankAccount[] accounts = new IBankAccount[2];
accounts[0] = new SaverAccount();
accounts[1] = new GoldAccount();
```

Note, however, that we'd get a compiler error if we tried something like this:

```
accounts[1] = new SomeOtherClass();    // SomeOtherClass does NOT implement
                                       // IBankAccount: WRONG!!
```

This causes a compilation error similar to this:

```
Cannot implicitly convert type 'Wrox.ProCSharp. SomeOtherClass' to 'Wrox.ProCSharp.
IBankAccount'
```

Derived Interfaces

It's possible for interfaces to inherit from each other in the same way that classes do. This concept is illustrated by defining a new interface, ITransferBankAccount, which has the same features as IBankAccount but also defines a method to transfer money directly to a different account:

```
namespace Wrox.ProCSharp
{
    public interface ITransferBankAccount : IBankAccount
    {
        bool TransferTo(IBankAccount destination, decimal amount);
    }
}
```

Because ITransferBankAccount is derived from IBankAccount, it gets all the members of IBankAccount as well as its own. That means that any class that implements (derives from) ITransferBankAccount must implement all the methods of IBankAccount, as well as the new TransferTo() method defined in ITransferBankAccount. Failure to implement all of these methods will result in a compilation error.

Note that the TransferTo() method uses an IBankAccount interface reference for the destination account. This illustrates the usefulness of interfaces: when implementing and then invoking this method, you don't need to know anything about what type of object you are transferring money to — all you need to know is that this object implements IBankAccount.

To illustrate ITransferBankAccount, assume that the Planetary Bank of Jupiter also offers a current account. Most of the implementation of the CurrentAccount class is identical to the implementations of SaverAccount and GoldAccount (again, this is just to keep this example simple — that won't normally be the case), so in the following code just the differences are highlighted:

```csharp
public class CurrentAccount : ITransferBankAccount
{
    private decimal balance;
    public void PayIn(decimal amount)
    {
        balance += amount;
    }
    public bool Withdraw(decimal amount)
    {
        if (balance >= amount)
        {
            balance -= amount;
            return true;
        }
        Console.WriteLine("Withdrawal attempt failed.");
        return false;
    }
    public decimal Balance
    {
        get
        {
            return balance;
        }
    }
    public bool TransferTo(IBankAccount destination, decimal amount)
    {
        bool result;
        result = Withdraw(amount);
        if (result)
        {
            destination.PayIn(amount);
        }
        return result;
    }
    public override string ToString()
    {
        return String.Format("Jupiter Bank Current Account: Balance = {0,6:C}",
            balance);
    }
}
```

The class can be demonstrated with this code:

```
static void Main()
{
    IBankAccount venusAccount = new SaverAccount();
    ITransferBankAccount jupiterAccount = new CurrentAccount();
    venusAccount.PayIn(200);
    jupiterAccount.PayIn(500);
    jupiterAccount.TransferTo(venusAccount, 100);
    Console.WriteLine(venusAccount.ToString());
    Console.WriteLine(jupiterAccount.ToString());
}
```

This code (`CurrentAccount.cs`) produces the following output, which, as you can verify, shows that the correct amounts have been transferred:

```
C:> CurrentAccount
Venus Bank Saver: Balance = £300.00
Jupiter Bank Current Account: Balance = £400.00
```

Summary

This chapter examined how to code inheritance in C#. You have seen that C# offers rich support for both multiple interface and single implementation inheritance. You have also learned that C# provides a number of useful syntactical constructs designed to assist in making code more robust, such as the override keyword, which indicates when a function should override a base function; the new keyword, which indicates when a function hides a base function; and rigid rules for constructor initializers that are designed to ensure that constructors are designed to interoperate in a robust manner.

5

Arrays

If you need to work with multiple objects of the same type, you can use collections and arrays. C# has a special notation to declare and use arrays. Behind the scenes, the `Array` class comes into play, which offers several methods to sort and filter the elements inside the array.

Using an enumerator, you can iterate through all the elements of an array.

This chapter discusses the following:

❑   Simple arrays

❑   Multidimensional arrays

❑   Jagged arrays

❑   The `Array` class

❑   Interfaces for arrays

❑   Enumerations

Simple Arrays

If you need to use multiple objects of the same type, you can use an array. An *array* is a data structure that contains a number of elements of the same type.

Array Declaration

An array is declared by defining the type of the elements inside the array followed by empty brackets and a variable name; for example, an array containing integer elements is declared like this:

```
int[] myArray;
```

Array Initialization

After declaring an array, memory must be allocated to hold all the elements of the array. An array is a reference type, so memory on the heap must be allocated. You do this by initializing the variable of the array using the `new` operator with the type and the number of elements inside the array. Here you specify the size of the array:

```
myArray = new int[4];
```

Value and reference types are covered in Chapter 3, "Objects and Types."

With this declaration and initialization, the variable `myArray` references four integer values that are allocated on the managed heap (see Figure 5-1).

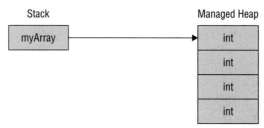

Figure 5-1

> The array cannot be resized after the size was specified without copying all
> elements. If you don't know the number of elements that should be in the array in
> advance, you can use a collection. Collections are covered in Chapter 10,
> "Collections."

Instead of using a separate line for the declaration and initialization, you can declare and initialize an array in a single line:

```
int[] myArray = new int[4];
```

You can also assign values to every array element using an array initializer. Array initializers can be used only while declaring an array variable, not after the array is declared.

```
int[] myArray = new int[4] {4, 7, 11, 2};
```

If you initialize the array using curly brackets, the size of the array can also be left out, because the compiler can count the number of elements itself:

```
int[] myArray = new int[] {4, 7, 11, 2};
```

There's even a shorter form using the C# compiler. Using curly brackets you can write the array declaration and initialization. The code generated from the compiler is the same as in the previous example.

```
int[] myArray = {4, 7, 11, 2};
```

Accessing Array Elements

After an array is declared and initialized, you can access the array elements using an indexer. Arrays only support indexers that have integer parameters.

With custom classes, you can also create indexers that support other types. You can read about creating custom indexers in Chapter 6, "Operators and Casts."

With the indexer, you pass the element number to access the array. The indexer always starts with a value of 0 for the first element. The highest number you can pass to the indexer is the number of elements minus one, because the index starts at zero. In the following example, the array `myArray` is declared and initialized with four integer values. The elements can be accessed with indexer values 0, 1, 2, and 3.

```
int[] myArray = new int[] {4, 7, 11, 2};
int v1 = myArray[0];    // read first element
int v2 = myArray[1];    // read second element
myArray[3] = 44;        // change fourth element
```

> **If you use a wrong indexer value where no element exists, an exception of type** `IndexOutOfRangeException` **is thrown.**

If you don't know the number of elements in the array, you can use the `Length` property that is used in this `for` statement:

```
for (int i = 0; i < myArray.Length; i++)
{
    Console.WriteLine(myArray[i]);
}
```

Instead of using a `for` statement to iterate through all elements of the array, you can also use the `foreach` statement:

```
foreach (int val in myArray)
{
    Console.WriteLine(val);
}
```

The `foreach` *statement makes use of the* `IEnumerable` *and* `IEnumerator` *interfaces, which are discussed later in this chapter.*

Using Reference Types

In addition to being able to declare arrays of predefined types, you can also declare arrays of custom types. Let's start with this `Person` class with two constructors, the properties `FirstName` and `LastName` using auto-implemented properties, and an override of the `ToString()` method from the `Object` class:

```
public class Person
{
    public Person()
    {
    }

    public Person(string firstName, string lastName)
```

(continued)

(continued)

```
    {
        this.FirstName = firstName;
        this.LastName = lastName;
    }

    public string FirstName { get; set; }

    public string LastName { get; set; }

    public override string ToString()
    {
        return String.Format("{0} {1}",
            FirstName, LastName);
    }
}
```

Declaring an array of two Person elements is similar to declaring an array of int:

```
Person[] myPersons = new Person[2];
```

However, you must be aware that if the elements in the array are reference types, memory must be allocated for every array element. In case you use an item in the array where no memory was allocated, a NullReferenceException is thrown.

> Chapter 14, "Errors and Exceptions," gives you all the information you need about errors and exceptions.

You can allocate every element of the array by using an indexer starting from 0:

```
myPersons[0] = new Person("Ayrton", "Senna");
myPersons[1] = new Person("Michael", "Schumacher");
```

Figure 5-2 shows the objects in the managed heap with the Person array. myPersons is a variable that is stored on the stack. This variable references an array of Person elements that is stored on the managed heap. This array has enough space for two references. Every item in the array references a Person object that is also stored in the managed heap.

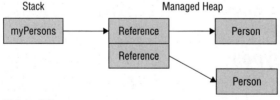

Figure 5-2

As with the int type, you can also use an array initializer with custom types:

```
Person[] myPersons = { new Person("Ayrton", "Senna"),
                       new Person("Michael",
                            "Schumacher") };
```

Multidimensional Arrays

Ordinary arrays (also known as 1-dimensional arrays) are indexed by a single integer. A multidimensional array is indexed by two or more integers.

Figure 5-3 shows the mathematical notation for a 2-dimensional array that has three rows and three columns. The first row has the values 1, 2, and 3, and the third row has the values 7, 8, and 9.

$$a = \begin{bmatrix} 1, \ 2, \ 3 \\ 4, \ 5, \ 6 \\ 7, \ 8, \ 9 \end{bmatrix}$$

Figure 5-3

Declaring this 2-dimensional array with C# is done by putting a comma inside the brackets. The array is initialized by specifying the size of every dimension (also known as rank). Then the array elements can be accessed by using two integers with the indexer:

```
int[,] twodim = new int[3, 3];
twodim[0, 0] = 1;
twodim[0, 1] = 2;
twodim[0, 2] = 3;
twodim[1, 0] = 4;
twodim[1, 1] = 5;
twodim[1, 2] = 6;
twodim[2, 0] = 7;
twodim[2, 1] = 8;
twodim[2, 2] = 9;
```

You cannot change the rank after declaring an array.

You can also initialize the 2-dimensional array by using an array indexer if you know the value for the elements in advance. For the initialization of the array, one outer curly bracket is used, and every row is initialized by using curly brackets inside the outer curly brackets.

```
int[,] twodim = {
                {1, 2, 3},
                {4, 5, 6},
                {7, 8, 9}
               };
```

When using an array initializer, you must initialize every element of the array. It is not possible to leave the initialization for some values.

By using two commas inside the brackets, you can declare a 3-dimensional array:

```
int[,,] threedim = {
                   { { 1, 2 }, { 3, 4 } },
                   { { 5, 6 }, { 7, 8 } },
                   { { 9, 10 }, { 11, 12 } }
                  };

Console.WriteLine(threedim[0, 1, 1]);
```

Jagged Arrays

A 2-dimensional array has a rectangular size (for example, 3 × 3 elements). A jagged array is more flexible in sizing the array. With a jagged array every row can have a different size.

Figure 5-4 contrasts a 2-dimensional array that has 3 × 3 elements with a jagged array. The jagged array shown contains three rows where the first row has two elements, the second row has six elements, and the third row has three elements.

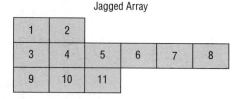

Figure 5-4

A jagged array is declared by placing one pair of opening and closing brackets after another. With the initialization of the jagged array, only the size that defines the number of rows in the first pair of brackets is set. The second brackets that define the number of elements inside the row are kept empty because every row has a different number of elements. Next, the element number of the rows can be set for every row:

```
int[][] jagged = new int[3][];
jagged[0] = new int[2] { 1, 2 };
jagged[1] = new int[6] { 3, 4, 5, 6, 7, 8 };
jagged[2] = new int[3] { 9, 10, 11 };
```

Iterating through all elements of a jagged array can be done with nested `for` loops. In the outer `for` loop every row is iterated, and the inner `for` loop iterates through every element inside a row.

```
for (int row = 0; row < jagged.Length; row++)
{
    for (int element = 0;
        element < jagged[row].Length; element++)
    {
        Console.WriteLine(
            "row: {0}, element: {1}, value: {2}",
            row, element, jagged[row][element]);
    }
}
```

The outcome of the iteration displays the rows and every element within the rows:

```
row: 0, element: 0, value: 1
row: 0, element: 1, value: 2
row: 1, element: 0, value: 3
row: 1, element: 1, value: 4
row: 1, element: 2, value: 5
row: 1, element: 3, value: 6
row: 1, element: 4, value: 7
row: 1, element: 5, value: 8
row: 2, element: 1, value: 9
row: 2, element: 2, value: 10
row: 2, element: 3, value: 11
```

Array Class

Declaring an array with brackets is a C# notation of using the Array class. Using the C# syntax behind the scenes creates a new class that derives from the abstract base class Array. It is possible, in this way, to use methods and properties that are defined with the Array class with every C# array. For example, you've already used the Length property or iterated through the array by using the foreach statement. By doing this, you are using the GetEnumerator() method of the Array class.

Properties

The Array class contains the properties listed in the following table that you can use with every array instance. More properties are available, which are discussed later in this chapter.

Property	Description
Length	The Length property returns the number of elements inside the array. If the array is a multidimensional array, you get the number of elements of all ranks. If you need to know the number of elements within a dimension, you can use the GetLength() method instead.
LongLength	The Length property returns an int value; the LongLength property returns the length in a long value. If the array contains more elements than fit into a 32-bit int value, you need to use the LongLength property to get the number of elements.
Rank	With the Rank property you get the number of dimensions of the array.

Creating Arrays

The Array class is abstract, so you cannot create an array by using a constructor. However, instead of using the C# syntax to create array instances, it is also possible to create arrays by using the static CreateInstance() method. This is extremely useful if you don't know the type of the elements in advance, because the type can be passed to the CreateInstance() method as a Type object.

The following example shows how to create an array of type int with a size of 5. The first argument of the CreateInstance() method requires the type of the elements, and the second argument defines the size. You can set values with the SetValue() method, and read values with the GetValue() method.

```
Array intArray1 = Array.CreateInstance(typeof(int), 5);
for (int i = 0; i < 5; i++)
{
    intArray1.SetValue(33, i);
}

for (int i = 0; i < 5; i++)
{
    Console.WriteLine(intArray1.GetValue(i));
}
```

You can also cast the created array to an array declared as int[]:

```
int[] intArray2 = (int[])intArray1;
```

The `CreateInstance()` method has many overloads to create multidimensional arrays and also to create arrays that are not 0-based. The following example creates a 2-dimensional array with 2 × 3 elements. The first dimension is 1-based; the second dimension is 10-based.

```
int[] lengths = { 2, 3 };
int[] lowerBounds = { 1, 10 };
Array racers = Array.CreateInstance(typeof(Person), lengths, lowerBounds);
```

Setting the elements of the array, the `SetValue()` method accepts indices for every dimension:

```
racers.SetValue(new Person("Alain", "Prost"), 1, 10);
racers.SetValue(new Person("Emerson", "Fittipaldi"), 1, 11);
racers.SetValue(new Person("Ayrton", "Senna"), 1, 12);
racers.SetValue(new Person("Ralf", "Schumacher"), 2, 10);
racers.SetValue(new Person("Fernando", "Alonso"), 2, 11);
racers.SetValue(new Person("Jenson", "Button"), 2, 12);
```

Although the array is not 0-based you can assign it to a variable with the normal C# notation. You just have to pay attention to not crossing the boundaries.

```
Person[,] racers2 = (Person[,])racers;
Person first = racers2[1, 10];
Person last = racers2[2, 12];
```

Copying Arrays

Because arrays are reference types, assigning an array variable to another one just gives you two variables referencing the same array. For copying arrays, the array implements the interface `ICloneable`. The `Clone()` method that is defined with this interface creates a shallow copy of the array.

If the elements of the array are value types, as in the following code segment, all values are copied, as you can see in Figure 5-5.

```
int[] intArray1 = {1, 2};
int[] intArray2 = (int[])intArray1.Clone();
```

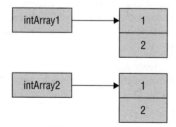

Figure 5-5

If the array contains reference types, only the references are copied; not the elements. Figure 5-6 shows the variables `beatles` and `beatlesClone`, where `beatlesClone` is created by calling the `Clone()` method from `beatles`. The `Person` objects that are referenced are the same with `beatles` and `beatlesClone`. If you change a property of an element of `beatlesClone`, you change the same object of `beatles`.

```
Person[] beatles = {
                    new Person("John", "Lennon"),
                    new Person("Paul", "McCartney")
                  };
Person[] beatlesClone = (Person[])beatles.Clone();
```

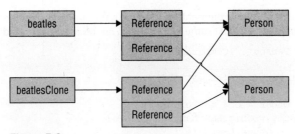

Figure 5-6

Instead of using the `Clone()` method, you can use the `Array.Copy()` method, which creates a shallow copy as well. But there's one important difference with `Clone()` and `Copy()`: `Clone()` creates a new array; with `Copy()` you have to pass an existing array with the same rank and enough elements.

If you need a deep copy of an array containing reference types, you have to iterate the array and create new objects.

Sorting

The `Array` class implements a bubble-sort for sorting the elements in the array. The `Sort()` method requires the interface `IComparable` to be implemented by the elements in the array. Simple types such as `System.String` and `System.Int32` implement `IComparable`, so you can sort elements containing these types.

With the sample program, the array name contains elements of type string, and this array can be sorted:

```
string[] names = {
                    "Christina Aguilera",
                    "Shakira",
                    "Beyonce",
                    "Gwen Stefani"
                  };

Array.Sort(names);

foreach (string name in names)
{
    Console.WriteLine(name);
}
```

The output of the application shows the sorted result of the array:

```
Beyonce
Christina Aguilera
Gwen Stefani
Shakira
```

If you are using custom classes with the array, you must implement the interface `IComparable`. This interface defines just one method, `CompareTo()`, that must return 0 if the objects to compare are equal, a value smaller than 0 if the instance should go before the object from the parameter, and a value larger than 0 if the instance should go after the object from the parameter.

Change the `Person` class to implement the interface `IComparable`. The comparison is done on the value of the `LastName`. Because the `LastName` is of type `string`, and the `String` class already implements the

`IComparable` interface, with the implementation you can rely on the `CompareTo()` method of the `String` class. If the `LastName` has the same value, the `FirstName` is compared:

```
public class Person : IComparable
{
    public int CompareTo(object obj)
    {
        Person other = obj as Person;
        int result = this.LastName.CompareTo(
                other.LastName);
        if (result == 0)
        {
            result = this.FirstName.CompareTo(
                other.FirstName);
        }
        return result;
    }
}
//...
```

Now it is possible to sort an array of `Person` objects by the last name:

```
Person[] persons = {
    new Person("Emerson", "Fittipaldi"),
    new Person("Niki", "Lauda"),
    new Person("Ayrton", "Senna"),
    new Person("Michael", "Schumacher")
};

Array.Sort(persons);
foreach (Person p in persons)
{
    Console.WriteLine(p);
}
```

Using the sort of the `Person` class, the output returns the names sorted by the last name:

```
Emerson Fittipaldi
Niki Lauda
Michael Schumacher
Ayrton Senna
```

If the `Person` object should be sorted differently, or if you don't have the option to change the class that is used as an element in the array, you can implement the interface `IComparer`. This interface defines the method `Compare()`. The interface `IComparable` must be implemented by the class that should be compared. The `IComparer` interface is independent of the class to compare. That's why the `Compare()` method defines two arguments that should be compared. The return value is similar to the `CompareTo()` method of the `IComparable` interface.

The class `PersonComparer` implements the `IComparer` interface to sort `Person` objects either by `firstName` or by `lastName`. The enumeration `PersonCompareType` defines the different sorting options that are available with the `PersonComparer`: `FirstName` and `LastName`. How the compare should happen is defined with the constructor of the class `PersonComparer` where a `PersonCompareType` value is set. The `Compare()` method is implemented with a `switch` statement to compare either by `LastName` or by `FirstName`.

```
public class PersonComparer : IComparer
{
    public enum PersonCompareType
    {
        FirstName,
        LastName
    }

    private PersonCompareType compareType;

    public PersonComparer(
            PersonCompareType compareType)
    {
        this.compareType = compareType;
    }

    public int Compare(object x, object y)
    {
        Person p1 = x as Person;
        Person p2 = y as Person;
        switch (compareType)
        {
            case PersonCompareType.FirstName:
                return p1.FirstName.CompareTo(
                        p2.FirstName);
            case PersonCompareType.LastName:
                return p1.LastName.CompareTo(
                        p2.LastName);
            default:
                throw new ArgumentException(
                        "unexpected compare type");
        }
    }
}
```

Now you can pass a `PersonComparer` object to the second argument of the `Array.Sort()` method. Here the persons are sorted by first name:

```
Array.Sort(persons,
    new PersonComparer(
                PersonComparer.PersonCompareType.
                FirstName));
foreach (Person p in persons)
{
    Console.WriteLine(p);
}
```

The `persons` array is now sorted by the first name:

```
Ayrton Senna
Emerson Fittipaldi
Michael Schumacher
Niki Lauda
```

The `Array` class also offers `Sort` methods that require a delegate as an argument. Chapter 7, "Delegates and Events," discusses how to use delegates.

Array and Collection Interfaces

The Array class implements the interfaces IEnumerable, ICollection, and IList for accessing and enumerating the elements of the array. Because with a custom array a class is created that derives from the abstract class Array, you can use the methods and properties of the implemented interfaces with an array variable.

IEnumerable

IEnumerable is an interface that is used by the foreach statement to iterate through the array. Because this is a very special feature, it is discussed in the next section, "Enumerations."

ICollection

The interface ICollection derives from the interface IEnumerable and has additional properties and methods as shown in the following table. This interface is mainly used to get the number of elements in a collection and for synchronization.

ICollection Interface Properties and Methods	Description
Count	The Count property gives you the number of elements inside the collection. The Count property returns the same value as the Length property.
IsSynchronized SyncRoot	The property IsSynchronized defines whether the collection is thread-safe. For arrays, this property always returns false. For synchronized access, the SyncRoot property can be used for thread-safe access. Chapter 19, "Threading and Synchronization," explains threads and synchronization, and there you can read how to implement thread safety with collections.
CopyTo()	With the CopyTo() method you can copy the elements of an array to an existing array. This is similar to the static method Array.Copy().

IList

The IList interface derives from the interface ICollection and defines additional properties and methods. The major reason why the Array class implements the IList interface is that the IList interface defines the Item property for accessing the elements using an indexer. Many of the other IList members are implemented by the Array class by throwing a NotSupportedException, because these do not apply to arrays. All the properties and methods of the IList interface are shown in the following table.

IList Interface	Description
Add()	The Add() method is used to add elements to a collection. With arrays, the method throws a NotSupportedException.
Clear()	The Clear() method empties all elements of the array. Value types are set to 0, reference types to null.

ILIst Interface	Description
Contains()	With the Contains() method, you can find out if an element is within the array. The return value is true or false. This method does a linear search through all elements of the array until the element is found.
IndexOf()	The IndexOf() method does a linear search through all elements of the array similar to the Contains() method. What's different is that the IndexOf() method returns the index of the first element found.
Insert() Remove() RemoveAt()	With collections, the Insert() method is used to insert elements; with Remove() and RemoveAt(), elements can be removed. With arrays, all these methods throw a NotSupportedException.
IsFixedSize	Because arrays are always fixed in size, this property always returns true.
IsReadOnly	Arrays are always read/write, so this property returns false. In Chapter 10, "Collections," you can read how to create a read-only collection from an array.
Item	The Item property allows accessing the array using an integer index.

Enumerations

By using the foreach statement you can iterate elements of a collection without the need to know the number of elements inside the collection. The foreach statement uses an enumerator. Figure 5-7 shows the relationship between the client invoking the foreach method and the collection. The array or collection implements the IEnumerable interface with the GetEnumerator() method. The GetEnumerator() method returns an enumerator implementing the IEnumerable interface. The interface IEnumerable then is used by the foreach statement to iterate through the collection.

> *The* GetEnumerator() *method is defined with the interface* IEnumerable. *The* foreach *statement doesn't really need this interface implemented in the collection class. It's enough to have a method with the name* GetEnumerator() *that returns an object implementing the* IEnumerator *interface.*

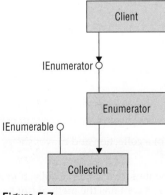

Figure 5-7

IEnumerator Interface

The foreach statement uses the methods and properties of the IEnumerator interface to iterate all elements in a collection. The properties and methods from this interface are defined in the following table.

IEnumerator Interface Properties and Methods	Description
MoveNext()	The MoveNext() method moves to the next element of the collection and returns true if there's an element. If the collection does not contain any more elements, the value false is returned.
Current	The property Current returns the element where the cursor is positioned.
Reset()	The method Reset() repositions the cursor to the beginning of the collection. Many enumerators throw a NotSupportedException.

foreach Statement

The C# foreach statement is not resolved to a foreach statement in the IL code. Instead, the C# compiler converts the foreach statement to methods and properties of the IEnumerable interface. Here's a simple foreach statement to iterate all elements in the persons array and to display them person by person:

```
foreach (Person p in persons)
{
    Console.WriteLine(p);
}
```

The foreach statement is resolved to the following code segment. First, the GetEnumerator() method is invoked to get an enumerator for the array. Inside a while loop — as long as MoveNext() returns true — the elements of the array are accessed using the Current property:

```
IEnumerator enumerator = persons.GetEnumerator();
while (enumerator.MoveNext())
{
    Person p = (Person)enumerator.Current;
    Console.WriteLine(p);
}
```

yield Statement

C# 1.0 made it easy to iterate through collections by using the foreach statement. With C# 1.0, it was still a lot of work to create an enumerator. C# 2.0 adds the yield statement for creating enumerators easily.

yield return returns one element of a collection and moves the position to the next element, and yield break stops the iteration.

The next example shows the implementation of a simple collection using the yield return statement. The class HelloCollection contains the method GetEnumerator(). The implementation of the GetEnumerator() method contains two yield return statements where the strings Hello and World are returned.

```
using System;
using System.Collections;

namespace Wrox.ProCSharp.Arrays
{
    public class HelloCollection
    {
        public IEnumerator GetEnumerator()
        {
            yield return "Hello";
            yield return "World";
        }
    }
}
```

A method or property that contains yield *statements is also known as an* iterator block. *An iterator block must be declared to return an* IEnumerator *or* IEnumerable *interface. This block may contain multiple* yield return *or* yield break *statements; a* return *statement is not allowed.*

Now it is possible to iterate through the collection using a foreach statement:

```
public class Program
{
    HelloCollection helloCollection =
        new HelloCollection();
    foreach (string s in helloCollection)
    {
        Console.WriteLine(s);
    }
}
```

With an iterator block the compiler generates a yield type, including a state machine, as shown with the following code segment. The yield type implements the properties and methods of the interfaces IEnumerator and IDisposable. In the sample, you can see the yield type as the inner class Enumerator. The GetEnumerator() method of the outer class instantiates and returns a new yield type. Within the yield type, the variable state defines the current position of the iteration and is changed every time the method MoveNext() is invoked. MoveNext() encapsulates the code of the iterator block and sets the value of the current variable so that the Current property returns an object depending on the position.

```
public class HelloCollection
{
    public IEnumerator GetEnumerator()
    {
        Enumerator enumerator = new Enumerator();
        return enumerator;
    }

    public class Enumerator : IEnumerator, IDisposable
    {
        private int state;
        private object current;

        public Enumerator(int state)
```

(continued)

(continued)

```
        {
            this.state = state;
        }
        bool System.Collections.IEnumerator.MoveNext()
        {
            switch (state)
            {
                case 0:
                    current = "Hello";
                    state = 1;
                    return true;
                case 1:
                    current = "World";
                    state = 2;
                    return true;
                case 2:
                    break;
            }

            return false;
        }

        void System.Collections.IEnumerator.Reset()
        {
            throw new NotSupportedException();
        }

        object System.Collections.IEnumerator.Current
        {
            get
            {
                return current;
            }
        }

        void IDisposable.Dispose()
        {
        }
    }
}
```

Now, using the `yield return` statement makes it easy to implement a class that allows iterating through a collection in different ways. The class `MusicTitles` allows iterating the titles in a default way with the `GetEnumerator()` method, in reverse order with the `Reverse()` method, and to iterate through a subset with the `Subset()` method:

```
public class MusicTitles
{
    string[] names = {
            "Tubular Bells", "Hergest Ridge",
            "Ommadawn", "Platinum" };

    public IEnumerator GetEnumerator()
```

```
        {
            for (int i = 0; i < 4; i++)
            {
                yield return names[i];
            }
        }

        public IEnumerable Reverse()
        {
            for (int i = 3; i >= 0; i--)
            {
                yield return names[i];
            }
        }

        public IEnumerable Subset(int index,
                int length)
        {
            for (int i = index; i < index + length;
                    i++)
            {
                yield return names[i];
            }
        }
    }
```

The client code to iterate through the string array first uses the `GetEnumerator()` method, which you don't have to write in your code because this one is used by default. Then the titles are iterated in reverse, and finally a subset is iterated by passing the index and number of items to iterate to the `Subset()` method:

```
MusicTitles titles = new MusicTitles();
foreach (string title in titles)
{
    Console.WriteLine(title);
}
Console.WriteLine();

Console.WriteLine("reverse");
foreach (string title in titles.Reverse())
{
    Console.WriteLine(title);
}
Console.WriteLine();

Console.WriteLine("subset");
foreach (string title in
        titles.Subset(2, 2))
{
    Console.WriteLine(title);
}
```

With the yield statement you can also do more complex things, for example, returning an enumerator from `yield return`.

With the TicTacToe game, players alternate putting a cross or a circle in one of nine fields. These moves are simulated by the `GameMoves` class. The methods `Cross()` and `Circle()` are the iterator blocks for creating iterator types. The variables `cross` and `circle` are set to `Cross()` and `Circle()` inside the constructor of the `GameMoves` class. By setting these fields the methods are not invoked, but set to the iterator types that are defined with the iterator blocks. Within the `Cross()` iterator block, information about the move is written to the console and the move number is incremented. If the move number is higher than 9, the iteration ends with `yield break`; otherwise, the enumerator object of the cross yield type is returned with each iteration. The `Circle()` iterator block is very similar to the `Cross()` iterator block; it just returns the circle iterator type with each iteration.

```
public class GameMoves
{
    private IEnumerator cross;
    private IEnumerator circle;

    public GameMoves()
    {
        cross = Cross();
        circle = Circle();
    }

    private int move = 0;

    public IEnumerator Cross()
    {
        while (true)
        {
            Console.WriteLine("Cross, move {0}",
                move);
            move++;
            if (move > 9)
                yield break;
            yield return circle;
        }
    }

    public IEnumerator Circle()
    {
        while (true)
        {
            Console.WriteLine("Circle, move {0}",
                move);
            move++;
            if (move > 9)
                yield break;
            yield return cross;
        }
    }
}
```

From the client program you can use the class `GameMoves` as follows. The first move is set by setting enumerator to the enumerator type returned by `game.Cross()`. `enumerator.MoveNext` invokes one iteration defined with the iterator block that returns the other enumerator. The returned value can be accessed with the `Current` property and is set to the `enumerator` variable for the next loop:

```
GameMoves game = new GameMoves();
IEnumerator enumerator = game.Cross();
while (enumerator.MoveNext())
```

```
        {
            enumerator =
                (IEnumerator)enumerator.Current;
        }
```

The outcome of this program shows alternating moves until the last move:

```
Cross, move 0
Circle, move 1
Cross, move 2
Circle, move 3
Cross, move 4
Circle, move 5
Cross, move 6
Circle, move 7
Cross, move 8
```

Summary

In this chapter, you've seen the C# notation to create and use simple, multidimensional, and jagged arrays. The `Array` class is used behind the scenes of C# arrays, and this way you can invoke properties and methods of this class with array variables.

You've seen how to sort elements in the array by using the `IComparable` and `IComparer` interfaces. The features of the `IEnumerable`, `ICollection`, and `IList` interfaces as implemented with the `Array` class were described, and finally, you've seen the advantages of the `yield` statement. Moving on, the next chapter focuses on operators and casts, in which you read about creating a custom indexer. Chapter 7 gives you information about delegates and events. Some methods of the `Array` class use delegates as parameters. Chapter 10 is about collection classes that already have been mentioned in this chapter. Collection classes give you more flexibility of the size, and there you can also read about other containers such as dictionaries and linked lists.

6

Operators and Casts

The preceding chapters have covered most of what you need to start writing useful programs using C#. This chapter completes the discussion of the essential language elements and begins to illustrate some powerful aspects of C# that allow you to extend the capabilities of the C# language. Specifically, this chapter discusses the following:

- ❏ The operators available in C#
- ❏ The idea of equality when dealing with reference and value types
- ❏ Data conversion between the primitive data types
- ❏ Converting value types to reference types using boxing
- ❏ Converting between reference types by casting
- ❏ Overloading the standard operators to support operations on the custom types you define
- ❏ Adding cast operators to the custom types you define to support seamless data type-conversions

Operators

Although most of C#'s operators should be familiar to C and C++ developers, this section discusses the most important operators for the benefit of new programmers and Visual Basic converts, as well as to shed light on some of the changes introduced with C#.

C# supports the operators listed in the following table.

Category	Operator
Arithmetic	+ - * / %
Logical	& | ^ ~ && || !
String concatenation	+
Increment and decrement	++ --
Bit shifting	<< >>
Comparison	== != < ><= >=
Assignment	= += -= *= /= %= &= |= ^= <<= >>=
Member access (for objects and structs)	.
Indexing (for arrays and indexers)	[]
Cast	()
Conditional (the ternary operator)	?:
Delegate concatenation and removal (discussed in Chapter 7, "Delegates and Events")	+ -
Object creation	new
Type information	sizeof is typeof as
Overflow exception control	checked unchecked
Indirection and address	[]
Namespace alias qualifier (discussed in Chapter 2, "C# Basics")	::
Null coalescing operator	??

Note that four specific operators (`sizeof`, `*`, `->`, and `&`, listed in the following table), however, are available only in unsafe code (code that bypasses C#'s type-safety checking), which is discussed in Chapter 12, "Memory Management and Pointers." It is also important to note that the `sizeof` operator keywords, when used with the .NET Framework 1.0 and 1.1, require the unsafe mode. This is not a requirement since the .NET Framework 2.0.

Category	Operator
Operator keywords	sizeof (for .NET Framework versions 1.0 and 1.1 only)
Operators	* -> &

One of the biggest pitfalls to watch out for when using C# operators is that, like other C-style languages, C# uses different operators for assignment (=) and comparison (==). For instance, the following statement means *let x equal three*:

```
x = 3;
```

If you now want to compare x to a value, you need to use the double equals sign ==:

```
if (x == 3)
{

}
```

Fortunately, C#'s strict type-safety rules prevent the very common C error where assignment is performed instead of comparison in logical statements. This means that in C# the following statement will generate a compiler error:

```
if (x = 3)
{

}
```

Visual Basic programmers who are accustomed to using the ampersand (&) character to concatenate strings will have to make an adjustment. In C#, the plus sign (+) is used instead for concatenation, whereas the & symbol denotes a bitwise AND between two different integer values. The symbol | allows you to perform a bitwise OR between two integers. Visual Basic programmers also might not recognize the modulus (%) arithmetic operator. This returns the remainder after division, so, for example, x % 5 returns 2 if x is equal to 7.

You will use few pointers in C#, and, therefore, few indirection operators. More specifically, the only place you will use them is within blocks of unsafe code, because that is the only place in C# where pointers are allowed. Pointers and unsafe code are discussed in Chapter 12, "Memory Management and Pointers."

Operator Shortcuts

The following table shows the full list of shortcut assignment operators available in C#.

Shortcut Operator	Equivalent To
x++, ++x	x = x + 1
x--, --x	x = x - 1
x += y	x = x + y
x -= y	x = x - y
x *= y	x = x * y
x /= y	x = x / y
x %= y	x = x % y
x >>= y	x = x >> y
x <<= y	x = x << y
x &= y	x = x & y
x |= y	x = x | y
x ^= y	x = x ^ y

You may be wondering why there are two examples each for the ++ increment and the -- decrement operators. Placing the operator *before* the expression is known as a *prefix*, placing the operator *after* the expression is known as a *postfix*, and it is important to note that there is a difference in the way they behave.

The increment and decrement operators can act both as whole expressions and within expressions. When used by themselves, the effect of both the prefix and postfix versions is identical and corresponds to the statement x = x + 1. When used within larger expressions, the prefix operator will increment the value of x *before* the expression is evaluated; in other words, x is incremented and the new value is used in the expression. In contrast, the postfix operator increments the value of x *after* the expression is evaluated — the expression is evaluated using the original value of x. The following example uses the increment operator (++) as an example to demonstrate the difference between the prefix and postfix behavior:

```
int x = 5;

if (++x == 6)   // true - x is incremented to 6 before the evaluation
{
    Console.WriteLine("This will execute");
}

if (x++ == 7) // false - x is incremented to 7 after the evaluation
{
    Console.WriteLine("This won't");
}
```

The first if condition evaluates to true, because x is incremented from 5 to 6 *before* the expression is evaluated. The condition in the second if statement is false, however, because x is incremented to 7 only after the entire expression has been evaluated (while x = 6).

The prefix and postfix operators --x and x-- behave in the same way, but decrement rather than increment the operand.

The other shortcut operators, such as += and -=, require two operands, and are used to modify the value of the first operand by performing an arithmetic, logical, or bitwise operation on it. For example, the next two lines are equivalent:

```
x += 5;
x = x + 5;
```

The following sections look at some of the primary and cast operators that you will frequently use within your C# code.

The Conditional Operator

The conditional operator (?:), also known as the ternary operator, is a shorthand form of the if...else construction. It gets its name from the fact that it involves three operands. It allows you to evaluate a condition, returning one value if that condition is true, or another value if it is false. The syntax is:

```
condition ? true_value : false_value
```

Here, *condition* is the Boolean expression to be evaluated, *true_value* is the value that will be returned if *condition* is true, and *false_value* is the value that will be returned otherwise.

When used sparingly, the conditional operator can add a dash of terseness to your programs. It is especially handy for providing one of a couple of arguments to a function that is being invoked. You can use it to quickly convert a Boolean value to a string value of true or false. It is also handy for displaying the correct singular or plural form of a word, for example:

```
int x = 1;
string s = x + " ";
s += (x == 1 ? "man" : "men");
Console.WriteLine(s);
```

This code displays 1 man if x is equal to one but will display the correct plural form for any other number. Note, however, that if your output needs to be localized to different languages, you will have to write more sophisticated routines to take into account the different grammatical rules of different languages.

The checked and unchecked Operators

Consider the following code:

```
byte b = 255;
b++;
Console.WriteLine(b.ToString());
```

The byte data type can hold values only in the range zero to 255, so incrementing the value of b causes an overflow. How the CLR handles this depends on a number of issues, including compiler options, so whenever there's a risk of an unintentional overflow, you need some way of making sure that you get the result you want.

To do this, C# provides the checked and unchecked operators. If you mark a block of code as checked, the CLR will enforce overflow checking, and throw an OverflowException if an overflow occurs. Let's change the code to include the checked operator:

```
byte b = 255;
checked
{
    b++;
}
Console.WriteLine(b.ToString());
```

When you try to run this code, you will get an error message like this:

```
Unhandled Exception: System.OverflowException: Arithmetic operation resulted in an
overflow.
    at Wrox.ProCSharp.Basics.OverflowTest.Main(String[] args)
```

You can enforce overflow checking for all unmarked code in your program by specifying the /checked *compiler option.*

If you want to suppress overflow checking, you can mark the code as unchecked:

```
byte b = 255;
unchecked
{
    b++;
}
Console.WriteLine(b.ToString());
```

In this case, no exception will be raised, but you will lose data — because the byte type cannot hold a value of 256, the overflowing bits will be discarded, and your b variable will hold a value of zero (0).

Note that unchecked is the default behavior. The only time you are likely to need to explicitly use the unchecked keyword is if you need a few unchecked lines of code inside a larger block that you have explicitly marked as checked.

The is Operator

The `is` operator allows you to check whether an object is compatible with a specific type. The phrase "is compatible" means that an object either is of that type or is derived from that type. For example, to check whether a variable is compatible with the `object` type, you could use the following bit of code:

```
int i = 10;
if (i is object)
{
    Console.WriteLine("i is an object");
}
```

`int`, like all C# data types, inherits from `object`; therefore the expression `i is object` will evaluate to `true` in this case, and the appropriate message will be displayed.

The as Operator

The `as` operator is used to perform explicit type conversions of reference types. If the type being converted is compatible with the specified type, conversion is performed successfully. However, if the types are incompatible, the `as` operator returns the value `null`. As shown in the following code, attempting to convert an `object` reference to a `string` will return `null` if the `object` reference does not actually refer to a `string` instance:

```
object o1 = "Some String";
object o2 = 5;

string s1 = o1 as string;    // s1 = "Some String"
string s2 = o2 as string;    // s2 = null
```

The `as` operator allows you to perform a safe type conversion in a single step without the need to first test the type using the `is` operator and then perform the conversion.

The sizeof Operator

You can determine the size (in bytes) required on the stack by a value type using the `sizeof` operator:

```
unsafe
{
    Console.WriteLine(sizeof(int));
}
```

This will display the number 4, because an `int` is 4 bytes long.

Notice that you can use the `sizeof` operator only in unsafe code. Chapter 12, "Memory Management and Pointers," looks at unsafe code in more detail.

The typeof Operator

The `typeof` operator returns a `System.Type` object representing a specified type. For example, `typeof(string)` will return a `Type` object representing the `System.String` type. This is useful when you want to use reflection to find information about an object dynamically. Chapter 13, "Reflection," looks at reflection.

Nullable Types and Operators

Looking at the Boolean type, you have a true or false value that you can assign to this type. However, what if you wanted to define the value of the type as undefined? This is where using nullable types can have a distinct value to your applications. If you use nullable types in your programs, you must always consider the effect a `null` value can have when used in conjunction with the various operators. Usually, when using a unary or binary operator with nullable types, the result will be `null` if one or both of the operands is `null`. For example:

```
int? a = null;

int? b = a + 4;      // b = null
int? c = a * 5;      // c = null
```

However, when comparing nullable types, if only one of the operands is `null`, the comparison will always equate to `false`. This means that you cannot assume a condition is `true` just because its opposite is `false`, as often happens in programs using non-nullable types. For example:

```
int? a = null;
int? b = -5;

if (a >= b)
    Console.WriteLine("a >= b");
else
    Console.WriteLine("a < b");
```

The possibility of a `null` value means that you cannot freely combine nullable and non-nullable types in an expression. This is discussed in the "Type Conversions" section later in this chapter.

The Null Coalescing Operator

The null coalescing operator (`??`) provides a shorthand mechanism to cater to the possibility of `null` values when working with nullable and reference types. The operator is placed between two operands — the first operand must be a nullable type or reference type, and the second operand must be of the same type as the first or of a type that is implicitly convertible to the type of the first operand. The null coalescing operator evaluates as follows: If the first operand is not `null`, then the overall expression has the value of the first operand. However, if the first operand is `null`, then the overall expression has the value of the second operand. For example:

```
int? a = null;
int b;

b = a ?? 10;      // b has the value 10
a = 3;
b = a ?? 10;      // b has the value 3
```

If the second operand cannot be implicitly converted to the type of the first operand, a compile-time error is generated.

Operator Precedence

The following table shows the order of precedence of the C# operators. The operators at the top of the table are those with the highest precedence (that is, the ones evaluated first in an expression containing multiple operators).

Group	Operators
Primary	`() . [] x++ x-- new typeof sizeof checked unchecked`
Unary	`+ - ! ~ ++x --x` and casts
Multiplication/division	`* / %`
Group	Operators
Addition/subtraction	`+ -`
Bitwise shift operators	`<< >>`
Relational	`< ><= >= is as`
Comparison	`== !=`
Bitwise AND	`&`
Bitwise XOR	`^`
Bitwise OR	`|`
Boolean AND	`&&`
Boolean OR	`||`
Conditional operator	`?:`
Assignment	`= += -= *= /= %= &= |= ^= <<= >>= >>>=`

In complex expressions, you should avoid relying on operator precedence to produce the correct result. Using parentheses to specify the order in which you want operators applied clarifies your code and prevents potential confusion.

Type Safety

Chapter 1, ".NET Architecture," noted that the Intermediate Language (IL) enforces strong type safety upon its code. Strong typing enables many of the services provided by .NET, including security and language interoperability. As you would expect from a language compiled into IL, C# is also strongly typed. Among other things, this means that data types are not always seamlessly interchangeable. This section looks at conversions between primitive types.

C# also supports conversions between different reference types and allows you to define how data types that you create behave when converted to and from other types. Both of these topics are discussed later in this chapter.

Generics, a feature included in C#, allows you to avoid some of the most common situations in which you would need to perform type conversions. See Chapter 9, "Generics," for details.

Type Conversions

Often, you need to convert data from one type to another. Consider the following code:

```
byte value1 = 10;
byte value2 = 23;
byte total;
total = value1 + value2;
Console.WriteLine(total);
```

When you attempt to compile these lines, you get the following error message:

```
Cannot implicitly convert type 'int' to 'byte'
```

The problem here is that when you add 2 bytes together, the result will be returned as an int, not as another byte. This is because a byte can contain only 8 bits of data, so adding 2 bytes together could very easily result in a value that cannot be stored in a single byte. If you do want to store this result in a byte variable, you are going to have to convert it back to a byte. The following sections discuss two conversion mechanisms supported by C# — *implicit* and *explicit*.

Implicit Conversions

Conversion between types can normally be achieved automatically (implicitly) only if you can guarantee that the value is not changed in any way. This is why the previous code failed; by attempting a conversion from an int to a byte, you were potentially losing 3 bytes of data. The compiler is not going to let you do that unless you explicitly tell it that that's what you want to do. If you store the result in a long instead of a byte, however, you will have no problems:

```
byte value1 = 10;
byte value2 = 23;
long total;                    // this will compile fine
total = value1 + value2;
Console.WriteLine(total);
```

Your program has compiled with no errors at this point because a long holds more bytes of data than a byte, so there is no risk of data being lost. In these circumstances, the compiler is happy to make the conversion for you, without your needing to ask for it explicitly.

The following table shows the implicit type conversions supported in C#.

From	To
sbyte	short, int, long, float, double, decimal
byte	short, ushort, int, uint, long, ulong, float, double, decimal
short	int, long, float, double, decimal
ushort	int, uint, long, ulong, float, double, decimal
int	long, float, double, decimal
uint	long, ulong, float, double, decimal
long, ulong	float, double, decimal
float	Double
char	ushort, int, uint, long, ulong, float, double, decimal

As you would expect, you can perform implicit conversions only from a smaller integer type to a larger one, not from larger to smaller. You can also convert between integers and floating-point values; however, the rules are slightly different here. Though you can convert between types of the same size, such as `int`/`uint` to `float` and `long`/`ulong` to `double`, you can also convert from `long`/`ulong` back to `float`. You might lose 4 bytes of data doing this, but this only means that the value of the `float` you receive will be less precise than if you had used a `double`; this is regarded by the compiler as an acceptable possible error because the magnitude of the value is not affected. You can also assign an unsigned variable to a signed variable as long as the limits of value of the unsigned type fit between the limits of the signed variable.

Nullable types introduce additional considerations when implicitly converting value types:

❑   Nullable types implicitly convert to other nullable types following the conversion rules described for non-nullable types in the previous table; that is, `int?` implicitly converts to `long?`, `float?`, `double?`, and `decimal?`.

❑   Non-nullable types implicitly convert to nullable types according to the conversion rules described in the preceding table; that is, `int` implicitly converts to `long?`, `float?`, `double?`, and `decimal?`.

❑   Nullable types *do not* implicitly convert to non-nullable types; you must perform an explicit conversion as described in the next section. This is because there is the chance a nullable type will have the value `null`, which cannot be represented by a non-nullable type.

Explicit Conversions

Many conversions cannot be implicitly made between types, and the compiler will give you an error if any are attempted. These are some of the conversions that cannot be made implicitly:

❑   `int` to `short` — Data loss is possible.

❑   `int` to `uint` — Data loss is possible.

❑   `uint` to `int` — Data loss is possible.

❑   `float` to `int` — You will lose everything after the decimal point.

❑   Any numeric type to `char` — Data loss is possible.

❑   `decimal` to any numeric type — The decimal type is internally structured differently from both integers and floating-point numbers.

❑   `int?` to `int` — The nullable type may have the value `null`.

However, you can explicitly carry out such conversions using *casts*. When you cast one type to another, you deliberately force the compiler to make the conversion. A cast looks like this:

```
long val = 30000;
int i = (int)val;    // A valid cast. The maximum int is 2147483647
```

You indicate the type to which you are casting by placing its name in parentheses before the value to be converted. If you are familiar with C, this is the typical syntax for casts. If you are familiar with the C++ special cast keywords such as `static_cast`, note that these do not exist in C# and that you have to use the older C-type syntax.

Casting can be a dangerous operation to undertake. Even a simple cast from a `long` to an `int` can cause problems if the value of the original `long` is greater than the maximum value of an `int`:

```
long val = 3000000000;
int i = (int)val;           // An invalid cast. The maximum int is 2147483647
```

In this case, you will not get an error, but you also will not get the result you expect. If you run this code and output the value stored in i, this is what you get:

```
-1294967296
```

It is good practice to assume that an explicit cast will not give the results you expect. As you saw earlier, C# provides a checked operator that you can use to test whether an operation causes an arithmetic overflow. You can use the checked operator to check that a cast is safe and to force the runtime to throw an overflow exception if it is not:

```
long val = 3000000000;
int i = checked((int)val);
```

Bearing in mind that all explicit casts are potentially unsafe, you should take care to include code in your application to deal with possible failures of the casts. Chapter 14, "Errors and Exceptions," introduces structured exception handling using the try and catch statements.

Using casts, you can convert most primitive data types from one type to another; for example, in this code, the value 0.5 is added to price, and the total is cast to an int:

```
double price = 25.30;
int approximatePrice = (int)(price + 0.5);
```

This will give the price rounded to the nearest dollar. However, in this conversion, data is lost — namely, everything after the decimal point. Therefore, such a conversion should never be used if you want to go on to do more calculations using this modified price value. However, it is useful if you want to output the approximate value of a completed or partially completed calculation — if you do not want to bother the user with lots of figures after the decimal point.

This example shows what happens if you convert an unsigned integer into a char:

```
ushort c = 43;
char symbol = (char)c;
Console.WriteLine(symbol);
```

The output is the character that has an ASCII number of 43, the + sign. You can try any kind of conversion you want between the numeric types (including char), and it will work, such as converting a decimal into a char, or vice versa.

Converting between value types is not restricted to isolated variables, as you have seen. You can convert an array element of type double to a struct member variable of type int:

```
struct ItemDetails
{
    public string Description;
    public int ApproxPrice;
}

//...

double[] Prices = { 25.30, 26.20, 27.40, 30.00 };

ItemDetails id;
id.Description = "Whatever";
id.ApproxPrice = (int)(Prices[0] + 0.5);
```

To convert a nullable type to a non-nullable type or another nullable type where data loss may occur, you must use an explicit cast. This is true even when converting between elements with the same basic underlying type, for example, int? to int or float? to float. This is because the nullable type may have the value null, which cannot be represented by the non-nullable type. As long as an explicit cast between two equivalent non-nullable types is possible, so is the explicit cast between nullable types. However, when casting from a nullable to non-nullable type and the variable has the value `null`, an `InvalidOperationException` is thrown. For example:

```
int? a = null;
int  b = (int)a;      // Will throw exception
```

Using explicit casts and a bit of care and attention, you can convert any instance of a simple value type to almost any other. However, there are limitations on what you can do with explicit type conversions — as far as value types are concerned, you can only convert to and from the numeric and `char` types and enum types. You cannot directly cast Booleans to any other type or vice versa.

If you need to convert between numeric and string, you can use methods provided in the .NET class library. The `Object` class implements a `ToString()` method, which has been overridden in all the .NET predefined types and which returns a string representation of the object:

```
int i = 10;
string s = i.ToString();
```

Similarly, if you need to parse a string to retrieve a numeric or Boolean value, you can use the `Parse()` method supported by all the predefined value types:

```
string s = "100";
int i = int.Parse(s);
Console.WriteLine(i + 50);    // Add 50 to prove it is really an int
```

Note that `Parse()` will register an error by throwing an exception if it is unable to convert the string (for example, if you try to convert the string `Hello` to an integer). Again, exceptions are covered in Chapter 14.

Boxing and Unboxing

In Chapter 2, "C# Basics," you learned that all types, both the simple predefined types such as `int` and `char`, and the complex types such as classes and structs, derive from the `object` type. This means that you can treat even literal values as though they were objects:

```
string s = 10.ToString();
```

However, you also saw that C# data types are divided into value types, which are allocated on the stack, and reference types, which are allocated on the heap. How does this square with the ability to call methods on an `int`, if the `int` is nothing more than a 4-byte value on the stack?

The way C# achieves this is through a bit of magic called *boxing*. Boxing and its counterpart, *unboxing*, allow you to convert value types to reference types and then back to value types. We include this in the section on casting because this is essentially what you are doing — you are casting your value to the `object` type. Boxing is the term used to describe the transformation of a value type to a reference type. Basically, the runtime creates a temporary reference-type box for the object on the heap.

This conversion can occur implicitly, as in the preceding example, but you can also perform it explicitly:

```
int myIntNumber = 20;
object myObject = myIntNumber;
```

Unboxing is the term used to describe the reverse process, where the value of a previously boxed value type is cast back to a value type. We use the term *cast* here, because this has to be done explicitly. The syntax is similar to explicit type conversions already described:

```
int myIntNumber = 20;
object myObject = myIntNumber;     // Box the int
int mySecondNumber = (int)myObject;   // Unbox it back into an int
```

You can only unbox a variable that has previously been boxed. If you execute the last line when `myObject` is not a boxed `int`, you will get an exception thrown at runtime.

One word of warning: when unboxing, you have to be careful that the receiving value variable has enough room to store all the bytes in the value being unboxed. C#'s ints, for example, are only 32 bits long, so unboxing a `long` value (64 bits) into an `int` as shown here will result in an `InvalidCastException`:

```
long myLongNumber = 333333423;
object myObject = (object)myLongNumber;
int myIntNumber = (int)myObject;
```

Comparing Objects for Equality

After discussing operators and briefly touching on the equality operator, it is worth considering for a moment what equality means when dealing with instances of classes and structs. Understanding the mechanics of object equality is essential for programming logical expressions and is important when implementing operator overloads and casts, which is the topic of the rest of this chapter.

The mechanisms of object equality are different depending on whether you are comparing reference types (instances of classes) or value types (the primitive data types, instances of structs or enums). The following sections present the equality of reference and value types independently.

Comparing Reference Types for Equality

You might be surprised to learn that `System.Object` defines three different methods for comparing objects for equality: `ReferenceEquals()` and two versions of `Equals()`. Add to this the comparison operator (==), and you actually have four ways of comparing for equality. Some subtle differences exist between the different methods, which are examined next.

The ReferenceEquals() Method

`ReferenceEquals()` is a `static` method that tests whether two references refer to the same instance of a class, specifically whether the two references contain the same address in memory. As a `static` method, it is not possible to override, so the `System.Object` implementation is what you always have. `ReferenceEquals()` will always return `true` if supplied with two references that refer to the same object instance, and `false` otherwise. It does, however, consider `null` to be equal to `null`:

```
SomeClass x, y;
x = new SomeClass();
y = new SomeClass();
bool B1 = ReferenceEquals(null, null);    // returns true
bool B2 = ReferenceEquals(null,x);        // returns false
bool B3 = ReferenceEquals(x, y);          // returns false because x and y
                                          // point to different objects
```

The virtual Equals() Method

The `System.Object` implementation of the virtual version of `Equals()` also works by comparing references. However, because this method is virtual, you can override it in your own classes in order to compare objects by value. In particular, if you intend instances of your class to be used as keys in a dictionary, you will need to override this method to compare values. Otherwise, depending on how you override `Object.GetHashCode()`, the dictionary class that contains your objects will either not work at all or will work very inefficiently. One point you should note when overriding `Equals()` is that your override should never throw exceptions. Once again, this is because doing so could cause problems for dictionary classes and possibly certain other .NET base classes that internally call this method.

The static Equals() Method

The `static` version of `Equals()` actually does the same thing as the virtual instance version. The difference is that the static version takes two parameters and compares them for equality. This method is able to cope when either of the objects is `null`, and, therefore, provides an extra safeguard against throwing exceptions if there is a risk that an object might be `null`. The `static` overload first checks whether the references it has been passed are `null`. If they are both `null`, it returns `true` (because `null` is considered to be equal to `null`). If just one of them is `null`, it returns `false`. If both references actually refer to something, it calls the virtual instance version of `Equals()`. This means that when you override the instance version of `Equals()`, the effect is as if you were overriding the static version as well.

Comparison Operator (==)

It is best to think of the comparison operator as an intermediate option between strict value comparison and strict reference comparison. In most cases, writing the following means that you are comparing references:

```
bool b = (x == y);    // x, y object references
```

However, it is accepted that there are some classes whose meanings are more intuitive if they are treated as values. In those cases, it is better to override the comparison operator to perform a value comparison. Overriding operators is discussed next, but the obvious example of this is the `System.String` class for which Microsoft has overridden this operator to compare the contents of the strings rather than their references.

Comparing Value Types for Equality

When comparing value types for equality, the same principles hold as for reference types: `ReferenceEquals()` is used to compare references, `Equals()` is intended for value comparisons, and the comparison operator is viewed as an intermediate case. However, the big difference is that value types need to be boxed in order to be converted to references so that methods can be executed on them. In addition, Microsoft has already overloaded the instance `Equals()` method in the `System.ValueType` class in order to test equality appropriate to value types. If you call `sA.Equals(sB)` where `sA` and `sB` are instances of some struct, the return value will be `true` or `false`, according to whether `sA` and `sB` contain the same values in all their fields. On the other hand, no overload of `==` is available by default for your own structs. Writing `(sA == sB)` in any expression will result in a compilation error unless you have provided an overload of `==` in your code for the struct in question.

Another point is that `ReferenceEquals()` always returns `false` when applied to value types because, to call this method, the value types will need to be boxed into objects. Even if you write the following, you will still get the answer of `false`:

```
bool b = ReferenceEquals(v,v);    // v is a variable of some value type
```

The reason for this is that `v` will be boxed separately when converting each parameter, which means you get different references. Because of this, there really is no reason to call `ReferenceEquals()` to compare value types because it doesn't make much sense.

Although the default override of `Equals()` supplied by `System.ValueType` will almost certainly be adequate for the vast majority of structs that you define, you might want to override it again for your own structs in order to improve performance. Also, if a value type contains reference types as fields, you might want to override `Equals()` to provide appropriate semantics for these fields because the default override of `Equals()` will simply compare their addresses.

Operator Overloading

This section looks at another type of member that you can define for a class or a struct: the *operator overload*.

Operator overloading is something that will be familiar to C++ developers. However, because the concept will be new to both Java and Visual Basic developers, we explain it here. C++ developers will probably prefer to skip ahead to the main operator overloading example.

The point of operator overloading is that you do not always just want to call methods or properties on objects. Often, you need to do things like adding quantities together, multiplying them, or performing logical operations such as comparing objects. Suppose that you had defined a class that represents a mathematical matrix. Now in the world of math, matrices can be added together and multiplied, just like numbers. Therefore, it is quite plausible that you would want to write code like this:

```
Matrix a, b, c;
// assume a, b and c have been initialized
Matrix d = c * (a + b);
```

By overloading the operators, you can tell the compiler what + and * do when used in conjunction with a `Matrix` object, allowing you to write code like the preceding. If you were coding in a language that did not support operator overloading, you would have to define methods to perform those operations. The result would certainly be less intuitive and would probably look something like this:

```
Matrix d = c.Multiply(a.Add(b));
```

With what you have learned so far, operators like + and * have been strictly for use with the predefined data types, and for good reason: The compiler knows what all the common operators mean for those data types. For example, it knows how to add two `long`s or how to divide one `double` by another `double`, and it can generate the appropriate intermediate language code. When you define your own classes or structs, however, you have to tell the compiler everything: what methods are available to call, what fields to store with each instance, and so on. Similarly, if you want to use operators with your own types, you will have to tell the compiler what the relevant operators mean in the context of that class. The way you do that is by defining overloads for the operators.

The other thing we should stress is that overloading is not concerned just with arithmetic operators. You also need to consider the comparison operators, ==, <, >, !=, >=, and <=. Take the statement `if (a==b)`. For classes, this statement will, by default, compare the references a and b. It tests to see if the references point to the same location in memory, rather than checking to see if the instances actually contain the same data. For the `string` class, this behavior is overridden so that comparing strings really does compare the contents of each string. You might want to do the same for your own classes. For structs, the == operator does not do anything at all by default. Trying to compare two structs to see if they are equal produces a compilation error unless you explicitly overload == to tell the compiler how to perform the comparison.

A large number of situations exist in which being able to overload operators will allow you to generate more readable and intuitive code, including:

❑   Almost any mathematical object such as coordinates, vectors, matrices, tensors, functions, and so on. If you are writing a program that does some mathematical or physical modeling, you will almost certainly use classes representing these objects.

❑   Graphics programs that use mathematical or coordinate-related objects when calculating positions onscreen.

❑   A class that represents an amount of money (for example, in a financial program).

❑ A word processing or text analysis program that uses classes representing sentences, clauses, and so on; you might want to use operators to combine sentences (a more sophisticated version of concatenation for strings).

However, there are also many types for which operator overloading would not be relevant. Using operator overloading inappropriately will make code that uses your types far more difficult to understand. For example, multiplying two `DateTime` objects just does not make any sense conceptually.

How Operators Work

To understand how to overload operators, it's quite useful to think about what happens when the compiler encounters an operator. Using the addition operator (+) as an example, suppose that the compiler processes the following lines of code:

```
int myInteger = 3;
uint myUnsignedInt = 2;
double myDouble = 4.0;
long myLong = myInteger + myUnsignedInt;
double myOtherDouble = myDouble + myInteger;
```

What happens when the compiler encounters the following line?

```
long myLong = myInteger + myUnsignedInt;
```

The compiler identifies that it needs to add two integers and assign the result to a `long`. However, the expression `myInteger + myUnsignedInt` is really just an intuitive and convenient syntax for calling a method that adds two numbers together. The method takes two parameters, `myInteger` and `myUnsignedInt`, and returns their sum. Therefore, the compiler does the same thing as it does for any method call — it looks for the best matching overload of the addition operator based on the parameter types — in this case, one that takes two integers. As with normal overloaded methods, the desired return type does not influence the compiler's choice as to which version of a method it calls. As it happens, the overload called in the example takes two `int` parameters and returns an `int`; this return value is subsequently converted to a `long`.

The next line causes the compiler to use a different overload of the addition operator:

```
double myOtherDouble = myDouble + myInteger;
```

In this instance, the parameters are a `double` and an `int`, but there is not an overload of the addition operator that takes this combination of parameters. Instead, the compiler identifies the best matching overload of the addition operator as being the version that takes two `double`s as its parameters, and it implicitly casts the `int` to a `double`. Adding two `double`s requires a different process from adding two integers. Floating-point numbers are stored as a mantissa and an exponent. Adding them involves bit-shifting the mantissa of one of the `double`s so that the two exponents have the same value, adding the mantissas, then shifting the mantissa of the result and adjusting its exponent to maintain the highest possible accuracy in the answer.

Now, you are in a position to see what happens if the compiler finds something like this:

```
Vector vect1, vect2, vect3;
// initialize vect1 and vect2
vect3 = vect1 + vect2;
vect1 = vect1*2;
```

Here, `Vector` is the struct, which is defined in the following section. The compiler will see that it needs to add two `Vector` instances, `vect1` and `vect2`, together. It will look for an overload of the addition operator, which takes two `Vector` instances as its parameters.

If the compiler finds an appropriate overload, it will call up the implementation of that operator. If it cannot find one, it will look to see if there is any other overload for + that it can use as a best match — perhaps something that has two parameters of other data types that can be implicitly converted to Vector instances. If the compiler cannot find a suitable overload, it will raise a compilation error, just as it would if it could not find an appropriate overload for any other method call.

Operator Overloading Example: The Vector Struct

This section demonstrates operator overloading through developing a struct named Vector that represents a 3-dimensional mathematical vector. Do not worry if mathematics is not your strong point — we will keep the vector example very simple. As far as you are concerned, a 3D-vector is just a set of three numbers (doubles) that tell you how far something is moving. The variables representing the numbers are called x, y, and z: x tells you how far something moves east, y tells you how far it moves north, and z tells you how far it moves upward (in height). Combine the three numbers and you get the total movement. For example, if x=3.0, y=3.0, and z=1.0 (which you would normally write as (3.0, 3.0, 1.0)), you're moving 3 units east, 3 units north, and rising upward by 1 unit.

You can add or multiply vectors by other vectors or by numbers. Incidentally, in this context, we use the term *scalar*, which is math-speak for a simple number — in C# terms that is just a double. The significance of addition should be clear. If you move first by the vector (3.0, 3.0, 1.0) then you move by the vector (2.0, -4.0, -4.0), the total amount you have moved can be worked out by adding the two vectors. Adding vectors means adding each component individually, so you get (5.0, -1.0, -3.0). In this context, mathematicians write c=a+b, where a and b are the vectors and c is the resulting vector. You want to be able to use the Vector struct the same way.

> *The fact that this example will be developed as a struct rather than a class is not significant. Operator overloading works in the same way for both structs and classes.*

The following is the definition for Vector — containing the member fields, constructors, a ToString() override so you can easily view the contents of a Vector, and, finally, that operator overload:

```
namespace Wrox.ProCSharp.OOCSharp
{
    struct Vector
    {
        public double x, y, z;

        public Vector(double x, double y, double z)
        {
            this.x = x;
            this.y = y;
            this.z = z;
        }

        public Vector(Vector rhs)
        {
            x = rhs.x;
            y = rhs.y;
            z = rhs.z;
        }

        public override string ToString()
        {
            return "( " + x + " , " + y + " , " + z + " )";
        }
    }
```

This example has two constructors that require the initial value of the vector to be specified, either by passing in the values of each component or by supplying another Vector whose value can be copied. Constructors like the second one that takes a single Vector argument are often termed *copy constructors* because they effectively allow you to initialize a class or struct instance by copying another instance. Note that to keep things simple, the fields are left as public. We could have made them private and written corresponding properties to access them, but it would not have made any difference to the example, other than to make the code longer.

Here is the interesting part of the Vector struct — the operator overload that provides support for the addition operator:

```csharp
public static Vector operator + (Vector lhs, Vector rhs)
{
    Vector result = new Vector(lhs);
    result.x += rhs.x;
    result.y += rhs.y;
    result.z += rhs.z;

    return result;
}
    }
}
```

The operator overload is declared in much the same way as a method, except that the operator keyword tells the compiler it is actually an operator overload you are defining. The operator keyword is followed by the actual symbol for the relevant operator, in this case the addition operator (+). The return type is whatever type you get when you use this operator. Adding two vectors results in a vector, therefore, the return type is also a Vector. For this particular override of the addition operator, the return type is the same as the containing class, but that is not necessarily the case as you will see later in this example. The two parameters are the things you are operating on. For binary operators (those that take two parameters), like the addition and subtraction operators, the first parameter is the value on the left of the operator, and the second parameter is the value on the right.

> Note that it is convention to name your left-hand parameters lhs (for left-hand side) and your right-hand parameters rhs (for right-hand side).

C# requires that all operator overloads be declared as public and static, which means that they are associated with their class or struct, not with a particular instance. Because of this, the body of the operator overload has no access to non-static class members and has no access to the this identifier. This is fine because the parameters provide all the input data the operator needs to know to perform its task.

Now that you understand the syntax for the addition operator declaration, you can look at what happens inside the operator:

```csharp
{
    Vector result = new Vector(lhs);
    result.x += rhs.x;
    result.y += rhs.y;
    result.z += rhs.z;

    return result;
}
```

This part of the code is exactly the same as if you were declaring a method, and you should easily be able to convince yourself that this really will return a vector containing the sum of lhs and rhs as defined. You simply add the members x, y, and z together individually.

Now all you need to do is write some simple code to test the `Vector` struct. Here it is:

```
static void Main()
{
    Vector vect1, vect2, vect3;

    vect1 = new Vector(3.0, 3.0, 1.0);
    vect2 = new Vector(2.0, -4.0, -4.0);
    vect3 = vect1 + vect2;

    Console.WriteLine("vect1 = " + vect1.ToString());
    Console.WriteLine("vect2 = " + vect2.ToString());
    Console.WriteLine("vect3 = " + vect3.ToString());
}
```

Saving this code as `Vectors.cs` and compiling and running it returns this result:

Vectors

```
vect1 = ( 3 , 3 , 1 )
vect2 = ( 2 , -4 , -4 )
vect3 = ( 5 , -1 , -3 )
```

Adding More Overloads

In addition to adding vectors, you can multiply and subtract them and compare their values. In this section, you develop the `Vector` example further by adding a few more operator overloads. You will not develop the complete set that you'd probably need for a fully functional `Vector` type, but just enough to demonstrate some other aspects of operator overloading. First, you'll overload the multiplication operator to support multiplying vectors by a scalar and multiplying vectors by another vector.

Multiplying a vector by a scalar simply means multiplying each component individually by the scalar: for example, `2 * (1.0, 2.5, 2.0)` returns `(2.0, 5.0, 4.0)`. The relevant operator overload looks like this:

```
public static Vector operator * (double lhs, Vector rhs)
{
    return new Vector(lhs * rhs.x, lhs * rhs.y, lhs * rhs.z);
}
```

This by itself, however, is not sufficient. If a and b are declared as type `Vector`, it will allow you to write code like this:

```
b = 2 * a;
```

The compiler will implicitly convert the integer 2 to a `double` in order to match the operator overload signature. However, code like the following will not compile:

```
b = a * 2;
```

The thing is that the compiler treats operator overloads exactly as method overloads. It examines all the available overloads of a given operator to find the best match. The preceding statement requires the first parameter to be a `Vector` and the second parameter to be an integer, or something that an integer can be implicitly converted to. You have not provided such an overload. The compiler cannot start swapping the order of parameters, so the fact that you've provided an overload that takes a `double` followed by a `Vector` is not sufficient. You need to explicitly define an overload that takes a `Vector` followed by a `double` as well. There are two possible ways of implementing this. The first way involves breaking down the vector multiplication operation in the same way that you have done for all operators so far:

```
public static Vector operator * (Vector lhs, double rhs)
{
    return new Vector(rhs * lhs.x, rhs * lhs.y, rhs *lhs.z);
}
```

Given that you have already written code to implement essentially the same operation, however, you might prefer to reuse that code by writing:

```
public static Vector operator * (Vector lhs, double rhs)
{
    return rhs * lhs;
}
```

This code works by effectively telling the compiler that if it sees a multiplication of a `Vector` by a `double`, it can simply reverse the parameters and call the other operator overload. The sample code for this chapter uses the second version, because it looks neater and illustrates the idea in action. This version also makes for more maintainable code because it saves duplicating the code to perform the multiplication in two separate overloads.

Next, you need to overload the multiplication operator to support vector multiplication. Mathematics provides a couple of ways of multiplying vectors together, but the one we are interested in here is known as the *dot product* or *inner product*, which actually gives a scalar as a result. That's the reason for this example, to demonstrate that arithmetic operators don't have to return the same type as the class in which they are defined.

In mathematical terms, if you have two vectors (x, y, z) and (X, Y, Z), then the inner product is defined to be the value of $x*X + y*Y + z*Z$. That might look like a strange way to multiply two things together, but it is actually very useful because it can be used to calculate various other quantities. Certainly, if you ever end up writing code that displays complex 3D graphics, for example using Direct3D or DirectDraw, you will almost certainly find your code needs to work out inner products of vectors quite often as an intermediate step in calculating where to place objects on the screen. What concerns us here is that we want people using your `Vector` to be able to write `double X = a*b` to calculate the inner product of two `Vector` objects (a and b). The relevant overload looks like this:

```
public static double operator * (Vector lhs, Vector rhs)
{
    return lhs.x * rhs.x + lhs.y * rhs.y + lhs.z * rhs.z;
}
```

Now that you understand the arithmetic operators, you can check that they work using a simple test method:

```
static void Main()
{
    // stuff to demonstrate arithmetic operations
    Vector vect1, vect2, vect3;
    vect1 = new Vector(1.0, 1.5, 2.0);
    vect2 = new Vector(0.0, 0.0, -10.0);

    vect3 = vect1 + vect2;

    Console.WriteLine("vect1 = " + vect1);
    Console.WriteLine("vect2 = " + vect2);
    Console.WriteLine("vect3 = vect1 + vect2 = " + vect3);
    Console.WriteLine("2*vect3 = " + 2*vect3);
```

```
        vect3 += vect2;

        Console.WriteLine("vect3+=vect2 gives " + vect3);

        vect3 = vect1*2;

        Console.WriteLine("Setting vect3=vect1*2 gives " + vect3);

        double dot = vect1*vect3;

        Console.WriteLine("vect1*vect3 = " + dot);
    }
```

Running this code (`Vectors2.cs`) produces the following result:

Vectors2

```
vect1 = ( 1 , 1.5 , 2 )
vect2 = ( 0 , 0 , -10 )
vect3 = vect1 + vect2 = ( 1 , 1.5 , -8 )
2*vect3 = ( 2 , 3 , -16 )
vect3+=vect2 gives ( 1 , 1.5 , -18 )
Setting vect3=vect1*2 gives ( 2 , 3 , 4 )
vect1*vect3 = 14.5
```

This shows that the operator overloads have given the correct results, but if you look at the test code closely, you might be surprised to notice that it actually used an operator that wasn't overloaded — the addition assignment operator, +=:

```
        vect3 += vect2;

        Console.WriteLine("vect3 += vect2 gives " + vect3);
```

Although += normally counts as a single operator, it can be broken down into two steps: the addition and the assignment. Unlike the C++ language, C# will not actually allow you to overload the = operator, but if you overload +, the compiler will automatically use your overload of + to work out how to perform a += operation. The same principle works for all of the assignment operators such as -=, *=, /=, &=, and so on.

Overloading the Comparison Operators

C# has six comparison operators, and they come in three pairs:

❑   == and !=

❑   > and <

❑   >= and <=

The C# language requires that you overload these operators in pairs. That is, if you overload ==, you must overload != too; otherwise, you get a compiler error. In addition, the comparison operators must return a `bool`. This is the fundamental difference between these operators and the arithmetic operators. The result of adding or subtracting two quantities, for example, can theoretically be any type depending on the quantities. You have already seen that multiplying two `Vector` objects can be implemented to give a scalar. Another example involves the .NET base class `System.DateTime`. It's possible to subtract two `DateTime` instances, but the result is not a `DateTime`; instead it is a `System.TimeSpan` instance. By contrast, it doesn't really make much sense for a comparison to return anything other than a `bool`.

If you overload == and !=, you must also override the Equals() *and* GetHashCode() *methods inherited from* System.Object; *otherwise, you'll get a compiler warning. The reasoning is that the* Equals() *method should implement the same kind of equality logic as the == operator.*

Apart from these differences, overloading the comparison operators follows the same principles as overloading the arithmetic operators. However, comparing quantities isn't always as simple as you might think. For example, if you simply compare two object references, you will compare the memory address where the objects are stored. This is rarely the desired behavior of a comparison operator, and so you must code the operator to compare the value of the objects and return the appropriate Boolean response. The following example overrides the == and != operators for the Vector struct. Here is the implementation of ==:

```
public static bool operator == (Vector lhs, Vector rhs)
{
    if (lhs.x == rhs.x && lhs.y == rhs.y && lhs.z == rhs.z)
        return true;
    else
        return false;
}
```

This approach simply compares two Vector objects for equality based on the values of their components. For most structs, that is probably what you will want to do, though in some cases you may need to think carefully about what you mean by equality. For example, if there are embedded classes, should you simply compare whether the references point to the same object (*shallow comparison*) or whether the values of the objects are the same (*deep comparison*)?

A shallow comparison is where the objects point to the same point in memory, whereas deep comparisons are working with values and properties of the object to deem equality. You want to perform equality checks depending on the depth to help you decide what you will want to verify.

Don't be tempted to overload the comparison operator by calling the instance version of the Equals() *method inherited from* System.Object. *If you do and then an attempt is made to evaluate* (objA == objB), *when* objA *happens to be* null, *you will get an exception as the .NET runtime tries to evaluate* null.Equals(objB). *Working the other way around (overriding* Equals() *to call the comparison operator) should be safe.*

You also need to override the != operator. The simple way to do this is:

```
public static bool operator != (Vector lhs, Vector rhs)
{
    return ! (lhs == rhs);
}
```

As usual, you should quickly check that your override works with some test code. This time you'll define three Vector objects and compare them:

```
static void Main()
{
    Vector vect1, vect2, vect3;

    vect1 = new Vector(3.0, 3.0, -10.0);
    vect2 = new Vector(3.0, 3.0, -10.0);
    vect3 = new Vector(2.0, 3.0, 6.0);

    Console.WriteLine("vect1==vect2 returns  " + (vect1==vect2));
    Console.WriteLine("vect1==vect3 returns  " + (vect1==vect3));
    Console.WriteLine("vect2==vect3 returns  " + (vect2==vect3));
```

```
        Console.WriteLine();

        Console.WriteLine("vect1!=vect2 returns  " + (vect1!=vect2));
        Console.WriteLine("vect1!=vect3 returns  " + (vect1!=vect3));
        Console.WriteLine("vect2!=vect3 returns  " + (vect2!=vect3));
    }
```

Compiling this code (the `Vectors3.cs` sample in the code download) generates the following compiler warning because you haven't overridden `Equals()` for your `Vector`. For our purposes here, that does not matter, so we will ignore it.

csc Vectors3.cs

```
Microsoft (R) Visual C# 2008 Compiler version 3.05.20706.1
for Microsoft (R) .NET Framework version 3.5
Copyright (C) Microsoft Corporation. All rights reserved.


Vectors3.cs(5,11): warning CS0660: 'Wrox.ProCSharp.OOCSharp.Vector' defines
        operator == or operator != but does not override Object.Equals(object o)
Vectors3.cs(5,11): warning CS0661: 'Wrox.ProCSharp.OOCSharp.Vector' defines
        operator == or operator != but does not override Object.GetHashCode()
```

Running the example produces these results at the command line:

Vectors3

```
vect1==vect2 returns  True
vect1==vect3 returns  False
vect2==vect3 returns  False

vect1!=vect2 returns  False
vect1!=vect3 returns  True
vect2!=vect3 returns  True
```

Which Operators Can You Overload?

It is not possible to overload all of the available operators. The operators that you can overload are listed in the following table.

Category	Operators	Restrictions
Arithmetic binary	+, *, /, -, %	None.
Arithmetic unary	+, -, ++, --	None.
Bitwise binary	&, |, ^, <<, >>	None.
Bitwise unary	!, ~true, false	The true and false operators must be overloaded as a pair.
Comparison	==, !=, >=, <=>, <,	Comparison operators must be overloaded in pairs.

Category	Operators	Restrictions
Assignment	+=, -=, *=, /=, >>=, <<=, %=, &=, |=, ^=	You cannot explicitly overload these operators; they are overridden implicitly when you override the individual operators such as +, -, %, and so on.
Index	[]	You cannot overload the index operator directly. The indexer member type, discussed in Chapter 2, "C# Basics," allows you to support the index operator on your classes and structs.
Cast	()	You cannot overload the cast operator directly. User-defined casts (discussed next) allow you to define custom cast behavior.

User-Defined Casts

Earlier in this chapter, you learned that you can convert values between predefined data types through a process of *casting*. You also saw that C# allows two different types of casts: implicit and explicit. This section looks at these types of casts.

For an explicit cast, you *explicitly* mark the cast in your code by writing the destination data type inside parentheses:

```
int I = 3;
long l = I;             // implicit
short s = (short)I;     // explicit
```

For the predefined data types, explicit casts are required where there is a risk that the cast might fail or some data might be lost. The following are some examples:

❑ When converting from an int to a short, the short might not be large enough to hold the value of the int.

❑ When converting from signed to unsigned data types, incorrect results will be returned if the signed variable holds a negative value.

❑ When converting from floating-point to integer data types, the fractional part of the number will be lost.

❑ When converting from a nullable type to a non-nullable type, a value of null will cause an exception.

By making the cast explicit in your code, C# forces you to affirm that you understand there is a risk of data loss, and therefore presumably you have written your code to take this into account.

Because C# allows you to define your own data types (structs and classes), it follows that you will need the facility to support casts to and from those data types. The mechanism is that you can define a cast as a member operator of one of the relevant classes. Your cast operator must be marked as either implicit or explicit to indicate how you are intending it to be used. The expectation is that you follow the same guidelines as for the predefined casts: If you know that the cast is always safe whatever the value held by the source variable, then you define it as implicit. If, however, you know there is a risk of something going wrong for certain values — perhaps some loss of data or an exception being thrown — then you should define the cast as `explicit`.

> **You should define any custom casts you write as explicit if there are any source data values for which the cast will fail or if there is any risk of an exception being thrown.**

The syntax for defining a cast is similar to that for overloading operators discussed earlier in this chapter. This is not a coincidence — a cast is regarded as an operator whose effect is to convert from the source type to the destination type. To illustrate the syntax, the following is taken from an example `struct` named `Currency`, which is introduced later in this section:

```
public static implicit operator float (Currency value)
{
    // processing
}
```

The return type of the operator defines the target type of the cast operation, and the single parameter is the source object for the conversion. The cast defined here allows you to implicitly convert the value of a `Currency` into a `float`. Note that if a conversion has been declared as `implicit`, the compiler will permit its use either implicitly or explicitly. If it has been declared as `explicit`, the compiler will only permit it to be used explicitly. In common with other operator overloads, casts must be declared as both `public` and `static`.

C++ developers will notice that this is different from what they are used to with C++, in which casts are instance members of classes.

Implementing User-Defined Casts

This section illustrates the use of implicit and explicit user-defined casts in an example called `SimpleCurrency` (which, as usual, is available in the code download). In this example, you define a struct, `Currency`, which holds a positive USD ($) monetary value. C# provides the `decimal` type for this purpose, but it is possible you will still want to write your own struct or class to represent monetary values if you want to perform sophisticated financial processing and therefore want to implement specific methods on such a class.

The syntax for casting is the same for structs and classes. This example happens to be for a struct, but would work just as well if you declared Currency as a class.

Initially, the definition of the `Currency` struct is:

```
struct Currency
{
    public uint Dollars;
    public ushort Cents;

    public Currency(uint dollars, ushort cents)
    {
        this.Dollars = dollars;
```

(continued)

(continued)

```
            this.Cents = cents;
        }

        public override string ToString()
        {
            return string.Format("${0}.{1,-2:00}", Dollars,Cents);
        }
    }
```

The use of unsigned data types for the `Dollar` and `Cents` fields ensures that a `Currency` instance can hold only positive values. It is restricted this way in order to illustrate some points about explicit casts later on. You might want to use a class like this to hold, for example, salary information for employees of a company (people's salaries tend not to be negative!). To keep the class simple, the fields are public, but usually you would make them `private` and define corresponding properties for the dollars and cents.

Start by assuming that you want to be able to convert `Currency` instances to `float` values, where the integer part of the `float` represents the dollars. In other words, you would like to be able to write code like this:

```
Currency balance = new Currency(10,50);
float f = balance; // We want f to be set to 10.5
```

To be able to do this, you need to define a cast. Hence, you add the following to your `Currency` definition:

```
public static implicit operator float (Currency value)
{
    return value.Dollars + (value.Cents/100.0f);
}
```

The preceding cast is implicit. It is a sensible choice in this case because, as should be clear from the definition of `Currency`, any value that can be stored in the currency can also be stored in a `float`. There is no way that anything should ever go wrong in this cast.

> *There is a slight cheat here — in fact, when converting a `uint` to a `float`, there can be a loss in precision, but Microsoft has deemed this error sufficiently marginal to count the `uint`-to-`float` cast as implicit.*

However, if you have a `float` that you would like to be converted to a `Currency`, the conversion is not guaranteed to work. A `float` can store negative values, which `Currency` instances can't, and a `float` can store numbers of a far higher magnitude than can be stored in the (`uint`) `Dollar` field of `Currency`. Therefore, if a `float` contains an inappropriate value, converting it to a `Currency` could give unpredictable results. Because of this risk, the conversion from `float` to `Currency` should be defined as explicit. Here is the first attempt, which will not give quite the correct results, but it is instructive to examine why:

```
public static explicit operator Currency (float value)
{
    uint dollars = (uint)value;
    ushort cents = (ushort)((value-dollars)*100);
    return new Currency(dollars, cents);
}
```

The following code will now successfully compile:

```
float amount = 45.63f;
Currency amount2 = (Currency)amount;
```

However, the following code, if you tried it, would generate a compilation error, because it attempts to use an explicit cast implicitly:

```
float amount = 45.63f;
Currency amount2 = amount;    // wrong
```

By making the cast explicit, you warn the developer to be careful because data loss might occur. However, as you will soon see, this is not how you want your Currency struct to behave. Try writing a test harness and running the sample. Here is the Main() method, which instantiates a Currency struct and attempts a few conversions. At the start of this code, you write out the value of balance in two different ways (this will be needed to illustrate something later in the example):

```
static void Main()
{
    try
    {
        Currency balance = new Currency(50,35);

        Console.WriteLine(balance);
        Console.WriteLine("balance is " + balance);
        Console.WriteLine("balance is (using ToString()) " + balance.ToString());

        float balance2= balance;

        Console.WriteLine("After converting to float, = " + balance2);

        balance = (Currency) balance2;

        Console.WriteLine("After converting back to Currency, = " + balance);
        Console.WriteLine("Now attempt to convert out of range value of " +
                    "-$100.00 to a Currency:");

        checked
        {
            balance = (Currency) (-50.5);
            Console.WriteLine("Result is " + balance.ToString());
        }
    }
    catch(Exception e)
    {
        Console.WriteLine("Exception occurred: " + e.Message);
    }
}
```

Notice that the entire code is placed in a try block to catch any exceptions that occur during your casts. In addition, the lines that test converting an out-of-range value to Currency are placed in a checked block in an attempt to trap negative values. Running this code gives this output:

SimpleCurrency

```
50.35
Balance is $50.35
Balance is (using ToString()) $50.35
After converting to float, = 50.35
After converting back to Currency, = $50.34
Now attempt to convert out of range value of -$100.00 to a Currency:
Result is $4294967246.60486
```

This output shows that the code did not quite work as expected. First, converting back from `float` to `Currency` gave a wrong result of $50.34 instead of $50.35. Second, no exception was generated when you tried to convert an obviously out-of-range value.

The first problem is caused by rounding errors. If a cast is used to convert from a `float` to a `uint`, the computer will *truncate* the number rather than *rounding* it. The computer stores numbers in binary rather than decimal, and the fraction 0.35 cannot be exactly represented as a binary fraction (just as 1/3 cannot be represented exactly as a decimal fraction; it comes out as 0.3333 recurring). The computer ends up storing a value very slightly lower than 0.35 that can be represented exactly in binary format. Multiply by 100 and you get a number fractionally less than 35, which is truncated to 34 cents. Clearly, in this situation, such errors caused by truncation are serious, and the way to avoid them is to ensure that some intelligent rounding is performed in numerical conversions instead. Luckily, Microsoft has written a class that will do this: `System.Convert`. The `System.Convert` object contains a large number of static methods to perform various numerical conversions, and the one that we want is `Convert.ToUInt16()`. Note that the extra care taken by the `System.Convert` methods does come at a performance cost. You should use them only when you need them.

Let's examine the second problem — why the expected overflow exception wasn't thrown. The issue here is this: The place where the overflow really occurs isn't actually in the `Main()` routine at all — it is inside the code for the cast operator, which is called from the `Main()` method. The code in this method was not marked as `checked`.

The solution is to ensure that the cast itself is computed in a `checked` context too. With both this change and the fix for the first problem, the revised code for the conversion looks like the following:

```
public static explicit operator Currency (float value)
{
    checked
    {
        uint dollars = (uint)value;
        ushort cents = Convert.ToUInt16((value-dollars)*100);
        return new Currency(dollars, cents);
    }
}
```

Note that you use `Convert.ToUInt16()` to calculate the cents, as described earlier, but you do not use it for calculating the dollar part of the amount. `System.Convert` is not needed when working out the dollar amount because truncating the `float` value is what you want there.

> *It is worth noting that the `System.Convert` methods also carry out their own overflow checking. Hence, for the particular case we are considering, there is no need to place the call to `Convert` .ToUInt16() inside the checked context. The checked context is still required, however, for the explicit casting of `value` to dollars.*

You won't see a new set of results with this new `checked` cast just yet because you have some more modifications to make to the `SimpleCurrency` example later in this section.

> *If you are defining a cast that will be used very often, and for which performance is at an absolute premium, you may prefer not to do any error checking. That is also a legitimate solution, provided that the behavior of your cast and the lack of error checking are very clearly documented.*

Casts Between Classes

The `Currency` example involves only classes that convert to or from `float` — one of the predefined data types. However, it is not necessary to involve any of the simple data types. It is perfectly legitimate to define casts to convert between instances of different structs or classes that you have defined. You need to be aware of a couple of restrictions, however:

❑ You cannot define a cast if one of the classes is derived from the other (these types of casts already exist, as you will see).

❑ The cast must be defined inside the definition of either the source or the destination data type.

To illustrate these requirements, suppose that you have the class hierarchy shown in Figure 6-1.

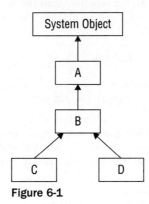

Figure 6-1

In other words, classes C and D are indirectly derived from A. In this case, the only legitimate user-defined cast between A, B, C, or D would be to convert between classes C and D, because these classes are not derived from each other. The code to do so might look like this (assuming that you want the casts to be explicit, which is usually the case when defining casts between user-defined casts):

```
public static explicit operator D(C value)
{
    // and so on
}
public static explicit operator C(D value)
{
    // and so on
}
```

For each of these casts, you have a choice of where you place the definitions — inside the class definition of C or inside the class definition of D, but not anywhere else. C# requires you to put the definition of a cast inside either the source class (or struct) or the destination class (or struct). A side effect of this is that you cannot define a cast between two classes unless you have access to edit the source code for at least one of them. This is sensible because it prevents third parties from introducing casts into your classes.

Once you have defined a cast inside one of the classes, you cannot also define the same cast inside the other class. Obviously, there should be only one cast for each conversion — otherwise, the compiler would not know which one to pick.

Casts Between Base and Derived Classes

To see how these casts work, start by considering the case where the source and destination are both reference types, and consider two classes, MyBase and MyDerived, where MyDerived is derived directly or indirectly from MyBase.

First, from `MyDerived` to `MyBase`, it is always possible (assuming the constructors are available) to write:

```
MyDerived derivedObject = new MyDerived();
MyBase baseCopy = derivedObject;
```

In this case, you are casting implicitly from `MyDerived` to `MyBase`. This works because of the rule that any reference to a type `MyBase` is allowed to refer to objects of class `MyBase` or to objects of anything derived from `MyBase`. In OO programming, instances of a derived class are, in a real sense, instances of the base class, plus something extra. All the functions and fields defined on the base class are defined in the derived class too.

Alternatively, you can write:

```
MyBase derivedObject = new MyDerived();
MyBase baseObject = new MyBase();
MyDerived derivedCopy1 = (MyDerived) derivedObject;    // OK
MyDerived derivedCopy2 = (MyDerived) baseObject;       // Throws exception
```

This code is perfectly legal C# (in a syntactic sense, that is) and illustrates casting from a base class to a derived class. However, the final statement will throw an exception when executed. When you perform the cast, the object being referred to is examined. Because a base class reference can in principle refer to a derived class instance, it is possible that this object is actually an instance of the derived class that you are attempting to cast to. If that is the case, the cast succeeds, and the derived reference is set to refer to the object. If, however, the object in question is not an instance of the derived class (or of any class derived from it), the cast fails and an exception is thrown.

Notice that the casts that the compiler has supplied, which convert between base and derived class, do not actually do any data conversion on the object in question. All they do is set the new reference to refer to the object if it is legal for that conversion to occur. To that extent, these casts are very different in nature from the ones that you will normally define yourself. For example, in the `SimpleCurrency` example earlier, you defined casts that convert between a `Currency` struct and a `float`. In the `float`-to-`Currency` cast, you actually instantiated a new `Currency` struct and initialized it with the required values. The predefined casts between base and derived classes do not do this. If you actually want to convert a `MyBase` instance into a real `MyDerived` object with values based on the contents of the `MyBase` instance, you would not be able to use the cast syntax to do this. The most sensible option is usually to define a derived class constructor that takes a base class instance as a parameter and have this constructor perform the relevant initializations:

```
class DerivedClass : BaseClass
{
    public DerivedClass(BaseClass rhs)
    {
        // initialize object from the Base instance
    }
    // etc.
```

Boxing and Unboxing Casts

The previous discussion focused on casting between base and derived classes where both participants were reference types. Similar principles apply when casting value types, although in this case it is not possible to simply copy references — some copying of data must take place.

It is not, of course, possible to derive from structs or primitive value types. Casting between base and derived structs invariably means casting between a primitive type or a struct and `System.Object`. (Theoretically, it is possible to cast between a struct and `System.ValueType`, though it is hard to see why you would want to do this.)

The cast from any struct (or primitive type) to `object` is always available as an implicit cast — because it is a cast from a derived to a base type — and is just the familiar process of *boxing*. For example, with the `Currency` struct:

```
Currency balance = new Currency(40,0);
object baseCopy = balance;
```

When this implicit cast is executed, the contents of `balance` are copied onto the heap into a boxed object, and the `baseCopy` object reference is set to this object. What actually happens behind the scenes is this: When you originally defined the `Currency` struct, the .NET Framework implicitly supplied another (hidden) class, a boxed `Currency` class, which contains all the same fields as the `Currency` struct, but it is a reference type, stored on the heap. This happens whenever you define a value type — whether it is a `struct` or enum, and similar boxed reference types exist corresponding to all the primitive value types of `int`, `double`, `uint`, and so on. It is not possible, or necessary, to gain direct programmatic access to any of these boxed classes in source code, but they are the objects that are working behind the scenes whenever a value type is cast to `object`. When you implicitly cast `Currency` to `object`, a boxed `Currency` instance gets instantiated and initialized with all the data from the `Currency` struct. In the preceding code, it is this boxed `Currency` instance that `baseCopy` will refer to. By these means, it is possible for casting from derived to base type to work syntactically in the same way for value types as for reference types.

Casting the other way is known as *unboxing*. Just as for casting between a base reference type and a derived reference type, it is an explicit cast because an exception will be thrown if the object being cast is not of the correct type:

```
object derivedObject = new Currency(40,0);
object baseObject = new object();
Currency derivedCopy1 = (Currency)derivedObject;   // OK
Currency derivedCopy2 = (Currency)baseObject;       // Exception thrown
```

This code works in a way similar to the code presented earlier for reference types. Casting `derivedObject` to `Currency` works fine because `derivedObject` actually refers to a boxed `Currency` instance — the cast will be performed by copying the fields out of the boxed `Currency` object into a new `Currency` struct. The second cast fails because `baseObject` does not refer to a boxed `Currency` object.

When using boxing and unboxing, it is important to understand that both processes actually copy the data into the new boxed or unboxed object. Hence, manipulations on the boxed object, for example, will not affect the contents of the original value type.

Multiple Casting

One thing you will have to watch for when you are defining casts is that if the C# compiler is presented with a situation in which no direct cast is available to perform a requested conversion, it will attempt to find a way of combining casts to do the conversion. For example, with the `Currency` struct, suppose the compiler encounters a few lines of code like this:

```
Currency balance = new Currency(10,50);
long amount = (long)balance;
double amountD = balance;
```

You first initialize a `Currency` instance, and then you attempt to convert it to a `long`. The trouble is that you haven't defined the cast to do that. However, this code will still compile successfully. What will happen is that the compiler will realize that you have defined an implicit cast to get from `Currency` to `float`, and the compiler already knows how to explicitly cast a `float` to a `long`. Hence, it will compile that line of code into IL code that converts `balance` first to a `float`, and then converts that result to a long. The same thing happens in the final line of the code, when you convert balance to a double. However, because the cast from Currency to float and the predefined cast from float to double are both implicit, you can write this conversion in your code as an implicit cast. If you had preferred, you could have specified the casting route explicitly:

```
Currency balance = new Currency(10,50);
long amount = (long)(float)balance;
double amountD = (double)(float)balance;
```

However, in most cases, this would be seen as needlessly complicating your code. The following code, by contrast, would produce a compilation error:

```
Currency balance = new Currency(10,50);
long amount = balance;
```

The reason is that the best match for the conversion that the compiler can find is still to convert first to float then to long. The conversion from float to long needs to be specified explicitly, though.

Not all of this by itself should give you too much trouble. The rules are, after all, fairly intuitive and designed to prevent any data loss from occurring without the developer knowing about it. However, the problem is that if you are not careful when you define your casts, it is possible for the compiler to figure out a path that leads to unexpected results. For example, suppose that it occurs to someone else in the group writing the Currency struct that it would be useful to be able to convert a uint containing the total number of cents in an amount into a Currency (cents, not dollars, because the idea is not to lose the fractions of a dollar). Therefore, this cast might be written to try to achieve this:

```
public static implicit operator Currency (uint value)
{
    return new Currency(value/100u, (ushort)(value%100));
} // Do not do this!
```

Note the u after the first 100 in this code to ensure that value/100u is interpreted as a uint. If you had written value/100, the compiler would have interpreted this as an int, not a uint.

The code comment Do not do this is clearly commented in this code, and here is why. Look at the following code snippet; all it does is convert a uint containing 350 into a Currency and back again. What do you think bal2 will contain after executing this?

```
uint bal = 350;
Currency balance = bal;
uint bal2 = (uint)balance;
```

The answer is not 350 but 3! Moreover, it all follows logically. You convert 350 implicitly to a Currency, giving the result balance.Dollars = 3, balance.Cents = 50. Then the compiler does its usual figuring out of the best path for the conversion back. Balance ends up being implicitly converted to a float (value 3.5), and this is converted explicitly to a uint with value 3.

Of course, other instances exist in which converting to another data type and back again causes data loss. For example, converting a float containing 5.8 to an int and back to a float again will lose the fractional part, giving you a result of 5, but there is a slight difference in principle between losing the fractional part of a number and dividing an integer by more than 100! Currency has suddenly become a rather dangerous class that does strange things to integers!

The problem is that there is a conflict between how your casts interpret integers. The casts between Currency and float interpret an integer value of 1 as corresponding to one dollar, but the latest uint-to-Currency cast interprets this value as one cent. This is an example of very poor design. If you want your classes to be easy to use, you should make sure that all of your casts behave in a way that is mutually compatible, in the sense that they intuitively give the same results. In this case, the solution is obviously to rewrite the `uint`-to-`Currency` cast so that it interprets an integer value of 1 as one dollar:

```
public static implicit operator Currency (uint value)
{
    return new Currency(value, 0);
}
```

Incidentally, you might wonder whether this new cast is necessary at all. The answer is that it could be useful. Without this cast, the only way for the compiler to carry out a `uint`-to-`Currency` conversion would be via a `float`. Converting directly is a lot more efficient in this case, so having this extra cast provides performance benefits, though you need to make sure it gives the same result as via a `float`, which you have now done. In other situations, you may also find that separately defining casts for different predefined data types allows more conversions to be implicit rather than explicit, though that is not the case here.

A good test of whether your casts are compatible is to ask whether a conversion will give the same results (other than perhaps a loss of accuracy as in `float`-to-`int` conversions), regardless of which path it takes. The `Currency` class provides a good example of this. Look at this code:

```
Currency balance = new Currency(50, 35);
ulong bal = (ulong) balance;
```

At present, there is only one way that the compiler can achieve this conversion: by converting the `Currency` to a `float` implicitly, then to a `ulong` explicitly. The `float`-to-`ulong` conversion requires an explicit conversion, but that is fine because you have specified one here.

Suppose, however, that you then added another cast, to convert implicitly from a `Currency` to a `uint`. You will actually do this by modifying the `Currency` struct by adding the casts both to and from `uint`. This code is available as the `SimpleCurrency2` example:

```
public static implicit operator Currency (uint value)
{
    return new Currency(value, 0);
}

public static implicit operator uint (Currency value)
{
    return value.Dollars;
}
```

Now the compiler has another possible route to convert from `Currency` to `ulong`: to convert from `Currency` to `uint` implicitly, then to `ulong` implicitly. Which of these two routes will it take? C# does have some precise rules to say how the compiler decides which is the best route if there are several possibilities. (The rules are not detailed in this book, but if you are interested, details are in the MSDN documentation.) The best answer is that you should design your casts so that all routes give the same answer (other than possible loss of precision), in which case it doesn't really matter which one the compiler picks. (As it happens in this case, the compiler picks the `Currency`-to-`uint`-to-`ulong` route in preference to `Currency`-to-`float`-to-`ulong`.)

To test the `SimpleCurrency2` sample, add this code to the test code for `SimpleCurrency`:

```
try
{
    Currency balance = new Currency(50,35);

    Console.WriteLine(balance);
    Console.WriteLine("balance is " + balance);
```

```
        Console.WriteLine("balance is (using ToString()) " + balance.ToString());

        uint balance3 = (uint) balance;

        Console.WriteLine("Converting to uint gives " + balance3);
```

Running the sample now gives you these results:

SimpleCurrency2

```
50
balance is $50.35
balance is (using ToString()) $50.35
Converting to uint gives 50
After converting to float, = 50.35
After converting back to Currency, = $50.34
Now attempt to convert out of range value of -$100.00 to a Currency:
Exception occurred: Arithmetic operation resulted in an overflow.
```

The output shows that the conversion to uint has been successful, though as expected, you have lost the cents part of the Currency in making this conversion. Casting a negative float to Currency has also produced the expected overflow exception now that the float-to-Currency cast itself defines a checked context.

However, the output also demonstrates one last potential problem that you need to be aware of when working with casts. The very first line of output has not displayed the balance correctly, displaying 50 instead of $50.35. Consider these lines:

```
        Console.WriteLine(balance);
        Console.WriteLine("balance is " + balance);
        Console.WriteLine("balance is (using ToString()) " + balance.ToString());
```

Only the last two lines correctly display the Currency as a string. So what is going on? The problem here is that when you combine casts with method overloads, you get another source of unpredictability. We will look at these lines in reverse order.

The third Console.WriteLine() statement explicitly calls the Currency.ToString() method, ensuring that the Currency is displayed as a string. The second does not do so. However, the string literal "balance is" passed to Console.WriteLine() makes it clear to the compiler that the parameter is to be interpreted as a string. Hence, the Currency.ToString() method will be called implicitly.

The very first Console.WriteLine() method, however, simply passes a raw Currency struct to Console.WriteLine(). Now, Console.WriteLine() has many overloads, but none of them takes a Currency struct. So the compiler will start fishing around to see what it can cast the Currency to in order to make it match up with one of the overloads of Console.WriteLine(). As it happens, one of the Console.WriteLine() overloads is designed to display uints quickly and efficiently, and it takes a uint as a parameter — you have now supplied a cast that converts Currency implicitly to uint.

In fact, Console.WriteLine() has another overload that takes a double as a parameter and displays the value of that double. If you look closely at the output from the first SimpleCurrency example, you will find the very first line of output displayed Currency as a double, using this overload. In that example, there wasn't a direct cast from Currency to uint, so the compiler picked Currency-to-float-to-double as its preferred way of matching up the available casts to the available Console .WriteLine() overloads. However, now that there is a direct cast to uint available in SimpleCurrency2, the compiler has opted for this route.

The upshot of this is that if you have a method call that takes several overloads, and you attempt to pass it a parameter whose data type doesn't match any of the overloads exactly, then you are forcing the compiler to decide not only what casts to use to perform the data conversion, but which overload, and hence which data conversion, to pick. The compiler always works logically and according to strict rules, but the results may not be what you expected. If there is any doubt, you are better off specifying which cast to use explicitly.

Summary

This chapter looked at the standard operators provided by C#, described the mechanics of object equality, and examined how the compiler converts the standard data types from one to another. It also demonstrated how you can implement custom operator support on your data types using operator overloads. Finally, the chapter looked at a special type of operator overload, the cast operator, which allows you to specify how instances of your types are converted to other data types.

Chapter 7 focuses on two closely related member types that you can implement in your types to support very clean event-based object models: delegates and events.

7

Delegates and Events

Callback functions are an important part of programming in Windows. If you have a background in C or C++ programming, you have seen callbacks used in many of the Windows APIs. With the addition of the `AddressOf` keyword, Visual Basic developers are now able to take advantage of the API that once was off limits. Callback functions are really pointers to a method call. Also known as function pointers, they are a very powerful programming feature. .NET has implemented the concept of a function pointer in the form of delegates. What makes them special is that, unlike the C function pointer, the .NET delegate is type-safe. What this means is that a function pointer in C is nothing but a pointer to a memory location. You have no idea what that pointer is really pointing to. Things like parameters and return types are not known. As you see in this chapter, .NET has made delegates a type-safe operation. Later in the chapter, you see how .NET uses delegates as the means of implementing events.

The main topics of this chapter are:

❑ Delegates

❑ Anonymous methods

❑ Lambda expressions

❑ Events

Delegates

Delegates exist for situations in which you want to pass methods around to other methods. To see what that means, consider this line of code:

```
int i = int.Parse("99");
```

You are so used to passing data to methods as parameters, as in this example, that you don't consciously think about it, and for this reason the idea of passing methods around instead of data might sound a little strange. However, there are cases in which you have a method that does something, and rather than operating on data, the method might need to do something that involves invoking another method. To complicate things further, you do not know at compile time what this second method is. That information is available only at runtime and hence will need to be passed in as a parameter to the first method. That might sound confusing but should become clearer with a couple of examples:

❑ **Starting threads** — It is possible in C# to tell the computer to start some new sequence of execution in parallel with what it is currently doing. Such a sequence is known as a thread, and starting one up is done using the `Start()` method on an instance of one of the base classes, `System.Threading.Thread`. If you tell the computer to start a new sequence of execution, you have to tell it where to start that sequence. You have to supply it with the details of a method in which execution can start. In other words, the constructor of the `Thread` class takes a parameter that defines the method to be invoked by the thread.

❑ **Generic library classes** — Many libraries contain code to perform various standard tasks. It is usually possible for these libraries to be self-contained, in the sense that you know when you write to the library exactly how the task must be performed. However, sometimes the task contains some subtask, which only the individual client code that uses the library knows how to perform. For example, say that you want to write a class that takes an array of objects and sorts them into ascending order. Part of the sorting process involves repeatedly taking two of the objects in the array and comparing them in order to see which one should come first. If you want to make the class capable of sorting arrays of any object, there is no way that it can tell in advance how to do this comparison. The client code that hands your class the array of objects will also have to tell your class how to do this comparison for the particular objects it wants sorted. The client code will have to pass your class details of an appropriate method that can be called and does the comparison.

❑ **Events** — The general idea here is that often you have code that needs to be informed when some event takes place. GUI programming is full of situations like this. When the event is raised, the runtime will need to know what method should be executed. This is done by passing the method that handles the event as a parameter to a delegate. This is discussed later in the chapter.

In C and C++, you can just take the address of a function and pass this as a parameter. There's no type safety with C. You can pass any function to a method where a function pointer is required. Unfortunately, this direct approach not only causes some problems with type safety but also neglects the fact that when you are doing object-oriented programming, methods rarely exist in isolation, but usually need to be associated with a class instance before they can be called. As a result of these problems, the .NET Framework does not syntactically permit this direct approach. Instead, if you want to pass methods around, you have to wrap up the details of the method in a new kind of object, a delegate. Delegates quite simply are a special type of object — special in the sense that, whereas all the objects defined up to now contain data, a delegate contains the address of a method.

Declaring Delegates in C#

When you want to use a class in C#, you do so in two stages. First, you need to define the class — that is, you need to tell the compiler what fields and methods make up the class. Then (unless you are using only static methods), you instantiate an object of that class. With delegates it is the same thing. You have to start off by defining the delegates you want to use. In the case of delegates, defining them means telling the compiler what kind of method a delegate of that type will represent. Then, you have to create one or more instances of that delegate. Behind the scenes, the compiler creates a class that represents the delegate.

The syntax for defining delegates looks like this:

```
delegate void IntMethodInvoker(int x);
```

In this case, you have defined a delegate called `IntMethodInvoker`, and you have indicated that each instance of this delegate can hold a reference to a method that takes one `int` parameter and returns void. The crucial point to understand about delegates is that they are type-safe. When you define the delegate, you have to give full details of the signature and the return type of the method that it is going to represent.

> **One good way of understanding delegates is by thinking of a delegate as something that gives a name to a method signature and the return type.**

Suppose that you wanted to define a delegate called TwoLongsOp that will represent a method that takes two longs as its parameters and returns a double. You could do it like this:

```
delegate double TwoLongsOp(long first, long second);
```

Or, to define a delegate that will represent a method that takes no parameters and returns a string, you might write this:

```
delegate string GetAString();
```

The syntax is similar to that for a method definition, except that there is no method body and the definition is prefixed with the keyword delegate. Because what you are doing here is basically defining a new class, you can define a delegate in any of the same places that you would define a class — that is to say either inside another class or outside of any class and in a namespace as a top-level object. Depending on how visible you want your definition to be, you can apply any of the normal access modifiers to delegate definitions — public, private, protected, and so on:

```
public delegate string GetAString();
```

We really mean what we say when we describe defining a delegate as defining a new class. Delegates are implemented as classes derived from the class System.MulticastDelegate, which is derived from the base class, System.Delegate. The C# compiler is aware of this class and uses its delegate syntax to shield you from the details of the operation of this class. This is another good example of how C# works in conjunction with the base classes to make programming as easy as possible.

After you have defined a delegate, you can create an instance of it so that you can use it to store details of a particular method.

There is an unfortunate problem with terminology here. With classes there are two distinct terms — class, which indicates the broader definition, and object, which means an instance of the class. Unfortunately, with delegates there is only the one term. When you create an instance of a delegate, what you have created is also referred to as a delegate. You need to be aware of the context to know which meaning we are using when we talk about delegates.

Using Delegates in C#

The following code snippet demonstrates the use of a delegate. It is a rather long-winded way of calling the ToString() method on an int:

```
private delegate string GetAString();

static void Main()
{
    int x = 40;
    GetAString firstStringMethod = new GetAString(x.ToString);
    Console.WriteLine("String is {0}", firstStringMethod());
```

(continued)

(continued)

```
        // With firstStringMethod initialized to x.ToString(),
        // the above statement is equivalent to saying
        // Console.WriteLine("String is {0}", x.ToString());
    }
```

In this code, you instantiate a delegate of type `GetAString`, and you initialize it so it refers to the `ToString()` method of the integer variable x. Delegates in C# always syntactically take a one-parameter constructor, the parameter being the method to which the delegate will refer. This method must match the signature with which you originally defined the delegate. So in this case, you would get a compilation error if you tried to initialize the variable `firstStringMethod` with any method that did not take any parameters and return a string. Notice that, because `int.ToString()` is an instance method (as opposed to a static one), you need to specify the instance (x) as well as the name of the method to initialize the delegate properly.

The next line actually uses the delegate to display the string. In any code, supplying the name of a delegate instance, followed by brackets containing any parameters, has exactly the same effect as calling the method wrapped by the delegate. Hence, in the preceding code snippet, the `Console.WriteLine()` statement is completely equivalent to the commented-out line.

In fact, supplying brackets to the delegate instance is the same as invoking the `Invoke()` method of the delegate class. Because `firstStringMethod` is a variable of a delegate type, the C# compiler replaces `firstStringMethod()` with `firstStringMethod.Invoke()`:

```
firstStringMethod();
firstStringMethod.Invoke();
```

For less typing, at every place where a delegate instance is needed, you can just pass the name of the address. This is known by the term *delegate inference*. This C# feature works as long as the compiler can resolve the delegate instance to a specific type. The example initialized the variable `firstStringMethod` of type `GetAString` with a new instance of the delegate `GetAString`:

```
GetAString firstStringMethod = new GetAString(x.ToString);
```

You can write the same just by passing the method name with the variable x to the variable `firstStringMethod`:

```
GetAString firstStringMethod = x.ToString;
```

The code that is created by the C# compiler is the same. The compiler detects that a delegate type is required with `firstStringMethod`, so it creates an instance of the delegate type `GetAString` and passes the address of the method with the object x to the constructor.

> *Be aware that you can't type the (and) as* `x.ToString()` *and pass it to the delegate variable. This would be an invocation of the method. The invocation of* `x.ToString()` *returns a string object that can't be assigned to the delegate variable. You can only assign the address of a method to the delegate variable.*

Delegate inference can be used any place a delegate instance is required. Delegate inference can also be used with events because events are based on delegates (as you can see later in this chapter).

One feature of delegates is that they are type-safe to the extent that they ensure the signature of the method being called is correct. However, interestingly, they do not care what type of object the method is being called against or even whether the method is a static method or an instance method.

> **An instance of a given delegate can refer to any instance or static method on any object of any type, provided that the signature of the method matches the signature of the delegate.**

To demonstrate this, the following example expands the previous code snippet so that it uses the firstStringMethod delegate to call a couple of other methods on another object — an instance method and a static method. For this, you use the Currency struct, which is defined as follows. The Currency struct has its own overload of ToString() and a static method with the same signature to GetCurrencyUnit(). This way the same delegate variable can be used to invoke these methods.

```
struct Currency
{
   public uint Dollars;
   public ushort Cents;

   public Currency(uint dollars, ushort cents)
   {
      this.Dollars = dollars;
      this.Cents = cents;
   }

   public override string ToString()
   {
      return string.Format("${0}.{1,-2:00}", Dollars,Cents);
   }

   public static string GetCurrencyUnit()
   {
      return "Dollar";
   }

   public static explicit operator Currency (float value)
   {
      checked
      {
         uint dollars = (uint)value;
         ushort cents = (ushort)((value-dollars)*100);
         return new Currency(dollars, cents);
      }
   }

   public static implicit operator float (Currency value)
   {
      return value.Dollars + (value.Cents/100.0f);
   }

   public static implicit operator Currency (uint value)
   {
      return new Currency(value, 0);
   }

   public static implicit operator uint (Currency value)
   {
      return value.Dollars;
   }
}
```

Now you can use your `GetAString` instance as follows:

```
private delegate string GetAString();

static void Main()
{
    int x = 40;
    GetAString firstStringMethod = x.ToString;
    Console.WriteLine("String is {0}", firstStringMethod());

    Currency balance = new Currency(34, 50);

    // firstStringMethod references an instance method
    firstStringMethod = balance.ToString;
    Console.WriteLine("String is {0}", firstStringMethod());

    // firstStringMethod references a static method
    firstStringMethod = new GetAString(Currency.GetCurrencyUnit);
    Console.WriteLine("String is {0}", firstStringMethod());
}
```

This code shows how you can call a method via a delegate and subsequently reassign the delegate to refer to different methods on different instances of classes, even static methods or methods against instances of different types of class, provided that the signature of each method matches the delegate definition.

When you run the application, you get the output from the different methods that are referenced by the delegate:

```
String is 40
String is $34.50
String is Dollar
```

However, you still haven't seen the process of actually passing a delegate to another method. Nor have you actually achieved anything particularly useful yet. It is possible to call the `ToString()` method of `int` and `Currency` objects in a much more straightforward way than using delegates! Unfortunately, the nature of delegates requires a fairly complex example before you can really appreciate their usefulness. The next section presents two delegate examples. The first one simply uses delegates to call a couple of different operations. It illustrates how to pass delegates to methods and how you can use arrays of delegates — although arguably it still doesn't do much that you couldn't do a lot more simply without delegates. Then, a second, much more complex example of a `BubbleSorter` class is presented, which implements a method to sort out arrays of objects into increasing order. This class would be difficult to write without delegates.

Simple Delegate Example

This example defines a `MathOperations` class that has a couple of static methods to perform two operations on doubles. Then you use delegates to call up these methods. The math class looks like this:

```
class MathOperations
{
    public static double MultiplyByTwo(double value)
    {
        return value * 2;
    }
```

```csharp
        public static double Square(double value)
        {
            return value * value;
        }
    }
```

You call up these methods like this:

```csharp
using System;

namespace Wrox.ProCSharp.Delegates
{
    delegate double DoubleOp(double x);

    class Program
    {
        static void Main()
        {
            DoubleOp[] operations =
                {
                    MathOperations.MultiplyByTwo,
                    MathOperations.Square
                };

            for (int i=0 ; i < operations.Length ; i++)
            {
                Console.WriteLine("Using operations[{0}]:", i);
                ProcessAndDisplayNumber(operations[i], 2.0);
                ProcessAndDisplayNumber(operations[i], 7.94);
                ProcessAndDisplayNumber(operations[i], 1.414);
                Console.WriteLine();
            }
        }

        static void ProcessAndDisplayNumber(DoubleOp action, double value)
        {
            double result = action(value);
            Console.WriteLine(
                "Value is {0}, result of operation is {1}", value, result);
        }
    }
}
```

In this code, you instantiate an array of DoubleOp delegates (remember that once you have defined a delegate class, you can basically instantiate instances just like you can with normal classes, so putting some into an array is no problem). Each element of the array gets initialized to refer to a different operation implemented by the MathOperations class. Then, you loop through the array, applying each operation to three different values. This illustrates one way of using delegates — that you can group methods together into an array using them, so that you can call several methods in a loop.

The key lines in this code are the ones in which you actually pass each delegate to the ProcessAndDisplayNumber() method, for example:

```csharp
            ProcessAndDisplayNumber(operations[i], 2.0);
```

Here, you are passing in the name of a delegate but without any parameters. Given that `operations[i]` is a delegate, syntactically:

❑ `operations[i]` means *the delegate* (that is, the method represented by the delegate).

❑ `operations[i](2.0)` means *actually call this method, passing in the value in parentheses.*

The `ProcessAndDisplayNumber()` method is defined to take a delegate as its first parameter:

```
static void ProcessAndDisplayNumber(DoubleOp action, double value)
```

Then, when in this method, you call:

```
double result = action(value);
```

This actually causes the method that is wrapped up by the `action` delegate instance to be called and its return result stored in `Result`.

Running this example gives you the following:

```
SimpleDelegate
Using operations[0]:
Value is 2, result of operation is 4
Value is 7.94, result of operation is 15.88
Value is 1.414, result of operation is 2.828

Using operations[1]:
Value is 2, result of operation is 4
Value is 7.94, result of operation is 63.0436
Value is 1.414, result of operation is 1.999396
```

BubbleSorter Example

You are now ready for an example that will show delegates working in a situation in which they are very useful. You are going to write a class called `BubbleSorter`. This class implements a static method, `Sort()`, which takes as its first parameter an array of objects, and rearranges this array into ascending order. For example, if you were to pass it this array of `int`s, `{0, 5, 6, 2, 1}`, it would rearrange this array into `{0, 1, 2, 5, 6}`.

The bubble-sorting algorithm is a well-known and very simple way of sorting numbers. It is best suited to small sets of numbers, because for larger sets of numbers (more than about 10) far more efficient algorithms are available). It works by repeatedly looping through the array, comparing each pair of numbers and, if necessary, swapping them, so that the largest numbers progressively move to the end of the array. For sorting `int`s, a method to do a bubble sort might look like this:

```
for (int i = 0; i < sortArray.Length; i++)
{
    for (int j = i + 1; j < sortArray.Length; j++)
    {
        if (sortArray[j] < sortArray[i])    // problem with this test
        {
            int temp = sortArray[i];    // swap ith and jth entries
            sortArray[i] = sortArray[j];
            sortArray[j] = temp;
        }
    }
}
```

This is all very well for ints, but you want your Sort() method to be able to sort any object. In other words, if some client code hands you an array of Currency structs or any other class or struct that it may have defined, you need to be able to sort the array. This presents a problem with the line if (sortArray [j]<sortArray[i]) in the preceding code, because that requires you to compare two objects on the array to see which one is greater. You can do that for ints, but how are you to do it for some new class that is unknown or undecided until runtime? The answer is the client code that knows about the class will have to pass in a delegate wrapping a method that will do the comparison.

You define the delegate like this:

```
delegate bool Comparison(object x, object y);
```

And you give your Sort method this signature:

```
static public void Sort(object[] sortArray, Comparison comparison)
```

The documentation for this method states that comparison must refer to a static method that takes two arguments, and returns true if the value of the second argument is *greater than* (that is, should come later in the array than) the first one.

Now you are all set. Here is the definition for the BubbleSorter class:

```
class BubbleSorter
{
    static public void Sort(object[] sortArray, Comparison comparison)
    {
        for (int i = 0 ; i < sortArray.Length ; i++)
        {
            for (int j = i + 1 ; j < sortArray.Length ; j++)
            {
                if (comparison(sortArray[j], sortArray[i]))
                {
                    object temp = sortArray[i];
                    sortArray[i] = sortArray[j];
                    sortArray[j] = temp;
                }
            }
        }
    }
}
```

To use this class, you need to define some other class, which you can use to set up an array that needs sorting. For this example, assume that the Mortimer Phones mobile phone company has a list of employees and wants them sorted according to salary. The employees are each represented by an instance of a class, Employee, which looks like this:

```
class Employee
{
    private string name;
    private decimal salary;

    public Employee(string name, decimal salary)
    {
        this.name = name;
        this.salary = salary;
    }
```

(continued)

(continued)

```
    public override string ToString()
    {
        return string.Format("{0}, {1:C}", name, salary);
    }

    public static bool CompareSalary(object x, object y)
    {
        Employee e1 = (Employee) x;
        Employee e2 = (Employee) y;
        return (e1.salary < e2.salary);
    }
}
```

Notice that in order to match the signature of the `Comparison` delegate, you had to define `CompareSalary` in this class as taking two object references, rather than `Employee` references, as parameters. This means that you had to cast the parameters into `Employee` references in order to perform the comparison.

> *Instead of using objects as parameters here, strong typing generics can also be used. Chapter 9 explains generics and generic delegates.*

Now you are ready to write some client code to request a sort:

```
using System;

namespace Wrox.ProCSharp.Delegates
{
    delegate bool Comparison(object x, object y);

    class Program
    {
        static void Main()
        {
            Employee[] employees =
                {
                    new Employee("Bugs Bunny", 20000),
                    new Employee("Elmer Fudd", 10000),
                    new Employee("Daffy Duck", 25000),
                    new Employee("Wiley Coyote", (decimal)1000000.38),
                    new Employee("Foghorn Leghorn", 23000),
                    new Employee("RoadRunner", 50000)};

            BubbleSorter.Sort(employees, Employee.CompareSalary);

            foreach (var employee in employees)
            {
                Console.WriteLine(employee);
            }
        }
    }
}
```

Running this code shows that the `Employees` are correctly sorted according to salary:

```
BubbleSorter
Elmer Fudd, $10,000.00
Bugs Bunny, $20,000.00
```

```
Foghorn Leghorn, $23,000.00
Daffy Duck, $25,000.00
RoadRunner, $50,000.00
Wiley Coyote, $1,000,000.38
```

Multicast Delegates

So far, each of the delegates you have used wraps just one single method call. Calling the delegate amounts to calling that method. If you want to call more than one method, you need to make an explicit call through a delegate more than once. However, it is possible for a delegate to wrap more than one method. Such a delegate is known as a *multicast delegate*. If a multicast delegate is called, it will successively call each method in order. For this to make sense, the delegate signature should return a void; otherwise, you would only get the result of the last method that is invoked by the delegate.

Consider the following code, which is adapted from the SimpleDelegate example. Although the syntax is the same as before, it is actually a multicast delegate, Operations, that gets instantiated:

```
    delegate void DoubleOp(double value);
//    delegate double DoubleOp(double value);    // can't do this now

    class MainEntryPoint
    {
       static void Main()
       {
          DoubleOp operations = MathOperations.MultiplyByTwo;
          operations += MathOperations.Square;
```

In the earlier example, you wanted to store references to two methods, so you instantiated an array of delegates. Here, you simply add both operations into the same multicast delegate. Multicast delegates recognize the operators + and +=. Alternatively, you can also expand the last two lines of the preceding code, as in this snippet:

```
    DoubleOp operation1 = MathOperations.MultiplyByTwo;
    DoubleOp operation2 = MathOperations.Square;
    DoubleOp operations = operation1 + operation2;
```

Multicast delegates also recognize the operators – and –= to remove method calls from the delegate.

> In terms of what's going on under the hood, a multicast delegate is a class derived from System .MulticastDelegate, which in turn is derived from System.Delegate. System .MulticastDelegate, and has additional members to allow chaining of method calls together into a list.

To illustrate the use of multicast delegates, the following code recasts the SimpleDelegate example into a new example, MulticastDelegate. Because you now need the delegate to refer to methods that return void, you have to rewrite the methods in the MathOperations class, so they display their results instead of returning them:

```
    class MathOperations
    {
       public static void MultiplyByTwo(double value)
       {
          double result = value * 2;
          Console.WriteLine(
             "Multiplying by 2: {0} gives {1}", value, result);
       }
```

(continued)

187

(continued)

```
        public static void Square(double value)
        {
            double result = value * value;
            Console.WriteLine("Squaring: {0} gives {1}", value, result);
        }
    }
```

To accommodate this change, you also have to rewrite ProcessAndDisplayNumber:

```
    static void ProcessAndDisplayNumber(DoubleOp action, double valueToProcess)
    {
        Console.WriteLine();
        Console.WriteLine("ProcessAndDisplayNumber called with value = {0}",
                          valueToProcess);
        action(valueToProcess);
    }
```

Now you can try out your multicast delegate like this:

```
        static void Main()
        {
            DoubleOp operations = MathOperations.MultiplyByTwo;
            operations += MathOperations.Square;

            ProcessAndDisplayNumber(operations, 2.0);
            ProcessAndDisplayNumber(operations, 7.94);
            ProcessAndDisplayNumber(operations, 1.414);
            Console.WriteLine();
        }
```

Now, each time ProcessAndDisplayNumber is called, it will display a message to say that it has been called. Then the following statement will cause each of the method calls in the action delegate instance to be called in succession:

```
        action(value);
```

Running this code produces this result:

```
    MulticastDelegate

    ProcessAndDisplayNumber called with value = 2
    Multiplying by 2: 2 gives 4
    Squaring: 2 gives 4

    ProcessAndDisplayNumber called with value = 7.94
    Multiplying by 2: 7.94 gives 15.88
    Squaring: 7.94 gives 63.0436

    ProcessAndDisplayNumber called with value = 1.414
    Multiplying by 2: 1.414 gives 2.828
    Squaring: 1.414 gives 1.999396
```

If you are using multicast delegates, you should be aware that the order in which methods chained to the same delegate will be called is formally undefined. You should, therefore, avoid writing code that relies on such methods being called in any particular order.

Invoking multiple methods by one delegate might cause an even bigger problem. The multicast delegate contains a collection of delegates to invoke one after the other. If one of the methods invoked by a delegate throws an exception, the complete iteration stops. Have a look at the following `MulticastIteration` example. Here, a simple delegate named `DemoDelegate` that returns `void` without arguments is defined. This delegate is meant to invoke the methods `One()` and `Two()` that fulfill the parameter and return type requirements of the delegate. Be aware that method `One()` throws an exception.

```
using System;

namespace Wrox.ProCSharp.Delegates
{
    public delegate void DemoDelegate();

    class Program
    {
        static void One()
        {
            Console.WriteLine("One");
            throw new Exception("Error in one");
        }

        static void Two()
        {
            Console.WriteLine("Two");
        }
```

In the `Main()` method, delegate d1 is created to reference method `One()`; next, the address of method `Two()` is added to the same delegate. d1 is invoked to call both methods. The exception is caught in a `try/catch` block.

```
        static void Main()
        {
            DemoDelegate d1 = One;
            d1 += Two;

            try
            {
                d1();
            }
            catch (Exception)
            {
                Console.WriteLine("Exception caught");
            }
        }
    }
}
```

Only the first method is invoked by the delegate. Because the first method throws an exception, iterating the delegates stops here and method `Two()` is never invoked. The result might differ because the order of calling the methods is not defined.

```
One
Exception Caught
```

Errors and exceptions are explained in detail in Chapter 14, "Errors and Exceptions."

In such a scenario, you can avoid the problem by iterating the list on your own. The `Delegate` class defines the method `GetInvocationList()` that returns an array of `Delegate` objects. You can now use this delegate to invoke the methods associated with them directly, catch exceptions, and continue with the next iteration:

```
static void Main()
{
    DemoDelegate d1 = One;
    d1 += Two;

    Delegate[] delegates = d1.GetInvocationList();
    foreach (DemoDelegate d in delegates)
    {
        try
        {
            d();
        }
        catch (Exception)
        {
            Console.WriteLine("Exception caught");
        }
    }
}
```

When you run the application with the code changes, you can see that the iteration continues with the next method after the exception is caught:

```
One
Exception caught
Two
```

Anonymous Methods

Up to this point, a method must already exist in order for the delegate to work (that is, the delegate is defined with the same signature as the method(s) it will be used with). However, there is another way to use delegates — with anonymous methods. An anonymous method is a block of code that is used as the parameter for the delegate.

The syntax for defining a delegate with an anonymous method doesn't change. It's when the delegate is instantiated that things change. The following is a very simple console application that shows how using an anonymous method can work:

```
using System;

namespace Wrox.ProCSharp.Delegates
{
    class Program
    {
        delegate string DelegateTest(string val);

        static void Main()
        {
            string mid = ", middle part,";

            DelegateTest anonDel = delegate(string param)
            {
                param += mid;
                param += " and this was added to the string.";
                return param;
            };
```

```
         Console.WriteLine(anonDel("Start of string"));

      }
   }
}
```

The delegate `DelegateTest` is defined inside the class `Program`. It takes a single string parameter. Where things become different is in the `Main` method. When `anonDel` is defined, instead of passing in a known method name, a simple block of code is used, prefixed by the delegate keyword, followed by a parameter:

```
delegate (string param)
{
  param += mid;
  param += " and this was added to the string.";
  return param;
};
```

As you can see, the block of code uses a method-level string variable, `mid`, which is defined outside of the anonymous method and adds it to the parameter that was passed in. The code then returns the string value. When the delegate is called, a string is passed in as the parameter and the returned string is output to the console.

The benefit of anonymous methods is to reduce the code you have to write. You don't have to define a method just to use it with a delegate. This becomes very evident when defining the delegate for an event. (Events are discussed later in this chapter.) This can help reduce the complexity of code, especially where there are several events defined. With anonymous methods, the code does not perform faster. The compiler still defines a method; the method just has an automatically assigned name that you don't need to know.

A couple of rules must be followed when using anonymous methods. You can't have a jump statement (`break`, `goto`, or `continue`) in an anonymous method that has a target outside of the anonymous method. The reverse is also true — a jump statement outside the anonymous method cannot have a target inside the anonymous method.

Unsafe code cannot be accessed inside an anonymous method. Also, `ref` and `out` parameters that are used outside of the anonymous method cannot be accessed. Other variables defined outside of the anonymous method can be used.

If you have to write the same functionality more than once, don't use anonymous methods. In this case, instead of duplicating the code, writing a named method is the preferred way. You only have to write it once and reference it by its name.

Lambda Expressions

C# 3.0 offers a new syntax for anonymous methods: Lambda expressions. Lambda expressions can be used with delegate types. The previous example using anonymous methods is changed to use a Lambda expression:

```
using System;

namespace Wrox.ProCSharp.Delegates
{
  class Program
  {
    delegate string DelegateTest(string val);

    static void Main()
```

(continued)

191

(continued)

```
        {
            string mid = ", middle part,";

            DelegateTest anonDel = param =>
                {
                    param += mid;
                    param += " and this was added to the string.";
                    return param;
                };

            Console.WriteLine(anonDel("Start of string"));
        }
    }
}
```

The left side of the Lambda operator => lists the parameters needed with the anonymous method. There are several ways to write this. For example, if a string parameter is needed as the delegate type defined in the sample code, one way to write this is by defining the type and variable name inside brackets:

```
(string param)
```

With Lambda expressions there's no need to add the variable type to the declaration because the compiler knows about the type:

```
(param)
```

If there's only one parameter, the brackets can be removed:

```
param
```

The right side of the Lambda expression lists the implementation. With the sample program the implementation was surrounded by curly brackets similar to the anonymous method earlier:

```
        {
            param += mid;
            param += " and this was added to the string.";
            return param;
        };
```

If the implementation consists of just a single line, you can also remove the curly brackets and the return statement because this is filled automatically by the compiler.

For example, with the following delegate that requires an int parameter and returns a bool:

```
public delegate bool Predicate(int obj)
```

you can declare a variable of the delegate and assign a Lambda expression. With the Lambda expression here, on the left side the variable x is defined. This variable is automatically of type int because this is as it is defined with the delegate. The implementation returns the Boolean result of comparing x > 5. If x is larger than 5, true is returned, otherwise false.

```
Predicate p1 = x => x > 5;
```

You can pass this Lambda expression to a method that requires a Predicate parameter:

```
list.FindAll(x => x > 5);
```

The same Lambda expression is shown here, without using variable type inference by defining the variable x of type int, and also adding the return statement to the implementation:

```
list.FindAll((int x) => { return x > 5; });
```

Using the older syntax, the same functionality is written by using an anonymous method:

```
list.FindAll(delegate(int x) { return x > 5; });
```

With all these different variants, the C# compiler always creates the same IL code.

Changing the `SimpleDelegate` sample shown earlier, you can eliminate the class `MathOperations` by using Lambda expressions. The `Main()` method would then look like this:

```
static void Main()
{
    DoubleOp multByTwo = val => val * 2;
    DoubleOp square = val => val * val;

    DoubleOp [] operations = {multByTwo, square};

    for (int i=0 ; i<operations.Length ; i++)
    {
        Console.WriteLine("Using operations[{0}]:", i);
        ProcessAndDisplayNumber(operations[i], 2.0);
        ProcessAndDisplayNumber(operations[i], 7.94);
        ProcessAndDisplayNumber(operations[i], 1.414);
        Console.WriteLine();
    }
}
```

Running this version will give you the same results as the previous example. The advantage is that it eliminated a class.

> *Lambda expressions can be used any place where the type is a delegate. Another use of Lambda expressions is when the type is* Expression *or* Expression<T>. *Here the compiler creates an expression tree. This feature is discussed in Chapter 11, "Language Integrated Query."*

Covariance and Contra-variance

The method that is invoked by the delegate does not need the exact same types as defined by the delegate declaration. Covariance and contra-variance are possible.

Return Type Covariance

The return type of a method can derive from the type defined by the delegate. In the example the delegate `MyDelegate1` is defined to return the type `DelegateReturn`. The method that is assigned to the delegate instance d1 returns the type `DelegateReturn2` that derives from the base class `DelegateReturn` and thus fulfills the requirements of the delegate. This behavior is known by the name *return type covariance*.

```
public class DelegateReturn
{
}

public class DelegateReturn2 : DelegateReturn
{
}

public delegate DelegateReturn MyDelegate1();

class Program
```

(continued)

(continued)

```
        {
            static void Main()
            {
                MyDelegate1 d1 = Method1;
                d1();
            }

            static DelegateReturn2 Method1()
            {
                DelegateReturn2 d2 = new DelegateReturn2();
                return d2;
            }
        }
```

Parameter Type Contra-variance

The term *parameter type contra-variance* means that the parameters defined by the delegate might differ in the method that is called by the delegate. Here it's different from the return type because the method might use a parameter type that derives from the type defined by the delegate. In the code sample the delegate uses the parameter type DelegateParam2, and the method that is assigned to the delegate instance d2 uses the parameter type DelegateParam that is the base type of DelegateParam2.

```
public class DelegateParam
{
}
public class DelegateParam2 : DelegateParam
{
}

public delegate void MyDelegate2(DelegateParam2 p);

class Program
{
    static void Main()
    {
        MyDelegate2 d2 = Method2;
        DelegateParam2 p = new DelegateParam2();
        d2(p);
    }

    static void Method2(DelegateParam p)
    {
    }
}
```

Events

Windows-based applications are message-based. This means that the application is communicating with Windows and Windows is communicating with the application by using predefined messages. These messages are structures that contain various pieces of information that the application and Windows will use to determine what to do next. Prior to libraries such as MFC (Microsoft Foundation Classes) or to development environments such as Visual Basic, the developer would have to handle the message that Windows sends to the application. Visual Basic and now .NET wrap some of these incoming messages as something called events. If you need to react to a specific incoming message, you would handle the corresponding event. A common example of this is when the user clicks a button on a form. Windows is sending a WM_MOUSECLICK message to the button's message handler (sometimes referred to as the Windows Procedure or WndProc). To the .NET developer, this is exposed as the Click event of the button.

In developing object-based applications, another form of communication between objects is required. When something of interest happens in one of your objects, chances are that other objects will want to be informed. Again, events come to the rescue. Just as the .NET Framework wraps up Windows messages in events, you can also utilize events as the communications medium between your objects.

Delegates are used as the means of wiring up the event when the message is received by the application. Believe it or not, in the preceding section on delegates, you learned just about everything you need to know to understand how events work. However, one of the great things about how Microsoft has designed C# events is that you don't actually need to understand anything about the underlying delegates in order to use them. So, this section starts off with a short discussion of events from the point of view of the client software. It focuses on what code you need to write in order to receive notifications of events, without worrying too much about what is happening behind the scenes — just so you can see how easy handling events really is. After that, you write an example that generates events, and as you do so, you should see how the relationship between events and delegates works.

The discussion in this section will be of most use to C++ developers because C++ does not have any concept similar to events. C# events, on the other hand, are quite similar in concept to Visual Basic events, although the syntax and the underlying implementation are different in C#.

In this context, the term "event" is used in two different senses. First, as something interesting that happens, and second, as a precisely defined object in the C# language — the object that handles the notification process. When we mean the latter, we will usually refer to it either as a C# event or, when the meaning is obvious from the context, simply as an event.

The Receiver's View of Events

The event receiver is any application, object, or component that wants to be notified when something happens. To go along with the receiver, there will of course be the event sender. The sender's job will be to raise the event. The sender can be either another object or assembly in your application, or in the case of system events such as mouse clicks or keyboard entry, the sender will be the .NET runtime. It is important to note that the sender of the event will not have any knowledge of who or what the receiver is. This is what makes events so useful.

Now, somewhere inside the event receiver will be a method that is responsible for handling the event. This event handler will be executed each time the event that it is registered to is raised. This is where the delegate comes in. Because the sender has no idea who the receiver(s) will be, there cannot be any type of reference set between the two. So the delegate is used as the intermediary. The sender defines the delegate that will be used by the receiver. The receiver registers the event handler with the event. The process of hooking up the event handler is known as wiring up an event. A simple example of wiring up the Click event will help illustrate this process.

First, create a simple Windows Forms application. Drag over a button control from the toolbox and place it on the form. In the properties window rename the button to buttonOne. In the code editor, add the following line of code in the Form1 constructor:

```csharp
public Form1()
{
    InitializeComponent();
    buttonOne.Click += new EventHandler(Button_Click);
}
```

Now in Visual Studio, you should have noticed that after you typed in the += operator, all you had to do was press the Tab key a couple of times and the editor did the rest of the work for you. In most cases this is fine. However, in this example the default handler name is not being used, so you should just enter the text yourself.

What is happening is that you are telling the runtime that when the Click event of buttonOne is raised, that Button_Click method should be executed. EventHandler is the delegate that the event uses to assign the handler (Button_Click) to the event (Click). Notice that you used the += operator to add this new method to the delegate list. This is just like the multicast example that you looked at earlier in this chapter. This means that you can add more than one handler for any event. Because this is a multicast delegate, all of the rules about adding multiple methods apply; however, there is no guarantee as to the order in which the methods are called. Go ahead and drag another button onto the form and rename it to buttonTwo. Now connect the buttonTwo Click event to the same Button_Click method, as shown here:

```
buttonOne.Click += new EventHandler(Button_Click);
buttonTwo.Click += new EventHandler(Button_Click);
```

With delegate inference you can also write the code as follows, where the compiler generates the same code as in the previous version:

```
buttonOne.Click += Button_Click;
buttonTwo.Click += Button_Click;
```

The EventHandler delegate is defined for you in the .NET Framework. It is in the System namespace, and all of the events that are defined in the .NET Framework use it. As discussed earlier, a delegate requires that all of the methods that are added to the delegate list must have the same signature. This obviously holds true for event delegates as well. Here is the Button_Click method defined:

```
private void Button_Click(object sender, EventArgs e)
{

}
```

A few things are important about this method. First, it always returns void. Event handlers cannot return a value. Next are the parameters. As long as you use the EventHandler delegate, your parameters will be object and EventArgs. The first parameter is the object that raised the event. In this example it is either buttonOne or buttonTwo, depending on which button is clicked. By sending a reference to the object that raised the event you can assign the same event handler to more than one object. For example, you can define one button click handler for several buttons and then determine which button was clicked by asking the sender parameter.

The second parameter, EventArgs, is an object that contains other potentially useful information about the event. This parameter could actually be any type as long as it is derived from EventArgs. The MouseDown event uses MouseDownEventArgs. It contains properties for which button was used, the X and Y coordinates of the pointer, and other information related to the event. Notice the naming pattern of ending the type with EventArgs. Later in the chapter, you'll see how to create and use a custom EventArgs-based object.

The name of the method should also be mentioned. As a convention, event handlers follow a naming convention of object_event. object is the object that is raising the event, and event is the event being raised. There is a convention and, for readability's sake, it should be followed.

The last thing to do in this example is to add some code to actually do something in the handler. Now remember that two buttons are using the same handler. So, first you have to determine which button raises the event, and then you can call the action that should be performed. In this example, you can just output some text to a label control on the form. Drag a label control from the toolbox onto the form and name it labelInfo. Then write the following code on the Button_Click method:

```
if(((Button)sender).Name == "buttonOne")
    labelInfo.Text = "Button One was pressed";
else
    labelInfo.Text = "Button Two was pressed";
```

Notice that because the sender parameter is sent as `object`, you will have to cast it to whatever object is raising the event, in this case `Button`. In this example, you use the `Name` property to determine what button raised the event; however, you can also use another property. The `Tag` property is handy to use in this scenario, because it can contain anything that you want to place in it. To see how the multicast capability of the event delegate works, add another method to the `Click` event of `buttonTwo`. The constructor of the form should look something like this now:

```
buttonOne.Click += new EventHandler(Button_Click);
buttonTwo.Click += new EventHandler(Button_Click);
buttonTwo.Click += new EventHandler(Button2_Click);
```

If you let Visual Studio create the stub for you, you will have the following method at the end of the source file. However, you have to add the call to the `MessageBox.Show()` function:

```
private void Button2_Click(object sender, EventArgs e)
{
    MessageBox.Show("This only happens in Button 2 click event");
}
```

If you go back and make use of Lambda expressions, the methods `Button_Click` and `Button2_Click` would not be needed. The code for the events would like this:

```
buttonOne.Click += (sender, e) => labelInfo.Text = "Button One was pressed";
buttonTwo.Click += (sender, e) => labelInfo.Text = "Button Two was pressed";
buttonTwo.Click += (sender, e) =>
    {
        MessageBox.Show("This only happens in Button 2 click event");
    };
```

When you run this example, clicking `buttonOne` will change the text in the label. Clicking `buttonTwo` will not only change the text but also display the `MessageBox`. Again, the important thing to remember is that there is no guarantee that the label text will change before the `MessageBox` appears, so be careful not to write dependent code in the handlers.

You might have had to learn a lot of concepts to get this far, but the amount of coding you need to do in the receiver is fairly trivial. Also bear in mind that you will find yourself writing event receivers a lot more often than you write event senders. At least in the field of the Windows user interface, Microsoft has already written all the event senders you are likely to need (these are in the .NET base classes, in the `Windows.Forms` namespace).

Defining Events

Receiving events and responding to them is only one side of the story. For events to be really useful, you need the ability to define them and raise them in your code. The example in this section looks at creating, raising, receiving, and optionally canceling an event.

The example has a form raise an event that will be listened to by another class. When the event is raised, the receiving object will determine if the process should execute and then cancel the event if the process cannot continue. The goal in this case is to determine whether the number of seconds of the current time is greater than or less than 30. If the number of seconds is less than 30, a property is set with a string that represents the current time; if the number of seconds is greater than 30, the event is canceled and the time string is set to an empty string.

The form used to generate the event has a button and a label on it. In the example code to download the button is named `buttonRaise` and the label is `labelInfo`. After you have created the form and added the two controls, you will be able to create the event and the corresponding delegate. Add the following code in the class declaration section of the form class:

```
public delegate void ActionEventHandler(object sender,
    ActionCancelEventArgs ev);

public static event ActionEventHandler Action;
```

So, what exactly is going on with these two lines of code? First, you are declaring a new delegate type of `ActionEventHandler`. The reason that you have to create a new one and not use one of the predefined delegates in the .NET Framework is that there will be a custom `EventArgs` class used. Remember that the method signature must match the delegate. So, you now have a delegate to use; the next line actually defines the event. In this case the `Action` event is defined, and the syntax for defining the event requires that you specify the delegate that will be associated with the event. You can also use a delegate that is defined in the .NET Framework. Nearly 100 classes are derived from the `EventArgs` class, so you might find one that works for you. Again, because a custom `EventArgs` class is used in this example, a new delegate type has to be created that matches it.

Defining the event in one line is a C# shorthand notation to add methods that add and remove handler methods and to declare a variable of a delegate. Instead of writing one line you can do the same with the following lines. A variable of the event type as well as methods to add and remove event handlers are declared. The syntax for defining the methods to add and remove event handlers is very similar to properties. The variable value is also defined similarly to add and remove the event handler.

```
private static ActionEventHandler action;

public static event ActionEventHandler Action
{
    add
    {
        action += value;
    }
    remove
    {
        action -= value;
    }
}
```

The long notation for defining an event is useful if more needs to be done than just adding and removing the event handler: for example, to add synchronization for multiple thread access. The WPF controls make use of the long notation to add bubbling and tunneling functionality with the events. You can read more about bubbling and tunneling events in Chapter 34, "Windows Presentation Foundation."

The new `EventArgs`-based class, `ActionCancelEventArgs`, is actually derived from `CancelEventArgs`, which is derived from `EventArgs`. `CancelEventArgs` and adds the `Cancel` property. `Cancel` is a Boolean that informs the sender object that the receiver wants to cancel or stop the event processing. In the `ActionCancelEventArgs` class a `Message` property has been added. This is a string property that will contain textual information on the processing state of the event. Here is the code for the `ActionCancelEventArgs` class:

```
public class ActionCancelEventArgs : System.ComponentModel.CancelEventArgs
{
    public ActionCancelEventArgs() : this(false)   {}

    public ActionCancelEventArgs(bool cancel) : this(cancel, String.Empty)   {}
    public ActionCancelEventArgs(bool cancel, string message) : base(cancel)
```

```
        {
            this.Message = message;
        }

        public string Message { get; set; }
    }
```

You can see that all an `EventArgs`-based class does is carry information about an event to and from the sender and receiver. Most times the information used from the `EventArgs` class will be used by the receiver object in the event handler. However, sometimes the event handler can add information into the `EventArgs` class and it will be available to the sender. This is how the example uses the `EventArgs` class. Notice that a couple of constructors are available in the `EventArgs` class. This extra flexibility adds to the usability of the class by others.

At this point, an event has been declared, the delegate has been defined, and the `EventArgs` class has been created. The next thing that has to happen is that the event needs to be raised. The only thing that you really need to do is make a call to the event with the proper parameters as shown in this example:

```
ActionCancelEventArgs e = new ActionCancelEventArgs();
Action(this, e);
```

This sounds simple enough. Create the new `ActionCancelEventArgs` class and pass it in as one of the parameters to the event. However, there is one small problem. What if the event hasn't been used anywhere yet? What if an event handler has not yet been defined for the event? The `Action` event would actually be null. If you tried to raise the event, you would get a null reference exception. If you wanted to derive a new form class and use the form that has the `Action` event defined as the base, you would have to do something else whenever the `Action` event were raised. Currently, you would have to enable another event handler in the derived form in order to get access to it. To make this process a little easier and to catch the null reference error, you have to create a method with the name `OnEventName` where `EventName` is the name of the event. The example has a method named `OnAction()`. Here is the complete code for the `OnAction()` method:

```
protected void OnAction(object sender, ActionCancelEventArgs e)
{
    if (Action != null)
    {
        Action(sender, e);
    }
}
```

Not much to it, but it does accomplish what is needed. By making the method protected, only derived classes have access to it. You can also see that the event is tested against null before it is raised. If you were to derive a new class that contains this method and event, you would have to override the `OnAction` method and then you would be hooked into the event. To do this, you would have to call `base.OnAction()` in the override. Otherwise, the event would not be raised. This naming convention is used throughout the .NET Framework and is documented in the .NET SDK documentation.

Notice the two parameters that are passed into the `OnAction` method. They should look familiar to you because they are the same parameters that will need to be passed to the event. If the event needed to be raised from another object other than the one that the method is defined in, you would need to make the accessor internal or public and not protected. Sometimes it makes sense to have a class that consists of nothing but event declarations, and that these events are called from other classes. You would still want to create the `OnEventName` methods. However, in that case they might be static methods.

So, now that the event has been raised, something needs to handle it. Create a new class in the project and call it BusEntity. Remember that the goal of this project is to check the seconds property of the current time, and if it is less than 30, set a string value to the time, and if it is greater than 30, set the string to : : and cancel the event. Here is the code:

```csharp
using System;
using System.IO;
using System.ComponentModel;

namespace Wrox.ProCSharp.Delegates
{
    public class BusEntity
    {
        string time = String.Empty;

        public BusEntity()
        {
            Form1.Action += new Form1.ActionEventHandler(Form1_Action);
        }

        private void Form1_Action(object sender, ActionCancelEventArgs e)
        {
            e.Cancel = !DoActions();
            if(e.Cancel)
                e.Message = "Wasn't the right time.";
        }

        private bool DoActions()
        {
            bool retVal = false;
            DateTime tm = DateTime.Now;

            if(tm.Second < 30)
            {
                time = "The time is " + DateTime.Now.ToLongTimeString();
                retVal = true;
            }
            else
                time = "";

            return retVal;
        }

        public string TimeString
        {
            get {return time;}
        }
    }
}
```

In the constructor, the handler for the Form1.Action event is declared. Notice that the syntax is very similar to the Click event that you registered earlier. Because you used the same pattern for declaring the event, the usage syntax stays consistent as well. Something else worth mentioning at this point is how you were able to get a reference to the Action event without having a reference to Form1 in the

BusEntity class. Remember that in the Form1 class the Action event is declared static. This isn't a requirement, but it does make it easier to create the handler. You could have declared the event public, but then an instance of Form1 would need to be referenced.

When you coded the event in the constructor, you called the method that was added to the delegate list Form1_Action, in keeping with the naming standards. In the handler a decision on whether or not to cancel the event needs to be made. The DoActions method returns a Boolean value based on the time criteria described earlier. DoAction also sets the time string to the proper value.

Next, the DoActions return value is set to the ActionCancelEventArgs Cancel property. Remember that EventArg classes generally do not do anything other than carry values to and from the event senders and receivers. If the event is canceled (e.Cancel = true), the Message property is also set with a string value that describes why the event was canceled.

Now if you look at the code in the buttonRaise_Click event handler again you will be able to see how the Cancel property is used:

```
private void buttonRaise_Click(object sender, EventArgs e)
{
    ActionCancelEventArgs cancelEvent = new ActionCancelEventArgs();
    OnAction(this, cancelEvent);
    if (cancelEvent.Cancel)
        labelInfo.Text = cancelEvent.Message;
    else
        labelInfo.Text = busEntity.TimeString;
}
```

Note that the ActionCancelEventArgs object is created. Next, the event Action is raised, passing in the newly created ActionCancelEventArgs object. When the OnAction method is called and the event is raised, the code in the Action event handler in the BusEntity object is executed. If there were other objects that had registered for the Action event, they too would execute. Something to keep in mind is that if there were other objects handling this event, they would all see the same ActionCancelEventArgs object. If you needed to keep up with which object canceled the event and whether more than one object canceled the event, you would need some type of list-based data structure in the ActionCancelEventArgs class.

After the handlers that have been registered with the event delegate have been executed, you can query the ActionCancelEventArgs object to see if it has been canceled. If it has been canceled, lblInfo will contain the Message property value. If the event has not been canceled, lblInfo will show the current time.

This should give you a basic idea of how you can utilize events and the EventArgs-based object in the events to pass information around in your applications.

Summary

This chapter gave you the basics of delegates and events. You learned how to declare a delegate and add methods to the delegate list. You also learned the process of declaring event handlers to respond to an event, as well as how to create a custom event and use the patterns for raising the event.

As a .NET developer, you will be using delegates and events extensively, especially when developing Windows Forms applications. Events are the means that the .NET developer has to monitor the various Windows messages that occur while the application is executing. Otherwise, you would have to monitor the WndProc and catch the WM_MOUSEDOWN message instead of getting the mouse Click event for a button.

The use of delegates and events in the design of a large application can reduce dependencies and the coupling of layers. This allows you to develop components that have a higher reusability factor.

Anonymous methods and Lambda expressions are C# language features on delegates. With these, you can reduce the amount of code you need to write. Lambda expressions are not only used with delegates, as you can see in Chapter 11, "Language Integrated Query."

The next chapter goes into the foundation of strings and regular expressions.

8

Strings and Regular Expressions

Since the beginning of this book, you have been using strings almost constantly and might not have realized that the stated mapping that the `string` keyword in C# actually refers to is the `System.String` .NET base class. `System.String` is a very powerful and versatile class, but it is by no means the only string-related class in the .NET armory. This chapter starts by reviewing the features of `System.String` and then looks at some nifty things you can do with strings using some of the other .NET classes — in particular those in the `System.Text` and `System.Text.RegularExpressions` namespaces. This chapter covers the following areas:

❑ **Building strings** — If you're performing repeated modifications on a string, for example, in order to build up a lengthy string prior to displaying it or passing it to some other method or application, the `String` class can be very inefficient. For this kind of situation, another class, `System.Text.StringBuilder`, is more suitable because it has been designed exactly for this situation.

❑ **Formatting expressions** — We also take a closer look at those formatting expressions that have been used in the `Console.WriteLine()` method throughout the past few chapters. These formatting expressions are processed using a couple of useful interfaces, `IFormatProvider` and `IFormattable`. By implementing these interfaces on your own classes, you can actually define your own formatting sequences so that `Console.WriteLine()` and similar classes will display the values of your classes in whatever way you specify.

❑ **Regular expressions** — .NET also offers some very sophisticated classes that deal with situations in which you need to identify or extract substrings that satisfy certain fairly sophisticated criteria; for example, finding all occurrences within a string where a character or set of characters is repeated, finding all words that begin with s and contain at least one n, or strings that adhere to employee ID or Social Security number constructions. Although you can write methods to perform this kind of processing using the `String` class, such methods are cumbersome to write. Instead, you can use some classes from `System.Text.RegularExpressions`, which are designed specifically to perform this kind of processing.

System.String

Before examining the other string classes, this section quickly reviews some of the available methods in the String class.

System.String is a class specifically designed to store a string and allow a large number of operations on the string. In addition, due to the importance of this data type, C# has its own keyword and associated syntax to make it particularly easy to manipulate strings using this class.

You can concatenate strings using operator overloads:

```
string message1 = "Hello";  // returns "Hello"
message1 += ", There"; // returns "Hello, There"
string message2 = message1 + "!"; // returns "Hello, There!"
```

C# also allows extraction of a particular character using an indexer-like syntax:

```
char char4 = message[4];   // returns 'a'. Note the char is zero-indexed
```

This enables you to perform such common tasks as replacing characters, removing whitespace, and capitalization. The following table introduces the key methods.

Method	Purpose
Compare	Compares the contents of strings, taking into account the culture (locale) in assessing equivalence between certain characters
CompareOrdinal	Same as Compare but doesn't take culture into account
Concat	Combines separate string instances into a single instance
CopyTo	Copies a specific number of characters from the selected index to an entirely new instance of an array
Format	Formats a string containing various values and specifiers for how each value should be formatted
IndexOf	Locates the first occurrence of a given substring or character in the string
IndexOfAny	Locates the first occurrence of any one of a set of characters in the string
Insert	Inserts a string instance into another string instance at a specified index
Join	Builds a new string by combining an array of strings
LastIndexOf	Same as IndexOf but finds the last occurrence
LastIndexOfAny	Same as IndexOfAny but finds the last occurrence
PadLeft	Pads out the string by adding a specified repeated character to the left side of the string
PadRight	Pads out the string by adding a specified repeated character to the right side of the string
Replace	Replaces occurrences of a given character or substring in the string with another character or substring

Method	Purpose
Split	Splits the string into an array of substrings, the breaks occurring wherever a given character occurs
Substring	Retrieves the substring starting at a specified position in the string
ToLower	Converts string to lowercase
ToUpper	Converts string to uppercase
Trim	Removes leading and trailing whitespace

Please note that this table is not comprehensive but is intended to give you an idea of the features offered by strings.

Building Strings

As you have seen, `String` is an extremely powerful class that implements a large number of very useful methods. However, the `String` class has a shortcoming that makes it very inefficient for making repeated modifications to a given string — it is actually an *immutable* data type, which means that once you initialize a string object, that string object can never change. The methods and operators that appear to modify the contents of a string actually create new strings, copying across the contents of the old string if necessary. For example, look at the following code:

```
string greetingText = "Hello from all the guys at Wrox Press. ";
greetingText += "We do hope you enjoy this book as much as we enjoyed writing it.";
```

What happens when this code executes is this: first, an object of type `System.String` is created and initialized to hold the text `Hello from all the guys at Wrox Press.`. Note the space *after* the period. When this happens, the .NET runtime allocates just enough memory in the string to hold this text (39 chars), and the variable `greetingText` is set to refer to this string instance.

In the next line, syntactically it looks like more text is being added onto the string — though it is not. Instead, what happens is that a new string instance is created with just enough memory allocated to store the combined text — that's 103 characters in total. The original text, `Hello from all the people at Wrox Press.`, is copied into this new string instance along with the extra text, `We do hope you enjoy this book as much as we enjoyed writing it.`. Then, the address stored in the variable `greetingText` is updated, so the variable correctly points to the new `String` object. The old `String` object is now unreferenced — there are no variables that refer to it — and so will be removed the next time the garbage collector comes along to clean out any unused objects in your application.

By itself, that does not look too bad, but suppose that you wanted to encode that string by replacing each letter (not the punctuation) with the character that has an ASCII code further on in the alphabet, as part of some extremely simple encryption scheme. This would change the string to `Ifmmp gspn bmm uif hvst bu Xspy Qsftt. Xf ep ipqf zpv fokpz uijt cppl bt nvdi bt xf fokpzfe xsjujoh ju.`. Several ways of doing this exist, but the simplest and (if you are restricting yourself to using the `String` class) almost certainly the most efficient way is to use the `String.Replace()` method, which replaces all occurrences of a given substring in a string with another substring. Using `Replace()`, the code to encode the text looks like this:

```
string greetingText = "Hello from all the guys at Wrox Press. ";
greetingText += "We do hope you enjoy this book as much as we enjoyed writing it.";

for(int i = 'z'; i>= 'a' ; i--)
{
    char old1 = (char)i;
    char new1 = (char)(i+1);
    greetingText = greetingText.Replace(old1, new1);
}

for(int i = 'Z'; i>='A' ; i--)
{
    char old1 = (char)i;
    char new1 = (char)(i+1);
    greetingText = greetingText.Replace(old1, new1);
}

Console.WriteLine("Encoded:\n" + greetingText);
```

For simplicity, this code does not wrap Z to A or z to a. These letters get encoded to [and {, respectively.

Here, the `Replace()` method works in a fairly intelligent way, to the extent that it won't actually create a new string unless it actually makes changes to the old string. The original string contained 23 different lowercase characters and 3 different uppercase ones. The `Replace` method will therefore have allocated a new string 26 times in total, with each new string storing 103 characters. That means that because of the encryption process, there will be string objects capable of storing a combined total of 2,678 characters now sitting on the heap waiting to be garbage-collected! Clearly, if you use strings to do text processing extensively, your applications will run into severe performance problems.

To address this kind of issue, Microsoft has supplied the `System.Text.StringBuilder` class. `StringBuilder` is not as powerful as `String` in terms of the number of methods it supports. The processing you can do on a `StringBuilder` is limited to substitutions and appending or removing text from strings. However, it works in a much more efficient way.

When you construct a string using the `String` class, just enough memory is allocated to hold the string. The `StringBuilder`, however, normally allocates more memory than is actually needed. You, as a developer, have the option to indicate how much memory the `StringBuilder` should allocate, but if you do not, the amount will default to some value that depends on the size of the string that the `StringBuilder` instance is initialized with. The `StringBuilder` class has two main properties:

- ❑   `Length`, which indicates the length of the string that it actually contains
- ❑   `Capacity`, which indicates the maximum length of the string in the memory allocation

Any modifications to the string take place within the block of memory assigned to the `StringBuilder` instance, which makes appending substrings and replacing individual characters within strings very efficient. Removing or inserting substrings is inevitably still inefficient because it means that the following part of the string has to be moved. Only if you perform some operation that exceeds the capacity of the string is it necessary to allocate new memory and possibly move the entire contained string. In adding extra capacity, based on our experiments the `StringBuilder` appears to double its capacity if it detects the capacity has been exceeded and no new value for the capacity has been set.

For example, if you use a `StringBuilder` object to construct the original greeting string, you might write this code:

```
StringBuilder greetingBuilder =
    new StringBuilder("Hello from all the guys at Wrox Press. ", 150);
greetingBuilder.AppendFormat("We do hope you enjoy this book as much as we enjoyed
                        writing it");
```

In order to use the StringBuilder *class, you will need a* System.Text *reference in your code.*

This code sets an initial capacity of 150 for the StringBuilder. It is always a good idea to set some capacity that covers the likely maximum length of a string, to ensure the StringBuilder does not need to relocate because its capacity was exceeded. Theoretically, you can set as large a number as you can pass in an int, although the system will probably complain that it does not have enough memory if you actually try to allocate the maximum of 2 billion characters (this is the theoretical maximum that a StringBuilder instance is in principle allowed to contain).

When the preceding code is executed, it first creates a StringBuilder object that looks like Figure 8-1.

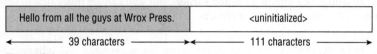

Figure 8-1

Then, on calling the AppendFormat() method, the remaining text is placed in the empty space, without the need for more memory allocation. However, the real efficiency gain from using a StringBuilder comes when you are making repeated text substitutions. For example, if you try to encrypt the text in the same way as before, you can perform the entire encryption without allocating any more memory whatsoever:

```
StringBuilder greetingBuilder =
    new StringBuilder("Hello from all the guys at Wrox Press. ", 150);
greetingBuilder.AppendFormat("We do hope you enjoy this book as much as we " +
    "enjoyed writing it");

Console.WriteLine("Not Encoded:\n" + greetingBuilder);

for(int i = 'z'; i>='a' ; i--)
{
    char old1 = (char)i;
    char new1 = (char)(i+1);
    greetingBuilder = greetingBuilder.Replace(old1, new1);
}

for(int i = 'Z'; i>='A' ; i--)
{
    char old1 = (char)i;
    char new1 = (char)(i+1);
    greetingBuilder = greetingBuilder.Replace(old1, new1);
}

Console.WriteLine("Encoded:\n" + greetingBuilder);
```

This code uses the StringBuilder.Replace() method, which does the same thing as String.Replace(), but without copying the string in the process. The total memory allocated to hold strings in the preceding code is 150 characters for the StringBuilder instance, as well as the memory allocated during the string operations performed internally in the final Console.WriteLine() statement.

Normally, you will want to use `StringBuilder` to perform any manipulation of strings and `String` to store or display the final result.

StringBuilder Members

You have seen a demonstration of one constructor of `StringBuilder`, which takes an initial string and capacity as its parameters. There are others. For example, you can supply only a string:

```
StringBuilder sb = new StringBuilder("Hello");
```

Or you can create an empty `StringBuilder` with a given capacity:

```
StringBuilder sb = new StringBuilder(20);
```

Apart from the `Length` and `Capacity` properties, there is a read-only `MaxCapacity` property that indicates the limit to which a given `StringBuilder` instance is allowed to grow. By default, this is given by `int.MaxValue` (roughly 2 billion, as noted earlier), but you can set this value to something lower when you construct the `StringBuilder` object:

```
// This will both set initial capacity to 100, but the max will be 500.
// Hence, this StringBuilder can never grow to more than 500 characters,
// otherwise it will raise exception if you try to do that.
StringBuilder sb = new StringBuilder(100, 500);
```

You can also explicitly set the capacity at any time, though an exception will be raised if you set it to a value less than the current length of the string or a value that exceeds the maximum capacity:

```
StringBuilder sb = new StringBuilder("Hello");
sb.Capacity = 100;
```

The following table lists the main `StringBuilder` methods.

Method	Purpose
Append()	Appends a string to the current string
AppendFormat()	Appends a string that has been worked out from a format specifier
Insert()	Inserts a substring into the current string
Remove()	Removes characters from the current string
Replace()	Replaces all occurrences of a character with another character or a substring with another substring in the current string
ToString()	Returns the current string cast to a `System.String` object (overridden from `System.Object`)

Several overloads of many of these methods exist.

> `AppendFormat()` *is actually the method that is ultimately called when you call* `Console.WriteLine()`, *which has responsibility for working out what all the format expressions like* `{0:D}` *should be replaced with. This method is examined in the next section.*

There is no cast (either implicit or explicit) from `StringBuilder` to `String`. If you want to output the contents of a `StringBuilder` as a `String`, you must use the `ToString()` method.

Now that you have been introduced to the `StringBuilder` class and have learned some of the ways in which you can use it to increase performance, you should be aware that this class will not always give you the increased performance that you are looking for. Basically, the `StringBuilder` class should be used when you are manipulating multiple strings. However, if you are just doing something as simple as concatenating two strings, you will find that `System.String` will be better-performing.

Format Strings

So far, a large number of classes and structs have been written for the code samples presented in this book, and they have normally implemented a `ToString()` method in order to be able to display the contents of a given variable. However, quite often users might want the contents of a variable to be displayed in different, often culture- and locale-dependent, ways. The .NET base class, `System.DateTime`, provides the most obvious example of this. For example, you might want to display the same date as 10 June 2008, 10 Jun 2008, 6/10/08 (USA), 10/6/08 (UK), or 10.06.2008 (Germany).

Similarly, the `Vector` struct in Chapter 6, "Operators and Casts" implements the `Vector.ToString()` method to display the vector in the format `(4, 56, 8)`. There is, however, another very common way of writing vectors, in which this vector would appear as `4i + 56j + 8k`. If you want the classes that you write to be user-friendly, they need to support the facility to display their string representations in any of the formats that users are likely to want to use. The .NET runtime defines a standard way in which this should be done: the `IFormattable` interface. Showing how to add this important feature to your classes and structs is the subject of this section.

As you probably know, you need to specify the format in which you want a variable displayed when you call `Console.WriteLine()`. Therefore, this section uses this method as an example, although most of the discussion applies to any situation in which you want to format a string. For example, if you want to display the value of a variable in a list box or text box, you will normally use the `String.Format()` method to obtain the appropriate string representation of the variable. However, the actual format specifiers you use to request a particular format are identical to those passed to `Console.WriteLine()`. Hence, you will focus on `Console.WriteLine()` as an example. You start by examining what actually happens when you supply a format string to a primitive type, and from this, you will see how you can plug format specifiers for your own classes and structs into the process.

Chapter 2, "C# Basics," uses format strings in `Console.Write()` and `Console.WriteLine()` like this:

```
double d = 13.45;
int i = 45;
Console.WriteLine("The double is {0,10:E} and the int contains {1}", d, i);
```

The format string itself consists mostly of the text to be displayed, but wherever there is a variable to be formatted, its index in the parameter list appears in braces. You might also include other information inside the braces concerning the format of that item. For example, you can include:

❑   The number of characters to be occupied by the representation of the item, prefixed by a comma. A negative number indicates that the item should be left-justified, whereas a positive number indicates that it should be right-justified. If the item actually occupies more characters than have been requested, it will still appear in full.

❑   A format specifier, preceded by a colon. This indicates how you want the item to be formatted. For example, you can indicate whether you want a number to be formatted as a currency or displayed in scientific notation.

The following table lists the common format specifiers for the numeric types, which were briefly discussed in Chapter 2.

Specifier	Applies To	Meaning	Example
C	Numeric types	Locale-specific monetary value	$4834.50 (USA) £4834.50 (UK)
D	Integer types only	General integer	4834
E	Numeric types	Scientific notation	4.834E+003
F	Numeric types	Fixed-point decimal	4384.50
G	Numeric types	General number	4384.5
N	Numeric types	Common locale-specific format for numbers	4,384.50 (UK/USA) | 4 384,50 (continental Europe)
P	Numeric types	Percentage notation	432,000.00%
X	Integer types only	Hexadecimal format	1120 (If you want to display 0x1120, you will have to write out the 0x separately)

If you want an integer to be padded with zeros, you can use the format specifier 0 (zero) repeated as many times as the number length is required. For example, the format specifier 0000 will cause 3 to be displayed as 0003, and 99 to be displayed as 0099, and so on.

It is not possible to give a complete list because other data types can add their own specifiers. Showing how to define your own specifiers for your own classes is the aim of this section.

How the String Is Formatted

As an example of how strings are formatted, if you execute the following statement:

```
Console.WriteLine("The double is {0,10:E} and the int contains {1}", d, i);
```

`Console.WriteLine()` just passes the entire set of parameters to the static method, `String.Format()`. This is the same method that you would call if you wanted to format these values for use in a string to be displayed in a text box, for example. The implementation of the three-parameter overload of `WriteLine()` basically does this:

```
// Likely implementation of Console.WriteLine()

public void WriteLine(string format, object arg0, object arg1)
{
    Console.WriteLine(string.Format(format, arg0, arg1));
}
```

The one-parameter overload of this method, which is in turn called in the preceding code sample, simply writes out the contents of the string it has been passed, without doing any further formatting on it.

`String.Format()` now needs to construct the final string by replacing each format specifier with a suitable string representation of the corresponding object. However, as you saw earlier, for this process of building up a string, you need a `StringBuilder` instance rather than a `string` instance. In this example, a `StringBuilder` instance is created and initialized with the first known portion of the string, the text "The double is". Next, the `StringBuilder.AppendFormat()` method is called, passing in the first format specifier, `{0,10:E}`, as well as the associated object, `double`, in order to add the string representation of this object to the string object being constructed. This process continues with `StringBuilder.Append()` and `StringBuilder.AppendFormat()` being called repeatedly until the entire formatted string has been obtained.

Now comes the interesting part: `StringBuilder.AppendFormat()` has to figure out how to format the object. First, it probes the object to find out whether it implements an interface in the `System` namespace called `IFormattable`. You can determine this quite simply by trying to cast an object to this interface and seeing whether the cast succeeds, or by using the C# `is` keyword. If this test fails, `AppendFormat()` calls the object's `ToString()` method, which all objects either inherit from `System.Object` or override. This is exactly what happens here because none of the classes written so far has implemented this interface. That is why the overrides of `Object.ToString()` have been sufficient to allow the structs and classes from earlier chapters such as `Vector` to get displayed in `Console.WriteLine()` statements.

However, all of the predefined primitive numeric types do implement this interface, which means that for those types, and in particular for `double` and `int` in the example, the basic `ToString()` method inherited from `System.Object` will not be called. To understand what happens instead, you need to examine the `IFormattable` interface.

`IFormattable` defines just one method, which is also called `ToString()`. However, this method takes two parameters as opposed to the `System.Object` version, which doesn't take any parameters. The following code shows the definition of `IFormattable`:

```
interface IFormattable
{
    string ToString(string format, IFormatProvider formatProvider);
}
```

The first parameter that this overload of `ToString()` expects is a string that specifies the requested format. In other words, it is the specifier portion of the string that appears inside the braces (`{}`) in the string originally passed to `Console.WriteLine()` or `String.Format()`. For example, in the example the original statement was:

```
Console.WriteLine("The double is {0,10:E} and the int contains {1}", d, i);
```

Hence, when evaluating the first specifier, `{0,10:E}`, this overload will be called against the `double` variable, d, and the first parameter passed to it will be E. `StringBuilder.AppendFormat()` will pass in here the text that appears after the colon in the appropriate format specifier from the original string.

We won't worry about the second `ToString()` parameter in this book. It is a reference to an object that implements the `IFormatProvider` interface. This interface gives further information that `ToString()` might need to consider when formatting the object, such as culture-specific details (a .NET culture is similar to a Windows locale; if you are formatting currencies or dates, you need this information). If you are calling this `ToString()` overload directly from your source code, you might want to supply such an object. However, `StringBuilder.AppendFormat()` passes in `null` for this parameter. If `formatProvider` is `null`, then `ToString()` is expected to use the culture specified in the system settings.

Getting back to the example, the first item you want to format is a `double`, for which you are requesting exponential notation, with the format specifier E. The `StringBuilder.AppendFormat()` method establishes that the `double` does implement `IFormattable`, and will therefore call the two-parameter `ToString()` overload, passing it the string E for the first parameter and `null` for the second parameter. It is now up to the `double`'s implementation of this method to return the string representation of the `double` in the appropriate format, taking into account the requested format and the current culture. `StringBuilder.AppendFormat()` will then sort out padding the returned string with spaces, if necessary, to fill the 10 characters the format string specified.

The next object to be formatted is an `int`, for which you are not requesting any particular format (the format specifier was simply `{1}`). With no format requested, `StringBuilder.AppendFormat()` passes in a null reference for the format string. The two-parameter overload of `int.ToString()` is expected to respond appropriately. No format has been specifically requested; therefore, it will call the no-parameter `ToString()` method.

This entire string formatting process is summarized in Figure 8-2.

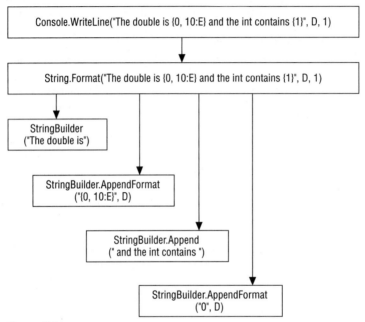

Figure 8-2

The FormattableVector Example

Now that you know how format strings are constructed, in this section you extend the `Vector` example from Chapter 6, so that you can format vectors in a variety of ways. You can download the code for this example from www.wrox.com. With your new knowledge of the principles involved now in hand, you will discover that the actual coding is quite simple. All you need to do is implement `IFormattable` and supply an implementation of the `ToString()` overload defined by that interface.

The format specifiers you are going to support are:

❑   N — Should be interpreted as a request to supply a quantity known as the Norm of the Vector. This is just the sum of squares of its components, which for mathematics buffs happens to be equal to the square of the length of the Vector, and is usually displayed between double vertical bars, like this: `||34.5||`.

❑   VE — Should be interpreted as a request to display each component in scientific format, just as the specifier E applied to a `double` indicates (`2.3E+01, 4.5E+02, 1.0E+00`).

❏ IJK — Should be interpreted as a request to display the vector in the form 23i + 450j + 1k.

❏ Anything else should simply return the default representation of the Vector (23, 450, 1.0).

To keep things simple, you are not going to implement any option to display the vector in combined IJK and scientific format. You will, however, make sure you test the specifier in a case-insensitive way, so that you allow ijk instead of IJK. Note that it is entirely up to you which strings you use to indicate the format specifiers.

To achieve this, you first modify the declaration of Vector so it implements IFormattable:

```
struct Vector : IFormattable
{
    public double x, y, z;

    // Beginning part of Vector
```

Now you add your implementation of the two-parameter ToString() overload:

```
public string ToString(string format, IFormatProvider formatProvider)
{
    if (format == null)
    {
        return ToString();
    }

    string formatUpper = format.ToUpper();

    switch (formatUpper)
    {
        case "N":
            return "|| " + Norm().ToString() + " ||";
        case "VE":
            return String.Format("( {0:E}, {1:E}, {2:E} )", x, y, z);
        case "IJK":
            StringBuilder sb = new StringBuilder(x.ToString(), 30);
            sb.AppendFormat(" i + ");
            sb.AppendFormat(y.ToString());
            sb.AppendFormat(" j + ");
            sb.AppendFormat(z.ToString());
            sb.AppendFormat(" k");
            return sb.ToString();
        default:
            return ToString();
    }
}
```

That is all you have to do! Notice how you take the precaution of checking whether format is null before you call any methods against this parameter — you want this method to be as robust as reasonably possible. The format specifiers for all the primitive types are case-insensitive, so that is the behavior that other developers are going to expect from your class, too. For the format specifier VE, you need each component to be formatted in scientific notation, so you just use String.Format() again to achieve this. The fields x, y, and z are all doubles. For the case of the IJK format specifier, there are quite a few substrings to be added to the string, so you use a StringBuilder object to improve performance.

For completeness, you also reproduce the no-parameter `ToString()` overload developed earlier:

```
public override string ToString()
{
    return "( " + x + " , " + y + " , " + z + " )";
}
```

Finally, you need to add a `Norm()` method that computes the square (norm) of the vector because you didn't actually supply this method when you developed the `Vector` struct:

```
public double Norm()
{
    return x*x + y*y + z*z;
}
```

Now you can try your formattable vector with some suitable test code:

```
static void Main()
{
    Vector v1 = new Vector(1,32,5);
    Vector v2 = new Vector(845.4, 54.3, -7.8);
    Console.WriteLine("\nIn IJK format,\nv1 is {0,30:IJK}\nv2 is {1,30:IJK}",
                      v1, v2);
    Console.WriteLine("\nIn default format,\nv1 is {0,30}\nv2 is {1,30}", v1, v2);
    Console.WriteLine("\nIn VE format\nv1 is {0,30:VE}\nv2 is {1,30:VE}", v1, v2);
    Console.WriteLine("\nNorms are:\nv1 is {0,20:N}\nv2 is {1,20:N}", v1, v2);
}
```

The result of running this sample is this:

```
FormattableVector
In IJK format,
v1 is                  1 i + 32 j + 5 k
v2 is          845.4 i + 54.3 j + -7.8 k

In default format,
v1 is                  ( 1 , 32 , 5 )
v2 is          ( 845.4 , 54.3 , -7.8 )

In VE format
v1 is ( 1.000000E+000, 3.200000E+001, 5.000000E+000 )
v2 is ( 8.454000E+002, 5.430000E+001, -7.800000E+000 )

Norms are:
v1 is                || 1050 ||
v2 is          || 717710.49 ||
```

This shows that your custom specifiers are being picked up correctly.

Regular Expressions

Regular expressions are part of those small technology areas that are incredibly useful in a wide range of programs, yet rarely used among developers. You can think of regular expressions as a mini-programming language with one specific purpose: to locate substrings within a large string expression. It is not a new technology; it originated in the Unix environment and is commonly used with the Perl programming language. Microsoft ported it onto Windows, where up until now it has been used mostly with scripting languages. Today, regular expressions are, however, supported by a number of .NET classes in the namespace System.Text.RegularExpressions. You can also find the use of regular expressions in various parts of the .NET Framework. For instance, you will find that they are used within the ASP.NET Validation server controls.

If you are not familiar with the regular expressions language, this section introduces both regular expressions and their related .NET classes. If you are already familiar with regular expressions, you will probably want to just skim through this section to pick out the references to the .NET base classes. You might like to know that the .NET regular expression engine is designed to be mostly compatible with Perl 5 regular expressions, although it has a few extra features.

Introduction to Regular Expressions

The regular expressions language is designed specifically for string processing. It contains two features:

❑ A set of *escape codes* for identifying specific types of characters. You will be familiar with the use of the * character to represent any substring in DOS expressions. (For example, the DOS command Dir Re* lists the files with names beginning with Re.) Regular expressions use many sequences like this to represent items such as *any one character, a word break, one optional character,* and so on.

❑ A system for grouping parts of substrings and intermediate results during a search operation.

With regular expressions, you can perform quite sophisticated and high-level operations on strings. For example, you can:

❑ Identify (and perhaps either flag or remove) all repeated words in a string (for example, "The computer books books" to "The computer books")

❑ Convert all words to title case (for example, "this is a Title" to "This Is A Title")

❑ Convert all words longer than three characters to title case (for example, "this is a Title" to "This is a Title")

❑ Ensure that sentences are properly capitalized

❑ Separate the various elements of a URI (for example, given http://www.wrox.com, extract the protocol, computer name, file name, and so on)

Of course, all of these tasks can be performed in C# using the various methods on System.String and System.Text.StringBuilder. However, in some cases, this would require writing a fair amount of C# code. If you use regular expressions, this code can normally be compressed to just a couple of lines. Essentially, you instantiate a System.Text.RegularExpressions.RegEx object (or, even simpler, invoke a static RegEx() method), pass it the string to be processed, and pass in a regular expression (a string containing the instructions in the regular expressions language), and you're done.

A regular expression string looks at first sight rather like a regular string, but interspersed with escape sequences and other characters that have a special meaning. For example, the sequence \b indicates the beginning or end of a word (a word boundary), so if you wanted to indicate you were looking for the characters th at the beginning of a word, you would search for the regular expression, \bth (that is, the sequence word boundary-t-h). If you wanted to search for all occurrences of th at the end of a word, you would write th\b (the sequence t-h-word boundary). However, regular expressions are much more sophisticated than that and include, for example, facilities to store portions of text that are found in a search operation. This section merely scratches the surface of the power of regular expressions.

For more on regular expressions, please review the book Beginning Regular Expressions *(ISBN 978-0-7645-7489-4).*

Suppose your application needed to convert U.S. phone numbers to an international format. In the United States, the phone numbers have this format: 314-123-1234, which is often written as (314) 123-1234. When converting this national format to an international format you have to include +1 (the country code of the United States) and add brackets around the area code: +1 (314) 123-1234. As find-and-replace operations go, that's not too complicated. It would still require some coding effort if you were going to use the `String` class for this purpose (which would mean that you would have to write your code using the methods available from `System.String`). The regular expressions language allows you to construct a short string that achieves the same result.

This section is intended only as a very simple example, so it concentrates on searching strings to identify certain substrings, not on modifying them.

The RegularExpressionsPlayaround Example

For the rest of this section, you develop a short example, called RegularExpressionsPlayaround, that illustrates some of the features of regular expressions and how to use the .NET regular expressions engine in C# by performing and displaying the results of some searches. The text you are going to use as your sample document is an introduction to a Wrox Press book on ASP.NET (*Professional ASP.NET 3.5: in C# and VB*, ISBN 978-0-470-18757-9).

```
string Text =
@"This comprehensive compendium provides a broad and thorough investigation of all
aspects of programming with ASP.NET. Entirely revised and updated for the 3.5
Release of .NET, this book will give you the information you need to master ASP.NET
and build a dynamic, successful, enterprise Web application.";
```

This code is valid C# code, despite all the line breaks. It nicely illustrates the utility of verbatim strings that are prefixed by the @ symbol.

This text is referred to as the *input string*. To get your bearings and get used to the regular expressions .NET classes, you start with a basic plain text search that does not feature any escape sequences or regular expression commands. Suppose that you want to find all occurrences of the string `ion`. This search string is referred to as the *pattern*. Using regular expressions and the `Text` variable declared previously, you can write this:

```
string Pattern = "ion";
MatchCollection Matches = Regex.Matches(Text, Pattern,
                                  RegexOptions.IgnoreCase |
                                  RegexOptions.ExplicitCapture);
foreach (Match NextMatch in Matches)
{
    Console.WriteLine(NextMatch.Index);
}
```

This code uses the static method `Matches()` of the `Regex` class in the `System.Text.RegularExpressions` namespace. This method takes as parameters some input text, a pattern, and a set of optional flags taken from the `RegexOptions` enumeration. In this case, you have specified that all searching should be case insensitive. The other flag, `ExplicitCapture`, modifies the way that the match is collected in a way that, for your purposes, makes the search a bit more efficient — you see why this is later (although it does have other uses that we won't explore here). `Matches()` returns a reference to a `MatchCollection` object. A *match* is the technical term for the results of finding an instance of the pattern in the expression. It is represented by the class `System.Text.RegularExpressions.Match`. Therefore, you return a `MatchCollection` that contains all the matches, each represented by a `Match` object. In the preceding code, you simply iterate over the collection and use the `Index` property of the `Match` class, which returns the index in the input text of where the match was found. Running this code results in three matches. The following table details some of the `RegexOptions` enumerations.

Member Name	Description
CultureInvariant	Specifies that the culture of the string is ignored
ExplicitCapture	Modifies the way the match is collected by making sure that valid captures are the ones that are explicitly named
IgnoreCase	Ignores the case of the string that is input
IgnorePatternWhitespace	Removes unescaped whitespace from the string and enables comments that are specified with the pound or hash sign
Multiline	Changes the characters ^ and $ so that they are applied to the beginning and end of each line and not just to the beginning and end of the entire string
RightToLeft	Causes the inputted string to be read from right to left instead of the default left to right (ideal for some Asian and other languages that are read in this direction)
Singleline	Specifies a single-line mode where the meaning of the dot (.) is changed to match every character

So far, nothing is really new from the preceding example apart from some .NET base classes. However, the power of regular expressions really comes from that pattern string. The reason is that the pattern string does not have to contain only plain text. As hinted earlier, it can also contain what are known as *meta-characters*, which are special characters that give commands, as well as escape sequences, which work in much the same way as C# escape sequences. They are characters preceded by a backslash (\) and have special meanings.

For example, suppose that you wanted to find words beginning with n. You could use the escape sequence \b, which indicates a word boundary (a word boundary is just a point where an alphanumeric character precedes or follows a whitespace character or punctuation symbol). You would write this:

```
string Pattern = @"\bn";
MatchCollection Matches = Regex.Matches(Text, Pattern,
                               RegexOptions.IgnoreCase |
                               RegexOptions.ExplicitCapture);
```

Notice the @ character in front of the string. You want the \b to be passed to the .NET regular expressions engine at runtime — you don't want the backslash intercepted by a well-meaning C# compiler that thinks it's an escape sequence intended for itself! If you want to find words ending with the sequence ion, you write this:

```
string Pattern = @"ion\b";
```

If you want to find all words beginning with the letter a and ending with the sequence ion (which has as its only match the word *application* in the example), you will have to put a bit more thought into your code. You clearly need a pattern that begins with \ba and ends with ion\b, but what goes in the middle? You need to somehow tell the application that between the a and the ion there can be any number of characters as long as none of them are whitespace. In fact, the correct pattern looks like this:

```
string Pattern = @"\ba\S*ion\b";
```

Eventually you will get used to seeing weird sequences of characters like this when working with regular expressions. It actually works quite logically. The escape sequence \S indicates any character that is not a whitespace character. The * is called a *quantifier*. It means that the preceding character can be repeated any number of times, including zero times. The sequence \S* means *any number of characters as long as they are not whitespace characters*. The preceding pattern will, therefore, match any single word that begins with a and ends with ion.

The following table lists some of the main special characters or escape sequences that you can use. It is not comprehensive, but a fuller list is available in the MSDN documentation.

Symbol	Meaning	Example	Matches
^	Beginning of input text	^B	B, but only if first character in text
$	End of input text	X$	X, but only if last character in text
.	Any single character except the new-line character (\n)	i.ation	isation, ization
*	Preceding character may be repeated zero or more times	ra*t	rt, rat, raat, raaat, and so on
+	Preceding character may be repeated one or more times	ra+t	rat, raat, raaat and so on, but not rt
?	Preceding character may be repeated zero or one time	ra?t	rt and rat only
\s	Any whitespace character	\sa	[space]a, \ta, \na (\t and \n have the same meanings as in C#)
\S	Any character that isn't a whitespace	\SF	aF, rF, cF, but not \tf
\b	Word boundary	ion\b	Any word ending in ion
\B	Any position that isn't a word boundary	\BX\B	Any X in the middle of a word

If you want to search for one of the meta-characters, you can do so by escaping the corresponding character with a backslash. For example, . (a single period) means any single character other than the newline character, whereas \. means a dot.

You can request a match that contains alternative characters by enclosing them in square brackets. For example, [1|c] means one character that can be either 1 or c. If you wanted to search for any occurrence of the words map or man, you would use the sequence ma[n|p]. Within the square brackets, you can also indicate a range, for example [a-z] to indicate any single lowercase letter, [A-E] to indicate any uppercase letter between A and E (including the letters A and E themselves), or [0-9] to represent a single digit. If you want to search for an integer (that is, a sequence that contains only the characters 0 through 9), you could write [0-9]+ (note the use of the + character to indicate there must be at least one such digit, but there may be more than one — so this would match 9, 83, 854, and so on).

Displaying Results

In this section, you code the `RegularExpressionsPlayaround` example, so you can get a feel for how the regular expressions work.

The core of the example is a method called `WriteMatches()`, which writes out all the matches from a `MatchCollection` in a more detailed format. For each match, it displays the index of where the match was found in the input string, the string of the match, and a slightly longer string, which consists of the match plus up to ten surrounding characters from the input text — up to five characters before the match and up to five afterward. (It is fewer than five characters if the match occurred within five characters of the beginning or end of the input text.) In other words, a match on the word `messaging` that occurs near the end of the input text quoted earlier would display `and messaging of d` (five characters before and after the match), but a match on the final word `data` would display `g of data.` (only one character after the match), because after that you get to the end of the string. This longer string lets you see more clearly where the regular expression locates the match:

```
static void WriteMatches(string text, MatchCollection matches)
{
    Console.WriteLine("Original text was: \n\n" + text + "\n");
    Console.WriteLine("No. of matches: " + matches.Count);
    foreach (Match nextMatch in matches)
    {
        int Index = nextMatch.Index;
        string result = nextMatch.ToString();
        int charsBefore = (Index < 5) ? Index : 5;
        int fromEnd = text.Length - Index - result.Length;
        int charsAfter = (fromEnd < 5) ? fromEnd : 5;
        int charsToDisplay = charsBefore + charsAfter + result.Length;

        Console.WriteLine("Index: {0}, \tString: {1}, \t{2}",
            Index, result,
            text.Substring(Index - charsBefore, charsToDisplay));
    }
}
```

The bulk of the processing in this method is devoted to the logic of figuring out how many characters in the longer substring it can display without overrunning the beginning or end of the input text. Note that you use another property on the `Match` object, `Value`, which contains the string identified for the match. Other than that, `RegularExpressionsPlayaround` simply contains a number of methods with names like `Find1`, `Find2`, and so on, which perform some of the searches based on the examples in this section. For example, `Find2` looks for any string that contains a at the beginning of a word:

```
static void Find2()
{
    string text = @"This comprehensive compendium provides a broad and thorough
        investigation of all aspects of programming with ASP.NET. Entirely revised and
        updated for the 3.5 Release of .NET, this book will give you the information
        you need to master ASP.NET and build a dynamic, successful, enterprise Web
        application.";
    string pattern = @"\ba";
    MatchCollection matches = Regex.Matches(text, pattern,
        RegexOptions.IgnoreCase);
    WriteMatches(text, matches);
}
```

Along with this comes a simple `Main()` method that you can edit to select one of the `Find<n>()` methods:

```
static void Main()
{
    Find1();
    Console.ReadLine();
}
```

The code also needs to make use of the `RegularExpressions` namespace:

```
using System;
using System.Text.RegularExpressions;
```

Running the example with the `Find1()` method shown previously gives these results:

```
RegularExpressionsPlayaround
Original text was:

This comprehensive compendium provides a broad and thorough investigation of all
aspects of programming with ASP.NET. Entirely revised and updated for the 3.5
Release of .NET, this book will give you the information you need to master ASP.NET
and build a dynamic, successful, enterprise Web application.

No. of matches: 1
Index: 291,      String: application,      Web application.
```

Matches, Groups, and Captures

One nice feature of regular expressions is that you can group characters. It works the same way as compound statements in C#. In C#, you can group any number of statements by putting them in braces, and the result is treated as one compound statement. In regular expression patterns, you can group any characters (including meta-characters and escape sequences), and the result is treated as a single character. The only difference is that you use parentheses instead of braces. The resultant sequence is known as a *group*.

For example, the pattern (an) + locates any recurrences of the sequence an. The + quantifier applies only to the previous character, but because you have grouped the characters together, it now applies to repeats of an treated as a unit. This means that if you apply (an) + to the input text, bananas came to Europe late in the annals of history, the anan from bananas is identified. Yet, if you write an+, the program selects the ann from annals, as well as two separate sequences of an from bananas. The expression (an) + identifies occurrences of an, anan, ananan, and so on, whereas the expression an+ identifies occurrences of an, ann, annn, and so on.

> You might wonder why with the preceding example (an) + picks out anan from the word banana but doesn't identify either of the two occurrences of an from the same word. The rule is that matches must not overlap. If there are a couple of possibilities that would overlap, then by default the longest possible sequence will be matched.

However, groups are actually more powerful than that. By default, when you form part of the pattern into a group, you are also asking the regular expression engine to remember any matches against just that group, as well as any matches against the entire pattern. In other words, you are treating that group as a pattern to be matched and returned in its own right. This can actually be extremely useful if you want to break up strings into component parts.

For example, URIs have the format `<protocol>://<address>:<port>`, where the port is optional. An example of this is `http://www.wrox.com:4355`. Suppose that you want to extract the protocol, the address, and the port from a URI, where you know that there may or may not be whitespace (but no punctuation) immediately following the URI. You could do so using this expression:

```
\b(\S+)://(\S+)(?::(\S+))?\b
```

Here is how this expression works: First, the leading and trailing `\b` sequences ensure that you consider only portions of text that are entire words. Within that, the first group, `(\S+)://`, identifies one or more characters that don't count as whitespace, and that are followed by `://` — the `http://` at the start of an HTTP URI. The brackets cause the `http` to be stored as a group. The subsequent `(\S+)` identifies the string `www.wrox.com` in the URI. This group will end either when it encounters the end of the word (the closing `\b`) or a colon (`:`) as marked by the next group.

The next group identifies the port (`:4355`). The following `?` indicates that this group is optional in the match — if there is no `:xxxx`, this won't prevent a match from being marked. This is very important because the port number is not always specified in a URI — in fact, it is absent most of the time. However, things are a bit more complicated than that. You want to indicate that the colon might or might not appear too, but you don't want to store this colon in the group. You've achieved this by having two nested groups. The inner `(\S+)` identifies anything that follows the colon (for example, `4355`). The outer group contains the inner group preceded by the colon, and this group in turn is preceded by the sequence `?:`. This sequence indicates that the group in question should not be saved (you only want to save `4355`; you don't need `:4355` as well!). Don't get confused by the two colons following each other — the first colon is part of the `?:` sequence that says "don't save this group," and the second is text to be searched for.

If you run this pattern on the following string, you'll get one match: `http://www.wrox.com`.

```
Hey I've just found this amazing URI at http:// what was it -- oh yes
http://www.wrox.com
```

Within this match, you will find the three groups just mentioned as well as a fourth group, which represents the match itself. Theoretically, it is possible that each group itself might return no, one, or more than one match. Each of these individual matches is known as a *capture*. So, the first group, `(\S+)`, has one capture, `http`. The second group also has one capture (`www.wrox.com`). The third group, however, has no captures, because there is no port number on this URI.

Notice that the string contains a second `http://`. Although this does match up to the first group, it will not be captured by the search because the entire search expression does not match this part of the text.

There isn't space to show examples of C# code that uses groups and captures, but you should know that the .NET `RegularExpressions` classes support groups and captures, through classes known as `Group` and `Capture`. Also, the `GroupCollection` and `CaptureCollection` classes represent collections of groups and captures. The `Match` class exposes the `Groups()` method, which returns the corresponding `GroupCollection` object. The `Group` class correspondingly implements the `Captures()` method, which returns a `CaptureCollection`. The relationship between the objects is shown in Figure 8-3.

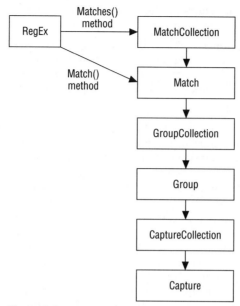

Figure 8-3

You might not want to return a `Group` object every time you just want to group some characters. A fair amount of overhead is involved in instantiating the object, which is not necessary if all you want is to group some characters as part of your search pattern. You can disable this by starting the group with the character sequence `?:` for an individual group, as was done for the URI example, or for all groups by specifying the `RegExOptions.ExplicitCaptures` flag on the `RegEx.Matches()` method, as was done in the earlier examples.

Summary

You have quite a number of available data types at your disposal when working with the .NET Framework. One of the most used types in your applications (especially applications that focus on the submission and retrieval of data) is the `string` data type. The importance of `string` is the reason that this book has a complete chapter focused on how to use the `string` data type and manipulate it in your applications.

When working with strings in the past, it was quite common to just slice and dice the strings as needed using concatenation. With the .NET Framework, you can use the `StringBuilder` class to accomplish a lot of this task with better performance than before.

Last, but hardly least, advanced string manipulation using regular expressions is an excellent tool to search through and validate your strings.

The next chapter takes a look at one of the more powerful features of C# — generics.

9

Generics

A new feature of the CLR 2.0 is the introduction of generics. With CLR 1.0, creating a flexible class or method that should use classes that are not known at compile time must be based on the `Object` class. With the `Object` class, there's no type safety during compile time. Casting is necessary. Also, using the `Object` class for value types has a performance impact.

CLR 2.0 (.NET 3.5 is based on the CLR 2.0) supports generics. With generics, the `Object` class is no longer necessary in such scenarios. Generic classes make use of generic types that are replaced with specific types as needed. This allows for type safety: the compiler complains if a specific type is not supported with the generic class.

Generics are a great feature, especially with collection classes. Most of the .NET 1.0 collection classes are based on the `Object` type. Starting with version 2.0, .NET offers collection classes that are implemented as generics.

Generics are not limited to classes; in this chapter, you also see generics with delegates, interfaces, and methods.

This chapter discusses the following:

❑ Generics overview

❑ Creating generic classes

❑ Features of generic classes

❑ Generic interfaces

❑ Generic methods

❑ Generic delegates

❑ Other generic framework types

Overview

Generics are not a completely new construct; similar concepts exist with other languages. For example, C++ templates can be compared to generics. However, there's a big difference between C++ templates and .NET generics. With C++ templates, the source code of the template is required when a template is instantiated with a specific type. Contrary to C++ templates, generics are not only a construct of the C# language; generics are defined with the CLR. This makes it possible to instantiate generics with a specific type in Visual Basic even though the generic class was defined with C#.

The following sections look into the advantages and disadvantages of generics, particularly:

❑ Performance

❑ Type safety

❑ Binary code reuse

❑ Code bloat

❑ Naming guidelines

Performance

One of the big advantages of generics is performance. In Chapter 10, you will see non-generic and generic collection classes from the namespaces `System.Collections` and `System.Collections.Generic`. Using value types with non-generic collection classes results in boxing and unboxing when the value type is converted to a reference type and vice versa.

> *Boxing and unboxing is discussed in Chapter 6, "Operators and Casts." Here is just a short refresher about these terms.*

> *Value types are stored on the stack. Reference types are stored on the heap. C# classes are reference types; structs are value types. .NET makes it easy to convert value types to reference types, and so you can use a value type everywhere an object (which is a reference type) is needed. For example, an int can be assigned to an object. The conversion from a value type to a reference type is known as boxing. Boxing happens automatically if a method requires an object as a parameter, and a value type is passed. On the other side, a boxed value type can be converted to a value type by using unboxing. With unboxing, the cast operator is required.*

The following example shows the `ArrayList` class from the namespace `System.Collections`. `ArrayList` stores objects, the `Add()` method is defined to require an object as a parameter, and so an integer type is boxed. When the values from an `ArrayList` are read, unboxing occurs when the object is converted to an integer type. This may be obvious with the cast operator that is used to assign the first element of the `ArrayList` collection to the variable `i1`, but also happens inside the `foreach` statement where the variable `i2` of type `int` is accessed:

```
ArrayList list = new ArrayList();
list.Add(44);    // boxing - convert a value type to a reference type

int i1 = (int)list[0];    // unboxing - convert a reference type to
                          // a value type

foreach (int i2 in list)
{
    Console.WriteLine(i2);    // unboxing
}
```

Boxing and unboxing are easy to use, but have a big performance impact, especially when iterating through many items.

Instead of using objects, the `List<T>` class from the namespace `System.Collections.Generic` allows you to define the type when it is used. In the example here, the generic type of the `List<T>` class is defined as `int`, so the `int` type is used inside the class that is generated dynamically from the JIT compiler. Boxing and unboxing no longer happens:

```
List<int> list = new List<int>();
list.Add(44);    // no boxing - value types are stored in the List<int>

int i1 = list[0];    // no unboxing, no cast needed

foreach (int i2 in list)
{
    Console.WriteLine(i2);
}
```

Type Safety

Another feature of generics is type safety. As with the ArrayList class, if objects are used, any type can be added to this collection. This example shows adding an integer, a string, and an object of type MyClass to the collection of type ArrayList:

```
ArrayList list = new ArrayList();
list.Add(44);
list.Add("mystring");
list.Add(new MyClass());
```

Now if this collection is iterated using the following foreach statement, which iterates using integer elements, the compiler accepts this code. However, because not all elements in the collection can be cast to an int, a runtime exception will occur:

```
foreach (int i in list)
{
    Console.WriteLine(i);
}
```

Errors should be detected as early as possible. With the generic class List<T>, the generic type T defines what types are allowed. With a definition of List<int>, only integer types can be added to the collection. The compiler doesn't compile this code because the Add() method has invalid arguments:

```
List<int> list = new List<int>();
list.Add(44);
list.Add("mystring");    // compile time error
list.Add(new MyClass());    // compile time error
```

Binary Code Reuse

Generics allow better binary code reuse. A generic class can be defined once and can be instantiated with many different types. Unlike C++ templates, it is not necessary to access the source code.

As an example, here the List<T> class from the namespace System.Collections.Generic is instantiated with an int, a string, and a MyClass type:

```
List<int> list = new List<int>();
list.Add(44);

List<string> stringList = new List<string>();
stringList.Add("mystring");

List<MyClass> myclassList = new List<MyClass>();
myClassList.Add(new MyClass());
```

Generic types can be defined in one language and used from any other .NET language.

Code Bloat

How much code is created with generics when instantiating them with different specific types?

Because a generic class definition goes into the assembly, instantiating generic classes with specific types doesn't duplicate these classes in the IL code. However, when the generic classes are compiled by the JIT compiler to native code, a new class for every specific value type is created. Reference types share all the same implementation of the same native class. This is because with reference types only a 4-byte memory address (with 32-bit systems) is needed within the generic instantiated class to reference a reference type. Value types are contained within the memory of the generic instantiated class, and because every value type can have different memory requirements, a new class for every value type is instantiated.

Naming Guidelines

If generics are used in the program, it helps when generic types can be distinguished from non-generic types. Here are naming guidelines for generic types:

- ❑ Generic type names should be prefixed with the letter T.

- ❑ If the generic type can be replaced by any class because there's no special requirement, and only one generic type is used, the character T is good as a generic type name:

```
public class List<T> { }

public class LinkedList<T> { }
```

- ❑ If there's a special requirement for a generic type (for example, it must implement an interface or derive from a base class), or if two or more generic types are used, descriptive names should be used for the type names:

```
public delegate void EventHandler<TEventArgs>(object sender, TEventArgs e);

public delegate TOutput Converter<TInput, TOutput>(TInput from);

public class SortedList<TKey, TValue> { }
```

Creating Generic Classes

First start with a normal, non-generic simplified linked list class that can contain objects of any kind, and later convert this class to a generic class.

With a linked list, one element references the next one. So, you must create a class that wraps the object inside the linked list and references the next object. The class `LinkedListNode` contains an object named `value` that is initialized with the constructor, and can be read with the `Value` property. In addition to that, the `LinkedListNode` class contains references to the next and previous elements in the list that can be accessed from properties.

```
public class LinkedListNode
{
    private object value;
    public LinkedListNode(object value)
    {
        this.value = value;
    }

    public object Value
```

```
    {
        get { return value; }
    }


    private LinkedListNode next;
    public LinkedListNode Next
    {
        get { return next; }
        internal set { next = value; }
    }

    private LinkedListNode prev;
    public LinkedListNode Prev
    {
        get { return prev; }
        internal set { prev = value; }
    }
}
```

The LinkedList class includes first and last fields of type LinkedListNode that mark the beginning and end of the list. The method AddLast() adds a new element to the end of the list. First, an object of type LinkedListNode is created. If the list is empty, the first and last fields are set to the new element; otherwise, the new element is added as the last element to the list. By implementing the GetEnumerator() method, it is possible to iterate through the list with the foreach statement. The GetEnumerator() method makes use of the yield statement for creating an enumerator type.

The yield statement is explained in Chapter 5, "Arrays."

```
public class LinkedList : IEnumerable
{
    private LinkedListNode first;
    public LinkedListNode First
    {
        get { return first; }
    }

    private LinkedListNode last;
    public LinkedListNode Last
    {
        get { return last; }
    }

    public LinkedListNode AddLast(object node)
    {
        LinkedListNode newNode = new LinkedListNode(node);
        if (first == null)
        {
            first = newNode;
            last = first;
        }
        else
```

(continued)

(continued)

```
            {
                last.Next = newNode;
                last = newNode;
            }
            return newNode;
        }

        public IEnumerator GetEnumerator()
        {
            LinkedListNode current = first;
            while (current != null)
            {
                yield return current.Value;
                current = current.Next;
            }
        }
    }
```

Now you can use the `LinkedList` class with any type. The following code segment instantiates a new
`LinkedList` object and adds two integer types and one string type. As the integer types are converted to
an object, boxing occurs as was discussed earlier. With the `foreach` statement unboxing happens. In the
`foreach` statement the elements from the list are cast to an integer, so with the third element in the list a
runtime exception occurs as casting to an `int` fails.

```
        LinkedList list1 = new LinkedList();
        list1.AddLast(2);
        list1.AddLast(4);
        list1.AddLast("6");

        foreach (int i in list1)
        {
            Console.WriteLine(i);
        }
```

Now let's make a generic version of the linked list. A generic class is defined similarly to a normal class
with the generic type declaration. The generic type can then be used within the class as a field member,
or with parameter types of methods. The class `LinkedListNode` is declared with a generic type `T`. The
field `value` is now type `T` instead of `object`; the constructor and property `Value` are changed as well to
accept and return an object of type `T`. A generic type can also be returned and set, so the properties `Next`
and `Prev` are now of type `LinkedListNode<T>`:

```
    public class LinkedListNode<T>
    {
        private T value;
        public LinkedListNode(T value)
        {
            this.value = value;
        }

        public T Value
        {
            get { return value; }
        }

        private LinkedListNode<T> next;
```

```
    public LinkedListNode<T> Next
    {
        get { return next; }
        internal set { next = value; }
    }

    private LinkedListNode<T> prev;
    public LinkedListNode<T> Prev
    {
        get { return prev; }
        internal set { prev = value; }
    }
}
```

In the following code the class LinkedList is changed to a generic class as well. LinkedList<T> contains LinkedListNode<T> elements. The type T from the LinkedList defines the type T of the containing fields first and last. The method AddLast() now accepts a parameter of type T and instantiates an object of LinkedListNode<T>.

Beside the interface IEnumerable, a generic version is also available: IEnumerable<T>. IEnumerable<T> derives from IEnumerable and adds the GetEnumerator() method that returns IEnumerator<T>. LinkedList<T> implements the generic interface IEnumerable<T>.

Enumerations and the interfaces IEnumerable *and* IEnumerator *are discussed in Chapter 5,* "Arrays."

```
    public class LinkedList<T> : IEnumerable<T>
    {
        private LinkedListNode<T> first;
        public LinkedListNode<T> First
        {
            get { return first; }
        }

        private LinkedListNode<T> last;
        public LinkedListNode<T> Last
        {
            get { return last; }
        }

        public LinkedListNode<T> AddLast(T node)
        {
            LinkedListNode<T> newNode = new LinkedListNode<T>(node);
            if (first == null)
            {
                first = newNode;
                last = first;
            }
            else
            {
                last.Next = newNode;
                last = newNode;
            }
```

(continued)

(continued)

```
            return newNode;
        }

        public IEnumerator<T> GetEnumerator()
        {
            LinkedListNode<T> current = first;

            while (current != null)
            {
                yield return current.Value;
                current = current.Next;
            }
        }

        IEnumerator IEnumerable.GetEnumerator()
        {
            return GetEnumerator();
        }
    }
```

Using the generic `LinkedList<T>`, you can instantiate it with an `int` type, and there's no boxing. Also, you get a compiler error if you don't pass an `int` with the method `AddLast()`. Using the generic `IEnumerable<T>`, the `foreach` statement is also type-safe, and you get a compiler error if that variable in the `foreach` statement is not an `int`.

```
            LinkedList<int> list2 = new LinkedList<int>();
            list2.AddLast(1);
            list2.AddLast(3);
            list2.AddLast(5);

            foreach (int i in list2)
            {
                Console.WriteLine(i);
            }
```

Similarly, you can use the generic `LinkedList<T>` with a `string` type and pass strings to the `AddLast()` method:

```
            LinkedList<string> list3 = new LinkedList<string>();
            list3.AddLast("2");
            list3.AddLast("four");
            list3.AddLast("foo");

            foreach (string s in list3)
            {
                Console.WriteLine(s);
            }
```

> Every class that deals with the object type is a possible candidate for a generic implementation. Also, if classes make use of hierarchies, generics can be very helpful in making casting unnecessary.

Generic Classes' Features

When creating generic classes, you might need some more C# keywords. For example, it is not possible to assign null to a generic type. In this case, the keyword default can be used. If the generic type does not require the features of the Object class, but you need to invoke some specific methods in the generic class, you can define constraints.

This section discusses the following topics:

- ❑ Default Values
- ❑ Constraints
- ❑ Inheritance
- ❑ Static members

Let's start this example with a generic document manager. The document manager is used to read and write documents from a queue. Start by creating a new Console project named DocumentManager and add the class DocumentManager<T>. The method AddDocument() adds a document to the queue. The read-only property IsDocumentAvailable returns true if the queue is not empty.

```
using System;
using System.Collections.Generic;

namespace Wrox.ProCSharp.Generics
{
    public class DocumentManager<T>
    {
        private readonly Queue<T> documentQueue = new Queue<T>();

        public void AddDocument(T doc)
        {
            lock (this)
            {
                documentQueue.Enqueue(doc);
            }
        }

        public bool IsDocumentAvailable
        {
            get { return documentQueue.Count > 0; }
        }
    }
}
```

Default Values

Now you add a GetDocument() method to the DocumentManager<T> class. Inside this method the type T should be assigned to null. However, it is not possible to assign null to generic types. The reason is that a generic type can also be instantiated as a value type, and null is allowed only with reference types. To circumvent this problem, you can use the default keyword. With the default keyword, null is assigned to reference types and 0 is assigned to value types.

```
public T GetDocument()
{
    T doc = default(T);
    lock (this)
    {
        doc = documentQueue.Dequeue();
    }
    return doc;
}
```

The default *keyword has multiple meanings depending on the context where it is used. The switch statement uses a default for defining the default case, and with generics the default is used to initialize generic types either to null or 0 depending on if it is a reference or value type.*

Constraints

If the generic class needs to invoke some methods from the generic type, you have to add constraints. With the DocumentManager<T>, all the titles of the documents should be displayed in the DisplayAllDocuments() method.

The Document class implements the interface IDocument with the properties Title and Content:

```
public interface IDocument
{
    string Title { get; set; }
    string Content { get; set; }
}

public class Document : IDocument
{
    public Document()
    {
    }

    public Document(string title, string content)
    {
        this.Title = title;
        this.Content = content;
    }

    public string Title { get; set; }
    public string Content { get; set; }
}
```

For displaying the documents with the DocumentManager<T> class, you can cast the type T to the interface IDocument to display the title:

```
public void DisplayAllDocuments()
{
    foreach (T doc in documentQueue)
    {
        Console.WriteLine(((IDocument)doc).Title);
    }
}
```

The problem is that doing a cast results in a runtime exception if the type T does not implement the interface IDocument. Instead, it would be better to define a constraint with the DocumentManager <TDocument> class that the type TDocument must implement the interface IDocument. To clarify the requirement in the name of the generic type, T is changed to TDocument. The where clause defines the requirement to implement the interface IDocument:

```
public class DocumentManager<TDocument>
    where TDocument : IDocument
{
```

This way you can write the foreach statement in such a way that the type T contains the property Title. You get support from Visual Studio IntelliSense and from the compiler:

```
public void DisplayAllDocuments()
{
    foreach (TDocument doc in documentQueue)
    {
        Console.WriteLine(doc.Title);
    }
}
```

In the Main() method the DocumentManager<T> class is instantiated with the type Document that implements the required interface IDocument. Then new documents are added and displayed, and one of the documents is retrieved:

```
static void Main()
{
    DocumentManager<Document> dm = new DocumentManager<Document>();
    dm.AddDocument(new Document("Title A", "Sample A"));
    dm.AddDocument(new Document("Title B", "Sample B"));

    dm.DisplayAllDocuments();

    if (dm.IsDocumentAvailable)
    {
        Document d = dm.GetDocument();
        Console.WriteLine(d.Content);
    }
}
```

The DocumentManager now works with any class that implements the interface IDocument.

In the sample application, you've seen an interface constraint. Generics support several constraint types:

Constraint	Description
where T : struct	With a struct constraint, type T must be a value type.
where T : class	The class constraint indicates that type T must be a reference type.
where T : IFoo	where T : IFoo specifies that type T is required to implement interface IFoo.
where T : Foo	where T : Foo specifies that type T is required to derive from base class Foo.
where T : new()	where T : new() is a constructor constraint and specifies that type T must have a default constructor.
where T1 : T2	With constraints it is also possible to specify that type T1 derives from a generic type T2. This constraint is known as *naked type constraint*.

With CLR 2.0 only constructor constraints for the default constructor can be defined. It is not possible to define a constructor constraint for other constructors.

With a generic type, you can also combine multiple constraints. The constraint where T : IFoo, new() with the MyClass<T> declaration specifies that type T implements the interface IFoo and has a default constructor:

```
public class MyClass<T>
    where T : IFoo, new()
{
    //...
```

> **One important restriction of the where clause with C# is that it's not possible to define operators that must be implemented by the generic type. Operators cannot be defined in interfaces. With the where clause, it is only possible to define base classes, interfaces, and the default constructor.**

Inheritance

The LinkedList<T> class created earlier implements the interface IEnumerable<T>:

```
public class LinkedList<T> : IEnumerable<T>
{
    //...
```

A generic type can implement a generic interface. The same is possible by deriving from a class. A generic class can be derived from a generic base class:

```
public class Base<T>
{
}

public class Derived<T> : Base<T>
{
}
```

The requirement is that the generic types of the interface must be repeated, or the type of the base class must be specified, as in this case:

```
public class Base<T>
{
}

public class Derived<T> : Base<string>
{
}
```

This way, the derived class can be a generic or non-generic class. For example, you can define an abstract generic base class that is implemented with a concrete type in the derived class. This allows you to do specialization for specific types:

```
        public abstract class Calc<T>
        {
            public abstract T Add(T x, T y);
```

```
        public abstract T Sub(T x, T y);
    }

    public class SimpleCalc : Calc<int>
    {
        public override int Add(int x, int y)
        {
            return x + y;
        }

        public override int Sub(int x, int y)
        {
            return x - y;
        }
    }
```

Static Members

Static members of generic classes require special attention. Static members of a generic class are only shared with one instantiation of the class. Let's have a look at one example. The class `StaticDemo<T>` contains the static field x:

```
public class StaticDemo<T>
{
    public static int x;
}
```

Because of using the class `StaticDemo<T>` both with a `string` type and an `int` type, two sets of static fields exist:

```
StaticDemo<string>.x = 4;
StaticDemo<int>.x = 5;
Console.WriteLine(StaticDemo<string>.x);     // writes 4
```

Generic Interfaces

Using generics, you can define interfaces that define methods with generic parameters. In the linked list sample, you've already implemented the interface `IEnumerable<T>`, which defines a `GetEnumerator()` method to return `IEnumerator<T>`. For many non-generic interfaces of .NET 1.0, new generic versions have been defined since .NET 2.0, for example `IComparable<T>`:

```
public interface IComparable<T>
{
    int CompareTo(T other);
}
```

In Chapter 5, "Arrays," the non-generic interface `IComparable` that requires an object with the `CompareTo()` method is implemented with the `Person` class to sort persons by `LastName`:

```
public class Person : IComparable
{
    public int CompareTo(object obj)
    {
        Person other = obj as Person;
        return this.lastname.CompareTo(other.LastName);
    }
//...
```

When implementing the generic version, it is no longer necessary to cast the object to a Person:

```
public class Person : IComparable<Person>
{
    public int CompareTo(Person other)
    {
        return this.LastName.CompareTo(other.LastName);
    }
    //...
```

Generic Methods

In addition to defining generic classes, it is also possible to define generic methods. With a generic method, the generic type is defined with the method declaration.

The method Swap<T> defines T as a generic type that is used for two arguments and a variable temp:

```
void Swap<T>(ref T x, ref T y)
{
    T temp;
    temp = x;
    x = y;
    y = temp;
}
```

A generic method can be invoked by assigning the generic type with the method call:

```
int i = 4;
int j = 5;
Swap<int>(ref i, ref j);
```

However, because the C# compiler can get the type of the parameters by calling the Swap method, it is not required to assign the generic type with the method call. The generic method can be invoked as simply as non-generic methods:

```
int i = 4;
int j = 5;
Swap(ref i, ref j);
```

Here's an example where a generic method is used to accumulate all elements of a collection. To show the features of generic methods, the following Account class that contains a name and a balance is used:

```
public class Account
{
    private string name;
    public string Name
    {
        get
        {
            return name;
        }
    }

    private decimal balance;
    public decimal Balance
```

```
    {
        get
        {
            return balance;
        }
    }

    public Account(string name, Decimal balance)
    {
        this.name = name;
        this.balance = balance;
    }
}
```

All the accounts where the balance should be accumulated are added to an accounts list of type List<Account>:

```
List<Account> accounts = new List<Account>();
accounts.Add(new Account("Christian", 1500));
accounts.Add(new Account("Sharon", 2200));
accounts.Add(new Account("Katie", 1800));
```

A traditional way to accumulate all Account objects is by looping through all Account objects with a foreach statement, as shown here. Because the foreach statement is using the IEnumerable interface to iterate the elements of a collection, the argument of the AccumulateSimple() method is of type IEnumerable. This way, the AccumulateSimple() method can be used with all collection classes that implement the interface IEnumerable<Account>. In the implementation of this method, the property Balance of the Account object is directly accessed:

```
public static class Algorithm
{
    public static decimal AccumulateSimple(IEnumerable<Account> e)
    {
        decimal sum = 0;
        foreach (Account a in e)
        {
            sum += a.Balance;
        }
        return sum;
    }
}
```

The AccumulateSimple() method is invoked this way:

```
decimal amount = Algorithm.AccumulateSimple(accounts);
```

The problem with the first implementation is that it works only with Account objects. This can be avoided by using a generic method.

The second version of the Accumulate() method accepts any type that implements the interface IAccount. As you've seen earlier with generic classes, generic types can be restricted with the where clause. The same clause that is used with generic classes can be used with generic methods. The parameter of the Accumulate() method is changed to IEnumerable<T>. IEnumerable<T> is a generic version of the interface IEnumerable that is implemented by the generic collection classes:

```
public static decimal Accumulate<TAccount>(IEnumerable<TAccount> coll)
    where TAccount : IAccount
{
    decimal sum = 0;

    foreach (TAccount a in coll)
    {
        sum += a.Balance;
    }
    return sum;
}
```

The `Account` class is now re-factored to implement the interface `IAccount`:

```
public class Account : IAccount
{
    //...
```

The `IAccount` interface defines the read-only properties `Balance` and `Name`:

```
public interface IAccount
{
    decimal Balance { get; }
    string Name { get; }
}
```

The new `Accumulate()` method can be invoked by defining the `Account` type as generic type parameter:

```
decimal amount = Algorithm.Accumulate<Account>(accounts);
```

Because the generic type parameter can be automatically inferred by the compiler from the parameter type of the method, it is valid to invoke the `Accumulate()` method this way:

```
decimal amount = Algorithm.Accumulate(accounts);
```

The requirement for the generic types to implement the interface `IAccount` may be too restrictive. This requirement can be changed by using generic delegates. In the next section, the `Accumulate()` method will be changed to be independent of any interface.

Generic Delegates

As discussed in Chapter 7, "Delegates and Events," delegates are type-safe references to methods. With generic delegates, the parameters of the delegate can be defined later.

The .NET Framework defines a generic `EventHandler` delegate with the second parameter of type `TEventArgs`, so it is no longer necessary to define a new delegate with every new parameter type:

```
public sealed delegate void EventHandler<TEventArgs>(object sender,
    TEventArgs e)
  where TEventArgs : EventArgs
```

Implementing Methods Called by Delegates

The method `Accumulate()` is changed to have two generic types. `TInput` is the type of the objects that are accumulated, and `TSummary` is the returned type. The first parameter of `Accumulate` is the interface

IEnumerable<T>, as it was before. The second parameter requires the Action delegate to reference a method that is invoked to accumulate all balances.

With the implementation, the method referenced by the Action delegate is now invoked for every element, and then the sum of the calculation is returned:

```
public delegate TSummary Action<TInput, TSummary>(TInput t, TSummary u);

public static TSummary Accumulate<TInput, TSummary>(
      IEnumerable<TInput> coll,
      Action<TInput, TSummary> action)
{
   TSummary sum = default(TSummary);

   foreach (TInput input in coll)
   {
      sum = action(input, sum);
   }
   return sum;
}
```

The method Accumulate() can be invoked using an anonymous method that specifies that the balance of the account should be added to the second parameter that is of type Action:

```
decimal amount = Algorithm.Accumulate<Account, decimal>(
      accounts,
      delegate(Account a, decimal d)
      { return a.Balance + d; });
```

Instead of using anonymous methods, you can use a Lambda expression to pass it to the second parameter:

```
decimal amount = Algorithm.Accumulate<Account, decimal>(
      accounts, (a, d) => a.Balance + d;);
```

Anonymous methods and Lambda expressions are explained in Chapter 7, "Delegates and Events."

If the addition of Account balances is needed more than once, it can be useful to move the functionality into a separate method, AccountAdder():

```
static decimal AccountAdder(Account a, decimal d)
{
   return a.Balance + d;
}
```

And use the address of the AccountAdder method with the Accumulate method:

```
decimal amount = Algorithm.Accumulate<Account, decimal>(
      accounts, AccountAdder);
```

The method referenced by the Action delegate can implement any logic; for example, a multiplication could be done instead of a summation.

The Accumulate() method is made more flexible with the AccumulateIf() method. With AccumulateIf(), an additional parameter of type Predicate<T> is used. The delegate Predicate<T> references the method that will be invoked to check whether the account should be part of the accumulation. In the `foreach` statement, the `action` method will be invoked only if the predicate `match` returns `true`:

```
public static TSummary AccumulateIf<TInput, TSummary>(
        IEnumerable<TInput> coll,
        Action<TInput, TSummary> action,
        Predicate<TInput> match)
{
    TSummary sum = default(TSummary);

    foreach (TInput a in coll)
    {
        if (match(a))
        {
            sum = action(a, sum);
        }
    }
    return sum;
}
```

Calling the method `AccumulateIf()` can have an implementation for the accumulation and an implementation for the predicate. Here, only the accounts with a balance higher than 2,000 are accumulated as defined by the second Lambda expression `a => a.Balance > 2000`:

```
decimal amount = Algorithm.AccumulateIf<Account, decimal>(
        accounts, (a, d) => a.Balance + d, a => a.Balance > 2000);
```

Using Generic Delegates with the Array Class

Chapter 5, "Arrays," demonstrated different sort techniques with the `Array` class by using the `IComparable` and `IComparer` interfaces. Starting with .NET 2.0, some methods of the `Array` class use generic delegate types as parameters. The following table shows these methods, the generic type, and the functionality.

Method	Generic Parameter Type	Description
Sort()	int Comparison<T> (T x, T y)	The Sort() method defines several overloads. One overload requires a parameter of type Comparison<T>. Sort() is using the method referenced by the delegate for ordering all elements in the collection.
ForEach()	void Action<T> (T obj)	The method ForEach() invokes the method referenced by the Action<T> delegate with every item in the collection.
FindAll() Find() FindLast() FindIndex() FindLastIndex()	bool Predicate<T> (T match)	The FindXXX() methods accept the Predicate<T> delegate as parameter. The method referenced by the delegate is invoked multiple times, and the elements of the collection are passed one after the other. The Find() method stops a search until the predicate returns true the first time and returns this

Method	Generic Parameter Type	Description
		element. `FindIndex()` returns the index of the first element found. `FindLast()` and `FindLastIndex()` invoke the predicate in the reversed order of the elements in the collection, and thus either return the last item or the last index. `FindAll()` returns a new list with all items where the predicate was true.
`ConvertAll()`	`TOutput Converter <TInput, TOutput> (TInput input)`	The `ConvertAll()` method invokes the `Converter<TInput, TOutput>` delegate for every element in the collection and returns a list of converted elements.
`TrueForAll()`	`bool Predicate<T> (T match)`	The method `TrueForAll()` invokes the predicate delegate for every element. If the predicate returns true for every element, `TrueForAll()` returns true as well. If the predicate returns false just for one of the elements, `TrueForAll()` returns false.

Let's get into how these methods can be used.

The `Sort()` method accepts this delegate as parameter:

```
public delegate int Comparison<T>(T x, T y);
```

This way, it is possible to sort the array by using a Lambda expression passing two `Person` objects. With an array of `Person` objects, parameter `T` is of type `Person`:

```
Person[] persons = {
    new Person("Emerson", "Fittipaldi"),
    new Person("Niki", "Lauda"),
    new Person("Ayrton", "Senna"),
    new Person("Michael", "Schumacher")
};

Array.Sort(persons, (p1, p2) => p1.FirstName.CompareTo(p2.FirstName);
```

The `Array.ForEach()` method accepts an `Action<T>` delegate as parameter to invoke the action for every element of the array:

```
public delegate void Action<T>(T obj);
```

This way, you can write every person to the console by passing the address of the method `Console.WriteLine`. One overload of the `WriteLine()` method accepts the `Object` class as parameter type. Because `Person` derives from `Object`, this fits with a `Person` array:

```
Array.ForEach(persons, Console.WriteLine);
```

The result of the `ForEach()` statement writes every person of the collection referenced by the `persons` variable to the console:

```
Emerson Fittipaldi
Niki Lauda
Ayrton Senna
Michael Schumacher
```

If more control is needed, you can pass a Lambda expression that fits the parameter defined by the delegate:

```
Array.ForEach(persons, p => Console.WriteLine("{0}", p.LastName);
```

Here, the result is the last name written to the console:

```
Fittipaldi
Lauda
Senna
Schumacher
```

The `Array.FindAll()` method requires the `Predicate<T>` delegate:

```
public delegate bool Predicate<T>(T match);
```

The `Array.FindAll()` method invokes the predicate for every element in the array and returns a new array where the predicate returns `true` for the element. In the example, `true` is returned for all `Person` objects where the `LastName` starts with the string "S":

```
Person[] sPersons = Array.FindAll(persons, p => p.LastName.StartsWith("S"));
```

Iterating through the returned collection `sPersons` to write it to the console gives this result:

```
Ayrton Senna
Michael Schumacher
```

The `Array.ConvertAll()` method used the generic delegate `Converter` with two generic types. The first generic type `TInput` is the input parameter, the second generic type `TOutput` is the return type:

```
public delegate TOutput Converter<TInput, TOutput>(TInput input);
```

The `ConvertAll()` method is very useful if an array of one type should be converted to an array of another type. Following is a `Racer` class that is unrelated to the `Person` class. The `Person` class contains the `FirstName` and `LastName` properties, while the `Racer` class defines for the name of the racer just one property `Name`:

```
public class Racer
{
    public Racer(string name)
    {
        this.Name = name;
    }

    public string Name { get; set; }
    public string Team { get; set; }
}
```

Using `Array.ConvertAll()` you can easily convert the person array `persons` to a `Racer` array. The delegate is invoked for every `Person` element. In the anonymous method implementation for every person, a new `Racer` object is created, and the `FirstName` and `LastName` are passed concatenated to the constructor, which accepts a string. The result is an array of `Racer` objects:

```
Racer[] racers =
        Array.ConvertAll<Person, Racer>(
                persons,
                p => new Racer(String.Format("{0} {1}", p.FirstName, p.LastName));
```

Other Generic Framework Types

In addition to the `System.Collections.Generic` namespace, the .NET Framework has other uses for generic types. The structs and delegates discussed here are all in the `System` namespace and serve different purposes.

This section discusses the following:

❑ The struct `Nullable<T>`

❑ The delegate `EventHandler<TEventArgs>`

❑ The struct `ArraySegment<T>`

Nullable<T>

A number in a database and a number in a programming language have an important difference in their characteristics, as a number in the database can be `null`. A number in C# cannot be `null`. `Int32` is a struct, and because structs are implemented as value types, they cannot be `null`.

The problem doesn't exist only with databases but also with mapping XML data to .NET types.

This difference often causes headaches and lot of additional work to map the data. One solution is to map numbers from databases and XML files to reference types, because reference types can have a `null` value. However, this also means additional overhead during runtime.

With the structure `Nullable<T>` this can be easily resolved. In the example, `Nullable<T>` is instantiated with `Nullable<int>`. The variable x can now be used like an `int`, assigning values and using operators to do some calculation. This behavior is made possible by casting operators of the `Nullable<T>` type. However, x can also be null. The `Nullable<T>` properties `HasValue` and `Value` can check if there is a value, and the value can be accessed:

```
Nullable<int> x;
x = 4;
x += 3;
if (x.HasValue)
{
    int y = x.Value;
}
x = null;
```

Because nullable types are used very often, C# has a special syntax for defining variables of this type. Instead of using the syntax with the generic structure, the `?` operator can be used. In the following example, the variables x1 and x2 both are instances of a nullable `int` type:

```
Nullable<int> x1;
int? x2;
```

A nullable type can be compared with null and numbers as shown. Here, the value of x is compared with null, and if it is not null, it is compared with a value smaller than 0:

```
int? x = GetNullableType();if (x == null)
{
    Console.WriteLine("x is null");
}
else if (x < 0)
{
    Console.WriteLine("x is smaller than 0");
}
```

Nullable types can also be used with arithmetic operators. The variable x3 is the sum of the variables x1 and x2. If any of the nullable types has a null value, the result is null:

```
int? x1 = GetNullableType();
int? x2 = GetNullableType();
int? x3 = x1 + x2;
```

The method GetNullableType() *that is called here is just a placeholder for any method that returns a nullable* int. *For testing you can implement it as simple to return* null *or to return any integer value.*

Non-nullable types can be converted to nullable types. With the conversion from a non-nullable type to a nullable type, an implicit conversion is possible where casting is not required. This conversion always succeeds:

```
int y1 = 4;
int? x1 = y1;
```

The other way around, the conversion from a nullable type to a non-nullable type, can fail. If the nullable type has a null value and the null value is assigned to a non-nullable type, an exception of type InvalidOperationException is thrown. That's the reason the cast operator is required to do an explicit conversion:

```
int? x1 = GetNullableType();
int y1 = (int)x1;
```

Instead of doing an explicit cast, it is also possible to convert a nullable type to a non-nullable type with the coalescing operator. The coalescing operator has the syntax ?? to define a default value for the conversion in case the nullable type has a value of null. Here, y1 gets the value 0 if x1 is null:

```
int? x1 = GetNullableType();
int y1 = x1 ?? 0;
```

EventHandler<TEventArgs>

With Windows Forms and Web applications, delegates for many different event handlers are defined. Some of the event handlers are listed here:

```
public sealed delegate void EventHandler(object sender, EventArgs e);
public sealed delegate void PaintEventHandler(object sender,
        PaintEventArgs e);
public sealed delegate void MouseEventHandler(object sender,
        MouseEventArgs e);
```

These delegates have in common that the first argument is always the sender, who was the origin of the event, and the second argument is of a type to contain information specific to the event.

With the new EventHandler<TEventArgs>, it is not necessary to define a new delegate for every event handler. As you can see, the first parameter is defined the same way as before, but the second parameter is a generic type TEventArgs. The where clause specifies that the type for TEventArgs must be derived from the base class EventArgs:

```
public sealed delegate void EventHandler<TEventArgs>(object sender,
        TEventArgs e)
    where TEventArgs : EventArgs
```

ArraySegment<T>

The struct ArraySegment<T> represents a segment of an array. If parts of an array are needed, a segment can be used. With the struct ArraySegment<T>, the information about the segment (the offset and count) is contained within this structure.

In the example, the variable arr is defined as an int array with eight elements. The variable segment of type ArraySegment<int> is used to represent a segment of the integer array. The segment is initialized with the constructor, where the array is passed together with an offset and an item count. Here, the offset is set to 2, so you start with the third element, and the count is set to 3, so 6 is the last element of the segment.

The array behind the array segment can be accessed with the Array property. ArraySegment<T> also has the properties Offset and Count that indicate the initialized values to define the segment. The for loop is used to iterate through the array segment. The first expression of the for loop is initialized to the offset where the iteration should begin. With the second expression, the count of the element numbers in the segment is used to check if the iteration should stop. Within the for loop, the elements contained by the segment are accessed with the Array property:

```
int[] arr = {1, 2, 3, 4, 5, 6, 7, 8};
ArraySegment<int> segment = new ArraySegment<int>(arr, 2, 3);

for (int i = segment.Offset; i < segment.Offset + segment.Count; i++)
{
    Console.WriteLine(segment.Array[i]);
}
```

With the example so far, you might question the usefulness of the ArraySegment<T> structure. However, the ArraySegment<T> can also be passed as an argument to methods. This way, just a single argument is needed instead of three that define the offset and count in addition to the array.

The method WorkWithSegment() gets an ArraySegment<string> as a parameter. In the implementation of this method, the properties Offset, Count, and Array are used as before:

```
void WorkWithSegment(ArraySegment<string> segment)
{
    for (int i = segment.Offset; i < segment.Offset + segment.Count; i++)
    {
        Console.WriteLine(segment.Array[i]);
    }
}
```

> It's important to note that array segments don't copy the elements of the originating array. Instead, the originating array can be accessed through ArraySegment<T>. If elements of the array segment are changed, the changes can be seen in the original array.

Summary

This chapter introduced a very important feature of the CLR 2.0: generics. With generic classes you can create type-independent classes, and generic methods allow type-independent methods. Interfaces, structs, and delegates can be created in a generic way as well. Generics make new programming styles possible. You've seen how algorithms, particularly actions and predicates, can be implemented to be used with different classes — and all type-safe. Generic delegates make it possible to decouple algorithms from -collections.

Other .NET Framework types include `Nullable<T>`, `EventHandler<TEventArgs>`, and `ArraySegment<T>`.

The next chapter makes use of generics showing collection classes.

10

Collections

In Chapter 5, "Arrays," you read information about arrays and the interfaces implemented by the Array class. The size of arrays is fixed. If the number of elements is dynamic, you should use a collection class.

List<T> and ArrayList are collection classes that can be compared to arrays. But there are also other kinds of collections: queues, stacks, linked lists, and dictionaries.

This chapter shows you how to work with groups of objects. It takes a close look at these topics:

- ❑ Collection interfaces and types
- ❑ Lists
- ❑ Queues
- ❑ Stacks
- ❑ Linked lists
- ❑ Sorted lists
- ❑ Dictionaries
- ❑ Lookups
- ❑ HashSets
- ❑ Bit arrays
- ❑ Performance

Collection Interfaces and Types

Collection classes can be grouped into collections that store elements of type Object and generic collection classes. Previous to CLR 2.0, generics didn't exist. Now the generic collection classes usually are the preferred type of collection. Generic collection classes are type-safe, and there is no boxing if value types are used. You need object-based collection classes only if you want to add objects of different types where the types are not based on each other, for example, adding int and string objects to one collection. Another group of collection classes is collections specialized for a specific type; for example, the StringCollection class is specialized for the string type.

You can read all about generics in Chapter 9, "Generics."

Object-type collections are located in the namespace System.Collections; generic collection classes are located in the namespace System.Collections.Generic. Collection classes that are specialized for a specific type are located in the namespace System.Collections.Specialized.

Of course, there are also other ways to group collection classes. Collections can be grouped into lists, collections, and dictionaries based on the interfaces that are implemented by the collection class. Interfaces and their functionalities are described in the following table. .NET 2.0 added new generic interfaces for collection classes, for example, IEnumerable<T> and IList<T>. Whereas the non-generic versions of these interfaces define an Object as a parameter of the methods, the generic versions of these interfaces use the generic type T.

You can read detailed information about the interfaces IEnumerable, ICollection, and IList in Chapter 5, "Arrays."

The following table describes interfaces implemented by collections and lists, and their methods and properties.

Interface	Methods and Properties	Description
IEnumerable, IEnumerable<T>	GetEnumerator()	The interface IEnumerable is required if a foreach statement is used with the collection. This interface defines the method GetEnumerator(), which returns an enumerator that implements IEnumerator. The generic interface IEnumerable<T> inherits from the non-generic interface IEnumerable, and defines a GetEnumerator method to return Enumerator<T>. Because of the inheritance with these two interfaces, with every method that requires a parameter of type IEnumerable, you can also pass IEnumerable<T> objects.
ICollection	Count, IsSynchronized, SyncRoot, CopyTo()	The interface ICollection is implemented by collection classes. With collections implementing this interface, you can get the number of elements and copy the collection to an array. The interface ICollection extends the functionality from the interface IEnumerable.
ICollection<T>	Count, IsReadOnly, Add(), Clear(), Contains(), CopyTo(), Remove()	ICollection<T> is the generic version of the ICollection interface. The generic version of this interface allows adding and removing elements as well as getting the element number.

Interface	Methods and Properties	Description
IList	IsFixedSize, IsReadOnly, Item, Add(), Clear(), Contains(), IndexOf(), Insert(), Remove(), RemoveAt()	The interface IList derives from the interface ICollection. IList allows you to access a collection using an indexer. It is also possible to insert or remove elements at any position of the collection.
IList<T>	Item, IndexOf(), Insert(), RemoveAt()	Similar to IList, the interface IList<T> inherits from ICollection<T>.
		In Chapter 5, "Arrays," you saw that the Array class implements this interface, but methods to add or remove elements throw a NotSupportedException. Collections that have a fixed size (for example, the Array class) and are read-only can throw a NotSupportedException with some of the methods defined in this interface.
		Comparing the non-generic and the generic version of the IList interfaces, the new generic interface just defines the methods and properties important for collections that offer an index. The other methods have been re-factored to the ICollection<T> interface.
IDictionary	IsFixedSize, IsReadOnly, Item, Keys, Values, Add(), Clear(), Contains(), GetEnumerator(), Remove()	The interface IDictionary is implemented by non-generic collections whose elements have a key and a value.
IDictionary<TKey, TValue>	Item, Keys, Values, Add(), ContainsKey(), Remove(), TryGetValue()	IDictionary<TKey, TValue> is implemented by generic collection classes that have a key and a value. This interface is simpler compared to IDictionary.
ILookup<TKey, TElement>	Count, Item, Contains()	ILookup<TKey, TElement> is a new interface with .NET 3.5 that is used by collections that have multiple values for a key. The indexer returns an enumeration for a specified key.
IComparer<T>	Compare()	The interface IComparer<T> is implemented by a comparer and used to sort elements inside a collection with the Compare() method.
IEquality Comparer<T>	Equals(), GetHashCode()	IEqualityComparer<T> is implemented by a comparer that can be used for keys in a dictionary. With this interface the objects can be compared for equality.

The non-generic interface `ICollection` *defines properties used to synchronize different threads accessing the same collection. These properties are no longer available with the new generic interfaces. The reason for this change was that these properties led to a false safety regarding synchronization, because the collection usually is not the only thing that must be synchronized. You can read information about synchronization with collections in Chapter 19, "Threading and Synchronization."*

The following table lists the collection classes and the collection interfaces that are implemented by these classes.

Collection Class	Collection Interfaces
ArrayList	IList, ICollection, IEnumerable
Queue	ICollection, IEnumerable
Stack	ICollection, IEnumerable
BitArray	ICollection, IEnumerable
Hashtable	IDictionary, ICollection, IEnumerable
SortedList	IDictionary, ICollection, IEnumerable
List<T>	IList<T>, ICollection<T>, IEnumerable<T>, IList, ICollection, IEnumerable
Queue<T>	IEnumerable<T>, ICollection, IEnumerable
Stack<T>	IEnumerable<T>, ICollection, IEnumerable
LinkedList<T>	ICollection<T>, IEnumerable<T>, ICollection, IEnumerable
HashSet<T>	ICollection<T>, IEnumerable<T>, IEnumerable
Dictionary<TKey, TValue>	IDictionary<TKey, TValue>, ICollection<KeyValuePair<TKey, TValue>>, IEnumerable<KeyValuePair<TKey, TValue>>, IDictionary, ICollection, IEnumerable
SortedDictionary<TKey, TValue>	IDictionary<TKey, TValue>, ICollection<KeyValuePair<TKey, TValue>>, IEnumerable<KeyValuePair<TKey, TValue>>, IDictionary, ICollection, IEnumerable
SortedList<TKey, TValue>	IDictionary<TKey, TValue>, ICollection<KeyValuePair<TKey, TValue>>, IEnumerable<KeyValuePair<TKey, TValue>>, IDictionary, ICollection, IEnumerable
Lookup<TKey, TElement>	ILookup<TKey, TElement>,IEnumerable<IGrouping<TKey, TElement>>,IEnumerable

Lists

For dynamic lists, the .NET Framework offers the classes `ArrayList` and `List<T>`. The class `List<T>` in the namespace `System.Collections.Generic` is very similar in its usage to the `ArrayList` class from the namespace `System.Collections`. This class implements the `IList`, `ICollection`, and

`IEnumerable` interfaces. Because Chapter 9, "Generics," already discussed the methods of these interfaces, this section looks at how to use the `List<T>` class.

The following examples use the members of the class `Racer` as elements to be added to the collection to represent a Formula-1 racer. This class has four fields: `firstName`, `lastName`, `country`, and the number of `wins`. The fields can be accessed with properties. With the constructor of the class, the name of the racer and the number of wins can be passed to set the members. The method `ToString()` is overridden to return the name of the racer. The class `Racer` also implements the generic interface `IComparer<T>` for sorting racer elements.

```
[Serializable]
public class Racer : IComparable<Racer>, IFormattable
{
    public Racer()
        : this(String.Empty, String.Empty,
                String.Empty) {}

    public Racer(string firstName, string lastName,
                string country)
        : this(firstName, lastName, country, 0) {}

    public Racer(string firstName, string lastName,
                string country, int wins)
    {
        this.FirstName = firstName;
        this.LastName = lastName;
        this.Country = country;
        this.Wins = wins;
    }

    public string FirstName { get; set; }
    public string LastName { get; set; }
    public string Country { get; set; }
    public int Wins { get; set; }

    public override string ToString()
    {
        return String.Format("{0} {1}",
            FirstName, LastName);
    }

    public string ToString(string format,
        IFormatProvider formatProvider)
    {
        switch (format.ToUpper())
        {
            case null:
            case "N": // name
                return ToString();
            case "F": // first name
                return FirstName;
            case "L": // last name
                return LastName;
            case "W": // Wins
```

(continued)

(continued)

```
                    return String.Format("{0}, Wins: {1}",
                            ToString(), Wins);
            case "C": // Country
                return String.Format(
                        "{0}, Country: {1}",
                        ToString(), Country);
            case "A": // All
                return String.Format(
                        "{0}, {1} Wins: {2}",
                        ToString(), Country, Wins);
            default:
                throw new FormatException(String.Format(
                        formatProvider,
                        "Format {0} is not supported",
                        format));
        }
    }

    public string ToString(string format)
    {
        return ToString(format, null);
    }

    public int CompareTo(Racer other)
    {
        int compare = this.LastName.CompareTo(
            other.LastName);
        if (compare == 0)
           return this.FirstName.CompareTo(
                  other.FirstName);
        return compare;
    }
}
```

Creating Lists

You can create list objects by invoking the default constructor. With the generic class List<T>, you must specify the type for the values of the list with the declaration. The code shows how to declare a List<T> with int and a list with Racer elements. ArrayList is a non-generic list that accepts any Object type for its elements.

Using the default constructor creates an empty list. As soon as elements are added to the list, the capacity of the list is extended to allow four elements. If the fifth element is added, the list is resized to allow eight elements. If eight elements are not enough, the list is resized again to contain 16 elements. With every resize the capacity of the list is doubled.

```
ArrayList objectList = new ArrayList();

List<int> intList = new List<int>();
List<Racer> racers = new List<Racer>();
```

If the capacity of the list changes, the complete collection is reallocated to a new memory block. With the implementation of List<T>, an array of type T is used. With reallocation, a new array is created, and Array.Copy() copies the elements from the old to the new array. To save time, if you know the number of elements in advance, that should be in the list; you can define the capacity with the constructor. Here a collection with a capacity of 10 elements is created. If the capacity is not large enough for the elements added, the capacity is resized to 20 and 40 elements — doubled again.

```
ArrayList objectList = new ArrayList(10);
List<int> intList = new List<int>(10);
```

You can get and set the capacity of a collection by using the Capacity property:

```
objectList.Capacity = 20;
intList.Capacity = 20;
```

The capacity is not the same as the number of elements in the collection. The number of elements in the collection can be read with the Count property. Of course, the capacity is always larger or equal to the number of items. As long as no element was added to the list, the count is 0.

```
Console.WriteLine(intList.Count);
```

If you are finished adding elements to the list and don't want to add any more elements, you can get rid of the unneeded capacity by invoking the TrimExcess() method. However, because the relocation takes time, TrimExcess() does nothing if the item count is more than 90 percent of capacity.

```
intList.TrimExcess();
```

Because with new applications usually you can use the generic List<T> class instead of the non-generic ArrayList class, and also because the methods of ArrayList are very similar, the reminder of this section focuses just on List<T>.

Collection Initializers

C# 3.0 allows you to assign values to collections using collection initializers. The syntax of collection initializers is similar to array initializers, which were explained in Chapter 5. With a collection initializer, values are assigned to the collection within curly brackets at the initialization of the collection:

```
List<int> intList = new List<int>() {1, 2};
List<string> stringList =
        new List<string>() {"one", "two"};
```

Collection initializers are a feature of the C# 3.0 programming language and are not reflected within the IL code of the compiled assembly. The compiler converts the collection initializer to invoking the Add() method for every item from the initializer list.

Adding Elements

You can add elements to the list with the Add() method as shown. The generic instantiated type defines the parameter type of the Add() method.

```
List<int> intList = new List<int>();
intList.Add(1);
intList.Add(2);

List<string> stringList = new List<string>();
stringList.Add("one");
stringList.Add("two");
```

The variable racers is defined as type List<Racer>. With the new operator, a new object of the same type is created. Because the class List<T> was instantiated with the concrete class Racer, now only Racer objects can be added with the Add() method. In the following sample code, five Formula-1 racers are created and added to the collection. The first three are added using the collection initializer, and the last two are added by invoking the Add() method explicitly.

```
Racer graham = new Racer("Graham", "Hill",
        "UK", 14);
Racer emerson = new Racer("Emerson",
        "Fittipaldi", "Brazil", 14);
Racer mario = new Racer("Mario", "Andretti",
        "USA", 12);
```

```
List<Racer> racers = new List<Racer>(20)
        {graham, emerson, mario};

racers.Add(new Racer("Michael", "Schumacher",
        "Germany", 91));
racers.Add(new Racer("Mika", "Hakkinen",
        "Finland", 20));
```

With the `AddRange()` method of the `List<T>` class, you can add multiple elements to the collection at once. The method `AddRange()` accepts an object of type `IEnumerable<T>`, so you can also pass an array as shown:

```
racers.AddRange(new Racer[] {
        new Racer("Niki", "Lauda", "Austria",
                25),
        new Racer("Alain", "Prost", "France",
                51)});
```

The collection initializer can be used only during declaration of the collection. The `AddRange()` method can be invoked after the collection is initialized.

If you know some elements of the collection when instantiating the list, you can also pass any object that implements `IEnumerable<T>` to the constructor of the class. This is very similar to the `AddRange()` method.

```
List<Racer> racers =
    new List<Racer>(new Racer[] {
        new Racer("Jochen", "Rindt", "Austria",
                6),
        new Racer("Ayrton", "Senna", "Brazil",
                41) });
```

Inserting Elements

You can insert elements at a specified position with the `Insert()` method:

```
racers.Insert(3, new Racer("Phil", "Hill",
        "USA", 3));
```

The method `InsertRange()` offers the capability to insert a number of elements, similarly to the `AddRange()` method shown earlier.

If the index set is larger than the number of elements in the collection, an exception of type `ArgumentOutOfRangeException` is thrown.

Accessing Elements

All classes that implement the `IList` and `IList<T>` interface offer an indexer, so you can access the elements by using an indexer and passing the item number. The first item can be accessed with an index value 0. By specifying `racers[3]`, you will access the fourth element of the list:

```
Racer r1 = racers[3];
```

Getting the number of elements with the `Count` property, you can do a `for` loop to iterate through every item in the collection, and use the indexer to access every item:

```
for (int i = 0; i < racers.Count; i++)
{
    Console.WriteLine(racers[i]);
}
```

> Indexed access to collection classes is available with `ArrayList`, `StringCollection`, and `List<T>`.

Because `List<T>` implements the interface `IEnumerable`, you can iterate through the items in the collection using the `foreach` statement as well:

```
foreach (Racer r in racers)
{
    Console.WriteLine(r);
}
```

How the `foreach` statement is resolved by the compiler to make use of the `IEnumerable` and `IEnumerator` interfaces is explained in Chapter 5, "Arrays."

Instead of using the `foreach` statement, the `List<T>` class also offers a `ForEach()` method that is declared with an `Action<T>` parameter:

```
public void ForEach(Action<T> action);
```

The implementation of `ForEach()` is shown next. `ForEach()` iterates through every item of the collection and invokes the method that is passed as parameter for every item.

```
public class List<T> : IList<T>
{
    private T[] items;

    //...

    public void ForEach(Action<T> action)
    {
        if (action == null) throw new ArgumentNullException("action");

        foreach (T item in items)
        {
            action(item);
        }
    }

    //...
}
```

For passing a method with `ForEach`, `Action<T>` is declared as a delegate that defines a method with `void` return type and parameter `T`:

```
public delegate void Action<T>(T obj);
```

With a list of `Racer` items, the handler for the `ForEach()` method must be declared with a `Racer` object as parameter and a `void` return type:

```
public void ActionHandler(Racer obj);
```

Because one overload of the `Console.WriteLine()` method accepts `Object` as parameter, you can pass the address of this method to the `ForEach()` method, and every racer of the collection is written to the console:

```
racers.ForEach(Console.WriteLine);
```

You can also write an anonymous method that accepts a `Racer` object as parameter. Here, the format A is used with the `ToString()` method of the `IFormattable` interface to display all information of the racer:

```
racers.ForEach(
    delegate(Racer r)
    {
        Console.WriteLine("{0:A}", r);
    });
```

With C# 3.0 you can also use Lambda expressions with methods accepting a delegate parameter. The same iteration that was implemented using an anonymous method is defined with a Lambda expression:

```
racers.ForEach(
        r => Console.WriteLine("{0:A}", r));
```

Anonymous methods and Lambda expressions are explained in Chapter 7, "Delegates and Events."

Removing Elements

You can remove elements by index or pass the item that should be removed. Here, the fourth element is removed by passing 3 to `RemoveAt()`:

```
racers.RemoveAt(3);
```

You can also directly pass a `Racer` object to the `Remove()` method to remove this element. Removing by index is faster, because here the collection must be searched for the item to remove. The `Remove()` method first searches in the collection to get the index of the item with the `IndexOf()` method, and then uses the index to remove the item. `IndexOf()` first checks if the item type implements the interface `IEquatable`. If it does, the `Equals()` method of this interface is invoked to find the item in the collection that is the same as the one passed to the method. If this interface is not implemented, the `Equals()` method of the `Object` class is used to compare the items. The default implementation of the `Equals()` method in the `Object` class does a bitwise compare with value types, but compares only references with reference types.

Chapter 6, "Operators and Casts," explains how you can override the `Equals()` method.

Here, the racer referenced by the variable `graham` is removed from the collection. The variable `graham` was created earlier when the collection was filled. Because the interface `IEquatable` and the `Object.Equals()` method are not overridden with the `Racer` class, you cannot create a new object with the same content as the item that should be removed and pass it to the `Remove()` method.

```
if (!racers.Remove(graham))
{
    Console.WriteLine(
            "object not found in collection");
}
```

The method `RemoveRange()` removes a number of items from the collection. The first parameter specifies the index where the removal of items should begin; the second parameter specifies the number of items to be removed.

```
int index = 3;
int count = 5;
racers.RemoveRange(index, count);
```

To remove all items with some specific characteristics from the collection, you can use the `RemoveAll()` method. This method uses the `Predicate<T>` parameter when searching for elements, which is discussed next. For removing all elements from the collection, use the `Clear()` method defined with the `ICollection<T>` interface.

Searching

There are different ways to search for elements in the collection. You can get the index to the found item, or the item itself. You can use methods such as `IndexOf()`, `LastIndexOf()`, `FindIndex()`, `FindLastIndex()`, `Find()`, and `FindLast()`. And for just checking if an item exists, the `List<T>` class offers the `Exists()` method.

The method `IndexOf()` requires an object as parameter and returns the index of the item if it is found inside the collection. If the item is not found, –1 is returned. Remember that `IndexOf()` is using the `IEquatable` interface for comparing the elements.

```
int index1 = racers.IndexOf(mario);
```

With the `IndexOf()` method, you can also specify that the complete collection should not be searched, but rather specify an index where the search should start and the number of elements that should be iterated for the comparison.

Instead of searching a specific item with the `IndexOf()` method, you can search for an item that has some specific characteristics that you can define with the `FindIndex()` method. `FindIndex()` requires a parameter of type `Predicate`:

```
public int FindIndex(Predicate<T> match);
```

The `Predicate<T>` type is a delegate that returns a Boolean value and requires type `T` as parameter. This delegate can be used similarly to the `Action` delegate shown earlier with the `ForEach()` method. If the predicate returns `true`, there's a match and the element is found. If it returns `false`, the element is not found and the search continues.

```
public delegate bool Predicate<T>(T obj);
```

With the `List<T>` class that is using `Racer` objects for type `T`, you can pass the address of a method that returns a `bool` and defines a parameter of type `Racer` to the `FindIndex()` method. Finding the first racer of a specific country, you can create the `FindCountry` class as shown. The `Find()` method has the signature and return type defined by the `Predicate<T>` delegate. The `Find()` method uses the variable `country` to search for a country that you can pass with the constructor of the class.

```
public class FindCountry
{
    public FindCountry(string country)
    {
        this.country = country;
    }
    private string country;

    public bool FindCountryPredicate(Racer racer)
    {
        if (racer == null)
            throw new ArgumentNullException("racer");
        return r.Country == country;
    }
}
```

With the `FindIndex()` method, you can create a new instance of the `FindCountry()` class, pass a country string to the constructor, and pass the address of the `Find` method. After `FindIndex()` completes successfully, index2 contains the index of the first item where the `Country` property of the racer is set to `Finland`.

```
int index2 = racers.FindIndex(
        new FindCountry("Finland").FindCountryPredicate);
```

Instead of creating a class with a handler method, you can use a Lambda expression here as well. The result is exactly the same as before. Now the Lambda expression defines the implementation to search for an item where the `Country` property is set to `Finland`.

```
int index3 = racers.FindIndex(
        r => r.Country == "Finland");
```

Similarly to the `IndexOf()` method, with the `FindIndex()` method, you can also specify the index where the search should start and the count of items that should be iterated through. To do a search for an index beginning from the last element in the collection, you can use the `FindLastIndex()` method.

The method `FindIndex()` returns the index of the found item. Instead of getting the index, you can also get directly to the item in the collection. The `Find()` method requires a parameter of type `Predicate<T>`, much like the `FindIndex()` method. The `Find()` method here is searching for the first racer in the list that has the `FirstName` property set to `Niki`. Of course, you can also do a `FindLast()` to find the last item that fulfills the predicate.

```
Racer r = racers.Find(
        r => r.FirstName == "Niki");
```

To get not only one, but all items that fulfill the requirements of a predicate, you can use the `FindAll()` method. The `FindAll()` method uses the same `Predicate<T>` delegate as the `Find()` and `FindIndex()` methods. The `FindAll()` method does not stop when the first item is found but instead iterates through every item in the collection and returns all items where the predicate returns `true`.

With the `FindAll()` method invoked here, all racer items are returned where the property `Wins` is set to more than 20. All racers that won more than 20 races are referenced from the `bigWinners` list.

```
List<Racer> bigWinners = racers.FindAll(
        r => r.Wins > 20);
```

Iterating through the variable `bigWinners` with a `foreach` statement gives the following result:

```
foreach (Racer r in bigWinners)
{
        Console.WriteLine("{0:A}", r);
}
```

```
Michael Schumacher, Germany Wins: 91
Niki Lauda, Austria Wins: 25
Alain Prost, France Wins: 51
```

The result is not sorted, but this is done next.

Sorting

The `List<T>` class allows sorting its elements by using the `Sort()` method. `Sort()` uses the quick sort algorithm where all elements are compared until the complete list is sorted.

You can use several overloads of the Sort() method. The arguments that can be passed are a generic delegate Comparison<T>, the generic interface IComparer<T>, and a range together with the generic interface IComparer<T>:

```
public void List<T>.Sort();
public void List<T>.Sort(Comparison<T>);
public void List<T>.Sort(IComparer<T>);
public void List<T>.Sort(Int32, Int32, IComparer<T>);
```

Using the Sort() method without arguments is possible only if the elements in the collection implement the interface IComparable.

The class Racer implements the interface IComparable<T> to sort racers by the last name:

```
racers.Sort();
racers.ForEach(Console.WriteLine);
```

If you need to do a sort other than the default supported by the item types, you need to use other techniques, for example passing an object that implements the IComparer<T> interface.

The class RacerComparer implements the interface IComparer<T> for Racer types. This class allows you to sort either by the first name, last name, country, or number of wins. The kind of sort that should be done is defined with the inner enumeration type CompareType. The CompareType is set with the constructor of the class RacerComparer. The interface IComparer<Racer> defines the method Compare that is required for sorting. In the implementation of this method, the CompareTo() method of the string and int types is used.

```
public class RacerComparer : IComparer<Racer>
{
    public enum CompareType
    {
        FirstName,
        LastName,
        Country,
        Wins
    }

    private CompareType compareType;
    public RacerComparer(CompareType compareType)
    {
        this.compareType = compareType;
    }

    public int Compare(Racer x, Racer y)
    {
        if (x == null)
            throw new ArgumentNullException("x");
        if (y == null)
            throw new ArgumentNullException("y");

        int result;
        switch (compareType)
        {
            case CompareType.FirstName:
                return
                    x.FirstName.CompareTo(y.FirstName);
```

(continued)

(continued)

```
            case CompareType.LastName:
                return x.LastName.CompareTo(y.LastName);
            case CompareType.Country:
                if ((result =
                    x.Country.CompareTo(y.Country) == 0)
                    return x.LastName.CompareTo(
                        y.LastName);
                else
                    return result;
            case CompareType.Wins:
                return x.Wins.CompareTo(y.Wins);
            default:
                throw new ArgumentException(
                    "Invalid Compare Type");
        }
    }
}
```

An instance of the `RacerComparer` class can now be used with the `Sort()` method. Passing the enumeration `RacerComparer.CompareType.Country` sorts the collection by the property `Country`:

```
    racers.Sort(new RacerComparer(
        RacerComparer.CompareType.Country));
    racers.ForEach(Console.WriteLine);
```

Another way to do the sort is by using the overloaded `Sort()` method, which requires a `Comparison<T>` delegate:

```
    public void List<T>.Sort(Comparison<T>);
```

`Comparison<T>` is a delegate to a method that has two parameters of type `T` and a return type `int`. If the parameter values are equal, the method must return 0. If the first parameter is less than the second, a value less than zero must be returned; otherwise, a value greater than zero is returned.

```
    public delegate int Comparison<T>(T x, T y);
```

Now you can pass a Lambda expression to the `Sort()` method to do a sort by the number of wins. The two parameters are of type `Racer`, and in the implementation the `Wins` properties are compared by using the `int` method `CompareTo()`. In the implementation, `r2` and `r1` are used in the reverse order, so the number of wins is sorted in descending order. After the method has been invoked, the complete racer list is sorted based on the number of wins of the racer.

```
    racers.Sort(
        (r1, r2) => r2.Wins.CompareTo(r1.Wins));
```

You can also reverse the order of a complete collection by invoking the `Reverse()` method.

Type Conversion

With the `List<T>` method `ConvertAll()`, all types of a collection can be converted to a different type. The `ConvertAll()` method uses a `Converter` delegate that is defined like this:

```
    public sealed delegate TOutput Converter<TInput, TOutput>(TInput from);
```

The generic types `TInput` and `TOutput` are used with the conversion. `TInput` is the argument of the delegate method, and `TOutput` is the return type.

In this example, all `Racer` types should be converted to `Person` types. Whereas the `Racer` type contains a `firstName`, `lastName`, `country`, and the number of `wins`, the `Person` type contains just a `name`. For the conversion, the country of the racer and race wins can be ignored, but the name must be converted:

```
[Serializable]
public class Person
{
    private string name;

    public Person(string name)
    {
        this.name = name;
    }

    public override string ToString()
    {
        return name;
    }
}
```

The conversion happens by invoking the `racers.ConvertAll<Person>()` method. The argument of this method is defined as a Lambda expression with an argument of type `Racer` and a `Person` type that is returned. In the implementation of the Lambda expression, a new `Person` object is created and returned. For the `Person` object, the `FirstName` and `LastName` are passed to the constructor:

```
List<Person> persons =
    racers.ConvertAll<Person>(
    r => new Person(r.FirstName + " " +
    r.LastName));
```

The result of the conversion is a list containing the converted `Person` objects: `persons` of type `List<Person>`.

Read-Only Collections

After collections are created they are read/write. Of course, they must be read/write; otherwise, you couldn't fill them with any values. However, after the collection is filled, you can create a read-only collection. The `List<T>` collection has the method `AsReadOnly()` that returns an object of type `ReadOnlyCollection<T>`. The class `ReadOnlyCollection<T>` implements the same interfaces as `List<T>`, but all methods and properties that change the collection throw a `NotSupportedException`.

Queues

A queue is a collection where elements are processed *first in, first out* (FIFO). The item that is put first in the queue is read first. Examples of queues are standing in the queue at the airport, a human resources queue to process employee applicants, print jobs waiting to be processed in a print queue, and a thread waiting for the CPU in a round-robin fashion. Often, there are queues where the elements processed differ in their priority. For example, in the queue at the airport, business passengers are processed before economy passengers. Here, multiple queues can be used, one queue for every priority. At the airport this can easily be found out, because there are separate check-in queues for business and economy passengers. The same is true for print queues and threads. You can have an array of a list of queues where one item in the array stands for a priority. Within every array item there's a queue, where processing happens with the FIFO principle.

Later in this chapter, a different implementation with a linked list is used to define a list of priorities.

With .NET you have the non-generic class Queue in the System.Collections namespace and the generic class Queue<T> in the System.Collections.Generic namespace. Both classes are very similar in their functionality with the exception that the generic class is strongly typed, defining type T, and the non-generic class is based on the object type.

Internally, the Queue<T> class is using an array of type T similar to the List<T> type. What's also similar is that the interfaces ICollection and IEnumerable are implemented. The Queue class implements the interfaces ICollection, IEnumerable, and ICloneable. The Queue<T> class implements the interfaces IEnumerable<T> and ICollection. The generic class Queue<T> does not implement the generic interface ICollection<T> because this interface defines methods to add and remove items to the collection with Add() and Remove() methods.

The big difference of the queue is that the interface IList is not implemented. You cannot access the queue using an indexer. The queue just allows you to add an item to the queue, where the item is put at the end of the queue (with the Enqueue() method), and to get items from the head of the queue (with the Dequeue() method).

Figure 10-1 shows the items of the queue. The Enqueue() method adds items to one end of the queue; the items are read and removed at the other end of the queue with the Dequeue() method. Reading items with the Dequeue() method also removes the items from the queue. Invoking the Dequeue() method once more removes the next item from the queue.

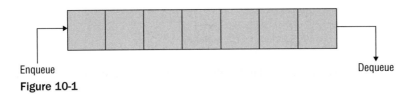

Enqueue   Dequeue

Figure 10-1

Methods of the Queue and Queue<T> classes are described in the following table.

Queue and Queue<T> Members	Description
Enqueue()	The Enqueue() method adds an item to the end of the queue.
Dequeue()	The Dequeue() method reads and removes an item from the head of the queue. If there are no more items in the queue when the Dequeue() method is invoked, an exception of type InvalidOperationException is thrown.
Peek()	The Peek() method reads an item from the head of the queue but does not remove the item.
Count	The property Count returns the number of items in the queue.
TrimExcess()	TrimExcess() resizes the capacity of the queue. The Dequeue() method removes items from the queue, but it doesn't resize the capacity of the queue. To get rid of the empty items at the beginning of the queue, use the TrimExcess() method.

Queue and Queue <T> Members	Description
Contains()	The Contains() method checks whether an item is in the queue and returns true if it is.
CopyTo()	With the CopyTo() method, you can copy the items from the queue to an existing array.
ToArray()	The method ToArray() returns a new array containing the elements of the queue.

When creating queues, you can use constructors similar to those used with the List<T> type. The default constructor creates an empty queue, but you can also use a constructor to specify the capacity. As items are added to the queue, the capacity is increased to hold 4, 8, 16, and 32 items if the capacity is not defined. Similarly to the List<T> class, the capacity is always doubled as required. The default constructor of the non-generic Queue class is different, because it creates an initial array of 32 empty items. With an overload of the constructor you can also pass any other collection that implements the IEnumerable<T> interface that is copied to the queue.

The sample application that demonstrates the use of the Queue<T> class is a document management application. One thread is used to add documents to the queue, and another thread reads documents from the queue and processes them.

The items stored in the queue are of type Document. The Document class defines a title and content:

```
public class Document
{
    private string title;
    public string Title
    {
        get
        {
            return title;
        }
    }

    private string content;
    public string Content
    {
        get
        {
            return content;
        }
    }

    public Document(string title, string content)
    {
        this.title = title;
        this.content = content;
    }
}
```

The `DocumentManager` class is a thin layer around the `Queue<T>` class. The class `DocumentManager` defines how to handle documents: adding documents to the queue with the `AddDocument()` method, and getting documents from the queue with the `GetDocument()` method.

Inside the `AddDocument()` method, the document is added to the end of the queue by using the `Enqueue()` method. The first document from the queue is read with the `Dequeue()` method inside `GetDocument()`. Because multiple threads can access the `DocumentManager` concurrently, access to the queue is locked with the `lock` statement.

Threading and the `lock` statement are discussed in Chapter 19, "Threading and Synchronization."

`IsDocumentAvailable` is a read-only Boolean property that returns `true` if there are documents in the queue, and `false` if not:

```csharp
public class DocumentManager
{
    private readonly Queue<Document> documentQueue = new Queue<Document>();

    public void AddDocument(Document doc)
    {
        lock (this)
        {
            documentQueue.Enqueue(doc);
        }
    }

    public Document GetDocument()
    {
        Document doc = null;
        lock (this)
        {
            doc = documentQueue.Dequeue();
        }
        return doc;
    }

    public bool IsDocumentAvailable
    {
        get
        {
            return documentQueue.Count > 0;
        }
    }
}
```

The class `ProcessDocuments` processes documents from the queue in a separate thread. The only method that can be accessed from the outside is `Start()`. In the `Start()` method, a new thread is instantiated. A `ProcessDocuments` object is created for starting the thread, and the `Run()` method is defined as the start method of the thread. `ThreadStart` is a delegate that references the method to be started by the thread. After creating the `Thread` object, the thread is started by calling the method `Thread.Start()`.

With the `Run()` method of the `ProcessDocuments` class, an endless loop is defined. Within this loop, the property `IsDocumentAvailable` is used to see if there is a document in the queue. If there is a document in the queue, the document is taken from the `DocumentManager` and processed. Processing here is writing information only to the console. In a real application, the document could be written to a file, written to the database, or sent across the network.

```
public class ProcessDocuments
{
    public static void Start(DocumentManager dm)
    {
        new Thread(new ProcessDocuments(dm).Run).Start();
    }

    protected ProcessDocuments(DocumentManager dm)
    {
        documentManager = dm;
    }

    private DocumentManager documentManager;

    protected void Run()
    {
        while (true)
        {
            if (documentManager.IsDocumentAvailable)
            {
                Document doc =
                    documentManager.GetDocument();
                Console.WriteLine(
                    "Processing document {0}",
                    doc.Title);
            }
            Thread.Sleep(new Random().Next(20));
        }
    }
}
```

In the Main() method of the application, a DocumentManager object is instantiated, and the document processing thread is started. Then 1,000 documents are created and added to the DocumentManager.

```
class Program
{
    static void Main()
    {
        DocumentManager dm = new DocumentManager();

        ProcessDocuments.Start(dm);

        // Create documents and add them to the
        // DocumentManager
        for (int i = 0; i < 1000; i++)
        {
            Document doc = new Document("Doc " +
                i.ToString(), "content");
            dm.AddDocument(doc);
            Console.WriteLine("Added document {0}",
                doc.Title);
            Thread.Sleep(new Random().Next(20));
        }
    }
}
```

When you start the application, the documents are added to and removed from the queue, and you get output similar to the following:

```
Added document Doc 279
Processing document Doc 236
Added document Doc 280
Processing document Doc 237
Added document Doc 281
Processing document Doc 238
Processing document Doc 239
Processing document Doc 240
Processing document Doc 241
Added document Doc 282
Processing document Doc 242
Added document Doc 283
Processing document Doc 243
```

A real-life scenario doing the task described with the sample application can be an application that processes documents received with a Web service.

Stacks

A stack is another container that is very similar to the queue. You just use different methods to access the stack. The item that is added last to the stack is read first. The stack is a *last in, first out* (LIFO) container.

Figure 10-2 shows the representation of a stack where the Push() method adds an item to the stack, and the Pop() method gets the item that was added last.

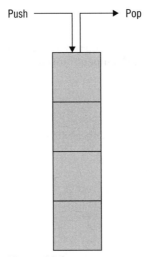

Figure 10-2

Similar to the queue classes, the non-generic Stack class implements the interfaces ICollection, IEnumerable, and ICloneable; the generic Stack<T> class implements the interfaces IEnumerable<T>, ICollection, and IEnumerable.

Members of the Stack and Stack<T> class are listed in the following table.

Stack and Stack<T> Members	Description
Push()	The Push() method adds an item on top of the stack.
Pop()	The Pop() method removes and returns an item from the top of the stack. If the stack is empty, an exception of type InvalidOperationException is thrown.
Peek()	The Peek() method returns an item from the top of the stack but does not remove the item.
Count	The property Count returns the number of items in the stack.
Contains()	The Contains() method checks whether an item is in the stack and returns true if it is.
CopyTo()	With the CopyTo() method, you can copy the items from the stack to an existing array.
ToArray()	The method ToArray() returns a new array containing the elements of the stack.

In this example, three items are added to the stack with the Push() method. With the foreach method, all items are iterated using the IEnumerable interface. The enumerator of the stack does not remove the items; it just returns item by item.

```
Stack<char> alphabet = new Stack<char>();
alphabet.Push('A');
alphabet.Push('B');
alphabet.Push('C');

foreach (char item in alphabet)
{
    Console.Write(item);
}
Console.WriteLine();
```

Because the items are read in the order from the last added to the first, the following result is produced:

```
CBA
```

Reading the items with the enumerator does not change the state of the items. With the Pop() method, every item that is read is also removed from the stack. This way you can iterate the collection using a while loop and verify the Count property if items are still existing:

```
Stack<char> alphabet = new Stack<char>();
alphabet.Push('A');
alphabet.Push('B');
alphabet.Push('C');

Console.Write("First iteration: ");
foreach (char item in alphabet)
{
    Console.Write(item);
}
```

(continued)

(continued)

```
            Console.WriteLine();

            Console.Write("Second iteration: ");
            while (alphabet.Count > 0)
            {
                Console.Write(alphabet.Pop());
            }
            Console.WriteLine();
```

The result gives CBA twice, once for each iteration. After the second iteration, the stack is empty because the second iteration used the `Pop()` method:

```
    First iteration: CBA
    Second iteration: CBA
```

Linked Lists

A collection class that has no similar version with a non-generic collection is `LinkedList<T>`. `LinkedList<T>` is a doubly linked list, where one element references the next and the previous one, as shown in Figure 10-3.

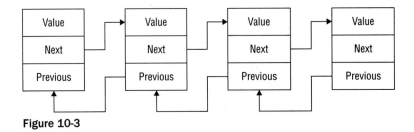

Figure 10-3

The advantage of a linked list is that if items are inserted in the middle of a list, the linked list is very fast. When an item is inserted, only the `Next` reference of the previous item and the `Previous` reference of the next item must be changed to reference the inserted item. With the `List<T>` and `ArrayList` classes, when an element is inserted all following elements must be moved.

Of course, there's also a disadvantage with linked lists. Items of linked lists can be accessed only one after the other. It takes a long time to find an item that's somewhere in the middle or at the end of the list.

A linked list cannot just store the items inside the list; together with every item, the linked list must have information about the next and previous items. That's why the `LinkedList<T>` contains items of type `LinkedListNode<T>`. With the class `LinkedListNode<T>`, you can get to the next and previous items in the list. The following table describes the properties of `LinkedListNode<T>`.

LinkedListNode<T> Properties	Description
List	The property List returns the LinkedList<T> that is associated with the node.
Next	The property Next returns the node that follows the current node. The return type is again of type LinkedListNode<T>.
Previous	The property Previous returns the node before the current node.
Value	The property Value returns the item that is associated with the node. Value is of type T.

The class LinkedList<T> implements the interfaces ICollection<T>, IEnumerable<T>, ICollection, IEnumerable, ISerializable, and IDeserializationCallback. Members of this class are explained in the following table.

LinkedList<T> Members	Description
Count	The property Count returns the number of items in the list.
First	The property First returns the first node in the list. The type returned is LinkedListNode<T>. Using this returned node, you can iterate through the other nodes of the collection.
Last	The property Last returns the last node in the list. Again, the type is LinkedListNode<T>. From here you can iterate through the list backwards.
AddAfter() AddBefore() AddFirst() AddLast()	With the AddXXX methods you can add items to the linked list. Use the corresponding Add method to add the item to a specific position inside the list. AddAfter() requires a LinkedListNode<T> object where you can specify the node after which the new item should be added. AddBefore() positions the new item before the node defined with the first parameter. AddFirst() and AddLast() just add the new item to the beginning or the end of the list. All these methods are overloaded to accept an object to add of either type LinkedListNode<T> or of type T. If you pass a T object, a new LinkedListNode<T> object is created.
Remove() RemoveFirst() RemoveLast()	The Remove(), RemoveFirst(), and RemoveLast() methods remove nodes from the list. RemoveFirst() removes the first item, and RemoveLast() removes the last item. The Remove() method requires an object that is searched and removes the first occurrence of this item in the list.
Clear()	The Clear() method removes all nodes from the list.

LinkedList<T> Members	Description
Contains()	The method Contains() searches for an item and returns true if the item is found, and false otherwise.
Find()	The Find() method searches the list from the beginning to find the item passed. The Find() method then returns a LinkedListNode<T>.
FindLast()	The FindLast() method is similar to Find(), but the search starts from the end of the list.

The sample application uses a linked list, LinkedList<T>, together with a list, List<T>. The linked list contains documents as in the previous example, but the documents have an additional priority associated with them. The documents will be sorted inside the linked list depending on the priority. If multiple documents have the same priority, the elements are sorted according to the time the document was inserted.

Figure 10-4 describes the collections of the sample application. LinkedList<Document> is the linked list containing all the Document objects. The figure shows the title and the priority of the documents. The title indicates when the document was added to the list: The first document added has the title One, the second document has the title Two, and so on. You can see that the documents One and Four have the same priority, 8, but because One was added before Four, it is earlier in the list.

When new documents are added to the linked list, they should be added after the last document that has the same priority. A LinkedList<Document> collection contains elements of type LinkedListNode <Document>. The class LinkedListNode<T> adds Next and Previous properties to walk from one node to the next. For referencing such elements, the List<T> is defined as List<LinkedListNode <Document>>. For fast access to the last document of every priority, the collection List<LinkedListNode> contains up to 10 elements, each referencing the last document of every priority. In the upcoming discussion, the reference to the last document of every priority is called the *priority node*.

From the previous example, the Document class is extended to contain the priority. The priority is set with the constructor of the class:

```
public class Document
{
    private string title;
    public string Title
    {
        get
        {
            return title;
        }
    }

    private string content;
    public string Content
    {
        get
        {
            return content;
        }
    }
```

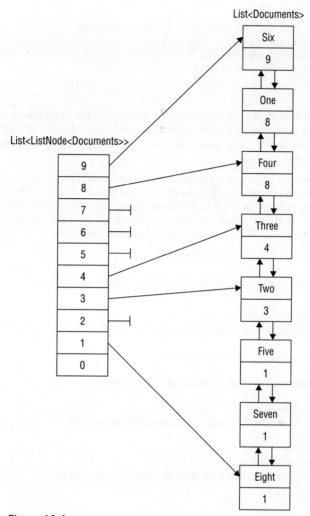

Figure 10-4

```
private byte priority;
public byte Priority
{
    get
    {
        return priority;
    }
}

public Document(string title, string content,
    byte priority)
```

(continued)

(continued)

```
        {
            this.title = title;
            this.content = content;
            this.priority = priority;
        }
    }
```

The heart of the solution is the `PriorityDocumentManager` class. This class is very easy to use. With the public interface of this class, new `Document` elements can be added to the linked list, the first document can be retrieved, and for testing purposes it also has a method to display all elements of the collection as they are linked in the list.

The class `PriorityDocumentManager` contains two collections. The collection of type `LinkedList<Document>` contains all documents. The collection of type `List<LinkedListNode <Document>>` contains references of up to 10 elements that are entry points for adding new documents with a specific priority. Both collection variables are initialized with the constructor of the class `PriorityDocumentManager`. The list collection is also initialized with `null`:

```
    public class PriorityDocumentManager
    {
        private readonly LinkedList<Document> documentList;

        // priorities 0..9
        private readonly List<LinkedListNode<Document>> priorityNodes;

        public PriorityDocumentManager()
        {
            documentList = new LinkedList<Document>();

            priorityNodes =
                    new List<LinkedListNode<Document>>(10);
            for (int i = 0; i < 10; i++)
            {
                priorityNodes.Add(
                    new LinkedListNode<Document>(null));
            }
        }
```

Part of the public interface of the class is the method `AddDocument()`. `AddDocument()` does nothing more than call the private method `AddDocumentToPriorityNode()`. The reason for having the implementation inside a different method is that `AddDocumentToPriorityNode()` may be called recursively, as you will see soon.

```
        public void AddDocument(Document d)
        {
            if (d == null)
                throw new ArgumentNullException("d");
            AddDocumentToPriorityNode(d, d.Priority);
        }
```

The first action that is done in the implementation of `AddDocumentToPriorityNode()` is a check to see if the priority fits in the allowed priority range. Here, the allowed range is between 0 and 9. If a wrong value is passed, an exception of type `ArgumentException` is thrown.

Next, you check if there's already a priority node with the same priority as the priority that was passed. If there's no such priority node in the list collection, `AddDocumentToPriorityNode()` is invoked recursively with the priority value decremented to check for a priority node with the next lower priority.

If there's no priority node with the same priority or any priority with a lower value, the document can be safely added to the end of the linked list by calling the method `AddLast()`. Also, the linked list node is referenced by the priority node that's responsible for the priority of the document.

If there's an existing priority node, you can get the position inside the linked list where the document should be inserted. Here, you must differentiate whether a priority node already exists with the correct priority, or if there's just a priority node that references a document with a lower priority. In the first case, you can just insert the new document after the position that's referenced by the priority node. Because the priority node always must reference the last document with a specific priority, the reference of the priority node must be set. It gets more complex if just a priority node referencing a document with a lower priority exists. Here, the document must be inserted before all documents with the same priority as the priority node. To get the first document of the same priority, a `while` loop iterates through all linked list nodes, using the `Previous` property, until a linked list node is reached that has a different priority. This way, you know the position where the document must be inserted, and the priority node can be set.

```
private void AddDocumentToPriorityNode(
    Document doc, int priority)
{
    if (priority > 9 || priority < 0)
        throw new ArgumentException(
            "Priority must be between 0 and 9");

    if (priorityNodes[priority].Value == null)
    {
        priority--;
        if (priority >= 0)
        {
            // check for the next lower priority
            AddDocumentToPriorityNode(doc,
                priority);
        }
        else // now no priority node exists with
             // the same priority or lower
             // add the new document to the end
        {
            documentList.AddLast(doc);
            priorityNodes[doc.Priority] =
                documentList.Last;
        }
        return;
    }
    else // a priority node exists
    {
        LinkedListNode<Document> prioNode =
            priorityNodes[priority];
        if (priority == doc.Priority)
            // priority node with the same
            // priority exists
```

(continued)

(continued)

```
        {
            documentList.AddAfter(prioNode, doc);

            // set the priority node to the last
            // document with the same priority
            priorityNodes[doc.Priority] =
                    prioNode.Next;
        }
        else // only priority node with a lower
             // priority exists
        {
            // get the first node of the lower
            // priority
            LinkedListNode<Document>
                    firstPrioNode = prioNode;

            while (firstPrioNode.Previous != null &&
                firstPrioNode.Previous.Value.Priority
                == prioNode.Value.Priority)
            {
                firstPrioNode =
                        prioNode.Previous;
            }

            documentList.AddBefore(firstPrioNode,
                    doc);

            // set the priority node to the
            // new value
            priorityNodes[doc.Priority] =
                    firstPrioNode.Previous;
        }
    }
}
```

Now only simple methods are left for discussion. `DisplayAllNodes()` just does a `foreach` loop to display the priority and the title of every document to the console.

The method `GetDocument()` returns the first document (the document with the highest priority) from the linked list and removes it from the list:

```
public void DisplayAllNodes()
{
    foreach (Document doc in documentList)
    {
        Console.WriteLine(
                "priority: {0}, title {1}",
                doc.Priority, doc.Title);
    }
}

// returns the document with the highest priority
// (that's first in the linked list)
public Document GetDocument()
```

```
        {
            Document doc = documentList.First.Value;
            documentList.RemoveFirst();
            return doc;
        }
    }
```

In the `Main()` method, the `PriorityDocumentManager` is used to demonstrate its functionality. Eight new documents with different priorities are added to the linked list, and then the complete list is displayed:

```
static void Main()
{
    PriorityDocumentManager pdm =
        new PriorityDocumentManager();
    pdm.AddDocument(new Document("one", "Sample",
        8));
    pdm.AddDocument(new Document("two", "Sample",
        3));
    pdm.AddDocument(new Document("three",
        "Sample", 4));
    pdm.AddDocument(new Document("four", "Sample",
        8));
    pdm.AddDocument(new Document("five", "Sample",
        1));
    pdm.AddDocument(new Document("six", "Sample",
        9));
    pdm.AddDocument(new Document("seven",
        "Sample", 1));
    pdm.AddDocument(new Document("eight",
        "Sample", 1));

    pdm.DisplayAllNodes();
}
```

With the processed result, you can see that the documents are sorted first by the priority and second by when the document was added:

```
priority: 9, title six
priority: 8, title one
priority: 8, title four
priority: 4, title three
priority: 3, title two
priority: 1, title five
priority: 1, title seven
priority: 1, title eight
```

Sorted Lists

If you need a sorted list, you can use `SortedList<TKey, TValue>`. This class sorts the elements based on a key.

The example creates a sorted list where both the key and the value are of type `string`. The default constructor creates an empty list, and then two books are added with the `Add()` method. With overloaded constructors, you can define the capacity of the list and also pass an object that implements the interface `IComparer<TKey>`, which is used to sort the elements in the list.

The first parameter of the Add() method is the key (the book title); the second parameter is the value (the ISBN number). Instead of using the Add() method, you can use the indexer to add elements to the list. The indexer requires the key as index parameter. If a key already exists, the Add() method throws an exception of type ArgumentException. If the same key is used with the indexer, the new value replaces the old value.

```
SortedList<string, string> books =
    new SortedList<string, string>();
books.Add(".NET 2.0 Wrox Box",
    "978-0-470-04840-5");
books.Add(
    "Professional C# 2005 with .NET 3.0",
    "978-0-470-12472-7");

books["Beginning Visual C# 2005"] =
    "978-0-7645-4382-1";
books["Professional C# 2008"] =
    "978-0-470-19137-6";
```

You can iterate through the list by using a foreach statement. Elements that are returned by the enumerator are of type KeyValuePair<TKey, TValue>, which contains both the key and the value. The key can be accessed with the Key property, and the value can be accessed with the Value property.

```
foreach (KeyValuePair<string, string> book in
    books)
{
    Console.WriteLine("{0}, {1}", book.Key,
        book.Value);
}
```

The iteration displays book titles and ISBN numbers ordered by the key:

```
.NET 2.0 Wrox Box, 978-0-470-04840-5
Beginning Visual C# 2005, 978-0-7645-4382-1
Professional C# 2005 with .NET 3.0, 978-0-470-12472-7
Professional C# 2008, 978-0-470-19137-6
```

You can also access the values and keys by using the Values and Keys properties. The Values property returns IList<TValue> and the Keys property returns IList<TKey>, so you can use these properties with a foreach:

```
foreach (string isbn in books.Values)
{
    Console.WriteLine(isbn);
}

foreach (string title in books.Keys)
{
    Console.WriteLine(title);
}
```

The first loop displays the values, and next the keys:

```
978-0-470-04840-5
978-0-7645-4382-1
978-0-470-12472-7
978-0-470-19137-6
.NET 2.0 Wrox Box
Beginning Visual C# 2005
Professional C# 2005 with .NET 3.0
Professional C# 2008
```

Properties of the `SortedList<TKey, TValue>` class are described in the following table.

SortedList<TKey, TValue> Properties	Description
Capacity	With the property `Capacity` you can get and set the number of elements the list can contain. The capacity behaves as `List<T>`: the default constructor creates an empty list; adding the first item allocates a capacity of four items, and then the capacity is doubled as needed.
Comparer	The property `Comparer` returns the comparer that is associated with the list. You can pass the comparer in the constructor. The default comparer compares the key items by invoking the method `CompareTo` of the `IComparable<TKey>` interface. Either the key type implements this interface or you have to create a custom comparer.
Count	The property `Count` returns the number of elements in the list.
Item	With the indexer you can access the elements in the list. The parameter type of the indexer is defined by the key type.
Keys	The property `Keys` returns `IList<TKey>` containing all keys.
Values	The property `Values` returns `IList<TValue>` containing all values.

Methods of the `SortedList<T>` type are similar to the other collections you've learned about in this chapter. The difference is that `SortedList<T>` requires a key and a value.

SortedList<TKey, TValue> Methods	Description
Add()	The `Add()` method adds an element with key and value to the list.
Remove() RemoveAt()	The `Remove()` method requires the key of the element to be removed from the list. With `RemoveAt()`, you can remove an element at a specified index.
Clear()	The method `Clear()` removes all elements from the list.
ContainsKey() ContainsValue()	The `ContainsKey()` and `ContainsValue()` methods check if the list contains a specified key or value, and return `true` or `false`.
IndexOfKey() IndexOfValue()	The `IndexOfKey()` and `IndexOfValue()` methods check if the list contains a specified key or value and return the integer-based index.
TrimExcess()	The method `TrimExcess()` resizes the collection and changes the capacity to the required item count.
TryGetValue()	With the method `TryGetValue()`, you can try to get the value for a specified key. If the key does not exist, this method returns `false`. If the key exists, `true` is returned, and the value is returned as `out` parameter.

In addition to the generic `SortedList<TKey, TValue>`, *a corresponding non-generic list named* `SortedList` *is available.*

Dictionaries

Dictionaries represent a sophisticated data structure that allows you to access an element based on a key. Dictionaries are also known as hash tables or maps. The main feature of dictionaries is fast lookup based on keys. You can also add and remove items freely, a bit like a `List<T>`, but without the performance overhead of having to shift subsequent items in memory.

Figure 10-5 shows a simplified representation of a dictionary. Here `employee-ids` such as B4711 are the keys added to the dictionary. The key is transformed into a hash. With the hash a number is created to associate an index with the values. The index then contains a link to the value. The figure is simplified because it is possible that a single index entry can be associated with multiple values, and the index can be stored as a tree.

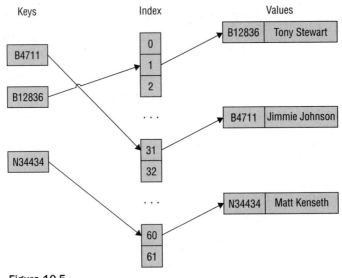

Figure 10-5

The .NET Framework offers several dictionary classes. The main class you can use is `Dictionary<TKey, TValue>`. This class offers nearly the same properties and methods as `SortedList<TKey, TValue>` discussed earlier; that's why they are not repeated here.

Key Type

A type that is used as a key in the dictionary must override the method `GetHashCode()` of the `Object` class. Whenever a dictionary class needs to work out where an item should be located, it calls the `GetHashCode()` method. The `int` that is returned by `GetHashCode()` is used by the dictionary to calculate an index of where to place the element. We don't go into this part of the algorithm. What you should know is that it involves prime numbers, so the capacity of a dictionary is a prime number.

The implementation of GetHashCode() must satisfy these requirements:

❑ The same object should always return the same value.

❑ Different objects can return the same value.

❑ It should execute as quickly as possible; it must be inexpensive to compute.

❑ It must not throw exceptions.

❑ It should use at least one instance field.

❑ The hash code value should be evenly distributed across the entire range of numbers that an int can store.

❑ At best, the hash code should not change during the lifetime of the object.

> **A good performance of the dictionary is based on a good implementation of the method** GetHashCode()**.**

What's the reason for having hash code values evenly distributed across the range of integers? If two keys return hashes that give the same index, the dictionary class needs to start looking for the nearest available free location to store the second item — and will have to do some searching in order to retrieve this item later on. This is obviously going to hurt performance, and clearly, if lots of your keys are tending to give the same indexes for where they should be stored, this kind of clash becomes more likely. However, because of the way that Microsoft's part of the algorithm works, this risk is minimized when the calculated hash values are evenly distributed between int.MinValue and int.MaxValue.

Besides having an implementation of GetHashCode(), the key type also must implement the IEquality.Equals() method or override the Equals() method from the Object class. Because different key objects may return the same hash code, the method Equals() is used by the dictionary comparing keys. The dictionary examines if two keys A and B are equal; it invokes A.Equals(B). This means that you must ensure that the following is always true:

If A.Equals(B) is true, then A.GetHashCode() and B.GetHashCode() must always return the same hash code.

This probably seems a fairly subtle point, but it is crucial. If you contrived some way of overriding these methods so that the preceding statement was not always true, a dictionary that uses instances of this class as its keys would simply not work properly. Instead, you'd find funny things happening. For example, you might place an object in the dictionary and then discover that you could never retrieve it, or you might try to retrieve an entry and have the wrong entry returned.

For this reason, the C# compiler will display a compilation warning if you supply an override for Equals() *but don't supply an override for* GetHashCode()*.*

For System.Object this condition is true, because Equals() simply compares references, and GetHashCode() actually returns a hash that is based solely on the address of the object. This means that hash tables based on a key that doesn't override these methods will work correctly. However, the problem with this way of doing things is that keys are regarded as equal only if they are the same object. That means that when you place an object in the dictionary, you then have to hang onto the reference to the key. You can't simply instantiate another key object later with the same value. If you don't override Equals() and GetHashCode(), the type is not very convenient to use in a dictionary.

Incidentally, System.String implements the interface IEquatable and overloads GetHashCode() appropriately. Equals() provides value comparison, and GetHashCode() returns a hash based on the value of the string. Strings can be used conveniently as keys in dictionaries.

Number types such as `Int32` also implement the interface `IEquatable` and overload `GetHashCode()`. However, the hash code returned by these types simply maps to the value. If the number you would like to use as a key is not itself distributed around the possible values of an integer, using integers as keys doesn't fulfill the rule of evenly distributing key values to get the best performance. `Int32` is not meant to be used in a dictionary.

If you need to use a key type that does not implement `IEquatable` and override `GetHashCode` according to the key values you store in the dictionary, you can create a comparer implementing the interface `IEqualityComparer<T>`. `IEqualityComparer<T>` defines the methods `GetHashCode()` and `Equals()` with an argument of the object passed, so you can offer an implementation different from the object type itself. An overload of the `Dictionary<TKey, TValue>` constructor allows passing an object implementing `IEqualityComparer<T>`. If such an object is assigned to the dictionary, this class is used to generate the hash codes and compare the keys.

Dictionary Example

The dictionary example is a program that sets up a dictionary of employees. The dictionary is indexed by `EmployeeId` objects, and each item stored in the dictionary is an `Employee` object that stores details of an employee.

The struct `EmployeeId` is implemented to define a key to be used in a dictionary. The members of the class are a prefix character and a number for the employee. Both of these variables are read-only and can be initialized only in the constructor. A key within the dictionary shouldn't change, and this way that is guaranteed. The fields are filled within the constructor. The `ToString()` method is overloaded to get a string representation of the employee ID. As required for a key type, `EmployeeId` implements the interface `IEquatable` and overloads the method `GetHashCode()`.

```
[Serializable]
public struct EmployeeId  : IEquatable<EmployeeId>
{
    private readonly char prefix;
    private readonly int number;

    public EmployeeId(string id)
    {
        if (id == null)
            throw new ArgumentNullException("id");

        prefix = (id.ToUpper())[0];
        int numLength = id.Length - 1;
        number = int.Parse(id.Substring(
            1, numLength > 6 ? 6 : numLength));
    }

    public override string ToString()
    {
        return prefix.ToString() +
            string.Format("{0,6:000000}", number);
    }

    public override int GetHashCode()
    {
        return (number ^ number << 16) * 0x15051505;
    }

    public bool Equals(EmployeeId other)
```

```
    {
        return (prefix == other.prefix &&
             number == other.number);
    }
}
```

The `Equals()` method that is defined by the `IEquatable<T>` interface compares the values of two `EmployeeId` objects and returns `true` if the both values are the same. Instead of implementing the `Equals()` method from the `IEquatable<T>` interface, you can also override the `Equals()` method from the `Object` class:

```
public bool Equals(EmployeeId other)
{
    if (other == null) return false;
    return (prefix == other.prefix &&
         number == other.number);
}
```

With the number variable, a value from 1 to around 190,000 is expected for the employees. This doesn't fill the range of an integer. The algorithm used by `GetHashCode()` shifts the number 16 bits to the left, then does an XOR with the original number, and finally multiplies the result by the hex value 15051505. The hash code is fairly distributed across the range of an integer.

```
public override int GetHashCode()
{
    return (number ^ number << 16) * 0x15051505;
}
```

On the Internet, you can find a lot more complex algorithms that have a better distribution across the integer range. You can also use the `GetHashCode()` method of a string to return a hash.

The `Employee` class is a simple entity class containing the name, salary, and ID of the employee. The constructor initializes all values, and the method `ToString()` returns a string representation of an instance. The implementation of `ToString()` uses a format string to create the string representation for performance reasons.

```
[Serializable]
public class Employee
{
    private string name;
    private decimal salary;
    private readonly EmployeeId id;

    public Employee(EmployeeId id, string name,
            decimal salary)
    {
        this.id = id;
        this.name = name;
        this.salary = salary;
    }

    public override string ToString()
    {
        return String.Format("{0}: {1, -20} {2:C}",
            id.ToString(), name, salary);
    }
}
```

In the `Main()` method of the sample application, a new `Dictionary<TKey, TValue>` instance is created, where the key is of type `EmployeeId` and the value is of type `Employee`. The constructor allocates a capacity of 31 elements. Remember, the capacity is based on prime numbers. However, when you assign a value that is not a prime number, you don't need to worry. The `Dictionary<TKey, TValue>` class itself takes the next prime number that follows the integer passed to the constructor to allocate the capacity. The employee objects and IDs are created and added to the dictionary with the `Add()` method. Instead of using the `Add()` method, you can also use the indexer to add keys and values to the dictionary, as shown with the employees Carl and Matt:

```
static void Main()
{
    Dictionary<EmployeeId, Employee> employees =
        new Dictionary<EmployeeId,
            Employee>(31);

    EmployeeId idJeff = new EmployeeId("C7102");
    Employee jeff = new Employee(idJeff,
        "Jeff Gordon", 5164580.00m);
    employees.Add(idJeff, jeff);
    Console.WriteLine(jeff);

    EmployeeId idTony = new EmployeeId("C7105");
    Employee tony = new Employee(idTony,
        "Tony Stewart", 4814200.00m);
    employees.Add(idTony, tony);
    Console.WriteLine(tony);

    EmployeeId idDenny = new EmployeeId("C8011");
    Employee denny = new Employee(idDenny,
        "Denny Hamlin", 3718710.00m);
    employees.Add(idDenny, denny);
    Console.WriteLine(denny);

    EmployeeId idCarl = new EmployeeId("F7908");
    Employee carl = new Employee(idCarl,
        "Carl Edwards", 3285710.00m);
    employees[idCarl] = carl;
    Console.WriteLine(carl);

    EmployeeId idMatt = new EmployeeId("F7203");
    Employee matt = new Employee(idMatt,
        "Matt Kenseth", 4520330.00m);
    employees[idMatt] = matt;
    Console.WriteLine(matt);
```

After the entries are added to the dictionary, inside a `while` loop employees are read from the dictionary. The user is asked to enter an employee number to store in the variable `userInput`. The user can exit the application by entering X. If the key is in the dictionary, it is examined with the `TryGetValue()` method of the `Dictionary<TKey, TValue>` class. `TryGetValue()` returns `true` if the key is found and `false` otherwise. If the value is found, the value associated with the key is stored in the employee variable. This value is written to the console.

You can also use an indexer of the `Dictionary<TKey, TValue>` class instead of `TryGetValue()` to access a value stored in the dictionary. However, if the key is not found, the indexer throws an exception of type `KeyNotFoundException`.

```
        while (true)
        {
            Console.Write(
                "Enter employee id (X to exit)> ");
            string userInput = Console.ReadLine();
            userInput = userInput.ToUpper();
            if (userInput == "X") break;

            EmployeeId id = new EmployeeId(userInput);

            Employee employee;
            if (!employees.TryGetValue(id,
                    out employee))
            {
                Console.WriteLine("Employee with id " +
                    "{0} does not exist", id);
            }
            else
            {
                Console.WriteLine(employee);
            }
        }
    }
```

Running the application produces the following output:

```
Enter employee ID (format:A999999, X to exit)> C7102
C007102: Jeff Gordon          $5,164,580.00
Enter employee ID (format:A999999, X to exit)> F7908
F007908: Carl Edwards         $3,285,710.00
Enter employee ID (format:A999999, X to exit)> X
```

Lookup

Dictionary<TKey, TValue> supports only one value per key. The new class Lookup<TKey, TElement> that is part of .NET 3.5 resembles a Dictionary<TKey, TValue> but maps keys to a collection of values. This class is implemented in the assembly System.Core and defined with the namespace System.Linq.

Properties and methods of Lookup<TKey, TElement> are described in the following table.

Lookup<TKey, TElement> Properties and Methods	Description
Count	The property Count returns the number of elements in the collection.
Item	With the indexer you can access specific elements based on the key. Because multiple values can exist with the same key, this property returns an enumeration of all values.
Contains()	The method Contains() returns a Boolean result depending on whether there's an element passed with the key parameter.
ApplyResultSelector()	ApplyResultSelector() returns a collection by transforming every item based on the transformation function that is passed to this method.

Lookup<TKey, TElement> cannot be created like a normal dictionary. Instead, you have to invoke the method ToLookup() that returns a Lookup<TKey, TElement> object. The method ToLookup() is an extension method that is available with every class implementing IEnumerable<T>. In the following example, a list of Racer objects is filled. Because List<T> implements IEnumerable<T>, the ToLookup() method can be invoked on the racers list. This method requires a delegate of type Func<TSource, TKey> that defines the selector of the key. Here the racers are selected based on the country by using the Lambda expression r => r.Country. The foreach loop accesses only the racers from Australia by using the indexer.

You can read more about extension methods in Chapter 11, "Language Integrated Query." Lambda expressions are explained in Chapter 7, "Delegates and Events."

```
List<Racer> racers = new List<Racer>();
racers.Add(new Racer("Jacques", "Villeneuve",
        "Canada", 11));
racers.Add(new Racer("Alan", "Jones",
        "Australia", 12));
racers.Add(new Racer("Jackie", "Stewart",
        "United Kingdom", 27));
racers.Add(new Racer("James", "Hunt",
        "United Kingdom", 10));
racers.Add(new Racer("Jack", "Brabham",
        "Australia", 14));

Lookup<string, Racer> lookupRacers =
        (Lookup<string, Racer>)
        racers.ToLookup(r => r.Country);

foreach (Racer r in lookupRacers["Australia"])
{
    Console.WriteLine(r);
}
```

The output shows the racers from Australia:

```
Alan Jones
Jack Brabham
```

Other Dictionary Classes

Dictionary<TKey, TValue> is the major dictionary class from the framework. There are some more classes, and of course there are also some non-generic dictionary classes.

Dictionaries that are based on the Object type and are available since .NET 1.0 are described in the following table.

Non-generic dictionary	Description
Hashtable	Hashtable is the most-used dictionary implementation of .NET 1.0. Keys and values are based on the Object type.
ListDictionary	ListDictionary is located in the namespace System.Collections.Specialized and is faster than the Hashtable if 10 or fewer items are used. ListDictionary is implemented as a linked list.

Non-generic dictionary	Description
HybridDictionary	HybridDictionary uses a ListDictionary if the collection is small and switches to a Hashtable as the collection grows. If you don't know the number of items in advance, you can use the HybridDictionary.
NameObjectCollectionBase	NameObjectCollectionBase is an abstract base class to associate keys of type string to values of type object. This can be used as a base class for custom string/object collections. This class uses a Hashtable internally.
NameValueCollection	NameValueCollection derives from NameObjectCollection. Here, both the key and value are of type string. This class has another feature where multiple values can use the same key.

Since .NET 2.0, generic dictionaries are preferred over object-based dictionaries:

Generic Dictionary	Description
Dictionary<TKey, TValue>	Dictionary<TKey, TValue> is the general-purpose dictionary for mapping keys to values.
SortedDictionary<TKey, TValue>	SortedDictionary<TKey, TValue> is a binary search tree where the items are sorted based on the key. The key type must implement the interface IComparable<TKey>. If the key type is not sortable, you can also create a comparer implementing IComparer<TKey> and assign the comparer as a constructor argument of the sorted dictionary.

SortedDictionary<TKey, TValue> and SortedList<TKey, TValue> have similar functionality. But because SortedList<TKey, TValue> is implemented as a list that is based on an array and SortedDictionary<TKey, TValue> is implemented as a dictionary, the classes have different characteristics:

❑ SortedList<TKey, TValue> uses less memory than SortedDictionary<TKey, TValue>.

❑ SortedDictionary<TKey, TValue> has faster insertion and removal of elements.

❑ When populating the collection with already sorted data, SortedList<TKey, TValue> is faster, if capacity changes are not needed.

> SortedList **consumes less memory than** SortedDictionary. SortedDictionary **is faster for inserts and the removal of unsorted data.**

HashSet

.NET 3.5 includes a new collection class in the `System.Collections.Generic` namespace: `HashSet<T>`. This collection class contains an unordered list of distinct items. Such a collection is known by the term *set*. Because *set* is a reserved word, the class has a different name: `HashSet<T>`. The name was easily decided because this collection is based on hash values; inserting elements is fast. There's no need to rearrange the collection as is necessary with the `List<T>` class.

The `HashSet<T>` class offers methods to create a union, an intersection of sets. The following table describes the methods that change the values of the set.

HashSet<T> Modification Methods	Description
`Add()`	The `Add()` method adds elements to the collection if the element is not already in the collection. With the Boolean return value, the information is returned if the element was added.
`Clear()`	The method `Clear()` removes all elements from the collection.
`Remove()`	The `Remove()` method removes the element specified.
`RemoveWhere()`	The `RemoveWhere()` method requires a `Predicate<T>` delegate as argument. This method removes all elements where the predicate condition matches.
`CopyTo()`	The method `CopyTo()` copies the elements of the set to an array.
`ExceptWith()`	The `ExceptWith()` method receives a collection as argument and removes all the elements from this collection from the set.
`IntersectWith()`	`IntersectWith()` changes the set to include only elements that are part of both the collection that is passed and the set.
`UnionWith()`	The `UnionWith()` method adds all elements from the collection passed with the argument to the set.

The next table lists the methods that just return information about the set without changing the elements.

HashSet<T> Verification Methods	Description
`Contains()`	The method `Contains()` returns `true` if the passed element is within the collection.
`IsSubsetOf()`	The method `IsSubsetOf()` returns `true` if the collection that is passed with the argument is a subset of the set.
`IsSupersetOf()`	The method `IsSupersetOf()` returns `true` if the collection that is passed with the argument is a superset of the set.

HashSet<T> Verification Methods	Description
Overlaps()	If there's at least one element in common with the collection that is passed with the argument and the set, true is returned.
SetEquals()	The SetEquals() method returns true if both the collection passed with the argument and the set contain the same elements.

With the sample code, three new sets of type string are created and filled with Formula-1 cars. The HashSet<T> class implements the ICollection<T> interface. However, the Add() method is implemented explicitly and a different Add() method is offered by the class as you can see here. The Add() method differs by the return type; a Boolean value is returned to give the information if the element was added. If the element was already in the set, it is not added, and false is returned.

```
HashSet<string> companyTeams =
      new HashSet<string>()
      { "Ferrari", "McLaren", "Toyota", "BMW",
        "Renault", "Honda" };
HashSet<string> traditionalTeams =
      new HashSet<string>()
      { "Ferrari", "McLaren" };
HashSet<string> privateTeams =
      new HashSet<string>()
      { "Red Bull", "Toro Rosso", "Spyker",
        "Super Aguri" };

if (privateTeams.Add("Williams"))
   Console.WriteLine("Williams added");
if (!companyTeams.Add("McLaren"))
   Console.WriteLine(
         "McLaren was already in this set");
```

The result of these two Add() methods is written to the console:

```
Williams added
McLaren was already in this set
```

The methods IsSubsetOf() and IsSupersetOf() compare a set with a collection that implements the IEnumerable<T> interface and returns a Boolean result. Here, IsSubsetOf() verifies if every element in traditionalTeams is contained in companyTeams, which is the case; IsSupersetOf() verifies if traditionalTeams does not have any additional element compared to companyTeams.

```
if (traditionalTeams.IsSubsetOf(companyTeams))
{
   Console.WriteLine("traditionalTeams is " +
         "subset of companyTeams");
}

if (companyTeams.IsSupersetOf(traditionalTeams))
{
   Console.WriteLine(
         "companyTeams is a superset of " +
         "traditionalTeams");
}
```

The output of this verification is shown here:

```
traditionalTeams is a subset of companyTeams
companyTeams is a superset of traditionalTeams
```

Williams is a traditional team as well, and that's why this team is added to the `traditionalTeams` collection:

```
traditionalTeams.Add("Williams");
if (privateTeams.Overlaps(traditionalTeams))
{
    Console.WriteLine("At least one team is " +
            "the same with the traditional " +
            "and private teams");
}
```

Because there's an overlap, this is the result:

```
At least one team is the same with the traditional and private teams.
```

The variable `allTeams` is filled with a union of `companyTeams`, `privateTeams`, and `traditionalTeams` by calling the `UnionWith()` method:

```
HashSet<string> allTeams =
        new HashSet<string>(companyTeams);
allTeams.UnionWith(privateTeams);
allTeams.UnionWith(traditionalTeams);

Console.WriteLine();
Console.WriteLine("all teams");
foreach (var team in allTeams)
{
    Console.WriteLine(team);
}
```

Here all teams are returned, but every team is listed just once because the set contains only unique values:

```
Ferrari
McLaren
Toyota
BMW
Renault
Honda
Red Bull
Toro Rosso
Spyker
Super Aguri
Williams
```

The method `ExceptWith()` removes all private teams from the `allTeams` set:

```
allTeams.ExceptWith(privateTeams);
Console.WriteLine();
Console.WriteLine("no private team left");
foreach (var team in allTeams)
{
    Console.WriteLine(team);
}
```

The remaining elements in the collection do not contain any private team:

```
Ferrari
McLaren
Toyota
BMW
Renault
Honda
```

Bit Arrays

If you need to deal with a number of bits, you can use the class BitArray and the struct BitVector32. BitArray is located in the namespace System.Collections; BitVector32 is in the namespace System.Collections.Specialized. The most important difference between these two types is that BitArray is resizable, which is useful if you don't know the number of bits needed in advance, and it can contain a large number of bits. BitVector32 is stack-based and therefore faster. BitVector32 contains only 32 bits, which are stored in an integer.

BitArray

The class BitArray is a reference type that contains an array of ints, where for every 32 bits a new integer is used. Members of this class are explained in the following table.

BitArray Members	Description
Count Length	The get accessor of both Count and Length return the number of bits in the array. With the Length property, you can also define a new size and resize the collection.
Item	You can use an indexer to read and write bits in the array. The indexer is of type bool.
Get() Set()	Instead of using the indexer, you can also use the Get() and Set() methods to access the bits in the array.
SetAll()	The method SetAll() sets the values of all bits according to the parameter passed to the method.
Not()	The method Not() generates the inverse of all bits of the array.
And() Or() Xor()	With the methods And(), Or(), and Xor(), you can combine two BitArray objects. The And() method does a binary AND, where the result bits are set only if the bits from both input arrays are set. The Or() method does a binary OR, where the result bits are set if one or both of the input arrays are set. The Xor() method is an exclusive OR, where the result is set if only one of the input bits is set.

In Chapter 6, "Operators and Casts," you can read about the C# operators for working with bits.

The helper method `DisplayBits()` iterates through a `BitArray` and displays 1 or 0 to the console, depending on whether or not the bit is set:

```
static void DisplayBits(BitArray bits)
{
    foreach (bool bit in bits)
    {
        Console.Write(bit ? 1 : 0);
    }
}
```

The example to demonstrate the `BitArray` class creates a bit array with 8 bits, indexed from 0 to 7. The `SetAll()` method sets all 8 bits to `true`. Then the `Set()` method changes bit 1 to `false`. Instead of the `Set` method, you can also use an indexer, as shown with index 5 and 7:

```
BitArray bits1 = new BitArray(8);
bits1.SetAll(true);
bits1.Set(1, false);
bits1[5] = false;
bits1[7] = false;
Console.Write("initialized: ");
DisplayBits(bits1);
Console.WriteLine();
```

This is the displayed result of the initialized bits:

```
initialized: 10111010
```

The `Not()` method generates the inverse of the bits of the `BitArray`:

```
Console.Write(" not ");
DisplayBits(bits1);
bits1.Not();
Console.Write(" = ");
DisplayBits(bits1);
Console.WriteLine();
```

The result of `Not()` is all bits inversed. If the bit was `true`, it is `false`, and if it was `false`, it is `true`:

```
not 10111010 = 01000101
```

Here, a new `BitArray` is created. With the constructor, the variable `bits1` is used to initialize the array, so the new array has the same values. Then the values for bits 0, 1, and 4 are set to different values. Before the `Or()` method is used, the bit arrays `bits1` and `bits2` are displayed. The `Or()` method changes the values of `bits1`.

```
BitArray bits2 = new BitArray(bits1);
bits2[0] = true;
bits2[1] = false;
bits2[4] = true;
DisplayBits(bits1);
Console.Write(" or ");
DisplayBits(bits2);
Console.Write(" = ");
bits1.Or(bits2);
DisplayBits(bits1);
Console.WriteLine();
```

With the Or() method, the set bits are taken from both input arrays. In the result, the bit is set if it was set with either the first or the second array:

```
01000101 or 10001101 = 11001101
```

Next, the And() method is used to operate on bits2 and bits1:

```
DisplayBits(bits2);
Console.Write(" and ");
DisplayBits(bits1);
Console.Write(" = ");
bits2.And(bits1);
DisplayBits(bits2);
Console.WriteLine();
```

The result of the And() method only sets the bits where the bit was set in both input arrays:

```
10001101 and 11001101 = 10001101
```

Finally the Xor() method is used for an exclusive OR:

```
DisplayBits(bits1);
Console.Write(" xor ");
DisplayBits(bits2);
bits1.Xor(bits2);
Console.Write(" = ");
DisplayBits(bits1);
Console.WriteLine();
```

With the Xor() method, the resultant bits are set only if the bit was set either in the first or the second input, but not both:

```
11001101 xor 10001101 = 01000000
```

BitVector32

If you know the number of bits you need in advance, you can use the BitVector32 structure instead of BitArray. BitVector32 is more efficient, because it is a value type and stores the bits on the stack inside an integer. With a single integer you have a place for 32 bits. If you need more bits, you can use multiple BitVector32 values or the BitArray. The BitArray can grow as needed; this is not an option with BitVector32.

The next table shows the members of BitVector that are very different from BitArray.

BitVector Members	Description
Data	The property Data returns the data behind the BitVector32 as integer.
Item	The values for the BitVector32 can be set using an indexer. The indexer is overloaded — you can get and set the values using a mask or a section of type BitVector32.Section.
CreateMask()	CreateMask() is a static method that you can use to create a mask for accessing specific bits in the BitVector32.
CreateSection()	CreateSection() is a static method that you can use to create several sections within the 32 bits.

The sample code creates a `BitVector32` with the default constructor, where all 32 bits are initialized to `false`. Then masks are created to access the bits inside the bit vector. The first call to `CreateMask()` creates a mask to access the first bit. After `CreateMask()` is invoked, `bit1` has a value of 1. Invoking `CreateMask()` once more and passing the first mask as a parameter to `CreateMask()` returns a mask to access the second bit, which is 2. `bit3` then has a value of 4 to access bit number 3. `bit4` has a value of 8 to access bit number 4.

Then the masks are used with the indexer to access the bits inside the bit vector and set fields accordingly:

```
BitVector32 bits1 = new BitVector32();
int bit1 = BitVector32.CreateMask();
int bit2 = BitVector32.CreateMask(bit1);
int bit3 = BitVector32.CreateMask(bit2);
int bit4 = BitVector32.CreateMask(bit3);
int bit5 = BitVector32.CreateMask(bit4);

bits1[bit1] = true;
bits1[bit2] = false;
bits1[bit3] = true;
bits1[bit4] = true;
bits1[bit5] = true;
Console.WriteLine(bits1);
```

The `BitVector32` has an overridden `ToString()` method that not only displays the name of the class but also 1 or 0 if the bits are set or not, respectively:

```
BitVector32{00000000000000000000000000011101}
```

Instead of creating a mask with the `CreateMask()` method, you can define the mask yourself; you can also set multiple bits at once. The hexadecimal value abcdef is the same as the binary value 1010 1011 1100 1101 1110 1111. All the bits defined with this value are set:

```
bits1[0xabcdef] = true;
Console.WriteLine(bits1);
```

With the output shown you can verify the bits that are set:

```
BitVector32{00000000101010111100110111101111}
```

Separating the 32 bits to different sections can be extremely useful. For example, an IPv4 address is defined as a 4-byte number that is stored inside an integer. You can split the integer by defining four sections. With a multicast IP message, several 32-bit values are used. One of these 32-bit values is separated in these sections: 16 bits for the number of sources, 8 bits for a querier's query interval code, 3 bits for a querier's robustness variable, a 1-bit suppress flag, and 4 bits that are reserved. You can also define your own bit meanings to save memory.

The example simulates receiving the value `0x79abcdef` and passes this value to the constructor of `BitVector32`, so that the bits are set accordingly:

```
int received = 0x79abcdef;

BitVector32 bits2 = new BitVector32(received);
Console.WriteLine(bits2);
```

The bits are shown on the console as initialized:

```
BitVector32{01111001101010111100110111101111}
```

Then six sections are created. The first section requires 12 bits, as defined by the hexadecimal value 0xfff (12 bits are set); section B requires 8 bits; section C, 4 bits; section D and E, 3 bits; and section F, 2 bits. The first call to CreateSection() just receives 0xfff to allocate the first 12 bits. With the second call to CreateSection(), the first section is passed as an argument, so that the next section continues where the first section ended. CreateSection() returns a value of type BitVector32.Section that contains the offset and the mask for the section.

```
// sections: FF EEE DDD CCCC BBBBBBBB
// AAAAAAAAAAAA
BitVector32.Section sectionA =
    BitVector32.CreateSection(0xfff);
BitVector32.Section sectionB =
    BitVector32.CreateSection(0xff,
    sectionA);
BitVector32.Section sectionC =
    BitVector32.CreateSection(0xf,
    sectionB);
BitVector32.Section sectionD =
    BitVector32.CreateSection(0x7,
    sectionC);
BitVector32.Section sectionE =
    BitVector32.CreateSection(0x7,
    sectionD);
BitVector32.Section sectionF =
    BitVector32.CreateSection(0x3,
    sectionE);
```

Passing a BitVector32.Section to the indexer of the BitVector32 returns an int just mapped to the section of the bit vector. Here, a helper method, IntToBinaryString(), retrieves a string representation of the int number:

```
Console.WriteLine("Section A: " +
    IntToBinaryString(bits2[sectionA],
    true));
Console.WriteLine("Section B: " +
    IntToBinaryString(bits2[sectionB],
    true));
Console.WriteLine("Section C: " +
    IntToBinaryString(bits2[sectionC],
    true));
Console.WriteLine("Section D: " +
    IntToBinaryString(bits2[sectionD],
    true));
Console.WriteLine("Section E: " +
    IntToBinaryString(bits2[sectionE],
    true));
Console.WriteLine("Section F: " +
    IntToBinaryString(bits2[sectionF],
    true));
```

The method IntToBinaryString() receives the bits in an integer and returns a string representation containing 0 and 1. With the implementation, 32 bits of the integer are iterated through. In the iteration, if the bit is set, 1 is appended to the StringBuilder; otherwise, 0 is appended. Within the loop, a bit shift happens to check if the next bit is set.

```
    static string IntToBinaryString(int bits,
        bool removeTrailingZero)
{
    StringBuilder sb = new StringBuilder(32);

    for (int i = 0; i < 32; i++)
    {
        if ((bits & 0x80000000) != 0)
        {
            sb.Append("1");
        }
        else
        {
            sb.Append("0");
        }
        bits = bits << 1;
    }
    string s = sb.ToString();
    if (removeTrailingZero)
    {
        return s.TrimStart('0');
    }
    else
    {
        return s;
    }
}
```

The result displays the bit representation of sections A to F, which you can now verify with the value that was passed into the bit vector:

```
Section A: 110111101111
Section B: 10111100
Section C: 1010
Section D: 1
Section E: 111
Section F: 1
```

Performance

Many collection classes offer the same functionality as others; for example, SortedList offers nearly the same features as SortedDictionary. However, often there's a big difference in performance. Whereas one collection consumes less memory, the other collection class is faster with retrieval of elements. In the MSDN documentation, you often find performance hints with methods of the collection giving you information about the time the operation represents in *big-O* notation:

```
O(1)
O(log n)
O(n)
```

O(1) means that the time this operation needs is constant no matter how many items are in the collection. For example, the ArrayList has an Add() method with O(1) behavior. No matter how many elements are in the list, it always takes the same time when adding a new element to the end of the list. The Count property gives the number of items, so it is easy to find the end of the list.

O(n) means that for every element in the collection the same amount of additional time is needed. The Add() method of ArrayList can be an O(n) operation if a reallocation of the collection is required. Changing the capacity causes the copying of the list, and the time for the copy increases linearly with every element.

O(log n) means that the time needed for the operation increases with every element in the collection. But the increase of time for every element is not linear but logarithmic. SortedDictionary<TKey,TValue> has O(log n) behavior for inserting operations inside the collection; SortedList<TKey,TValue> has O(n) behavior for the same functionality. Here, SortedDictionary<TKey,TValue> is a lot faster because it is more efficient to insert elements into a tree structure than into a list.

The following table lists collection classes and their performance for different actions such as adding, inserting, and removing items. Using this table you can select the best collection class for the purpose of your use. The left column lists the collection class. The Add column gives timing information about adding items to the collection. The List<T> and the HashSet<T> classes define Add methods to add items to the collection. With other collection classes, there's a different method to add elements to the collection; for example, the Stack<T> class defines a Push() method, and the Queue<T> class defines an Enqueue() method. You can find this information in the table as well.

If there are multiple big-O values in a cell the reason is that if a collection needs to be resized, resizing takes a while. For example, with the List<T> class, adding items needs O(1). If the capacity of the collection is not large enough and the collection needs to be resized, the resize requires O(n) time. The larger the collection is, the longer the resize operation takes. It's best to avoid resizes by setting the capacity of the collection to a value that can hold all elements.

If the cell content is *na*, this means that this operation is *not applicable* with this collection type.

Collection	Add	Insert	Remove	Item	Sort	Find
List<T>	O(1) or O(n) if the collection must be resized	O(n)	O(n)	O(1)	O (n log n), worst case O(n ^ 2)	O(n)
Stack<T>	Push(), O(1) or O(n) if the stack must be resized	na	Pop(), O(1)	na	na	na
Queue<T>	Enqueue(), O(1) or O(n) if the queue must be resized	na	Dequeue(), O(1)	na	na	na
HashSet<T>	O(1) or O(n) if the set must be resized	Add() O(1) or O(n)	O(1)	na	na	na
LinkedList<T>	AddLast() O(1)	Add After() O(1)	O(1)	na	na	O(n)

Collection	Add	Insert	Remove	Item	Sort	Find
Dictionary <TKey, TValue>	O(1) or O(n)	na	O(1)	O(1)	na	na
SortedDictionary <TKey, TValue>	O(log n)	na	O(log n)	O(log n)	na	na
SortedList <TKey, TValue>	O(n) for unsorted data, O(log n) for end of list O(n) if resize is needed	na	O(n)	O(log n) to read, write O(log n) if the key is in the list, O(n) if the key is not in the list	na	na

Summary

This chapter took a look at working with different kinds of collections. Arrays are fixed in size, but you can use lists for dynamically growing collections. For accessing elements on a first-in, first-out basis, there's a queue, and there's a stack for last-in, first-out operations. Linked lists allow for fast inserting and removing of elements but are slow for searching. With keys and value, you can use dictionaries, which are fast for searching and inserting elements. A set (which has the name HashSet<T>) is for unique items that are not ordered.

In this chapter, you've seen a lot of interfaces and their use for accessing and sorting collections. You've also seen some specialized collections, such as BitArray and BitVector32, which are optimized for working with a collection of bits.

Chapter 11 gives you details about Language Integrated Query (LINQ), the major new language extensions of C# 3.0.

11

Language Integrated Query

LINQ (Language Integrated Query) is the most important new feature of C# 3.0 and .NET 3.5. LINQ integrates query syntax inside the C# programming language and makes it possible to access different data sources with the same syntax. LINQ makes this possible by offering an abstraction layer.

This chapter gives you the core foundation of LINQ and the language extensions for C# 3.0 that make the new features possible. The topics of this chapter are:

- ❑ Traditional queries across objects using `List<T>`
- ❑ Extension methods
- ❑ Lambda expressions
- ❑ LINQ query
- ❑ Standard query operators
- ❑ Expression trees
- ❑ LINQ providers

This chapter gives you the core foundation of LINQ. For using LINQ across the database you should read Chapter 27, "LINQ to SQL." To query XML data read Chapter 29, "LINQ to XML," after reading this chapter.

LINQ Overview

Before getting into the features of LINQ, this section uses an example to show how queries across objects were done before LINQ was available. As you read on, the query will evolve to show how the LINQ query is reached. By going through the steps you will know what's behind the LINQ query.

The example in this chapter is based on Formula-1 world champions. Queries are done across a list of `Racer` objects. The first query gets all Formula-1 champions from Brazil in the order of races won.

Query using List<T>

The first variant of a filter and sort is to search data in a list of type `List<T>`. Before the search can start, the object type and the list must be prepared.

For the object, the type `Racer` is defined. `Racer` defines several properties and an overloaded `ToString()` method to display a racer in a string format. This class implements the interface `IFormattable` to support different variants of format strings, and the interface `IComparable<Racer>`, which can be used to sort a list of racers based on the `LastName`. For doing more advanced queries, the class `Racer` contains not only single value properties such as `FirstName`, `LastName`, `Wins`, `Country`, and `Starts`, but also multivalue properties such as `Cars` and `Years`. The `Years` property lists all the years of the championship title. Some racers have won more than one title. The `Cars` property is used to list all the cars that have been used by the driver during the title years.

```csharp
using System;
using System.Text;

namespace Wrox.ProCSharp.LINQ
{
    [Serializable]
    public class Racer : IComparable<Racer>, IFormattable
    {
        public string FirstName {get; set;}
        public string LastName {get; set;}
        public int Wins {get; set;}
        public string Country {get; set;}
        public int Starts {get; set;}
        public string[] Cars { get; set; }
        public int[] Years { get; set; }

        public override string ToString()
        {
            return String.Format("{0} {1}",
                FirstName, LastName);
        }

        public int CompareTo(Racer other)
        {
            return this.LastName.CompareTo(
                other.LastName);
        }

        public string ToString(string format)
        {
            return ToString(format, null);
        }

        public string ToString(string format,
                IFormatProvider formatProvider)
        {
            switch (format)
            {
                case null:
                case "N":
                    return ToString();
```

```
            case "F":
                return FirstName;
            case "L":
                return LastName;
            case "C":
                return Country;
            case "S":
                return Starts.ToString();
            case "W":
                return Wins.ToString();
            case "A":
                return String.Format("{0} {1}, {2};" +
                        " starts: {3}, wins: {4}",
                        FirstName, LastName, Country,
                        Starts, Wins);
            default:
                throw new FormatException(String.Format(
                    "Format {0} not supported", format));
            }
        }
    }
}
```

The class `Formula1` returns a list of racers in the method `GetChampions()`. The list is filled with all Formula-1 champions from the years 1950 to 2007:

```
using System;
using System.Collections.Generic;

namespace Wrox.ProCSharp.LINQ
{
    public static class Formula1
    {
        public static IList<Racer> GetChampions()
        {
            List<Racer> racers = new List<Racer>(40);
            racers.Add(new Racer() { FirstName = "Nino",
                    LastName = "Farina", Country = "Italy",
                            Starts = 33, Wins = 5,
                    Years = new int[] { 1950 },
                    Cars = new string[] { "Alfa Romeo" } });
            racers.Add(new Racer() {
                            FirstName = "Alberto",
                    LastName = "Ascari", Country = "Italy",
                    Starts = 32, Wins = 10,
                    Years = new int[] { 1952, 1953 },
                    Cars = new string[] { "Ferrari" } });
            racers.Add(new Racer() {
                    FirstName = "Juan Manuel",
                    LastName = "Fangio",
                    Country = "Argentina", Starts = 51,
                    Wins = 24, Years = new int[]
                            { 1951, 1954, 1955, 1956, 1957 },
                    Cars = new string[] { "Alfa Romeo",
```

(continued)

(continued)

```
                    "Maserati", "Mercedes",
                    "Ferrari" } });
        racers.Add(new Racer() { FirstName = "Mike",
            LastName = "Hawthorn", Country = "UK",
            Starts = 45, Wins = 3,
            Years = new int[] { 1958 },
            Cars = new string[] { "Ferrari" } });
        racers.Add(new Racer() { FirstName = "Phil",
            LastName = "Hill", Country = "USA",
            Starts = 48, Wins = 3,
            Years = new int[] { 1961 },
            Cars = new string[] { "Ferrari" } });
        racers.Add(new Racer() { FirstName = "John",
            LastName = "Surtees", Country = "UK",
            Starts = 111, Wins = 6,
            Years = new int[] { 1964 },
            Cars = new string[] { "Ferrari" } });
        racers.Add(new Racer() { FirstName = "Jim",
            LastName = "Clark", Country = "UK",
            Starts = 72, Wins = 25,
            Years = new int[] { 1963, 1965 },
            Cars = new string[] { "Lotus" } });
        racers.Add(new Racer() { FirstName = "Jack",
            LastName = "Brabham",
                    Country = "Australia", Starts = 125,
                    Wins = 14,
            Years = new int[] { 1959, 1960, 1966 },
            Cars = new string[] { "Cooper",
                "Brabham" } });
        racers.Add(new Racer() { FirstName = "Denny",
            LastName = "Hulme",
            Country = "New Zealand", Starts = 112,
            Wins = 8,
            Years = new int[] { 1967 },
            Cars = new string[] { "Brabham" } });
        racers.Add(new Racer() { FirstName = "Graham",
            LastName = "Hill", Country = "UK",
            Starts = 176, Wins = 14,
            Years = new int[] { 1962, 1968 },
            Cars = new string[] { "BRM", "Lotus" }
            });
        racers.Add(new Racer() { FirstName = "Jochen",
            LastName = "Rindt", Country = "Austria",
            Starts = 60, Wins = 6,
            Years = new int[] { 1970 },
            Cars = new string[] { "Lotus" } });
        racers.Add(new Racer() { FirstName = "Jackie",
            LastName = "Stewart", Country = "UK",
            Starts = 99, Wins = 27,
            Years = new int[] { 1969, 1971, 1973 },
            Cars = new string[] { "Matra",
                "Tyrrell" } });
```

```
racers.Add(new Racer() {
      FirstName = "Emerson",
      LastName = "Fittipaldi",
      Country = "Brazil", Starts = 143,
      Wins = 14, Years = new int[] { 1972,
           1974 },
      Cars = new string[] { "Lotus",
           "McLaren" } });
racers.Add(new Racer() { FirstName = "James",
      LastName = "Hunt", Country = "UK",
      Starts = 91, Wins = 10,
      Years = new int[] { 1976 },
      Cars = new string[] { "McLaren" } });
racers.Add(new Racer() { FirstName = "Mario",
      LastName = "Andretti", Country = "USA",
      Starts = 128, Wins = 12,
      Years = new int[] { 1978 },
      Cars = new string[] { "Lotus" } });
racers.Add(new Racer() { FirstName = "Jody",
      LastName = "Scheckter",
      Country = "South Africa", Starts = 112,
      Wins = 10,
      Years = new int[] { 1979 },
      Cars = new string[] { "Ferrari" } });
racers.Add(new Racer() { FirstName = "Alan",
      LastName = "Jones",
      Country = "Australia", Starts = 115,
      Wins = 12,
      Years = new int[] { 1980 },
      Cars = new string[] { "Williams" } });
racers.Add(new Racer() { FirstName = "Keke",
      LastName = "Rosberg",
                Country = "Finland", Starts = 114,
                Wins = 5,
      Years = new int[] { 1982 },
      Cars = new string[] { "Williams" } });
racers.Add(new Racer() { FirstName = "Niki",
      LastName = "Lauda", Country = "Austria",
      Starts = 173, Wins = 25,
      Years = new int[] { 1975, 1977, 1984 },
      Cars = new string[] { "Ferrari",
      "McLaren" } });
racers.Add(new Racer() { FirstName = "Nelson",
      LastName = "Piquet", Country = "Brazil",
      Starts = 204, Wins = 23,
      Years = new int[] { 1981, 1983, 1987 },
      Cars = new string[] { "Brabham",
      "Williams" } });
racers.Add(new Racer() { FirstName = "Ayrton",
      LastName = "Senna", Country = "Brazil",
      Starts = 161, Wins = 41,
      Years = new int[] { 1988, 1990, 1991 },
      Cars = new string[] { "McLaren" } });
racers.Add(new Racer() { FirstName = "Nigel",
      LastName = "Mansell", Country = "UK",
```

(continued)

(continued)

```
                    Starts = 187, Wins = 31,
                    Years = new int[] { 1992 },
                    Cars = new string[] { "Williams" } });
        racers.Add(new Racer() { FirstName = "Alain",
                    LastName = "Prost", Country = "France",
                    Starts = 197, Wins = 51,
                    Years = new int[] { 1985, 1986, 1989,
                    1993 },
                    Cars = new string[] { "McLaren",
                    "Williams" } });
        racers.Add(new Racer() { FirstName = "Damon",
                    LastName = "Hill", Country = "UK",
                    Starts = 114, Wins = 22,
                    Years = new int[] { 1996 },
                    Cars = new string[] { "Williams" } });
        racers.Add(new Racer() {
                    FirstName = "Jacques",
                    LastName = "Villeneuve",
                    Country = "Canada", Starts = 165,
                    Wins = 11, Years = new int[] { 1997 },
                    Cars = new string[] { "Williams" } });
        racers.Add(new Racer() { FirstName = "Mika",
                    LastName = "Hakkinen",
                    Country = "Finland", Starts = 160,
                    Wins = 20, Years = new int[] { 1998,
                    1999 },
                    Cars = new string[] { "McLaren" } });
        racers.Add(new Racer() {
                    FirstName = "Michael",
                    LastName = "Schumacher",
                    Country = "Germany", Starts = 250,
                    Wins = 91,
                    Years = new int[] { 1994, 1995, 2000,
                    2001, 2002, 2003, 2004 },
                    Cars = new string[] { "Benetton",
                    "Ferrari" } });
        racers.Add(new Racer() {
                    FirstName = "Fernando",
                    LastName = "Alonso", Country = "Spain",
                    Starts = 105, Wins = 19,
                    Years = new int[] { 2005, 2006 },
                    Cars = new string[] { "Renault" } });
        racers.Add(new Racer() { FirstName = "Kimi",
                    LastName = "Räikkönen",
                    Country = "Finland", Starts = 122,
                    Wins = 15, Years = new int[] { 2007 },
                    Cars = new string[] { "Ferrari" } });
        return racers;
    }
  }
}
```

For later queries where queries are done across multiple lists, the GetConstructorChampions() method that follows returns the list of all constructor championships. Constructor championships have been around since 1958.

```
public static IList<Team>
    GetConstructorChampions()
{
    List<Team> teams = new List<Team>(20);
    teams.Add(new Team() { Name = "Vanwall",
        Years = new int[] { 1958 } });
    teams.Add(new Team() { Name = "Cooper",
        Years = new int[] { 1959, 1960 } });
    teams.Add(new Team() { Name = "Ferrari",
        Years = new int[] { 1961, 1964, 1975,
        1976, 1977, 1979, 1982, 1983, 1999,
        2000, 2001, 2002, 2003, 2004, 2007 } });
    teams.Add(new Team() { Name = "BRM",
        Years = new int[] { 1962 } });
    teams.Add(new Team() { Name = "Lotus",
        Years = new int[] { 1963, 1965, 1968,
        1970, 1972, 1973, 1978 } });
    teams.Add(new Team() { Name = "Brabham",
        Years = new int[] { 1966, 1967 } });
    teams.Add(new Team() { Name = "Matra",
        Years = new int[] { 1969 } });
    teams.Add(new Team() { Name = "Tyrrell",
        Years = new int[] { 1971 } });
    teams.Add(new Team() { Name = "McLaren",
        Years = new int[] { 1974, 1984, 1985,
        1988, 1989, 1990, 1991, 1998 } });
    teams.Add(new Team() { Name = "Williams",
        Years = new int[] { 1980, 1981, 1986,
        1987, 1992, 1993, 1994, 1996, 1997 } });
    teams.Add(new Team() { Name = "Benetton",
        Years = new int[] { 1995 } });
    teams.Add(new Team() { Name = "Renault",
        Years = new int[] { 2005, 2006 } });
    return teams;
}
```

Now let's get into the heart of the object query. First, you need to get the list of objects with the static method GetChampions(). The list is filled into the generic class List<T>. The FindAll() method of this class accepts a Predicate<T> delegate that can be implemented as an anonymous method. Only the racers whose Country property is set to Brazil should be returned. Next, the resulting list is sorted with the Sort() method. The sort should not be done by the LastName property as is the default sort implementation of the Racer class, but you can pass a delegate of type Comparison<T>. It is again implemented as an anonymous method to compare the number of wins. Using the r2 object and comparing it with r1 does a descending sort as is required. The foreach statement finally iterates through all Racer objects in the resulting sorted collection.

```
private static void TraditionalQuery()
{
    List<Racer> racers =
        new List<Racer>(Formula1.GetChampions());
    List<Racer> brazilRacers = racers.FindAll(
        delegate(Racer r)
        {
            return r.Country == "Brazil";
        });
    brazilRacers.Sort(
        delegate(Racer r1, Racer r2)
        {
            return r2.Wins.CompareTo(r1.Wins);
        });

    foreach (Racer r in brazilRacers)
    {
        Console.WriteLine("{0:A}", r);
    }
}
```

The list displayed shows all champions from Brazil, sorted by the number of wins:

```
Ayrton Senna, Brazil; starts: 161, wins: 41
Nelson Piquet, Brazil; starts: 204, wins: 23
Emerson Fittipaldi, Brazil; starts: 143, wins: 14
```

Sorting and filtering object lists is discussed in Chapter 10, "Collections."

In the previous sample, methods from the List<T> class, FindAll() and Sort() have been used. It would be great to get the functionality of these methods with any collection and not just List<T>. This is where extension methods come into play. Extension methods are new to C# 3.0. This is the first change of the previous sample that will lead toward LINQ.

Extension Methods

Extension methods make it possible to write a method to a class that doesn't offer the method at first. You can also add a method to any class that implements a specific interface, so multiple classes can make use of the same implementation.

For example, wouldn't you like to have a Foo() method with the String class? The String class is sealed, so it is not possible to inherit from this class. You can do an extension method, as shown:

```
public static class StringExtension
{
    public static void Foo(this string s)
    {
        Console.WriteLine("Foo invoked for {0}", s);
    }
}
```

An extension method is declared in a static class. An extension method is defined as a static method where the first parameter defines the type it extends. The Foo() method extends the string class, as is defined with the first parameter. For differentiating extension methods from normal static methods, the extension method also requires the this keyword with the first parameter.

Indeed, it is now possible to use the Foo() method with the string type:

```
string s = "Hello";
s.Foo();
```

The result shows `Foo invoked for Hello` in the console, because `Hello` is the string passed to the `Foo()` method.

This might appear to be breaking object-oriented rules because a new method is defined for a type without changing the type. However, this is not the case. The extension method cannot access private members of the type it extends. Calling an extension method is just a new syntax of invoking a static method. With the string you can get the same result by calling the method `Foo()` this way:

```
string s = "Hello";
StringExtension.Foo(s);
```

To invoke the static method, write the class name followed by the method name. Extension methods are a different way to invoke static methods. You don't have to supply the name of the class where the static method is defined. Instead, the static method is taken because of the parameter type. You just have to import the namespace that contains the class to get the `Foo()` extension method in the scope of the `String` class.

One of the classes that define LINQ extension methods is `Enumerable` in the namespace `System.Linq`. You just have to import the namespace to open the scope of the extension methods of this class. A sample implementation of the `Where()` extension method is shown here. The first parameter of the `Where()` method that includes the `this` keyword is of type `IEnumerable<T>`. This way the `Where()` method can be used with every type that implements `IEnumerable<T>`. To mention just a few examples, arrays and `List<T>` implement `IEnumerable<T>`. The second parameter is a `Func<T, bool>` delegate that references a method that returns a Boolean value and requires a parameter of type `T`. This predicate is invoked within the implementation to examine if the item from the `IEnumerable<T>` source should go into the destination collection. If the method is referenced by the delegate, the `yield return` statement returns the item from the source to the destination.

```
public static IEnumerable<TSource> Where<TSource>(
     this IEnumerable<TSource> source,
     Func<TSource, bool> predicate)
{
   foreach (TSource item in source)
      if (predicate(item))
         yield return item;
}
```

Because `Where()` is implemented as a generic method, it works with any type that is contained in a collection. Any collection implementing `IEnumerable<T>` is supported.

> The extension methods here are defined in the namespace `System.Linq` in the assembly `System.Core`.

Now it's possible to use the extension methods `Where()`, `OrderByDescending()`, and `Select()` from the class `Enumerable`. Because each of these methods returns `IEnumerable<TSource>`, it is possible to invoke one method after the other by using the previous result. With the arguments of the extension methods, anonymous methods that define the implementation for the delegate parameters are used.

```
private static void ExtensionMethods()
{
   List<Racer> champions =
      new List<Racer>(
         Formula1.GetChampions());
   IEnumerable<Racer> brazilChampions =
      champions.Where(
      delegate(Racer r)
```

(continued)

(continued)

```
        {
            return r.Country == "Brazil";
        }).OrderByDescending(
        delegate(Racer r)
        {
            return r.Wins;
        }).Select(
        delegate(Racer r)
        {
            return r;
        });

    foreach (Racer r in brazilChampions)
    {
        Console.WriteLine("{0:A}", r);
    }
}
```

Lambda Expressions

C# 3.0 has a new syntax for anonymous methods — Lambda expressions. Instead of passing anonymous methods to the `Where()`, `OrderByDescending()`, and `Select()` methods, the same can be done using Lambda expressions.

Here the previous example is changed to make use of Lambda expressions. Now the syntax is shorter and also easier to understand due to the removal of the `return` statement, the parameter types, and the curly brackets.

Lambda expressions are covered in detail in Chapter 7, "Delegates and Events." Because of the importance of Lambda expressions with LINQ, here's a reminder about the syntax. For more details you should read Chapter 7.

By comparing Lambda expressions to anonymous delegates you can find many similarities. To the left of the Lambda operator => are parameters. It's ok not to add the parameter types because they are resolved by the compiler. The right side of the Lambda operator defines the implementation. With anonymous methods, curly brackets and the return statement are required. With Lambda expressions the syntax elements are not required because they are done by the compiler in any case. If you have more than one statement on the right side of the Lambda operator, curly brackets and the return statement are possible.

```
private static void LambdaExpressions()
{
    IEnumerable<Racer> brazilChampions =
        Formula1.GetChampions().
        Where(r => r.Country == "Brazil").
        OrderByDescending(r => r.Wins).
        Select(r => r);

    foreach (Racer r in brazilChampions)
    {
        Console.WriteLine("{0:A}", r);
    }
}
```

Return statements and curly brackets are optional when using Lambda expressions without parameter types. You can still use these language constructs with Lambda expressions. This is explained in Chapter 7, "Delegates and Events," where Lambda expressions are introduced.

LINQ Query

The last change that needs to be done is to define the query using the new LINQ query notation. The statement `from r in Formula1.GetChampions() where r.Country == "Brazil" orderby r .Wins descending select r;` is a LINQ query. The clauses `from`, `where`, `orderby`, `descending`, and `select` are predefined keywords in this query. The compiler maps these clauses to extension methods. The syntax used here is using the extension methods `Where()`, `OrderByDescending()`, and `Select()`. Lambda expressions are passed to the parameters.

`where r.Country == "Brazil"` is converted to `Where(r => r.Country == "Brazil")` `.orderby r.Wins descending` is converted to `OrderByDescending(r => r.Wins)`.

```
private static void LinqQuery()
{
    var query = from r in Formula1.GetChampions()
                where r.Country == "Brazil"
                orderby r.Wins descending
                select r;

    foreach (Racer r in query)
    {
        Console.WriteLine("{0:A}", r);
    }
}
```

The LINQ query is a simplified query notation inside the C# language. The compiler compiles the query expression to invoke extension methods. The query expression is just a nice syntax from C#, but changes to the underlying IL code are not needed.

The query expression must begin with a `from` clause and end with a `select` or `group` clause. In between you can optionally use `where`, `orderby`, `join`, `let`, and additional `from` clauses.

It is important to note that the variable `query` just has the LINQ query assigned to it. The query is not done by this assignment. The query is done as soon as the query is accessed using the `foreach` loop. This is discussed in more detail later.

With the samples so far you've seen new C# 3.0 language features and how they relate to the LINQ query. Now is the time to dig deeper into the features of LINQ.

Deferred Query Execution

When the query expression is defined during runtime, the query does not run. The query runs when the items are iterated.

Let's have a look once more at the extension method `Where()`. This extension method makes use of the `yield return` statement to return the elements where the predicate is true. Because the `yield return` statement is used, the compiler creates an enumerator and returns the items as soon as they are accessed from the enumeration.

```
public static IEnumerable<T> Where<T>(this IEnumerable<T> source,
Func<T, bool> predicate)
{
    foreach (T item in source)
        if (predicate(item))
            yield return item;
}
```

This has a very interesting and important effect. With the following example a collection of `String` elements is created and filled with the name `arr`. Next, a query is defined to get all names from the collection where the item starts with the letter `J`. The collection should also be sorted. The iteration does not happen when the query is defined. Instead, the iteration happens with the `foreach` statement, where all items are iterated. Only one element of the collection fulfills the requirements of the `where` expression by starting with the letter J: `Juan`. After the iteration is done and `Juan` is written to the console, four new names are added to the collection. Then the iteration is done once more.

```
List<string> names = new List<string>
        { "Nino", "Alberto", "Juan", "Mike",
          "Phil" };

var namesWithJ = from n in names
    where n.StartsWith("J")
    orderby n
    select n;

Console.WriteLine("First iteration");
foreach (string name in namesWithJ)
{
    Console.WriteLine(name);
}
Console.WriteLine();

names.Add("John");
names.Add("Jim");
names.Add("Jack");
names.Add("Denny");

Console.WriteLine("Second iteration");
foreach (string name in namesWithJ)
{
    Console.WriteLine(name);
}
```

Because the iteration does not happen when the query is defined, but it does happen with every `foreach`, changes can be seen, as the output from the application demonstrates:

```
First iteration
Juan

Second iteration
Jack
Jim
John
Juan
```

Of course, you also must be aware that the extension methods are invoked every time the query is used within an iteration. Most of the time this is very practical, because you can detect changes in the source data. However, there are situations where this is impractical. You can change this behavior by invoking the extension methods `ToArray()`, `ToEnumerable()`, `ToList()`, and the like. In the example, you can see that `ToList` iterates through the collection immediately and returns a collection implementing `IList<string>`. The returned list is then iterated through twice; in between iterations, the data source gets new names.

```
List<string> names = new List<string>
        { "Nino", "Alberto", "Juan", "Mike",
        "Phil" };

IList<string> namesWithJ = (from n in names
    where n.StartsWith("J")
    orderby n
    select n).ToList();


Console.WriteLine("First iteration");
foreach (string name in namesWithJ)
{
    Console.WriteLine(name);
}
Console.WriteLine();

names.Add("John");
names.Add("Jim");
names.Add("Jack");
names.Add("Denny");

Console.WriteLine("Second iteration");
foreach (string name in namesWithJ)
{
    Console.WriteLine(name);
}
```

In the result, you can see that in between the iterations the output stays the same although the collection values changed:

```
First iteration
Juan

Second iteration
Juan
```

Standard Query Operators

`Where`, `OrderByDescending`, and `Select` are only few of the query operators defined by LINQ. The LINQ query defines a declarative syntax for the most common operators. There are many more standard query operators available.

The following table lists the standard query operators defined by LINQ.

Standard Query Operators	Description
Where OfType<TResult>	*Filtering* operators define a restriction to the elements returned. With the Where query operator you can use a predicate, for example, defined by a Lambda expression that returns a bool. OfType<TResult> filters the elements based on the type and returns only the elements of the type TResult.
Select SelectMany	*Projection* operators are used to transform an object into a new object of a different type. Select and SelectMany define a projection to select values of the result based on a selector function.
OrderBy ThenBy OrderByDescending ThenByDescending Reverse	*Sorting* operators change the order of elements returned. OrderBy sorts values in ascending order; OrderByDescending sorts values in descending order. ThenBy and ThenByDescending operators are used for a secondary sort if the first sort gives similar results. Reverse reverses the elements in the collection.
Join GroupJoin	*Join* operators are used to combine collections that might not be directly related to each other. With the Join operator a join of two collections based on key selector functions can be done. This is similar to the JOIN you know from SQL. The GroupJoin operator joins two collections and groups the results.
GroupBy	*Grouping* operators put the data into groups. The GroupBy operator groups elements with a common key.
Any All Contains	*Quantifier* operators return a Boolean value if elements of the sequence satisfy a specific condition. Any, All, and Contains are quantifier operators. Any determines if any element in the collection satisfies a predicate function; All determines if all elements in the collection satisfy a predicate. Contains checks whether a specific element is in the collection. These operators return a Boolean value.
Take Skip TakeWhile SkipWhile	*Partitioning* operators return a subset of the collection. Take, Skip, TakeWhile, and SkipWhile are partitioning operators. With these, you get a partial result. With Take, you have to specify the number of elements to take from the collection; Skip ignores the specified number of elements and takes the rest. TakeWhile takes the elements as long as a condition is true.
Distinct Union Intersect Except	*Set* operators return a collection set. Distinct removes duplicates from a collection. With the exception of Distinct, the other set operators require two collections. Union returns unique elements that appear in either of the two collections. Intersect returns elements that appear in both collections. Except returns elements that appear in just one collection.

Standard Query Operators	Description
First FirstOrDefault Last LastOrDefault ElementAt ElementAtOrDefault Single SingleOrDefault	*Element* operators return just one element. First returns the first element that satisfies a condition. FirstOrDefault is similar to First, but it returns a default value of the type if the element is not found. Last returns the last element that satisfies a condition. With ElementAt, you specify the position of the element to return. Single returns only the one element that satisfies a condition. If more than one element satisfies the condition, an exception is thrown.
Count Sum Min Max Average Aggregate	*Aggregate* operators compute a single value from a collection. With aggregate operators, you can get the sum of all values, the number of all elements, the element with the lowest or highest value, an average number, and so on.
ToArray AsEnumerable ToList ToDictionary Cast<TResult>	*Conversion* operators convert the collection to an array: IEnumerable, IList, IDictionary, and so on.
Empty Range Repeat	*Generation* operators return a new sequence. The collection is empty using the Empty operator, Range returns a sequence of numbers, and Repeat returns a collection with one repeated value.

Following are examples of using these operators.

Filtering

Have a look at some examples for a query.

With the where clause, you can combine multiple expressions; for example, get only the racers from Brazil and Austria who won more than 15 races. The result type of the expression passed to the where clause just needs to be of type bool:

```
var racers = from r in Formula1.GetChampions()
             where r.Wins > 15 &&
                 (r.Country == "Brazil" ||
                  r.Country == "Austria")
             select r;
```

```
foreach (var r in racers)
{
    Console.WriteLine("{0:A}", r);
}
```

Starting the program with this LINQ query returns Niki Lauda, Nelson Piquet, and Ayrton Senna as shown:

```
Niki Lauda, Austria, Starts: 173, Wins: 25
Nelson Piquet, Brazil, Starts: 204, Wins: 23
Ayrton Senna, Brazil, Starts: 161, Wins: 41
```

Not all queries can be done with the LINQ query. Not all extension methods are mapped to LINQ query clauses. Advanced queries require using extension methods. To better understand complex queries with extension methods it's good to see how simple queries are mapped. Using the extension methods `Where()` and `Select()` produces a query very similar to the LINQ query done before:

```
var racers = Formula1.GetChampions().
    Where(r => r.Wins > 15 &&
        (r.Country == "Brazil" ||
         r.Country == "Austria")).
    Select(r => r);
```

Filtering with Index

One example where you can't use the LINQ query is an overload of the `Where()` method. With an overload of the `Where()` method you can a pass a second parameter that is the index. The index is a counter for every result returned from the filter. You can use the index within the expression to do some calculation based on the index. Here the index is used within the code that is called by the `Where()` extension method to return only racers whose last name starts with A if the index is even:

```
var racers = Formula1.GetChampions().
    Where((r, index) =>
        r.LastName.StartsWith("A") &&
        index % 2 != 0);

foreach (var r in racers)
{
    Console.WriteLine("{0:A}", r);
}
```

All the racers with last names beginning with the letter A are Alberto Ascari, Mario Andretti, and Fernando Alonso. Because Mario Andretti is positioned within an index that is odd, he is not in the result:

```
Alberto Ascari, Italy; starts: 32, wins: 10
Fernando Alsonso, Spain; starts: 105, wins: 19
```

Type Filtering

For filtering based on a type you can use the `OfType()` extension method. Here the array data contains both `string` and `int` objects. Using the extension method `OfType()`, passing the string class to the generic parameter returns only the strings from the collection:

```
object[] data = { "one", 2, 3, "four", "five",
    6 };
var query = data.OfType<string>();
foreach (var s in query)
{
    Console.WriteLine(s);
}
```

Running this code, the strings one, four, and five are displayed:

```
one
four
five
```

Compound from

If you need to do a filter based on a member of the object that itself is a sequence, you can use a compound `from`. The `Racer` class defines a property `Cars` where `Cars` is a string array. For a filter of all racers who were champions with a Ferrari, you can use the LINQ query as shown. The first `from` clause accesses the `Racer` objects returned from `Formula1.GetChampions()`. The second `from` clause accesses the `Cars` property of the `Racer` class to return all cars of type `string`. Next the cars are used with the `where` clause to filter only the racers who were champions with a Ferrari.

```
var ferrariDrivers = from r in
                        Formula1.GetChampions()
                     from c in r.Cars
                     where c == "Ferrari"
                     orderby r.LastName
                     select r.FirstName + " "
                        + r.LastName;
```

If you are curious about the result of this query, all Formula-1 champions driving a Ferrari are:

```
Alberto Ascari
Juan Manuel Fangio
Mike Hawthorn
Phil Hill
Niki Lauda
Jody Scheckter
Michael Schumacher
John Surtees
```

The C# compiler converts a compound `from` clause with a LINQ query to the `SelectMany()` extension method. `SelectMany()` can be used to iterate a sequence of a sequence. The overload of the `SelectMany` method that is used with the example is shown here:

```
public static IEnumerable<TResult> SelectMany<TSource, TCollection, TResult> (
    this IEnumerable<TSource> source,
    Func<TSource,
    IEnumerable<TCollection>> collectionSelector,
    Func<TSource, TCollection, TResult>
       resultSelector);
```

The first parameter is the implicit parameter that receives the sequence of `Racer` objects from the `GetChampions()` method. The second parameter is the `collectionSelector` delegate where the inner sequence is defined. With the Lambda expression `r => r.Cars` the collection of cars should be returned. The third parameter is a delegate that is now invoked for every car and receives the `Racer` and `Car` objects. The Lambda expression creates an anonymous type with a `Racer` and a `Car` property. As a result of this `SelectMany()` method the hierarchy of racers and cars is flattened and a collection of new objects of an anonymous type for every car is returned.

This new collection is passed to the `Where()` method so that only the racers driving a Ferrari are filtered. Finally, the `OrderBy()` and `Select()` methods are invoked.

```
var ferrariDrivers = Formula1.GetChampions().
    SelectMany(
      r => r.Cars,
      (r, c) => new { Racer = r, Car = c }).
    Where(r => r.Car == "Ferrari").
    OrderBy(r => r.Racer.LastName).
    Select(r => r.Racer.FirstName + " " +
       r.Racer.LastName);
```

Resolving the generic `SelectMany()` method to the types that are used here, the types are resolved as follows. In this case the source is of type `Racer`, the filtered collection is a `string` array, and of course the name of the anonymous type that is returned is not known and shown here as `TResult`:

```
public static IEnumerable<TResult> SelectMany<Racer, string, TResult> (
      this IEnumerable<Racer> source,
      Func<Racer, IEnumerable<string>> collectionSelector,
      Func<Racer, string, TResult> resultSelector);
```

Because the query was just converted from a LINQ query to extension methods, the result is the same as before.

Sorting

For sorting a sequence, the `orderby` clause was used already. Let's review the example from before with the `orderby descending` clause. Here the racers are sorted based on the number of wins as specified by the key selector in a descending order:

```
var racers = from r in Formula1.GetChampions()
              where r.Country == "Brazil"
              orderby r.Wins descending
              select r;
```

The `orderby` clause is resolved to the `OrderBy()` method, and the `orderby descending` clause is resolved to the `OrderBy Descending()` method:

```
var racers = Formula1.GetChampions().
      Where(r => r.Country == "Brazil").
      OrderByDescending(r => r.Wins).
      Select(r => r);
```

The `OrderBy()` and `OrderByDescending()` methods return `IOrderedEnumerable<TSource>`. This interface derives from the interface `IEnumerable<TSource>` but contains an additional method `CreateOrderedEnumerable<TSource>()`. This method is used for further ordering of the sequence. If two items are the same based on the key selector, ordering can continue with the `ThenBy()` and `ThenByDescending()` methods. These methods require an `IOrderedEnumerable<TSource>` to work on, but return this interface as well. So, you can add any number of `ThenBy()` and `ThenByDescending()` to sort the collection.

Using the LINQ query you just have to add all the different keys (with commas) for sorting to the `orderby` clause. Here the sort of all racers is done first based on the country, next on the last name, and finally on the first name. The `Take()` extension method that is added to the result of the LINQ query is used to take just the first 10 results.

```
var racers = (from r in
              Formula1.GetChampions()
              orderby r.Country, r.LastName,
                 r.FirstName
              select r).Take(10);
```

The sorted result is shown here:

```
Argentina: Fangio, Juan Manuel
Australia: Brabham, Jack
Australia: Jones, Alan
Austria: Lauda, Niki
Austria: Rindt, Jochen
Brazil: Fittipaldi, Emerson
```

```
Brazil: Piquet, Nelson
Brazil: Senna, Ayrton
Canada: Villeneuve, Jacques
Finland: Hakkinen, Mika
```

Doing the same with extension methods makes use of the `OrderBy()` and `ThenBy()` methods:

```
var racers = Formula1.GetChampions().
    OrderBy(r => r.Country).
    ThenBy(r => r.LastName).
    ThenBy(r => r.FirstName).
    Take(10);
```

Grouping

To group query results based on a key value, the `group` clause can be used. Now the Formula-1 champions should be grouped by the country, and the number of champions within a country should be listed. The clause `group r by r.Country into g` groups all the racers based on the `Country` property and defines a new identifier `g` that can be used later to access the group result information. The result from the `group` clause is ordered based on the extension method `Count()` that is applied on the group result, and if the count is the same the ordering is done based on the key, which is the country because this was the key used for grouping. The `where` clause filters the results based on groups that have at least two items, and the `select` clause creates an anonymous type with `Country` and `Count` properties.

```
var countries = from r in
    Formula1.GetChampions()
    group r by r.Country into g
    orderby g.Count() descending, g.Key
    where g.Count() >= 2
    select new { Country = g.Key,
                 Count = g.Count() };
```

```
foreach (var item in countries)
{
    Console.WriteLine("{0, -10} {1}",
        item.Country, item.Count);
}
```

The result displays the collection of objects with the `Country` and `Count` property:

```
UK          9
Brazil      3
Australia   2
Austria     2
Finland     2
Italy       2
USA         2
```

Doing the same with extension methods, the `groupby` clause is resolved to the `GroupBy()` method. What's interesting with the declaration of the `GroupBy()` method is that it returns an enumeration of objects implementing the `IGrouping` interface. The `IGrouping` interface defines the `Key` property, so you can access the key of the group after defining the call to this method:

```
public static IEnumerable<IGrouping<TKey, TSource>> GroupBy<TSource, TKey>(
    this IEnumerable<TSource> source,
    Func<TSource, TKey> keySelector);
```

The `group r by r.Country into g` clause is resolved to `GroupBy(r => r.Country)` and returns the group sequence. The group sequence is first ordered by the `OrderByDescending()` method, then by the `ThenBy()` method. Next the `Where()` and `Select()` methods that you already know are invoked.

```
var countries = Formula1.GetChampions().
    GroupBy(r => r.Country).
    OrderByDescending(g => g.Count()).
    ThenBy(g => g.Key).
    Where(g => g.Count() >= 2).
    Select(g => new { Country = g.Key,
                      Count = g.Count() });
```

Grouping with Nested Objects

If the grouped objects should contain nested sequences, you can do that by changing the anonymous type created by the `select` clause. With this example the returned countries should contain not only the properties for the name of the country and the number of racers, but also a sequence of the names of the racers. This sequence is assigned by using an inner `from/in` clause assigned to the `Racers` property. The inner `from` clause is using the group g to get all racers from the group, order them by the last name, and create a new string based on the first and last name.

```
var countries = from r in
        Formula1.GetChampions()
    group r by r.Country into g
    orderby g.Count() descending, g.Key
    where g.Count() >= 2
    select new
    {
        Country = g.Key,
        Count = g.Count(),
        Racers = from r1 in g
                 orderby r1.LastName
                 select r1.FirstName + " "
                    + r1.LastName
    };

foreach (var item in countries)
{
    Console.WriteLine("{0, -10} {1}",
        item.Country, item.Count);
    foreach (var name in item.Racers)
    {
        Console.Write("{0}; ", name);
    }
    Console.WriteLine();
}
```

The output now lists all champions from the specified countries:

```
UK         8
Jim Clark; Mike Hawthorn; Graham Hill; Damon Hill; James Hunt; Nigel Mansell;
Jackie Stewart; John Surtees;
Brazil     3
Emerson Fittipaldi; Nelson Piquet; Ayrton Senna;
Australia  2
```

```
Jack Brabham; Alan Jones;
Austria    2
Niki Lauda; Jochen Rindt;
Finland    3
Mika Hakkinen; Kimi Raikkonen; Keke Rosberg;
Italy      2
Alberto Ascari; Nino Farina;
USA        2
Mario Andretti; Phil Hill;
```

Join

You can use the join clause to combine two sources based on specific criteria. But first, let's get two lists that should be joined. With Formula-1 there's a drivers and a constructors championship. The drivers are returned from the method GetChampions(), and the constructors are returned from the method GetConstructorChampions(). Now it would be interesting to get a list by the year where every year lists the driver and the constructor champion.

For doing this, first two queries for the racers and the teams are defined:

```
var racers = from r in Formula1.GetChampions()
             from y in r.Years
             where y > 2003
             select new
             {
                 Year = y,
                 Name = r.FirstName + " " +
                     r.LastName
             };

var teams = from t in
            Formula1.GetContructorChampions()
            from y in t.Years
            where y > 2003
            select new { Year = y,
                         Name = t.Name };
```

Using these two queries, a join is done based on the year of the driver champion and the year of the team champion with the clause join t in teams on r.Year equals t.Year. The select clause defines a new anonymous type containing Year, Racer, and Team properties.

```
var racersAndTeams =
    from r in racers
    join t in teams on r.Year equals t.Year
    select new
    {
        Year = r.Year,
        Racer = r.Name,
        Team = t.Name
    };

Console.WriteLine("Year  Champion " +
    "Constructor Title");
foreach (var item in racersAndTeams)
{
    Console.WriteLine("{0}: {1,-20} {2}",
        item.Year, item.Racer, item.Team);
}
```

Of course you can also combine this to one LINQ query, but that's a matter of taste:

```
int year = 2003;
```

```
var racersAndTeams =
    from r in
        from r1 in Formula1.GetChampions()
        from yr in r1.Years
        where yr > year
        select new
        {
            Year = yr,
            Name = r1.FirstName + " " +
                r1.LastName
        }
    join t in
        from t1 in
            Formula1.GetContructorChampions()
        from yt in t1.Years
        where yt > year
        select new { Year = yt,
                     Name = t1.Name }
    on r.Year equals t.Year
    select new
    {
        Year = r.Year,
        Racer = r.Name,
        Team = t.Name
    };
```

The output displays data from the anonymous type:

```
Year    Champion            Constructor Title
2004    Michael Schumacher  Ferrari
2005    Fernando Alonso     Renault
2006    Fernando Alonso     Renault
2007    Kimi Räikkönen      Ferrari
```

Set Operations

The extension methods `Distinct()`, `Union()`, `Intersect()`, and `Except()` are set operations. Let's create a sequence of Formula-1 champions driving a Ferrari and another sequence of Formula-1 champions driving a McLaren, and then let's find out if any driver has been a champion driving both of these cars. Of course, that's where the `Intersect()` extension method can help.

First get all champions driving a Ferrari. This is just using a simple LINQ query with a compound `from` to access the property `Cars` that's returning a sequence of string objects.

```
var ferrariDrivers = from r in
                         Formula1.GetChampions()
                     from c in r.Cars
                     where c == "Ferrari"
                     orderby r.LastName
                     select r;
```

Now the same query with a different parameter of the `where` clause would be needed to get all McLaren racers. It's not a good idea to write the same query another time. You have one option to create a method where you can pass the parameter `car`:

```
private static IEnumerable<Racer>
    GetRacersByCar(string car)
{
    return from r in Formula1.GetChampions()
           from c in r.Cars
           where c == car
           orderby r.LastName
           select r;
}
```

However, because the method wouldn't be needed in other places, defining a variable of a delegate type to hold the LINQ query is a good approach. The variable `racersByCar` needs to be of a delegate type that requires a string parameter and returns `IEnumerable<Racer>`, similar to the method that was implemented before. For doing this several generic `Func<>` delegates are defined, so you do not need to declare your own delegate. A Lambda expression is assigned to the variable `racersByCar`. The left side of the Lambda expression defines a `car` variable of the type that is the first generic parameter of the `Func` delegate (a string). The right side defines the LINQ query that uses the parameter with the `where` clause.

```
Func<string, IEnumerable<Racer>> racersByCar =
    Car => from r in Formula1.GetChampions()
           from c in r.Cars
           where c == car
           orderby r.LastName
           select r;
```

Now you can use the `Intersect()` extension method to get all racers that won the championship with a Ferrari and a McLaren:

```
Console.WriteLine("World champion with " +
    "Ferrari and McLaren");
foreach (var racer in racersByCar("Ferrari").
        Intersect(racersByCar("McLaren")))
{
    Console.WriteLine(racer);
}
```

The result is just one racer, Niki Lauda:

```
World champion with Ferrari and McLaren
Niki Lauda
```

Partitioning

Partitioning operations such as the extension methods `Take()` and `Skip()` can be used for easily paging, for example, to display 5 by 5 racers.

With the LINQ query shown here, the extension methods `Skip()` and `Take()` are added to the end of the query. The `Skip()` method first ignores a number of items calculated based on the page size and the actual page number; the `Take()` method then takes a number of items based on the page size:

```csharp
int pageSize = 5;

int numberPages = (int)Math.Ceiling(
        Formula1.GetChampions().Count() /
        (double)pageSize);

for (int page = 0; page < numberPages; page++)
{
    Console.WriteLine("Page {0}", page);

    var racers =
        (from r in Formula1.GetChampions()
         orderby r.LastName
         select r.FirstName + " " + r.LastName).
        Skip(page * pageSize).Take(pageSize);

    foreach (var name in racers)
    {
        Console.WriteLine(name);
    }
    Console.WriteLine();
}
```

Here is the output of the first three pages:

```
Page 0
Fernando Alonso
Mario Andretti
Alberto Ascari
Jack Brabham
Jim Clark

Page 1
Juan Manuel Fangio
Nino Farina
Emerson Fittipaldi
Mika Hakkinen
Mike Hawthorn

Page 2
Phil Hill
Graham Hill
Damon Hill
Denny Hulme
James Hunt
```

Paging can be extremely useful with Windows or Web applications showing the user only a part of the data.

An important behavior of this paging mechanism that you will notice: because the query is done with every page, changing the underlying data affects the results. New objects are shown as paging continues. Depending on your scenario this can be advantageous to your application. If this behavior is not what you need you can do the paging not over the original data source, but by using a cache that maps to the original data.

With the `TakeWhile()` and `SkipWhile()` extension methods you can also pass a predicate to take or skip items based on the result of the predicate.

Aggregate Operators

The aggregate operators such as `Count()`, `Sum()`, `Min()`, `Max()`, `Average()`, and `Aggregate()` do not return a sequence but a single value instead.

The `Count()` extension method returns the number of items in the collection. Here the `Count()` method is applied to the `Years` property of a `Racer` to filter the racers and return only the ones who won more than three championships:

```
var query = from r in Formula1.GetChampions()
            where r.Years.Count() > 3
            orderby r.Years.Count() descending
            select new
            {
                Name = r.FirstName + " " +
                    r.LastName,
                TimesChampion = r.Years.Count()
            };
```

```
foreach (var r in query)
{
    Console.WriteLine("{0} {1}", r.Name,
        r.TimesChampion);
}
```

The result is shown here:

```
Michael Schumacher 7
Juan Manuel Fangio 5
Alain Prost 4
```

The `Sum()` method summarizes all numbers of a sequence and returns the result. Here, `Sum()` is used to calculate the sum of all race wins for a country. First the racers are grouped based on the country, then with the new anonymous type created the `Wins` property is assigned to the sum of all wins from a single country:

```
var countries =
    (from c in
        from r in Formula1.GetChampions()
        group r by r.Country into c
        select new
        {
            Country = c.Key,
            Wins = (from r1 in c
                    select r1.Wins).Sum()
        }
        orderby c.Wins descending, c.Country
        select c).Take(5);
```

(continued)

(continued)

```
            foreach (var country in countries)
            {
                Console.WriteLine("{0} {1}",
                    country.Country, country.Wins);
            }
```

The most successful countries based on the race wins by the Formula-1 champions are:

```
UK 138
Germany 91
Brazil 78
France 51
Finland 40
```

The methods `Min()`, `Max()`, `Average()`, and `Aggregate()` are used in the same way as `Count()` and `Sum()`. `Min()` returns the minimum number of the values in the collection, and `Max()` returns the maximum number. `Average()` calculates the average number. With the `Aggregate()` method you can pass a Lambda expression that should do an aggregation with all the values.

Conversion

In this chapter you've already seen that the query execution is deferred until the items are accessed. Using the query within an iteration, the query is executed. With conversion operator the query is executed immediately and you get the result in an array, a list, or a dictionary.

In this example the `ToList()` extension method is invoked to immediately execute the query and get the result into a `List<T>`:

```
List<Racer> racers =
    (from r in Formula1.GetChampions()
    where r.Starts > 150
    orderby r.Starts descending
    select r).ToList();

foreach (var racer in racers)
{
    Console.WriteLine("{0} {0:S}", racer);
}
```

It's not that simple to just get the returned objects to the list. For example, for a fast access from a car to a racer within a collection class, you can use the new class `Lookup<TKey, TElement>`.

The `Dictionary<TKey, TValue>` supports only a single value for a key. With the class `Lookup<TKey TElement>` from the namespace `System.Linq` you can have multiple values for a single key. These classes are covered in detail in Chapter 10, "Collections."

Using the compound `from` query, the sequence of racers and cars is flattened, and an anonymous type with the properties `Car` and `Racer` gets created. With the lookup that is returned, the key should be of type `string` referencing the car, and the value should be of type `Racer`. To make this selection, you can pass a key and an element selector to one overload of the `ToLookup()` method. The key selector references the `Car` property, and the element selector references the `Racer` property.

```
ILookup<string, Racer> racers =
    (from r in Formula1.GetChampions()
    from c in r.Cars
    select new
    {
        Car = c,
        Racer = r
    }).ToLookup(cr => cr.Car, cr => cr.Racer);
```

```
if (racers.Contains("Williams"))
{
    foreach (var williamsRacer in
        racers["Williams"])
    {
        Console.WriteLine(williamsRacer);
    }
}
```

The result of all "Williams" champions that are accessed using the indexer of the `Lookup` class is shown here:

```
Alan Jones
Keke Rosberg
Nigel Mansell
Alain Prost
Damon Hill
Jacques Villeneuve
```

In case you need to use a LINQ query over an untyped collection, for example the `ArrayList`, you can use the `Cast()` method. With the following sample an `ArrayList` collection that is based on the `Object` type is filled with `Racer` objects. To make it possible to define a strongly typed query, you can use the `Cast()` method:

```
System.Collections.ArrayList list =
    new System.Collections.ArrayList(
    Formula1.GetChampions() as
    System.Collections.ICollection);
```

```
var query = from r in list.Cast<Racer>()
            where r.Country == "USA"
            orderby r.Wins descending
            select r;
```

```
foreach (var racer in query)
{
    Console.WriteLine("{0:A}", racer);
}
```

Generation Operators

The generation operators `Range()`, `Empty()`, and `Repeat()` are not extension methods but normal static methods that return sequences. With LINQ to objects, these methods are available with the `Enumerable` class.

Have you ever needed a range of numbers filled? Nothing is easier than with the `Range()` method. This method receives the start value with the first parameter and the number of items with the second parameter:

```
var values = Enumerable.Range(1, 20);
foreach (var item in values)
{
    Console.Write("{0} ", item);
}
Console.WriteLine();
```

Of course the result now looks like this:

```
1 2 3 4 5 6 7 8 9 10 11 12 13 14 15 16 17 18 19 20
```

The `Range()` *method does not return a collection filled with the values as defined. This method does a deferred query execution similar to the other methods. The method returns a* `RangeEnumerator` *that just does a* `yield return` *with the values incremented.*

You can combine the result with other extension methods to get a different result, for example using the `Select()` extension method:

```
var values = Enumerable.Range(1, 20).
    Select(n => n * 3);
```

The `Empty()` method returns an iterator that does not return values. This can be used for parameters that require a collection where you can pass an empty collection.

The `Repeat()` method returns an iterator that returns the same value a specific number of times.

Expression Trees

With LINQ to objects, the extension methods require a delegate type as parameter; this way, a Lambda expression can be assigned to the parameter. Lambda expressions can also be assigned to parameters of type `Expression<T>`. The type `Expression<T>` specifies that an expression tree made from the Lambda expression is stored in the assembly. This way the expression can be analyzed during runtime and optimized for doing the query to the data source.

Let's turn to a query expression that was used previously:

```
var brazilRacers = from r in racers
                   where r.Country == "Brazil"
                   orderby r.Wins
                   select r;
```

This query expression is using the extension methods `Where`, `OrderBy`, and `Select`. The `Enumerable` class defines the `Where()` extension method with the delegate type `Func<T, bool>` as parameter predicate:

```
public static IEnumerable<TSource> Where<TSource> (
    this IEnumerable<TSource> source,
    Func<TSource, bool> predicate);
```

This way, the Lambda expression is assigned to the predicate. Here, the Lambda expression is similar to an anonymous method, as was explained earlier:

```
Func<Racer, bool> predicate = r => r.Country == "Brazil";
```

The `Enumerable` class is not the only class to define the `Where()` extension method. The `Where()` extension method is also defined by the class `Queryable<T>`. This class has a different definition of the `Where()` extension method:

```
public static IQueryable<TSource> Where<TSource> (
    this IQueryable<TSource> source,
    Expression<Func<TSource, bool>> predicate);
```

Here, the Lambda expression is assigned to the type `Expression<T>`, which behaves differently:

```
Expression<Func<Racer, bool>> predicate =
    r => r.Country == "Brazil";
```

Instead of using delegates, the compiler emits an expression tree to the assembly. The expression tree can be read during runtime. Expression trees are built from classes that are derived from the abstract base class `Expression`. The `Expression` class is not the same as `Expression<T>`. Some of the expression classes that inherit from `Expression` are `BinaryExpression`, `ConstantExpression`, `InvocationExpression`, `LambdaExpression`, `NewExpression`, `NewArrayExpression`, `TernaryExpression`, `UnaryExpression`, and so on. The compiler creates an expression tree resulting from the Lambda expression.

For example, the Lambda expression `r.Country == "Brazil"` makes use of `ParameterExpression`, `MemberExpression`, `ConstantExpression`, and `MethodCallExpression` to create a tree and store the tree in the assembly. This tree is then used during runtime to create an optimized query to the underlying data source.

The method `DisplayTree()` is implemented to display an expression tree graphically on the console. Here an `Expression` object can be passed, and depending on the expression type some information about the expression is written to the console. Depending on the type of the expression, `DisplayTree()` is called recursively.

With this method not all expression types are dealt with; only the types that are used with the next sample expression.

```
private static void DisplayTree(int indent,
    string message, Expression expression)
{
    string output = String.Format("{0} {1}" +
        "! NodeType: {2}; Expr: {3} ",
        "".PadLeft(indent, '>'), message,
        expression.NodeType, expression);

    indent++;
    switch (expression.NodeType)
    {
        case ExpressionType.Lambda:
            Console.WriteLine(output);
            LambdaExpression lambdaExpr =
                (LambdaExpression)expression;
            foreach (var parameter in
                lambdaExpr.Parameters)
            {
                DisplayTree(indent, "Parameter",
                    parameter);
            }
            DisplayTree(indent, "Body",
                lambdaExpr.Body);
            break;
```

(continued)

(continued)

```csharp
                case ExpressionType.Constant:
                    ConstantExpression constExpr =
                        (ConstantExpression)expression;
                    Console.WriteLine("{0} Const Value: " +
                        "{1}", output, constExpr.Value);
                    break;
                case ExpressionType.Parameter:
                    ParameterExpression paramExpr =
                            (ParameterExpression)expression;
                    Console.WriteLine("{0} Param Type: {1}",
                        output, paramExpr.Type.Name);
                    break;
                case ExpressionType.Equal:
                case ExpressionType.AndAlso:
                case ExpressionType.GreaterThan:
                    BinaryExpression binExpr =
                        (BinaryExpression)expression;
                    if (binExpr.Method != null)
                    {
                        Console.WriteLine("{0} Method: {1}",
                            output, binExpr.Method.Name);
                    }
                    else
                    {
                        Console.WriteLine(output);
                    }
                    DisplayTree(indent, "Left",
                        binExpr.Left);
                    DisplayTree(indent, "Right",
                        binExpr.Right);
                    break;
                case ExpressionType.MemberAccess:
                    MemberExpression memberExpr =
                        (MemberExpression)expression;
                    Console.WriteLine("{0} Member Name: " +
                        "{1}, Type: {2}", output,
                        memberExpr.Member.Name,
                        memberExpr.Type.Name);
                    DisplayTree(indent, "Member Expr",
                        memberExpr.Expression);
                    break;
                default:
                    Console.WriteLine();
                    Console.WriteLine("....{0} {1}",
                        expression.NodeType,
                        expression.Type.Name);
                    break;
            }
    }
```

The expression that is used for showing the tree is already well known. It's a Lambda expression with a `Racer` parameter, and the body of the expression takes racers from Brazil only if they have won more than six races:

```
Expression<Func<Racer, bool>> expression =
    r => r.Country == "Brazil" && r.Wins > 6;

DisplayTree(0, "Lambda", expression);
```

Let's look at the tree result. As you can see from the output, the Lambda expression consists of a `Parameter` and an `AndAlso` node type. The `AndAlso` node type has an `Equal` node type to the left and a `GreaterThan` node type to the right. The `Equal` node type to the left of the `AndAlso` node type has a `MemberAccess` node type to the left and a `Constant` node type to the right, and so on.

```
Lambda! NodeType: Lambda; Expr: r => ((r.Country = "Brazil") && (r.Wins > 6))
> Parameter! NodeType: Parameter; Expr: r  Param Type: Racer
> Body! NodeType: AndAlso; Expr: ((r.Country = "Brazil") && (r.Wins > 6))
>> Left! NodeType: Equal; Expr: (r.Country = "Brazil")  Method: op_Equality
>>> Left! NodeType: MemberAccess; Expr: r.Country  Member Name: Country, Type:
String
>>>> Member Expr! NodeType: Parameter; Expr: r  Param Type: Racer
>>> Right! NodeType: Constant; Expr: "Brazil"  Const Value: Brazil
>> Right! NodeType: GreaterThan; Expr: (r.Wins > 6)
>>> Left! NodeType: MemberAccess; Expr: r.Wins  Member Name: Wins, Type: Int32
>>>> Member Expr! NodeType: Parameter; Expr: r  Param Type: Racer
>>> Right! NodeType: Constant; Expr: 6  Const Value: 6
```

One example where the `Expression<T>` type is used is with LINQ to SQL. LINQ to SQL defines extension methods with `Expression<T>` parameters. This way the LINQ provider accessing the database can create a runtime-optimized query by reading the expressions to get the data from the database.

LINQ Providers

.NET 3.5 includes several LINQ providers. A LINQ provider implements the standard query operators for a specific data source. LINQ providers might implement more extension methods that are defined by LINQ, but the standard operators at least must be implemented. LINQ to XML implements more methods that are particularly useful with XML, for example the methods `Elements()`, `Descendants`, and `Ancestors` are defined by the class `Extensions` in the `System.Xml.Linq` namespace.

The implementation of the LINQ provider is selected based on the namespace and on the type of the first parameter. The namespace of the class that implements the extension methods must be opened, otherwise the extension class is not in scope. The parameter of the `Where()` method that is defined by LINQ to objects and the `Where()` method that is defined by LINQ to SQL is different.

The `Where()` method of LINQ to objects is defined with the `Enumerable` class:

```
public static IEnumerable<TSource> Where<TSource>(
    this IEnumerable<TSource> source,
    Func<TSource, bool> predicate);
```

Inside the `System.Linq` namespace there's another class that implements the operator `Where`. This implementation is used by LINQ to SQL. You can find the implementation in the class `Queryable`:

```
public static IQueryable<TSource> Where<TSource>(
    this IQueryable<TSource> source,
    Expression<Func<TSource, bool>> predicate);
```

Both of these classes are implemented in the System.Core assembly in the System.Linq namespace. How is it defined and what method is used? The Lambda expression is the same no matter whether it is passed with a Func<TSource, bool> parameter or with an Expression<Func<TSource, bool>> parameter. Just the compiler behaves differently. The selection is done based on the source parameter. The method that matches best based on its parameters is chosen by the compiler. The GetTable() method of the DataContext class that is defined by LINQ to SQL returns IQueryable<TSource>, and thus LINQ to SQL uses the Where() method of the Queryable class.

The LINQ to SQL provider is a provider that makes use of expression trees and implements the interfaces IQueryable and IQueryProvider.

Summary

In this chapter, you've probably seen the most important enhancements of the 3.0 version of C#. C# is continuously extended. With C# 2.0 the major new feature was generics, which provide the foundation for generic type-safe collection classes, as well as generic interfaces and delegates. The major feature of C# 3.0 is LINQ. You can use a syntax that is integrated with the language to query any data source, as long there's a provider for the data source.

You have now seen the LINQ query and the language constructs that the query is based on, such as extension methods and Lambda expressions. You've seen the various LINQ query operators not just for filtering and ordering of data sources, but also for partitioning, grouping, doing conversions, joins, and so on.

LINQ is a very in-depth topic, and you should see Chapters 27, 29, and Appendix A for more information. Other third-party providers are available for download; for example, LINQ to MySQL, LINQ to Amazon, LINQ to Flickr, and LINQ to SharePoint. No matter what data source you have, with LINQ you can use the same query syntax.

Another important concept not to be forgotten is the expression tree. Expression trees allow building the query to the data source at runtime because the tree is stored in the assembly. You can read about the great advantages of it in Chapter 27, "LINQ to SQL."

12

Memory Management and Pointers

This chapter presents various aspects of memory management and memory access. Although the runtime takes much of the responsibility for memory management away from the programmer, it is useful to understand how memory management works and important to know how to work with unmanaged resources efficiently.

A good understanding of memory management and knowledge of the pointer capabilities provided by C# will better enable you to integrate C# code with legacy code and perform efficient memory manipulation in performance-critical systems.

Specifically, this chapter discusses:

- ❑ How the runtime allocates space on the stack and the heap
- ❑ How garbage collection works
- ❑ How to use destructors and the `System.IDisposable` interface to ensure unmanaged resources are released correctly
- ❑ The syntax for using pointers in C#
- ❑ How to use pointers to implement high-performance stack-based arrays

Memory Management Under the Hood

One of the advantages of C# programming is that the programmer does not need to worry about detailed memory management; in particular, the garbage collector deals with the problem of memory cleanup on your behalf. The result is that you get something that approximates the efficiency of languages like C++ without the complexity of having to handle memory management yourself as you do in C++. However, although you do not have to manage memory manually, it still pays to understand what is going on behind the scenes. This section looks at what happens in the computer's memory when you allocate variables.

The precise details of much of the content of this section are undocumented. You should interpret this section as a simplified guide to the general processes rather than as a statement of exact implementation.

Value Data Types

Windows uses a system known as *virtual addressing*, in which the mapping from the memory address seen by your program to the actual location in hardware memory is entirely managed by Windows. The result of this is that each process on a 32-bit processor sees 4GB of available memory, regardless of how much hardware memory you actually have in your computer (on 64-bit processors this number will be greater). This 4GB of memory contains everything that is part of the program, including the executable code, any DLLs loaded by the code, and the contents of all variables used when the program runs. This 4GB of memory is known as the *virtual address space* or *virtual memory*. For convenience, in this chapter, we call it simply *memory*.

Each memory location in the available 4GB is numbered starting from zero. To access a value stored at a particular location in memory, you need to supply the number that represents that memory location. In any compiled high-level language, including C#, Visual Basic, C++, and Java, the compiler converts human-readable variable names into memory addresses that the processor understands.

Somewhere inside a processor's virtual memory is an area known as the *stack*. The stack stores value data types that are not members of objects. In addition, when you call a method, the stack is used to hold a copy of any parameters passed to the method. To understand how the stack works, you need to understand the importance of variable scope in C#. It is *always* the case that if a variable a goes into scope before variable b, then b will go out of scope first. Look at this code:

```
{
    int a;
    // do something
    {
        int b;
        // do something else
    }
}
```

First, a gets declared. Then, inside the inner code block, b gets declared. Then the inner code block terminates and b goes out of scope, then a goes out of scope. So, the lifetime of b is entirely contained within the lifetime of a. The idea that you always deallocate variables in the reverse order to how you allocate them is crucial to the way the stack works.

You do not know exactly where in the address space the stack is — you don't need to know for C# development. A *stack pointer* (a variable maintained by the operating system) identifies the next free location on the stack. When your program first starts running, the stack pointer will point to just past the end of the block of memory that is reserved for the stack. The stack actually fills downward, from high memory addresses to low addresses. As data is put on the stack, the stack pointer is adjusted accordingly, so it always points to just past the next free location. This is illustrated in Figure 12-1, which shows a stack pointer with a value of 800000 (0xC3500 in hex); the next free location is the address 799999.

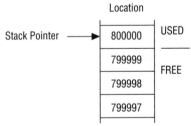

Figure 12-1

The following code instructs the compiler that you need space in memory to store an integer and a double, and these memory locations are referred to as nRacingCars and engineSize. The line that declares each variable indicates the point at which you will start requiring access to this variable. The closing curly brace of the block in which the variables are declared identifies the point at which both variables go out of scope.

```
{
    int nRacingCars = 10;
    double engineSize = 3000.0;
    // do calculations;
}
```

Assuming that you use the stack shown in Figure 12-1, when the variable nRacingCars comes into scope and is assigned the value 10, the value 10 is placed in locations 799996 through 799999, the 4 bytes just below the location pointed to by the stack pointer. (Four bytes because that's how much memory is needed to store an int.) To accommodate this, 4 is subtracted from the value of the stack pointer, so it now points to the location 799996, just after the new first free location (799995).

The next line of code declares the variable engineSize (a double) and initializes it to the value 3000.0. A double occupies 8 bytes, so the value 3000.0 will be placed in locations 799988 through 799995 on the stack, and the stack pointer is decremented by 8, so that once again, it points to the location just after the next free location on the stack.

When engineSize goes out of scope, the computer knows that it is no longer needed. Because of the way variable lifetimes are always nested, you can guarantee that, whatever has happened while engineSize was in scope, the stack pointer is now pointing to the location where engineSize is stored. To remove engineSize from the stack, the stack pointer is incremented by 8, so that it now points to the location immediately after the end of engineSize. At this point in the code, you are at the closing curly brace, so nRacingCars also goes out of scope. The stack pointer is incremented by 4. When another variable comes into scope after engineSize and nRacingCars have been removed from the stack, it will overwrite the memory descending from location 799999, where nRacingCars used to be stored.

If the compiler hits a line like int i, j, then the order of variables coming into scope looks indeterminate. Both variables are declared at the same time and go out of scope at the same time. In this situation, it does not matter in what order the two variables are removed from memory. The compiler internally always ensures that the one that was put in memory first is removed last, thus preserving the rule about no crossover of variable lifetimes.

Reference Data Types

Although the stack gives very high performance, it is not flexible enough to be used for all variables. The requirement that the lifetimes of variables must be nested is too restrictive for many purposes. Often, you will want to use a method to allocate memory to store some data and be able to keep that data available long after that method has exited. This possibility exists whenever storage space is requested with the new operator — as is the case for all reference types. That is where the *managed heap* comes in.

If you have done any C++ coding that required low-level memory management, you will be familiar with the heap. The managed heap is not quite the same as the heap C++ uses; the managed heap works under the control of the garbage collector and provides significant benefits when compared to traditional heaps.

The managed heap (or heap for short) is just another area of memory from the processor's available 4GB. The following code demonstrates how the heap works and how memory is allocated for reference data types:

```
void DoWork()
{
    Customer arabel;
    arabel = new Customer();
    Customer otherCustomer2 = new EnhancedCustomer();
}
```

This code assumes the existence of two classes, Customer and EnhancedCustomer. The EnhancedCustomer class extends the Customer class.

First, you declare a Customer reference called arabel. The space for this will be allocated on the stack, but remember that this is only a reference, not an actual Customer object. The arabel reference takes up 4 bytes, enough space to hold the address at which a Customer object will be stored. (You need 4 bytes to represent a memory address as an integer value between 0 and 4GB.)

The next line,

```
arabel = new Customer();
```

does several things. First, it allocates memory on the heap to store a Customer object (a real object, not just an address). Then it sets the value of the variable arabel to the address of the memory it has allocated to the new Customer object. (It also calls the appropriate Customer() constructor to initialize the fields in the class instance, but we won't worry about that here.)

The Customer instance is not placed on the stack — it is placed on the heap. In this example, you don't know precisely how many bytes a Customer object occupies, but assume for the sake of argument that it is 32. These 32 bytes contain the instance fields of Customer as well as some information that .NET uses to identify and manage its class instances.

To find a storage location on the heap for the new Customer object, the .NET runtime will look through the heap and grab the first adjacent, unused block of 32 bytes. Again for the sake of argument, assume that this happens to be at address 200000, and that the arabel reference occupied locations 799996 through 799999 on the stack. This means that before instantiating the arabel object, the memory contents will look similar to Figure 12-2.

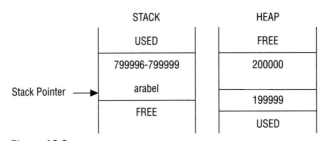

Figure 12-2

After allocating the new Customer object, the contents of memory will look like Figure 12-3. Note that unlike the stack, memory in the heap is allocated upward, so the free space can be found above the used space.

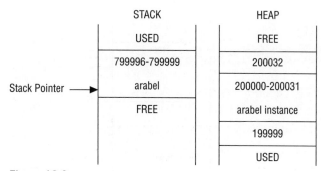

Figure 12-3

The next line of code both declares a `Customer` reference and instantiates a `Customer` object. In this instance, space on the stack for the `otherCustomer2` reference is allocated and space for the `mrJones` object is allocated on the heap in a single line of code:

```
Customer otherCustomer2 = new EnhancedCustomer();
```

This line allocates 4 bytes on the stack to hold the `otherCustomer2` reference, stored at locations `799992` through `799995`. The `otherCustomer2` object is allocated space on the heap starting at location `200032`.

It is clear from the example that the process of setting up a reference variable is more complex than that for setting up a value variable, and there is a performance overhead. In fact, the process is somewhat oversimplified here, because the .NET runtime needs to maintain information about the state of the heap, and this information needs to be updated whenever new data is added to the heap. Despite this overhead, you now have a mechanism for allocating variables that is not constrained by the limitations of the stack. By assigning the value of one reference variable to another of the same type, you have two variables that reference the same object in memory. When a reference variable goes out of scope, it is removed from the stack as described in the previous section, but the data for a referenced object is still sitting on the heap. The data will remain on the heap until either the program terminates or the garbage collector removes it, which will happen only when it is no longer referenced by any variables.

That is the power of reference data types, and you will see this feature used extensively in C# code. It means that you have a high degree of control over the lifetime of your data, because it is guaranteed to exist in the heap as long as you are maintaining some reference to it.

Garbage Collection

The previous discussion and diagrams show the managed heap working very much like the stack, to the extent that successive objects are placed next to each other in memory. This means that you can work out where to place the next object by using a heap pointer that indicates the next free memory location and that is adjusted as you add more objects to the heap. However, things are complicated because the lives of the heap-based objects are not coupled to the scope of the individual stack-based variables that reference them.

When the garbage collector runs, it will remove all those objects from the heap that are no longer referenced. Immediately after it has done this, the heap will have objects scattered on it, mixed up with memory that has just been freed (see Figure 12-4).

Figure 12-4

If the managed heap stayed like this, allocating space for new objects would be an awkward process, with the runtime having to search through the heap for a block of memory big enough to store each new object. However, the garbage collector does not leave the heap in this state. As soon as the garbage collector has freed up all the objects it can, it compacts the heap by moving all remaining objects to form one continuous block of memory. This means that the heap can continue working just like the stack as far as locating where to store new objects. Of course, when the objects are moved about, all the references to those objects need to be updated with the correct new addresses, but the garbage collector handles that too.

This action of compacting by the garbage collector is where the managed heap really works differently from old unmanaged heaps. With the managed heap, it is just a question of reading the value of the heap pointer, rather than iterating through a linked list of addresses to find somewhere to put the new data. For this reason, instantiating an object under .NET is much faster. Interestingly, accessing objects tends to be faster too, because the objects are compacted toward the same area of memory on the heap, resulting in less page swapping. Microsoft believes that these performance gains more than compensate for the performance penalty that you get whenever the garbage collector needs to do some work to compact the heap and change all those references to objects it has moved.

Generally, the garbage collector runs when the .NET runtime determines that garbage collection is required. You can force the garbage collector to run at a certain point in your code by calling System `.GC.Collect()`. *The* System.GC *class is a .NET class that represents the garbage collector, and the* Collect() *method initiates a garbage collection. The* GC *class is intended for rare situations in which you know that it's a good time to call the garbage collector; for example, if you have just de-referenced a large number of objects in your code. However, the logic of the garbage collector does not guarantee that all unreferenced objects will be removed from the heap in a single garbage collection pass.*

Freeing Unmanaged Resources

The presence of the garbage collector means that you will usually not worry about objects that you no longer need; you will simply allow all references to those objects to go out of scope and allow the garbage collector to free memory as required. However, the garbage collector does not know how to free unmanaged resources (such as file handles, network connections, and database connections). When managed classes encapsulate direct or indirect references to unmanaged resources, you need to make special provision to ensure that the unmanaged resources are released when an instance of the class is garbage collected.

When defining a class, you can use two mechanisms to automate the freeing of unmanaged resources. These mechanisms are often implemented together because each provides a slightly different approach to the solution of the problem. The mechanisms are:

❑ Declaring a destructor (or finalizer) as a member of your class

❑ Implementing the System.IDisposable interface in your class

The following sections discuss each of these mechanisms in turn, and then look at how to implement them together for best effect.

Destructors

You have seen that constructors allow you to specify actions that must take place whenever an instance of a class is created. Conversely, destructors are called before an object is destroyed by the garbage collector. Given this behavior, a destructor would initially seem like a great place to put code to free unmanaged resources and perform a general cleanup. Unfortunately, things are not so straightforward.

Although we talk about destructors in C#, in the underlying .NET architecture these are known as finalizers. When you define a destructor in C#, what is emitted into the assembly by the compiler is actually a method called Finalize(). That is something that doesn't affect any of your source code, but you'll need to be aware of the fact if you need to examine the contents of an assembly.

The syntax for a destructor will be familiar to C++ developers. It looks like a method, with the same name as the containing class, but prefixed with a tilde (~). It has no return type, and takes no parameters and no access modifiers. Here is an example:

```
class MyClass
{
    ~MyClass()
    {
        // destructor implementation
    }
}
```

When the C# compiler compiles a destructor, it implicitly translates the destructor code to the equivalent of a Finalize() method, which ensures that the Finalize() method of the parent class is executed. The following example shows the C# code equivalent to the Intermediate Language (IL) that the compiler would generate for the ~MyClass destructor:

```
protected override void Finalize()
{
    try
    {
        // destructor implementation
    }
    finally
    {
        base.Finalize();
    }
}
```

As shown, the code implemented in the ~MyClass destructor is wrapped in a try block contained in the Finalize() method. A call to the parent's Finalize() method is ensured by placing the call in a finally block. We discuss try and finally blocks in Chapter 14, "Errors and Exceptions."

Experienced C++ developers make extensive use of destructors, sometimes not only to clean up resources but also to provide debugging information or perform other tasks. C# destructors are used far less than their C++ equivalents. The problem with C# destructors as compared to their C++ counterparts is that they are nondeterministic. When a C++ object is destroyed, its destructor runs immediately. However, because of the way the garbage collector works when using C#, there is no way to know when an object's destructor will actually execute. Hence, you cannot place any code in the destructor that relies on being run at a certain time, and you should not rely on the destructor being called for different class instances in any particular order. When your object is holding scarce and critical resources that need to be freed as soon as possible, you do not want to wait for garbage collection.

Another problem with C# destructors is that the implementation of a destructor delays the final removal of an object from memory. Objects that do not have a destructor are removed from memory in one pass of the garbage collector, but objects that have destructors require two passes to be destroyed: The first pass calls the destructor without removing the object, and the second pass actually deletes the object. In addition, the runtime uses a single thread to execute the Finalize() methods of all objects. If you use destructors frequently, and use them to execute lengthy cleanup tasks, the impact on performance can be noticeable.

The IDisposable Interface

In C#, the recommended alternative to using a destructor is using the System.IDisposable interface. The IDisposable interface defines a pattern (with language-level support) that provides a deterministic mechanism for freeing unmanaged resources and avoids the garbage collector–related problems inherent with destructors. The IDisposable interface declares a single method named Dispose(), which takes no parameters and returns void. Here is an implementation for MyClass:

```
class MyClass : IDisposable
{
    public void Dispose()
    {
        // implementation
    }
}
```

The implementation of Dispose() should explicitly free all unmanaged resources used directly by an object and call Dispose() on any encapsulated objects that also implement the IDisposable interface. In this way, the Dispose() method provides precise control over when unmanaged resources are freed.

Suppose that you have a class named ResourceGobbler, which relies on the use of some external resource and implements IDisposable. If you want to instantiate an instance of this class, use it, and then dispose of it, you could do it like this:

```
ResourceGobbler theInstance = new ResourceGobbler();

// do your processing

theInstance.Dispose();
```

Unfortunately, this code fails to free the resources consumed by theInstance if an exception occurs during processing, so you should write the code as follows using a try block (which is discussed fully in Chapter 14):

```
ResourceGobbler theInstance = null;

try
{
    theInstance = new ResourceGobbler();
```

```
      // do your processing
   }
   finally
   {
      if (theInstance != null)
      {
         theInstance.Dispose();
      }
   }
```

This version ensures that `Dispose()` is always called on `theInstance` and that any resources consumed by it are always freed, even if an exception occurs during processing. However, it would make for confusing code if you always had to repeat such a construct. C# offers a syntax that you can use to guarantee that `Dispose()` will automatically be called against an object that implements `IDisposable` when its reference goes out of scope. The syntax to do this involves the `using` keyword — though now in a very different context, which has nothing to do with namespaces. The following code generates IL code equivalent to the `try` block just shown:

```
using (ResourceGobbler theInstance = new ResourceGobbler())
{
   // do your processing
}
```

The `using` statement, followed in brackets by a reference variable declaration and instantiation, will cause that variable to be scoped to the accompanying statement block. In addition, when that variable goes out of scope, its `Dispose()` method will be called automatically, even if an exception occurs. However, if you are already using `try` blocks to catch other exceptions, it is cleaner and avoids additional code indentation if you avoid the `using` statement and simply call `Dispose()` in the `Finally` clause of the existing `try` block.

> *For some classes, the notion of a `Close()` method is more logical than `Dispose()`; for example, when dealing with files or database connections. In these cases, it is common to implement the `IDisposable` interface and then implement a separate `Close()` method that simply calls `Dispose()`. This approach provides clarity in the use of your classes but also supports the `using` statement provided by C#.*

Implementing IDisposable and a Destructor

The previous sections discussed two alternatives for freeing unmanaged resources used by the classes you create:

❑   The execution of a destructor is enforced by the runtime but is nondeterministic and places an unacceptable overhead on the runtime because of the way garbage collection works.

❑   The `IDisposable` interface provides a mechanism that allows users of a class to control when resources are freed but requires discipline to ensure that `Dispose()` is called.

In general, the best approach is to implement both mechanisms in order to gain the benefits of both while overcoming their limitations. You implement `IDisposable` on the assumption that most programmers will call `Dispose()` correctly, but implement a destructor as a safety mechanism in case `Dispose()` is not called. Here is an example of a dual implementation:

```
using System;

public class ResourceHolder : IDisposable
```

(continued)

(continued)

```csharp
    {

        private bool isDisposed = false;

        public void Dispose()
        {
            Dispose(true);
            GC.SuppressFinalize(this);
        }

        protected virtual void Dispose(bool disposing)
        {
            if (!isDisposed)
            {
                if (disposing)
                {
                    // Cleanup managed objects by calling their
                    // Dispose() methods.
                }
                // Cleanup unmanaged objects
            }
            isDisposed = true;
        }

        ~ResourceHolder()
        {
            Dispose (false);
        }

        public void SomeMethod()
        {
            // Ensure object not already disposed before execution of any method
            if(isDisposed)
            {
                throw new ObjectDisposedException("ResourceHolder");
            }

            // method implementation…
        }
    }
```

You can see from this code that there is a second `protected` overload of `Dispose()`, which takes one `bool` parameter — and this is the method that does all cleaning up. `Dispose(bool)` is called by both the destructor and by `IDisposable.Dispose()`. The point of this approach is to ensure that all cleanup code is in one place.

The parameter passed to `Dispose(bool)` indicates whether `Dispose(bool)` has been invoked by the destructor or by `IDisposable.Dispose()` — `Dispose(bool)` should not be invoked from anywhere else in your code. The idea is this:

❑ If a consumer calls `IDisposable.Dispose()`, that consumer is indicating that all managed and unmanaged resources associated with that object should be cleaned up.

❑ If a destructor has been invoked, all resources still need to be cleaned up. However, in this case, you know that the destructor must have been called by the garbage collector and you should not attempt to access other managed objects because you can no longer be certain of their state. In this situation, the best you can do is clean up the known unmanaged resources and hope that any referenced managed objects also have destructors that will perform their own cleaning up.

The `isDisposed` member variable indicates whether the object has already been disposed of and allows you to ensure that you do not try to dispose of member variables more than once. It also allows you to test whether an object has been disposed of before executing any instance methods, as shown in `SomeMethod()`. This simplistic approach is not thread-safe and depends on the caller ensuring that only one thread is calling the method concurrently. Requiring a consumer to enforce synchronization is a reasonable assumption and one that is used repeatedly throughout the .NET class libraries (in the `Collection` classes, for example). Threading and synchronization are discussed in Chapter 19, "Threading and Synchronization."

Finally, `IDisposable.Dispose()` contains a call to the method `System.GC.SuppressFinalize()`. `GC` is the class that represents the garbage collector, and the `SuppressFinalize()` method tells the garbage collector that a class no longer needs to have its destructor called. Because your implementation of `Dispose()` has already done all the cleanup required, there's nothing left for the destructor to do. Calling `SuppressFinalize()` means that the garbage collector will treat that object as if it doesn't have a destructor at all.

Unsafe Code

As you have just seen, C# is very good at hiding much of the basic memory management from the developer, thanks to the garbage collector and the use of references. However, sometimes you will want direct access to memory. For example, you might want to access a function in an external (non-.NET) DLL that requires a pointer to be passed as a parameter (as many Windows API functions do), or possibly for performance reasons. This section examines C#'s facilities that provide direct access to the contents of memory.

Accessing Memory Directly with Pointers

Although we are introducing *pointers* as if they were a new topic, in reality pointers are not new at all. You have been using references freely in your code, and a reference is simply a type-safe pointer. You have already seen how variables that represent objects and arrays actually store the memory address of where the corresponding data (the *referent*) is stored. A pointer is simply a variable that stores the address of something else in the same way as a reference. The difference is that C# does not allow you direct access to the address contained in a reference variable. With a reference, the variable is treated syntactically as if it stores the actual contents of the referent.

C# references are designed to make the language simpler to use and to prevent you from inadvertently doing something that corrupts the contents of memory. With a pointer, however, the actual memory address is available to you. This gives you a lot of power to perform new kinds of operations. For example, you can add 4 bytes to the address, so that you can examine or even modify whatever data happens to be stored 4 bytes further on in memory.

The two main reasons for using pointers are:

❑ **Backward compatibility** — Despite all of the facilities provided by the .NET runtime, it is still possible to call native Windows API functions, and for some operations this may be the only way to accomplish your task. These API functions are generally written in C and often require pointers as parameters. However, in many cases it is possible to write the `DllImport` declaration in a way that avoids use of pointers; for example, by using the `System.IntPtr` class.

❑ **Performance** — On those occasions where speed is of the utmost importance, pointers can provide a route to optimized performance. If you know what you are doing, you can ensure that data is accessed or manipulated in the most efficient way. However, be aware that, more often than not, there are other areas of your code where you can make the necessary performance improvements without resorting to using pointers. Try using a code profiler to look for the bottlenecks in your code — one comes with Visual Studio 2008.

Low-level memory access comes at a price. The syntax for using pointers is more complex than that for reference types, and pointers are unquestionably more difficult to use correctly. You need good programming skills and an excellent ability to think carefully and logically about what your code is doing in order to use pointers successfully. If you are not careful, it is very easy to introduce subtle, difficult-to-find bugs into your program when using pointers. For example, it is easy to overwrite other variables, cause stack overflows, access areas of memory that don't store any variables, or even overwrite information about your code that is needed by the .NET runtime, thereby crashing your program.

In addition, if you use pointers your code must be granted a high level of trust by the runtime's code access security mechanism or it will not be allowed to execute. Under the default code access security policy, this is only possible if your code is running on the local machine. If your code must be run from a remote location, such as the Internet, users must grant your code additional permissions for it to work. Unless the users trust you and your code, they are unlikely to grant these permissions. Code access security is discussed more in Chapter 20, "Security."

Despite these issues, pointers remain a very powerful and flexible tool in the writing of efficient code.

> We strongly advise against using pointers unnecessarily because your code will not only be harder to write and debug, but it will also fail the memory type-safety checks imposed by the CLR, which is discussed in Chapter 1, ".NET Architecture."

Writing Unsafe Code with the unsafe Keyword

As a result of the risks associated with pointers, C# allows the use of pointers only in blocks of code that you have specifically marked for this purpose. The keyword to do this is unsafe. You can mark an individual method as being unsafe like this:

```
unsafe int GetSomeNumber()
{
    // code that can use pointers
}
```

Any method can be marked as unsafe, regardless of what other modifiers have been applied to it (for example, static methods or virtual methods). In the case of methods, the unsafe modifier applies to the method's parameters, allowing you to use pointers as parameters. You can also mark an entire class or struct as unsafe, which means that all of its members are assumed unsafe:

```
unsafe class MyClass
{
    // any method in this class can now use pointers
}
```

Similarly, you can mark a member as unsafe:

```
class MyClass
{
    unsafe int* pX;    // declaration of a pointer field in a class
}
```

Or you can mark a block of code within a method as unsafe:

```
void MyMethod()
{
    // code that doesn't use pointers
    unsafe
```

```
    {
        // unsafe code that uses pointers here
    }
    // more 'safe' code that doesn't use pointers
}
```

Note, however, that you cannot mark a local variable by itself as `unsafe`:

```
int MyMethod()
{
    unsafe int *pX;    // WRONG
}
```

If you want to use an unsafe local variable, you will need to declare and use it inside a method or block that is unsafe. There is one more step before you can use pointers. The C# compiler rejects unsafe code unless you tell it that your code includes unsafe blocks. The flag to do this is `unsafe`. Hence, to compile a file named `MySource.cs` that contains unsafe blocks (assuming no other compiler options), the command is:

```
csc /unsafe MySource.cs
```

or:

```
csc -unsafe MySource.cs
```

If you are using Visual Studio 2005 or 2008, you will also find the option to compile unsafe code in the Build tab of the project properties window.

Pointer Syntax

Once you have marked a block of code as `unsafe`, you can declare a pointer using this syntax:

```
int* pWidth, pHeight;
double* pResult;
byte*[] pFlags;
```

This code declares four variables: `pWidth` and `pHeight` are pointers to integers, `pResult` is a pointer to a `double`, and `pFlags` is an array of pointers to bytes. It is common practice to use the prefix `p` in front of names of pointer variables to indicate that they are pointers. When used in a variable declaration, the symbol `*` indicates that you are declaring a pointer (that is, something that stores the address of a variable of the specified type).

C++ developers should be aware of the syntax difference between C++ and C#. The C# statement `int* pX, pY;` corresponds to the C++ statement `int *pX, *pY;`. In C#, the `*` symbol is associated with the type rather than the variable name.

Once you have declared variables of pointer types, you can use them in the same way as normal variables, but first you need to learn two more operators:

❑ `&` means *take the address of*, and converts a value data type to a pointer, for example `int` to `*int`. This operator is known as the *address operator*.

❑ `*` means *get the contents of this address*, and converts a pointer to a value data type (for example, `*float` to `float`). This operator is known as the *indirection operator* (or sometimes as the *dereference operator*).

You will see from these definitions that `&` and `*` have opposite effects.

You might be wondering how it is possible to use the symbols `&` and `*` in this manner because these symbols also refer to the operators of bitwise AND (`&`) and multiplication (`*`). Actually, it is always possible for both you and the compiler to know what is meant in each case because with the new pointer *meanings, these symbols always appear as unary operators — they act on only one variable and appear in front of that variable in your code. By contrast, bitwise AND and multiplication are binary operators — they require two operands.*

The following code shows examples of how to use these operators:

```
int x = 10;
int* pX, pY;
pX = &x;
pY = pX;
*pY = 20;
```

You start by declaring an integer, x, with the value 10 followed by two pointers to integers, pX and pY. You then set pX to point to x (that is, you set the contents of pX to be the address of x). Then you assign the value of pX to pY, so that pY also points to x. Finally, in the statement *pY = 20, you assign the value 20 as the contents of the location pointed to by pY — in effect changing x to 20 because pY happens to point to x. Note that there is no particular connection between the variables pY and x. It is just that at the present time, pY happens to point to the memory location at which x is held.

To get a better understanding of what is going on, consider that the integer x is stored at memory locations 0x12F8C4 through 0x12F8C7 (1243332 to 1243335 in decimal) on the stack (there are four locations because an int occupies 4 bytes). Because the stack allocates memory downward, this means that the variables pX will be stored at locations 0x12F8C0 to 0x12F8C3, and pY will end up at locations 0x12F8BC to 0x12F8BF. Note that pX and pY also occupy 4 bytes each. That is not because an int occupies 4 bytes. It is because on a 32-bit processor you need 4 bytes to store an address. With these addresses, after executing the previous code, the stack will look like Figure 12-5.

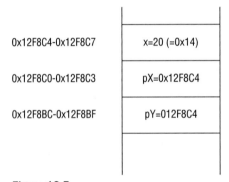

0x12F8C4-0x12F8C7	x=20 (=0x14)
0x12F8C0-0x12F8C3	pX=0x12F8C4
0x12F8BC-0x12F8BF	pY=012F8C4

Figure 12-5

Although this process is illustrated with integers, which will be stored consecutively on the stack on a 32-bit processor, this does not happen for all data types. The reason is that 32-bit processors work best when retrieving data from memory in 4-byte chunks. Memory on such machines tends to be divided into 4-byte blocks, and each block is sometimes known under Windows as a DWORD because this was the name of a 32-bit unsigned int in pre-.NET days. It is most efficient to grab DWORDs from memory — storing data across DWORD boundaries normally results in a hardware performance hit. For this reason, the .NET runtime normally pads out data types so that the memory they occupy is a multiple of 4. For example, a short occupies 2 bytes, but if a short is placed on the stack, the stack pointer will still be decremented by 4, not 2, so that the next variable to go on the stack will still start at a DWORD boundary.

You can declare a pointer to any value type (that is, any of the predefined types `uint`, `int`, `byte`, and so on, or to a struct). However, it is not possible to declare a pointer to a class or an array; this is because doing so could cause problems for the garbage collector. In order to work properly, the garbage collector needs to know exactly what class instances have been created on the heap, and where they are, but if your code started manipulating classes using pointers, you could very easily corrupt the information on the heap concerning classes that the .NET runtime maintains for the garbage collector. In this context, any data type that the garbage collector can access is known as a *managed type*. Pointers can only be declared as *unmanaged types* because the garbage collector cannot deal with them.

Casting Pointers to Integer Types

Because a pointer really stores an integer that represents an address, you won't be surprised to know that the address in any pointer can be converted to or from any integer type. Pointer-to-integer-type conversions must be explicit. Implicit conversions are not available for such conversions. For example, it is perfectly legitimate to write the following:

```
int x = 10;
int* pX, pY;
pX = &x;
pY = pX;
*pY = 20;
uint y = (uint)pX;
int* pD = (int*)y;
```

The address held in the pointer `pX` is cast to a `uint` and stored in the variable `y`. You have then cast `y` back to an `int*` and stored it in the new variable `pD`. Hence, now `pD` also points to the value of `x`.

The primary reason for casting a pointer value to an integer type is to display it. The `Console.Write()` and `Console.WriteLine()` methods do not have any overloads that can take pointers, but will accept and display pointer values that have been cast to integer types:

```
Console.WriteLine("Address is " + pX);      // wrong -- will give a
                                            // compilation error
Console.WriteLine("Address is " + (uint)pX);   // OK
```

You can cast a pointer to any of the integer types. However, because an address occupies 4 bytes on 32-bit systems, casting a pointer to anything other than a `uint`, `long`, or `ulong` is almost certain to lead to overflow errors. (An `int` causes problems because its range is from roughly –2 billion to 2 billion, whereas an address runs from zero to about 4 billion.) When C# is released for 64-bit processors, an address will occupy 8 bytes. Hence, on such systems, casting a pointer to anything other than `ulong` is likely to lead to overflow errors. It is also important to be aware that the `checked` keyword does not apply to conversions involving pointers. For such conversions, exceptions will not be raised when overflows occur, even in a `checked` context. The .NET runtime assumes that if you are using pointers you know what you are doing and are not worried about possible overflows.

Casting Between Pointer Types

You can also explicitly convert between pointers pointing to different types. For example:

```
byte aByte = 8;
byte* pByte= &aByte;
double* pDouble = (double*)pByte;
```

This is perfectly legal code, though again, if you try something like this, be careful. In this example, if you look at the `double` value pointed to by `pDouble`, you will actually be looking up some memory that contains a `byte` (`aByte`), combined with some other memory, and treating it as if this area of memory contained a `double`, which will not give you a meaningful value. However, you might want to convert between types in order to implement the equivalent of a C union, or you might want to cast pointers from other types into pointers to sbyte in order to examine individual bytes of memory.

void Pointers

If you want to maintain a pointer, but do not want to specify what type of data it points to, you can declare it as a pointer to a void:

```
int* pointerToInt;
void* pointerToVoid;
pointerToVoid = (void*)pointerToInt;
```

The main use of this is if you need to call an API function that requires void* parameters. Within the C# language, there isn't a great deal that you can do using void pointers. In particular, the compiler will flag an error if you attempt to dereference a void pointer using the * operator.

Pointer Arithmetic

It is possible to add or subtract integers to and from pointers. However, the compiler is quite clever about how it arranges for this to be done. For example, suppose that you have a pointer to an int and you try to add 1 to its value. The compiler will assume that you actually mean you want to look at the memory location following the int, and hence it will increase the value by 4 bytes — the size of an int. If it is a pointer to a double, adding 1 will actually increase the value of the pointer by 8 bytes, the size of a double. Only if the pointer points to a byte or sbyte (1 byte each) will adding 1 to the value of the pointer actually change its value by 1.

You can use the operators +, -, +=, -=, ++, and -- with pointers, with the variable on the right-hand side of these operators being a long or ulong.

It is not permitted to carry out arithmetic operations on void pointers.

For example, assume these definitions:

```
uint u = 3;
byte b = 8;
double d = 10.0;
uint* pUint= &u;        // size of a uint is 4
byte* pByte = &b;       // size of a byte is 1
double* pDouble = &d;   // size of a double is 8
```

Next, assume the addresses to which these pointers point are:

❑   pUint: 1243332

❑   pByte: 1243328

❑   pDouble: 1243320

Then execute this code:

```
++pUint;                // adds (1*4) = 4 bytes to pUint
pByte -= 3;             // subtracts (3*1) = 3 bytes from pByte
double* pDouble2 = pDouble + 4; // pDouble2 = pDouble + 32 bytes (4*8 bytes)
```

The pointers now contain:

❑   pUint: 1243336

❑   pByte: 1243325

❑   pDouble2: 1243352

> The general rule is that adding a number *X* to a pointer to type *T* with value *P* gives the result *P* + *X**(sizeof(*T*)).

You need to be aware of the previous rule. If successive values of a given type are stored in successive memory locations, pointer addition works very well to allow you to move pointers between memory locations. If you are dealing with types such as `byte` *or* `char`, *though, whose sizes are not multiples of 4, successive values will not, by default, be stored in successive memory locations.*

You can also subtract one pointer from another pointer, if both pointers point to the same data type. In this case, the result is a `long` whose value is given by the difference between the pointer values divided by the size of the type that they represent:

```
double* pD1 = (double*)1243324;    // note that it is perfectly valid to
                                   // initialize a pointer like this.
double* pD2 = (double*)1243300;
long L = pD1-pD2;                  // gives the result 3 (=24/sizeof(double))
```

The sizeof Operator

This section has been referring to the sizes of various data types. If you need to use the size of a type in your code, you can use the `sizeof` operator, which takes the name of a data type as a parameter and returns the number of bytes occupied by that type. For example:

```
int x = sizeof(double);
```

This will set x to the value 8.

The advantage of using `sizeof` is that you don't have to hard-code data type sizes in your code, making your code more portable. For the predefined data types, `sizeof` returns the following values:

```
sizeof(sbyte) = 1;   sizeof(byte) = 1;
sizeof(short) = 2;   sizeof(ushort) = 2;
sizeof(int) = 4;     sizeof(uint) = 4;
sizeof(long) = 8;    sizeof(ulong) = 8;
sizeof(char) = 2;    sizeof(float) = 4;
sizeof(double) = 8;  sizeof(bool) = 1;
```

You can also use `sizeof` for structs that you define yourself, although in that case, the result depends on what fields are in the struct. You cannot use `sizeof` for classes, and it can only be used in an `unsafe` code block.

Pointers to Structs: The Pointer Member Access Operator

Pointers to structs work in exactly the same way as pointers to the predefined value types. There is, however, one condition — the struct must not contain any reference types. This is due to the restriction mentioned earlier that pointers cannot point to any reference types. To avoid this, the compiler will flag an error if you create a pointer to any struct that contains any reference types.

Suppose that you had a struct defined like this:

```
struct MyStruct
{
    public long X;
    public float F;
}
```

You could define a pointer to it like this:

```
MyStruct* pStruct;
```

Then you could initialize it like this:

```
MyStruct Struct = new MyStruct();
pStruct = &Struct;
```

It is also possible to access member values of a struct through the pointer:

```
(*pStruct).X = 4;
(*pStruct).F = 3.4f;
```

However, this syntax is a bit complex. For this reason, C# defines another operator that allows you to access members of structs through pointers using a simpler syntax. It is known as the *pointer member access operator*, and the symbol is a dash followed by a greater-than sign, so it looks like an arrow: ->.

> C++ developers will recognize the pointer member access operator because C++ uses the same symbol for the same purpose.

Using the pointer member access operator, the previous code can be rewritten:

```
pStruct->X = 4;
pStruct->F = 3.4f;
```

You can also directly set up pointers of the appropriate type to point to fields within a struct:

```
long* pL = &(Struct.X);
float* pF = &(Struct.F);
```

or

```
long* pL = &(pStruct->X);
float* pF = &(pStruct->F);
```

Pointers to Class Members

As indicated earlier, it is not possible to create pointers to classes. That is because the garbage collector does not maintain any information about pointers, only about references, so creating pointers to classes could cause garbage collection to not work properly.

However, most classes do contain value type members, and you might want to create pointers to them. This is possible but requires a special syntax. For example, suppose that you rewrite the struct from the previous example as a class:

```
class MyClass
{
    public long X;
    public float F;
}
```

Then you might want to create pointers to its fields, X and F, in the same way as you did earlier. Unfortunately, doing so will produce a compilation error:

```
MyClass myObject = new MyClass();
long* pL = &(myObject.X);    // wrong -- compilation error
float* pF = &(myObject.F);   // wrong -- compilation error
```

Although X and F are unmanaged types, they are embedded in an object, which sits on the heap. During garbage collection, the garbage collector might move MyObject to a new location, which would leave pL and pF pointing to the wrong memory addresses. Because of this, the compiler will not let you assign addresses of members of managed types to pointers in this manner.

The solution is to use the `fixed` keyword, which tells the garbage collector that there may be pointers referencing members of certain objects, so those objects must not be moved. The syntax for using `fixed` looks like this if you just want to declare one pointer:

```
MyClass myObject = new MyClass();
fixed (long* pObject = &(myObject.X))
{
    // do something
}
```

You define and initialize the pointer variable in the brackets following the keyword `fixed`. This pointer variable (`pObject` in the example) is scoped to the `fixed` block identified by the curly braces. As a result, the garbage collector knows not to move the `myObject` object while the code inside the `fixed` block is executing.

If you want to declare more than one pointer, you can place multiple `fixed` statements before the same code block:

```
MyClass myObject = new MyClass();
fixed (long* pX = &(myObject.X))
fixed (float* pF = &(myObject.F))
{
    // do something
}
```

You can nest entire `fixed` blocks if you want to fix several pointers for different periods:

```
MyClass myObject = new MyClass();
fixed (long* pX = &(myObject.X))
{
    // do something with pX
    fixed (float* pF = &(myObject.F))
    {
        // do something else with pF
    }
}
```

You can also initialize several variables within the same `fixed` block, if they are of the same type:

```
MyClass myObject = new MyClass();
MyClass myObject2 = new MyClass();
fixed (long* pX = &(myObject.X), pX2 = &(myObject2.X))
{
    // etc.
}
```

In all these cases, it is immaterial whether the various pointers you are declaring point to fields in the same or different objects or to static fields not associated with any class instance.

Pointer Example: PointerPlayaround

This section presents an example that uses pointers. The following code is an example named `PointerPlayaround`. It does some simple pointer manipulation and displays the results, allowing you to see what is happening in memory and where variables are stored:

```
using System;

namespace Wrox.ProCSharp.Memory
{
    class MainEntryPoint
    {
        static unsafe void Main()
```

(continued)

(continued)

```
        {
            int x=10;
            short y = -1;
            byte y2 = 4;
            double z = 1.5;
            int* pX = &x;
            short* pY = &y;
            double* pZ = &z;

            Console.WriteLine(
                "Address of x is 0x{0:X}, size is {1}, value is {2}",
                (uint)&x, sizeof(int), x);
            Console.WriteLine(
                "Address of y is 0x{0:X}, size is {1}, value is {2}",
                (uint)&y, sizeof(short), y);
            Console.WriteLine(
                "Address of y2 is 0x{0:X}, size is {1}, value is {2}",
                (uint)&y2, sizeof(byte), y2);
            Console.WriteLine(
                "Address of z is 0x{0:X}, size is {1}, value is {2}",
                (uint)&z, sizeof(double), z);
            Console.WriteLine(
                "Address of pX=&x is 0x{0:X}, size is {1}, value is 0x{2:X}",
                (uint)&pX, sizeof(int*), (uint)pX);
            Console.WriteLine(
                "Address of pY=&y is 0x{0:X}, size is {1}, value is 0x{2:X}",
                (uint)&pY, sizeof(short*), (uint)pY);
            Console.WriteLine(
                "Address of pZ=&z is 0x{0:X}, size is {1}, value is 0x{2:X}",
                (uint)&pZ, sizeof(double*), (uint)pZ);

            *pX = 20;
            Console.WriteLine("After setting *pX, x = {0}", x);
            Console.WriteLine("*pX = {0}", *pX);

            pZ = (double*)pX;
            Console.WriteLine("x treated as a double = {0}", *pZ);

            Console.ReadLine();
        }
    }
}
```

This code declares four value variables:

❑ An int x

❑ A short y

❑ A byte y2

❑ A double z

It also declares pointers to three of these values: pX, pY, and pZ.

Next, you display the values of these variables as well as their sizes and addresses. Note that in taking the address of pX, pY, and pZ, you are effectively looking at a pointer *to* a pointer — an address of an address of a value. Notice that, in accordance with the usual practice when displaying addresses, you have used the `{0:X}` format specifier in the `Console.WriteLine()` commands to ensure that memory addresses are displayed in hexadecimal format.

Finally, you use the pointer pX to change the value of x to 20 and do some pointer casting to see what happens if you try to treat the content of x as if it were a `double`.

Compiling and running this code results in the following output. This screen output demonstrates the effects of attempting to compile both with and without the `/unsafe` flag:

```
csc PointerPlayaround.cs
Microsoft (R) Visual C# 2008 Compiler version 3.05.20706.1
for Microsoft (R) .NET Framework version 3.5
Copyright (C) Microsoft Corporation. All rights reserved.

PointerPlayaround.cs(7,26): error CS0227: Unsafe code may only appear if
          compiling with /unsafe

csc /unsafe PointerPlayaround.cs
Microsoft (R) Visual C# 2008 Compiler version 3.05.20706.1
for Microsoft (R) .NET Framework version 3.5
Copyright (C) Microsoft Corporation. All rights reserved.

PointerPlayaround
Address of x is 0x12F4B0, size is 4, value is 10
Address of y is 0x12F4AC, size is 2, value is -1
Address of y2 is 0x12F4A8, size is 1, value is 4
Address of z is 0x12F4A0, size is 8, value is 1.5
Address of pX=&x is 0x12F49C, size is 4, value is 0x12F4B0
Address of pY=&y is 0x12F498, size is 4, value is 0x12F4AC
Address of pZ=&z is 0x12F494, size is 4, value is 0x12F4A0
After setting *pX, x = 20
*pX = 20
x treated as a double = 2.86965129997082E-308
```

Checking through these results confirms the description of how the stack operates that was given in the "Memory Management under the Hood" section earlier in this chapter. It allocates successive variables moving downward in memory. Notice how it also confirms that blocks of memory on the stack are always allocated in multiples of 4 bytes. For example, y is a `short` (of size 2), and has the (decimal) address `1242284`, indicating that the memory locations reserved for it are locations `1242284` through `1242287`. If the .NET runtime had been strictly packing up variables next to each other, Y would have occupied just two locations, `1242284` and `1242285`.

The next example illustrates pointer arithmetic, as well as pointers to structs and class members. This example is named `PointerPlayaround2`. To start, you define a struct named `CurrencyStruct`, which represents a currency value as dollars and cents. You also define an equivalent class named `CurrencyClass`:

```
internal struct CurrencyStruct
{
    public long Dollars;
    public byte Cents;

    public override string ToString()
    {
        return "$" + Dollars + "." + Cents;
```

(continued)

(continued)

```
        }
    }

    internal class CurrencyClass
    {
        public long Dollars;
        public byte Cents;

        public override string ToString()
        {
            return "$" + Dollars + "." + Cents;
        }
    }
```

Now that you have your struct and class defined, you can apply some pointers to them. Following is the code for the new example. Because the code is fairly long, we will go through it in detail. You start by displaying the size of `CurrencyStruct`, creating a couple of `CurrencyStruct` instances and creating some `CurrencyStruct` pointers. You use the `pAmount` pointer to initialize the members of the `amount1` `CurrencyStruct` and then display the addresses of your variables:

```
public static unsafe void Main()
{
    Console.WriteLine(
        "Size of CurrencyStruct struct is " + sizeof(CurrencyStruct));
    CurrencyStruct amount1, amount2;
    CurrencyStruct* pAmount = &amount1;
    long* pDollars = &(pAmount->Dollars);
    byte* pCents = &(pAmount->Cents);

    Console.WriteLine("Address of amount1 is 0x{0:X}", (uint)&amount1);
    Console.WriteLine("Address of amount2 is 0x{0:X}", (uint)&amount2);
    Console.WriteLine("Address of pAmount is 0x{0:X}", (uint)&pAmount);
    Console.WriteLine("Address of pDollars is 0x{0:X}", (uint)&pDollars);
    Console.WriteLine("Address of pCents is 0x{0:X}", (uint)&pCents);
    pAmount->Dollars = 20;
    *pCents = 50;
    Console.WriteLine("amount1 contains " + amount1);
```

Now you do some pointer manipulation that relies on your knowledge of how the stack works. Due to the order in which the variables were declared, you know that `amount2` will be stored at an address immediately below `amount1`. The `sizeof(CurrencyStruct)` operator returns 16 (as demonstrated in the screen output coming up), so `CurrencyStruct` occupies a multiple of 4 bytes. Therefore, after you decrement your currency pointer, it will point to `amount2`:

```
    --pAmount;    // this should get it to point to amount2
    Console.WriteLine("amount2 has address 0x{0:X} and contains {1}",
        (uint)pAmount, *pAmount);
```

Notice that when you call `Console.WriteLine()` you display the contents of `amount2`, but you haven't yet initialized it. What gets displayed will be random garbage — whatever happened to be stored at that location in memory before execution of the example. There is an important point here: Normally, the C# compiler would prevent you from using an uninitialized variable, but when you start using pointers, it is very easy to circumvent many of the usual compilation checks. In this case, you have done so because the compiler has no way of knowing that you are actually displaying the contents of `amount2`. Only you know that, because your knowledge of the stack means that you can tell what the effect of decrementing pAmount will be. Once you start doing pointer arithmetic, you will find that you can access all sorts of variables and memory locations that the compiler would usually stop you from accessing, hence the description of pointer arithmetic as unsafe.

Next, you do some pointer arithmetic on your pCents pointer. pCents currently points to amount1 .Cents, but the aim here is to get it to point to amount2.Cents, again using pointer operations instead of directly telling the compiler that's what you want to do. To do this, you need to decrement the address pCents contains by sizeof(Currency):

```
// do some clever casting to get pCents to point to cents
// inside amount2
CurrencyStruct* pTempCurrency = (CurrencyStruct*)pCents;
pCents = (byte*) ( --pTempCurrency );
Console.WriteLine("Address of pCents is now 0x{0:X}", (uint)&pCents);
```

Finally, you use the fixed keyword to create some pointers that point to the fields in a class instance and use these pointers to set the value of this instance. Notice that this is also the first time that you have been able to look at the address of an item stored on the heap rather than the stack:

```
Console.WriteLine("\nNow with classes");
// now try it out with classes
CurrencyClass amount3 = new CurrencyClass();

fixed(long* pDollars2 = &(amount3.Dollars))
fixed(byte* pCents2 = &(amount3.Cents))
{
    Console.WriteLine(
        "amount3.Dollars has address 0x{0:X}", (uint)pDollars2);
    Console.WriteLine(
        "amount3.Cents has address 0x{0:X}", (uint) pCents2);
    *pDollars2 = -100;
    Console.WriteLine("amount3 contains " + amount3);
}
```

Compiling and running this code gives output similar to this:

```
csc /unsafe PointerPlayaround2.cs
Microsoft (R) Visual C# 2008 Compiler version 3.05.20706.1
for Microsoft (R) .NET Framework version 3.5
Copyright (C) Microsoft Corporation. All rights reserved.

PointerPlayaround2
Size of CurrencyStruct struct is 16
Address of amount1 is 0x12F4A4
Address of amount2 is 0x12F494
Address of pAmount is 0x12F490
Address of pDollars is 0x12F48C
Address of pCents is 0x12F488
amount1 contains $20.50
amount2 has address 0x12F494 and contains $0.0
Address of pCents is now 0x12F488

Now with classes
amount3.Dollars has address 0xA64414
amount3.Cents has address 0xA6441C
amount3 contains $-100.0
```

Notice in this output the uninitialized value of `amount2` that is displayed, and notice that the size of the `CurrencyStruct` struct is `16` — somewhat larger than you would expect given the sizes of its fields (a `long` and a `byte` should total 9 bytes).

Using Pointers to Optimize Performance

Until now, all of the examples have been designed to demonstrate the various things that you can do with pointers. We have played around with memory in a way that is probably interesting only to people who like to know what's happening under the hood but that doesn't really help you to write better code. Here you're going to apply your understanding of pointers and see an example of how judicious use of pointers has a significant performance benefit.

Creating Stack-Based Arrays

This section explores one of the main areas in which pointers can be useful: creating high-performance, low-overhead arrays on the stack. As discussed in Chapter 2, "C# Basics," C# includes rich support for handling arrays. Although C# makes it very easy to use both 1-dimensional and rectangular or jagged multidimensional arrays, it suffers from the disadvantage that these arrays are actually objects; they are instances of `System.Array`. This means that the arrays are stored on the heap with all of the overhead that this involves. There may be occasions when you need to create a short-lived high-performance array and don't want the overhead of reference objects. You can do this using pointers, although as you see in this section, this is easy for only 1-dimensional arrays.

To create a high-performance array, you need to use a new keyword: `stackalloc`. The `stackalloc` command instructs the .NET runtime to allocate an amount of memory on the stack. When you call `stackalloc`, you need to supply it with two pieces of information:

❑   The type of data you want to store

❑   The number of these data items you need to store

For example, to allocate enough memory to store 10 `decimal` data items, you can write:

```
decimal* pDecimals = stackalloc decimal[10];
```

This command simply allocates the stack memory; it does not attempt to initialize the memory to any default value. This is fine for the purpose of this example because you are creating a high-performance array, and initializing values unnecessarily would hurt performance.

Similarly, to store 20 `double` data items, you write:

```
double* pDoubles = stackalloc double[20];
```

Although this line of code specifies the number of variables to store as a constant, this can equally be a quantity evaluated at runtime. So, you can write the previous example like this:

```
int size;
size = 20;    // or some other value calculated at run-time
double* pDoubles = stackalloc double[size];
```

You will see from these code snippets that the syntax of `stackalloc` is slightly unusual. It is followed immediately by the name of the data type you want to store (and this must be a value type) and then by the number of items you need space for in square brackets. The number of bytes allocated will be this number multiplied by `sizeof`(data type). The use of square brackets in the preceding code sample suggests an array, which is not too surprising. If you have allocated space for 20 doubles, then what you have is an array of 20 doubles. The simplest type of array that you can have is a block of memory that stores one element after another (see Figure 12-6).

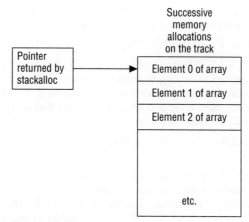

Figure 12-6

This diagram also shows the pointer returned by `stackalloc`, which is always a pointer to the allocated data type that points to the top of the newly allocated memory block. To use the memory block, you simply dereference the returned pointer. For example, to allocate space for 20 doubles and then set the first element (element 0 of the array) to the value 3.0, write this:

```
double* pDoubles = stackalloc double [20];
*pDoubles = 3.0;
```

To access the next element of the array, you use pointer arithmetic. As described earlier, if you add 1 to a pointer, its value will be increased by the size of whatever data type it points to. In this case, this will be just enough to take you to the next free memory location in the block that you have allocated. So, you can set the second element of the array (element number 1) to the value 8.4 like this:

```
double* pDoubles = stackalloc double [20];
*pDoubles = 3.0;
*(pDoubles+1) = 8.4;
```

By the same reasoning, you can access the element with index X of the array with the expression `*(pDoubles+X)`.

Effectively, you have a means by which you can access elements of your array, but for general-purpose use, this syntax is too complex. Fortunately, C# defines an alternative syntax using square brackets. C# gives a very precise meaning to square brackets when they are applied to pointers; if the variable p is any pointer type and X is an integer, then the expression `p[X]` is always interpreted by the compiler as meaning `*(p+X)`. This is true for all pointers, not only those initialized using `stackalloc`. With this shorthand notation, you now have a very convenient syntax for accessing your array. In fact, it means that you have exactly the same syntax for accessing 1-dimensional stack-based arrays as you do for accessing heap-based arrays that are represented by the `System.Array` class:

```
double* pDoubles = stackalloc double [20];
pDoubles[0] = 3.0;    // pDoubles[0] is the same as *pDoubles
pDoubles[1] = 8.4;    // pDoubles[1] is the same as *(pDoubles+1)
```

This idea of applying array syntax to pointers is not new. It has been a fundamental part of both the C and the C++ languages ever since those languages were invented. Indeed, C++ developers will recognize the stack-based arrays they can obtain using `stackalloc` as being essentially identical to classic stack-based C and C++ arrays. It is this syntax and the way it links pointers and arrays that was one of the reasons why the C language became popular in the 1970s, and the main reason why the use of pointers became such a popular programming technique in C and C++.

Although your high-performance array can be accessed in the same way as a normal C# array, a word of caution is in order. The following code in C# raises an exception:

```
double[] myDoubleArray = new double [20];
myDoubleArray[50] = 3.0;
```

The exception occurs because you are trying to access an array using an index that is out of bounds; the index is 50, whereas the maximum allowed value is 19. However, if you declare the equivalent array using stackalloc, there is no object wrapped around the array that can perform bounds checking. Hence, the following code will *not* raise an exception:

```
double* pDoubles = stackalloc double [20];
pDoubles[50] = 3.0;
```

In this code, you allocate enough memory to hold 20 doubles. Then you set sizeof(double) memory locations starting at the location given by the start of this memory + 50*sizeof(double) to hold the double value 3.0. Unfortunately, that memory location is way outside the area of memory that you have allocated for the doubles. There is no knowing what data might be stored at that address. At best, you may have used some currently unused memory, but it is equally possible that you may have just overwritten some locations in the stack that were being used to store other variables or even the return address from the method currently being executed. Once again, you see that the high performance to be gained from pointers comes at a cost; you need to be certain you know what you are doing, or you will get some very strange runtime bugs.

QuickArray Example

Our discussion of pointers ends with a stackalloc example called QuickArray. In this example, the program simply asks users how many elements they want to be allocated for an array. The code then uses stackalloc to allocate an array of longs that size. The elements of this array are populated with the squares of the integers starting with 0 and the results displayed on the console:

```
using System;

namespace QuickArray
{
    internal class Program
    {
        private static unsafe void Main()
        {
            Console.Write("How big an array do you want? \n> ");
            string userInput = Console.ReadLine();
            uint size = uint.Parse(userInput);

            long* pArray = stackalloc long[(int) size];
            for (int i = 0; i < size; i++)
            {
                pArray[i] = i*i;
            }

            for (int i = 0; i < size; i++)
            {
                Console.WriteLine("Element {0} = {1}", i, *(pArray + i));
            }

            Console.ReadLine();
        }
    }
}
```

Here is the output for the `QuickArray` example:

```
QuickArray
How big an array do you want?
> 15
Element 0 = 0
Element 1 = 1
Element 2 = 4
Element 3 = 9
Element 4 = 16
Element 5 = 25
Element 6 = 36
Element 7 = 49
Element 8 = 64
Element 9 = 81
Element 10 = 100
Element 11 = 121
Element 12 = 144
Element 13 = 169
Element 14 = 196
```

Summary

Remember, to become a truly proficient C# programmer, you must have a solid understanding of how memory allocation and garbage collection work. This chapter described how the CLR manages and allocates memory on the heap and the stack. It also illustrated how to write classes that free unmanaged resources correctly, and how to use pointers in C#. These are both advanced topics that are poorly understood and often implemented incorrectly by novice programmers.

This chapter should be treated as a companion to what you learn from Chapter 14 on error handling and in Chapter 19 when dealing with threading. The next chapter of this book looks at reflection in C#.

13

Reflection

Reflection is a generic term that describes the ability to inspect and manipulate program elements at runtime. For example, reflection allows you to:

❑ Enumerate the members of a type

❑ Instantiate a new object

❑ Execute the members of an object

❑ Find out information about a type

❑ Find out information about an assembly

❑ Inspect the custom attributes applied to a type

❑ Create and compile a new assembly

This list represents a great deal of functionality and encompasses some of the most powerful and complex capabilities provided by the .NET Framework class library. Although this chapter does not have the space to cover all the capabilities of reflection, it focuses on those elements that you are likely to use most frequently.

This chapter is about:

❑ Custom attributes, a mechanism that allows you to associate custom metadata with program elements. This metadata is created at compile time and embedded in an assembly.

❑ Inspecting the metadata at runtime using some of the capabilities of reflection.

❑ Some of the fundamental classes that enable reflection, including the `System.Type` and `System.Reflection.Assembly` classes, which provide the access points for much of what you can do with reflection.

To demonstrate custom attributes and reflection, you develop an example based on a company that regularly ships upgrades of its software and wants to have details of these upgrades documented automatically. In the example, you define custom attributes that indicate the date when program elements were last modified, and what changes were made. You then use reflection to develop an application that looks for these attributes in an assembly, and can automatically display all the details about what upgrades have been made to the software since a given date.

Another example in this chapter considers an application that reads from or writes to a database and uses custom attributes as a way of marking which classes and properties correspond to which database tables and columns. By reading these attributes from the assembly at runtime, the program is able to automatically retrieve or write data to the appropriate location in the database, without requiring specific logic for each table or column.

Custom Attributes

From this book, you have seen how you can define attributes on various items within your program. These attributes have been defined by Microsoft as part of the .NET Framework class library, and many of them receive special support from the C# compiler. This means that for those particular attributes, the compiler could customize the compilation process in specific ways; for example, laying out a struct in memory according to the details in the `StructLayout` attributes.

The .NET Framework also allows you to define your own attributes. Clearly, these attributes will not have any effect on the compilation process, because the compiler has no intrinsic awareness of them. However, these attributes will be emitted as metadata in the compiled assembly when they are applied to program elements.

By itself, this metadata might be useful for documentation purposes, but what makes attributes really powerful is that by using reflection, your code can read this metadata and use it to make decisions at runtime. This means that the custom attributes that you define can directly affect how your code runs. For example, custom attributes can be used to enable declarative code access security checks for custom permission classes, to associate information with program elements that can then be used by testing tools, or when developing extensible frameworks that allow the loading of plugins or modules.

Writing Custom Attributes

To understand how to write your own custom attributes, it is useful to know what the compiler does when it encounters an element in your code that has a custom attribute applied to it. To take the database example, suppose that you have a C# property declaration that looks like this:

```
[FieldName("SocialSecurityNumber")]
public string SocialSecurityNumber
{
    get {
        // etc.
```

When the C# compiler recognizes that this property has an attribute applied to it (`FieldName`), it will start by appending the string `Attribute` to this name, forming the combined name `FieldNameAttribute`. The compiler will then search all the namespaces in its search path (those namespaces that have been mentioned in a `using` statement) for a class with the specified name. Note that if you mark an item with an attribute whose name already ends in the string `Attribute`, the compiler will not add the string to the name a second time; it will leave the attribute name unchanged. Therefore, the preceding code is equivalent to this:

```
[FieldNameAttribute("SocialSecurityNumber")]
public string SocialSecurityNumber
{
    get {
    // etc.
```

The compiler expects to find a class with this name, and it expects this class to be derived directly or indirectly from System.Attribute. The compiler also expects that this class contains information that governs the use of the attribute. In particular, the attribute class needs to specify the following:

❑   The types of program elements to which the attribute can be applied (classes, structs, properties, methods, and so on)

❑   Whether it is legal for the attribute to be applied more than once to the same program element

❑   Whether the attribute, when applied to a class or interface, is inherited by derived classes and interfaces

❑   The mandatory and optional parameters the attribute takes

If the compiler cannot find a corresponding attribute class, or it finds one but the way that you have used that attribute does not match the information in the attribute class, the compiler will raise a compilation error. For example, if the attribute class indicates that the attribute can be applied only to classes, but you have applied it to a struct definition, a compilation error will occur.

To continue with the example, assume that you have defined the FieldName attribute like this:

```
[AttributeUsage(AttributeTargets.Property,
    AllowMultiple=false,
    Inherited=false)]
public class FieldNameAttribute : Attribute
{
    private string name;
    public FieldNameAttribute(string name)
    {
        this.name = name;
    }
}
```

The following sections discuss each element of this definition.

AttributeUsage Attribute

The first thing to note is that the attribute class itself is marked with an attribute — the System. AttributeUsage attribute. This is an attribute defined by Microsoft for which the C# compiler provides special support. (You could argue that AttributeUsage isn't an attribute at all; it is more like a meta-attribute, because it applies only to other attributes, not simply to any class.) The primary purpose of AttributeUsage is to identify the types of program elements to which your custom attribute can be applied. This information is given by the first parameter of the AttributeUsage attribute — this parameter is mandatory, and is of an enumerated type, AttributeTargets. In the previous example, you have indicated that the FieldName attribute can be applied only to properties, which is fine, because that is exactly what you have applied it to in the earlier code fragment. The members of the AttributeTargets enumeration are:

❑   All

❑   Assembly

❑   Class

❑   Constructor

❑   Delegate

❑   Enum

❑   Event

❑   Field

❑   GenericParameter (from .NET 2.0 on only)

❑   Interface

❑   Method

❑   Module

❑   Parameter

❑   Property

❑   ReturnValue

❑   Struct

This list identifies all of the program elements to which you can apply attributes. Note that when applying the attribute to a program element, you place the attribute in square brackets immediately before the element. However, two values in the preceding list do not correspond to any program element: `Assembly` and `Module`. An attribute can be applied to an assembly or module as a whole instead of to an element in your code; in this case the attribute can be placed anywhere in your source code, but needs to be prefixed with the `Assembly` or `Module` keyword:

```
[assembly:SomeAssemblyAttribute(Parameters)]
[module:SomeAssemblyAttribute(Parameters)]
```

When indicating the valid target elements of a custom attribute, you can combine these values using the bitwise OR operator. For example, if you wanted to indicate that your `FieldName` attribute can be applied to both properties and fields, you would write:

```
[AttributeUsage(AttributeTargets.Property | AttributeTargets.Field,
    AllowMultiple=false,
    Inherited=false)]
public class FieldNameAttribute : Attribute
```

You can also use `AttributeTargets.All` to indicate that your attribute can be applied to all types of program elements. The `AttributeUsage` attribute also contains two other parameters, `AllowMultiple` and `Inherited`. These are specified using the syntax of `<ParameterName>=<ParameterValue>`, instead of simply giving the values for these parameters. These parameters are optional — you can omit them if you want.

The `AllowMultiple` parameter indicates whether an attribute can be applied more than once to the same item. The fact that it is set to `false` here indicates that the compiler should raise an error if it sees something like this:

```
[FieldName("SocialSecurityNumber")]
[FieldName("NationalInsuranceNumber")]
public string SocialSecurityNumber
{

    // etc.
```

If the `Inherited` parameter is set to `true`, an attribute applied to a class or interface will also automatically be applied to all derived classes or interfaces. If the attribute is applied to a method or property, it will automatically apply to any overrides of that method or property, and so on.

Specifying Attribute Parameters

This section examines how you can specify the parameters that your custom attribute takes. The way it works is that when the compiler encounters a statement such as the following,

```
[FieldName("SocialSecurityNumber")]
public string SocialSecurityNumber
{

    // etc.
```

the compiler examines the parameters passed into the attribute — which is a string — and looks for a constructor for the attribute that takes exactly those parameters. If the compiler finds an appropriate constructor, the compiler will emit the specified metadata to the assembly. If the compiler does not find an appropriate constructor, a compilation error occurs. As discussed later in this chapter, reflection involves reading metadata (attributes) from assemblies and instantiating the attribute classes they represent. Because of this, the compiler must ensure that an appropriate constructor exists that will allow the runtime instantiation of the specified attribute.

In the example, you have supplied just one constructor for FieldNameAttribute, and this constructor takes one string parameter. Therefore, when applying the FieldName attribute to a property, you must supply one string as a parameter, as was done in the preceding sample code.

If you want to allow a choice of what types of parameters should be supplied with an attribute, you can provide different constructor overloads, although normal practice is to supply just one constructor and use properties to define any other optional parameters, as explained next.

Specifying Optional Attribute Parameters

As demonstrated with reference to the AttributeUsage attribute, an alternative syntax exists by which optional parameters can be added to an attribute. This syntax involves specifying the names and values of the optional parameters. It works through public properties or fields in the attribute class. For example, suppose that you modified the definition of the SocialSecurityNumber property as follows:

```
[FieldName("SocialSecurityNumber", Comment="This is the primary key field")]
public string SocialSecurityNumber
{

    // etc.
```

In this case, the compiler recognizes the <ParameterName>=<ParameterValue> syntax of the second parameter and does not attempt to match this parameter to a FieldNameAttribute constructor. Instead, it looks for a public property or field (although public fields are not considered good programming practice, so normally you will work with properties) of that name that it can use to set the value of this parameter. If you want the previous code to work, you have to add some code to FieldNameAttribute:

```
[AttributeUsage(AttributeTargets.Property,
    AllowMultiple=false,
    Inherited=false)]
public class FieldNameAttribute : Attribute
{
    private string comment;
    public string Comment
```

(continued)

(continued)

```
        {
            get
            {
                return comment;
            }
            set
            {
                comment = value;
            }
        }

            // etc
    }
```

Custom Attribute Example: WhatsNewAttributes

In this section, you start developing the example mentioned at the beginning of the chapter. `WhatsNewAttributes` provides for an attribute that indicates when a program element was last modified. This is a more ambitious code sample than many of the others in that it consists of three separate assemblies:

- ❑ The `WhatsNewAttributes` assembly, which contains the definitions of the attributes
- ❑ The `VectorClass` assembly, which contains the code to which the attributes have been applied
- ❑ The `LookUpWhatsNew` assembly, which contains the project that displays details of items that have changed

Of these, only `LookUpWhatsNew` is a console application of the type that you have used up until now. The remaining two assemblies are libraries — they each contain class definitions but no program entry point. For the `VectorClass` assembly, this means that the entry point and test harness class have been removed from the `VectorAsCollection` sample, leaving only the `Vector` class. These classes are represented later in this chapter.

Managing three related assemblies by compiling at the command line is tricky. Although the commands for compiling all these source files are provided separately, you might prefer to edit the code sample (which you can download from the Wrox Web site at www.wrox.com) as a combined Visual Studio solution, as discussed in Chapter 15, "Visual Studio 2008." The download includes the required Visual Studio 2008 solution files.

The WhatsNewAttributes Library Assembly

This section starts with the core `WhatsNewAttributes` assembly. The source code is contained in the file `WhatsNewAttributes.cs`, which is located in the WhatsNewAttributes project of the `WhatsNewAttributes` solution in the example code for this chapter. The syntax for doing this is quite simple. At the command line, you supply the flag `target:library` to the compiler. To compile `WhatsNewAttributes`, type the following:

```
csc /target:library WhatsNewAttributes.cs
```

The `WhatsNewAttributes.cs` file defines two attribute classes, `LastModifiedAttribute` and `SupportsWhatsNewAttribute`. The attribute, `LastModifiedAttribute`, is the attribute that you can use to mark when an item was last modified. It takes two mandatory parameters (parameters that are passed to the constructor): the date of the modification and a string containing a description of the changes. There is also one optional parameter named `issues` (for which a `public` property exists), which can be used to describe any outstanding issues for the item.

In practice, you would probably want this attribute to apply to anything. To keep the code simple, its usage is limited here to classes and methods. You will allow it to be applied more than once to the same item (AllowMultiple=true) because an item might be modified more than once, and each modification will have to be marked with a separate attribute instance.

SupportsWhatsNew is a smaller class representing an attribute that doesn't take any parameters. The idea of this attribute is that it is an assembly attribute that is used to mark an assembly for which you are maintaining documentation via the LastModifiedAttribute. This way, the program that will examine this assembly later on knows that the assembly it is reading is one on which you are actually using your automated documentation process. Here is the complete source code for this part of the example:

```
using System;

namespace Wrox.ProCSharp.WhatsNewAttributes
{
    [AttributeUsage(
        AttributeTargets.Class | AttributeTargets.Method,
        AllowMultiple=true, Inherited=false)]
    public class LastModifiedAttribute : Attribute
    {
        private readonly DateTime dateModified;
        private readonly string changes;
        private string issues;

        public LastModifiedAttribute(string dateModified, string changes)
        {
            this.dateModified = DateTime.Parse(dateModified);
            this.changes = changes;
        }

        public DateTime DateModified
        {
            get { return dateModified; }
        }

        public string Changes
        {
            get { return changes; }
        }

        public string Issues
        {
            get { return issues; }
            set { issues = value; }
        }    }

    [AttributeUsage(AttributeTargets.Assembly)]
    public class SupportsWhatsNewAttribute : Attribute
    {
    }
}
```

This code should be clear with reference to previous descriptions. Notice, however, that we have not bothered to supply set accessors to the Changes and DateModified properties. There is no need for these accessors because you are requiring these parameters to be set in the constructor as mandatory parameters. You need the get accessors so that you can read the values of these attributes.

The VectorClass Assembly

Next, you need to use these attributes. To this end, you use a modified version of the earlier `VectorAsCollection` sample. Note that you need to reference the `WhatsNewAttributes` library that you have just created. You also need to indicate the corresponding namespace with a `using` statement so that the compiler can recognize the attributes:

```
using System;
using System.Collections;
using System.Text;
using Wrox.ProCSharp.WhatsNewAttributes;

[assembly: SupportsWhatsNew]
```

In this code, you have also added the line that will mark the assembly itself with the `SupportsWhatsNew` attribute.

Now for the code for the `Vector` class. You are not making any major changes to this class; you only add a couple of `LastModified` attributes to mark out the work that you have done on this class in this chapter. Then `Vector` is defined as a class instead of a struct to simplify the code (of the next iteration of the sample) that displays the attributes. (In the `VectorAsCollection` sample, `Vector` is a struct, but its enumerator is a class. This means that the next iteration of the sample would have had to pick out both classes and structs when looking at the assembly, which would have made the example less straightforward.)

```
namespace Wrox.ProCSharp.VectorClass
{
    [LastModified("14 Feb 2008", "IEnumerable interface implemented " +
        "So Vector can now be treated as a collection")]
    [LastModified("10 Feb 2008", "IFormattable interface implemented " +
        "So Vector now responds to format specifiers N and VE")]
    class Vector : IFormattable, IEnumerable
    {
        public double x, y, z;

        public Vector(double x, double y, double z)
        {
            this.x = x;
            this.y = y;
            this.z = z;
        }

        [LastModified("10 Feb 2008",
                    "Method added in order to provide formatting support")]
        public string ToString(string format, IFormatProvider formatProvider)
        {
            if (format == null)
            {
                return ToString();
            }
```

You also mark the contained `VectorEnumerator` class as new:

```
    [LastModified("14 Feb 2008",
                "Class created as part of collection support for Vector")]
    private class VectorEnumerator : IEnumerator
    {
```

To compile this code from the command line, type the following:

```
csc /target:library /reference:WhatsNewAttributes.dll VectorClass.cs
```

That's as far as you can get with this example for now. You are unable to run anything yet because all you have are two libraries. You will develop the final part of the example, in which you look up and display these attributes, as soon as you have had a look at how reflection works.

Reflection

In this section, we take a closer look at the `System.Type` class, which lets you access information concerning the definition of any data type. We then discuss the `System.Reflection.Assembly` class, which you can use to access information about an assembly or to load that assembly into your program. Finally, you will combine the code in this section with the code in the previous section to complete the `WhatsNewAttributes` sample.

The System.Type Class

So far you have used the `Type` class only to hold the reference to a type as follows:

```
Type t = typeof(double);
```

Although previously referred to as a class, `Type` is an abstract base class. Whenever you instantiate a `Type` object, you are actually instantiating a class derived from `Type`. `Type` has one derived class corresponding to each actual data type, though in general the derived classes simply provide different overloads of the various `Type` methods and properties that return the correct data for the corresponding data type. They do not generally add new methods or properties. In general, there are three common ways to obtain a `Type` reference that refers to any given type:

1. You can use the C# `typeof` operator as in the preceding code. This operator takes the name of the type (not in quotation marks, however) as a parameter.

2. You can use the `GetType()` method, which all classes inherit from `System.Object`:

```
double d = 10;
Type t = d.GetType();
```

GetType() is called against a variable, rather than taking the name of a type. Note, however, that the `Type` object returned is still associated with only that data type. It does not contain any information that relates to that instance of the type. The `GetType()` method can be useful if you have a reference to an object but are not sure what class that object is actually an instance of.

3. You can call the `static` method of the `Type` class, `GetType()`:

```
Type t = Type.GetType("System.Double");
```

`Type` is really the gateway to much of the reflection functionality. It implements a huge number of methods and properties — far too many to provide a comprehensive list here. However, the following subsections should give you some idea of the kinds of things you can do with the `Type` class. Note that the available properties are all read-only; you use `Type` to find out about the data type — you cannot use it to make any modifications to the type!

Type Properties

You can split the properties implemented by `Type` into three categories:

❑   A number of properties retrieve the strings containing various names associated with the class, as shown in the following table:

Property	Returns
Name	The name of the data type
FullName	The fully qualified name of the data type (including the namespace name)
Namespace	The name of the namespace in which the data type is defined

❑ It is also possible to retrieve references to further type objects that represent related classes, as shown in the following table:

Property	Returns Type Reference Corresponding To
BaseType	Immediate base type of this type
UnderlyingSystemType	The type that this type maps to in the .NET runtime (recall that certain .NET base types actually map to specific predefined types recognized by IL)

❑ A number of Boolean properties indicate whether this type is, for example, a class, an enum, and so on. These properties include `IsAbstract`, `IsArray`, `IsClass`, `IsEnum`, `IsInterface`, `IsPointer`, `IsPrimitive` (one of the predefined primitive data types), `IsPublic`, `IsSealed`, and `IsValueType`.

For example, using a primitive data type:

```
Type intType = typeof(int);
Console.WriteLine(intType.IsAbstract);      // writes false
Console.WriteLine(intType.IsClass);         // writes false
Console.WriteLine(intType.IsEnum);          // writes false
Console.WriteLine(intType.IsPrimitive);     // writes true
Console.WriteLine(intType.IsValueType);     // writes true
```

Or using the `Vector` class:

```
Type vecType = typeof(Vector);
Console.WriteLine(vecType.IsAbstract);      // writes false
Console.WriteLine(vecType.IsClass);         // writes true
Console.WriteLine(vecType.IsEnum);          // writes false
Console.WriteLine(vecType.IsPrimitive);     // writes false
Console.WriteLine(vecType.IsValueType);     // writes false
```

You can also retrieve a reference to the assembly that the type is defined in. This is returned as a reference to an instance of the `System.Reflection.Assembly` class, which is examined shortly:

```
Type t = typeof(Vector);
Assembly containingAssembly = new Assembly(t);
```

Methods

Most of the methods of `System.Type` are used to obtain details of the members of the corresponding data type — the constructors, properties, methods, events, and so on. Quite a large number of methods exist, but they all follow the same pattern. For example, two methods retrieve details of the methods of the data type: GetMethod() and GetMethods(). GetMethod() returns a reference to a System. Reflection.MethodInfo object, which contains details of a method. GetMethods() returns an array of such references. The difference is that GetMethods() returns details of all the methods, whereas GetMethod() returns details of just one method with a specified parameter list. Both methods have overloads that take an extra parameter, a BindingFlags enumerated value that indicates which members should be returned — for example, whether to return public members, instance members, static members, and so on.

For example, the simplest overload of GetMethods() takes no parameters and returns details of all the public methods of the data type:

```
Type t = typeof(double);
MethodInfo[] methods = t.GetMethods();
foreach (MethodInfo nextMethod in methods)
{
    // etc.
    }
```

The member methods of Type that follow the same pattern are shown in the following table.

Type of Object Returned	Methods (The Method with the Plural Name Returns an Array)
ConstructorInfo	GetConstructor(), GetConstructors()
EventInfo	GetEvent(), GetEvents()
FieldInfo	GetField(), GetFields()
InterfaceInfo	GetInterface(), GetInterfaces()
MemberInfo	GetMember(), GetMembers()
MethodInfo	GetMethod(), GetMethods()
PropertyInfo	GetProperty(), GetProperties()

The GetMember() and GetMembers() methods return details of any or all members of the data type, regardless of whether these members are constructors, properties, methods, and so on. Finally, note that it is possible to invoke members either by calling the InvokeMember() method of Type or by calling the Invoke() method of the MethodInfo, PropertyInfo, and the other classes.

The TypeView Example

This section demonstrates some of the features of the Type class with a short example, TypeView, which you can use to list the members of a data type. The example demonstrates how to use TypeView for a double; however, you can swap this type with any other data type just by changing one line of the code in the sample. TypeView displays far more information than can be displayed in a console window, so we're going to take a break from our normal practice and display the output in a message box. Running TypeView for a double produces the results shown in Figure 13-1.

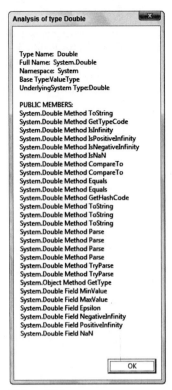

Analysis of type Double

Type Name: Double
Full Name: System.Double
Namespace: System
Base Type:ValueType
UnderlyingSystem Type:Double

PUBLIC MEMBERS:
System.Double Method ToString
System.Double Method GetTypeCode
System.Double Method IsInfinity
System.Double Method IsPositiveInfinity
System.Double Method IsNegativeInfinity
System.Double Method IsNaN
System.Double Method CompareTo
System.Double Method CompareTo
System.Double Method Equals
System.Double Method Equals
System.Double Method GetHashCode
System.Double Method ToString
System.Double Method ToString
System.Double Method ToString
System.Double Method Parse
System.Double Method Parse
System.Double Method Parse
System.Double Method Parse
System.Double Method TryParse
System.Double Method TryParse
System.Object Method GetType
System.Double Field MinValue
System.Double Field MaxValue
System.Double Field Epsilon
System.Double Field NegativeInfinity
System.Double Field PositiveInfinity
System.Double Field NaN

OK

Figure 13-1

The message box displays the name, full name, and namespace of the data type as well as the name of the underlying type and the base type. Next, it simply iterates through all the public instance members of the data type, displaying for each member the declaring type, the type of member (method, field, and so on), and the name of the member. The *declaring type* is the name of the class that actually declares the type member (for example, System.Double if it is defined or overridden in System.Double, or the name of the relevant base type if the member is simply inherited from some base class).

TypeView does not display signatures of methods because you are retrieving details of all public instance members through MemberInfo objects, and information about parameters is not available through a MemberInfo object. In order to retrieve that information, you would need references to MethodInfo and other more specific objects, which means that you would need to obtain details of each type of member separately.

TypeView does display details of all public instance members, but for doubles, the only ones defined are fields and methods. For this example, you will compile TypeView as a console application — there is no problem with displaying a message box from a console application. However, the fact that you are using a message box means that you need to reference the base class assembly System.Windows.Forms.dll, which contains the classes in the System.Windows.Forms namespace in which the MessageBox class that you will need is defined. The code for TypeView is as follows. To begin, you need to add a few using statements:

```
using System;
using System.Text;
```

```
using System.Windows.Forms;
using System.Reflection;
```

You need System.Text because you will be using a StringBuilder object to build up the text to be displayed in the message box, and System.Windows.Forms for the message box itself. The entire code is in one class, MainClass, which has a couple of static methods and one static field, a StringBuilder instance called OutputText, which will be used to build up the text to be displayed in the message box. The main method and class declaration look like this:

```
class MainClass
{
    static StringBuilder OutputText = new StringBuilder();

    static void Main()
    {
        // modify this line to retrieve details of any
        // other data type
        Type t = typeof(double);

        AnalyzeType(t);
        MessageBox.Show(OutputText.ToString(), "Analysis of type "
                                               + t.Name);
        Console.ReadLine();
    }
```

The Main() method implementation starts by declaring a Type object to represent your chosen data type. You then call a method, AnalyzeType(), which extracts the information from the Type object and uses it to build up the output text. Finally, you show the output in a message box. Using the MessageBox class is fairly intuitive. You just call its static Show() method, passing it two strings, which will, respectively, be the text in the box and the caption. AnalyzeType() is where the bulk of the work is done:

```
    static void AnalyzeType(Type t)
    {
        AddToOutput("Type Name:   " + t.Name);
        AddToOutput("Full Name:   " + t.FullName);
        AddToOutput("Namespace:   " + t.Namespace);

        Type tBase = t.BaseType;

        if (tBase != null)
        {
            AddToOutput("Base Type:" + tBase.Name);
        }

        Type tUnderlyingSystem = t.UnderlyingSystemType;

        if (tUnderlyingSystem != null)
        {
            AddToOutput("UnderlyingSystem Type:" + tUnderlyingSystem.Name);
        }

        AddToOutput("\nPUBLIC MEMBERS:");
        MemberInfo [] Members = t.GetMembers();

        foreach (MemberInfo NextMember in Members)
```

(continued)

369

(continued)

```
        {
            AddToOutput(NextMember.DeclaringType + " " +
            NextMember.MemberType + " " + NextMember.Name);
        }
    }
```

You implement the `AnalyzeType()` method by calling various properties of the `Type` object to get the information you need concerning the type names, then call the `GetMembers()` method to get an array of `MemberInfo` objects that you can use to display the details of each member. Note that you use a helper method, `AddToOutput()`, to build up the text to be displayed in the message box:

```
static void AddToOutput(string Text)
{
    OutputText.Append("\n" + Text);
}
```

Compile the `TypeView` assembly using this command:

```
csc /reference:System.Windows.Forms.dll TypeView.cs
```

The Assembly Class

The `Assembly` class is defined in the `System.Reflection` namespace and provides access to the metadata for a given assembly. It also contains methods to allow you to load and even execute an assembly — assuming that the assembly is an executable. Like the `Type` class, `Assembly` contains a large number of methods and properties — too many to cover here. Instead, this section is confined to covering those methods and properties that you need to get started and that you will use to complete the `WhatsNewAttributes` example.

Before you can do anything with an `Assembly` instance, you need to load the corresponding assembly into the running process. You can do this with either the `static` members `Assembly.Load()` or `Assembly.LoadFrom()`. The difference between these methods is that `Load()` takes the name of the assembly, and the runtime searches in a variety of locations in an attempt to locate the assembly. These locations include the local directory and the global assembly cache. `LoadFrom()` takes the full path name of an assembly and does not attempt to find the assembly in any other location:

```
Assembly assembly1 = Assembly.Load("SomeAssembly");
Assembly assembly2 = Assembly.LoadFrom
    (@"C:\My Projects\Software\SomeOtherAssembly");
```

A number of other overloads of both methods exist, which supply additional security information. Once you have loaded an assembly, you can use various properties on it to find out, for example, its full name:

```
string name = assembly1.FullName;
```

Finding Out About Types Defined in an Assembly

One nice feature of the `Assembly` class is that it allows you to obtain details of all the types that are defined in the corresponding assembly. You simply call the `Assembly.GetTypes()` method, which returns an array of `System.Type` references containing details of all the types. You can then manipulate these `Type` references as explained in the previous section.

```
Type[] types = theAssembly.GetTypes();

foreach(Type definedType in types)
{
    DoSomethingWith(definedType);
}
```

Finding Out About Custom Attributes

The methods you use to find out which custom attributes are defined on an assembly or type depend on what type of object the attribute is attached to. If you want to find out what custom attributes are attached to an assembly as a whole, you need to call a `static` method of the `Attribute` class, `GetCustomAttributes()`, passing in a reference to the assembly:

```
Attribute[] definedAttributes =
         Attribute.GetCustomAttributes(assembly1);
         // assembly1 is an Assembly object
```

This is actually quite significant. You may have wondered why, when you defined custom attributes, you had to go to all the trouble of actually writing classes for them, and why Microsoft hadn't come up with some simpler syntax. Well, the answer is here. The custom attributes do genuinely exist as objects, and when an assembly is loaded you can read in these attribute objects, examine their properties, and call their methods.

`GetCustomAttributes()`, which is used to get assembly attributes, has a few overloads. If you call it without specifying any parameters other than an assembly reference, it will simply return all the custom attributes defined for that assembly. You can also call `GetCustomAttributes()` specifying a second parameter, which is a `Type` object that indicates the attribute class in which you are interested. In this case, `GetCustomAttributes()` returns an array consisting of all the attributes present that are of the specified type.

Note that all attributes are retrieved as plain `Attribute` references. If you want to call any of the methods or properties you defined for your custom attributes, you will need to cast these references explicitly to the relevant custom attribute classes. You can obtain details of custom attributes that are attached to a given data type by calling another overload of `Assembly.GetCustomAttributes()`, this time passing a `Type` reference that describes the type for which you want to retrieve any attached attributes. If you want to obtain attributes that are attached to methods, constructors, fields, and so on, however, you will need to call a `GetCustomAttributes()` method that is a member of one of the classes `MethodInfo`, `ConstructorInfo`, `FieldInfo`, and so on.

If you expect only a single attribute of a given type, you can call the `GetCustomAttribute()` method instead, which returns a single `Attribute` object. You will use `GetCustomAttribute()` in the `WhatsNewAttributes` example to find out whether the `SupportsWhatsNew` attribute is present in the assembly. To do this, you call `GetCustomAttribute()`, passing in a reference to the `WhatsNewAttributes` assembly, and the type of the `SupportsWhatsNewAttribute` attribute. If this attribute is present, you get an `Attribute` instance. If no instances of it are defined in the assembly, you get `null`. And if two or more instances are found, `GetCustomAttribute()` throws a `System.Reflection.AmbiguousMatchException`.

```
Attribute supportsAttribute =
         Attribute.GetCustomAttributes(assembly1,
         typeof(SupportsWhatsNewAttribute));
```

Completing the WhatsNewAttributes Example

You now have enough information to complete the `WhatsNewAttributes` example by writing the source code for the final assembly in the sample, the `LookUpWhatsNew` assembly. This part of the application is a console application. However, it needs to reference the other assemblies of `WhatsNewAttributes` and `VectorClass`. Although this is going to be a command-line application, you will follow the previous `TypeView` sample in actually displaying your results in a message box because there is a lot of text output — too much to show in a console window screenshot.

The file is called `LookUpWhatsNew.cs,` and the command to compile it is:

```
csc /reference:WhatsNewAttributes.dll /reference:VectorClass.dll LookUpWhatsNew.cs
```

In the source code of this file, you first indicate the namespaces you want to infer. `System.Text` is there because you need to use a `StringBuilder` object again:

```
using System;
using System.Reflection;
using System.Windows.Forms;
using System.Text;
using Wrox.ProCSharp.VectorClass;
using Wrox.ProCSharp.WhatsNewAttributes;

namespace Wrox.ProCSharp.LookUpWhatsNew
{
```

The class that contains the main program entry point as well as the other methods is `WhatsNewChecker`. All the methods you define are in this class, which also has two static fields: `outputText`, which contains the text as you build it up in preparation for writing it to the message box, and `backDateTo`, which stores the date you have selected. All modifications made since this date will be displayed. Normally, you would display a dialog box inviting the user to pick this date, but we don't want to get sidetracked into that kind of code. For this reason, `backDateTo` is hard-coded to a value of 1 Feb 2008. You can easily change this date if you want when you download the code:

```
class WhatsNewChecker
{
    static StringBuilder outputText = new StringBuilder(1000);
    static readonly DateTime backDateTo = new DateTime(2008, 2, 1);

    static void Main()
    {
        Assembly theAssembly = Assembly.Load("VectorClass");
        Attribute supportsAttribute =
            Attribute.GetCustomAttribute(
                theAssembly, typeof(SupportsWhatsNewAttribute));
        string Name = theAssembly.FullName;

        AddToMessage("Assembly: " + Name);

        if (supportsAttribute == null)
        {
            AddToMessage(
                "This assembly does not support WhatsNew attributes");
            return;
        }
        else
        {
            AddToMessage("Defined Types:");
        }

        Type[] types = theAssembly.GetTypes();

        foreach(Type definedType in types)
            DisplayTypeInfo(theAssembly, definedType);
```

```
        MessageBox.Show(outputText.ToString(),
            "What\'s New since " + backDateTo.ToLongDateString());
        Console.ReadLine();
}
```

The `Main()` method first loads the `VectorClass` assembly, and verifies that it is marked with the `SupportsWhatsNew` attribute. You know `VectorClass` has the `SupportsWhatsNew` attribute applied to it because you have only recently compiled it, but this is a check that would be worth making if users were given a choice of what assembly they wanted to check.

Assuming that all is well, you use the `Assembly.GetTypes()` method to get an array of all the types defined in this assembly, and then loop through them. For each one, you call a method, `DisplayTypeInfo()`, which will add the relevant text, including details of any instances of `LastModifiedAttribute`, to the `outputText` field. Finally, you show the message box with the complete text. The `DisplayTypeInfo()` method looks like this:

```
static void DisplayTypeInfo(Assembly theAssembly, Type type)
{
    // make sure we only pick out classes
    if (!(type.IsClass))
    {
        return;
    }

    AddToMessage("\nclass " + type.Name);

    Attribute [] attribs = Attribute.GetCustomAttributes(type);

    if (attribs.Length == 0)
    {
        AddToMessage("No changes to this class\n");
    }
    else
    {
        foreach (Attribute attrib in attribs)
        {
            WriteAttributeInfo(attrib);
        }
    }

    MethodInfo [] methods = type.GetMethods();
    AddToMessage("CHANGES TO METHODS OF THIS CLASS:");

    foreach (MethodInfo nextMethod in methods)
    {
        object [] attribs2 =
            nextMethod.GetCustomAttributes(
                typeof(LastModifiedAttribute), false);

        if (attribs2 != null)
        {
            AddToMessage(
                nextMethod.ReturnType + " " + nextMethod.Name + "()");
            foreach (Attribute nextAttrib in attribs2)
```

(continued)

(continued)

```
                        {
                            WriteAttributeInfo(nextAttrib);
                        }
                    }
                }
            }
```

Notice that the first thing you do in this method is check whether the Type reference you have been passed actually represents a class. Because, in order to keep things simple, you have specified that the LastModified attribute can be applied only to classes or member methods, you would be wasting your time doing any processing if the item is not a class (it could be a class, delegate, or enum).

Next, you use the Attribute.GetCustomAttributes() method to find out if this class does have any LastModifiedAttribute instances attached to it. If it does, you add their details to the output text, using a helper method, WriteAttributeInfo().

Finally, you use the Type.GetMethods() method to iterate through all the member methods of this data type, and then do the same with each method as you did for the class — check if it has any LastModifiedAttribute instances attached to it and, if so, display them using WriteAttributeInfo().

The next bit of code shows the WriteAttributeInfo() method, which is responsible for working out what text to display for a given LastModifiedAttribute instance. Note that this method is passed an Attribute reference, so it needs to cast this to a LastModifiedAttribute reference first. After it has done that, it uses the properties that you originally defined for this attribute to retrieve its parameters. It checks that the date of the attribute is sufficiently recent before actually adding it to the text for display:

```
static void WriteAttributeInfo(Attribute attrib)
{

    LastModifiedAttribute lastModifiedAttrib =
        attrib as LastModifiedAttribute;

    if (lastModifiedAttrib == null)
    {
        return;
    }

    // check that date is in range
    DateTime modifiedDate = lastModifiedAttrib.DateModified;

    if (modifiedDate < backDateTo)
    {
        return;
    }

    AddToMessage("  MODIFIED: " +
        modifiedDate.ToLongDateString() + ":");
    AddToMessage("      " + lastModifiedAttrib.Changes);

    if (lastModifiedAttrib.Issues != null)
    {
        AddToMessage("    Outstanding issues:" +
```

```
                        lastModifiedAttrib.Issues);
            }
        }
```

Finally, here is the helper `AddToMessage()` method:

```
        static void AddToMessage(string message)
        {
            outputText.Append("\n" + message);
        }
    }
}
```

Running this code produces the results shown in Figure 13-2.

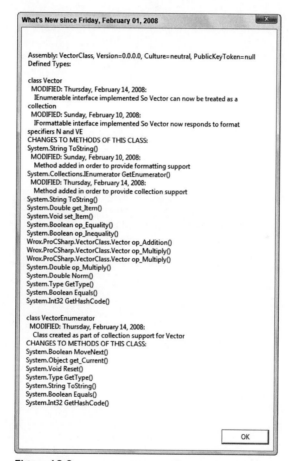

Figure 13-2

Notice that when you list the types defined in the `VectorClass` assembly, you actually pick up two classes: `Vector` and the embedded `VectorEnumerator` class. Also notice that because the `backDateTo` date of 1 Feb is hard-coded in this example, you actually pick up the attributes that are dated 14 Feb (when you added the collection support) but not those dated 14 Jan (when you added the `IFormattable` interface).

Summary

This chapter did not attempt to cover the entire topic of reflection. Reflection is an extensive subject worthy of a book of its own. Instead, it illustrated the `Type` and `Assembly` classes, which are the primary entry points through which you can access the extensive capabilities provided by reflection.

In addition, this chapter demonstrated a specific aspect of reflection that you are likely to use more often than any other — the inspection of custom attributes. You learned how to define and apply your own custom attributes, and how to retrieve information about custom attributes at runtime.

Chapter 14 explores exceptions and structured exception handling.

14

Errors and Exceptions

Errors happen, and they are not always caused by the person who coded the application. Sometimes your application will generate an error because of an action that was initiated by the end user of your application or it might be simply due to the environmental context in which your code is running. In any case, you should anticipate errors occurring in your applications and code accordingly.

The .NET Framework has enhanced the ways in which you deal with errors. C#'s mechanism for handling error conditions allows you to provide custom handling for each type of error condition as well as to separate code that identifies errors from the code that handles them.

The main topics covered in this chapter include:

❑ Looking at the exception classes

❑ Using `try` - `catch` - `finally` to capture exceptions

❑ Creating user-defined exceptions

By the end of the chapter, you will have a good grasp on advanced exception handling in your C# applications.

No matter how good your coding is, your programs should have the ability to handle any possible errors that may occur. For example, in the middle of some complex processing your code may discover that it doesn't have permission to read a file, or, while it is sending network requests, the network may go down. In such exceptional situations, it is not enough for a method to simply return an appropriate error code — there might be 15 or 20 nested method calls, so what you really want the program to do is jump back up through all those 15 or 20 calls in order to exit the task completely and take the appropriate counteractions. The C# language has very good facilities to handle this kind of situation, through the mechanism known as *exception handling*.

> *Error-handling facilities in Visual Basic 6 are very restricted and essentially limited to the* On Error GoTo *statement. If you are coming from a Visual Basic 6 background, you will find that C# exceptions open a completely new world of error handling in your programs. Java and C++ developers, however, will be familiar with the principle of exceptions because these languages handle errors in a similar way to C#. Developers using C++ are sometimes wary of exceptions because of possible C++ performance implications, but this is not the case in C#. Using exceptions in C# code in general does not adversely affect performance. Visual Basic developers will find that working with exceptions in C# is very similar to using exceptions in Visual Basic (except for the syntax differences).*

Exception Classes

In C#, an exception is an object created (or *thrown*) when a particular exceptional error condition occurs. This object contains information that should help track down the problem. Although you can create your own exception classes (and you will be doing so later), .NET provides you with many predefined exception classes.

This section provides a quick survey of some of the exceptions available in the .NET base class library. Microsoft has provided a large number of exception classes in .NET — too many to provide a comprehensive list here. This class hierarchy diagram in Figure 14-1 shows a few of these classes to give you a sense of the general pattern.

All the classes in Figure 14-1 are part of the `System` namespace, except for `IOException` and the classes derived from `IOException`, which are part of the namespace `System.IO`. The `System.IO` namespace deals with reading and writing data to files. In general, there is no specific namespace for exceptions. Exception classes should be placed in whatever namespace is appropriate to the classes that can generate them — hence IO-related exceptions are in the `System.IO` namespace. You will find exception classes in quite a few of the base class namespaces.

The generic exception class, `System.Exception`, is derived from `System.Object`, as you would expect for a .NET class. In general, you should not throw generic `System.Exception` objects in your code, because they provide no specifics about the error condition.

Two important classes in the hierarchy are derived from `System.Exception`:

❑ `System.SystemException` — This class is for exceptions that are usually thrown by the .NET runtime or that are considered to be of a generic nature and might be thrown by almost any application. For example, `StackOverflowException` will be thrown by the .NET runtime if it detects the stack is full. However, you might choose to throw `ArgumentException` or its subclasses in your own code, if you detect that a method has been called with inappropriate arguments. Subclasses of `System.SystemException` include classes that represent both fatal and nonfatal errors.

❑ `System.ApplicationException` — This class is important, because it is the intended base for any class of exception defined by third parties. If you define any exceptions covering error conditions unique to your application, you should derive these directly or indirectly from `System.ApplicationException`.

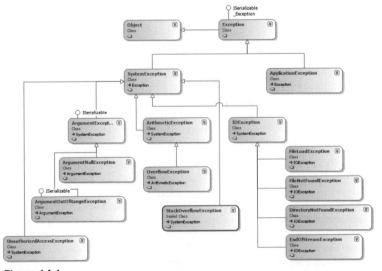

Figure 14-1

Other exception classes that might come in handy include the following:

❑   `StackOverflowException` — This exception is thrown when the area of memory allocated to the stack is full. A stack overflow can occur if a method continuously calls itself recursively. This is generally a fatal error, because it prevents your application from doing anything apart from terminating (in which case it is unlikely that even the `finally` block will execute). Trying to handle errors like this yourself is usually pointless; instead, you should get the application to gracefully exit.

❑   `EndOfStreamException` — The usual cause of an `EndOfStreamException` is an attempt to read past the end of a file. A *stream* represents a flow of data between data sources. Streams are covered in detail in Chapter 41, "Accessing the Internet."

❑   `OverflowException` — An `OverflowException` is what happens if you attempt to cast an `int` containing a value of `-40` to a `uint` in a `checked` context.

The other exception classes shown in Figure 14-1 are not discussed here.

The class hierarchy for exceptions is somewhat unusual in that most of these classes do not add any functionality to their respective base classes. However, in the case of exception handling, the common reason for adding inherited classes is to indicate more specific error conditions. There is often no need to override methods or add any new ones (although it is not uncommon to add extra properties that carry extra information about the error condition). For example, you might have a base `ArgumentException` class intended for method calls where inappropriate values are passed in, and an `ArgumentNullException` class derived from it, which is intended to handle a `null` argument if passed.

Catching Exceptions

Given that the .NET Framework includes a selection of predefined base class exception objects, how do you use them in your code to trap error conditions? To deal with possible error conditions in C# code, you will normally divide the relevant part of your program into blocks of three different types:

❑   `try` blocks encapsulate the code that forms part of the normal operation of your program and that might encounter some serious error conditions.

❑   `catch` blocks encapsulate the code that deals with the various error conditions that your code might have encountered by working through any of the code in the accompanying `try` block. This place could also be used for logging errors.

❑   `finally` blocks encapsulate the code that cleans up any resources or takes any other action that you will normally want done at the end of a `try` or `catch` block. It is important to understand that the `finally` block is executed whether or not an exception is thrown. Because the aim is that the `finally` block contains cleanup code that should always be executed, the compiler will flag an error if you place a `return` statement inside a `finally` block. For an example of using the `finally` block, you might close any connections that were opened in the `try` block. It is also important to understand that the `finally` block is completely optional. If you do not have a requirement for any cleanup code (such as disposing or closing any open objects), then there is no need for this block.

So how do these blocks fit together to trap error conditions? Here is how:

1.   The execution flow first enters the `try` block.

2.   If no errors occur in the `try` block, execution proceeds normally through the block, and when the end of the `try` block is reached, the flow of execution jumps to the `finally` block if one is present (Step 5). However, if an error does occur within the `try` block, execution jumps to a `catch` block (Step 3).

3. The error condition is handled in the `catch` block.

4. At the end of the `catch` block, execution automatically transfers to the `finally` block if one is present.

5. The `finally` block is executed (if present).

The C# syntax used to bring all of this about looks roughly like this:

```
try
{
    // code for normal execution
}
catch
{
    // error handling
}
finally
{
    // clean up
}
```

Actually, a few variations on this theme exist:

❑ You can omit the `finally` block because it is optional.

❑ You can also supply as many `catch` blocks as you want to handle specific types of errors. However, the idea is not to get too carried away and have a huge number of `catch` blocks, because this can hurt the performance of your application.

❑ You can omit the `catch` blocks altogether, in which case the syntax serves not to identify exceptions, but as a way of guaranteeing that code in the `finally` block will be executed when execution leaves the `try` block. This is useful if the `try` block contains several exit points.

So far so good, but the question that has yet to be answered is this: If the code is running in the `try` block, how does it know when to switch to the `catch` block if an error has occurred? If an error is detected, the code does something known as *throwing an exception*. In other words, it instantiates an exception object class and throws it:

```
throw new OverflowException();
```

Here, you have instantiated an exception object of the `OverflowException` class. As soon as the computer encounters a `throw` statement inside a `try` block, it immediately looks for the `catch` block associated with that `try` block. If there is more than one `catch` block associated with the `try` block, it identifies the correct `catch` block by checking which exception class the `catch` block is associated with. For example, when the `OverflowException` object is thrown, execution jumps to the following `catch` block:

```
catch (OverflowException ex)
{
    // exception handling here
}
```

In other words, the computer looks for the `catch` block that indicates a matching exception class instance of the same class (or of a base class).

With this extra information, you can expand the `try` block just demonstrated. Assume, for the sake of argument, that there are two possible serious errors that can occur in the `try` block: an overflow and an array out of bounds. Assume that your code contains two Boolean variables, `Overflow` and `OutOfBounds`, which indicate whether these conditions exist. You have already seen that a predefined exception class exists to indicate overflow (`OverflowException`); similarly, an `IndexOutOfRangeException` class exists to handle an array that is out of bounds.

Now your `try` block looks like this:

```
try
{
    // code for normal execution

    if (Overflow == true)
    {
        throw new OverflowException();
    }

    // more processing

    if (OutOfBounds == true)
    {
        throw new IndexOutOfRangeException();
    }

    // otherwise continue normal execution
}
catch (OverflowException ex)
{
    // error handling for the overflow error condition
}
catch (IndexOutOfRangeException ex)
{
    // error handling for the index out of range error condition
}
finally
{
    // clean up
}
```

So far, this might not look that much different from what you could have done with the Visual Basic 6 `On Error GoTo` statement (with the exception perhaps that the different parts in the code are separated). C#, however, provides a far more powerful and flexible mechanism for error handling.

This is because you can have `throw` statements that are nested in several method calls inside the `try` block, but the same `try` block continues to apply even as execution flow enters these other methods. If the computer encounters a `throw` statement, it immediately goes back up through all the method calls on the stack, looking for the end of the containing `try` block and the start of the appropriate `catch` block. During this process, all the local variables in the intermediate method calls will correctly go out of scope. This makes the `try...catch` architecture well suited to the situation described at the beginning of this section, where the error occurs inside a method call that is nested inside 15 or 20 method calls, and processing has to stop immediately.

As you can probably gather from this discussion, `try` blocks can play a very significant part in controlling the flow of execution of your code. However, it is important to understand that exceptions are intended for exceptional conditions, hence their name. You wouldn't want to use them as a way of controlling when to exit a `do...while` loop.

Implementing Multiple Catch Blocks

The easiest way to see how `try...catch...finally` blocks work in practice is with a couple of examples. The first example is called `SimpleExceptions`. It repeatedly asks the user to type in a number and then displays it. However, for the sake of this example, imagine that the number has to be between 0 and 5; otherwise, the program won't be able to process the number properly. Therefore, you will throw an exception if the user types in anything outside of this range.

The program then continues to ask for more numbers for processing until the user simply presses the Enter key without entering anything.

> *You should note that this code does not provide a good example of when to use exception handling. As already indicated, the idea of exceptions is that they are provided for exceptional circumstances. Users are always typing in silly things, so this situation doesn't really count. Normally, your program will handle incorrect user input by performing an instant check and asking the user to retype the input if there is a problem. However, generating exceptional situations is difficult in a small example that you can read through in a few minutes! So, we will tolerate this bad practice for now in order to demonstrate how exceptions work. The examples that follow present more realistic situations.*

The code for `SimpleExceptions` looks like this:

```csharp
using System;

namespace Wrox.ProCSharp.AdvancedCSharp
{
    public class MainEntryPoint
    {
        public static void Main()
        {
            while (true)
            {
                try
                {
                    string userInput;

                    Console.Write("Input a number between 0 and 5 " +
                        "(or just hit return to exit)> ");
                    userInput = Console.ReadLine();

                    if (userInput == "")
                    {
                        break;
                    }

                    int index = Convert.ToInt32(userInput);

                    if (index < 0 || index > 5)
                    {
                        throw new IndexOutOfRangeException(
                            "You typed in " + userInput);
                    }

                    Console.WriteLine("Your number was " + index);
                }
```

```
            catch (IndexOutOfRangeException ex)
            {
                Console.WriteLine("Exception: " +
                    "Number should be between 0 and 5. {0}", ex.Message);
            }
            catch (Exception ex)
            {
                Console.WriteLine(
                    "An exception was thrown. Message was: {0}", ex.Message);
            }
            catch
            {
                Console.WriteLine("Some other exception has occurred");
            }
            finally
            {
                Console.WriteLine("Thank you");
            }
        }
    }
}
```

The core of this code is a `while` loop, which continually uses `Console.ReadLine()` to ask for user input. `ReadLine()` returns a string, so your first task is to convert it to an `int` using the `System.Convert.ToInt32()` method. The `System.Convert` class contains various useful methods to perform data conversions and provides an alternative to the `int.Parse()` method. In general, `System.Convert` contains methods to perform various type conversions. Recall that the C# compiler resolves `int` to instances of the `System.Int32` base class.

> *It is also worth pointing out that the parameter passed to the `catch` block is scoped to that `catch`*
> *block — which is why you are able to use the same parameter name, ex, in successive `catch` blocks in*
> *the preceding code.*

In the preceding example, you also check for an empty string, because this is your condition for exiting the `while` loop. Notice how the `break` statement actually breaks right out of the enclosing `try` block as well as the `while` loop because this is valid behavior. Of course, once execution breaks out of the `try` block, the `Console.WriteLine()` statement in the `finally` block is executed. Although you just display a greeting here, more commonly, you will be doing tasks like closing file handles and calling the `Dispose()` method of various objects in order to perform any cleaning up. Once the computer leaves the `finally` block, it simply carries on executing unto the next statement that it would have executed had the `finally` block not been present. In the case of this example, though, you iterate back to the start of the `while` loop, and enter the `try` block once again (unless the `finally` block was entered as a result of executing the `break` statement in the `while` loop, in which case you simply exit the `while` loop).

Next, you check for your exception condition:

```
if (index < 0 || index > 5)
{
    throw new IndexOutOfRangeException("You typed in " + userInput);
}
```

When throwing an exception, you need to choose what type of exception to throw. Although the class `System.Exception` is available, it is intended only as a base class. It is considered bad programming practice to throw an instance of this class as an exception, because it conveys no information about the nature of the error condition. Instead, the .NET Framework contains many other exception classes that are derived from `System.Exception`. Each of these matches a particular type of exception condition, and you are free to define your own ones as well. The idea is that you give as much information as possible about the particular exception condition by throwing an instance of a class that matches the particular error condition. In the preceding example, `System.IndexOutOfRangeException` is the best choice for the circumstances. `IndexOutOfRangeException` has several constructor overloads. The one chosen in the example takes a string, which describes the error. Alternatively, you might choose to derive your own custom `Exception` object that describes the error condition in the context of your application.

Suppose that the user then types a number that is not between 0 and 5. This will be picked up by the `if` statement and an `IndexOutOfRangeException` object will be instantiated and thrown. At this point, the computer will immediately exit the `try` block and hunt for a `catch` block that handles `IndexOutOfRangeException`. The first `catch` block it encounters is this:

```
catch (IndexOutOfRangeException ex)
{
    Console.WriteLine(
        "Exception: Number should be between 0 and 5. {0}", ex.Message);
}
```

Because this `catch` block takes a parameter of the appropriate class, the `catch` block will be passed the exception instance and executed. In this case, you display an error message and the `Exception`. `Message` property (which corresponds to the string you passed to the `IndexOutOfRangeException`'s constructor). After executing this `catch` block, control then switches to the `finally` block, just as if no exception had occurred.

Notice that in the example, you have also provided another `catch` block:

```
catch (Exception ex)
{
    Console.WriteLine("An exception was thrown. Message was: {0}", ex.Message);
}
```

This `catch` block would also be capable of handling an `IndexOutOfRangeException` if it weren't for the fact that such exceptions will already have been caught by the previous `catch` block. A reference to a base class can also refer to any instances of classes derived from it, and all exceptions are derived from `System.Exception`. So why isn't this `catch` block executed? The answer is that the computer executes only the first suitable `catch` block it finds from the list of available `catch` blocks. So why is this second `catch` block even here? Well, it is not only your code that is covered by the `try` block. Inside the block, you actually make three separate calls to methods in the `System` namespace (`Console.ReadLine()`, `Console.Write()`, and `Convert.ToInt32()`), and any of these methods might throw an exception.

If you type in something that is not a number — say a or hello — the `Convert.ToInt32()` method will throw an exception of the class `System.FormatException` to indicate that the string passed into `ToInt32()` is not in a format that can be converted to an `int`. When this happens, the computer will trace back through the method calls, looking for a handler that can handle this exception. Your first `catch` block (the one that takes an `IndexOutOfRangeException`) will not do. The computer then looks at the second `catch` block. This one will do because `FormatException` is derived from `Exception`, so a `FormatException` instance can be passed in as a parameter here.

The structure of the example is actually fairly typical of a situation with multiple `catch` blocks. You start off with `catch` blocks that are designed to trap very specific error conditions. Then, you finish with more general blocks that will cover any errors for which you have not written specific error handlers. Indeed, the order of the `catch` blocks is important. If you had written the previous two blocks in the opposite order, the code would not have compiled, because the second `catch` block is unreachable (the `Exception` catch block would catch all exceptions). Therefore, the uppermost `catch` blocks should be the most granular options available and ending with the most general options.

However, in the previous example, you have a third catch block listed in the code:

```
catch
{
    Console.WriteLine("Some other exception has occurred");
}
```

This is the most general catch block of all — it does not take any parameter. The reason this catch block is here is to catch exceptions thrown by other code that is not written in C# or is not even managed code at all. You see, it is a requirement of the C# language that only instances of classes derived from System. Exception can be thrown as exceptions, but other languages might not have this restriction — C++, for example, allows any variable whatsoever to be thrown as an exception. If your code calls into libraries or assemblies that have been written in other languages, it might find that an exception has been thrown that is not derived from System.Exception, although in many cases, the .NET PInvoke mechanism will trap these exceptions and convert them into .NET Exception objects. However, there is not that much that this catch block can do, because you have no idea what class the exception might represent.

> *For this particular example, there is no point in adding this catch-all catch handler. Doing this is useful if you are calling into some other libraries that are not .NET-aware and that might throw exceptions. However, it is included in the example to illustrate the principle.*

Now that you have analyzed the code for the example, you can run it. The following output illustrates what happens with different inputs and demonstrates both the IndexOutOfRangeException and the FormatException being thrown:

```
SimpleExceptions
Input a number between 0 and 5 (or just hit return to exit)>4
Your number was 4
Thank you
Input a number between 0 and 5 (or just hit return to exit)>0
Your number was 0
Thank you
Input a number between 0 and 5 (or just hit return to exit)>10
Exception: Number should be between 0 and 5. You typed in 10
Thank you
Input a number between 0 and 5 (or just hit return to exit)>hello
An exception was thrown. Message was: Input string was not in a correct format.
Thank you
Input a number between 0 and 5 (or just hit return to exit)>
Thank you
```

Catching Exceptions from Other Code

The previous example demonstrated the handling of two exceptions. One of them, IndexOutOfRangeException, was thrown by your own code. The other, FormatException, was thrown from inside one of the base classes. It is very common for code in a library to throw an exception if it detects that some problem has occurred, or if one of the methods has been called inappropriately by being passed the wrong parameters. However, library code rarely attempts to catch exceptions; this is regarded as the responsibility of the client code.

Often, you will find that exceptions are thrown from the base class libraries while you are debugging. The process of debugging to some extent involves determining why exceptions have been thrown and removing the causes. Your aim should be to ensure that by the time the code is actually shipped, exceptions do occur only in very exceptional circumstances, and if at all possible, are handled in some appropriate way in your code.

System.Exception Properties

The example has illustrated the use of only the `Message` property of the exception object. However, a number of other properties are available in `System.Exception`, as shown in the following table.

Property	Description
Data	This provides you with the ability to add key/value statements to the exception that can be used to supply extra information about the exception.
HelpLink	This is a link to a help file that provides more information about the exception.
InnerException	If this exception was thrown inside a `catch` block, then `InnerException` contains the exception object that sent the code into that `catch` block.
Message	This is text that describes the error condition.
Source	This is the name of the application or object that caused the exception.
StackTrace	This provides details of the method calls on the stack (to help track down the method that threw the exception).
TargetSite	This is a .NET reflection object that describes the method that threw the exception.

Of these properties, `StackTrace` and `TargetSite` are supplied automatically by the .NET runtime if a stack trace is available. `Source` will always be filled in by the .NET runtime as the name of the assembly in which the exception was raised (though you might want to modify the property in your code to give more specific information), whereas `Data`, `Message`, `HelpLink`, and `InnerException` must be filled in by the code that threw the exception, by setting these properties immediately before throwing the exception. For example, the code to throw an exception might look something like this:

```
if (ErrorCondition == true)
{
    Exception myException = new ClassMyException("Help!!!!");
    myException.Source = "My Application Name";
    myException.HelpLink = "MyHelpFile.txt";
    myException.Data["ErrorDate"] = DateTime.Now;
    myException.Data.Add("AdditionalInfo", "Contact Bill from the Blue Team");
    throw myException;
}
```

Here, `ClassMyException` is the name of the particular exception class you are throwing. Note that it is common practice for the names of all exception classes to end with `Exception`. Also note that the `Data` property is assigned in two possible ways.

What Happens If an Exception Isn't Handled?

Sometimes an exception might be thrown, but there might not be a `catch` block in your code that is able to handle that kind of exception. The `SimpleExceptions` example can serve to illustrate this. Suppose, for example, that you omitted the `FormatException` and catch-all `catch` blocks, and supplied only the block that traps an `IndexOutOfRangeException`. In that circumstance, what would happen if a `FormatException` were thrown?

The answer is that the .NET runtime would catch it. Later in this section, you learn how you can nest `try` blocks, and in fact, there is already a nested `try` block behind the scenes in the example. The .NET runtime has effectively placed the entire program inside another huge `try` block — it does this for every .NET program. This `try` block has a `catch` handler that can catch any type of exception. If an exception occurs that your code does not handle, the execution flow will simply pass right out of your program and be trapped by this `catch` block in the .NET runtime. However, the results of this probably will not be what you want. What happens is that the execution of your code will be terminated promptly; the user will see a dialog box that complains that your code has not handled the exception, and that provides any details about the exception the .NET runtime was able to retrieve. At least the exception will have been caught though! This is what actually happened earlier in Chapter 2, "C# Basics," in the `Vector` example when the program threw an exception.

In general, if you are writing an executable, try to catch as many exceptions as you reasonably can and handle them in a sensible way. If you are writing a library, it is normally best not to handle exceptions (unless a particular exception represents something wrong in your code that you can handle), but instead, assume that the calling code will handle any errors it encounters. However, you may nevertheless want to catch any Microsoft-defined exceptions, so that you can throw your own exception objects that give more specific information to the client code.

Nested try Blocks

One nice feature of exceptions is that you can nest `try` blocks inside each other, like this:

```
try
{
    // Point A
    try
    {
        // Point B
    }
    catch
    {
        // Point C
    }
    finally
    {
        // clean up
    }
    // Point D
}
catch
{
    // error handling
}
finally
{
    // clean up
}
```

Although each `try` block is accompanied by only one `catch` block in this example, you could string several `catch` blocks together, too. This section takes a closer look at how nested `try` blocks work.

If an exception is thrown inside the outer `try` block but outside the inner `try` block (points A and D), the situation is no different from any of the scenarios you have seen before: either the exception is caught by the outer `catch` block and the outer `finally` block is executed, or the `finally` block is executed and the .NET runtime handles the exception.

If an exception is thrown in the inner `try` block (point B), and there is a suitable inner `catch` block to handle the exception, then, again, you are in familiar territory: the exception is handled there, and the inner `finally` block is executed before execution resumes inside the outer `try` block (at point D).

Now suppose that an exception occurs in the inner `try` block, but there *isn't* a suitable inner `catch` block to handle it. This time, the inner `finally` block is executed as usual, but then the .NET runtime will have no choice but to leave the entire inner `try` block in order to search for a suitable exception handler. The next obvious place to look is in the outer `catch` block. If the system finds one here, then that handler will be executed and then the outer `finally` block will be executed after. If there is no suitable handler here, the search for one will go on. In this case, it means the outer `finally` block will be executed, and then, because there are no more `catch` blocks, control will be transferred to the .NET runtime. Note that at no point is the code beyond point D in the outer `try` block executed.

An even more interesting thing happens if an exception is thrown at point C. If the program is at point C, it must be already processing an exception that was thrown at point B. It is quite legitimate to throw another exception from inside a `catch` block. In this case, the exception is treated as if it had been thrown by the outer `try` block, so flow of execution will immediately leave the inner `catch` block, and execute the inner `finally` block, before the system searches the outer `catch` block for a handler. Similarly, if an exception is thrown in the inner `finally` block, control will immediately be transferred to the best appropriate handler, with the search starting at the outer `catch` block.

> **It is perfectly legitimate to throw exceptions from `catch` and `finally` blocks.**

Although the situation has been shown with just two `try` blocks, the same principles hold no matter how many `try` blocks you nest inside each other. At each stage, the .NET runtime will smoothly transfer control up through the `try` blocks, looking for an appropriate handler. At each stage, as control leaves a `catch` block, any cleanup code in the corresponding `finally` block (if present) will be executed, but no code outside any `finally` block will be run until the correct `catch` handler has been found and run.

The nesting of `try` blocks can also occur between methods themselves. For example, if method A calls method B from within a `try` block, then method B itself has a `try` block within it as well.

You have now seen how having nested `try` blocks can work. The obvious next question is why would you want to do that? There are two reasons:

❑   To modify the type of exception thrown

❑   To enable different types of exception to be handled in different places in your code

Modifying the Type of Exception

Modifying the type of the exception can be useful when the original exception thrown does not adequately describe the problem. What typically happens is that something — possibly the .NET runtime — throws a fairly low-level exception that says something like an overflow occurred (`OverflowException`) or an argument passed to a method was incorrect (a class derived from `ArgumentException`). However, because of the context in which the exception occurred, you will know that this reveals some other underlying problem (for example, an overflow can only have happened at that point in your code because a file you have just read contained incorrect data). In that case, the most appropriate thing that your handler for the first exception can do is throw another exception that more accurately describes the problem, so that another `catch` block further along can deal with it more appropriately. In this case, it can also forward the original exception through a property implemented by `System.Exception` called `InnerException`. `InnerException` simply contains a reference to any other related exception that was thrown — in case the ultimate handler routine will need this extra information.

Of course, the situation also exists where an exception occurs inside a `catch` block. For example, you might normally read in some configuration file that contains detailed instructions for handling the error, and it might turn out that this file is not there.

Handling Different Exceptions in Different Places

The second reason for having nested `try` blocks is so that different types of exceptions can be handled at different locations in your code. A good example of this is if you have a loop where various exception conditions can occur. Some of these might be serious enough that you need to abandon the entire loop, whereas others might be less serious and simply require that you abandon that iteration and move on to the next iteration around the loop. You could achieve this by having one `try` block inside the loop, which handles the less serious error conditions, and an outer `try` block outside the loop, which handles the more serious error conditions. You will see how this works in the next exceptions example.

User-Defined Exception Classes

You are now ready to look at a second example that illustrates exceptions. This example, called `SolicitColdCall`, contains two nested `try` blocks and also illustrates the practice of defining your own custom exception classes and throwing another exception from inside a `try` block.

This example assumes that a sales company wants to have additional customers on its sales list. The company's sales team is going to phone a list of people to invite them to become customers, a practice known in sales jargon as *cold calling*. To this end, you have a text file available that contains the names of the people to be cold called. The file should be in a well-defined format in which the first line contains the number of people in the file and each subsequent line contains the name of the next person. In other words, a correctly formatted file of names might look like this:

```
4
George Washington
Benedict Arnold
John Adams
Thomas Jefferson
```

This version of cold calling is designed to display the name of the person on the screen (perhaps for the salesperson to read). That is why only names and not phone numbers of the individuals are contained in the file.

For this example, your program will ask the user for the name of the file and will then simply read it in and display the names of people. That sounds like a simple task, but even so, a couple of things can go wrong and require you to abandon the entire procedure:

❑   The user might type the name of a file that does not exist. This will be caught as a `FileNotFound` exception.

❑   The file might not be in the correct format. There are two possible problems here. First, the first line of the file might not be an integer. Second, there might not be as many names in the file as the first line of the file indicates. In both cases, you want to trap this oddity as a custom exception that has been written specially for this purpose, `ColdCallFileFormatException`.

There is something else that can go wrong that, while not causing you to abandon the entire process, will mean that you need to abandon that person and move on to the next person in the file (and therefore will need to be trapped by an inner `try` block). Some people are spies working for rival sales companies, and obviously, you would not want to let these people know what you are up to by accidentally phoning one of them. Your research has indicated that you can identify who the spies are because their names begin with B. Such people should have been screened out when the data file was first prepared, but just in case any have slipped through, you will need to check each name in the file and throw a `SalesSpyFoundException` if you detect a sales spy. This, of course, is another custom exception object.

Finally, you will implement this example by coding a class, `ColdCallFileReader`, which maintains the connection to the cold-call file and retrieves data from it. You will code this class in a very safe way, which means that its methods will all throw exceptions if they are called inappropriately; for example, if a method that will read a file is called before the file has even been opened. For this purpose, you will write another exception class, `UnexpectedException`.

Catching the User-Defined Exceptions

Let's start with the `Main()` method of the `SolicitColdCall` sample, which catches your user-defined exceptions. Note that you will need to call up file-handling classes in the `System.IO` namespace as well as the `System` namespace.

```
using System;
using System.IO;

namespace Wrox.ProCSharp.AdvancedCSharp
{
    class MainEntryPoint
    {
        static void Main()
        {
            string fileName;
            Console.Write("Please type in the name of the file " +
                "containing the names of the people to be cold called > ");
            fileName = Console.ReadLine();
            ColdCallFileReader peopleToRing = new ColdCallFileReader();

            try
            {
                peopleToRing.Open(fileName);
                for (int i=0 ; i<peopleToRing.NPeopleToRing; i++)
                {
                    peopleToRing.ProcessNextPerson();
                }
                Console.WriteLine("All callers processed correctly");
            }
            catch(FileNotFoundException)
            {
                Console.WriteLine("The file {0} does not exist", fileName);
            }
            catch(ColdCallFileFormatException ex)
            {
                Console.WriteLine(
               "The file {0} appears to have been corrupted", fileName);
                Console.WriteLine("Details of problem are: {0}", ex.Message);
                if (ex.InnerException != null)
```

```
        {
            Console.WriteLine(
                "Inner exception was: {0}", ex.InnerException.Message);
        }
    }
    catch(Exception ex)
    {
        Console.WriteLine("Exception occurred:\n" + ex.Message);
    }
    finally
    {
        peopleToRing.Dispose();
    }
    Console.ReadLine();
    }
}
```

This code is a little more than just a loop to process people from the file. You start by asking the user for the name of the file. Then you instantiate an object of a class called `ColdCallFileReader`, which is defined shortly. The `ColdCallFileReader` class is the class that handles the file reading. Notice that you do this outside the initial `try` block — that's because the variables that you instantiate here need to be available in the subsequent `catch` and `finally` blocks, and if you declared them inside the `try` block they would go out of scope at the closing curly brace of the `try` block, which would not be a good thing.

In the `try` block, you open the file (using the `ColdCallFileReader.Open()` method) and loop over all the people in it. The `ColdCallFileReader.ProcessNextPerson()` method reads in and displays the name of the next person in the file, and the `ColdCallFileReader.NPeopleToRing` property tells you how many people should be in the file (obtained by reading the first line of the file). There are three `catch` blocks: one for `FileNotFoundException`, one for `ColdCallFileFormatException`, and one to trap any other .NET exceptions.

In the case of a `FileNotFoundException`, you display a message to that effect. Notice that in this `catch` block, the exception instance is not actually used at all. This `catch` block is used to illustrate the user-friendliness of the application. Exception objects generally contain technical information that is useful for developers, but not the sort of stuff you want to show to your end users. So in this case, you create a simpler message of your own.

For the `ColdCallFileFormatException` handler, you have done the opposite, and illustrated how to give fuller technical information, including details of the inner exception, if one is present.

Finally, if you catch any other generic exceptions, you display a user-friendly message, instead of letting any such exceptions fall through to the .NET runtime. Note that you have chosen not to handle any other exceptions not derived from `System.Exception`, because you are not calling directly into non-.NET code.

The `finally` block is there to clean up resources. In this case, this means closing any open file — performed by the `ColdCallFileReader.Dispose()` method.

Throwing the User-Defined Exceptions

Now take a look at the definition of the class that handles the file reading and (potentially) throws your user-defined exceptions: `ColdCallFileReader`. Because this class maintains an external file connection, you will need to make sure that it is disposed of correctly in accordance with the principles laid down for the disposing of objects in Chapter 4, "Inheritance." Therefore, you derive this class from `IDisposable`.

First, you declare some variables:

```
class ColdCallFileReader : IDisposable
{
    FileStream fs;
    StreamReader sr;
    uint nPeopleToRing;
    bool isDisposed = false;
    bool isOpen = false;
```

`FileStream` and `StreamReader`, both in the `System.IO` namespace, are the base classes that you will use to read the file. `FileStream` allows you to connect to the file in the first place, whereas `StreamReader` is specially geared up to reading text files and implements a method, `ReadLine()`, which reads a line of text from a file. You look at `StreamReader` more closely in Chapter 25, "Manipulating Files and the Registry," which discusses file handling in depth.

The `isDisposed` field indicates whether the `Dispose()` method has been called. `ColdCallFileReader` is implemented so that once `Dispose()` has been called, it is not permitted to reopen connections and reuse the object. `isOpen` is also used for error checking — in this case, checking whether the `StreamReader` actually connects to an open file.

The process of opening the file and reading in that first line — the one that tells you how many people are in the file — is handled by the `Open()` method:

```
public void Open(string fileName)
{
    if (isDisposed)
        throw new ObjectDisposedException("peopleToRing");

    fs = new FileStream(fileName, FileMode.Open);
    sr = new StreamReader(fs);

    try
    {
        string firstLine = sr.ReadLine();
        nPeopleToRing = uint.Parse(firstLine);
        isOpen = true;
    }
    catch (FormatException ex)
    {
        throw new ColdCallFileFormatException(
            "First line isn\'t an integer", ex);
    }
}
```

The first thing you do in this method (as with all other `ColdCallFileReader` methods) is check whether the client code has inappropriately called it after the object has been disposed of, and if so, throw a predefined `ObjectDisposedException` object. The `Open()` method checks the `isDisposed` field to see whether `Dispose()` has already been called. Because calling `Dispose()` implies that the caller has now finished with this object, you regard it as an error to attempt to open a new file connection if `Dispose()` has been called.

Next, the method contains the first of two inner `try` blocks. The purpose of this one is to catch any errors resulting from the first line of the file not containing an integer. If that problem arises, the .NET runtime will throw a `FormatException`, which you trap and convert to a more meaningful exception that indicates there is actually a problem with the format of the cold-call file. Note that `System.FormatException` is there to indicate format problems with basic data types, not with files, and so is not a particularly useful exception to pass back to the calling routine in this case. The new exception thrown will be trapped by the outermost `try` block. Because no cleanup is needed here, there is no need for a `finally` block.

If everything is fine, you set the `isOpen` field to `true` to indicate that there is now a valid file connection from which data can be read.

The `ProcessNextPerson()` method also contains an inner `try` block:

```
public void ProcessNextPerson()
{
    if (isDisposed)
    {
        throw new ObjectDisposedException("peopleToRing");
    }

    if (!isOpen)
    {
        throw new UnexpectedException(
            "Attempted to access cold-call file that is not open");
    }

    try
    {
        string name;
        name = sr.ReadLine();
        if (name == null)
            throw new ColdCallFileFormatException("Not enough names");
        if (name[0] == 'B')
        {
            throw new SalesSpyFoundException(name);
        }
        Console.WriteLine(name);
    }
    catch(SalesSpyFoundException ex)
    {
        Console.WriteLine(ex.Message);
    }

    finally
    {
    }
}
```

Two possible problems exist with the file here (assuming that there actually is an open file connection; the `ProcessNextPerson()` method checks this first). First, you might read in the next name and discover that it is a sales spy. If that condition occurs, the exception is trapped by the first of the `catch` blocks in this method. Because that exception has been caught here, inside the loop, it means that execution can subsequently continue in the `Main()` method of the program, and the subsequent names in the file will continue to be processed.

A problem might also occur if you try to read the next name and discover that you have already reached the end of the file. The way that the `StreamReader` object's `ReadLine()` method works is if it has gone past the end of the file, it doesn't throw an exception, but simply returns `null`. Therefore, if you find a null string, you know that the format of the file was incorrect because the number in the first line of the file indicated a larger number of names than were actually present in the file. If that happens, you throw a `ColdCallFileFormatException`, which will be caught by the outer exception handler (which will cause execution to terminate).

Once again, you don't need a `finally` block here because there is no cleanup to do; however, this time an empty `finally` block is included, just to show that you can do so, if you want.

The example is nearly finished. You have just two more members of `ColdCallFileReader` to look at: the `NPeopleToRing` property, which returns the number of people supposed to be in the file, and the `Dispose()` method, which closes an open file. Notice that the `Dispose()` method just returns if it has already been called — this is the recommended way of implementing it. It also checks that there actually is a file stream to close before closing it. This example is shown here to illustrate defensive coding techniques, so that's what you are doing!

```csharp
public uint NPeopleToRing
{
    get
    {
        if (isDisposed)
        {
            throw new ObjectDisposedException("peopleToRing");
        }

        if (!isOpen)
        {
            throw new UnexpectedException(
                "Attempted to access cold-call file that is not open");
        }

        return nPeopleToRing;
    }
}

public void Dispose()
{
    if (isDisposed)
    {
        return;
    }

    isDisposed = true;
    isOpen = false;

    if (fs != null)
    {
        fs.Close();
        fs = null;
    }
}
```

Defining the User-Defined Exception Classes

Finally, you need to define your own three exception classes. Defining your own exception is quite easy because there are rarely any extra methods to add. It is just a case of implementing a constructor to ensure that the base class constructor is called correctly. Here is the full implementation of `SalesSpyFoundException`:

```
class SalesSpyFoundException : ApplicationException
{
    public SalesSpyFoundException(string spyName)
        :   base("Sales spy found, with name " + spyName)
    {
    }

    public SalesSpyFoundException(
        string spyName, Exception innerException)
        :   base(
            "Sales spy found with name " + spyName, innerException)
    {
    }
}
```

Notice that it is derived from `ApplicationException`, as you would expect for a custom exception. In fact, in practice, you would probably have put in an intermediate class, something like `ColdCallFileException`, derived from `ApplicationException`, and derived both of your exception classes from this class. This would ensure that the handling code has that extra-fine degree of control over which exception handler handles which exception. However, to keep the example simple, you will not do that.

You have done one bit of processing in `SalesSpyFoundException`. You have assumed that the message passed into its constructor is just the name of the spy found, so you turn this string into a more meaningful error message. You have also provided two constructors, one that simply takes a message, and one that also takes an inner exception as a parameter. When defining your own exception classes, it is best to include, at a minimum, at least these two constructors (although you will not actually be using the second `SalesSpyFoundException` constructor in this example).

Now for the `ColdCallFileFormatException`. This follows the same principles as the previous exception, except that you don't do any processing on the message:

```
class ColdCallFileFormatException : ApplicationException
{
    public ColdCallFileFormatException(string message)
        :   base(message)
    {
    }

    public ColdCallFileFormatException(
        string message, Exception innerException)
        :   base(message, innerException)
    {
    }
}
```

And finally, `UnexpectedException`, which looks much the same as `ColdCallFileFormatException`:

```
class UnexpectedException : ApplicationException
{
    public UnexpectedException(string message)
        :   base(message)
```

(continued)

(continued)

```
            {
            }

        public UnexpectedException(string message, Exception innerException)
            :    base(message, innerException)
            {
            }
    }
```

Now you are ready to test the program. First, try the `people.txt` file whose contents are defined here.

```
4
George Washington
Benedict Arnold
John Adams
Thomas Jefferson
```

This has four names (which match the number given in the first line of the file), including one spy. Then try the following `people2.txt` file, which has an obvious formatting error:

```
49
George Washington
Benedict Arnold
John Adams
Thomas Jefferson
```

Finally, try the example but specify the name of a file that does not exist, say, `people3.txt`. Running the program three times for the three file names gives these results:

```
SolicitColdCall
Please type in the name of the file containing the names of the people to be cold
called > people.txt
George Washington
Sales spy found, with name Benedict Arnold
John Adams
Thomas Jefferson
All callers processed correctly


SolicitColdCall
Please type in the name of the file containing the names of the people to be cold
called > people2.txt
George Washington
Sales spy found, with name Benedict Arnold
John Adams
Thomas Jefferson
The file people2.txt appears to have been corrupted.
Details of the problem are: Not enough names


SolicitColdCall
Please type in the name of the file containing the names of the people to be cold
called > people3.txt
The file people3.txt does not exist.
```

In the end, this application shows you a number of different ways in which you can handle the errors and exceptions that you might find in your own applications.

Summary

This chapter examined the rich mechanism C# has for dealing with error conditions through exceptions. You are not limited to the generic error codes that could be output from your code; instead, you have the ability to go in and uniquely handle the most granular of error conditions. Sometimes these error conditions are provided to you through the .NET Framework itself, but at other times, you might want to go in and code your own error conditions as illustrated in this chapter. In either case, you have many ways of protecting the workflow of your applications from unnecessary and dangerous faults.

The next chapter allows you to take a lot of what you learned so far in this book and works at implementing these lessons within the .NET developers IDE — Visual Studio 2008.

Part II
Visual Studio

15

Visual Studio 2008

At this point, you should be familiar with the C# language and almost ready to move on to the applied sections of the book, which cover how to use C# to program a variety of applications. Before doing that, however, you need to examine how you can use Visual Studio and some of the features provided by the .NET environment to get the best from your programs.

This chapter explains what programming in the .NET environment means in practice. It covers Visual Studio, the main development environment in which you will write, compile, debug, and optimize your C# programs, and provides guidelines for writing good applications. Visual Studio is the main IDE used for everything from writing Web Forms and Windows Forms to XML Web services, and more. For more details on Windows Forms and how to write user interface code, see Chapter 31, "Windows Forms." This chapter takes a strong look at the following:

❑   Using Visual Studio 2008

❑   Refactoring with Visual Studio

❑   Visual Studio 2008's multi-targeting capabilities

❑   Working with the new technologies WPF, WCF, WF, and more.

This chapter also explores what it takes to build applications that are targeted at the .NET Framework 3.0 or 3.5. The types of applications provided ever since the .NET Framework 3.0 class library include the Windows Presentation Foundation (WPF), the Windows Communication Foundation (WCF), and the Windows Workflow Foundation (WF). Working with Visual Studio 2008 will provide you the ability to work with these new application types directly.

Working with Visual Studio 2008

Visual Studio 2008 is a fully integrated development environment. It is designed to make the process of writing your code, debugging it, and compiling it to an assembly to be shipped as easy as possible. What this means is that Visual Studio gives you a very sophisticated multiple-document-interface application in which you can do just about everything related to developing your code. It offers these features:

❑   Text editor — Using this editor, you can write your C# (as well as Visual Basic 2008 and Visual C++) code. This text editor is quite sophisticated. For example, as you type, it automatically lays out your code by indenting lines, matching start and end brackets of code blocks, and color-coding keywords. It also performs some syntax checks as you type, and it underlines code that causes compilation errors, also known as design-time debugging. In addition, it features IntelliSense, which automatically displays the names of classes, fields, or methods as you begin to type them. As you start typing parameters to methods, it will also show you the parameter lists for the available overloads. Figure 15-1 shows the IntelliSense feature in action with one of the .NET base classes, ListBox.

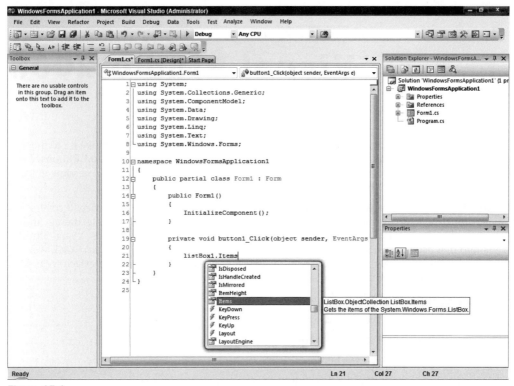

Figure 15-1

> By pressing Ctrl+Space, you can bring back the IntelliSense list box if you need it
> and if for any reason it is not visible.

❑   Design view editor — This editor enables you to place user-interface and data-access controls in your project; Visual Studio automatically adds the necessary C# code to your source files to instantiate these controls in your project. (This is possible because all .NET controls are instances of particular base classes.)

❑   Supporting windows — These windows allow you to view and modify aspects of your project, such as the classes in your source code, as well as the available properties (and their startup values) for Windows Forms and Web Forms classes. You can also use these windows to specify compilation options, such as which assemblies your code needs to reference.

❑ The ability to compile from within the environment — Instead of needing to run the C# compiler from the command line, you can simply select a menu option to compile the project, and Visual Studio will call the compiler for you and pass all the relevant command-line parameters to the compiler, detailing such things as which assemblies to reference and what type of assembly you want to be emitted (executable or library .dll, for example). If you want, it can also run the compiled executable for you so that you can see whether it runs satisfactorily. You can even choose between different build configurations (for example, a release or debug build).

❑ Integrated debugger — It is in the nature of programming that your code will not run correctly the first time you try it. Or the second time. Or the third time. Visual Studio seamlessly links up to a debugger for you, allowing you to set breakpoints and watches on variables from within the environment.

❑ Integrated MSDN help — Visual Studio enables you to access the MSDN documentation from within the IDE. For example, if you are not sure of the meaning of a keyword while using the text editor, simply select the keyword and press the F1 key, and Visual Studio will access MSDN to show you related topics. Similarly, if you are not sure what a certain compilation error means, you can bring up the documentation for that error by selecting the error message and pressing F1.

❑ Access to other programs — Visual Studio can also access a number of other utilities that allow you to examine and modify aspects of your computer or network, without your having to leave the developer environment. Among the tools available, you can check running services and database connections, look directly into your SQL Server tables, and even browse the Web using an Internet Explorer window.

If you have developed previously using C++ or Visual Basic, you will already be familiar with the relevant Visual Studio 6 version of the IDE, and many of the features in the preceding list will not be new to you. What is new in Visual Studio is that it combines all the features that were previously available across all Visual Studio 6 development environments. This means that whatever language you used in Visual Studio 6, you will find some new features in Visual Studio. For example, in the older Visual Basic environment, you could not compile separate debug and release builds. If you are coming to C# from a background of C++, though, then much of the support for data access and the ability to drop controls into your application with a click of the mouse, which has long been part of the Visual Basic developer's experience, will be new to you. In the C++ development environment, drag-and-drop support is limited to the most common user-interface controls.

C++ developers will miss two Visual Studio 6 features in Visual Studio 2008: edit-and-continue debugging and an integrated profiler. Visual Studio 2008 also does not include a full profiler application. Instead, you will find a number of .NET classes that assist with profiling in the System .Diagnostics *namespace. The perfmon profiling tool is available from the command line (just type perfmon) and has a number of new .NET-related performance monitors.*

Whatever your background, you will find that the overall look of the Visual Studio 2008 developer environment has changed since the days of Visual Studio 6 to accommodate the new features, the single cross-language IDE, and the integration with .NET. There are new menu and toolbar options, and many of the existing ones from Visual Studio 6 have been renamed. Therefore, you will need to spend some time familiarizing yourself with the layout and commands available in Visual Studio 2008.

The differences between Visual Studio 2005 and Visual Studio 2008 are a few nice additions that facilitate working in Visual Studio 2008. The biggest changes in Visual Studio 2008 include the ability to target specific versions of the .NET Framework (including the .NET Framework versions 2.0, 3.0, or 3.5), JavaScript IntelliSense support, and new abilities to work with CSS. You will also find new built-in features that allow you to build ASP.NET AJAX applications as well as applications using some of the newest technical capabilities coming out of Microsoft, including the Windows Communication Foundation, Windows Workflow Foundation, and the Windows Presentation Foundation.

One of the biggest items to notice with your installation of Visual Studio 2008 is that this new IDE works with the .NET Framework 3.5. In fact, when you install Visual Studio 2008, you will also be installing the .NET Framework 3.0 and 3.5 if they aren't already installed. Like Visual Studio 2005, this new IDE, Visual Studio 2008, is not built to work with version 1.0 or 1.1 of the .NET Framework, which means that if you still want to develop 1.0 or 1.1 applications, you will want to keep Visual Studio 2002 or 2003, respectively, installed on your machine. Installing Visual Studio 2008 installs a complete and new copy of Visual Studio and does not upgrade the previous Visual Studio 2002, 2003, or 2005 IDEs. The three copies of Visual Studio will then run side by side on your machine if required.

Note that if you attempt to open your Visual Studio 2002, 2003, or 2005 projects using Visual Studio 2008, the IDE will warn you that your solution will be upgraded to Visual Studio 2008 if you continue by popping up the Visual Studio Conversion Wizard (see Figure 15-2).

Figure 15-2

The upgrade wizard has been dramatically improved from Visual Studio 2003 to this newer one provided by Visual Studio 2008. This wizard can make backup copies of the solutions that are being backed up (see Figure 15-3), and it can also back up solutions that are contained within source control.

It is also possible to have Visual Studio generate a conversion report for you in the conversion process's final step. The report will then be viewable directly in the document window of Visual Studio. This report is illustrated (done with a simple conversion) in Figure 15-4.

Because this is a professional-level book, it does not look in detail at every feature or menu option available in Visual Studio 2008. Surely, you will be able to find your way around the IDE. The real aim of this Visual Studio coverage is to ensure that you are sufficiently familiar with the concepts involved when building and debugging a C# application that you can make the most of working with Visual Studio 2008. Figure 15-5 shows what your screen might look like when working in Visual Studio 2008. (Note that because the appearance of Visual Studio is highly customizable, the windows might not be in the same locations, or different windows might be visible when you launch this development environment.)

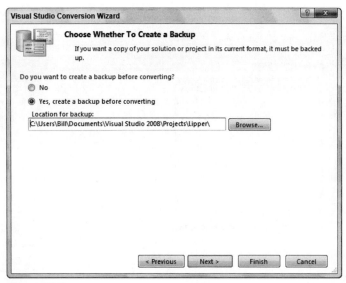

Figure 15-3

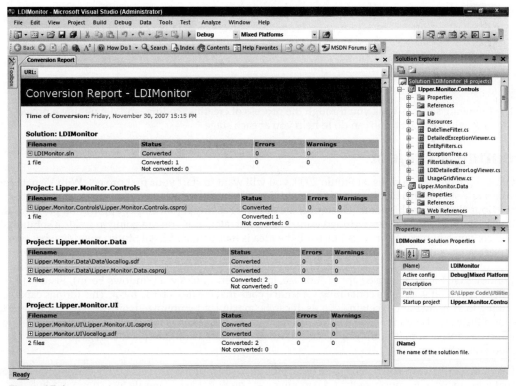

Figure 15-4

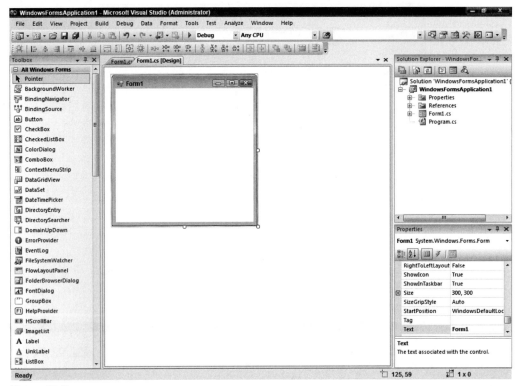

Figure 15-5

The following sections walk you through the process of creating, coding, and debugging a project, showing what Visual Studio can do to help you at each stage.

Creating a Project

Once you have installed Visual Studio 2008, you will want to start your first project. With Visual Studio, you rarely start with a blank file and then add C# code, in the way that you have been doing in the previous chapters in this book. (Of course, the option of asking for an empty application project is there if you really do want to start writing your code from scratch or if you are going to create a solution that will contain a number of projects.) Instead, the idea is that you tell Visual Studio roughly what type of project you want to create, and it will generate the files and C# code that provide a framework for that type of project. You then work by adding your code to this outline. For example, if you want to build a Windows GUI-interface-based application (or, in .NET terminology, a Windows Form), Visual Studio will start you off with a file containing C# source code that creates a basic form. This form is capable of talking to Windows and receiving events. It can be maximized, minimized, or resized; all you need to do is add the controls and functionality you want. If your application is intended to be a command-line utility (a console application), Visual Studio will give you a basic namespace, class, and a `Main()` method to start you off.

Last, but hardly least, when you create your project, Visual Studio also sets up the compilation options that you are likely to supply to the C# compiler — whether it is to compile to a command-line application, a library, or a Windows application. It will also tell the compiler which base class libraries you will need to reference (a Windows GUI application will need to reference many of the `Windows` `.Forms`-related libraries; a console application probably will not). You can, of course, modify all these settings as you are editing, if you need to.

The first time you start Visual Studio, you will be presented with a blank IDE (see Figure 15-6). The Start Page is an HTML page that contains various links to useful Web sites and enables you to open existing projects or start a new project altogether.

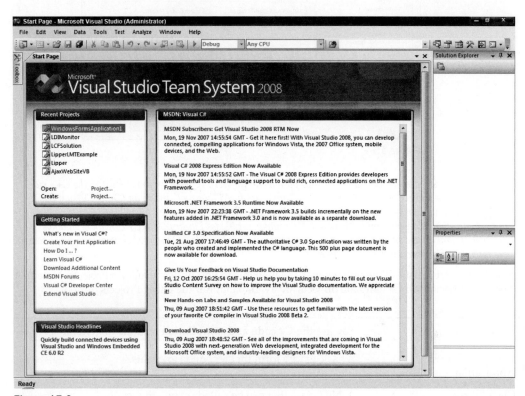

Figure 15-6

Figure 15-6 shows the type of Start Page you get after you have used Visual Studio 2008; it includes a list of the most recently edited projects. You can just click one of these projects to open it again.

Selecting a Project Type

You can create a new project by selecting File ⇨ New Project from the Visual Studio menu. From there you will get the New Project dialog box (see Figure 15-7) — and your first inkling of the variety of different projects you can create.

Using this dialog box, you effectively select the initial framework files and code you want Visual Studio to generate for you, the type of compilation options you want, and the compiler you want to compile your code with — either the Visual C#, Visual Basic 2008, or Visual C++ compiler. You can immediately see the language integration that Microsoft has promised for .NET at work here! This particular example uses a C# console application.

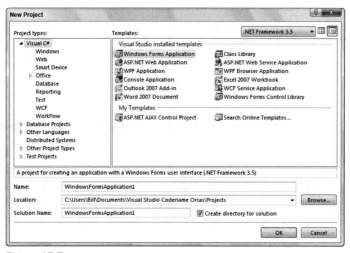

Figure 15-7

We do not have space to cover all the various options for different types of projects here. On the C++ side, all the old C++ project types are there — MFC application, ATL project, and so on. On the Visual Basic 2008 side, the options have changed somewhat. For example, you can create a Visual Basic 2008 command-line application (Console Application), a .NET component (Class Library), a .NET control (Windows Control Library), and more. However, you cannot create an old-style COM-based control (the .NET control is intended to replace such ActiveX controls).

The following table lists all the options that are available to you under Visual C# Projects. Note that some other, more specialized C# template projects are available under the Other Projects option.

If you choose . . .	You get the C# code and compilation options to generate . . .
Windows Forms Application	A basic empty form that responds to events.
Class Library	A .NET class that can be called up by other code.
WPF Application	A basic empty form that responds to events. Though the project type is similar to the Windows Forms Application project type (Windows Forms), this Windows Application project type allows you to build an XAML-based smart client solution.
WPF Browser Application	Quite similar to the Windows Application for WPF, this variant allows you to build an XAML-based application that is targeted at the browser.
ASP.NET Web Application	An ASP.NET-based Web site: ASP.NET pages and C# classes that generate the HTML response sent to browsers from those pages.
ASP.NET Web Service Application	A C# class that acts as a fully operational Web service.
ASP.NET AJAX Server Control	Allows you to build a custom server control for use within ASP.NET applications.

If you choose . . .	You get the C# code and compilation options to generate . . .
Web Control Library	A control that can be called up by ASP.NET pages, to generate the HTML code that gives the appearance of a control when displayed on a browser.
WPF Custom Control Library	A custom control that can be used in a Windows Presentation Foundation application.
WPF User Control Library	A user control library built using the Windows Presentation Foundation.
Windows Forms Control Library	A project for creating controls to use in Windows Forms applications.
Console Application	An application that runs at the command-line prompt, or in a console window.
WCF Service Application	A project type for Windows Communication Foundation services.
Windows Service	A service that runs in the background on a Windows operating system.
Reports Application	A project for creating an application with a Windows user interface and a Report.
Crystal Reports Windows Application	A project for creating a C# application with a Windows user interface and a sample Crystal Report.
SQL Server Project	A project for creating classes to use in SQL Server.
Smart Device	A project type that allows you to target a specific type of mobile device.
Sequential Workflow Service Library	A project that provides a sequential workflow exposed as a WCF service.
State Machine Workflow Service Library	A project that provides a state machine workflow exposed as a WCF service.
Syndication Service Library	A project that provides a syndication service exposed as a WCF service
WCF Service Library	A project that provides for creating a WCF service class library (.dll) that has endpoints controlled via XML configuration files.
Empty Workflow Project	A project that provides an empty project for creating a workflow.
Sequential Workflow Console Application	A project that provides for creating a sequential workflow console application.
Sequential Workflow Library	A project for creating a sequential workflow library.
SharePoint 2007 Sequential Workflow	A project that provides for creating a SharePoint sequential workflow.
SharePoint 2007 State Machine Workflow	A project that provides for creating a SharePoint state machine workflow.
State Machine Workflow Console Application	A project that provides for creating a state machine workflow console application.

If you choose . . .	You get the C# code and compilation options to generate . . .
State Machine Workflow Library	A project that provides for creating a state machine workflow library.
Workflow Activity Library	A project that provides for creating a library of activities that can later be reused as building blocks in workflows.
Office	A series of projects that are aimed at building applications or add-ins targeted at the Microsoft Office applications (Word, Excel, PowerPoint, InfoPath, Outlook, and SharePoint).

As mentioned, this is not a full list of the .NET Framework 3.5 projects, but it is a good start. The big additions to this project table are the new projects that are aimed at the Windows Presentation Foundation (WPF), the Windows Communication Foundation (WCF), and the Windows Workflow Foundation (WF). You will find chapters covering these new capabilities later in this book. Be sure to look at Chapter 34, "Windows Presentation Foundation," Chapter 42, "Windows Communication Foundation," and Chapter 43, "Windows Workflow Foundation."

The Newly Created Console Project

When you click OK after selecting the Console Application option, Visual Studio gives you a couple of files, including a source code file, `Program.cs`, which contains the initial framework code. Figure 15-8 shows what code Visual Studio has written for you.

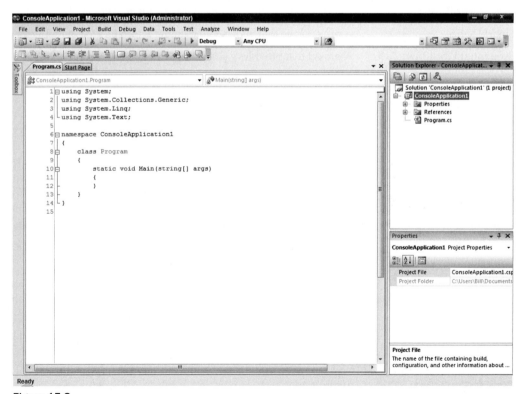

Figure 15-8

As you can see, you have a C# program that does not do anything yet but contains the basic items required in any C# executable program: a namespace and a class that contains the `Main()` method, which is the program's entry point. (Strictly speaking, the namespace is not necessary, but it would be very bad programming practice not to declare one.) This code is all ready to compile and run, which you can do immediately by pressing the F5 key or by selecting the Debug menu and choosing Start. However, before you do that, add the following line of code — to make your application actually do something!

```
static void Main(string[] args)
    {
        Console.WriteLine("Hello from all the authors of Professional C#");
    }
```

If you compile and run the project, you will see a console window that stays onscreen barely long enough to read the message. The reason this happens is that Visual Studio, remembering the settings you specified when you created the project, arranged for it to be compiled and run as a console application. Windows then realizes that it has to run a console application but does not have a console window to run it from. Therefore, Windows creates a console window and runs the program. As soon as the program exits, Windows recognizes that it does not need the console window anymore and promptly removes it. That is all very logical but does not help you very much if you actually want to look at the output from your project!

A good way to prevent this problem is to insert the following line just before the `Main()` method returns in your code:

```
static void Main(string[] args)
    {
        Console.WriteLine("Hello from all the folks at Wrox Press");
        Console.ReadLine();
    }
```

That way, your code will run, display its output, and come across the `Console.ReadLine()` statement, at which point it will wait for you to press the Return (or Enter) key before the program exits. This means that the console window will hang around until you press Return.

Note that all this is only an issue for console applications that you test-run from Visual Studio — if you are writing a Windows application, the window displayed by the application will automatically remain onscreen until you exit it. Similarly, if you run a console application from the command-line prompt, you will not have any problems with the window disappearing.

Other Files Created

The `Program.cs` source code file is not the only file that Visual Studio has created for you. Looking in the folder in which you asked Visual Studio to create your project, you will see not just the C# file, but a complete directory structure that looks like what is shown in Figure 15-9.

The two folders, `bin` and `obj`, store compiled and intermediate files. Subfolders of `obj` hold various temporary or intermediate files; subfolders of `bin` hold the compiled assemblies.

> Traditionally, Visual Basic developers would simply write the code and then run it. Before shipping, the code would then need to be compiled into an executable; Visual Basic tended to hide the process of compilation when debugging. In C#, it is more explicit: to run the code, you have to compile (or build) it first, which means that an assembly must be created somewhere.

You will also find a `Properties` folder that holds the `AssemblyInfo.cs` file. The remaining files in the project's main folder, `ConsoleApplication1`, are there for Visual Studio's benefit. They contain information about the project (for example, the files it contains) so that Visual Studio knows how to have the project compiled and how to read it in the next time you open the project.

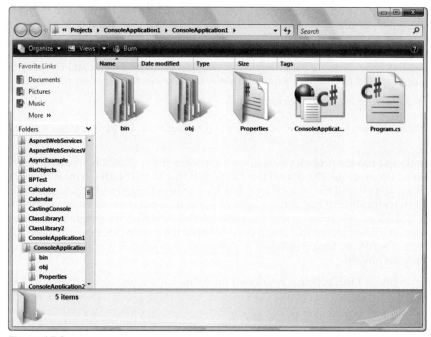

Figure 15-9

Solutions and Projects

One important distinction you must understand is that between a project and a solution:

❑ A *project* is a set of all the source code files and resources that will compile into a single assembly (or in some cases, a single module). For example, a project might be a class library or a Windows GUI application.

❑ A *solution* is the set of all the projects that make up a particular software package (application).

To understand this distinction, look at what happens when you ship a project — the project consists of more than one assembly. For example, you might have a user interface, custom controls, and other components that ship as libraries of the parts of the application. You might even have a different user interface for administrators. Each of these parts of the application might be contained in a separate assembly, and hence, they are regarded by Visual Studio as a separate project. However, it is quite likely that you will be coding these projects in parallel and in conjunction with each other. Thus, it is quite useful to be able to edit them all as one single unit in Visual Studio. Visual Studio allows this by regarding all the projects as forming one solution and by treating the solution as the unit that it reads in and allows you to work on.

Up until now, we have been loosely talking about creating a console project. In fact, in the example you are working on, Visual Studio has actually created a solution for you — though this particular solution contains just one project. You can see the situation in a window in Visual Studio known as the Solution Explorer (see Figure 15-10), which contains a tree structure that defines your solution.

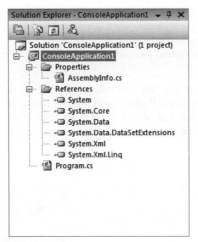

Figure 15-10

Figure 15-10 shows that the project contains your source file, `Program.cs`, as well as another C# source file, `AssemblyInfo.cs` (found in the `Properties` folder), which allows you to provide information that describes the assembly as well as the ability to specify versioning information. (You look at this file in detail in Chapter 17, "Assemblies.") The Solution Explorer also indicates the assemblies that your project references according to namespace. You can see this by expanding the `References` folder in the Solution Explorer.

If you have not changed any of the default settings in Visual Studio, you will probably find the Solution Explorer in the top-right corner of your screen. If you cannot see it, just go to the View menu and select Solution Explorer.

The solution is described by a file with the extension `.sln` — in this example, it is `ConsoleApplication1.sln`. The project is described by various other files in the project's main folder. If you attempt to edit these files using Notepad, you will find that they are mostly plain-text files, and, in accordance with the principle that .NET and .NET tools rely on open standards wherever possible, they are mostly in XML format.

> *C++ developers will recognize that a Visual Studio solution corresponds to an old Visual C++ project workspace (stored in a `.dsw` file), and a Visual Studio project corresponds to an old C++ project (`.dsp` file). By contrast, Visual Basic developers will recognize that a solution corresponds to an old Visual Basic project group (`.vbg` file), and the .NET project corresponds to an old Visual Basic project (`.vbp` file). Visual Studio differs from the old Visual Basic IDE in that it always creates a solution for you automatically. In Visual Studio 6, Visual Basic developers would get a project; however, they would need to request a project group from the IDE separately.*

Adding Another Project to the Solution

As you work through the following sections, you will see how Visual Studio works with Windows applications as well as with console applications. To that end, you create a Windows project called `BasicForm` that you will add to your current solution, `ConsoleApplication1`.

413

This means that you will end up with a solution containing a Windows application and a console application. That is not a very common scenario — you are more likely to have one application and a number of libraries — but it allows you to see more code! You might, however, create a solution like this if, for example, you are writing a utility that you want to run either as a Windows application or as a command-line utility.

You can create the new project in two ways. You can select New Project from the File menu (as you have done already) or you can select Add ⇨ New Project from the File menu. If you select New Project from the File menu, this will bring up the familiar New Project dialog box; this time, however, you will notice that Visual Studio wants to create the new project in the preexisting `ConsoleApplication1` project location (see Figure 15-11).

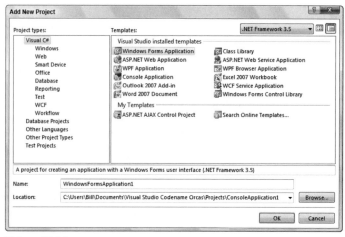

Figure 15-11

If you select this option, a new project is added so that the `ConsoleApplication1` solution now contains a console application and a Windows application.

In accordance with the language-independence of Visual Studio, the new project does not need to be a C# project. It is perfectly acceptable to put a C# project, a Visual Basic 2008 project, and a C++ project in the same solution. However, we will stick with C# here because this is a C# book!

Of course, this means that `ConsoleApplication1` is not really an appropriate name for the solution anymore! To change the name, you can right-click the name of the solution and select Rename from the context menu. Call the new solution `DemoSolution`. The Solution Explorer window now looks like Figure 15-12.

You can see from this that Visual Studio has made your newly added Windows project automatically reference some of the extra base classes that are important for Windows Forms functionality.

You will notice if you look in Windows Explorer that the name of the solution file has changed to `DemoSolution.sln`. In general, if you want to rename any files, the Solution Explorer window is the best place to do so, because Visual Studio will then automatically update any references to that file in the other project files. If you rename files using just Windows Explorer, you might break the solution because Visual Studio will not be able to locate all the files it needs to read in. You will then need to manually edit the project and solution files to update the file references.

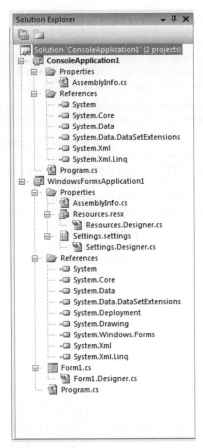

Figure 15-12

Setting the Startup Project

Bear in mind that if you have multiple projects in a solution only one of them can be run at a time! When you compile the solution, all the projects in it will be compiled. However, you must specify which one you want Visual Studio to start running when you press F5 or select Start. If you have one executable and several libraries that it calls, this will clearly be the executable. In this case, where you have two independent executables in the project, you would simply need to debug each in turn.

You can tell Visual Studio which project to run by right-clicking that project in the Solution Explorer window and selecting Set as Startup Project from the context menu. You can tell which one is the current startup project — it is the one that appears in bold in the Solution Explorer window (WindowsFormsApplication1 in Figure 15-12).

Windows Application Code

A Windows application contains a lot more code right from the start than a console application when Visual Studio first creates it. That is because creating a window is an intrinsically more complex process. Chapter 31, "Windows Forms," discusses the code for a Windows application in detail. For now, look at the code in the Form1 class in the WindowsApplication1 project to see for yourself how much is auto-generated.

Reading in Visual Studio 6 Projects

If you are coding in C#, you will not need to read in any old Visual Studio 6 projects because C# does not exist in Visual Studio 6. However, language interoperability is a key part of the .NET Framework, so you might want your C# code to work alongside code written in Visual Basic or in C++. In that situation, you might need to edit projects that were created with Visual Studio 6.

Visual Studio has no problems reading in and upgrading Visual Studio 6 projects and workspaces. The situation is different for pre-Visual Studio C++ and Visual Basic projects:

❑   In Visual C++, no change to the source code is needed. All your old Visual C++ code still works fine with the new C++ compiler. Obviously, it is not managed code, but it will still compile to code that runs outside the .NET runtime; if you want your code to integrate with the .NET Framework, you will need to edit it. If you get Visual Studio to read in an old Visual C++ project, it will simply add a new solution file and updated project files. It will leave the old .dsw and .dsp files unchanged so that the project can still be edited by Visual Studio 6, if necessary.

❑   In Visual Basic, things are a bit more complicated. As mentioned in Chapter 1, ".NET Architecture," although Visual Basic 2008 has been designed very much around Visual Basic 6.0 and shares much of the same syntax, it is in many ways a new language. In Visual Basic 6.0, the source code largely consisted of the event handlers for the controls. In Visual Basic 2008, the code that actually instantiates the main window and many of its controls is not part of Visual Basic but is instead hidden behind the scenes as part of the configuration of your project. In contrast, Visual Basic 2008 works in the same way as C#, by putting the entire program out in the open as source code, so all the code that displays in the main window and all the controls on it need to be in the source file. Also, like C#, Visual Basic 2008 requires everything to be object oriented and part of a class, whereas VB did not even recognize the concept of classes in the .NET sense. If you try to read a Visual Basic project with Visual Studio, it will need to upgrade the entire source code to Visual Basic 2008 before it can handle it — and this involves making a lot of changes to the Visual Basic code. Visual Studio can largely make these changes automatically and will then create a new Visual Basic 2008 solution for you. You will find that the source code it gives you looks very different from the corresponding Visual Basic code, and you will still need to check carefully through the generated code to make sure that the project still works correctly. You might even find areas in the code where Visual Studio has left comments to the effect that it cannot figure out exactly what you wanted the code to do, and you might need to edit the code manually.

Exploring and Coding a Project

This section looks at the features that Visual Studio provides to help you add code to your project.

The Folding Editor

One really exciting feature of Visual Studio is its use of a folding editor as its default code editor (see Figure 15-13).

Figure 15-13 shows the code for the console application that you generated earlier. Notice those little minus signs on the left-hand side of the window. These signs mark the points where the editor assumes that a new block of code (or documentation comment) begins. You can click these icons to close up the view of the corresponding block of code just as you would close a node in a tree control (see Figure 15-14).

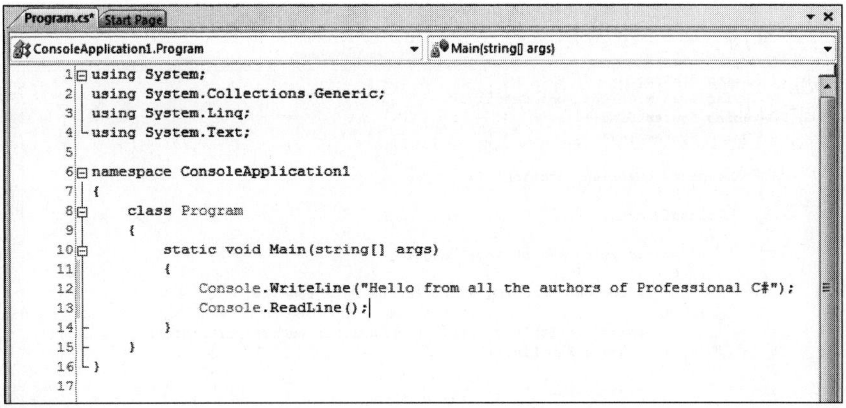

Figure 15-13

This means that while you are editing you can focus on just the areas of code you want to look at, and you can hide the bits of code you are not interested in working with at that moment. If you do not like the way the editor has chosen to block off your code, you can indicate your own blocks of collapsing code with the C# preprocessor directives, `#region` and `#endregion`, which were examined earlier in the book. For example, to collapse the code inside the `Main()` method, you would add the code shown in Figure 15-15.

The code editor will automatically detect the `#region` block and place a new minus sign by the `#region` directive, as shown in Figure 15-15, allowing you to close the region. Enclosing this code in a region means that you can get the editor to close the block of code (see Figure 15-16), marking the area with the comment you specified in the `#region` directive. The compiler, however, ignores the directives and compiles the `Main()` method as normal.

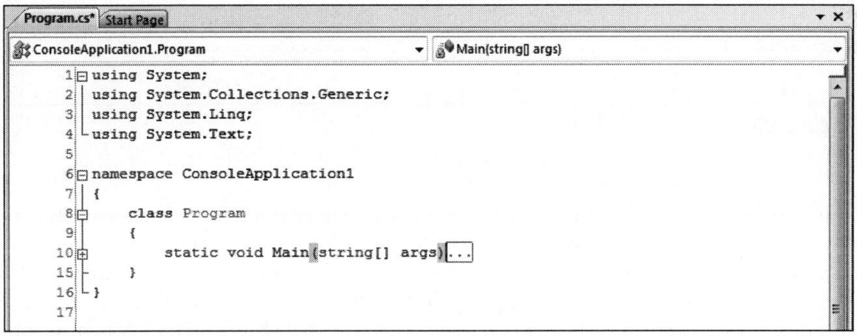

Figure 15-14

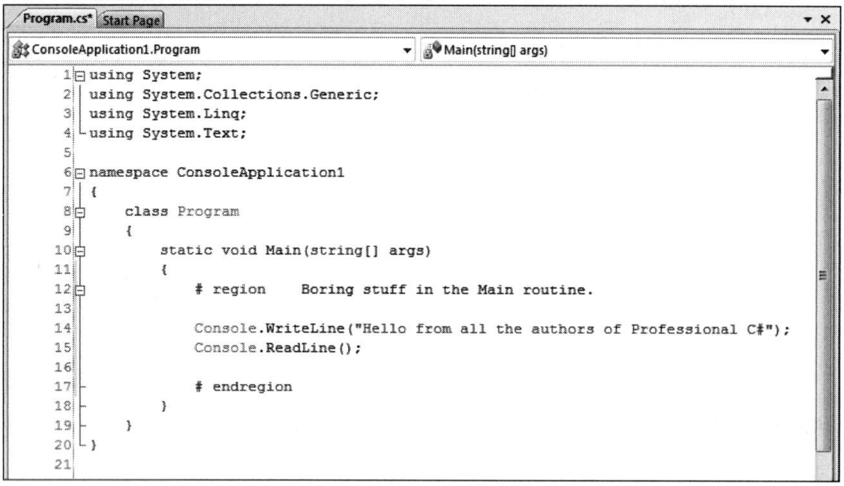

Figure 15-15

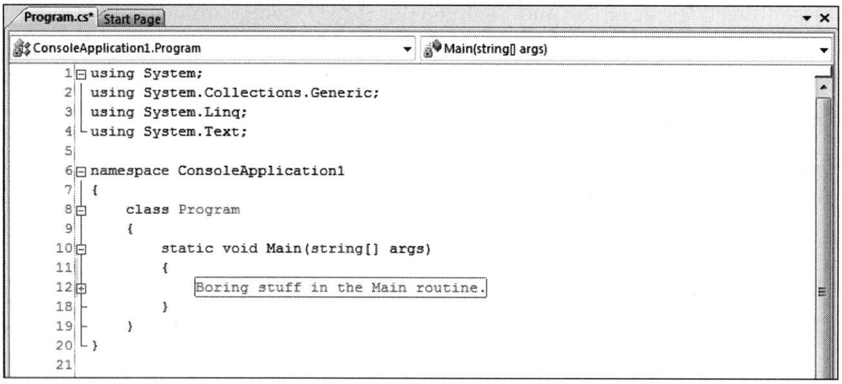

Figure 15-16

In addition to the folding editor feature, Visual Studio's code editor brings across all the familiar functionality from Visual Studio 6. In particular, it features IntelliSense, which not only saves you typing, but also ensures that you use the correct parameters. C++ developers will notice that the Visual Studio IntelliSense feature is a bit more robust than the Visual Studio 6 version and also works more quickly. You will also notice that IntelliSense has been improved in Visual Studio 2008. It is now smarter in that it remembers your preferred choices and starts with one of these choices instead of starting directly at the beginning of the sometimes rather lengthy lists that IntelliSense can now provide.

The code editor also performs some syntax checking on your code and underlines most syntax errors with a short wavy line, even before you compile the code. Hovering the mouse pointer over the underlined text brings up a small box telling you what the error is. Visual Basic developers have been familiar with this feature, known as *design-time debugging*, for years; now C# and C++ developers can benefit from it as well.

Other Windows

In addition to the code editor, Visual Studio provides a number of other windows that allow you to view your project from different points of view.

The rest of this section describes several other windows. If one of these windows is not visible on your screen, you can select it from the View menu. To show the design view and code editor, right-click the file name in the Solution Explorer and select View Designer or View Code from the context menu, or select the item from the toolbar at the top of the Solution Explorer. The design view and code editor share the same tabbed window.

The Design View Window

If you are designing a user interface application, such as a Windows application, Windows control library, or an ASP.NET application, you will use the Design View window. This window presents a visual overview of what your form will look like. You normally use the Design View window in conjunction with a window known as the toolbox. The toolbox contains a large number of .NET components that you can drag onto your program (see Figure 15-17).

Figure 15-17

The principle of the toolbox was applied in all development environments in Visual Studio 6, but with .NET, the number of components available from the toolbox has vastly increased. The categories of components available through the toolbox depend, to some extent, on the type of project you are editing — for example, you will get a far wider range when you are editing the `WindowsFormsApplication1` project in the `DemoSolution` solution than you will when you are editing the `ConsoleApplication1` project. The most important ranges of items available include the following:

- ❑ Data — Classes that allow you to connect to data sources and manage the data they contain. Here, you will find components for working with Microsoft SQL Server, Oracle, and any OleDb data source.

- ❑ Windows Forms Controls (labeled as Common Controls) — Classes that represent visual controls such as text boxes, list boxes, or tree views for working with thick-client applications.

- ❑ Web Forms Controls (labeled as Standard) — Classes that basically do the same thing as Windows controls, but that work in the context of Web browsers, and that work by sending HTML output to simulate the controls to the browser. (You will see this only when working with ASP.NET applications.)

- ❑ Components — Miscellaneous .NET classes that perform various useful tasks on your machine, such as connecting to directory services or to the event log.

You can also add your own custom categories to the toolbox by right-clicking any category and selecting Add Tab from the context menu. You can also place other tools in the toolbox by selecting Choose Items from the same context menu — this is particularly useful for adding your favorite COM components and ActiveX controls, which are not present in the toolbox by default. If you add a COM control, you can still click to place it in your project just as you would with a .NET control. Visual Studio automatically adds all the required COM interoperability code to allow your project to call up the control. In this case, what is actually added to your project is a .NET control that Visual Studio creates behind the scenes and that acts as a wrapper for your COM control.

> *C++ developers will recognize the toolbox as Visual Studio's (much-enhanced) version of the resource editor. Visual Basic developers might not be that impressed at first; after all, Visual Studio 6 also has a toolbox. However, the toolbox in Visual Studio has a dramatically different effect on your source code than its precursor.*

To see how the toolbox works, place a text box in your basic form project. You simply click the `TextBox` control contained within the toolbox and then click again to place it in the form in the design view (or if you prefer, you can simply drag and drop the control directly onto the design surface). Now the design view looks like Figure 15-18, showing roughly what `WindowsFormsApplication1` will look like if you compile and run it.

If you look at the code view of your form, you see that Visual Studio 2008 does not add the code that instantiates a `TextBox` object to go on the form directly here as it did in the early versions of the IDE. Instead, you will need to expand the plus sign next to `Form1.cs` in the Visual Studio Solution Explorer. Here, you will find a file that is dedicated to the design of the form and the controls that are placed on the form — `Form1.Designer.cs`. In this class file, you will find a new member variable in the `Form1` class:

```
partial class Form1
{
    private System.Windows.Forms.TextBox textBox1;
```

There is also some code to initialize it in the method, `InitializeComponent()`, which is called from the `Form1` constructor:

```
/// <summary>
/// Required method for Designer support - do not modify
/// the contents of this method with the code editor.
/// </summary>
```

```
private void InitializeComponent()
{
        this.textBox1 = new System.Windows.Forms.TextBox();
        this.SuspendLayout();
        //
        // textBox1
        //
        this.textBox1.Location = new System.Drawing.Point(0, 0);
        this.textBox1.Name = "textBox1";
        this.textBox1.Size = new System.Drawing.Size(100, 20);
        this.textBox1.TabIndex = 0;
        //
        // Form1
        //
        this.AutoScaleDimensions = new System.Drawing.SizeF(6F, 13F);
        this.AutoScaleMode = System.Windows.Forms.AutoScaleMode.Font;
        this.ClientSize = new System.Drawing.Size(284, 264);
        this.Controls.Add(this.textBox1);
        this.Name = "Form1";
        this.Text = "Form1";
        this.ResumeLayout(false);
        this.PerformLayout();

}
```

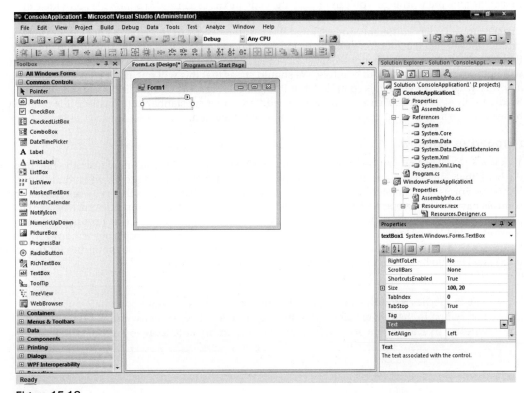

Figure 15-18

In one sense, there is no difference between the code editor and the design view; they simply present different views of the same code. What actually happened when you clicked to add the `TextBox` to the design view is that the editor placed the preceding extra code in your C# source file for you. The design view simply reflects this change because Visual Studio is able to read your source code and determine from it what controls should be around when the application starts up. This is a fundamental shift from the old Visual Basic way of looking at things, in which everything was based around the visual design. Now, your C# source code is what fundamentally controls your application, and the design view is just a different way of viewing the source code. Incidentally, if you do write any Visual Basic 2008 code with Visual Studio, you will find the same principles at work.

If you had wanted to, you could have worked the other way around. If you manually added the same code to your C# source files, Visual Studio would have automatically detected from the code that your application contained a `TextBox` control, and would have shown it in the design view at the designated position. It is best to add these controls visually, and let Visual Studio handle the initial code generation — it is a lot quicker and less error-prone to click the mouse button a couple of times than to type a few lines of code!

Another reason for adding these controls visually is that, to recognize that they are there, Visual Studio does need the relevant code to conform to certain criteria — and code that you write by hand might not do so. In particular, you will notice that the `InitializeComponent()` method that contains the code to initialize the `TextBox` is commented to warn you against modifying it. That is because this is the method that Visual Studio looks at to determine what controls are around when your application starts up. If you create and define a control somewhere else in your code, Visual Studio will not be aware of it, and you will not be able to edit it in the design view or in certain other useful windows.

In fact, despite the warnings, you can modify the code in `InitializeComponent()`, provided that you are careful. There is generally no harm in changing the values of some of the properties, for example, so that a control displays different text or so that it is a different size. In practice, the developer studio is pretty robust when it comes to working around any other code you place in this method. Just be aware that if you make too many changes to `InitializeComponent()`, you do run the risk that Visual Studio will not recognize some of your controls. We should stress that this will not affect your application in any way whatsoever when it is compiled, but it might disable some of the editing features of Visual Studio for those controls. Hence, if you want to add any other substantial initialization, it is probably better to do so in the `Form1` constructor or in some other method.

The Properties Window

This is another window that has its origins in the old Visual Basic IDE. You know from the first part of the book that .NET classes can implement properties. In fact, as you will discover when building Windows Forms (see Chapter 31, "Windows Forms"), the .NET base classes that represent forms and controls have a lot of properties that define their action or appearance — properties such as `Width`, `Height`, `Enabled` (whether the user can type input to the control), and `Text` (the text displayed by the control) — and Visual Studio knows about many of these properties. The Properties window, shown in Figure 15-19, displays and allows you to edit the initial values of most of these properties for the controls that Visual Studio has been able to detect by reading your source code.

> The Properties window can also show events. You can view events for what you are focused on in the IDE or selected in the drop-down list box directly in the Properties window by clicking the icon that looks like a lightning bolt at the top of the window.

Figure 15-19

At the top of the Properties window is a list box that allows you to select which control you want to view. In the example in this chapter, you have selected Form1, the main form class for your WindowsFormsApplication1 project, and have edited the text to "Basic Form — Hello!" If you now check the source code, you can see that what you have actually done is edit the source code — using a friendlier user interface:

```
this.AutoScaleDimensions = new System.Drawing.SizeF(6F, 13F);
this.AutoScaleMode = System.Windows.Forms.AutoScaleMode.Font;
this.ClientSize = new System.Drawing.Size(284, 264);
this.Controls.Add(this.textBox1);
this.Name = "Form1";
this.Text = "Basic Form - Hello";
this.ResumeLayout(false);
this.PerformLayout();
```

Not all the properties shown in the Properties window are explicitly mentioned in your source code. For those that are not, Visual Studio will display the default values that were set when the form was created and that are set when the form is actually initialized. Obviously, if you change a value for one of these properties in the Properties window, a statement explicitly setting that property will magically appear in your source code — and vice versa. It is interesting to note that if a property is changed from its original value, this property will then appear in bold type within the list box of the Properties window. Sometimes double-clicking the property in the Properties window returns the value to its original value.

The Properties window provides a convenient way to get a broad overview of the appearance and properties of a particular control or window.

It is interesting to note that the Properties window is implemented as a System.Windows.Forms *.*PropertyGrid *instance, which will internally use the reflection technology described in Chapter 13, "Reflection," to identify the properties and property values to display.*

The Class View Window

Unlike the Properties window, the Class View window, shown in Figure 15-20, owes its origins to the C++ (and J++) developer environments. This window will be new to Visual Basic developers because Visual Basic 6 did not even support the concept of the class, other than in the sense of a COM component. The class view is not actually treated by Visual Studio as a window in its own right — rather it is an additional tab to the Solution Explorer window. By default, the class view will not even appear in the Visual Studio Solution Explorer. To invoke the class view, select View ⇨ Class View. The class view (see Figure 15-20) shows the hierarchy of the namespaces and classes in your code. It gives you a tree view that you can expand to see what namespaces contain what classes and what classes contain what members.

A nice feature of the class view is that if you right-click the name of any item for which you have access to the source code, then the context menu features the Go To Definition option, which takes you to the definition of the item in the code editor. Alternatively, you can do this by double-clicking the item in class view (or, indeed, by right-clicking the item you want in the source code editor and choosing the same option from the resulting context menu). The context menu also gives you the option to add a field, method, property, or indexer to a class. This means that you specify the details of the relevant member in a dialog box, and the code is added for you. This might not be that useful for fields or methods, which can be quickly added to your code; however, you might find this feature helpful for properties and indexers, where it can save you quite a bit of typing.

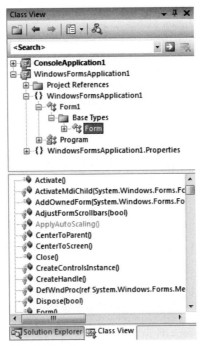

Figure 15-20

The Object Browser Window

One important aspect of programming in the .NET environment is being able to find out what methods and other code items are available in the base classes and any other libraries that you are referencing from your assembly. This feature is available through a window called the Object Browser. You can access this window by selecting Object Browser from the View menu in Visual Studio 2008.

The Object Browser window is quite similar to the Class View window in that it displays a tree view that gives the class structure of your application, allowing you to inspect the members of each class. The user interface is slightly different in that it displays class members in a separate pane rather than in the tree view itself. The real difference is that it lets you look at not just the namespaces and classes in your project but also the ones in all the assemblies referenced by the project. Figure 15-21 shows the Object Browser viewing the SystemException class from the .NET base classes.

One note of caution with the Object Browser is that it groups classes by the assembly in which they are located first and by namespace second. Unfortunately, because namespaces for the base classes are often spread across several assemblies, this means you might have trouble locating a particular class unless you know what assembly it is in.

The Object Browser is there to view .NET objects. If for any reason you want to investigate installed COM objects, you will find that the OLEView tool previously used in the C++ IDE is still available — it is located in the folder C:\Program Files\Microsoft SDKs\Windows\v6.0A\bin along with several other similar utilities.

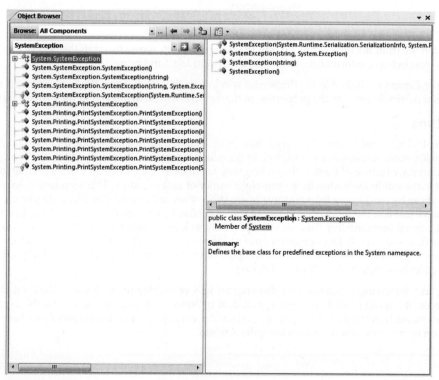

Figure 15-21

Visual Basic developers should not confuse the .NET Object Browser with the Object Browser of the Visual Basic 6 IDE. The .NET Object Browser is there to view .NET classes, whereas the tool of that name in Visual Basic 6 is used to view COM components. If you want the functionality of the old Object Browser, you should now use the OLEView tool.

The Server Explorer Window

You can use the Server Explorer window, shown in Figure 15-22, to find out about aspects of the computers in your network while coding.

Figure 15-22

As you can see from the screenshot, among the things you can access through the Server Explorer are database connections, information about services, event logs, and more.

The Server Explorer is linked to the Properties window so that if you open the Services node, for example, and click a particular service, the properties of that service will be displayed in the Properties window.

Pin Buttons

While exploring Visual Studio, you might have noticed that many of the windows have some interesting functionality more reminiscent of toolbars. In particular, apart from the code editor, they can all be docked. Another feature of them is that when they are docked, they have an extra icon that looks like a pin next to the minimize button in the top-right corner of each window. This icon really does act like a pin — it can be used to pin the windows open. When they are pinned (the pin is displayed vertically), they behave just like the regular windows that you are used to. When they are unpinned, however (the pin is displayed horizontally), they remain open only as long as they have the focus. As soon as they lose the focus (because you clicked or moved your mouse somewhere else), they smoothly retreat into the main border around the entire Visual Studio application. (You can also feel the speed of your computer by how quickly or slowly they open and close.)

Pinning and unpinning windows provides another way of making the best use of the limited space on your screen. It has not really been seen a great deal in Windows before, though a few third-party applications, such as PaintShop Pro, have used similar concepts. Pinned windows have, however, been around on many Unix-based systems for quite a while.

Building a Project

This section examines the options that Visual Studio gives you for building your project.

Building, Compiling, and Making

Before examining the various build options, it is important to clarify some terminology. You will often see three different terms used in connection with the process of getting from your source code to some sort of executable code: compiling, building, and making. The origin of these various terms comes from the fact that until recently, the process of getting from source code to executable code involved more than one step (and this is still the case in C++). This was due in large part to the number of source files in a program. In C++, for example, each source file needs to be compiled individually. This leads to what are known as object files, each containing something like executable code, but where each object file relates to only one source file. To generate an executable, these object files need to be linked together, a process that is officially known as linking. The combined process was usually referred to — at least on the Windows platform — as building your code. However, in C# terms the compiler is more sophisticated and is able to read in and treat all your source files as one block. Hence, there is not really a separate linking stage, so in the context of C# the terms *compile* and *build* are used interchangeably.

In addition to this, the term *make* basically means the same as *build*, though it is not really used in the context of C#. The term originated on old mainframe systems on which, when a project was composed of many source files, a separate file would be written that contained instructions to the compiler on how to build a project — which files to include and what libraries to link to and so on. This file was generally known as a make file and is still quite standard on Unix systems. Make files are not normally needed on Windows, though you can still write them (or get Visual Studio to generate them) if you need to.

Debug and Release Builds

The idea of having separate builds is very familiar to C++ developers and less so to those with a Visual Basic background. The point here is that when you are debugging, you typically want your executable to behave differently from when you are ready to ship the software. When you are ready to ship your software, you want the size of the executable to be as small as possible and the executable itself to be as fast as possible. Unfortunately, these requirements are not really compatible with your needs when you are debugging code, as explained in the following sections.

Optimization

High performance is achieved partly by the compiler doing many optimizations on the code. This means that the compiler actively looks at your source code as it is compiling to identify places where it can modify the precise details of what you are doing in a way that does not change the overall effect but that makes things more efficient. For example, if the compiler encountered the following source code:

```
double InchesToCm(double Ins)
{
    return Ins*2.54;
}

// later on in the code

Y = InchesToCm(X);
```

it might replace it with this:

```
Y = X * 2.54;
```

Or it might replace this code:

```
{
    string Message = "Hi";
    Console.WriteLine(Message);
}
```

with this:

```
Console.WriteLine("Hi");
```

By doing so, it bypasses having to declare an unnecessary object reference in the process.

It is not possible to exactly pin down what optimizations the C# compiler does — nor whether the two previous examples actually would occur with any particular example — because those kinds of details are not documented. (Chances are that for managed languages such as C#, the previous optimizations would occur at JIT compilation time, not when the C# compiler compiles source code to assembly.) For obvious commercial reasons, companies that write compilers are usually quite reluctant to give too many details about the tricks that their compilers use. We should stress that optimizations do not affect your source code — they affect only the contents of the executable code. However, the previous examples should give you a good idea of what to expect from optimizations.

The problem is that although optimizations like the previous ones help a great deal in making your code run faster, they are not that helpful for debugging. Suppose with the first example that you want to set a breakpoint inside the InchesToCm() method to see what's going on in there. How can you possibly do that if the executable code does not actually have an InchesToCm() method because the compiler has removed it? Moreover, how can you set a watch on the Message variable when that does not exist in the compiled code either?

Debugger Symbols

When you are debugging, you often have to look at values of variables, and you will specify them by their source code names. The trouble is that executable code generally does not contain those names — the compiler replaces the names with memory addresses. .NET has modified this situation somewhat, to the extent that certain items in assemblies are stored with their names, but this is only true of a small minority of items — such as public classes and methods — and those names will still be removed when the assembly is JIT-compiled. Asking the debugger to tell you what the value is in the variable called HeightInInches is not going to get you very far if, when the debugger examines the executable code, it sees only addresses and no reference to the name HeightInInches anywhere. Therefore, to debug properly, you need to have extra debugging information made available in the executable. This information includes, among other things, names of variables and line information that allows the debugger to match up which executable machine assembly language instructions correspond to those of your original source code instructions. You will not, however, want that information in a release build, both for commercial reasons (debugging information makes it a lot easier for other people to disassemble your code) and because it increases the size of the executable.

Extra Source Code Debugging Commands

A related issue is that quite often while you are debugging there will be extra lines in your code to display crucial debugging-related information. Obviously, you want the relevant commands removed entirely from the executable before you ship the software. You could do this manually, but wouldn't it be so much easier if you could simply mark those statements in some way so that the compiler ignores them when it is compiling your code to be shipped? You've already seen in the first part of the book how this can be done in C# by defining a suitable processor symbol, and possibly using this in conjunction with the Conditional attribute, giving you what is known as *conditional compilation*.

What all these factors add up to is that you need to compile almost all commercial software in a slightly different way when debugging than in the final product that is shipped. Visual Studio is able to consider this because, as you have already seen, it stores details of all the options that it is supposed to pass to the compiler when it has your code compiled. All that Visual Studio has to do to support different types of builds is to store more than one set of such details. The different sets of build information are referred to as configurations. When you create a project, Visual Studio automatically gives you two configurations, called Debug and Release:

❑ The Debug configuration commonly specifies that no optimizations are to take place, extra debugging information is to be present in the executable, and the compiler is to assume that the debug preprocessor symbol Debug is present unless it is explicitly #undefined in the source code.

❑ The Release configuration specifies that the compiler should optimize, that there should be no extra debugging information in the executable, and that the compiler should not assume that any particular preprocessor symbol is present.

You can define your own configurations as well. You might want to do this, for example, if you want to set up professional-level builds and enterprise-level builds so that you can ship two versions of the software. In the past, because of issues concerning the Unicode character encodings being supported on Windows NT but not on Windows 95, it was common for C++ projects to feature a Unicode configuration and an MBCS (multi-byte character set) configuration.

Selecting a Configuration

One obvious question is that, because Visual Studio stores details of more than one configuration, how does it determine which one to use when arranging for a project to be built? The answer is that there is always an active configuration, which is the configuration that will be used when you ask Visual Studio to build a project. (Note that configurations are set for each project rather than for each solution.)

By default, when you create a project, the Debug configuration is the active configuration. You can change which configuration is the active one by clicking the Build menu option and selecting the Configuration Manager item. It is also available through a drop-down menu in the main Visual Studio toolbar.

Editing Configurations

In addition to choosing the active configuration, you can also examine and edit the configurations. To do this, you select the relevant project in the Solution Explorer and then select the Properties from the Project menu. This brings up a very sophisticated dialog box. (Alternatively, you can access the same dialog box by right-clicking the name of the project in the Solution Explorer and then selecting Properties from the context menu.)

This dialog contains a tree view, which allows you to select many different general areas to examine or edit. We do not have space to show all of these areas, but we will show a couple of the most important ones.

Figure 15-23 shows a tabbed view of the available properties for a particular application. This screenshot shows the general application settings for the ConsoleApplication1 project that you created earlier in the chapter.

Among the points to note are that you can select the name of the assembly as well as the type of assembly to be generated. The options here are Console Application, Windows Application, and Class Library. You can, of course, change the assembly type if you want. (Though arguably, if you want, you might wonder why you did not pick the correct project type at the time that you asked Visual Studio to generate the project for you in the first place!)

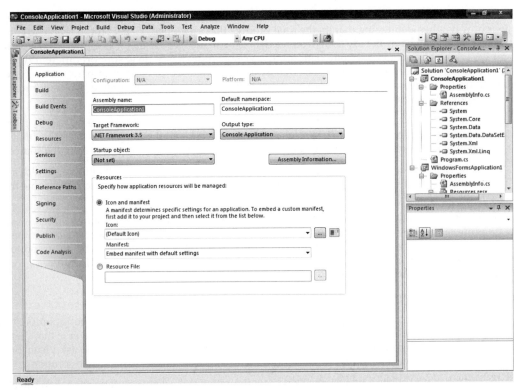

Figure 15-23

Figure 15-24 shows the build configuration properties. You will notice that a list box near the top of the dialog box allows you to specify which configuration you want to look at. You can see — in the case of the Debug configuration — that the compiler assumes that the DEBUG and TRACE preprocessor symbols have been defined. In addition, the code is not optimized and extra debugging information is generated.

In general, it is not that often that you will need to adjust the configuration settings. However, if you ever do need to use them, you now know the difference between the available configuration properties.

Debugging

After the long discussion about building and build configurations, you might be surprised to learn that this chapter is not going to spend a great deal of time discussing debugging itself. The reason for that is that the principles and the process of debugging — setting breakpoints and examining the values of variables — is not really significantly different in Visual Studio from any of the various Visual Studio 6 IDEs. Instead, this section briefly reviews the features offered by Visual Studio, focusing on those areas that might be new to some developers. It also discusses how to deal with exceptions, because these can cause problems during debugging.

In C#, as in pre-.NET languages, the main technique involved in debugging is simply setting breakpoints and using them to examine what is going on in your code at a certain point in its execution.

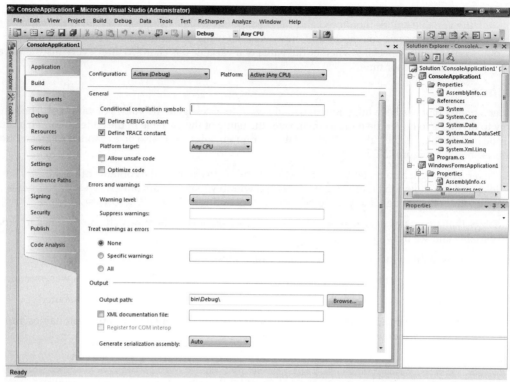

Figure 15-24

Breakpoints

You can set breakpoints from Visual Studio on any line of your code that is actually executed. The simplest way is to click the line in the code editor, within the shaded area toward the far left of the document window (or press the F9 key when the appropriate line is selected). This sets up a breakpoint on that particular line, which causes execution to break and control to be transferred to the debugger as soon as that line is reached in the execution process. As in previous versions of Visual Studio, a breakpoint is indicated by a large circle to the left of the line in the code editor. Visual Studio also highlights the line by displaying the text and background in a different color. Clicking the circle again removes the breakpoint.

If breaking every time at a particular line is not adequate for your particular problem, you can also set conditional breakpoints. To do this, select Debug ⇨ Windows ⇨ Breakpoints. This brings up a dialog box asking you for details of the breakpoint you want to set. Among the options available, you can:

❑   Specify that execution should break only after the breakpoint has been passed a certain number of times.

❑   Specify that the breakpoint should come into effect only every so many times that the line is reached, for example, every twentieth time that a line is executed. (This is useful when debugging large loops.)

❑ Set the breakpoints relative to a variable rather than to an instruction. In this case, the value of the variable will be monitored and the breakpoints will be triggered whenever the value of this variable changes. You might find, however, that using this option slows down your code considerably. Checking whether the value of a variable has changed after every instruction adds a lot of processor time.

Watches

After a breakpoint has been hit, you will usually want to investigate the values of variables. The simplest way to do this is to hover the mouse cursor over the name of the variable in the code editor. This causes a little box that shows the value of that variable to pop up, which can also be expanded to greater detail. This is shown in Figure 15-25.

However, you might also prefer to use the Autos window to examine the contents of variables. The Autos window (shown in Figure 15-26) is a tabbed window that appears only when the program is running under the debugger. If you do not see it, try selecting Debug ⇨ Windows ⇨ Autos.

Variables that are classes or structs are shown with a + icon next to them, which you can click to expand the variable and see the values of its fields.

The three tabs to this window are each designed to monitor different variables:

❑ **Autos** monitors the last few variables that have been accessed as the program was executing.

❑ **Locals** monitors variables that are accessible in the method currently being executed.

❑ **Watch** monitors any variables that you have explicitly specified by typing their names into the Watch window.

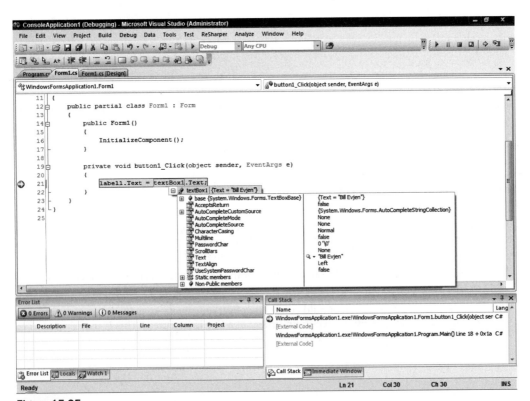

Figure 15-25

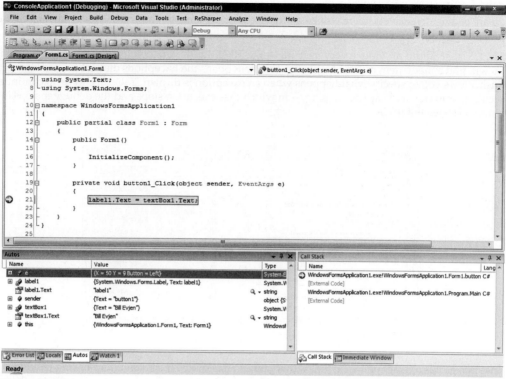

Figure 15-26

Exceptions

Exceptions are great when you ship your application and for making sure that error conditions are handled in an appropriate way within your application. Used well, they can ensure that your application copes with difficulties well and that the user is never presented with a technical dialog box. Unfortunately, exceptions are not so great when you are trying to debug your application. The problem is twofold:

❑   If an exception occurs when you are debugging, you often do not want it to be handled automatically — especially if automatically handling it means retiring gracefully and terminating execution! Rather, you want the debugger to help you find why the exception has occurred. Of course, the trouble is that if you have written good, robust, defensive code, your program will automatically handle almost anything — including the bugs that you want to detect!

❑   If an exception occurs that you have not written a handler for, the .NET runtime will still go off looking for a handler. However, by the time it discovers that there is not one, it will have terminated your program. There will not be a call stack left, and you will not be able to look at the values of any of your variables because they will all have gone out of scope.

Of course, you can set breakpoints in your catch blocks, but that often does not help very much because when the `catch` block is reached, flow of execution will, by definition, have exited the corresponding `try` block. That means that the variables you probably wanted to examine the values of to figure out what has gone wrong will have gone out of scope. You will not even be able to look at the stack trace to find what method was being executed when the `throw` statement occurred — because control will have left that method. Setting the breakpoints at the `throw` statement will of course solve this, except that if you are coding defensively, there will be many `throw` statements in your code. How can you tell which one is the one that threw the exception?

In fact, Visual Studio provides a very neat answer to all of this. If you look into the main Debug menu, you will find a menu item called Exceptions. This item opens the Exceptions dialog box (see Figure 15-27), which allows you to specify what happens when an exception is thrown. You can choose to continue execution or to stop and start debugging — in which case execution stops and the debugger steps in at the `throw` statement itself.

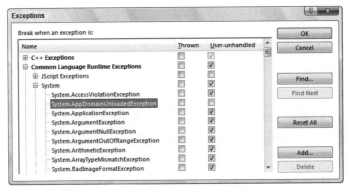

Figure 15-27

What makes this a really powerful tool is that you can customize the behavior according to which class of exception is thrown. For example, in Figure 15-27, we have told Visual Studio to break into the debugger whenever it encounters any exception thrown by a .NET base class, but not to break into the debugger if the exception is an `AppDomainUnloadedException`.

Visual Studio knows about all the exception classes available in the .NET base classes, and about quite a few exceptions that can be thrown outside the .NET environment. Visual Studio is not automatically aware of your own custom exception classes that you write, but you can manually add your exception classes to the list and thereby specify which of your exceptions should cause execution to stop immediately. To do this, just click the Add button (which is enabled when you have selected a top-level node from the tree) and type in the name of your exception class.

Refactoring

Many developers develop their applications first for functionality and then, once the functionality is in place, they *rework* their applications to make them more manageable and more readable. This is called *refactoring*. Refactoring is the process of reworking code for readability, performance, providing type safety, and lining applications up to better adhere to standard OO (object-oriented) programming practices.

For this reason, the C# environment of Visual Studio 2008 now includes a set of refactoring tools. You can find these tools under the Refactoring option in the Visual Studio menu. To show this in action, create a new class called `Car` in Visual Studio:

```
using System;
using System.Collections.Generic;
using System.Text;

namespace ConsoleApplication1
```

```
    {
        public class Car
        {
            public string _color;
            public string _doors;

            public int Go()
            {
                int speedMph = 100;
                return speedMph;
            }
        }
    }
```

Now, suppose that in the idea of refactoring, you want to change the code a bit so that the color and the door variables are encapsulated into public .NET properties. The refactoring capabilities of Visual Studio 2008 allow you to simply right-click either of these properties in the document window and select Refactor ⇨ Encapsulate Field. This will pull up the Encapsulate Field dialog shown in Figure 15-28.

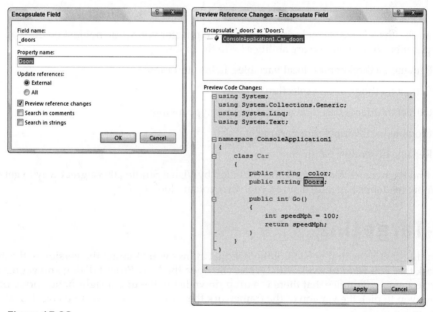

Figure 15-28

From this dialog, you can provide the name of the property and click the OK button. This will turn the selected public field into a private field, while also encapsulating the field into a public .NET property. After clicking OK, the code will have been reworked to the following (after redoing both fields):

```
namespace ConsoleApplication1
{
    public class Car
    {
        private string _color;

        public string Color
```

(continued)

(continued)

```
        {
            get { return _color; }
            set { _color = value; }
        }
        private string _doors;

        public string Doors
        {
            get { return _doors; }
            set { _doors = value; }
        }

        public int Go()
        {
            int speedMph = 100;
            return speedMph;
        }
    }
}
```

As you can see, these wizards make it quite simple to refactor your code not just on one page but for an entire application. Also included are abilities to do the following:

❑   Rename method names, local variables, fields, and more

❑   Extract methods from a selection of code

❑   Extract interfaces based on a set of existing type members

❑   Promote local variables to parameters

❑   Rename or reorder parameters

You will find the new refactoring abilities provided by Visual Studio 2008 a great way to get you the cleaner, more readable, better-structured code that you are looking for.

Multi-Targeting

Visual Studio 2008 is the first version of the IDE that allows you to target the version of the .NET Framework that you want to work with. When you open the New Project dialog and get ready to create a new project, you will notice that there is a drop-down list in the upper right-hand corner of the dialog that allows you to pick the version of the framework that you are interested in using. This dialog is presented in Figure 15-29.

From this figure, you can see that the drop-down list provides you the ability to target the .NET Framework 2.0, 3.0, or 3.5. This is possible only because the 3.0 and 3.5 versions of the framework are extensions of the .NET Framework 2.0. When you use the upgrade dialog to upgrade a Visual Studio 2005 solution to Visual Studio 2008, it is important that you are only upgrading the solution to *use* Visual Studio 2008 and that you are not upgrading your project to the .NET Framework 3.5. Your project will stay on the framework version you were using, but now, you will be able use the new Visual Studio 2008 to work on your project.

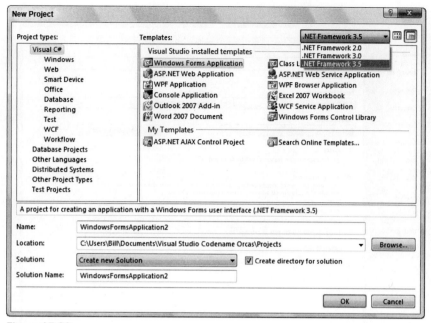

Figure 15-29

If you want to change the version of the framework the solution is using, right-click the solution and select the properties of the solution. If you are working with an ASP.NET project, you will get a dialog as shown in Figure 15-30.

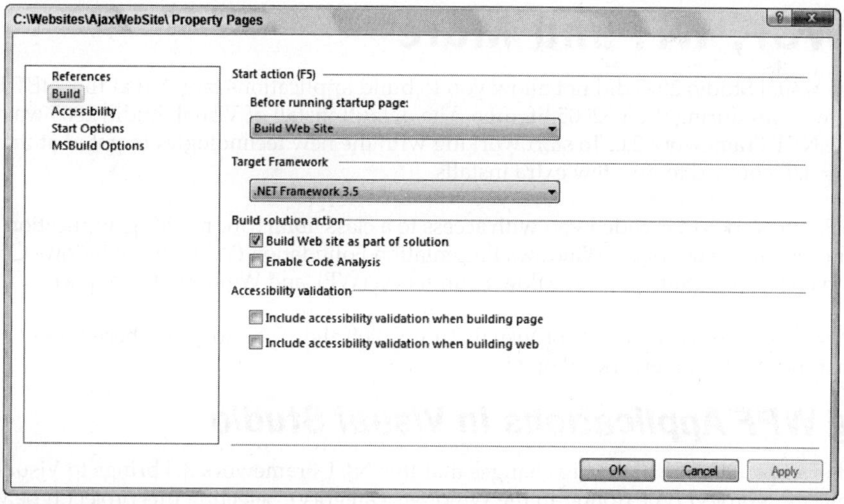

Figure 15-30

From this dialog, the Build tab will provide you the ability to change the version of the framework that the application is using. If you are working with a Windows Forms application's property pages, you will find the ability to target another version of the framework on the Application tab (the first tab). This is presented in Figure 15-31.

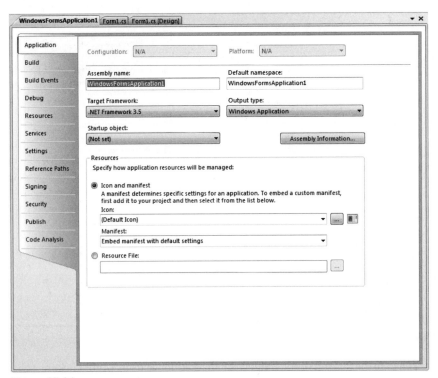

Figure 15-31

WPF, WCF, WF, and More

By default, Visual Studio 2005 did not allow you to build applications targeted at the .NET Framework 3.0, which was out during the VS2005 lifetime. The default install of Visual Studio 2005 was targeted only at the .NET Framework 2.0. To start working with the new technologies targeted at the .NET Framework 3.0, you had to do a few extra installs.

The .NET Framework 3.0 provided you with access to a class library for building application types such as applications that make use of the Windows Presentation Foundation (WPF), the Windows Communication Foundation (WCF), the Windows Workflow Foundation (WF), and Windows CardSpace.

The targeted framework capabilities of Visual Studio 2008 allow you to build these types of applications using either the .NET Framework 3.0 or 3.5.

Building WPF Applications in Visual Studio

One good example of some of the big changes that the .NET Framework 3.5 brings to Visual Studio is the WPF Application project type (found in the Windows category). Selecting this project type will create a `Window1.xaml` and `Window1.xaml.cs` file for you to work from. Everything that is created by default with this project type in the Solution Explorer is presented in Figure 15-32 (shown here with the new and searchable Properties dialog).

Figure 15-32

Right away, the biggest change you will notice in Visual Studio 2008 is contained within the document window. The default view of the document window after creating this project is presented in Figure 15-33.

The document window has two views — a design view and an XAML view. Making changes in the design view will make the appropriate changes in the XAML view, and vice versa. As with traditional Windows Forms applications, WPF applications also include the ability to use controls that are contained within Visual Studio's toolbox. This new toolbox of controls is presented in Figure 15-34.

Building WF Applications in Visual Studio

Another dramatically different application style (when it comes to building the application from within Visual Studio) is the Windows Workflow application type. For an example of this, select the Sequential Workflow Console Application project type from the Workflow section of the New Project dialog. This will create a console application as illustrated here with a view of the Solution Explorer (see Figure 15-35).

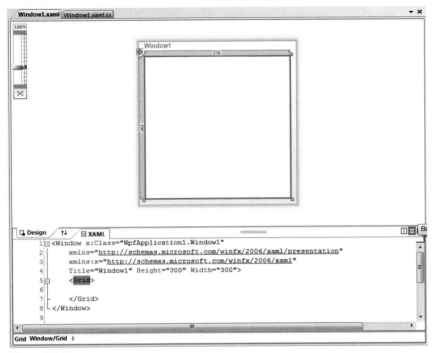

Figure 15-33

Figure 15-34

Figure 15-35

One big change you see when building applications that make use of the Windows Workflow Foundation is that there is a heavy dependency on the design view. Looking closely at the workflow (see Figure 15-36), you can see that it is made up of multiple sequential steps and even includes actions based on conditions (such as an `if-else` statement).

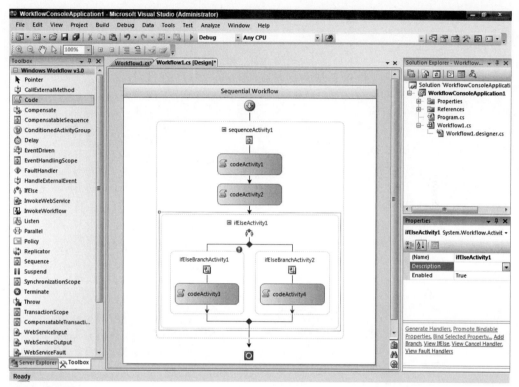

Figure 15-36

Summary

This chapter explored one of the most important programming tools in the .NET environment — Visual Studio 2008. The bulk of the chapter examined how this tool facilitates writing code in C# (and C++ and Visual Basic 2008).

Visual Studio 2008 is one of the easiest development environments to work with in the programming world. You will find that Visual Studio makes Rapid Application Development (RAD) easy to achieve, but at the same time, you can dig deep into the mechanics of how your applications are created. This chapter focused on using Visual Studio for everything from refactoring to multi-targeting to reading in Visual Studio 6 projects and to debugging. It also covered many of the windows available to Visual Studio.

This chapter also looked at the new projects available to you through the .NET Framework 3.5. These new project types focused on the Windows Presentation Foundation, the Windows Communication Foundation, and the Windows Workflow Foundation.

Chapter 16 presents the deployment situation in detail.

16

Deployment

The development process does not end when the source code is compiled and testing is complete. At that stage, the job of getting the application into the user's hands begins. Whether it's an ASP.NET application, a smart client application, or an application built using the Compact Framework, the software must be deployed to a target environment. The .NET Framework has made deployment much easier than it was in the past. The pains of registering COM components and writing new hives to the registry are all gone.

This chapter looks at the options that are available for application deployment, both from an ASP.NET perspective and from the smart client perspective. The following topics are discussed:

- ❑ Deployment requirements
- ❑ Simple deployment scenarios
- ❑ Windows Installer–based projects
- ❑ ClickOnce

Designing for Deployment

Often, deployment is an afterthought in the development process that can lead to nasty, if not costly, surprises. To avoid grief in deployment scenarios, the deployment process should be planned out during the initial design stage. Any special deployment considerations — such as server capacity, desktop security, or where assemblies will be loaded from — should be built into the design from the start, resulting in a much smoother deployment process.

Another issue that must be addressed early in the development process is the environment in which to test the deployment. Whereas unit testing of application code and of deployment options can be done on the developer's system, the deployment must be tested in an environment that resembles the target system. This is important to eliminate the dependencies that don't exist on a targeted computer. An example of this might be a third-party library that has been installed on the developer's computer early in the project. The target computer might not have this library on it. It can be easy to forget to include it in the deployment package. Testing on the developer's system would not uncover the error because the library already exists. Documenting dependencies can help in eliminating this potential problem.

Deployment processes can be very complex for a large application. Planning for the deployment can save time and effort when the deployment process is implemented.

Deployment Options

This section provides an overview of the deployment options that are available to .NET developers. Most of these options are discussed in greater detail later in this chapter.

Xcopy

The xcopy utility enables you to copy an assembly or group of assemblies to an application folder, cutting down on your development time. Because assemblies are self-discovering (that is, the metadata that describes the assembly is included in the assembly), there is no need to register anything in the registry. Each assembly keeps track of what other assemblies it requires to execute. By default, the assembly looks in the current application folder for the dependencies. The process of moving (or probing) assemblies to other folders is discussed later in this chapter.

Copy Web Tool

If you are developing a Web project, using the Copy Web tool option on the Web site menu will copy the components needed to run the application to the server.

Publishing Web Sites

When a Web site is published, the entire site is compiled and then copied to a specified location. As a result of precompiling, all source code is removed from the final output and all compile errors can be found and dealt with.

Deployment Projects

Visual Studio 2008 has the capability to create setup programs for an application. There are four options based on Microsoft Windows Installer technology: creating merge modules, creating a setup for client applications, creating a setup for Web applications, and creating a setup for Smart Device (Compact Framework) based applications. The ability to create cab files is also available. Deployment projects offer a great deal of flexibility and customization for the setup process. One of these deployment options will be useful for larger applications.

ClickOnce

ClickOnce is a way to build self-updating Windows-based applications. ClickOnce allows an application to be published to a Web site, file share, or even a CD. As updates and new builds are made to the application they can be published to the same location or site by the development team. As the application is used by the end user, it will check the location and see if an update is available. If there is, an update is attempted.

Deployment Requirements

It is instructive to look at the runtime requirements of a .NET-based application. The CLR does have certain requirements on the target platform before any managed application can execute.

The first requirement that must be met is the operating system. Currently, the following operating systems can run .NET-based applications:

- ❑ Windows 98
- ❑ Windows 98 Second Edition (SE)
- ❑ Windows Millennium Edition (ME)
- ❑ Windows NT 4.0 (Service Pack 6a)
- ❑ Windows 2000
- ❑ Windows XP Home
- ❑ Windows XP Professional
- ❑ Windows XP Professional TabletPC Edition
- ❑ Windows Vista

The following server platforms are supported:

- ❑ Windows 2000 Server and Advanced Server
- ❑ Windows 2003 Server Family

Other requirements are Windows Internet Explorer version 5.01 or later, MDAC version 2.6 or later (if the application is designed to access data), and Internet Information Services (IIS) for ASP.NET applications.

You also must consider hardware requirements when deploying .NET applications. The minimum requirements for hardware are as follows:

- ❑ **Client** — Pentium 90 MHz and 32 MB RAM
- ❑ **Server** — Pentium 133 MHz and 128 MB RAM

For best performance, increase the amount of RAM — the more RAM the better your .NET application runs. This is especially true for server applications.

If you want to run .NET 3.0 applications that make use of Windows Presentation Foundation (WPF), Windows Communication Foundation (WCF), or Windows Workflow Foundation (WF) the requirements are a little more strict. .NET 3.0 requires at least Windows XP SP2. The previous list is trimmed to the following:

- ❑ Windows XP Home (SP2)
- ❑ Windows XP Professional (SP2)
- ❑ Windows XP Professional TabletPC Edition (SP2)
- ❑ Windows Vista (not including IA64 platform)

The following server platforms are supported:

- ❑ Windows 2003 Server Family (SP1)
- ❑ Windows Server 2008 IA64 Edition

The minimum hardware requirements also change. They become Pentium 400 MHz and 96 MB RAM for both client and server.

Deploying the .NET Runtime

When an application is developed using .NET, there is a dependency on the .NET runtime. This may seem rather obvious, but sometimes the obvious can be overlooked. If the application does not use any .NET 3.0 features, then `dotnetfx.exe` (`netfx64.exe for 64 bit OS`) will be the only runtime installation required. If .NET 3.0 features are used, then `dotnetfx3.exe` will need to be used as well. If .NET 3.5 features are used, then `netfx35_x86.exe` will also have to be used.

In the following discussions on creating deployment packages, the inclusion of the runtime is optional. The installer can check to see if the proper runtime is installed, and if it isn't, the installer can then install the runtime from local media or even go to a specified download site and download and install the runtime.

Simple Deployment

If deployment is part of an application's original design considerations, deployment can be as simple as copying a set of files to the target computer. For a Web application, it can be a simple menu choice in Visual Studio 2008. This section discusses these simple deployment scenarios.

To see how the various deployment options are set up, you must have an application to deploy. The sample download at www.wrox.com contains three projects: `SampleClientApp`, `SampleWebApp`, and `AppSupport`. `SampleClientApp` is a smart client application. `SampleWebApp` is a simple Web app. `AppSupport` is a class library that contains one simple class that returns a string with the current date and time. `SampleClientApp` and `SampleWebApp` use `AppSupport` to fill a label with the output of `AppSupport`. To use the examples, first load and build `AppSupport`. Then, in each of the other applications, set a reference to the newly built `AppSupport.dll`.

Here is the code for the `AppSupport` assembly:

```
using System;

namespace AppSupport
  {
  /// <summary>
  /// Simple assembly to return date and time string.
  /// </summary>
  public class Support
  {
    private Support()
    {
    }

    public static string GetDateTimeInfo()
    {
      DateTime dt = DateTime.Now;
      return string.Concat(dt.ToLongDateString(), " ", dt.ToLongTimeString());
    }
  }
}
```

This simple assembly suffices to demonstrate the deployment options available to you.

Xcopy

Xcopy deployment is a term used for the process of copying a set of files to a folder on the target machine and then executing the application on the client. The term comes from the DOS command `xcopy.exe`. Regardless of the number of assemblies, if the files are copied into the same folder, the application will execute — rendering the task of editing the configuration settings or registry obsolete.

To see how an xcopy deployment works, execute the following steps:

1. Open the `SampleClientApp` solution (`SampleClientApp.sln`) that is part of the sample download file.

2. Change the target to Release and do a full compile.

3. Next, use either My Computer or File Explorer to navigate to the project folder `\SampleClientApp\bin\Release` and double-click `SampleClientApp.exe` to run the application.

4. Now, click the button to open another dialog. This verifies that the application functions properly. Of course, this folder is where Visual Studio placed the output, so you would expect the application to work.

5. Create a new folder and call it `ClientAppTest`. Copy the two files from the release folder to this new folder and then delete the release folder. Again, double-click the `SampleClientApp.exe` file to verify that it's working.

That's all there is to it; xcopy deployment provides the ability to deploy a fully functional application simply by copying the assemblies to the target machine. Just because the example that is used here is simple does not mean that this process cannot work for more complex applications. There really is no limit to the size or number of assemblies that can be deployed using this method. The reason that you might not want to use xcopy deployment is the ability to place assemblies in the global assembly cache (GAC) or the ability to add icons to the Start Menu. Also, if your application still relies on a COM library of some type, you will not be able to register the COM components easily.

Xcopy and Web Applications

Xcopy deployment can also work with Web applications with the exception of the folder structure. You must establish the virtual directory of your Web application and configure the proper user rights. This process is generally accomplished with the IIS administration tool. After the virtual directory is set up, the Web application files can be copied to the virtual directory. Copying a Web application's files can be a bit tricky. A couple of configuration files, as well as the images that the pages might be using, need to be accounted for.

Copy Web Tool

A better way would be to use the Copy Web tool. The Copy Web tool is accessed from the Website ⇨ Copy Web Site menu choice in Visual Studio 2008. It is basically an FTP client for transferring files to and from a remote location. The remote location can be any FTP or Web site including local Web sites, IIS Web sites, and Remote (FrontPage) Web sites. Another feature of the Copy Web tool is that it will synchronize files on the remote server with the source site. The source site will always be the site that is currently open in Visual Studio 2008. If the current project has multiple developers this tool can be used to keep changes in sync with the local development site. Changes can be synced back with a common server for testing.

Publishing a Web Site

Another deployment option for Web projects is to publish the Web site. Publishing a Web site will precompile the entire site and place the compiled version into a specified location. The location can be a file share, FTP location, or any other location that can be accessed via HTTP. The compilation process strips all source code from the assemblies and creates the DLLs for deployment. This also includes the markup contained in the `.ASPX` source files. Instead of containing the normal markup, the `.ASPX` files contain a pointer to an assembly. Each `.ASPX` file relates to an assembly. This process works regardless of the model: code behind or single file.

The advantages of publishing a Web site are speed and security. Speed is enhanced because all of the assemblies are already compiled. Otherwise, the first time a page is accessed there is a delay while the page and dependent code is compiled and cached. The security is enhanced because the source code is not deployed. Also, because everything is precompiled before deployment all compilation errors will be found.

You publish a Web site from the Website ⇨ Publish Web Site menu choice. You need to supply the location to publish to. Again, this can be a file share, FTP location, Web site, or local disk path. After the compilation is finished, the files are placed in the specified location. From there, they can be copied to a staging server, test server, or the production server.

Installer Projects

Xcopy deployment can be easy to use, but there are times when the lack of functionality becomes an issue. To overcome this shortcoming, Visual Studio 2008 has six installer project types. Four of these options are based on the Windows Installer technology. The following table lists the project types.

Project Type	Description
Setup Project	Used for the installation of client applications, middle-tier applications, and applications that run as a Windows Service.
Web Setup Project	Used for the installation of Web-based applications.
Merge Module Project	Creates `.msm` merge modules that can be used with other Windows Installer–based setup applications.
Cab Project	Creates `.cab` files for distribution through older deployment technologies.
Setup Wizard	Aids in the creation of a deployment project.
Smart Device CAB Project	CAB project for Pocket PC, Smartphone, and other CE-based applications.

Setup and Web Setup Projects are very similar. The key difference is that with Web Setup the project is deployed to a virtual directory on a Web server, whereas with Setup Project it is deployed to a folder structure. Both project types are based on Windows Installer and have all of the features of a Windows Installer–based setup program. Merge Module Project is generally used when you have created a component or library of functionality that is included in a number of deployment projects. By creating a merge module, you can set any configuration items specific to the component and without having to worry about them in the creation of the main deployment project. The Cab Project type simply creates cab files for the application. `.cab` files are used by older installation technologies as well as some Web-based installation processes. The Setup Wizard project type steps through the process of creating a deployment project, asking specific questions along the way. The following sections discuss how to create each of these deployment projects, what settings and properties can be changed, and what customization you can add.

What Is Windows Installer?

Windows Installer is a service that manages the installation, update, repair, and removal of applications on most Windows operating systems. It is part of Windows ME, Windows 2000, Windows XP, and Windows Vista and is available for Windows 95, Windows 98, and Windows NT 4.0. The current version of Windows Installer is 3.0.

Windows Installer tracks the installation of applications in a database. When an application has to be uninstalled, you can easily track and remove the registry settings that were added, the files that were copied to the hard drive, and the desktop and Start Menu icons that were added. If a particular file is still referenced by another application, the installer will leave it on the hard drive so that the other application doesn't break. The database also makes it possible to perform repairs. If a registry setting or a DLL associated with an application becomes corrupt or is accidentally deleted, you can repair the installation. During a repair, the installer reads the database from the last install and replicates that installation.

The deployment projects in Visual Studio 2008 give you the ability to create a Windows Installation package. The deployment projects give you access to most of what you will need to do in order to install a given application. However, if you need even more control, check out the Windows Installer SDK, which is part of the Platform SDK — it contains documentation on creating custom installation packages for your application. The following sections deal with creating these installation packages using the Visual Studio 2008 deployment projects.

Creating Installers

Creating installation packages for client applications or for Web applications is not that difficult. One of the first tasks is to identify all of the external resources your application requires, including configuration files, COM components, third-party libraries, and controls and images. Including a list of dependencies in the project documentation was discussed earlier. This is where having that documentation can prove to be very useful. Visual Studio 2008 can do a reasonable job of interrogating an assembly and retrieving the dependencies for it, but you still have to audit the findings to make sure that nothing is missing.

Another concern might be when in the overall process the install package is created. If you have an automated build process set up, you can include the building of the installation package upon a successful build of the project. Automating the process greatly reduces the chance for errors in what can be a time-consuming and complicated process for large projects. What you can do is to include the deployment project with the project solution. The Solution Property Pages dialog box has a setting for Configuration Properties. You can use this setting to select the projects that will be included for your various build configurations. If you select the Build check box under Release builds but not for the Debug builds, the installation package will be created only when you are creating a release build. This is the process used in the following examples. Figure 16-1 shows the Solution Property Pages dialog box of the SampleClientApp solution. Notice that the Debug configuration is displayed and that the Build check box is unchecked for the setup project.

Simple Client Application

In the following example, you create an installer for the SimpleClientApp solution (which is included in the sample download, together with the completed installer projects).

For the SimpleClientApp you create two deployment projects. One is done as a separate solution; the other is done in the same solution. This enables you to see the pros and cons of choosing each option.

The first example shows you how to create the deployment project in a separate solution. Before you get started on creating the deployment project, make sure that you have a release build of the application

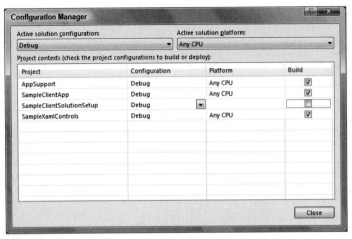

Figure 16-1

that will be deployed. Next, create a new project in Visual Studio 2008. In the New Project dialog box, select Setup and Deployment Projects on the left. On the right, select Setup Project and assign it a name of your choice (for example, `SampleClientStandaloneSetup`).

In the Solution Explorer window, click the project and then the Properties window. You will see a list of properties. These properties will be displayed during the setup of your application. Some of these properties are also displayed in the Add/Remove Programs Control Panel applet. Because most of these properties are visible to users during the installation process (or when they are looking at your installation in Add or Remove Programs), setting them correctly will add a professional touch to your application. The list of properties is important, especially if your application will be deployed commercially. The following table describes the properties and the values that you should enter.

Project Property	Description
AddRemoveProgramsIcon	The icon that appears in the Add/Remove dialog box.
Author	The author of the application. Generally this property setting is the same as the manufacturer. It is displayed on the Summary page of the Properties dialog of the `msi` package, as well as the Contact field of the SupportInfo page on the Add/Remove dialog box.
Description	A freeform text field that describes the application or component that is being installed. This information is displayed on the Summary page of the Properties dialog of the `msi` package, as well as the Comment field of the SupportInfo page on the Add/Remove dialog box.
DetectNewerInstalled Version	A Boolean value that, when set to `true`, will check to see if a newer version of the application is already installed. If so, the installation process will stop.
InstallAllUsers	Boolean value that, when set to `true`, will install that application for all users of the computer. If set to `false`, only the current user will have access.

Project Property	Description
Keywords	Keywords that can be used to search for the `.msi` file on the target computer. This information is displayed on the Summary page of the Properties dialog of the `msi` package.
Localization	The locale used for string resources and registry settings. This affects the user interface of the installer.
Manufacturer	Name of the company that manufactured the application or component. Typically, this is the same information as specified in the `Author` property. This information is displayed on the Summary page of the Properties dialog box of the `msi` package as well as the Publisher field of the SupportInfo page in the Add/Remove dialog box. It is used as part of the default installation path of the application.
ManufacturerURL	The URL for a Web site that relates to the application or component being installed.
PostBuildEvent	A command that is executed after the build ends.
PreBuildEvent	A command that is executed before the build begins.
ProductCode	A string GUID that is unique to this application or component. Windows Installer uses this property to identify the application for subsequent upgrades or installs.
ProductName	A name that describes the application. Used as the description of an application in the Add/Remove dialog box as well as part of the default install path: `C:\Program Files\Manufacturer\ProductName`.
RemovePrevious-Versions	Boolean value that, if set to `true`, will check for a previous version of the application. If yes, the uninstall function of the previous version is called before installation continues. This property uses `ProductCode` and `UpgradeCode` to determine if uninstall should occur. `UpgradeCode` should be the same; `ProductCode` should be different.
RunPostBuildEvent	When the `PostBuildEvent` should be run. Options are On successful build or Always.
SearchPath	A string that represents the search path for dependent assemblies, files, or merge modules. Used when the installer package is built on the development machine.
Subject	Additional information regarding the application. This information is displayed on the Summary page of the Properties dialog box of the `msi` package.
SupportPhone	A phone number for support of the application or component. This information is displayed in the Support Information field of the SupportInfo page on the Add/Remove dialog box.
SupportURL	A URL for support of the application or component. This information is displayed in the Support Information field of the SupportInfo page in the Add/Remove dialog box.
TargetPlatform	Supports the 32- or 64-bit versions of Windows.

Project Property	Description
Title	The title of the installer. This is displayed on the Summary page of the Properties dialog box of the msi package.
UpgradeCode	A string GUID that represents a shared identifier of different versions of the same application. The UpgradeCode should not change for different versions or different language versions of the application. Used by DetectNewerInstalledVersion and RemovePreviousVersion.
Version	The version number of the installer, .cab file, or merge module. Note that this is not the version of the application being installed.

After you have set the properties, you can start to add assemblies. In this example, the only assembly you have to add is the main executable (SampleClientApp.exe). To do this, you can either right-click the project in the Solution Explorer or select Add from the Project menu. You have four options:

❑ Project Output —You explore this option in the next example.

❑ File — This is used for adding a readme text file or any other file that is not part of the build process.

❑ Merge Module — A merge module that was created separately.

❑ Assembly — Use this option to select an assembly that is part of the installation.

Choose Assembly for this example. You will be presented with the Component Selector dialog box, which resembles the dialog box you use for adding references to a project. Browse to the \bin\release folder of your application. Select SampleClientApp.exe and click OK in the Component Selector dialog box. You can now see SampleClientApp.exe listed in the Solution Explorer of the deployment project. In the Detected Dependencies section, you can see that Visual Studio interrogated SampleClientApp.exe to find the assemblies on which it depends; in this case AppSupport.dll is included automatically. You would continue this process until all of the assemblies in your application are accounted for in the Solution Explorer of the deployment project.

Next, you have to determine where the assemblies will be deployed. By default, the File System editor is displayed in Visual Studio 2008. The File System editor is split into two panes: the left pane shows the hierarchical structure of the file system on the target machine; the right pane provides a detail view of the selected folder. The folder names might not be what you expect to see, but keep in mind that these are for the target machine. For example, the folder labeled User's Programs Menu maps to the C:\Documents and Settings\User Name\Start Menu\Programs folder on the target client.

You can add other folders at this point, either special folders or a custom folder. To add a special folder make sure that File System on Target Machine is highlighted in the left pane, and select Action menu on the main menu. The Add Special Folder menu choice provides a list of folders that can be added. For example, if you want to add a folder under the Application folder, you can select the Application Folder folder in the left pane of the editor and then select the Action menu. This time, there will be an Add menu that enables you to create the new folder. Rename the new folder and it will be created for you on the target machine.

One of the special folders that you might want to add is a folder for the GAC. AppSupport.dll can be installed to the GAC if it is used by several different applications. In order to add an assembly to the GAC, it does have to have a strong name. The process for adding the assembly to the GAC is to add the GAC from the Special Folder menu as described previously and then drag the assembly that you want in the GAC from the current folder to the Global Assembly Cache folder. If you try to do this with an assembly that is not strongly named, the deployment project will not compile.

If you select Application Folder, you will see on the right pane that the assemblies that you added are automatically added to the Application folder. You can move the assemblies to other folders, but keep in mind that the assemblies have to be able to find each other. (For more details on probing, see Chapter 17, "Assemblies.")

If you want to add a shortcut to the application on the user's desktop or to the Start Menu, drag the items to the appropriate folders. To create a desktop shortcut, go to the Application folder. On the right side of the editor select the application. Go to the Action menu, and select the Create Shortcut item to create a shortcut to the application. After the shortcut is created, drag it to the User's Desktop folder. Now when the application is installed, the shortcut will appear on the desktop. Typically, it is up to the user to decide if he or she wants a desktop shortcut to your application. The process of asking the user for input and taking conditional steps is explored later in this chapter. The same process can be followed to create an item in the Start Menu. Also, if you look at the properties for the shortcut that you just created, you will see that you can configure the basic shortcut properties such as Arguments and what icon to use. The application icon is the default icon.

Before you build the deployment project you might have to check some project properties. If you select Project menu, then SampleClientStandaloneSetup Properties, you will see the project Property Pages dialog box. These are properties that are specific to a current configuration. After selecting the configuration in the Configuration drop-down, you can change the properties listed in the following table.

Property	Description
Output file name	The name of the .msi or .msm file that is generated when the project is compiled.
Package files	This property enables you to specify how the files are packaged. Your options are:
	As loose uncompressed files — All of the deployment files are stored in the same directory as the .msi file.
	In setup file — Files are packaged in the .msi file (default setting).
	In cabinet file(s) — Files are in one or more .cab files in the same directory. When this is selected the CAB file size option becomes available.
Prerequisites URL	Allows you to specify where prerequisites such as the .NET Framework or Windows Installer 2.0 can be found. Clicking the Settings button will display a dialog that has the following technologies available to include in the setup:
	Windows Installer 2.0 .NET Framework Microsoft Visual J# .NET Redistributable Package 2.0 SQL Server 2008 Express Edition Microsoft Data Access Components 2.8
	There is also an option to have the prerequisites downloaded from a predefined URL or to have them loaded from the same location as the setup.
Compression	This specifies the compression style for the files included. Your options are:
	Optimized for speed — Larger files but faster installation time (default setting).
	Optimized for size — Smaller files but slower installation time.
	None — No compression applied.
CAB size	This is enabled when the Package file setting is set to In cabinet files. Unlimited creates one single cabinet file; custom allows you to set the maximum size for each .cab file.

Property	Description
Authenticode signature	When this is checked, the deployment project output is signed using Authenticode; the default setting is unchecked.
Certificate file	The certificate used for signing.
Private key file	The private key that contains the digital encryption key for the signed files.
Timestamp server URL	URL for timestamp server. This is also used for Authenticode signing.

After you have set the project properties, you should be able to build the deployment project and create the setup for the SampleClientApp application. After you build the project, you can test the installation by right-clicking the project name in the Solution Explorer. This enables you to access an Install and Uninstall choice in the context menu. If you have done everything correctly, you should be able to install and uninstall SampleClientApp successfully.

Same Solution Project

The previous example works well for creating a deployment package, but it does have a couple of downsides. For example, what happens when a new assembly is added to the original application? The deployment project will not automatically recognize any changes; you will have to add the new assemblies and verify that any new dependencies are covered. In smaller applications (like the example), this isn't that big of a deal. However, when you're dealing with an application that contains dozens or maybe hundreds of assemblies, this can become quite tedious to maintain. Visual Studio 2008 has a simple way of resolving this potential headache. Include the deployment project in your application's solution. You can then capture the output of the main project as your deployment assemblies. You can look at the SimpleClientApp as an example.

Open the SimpleClientApp solution in Visual Studio 2008. Add a new project using Solution Explorer. Select Deployment and Setup Projects and then select Setup Project, following the steps outlined in the previous section. You can name this project SimpleAppSolutionSetup. In the previous example, you added the assemblies by selecting Add ⇨ Assemblies from the Project menu. This time, select Add ⇨ Project Output from the Project menu. This opens the Add Project Output Group dialog box (see Figure 16-2).

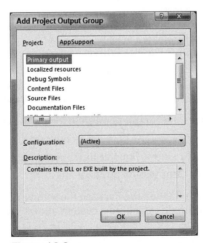

Figure 16-2

The top part of the dialog box has a drop-down list box that shows all projects in the current solution. Select the main startup project. Then select the items you want to include in your project from the list below. Your options are Documentation, Primary Output, Localized Resources, Debug Symbols, Content Files, and Source Files. First, select Primary Output. This includes the output and all dependencies when the application is built. Another drop-down list box lists the valid configurations: Debug and Release, plus any custom configurations you might have added. This also determines what outputs are picked up. For deployment, you will most likely want to use the Release configuration.

After you make these selections, a new item is added to your deployment project in Solution Explorer. The name of the item is Primary output from SampleClientApp (Release .NET). You will also see the file AppSupport.dll listed under the dependencies. As before, no need to search for the dependent assemblies.

At this point, all of the various project properties discussed in the previous section still apply. You can change the Name, Manufacturer, .cab file size, and other properties. After setting the properties, do a release build of the solution and test the installation. Everything should work as expected.

To see the advantage of adding the deployment package to the applications solution, add a new project to the solution. In the example it is called AppSupportII. In it is a simple test method that returns the string Hello World. Set a reference in SampleTestApp to the newly added project, and do another release build of the solution. You should see that the deployment project picked up the new assembly without you having to do anything. If you go back and open up the standalone deployment project from the previous example, unless you specifically add the assembly, it will not be picked up.

Simple Web Application

Creating an installation package for a Web application is not that different than creating a client install package. The download examples include a SimpleWebApp that also utilizes the AppSupport.dll assembly. You can create the deployment project the same way that the client deployment projects are created, either standalone or in the same solution. In this example, the deployment project is built in the same solution.

Start the SimpleWebApp solution and add a new deployment and setup project. This time, be sure to choose Web Setup Project in the Templates window. If you look at the properties view for the project, you will see that all of the same properties exist for Web applications that existed for client applications. The only addition is RestartWWWService. This is a Boolean value that will restart IIS during the install. If you're using ASP.NET components and not replacing any ATL or ISAPI DLLs, you shouldn't have to do this.

If you look at the File System editor, you will notice that there is only one folder. The Web Application folder will be your virtual directory. By default, the name of the directory is the name of the deployment project, and it is located below the Web root directory. The following table explains the properties that can be set from the installer. The properties discussed in the previous section are not included.

Property	Description
AllowDirectoryBrowsing	A Boolean value that, if true, allows an HTML listing of the files and subfolders of the virtual directory. Maps to the Directory browsing property of IIS.
AllowReadAccess	A Boolean value that, if true, allows users to read or download files. Maps to the Read property of IIS.
AllowScriptSourceAccess	A Boolean value that, if true, allows users to access source code, including scripts. Maps to Script source access in IIS.

Property	Description
AllowWriteAccess	A Boolean value that, if `true`, allows users to change content in write-enabled files. Maps to the Write property of IIS.
ApplicationProtection	Determines the protection level of applications that are run on the server. The valid values are: Low — Applications run in the same process as Web services. Medium — Applications run in same process but not the same as Web services. High — Application runs in its own process. Maps to the Application Protection property in IIS. Has no effect if the `IsApplication` property is `false`.
AppMappings	A list of application names and document or data files that are associated with the applications. Maps to the Application Mappings property of IIS.
Condition	A Windows Installer condition that must be met in order for the item to be installed.
DefaultDocument	The default or startup document when the user first browses to the site.
ExecutePermissions	The level of permissions that a user has to execute applications. The valid values are: None — Only static content can be accessed. ScriptsOnly — Only scripts can be accessed. Includes ASP. ScriptsAndExecutables — Any files can be accessed. Maps to Execute Permissions in IIS.
Index	Boolean value that, if `true`, would allow indexing of the content for Microsoft Indexing Service. Maps to the Index this resource property of IIS.
IsApplication	Boolean value that, if `true`, instructs IIS to create the application root for the folder.
LogVisits	Boolean value that, if `true`, logs visits to the Web site in a log file. Maps to the Log visits property of IIS.
Property	The named property that can be accessed at installation time.
VirtualDirectory	The virtual directory for the application. This is relative to the Web server.

You might notice that most of these properties are properties of IIS and can be set in the IIS administrator tool. So, the logical assumption is that in order to set these properties in the installer, the installer will need to run with administrator privileges. The settings made here can compromise security, so the changes should be well documented.

Other than these properties, the process of creating the deployment package is very similar to the previous client example. The main difference between the two projects is the ability to modify IIS from the installation process. As you can see, you have a great deal of control over the IIS environment.

Client from Web Server

Another installation scenario is either running the install program from a Web site or actually running the application from a Web site. Both of these are attractive options if you must deploy an application to a large number of users. By deploying from a Web site, you eliminate the need for a distribution medium such as CD-ROM, DVD, or even floppy disks. By running the application from a Web site or even a network share, you eliminate the need to distribute a setup program at all.

Running an installer from a Web site is fairly simple. You use the Web Bootstrapper project compile option. You will be asked to provide the URL of the setup folder. This is the folder in which the setup program is going to look for the `.msi` and other files necessary for the setup to work. After you set this option and compile the deployment package you can copy it to the Web site that you specify in the Setup folder URL property. At this point, when the user navigates to the folder, she will be able to either run the setup or download it and then run it. In both instances, the user must be able to connect to the same site to finish the installation.

No-Touch Deployment

You can also run the application from a Web site or network share. This process becomes a little more involved and is a prime reason that you should design the application with deployment in mind. This is sometimes referred to as *no-touch deployment* (NTD).

To make this process work, the application code must be written in a way to support it. A couple of ways exist to architect the application to take advantage of NTD. One way is to write the majority of the application code into DLL assemblies. The DLLs will live on a Web server or file share on the network. Then you create a smaller application `.exe` that will be deployed to the client PC's. This stub program will start the application by calling into one of the DLL assemblies, using the `LoadFrom` method. The only thing that the stub program will see is the main entry point in the DLL. Once the DLL assembly has been loaded, the application will continue loading other assemblies from the same URL or network share. Remember that an assembly first looks for dependent assemblies in the application directory (that is, the URL that was used to start the application). Here is the code used in the stub application on the user's client. This example calls the `AppSupportII` DLL assembly and puts the output of the `TestMethod` call in `label1`:

```
Assembly testAssembly =

Assembly.LoadFrom("http://localhost/AppSupport/AppSupportII.dll");
Type type = testAssembly.GetType("AppSupportII.TestClass");
object testObject = Activator.CreateInstance(type);
label1.Text = (string)type.GetMethod("TestMethod").Invoke(testObject,null);
```

This process uses reflection to first load the assembly from the Web server. In this example, the Web site is a folder on the local machine (`localhost`). Next, the type of the class is retrieved (here: `TestClass`). Now that you have type information the object can be created using the `Activator.CreateInstance` method. The last step is to get a `MethodInfo` object (the output of `GetMethod`) and call the `Invoke` method. In a more complex application this is the main entry point of the application. From this point on, the stub is not needed anymore.

Alternatively, you can also deploy the entire application to a Web site. For this method, create a simple Web page that contains a link to the application's setup executable or perhaps a shortcut on the user's desktop that has the Web site link. When the link is clicked, the application will be downloaded to the user's assembly download cache, which is located in the global assembly cache. The application will run from the download cache. Each time a new assembly is requested, it will go to the download cache first to see if it exists; if not, it will go to the URL that the main application came from.

The advantage to deploying the application in this way is that when an update is made available for the application, it has to be deployed in only one place. You place the new assemblies in the Web folder and when the user starts the application, the runtime will actually look at the assemblies in the URL and the assemblies in the download cache to compare versions. If a new version is found at the URL, it is then downloaded to replace the current one in the download cache. This way, the user always has access to the most current version of the application. The downside is that security is difficult to set up. The assemblies have to have a wide set of permissions in order to operate. This has the effect of making the application very insecure.

For more control over the update process and over security, ClickOnce is probably a better choice.

ClickOnce

ClickOnce is a deployment technology that allows applications to be self-updating. Applications are published to a file share, Web site, or media such as a CD. Once published, ClickOnce apps can be automatically updated with minimal user input.

ClickOnce also solves the security permission problem. Normally, to install an application the user would need Administrative rights. With ClickOnce a user can install and run an application with only the absolute minimum permissions required to run the application.

ClickOnce Operation

ClickOnce applications have two XML-based manifest files associated with them. One is the application manifest, and the other is the deployment manifest. These two files describe everything that is required to know to deploy an application.

The application manifest contains information about the application such as permissions required, assemblies to include, and other dependencies. The deployment manifest is about the deployment of the app. Items such as the location of the application manifest are contained in the deployment manifest. The complete schemas for the manifests are in the .NET SDK documentation.

ClickOnce has some limitations. Assemblies cannot be added to the GAC, for example. The following table compares ClickOnce and Windows Installer.

	ClickOnce	Windows Installer
Application installation location	ClickOnce application cache	Program Files folder
Install for multiple users	No	Yes
Install Shared files	No	Yes
Install drivers	No	Yes
Install to the GAC	No	Yes
Add application to Startup group	No	Yes
Add application to the favorites menu	No	Yes
Register file types	No	Yes
Access registry	No. The HKLM can be accessed with Full Trust permissions.	Yes
Binary patching of files	Yes	No
Install assemblies on demand	Yes	No

Some situations certainly exist where using Windows Installer is clearly a better choice; however, ClickOnce can be used for a large number of applications.

Publishing an Application

Everything that ClickOnce needs to know is contained in the two manifest files. The process of publishing an application for ClickOnce deployment is simply generating the manifests and placing the files in the proper location. The manifest files can be generated in Visual Studio 2008. There is also a command-line tool (mage.exe) and a version with a GUI (mageUI.exe).

You can create the manifest files in Visual Studio 2008 in two ways. At the bottom of the Publish tab on the Project Properties dialog are two buttons. One is the Publish Wizard and the other is Publish Now. The Publish Wizard asks several questions about the deployment of the application and then generates the manifest files and copies all of the needed files to the deployment location. The Publish Now button uses the values that have been set in the Publish tab to create the manifest files and copies the files to the deployment location.

In order to use the command-line tool, mage.exe, the values for the various ClickOnce properties must be passed in. Manifest files can be both created and updated using mage.exe. Typing **mage.exe -help** at the command prompt will give the syntax for passing in the values required.

The GUI version of mage.exe (mageUI.exe) is similar in appearance to the Publish tab in Visual Studio 2008. An application and deployment manifest file can be created and updated using the GUI tool.

ClickOnce applications appear in the Add/Remove Control Panel applet just like any other installed application. One big difference is that the user is presented with the choice of either uninstalling the application or rolling back to the previous version. ClickOnce keeps the previous version in the ClickOnce application cache.

ClickOnce Settings

Several properties are available for both manifest files. The most important property is where the application should be deployed from. The dependencies for the application must be specified. The Publish tab has an Application Files button that shows a dialog for entering all of the assemblies required by the application. The Prerequisite button displays a list of common prerequisites that can be installed along with the application. You have the choice of installing the prerequisites from the same location that the application is being published to or optionally having the prerequisites installed from the vendor's Web site.

The Update button displays a dialog that has the information about how the application should be updated. As new versions of an application are made available, ClickOnce can be used to update the application. Options include to check for updates every time the application starts or to check in the background. If the background option is selected, a specified period of time between checks can be entered. Options for allowing the user to be able to decline or accept the update are available. This can be used to force an update in the background so that the user is never aware that the update is occurring. The next time the application is run, the new version will be used instead of the older version. A separate location for the update files can be used as well. This way the original installation package can be located in one location and installed for new users, and all of the updates can be staged in another location.

The application can be set up so that it will run in either online or offline mode. In offline mode the application can be run from the Start Menu and acts as if it were installed using the Windows Installer. Online mode means that the application will run only if the installation folder is available.

Application Cache

Applications distributed with ClickOnce are not installed in the Program Files folder. Instead, they are placed in an application cache that resides in the Local Settings folder under the current user's Documents and Settings folder. Controlling this aspect of the deployment means that multiple versions of an application can reside on the client PC at the same time. If the application is set to run online, every version that the user has accessed is retained. For applications that are set to run locally, the current and previous versions are retained.

Because of this, it is a very simple process to roll back a ClickOnce application to its previous version. If the user goes to the Add/Remove Programs Control Panel applet, the dialog presented will contain the choice of removing the ClickOnce application or rolling back to the previous version. An Administrator can change the manifest file to point to the previous version. If the administrator does this, the next time the user runs that application, a check will be made for an update. Instead of finding new assemblies to deploy, the application will restore the previous version without any interaction from the user.

Security

Applications deployed over the Internet or intranet have a lower security or trust setting than applications that have been installed to the local drive have. For example, by default if an application is launched or deployed from the Internet it is in the Internet Security Zone. This means that it cannot access the file system, among other things. If the application is installed from a file share, it will run in the Intranet Zone.

If the application requires a higher level of trust than the default, the user will be prompted to grant the permissions required for the application to run. These permissions are set in the `trustInfo` element of the application manifest. Only the permissions asked for in this setting will be granted. So, if an application asks for file access permissions, Full Trust will not be granted, only the specific permissions requested.

Another option is to use Trusted Application Deployment. Trusted Application Deployment is a way to grant permissions on an enterprise-wide basis without having to prompt the user. A trust license issuer is identified to each client machine. This is done with public key cryptography. Typically, an organization will have only one issuer. It is important to keep the private key for the issuer in a safe, secure location.

A trust license is requested from the issuer. The level of trust that is being requested is part of the trust license configuration. A public key used to sign the application must also be supplied to the license issuer. The license created contains the public key used to sign the application and the public key of the license issuer. This trust license is then embedded in the deployment manifest. The last step is to sign the deployment manifest with your own key pair. The application is now ready to deploy.

When the client opens the deployment manifest the Trust Manager will determine if the ClickOnce application has been given a higher trust. The issuer license is looked at first. If it is valid, the public key in the license is compared to the public key that was used to sign the application. If these match, the application is granted the requested permissions.

Advanced Options

The installation processes discussed so far are very powerful and can do quite a bit. But there is much more that you can control in the installation process. For example, you can use the various editors in Visual Studio 2008 to build conditional installations or add registry keys and custom dialog boxes. The `SampleClientSetupSolution` example has all of these advanced options enabled.

File System Editor

The File System editor enables you to specify where in the target the various files and assemblies that make up the application will be deployed. By default, a standard set of deployment folders is displayed.

You can add any number of custom and special folders with the editor. This is also where you would add desktop and Start Menu shortcuts to the application. Any file that must be part of the deployment must be referenced in the File System editor.

Registry Editor

The Registry editor allows you to add keys and data to the registry. When the editor is first displayed, a standard set of main keys is displayed:

- ❑ HKEY_CLASSES_ROOT
- ❑ HKEY_CURRENT_USER
- ❑ HKEY_LOCAL_MACHINE
- ❑ HKEY_USERS

HKEY_CURRENT_USER and HKEY_LOCAL_MACHINE contain additional entries in the Software/[Manufacturer] key where Manufacturer is the information you entered in the Manufacturer property of the deployment project.

To add additional keys and values, highlight one of the main keys on the left side of the editor. Select Action from the main menu and then select New. Select the key or the value type that you want to add. Repeat this step until you have all of the registry settings that you want. If you select the Registry on Target Machine item on the left pane and then select the Action menu, you will see an Import option, which enables you to import an already defined *.reg file.

To create a default value for a key you must first enter a value for the key, then select the value name in the right or value pane. Select Rename from the File menu and delete the name. Press Enter, and the value name is replaced with (Default).

You can also set some properties for the subkeys and values in the editor. The only one that hasn't been discussed already is the DeleteAtUninstall property. A well-designed application should remove all keys that have been added by the application at uninstall time. The default setting is not to delete the keys.

One thing to keep in mind is that the preferred method for maintaining application settings is to use XML-based configuration files. These files offer a great deal more flexibility and are much easier to restore and back up than registry entries.

File Types Editor

The File Types editor is used to establish associations between files and applications. For example, when you double-click a file with the .doc extension, the file is opened in Word. You can create these same associations for your application.

To add an association, execute the following steps:

1. Select File Types on Target Machine from the Action menu.

2. Then select Add File Type. In the properties window, you can now set the name of the association.

3. In the Extension property, add the file extension that should be associated with the application. Do not enter the periods; you can separate multiple extensions with a semicolon, like this: **ex1;ex2**.

4. In the Command property, select the ellipse button.

5. Now, select the file (typically an executable) that you want to associate with the specified file types. Keep in mind that any one extension should be associated with only one application.

By default, the editor shows &Open as the Document Action. You can add others. The order in which the actions appear in the editor is the order in which they will appear in the context menu when the user right-clicks the file type. Keep in mind that the first item is always the default action. You can set the `Arguments` property for the actions. This is the command-line argument used to start the application.

User Interface Editor

Sometimes you might want to ask the user for more information during the installation process. The User Interface editor is used to specify properties for a set of predefined dialog boxes. The editor is separated into two sections, Install and Admin. One is for the standard installation and the other is used for an administrator's installation. Each section is broken up into three subsections: Start, Progress, and End. These subsections represent the three basic stages of the installation process (see Figure 16-3).

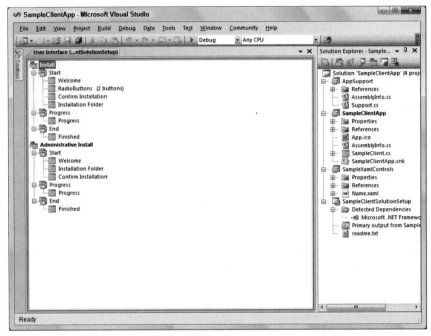

Figure 16-3

The following table lists the types of dialog boxes that you can add to the project.

Dialog Box	Description
Checkboxes	Contains up to four check boxes. Each check box has a `Label`, `Value`, and `Visible` property.
Confirm Installation	Gives the user the ability to confirm the various settings before installation takes place.
Customer Information	Has edit fields for the collection name, organization name, and serial number. Organization name and serial number are optional.
Finished	Displayed at the end of the setup process.

Dialog Box	Description
Installation Address	For Web applications, displays a dialog box so that users can choose an alternate installation URL.
Installation Folder	For client applications, displays a dialog box so that users can select an alternate installation folder.
License Agreement	Displays the license agreement that is located in a file specified by the `LicenseFile` property.
Progress	Displays a progress indicator during the installation process that shows the current installation status.
RadioButtons	Contains up to four radio buttons. Each radio button has a `Label` and `Value` property.
Read Me	Shows the readme information contained in the file specified by the `ReadMe` property.
Register User	Executes an application that will guide the user through the registration process. This application must be supplied in the setup project.
Splash	Displays a bitmap image.
TextBoxes	Contains up to four text box fields. Each text box has a `Label`, `Value`, and `Visible` property.
Welcome	Contains two properties: the `WelcomeText` property and the `CopyrightWarning`. Both are string properties.

Each of these dialog boxes also contains a property for setting the banner bitmap, and most have a property for banner text. You can also change the order in which the dialog boxes appear by dragging them up or down in the editor window.

Now that you can capture some of this information, the question is, how do you make use of it? This is where the `Condition` property that appears on most of the objects in the project comes in. The `Condition` property must evaluate to true for the installation step to proceed. For example, say the installation comes with three optional installation components. In this case, you would add a dialog box with three check boxes. The dialog should be somewhere after the Welcome and before the Confirm Installation dialog box. Change the `Label` property of each check box to describe the action. The first action could be "Install Component A," the second could be "Install Component B," and so on. In the File System editor select the file that represents Component A. Assuming that the name of the check box on the dialog box is CHECKBOXA1, the `Condition` property of the file would be CHECKBOXA1=Checked — that is, if CHECKBOXA1 is checked, install the file; otherwise, don't install it.

Custom Actions Editor

The Custom Actions editor allows you to define custom steps that will take place during certain phases of the installation. Custom actions are created beforehand and consist of a DLL, EXE, script, or Installer class. The action would contain special steps to perform that can't be defined in the standard deployment project. The actions will be performed at four specific points in the deployment. When the editor is first started, you will see the four points in the project (see Figure 16-4):

❑ Install — Actions will be executed at the end of the installation phase.

❑ Commit — Actions will be executed after the installation has finished and no errors have been recorded.

❑ Rollback — Actions occur after the rollback phase has completed.

❑ Uninstall — Actions occur after uninstall has completed.

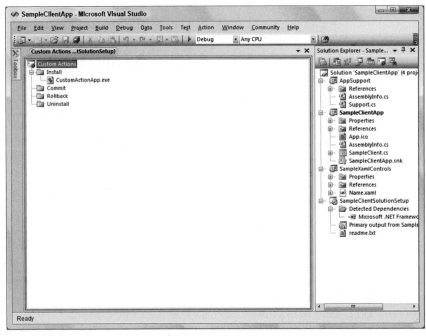

Figure 16-4

To add an action, you first select the phase of the installation in which you want the action to occur. Select the Add Custom Action menu option from the Action menu to open the file system dialog box. This means that the component that contains the action must be part of the deployment project. Because it will be executing on the target machine it has to be deployed; therefore, it should be listed in the File System editor.

After you have added the action, you can select one or more of the properties listed in the following table.

Arguments	Command-Line Arguments
Condition	A Windows Installer condition that must be evaluated and result in true for the action to execute.
CustomDataAction	Custom data that will be available to the action.
EntryPoint	The entry point for the custom DLL that contains the action. If the action is contained in an executable, this property does not apply.
InstallerClass	A Boolean value that, if true, specifies that the action is a .NET ProjectInstaller class.
Name	Name of the action. Defaults to the file name of the action.
SourcePath	The path to action on the development machine.

Because the action is code that you develop outside of the deployment project, you have the freedom to add just about anything that adds a professional touch to your application. The thing to remember is that such an action happens after the phase it is associated with is complete. If you select the Install phase, the action will not execute until after the install phase has completed. If you want to make determinations before the process, you will want to create a launch condition.

Launch Conditions Editor

The Launch Conditions editor allows you to specify that certain conditions must be met before installation can continue. Launch conditions are organized into types of conditions. The basic launch conditions are File Search, Registry Search, and Windows Installer Search. When the editor is first started you see two groups (see Figure 16-5): Search Target Machine and Launch Conditions. Typically, a search is conducted, and, based on the success or failure of that search, a condition is executed. This happens by setting the Property property of the search. The Property property can be accessed by the installation process. It can be checked in the Condition property of other actions, for example. You can also add a launch condition in the editor. In this condition, you set the Condition property to the value of the Property property in the search. In the condition, you can specify a URL that will download the file, registry key, or installer component that was being searched for. Notice in Figure 16-5 that a .NET Framework condition is added by default.

File Search will search for a file or type of file. You can set many different file-related properties that determine how files are searched, including file name, folder location, various date values, version information, and size. You can also set the number of subfolders that are searched.

Registry Search allows you to search for keys and values. It also allows you to set the root key for searching.

Windows Installer Search looks for the specified Installer component. The search is conducted by GUID.

The Launch Conditions editor provides two prepackaged launch conditions: the .NET Framework Launch Condition, which allows you to search for a specific version of the runtime, and a search for a specific version of MDAC, which uses the registry search to find the relevant MDAC registry entries.

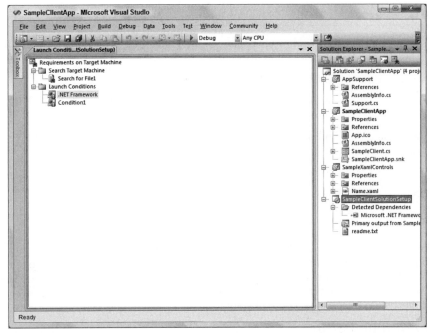

Figure 16-5

Summary

Deploying software has become difficult for developers of desktop software. As Web sites have grown more complex, the deployment of server-based software has become more difficult. This chapter looked at the options and capabilities that Visual Studio 2008 and version 3.5 of the .NET Framework provide to help make deployment easier and less error-prone.

After reading this chapter, you should be able to create a deployment package that resolves almost any deployment issue that you might have. Client applications can be deployed locally or via the Internet or an intranet. The extensive features of deployment projects and the ways that deployment projects can be configured were covered. You can also use no-touch deployment and ClickOnce to deploy applications. The security features of ClickOnce will make this a secure and efficient way of deploying client applications. Using deployment projects to install Web applications can make the process of configuring IIS much easier as well. Publishing a Web site provides the added benefit of precompiling the application.

Part III
Base Class Libraries

17

Assemblies

An *assembly* is the .NET term for a deployment and configuration unit. This chapter discusses exactly what assemblies are, how they can be applied, and why they are such a useful feature. In particular, this chapter covers the following topics:

- ❑ Overview
- ❑ Creating assemblies
- ❑ Application domains
- ❑ Shared assemblies
- ❑ Versioning

The chapter begins with an overview of assemblies.

What Are Assemblies?

Assemblies are the deployment units of .NET applications. .NET applications consist of one or more assemblies. .NET executables with the usual extension EXE or DLL are known by the term *assembly*. What's the difference between an assembly and a native DLL or EXE? Though they both have the same file extension, .NET assemblies include metadata that describe all the types that are defined in the assembly with information about its members — methods, properties, events, and fields.

The metadata of .NET assemblies also give information about the files that belong to the assembly, version information, and the exact information about assemblies that are used. .NET assemblies are the answer to the DLL hell we've seen previously with native DLLs.

Assemblies are self-describing installation units, consisting of one or more files. One assembly could be a single DLL or EXE that includes metadata, or it can be made of different files, for example, resource files, modules, and an EXE.

Assemblies can be private or shared. With simple .NET applications, using just private assemblies is the best way to work. No special management, registration, versioning, and so on is needed with private assemblies. The only application that could have version problems with private assemblies is your own application. Other applications are not influenced because they have their own copies of the assemblies. The private components you use within your application are installed at the same time as the application itself. Private assemblies are located in the same directory as the application or subdirectories thereof. This way you shouldn't have any versioning problems with the application. No other application will ever overwrite your private assemblies. Of course, it is still a good idea to use version numbers for private assemblies too. This helps a lot with code changes, but it's not a requirement of .NET.

With shared assemblies, several applications can use the same assembly and have a dependency on it. Shared assemblies reduce the need for disk and memory space. With shared assemblies, many rules must be fulfilled — a shared assembly must have a version number, a unique name, and usually it's installed in the *global assembly cache* (GAC).

Features of Assemblies

The features of assemblies can be summarized as follows:

❑ Assemblies are *self-describing*. It's no longer necessary to pay attention to registry keys for apartments, to get the type library from some other place, and so on. Assemblies include metadata that describes the assembly. The metadata includes the types exported from the assembly and a manifest; the next section describes the function of a manifest.

❑ *Version dependencies* are recorded inside an assembly manifest. Storing the version of any referenced assemblies in the manifest makes it possible to easily find deployment faults because of wrong versions available. The version of the referenced assembly that will be used can be configured by the developer and the system administrator. Later in this chapter, you learn which version policies are available and how they work.

❑ Assemblies can be loaded *side by side*. With Windows 2000 you already have a side-by-side feature where different versions of the same DLL can be used on a system. .NET extends this functionality of Windows 2000, allowing different versions of the same assembly to be used inside a single process! How is this useful? If assembly A references version 1 of the shared assembly Shared, and assembly B uses version 2 of the shared assembly Shared, and you are using both assembly A and B, you need both versions of the shared assembly Shared in your application — and with .NET both versions are loaded and used.

❑ Application isolation is ensured using *application domains*. With application domains a number of applications can run independently inside a single process. Faults in one application cannot directly affect other applications inside the same process.

❑ Installation can be as easy as copying the files that belong to an assembly. An xcopy can be enough. This feature is named *ClickOnce deployment*. However, there are cases in which ClickOnce deployment cannot be applied, and a normal Windows installation is required. Deployment of applications is discussed in Chapter 16, "Deployment."

Assembly Structure

An assembly consists of assembly metadata describing the complete assembly, type metadata describing the exported types and methods, MSIL code, and resources. All these parts can be inside of one file or spread across several files.

In the first example (see Figure 17-1), the assembly metadata, type metadata, MSIL code, and resources are all in one file — Component.dll. The assembly consists of a single file.

The second example shows a single assembly spread across three files (see Figure 17-2). Component.dll has assembly metadata, type metadata, and MSIL code, but no resources. The assembly uses a picture from `picture.jpeg` that is not embedded inside `Component.dll`, but is referenced from within the assembly metadata. The assembly metadata also references a module called `util.netmodule`, which itself includes only type metadata and MSIL code for a class. A module has no assembly metadata, thus the module itself has no version information; it also cannot be installed separately. All three files in this example make up a single assembly; the assembly is the installation unit. It would also be possible to put the manifest in a different file.

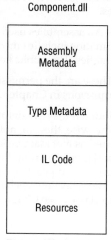

Figure 17-1

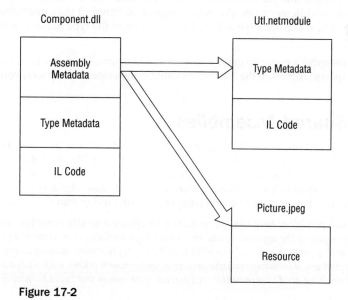

Figure 17-2

Assembly Manifests

An important part of an assembly is a *manifest*, which is part of the metadata. It describes the assembly with all the information that's needed to reference it and lists all its dependencies. The parts of the manifest are as follows:

❑ Identity — Name, version, culture, and public key.

❑ A list of files — Files belonging to this assembly. A single assembly must have at least one file but may contain a number of files.

❑ A list of referenced assemblies — All assemblies used from the assembly are documented inside the manifest. This reference information includes the version number and the public key, which is used to uniquely identify assemblies. The public key is discussed later in this chapter.

❑ A set of permission requests — These are the permissions needed to run this assembly. You can find more information about permissions in Chapter 20, " Security."

❑ Exported types — These are included if they are defined within a module and the module is referenced from the assembly; otherwise, they are not part of the manifest. A module is a unit of reuse. The type description is stored as metadata inside the assembly. You can get the structures and classes with the properties and methods from the metadata. This replaces the type library that was used with COM to describe the types. For the use of COM clients it's easy to generate a type library out of the manifest. The reflection mechanism uses the information about the exported types for late binding to classes. See Chapter 13, "Reflection," for more information about reflection.

Namespaces, Assemblies, and Components

You might be a little bit confused by the meanings of namespaces, types, assemblies, and components. How does a namespace fit into the assembly concept? The namespace is completely independent of an assembly. You can have different namespaces in a single assembly, but the same namespace can be spread across assemblies. The namespace is just an extension of the type name — it belongs to the name of the type.

For example, the assemblies mscorlib and system contain the namespace System.Threading among many other namespaces. Although the assemblies contain the same namespaces, you will not find the same class names.

Private and Shared Assemblies

Assemblies can be shared or private. A *private assembly* is found either in the same directory as the application, or within one of its subdirectories. With a private assembly, it's not necessary to think about naming conflicts with other classes or versioning problems. The assemblies that are referenced during the build process are copied to the application directory. Private assemblies are the usual way to build assemblies, especially when applications and components are built within the same company.

Although it is still possible to have naming conflicts with private assemblies (multiple private assemblies may be part of the application and they could have conflicts, or a name in a private assembly might conflict with a name in a shared assembly used by the application), naming conflicts are greatly reduced. If you find you'll be using multiple private assemblies or working with shared assemblies in other applications, it's a good idea to utilize well-named namespaces and types to minimize naming conflicts.

When using *shared assemblies*, you have to be aware of some rules. The assembly must be unique and therefore must also have a unique name called a *strong name*. Part of the strong name is a mandatory version number. Shared assemblies will mostly be used when a vendor, different from that of the application, builds the component, or when a large application is split into subprojects. Also, some technologies such as .NET Enterprise Services require shared assemblies in specific scenarios.

Satellite Assemblies

A satellite assembly is an assembly that only contains resources. This is extremely useful for localization. Because an assembly has a culture associated, the resource manager looks for satellite assemblies containing the resources of a specific culture.

> You can read more about satellite assemblies in Chapter 21, "Localization."

Viewing Assemblies

Assemblies can be viewed using the command-line utility ildasm, the MSIL disassembler. You can open an assembly by starting ildasm from the command line with the assembly as an argument or by selecting the File ⇨ Open menu.

Figure 17-3 shows ildasm opening the example that you build a little later in the chapter, SharedDemo .dll. ildasm shows the manifest and the SharedDemo type in the Wrox.ProCSharp.Assemblies .Sharing namespace. When you open the manifest, you can see the version number and the assembly attributes, as well as the referenced assemblies and their versions. You can see the MSIL code by opening the methods of the class.

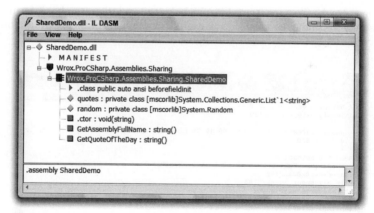

Figure 17-3

> In addition to using ildasm, the .NET Reflector is another great tool to use to analyze assemblies. The .NET Reflector allows type and member search, and call and callee graphs, and decompiles IL code to C#, C++, or Visual Basic. You can download this tool from www.aisto.com/roeder/dotnet.

Creating Assemblies

Now that you know what assemblies are, it is time to build some. Of course, you have already built assemblies in previous chapters, because a .NET executable counts as an assembly. This section looks at special options for assemblies.

Creating Modules and Assemblies

All C# project types in Visual Studio create an assembly. Whether you choose a DLL or EXE project type, an assembly is always created. With the command-line C# compiler *csc*, it's also possible to create modules. A module is a DLL without assembly attributes (so it's not an assembly, but it can be added to assemblies at a later time). The command

```
csc /target:module hello.cs
```

creates a module `hello.netmodule`. You can view this module using `ildasm`.

A module also has a manifest, but there is no `.assembly` entry inside the manifest (except for the external assemblies that are referenced) because a module has no assembly attributes. It's not possible to configure versions or permissions with modules; that can be done only at the assembly scope. You can find references to assemblies in the manifest of the module. With the `/addmodule` option of `csc`, it's possible to add modules to existing assemblies.

To compare modules to assemblies, create a simple class A and compile it by using the following command:

```
csc /target:module A.cs
```

The compiler generates the file `A.netmodule`, which doesn't include assembly information (as you can see using `ildasm` to look at the manifest information). The manifest of the module shows the referenced assembly `mscorlib` and the `.module` entry in Figure 17-4.

Figure 17-4

Next, create an assembly B, which includes the module `A.netmodule`. It's not necessary to have a source file to generate this assembly. The command to build the assembly is:

```
csc /target:library /addmodule:A.netmodule /out:B.dll
```

Looking at the assembly using `ildasm`, you can find only a manifest. In the manifest, the assembly `mscorlib` is referenced. Next, you see the assembly section with a hash algorithm and the version. The number of the algorithm defines the type of the algorithm that was used to create the hash code of the assembly. When creating an assembly programmatically it is possible to select the algorithm. Part of the manifest is a list of all modules belonging to the assembly. In Figure 17-5 you see `.module A .netmodule`, which belongs to the assembly. Classes exported from modules are part of the assembly manifest; classes exported from the assembly itself are not.

What's the purpose of modules? Modules can be used for faster startup of assemblies because not all types are inside a single file. The modules are loaded only when needed. Another reason to use modules is if you want to create an assembly with more than one programming language. One module could be written using Visual Basic, another module could be written using C#, and these two modules could be included in a single assembly.

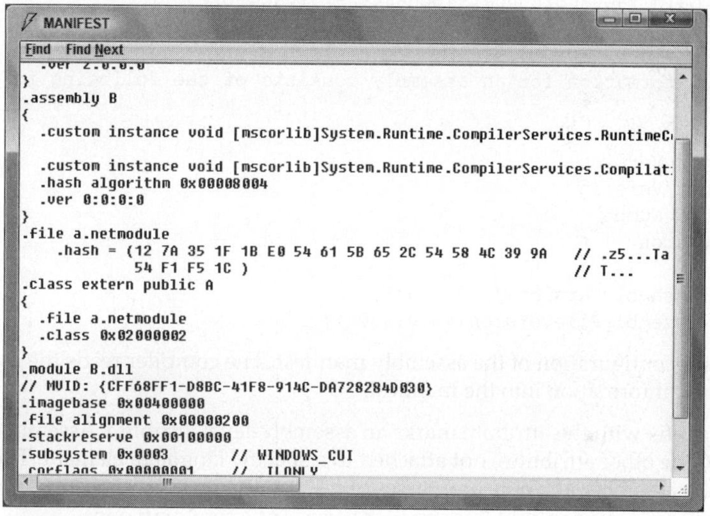

Figure 17-5

Assembly Attributes

When creating a Visual Studio project, the source file `AssemblyInfo.cs` is generated automatically. You can find this file below Properties in Solution Explorer. You can use the normal Source Code editor to configure the assembly attributes in this file. This is the file generated from the project template:

```csharp
using System.Reflection;
using System.Runtime.CompilerServices;
using System.Runtime.InteropServices;
//
// General Information about an assembly is controlled through the
// following set of attributes. Change these attribute values to modify
// the information associated with an assembly.
//
[assembly: AssemblyTitle("DomainTest")]
[assembly: AssemblyDescription("")]
[assembly: AssemblyConfiguration("")]
```

(continued)

(continued)

```
[assembly: AssemblyCompany("")]
[assembly: AssemblyProduct("DomainTest")]
[assembly: AssemblyCopyright("Copyright @ Wrox Press 2007")]
[assembly: AssemblyTrademark("")]
[assembly: AssemblyCulture("")]

// Setting ComVisible to false makes the types in this assembly not visible
// to COM components.  If you need to access a type in this assembly from
// COM, set the ComVisible attribute to true on that type.
[assembly: ComVisible(false)]

// The following GUID is for the ID of the typelib if this project is exposed
// to COM
[assembly: Guid("ae0acc2c-0daf-4bb0-84a3-f9f6ac48bfe9")]

//
// Version information for an assembly consists of the following four
// values:
//
//       Major Version
//       Minor Version
//       Build Number
//       Revision
//
[assembly: AssemblyVersion("1.0.0.0")]
[assembly: AssemblyFileVersion("1.0.0.0")]
```

This file is used for configuration of the assembly manifest. The compiler reads the assembly attributes to inject the specific information into the manifest.

The `assembly:` prefix with the attribute marks an assembly-level attribute. Assembly-level attributes are, in contrast to the other attributes, not attached to a specific language element. The arguments that can be used for the assembly attribute are classes of the namespaces `System.Reflection`, `System .Runtime.CompilerServices`, and `System.Runtime.InteropServices`.

> *You can read more about attributes and how to create and use custom attributes in Chapter 13, "Reflection."*

The following table contains a list of assembly attributes defined within the `System.Reflection` namespace.

Assembly Attribute	Description
`AssemblyCompany`	Specifies the company name.
`AssemblyConfiguration`	Specifies build information such as retail or debugging information.
`AssemblyCopyright` and `AssemblyTrademark`	Hold the copyright and trademark information.
`AssemblyDefaultAlias`	Can be used if the assembly name is not easily readable (such as a GUID when the assembly name is created dynamically). With this attribute an alias name can be specified.

Assembly Attribute	Description
AssemblyDescription	Describes the assembly or the product. Looking at the properties of the executable file this value shows up as Comments.
AssemblyProduct	Specifies the name of the product where the assembly belongs.
AssemblyTitle	Used to give the assembly a friendly name. The friendly name can include spaces. With the file properties you can see this value as Description.
AssemblyCulture	Defines the culture of the assembly. This attribute is important for satellite assemblies.
AssemblyInformationalVersion	This attribute isn't used for version checking when assemblies are referenced; it is for information only. It is very useful to specify the version of an application that uses multiple assemblies. Opening the properties of the executable you can see this value as the Product Version.
AssemblyVersion	This attribute gives the version number of the assembly. Versioning is discussed later in this chapter.
AssemblyFileVersion	This attribute defines the version of the file. The value shows up with the Windows file properties dialog, but it doesn't have any influence on the .NET behavior.

Here's an example of how these attributes might be configured:

```
[assembly: AssemblyTitle("Professional C#")]
[assembly: AssemblyDescription("Sample Application")]
[assembly: AssemblyConfiguration("Retail version")]
[assembly: AssemblyCompany("Wrox Press")]
[assembly: AssemblyProduct("Wrox Professional Series")]
[assembly: AssemblyCopyright("Copyright (C) Wrox Press 2008")]
[assembly: AssemblyTrademark("Wrox is a registered trademark of " +
    "John Wiley & Sons, Inc.")]
[assembly: AssemblyCulture("")]

[assembly: AssemblyVersion("1.0.0.0")]
[assembly: AssemblyFileVersion("1.0.0.0")]
```

With Visual Studio 2008 you can configure these attributes with the project properties, Application settings, and Assembly Information, as you can see in Figure 17-6.

Figure 17-6

Dynamic Loading and Creating Assemblies

During development time you add a reference to an assembly so it gets included with the assembly references and the types of the assembly are available to the compiler. During runtime the referenced assembly gets loaded as soon as a type of the assembly is instantiated or a method of the type is used. Instead of using this automatic behavior, you can also load assemblies programmatically. To load assemblies programmatically you can use the class `Assembly` with the static method `Load()`. This method is overloaded where you can pass the name of the assembly using `AssemblyName`, the name of the assembly, or a byte array.

It is also possible to create an assembly on the fly as shown with the next example. This sample demonstrates how C# code can be entered in a text box, a new assembly is dynamically created by starting the C# compiler, and the compiled code is invoked.

To compile C# code dynamically you can use the class `CSharpCodeProvider` from the namespace `Microsoft.CSharp`. Using this class, you can compile code and generate assemblies from a DOM tree, from a file, and from source code.

The UI of the application is done using WPF. You can see the UI in Figure 17-7. The window is made up of a `TextBox` to enter C# code, a `Button`, and a `TextBlock` WPF control that spans all columns of the last row to display the result as shown in Figure 17-7.

Figure 17-7

To dynamically compile and run C# code, the class `CodeDriver` defines the method `CompileAndRun()`. This method compiles the code from the text box and starts the generated method.

```csharp
using System;
using System.CodeDom.Compiler;
using System.IO;
using System.Reflection;
using System.Text;
using Microsoft.CSharp;

namespace Wrox.ProCSharp.Assemblies
{

    public class CodeDriver
    {
        private string prefix =
            "using System;" +
            "public static class Driver" +
            "{" +
            "    public static void Run()" +
            "    {";

        private string postfix =
            "    }" +
            "}";


        public string CompileAndRun(string input, out bool hasError)
        {
            hasError = false;
            string returnData = null;

            CompilerResults results = null;
            using (CSharpCodeProvider provider = new CSharpCodeProvider())
            {
                CompilerParameters options = new CompilerParameters();
                options.GenerateInMemory = true;

                StringBuilder sb = new StringBuilder();
                sb.Append(prefix);
                sb.Append(input);
                sb.Append(postfix);

                results = provider.CompileAssemblyFromSource(
                        options, sb.ToString());
            }

            if (results.Errors.HasErrors)
            {
                hasError = true;
                StringBuilder errorMessage = new StringBuilder();
                foreach (CompilerError error in results.Errors)
```

(continued)

(continued)

```
                {
                    errorMessage.AppendFormat("{0} {1}", error.Line,
                        error.ErrorText);
                }
                returnData = errorMessage.ToString();
            }
            else
            {
                TextWriter temp = Console.Out;
                StringWriter writer = new StringWriter();
                Console.SetOut(writer);
                Type driverType = results.CompiledAssembly.GetType("Driver");

                driverType.InvokeMember("Run", BindingFlags.InvokeMethod |
                    BindingFlags.Static | BindingFlags.Public,
                    null, null, null);
                Console.SetOut(temp);

                returnData = writer.ToString();
            }

            return returnData;
        }
    }
}
```

The method `CompileAndRun()` requires a string input parameter where one or multiple lines of C# code can be passed. Because every method that is called must be included in a method and a class, the variables `prefix` and `postfix` define the structure of the dynamically created class `Driver` and the method `Run()` that surround the code from the parameter. Using a `StringBuilder`, the `prefix`, `postfix`, and the code from the `input` variable are merged to create a complete class that can be compiled. Using this resultant string, the code is compiled with the `CSharpCodeProvider` class. The method `CompileAssemblyFromSource()` dynamically creates an assembly. Because this assembly is just needed in memory, the compiler parameter option `GenerateInMemory` is set.

If the source code that was passed contains some errors, these will show up in the `Errors` collection of `CompilerResults`. The errors are returned with the return data, and the variable `hasError` is set to `true`.

If the source code compiled successfully, the `Run()` method of the new `Driver` class is invoked. The invocation of this method is done using reflection. From the newly compiled assembly that can be accessed using `CompilerResults.CompiledType`, the new class `Driver` is referenced by the `driverType` variable. Then the `InvokeMember()` method of the `Type` class is used to invoke the method `Run()`. Because this method is defined as a public static method, the `BindingFlags` must be set accordingly. To see a result of the program that is written to the console, the console is redirected to a `StringWriter` to finally return the complete output of the program with the `returnData` variable.

> *Running the code with the `InvokeMember()` method makes use of .NET reflection. Reflection is discussed in Chapter 13.*

The `Click` event of the WPF button is connected to the `Compile_Click()` method where the `CodeDriver` class is instantiated, and the `CompileAndRun()` method is invoked. The input is taken from the `TextBox` named `textCode`, and the result is written to the `TextBlock` `textOutput`.

```
private void Compile_Click(object sender, RoutedEventArgs e)
{
    CodeDriver driver = new CodeDriver ();
    bool isError;
    textOutput.Text = driver.CompileAndRun(textCode.Text, out isError);
    if (isError)
    {
        textOutput.Background = Brushes.Red;
    }
}
```

Now you can start the application, enter C# code in the TextBox as shown in Figure 17-8, and compile and run the code.

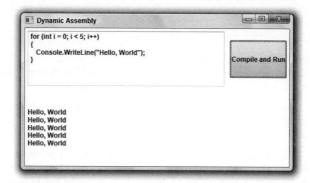

Figure 17-8

The program as written so far has the disadvantage that every time you click the Compile and Run button, a new assembly is created and loaded, and the program always needs more and more memory. You cannot unload an assembly from the application. To unload assemblies, application domains are needed.

Application Domains

Before .NET, processes were used as isolation boundaries, with every process having its private virtual memory; an application running in one process could not write to the memory of another application and thereby crash the other application. The process was used as an isolation and security boundary between applications. With the .NET architecture you have a new boundary for applications: *application domains*. With managed IL code, the runtime can ensure that access to the memory of another application inside a single process can't happen. Multiple applications can run in a single process within multiple application domains (see Figure 17-9).

An assembly is loaded into an application domain. In Figure 17-9 you can see process 4711 with two application domains. In application domain A, the objects one and two are instantiated, one in assembly One, and two in assembly Two. The second application domain in process 4711 has an instance one. To minimize memory consumption, the code of assemblies is only loaded once into an application domain. Instance and static members are not shared between application domains. It's not possible to directly access objects within another application domain; a proxy is needed instead. So in Figure 17-9,

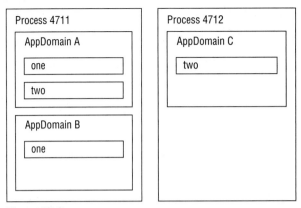

Figure 17-9

the object one in application domain B cannot directly access the objects one or two in application domain A without a proxy.

The AppDomain class is used to create and terminate application domains, load and unload assemblies and types, and enumerate assemblies and threads in a domain. In this section, you program a small example to see application domains in action.

First, create a C# console application called AssemblyA. In the Main() method add a Console .WriteLine() so that you can see when this method is called. In addition, add the class Demo with a constructor with two int values as arguments, which will be used to create instances with the AppDomain class. The AssemblyA.exe assembly will be loaded from the second application that will be created:

```csharp
using System;

namespace Wrox.ProCSharp.Assemblies.AppDomains
{
    public class Demo
    {
        public Demo(int val1, int val2)
        {
            Console.WriteLine("Constructor with the values {0}, {1}" +
                " in domain {2} called", val1, val2,
                AppDomain.CurrentDomain.FriendlyName);
        }
    }

    class Program
    {
        static void Main()
        {
            Console.WriteLine("Main in domain {0} called",
                AppDomain.CurrentDomain.FriendlyName);
        }
    }
}
```

Running the application produces this output:

```
Main in domain AssemblyA.exe called.
Press any key to continue ...
```

The second project you create is again a C# console application: DomainTest. First, display the name of the current domain using the property FriendlyName of the AppDomain class. With the CreateDomain() method, a new application domain with the friendly name New AppDomain is created. Then load the assembly AssemblyA into the new domain and call the Main() method by calling ExecuteAssembly():

```csharp
using System;

namespace Wrox.ProCSharp.Assemblies.AppDomains
{
    class Program
    {
        static void Main()
        {
            AppDomain currentDomain = AppDomain.CurrentDomain;
            Console.WriteLine(currentDomain.FriendlyName);
            AppDomain secondDomain =
                    AppDomain.CreateDomain("New AppDomain");
            secondDomain.ExecuteAssembly("AssemblyA.exe");
        }
    }
}
```

Before starting the program DomainTest.exe, reference the assembly AssemblyA.exe with the DomainTest project. Referencing the assembly with Visual Studio 2008 copies the assembly to the project directory, so that the assembly can be found. If the assembly cannot be found, a System .IO.FileNotFoundException exception is thrown.

When DomainTest.exe is run, you get the following console output. DomainTest.exe is the friendly name of the first application domain. The second line is the output of the newly loaded assembly in the New AppDomain. With a process viewer, you will not see the process AssemblyA.exe executing because there's no new process created. AssemblyA is loaded into the process DomainTest.exe.

```
DomainTest.exe
Main in domain New AppDomain called
Press any key to continue ...
```

Instead of calling the Main() method in the newly loaded assembly, you can also create a new instance. In the following example, replace the ExecuteAssembly() method with a CreateInstance(). The first argument is the name of the assembly, AssemblyA. The second argument defines the type that should be instantiated: Wrox.ProCSharp.Assemblies.AppDomains.Demo. The third argument, true, means that case is ignored. System.Reflection.BindingFlags.CreateInstance is a binding flag enumeration value to specify that the constructor should be called:

```csharp
            AppDomain secondDomain =
                AppDomain.CreateDomain("New AppDomain");
            // secondDomain.ExecuteAssembly("AssemblyA.exe");
            secondDomain.CreateInstance("AssemblyA",
                "Wrox.ProCSharp.Assemblies.AppDomains.Demo", true,
                System.Reflection.BindingFlags.CreateInstance,
                null, new object[] {7, 3}, null, null, null);
```

The results of a successful run of the application are as follows:

```
DomainTest.exe
Constructor with the values 7, 3 in domain New AppDomain called
Press any key to continue ...
```

Now you have seen how to create and call application domains. In runtime hosts, application domains are created automatically. ASP.NET creates an application domain for each Web application that runs on a Web server. Internet Explorer creates application domains in which managed controls will run. For applications, it can be useful to create application domains if you want to unload an assembly. You can unload assemblies only by terminating an application domain.

> **Application domains are an extremely useful construct if assemblies are loaded dynamically, and the requirement exists to unload assemblies after use. Within the primary application domain it is not possible to get rid of loaded assemblies. However, it is possible to end application domains where all assemblies loaded just within the application domain are cleaned from the memory.**

With this knowledge about application domains it is now possible to change the WPF program created earlier. The new class `CodeDriverInAppDomain` creates a new application domain using `AppDomain.CreateDomain`. Inside this new application domain the class `CodeDriver` is instantiated using `CreateInstanceAndUnwrap()`. Using the `CodeDriver` instance, the `CompileAndRun()` method is invoked before the new app-domain is unloaded again.

```csharp
using System;
using System.Runtime.Remoting;

namespace Wrox.ProCSharp.Assemblies
{
    public class CodeDriverInAppDomain
    {
        public string CompileAndRun(string code, out bool hasError)
        {
            AppDomain codeDomain = AppDomain.CreateDomain("CodeDriver");

            CodeDriver codeDriver = (CodeDriver)
                    codeDomain.CreateInstanceAndUnwrap("DynamicCompileWPF",
                        "Wrox.ProCSharp.Assemblies.CodeDriver");

            string result = codeDriver.CompileAndRun(code, out hasError);

            AppDomain.Unload(codeDomain);

            return result;
        }
    }
}
```

The class `CodeDriver` itself now is used both in the main app-domain and in the new app-domain, that's why it is not possible to get rid of the code that this class is using. If you would like to do that you can define an interface that is implemented by the `CodeDriver` and just use the interface in the main app-domain. However, here this is not an issue because there's only the need to get rid of the dynamically created assembly with the `Driver` class.

To access the class `CodeDriver` from a different app-domain, the class `CodeDriver` must derive from the base class `MarshalByRefObject`. Only classes that derive from this base type can be accessed across another app-domain. In the main app-domain a proxy is instantiated to invoke the methods of this class across an inter-appdomain channel.

```
using System;
using System.CodeDom.Compiler;
using System.IO;
using System.Reflection;
using System.Text;
using Microsoft.CSharp;

namespace Wrox.ProCSharp.Assemblies
{

    public class CodeDriver : MarshalByRefObject
    {
```

The `Compile_Click()` event handler can now be changed to use the `CodeDriverInAppDomain` class instead of the `CodeDriver` class:

```
private void Compile_Click(object sender, RoutedEventArgs e)
{
    CodeDriverInAppDomain driver = new CodeDriverInAppDomain();
    bool isError;
    textOutput.Text = driver.CompileAndRun(textCode.Text, out isError);
    if (isError)
    {
        textOutput.Background = Brushes.Red;
    }
}
```

Now you can click the Compile and Run button of the application any number of times, and the generated assembly is always unloaded.

You can see the loaded assemblies in an app-domain with the `GetAssemblies()` *method of the* `AppDomain` *class.*

Shared Assemblies

Assemblies can be isolated for use by a single application — not sharing an assembly is the default. When using shared assemblies there are specific requirements that must be followed.

This section explores the following:

❑   Strong names as a requirement for shared assemblies

❑   Global assembly cache

❑   Creating shared assemblies

❑   Installing shared assemblies in the GAC

❑   Delayed signing of shared assemblies

Strong Names

The goal of a shared assembly name is that it must be globally unique, and it must be possible to protect the name. At no time can any other person create an assembly using the same name.

COM solved the first problem by using a globally unique identifier (GUID). The second problem, however, still existed because anyone could steal the GUID and create a different object with the same identifier. Both problems are solved with *strong names* of .NET assemblies.

A strong name is made of these items:

- ❑ The *name* of the assembly itself.

- ❑ A *version number*. This allows it to use different versions of the same assembly at the same time. Different versions can also work side by side and can be loaded concurrently inside the same process.

- ❑ A *public key* guarantees that the strong name is unique. It also guarantees that a referenced assembly cannot be replaced from a different source.

- ❑ A *culture*. Cultures are discussed in Chapter 21, "Localization."

> **A shared assembly must have a strong name to uniquely identify the assembly.**

A strong name is a simple text name accompanied by a version number, a public key, and a culture. You wouldn't create a new public key with every assembly, but you'd have one in your company, so the key uniquely identifies your company's assemblies.

However, this key cannot be used as a trust key. Assemblies can carry Authenticode signatures to build up a trust. The key for the Authenticode signature can be a different one from the key used for the strong name.

For development purposes, a different public key can be used and later be exchanged easily with the real key. This feature is discussed later in the section "Delayed Signing of Assemblies."

To uniquely identify the assemblies in your companies, a useful namespace hierarchy should be used to name your classes. Here is a simple example showing how to organize namespaces: Wrox Press can use the major namespace `Wrox` for its classes and namespaces. In the hierarchy below the namespace, the namespaces must be organized so that all classes are unique. Every chapter of this book uses a different namespace of the form `Wrox.ProCSharp.<Chapter>`; this chapter uses `Wrox.ProCSharp.Assemblies`. So, if there is a class `Hello` in two different chapters, there's no conflict because of different namespaces. Utility classes that are used across different books can go into the namespace `Wrox.Utilities`.

A company name commonly used as the first part of the namespace is not necessarily unique, so something more must be used to build a strong name. For this the public key is used. Because of the public/private key principle in strong names, no one without access to your private key can destructively create an assembly that could be unintentionally called by the client.

Integrity Using Strong Names

A public/private key pair must be used to create a shared component. The compiler writes the public key to the manifest, creates a hash of all files that belong to the assembly, and signs the hash with the private key, which is not stored within the assembly. It is then guaranteed that no one can change your assembly. The signature can be verified with the public key.

During development, the client assembly must reference the shared assembly. The compiler writes the public key of the referenced assembly to the manifest of the client assembly. To reduce storage, it is not the public key that is written to the manifest of the client assembly, but a public key token. The public key token consists of the last 8 bytes of a hash of the public key and is unique.

At runtime, during loading of the shared assembly (or at install time if the client is installed using the native image generator), the hash of the shared component assembly can be verified by using the public key stored inside the client assembly. Only the owner of the private key can change the shared component assembly. There is no way a component Math that was created by vendor A and referenced from a client can be replaced by a component from a hacker. Only the owner of the private key can replace the shared component with a new version. Integrity is guaranteed insofar as the shared assembly comes from the expected publisher.

Figure 17-10 shows a shared component with a public key referenced by a client assembly that has a public key token of the shared assembly inside the manifest.

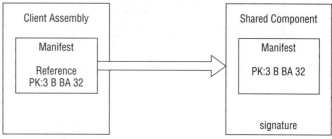

Figure 17-10

Global Assembly Cache

The *global assembly cache* (GAC) is, as the name implies, a cache for globally available assemblies. Most shared assemblies are installed inside this cache; otherwise a shared directory (also on a server) can be used.

The GAC can be displayed using shfusion.dll, which is a Windows shell extension to view and manipulate the contents of the cache. A Windows shell extension is a COM DLL that integrates with Windows Explorer. You just have to start Explorer and go to the <windir>/assembly directory.

With the Assembly Cache Viewer (see Figure 17-11), you can see the global assembly name, type, version, culture, and the public key token. Under Type you can see if the assembly was installed using the native image generator. When you select an assembly using the context menu, it's possible to delete an assembly and to view its properties (see Figure 17-12).

You can see the real files and directories behind the assembly cache by checking the directory from the command line. Inside the <windir>\assembly directory, you can find multiple GACxxx directories and a NativeImages_<runtime version> directory. The GACxxx directories contain shared assemblies. GAC_MSIL contains the assemblies with pure .NET code; GAC_32 contains the assemblies that are specific to a 32-bit platform. On a 64-bit system, you can also find the directory GAC_64 with assemblies specific for 64 bit. The directory GAC is for .NET 1.0 and 1.1. In the directory NativeImages_<runtime version>, you can find the assemblies compiled to native code. If you go deeper in the directory structure, you will find directory names that are similar to the assembly names, and below that a version directory and the assemblies themselves. This allows the installation of different versions of the same assembly.

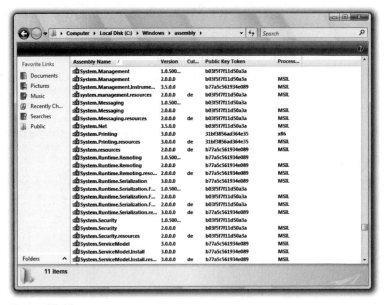

Figure 17-11

Figure 17-12

The assembly viewer can be used to view and delete assemblies with Windows Explorer. `gacutil.exe` is a utility to install, uninstall, and list assemblies using the command line.

The following list explains some of the `gacutil` options:

❑   `gacutil /l` lists all assemblies from the assembly cache.

❑   `gacutil /i mydll` installs the shared assembly `mydll` into the assembly cache.

❑   `gacutil /u mydll` uninstalls the assembly `mydll`.

For production you should use an installer program to install shared assemblies to the GAC. Deployment is covered in Chapter 16, "Deployment."

Creating a Shared Assembly

In the next example, you create a shared assembly and a client that uses it.

Creating shared assemblies is not much different from creating private assemblies. Create a simple Visual C# class library project with the name `SharedDemo`. Change the namespace to `Wrox.ProCSharp` `.Assemblies.Sharing` and the class name to `SharedDemo`. Enter the following code. In the constructor of the class, all lines of a file are read into a collection. The name of the file is passed as an argument to the constructor. The method `GetQuoteOfTheDay()` just returns a random string of the collection.

```
using System;
using System.Collections.Generic;
using System.IO;

namespace Wrox.ProCSharp.Assemblies.Sharing
{
    public class SharedDemo
    {
        private List<string> quotes;
        private Random random;

        public SharedDemo(string filename)
        {
            quotes = new List<string>();
            Stream stream = File.OpenRead(filename);
            StreamReader streamReader = new StreamReader(stream);
            string quote;
            while ((quote = streamReader.ReadLine()) != null)
            {
                quotes.Add(quote);
            }
            streamReader.Close();
            stream.Close();
            random = new Random();
        }

        public string GetQuoteOfTheDay()
        {
            int index = random.Next(1, quotes.Count);
            return quotes[index];
        }
    }
}
```

Create a Strong Name

A strong name is needed to share this assembly. You can create such a name with the *strong name tool* (sn):

```
sn -k mykey.snk
```

The strong name utility generates and writes a public/private key pair, and writes this pair to a file; here the file is `mykey.snk`.

With Visual Studio 2008, you can sign the assembly with the project properties by selecting the Signing tab, as shown in Figure 17-13. You can also create keys with this tool. However, you should not create a key file for every project. Just a few keys for the complete company can be used instead. It is useful to create different keys depending on security requirements (see Chapter 20, "Security").

Setting the signing option with Visual Studio adds the /keyfile option to the compiler setting. Visual Studio also allows you to create a keyfile that is secured with a password. Such a file has the file extension .pfx (see Figure 17-13).

Figure 17-13

After rebuilding, the public key can be found inside the manifest. You can verify this using ildasm, as shown in Figure 17-14.

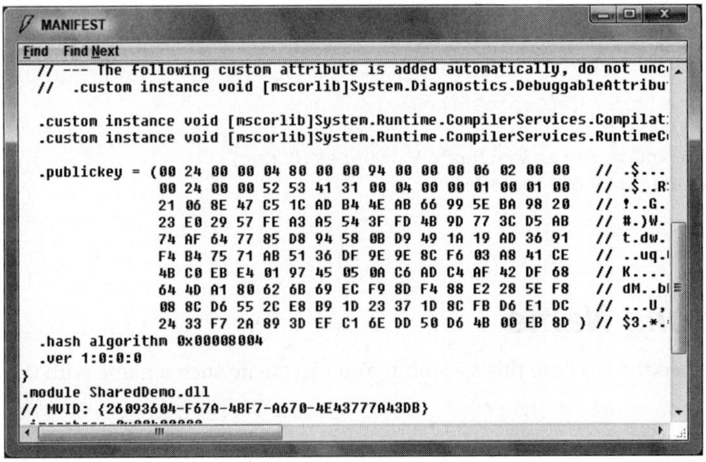

Figure 17-14

Install the Shared Assembly

With a public key in the assembly, you can now install it in the global assembly cache using the global assembly cache tool `gacutil` with the `/i` option:

```
gacutil /i SharedDemo.dll
```

By configuring a post-build event command line with Visual Studio (see Figure 17-15), the assembly can be installed in the GAC with each successful build.

Figure 17-15

If you're using Windows Vista to install an assembly to the GAC from Visual Studio, Visual Studio must be started with elevated rights. Installing assemblies to the GAC requires admin privileges.

Then you can use the Global Assembly Cache Viewer to check the version of the shared assembly and see if it is successfully installed.

Using the Shared Assembly

To use the shared assembly, create a C# console application called `Client`. Change the name of the namespace to `Wrox.ProCSharp.Assemblies.Sharing`. The shared assembly can be referenced in the same way as a private assembly: by using the Project ➪ Add Reference menu.

> With shared assemblies the reference property `Copy Local` **can be set to** `false`.
> **This way the assembly is not copied to the directory of the output files but will be**
> **loaded from the GAC instead.**

Here's the code for the `Client` application:

```
using System;
namespace Wrox.ProCSharp.Assemblies.Sharing
{
    class Program
    {
        static void Main()
        {
            SharedDemo quotes =
                new SharedDemo(@"C:\ProCSharp\Assemblies\Quotes.txt");
            for (int i=0; i < 3; i++)
```

(continued)

(continued)

```
        {
            Console.WriteLine(quotes.GetQuoteOfTheDay());
            Console.WriteLine();
        }
    }
  }
}
```

Looking at the manifest in the client assembly using `ildasm` (see Figure 17-16), you can see the reference to the shared assembly `SharedDemo`: `.assembly extern SharedDemo`. Part of this referenced information is the version number, discussed next, and the token of the public key.

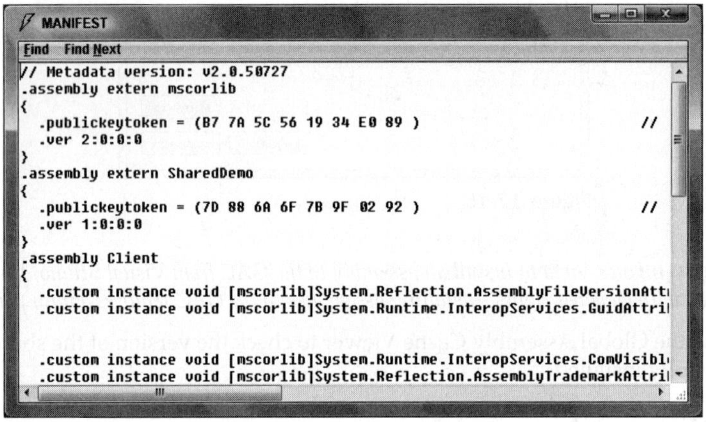

Figure 17-16

The token of the public key can also be seen within the shared assembly using the strong name utility: `sn -T` shows the token of the public key in the assembly, and `sn -Tp` shows the token and the public key. Pay attention to the use of the uppercase T!

The result of your program with a sample quotes file is shown here:

```
"We don't like their sound. And guitar music is on the way out." - Decca Recording,
Co., in rejecting the Beatles, 1962

"The ordinary 'horseless carriage' is at present a luxury for the wealthy; and
although its price will probably fall in the future, it will never come into as
common use as the bicycle."   -   The Literary Digest, 1889

"Landing and moving around the moon offer so many serious problems for human beings
that it may take science another 200 years to lick them", Lord Kelvin (1824-1907)

Press any key to continue ...
```

Delayed Signing of Assemblies

The private key of a company should be safely stored. Most companies don't give all developers access to the private key; only a few security people have it. That's why the signature of an assembly can be added at a later date, such as before distribution. When the assembly attribute `AssemblyDelaySign` is set to `true`, no signature is stored in the assembly, but enough free space is reserved so that it can be added later. Without using a key, you cannot test the assembly and install it in the GAC; however, you can use a temporary key for testing purposes, and replace this key with the real company key later.

The following steps are required to delay signing of assemblies:

1. Create a public/private key pair with the strong name utility `sn`. The generated file `mykey.snk` includes both the public and private key.

```
sn -k mykey.snk
```

2. Extract the public key to make it available to developers. The option `-p` extracts the public key of the keyfile. The file `mykeypub.snk` only holds the public key.

```
sn -p mykey.snk mykeypub.snk
```

All developers in the company can use this keyfile `mykeypub.snk` and compile the assembly with the `/delaysign+` option. This way the signature is not added to the assembly, but it can be added afterward. In Visual Studio 2008, the delay sign option can be set with a check box in the Signing settings.

3. Turn off the verification of the signature, because the assembly doesn't have a signature:

```
sn -Vr SharedDemo.dll
```

4. Before distribution the assembly can be re-signed with the `sn` utility. Use the `-R` option to re-sign previously signed or delayed signed assemblies. Resigning of the assembly can be done by the person doing the deployment package for the application and having access to the private key that is used for distribution.

```
sn -R MyAssembly.dll mykey.snk
```

> **The signature verification should be turned off only during the development process. Never distribute an assembly without verification, because it would be possible for this assembly to be replaced by a malicious one.**

Re-signing of assemblies can be automated by defining the tasks in an MSBuild file. This is discussed in Chapter 15, "Visual Studio 2008."

References

Properties lists a reference count. This reference count is responsible for the fact that a cached assembly cannot be deleted if it is still needed by an application. For example, if a shared assembly is installed by a Microsoft installer package (`.msi` file), it can only be deleted by uninstalling the application, but not by deleting it from the GAC. Trying to delete the assembly from the GAC results in the error message "`Assembly <name> could not be uninstalled because it is required by other applications.`"

A reference to the assembly can be set using the `gacutil` utility with the option `/r`. The option `/r` requires a reference type, a reference ID, and a description. The type of the reference can be one of three options: `UNINSTALL_KEY`, `FILEPATH`, or `OPAQUE`. `UNINSTALL_KEY` is used by MSI where a registry key is defined that is also needed with the uninstallation. A directory can be specified with `FILEPATH`. A useful directory would be the root directory of the application. The `OPAQUE` reference type allows you to set any type of reference.

The command line

```
gacutil /i shareddemo.dll /r FILEPATH c:\ProCSharp\Assemblies\Client "Shared Demo"
```

installs the assembly `shareddemo` in the GAC with a reference to the directory of the client application. Another installation of the same assembly can happen with a different path, or an OPAQUE ID like in this command line:

```
gacutil /i shareddemo.dll /r OPAQUE 4711 "Opaque installation"
```

Now, the assembly is in the GAC only once, but it has two references. To delete the assembly from the GAC, both references must be removed:

```
gacutil /u shareddemo /r OPAQUE 4711 "Opaque installation"
gacutil /u shareddemo /r FILEPATH c:\ProCSharp\Assemblies\Client "Shared Demo"
```

> **To remove a shared assembly, the option /u requires the assembly name without the file extension DLL. On the contrary, the option /i to install a shared assembly requires the complete file name including the file extension.**

Chapter 16, "Deployment," deals with deployment of assemblies, where the reference count is being dealt with in an MSI package.

Native Image Generator

With the native image generator, `Ngen.exe`, you can compile the IL code to native code at installation time. This way the program can start faster because the compilation during runtime is no longer necessary. Comparing precompiled assemblies to assemblies where the JIT compiler needs to run is not different from a performance view after the IL code is compiled. The only improvement you get with the native image generator is that the application starts faster because there's no need to run JIT. Reducing the startup time of the application might be enough reason for using the native image generator. In case you create a native image from the executable, you should also create native images from all the DLLs that are loaded by the executable. Otherwise the JIT compiler still needs to run.

The `ngen` utility installs the native image in the native image cache. The physical directory of the native image cache is `<windows>\assembly\NativeImages<RuntimeVersion>`.

With `ngen install myassembly`, you can compile the MSIL code to native code and install it into the native image cache. This should be done from an installation program if you would like to put the assembly in the native image cache.

With `ngen` you can also display all assemblies from the native image cache with the option `display`. If you add an assembly name to the `display` option you get the information about all installed versions of this assembly and the assemblies that are dependent on the native assembly:

```
C:\> ngen display System.Windows.Forms
Microsoft (R) CLR Native Image Generator - Version 2.0.50727.3178
Copyright (C) Microsoft Corporation. All rights reserved.

NGEN Roots:

System.Windows.Forms, Version=2.0.0.0, Culture=Neutral,
PublicKeyToken=b77a5c561934e089, processorArchitecture=msil

NGEN Roots that depend on "System.Windows.Forms":

ComSvcConfig, Version=3.0.0.0, Culture=Neutral,
```

```
PublicKeyToken=b03f5f7f11d50a3a, processorArchitecture=msil
ehepg, Version=6.0.6000.0, Culture=Neutral,
PublicKeyToken=31bf3856ad364e35, processorArchitecture=msil
ehepgdat, Version=6.0.6000.0, Culture=Neutral,
PublicKeyToken=31bf3856ad364e35, processorArchitecture=msil
ehExtCOM, Version=6.0.6000.0, Culture=Neutral,
PublicKeyToken=31bf3856ad364e35, processorArchitecture=msil
ehexthost, Version=6.0.6000.0, Culture=Neutral,
PublicKeyToken=31bf3856ad364e35, processorArchitecture=msil
ehRecObj, Version=6.0.6000.0, Culture=Neutral,
PublicKeyToken=31bf3856ad364e35, processorArchitecture=msil
ehshell, Version=6.0.6000.0, Culture=Neutral,
PublicKeyToken=31bf3856ad364e35, processorArchitecture=msil
EventViewer, Version=6.0.0.0, Culture=Neutral,
PublicKeyToken=31bf3856ad364e35, processorArchitecture=msil
```

If the security of the system changes, it's not sure if the native image has the security requirements it needs for running the application. This is why the native images become invalid with a system configuration change. With the command ngen update all native images are rebuilt to include the new configurations.

Installing CLR 2.0 runtime also installs the Native Image Service (or the Window Service CLR Optimization Service), with the name Microsoft .NET Framework NGEN v2.0.50727_X86. This service can be used to defer compilation of native images and regenerates native images that have been invalidated.

The command ngen install myassembly /queue can be used by an installation program to defer compilation of myassembly to a native image using the Native Image Service. ngen update /queue regenerates all native images that have been invalidated. With the ngen queue options pause, continue, and status you can control the service and get status information.

You might ask why the native images cannot be created on the developer system, and you just distribute the native image to the production system. The reason is that the native image generator takes care of the CPU that is installed with the target system and compiles the code optimized for the CPU type. During installation of the application, the CPU is known.

Configuring .NET Applications

COM components used the registry to configure components. Configuration of .NET applications is done by using configuration files. With registry configurations, an xcopy deployment is not possible. Configuration files can simply be copied. The configuration files use XML syntax to specify startup and runtime settings for applications.

This section explores the following:

❑   What you can configure using the XML base configuration files

❑   How you can redirect a strong named referenced assembly to a different version

❑   How you can specify the directory of assemblies to find private assemblies in subdirectories and shared assemblies in common directories or on a server

Configuration Categories

The configuration can be grouped into these categories:

❑ **Startup settings** enable you to specify the version of the required runtime. It's possible that different versions of the runtime could be installed on the same system. The version of the runtime can be specified with the `<startup>` element.

❑ **Runtime settings** enable you to specify how garbage collection is performed by the runtime, and how the binding to assemblies works. You can also specify the version policy and the code base with these settings. You take a more detailed look into the runtime settings later in this chapter.

❑ **WCF settings** are used to configure applications using WCF. You deal with these configurations in Chapter 42, "Windows Communication Foundation."

❑ **Security settings** are introduced in Chapter 20, " Security," and configuration for cryptography and permissions is done there.

These settings can be provided in three types of configuration files:

❑ **Application configuration files** include specific settings for an application, such as binding information to assemblies, configuration for remote objects, and so on. Such a configuration file is placed into the same directory as the executable; it has the same name as the executable with a `.config` extension appended. ASP.NET configuration files are named `web.config`.

❑ **Machine configuration files** are used for system-wide configurations. You can also specify assembly binding and remoting configurations here. During a binding process, the machine configuration file is consulted before the application configuration file. The application configuration can override settings from the machine configuration. The application configuration file should be the preferred place for application-specific settings so that the machine configuration file stays smaller and more manageable. A machine configuration file is located in `%runtime_install_path%\config\Machine.config`.

❑ **Publisher policy files** can be used by a component creator to specify that a shared assembly is compatible with older versions. If a new assembly version just fixes a bug of a shared component, it is not necessary to put application configuration files in every application directory that uses this component; the publisher can mark it as compatible by adding a publisher policy file instead. In case the component doesn't work with all applications, it is possible to override the publisher policy setting in an application configuration file. In contrast to the other configuration files, publisher policy files are stored in the GAC.

How are these configuration files used? How a client finds an assembly (also called *binding*) depends on whether the assembly is private or shared. Private assemblies must be in the directory of the application or in a subdirectory thereof. A process called *probing* is used to find such an assembly. If the assembly doesn't have a strong name, the version number is not used with probing.

Shared assemblies can be installed in the GAC or placed in a directory, on a network share, or on a Web site. You specify such a directory with the configuration of the `codeBase` shortly. The public key, version, and culture are all important aspects when binding to a shared assembly. The reference of the required assembly is recorded in the manifest of the client assembly, including the name, the version, and the public key token. All configuration files are checked to apply the correct version policy. The GAC and code bases specified in the configuration files are checked, followed by the application directories, and probing rules are then applied.

Configuring Directories for Assembly Searches

You've already seen how to install a shared assembly to the GAC. Instead of installing a shared assembly to the GAC, you can configure a specific shared directory by using configuration files. This feature can be used if you want to make the shared components available on a server. Another possible scenario arises if you want to share an assembly between your applications, but you don't want to make it publicly available in the GAC, so you put it into a shared directory instead.

There are two ways to find the correct directory for an assembly: the `codeBase` element in an XML configuration file, or through probing. The `codeBase` configuration is available only for shared assemblies, and probing is done for private assemblies.

<codeBase>

The `<codeBase>` can also be configured using the .NET Configuration utility. Code bases can be configured by selecting the properties of the configured application, `SimpleShared`, inside the Configured Assemblies in the Applications tree. Similarly to the Binding Policy, you can configure lists of versions with the Codebases tab. Figure 17-17 shows that the version 1.1 should be loaded from the Web server `http://www.christiannagel.com/WroxUtils`.

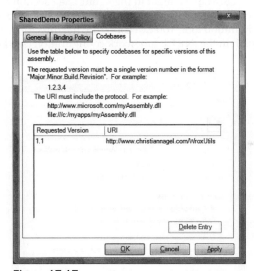

Figure 17-17

The .NET Configuration utility creates this application configuration file:

```xml
<?xml version="1.0"?>
<configuration>
  <runtime>
    <assemblyBinding xmlns="urn:schemas-microsoft-com:asm.v1">
      <dependentAssembly xmlns="">
        <assemblyIdentity name="SimpleShared"
                          publicKeyToken="7d886a6f7b9f0292" />
        <codeBase version="1.1"
              href="http://www.christiannagel.com/WroxUtils" />
```

(continued)

(continued)

```
        </dependentAssembly>
      </assemblyBinding>
    </runtime>
  </configuration>
```

The `<codeBase>` element has the attributes `version` and `href`. With `version`, the original referenced version of the assembly must be specified. With `href`, you can define the directory from where the assembly should be loaded. In the example, a path using the HTTP protocol is used. A directory on a local system or a share is specified using `href="file:C:/WroxUtils"`.

> *Using that assembly loaded from the network causes a* `System.Security.Permissions` *exception to occur. You must configure the required permissions for assemblies loaded from the network. In Chapter 20, "Security," you learn how to configure security for assemblies.*

<probing>

When the `<codeBase>` is not configured and the assembly is not stored in the GAC, the runtime tries to find an assembly through probing. The .NET runtime tries to find assemblies with either a `.dll` or an `.exe` file extension in the application directory, or in one of its subdirectories, that has the same name as the assembly searched for. If the assembly is not found here, the search continues. You can configure search directories with the `<probing>` element in the `<runtime>` section of application configuration files. This XML configuration can also be done easily by selecting the properties of the application with the .NET Framework Configuration tool. You can configure the directories where the probing should occur by using the search path in the .NET Framework configuration (see Figure 17-18).

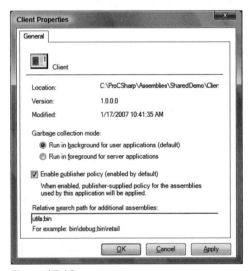

Figure 17-18

The XML file produced has these entries:

```
<?xml version="1.0"?>
<configuration>
    <runtime>
        <gcConcurrent enabled="true" />
        <assemblyBinding xmlns="urn:schemas-microsoft-com:asm.v1">
```

```
                <probing privatePath="bin;utils;" xmlns="" />
            </assemblyBinding>
        </runtime>
    </configuration>
```

The <probing> element has just a single required attribute: privatePath. This application configuration file tells the runtime that assemblies should be searched for in the base directory of the application, followed by the bin and the util directory. Both directories are subdirectories of the application base directory. It's not possible to reference a private assembly outside the application base directory or a subdirectory thereof. An assembly outside of the application base directory must have a shared name and can be referenced using the <codeBase> element, as you saw earlier.

Versioning

For private assemblies, versioning is not important because the referenced assemblies are copied with the client. The client uses the assembly it has in its private directories.

This is, however, different for shared assemblies. This section looks at the traditional problems that can occur with sharing. With shared components, more than one client application can use the same component. The new version can break existing clients when updating a shared component with a newer version. You can't stop shipping new versions because new features are requested and introduced with new versions of existing components. You can try to program carefully to be backward compatible, but that's not always possible.

A solution to this dilemma could be an architecture that allows installation of different versions of shared components, with clients using the version that they referenced during the build process. This solves a lot of problems but not all of them. What happens if you detect a bug in a component that's referenced from the client? You would like to update this component and make sure that the client uses the new version instead of the version that was referenced during the build process.

Therefore, depending on the type in the fix of the new version, you sometimes want to use a newer version, and you also want to use the older referenced version as well. The .NET architecture enables both scenarios.

In .NET, the original referenced assembly is used by default. You can redirect the reference to a different version using configuration files. Versioning plays a key role in the binding architecture — how the client gets the right assembly where the components live.

Version Numbers

Assemblies have a four-part version number, for example, 1.1.400.3300. The parts are <Major>.<Minor>.<Build>.<Revision>.

How these numbers are used depends on your application configuration.

> **A good policy is to change the major or minor number on changes incompatible with the previous version, but just the build or revision number with compatible changes. This way, it can be assumed that redirecting an assembly to a new version where just the build and revision changed is safe.**

With Visual Studio 2008, you can define the version number of the assembly with the assembly information in the project settings. The project settings write the assembly attribute [AssemblyVersion] to the file AssemblyInfo.cs:

```
[assembly: AssemblyVersion("1.0.0.0")]
```

Instead of defining all four version numbers you can also place an asterisk in the third or fourth place:

```
[assembly: AssemblyVersion("1.0.*")]
```

With this setting, the first two numbers specify the major and minor version, and the asterisk (*) means that the build and revision numbers are auto-generated. The build number is the number of days since January 1, 2000, and the revision is the number of seconds since midnight divided by two. Though the automatic versioning might help during development time, before shipping it is a good practice to define a specific version number.

This version is stored in the .assembly section of the manifest.

Referencing the assembly in the client application stores the version of the referenced assembly in the manifest of the client application.

Getting the Version Programmatically

To make it possible to check the version of the assembly that is used from the client application, add the method GetAssemblyFullName() to the SharedDemo class created earlier to return the strong name of the assembly. For easy use of the Assembly class, you have to import the System.Reflection namespace:

```
public string GetAssemblyFullName()
{
    return Assembly.GetExecutingAssembly().FullName;
}
```

The FullName property of the Assembly class holds the name of the class, the version, the locality, and the public key token, as you see in the following output, when calling GetAssemblyFullName() in your client application.

In the client application, just add a call to GetAssemblyFullName() in the Main() method after creating the shared component:

```
static void Main()
{
    SharedDemo quotes = new
        SharedDemo(@"C:\ProCSharp\Assemblies\Quotes.txt");
    Console.WriteLine(quotes.GetAssemblyFullName());
```

Be sure to register the new version of the shared assembly SharedDemo again in the GAC using gacutil. If the referenced version cannot be found, you will get a System.IO.FileLoadException, because the binding to the correct assembly failed.

With a successful run, you can see the full name of the referenced assembly:

```
SharedDemo, Version=1.0.0.0, Culture=neutral, PublicKeyToken=7d886a6f7b9f0292
Press any key to continue ...
```

This client program can now be used to test different configurations of this shared component.

Application Configuration Files

With a configuration file, you can specify that the binding should happen to a different version of a shared assembly. Assume that you create a new version of the shared assembly SharedDemo with major and minor versions 1.1. Maybe you don't want to rebuild the client but just want the new version of the assembly to be used with the existing client instead. This is useful in cases where either a bug is fixed with the shared assembly or you just want to get rid of the old version because the new version is compatible.

Figure 17-19 shows the Global Assembly Cache Viewer, where the versions 1.0.0.0 and 1.0.3300.0 are installed for the SharedDemo assembly.

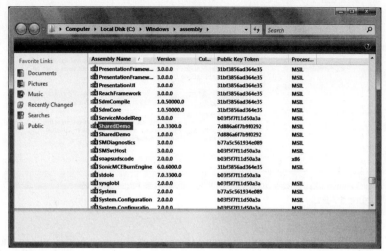

Figure 17-19

Figure 17-20 shows the manifest of the client application where the client references version 1.0.0.0 of the assembly SharedDemo.

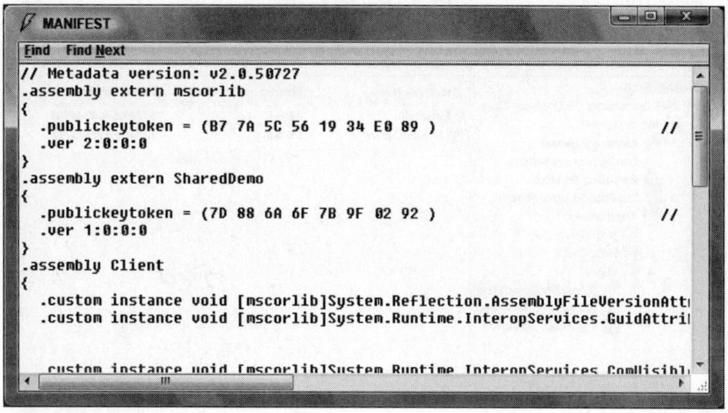

Figure 17-20

Now an application configuration file is needed. It is not necessary to work directly with XML; the .NET Framework Configuration tool can create application and machine configuration files. Figure 17-21 shows the .NET Framework Configuration tool, which is an MMC Snap-in. You can start this tool from Administrative Tools in the Control Panel.

This tool is shipped with Framework SDK and not with the .NET runtime, so don't expect this tool to be available to system administrators.

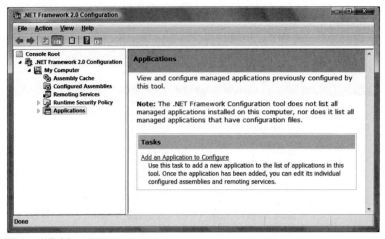

Figure 17-21

When you select Applications on the left side, and then select Action ⇨ Add, you can choose a .NET application to configure. If the `Client.exe` application does not show up with the list, click the Other . . . button and browse to the executable. Select the application `Client.exe` to create an application configuration file for this application. After adding the client application to the .NET Configuration utility, the assembly dependencies can be listed, as shown in Figure 17-22.

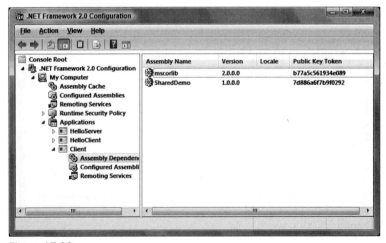

Figure 17-22

Select Configured Assemblies in the tree view and the menu Action ⇨ Add . . . to configure the dependency of the assembly `SharedDemo` from the dependency list. Select the Binding Policy tab to define the version that should be used as shown in Figure 17-23.

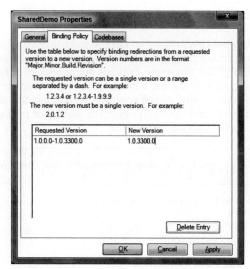

Figure 17-23

For the requested version, specify the version referenced in the manifest of the client assembly. newVersion specifies the new version of the shared assembly. In Figure 17-23, it is specified that the version 1.0.3300.0 should be used instead of any version in the range of 1.0.0.0 to 1.0.3300.0.

Now you can find the application configuration file Client.exe.config in the directory of the Client.exe application that includes this XML code:

```xml
<?xml version="1.0"?>
<configuration>
    <runtime>
        <assemblyBinding xmlns="urn:schemas-microsoft-com:asm.v1">
            <dependentAssembly>
                <assemblyIdentity name="SharedDemo"
                    publicKeyToken="7d886a6f7b9f0292" />
                <publisherPolicy apply="yes" />
                <bindingRedirect oldVersion="1.0.0.0-1.0.3300.0"
                    newVersion="1.0.3300.0" />
            </dependentAssembly>
        </assemblyBinding>
    </runtime>
</configuration>
```

Runtime settings can be configured with the <runtime> element. The subelement of <runtime> is <assemblyBinding>, which in turn has a subelement <dependentAssembly>. <dependentAssembly> has a required subelement <assemblyIdentity>. You specify the name of the referenced assembly with <assemblyIdentity>. name is the only mandatory attribute for <assemblyIdentity>. The optional attributes are publicKeyToken and culture. The other subelement of <dependentAssembly> that's needed for version redirection is <bindingRedirect>. The old and the new versions of the dependent assembly are specified with this element.

When you start the client with this configuration file, you will get the new version of the referenced shared assembly.

Publisher Policy Files

Using assemblies shared from the GAC allows you to use publisher policies to override versioning issues. Assume that you have an assembly used by some applications. What can be done if a critical bug is found in the shared assembly? You have seen that it is not necessary to rebuild all the applications that use this shared assembly, because you can use configuration files to redirect to the new version of this shared assembly. Maybe you don't know all the applications that use this shared assembly, but you want to get the bug fix to all of them. In that case, you can create publisher policy files to redirect all applications to the new version of the shared assembly.

> Publisher policy files apply only to shared assemblies installed in the GAC.

To set up publisher policies, you have to do the following:

❏   Create a publisher policy file

❏   Create a publisher policy assembly

❏   Add the publisher policy assembly to the GAC

Create a Publisher Policy File

A publisher policy file is an XML file that redirects an existing version or version range to a new version. The syntax used here is the same as for application configuration files, so you can use the same file you created earlier to redirect the old versions 1.0.0.0 through 1.0.3300.0 to the new version 1.0.3300.0.

Rename the previously created file to `mypolicy.config` to use it as a publisher policy file and remove the element `<publisherPolicy>`:

```xml
<?xml version="1.0"?>
<configuration>
   <runtime>
      <assemblyBinding xmlns="urn:schemas-microsoft-com:asm.v1">
         <dependentAssembly>
            <assemblyIdentity name="SharedDemo"
                              publicKeyToken="7d886a6f7b9f0292" />
            <bindingRedirect oldVersion="1.0.0.0-1.0.3300.0"
                             newVersion="1.0.3300.0" />
         </dependentAssembly>
      </assemblyBinding>
   </runtime>
</configuration>
```

Create a Publisher Policy Assembly

To associate the publisher policy file with the shared assembly, it is necessary to create a publisher policy assembly, and to put it into the GAC. The tool that can be used to create such files is the assembly linker `al`. The option `/linkresource` adds the publisher policy file to the generated assembly. The name of the generated assembly must start with policy, followed by the major and minor version number of the assembly that should be redirected, and the file name of the shared assembly. In this case the publisher policy assembly must be named `policy.1.0.SharedDemo.dll` to redirect the assemblies `SharedDemo` with the major version 1 and minor version 0. The key that must be added to this publisher key with the option `/keyfile` is the same key that was used to sign the shared assembly `SharedDemo` to guarantee that the version redirection is from the same publisher.

```
al /linkresource:mypolicy.config /out:policy.1.0.SharedDemo.dll
/keyfile:..\..\mykey.snk
```

Add the Publisher Policy Assembly to the GAC

The publisher policy assembly can now be added to the GAC with the utility `gacutil`:

```
gacutil -i policy.1.0.SharedDemo.dll
```

Now remove the application configuration file that was placed in the directory of the client application and start the client application. Although the client assembly references 1.0.0.0, you use the new version 1.0.3300.0 of the shared assembly because of the publisher policy.

Overriding Publisher Policies

With a publisher policy, the publisher of the shared assembly guarantees that a new version of the assembly is compatible with the old version. As you know, from changes of traditional DLLs, such guarantees don't always hold. Maybe all except one application is working with the new shared assembly. To fix the one application that has a problem with the new release, the publisher policy can be overridden by using an application configuration file.

With the .NET Framework Configuration tool you can override the publisher policy by deselecting the Enable Publisher Policy check box, as shown in Figure 17-24.

Figure 17-24

Disabling the publisher policy with the .NET Framework Configuration results in a configuration file with the XML element `<publisherPolicy>` and the attribute `apply="no"`.

```xml
<?xml version="1.0"?>
<configuration>
  <runtime>
    <assemblyBinding xmlns="urn:schemas-microsoft-com:asm.v1">
      <dependentAssembly>
        <assemblyIdentity name="SharedDemo"
            publicKeyToken="7d886a6f7b9f0292" />
```

(continued)

(continued)

```
            <publisherPolicy apply="no" />
        </dependentAssembly>
      </assemblyBinding>
    </runtime>
  </configuration>
```

By disabling the publisher policy, you can configure different version redirection in the application configuration file.

Runtime Version

Installing and using multiple versions is not only possible with assemblies but also with the .NET runtime (CLR). The versions 1.0, 1.1, and 2.0 (and later versions) of the CLR can be installed on the same operating system side by side. Visual Studio 2008 targets applications running on CLR 2.0 with .NET 2.0, 3.0, and 3.5. With CLR 2.0 the assembly file format changed, so it is not possible to run CLR 2.0 applications with CLR 1.1.

If the application is built with CLR 1.1, it is possible to target systems that have only the CLR 1.0 runtime installed. The same can be expected about future minor releases in that they can target CLR 2.0 runtime versions.

An application that was built using CLR 1.0 may run without changes on CLR 1.1. If an operating system has both versions of the runtime installed, the application will use the version with which it was built. However, if only version 1.1 is installed with the operating system, and the application was built with version 1.0, it tries to run with the newer version. There's a good chance the application runs without problems. The registry key HKEY_LOCAL_MACHINE\Software\Microsoft\.NETFramework\policy lists the ranges of the versions that will be used for a specific runtime.

If an application was built using .NET 1.1, it may run without changes on .NET 1.0, in case no classes or methods are used that are available only with .NET 1.1. Here an application configuration file is needed to make this possible.

In an application configuration file, it's not only possible to redirect versions of referenced assemblies; you can also define the required version of the runtime. Different .NET runtime versions can be installed on a single machine. You can specify the version that's required for the application in an application configuration file. The element `<supportedVersion>` marks the runtime versions that are supported by the application:

```
<?xml version="1.0"?>
<configuration>
    <startup>
        <supportedRuntime version="v1.1.4322" />
        <supportedRuntime version="v1.0.3512" />
    </startup>
</configuration>
```

There is one major point in case you still have .NET 1.0 applications that should run on .NET 1.1 runtime versions. The element `<supportedVersion>` was new with .NET 1.1. .NET 1.0 used the element `<requiredRuntime>` to specify the needed runtime. So for .NET 1.0 applications, both configurations must be done as shown here:

```
<?xml version="1.0"?>
<configuration>
    <startup>
```

```
        <supportedRuntime version="v1.1.4322"/>
        <supportedRuntime version="v1.0.3705"/>
        <requiredRuntime version="v1.0.3512" safeMode="true" />
    </startup>
</configuration>
```

<requiredRuntime> *does not overrule the configuration for* <supportedRuntime> *as it may look like, because* <requiredRuntime> *is used only with .NET 1.0, whereas* <supportedRuntime> *is used by .NET 1.1 and later versions.*

> **You cannot configure a supported runtime for a library. The library always uses the runtime selected by the application process.**

Summary

Assemblies are the new installation unit for the .NET platform. Microsoft learned from problems with previous architectures and did a complete redesign to avoid the old problems. This chapter discussed the features of assemblies: they are self-describing, and no type library and registry information is needed. Version dependencies are exactly recorded so that with assemblies, the DLL hell with old DLLs no longer exists. Because of these features, both development and deployment and administration have become a lot easier.

You learned the differences between private and shared assemblies and saw how shared assemblies can be created. With private assemblies, you don't have to pay attention to uniqueness and versioning issues because these assemblies are copied and only used by a single application. Sharing assemblies requires you to use a key for uniqueness and to define the version. You looked at the GAC, which can be used as an intelligent store for shared assemblies.

You can have faster application startups by using the native image generator. With this the JIT compiler does not need to run because the native code is created during installation time.

You looked at overriding versioning issues to use a version of an assembly different from the one that was used during development; this is done through publisher policies and application configuration files. Finally, you learned how probing works with private assemblies.

The chapter also discussed loading assemblies dynamically and creating assemblies during runtime. If you want to get more information on this, you should read Chapter 36 about the Add-In model of .NET 3.5.

18

Tracing and Events

Chapter 14 covered errors and exception handling. Besides handling exceptional code, it might be really interesting to get some live information about your running application to find the reason for some issues that application might have during production, or to monitor resources needed to early adapt to higher user loads. This is where the namespace `System.Diagnostics` comes into play.

The application doesn't throw exceptions, but sometimes it doesn't behave as expected. The application might be running well on most systems but might have a problem on a few. On the live system, you change the log behavior by changing a configuration value and get detailed live information about what's going on in the application. This can be done with *tracing*.

If there are problems with applications, the system administrator needs to be informed. With the Event Viewer, the system administrator both interactively monitors problems with applications and gets informed about specific events that happen by adding subscriptions. The *event-logging* mechanism allows you to write information about the application.

To analyze resources needed from applications, monitor applications with specified time intervals, and plan for a different application distribution or extending of system resources, the system administrator uses the performance monitor. You can write live data of your application using *performance counts*.

This chapter explains these three facilities and demonstrates how you can use them from your applications:

- ❑ Tracing
- ❑ Event logging
- ❑ Performance monitoring

Tracing

With tracing you can see messages from the running application. To get some information about a running application, you can start the application in the debugger. During debugging, you can walk through the application step by step and set breakpoints at specific lines and when you reach specific conditions. The problem with debugging is that a released program can behave differently. For example, while the program is stopping at a breakpoint, other threads of the application are suspended as well. Also, with a release build, the compiler-generated output is optimized and thus different effects can occur. There is a need to have information from a release build as well. Trace messages are written both with debug and release code.

A scenario showing how tracing helps is described here. After an application is deployed, it runs on one system without problems, while on another system intermediate problems occur. Turning on verbose tracing on the system with the problems gives you detailed information about what's happening inside the application. The system that is running without problems has tracing configured just for error messages redirected to the Windows event log system. Critical errors are seen by the system administrator. The overhead of tracing is very small, because you configure a trace level only when needed.

The tracing architecture has four major parts:

❑   The *source* is the originator of the trace information. You use the source to send trace messages.

❑   The *switch* defines the level of information to log. For example, you can request just error information or detailed verbose information.

❑   Trace *listeners* define where the trace messages should be written.

❑   Listeners can have *filters* attached. The filter defines what trace messages should be written by the listener. This way, you can have different listeners for the same source that write different levels of information.

Figure 18-1 shows the major classes for tracing and how they are connected in a Visual Studio class diagram. The `TraceSource` uses a switch to define what information to log. The `TraceSource` has a `TraceListenerCollection` associated where trace messages are forwarded to. The collection consists of `TraceListener` objects, and every listener has a `TraceFilter` connected.

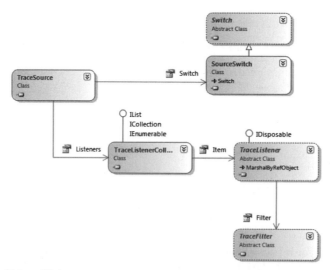

Figure 18-1

Trace Sources

You can write trace messages with the `TraceSource` class. Tracing requires the `Trace` flag of the compiler settings. With a Visual Studio project, the `Trace` flag is set by default with debug and release builds, but you can change it through the `Build` properties of the project.

The `TraceSource` class is more difficult to use compared to the `Trace` class writing trace messages, but it provides more options.

To write trace messages, you need to create a new `TraceSource` instance. In the constructor, the name of the trace source is defined. The method `TraceInformation()` writes an information message to the trace output. Instead of just writing informational messages, the `TraceEvent()` method requires an enumeration value of type `TraceEventType` to define the type of the trace message. `TraceEventType` `.Error` specifies the message as an error message. You can define it with a trace switch to see only error messages. The second argument of the `TraceEvent()` method requires an identifier. The ID can be used within the application itself. For example, you can use `id 1` for entering a method and `id 2` for exiting a method. The method `TraceEvent()` is overloaded, so the `TraceEventType` and the ID are the only required parameters. Using the third parameter of an overloaded method, you can pass the message written to the trace. `TraceEvent()` also supports passing a format string with any number of parameters in the same way as `Console.WriteLine()`. `TraceInformation()` does nothing more than invoke `TraceEvent()` with an identifier of 0. `TraceInformation()` is just a simplified version of `TraceEvent()`. With the `TraceData()` method, you can pass any object, for example an exception instance, instead of a message. To make sure that data is written by the listeners and does not stay in memory, you need to do a `Flush()`. If the source is no longer needed, you can invoke the `Close()` method that closes all listeners associated with the trace source. `Close()` does a `Flush()` as well.

```
TraceSource source1 = new TraceSource("Wrox.ProCSharp.Tracing");
source1.TraceInformation("Info message");
source1.TraceEvent(TraceEventType.Error, 3, "Error message");
source1.TraceData(TraceEventType.Information, 2,
                  new int[] { 1, 2, 3 });
source1.Flush();
source1.Close();
```

> You can use different trace sources within your application. It makes sense to define different sources for different libraries, so that you can turn on different trace levels for different parts of your application. To use a trace source you need to know its name. A commonly used name for the trace source is the same name as the namespace.

The `TraceEventType` enumeration that is passed as an argument to the `TraceEvent()` method defines the following levels to specify the severity of the problem: `Verbose`, `Information`, `Warning`, `Error`, and `Critical`. `Critical` defines a fatal error or application crash; `Error` defines a recoverable error. Trace messages at the `Verbose` level give you detailed debugging information. `TraceEventType` also defines action levels `Start`, `Stop`, `Suspend`, and `Resume`. These levels define timely events inside a logical operation.

The code, as it is written now, does not display any trace message because the switch associated with the trace source is turned off.

Trace Switches

To enable or disable trace messages, you can configure a trace switch. Trace switches are classes that are derived from the abstract base class `Switch`. Derived classes are `BooleanSwitch`, `TraceSwitch`, and `SourceSwitch`. The class `BooleanSwitch` can be turned on and off, and the other two classes provide a range level that is defined by the `TraceLevel` enumeration. To configure trace switches, you must know the values associated with the `TraceLevel` enumeration. `TraceLevel` defines the values `Off`, `Error`, `Warning`, `Info`, and `Verbose`.

You can associate a trace switch programmatically by setting the `Switch` property of the `TraceSource`. Here the switch associated is of type `SourceSwitch`, has the name `MySwitch`, and has the level `Verbose`:

```
TraceSource source1 = new TraceSource("Wrox.ProCSharp.Tracing");
source1.Switch = new SourceSwitch("MySwitch", "Verbose");
```

Setting the level to `Verbose` means that all trace messages should be written. If you set the value to `Error`, only error messages should show up. Setting the value to `Information` means that error, warning, and info messages are shown. Writing the trace messages once more, you can see the messages while running the debugger in the Output window.

Usually, you would want to change the switch level not by recompiling the application, but instead by changing the configuration. The trace source can be configured in the application configuration file. Tracing is configured within the `<system.diagnostics>` element. The trace source is defined with the `<source>` element as a child element of `<sources>`. The name of the source in the configuration file must exactly match the name of the source in the program code. Here, the trace source has a switch of type `System.Diagnostics.SourceSwitch` associated with the name `MySourceSwitch`. The switch itself is defined within the `<switches>` section, and the level of the switch is set to `verbose`.

```xml
<?xml version="1.0" encoding="utf-8" ?>
<configuration>
  <system.diagnostics>
    <sources>
      <source name="Wrox.ProCSharp.Tracing" switchName="MySourceSwitch"
          switchType="System.Diagnostics.SourceSwitch" />
    </sources>
    <switches>
      <add name="MySourceSwitch" value="Verbose"/>
    </switches>
  </system.diagnostics>
</configuration>
```

Now, you can change the trace level just by changing the configuration file without the need to recompile the code. After the configuration file is changed, you must restart the application.

Currently, trace messages are written to just the Output window of Visual Studio while you are running it in a debug session. Adding trace listeners changes this.

Trace Listeners

By default, trace information is written to the Output window of the Visual Studio debugger. Just by changing the application configuration, you can redirect the trace output to different locations.

Where tracing should be written to is defined by trace listeners. A trace listener is derived from the abstract base class `TraceListener`.

Trace listeners defined by the .NET Framework are described in the following table.

Trace Listener	Description
DefaultTraceListener	A default trace listener is automatically added to the listeners collection of the Trace class. Default output goes to the attached debugger. In Visual Studio, this is shown in the Output window during a debugging session.
EventLogTraceListener	The EventLogTraceListener writes trace information to the event log. With the constructor of the EventLogTraceListener, you can specify an event log source or an object of type EventLog. Event logging is described later in this chapter.
TextWriterTraceListener	With the TextWriterTraceListener trace, output can be written to a file, a TextWriter, or a Stream. See Chapter 25, "Manipulating Files and the Registry," for file manipulation information.
	Text WriterTraceListener is the base class of ConsoleTraceListener, DelimitedListTraceListener, and XmlWriterTraceListener.
ConsoleTraceListener	ConsoleTraceListener writes trace messages to the console.
DelimitedListTraceListener	DelimitedListTraceListener writes trace messages to a delimited file. With trace output options, you can define a lot of separate tracing information such as process ID, time, and the like, which can be read more easily with a delimited file.
XmlWriterTraceListener	Instead of using a delimited file, you can redirect the trace information to an XML file with the XmlWriterTraceListener.
IisTraceListener	The IisTraceListener was added in .NET 3.0.
WebPageTraceListener	ASP.NET has another tracing option to get ASP.NET trace information about Web pages in a dynamically created output file trace.axd. If you configure the WebPageTraceListener, then System.Diagnostics trace information goes into trace.axd as well.

.NET Framework delivers many listeners to which trace information can be written. In case the listeners don't fulfill your requirements, you can create a custom listener by deriving a class from the base class TraceListener. With a custom listener, you can, for example, write trace information to a Web service, write messages to your mobile phone . . . I guess it's not that interesting to receive hundreds of messages to your phone in your spare time. And with verbose tracing this can become really expensive.

You can configure a trace listener programmatically by creating a listener object and assigning it to the Listeners property of the TraceSource class. However, usually it is more interesting to just change a configuration to define a different listener.

You can configure listeners as child elements of the <source> element. With the listener, you define the type of the listener class and use initializeData to specify where the output of the listener should go. The configuration here defines the XmlWriterTraceListener to write to the file demotrace.xml and the DelimitedListTraceListener to write to the file demotrace.txt:

```xml
<?xml version="1.0" encoding="utf-8" ?>
<configuration>
  <system.diagnostics>
    <sources>
      <source name="Wrox.ProCSharp.Tracing" switchName="MySourceSwitch"
          switchType="System.Diagnostics.SourceSwitch">
        <listeners>
          <add name="xmlListener"
              type="System.Diagnostics.XmlWriterTraceListener"
              traceOutputOptions="None"
              initializeData="c:/logs/demotrace.xml" />

          <add name="delimitedListener" delimiter=":"
              type="System.Diagnostics.DelimitedListTraceListener"
              traceOutputOptions="DateTime, ProcessId"
              initializeData="c:/logs/demotrace.txt" />
        </listeners>
      </source>
    </sources>
    <switches>
      <add name="MySourceSwitch" value="Verbose"/>
    </switches>
  </system.diagnostics>
</configuration>
```

You might get a warning from the XML schema regarding the delimiter attribute declaration. You can ignore it.

With the listener, you can also specify what additional information should be written to the trace log. This information is defined with the `traceOutputOptions` XML attribute and is defined by the `TraceOptions` enumeration. The enumeration defines `Callstack`, `DateTime`, `LogicalOperationStack`, `ProcessId`, `ThreadId`, and `None`. The information needed can be added with comma separation to the `traceOutputOptions` XML attribute, as shown with the delimited trace listener.

The delimited file output from the `DelimitedListTraceListener`, including the process ID and date/time, is shown here:

```
"Wrox.ProCSharp.Tracing":Information:0:"Info message"::4188:""::
"2007-01-23T12:38:31.3750000Z"::
"Wrox.ProCSharp.Tracing":Error:3:"Error message"::4188:""::
"2007-01-23T12:38:31.3810000Z"::
```

The XML output from the `XmlWriterTraceListener` always contains the name of the computer, the process ID, the thread ID, the message, the time created, the source, and the activity ID. Other fields, such as the call stack, logical operation stack, and timestamp, depend on the trace output options.

You can use the `XmlDocument` and `XPathNavigator` classes to analyze the content from the XML file. These classes are covered in Chapter 28, "Manipulating XML."

If a listener should be used by multiple trace sources, you can add the listener configuration to the element `<sharedListeners>`, which is independent of the trace source. The name of the listener that is configured with a shared listener must be referenced from the listeners of the trace source:

```xml
<?xml version="1.0" encoding="utf-8" ?>
<configuration>
  <system.diagnostics>
    <sources>
      <source name="Wrox.ProCSharp.Tracing" switchName="MySourceSwitch"
```

```
            switchType="System.Diagnostics.SourceSwitch">
          <listeners>
            <add name="xmlListener"
                type="System.Diagnostics.XmlWriterTraceListener"
                traceOutputOptions="None"
                initializeData="c:/logs/demotrace.xml" />
            <add name="delimitedListener" />
          </listeners>
        </source>
      </sources>
      <sharedListeners>
  <add name="delimitedListener" delimiter=":"
            type="System.Diagnostics.DelimitedListTraceListener"
            traceOutputOptions="DateTime, ProcessId"
            initializeData="c:/logs/demotrace.txt" />
      </sharedListeners>
      <switches>
        <add name="MySourceSwitch" value="Verbose"/>
      </switches>
    </system.diagnostics>
</configuration>
```

Filters

Every listener has a `Filter` property that defines whether the listener should write the trace message. For example, multiple listeners can be used with the same trace source. One of the listeners writes verbose messages to a log file, and another listener writes error messages to the event log. Before a listener writes a trace message, it invokes the `ShouldTrace()` method of the associated filter object to decide if the trace message should be written.

A filter is a class that is derived from the abstract base class `TraceFilter`. .NET 3.0 offers two filter implementations: `SourceFilter` and `EventTypeFilter`. With the source filter, you can specify that trace messages are to be written only from specific sources. The event type filter is an extension to the switch functionality. With a switch, it is possible to define, according to the trace severity level, if the event source should forward the trace message to the listeners. If the trace message is forwarded, the listener now can use the filter to decide if the message should be written.

The changed configuration now defines that the delimited listener should write trace messages only if the severity level is of type warning or higher, because of the defined `EventTypeFilter`. The XML listener specifies a `SourceFilter` and accepts trace messages only from the source `Wrox.ProCSharp.Tracing`. In case you have a large number of sources defined to write trace messages to the same listener, you can change the configuration for the listener to concentrate on trace messages from a specific source.

```
<?xml version="1.0" encoding="utf-8" ?>
<configuration>
  <system.diagnostics>
    <sources>
      <source name="Wrox.ProCSharp.Tracing" switchName="MySourceSwitch"
          switchType="System.Diagnostics.SourceSwitch">
        <listeners>
          <add name="xmlListener" />
          <add name="delimitedListener" />
        </listeners>
      </source>
```

(continued)

(continued)

```
        </sources>
        <sharedListeners>
            <add name="delimitedListener" delimiter=":"
                type="System.Diagnostics.DelimitedListTraceListener"
                traceOutputOptions="DateTime, ProcessId"
                initializeData="c:/logs/demotrace.txt">
              <filter type="System.Diagnostics.EventTypeFilter"
                  initializeData="Warning" />
            </add>
            <add name="xmlListener"
                type="System.Diagnostics.XmlWriterTraceListener"
                traceOutputOptions="None"
                initializeData="c:/logs/demotrace.xml">
              <filter type="System.Diagnostics.SourceFilter"
                  initializeData="Wrox.ProCSharp.Tracing" />
            </add>
        </sharedListeners>
        <switches>
          <add name="MySourceSwitch" value="Verbose"/>
        </switches>
      </system.diagnostics>
    </configuration>
```

The tracing architecture can be extended. Just as you can write a custom listener derived from the base class `TraceListener`, you can also create a custom filter derived from `TraceFilter`. With that capability, you can create a filter that specifies to write trace messages, for example, depending on the time, depending on an exception that occurred lately, or depending on the weather.

Asserts

Another feature that belongs to tracing are asserts. Asserts are critical problems within the program path. With asserts, a message is displayed with the error, and you can abort or continue the application. Asserts are very helpful when you write a library that is used by another developer.

With the `Foo()` method, `Trace.Assert()` examines parameter o to see if it is not null. If the condition is `false`, the error message as shown in Figure 18-2 is issued. If the condition is `true`, the program

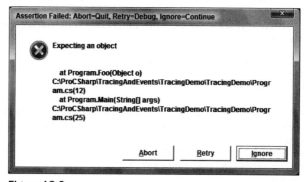

Figure 18-2

continues. The `Bar()` method includes a `Trace.Assert()` example where it is verified that the parameter is larger than 10 and smaller than 20. If the condition is `false`, an error message is shown again.

```
static void Foo(object o)
{
    Trace.Assert(o != null, "Expecting an object");
    Console.WriteLine(o);
}

static void Bar(int x)
{
    Trace.Assert(x > 10 && x < 20, "x should be between 10 and 20");
    Console.WriteLine(x);
}

static void Main()
{
    Foo(null);
    Bar(3);
}
```

You can create an application configuration file with the `<assert>` element to disable assert messages:

```
<?xml version="1.0" encoding="utf-8" ?>
<configuration>
  <system.diagnostics>
    <assert assertuienabled="false"/>
  </system.diagnostics>
</configuration>
```

Event Logging

The system administrator uses the Event Viewer to get critical and warning information about the system and applications. You should write error messages from your application to the event log so that the information can be read with the Event Viewer.

Trace messages can be written to the event log if you configure the `EventLogTraceListener` class. The `EventLogTraceListener` has an `EventLog` object associated with it to write the event log entry. You can also use the `EventLog` class directly to write and read event logs.

In this section, you explore the following:

❑   Event-logging architecture

❑   Classes for event logging from the `System.Diagnostics` namespace

❑   Adding event logging to services and to other application types

❑   Creating an event log listener with the `EnableRaisingEvents` property of the `EventLog` class

Figure 18-3 shows an example of a log entry from a modem.

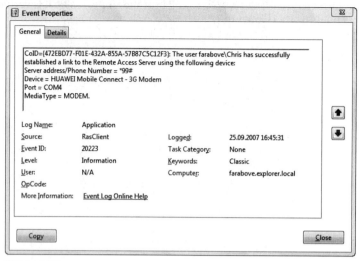

Figure 18-3

For custom event logging, you can use classes from the System.Diagnostics namespace.

Event-Logging Architecture

The event log information is stored in several log files. The most important ones are application, security, and system. Looking at the registry configuration of the event log service, you will notice several entries under HKEY_LOCAL_MACHINE\System\CurrentControlSet\Services\Eventlog with configurations pointing to the specific files. The system log file is used from the system and device drivers. Applications and services write to the application log. The security log is a read-only log for applications. The auditing feature of the operating system uses the security log. Every application can also create a custom category and log file to write event log entries there. For example, this is done by Windows OneCare and Media Center.

You can read these events by using the administrative tool Event Viewer. The Event Viewer can be started directly from the Server Explorer of Visual Studio by right-clicking the Event Logs item and selecting the Launch Event Viewer entry from the context menu. The Event Viewer is shown in Figure 18-4.

In the event log, you can see this information:

❑ **Type** — The type can be Information, Warning, or Error. Information is an infrequent successful operation; Warning is a problem that is not immediately significant; and Error is a major problem. Additional types are FailureAudit and SuccessAudit, but these types are used only for the security log.

❑ **Date** — Date and Time show the time when the event occurred.

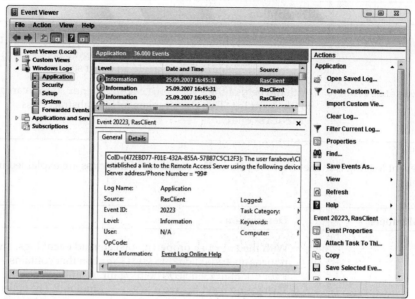

Figure 18-4

❑ **Source** — The Source is the name of the software that logs the event. The source for the application log is configured in:

```
HKEY_LOCAL_MACHINE\System\CurrentControlSet\Services\Eventlog\Application\
[ApplicationName]
```

Below this key, the value `EventMessageFile` is configured to point to a resource DLL that holds error messages.

❑ **Category** — A Category can be defined so that event logs can be filtered when using the Event Viewer. Categories can be defined by an event source.

❑ **Event identifier** — The Event identifier specifies a particular event message.

Event-Logging Classes

The `System.Diagnostics` namespace has some classes for event logging, which are shown in the following table.

Class	Description
EventLog	With the `EventLog` class, you can read and write entries in the event log, and establish applications as event sources.
EventLogEntry	The `EventLogEntry` class represents a single entry in the event log. With the `EventLogEntryCollection`, you can iterate through `EventLogEntry` items.

Class	Description
EventLogInstaller	The EventLogInstaller class is the installer for an EventLog component. EventLogInstaller calls EventLog .CreateEventSource() to create an event source.
EventLogTraceListener	With the help of the EventLogTraceListener, traces can be written to the event log. This class implements the abstract class TraceListener.

The heart of event logging is in the EventLog class. The members of this class are explained in the following table.

EventLog Members	Description
Entries	With the Entries property, you can read event logs. Entries returns an EventLogEntryCollection that contains EventLogEntry objects holding information about the events. There is no need to invoke a Read() method. The collection is filled as soon as you access this property.
Log	Specify the log for reading or writing event logs with the Log property.
LogDisplayName	LogDisplayName is a read-only property that returns the display name of the log.
MachineName	With the MachineName, you can specify the system on which to read or write log entries.
Source	The Source property specifies the source of the event entries to write.
CreateEventSource()	The CreateEventSource() creates a new event source and a new log file, if a new log file is specified with this method.
DeleteEventSource()	To get rid of an event source, you can invoke DeleteEventSource().
SourceExists()	Before creating an event source, you can verify if the source already exists by using this element.
WriteEntry()WriteEvent()	Write event log entries with either the WriteEntry() or WriteEvent() method. WriteEntry() is simpler, because you just need to pass a string. WriteEvent() is more flexible, because you can use message files that are independent of the application and that support localization.
Clear()	The Clear() method removes all entries from an event log.
Delete()	The Delete() method deletes a complete event log.

Creating an Event Source

Before writing events, you must create an event source. You can use either the `CreateEventSource()` method of the `EventLog` class or the class `EventLogInstaller`. Because you need administrative privileges when creating an event source, an installation program would be best for defining the new source.

Chapter 16, "Deployment," explains how to create installation programs.

The following sample verifies that an event log source named `EventLogDemoApp` already exists. If it doesn't exist, an object of type `EventSourceCreationData` is instantiated that defines the source name `EventLogDemoApp` and the log name `ProCSharpLog`. Here, all events of this source are written to the `ProCSharpLog` event log. The default is the application log.

```
if (!EventLog.SourceExists("EventLogDemoApp"))
{
    EventSourceCreationData eventSourceData =
        new EventSourceCreationData("EventlogDemoApp",
        "ProCSharpLog");

    EventLog.CreateEventSource(eventSourceData);
}
```

The name of the event source is an identifier of the application that writes the events. For the system administrator reading the log, the information helps in identifying the event log entries to map them to application categories. Examples of names for event log sources are `LoadPerf` for the performance monitor, `MSSQLSERVER` for Microsoft SQL Server, `MsiInstaller` for the Windows Installer, `Winlogon`, `Tcpip`, `Time-Service`, and so on.

Setting the name Application for the event log writes event log entries to the application log. You can also create your own log by specifying a different application log name. Log files are located in the directory `<windows>\System32\WinEvt\Logs`.

With the `EventSourceCreationData`, you can also specify several more characteristics for the event log, as shown in the following table.

EventSourceCreationData	Description
Source	The property `Source` gets or sets the name of the event source.
LogName	`LogName` defines the log where event log entries are written. The default is the application log.
MachineName	With `MachineName`, you can define the system to read or write log entries.
CategoryResourceFile	With the `CategoryResourceFile` property, you can define a resource file for categories. Categories can be used for an easier filtering of event log entries within a single source.
CategoryCount	The `CategoryCount` property defines the number of categories in the category resource file.

EventSourceCreationData	Description
`MessageResourceFile`	Instead of specifying that the message should be written to the event log in the program that writes the events, messages can be defined in a resource file that is assigned to the `MessageResourceFile` property. Messages from the resource file are localizable.
`ParameterResourceFile`	Messages in a resource file can have parameters. The parameters can be replaced by strings defined in a resource file that is assigned to the `ParameterResourceFile` property.

Writing Event Logs

For writing event log entries, you can use the `WriteEntry()` or `WriteEvent()` methods of the `EventLog` class.

The `EventLog` class has both a static and an instance method `WriteEntry()`. The static method `WriteEntry()` requires a parameter of the source. The source can also be set with the constructor of the `EventLog` class. Here in the constructor, the log name, the local machine, and the event source name are defined. Next, three event log entries are written with the message as the first parameter of the `WriteEntry()` method. `WriteEntry()` is overloaded. The second parameter you can assign is an enumeration of type `EventLogEntryType`. With `EventLogEntryType`, you can define the severity of the event log entry. Possible values are `Information`, `Warning`, and `Error`, and for auditing `SuccessAudit` and `FailureAudit`. Depending on the type, different icons are shown in the Event Viewer. With the third parameter, you can specify an application-specific event ID that can be used by the application itself. In addition to that, you can also pass application-specific binary data and a category.

```
using (EventLog log = new EventLog("ProCSharpLog", ".",
    "EventLogDemoApp"))
{
    log.WriteEntry("Message 1");
    log.WriteEntry("Message 2", EventLogEntryType.Warning);
    log.WriteEntry("Message 3", EventLogEntryType.Information, 33);
}
```

Resource Files

Instead of defining the messages for the event log in the C# code and passing it to the `WriteEntry()` method, you can create a *message resource file*, define messages in the resource file, and pass message identifiers to the `WriteEvent()` method. Resource files also support localization.

> *Message resource files are native resource files that have nothing in common with .NET resource files. .NET resource files are covered in Chapter 21, "Localization."*

A message file is a text file with the `mc` file extension. The syntax that this file uses to define messages is very strict. The sample file `EventLogMessages.mc` contains four categories followed by event messages. Every message has an ID that can be used by the application writing event entries. Parameters that can be passed from the application are defined with `%` syntax in the message text.

For the exact syntax of message files, check the MSDN documentation for Message Text Files.

```
;  //  EventLogDemoMessages.mc
;  //  *********************************************************

;  //  - Event categories -
;  //  Categories must be numbered consecutively starting at 1.
;  //  *********************************************************

MessageId=0x1
Severity=Success
SymbolicName=INSTALL_CATEGORY
Language=English
Installation
.

MessageId=0x2
Severity=Success
SymbolicName=DATA_CATEGORY
Language=English
Database Query
.

MessageId=0x3
Severity=Success
SymbolicName=UPDATE_CATEGORY
Language=English
Data Update
.

MessageId=0x4
Severity=Success
SymbolicName=NETWORK_CATEGORY
Language=English
Network Communication
.

;  //  - Event messages -
;  //  ******************************

MessageId = 1000
Severity = Success
Facility = Application
SymbolicName = MSG_CONNECT_1000
Language=English
Connection successful.
.

MessageId = 1001
Severity = Error
Facility = Application
SymbolicName = MSG_CONNECT_FAILED_1001
Language=English
Could not connect to server %1.
.
```

(continued)

(continued)

```
MessageId = 1002
Severity = Error
Facility = Application
SymbolicName = MSG_DB_UPDATE_1002
Language=English
Database update failed.
.


MessageId = 1003
Severity = Success
Facility = Application
SymbolicName = APP_UPDATE
Language=English
Application %%5002 updated.
.


; // - Event log display name -
; // ********************************************************

MessageId = 5001
Severity = Success
Facility = Application
SymbolicName = EVENT_LOG_DISPLAY_NAME_MSGID
Language=English
Professional C# Sample Event Log
.


; // - Event message parameters -
; //    Language independent insertion strings
; // ********************************************************


MessageId = 5002
Severity = Success
Facility = Application
SymbolicName = EVENT_LOG_SERVICE_NAME_MSGID
Language=English
EventLogDemo.EXE
.
```

Use the Messages Compiler, mc.exe, to create a binary message file. mc -s EventLogDemoMessages
.mc compiles the source file containing the messages to a messages file with the .bin extension and the
file Messages.rc, which contains a reference to the binary message file:

```
mc -s EventLogDemoMessages.mc
```

Next, you must use the Resource Compiler, rc.exe. rc EventLogDemoMessages.rc creates the
resource file EventLogDemoMessages.RES:

```
rc EventLogDemoMessages.rc
```

With the linker, you can bind the binary message file EventLogDemoMessages.RES to a native DLL:

```
link /DLL /SUBSYSTEM:WINDOWS /NOENTRY /MACHINE:x86 EventLogDemoMessages.RES
```

Now, you can register an event source that defines the resource files as shown in the following code. First, a check is done if the event source named `EventLogDemoApp` exists. If the event log must be created because it does not exist, the next check verifies if the resource file is available. Some samples in the MSDN documentation demonstrate writing the message file to the `<windows>\system32` directory, but you shouldn't do that. Copy the message DLL to a program-specific directory that you can get with the `SpecialFolder` enumeration value `ProgramFiles`. If you need to share the messages file among multiple applications, you can put it into `Environment.SpecialFolder.CommonProgramFiles`. If the file exists, a new object of type `EventSourceCreationData` is instantiated. In the constructor, the name of the source and the name of the log are defined. You use the properties `CategoryResourceFile`, `MessageResourceFile`, and `ParameterResourceFile` to define a reference to the resource file. After the event source is created, you can find the information on the resource files in the registry with the event source. The method `CreateEventSource` registers the new event source and log file. Finally, the method `RegisterDisplayName()` from the `EventLog` class specifies the name of the log as it is displayed in the Event Viewer. The ID 5001 is taken from the message file.

> *If you want to delete a previously created event source, you can do so with* `EventLog.DeleteEventS` `ource(sourceName);`. *To delete a log, you can invoke* `EventLog.Delete(logName);`.

```
string logName = "ProCSharpLog";
string sourceName = "EventLogDemoApp";
string resourceFile = Environment.GetFolderPath(
        Environment.SpecialFolder.ProgramFiles) +
        @"\procsharp\EventLogDemoMessages.dll";

if (!EventLog.SourceExists(sourceName))
{
    if (!File.Exists(resourceFile))
    {
        Console.WriteLine("Message resource file does not exist");
        return;
    }

    EventSourceCreationData eventSource =
            new EventSourceCreationData(sourceName, logName);

    eventSource.CategoryResourceFile = resourceFile;
    eventSource.CategoryCount = 4;
    eventSource.MessageResourceFile = resourceFile;
    eventSource.ParameterResourceFile = resourceFile;

    EventLog.CreateEventSource(eventSource);
}
else
{
    logName = EventLog.LogNameFromSourceName(sourceName, ".");
}

EventLog evLog = new EventLog(logName, ".", sourceName);
evLog.RegisterDisplayName(resourceFile, 5001);
```

Now, you can use the `WriteEvent()` method instead of `WriteEntry()` to write the event log entry. `WriteEvent()` requires an object of type `EventInstance` as parameter. With the `EventInstance`, you can assign the message ID, the category, and the severity of type `EventLogEntryType`. In addition to the `EventInstance` parameter, `WriteEvent()` accepts parameters for messages that have parameters and binary data as byte array.

```
EventLog log = new EventLog(logName, ".", sourceName);
EventInstance info1 = new EventInstance(1000, 4,
        EventLogEntryType.Information);

log.WriteEvent(info1);
EventInstance info2 = new EventInstance(1001, 4,
        EventLogEntryType.Error);
log.WriteEvent(info2, "avalon");

EventInstance info3 = new EventInstance(1002, 3,
        EventLogEntryType.Error);
byte[] addionalInfo = { 1, 2, 3 };
log.WriteEvent(info3, addionalInfo);

log.Dispose();
```

For the message identifiers, it is useful to define a class with const values that provide a more meaning-ful name for the identifiers in the application.

You can read the event log entries with the Event Viewer.

Event Log Listener

Instead of using the Event Viewer to read event log entries, you can create a custom event log reader that listens for events of specified types as needed. You can create a reader where important messages pop up to the screen, or send SMS to a system administrator.

Next, you write an application that receives an event when a service encounters a problem. Create a simple Windows application that monitors the events of your Quote service. This Windows application consists of a list box and an Exit button only, as shown in Figure 18-5.

Figure 18-5

Add an EventLog component to the design view by dragging and dropping it from the toolbox. Set the Log property to Application. You can set the Source property to a specific source to receive event log entries from only this source, for example the source EventLogDemoApp for receiving the event logs from the application created previously. If you leave the Source property empty, you will receive events from every source. You also need to change the property `EnableRaisingEvents`. The default value is `false`; setting it to `true` means that an event is generated each time this event occurs, and you can add an event handler for the `EntryWritten` event of the `EventLog` class. Add a handler with the name `OnEntryWritten()` to this event.

The `OnEntryWritten()` handler receives an `EntryWrittenEventArgs` object as argument, from which you can get the complete information about an event. With the `Entry` property, an `EventLogEntry` object with information about the time, event source, type, category, and so on is returned:

```
protected void OnEntryWritten (object sender,
    System.Diagnostics.EntryWrittenEventArgs e)
{
    StringBuilder sb = new StringBuilder();
    sb.AppendFormat("{0} {1} {2}",
            e.Entry.TimeGenerated.ToShortTimeString(),
            e.Entry.Source,
            e.Entry.Message);
    listBoxEvents.Items.Add(sb.ToString());
}
```

The running application displays event log information, as shown in Figure 18-6.

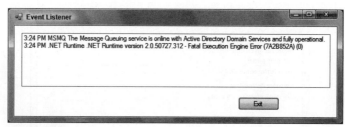

Figure 18-6

Performance Monitoring

Performance monitoring can be used to get information about the normal behavior of applications. Performance monitoring is a great tool that helps you understand the workload of the system and observe changes and trends, particularly in applications running on the server.

Microsoft Windows has many performance objects, such as `System`, `Memory`, `Objects`, `Process`, `Processor`, `Thread`, `Cache`, and so on. Each of these objects has many counts to monitor. For example, with the `Process` object, the user time, handle count, page faults, thread count, and so on can be monitored for all processes or for specific process instances. Some applications, such as SQL Server, also add application-specific objects.

For the quote service sample application, it might be interesting to get information about the number of client requests, the size of the data sent over the wire, and so on.

Performance-Monitoring Classes

The `System.Diagnostics` namespace provides these classes for performance monitoring:

❑ `PerformanceCounter` can be used both to monitor counts and to write counts. New performance categories can also be created with this class.

❑ `PerformanceCounterCategory` enables you to step through all existing categories as well as create new ones. You can programmatically get all the counters in a category.

❑ `PerformanceCounterInstaller` is used for the installation of performance counters. Its use is similar to that of the `EventLogInstaller` discussed previously.

Performance Counter Builder

The sample application is a simple Windows application with just one button so that you can see how to write performance counts. In a similar way, you can add performance counters to a Windows Service (see Chapter 23, "Windows Services"), to a network application (see Chapter 41, "Accessing the Internet"), or to any other application from which you would like to receive live counts.

Using Visual Studio, you can create a new performance counter category by selecting the performance counters in the Server Explorer and by selecting the menu entry Create New Category on the context menu. This launches the Performance Counter Builder (see Figure 18-7).

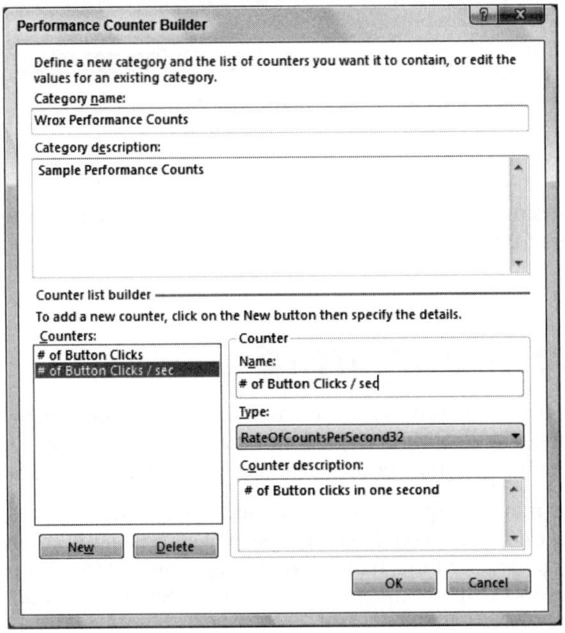

Figure 18-7

Set the name of the performance counter category to `Wrox Performance Counters`. The following table shows all performance counters of the quote service.

Name	Description	Type
# of Button clicks	Total # of button clicks	`NumberOfItems32`
# of Button clicks/sec	# of button clicks in one second	`RateOfCountsPerSecond32`
# of Mouse move events	Total # of mouse move events	`NumberOfItems32`
# of Mouse move events/sec	# of mouse move events in one second	`RateOfCountsPerSecond32`

The Performance Counter Builder writes the configuration to the performance database. This can also be done dynamically by using the `Create()` method of the `PerformanceCounterCategory` class in the `System.Diagnostics` namespace. An installer for other systems can easily be added later using Visual Studio.

Adding PerformanceCounter Components

Now you can add `PerformanceCounter` components from the toolbox. Instead of using the components from the toolbox category Components, you can directly drag and drop the previously created performance counters from the Server Explorer to the design view. This way, the instances are configured automatically; the `CategoryName` property is set to "Wrox Performance Counters" for all objects, and the `CounterName` property is set to one of the values available in the selected category. Because with this application the performance counts will not be read but written, you must set the `ReadOnly` property to `false`. Also, set the `MachineName` property to . so that the application writes performance counts locally.

Here is a part of the code generated into `InitalizeComponent()` by adding the `PerformanceCounter` components to the Designer and by setting the properties as indicated previously:

```
private void InitializeComponent()
{
    //...

    //
    // performanceCounterButtonClicks
    //
    this.performanceCounterButtonClicks.CategoryName =
        "Wrox Performance Counts";
    this.performanceCounterButtonClicks.CounterName =
        "# of Button Clicks";
    this.performanceCounterButtonClicks.ReadOnly = false;
    //
    // performanceCounterButtonClicksPerSec
    //
    this.performanceCounterButtonClicksPerSec.CategoryName =
        "Wrox Performance Counts";
    this.performanceCounterButtonClicksPerSec.CounterName =
        "# of Button Clicks / sec";
```

(continued)

(continued)

```
            this.performanceCounterButtonClicksPerSec.ReadOnly = false;
            //
            // performanceCounterMouseMoveEvents
            //
            this.performanceCounterMouseMoveEvents.CategoryName =
                 "Wrox Performance Counts";
            this.performanceCounterMouseMoveEvents.CounterName =
                 "# of Mouse Move Events";
            this.performanceCounterMouseMoveEvents.ReadOnly = false;
            //
            // performanceCounterMouseMoveEventsPerSec
            //
            this.performanceCounterMouseMoveEventsPerSec.CategoryName =
                 "Wrox Performance Counts";
            this.performanceCounterMouseMoveEventsPerSec.CounterName =
                 "# of Mouse Move Events / sec";
            this.performanceCounterMouseMoveEventsPerSec.ReadOnly = false;
            //...
        }
```

For the calculation of the performance values, you need to add the fields `clickCountPerSec` and `mouseMoveCountPerSec` to the class `Form1`:

```
        public partial class Form1 : Form
        {
            // Performance monitoring counter values
            private int clickCountPerSec = 0;
            private int mouseMoveCountPerSec = 0;
```

Add an event handler to the `Click` event of the button and an event handler to the `MouseMove` event to the form, and add the following code to the handlers:

```
        private void button1_Click(object sender, EventArgs e)
        {
            performanceCounterButtonClicks.Increment();
            clickCountPerSec++;
        }

        private void OnMouseMove(object sender, MouseEventArgs e)
        {
            performanceCounterMouseMoveEvents.Increment();
            mouseMoveCountPerSec++;
        }
```

The `Increment()` method of the `PerformanceCounter` object increments the counter by one. If you need to increment the counter by more than one, for example to add information about a byte count sent or received, you can use the `IncrementBy()` method. For the performance counts that show the value in seconds, just the two variables, `clickCountPerSec` and `mouseMovePerSec`, are incremented.

To show updated values every second, add a `Timer` component. Set the `OnTimer()` method to the `Elapsed` event of this component. The `OnTimer()` method is called once per second if you set the Interval property to 1000. In the implementation of this method, set the performance counts by using the `RawValue` property of the `PerformanceCounter` class:

```
protected void OnTimer (object sender, System.Timers.ElapsedEventArgs e)
{
    performanceCounterButtonClicksPerSec.RawValue = clickCountPerSec;
    clickCountPerSec = 0;

    performanceCounterMouseMoveEventsPerSec.RawValue =
            mouseMoveCountPerSec;
    mouseMoveCountPerSec = 0;
}
```

The timer must be started:

```
public Form1()
{
    InitializeComponent();

    this.timer1.Start();
}
```

perfmon.exe

Now you can monitor the application. You can start the Performance tool by selecting Administrative
Tools ⇨ Performance with Windows XP or Reliability and Performance Monitor with Windows Vista.
Select the Performance Monitor, and click the + button in the toolbar where you can add performance
counts. The Quote Service shows up as a performance object. All the counters that have been configured
show up in the counter list, as shown in Figure 18-8.

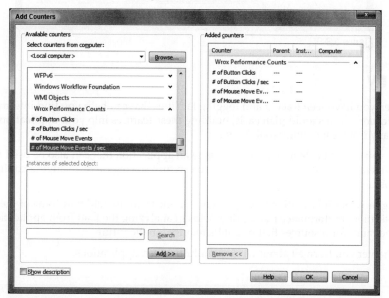

Figure 18-8

After you have added the counters to the performance monitor, you can see the actual values of the service over time (see Figure 18-9). Using this performance tool, you can also create log files to analyze the performance at a later time.

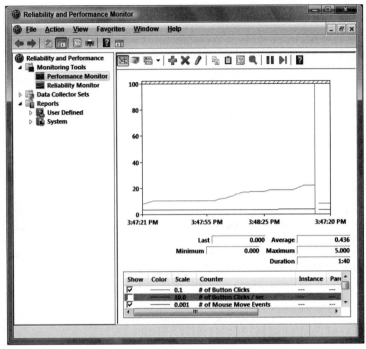

Figure 18-9

Summary

In this chapter, you have seen tracing and logging facilities that can help you find intermediate problems in your applications. You should plan early, building these features into your applications. This will help you avoid many troubleshooting problems later.

With tracing, you can write debugging messages to an application that can also be used for the final product delivered. In case there are problems, you can turn tracing on by changing configuration values, and find the issues.

Event logging provides information to the system administrator to help find some of the critical issues with the application. Performance monitoring helps in analyzing the load from applications and in planning in advance for resources that might be required in the future.

In the next chapter you learn all about writing multithreaded applications.

19

Threading and Synchronization

There are several reasons for using threading. Suppose that you are making a network call from an application that might take some time. You don't want to stall the user interface and just let the user wait until the response is returned from the server. The user could do some other actions in the meantime or even cancel the request that was sent to the server. Using threads can help.

For all activities that require a wait — for example, because of a file, database, or network access — a new thread can be started to fulfill other tasks at the same time. Even if you have only processing-intensive tasks to do, threading can help. Multiple threads of a single process can run on different CPUs, or, nowadays, on different cores of a multiple-core CPU, at the same time.

You must be aware of some issues when running multiple threads, however. Because they can run during the same time, you can easily get into problems if the threads access the same data. You must implement synchronization mechanisms.

This chapter provides the foundation you will need when programming applications with multiple threads, including:

- ❑   An overview of threading
- ❑   Lightweight threading using delegates
- ❑   Thread class
- ❑   Thread pools
- ❑   Threading issues
- ❑   Synchronization techniques
- ❑   Timers
- ❑   COM apartments
- ❑   Event-based asynchronous pattern

Overview

A thread is an independent stream of instructions in a program. All your C# programs up to this point have one entry point — the Main() method. Execution starts with the first statement in the Main() method and continues until that method returns.

This program structure is all very well for programs, in which there is one identifiable sequence of tasks, but often a program needs to do more than one thing at the same time. Threads are important both for client-side and for server-side applications. While you type C# code in the Visual Studio editor, the Dynamic Help window immediately shows the topics that fit to the code you type. A background thread is searching through help. The same thing is done by the spell checker in Microsoft Word. One thread is waiting for input from the user, while the other does some background research. A third thread can store the written data in an interim file, while another one downloads some additional data from the Internet.

In an application that is running on the server, one thread, the listener thread, waits for a request from a client. As soon as the request comes in, the request is forwarded to a separate worker thread, which continues the communication with the client. The listener thread immediately comes back to get the next request from the next client.

With the Windows Task Manager, you can turn on the column Threads from the menu View ➪ Select Columns and see the processes and the number of threads for every process. Only cmd.exe is running inside a single thread; all the other applications shown in Figure 19-1 use multiple threads. You can see one instance of Internet Explorer running 51 threads.

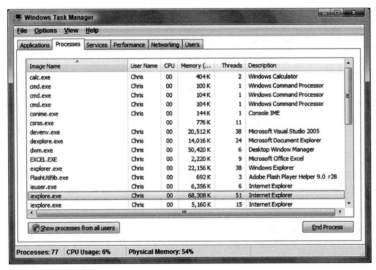

Figure 19-1

A process contains resources, such as Window handles, handles to the file system, or other kernel objects. Every process has virtual memory allocated. A process contains at least one thread. The operating system schedules threads. A thread has a priority, a program counter for the program location where it is actually processing, and a stack to store its local variables. Every thread has its own stack, but the memory for the program code and the heap are shared among all threads of a single process. This makes communication among threads of one process fast — the same virtual memory is addressed by all threads of a process. However, this also makes things difficult because multiple threads can change the same memory location.

A process manages resources that include virtual memory and Window handles, and contains at least one thread. A thread is required to run the program.

With .NET, a managed thread is defined by the Thread class. A managed thread does not necessarily map to one operating system thread. This can be the case, but it is the work of the .NET runtime host to map managed threads to the physical threads of the operating system. Here, the runtime host of SQL Server 2005 behaves very differently from the runtime host for Windows applications. You can get information about the native thread with the ProcessThread class, but with managed applications, it is usually just fine to use managed threads.

Asynchronous Delegates

A simple way to create a thread is by defining a delegate and invoking the delegate asynchronously. In Chapter 7, "Delegates and Events," you saw delegates as type-safe references to methods. The Delegate class also supports invoking the methods asynchronously. Behind the scenes, the Delegate class creates a thread that fulfills the task.

> *The delegate uses a thread pool for asynchronous tasks. Thread pools are discussed later.*

To demonstrate the asynchronous features of delegates, start with a method that takes a while to complete. The method TakesAWhile() needs at least the number of milliseconds passed with the second argument to finish because of the Thread.Sleep() method:

```
static int TakesAWhile(int data, int ms)
{
    Console.WriteLine("TakesAWhile started");
    Thread.Sleep(ms);
    Console.WriteLine("TakesAWhile completed");
    return ++data;
}
```

To invoke this method from a delegate, a delegate with the same parameter and return types must be defined, as shown by the delegate TakesAWhileDelegate:

```
public delegate int TakesAWhileDelegate(int data, int ms);
```

Now you can use different techniques, invoking the delegate asynchronously and having the result returned.

Polling

One technique is to poll and check if the delegate has already finished its work. The created delegate class provides the method BeginInvoke(), where you can pass the input parameters defined with the delegate type. BeginInvoke() always has two additional parameters of type AsyncCallback and object, which are discussed later. What's important now is the return type of BeginInvoke(): IAsyncResult. With IAsyncResult, you can get information about the delegate, and also verify if the delegate already finished its work, as is done with the IsCompleted property. The main thread of the program continues the while loop as long as the delegate hasn't completed its work.

```
static void Main()
{
    // synchronous method call
    // TakesAWhile(1, 3000);

    // asynchronous by using a delegate
```

(continued)

(continued)

```
            TakesAWhileDelegate d1 = TakesAWhile;

            IAsyncResult ar = d1.BeginInvoke(1, 3000, null, null);
            while (!ar.IsCompleted)
            {
                // doing something else in the main thread
                Console.Write(".");
                Thread.Sleep(50);
            }
            int result = d1.EndInvoke(ar);
            Console.WriteLine("result: {0}", result);
        }
```

When you run the application, you can see the main thread and the thread of the delegate running concurrently, and the main thread stops looping after the delegate thread completes:

```
.TakesAWhile started
.....................................................TakesAWhile completed
result: 2
```

Instead of examining if the delegate is completed, you can also just invoke the `EndInvoke()` method of the delegate type after you are finished with the work that can be done by the main thread. `EndInvoke()` itself waits until the delegate has completed its work.

> **If you don't wait for the delegate to complete its work and end the main thread before the delegate is finished, the thread of the delegate will be stopped.**

Wait Handle

Another way to wait for the result from the asynchronous delegate is by using the wait handle that is associated with `IAsyncResult`. You can access the wait handle with the `AsyncWaitHandle` property. This property returns an object of type `WaitHandle`, where you can wait for the delegate thread to finish its work. The method `WaitOne()` accepts a timeout with the optional first parameter, where you can define the maximum time you want to wait; here it is set to 50 milliseconds. If a timeout occurs, `WaitOne()` returns with a `false` and the `while` loop continues. If the wait is successful, the `while` loop is exited with a break, and the result is received with the delegate `EndInvoke()` method.

```
        static void Main()
        {
            TakesAWhileDelegate d1 = TakesAWhile;

            IAsyncResult ar = d1.BeginInvoke(1, 3000, null, null);
            while (true)
            {
                Console.Write(".");
                if (ar.AsyncWaitHandle.WaitOne(50, false))
                {
                    Console.WriteLine("Can get the result now");
                    break;
                }
            }
```

```
        int result = d1.EndInvoke(ar);
        Console.WriteLine("result: {0}", result);
    }
```

You can read more information about wait handles later in the synchronization section of this chapter.

Asynchronous Callback

The third version of waiting for the result from the delegate uses an asynchronous callback. With the third parameter of `BeginInvoke()`, you can pass a method that fulfills the requirements of the `AsyncCallback` delegate. The `AsyncCallback` delegate defines a parameter of `IAsnycResult` and a `void` return type. Here, the address of the method `TakesAWhileCompleted` is assigned to the third parameter that fulfills the requirements of the `AsyncCallback` delegate. With the last parameter, you can pass any object for accessing it from the callback method. It is useful to pass the delegate instance itself, so the callback method can use it to get the result of the asynchronous method.

Now the method `TakesAWhileCompleted()` is invoked as soon as the delegate `TakesAWhileDelegate` has completed its work. There is no need to wait for a result inside the main thread. However, you may not end the main thread before the work of the delegate threads is finished unless you don't have a problem with delegate threads stopping when the main thread ends.

```
static void Main()
{
    TakesAWhileDelegate d1 = TakesAWhile;

    d1.BeginInvoke(1, 3000, TakesAWhileCompleted, d1);
    for (int i = 0; i < 100; i++)
    {
        Console.Write(".");
        Thread.Sleep(50);
    }
}
```

The method `TakesAWhileCompleted()` is defined with the parameter and return type specified by the `AsyncCallback` delegate. The last parameter passed with the `BeginInvoke()` method can be read here using `ar.AsyncState`. With the `TakesAWhileDelegate` you can invoke the `EndInvoke` method to get the result.

```
static void TakesAWhileCompleted(IAsyncResult ar)
{
    if (ar == null) throw new ArgumentNullException("ar");

    TakesAWhileDelegate d1 = ar.AsyncState as TakesAWhileDelegate;
    Trace.Assert(d1 != null, "Invalid object type");

    int result = d1.EndInvoke(ar);
    Console.WriteLine("result: {0}", result);
}
```

> With a callback method, you need to pay attention to the fact that this method is invoked from the thread of the delegate and not from the main thread.

Instead of defining a separate method and passing it to the `BeginInvoke()` method, Lambda expressions can be used. The parameter `ar` is of type `IAsyncResult`. With the implementation, there is no need to assign a value to the last parameter of the `BeginInvoke()` method because the Lambda expression can directly access variable `d1` that is in the outer scope. However, the implementation block of the Lambda expression is still invoked from the thread of the delegate, which might not be clear immediately when defining the method this way.

```csharp
static void Main()
{
    TakesAWhileDelegate d1 = TakesAWhile;

    d1.BeginInvoke(1, 3000,
        ar =>
        {
            int result = d1.EndInvoke(ar);
            Console.WriteLine("result: {0}", result);
        },
        null);
    for (int i = 0; i < 100; i++)
    {
        Console.Write(".");
        Thread.Sleep(50);
    }
}
```

You should use Lambda expressions only if the code within is not too big, and the implementation is not required in different places. In such cases, defining a separate method is preferred. Lambda expressions are explained in Chapter 7, "Delegates and Events."

The programming model and all of these options with asynchronous delegates — polling, wait handles, and asynchronous callbacks — are not only available with delegates. The same programming model — this is the asynchronous pattern — can be found in various places in the .NET Framework. For example, you can send an HTTP Web request asynchronously with the `BeginGetResponse()` method of the `HttpWebRequest` class. You can send an asynchronous request to the database with the `BeginExecuteReader()` of the `SqlCommand` class. The parameters are similar to those of the `BeginInvoke()` class of the delegate, and you can use the same mechanisms to get the result.

`HttpWebRequest` is covered in Chapter 41, "Accessing the Internet," and `SqlCommand` is discussed in Chapter 26, "Data Access."

Instead of using the delegate for creating threads, you can create threads with the `Thread` class, which is covered in the next section.

The Thread Class

With the `Thread` class you can create and control threads. The code here is a very simple example of creating and starting a new thread. The constructor of the `Thread` class accepts a delegate parameter of type `ThreadStart` and `ParameterizedThreadStart`. The `ThreadStart` delegate defines a method with a void return type and without arguments. After the `Thread` object is created, you can start the thread with the `Start()` method:

```csharp
using System;
using System.Threading;

namespace Wrox.ProCSharp.Threading
```

```
{
    class Program
    {
        static void Main()
        {
            Thread t1 = new Thread(ThreadMain);
            t1.Start();
            Console.WriteLine("This is the main thread.");
        }

        static void ThreadMain()
        {
            Console.WriteLine("Running in a thread.");
        }
    }
}
```

When you run the application, you get the output of the two threads:

```
This is the main thread.
Running in a thread.
```

There is no guarantee as to what output comes first. Threads are scheduled by the operating system; which thread comes first can be different each time.

You have seen how a Lambda expression can be used with an asynchronous delegate. You can use it with the Thread class as well by passing the implementation of the thread method to the argument of the Thread constructor:

```
using System;
using System.Threading;

namespace Wrox.ProCSharp.Threading
{
    class Program
    {
        static void Main()
        {
            Thread t1 = new Thread(() => Console.WriteLine(
                "running in a thread"));
            t1.Start();
            Console.WriteLine("This is the main thread.");
        }
    }
}
```

If you don't need a variable referencing the thread to control the thread object after it was created, you can also write the code in a shorter way. Create a new Thread object with the constructor, pass a Lambda expression to the constructor, and with the Thread object returned, invoke the Start() method directly:

```
using System.Threading;

namespace Wrox.ProCSharp.Threading
{
    class Program
```

(continued)

(continued)

```
    {
        static void Main()
        {
            new Thread(() => Console.WriteLine("running in a thread")).Start();
            Console.WriteLine("This is the main thread.");
        }
    }
}
```

There are some good reasons for having a variable to reference the `Thread` object. One example, for better control of the threads, is that you can assign a name to the thread by setting the `Name` property before starting the thread. To get the name of the current thread, you can use the static property `Thread.CurrentThread` to get to the `Thread` instance of the current thread and access the `Name` property for read access. The thread also has a managed thread ID that you can read with the property `ManagedThreadId`.

```
static void Main()
{
    Thread t1 = new Thread(ThreadMain);
    t1.Name = "MyNewThread1";
    t1.Start();
    Console.WriteLine("This is the main thread.");
}

static void ThreadMain()
{
    Console.WriteLine("Running in the thread {0}, id: {1}.",
            Thread.CurrentThread.Name,
            Thread.CurrentThread.ManagedThreadId);
}
```

With the output of the application, now you can also see the thread name and ID:

```
This is the main thread.
Running in the thread MyNewThread1, id: 3.
```

> Assigning a name to the thread helps a lot with debugging threads. During your debugging session with Visual Studio, you can turn on the Debug Location toolbar that shows the name of the thread.

Passing Data to Threads

There are two ways to pass some data to a thread. You can either use the `Thread` constructor with the `ParameterizedThreadStart` delegate, or you can create a custom class and define the method of the thread as an instance method so that you can initialize data of the instance before starting the thread.

For passing data to a thread, any class or struct that holds the data is needed. Here, the struct `Data` containing a string is defined, but you can pass any object you want:

```
public struct Data
{
    public string Message;
}
```

If the `ParameterizedThreadStart` delegate is used, the entry point of the thread must have a parameter of type object and a void return type. The object can be cast to what it is, and here the message is written to the console:

```
static void ThreadMainWithParameters(object o)
{
    Data d = (Data)o;
    Console.WriteLine("Running in a thread, received {0}", d.Message);
}
```

With the constructor of the `Thread` class, you can assign the new entry point `ThreadMainWithParameters` and invoke the `Start()` method passing the variable d:

```
static void Main()
{
    Data d = new Data();
    d.Message = "Info";
    Thread t2 = new Thread(ThreadMainWithParameters);
    t2.Start(d);
}
```

Another way to pass data to the new thread is to define a class (see the class `MyThread`), where you define the fields that are needed as well as the main method of the thread as an instance method of the class:

```
public class MyThread
{
    private string data;

    public MyThread(string data)
    {
        this.data = data;
    }

    public void ThreadMain()
    {
        Console.WriteLine("Running in a thread, data: {0}", data);
    }
}
```

This way, you can create an object of `MyThread`, and pass the object and the method `ThreadMain()` to the constructor of the `Thread` class. The thread can access the data.

```
MyThread obj = new MyThread("info");
Thread t3 = new Thread(obj.ThreadMain);
t3.Start();
```

Background Threads

The process of the application keeps running as long as at least one foreground thread is running. If more than one foreground thread is running and the `Main()` method ends, the process of the application keeps active until all foreground threads finish their work.

A thread you create with the `Thread` class, by default, is a foreground thread. Thread pool threads are always background threads.

When you create a thread with the `Thread` class, you can define whether it should be a foreground or background thread by setting the property `IsBackground`. The `Main()` method sets the `IsBackground` property of the thread `t1` to `false` (which is the default). After starting the new thread, the main thread just writes to the console an end message. The new thread writes a start and an end message, and in between it sleeps for 3 seconds. The 3 seconds provide a good chance for the main thread to finish before the new thread completes its work.

```
class Program
{
    static void Main()
    {
        Thread t1 = new Thread(ThreadMain);
        t1.Name = "MyNewThread1";
        t1.IsBackground = false;
        t1.Start();
        Console.WriteLine("Main thread ending now...");
    }

    static void ThreadMain()
    {
        Console.WriteLine("Thread {0} started", Thread.CurrentThread.Name);
        Thread.Sleep(3000);
        Console.WriteLine("Thread {0} completed", Thread.CurrentThread.Name);
    }
}
```

When you start the application, you will still see the completion message written to the console, although the main thread completed its work earlier. The reason is that the new thread is a foreground thread as well.

```
Main thread ending now...
Thread MyNewThread1 started
Thread MyNewThread1 completed
```

If you change the `IsBackground` property to start the new thread to `true`, the result shown at the console is different. You can have the same result as shown here — the start message of the new thread is shown but never the end message. You might not see the start message either, if the thread was prematurely ended before it had a chance to kick off.

```
Main thread ending now...
Thread MyNewThread1 started
```

Background threads are very useful for background tasks. For example, when you close the Word application, it doesn't make sense for the spell checker to keep its process running. The spell checker thread can be killed when the application is closed. However, the thread organizing the Outlook message store should remain active until it is finished even if Outlook is closed.

Thread Priority

You have learned that the operating system schedules threads. You have had a chance to influence the scheduling by assigning a priority to the thread.

Before changing the priority, you must understand the thread scheduler. The operating system schedules threads based on a priority, and the thread with the highest priority is scheduled to run in the CPU. A thread stops running and gives up the CPU if it waits for a resource. There are several reasons why a thread must wait; for example, in response to a sleep instruction, while waiting for disk I/O to complete, while waiting for a network packet to arrive, and so on. If the thread does not give up the CPU on its own, it is preempted by the thread scheduler. If a thread does have a *time quantum*, it can use the CPU continuously. If there are multiple threads running with the same priority waiting to get the CPU, the thread scheduler uses a *round-robin* scheduling principle to give the CPU to one thread after the other. If a thread is preempted, it goes last to the queue.

The time quantum and round-robin principles are used only if multiple threads are running at the same priority. The priority is dynamic. If a thread is CPU-intensive (requires the CPU continuously without waiting for resources), the priority is lowered to the level of the base priority that is defined with the thread. If a thread is waiting for a resource, the thread gets a priority boost and the priority is increased. Because of the boost, there is a good chance that the thread gets the CPU the next time that the wait ends.

With the `Thread` class, you can influence the base priority of the thread by setting the `Priority` property. The `Priority` property requires a value that is defined by the `ThreadPriority` enumeration. The levels defined are `Highest`, `AboveNormal`, `Normal`, `BelowNormal`, and `Lowest`.

> *Be careful when giving a thread a higher priority, because this may decrease the chance for other threads to run. You can change the priority for a short time if needed.*

Controlling Threads

The thread is created by invoking the `Start()` method of a `Thread` object. However, after invoking the `Start()` method, the new thread is still not in the `Running` state, but in the `Unstarted` state instead. The thread changes to the `Running` state as soon as the operating system thread scheduler selects the thread to run. You can read the current state of a thread by reading the property `Thread.ThreadState`.

With the `Thread.Sleep()` method, a thread goes into the `WaitSleepJoin` state and waits until it is woken up again after the time span defined with the `Sleep()` method has elapsed.

To stop another thread, you can invoke the method `Thread.Abort()`. When this method is called, an exception of type `ThreadAbortException` is thrown in the thread that receives the abort. With a handler to catch this exception, the thread can do some cleanup before it ends. The thread also has a chance to continue running after receiving the `ThreadAbortException` as a result of invoking `Thread.ResetAbort()`. The state of the thread receiving the abort request changes from `AbortRequested` to the `Aborted` state if the thread does not reset the abort.

If you need to wait for a thread to end, you can invoke the `Thread.Join()` method. `Thread.Join()` blocks the current thread and sets it to the `WaitSleepJoin` state until the thread that is joined is completed.

.NET 1.0 also supported `Thread.Suspend()` and `Thread.Resume()` methods to pause and continue a thread, respectively. However, you don't know what the thread is doing when it gets the `Suspend` request, and the thread might be in a synchronized section holding locks. This can easily result in deadlocks. That's why these methods are now obsolete. Instead, you can signal a thread, using synchronization objects, so it can suspend itself. This way, the thread knows best when to go into a waiting state.

Thread Pools

Creating threads takes time. When you have different short tasks to do, you can create a number of threads in advance and send requests as they should be done. It would be nice if this number increased as more threads were needed and decreased as needed to release resources.

There is no need to create such a list on your own. The list is managed by the `ThreadPool` class. This class increases and decreases the number of threads in the pool as they are needed, up to the maximum number of threads. The maximum number of threads in a pool is configurable. With a dual-core CPU, the default number is set to 50 worker threads and 1,000 I/O threads. You can specify the minimum number of threads that should be started immediately when the pool is created and the maximum number of threads that are available in the pool. If there are more jobs to process, and the maximum number of threads in the pool has already been reached, the newest jobs are queued and must wait for a thread to complete its work.

The sample application first reads the maximum number of worker and I/O threads and writes this information to the console. Then in a `for` loop, the method `JobForAThread()` is assigned to a thread from the thread pool by invoking the method `ThreadPool.QueueUserWorkItem()` and passing a delegate of type `WaitCallback`. The thread pool receives this request and selects one of the threads from the pool to invoke the method. If the pool is not already running, the pool is created and the first thread is started. If the pool is already running and one thread is free to do the task, the job is forwarded to this thread.

```
using System;
using System.Threading;

namespace Wrox.ProCSharp.Threading
{
    class Program
    {
        static void Main()
        {
            int nWorkerThreads;
            int nCompletionPortThreads;
            ThreadPool.GetMaxThreads(out nWorkerThreads,
                                     out nCompletionPortThreads);
            Console.WriteLine("Max worker threads: {0}, " +
                            "I/O completion threads: {1}",
                            nWorkerThreads, nCompletionPortThreads);

            for (int i = 0; i < 5; i++)
            {
                ThreadPool.QueueUserWorkItem(JobForAThread);
            }
            Thread.Sleep(3000);
        }

        static void JobForAThread(object state)
        {
            for (int i = 0; i < 3; i++)
            {
                Console.WriteLine("loop {0}, running inside pooled thread {1}",
                    i, Thread.CurrentThread.ManagedThreadId);
                Thread.Sleep(50);
            }
        }
    }
}
```

When you run the application, you can see that 50 worker threads are possible with the current settings. The five jobs are processed by just two pooled threads. Your experience may be different, and you can also change the sleep time with the job and the number of jobs to process to get very different results.

```
Max worker threads: 50, I/O completion threads: 1000
loop 0, running inside pooled thread 4
loop 0, running inside pooled thread 3
loop 1, running inside pooled thread 4
loop 1, running inside pooled thread 3
loop 2, running inside pooled thread 4
loop 2, running inside pooled thread 3
loop 0, running inside pooled thread 4
loop 0, running inside pooled thread 3
loop 1, running inside pooled thread 4
loop 1, running inside pooled thread 3
loop 2, running inside pooled thread 4
loop 2, running inside pooled thread 3
loop 0, running inside pooled thread 4
loop 1, running inside pooled thread 4
loop 2, running inside pooled thread 4
```

Thread pools are very easy to use. However, there are some restrictions:

❑ All thread pool threads are background threads. If all foreground threads of a process are finished, all background threads are stopped. You cannot change a pooled thread to a foreground thread.

❑ You cannot set the priority or name of a pooled thread.

❑ For COM objects, all pooled threads are multithreaded apartment (MTA) threads. Many COM objects require a single-threaded apartment (STA) thread.

❑ Use pooled threads only for a short task. If a thread should run all the time (for example, the spell-checker thread of Word), create a thread with the Thread class.

Threading Issues

Programming with multiple threads is not easy. When starting multiple threads that access the same data, you can get intermittent problems that are hard to find. To avoid getting into trouble, you must pay attention to synchronization issues and the problems that can happen with multiple threads. We discuss two in particular next: race conditions and deadlocks.

Race Condition

A race condition can occur if two or more threads access the same objects and access to the shared state is not synchronized.

To demonstrate a race condition, the class StateObject with an int field and the method ChangeState are defined. In the implementation of ChangeState, the state variable is verified if it contains 5; if it does, the value is incremented. Trace.Assert is the next statement that immediately verifies that state now contains the value 6. After incrementing a variable by 1 that contains the value 5, you might expect that the variable now has the value 6. But this is not necessarily the case. For example, if one thread has just completed the if (state == 5) statement, it might be preempted, and the scheduler will run another thread. The second thread now goes into the if body and, because the state still has the value 5, the state is incremented by 1 to 6. The first thread is now scheduled again, and in the next statement the state is incremented to 7. This is when the race condition occurs and the assert message is shown.

```
public class StateObject
{
    private int state = 5;

    public void ChangeState(int loop)
    {
        if (state == 5)
        {
            state++;
            Trace.Assert(state == 6, "Race condition occurred after " +
                    loop + " loops");
        }
        state = 5;
    }
}
```

Let's verify this by defining a thread method. The method `RaceCondition()` of the class `SampleThread` gets a `StateObject` as a parameter. Inside an endless `while` loop, the `ChangeState()` method is invoked. The variable `i` is used just to show the loop number in the assert message:

```
public class SampleThread
{
    public void RaceCondition(object o)
    {
        Trace.Assert(o is StateObject, "o must be of type StateObject");
        StateObject state = o as StateObject;

        int i = 0;
        while (true)
        {
            state.ChangeState(i++);
        }
    }
}
```

In the `Main()` method of the program, a new `StateObject` is created that is shared between all the threads. `Thread` objects are created by passing the address of `RaceCondition` with an object of type `SampleThread` in the constructor of the `Thread` class. The thread is then started with the `Start()` method, passing the `state` object.

```
static void Main()
{
    StateObject state = new StateObject();
    for (int i = 0; i < 20; i++)
    {
        new Thread(new SampleThread().RaceCondition).Start(state);
    }
}
```

When you start the program, you will get race conditions. How long it takes until the first race condition happens depends on your system and whether you build the program as a release or debug build. With a release build, the problem will happen more often because the code is optimized. If you have multiple CPUs in your system or dual-core CPUs where multiple threads can run concurrently, the problem will also occur more often than with a single-core CPU. The problem will occur with a single-core CPU because thread scheduling is preemptive, but not that often.

Figure 19-2 shows an assert of the program where the race condition occurred after 3,816 loops. You can start the application multiple times, and you will always get different results.

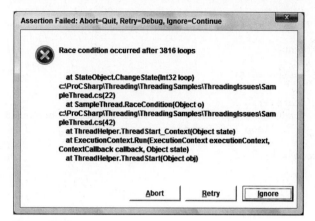

Figure 19-2

You can avoid the problem by locking the shared object. You can do this inside the thread by locking variable state that is shared between the threads with the `lock` statement as shown. Only one thread can be inside the lock block for the state object. Because this object is shared between all threads, a thread must wait at the lock if another thread has the lock for state. As soon as the lock is accepted, the thread owns the lock and gives it up with the end of the lock block. If every thread changing the object referenced with the state variable is using a lock, the race condition no longer occurs.

```
public class SampleThread
{
    public void RaceCondition(object o)
    {
        Trace.Assert(o is StateObject, "o must be of type StateObject");
        StateObject state = o as StateObject;

        int i = 0;
        while (true)
        {
            lock (state)   // no race condition with this lock
            {
                state.ChangeState(i++);
            }
        }
    }
}
```

Instead of doing the lock when using the shared object, you can make the shared object thread-safe. Here, the `ChangeState()` method contains a `lock` statement. Because you cannot lock the `state` variable itself (only reference types can be used for a lock), the variable `sync` of type `object` is defined and used with the `lock` statement. If a lock is done using the same synchronization object every time the value state is changed, race conditions no longer happen.

```
public class StateObject
{
    private int state = 5;
    private object sync = new object();

    public void ChangeState(int loop)
    {
        lock (sync)
        {
            if (state == 5)
            {
                state++;
                Trace.Assert(state == 6, "Race condition occurred after " +
                    loop + " loops");
            }
            state = 5;
        }
    }
}
```

Deadlock

Too much locking can get you in trouble as well. In a deadlock, at least two threads halt and wait for each other to release a lock. As both threads wait for each other, a deadlock occurs and the threads wait endlessly.

To demonstrate deadlocks, two objects of type `StateObject` are instantiated and passed with the constructor of the `SampleThread` class. Two threads are created: one thread running the method `Deadlock1()` and the other thread running the method `Deadlock2()`:

```
StateObject state1 = new StateObject();
StateObject state2 = new StateObject();
new Thread(new SampleThread(state1, state2).Deadlock1).Start();
new Thread(new SampleThread(state1, state2).Deadlock2).Start();
```

The methods `Deadlock1()` and `Deadlock2()` now change the state of two objects s1 and s2. That's why two locks are done. The method `Deadlock1()` first does a lock for s1 and next for s2. The method `Deadlock2()` first does a lock for s2 and then for s1. Now it may happen from time to time that the lock for s1 in `Deadlock1()` is resolved. Next, a thread switch occurs, and `Deadlock2()` starts to run and gets the lock for s2. The second thread now waits for the lock of s1. Because it needs to wait, the thread scheduler schedules the first thread again, which now waits for s2. Both threads now wait and don't release the lock as long as the lock block is not ended. This is a typical deadlock.

```
public class SampleThread
{
    public SampleThread(StateObject s1, StateObject s2)
    {
        this.s1 = s1;
        this.s2 = s2;
    }

    private StateObject s1;
    private StateObject s2;
```

```
public void Deadlock1()
{
    int i = 0;
    while (true)
    {
        lock (s1)
        {
            lock (s2)
            {
                s1.ChangeState(i);
                s2.ChangeState(i++);
                Console.WriteLine("still running, {0}", i);
            }
        }
    }
}

public void Deadlock2()
{
    int i = 0;
    while (true)
    {
        lock (s2)
        {
            lock (s1)
            {
                s1.ChangeState(i);
                s2.ChangeState(i++);
                Console.WriteLine("still running, {0}", i);
            }
        }
    }
}
```

As a result, the program will run a number of loops and will soon be unresponsive. The message still running is just written a few times to the console. Again, how soon the problem happens depends on your system configuration. And the result will differ from time to time.

The problem of deadlocks is not always as obvious as it is here. One thread locks s1 and then s2; the other thread locks s2 and then s1. You just need to change the order so that both threads do the lock in the same order. However, the locks might be hidden deeply inside a method. You can prevent this problem by designing a good lock order from the beginning in the architecture of the application, and also by defining timeouts for the locks, which we show in the next section.

Synchronization

It is best to avoid synchronization issues by not sharing data between threads. Of course, this is not always possible. If data sharing is necessary, you must use synchronization techniques so that only one thread at a time accesses and changes shared state. Remember the synchronization issues with race conditions and deadlocks. If you don't pay attention to these issues, the reason for problems in applications is hard to find because threading issues occur just from time to time.

This section discusses synchronization technologies that you can use with multiple threads:

- ❏ `lock` statement
- ❏ `Interlocked` class
- ❏ `Monitor` class
- ❏ Wait handles
- ❏ Mutex
- ❏ Semaphore
- ❏ Events
- ❏ `ReaderWriterLockSlim`

`lock`, `Interlocked`, and `Monitor` can be used for synchronization within a process. The classes `Mutex`, `Event`, `Semaphore`, and `ReaderWriterLockSlim` also offer synchronization between threads of multiple processes.

lock Statement and Thread Safety

C# has its own keyword for the synchronization of multiple threads: the `lock` statement. The `lock` statement is an easy way to hold for a lock and release it.

Before adding `lock` statements, let's go into another race condition. The class `SharedState` just demonstrates using shared state between threads, and keeps an integer value:

```
public class SharedState
{
    public int State { get; set; }
}
```

The class `Task` contains the method `DoTheTask()`, which is the entry point for a new thread. With the implementation, the `State` of `SharedState` is incremented 50,000 times. The variable `sharedState` is initialized in the constructor of this class.

```
public class Task
{
    SharedState sharedState;
    public Task(SharedState sharedState)
    {
        this.sharedState = sharedState;
    }
    public void DoTheTask()
    {
        for (int i = 0; i < 50000; i++)
        {
            sharedState.State += 1;
        }
    }
}
```

In the `Main()` method, a `SharedState` object is created and passed to the constructor of 20 `Thread` objects. All threads are started. After starting the threads, the `Main()` method does another loop to join every one of the 20 threads to wait until all threads are completed. After the threads are completed, the summarized value of the shared state is written to the console. Having 50,000 loops and 20 threads, a value of 1,000,000 could be expected. Often, however, this is not the case.

```
class Program
{
    static void Main()
    {
        int numThreads = 20;
        SharedState state = new SharedState();
        Thread[] threads = new Thread[numThreads];

        for (int i = 0; i < numThreads; i++)
        {
            threads[i] = new Thread(new Task(state).DoTheTask);
            threads[i].Start();
        }

        for (int i = 0; i < numThreads; i++)
        {
            threads[i].Join();
        }
        Console.WriteLine("summarized {0}", state.State);
    }
}
```

Results received from multiple runs of the application are as shown here:

```
summarized 939270
summarized 993799
summarized 998304
summarized 937630
```

The behavior is different every time, but none of the results is correct. You get big differences between debug and release builds, and on the types of CPUs you are using. If you change the loop count for smaller values, you will get correct values many times — but not every time. The application is small enough to see the problem easily; the reason for such a problem can be hard to find in a large application.

You must add synchronization to this program. This can be done with the lock keyword.

The object defined with the lock statement means you wait to get the lock for the specified object. You can pass only a reference type. Locking a value type would just lock a copy, and this wouldn't make any sense. Anyway, the C# compiler provides an error if value types are used with the lock statement. As soon as the lock is granted — only one thread gets the lock — the block of the lock statement can run. At the end of the lock statement block, the lock for the object is released, and another thread waiting for the lock can be granted.

```
lock (obj)
{
    // synchronized region
}
```

To lock static members, you can place the lock on the type object:

```
lock (typeof(StaticClass))
{
}
```

You can make the instance members of a class thread-safe by using the lock keyword. This way, only one thread at a time can access the methods DoThis() and DoThat() for the same instance.

```
public class Demo
{
    public void DoThis()
    {
        lock (this)
        {
            // only one thread at a time can access the DoThis and DoThat methods
        }
    }
    public void DoThat()
    {
        lock (this)
        {
        }
    }
}
```

However, because the object of the instance can also be used for synchronized access from the outside, and you can't control this from the class itself, you can apply the SyncRoot pattern. With the SyncRoot pattern, a private object named syncRoot is created, and this object is used with the lock statements:

```
public class Demo
{
    private object syncRoot = new object();

    public void DoThis()
    {
        lock (syncRoot)
        {
            // only one thread at a time can access the DoThis and DoThat methods
        }
    }
    public void DoThat()
    {
        lock (syncRoot)
        {
        }
    }
}
```

Using locks costs time and is not always needed. You can create two versions of a class: a synchronized and a nonsynchronized version. This is demonstrated here by changing the class Demo. The class Demo itself is not synchronized, as you can see in the implementation of the DoThis() and DoThat() methods. The class also defines the IsSynchronized property, where the client can get information about the synchronization option of the class. To make a synchronized variant of the class, the static method Synchronized() can be used to pass a nonsynchronized object, and this method returns an object of type SynchronizedDemo. SynchronizedDemo is implemented as an inner class that is derived from the base class Demo and overrides the virtual members of the base class. The overridden members make use of the SyncRoot pattern.

```
public class Demo
{
    private class SynchronizedDemo : Demo
    {
        private object syncRoot = new object();
        private Demo d;
```

```
        public SynchronizedDemo(Demo d)
        {
            this.d = d;
        }

        public override bool IsSynchronized
        {
            get { return true; }
        }

        public override void DoThis()
        {
            lock (syncRoot)
            {
                d.DoThis();
            }
        }

        public override void DoThat()
        {
            lock (syncRoot)
            {
                d.DoThat();
            }
        }
    }

    public virtual bool IsSynchronized
    {
        get { return false; }
    }

    public static Demo Synchronized(Demo d)
    {
        if (!d.IsSynchronized)
        {
            return new SynchronizedDemo(d);
        }
        return d;
    }

    public virtual void DoThis()
    {
    }

    public virtual void DoThat()
    {
    }
}
```

You must bear in mind that when using the SynchronizedDemo class, only methods are synchronized. There is no synchronization for invoking two members of this class.

> The SyncRoot pattern might lead to a false sense of thread safety. The .NET 1.0
> collection classes implement the SyncRoot pattern; the .NET 2.0 generic collection
> classes don't implement this pattern anymore.

Let's compare this with the example shown earlier. If you try to make the `SharedState` class thread-
safe by locking access to the properties with the SyncRoot pattern, you still get the race condition
shown earlier.

```
public class SharedState
{
    private int state = 0;
    private object syncRoot = new object();

    public int State // there's still a race condition,
                     // don't do this!
    {
        get { lock (syncRoot) {return state; }}
        set { lock (syncRoot) {state = value; }}
    }
}
```

The thread invoking the `DoTheTask` method is accessing the get accessor of the `SharedState` class
to get the current value of the state, and then the get accessor sets the new value for the state. In
between calling the get and the set accessor the object is not locked, and another thread can be the
interim value.

```
public void DoTheTask()
{
    for (int i = 0; i < 50000; i++)
    {
        sharedState.State += 1;
    }
}
```

So, it is better to leave the `SharedState` class as it was earlier without thread safety:

```
public class SharedState
{
    public int State { get; set; }
}
```

and to add the `lock` statement where it belongs, inside the method `DoTheTask()`:

```
public void DoTheTask()
{
    for (int i = 0; i < 50000; i++)
    {
        lock (sharedState)
        {
            sharedState.State += 1;
        }
    }
}
```

This way, the results of the application are always as expected:

```
summarized 1000000
```

> Using the `lock` statement in one place does not mean that all other threads accessing the object are waiting. You have to explicitly use synchronization with every thread accessing the shared state.

Of course, you can also change the design of the `SharedState` class and offer increment as an atomic operation. This is a design question — what should be an atomic functionality of the class?

```
public class SharedState
{
    private int state = 0;
    private object syncRoot = new object();

    public int State
    {
        get { return state; }
    }

    public int IncrementState()
    {
        lock (syncRoot)
        {
            return ++state;
        }
    }
}
```

There is, however, a faster way to lock the increment of the state, as shown next.

Interlocked

The `Interlocked` class is used to make simple statements for variables atomic. `i++` is not thread-safe. `i++` consists of getting a value from the memory, incrementing the value by 1, and storing the value back into memory. These operations can be interrupted by the thread scheduler. The `Interlocked` class provides methods for incrementing, decrementing, and exchanging values in a thread-safe manner.

The methods provided by the `Interlocked` class are described in the following table.

Interlocked Member	Description
Increment()	The `Increment()` method increments a variable and stores the result in an atomic operation.
Decrement()	`Decrement()` decrements a variable and stores the result.
Exchange()	`Exchange()` sets a variable to the specified value and returns the original value of the variable.

Interlocked Member	Description
CompareExchange()	CompareExchange() compares two variables for equality, and if they are the same, the specified value is set and the original value returned.
Add()	The Add() method adds two values and replaces the first variable with the result.
Read()	The Read() method is used to read 64-bit values from memory in an atomic operation. On a 32-bit system, reading 64 bits is not atomic; here, values from two memory addresses are read.
	On a 64-bit system, the Read() method is not required because accessing 64 bit values is an atomic operation.

Using the Interlocked class in contrast to other synchronization techniques is much faster. However, you can use it only for simple synchronization issues.

For example, instead of using the lock statement to lock access to the variable someState when setting it to a new value, in case it is null, you can use the Interlocked class, which is faster:

```
lock (this)
{
    if (someState == null)
    {
        someState = newState;
    }
}
```

The faster version with the same functionality uses the Interlocked.CompareExchange() method:

```
Interlocked.CompareExchange<SomeState>(ref someState, newState,
                                       null);
```

And instead of doing an increment inside a lock statement:

```
public int State
{
    get
    {
        lock (this)
        {
            return ++state;
        }
    }
}
```

Interlocked.Increment() is faster:

```
public int State
{
    get
    {
        return Interlocked.Increment(ref state);
    }
}
```

Monitor

The C# compiler resolves the `lock` statement to use the `Monitor` class. The following `lock` statement

```
lock (obj)
{
    // synchronized region for obj
}
```

is resolved to invoking the `Enter()` method that waits until the thread gets the lock of the object. Only one thread at a time may be the owner of the object lock. As soon as the lock is resolved, the thread can enter the synchronized section. The `Exit()` method of the `Monitor` class releases the lock. The compiler puts the `Exit()` method into a finally handler of a try block so that the lock is also released if an exception is thrown.

`try/finally` is covered in Chapter 14, "Errors and Exceptions."

```
Monitor.Enter(obj);
try
{
    // synchronized region for obj
}
finally
{
    Monitor.Exit(obj);
}
```

The class `Monitor` has a big advantage compared to the `lock` statement of C#: you can add a timeout value waiting to get the lock. So instead of endlessly waiting to get the lock, you can use the `TryEnter()` method, where you can pass a timeout value that defines the maximum amount of time waiting to get the lock. If the lock for `obj` is acquired, `TryEnter()` returns `true` and performs synchronized access to the state guarded by the object `obj`. If `obj` is locked for more than 500 milliseconds by another thread, `TryEnter()` returns `false`, and the thread does not wait any longer but is used to do something else. Maybe at a later time, the thread can try to acquire the lock once more.

```
if (Monitor.TryEnter(obj, 500))
{
    try
    {
        // acquired the lock
        // synchronized region for obj
    }
    finally
    {
        Monitor.Exit(obj);
    }

}
else
{
    // didn't get the lock, do something else
}
```

Wait Handle

`WaitHandle` is an abstract base class that you can use to wait for a signal to be set. There are different things you can wait for, because `WaitHandle` is a base class and some classes are derived from it.

In the use of asynchronous delegates early in this chapter, the WaitHandle was already in use. The method BeginInvoke() of the asynchronous delegate returns an object that implements the interface IAsyncResult. Using IAsyncResult, you can access a WaitHandle with the property AsyncWaitHandle. When you invoke the method WaitOne(), the thread waits until a signal is received that is associated with the wait handle.

```
static void Main()
{
    TakesAWhileDelegate d1 = TakesAWhile;

    IAsyncResult ar = d1.BeginInvoke(1, 3000, null, null);
    while (true)
    {
        Console.Write(".");
        if (ar.AsyncWaitHandle.WaitOne(50, false))
        {
            Console.WriteLine("Can get the result now");
            break;
        }
    }
    int result = d1.EndInvoke(ar);
    Console.WriteLine("result: {0}", result);
}
```

The methods that are defined by the class WaitHandle to perform a wait are described in the following table.

WaitHandle Member	Description
WaitOne()	WaitOne() is an instance method where you can wait for a signal to occur. Optionally, you can specify a timeout value for the maximum amount of time to wait.
WaitAll()	WaitAll() is a static method used to pass an array of WaitHandle objects and wait until all of these handles are signaled.
WaitAny()	WaitAny() is a static method used to pass an array of WaitHandle objects and to wait until one of these handles is signaled. This method returns the index of the wait handle object that was signaled, so you know with what functionality you can continue in the program. If the timeout occurred before one handle was signaled, WaitAny() returns WaitTimeout.

With the SafeWaitHandle property, you can also assign a native handle to an operating system resource and wait for that handle. For example, you can assign a SafeFileHandle to wait for a file I/O operation to complete, or a custom SafeTransactionHandle as shown in Chapter 22, "Transactions."

The classes Mutex, Event, and Semaphore are derived from the base class WaitHandle, so you can use all of these with waits.

Mutex

Mutex (mutual exclusion) is one of the classes of the .NET Framework that offers synchronization across multiple processes. It is very similar to the Monitor class in that there is just one owner. Just one thread can get a lock of the mutex and access the synchronized code regions that are secured by the mutex.

With the constructor of the Mutex class, you can define if the mutex should initially be owned by the calling thread, define a name of the mutex, and get the information if the mutex already existed. In the sample code, the third parameter is defined as an out parameter to receive a Boolean value if the mutex was newly created. If the value returned is false, the mutex was already defined. The mutex might be defined in a different process, because a mutex with a name is known for the operating system and is shared between different processes. If there is not a name assigned to the mutex, the mutex is unnamed and not shared between different processes.

```
bool createdNew;
Mutex mutex = new Mutex(false, "ProCSharpMutex", out createdNew);
```

To open an existing mutex, you can also use the method Mutex.OpenExisting(), which doesn't require the same .NET privileges as creating the mutex with the constructor.

Because the Mutex class derives from the base class WaitHandle, you can do a WaitOne() to acquire the mutex lock and be the owner of the mutex during that time. The mutex is released by invoking the ReleaseMutex() method.

```
if (mutex.WaitOne())
{
    try
    {
        // synchronized region
    }
    finally
    {
        mutex.ReleaseMutex();
    }
}
else
{
    // some problem happened while waiting
}
```

Because a named mutex is known system-wide, you can use it to not allow an application to be started twice. In the following Windows Forms application, the constructor of the Mutex object is invoked. Then it is verified if the mutex with the name SingletonWinAppMutex exists already. If it does, the application exits.

```
static class Program
{
    [STAThread]
    static void Main()
    {
        bool createdNew;
        Mutex mutex = new Mutex(false, "SingletonWinAppMutex",
                        out createdNew);
        if (!createdNew)
        {
            MessageBox.Show("You can only start one instance " +
                        "of the application");
```

(continued)

(continued)

```
                    Application.Exit();
                    return;
            }

            Application.EnableVisualStyles();
            Application.SetCompatibleTextRenderingDefault(false);
            Application.Run(new Form1());
        }
    }
```

Semaphore

A semaphore is very similar to a mutex, but, in contrast, the semaphore can be used by multiple threads at once. A semaphore is a counting mutex, meaning that with a semaphore you can define the number of threads that are allowed to access the resource guarded by the semaphore simultaneously. This can be used if you have several of the resources available and can allow only a specific number of threads access to the resource. For example, say that you want to access physical I/O ports on the system and there are three ports available. So, three threads can access the I/O ports simultaneously, but the fourth thread needs to wait until the resource is released by one of the other threads.

In the sample application, in the Main() method six threads are created and one semaphore with a count of 4. In the constructor of the Semaphore class, you can define count for the number of locks that can be acquired with the semaphore (the second parameter) and the number of locks that are free initially (the first parameter). If the first parameter has a lower value than the second parameter, the difference between the values defines the already allocated semaphore count. As with the mutex, you can also assign a name to the semaphore to share it between different processes. Here, no name is defined with the semaphore, so it is used only within this process. After the Semaphore object is created, six threads are started, and they all get the same semaphore.

```csharp
using System;
using System.Threading;
using System.Diagnostics;

namespace Wrox.ProCSharp.Threading
{
    class Program
    {
        static void Main()
        {
            int threadCount = 6;
            int semaphoreCount = 4;
            Semaphore semaphore = new Semaphore(semaphoreCount, semaphoreCount);
            Thread[] threads = new Thread[threadCount];

            for (int i = 0; i < threadCount; i++)
            {
                threads[i] = new Thread(ThreadMain);
                threads[i].Start(semaphore);
            }

            for (int i = 0; i < threadCount; i++)
```

```
        {
            threads[i].Join();
        }
        Console.WriteLine("All threads finished");
    }
```

In the thread's main method, ThreadMain(), the thread does a WaitOne() to lock the semaphore. Remember, the semaphore has a count of 4, so four threads can acquire the lock. Thread 5 must wait and, here, the timeout of 600 milliseconds is defined for a maximum wait time. If the lock cannot be acquired after the wait time, the thread writes a message to the console and repeats the wait in a loop. As soon as the lock is made, the thread writes a message to the console, sleeps for some time, and releases the lock. Again, with the release of the lock it is important that the resource be released in all cases. That's why the Release() method of the Semaphore class is invoked in a finally handler.

```
static void ThreadMain(object o)
{
    Semaphore semaphore = o as Semaphore;
    Trace.Assert(semaphore != null, "o must be a Semaphore type");
    bool isCompleted = false;
    while (!isCompleted)
    {
        if (semaphore.WaitOne(600, false))
        {
            try
            {
                Console.WriteLine("Thread {0} locks the semaphore",
                    Thread.CurrentThread.ManagedThreadId);
                Thread.Sleep(2000);
            }
            finally
            {
                semaphore.Release();
                Console.WriteLine("Thread {0} releases the semaphore",
                    Thread.CurrentThread.ManagedThreadId);
                isCompleted = true;
            }
        }
        else
        {
            Console.WriteLine("Timeout for thread {0}; wait again",
                Thread.CurrentThread.ManagedThreadId);
        }
    }
}
```

When you run the application, you can indeed see that with four threads the lock is made immediately. The threads with IDs 7 and 8 must wait. The wait continues in the loop until one of the other threads releases the semaphore.

```
Thread 3 locks the semaphore
Thread 4 locks the semaphore
Thread 5 locks the semaphore
Thread 6 locks the semaphore
```

(continued)

(continued)

```
Timeout for thread 8; wait again
Timeout for thread 7; wait again
Timeout for thread 8; wait again
Timeout for thread 7; wait again
Timeout for thread 7; wait again
Timeout for thread 8; wait again
Thread 3 releases the semaphore
Thread 8 locks the semaphore
Thread 4 releases the semaphore
Thread 7 locks the semaphore
Thread 5 releases the semaphore
Thread 6 releases the semaphore
Thread 8 releases the semaphore
Thread 7 releases the semaphore
All threads finished
```

Events

Events are the next of the system-wide synchronization resources. For using system events from managed code, the .NET Framework offers the classes `ManualResetEvent` and `AutoResetEvent` in the namespace `System.Threading`.

The `event` keyword from C# that was covered in Chapter 7 has nothing to do with the event classes from the namespace `System.Threading`. The `event` keyword is based on delegates, whereas both event classes are .NET wrappers to the system-wide native event resource for synchronization.

You can use events to inform other threads that some data is here, something is completed, and so on. An event can be signaled or not signaled. A thread can wait for the event to be in a signaled state with the help of the `WaitHandle` class, which was already discussed.

A `ManualResetEvent` is signaled by invoking the `Set()` method and turned back to a non-signaled state with the `Reset()` method. If multiple threads are waiting for an event to be signaled, and the `Set()` method is invoked, then all threads waiting are released. Also, if a thread just invokes the `WaitOne()` method, but the event is already signaled, the waiting thread can continue immediately.

An `AutoResetEvent` is also signaled by invoking the `Set()` method. It is also possible to set it back to a non-signaled state with the `Reset()` method. However, if a thread is waiting for an auto-reset event to be signaled, the event is automatically changed into a non-signaled state when the wait state of the first thread is finished. The event changes automatically back into a non-signaled state. This way, if multiple threads are waiting for the event to be set, only one thread is released from its wait state. It is not the thread that has been waiting the longest for the event to be signaled but the thread waiting with the highest priority.

To demonstrate events with the `AutoResetEvent` class, the class `ThreadTask` defines the method `Calculation()`, which is the entry point for a thread. With this method, the thread receives input data for calculation (defined with the struct `InputData`) and writes the result to the variable result that can be accessed from the `Result` property. As soon as the result is completed (after a random amount of time), the event is signaled by invoking the `Set()` method of the `AutoResetEvent`.

```
public struct InputData
{
    public int X;
    public int Y;

    public InputData(int x, int y)
```

```
        {
            this.X = x;
            this.Y = y;
        }
    }

    public class ThreadTask
    {
        private AutoResetEvent autoEvent;

        public int Result { get; private set; }

        public ThreadTask(AutoResetEvent ev)
        {
            this.autoEvent = ev;
        }

        public void Calculation(object obj)
        {
            InputData data = (InputData)obj;
            Console.WriteLine("Thread {0} starts calculation",
                Thread.CurrentThread.ManagedThreadId);
            Thread.Sleep(new Random().Next(3000));
            Result = data.X + data.Y;

            // signal the event - completed!
            Console.WriteLine("Thread {0} is ready",
                Thread.CurrentThread.ManagedThreadId);
            autoEvent.Set();
        }
    }
```

The `Main()` method of the program defines arrays of four `AutoResetEvent` objects and four `ThreadTask` objects. Every `ThreadTask` is initialized in the constructor with an `AutoResetEvent` object, so that every thread gets its own event object to signal when it is completed. Now the `ThreadPool` class is used to have background threads running the calculation tasks by invoking the method `QueueUserWorkItem()`.

```
    class Program
    {
        static void Main()
        {
            int taskCount = 4;

            AutoResetEvent[] autoEvents = new AutoResetEvent[taskCount];
            ThreadTask[] tasks = new ThreadTask[taskCount];

            for (int i = 0; i < taskCount; i++)
            {
                autoEvents[i] = new AutoResetEvent(false);
                tasks[i] = new ThreadTask(mevents[i]);

                ThreadPool.QueueUserWorkItem(tasks[i].Calculation,
                    new InputData(i + 1, i + 3));
            }
            //...
```

The WaitHandle class is now used to wait for any one of the events in the array. WaitAny() waits until any one of the events is signaled. WaitAny() returns an index value that provides information about the event that was signaled. The returned value matches the index of the event array that is passed to WaitAny(). Using this index the information from the signaled event can be read.

```
for (int i = 0; i < taskCount; i++)
{
    int index = WaitHandle.WaitAny(autoEvents);
    if (index == WaitHandle.WaitTimeout)
    {
        Console.WriteLine("Timeout!!");
    }
    else
    {
        Console.WriteLine("finished task for {0}, result: {1}",
                          index, tasks[index].Result);
    }
}
```

Starting the application, you can see the threads doing the calculation and setting the event to inform the main thread that it can read the result. Depending on random times, whether the build is a debug or release build, and your hardware, you might see different orders and also a different number of threads from the pool doing the tasks. Here, thread 4 was reused from the pool for doing two tasks because it was fast enough to finish the calculation first:

```
Thread 3 starts calculation
Thread 4 starts calculation
Thread 5 starts calculation
Thread 4 is ready
finished task for 1, result: 6
Thread 4 starts calculation
Thread 3 is ready
finished task for 0, result: 4
Thread 4 is ready
finished task for 3, result: 10
Thread 5 is ready
finished task for 2, result: 8
```

ReaderWriterLockSlim

For a locking mechanism to allow multiple readers, but just one writer, to a resource, the class ReaderWriterLockSlim can be used. This class offers a locking functionality in which multiple readers can access the resource if no writer locked it, and only a single writer can lock the resource.

> ReaderWriterLockSlim is new with .NET 3.0. The .NET 1.0 class with similar functionality is ReaderWriterLock. ReaderWriterLockSlim was redesigned to prevent deadlocks and to offer better performance.

The methods and properties of ReaderWriterLockSlim are explained in the following tables.

ReaderWriterLockSlim Methods	Description
TryEnterReadLock() EnterReadLock() ExitReadLock()	With TryEnterReadLock() and EnterReadLock() a read lock is done to access the resource. As long as there is no write lock, the read lock is successful. Multiple reads are allowed concurrently. With TryEnterReadLock() a time-out value can be specified for a maximum amount of time to wait for the lock to be acquired. ExitReadLock() releases the lock.
TryEnterUpgradableReadLock() EnterUpgradableReadLock() ExitUpgradableReadLock()	If the read lock needs to be changed to a write lock after doing a read access to the resource, TryEnterUpgradableReadLock() and EnterUpgradableReadLock() can be used. The thread having a read lock can acquire a write lock without releasing the read lock.
TryEnterWriteLock() EnterWriteLock() ExitWriteLock()	TryEnterWriteLock() and EnterWriteLock() are used to acquire a write lock to the resource. Only one thread acquiring the lock gets the lock. Also, there may not be any thread holding a read lock. When waiting for a write lock, it is also necessary that all read locks have been released. If one thread holding a write lock tries to get a write lock once again, the lock is acquired if the ReaderWriterLockSlim was created with the RecursionPolicy set to LockRecursionPolicy.SupportsRecursion.

Properties of the ReaderWriterLockSlim class give some status information about the current locks.

ReaderWriterLockSlim Properties	Description
CurrentReadCount	This returns the number of threads that acquired a read lock.
IsReadLockHeld IsUpgradableReadLockHeld IsWriteLockHeld	These properties return a Boolean value about the corresponding lock type.
WaitingReadCount WaitingUpgradableReadCount WaitingWriteCount	These properties return the number of threads that wait for the corresponding lock type.
RecursionPolicy RecursiveReadCount RecursiveUpgradableReadCount RecursiveWriteCount	With recursion, it is possible that one thread can acquire a lock again. The property RecursionPolicy is a read-only property to return the LockRecursionPolicy. The recursion policy can be configured with the ReaderWriterLockSlim constructor to NoRecursion or SupportsRecursion.

The sample program creates a collection containing six items and a `ReaderWriterLockSlim` object. The method `ReaderMethod()` acquired a read lock to read all items of the list and write it to the console. The method `WriterMethod()` tries to acquire a write lock to change all values of the collection. In the `Main()` method six threads are started that invoke either the method `ReaderMethod()` or the method `WriterMethod()`.

```csharp
using System;
using System.Collections.Generic;
using System.Threading;

namespace Wrox.ProCSharp.Threading
{
    class Program
    {
        private static List<int> items = new List<int>()
                { 0, 1, 2, 3, 4, 5};
        private static ReaderWriterLockSlim rwl = new
                ReaderWriterLockSlim(LockRecursionPolicy.SupportsRecursion);

        static void ReaderMethod(object reader)
        {
            try
            {
                rwl.EnterReadLock();

                for (int i = 0; i < items.Count; i++)
                {
                    Console.WriteLine("reader {0}, loop: {1}, item: {2}",
                            reader, i, items[i]);
                    Thread.Sleep(40);
                }
            }
            finally
            {
                rwl.ExitReadLock();
            }
        }

        static void WriterMethod(object writer)
        {
            try
            {
                while (!rwl.TryEnterWriteLock(50))
                {
                    Console.WriteLine("Writer {0} waiting for the write lock",
                            writer);
                    Console.WriteLine("current reader count: {0}",
                            rwl.CurrentReadCount);
                }
                Console.WriteLine("Writer {0} acquired the lock", writer);
                for (int i = 0; i < items.Count; i++)
                {
                    items[i]++;
                    Thread.Sleep(50);
                }
```

```
                Console.WriteLine("Writer {0} finished", writer);
            }
            finally
            {
                rwl.ExitWriteLock();
            }
        }

        static void Main()
        {
            new Thread(WriterMethod).Start(1);
            new Thread(ReaderMethod).Start(1);
            new Thread(ReaderMethod).Start(2);
            new Thread(WriterMethod).Start(2);
            new Thread(ReaderMethod).Start(3);
            new Thread(ReaderMethod).Start(4);
        }
    }
}
```

With a run of the application here the first writer gets the lock first. The second writer and all readers need to wait. Next, the readers can work concurrently while the second writer still waits for the resource.

```
Writer 1 acquired the lock
Writer 2 waiting for the write lock
current reader count: 0
Writer 2 waiting for the write lock
current reader count: 0
Writer 2 waiting for the write lock
current reader count: 0
Writer 2 waiting for the write lock
current reader count: 0
Writer 1 finished
reader 4, loop: 0, item: 1
reader 1, loop: 0, item: 1
Writer 2 waiting for the write lock
current reader count: 4
reader 2, loop: 0, item: 1
reader 3, loop: 0, item: 1
reader 4, loop: 1, item: 2
reader 1, loop: 1, item: 2
reader 3, loop: 1, item: 2
reader 2, loop: 1, item: 2
Writer 2 waiting for the write lock
current reader count: 4
reader 4, loop: 2, item: 3
reader 1, loop: 2, item: 3
reader 2, loop: 2, item: 3
reader 3, loop: 2, item: 3
Writer 2 waiting for the write lock
current reader count: 4
reader 4, loop: 3, item: 4
reader 1, loop: 3, item: 4
reader 2, loop: 3, item: 4
```

(continued)

(continued)

```
reader 3, loop: 3, item: 4
reader 4, loop: 4, item: 5
reader 1, loop: 4, item: 5
Writer 2 waiting for the write lock
current reader count: 4
reader 2, loop: 4, item: 5
reader 3, loop: 4, item: 5
reader 4, loop: 5, item: 6
reader 1, loop: 5, item: 6
reader 2, loop: 5, item: 6
reader 3, loop: 5, item: 6
Writer 2 waiting for the write lock
current reader count: 4
Writer 2 acquired the lock
Writer 2 finished
```

Timers

The .NET Framework offers several `Timer` classes that can be used to invoke a method after some time interval. The following table lists the `Timer` classes and their namespaces, as well as their functionality.

Namespace	Description
System.Threading	The `Timer` class from the `System.Threading` namespace offers core functionality. In the constructor, you can pass a delegate that should be invoked at the time interval specified.
System.Timers	The `Timer` class from the `System.Timers` namespace is a component, because it derives from the `Component` base class. This way, you can drag and drop it from the Toolbox to the design surface of a server-application such as a Windows Service. This `Timer` class uses `System.Threading.Timer` but offers an event-based mechanism instead of a delegate.
System.Windows.Forms	With the `Timer` classes from the namespaces `System.Threading` and `System.Timers`, the callback or event methods are invoked from a different thread than the calling thread. Windows Forms controls are bound to the creator thread. Calling back into this thread is done by the `Timer` class from the `System.Windows.Forms` namespace.
System.Web.UI	The `Timer` from the `System.Web.UI` namespace is an Ajax extension that can be used with Web pages.

Using the `System.Threading.Timer` class, you can pass the method to be invoked as the first parameter in the constructor. This method must fulfill the requirements of the `TimerCallback` delegate that defines a void return type and an `object` parameter. With the second parameter, you can pass any object that is then received with the object argument in the callback method. For example, you can pass an `Event` object to signal the caller. The third parameter specifies the time span when the callback should be invoked the first time. With the last parameter, you specify the repeating interval for the callback. If the timer should fire only once, set parameter four to the value –1.

If the time interval should be changed after creating the Timer object, you can pass new values with the Change() method.

```
private static void ThreadingTimer()
{
    System.Threading.Timer t1 = new System.Threading.Timer(
        TimeAction, null, TimeSpan.FromSeconds(2),
        TimeSpan.FromSeconds(3));

    Thread.Sleep(15000);

    t1.Dispose();
}

static void TimeAction(object o)
{
    Console.WriteLine("System.Threading.Timer {0:T}", DateTime.Now);
}
```

The constructor of the Timer class from the System.Timers namespace requires just a time interval. The method that should be invoked after the interval is specified by the Elapsed event. This event requires a delegate of type ElapsedEventHandler that requires object and ElapsedEventArgs parameters as you can see with the TimeAction method. The AutoReset property specifies whether the timer should be fired repeatedly. Setting this property to false, the event is fired only once. Calling the Start method enables the timer to fire the events. Instead of calling the Start method you can set the Enabled property to true. Behind the scenes Start() does nothing else. The Stop() method sets the Enabled property to false to stop the timer.

```
private static void TimersTimer()
{
    System.Timers.Timer t1 = new System.Timers.Timer(1000);
    t1.AutoReset = true;
    t1.Elapsed += TimeAction;
    t1.Start();
    Thread.Sleep(10000);
    t1.Stop();

    t1.Dispose();
}

static void TimeAction(object sender, System.Timers.ElapsedEventArgs e)
{
    Console.WriteLine("System.Timers.Timer {0:T}", e.SignalTime );
}
```

COM Apartments

Threading has always been an important topic with COM objects. COM defines apartment models for synchronization. With a single-threaded apartment (STA), the COM runtime does the synchronization. A multithreaded apartment (MTA) means better performance but without synchronization by the COM runtime.

A COM component defines the apartment model it requires by setting a configuration value in the registry. A COM component that is developed in a thread-safe manner supports the MTA. Multiple threads can access this component at once, and the component must do synchronization on its own.

A COM component that doesn't deal with multiple threads requires an STA. Here, just one (and always the same) thread accesses the component. Another thread can access the component only by using a proxy that sends a Windows message to the thread that is connected to the COM object. STAs use Windows messages for synchronization.

Visual Basic 6 components supported only the STA model. A COM component that is configured with the option `both` supports both STA and MTA.

Whereas the COM component defines the requirements for the apartment, the thread that instantiates the COM object defines the apartment it is running in. This apartment should be the same one that the COM component requires.

A .NET thread, by default, runs in a MTA. You have probably already seen the attribute `[STAThread]` with the `Main()` method of a Windows application. This attribute specifies that the main thread joins an STA. Windows Forms applications require an STA thread.

```
[STAThread]
static void Main()
{
    //...
```

When creating a new thread, you can define the apartment model either by applying the attribute `[STAThread]` or `[MTAThread]` to the entry point method of the thread or by invoking the `SetApartmentState()` method of the `Thread` class before starting the thread:

```
Thread t1 = new Thread(DoSomeWork);
t1.SetApartmentState(ApartmentState.STA);
t1.Start();
```

You can get the apartment of the thread with the `GetApartmentThread()` method.

In Chapter 24, "Interoperability," you can read about .NET interop with COM components and more about COM apartment models.

Event-Based Asynchronous Pattern

Earlier in this chapter, you saw the asynchronous pattern based on the `IAsyncResult` interface. With an asynchronous callback, the callback thread is different from the calling thread. Using Windows Forms or WPF, this is a problem, because Windows Forms and WPF controls are bound to a single thread. With every control, you can invoke methods only from the thread that created the control. This also means that if you have a background thread, you cannot directly access the UI controls from this thread.

The only methods with Windows Forms controls that you can invoke from a different thread than the creator thread are `Invoke()`, `BeginInvoke()`, `EndInvoke()`, and the property `InvokeRequired`. `BeginInvoke()` and `EndInvoke()` are asynchronous variants of `Invoke()`. These methods switch to the creator thread to invoke the method that is assigned to a delegate parameter that you can pass to these methods. Using these methods is not that easy, which is why, since .NET 2.0, a new component together with a new asynchronous pattern was invented: the event-based asynchronous pattern.

With the event-based asynchronous pattern, the asynchronous component offers a method with the suffix `Async`; for example, the synchronous method `DoATask()` has the name `DoATaskAsync()` in the asynchronous version. To get the result information, the component also needs to define an event that has the suffix `Completed`, for example, `DoATaskCompleted`. While the action happening in the `DoATaskAsync()` method is running in a background thread, the event `DoATaskCompleted` is fired in the same thread as the caller.

With the event-based asynchronous pattern, the asynchronous component optionally can support cancellation and information about progress. For cancellation, the method should have the name `CancelAsync()`, and for progress information, an event with the suffix `ProgressChanged`, for example, `DoATaskProgressChanged`, is offered.

> *If you haven't written any Windows applications until now, you can skip this section of the chapter and keep it for later. Just remember, using threads from Windows applications adds another complexity, and you should come back here after reading the Windows Forms chapters (Chapters 31 to 33) or WPF chapters (Chapters 34 and 35). In any case, the Windows Forms application demonstrated here is very simple from a Windows Forms viewpoint.*

BackgroundWorker

The `BackgroundWorker` class is one implementation of the asynchronous event pattern. This class implements methods, properties, and events, as described in the following table.

> *Another class that implements the asynchronous event pattern is the component `WebClient` in the `System.Net` namespace. This class uses the `WebRequest` and `WebResponse` classes but offers an easier-to-use interface. The `WebRequest` and `WebResponse` classes also offer asynchronous programming, but here it is based on the asynchronous pattern with the `IAsyncResult` interface.*

BackgroundWorker Members	Description
`IsBusy`	The property `IsBusy` returns `true` while an asynchronous task is active.
`CancellationPending`	The property `CancellationPending` returns `true` after the `CancelAsync()` method is invoked. If this property is set to `true`, the asynchronous task should stop its work.
`RunWorkerAsync()` `DoWork`	The method `RunWorkerAsync()` fires the `DoWork` event to start the asynchronous task in a separate thread.
`CancelAsync()` `WorkerSupportsCancellation`	If cancellation is enabled (by setting the `WorkerSupportsCancellation` property to `true`), the asynchronous task can be canceled with the `CancelAsync()` method.

`ReportProgress()`
`ProgressChanged`
`WorkerReportsProgress`
	If the `WorkerReportsProgress` property is set to `true`, the `BackgroundWorker` can give interim feedback about the progress of the asynchronous task. The asynchronous task provides feedback about the percentage of work completed, by invoking the method `ReportProgress()`. This method then fires the `ProgressChanged` event.

`RunWorkerCompleted`	The `RunWorkerCompleted` event is fired as soon as the asynchronous task is completed, regardless of whether it was canceled.

The sample application demonstrates the use of the `BackgroundWorker` control in a Windows Forms application by doing a task that takes some time. Create a new Windows Forms application and add three `Label` controls, three `TextBox` controls, two `Button` controls, one `ProgressBar`, and one `BackgroundWorker` to the form, as shown in Figure 19-3.

Figure 19-3

Configure the properties of the controls as listed in the following table.

Control	Property and Events	Value
Label	Text	X:
TextBox	Name	textbox
Label	Text	Y:
TextBox	Name	textBoxY
Label	Text	Result:
TextBox	Name	textBoxResult
Button	Name	buttonCalculate
Text	Calculate	
Click	OnCalculate	
Button	Name	buttonCancel
Text	Cancel	
Enabled	False	
Click	OnCancel	
ProgressBar	Name	progressBar
BackgroundWorker	Name	backgroundWorker
DoWork	OnDoWork	
RunWorkerCompleted	OnWorkCompleted	

Add the struct CalcInput to the project. This struct will be used to contain the input data from the TextBox controls.

```
public struct CalcInput
{
    public CalcInput(int x, int y)
    {
        this.x = x;
        this.y = y;
    }
    public int x;
    public int y;
}
```

The method OnCalculate() is the event handler for the Click event from the Button control named buttonCalculate. In the implementation buttonCalculate is disabled, so the user cannot click the button once more until the calculation is completed. To start the BackgroundWorker, invoke the method RunWorkerAsync(). The BackgroundWorker uses a thread pool thread to do the calculation. RunWorkerAsync() requires the input parameters that are passed to the handler that is assigned to the DoWork event.

```
private void OnCalculate(object sender, EventArgs e)
{
    this.buttonCalculate.Enabled = false;
    this.textBoxResult.Text = String.Empty;
    this.buttonCancel.Enabled = true;
    this.progressBar.Value = 0;

    backgroundWorker.RunWorkerAsync(new CalcInput(
        int.Parse(this.textBoxX.Text), int.Parse(this.textBoxY.Text)));
}
```

The method OnDoWork() is connected to the DoWork event of the BackgroundWorker control. With the DoWorkEventArgs, the input parameters are received with the property Argument. The implementation simulates functionality that takes some time with a sleep time of 5 seconds. After sleeping, the result of the calculation is written to the Result property of DoEventArgs. If you add the calculation and sleep to the OnCalculate() method instead, the Windows application is blocked from user input while this is active. However, here, a separate thread is used and the user interface is still active.

```
private void OnDoWork(object sender, DoWorkEventArgs e)
{
    CalcInput input = (CalcInput)e.Argument;

    Thread.Sleep(5000);
    e.Result = input.x + input.y;
}
```

After OnDoWork is completed, the background worker fires the RunWorkerCompleted event. The method OnWorkCompleted() is associated with this event. Here, the result is received from the Result property of the RunWorkerCompletedEventArgs parameter, and this result is written to the result TextBox control. When firing the event, the BackgroundWorker control changes control to the creator thread, so there is no need to use the Invoke methods of the Windows Forms controls, and you can invoke properties and methods of Windows Forms controls directly.

```
        private void OnWorkCompleted(object sender,
                                 RunWorkerCompletedEventArgs e)
        {
            this.textBoxResult.Text = e.Result.ToString();

            this.buttonCalculate.Enabled = true;
            this.buttonCancel.Enabled = false;
            this.progressBar.Value = 100;
        }
```

Now you can test the application and see that the calculation runs independently of the UI thread, the UI is still active, and the Form can be moved around. However, the cancel and progress bar functionality still needs implementation.

Enable Cancel

To enable the cancel functionality to stop the thread's progress while it is running, you must set the BackgroundWorker property WorkerSupportsCancellation to True. Next, you have to implement the OnCancel handler that is connected to the Click event of the control buttonCancel. The BackGroundWorker control has the CancelAsync() method to cancel an asynchronous task that is going on.

```
        private void OnCancel(object sender, EventArgs e)
        {
            backgroundWorker.CancelAsync();
        }
```

The asynchronous task is not canceled automatically. In the OnDoWork() handler that does the asynchronous task, you must change the implementation to examine the CancellationPending property of the BackgroundWorker control. This property is set as soon as CancelAsync() is invoked. If a cancellation is pending, set the Cancel property of DoWorkEventArgs to true and exit the handler.

```
        private void OnDoWork(object sender, DoWorkEventArgs e)
        {
            CalcInput input = (CalcInput)e.Argument;

            for (int i = 0; i < 10; i++)
            {
                Thread.Sleep(500);

                if (backgroundWorker.CancellationPending)
                {
                    e.Cancel = true;
                    return;
                }
            }

            e.Result = input.x + input.y;
        }
```

The completion handler OnWorkCompleted() is invoked if the asynchronous method has completed successfully or if it was canceled. If it was canceled, you cannot access the Result property, because this throws an InvalidOperationException with the information that the operation has been canceled. So, you have to check the Cancelled property of RunWorkerCompletedEventArgs and behave accordingly.

```
private void OnWorkCompleted(object sender,
                             RunWorkerCompletedEventArgs e)
{
    if (e.Cancelled)
    {
        this.textBoxResult.Text = "Cancelled";
    }
    else
    {
        this.textBoxResult.Text = e.Result.ToString();
    }
    this.buttonCalculate.Enabled = true;
    this.buttonCancel.Enabled = false;
}
```

Running the application once more, you can cancel the asynchronous progress from the user interface.

Enable Progress

To get progress information to the user interface, you must set the BackgroundWorker property WorkerReportsProgress to True.

With the OnDoWork method, you can report the progress to the BackgroundWorker control with the ReportProgress() method:

```
private void OnDoWork(object sender, DoWorkEventArgs e)
{
    CalcInput input = (CalcInput)e.Argument;

    for (int i = 0; i < 10; i++)
    {
        Thread.Sleep(500);
        backgroundWorker.ReportProgress(i * 10);
        if (backgroundWorker.CancellationPending)
        {
            e.Cancel = true;
            return;
        }
    }

    e.Result = input.x + input.y;
}
```

The method ReportProgress() fires the ProgressChanged event of the BackgroundWorker control. This event changes the control to the UI thread.

Add the method OnProgressChanged() to the ProgressChanged event, and in the implementation set a new value to the progress bar control that is received from the property ProgressPercentage of ProgressChangedEventArgs:

```
private void OnProgressChanged(object sender,
                               ProgressChangedEventArgs e)
{
    this.progressBar.Value = e.ProgressPercentage;
}
```

In the `OnWorkCompleted()` event handler, the progress bar finally is set to the 100% value:

```
private void OnWorkCompleted(object sender,
                             RunWorkerCompletedEventArgs e)
{
    if (e.Cancelled)
    {
        this.textBoxResult.Text = "Cancelled";
    }
    else
    {
        this.textBoxResult.Text = e.Result.ToString();
    }
    this.buttonCalculate.Enabled = true;
    this.buttonCancel.Enabled = false;
    this.progressBar.Value = 100;
}
```

Figure 19-4 shows the running application while the calculation is just active.

Figure 19-4

Creating an Event-Based Asynchronous Component

To create a custom component that supports the event-based asynchronous pattern, more work needs to be done. To demonstrate this with a simple scenario, the class `AsyncComponent` just returns a converted input string after a time span, as you can see with the synchronous method `LongTask()`. To offer asynchronous support, the public interface offers the asynchronous method `LongTaskAsync()` and the event `LongTaskCompleted`. This event is of type `LongTaskCompletedEventHandler` that defines the parameters `object sender` and `LongTaskCompletedEventArgs e`. `LongTaskCompletedEventArgs` is a new type where the caller can read the result of the asynchronous operation.

In addition, some helper methods such as `DoLongTask` and `CompletionMethod` are needed; these are discussed next.

```
using System;
using System.Collections.Generic;
using System.ComponentModel;
using System.Threading;

namespace Wrox.ProCSharp.Threading
{
    public delegate void LongTaskCompletedEventHandler(object sender,
        LongTaskCompletedEventArgs e);

    public partial class AsyncComponent : Component
    {
        private Dictionary<object, AsyncOperation> userStateDictionary =
            new Dictionary<object, AsyncOperation>();
        private SendOrPostCallback onCompletedDelegate;

        public AsyncComponent()
        {
            InitializeComponent();
            InitializeDelegates();
        }

        public AsyncComponent(IContainer container)
        {
            container.Add(this);

            InitializeComponent();
            InitializeDelegates();
        }

        private void InitializeDelegates()
        {
            onCompletedDelegate = LongTaskCompletion;
        }

        public string LongTask(string input)
        {
            Console.WriteLine("LongTask started");
            Thread.Sleep(5000);
            Console.WriteLine("LongTask finished");
            return input.ToUpper();
        }

        public void LongTaskAsync(string input, object taskId)
        {
            //...
        }

        public event LongTaskCompletedEventHandler LongTaskCompleted;

        private void LongTaskCompletion(object operationState)
        {
            //...
        }
```

(continued)

(continued)

```
        protected void OnLongTaskCompleted(LongTaskCompletedEventArgs e)
        {
            //...
        }

        private delegate void LongTaskWorkHandler(string input,
                AsyncOperation asyncOp);

        // running in a background thread
        private void DoLongTask(string input, AsyncOperation asyncOp)
        {
            //...
        }

        private void CompletionMethod(string output, Exception ex,
                bool cancelled, AsyncOperation asyncOp)
        {
            //...
        }
    }

    public class LongTaskCompletedEventArgs : AsyncCompletedEventArgs
    {
        //...
    }
}
```

The method `LongTaskAsync` needs to start the synchronous operation asynchronously. If the component allows starting the asynchronous task several times concurrently, the client needs to have an option to map the different results to the tasks started. This is why the second parameter of `LongTaskAsync` requires a `taskId` that can be used by the client to map the results. Of course, inside the component itself the task ID needs to be remembered to map the results. .NET offers the class `AsyncOperationManager` to create `AsyncOperationObjects` to help keep track of the state of operations. The class `AsyncOperationManager` has one method, `CreateOperation`, where a task identifier can be passed, and an `AsyncOperation` object is returned. This operation is kept as an item in the dictionary `userStateDictionary` that was created earlier.

Then, a delegate of type `LongTaskWorkHandler` is created, and the method `DoLongTask` is assigned to that delegate instance. `BeginInvoke()` is the method of the delegate to start the method `DoLongTask()` asynchronously using a thread from the thread pool.

```
        public void LongTaskAsync(string input, object taskId)
        {
            AsyncOperation asyncOp =
                    AsyncOperationManager.CreateOperation(taskId);

            lock (userStateDictionary)
            {
                if (userStateDictionary.ContainsKey(taskId))
                    throw new ArgumentException("taskId must be unique", "taskId");

                userStateDictionary[taskId] = asyncOp;
            }
```

```
        LongTaskWorkHandler longTaskDelegate = DoLongTask;
        longTaskDelegate.BeginInvoke(input, asyncOp, null, null);
    }
```

The delegate type `LongTaskWorkHandler` is just defined within the class `AsyncComponent` with a private access modifier because it is not needed outside. The parameters needed with this delegate are all input parameters from the caller plus the `AsyncOperation` parameter for getting the status and mapping the result of the operation.

```
        private delegate void LongTaskWorkHandler(string input,
            AsyncOperation asyncOp);
```

The method `DoLongTask()` is now called asynchronously by using the delegate. The synchronous method `LongTask()` can now be invoked to get the output value.

Because an exception that might happen inside the synchronous method should not just blow up the background thread, any exception is caught and remembered with the variable e of type `Exception`. Finally, the `CompletionMethod()` is invoked to inform the caller about the result.

```
        // running in a background thread
        private void DoLongTask(string input, AsyncOperation asyncOp)
        {
            Exception e = null;
            string output = null;
            try
            {
                output = LongTask(input);
            }
            catch (Exception ex)
            {
                e = ex;
            }

            this.CompletionMethod(output, e, false, asyncOp);
        }
```

With the implementation of the `CompletionMethod`, the `userStateDictionary` is cleaned up as the operation is removed. The `PostOperationCompleted()` method of the `AsyncOperation` object ends the lifetime of the asynchronous operation and informs the caller using the `onCompletedDelegate` method. This method ensures that the delegate is invoked on the thread as needed for the application type. To get information to the caller, an object of type `LongTaskCompletedEventArgs` is created and passed to the method `PostOperationCompleted()`.

```
        private void CompletionMethod(string output, Exception ex,
            bool cancelled, AsyncOperation asyncOp)
        {
            lock (userStateDictionary)
            {
                userStateDictionary.Remove(asyncOp.UserSuppliedState);
            }

            // results of the operation
            LongTaskCompletedEventArgs e = new LongTaskCompletedEventArgs(
                output, ex, cancelled, asyncOp.UserSuppliedState);

            asyncOp.PostOperationCompleted(onCompletedDelegate, e);
        }
    }
```

For passing information to the caller, the class `LongTaskCompletedEventArgs` derives from the base class `AsyncCompletedEventArgs` and adds a property containing output information. In the constructor, the base constructor is invoked to pass exception, cancellation, and user state information.

```csharp
public class LongTaskCompletedEventArgs : AsyncCompletedEventArgs
{
    public LongTaskCompletedEventArgs(string output, Exception e,
        bool cancelled, object state)
        : base(e, cancelled, state)
    {
        this.output = output;
    }

    private string output;

    public string Output
    {
        get
        {
            RaiseExceptionIfNecessary();

            return output;
        }
    }
}
```

The method `asyncOp.PostOperationCompleted()` uses the `onCompletedDelegate`. This delegate was initialized to reference the method `LongTaskCompletion`. `LongTaskCompletion` needs to fulfill the parameter requirements of the `SendOrPostCallbackDelegate`. The implementation just casts the parameter to `LongTaskCompletedEventArgs`, which was the type of the object that was passed to the `PostOperationCompleted` method, and calls the method `OnLongTaskCompleted`.

```csharp
private void LongTaskCompletion(object operationState)
{
    LongTaskCompletedEventArgs e =
        operationState as LongTaskCompletedEventArgs;

    OnLongTaskCompleted(e);
}
```

`OnLongTaskCompleted` then just fires the event `LongTaskCompleted` to return the `LongTaskCompletedEventArgs` to the caller.

```csharp
protected void OnLongTaskCompleted(LongTaskCompletedEventArgs e)
{
    if (LongTaskCompleted != null)
    {
        LongTaskCompleted(this, e);
    }
}
```

After creating the component, it is really easy to use it. The event `LongTaskCompleted` is assigned to the method `Comp_LongTaskCompleted`, and the method `LongTaskAsync()` is invoked. With a simple console application, you will see that the event handler `Comp_LongTaskCompleted` is called from a thread different from the main thread. (This is different from Windows Forms applications, as you will see next.)

```
static void Main()
{
    Console.WriteLine("Main thread: {0}",
        Thread.CurrentThread.ManagedThreadId);

    AsyncComponent comp = new AsyncComponent();
    comp.LongTaskCompleted += Comp_LongTaskCompleted;

    comp.LongTaskAsync("input", 33);

    Console.ReadLine();
}

static void Comp_LongTaskCompleted(object sender,
        LongTaskCompletedEventArgs e)
{
    Console.WriteLine("completed, result: {0}, thread: {1}", e.Output,
        Thread.CurrentThread.ManagedThreadId);
}
```

With a Windows Forms application the `SynchronizationContext` is set to `WindowsFormsSynchronizationContext` — that's why the event handler code is invoked in the same thread:

```
WindowsFormsSynchronizationContext syncContext =
        new WindowsFormsSynchronizationContext();
SynchronizationContext.SetSynchronizationContext(syncContext);
```

Summary

This chapter explored how to code applications that use multiple threads using the `System.Threading` namespace. Using multithreading in your applications takes careful planning. Too many threads can cause resource issues, and not enough threads can cause your application to seem sluggish and to perform poorly.

You've seen various ways to create multiple threads such as using the delegate, timers, a `ThreadPool`, and the `Thread` class. Various synchronization techniques have been explored such as a simple `lock` statement but also the `Monitor`, `Semaphore`, and `Event` classes. You've seen how to program the asynchronous pattern with the `IAsyncResult` interface, and the event-based asynchronous pattern.

The `System.Threading` namespace in the .NET Framework gives you multiple ways to manipulate threads; however, this does not mean that the .NET Framework handles all the difficult tasks of multithreading for you. You need to consider thread priority and synchronization issues. This chapter discussed these issues and how to code for them in your C# applications. It also looked at the problems associated with deadlocks and race conditions.

Just remember that if you are going to use multithreading in your C# applications, careful planning needs to be a major part of your efforts.

Some final guidelines regarding threading:

❏ Try to keep synchronization requirements to a minimum. Synchronization is complex and blocks threads. You can avoid it if you try to avoid sharing state. Of course, this is not always possible.

❏ Static members of a class should be thread-safe. Usually, this is the case with classes in the .NET Framework.

❏ Instance state does not need to be thread-safe. For best performance, synchronization is better used outside of the class where it is needed and not with every member of the class. Instance members of .NET Framework classes usually are not thread-safe. In the MSDN library you can find this information documented for every class of the Framework in the Thread Safety section.

The next chapter gives information on another core .NET topic: security.

20

Security

Security has several key aspects to consider. One is the user of the application. Is it really the user, or someone posing as the user, who is accessing the application? How can this user be trusted? As you will see in this chapter, the user first needs to be authenticated, and then authorization occurs to verify if the user is allowed to use the requested resources.

What about data that is stored or sent across the network? Is it possible that someone accesses this data, for example, by using a network sniffer? Encryption of data is important here.

Yet another aspect is the application itself. How can you trust the application? What is the origin or evidence from the application? This is extremely important, for example, in a Web hosting scenario. A Web hosting provider does not allow its customers to access all resources from the system. Depending on the evidence of the assembly, different permissions for the application apply.

This chapter explores the features available in .NET to help you manage security, including how .NET protects you from malicious code, how to administer security policies, and how to access the security subsystem programmatically. The topics of this chapter are:

❑ Authentication and authorization

❑ Cryptography

❑ Access control to resources

❑ Code access security

❑ Managing security policies

Authentication and Authorization

Authentication is the process of identifying the user, and authorization occurs afterward to verify if the identified user is allowed to access a specific resource.

Identity and Principal

You can identify the user running the application by using an identity. The `WindowsIdentity` class represents a Windows user. If you don't identify the user with a Windows account, you can use other classes that implement the interface IIdentity. With this interface you have access to the name of the user, information about whether the user is authenticated, and the authentication type.

A principal is an object that contains the identity of the user and the roles that the user belongs to. The interface IPrincipal defines the property Identity that returns an IIdentity object and the method IsInRole in which you can verify if the user is a member of a specific role. A role is a collection of users who have the same security permissions, and it is the unit of administration for users. Roles can be Windows groups or just a collection of strings that you define.

Principal classes available with .NET are WindowsPrincipal and GenericPrincipal. You can also create a custom principal class that implements the interface IPrincipal.

In the following example, you create a console application that provides access to the principal in an application that, in turn, enables you to access the underlying Windows account. You need to import the System.Security.Principal and System.Threading namespaces. First of all, you must specify that .NET automatically hooks up the principal with the underlying Windows account. This is because .NET does not automatically populate the thread's CurrentPrincipal property for security reasons. You can do it like this:

```
using System;
using System.Security.Principal;
using System.Threading;

namespace Wrox.ProCSharp.Security
{
    class Program
    {
        static void Main()
        {
            AppDomain.CurrentDomain.SetPrincipalPolicy(
                PrincipalPolicy.WindowsPrincipal);
```

It is possible to use WindowsIdentity.GetCurrent() to access the Windows account details; however, that method is best used when you are going to look at the principal only once. If you want to access the principal a number of times, it is more efficient to set the policy so that the current thread provides access to the principal for you. If you use the SetPrincipalPolicy method, it is specified that the principal in the current thread should hold a WindowsIdentity object. All identity classes, such as WindowsIdentity, implement the IIdentity interface. The interface contains three properties (AuthenticationType, IsAuthenticated, and Name) for all derived identity classes to implement.

Add code to access the principal's properties from the Thread object:

```
WindowsPrincipal principal =
    (WindowsPrincipal)Thread.CurrentPrincipal;
WindowsIdentity identity = (WindowsIdentity)principal.Identity;
Console.WriteLine("IdentityType: " + identity.ToString());
Console.WriteLine("Name: {0}", identity.Name);
Console.WriteLine("'Users'?: {0} ",
    principal.IsInRole("BUILTIN\\Users"));
Console.WriteLine("'Administrators'? {0}",
    principal.IsInRole(WindowsBuiltInRole.Administrator));
Console.WriteLine("Authenticated: {0}", identity.IsAuthenticated);
Console.WriteLine("AuthType: {0}", identity.AuthenticationType);
Console.WriteLine("Anonymous? {0}", identity.IsAnonymous);
Console.WriteLine("Token: {0}", identity.Token);
        }
    }
}
```

The output from this console application looks similar to the following lines; it will vary according to your machine's configuration and the roles associated with the account under which you are signed in:

```
IdentityType:System.Security.Principal.WindowsIdentity
Name: farabove\christian
'Users'? True
'Administrators'? True
Authenticated: True
AuthType: NTLM
Anonymous? False
Token: 368
```

It is enormously beneficial to be able to easily access details about the current users and their roles. With this information, you can make decisions about what actions should be permitted or denied. The ability to make use of roles and Windows user groups provides the added benefit that administration can be done by using standard user administration tools, and you can usually avoid altering the code when user roles change. The following section looks at roles in more detail.

Roles

Role-based security is especially useful in situations in which access to resources is an issue. A primary example is the finance industry, in which employees' roles define what information they can access and what actions they can perform.

Role-based security is also ideal for use in conjunction with Windows accounts, or a custom user directory to manage access to Web-based resources. For example, a Web site could restrict access to its content until a user registers with the site, and then additionally provide access to special content only, if the user is a paying subscriber. In many ways, ASP.NET makes role-based security easier because much of the code is based on the server.

For example, to implement a Web service that requires authentication, you could use the account subsystem of Windows and write the Web method in such a way that it ensures the user is a member of a specific Windows user group before allowing access to the method's functionality.

Imagine a scenario with an intranet application that relies on Windows accounts. The system has a group called `Manager` and one called `Assistant`; users are assigned to these groups according to their role within the organization. Say that the application contains a feature that displays information about employees that should be accessed only by users in the `Managers` group. You can easily use code that checks whether the current user is a member of the `Managers` group and whether he is permitted or denied access.

However, if you decide later to rearrange the account groups and to introduce a group called `Personnel` that also has access to employee details, you will have a problem. You will need to go through all the code and update it to include rules for this new group.

A better solution would be to create a permission called something like `ReadEmployeeDetails` and assign it to groups where necessary. If the code applies a check for the `ReadEmployeeDetails` permission, updating the application to allow those in the `Personnel` group access to employee details is simply a matter of creating the group, placing the users in it, and assigning the `ReadEmployeeDetails` permission.

Declarative Role-Based Security

Just as with code access security, you can implement role-based security requests ("the user must be in the Administrators group") using imperative requests by calling the `IsInRole()` method from the

`IPrincipal` class, or using attributes. You can state permission requirements declaratively at the class or method level using the `[PrincipalPermission]` attribute:

```
using System;
using System.Security;
using System.Security.Principal;
using System.Security.Permissions;

namespace Wrox.ProCSharp.Security
{
    class Program
    {
        static void Main()
        {
            AppDomain.CurrentDomain.SetPrincipalPolicy(
                PrincipalPolicy.WindowsPrincipal);
            try
            {
                ShowMessage();
            }
            catch (SecurityException exception)
            {
                Console.WriteLine("Security exception caught (" +
                                   exception.Message + ")");
                Console.WriteLine("The current principal must be in the local"
                                   + "Users group");
            }
            Console.ReadLine();
        }

        [PrincipalPermission(SecurityAction.Demand,
                                Role = "BUILTIN\\Users")]
        static void ShowMessage()
        {
            Console.WriteLine("The current principal is logged in locally ");
            Console.WriteLine("(member of the local Users group)");
        }
    }
}
```

The `ShowMessage()` method will throw an exception unless you execute the application in the context of a user in the Windows local Users group. For a Web application, the account under which the ASP.NET code is running must be in the group, although in a "real-world" example you would certainly avoid adding this account to the administrators group!

If you run the preceding code using an account in the local Users group, the output will look like this:

```
The current principal is logged in locally
(member of the local Users group)
```

Client Application Services

Visual Studio 2008 makes it easy to use authentication services that previously have been built for ASP.NET Web applications. With this service, it is possible to use the same authentication mechanism both with Windows and Web applications. This is a provider model that is primarily based on the classes `Membership` and `Roles` in the namespace `System.Web.Security`. With the `Membership` class you can validate, create, delete, find users, change the password, and other various things related to users. With the `Roles` class you can add and delete roles, get the roles for a user, and change roles from a user. Where the roles and users are stored depends on the provider. The `ActiveDirectoryMembershipProvider` accesses users and roles in the Active Directory; the `SqlMembershipProvider` uses a SQL Server database. For client application services new providers exist with .NET 3.5: `ClientFormsAuthenticationMembershipProvider` and `ClientWindowsAuthenticationMembershipProvider`.

Next, you use client application services with Forms authentication. To do this, first you need to start an application server, and then you can use this service from Windows Forms or WPF.

Application Services

For using client application services, you can create an ASP.NET Web service project that offers application services.

With the project a membership provider is needed. The sample code here defines the class `SampleMembershipProvider` that derives from the base class `MembershipProvider`. You must override all abstract methods from the base class. For login, the only implementation needed is the method `ValidateUser`. All other methods can throw a `NotSupportedException` as shown with the property `ApplicationName`. The sample code here uses a `Dictionary<string, string>` that contains usernames and passwords. Of course, you can change it to your own implementation, for example, to read username and password from the database.

```csharp
using System;
using System.Collections.Generic;
using System.Collections.Specialized;
using System.Web.Security;

namespace Wrox.ProCSharp.Security
{
    public class SampleMembershipProvider : MembershipProvider
    {
        private Dictionary<string, string> users = null;
        internal static string ManagerUserName = "Manager".ToLowerInvariant();
        internal static string EmployeeUserName = "Employee".ToLowerInvariant();


        public override void Initialize(string name, NameValueCollection config)
        {
            users = new Dictionary<string, string>();
            users.Add(ManagerUserName, "secret@Pa$$w0rd");
            users.Add(EmployeeUserName, "s0me@Secret");

            base.Initialize(name, config);
        }

        public override string ApplicationName
        {
            get
            {
                throw new NotImplementedException();
            }
```

(continued)

(continued)

```
            set
            {
                throw new NotImplementedException();
            }
        }

        // override abstract Membership members
        // ...

        public override bool ValidateUser(string username, string password)
        {
            if (users.ContainsKey(username.ToLowerInvariant()))
            {
                return password.Equals(users[username.ToLowerInvariant()]);
            }
            return false;
        }
    }
}
```

For using roles, you also need to implement a role provider. The class `SampleRoleProvider` derives from the base class `RoleProvider` and implements the methods `GetRolesForUser()` and `IsUserInRole()`:

```
using System;
using System.Collections.Specialized;
using System.Web.Security;

namespace Wrox.ProCSharp.Security
{
    public class SampleRoleProvider : RoleProvider
    {
        internal static string ManagerRoleName =
            "Manager".ToLowerInvariant();
        internal static string EmployeeRoleName =
            "Employee".ToLowerInvariant();

        public override void Initialize(string name, NameValueCollection config)
        {
            base.Initialize(name, config);
        }

        public override void AddUsersToRoles(string[] usernames,
                string[] roleNames)
        {
            throw new NotImplementedException();
        }

        //... override abstract RoleProvider members

        public override string[] GetRolesForUser(string username)
        {
            if (string.Compare(username,
                SampleMembershipProvider.ManagerUserName, true) == 0)
```

```csharp
        {
            return new string[] { ManagerRoleName };
        }
        else if (string.Compare(username,
            SampleMembershipProvider.EmployeeUserName, true) == 0)
        {
            return new string[] { EmployeeRoleName };
        }
        else
        {
            return new string[0];
        }
    }

    public override bool IsUserInRole(string username, string roleName)
    {
        string[] roles = GetRolesForUser(username);
        foreach (string role in roles)
        {
            if (string.Compare(role, roleName, true) == 0)
            {
                return true;
            }
        }
        return false;
    }
  }
}
```

Authentication services must be configured in the Web.config file. On the production system, it would be useful from a security standpoint to configure SSL with the server hosting application services.

```xml
<system.web.extensions>
  <scripting>
    <webServices>
      <authenticationService enabled="true" requireSSL="false"/>
      <roleService enabled="true"/>
    </webServices>
  </scripting>
</system.web.extensions>
```

Within the <system.web> section, the membership and roleManager elements must be configured to reference the classes that implement the membership and role provider:

```xml
<system.web>
  <membership defaultProvider="SampleMembershipProvider">
    <providers>
      <add name="SampleMembershipProvider"
           type="Wrox.ProCSharp.Security.SampleMembershipProvider"/>
    </providers>
  </membership>
  <roleManager enabled="true" defaultProvider="SampleRoleProvider">
    <providers>
      <add name="SampleRoleProvider"
           type="Wrox.ProCSharp.Security.SampleRoleProvider"/>
    </providers>
  </roleManager>
```

For debugging, you can assign a port number and virtual path with the Web tab of project properties. The sample application uses the port 55555 and the virtual path /AppServices. If you use different values, you need to change the configuration of the client application accordingly.

Now the application service can be used from a client application.

Client Application

With the client application WPF is used. Windows Forms can be used in the same way. Visual Studio 2008 has a new project setting named Services that allows using client application services. Here you can set Forms authentication and the location of the authentication and roles service to the address defined previously: `http://localhost:55555/AppServices`. All that's done from this project configuration is referencing the assemblies `System.Web` and `System.Web.Extensions`, and changing the application configuration file to configure membership and role providers that use the classes `ClientFormsAuthenticationMembershipProvider` and `ClientRoleProvider` and the address of the Web service that is used by these providers.

```xml
<?xml version="1.0" encoding="utf-8"?>
<configuration>
  <system.web>
    <membership defaultProvider="ClientAuthenticationMembershipProvider">
      <providers>
        <add name="ClientAuthenticationMembershipProvider"
            type="System.Web.ClientServices.Providers.
            ClientFormsAuthenticationMembershipProvider,
            System.Web.Extensions, Version=3.5.0.0, Culture=neutral,
            PublicKeyToken=31bf3856ad364e35" serviceUri=
"http://localhost:55555/AppServices/Authentication_JSON_AppService.axd" />
      </providers>
    </membership>
    <roleManager defaultProvider="ClientRoleProvider" enabled="true">
      <providers>
        <add name="ClientRoleProvider"
            type="System.Web.ClientServices.Providers.ClientRoleProvider,
            System.Web.Extensions, Version=3.5.0.0, Culture=neutral,
            PublicKeyToken=31bf3856ad364e35" serviceUri=
            "http://localhost:55555/AppServices/Role_JSON_AppService.axd"
            cacheTimeout="86400" />
      </providers>
    </roleManager>
  </system.web>
</configuration>
```

The Windows application just uses `Label`, `TextBox`, `PasswordBox`, and `Button` controls as shown in Figure 20-1. The `Label` with the content User Validated shows up only when the logon is successful.

Figure 20-1

The handler of the `Button.Click` event invokes the `ValidateUser()` method of the `Membership` class. Because of the configured provider `ClientAuthenticationMembershipProvider`, the provider in turn invokes the Web service and calls the method `ValidateUser()` of the `SampleMembershipProvider` class to verify a successful logon. With success, the Label `labelValidatedInfo` is made visible; otherwise a message box pops up:

```
private void buttonLogin_Click(object sender, RoutedEventArgs e)
{
    try
    {
        if (Membership.ValidateUser(textUsername.Text,
            textPassword.Password))
        {
            // user validated!
            labelValidatedInfo.Visibility = Visibility.Visible;
        }
        else
        {
            MessageBox.Show("Username or password not valid",
                    "Client Authentication Services", MessageBoxButton.OK,
                    MessageBoxImage.Warning);
        }
    }
    catch (WebException ex)
    {
        MessageBox.Show(ex.Message, "Client Application Services",
            MessageBoxButton.OK, MessageBoxImage.Error);
    }
}
```

Encryption

Confidential data should be secured so that it cannot be read by unprivileged users. This is valid both for data that is sent across the network, or data that is stored somewhere. You can encrypt such data with symmetric or asymmetric encryption keys.

With a symmetric key, the same key can be used for encryption and decryption. With asymmetric encryption, different keys are used for encryption and decryption: a public and a private key. Something encrypted using a public key can be decrypted with the corresponding private key. This also works the other way around: something encrypted using a private key can be decrypted by using the corresponding public key but not the private key.

Public and private keys are always created as a pair. The public key can be made available to everybody, and it can even be put on a Web site, but the private key must be safely locked away. Following are some examples where these public and private keys are used to explain encryption.

If Alice sends a message to Bob (see Figure 20-2), and Alice wants to make sure that no one else but Bob can read the message, she uses Bob's public key. The message is encrypted using Bob's public key. Bob opens the message and can decrypt it using his secretly stored private key. This key exchange guarantees that no one but Bob can read Alice's message.

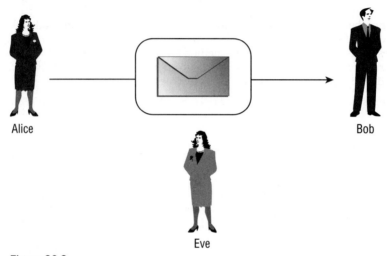

Figure 20-2

There is one problem left: Bob can't be sure that the mail comes from Alice. Eve can use Bob's public key to encrypt messages sent to Bob and pretend to be Alice. We can extend this principle using public/private keys. Let's start again with Alice sending a message to Bob. Before Alice encrypts the message using Bob's public key, she adds her signature and encrypts the signature using her own private key. Then she encrypts the mail using Bob's public key. Therefore, it is guaranteed that no one else but Bob can read the mail. When Bob decrypts the message, he detects an encrypted signature. The signature can be decrypted using Alice's public key. For Bob, it is not a problem to access Alice's public key because the key is public. After decrypting the signature, Bob can be sure that it was Alice who sent the message.

The encryption and decryption algorithms using symmetric keys are a lot faster than using asymmetric keys. The problem with symmetric keys is that the keys must be exchanged in a safe manner. With network communication, one way to do this is by using asymmetric keys first for the key exchange, and then symmetric keys for encryption of the data that is sent across the wire.

With the .NET Framework, you find classes for encryption in the namespace `System.Security .Cryptography`. Several symmetric and asymmetric algorithms are implemented. You can find different algorithm classes for many different purposes. Some of the new classes with .NET 3.5 have a `Cng` prefix or suffix. Cng is short for *Cryptography Next Generation*, which can be used with Windows Vista and Windows Server 2008. This API makes it possible to write a program independent of the algorithm by using a provider-based model. If you are targeting Windows Server 2003 as well, you need to pay attention to what encryption classes to use.

The following table lists encryption classes from the namespace `System.Security.Cryptography` and their purposes. The classes without a `Cng`, `Managed`, or `CryptoServiceProvider` suffix are abstract base classes, such as `MD5`. The `Managed` suffix means this algorithm is implemented with managed code; other classes might wrap native Windows API calls. The suffix `CryptoServiceProvider` is used with classes that implement the abstract base class. The `Cng` suffix is used with classes that make use of the new Cryptography CNG API that is available only with Windows Vista and Windows Server 2008.

Category	Classes	Description

Hash	`MD5, MD5Cng`
	`SHA1, SHA1Managed,`
	`SHA1Cng`
	`SHA256, SHA256Managed, SHA256Cng`
	`SHA384, SHA384Managed, SHA384Cng`
	`SHA512, SHA512Managed, SHA512Cng`
		Hash algorithms have the purpose of creating a fixed-length hash value from binary strings of arbitrary length. These algorithms are used with digital signatures and for data integrity. If the same binary string is hashed again, the same hash result is returned.

		MD5 (Message Digest Algorithm 5) was developed at RSA Laboratories and is faster than SHA1. SHA1 is stronger against brute force attacks. The SHA algorithms have been designed by the National Security Agency (NSA). MD5 uses a 128-bit hash size; SHA1 uses 160 bit. The other SHA algorithms contain the hash size in the name. SHA512 is the strongest of these algorithms; with a hash size of 512 bits, it is also the slowest.

Symmetric	`DES, DESCryptoServiceProvider`
	`TripleDES,`
	`TripleDESCryptoServiceProvider`
	`Aes, AesCryptoServiceProvider,`
	`AesManaged`
	`RC2, RC2CryptoServiceProvider`
	`Rijandel, RijandelManaged`
		Symmetric key algorithms use the same key for encryption and decryption of data. DES (Data Encryption Standard) is now considered insecure because it uses just 56 bits for the key size and can be broken in less than 24 hours. Triple-DES is the successor of DES and has a key length of 168 bits, but the effective security it provides is only 112 bit. AES (Advanced Encryption Standard) has a key size of 128, 192, or 256 bits. Rijandel is very similar to AES; it just has more options with the key size. AES is an encryption standard adopted by the U.S. government.

Category	Classes	Description
Asymmetric	DSA, DSACryptoServiceProvider ECDsa, ECDsaCng ECDiffieHellman, ECDiffieHellmanCng RSA, RSACryptoServiceProvider	Asymmetric algorithms use different keys for encryption and decryption. RSA (Rivest, Shamir, Adleman) was the first algorithm used for signing as well as encryption. This algorithm is widely used in e-commerce protocols.
		DSA (Digital Signature Algorithm) is a United States Federal Government standard for digital signatures.
		ECDSA (Elliptic Curve DSA) and ECDiffieHellman use algorithms based on elliptic curve groups. These algorithms are more secure with shorter key sizes. For example, having a key size of 1024 bits for DSA is similar in security with 160 bits for ECDSA. As a result, ECDSA is much faster.
		ECDiffieHellman is an algorithm used to exchange private keys in a secure way over a public channel.

Let's get into examples of how these algorithms can be used programmatically.

Signature

The first example demonstrates a signature using the ECDSA algorithm for signing. Alice creates a signature that is encrypted with her private key and can be accessed using her public key. This way, it is guaranteed that the signature is from Alice.

First, take a look at the major steps in the Main() method: Alice's keys are created, and the string Alice is signed and finally verified if the signature is really from Alice by using the public key. The message that is signed is converted to a byte array by using the Encoding class. To write the encrypted signature to the console, the byte array that contains the signature is converted to a string with the method Convert.ToBase64String().

Never convert encrypted data to a string using the Encoding *class. The* Encoding *class verifies and converts invalid values that are not allowed with Unicode, and thus converting the string back to a byte array yields a different result.*

```
using System;
using System.Security.Cryptography;
using System.Text;

namespace Wrox.ProCSharp.Security
{
    class Program
    {
        internal static CngKey aliceKeySignature;
```

```
        internal static byte[] alicePubKeyBlob;

    static void Main()
    {
        CreateKeys();

        byte[] aliceData = Encoding.UTF8.GetBytes("Alice");
        byte[] aliceSignature = CreateSignature(aliceData,
                aliceKeySignature);
        Console.WriteLine("Alice created signature: {0}",
                Convert.ToBase64String(aliceSignature));

        if (VerifySignature(aliceData, aliceSignature, alicePubKeyBlob))
        {
            Console.WriteLine("Alice signature verified successfully");
        }
    }
```

CreateKeys() is the method that creates a new key pair for Alice. This key pair is stored in a static field so it can be accessed from the other methods. The Create() method of CngKey gets the algorithm as an argument to define a key pair for the algorithm. With the Export() method, the public key of the key pair is exported. This public key can be given to Bob for the verification of the signature. Alice keeps the private key. Instead of creating a key pair with the CngKey class, you can open existing keys that are stored in the key store. Usually Alice would have a certificate containing a key pair in her private store, and the store could be accessed with CngKey.Open().

```
    static void CreateKeys()
    {
        aliceKeySignature = CngKey.Create(CngAlgorithm.ECDsaP256);
        alicePubKeyBlob = aliceKeySignature.Export(
                            CngKeyBlobFormat.GenericPublicBlob);
    }
```

With the key pair, Alice can create the signature using the ECDsaCng class. The constructor of this class receives the CngKey from Alice that contains both the public and private key. The private key is used, signing the data with the SignData() method.

```
    static byte[] CreateSignature(byte[] data, CngKey key)
    {
        ECDsaCng signingAlg = new ECDsaCng(key);
        byte[] signature = signingAlg.SignData(data);
        signingAlg.Clear();

        return signature;
    }
```

For verification if the signature was really from Alice, Bob checks the signature by using the public key from Alice. The byte array containing the public key blob can be imported to a CngKey object with the static Import() method. The ECDsaCng class is then used to verify the signature by invoking VerifyData().

```
    static bool VerifySignature(byte[] data, byte[] signature,
            byte[] pubKey)
    {
        bool retValue = false;
```

(continued)

(continued)

```
            using (CngKey key = CngKey.Import(pubKey,
                CngKeyBlobFormat.GenericPublicBlob))
            {
                ECDsaCng signingAlg = new ECDsaCng(key);
                retValue = signingAlg.VerifyData(data, signature);
                signingAlg.Clear();
            }
            return retValue;
        }
    }
}
```

Key Exchange and Secure Transfer

Let's get into a more complex example to exchange a symmetric key for a secure transfer by using the Diffie Hellman algorithm. In the `Main()` method, you can see the main functionality. Alice creates an encrypted message and sends the encrypted message to Bob. Before that, key pairs are created for Alice and Bob. Bob gets access only to Alice's public key, and Alice gets access only to Bob's public key.

```
using System;
using System.IO;
using System.Security.Cryptography;
using System.Text;

namespace Wrox.ProCSharp.Security
{
    class Program
    {
        static CngKey aliceKey;
        static CngKey bobKey;
        static byte[] alicePubKeyBlob;
        static byte[] bobPubKeyBlob;

        static void Main()
        {
            CreateKeys();
            byte[] encrytpedData = AliceSendsData("secret message");
            BobReceivesData(encrytpedData);

        }
```

In the implementation of the `CreateKeys()` method, keys are created to be used with the EC Diffie Hellman 256 algorithm.

```
        private static void CreateKeys()
        {
            aliceKey = CngKey.Create(CngAlgorithm.ECDiffieHellmanP256);
            bobKey = CngKey.Create(CngAlgorithm.ECDiffieHellmanP256);
            alicePubKeyBlob = aliceKey.Export(CngKeyBlobFormat.EccPublicBlob);
            bobPubKeyBlob = bobKey.Export(CngKeyBlobFormat.EccPublicBlob);
        }
```

In the method `AliceSendsData()`, the string that contains text characters is converted to a byte array by using the `Encoding` class. An `ECDiffieHellmanCng` object is created and initialized with the key pair from Alice. Alice creates a symmetric key by using her key pair and the public key from Bob calling the method `DeriveKeyMaterial()`. The returned symmetric key is used with the symmetric algorithm AES to encrypt the data. `AesCryptoServiceProvider` requires the key and an initialization vector (IV). The IV is generated dynamically from the method `GenerateIV()`. The symmetric key is exchanged with the help of the EC Diffie Hellman algorithm, but the IV must also be exchanged. From the security standpoint, it is okay to transfer the IV unencrypted across the network — just the key exchange must be secured. The IV is stored as first content in the memory stream followed by the encrypted data where the `CryptoStream` class uses the `encryptor` created by the `AesCryptoServiceProvider` class. Before the encrypted data is accessed from the memory stream, the crypto stream must be closed. Otherwise, end bits would be missing from the encrypted data.

```
private static byte[] AliceSendsData(string message)
{
    Console.WriteLine("Alice sends message: {0}", message);
    byte[] rawData = Encoding.UTF8.GetBytes(message);
    byte[] encryptedData = null;

    ECDiffieHellmanCng aliceAlgorithm = new ECDiffieHellmanCng(aliceKey);
    using (CngKey bobPubKey = CngKey.Import(bobPubKeyBlob,
        CngKeyBlobFormat.EccPublicBlob))
    {
        byte[] symmKey = aliceAlgorithm.DeriveKeyMaterial(bobPubKey);
        Console.WriteLine("Alice creates this symmetric key with " +
            "Bobs public key information: {0}",
            Convert.ToBase64String(symmKey));

        AesCryptoServiceProvider aes = new AesCryptoServiceProvider();
        aes.Key = symmKey;
        aes.GenerateIV();
        using (ICryptoTransform encryptor = aes.CreateEncryptor())
        using (MemoryStream ms = new MemoryStream())
        {
            // create CryptoStream and encrypt data to send
            CryptoStream cs = new CryptoStream(ms, encryptor,
                CryptoStreamMode.Write);

            // write initialization vector not encrypted
            ms.Write(aes.IV, 0, aes.IV.Length);
            cs.Write(rawData, 0, rawData.Length);
            cs.Close();
            encryptedData = ms.ToArray();
        }
        aes.Clear();
    }
    Console.WriteLine("Alice: message is encrypted: {0}",
        Convert.ToBase64String(encryptedData)); ;
    Console.WriteLine();
    return encryptedData;
}
```

Bob receives encrypted data in the argument of the method `BobReceivesData()`. First, the unencrypted initialization vector must be read. The `BlockSize` property of the class `AesCryptoServiceProvider` returns the number of bits for a block. The number of bytes can be calculated by doing a divide by 8, and the fastest way to do this is by doing a bit shift of 3 bits. Shifting by 1 bit is a division by 2, 2 bits by 4, and 3 bits by 8. With the `for` loop, the first bytes of the raw bytes that contain the IV unencrypted are written to the array `iv`. Next, an `ECDiffieHellmanCng` object is instantiated with the key pair from Bob. Using the public key from Alice, the symmetric key is returned from the method `DeriveKeyMaterial()`. Comparing the symmetric keys created from Alice and Bob shows that the same key value gets created. Using this symmetric key and the initialization vector, the message from Alice can be decrypted with the `AesCryptoServiceProvider` class.

```
private static void BobReceivesData(byte[] encryptedData)
{
    Console.WriteLine("Bob receives encrypted data");
    byte[] rawData = null;

    AesCryptoServiceProvider aes = new AesCryptoServiceProvider();

    int nBytes = aes.BlockSize >> 3;
    byte[] iv = new byte[nBytes];
    for (int i = 0; i < iv.Length; i++)
        iv[i] = encryptedData[i];

    ECDiffieHellmanCng bobAlgorithm = new ECDiffieHellmanCng(bobKey);

    using (CngKey alicePubKey = CngKey.Import(alicePubKeyBlob,
        CngKeyBlobFormat.EccPublicBlob))
    {
        byte[] symmKey = bobAlgorithm.DeriveKeyMaterial(alicePubKey);
        Console.WriteLine("Bob creates this symmetric key with " +
            "Alices public key information: {0}",
            Convert.ToBase64String(symmKey));

        aes.Key = symmKey;
        aes.IV = iv;

        using (ICryptoTransform decryptor = aes.CreateDecryptor())
        using (MemoryStream ms = new MemoryStream())
        {
            CryptoStream cs = new CryptoStream(ms, decryptor,
                CryptoStreamMode.Write);
            cs.Write(encryptedData, nBytes, encryptedData.Length - nBytes);
            cs.Close();

            rawData = ms.ToArray();

            Console.WriteLine("Bob decrypts message to: {0}",
                Encoding.UTF8.GetString(rawData));
        }
        aes.Clear();
    }
}
```

When you run the application you can see similar output on the console. The message from Alice is encrypted, and decrypted by Bob with the securely exchanged symmetric key.

```
Alice sends message: secret message
Alice creates this symmetric key with Bobs public key information:
5NWat8AemzFCYo1IIae9S3Vn4AXyai4aL8ATFo41vbw=
Alice: message is encrypted: 3C5U9CpYxnoFTk3Ew2V0T5Po0Jgryc5R7Te8ztau5N0=

Bob receives encrypted message
Bob creates this symmetric key with Alices public key information:
5NWat8AemzFCYo1IIae9S3Vn4AXyai4aL8ATFo41vbw=
Bob decrypts message to: secret message
```

Access Control to Resources

With the operating system, resources such as files and registry keys, as well as handles of a named pipe, are secured by using an access control list. Figure 20-3 shows the structure of how this maps. The resource has a security descriptor associated. The security descriptor contains information about the owner of the resource and references two access control lists: a discretionary access-control list (DACL) and a system access-control list (SACL). The DACL defines who has access or no access; the SACL defines audit rules for security event logging. An ACL contains a list of access-control entries (ACE). The ACE contains a type, a security identifier, and rights. With the DACL, the ACE can be of type access allowed or access denied. Some of the rights that you can set and get with a file are create, read, write, delete, modify, change permissions, and take ownership.

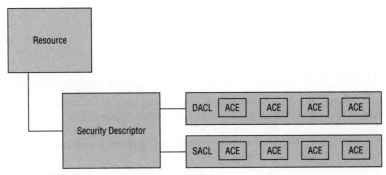

Figure 20-3

Classes to read and modify access control are in the namespace `System.Security.AccessControl`.

The following program demonstrates reading the access control list from a file.

The `FileStream` class defines the `GetAccessControl()` method that returns a `FileSecurity` object. `FileSecurity` is the .NET class that represents a security descriptor for files. `FileSecurity` derives from the base classes `ObjectSecurity`, `CommonObjectSecurity`, `NativeObjectSecurity`, and `FileSystemSecurity`. Other classes that represent a security descriptor are `CryptoKeySecurity`, `EventWaitHandleSecurity`, `MutexSecurity`, `RegistrySecurity`, `SemaphoreSecurity`, `PipeSecurity`, and `ActiveDirectorySecurity`. All of these objects can be secured using an access control list. In general, the corresponding .NET class defines the method `GetAccessControl` to return the corresponding security class; for example, the `Mutex.GetAccessControl()` method returns a `MutexSecurity`, and the `PipeStream.GetAccessControl()` method returns a `PipeSecurity`.

The `FileSecurity` class defines methods to read and change the DACL and SACL. The method `GetAccessRules()` returns the DACL in the form of the class `AuthorizationRuleCollection`. To access the SACL, you can use the method `GetAuditRules()`.

With the method `GetAccessRules()`, you can define if inherited access rules, and not only access rules directly defined with the object, should be used. The last parameter defines the type of the security identifier that should be returned. This type must derive from the base class `IdentityReference`. Possible types are `NTAccount` and `SecurityIdentifier`. Both of these classes represent users or groups; the `NTAccount` class finds the security object by its name and the `SecurityIdentifier` class finds the security object by a unique security identifier.

The returned `AuthorizationRuleCollection` contains `AuthorizationRule` objects. The `AuthorizationRule` is the .NET representation of an ACE. With the sample here, a file is accessed, so the `AuthorizationRule` can be cast to a `FileSystemAccessRule`. With ACEs of other resources, different .NET representations exist, such as `MutexAccessRule` and `PipeAccessRule`. With the `FileSystemAccessRule` class, the properties `AccessControlType`, `FileSystemRights`, and `IdentityReference` return information about the ACE.

```csharp
using System;
using System.IO;
using System.Security.AccessControl;
using System.Security.Principal;

namespace Wrox.ProCSharp.Security
{
    class Program
    {
        static void Main(string[] args)
        {
            string filename = null;
            if (args.Length == 0)
                return;

            filename = args[0];

            FileStream stream = File.Open(filename, FileMode.Open);
            FileSecurity securityDescriptor = stream.GetAccessControl();
            AuthorizationRuleCollection rules =
                    securityDescriptor.GetAccessRules(true, true,
                        typeof(NTAccount));

            foreach (AuthorizationRule rule in rules)
            {
                FileSystemAccessRule fileRule = rule as FileSystemAccessRule;
                Console.WriteLine("Access type: {0}", fileRule.AccessControlType);
                Console.WriteLine("Rights: {0}", fileRule.FileSystemRights);
                Console.WriteLine("Identity: {0}",
                        fileRule.IdentityReference.Value);
                Console.WriteLine();
            }
        }
    }
}
```

By running the application and passing a filename, you can see the access control list for the file. The output shown here lists full control to Administrators and System, modification rights to authenticated users, and read and execute rights to all users belonging to the group Users:

```
Access type: Allow
Rights: FullControl
Identity: BUILTIN\Administrators

Access type: Allow
Rights: FullControl
Identity: NT AUTHORITY\SYSTEM

Access type: Allow
Rights: Modify, Synchronize
Identity: NT AUTHORITY\Authenticated Users

Access type: Allow
Rights: ReadAndExecute, Synchronize
Identity: BUILTIN\Users
```

Setting access rights is very similar to reading access rights. To set access rights, several resource classes that can be secured offer the `SetAccessControl()` and `ModifyAccessControl()` methods. The sample code here modifies the access control list of a file by invoking the `SetAccessControl()` method from the `File` class. To this method a `FileSecurity` object is passed. The `FileSecurity` object is filled with `FileSystemAccessRule` objects. The access rules listed here deny write access to the Sales group, give read access to the Everyone group, and give full control to the Developers group.

This program runs on your system only if the Windows groups Sales and Developers are defined. You can change the program to use groups that are available in your environment.

```
private static void WriteAcl(string filename)
{
    NTAccount salesIdentity = new NTAccount("Sales");
    NTAccount developersIdentity = new NTAccount("Developers");
    NTAccount everyOneIdentity = new NTAccount("Everyone");

    FileSystemAccessRule salesAce = new FileSystemAccessRule(
            salesIdentity, FileSystemRights.Write, AccessControlType.Deny);
    FileSystemAccessRule everyoneAce = new FileSystemAccessRule(
            everyOneIdentity, FileSystemRights.Read,
            AccessControlType.Allow);
    FileSystemAccessRule developersAce = new FileSystemAccessRule(
            developersIdentity, FileSystemRights.FullControl,
            AccessControlType.Allow);

    FileSecurity securityDescriptor = new FileSecurity();
    securityDescriptor.SetAccessRule(everyoneAce);
    securityDescriptor.SetAccessRule(developersAce);
    securityDescriptor.SetAccessRule(salesAce);

    File.SetAccessControl(filename, securityDescriptor);
}
```

You can verify the access rules by opening the Properties and selecting a file in the Windows Explorer. Selecting the Security tab lists the access control list.

Code Access Security

What is the importance of code access security? With role-based security, you can define what the user is allowed to do. Code access security defines what the code is allowed to do. It depends on the evidence of the code — where is the code coming from? Depending on the origin of the code, different permissions apply. Of course, role-based security still applies. The code cannot do more than the user is allowed to do.

Code access security is a feature of the runtime that manages code, according to your level of trust. If the CLR trusts the code enough to allow it to run, it will begin executing the code. Depending on the permissions given to the assembly, however, it might run within a restricted environment. If the code is not trusted enough to run, or if it runs but then attempts to perform an action for which it does not have the relevant permissions, a security exception (of type SecurityException or a subclass of it) is thrown. The code access security system means that you can stop malicious code from running, but you can also allow code to run within a protected environment where you are confident that it cannot do any damage.

There are different scenarios in which code access security becomes important. With ClickOnce deployment, in many scenarios it is okay to use full trust, meaning the code is allowed to do anything that the user is allowed to do. If the ClickOnce deployed application is installed within the company, then maybe you trust your own application. An application certificate that is coming with the application can also give enough information about a vendor that you trust, so you can deploy the vendor's application using ClickOnce with full rights to your own system. Of course, restricted rights are also possible with ClickOnce. Scenarios in which code access security becomes more important than with ClickOnce are in hosting environments and with add-ins. If you create an add-in host, you might not want to give all your rights to the add-ins that are loaded from your application. You can restrict the permissions for assemblies that are called. A Web site hosting company does not want Web applications from different customers running on the server to have full rights to the system. They could break a server that might run hundreds or thousands of Web applications. Restricting permissions for Web applications is a good option.

> Chapter 16, "Deployment," explains ClickOnce in detail. Creating add-ins is discussed in Chapter 36, "Add-Ins."

Code access security is based on these concepts: permissions, permission sets, code groups, and policies. Take a look at them now, because they form the foundations of the sections that follow:

❑ **Permissions** are the actions that you allow each code group to perform. For example, permissions include "read files from the file system," "write to the Active Directory," and "use sockets to open network connections." Several predefined permissions exist, but you can also create your own permissions.

❑ **Permission sets** are collections of permissions. With permission sets, it is not necessary to apply every single permission to code; permissions are grouped to permission sets. Some examples of permission sets are FullTrust, LocalIntranet, and Internet. You can create a permission set that includes required permissions. An assembly that has FullTrust permissions has full access to all resources. With LocalIntranet, the assembly is restricted, that is, it is not allowed to write to the file system other than using the isolated storage.

❑ **Code groups** bring together code with similar characteristics. A code group defines the origin of the code. Examples for existing code groups are Internet and Intranet. The group Internet defines code that is sourced from the Internet, and the group Intranet defines code sourced from the LAN. The information used to place assemblies into code groups is called *evidence*. Other evidence is collected by the CLR, including the publisher of the code, the strong name, and (where applicable) the URI from which it was downloaded. Code groups are arranged in a hierarchy, and assemblies are nearly always matched to several code groups. The code group at the root of the hierarchy is called All Code and contains all other code groups. The hierarchy is used for deciding which code groups an assembly belongs to; if an assembly does not provide evidence that matches it to a group in the tree, no attempt is made to match it to code groups below.

❑ **Policies** allow the system administrator to define different levels of permissions for the complete company, machines, and users. Code groups are defined within all of these policies, and the permissions are combined.

Permissions

.NET permissions are independent of operating system permissions. .NET permissions are just verified by the CLR. An assembly demands a permission for a specific operation (for example, the `File` class demands the `FileIOPermission`), and the CLR verifies if the assembly has the permission granted so that it can continue.

There is a very fine-grained list of permissions that you can apply to an assembly or request from code. The following list shows a few of the code access permissions provided by the CLR; as you can see, you have great control of what code is or is not permitted to do:

❑ **DirectoryServicesPermission** controls the ability to access Active Directory through the `System.DirectoryServices` classes.

❑ **DnsPermission** controls the ability to use the TCP/IP Domain Name System (DNS).

❑ **EnvironmentPermission** controls the ability to read and write environment variables.

❑ **EventLogPermission** controls the ability to read and write to the event log.

❑ **FileDialogPermission** controls the ability to access files that have been selected by the user in the Open dialog box. This permission is commonly used when `FileIOPermission` is not granted to allow limited access to files.

❑ **FileIOPermission** controls the ability to work with files (reading, writing, and appending to files, as well as creating, altering, and accessing folders).

❑ **IsolatedStorageFilePermission** controls the ability to access private virtual file systems.

❑ **IsolatedStoragePermission** controls the ability to access isolated storage; storage that is associated with an individual user and with some aspect of the code's identity. Isolated storage is discussed in Chapter 25, "Manipulating Files and the Registry."

❑ **MessageQueuePermission** controls the ability to use message queues through the Microsoft Message Queue.

❑ **PerformanceCounterPermission** controls the ability to make use of performance counters.

❑ **PrintingPermission** controls the ability to print.

❑ **ReflectionPermission** controls the ability to discover information about a type at runtime by using `System.Reflection`.

❑ **RegistryPermission** controls the ability to read, write, create, or delete registry keys and values.

❑ **SecurityPermission** controls the ability to execute, assert permissions, call into unmanaged code, skip verification, and other rights.

❑ **ServiceControllerPermission** controls the ability to control Windows services.

❑ **SocketPermission** controls the ability to make or accept TCP/IP connections on a network transport address.

❑ **SQLClientPermission** controls the ability to access SQL Server databases with the .NET data provider for SQL Server.

❑ **UIPermission** controls the ability to access the user interface.

❑ **WebPermission** controls the ability to make or accept connections to or from the Web.

With each of these permission classes, it is often possible to specify an even deeper level of granularity; for example, the `DirectoryServicesPermission` allows you to differentiate between read and write access, and also allows you to define which entries in the directory services are allowed or denied access.

In terms of best practice, you should ensure that any attempts to use resources require permissions to be enclosed within `try/catch` error-handling blocks, so that your application degrades gracefully, should it be running under restricted permissions. The design of your application should specify how your application should act under these circumstances. Do not assume that it will be running under the same security policy under which it has been developed. For example, if your application cannot access the local drive, should it exit or operate in an alternative fashion?

Another set of permissions is assigned by the CLR on the basis of the identity of the code, which cannot be granted. These permissions relate to the evidence the CLR has collated about the assembly and are called *identity permissions*. Here are the names of the classes for the identity permissions:

❑ **PublisherIdentityPermission** refers to the software publisher's digital signature.

❑ **SiteIdentityPermission** refers to the name of the Web site from which the code originated.

❑ **StrongNameIdentityPermission** refers to the assembly's strong name.

❑ **URLIdentityPermission** refers to the URL from which the code came (including the protocol, for example, `https://`).

❑ **ZoneIdentityPermission** refers to the zone from which the assembly originates.

By assigning the permission to code groups, there is no need to deal with every single permission. Instead, the permissions are applied in blocks, which is why .NET has the concept of permission sets. These are lists of code access permissions grouped into a named set. The following list explains the named permission sets you get out of the box:

❑ **FullTrust** means no permission restrictions.

❑ **SkipVerification** means that verification is not done.

❑ **Execution** grants the ability to run, but not to access any protected resources.

❑ **Nothing** grants no permissions and prevents the code from executing.

❑ **LocalIntranet** specifies the default policy for the local intranet, a subset of the full set of permissions. For example, file IO is restricted to read access on the share where the assembly originates.

❑ **Internet** specifies the default policy for code of unknown origin. This is the most restrictive policy listed. For example, code executing in this permission set has no file IO capability, cannot read or write event logs, and cannot read or write environment variables.

❑ **Everything** grants all the permissions that are listed under this set, except the permission to skip code verification. The administrator can alter any of the permissions in this permission set. This is useful when the default policy needs to be tighter.

Note that of these you can change the definitions of only the Everything permission set — the other sets are fixed and cannot be changed. Of course, you can also create your own permission set.

Identity permissions cannot be included in permission sets because the CLR is the only body able to grant identity permissions to code. For example, if a piece of code is from a specific publisher, it would make little sense for the administrator to assign the identity permissions associated with another publisher. The CLR grants identity permissions where necessary, and if you want, you can use them.

Demanding Permissions Programmatically

An assembly can demand permissions declaratively or programmatically. To see how demanding permissions works, create a Windows Forms application that contains just a button. When the button is clicked, a file on the local file system is accessed. If the application does not have the relevant permission to access the local drive (`FileIOPermission`), the button will be marked as disabled (dimmed).

If you import the namespace `System.Security.Permissions`, you can change the constructor of the class `Form1` to check for permissions by creating a `FileIOPermission` object, calling its `Demand()` method, and then acting on the result:

```
public Form1()
{
    InitializeComponent();

    try
    {
        FileIOPermission fileIOPermission = new
            FileIOPermission(FileIOPermissionAccess.AllAccess,@"c:\");
        fileIOPermission.Demand();
    }
    catch (SecurityException)
    {
        button1.Enabled = false;
    }
}
```

`FileIOPermission` is contained within the `System.Security.Permissions` namespace, which is home to the full set of permissions and also provides classes for declarative permission attributes and enumerations for the parameters that are used to create permissions objects (for example, creating a `FileIOPermission` specifying whether read-only or full access is needed).

If you run the application from the local drive where the default security policy allows access to local storage, you will see a dialog box with a button that is enabled. However, if you copy the executable to a network share and run it again, you are operating within the `LocalIntranet` permission set, which blocks access to local storage, and the button will be disabled.

Within the implementation of the click event handler, there is no need to check the required security because the relevant class in the .NET Framework already demands the file permission, and the CLR ensures that each caller up the stack has those permissions before proceeding. If you run the application from the intranet, and it attempts to open a file on the local disk, you will see an exception unless the security policy has been altered to grant access to the local drive.

To catch exceptions thrown by the CLR when code attempts to act contrary to its granted permissions, you can catch the exception of the type `SecurityException`, which provides access to a number of useful pieces of information, including a human-readable stack trace (`SecurityException.StackTrace`) and a reference to the method that threw the exception (`SecurityException.TargetSite`). `SecurityException` even provides you with the `SecurityException.PermissionType` property, which returns the type of `Permission` object that caused the security exception to occur. If you have problems with security exceptions, this should be one of your first parts to diagnose. Simply remove the `try` and `catch` blocks from the previous code to see the security exception.

Declarative Permissions

You can deny, demand, and assert permissions by invoking permission classes programmatically. However, you can also use attributes and specify permission requirements declaratively.

The main benefit of using declarative security is that the settings are accessible through reflection. This can be of enormous benefit to system administrators, who often will want to view the security requirements of applications.

For example, you can specify that a method must have permission to read from `C:\` to execute:

```csharp
using System;
using System.Security.Permissions;

namespace Wrox.ProCSharp.Security
{
    class Program
    {
        static void Main()
        {
            MyClass.Method();
        }
    }

    class MyClass
    {
        [FileIOPermission(SecurityAction.Demand, Read="C:/")]
        public static void Method()
        {
            // implementation goes here
        }
    }
}
```

Be aware that if you use attributes to assert or demand permissions, you cannot catch any exceptions that are raised if the action fails, because there is no imperative code around in which you can place a `try-catch-finally` clause.

Requesting Permissions

As discussed in the previous section, demanding permissions (either by code or declaratively) is where you state clearly what you need at runtime; however, you can configure an assembly so it makes a softer request for permissions right at the start of execution. The assembly can specify the required permissions before it begins executing.

You can request permissions in three ways:

❑ **Minimum** permissions specify the permissions your code must run.

❑ **Optional** permissions specify the permissions your code can use but is able to run effectively without.

❑ **Refused** permissions specify the permissions that you want to ensure are not granted to your code.

Why would you want to request permissions when your assembly starts? There are several reasons:

❑ If your assembly needs certain permissions to run, it makes sense to state this at the start of execution rather than during execution to ensure that the user does not experience a road block after beginning to work in your program.

❑ You will be granted only the permissions you request and nothing more. Without explicitly requesting permissions your assembly might be granted more permissions than it needs to execute. This increases the risk of your assembly being used for malicious purposes by other code.

❑ If you request only a minimum set of permissions, you are increasing the probability that your assembly will run, because you cannot predict the security policies that are effective at the user's location.

Requesting permissions is likely to be most useful if you are doing more complex deployment, and there is a higher risk that your application will be installed on a machine that does not grant the required permissions. It is usually preferable for the application to know right at the start if it will not be granted permissions, rather than halfway through execution.

With Visual Studio, you can get help to calculate the required permissions of an application by selecting the Security tab with the properties (see Figure 20-4). Clicking the Calculate Permissions button checks the code of the assembly and lists all required permissions.

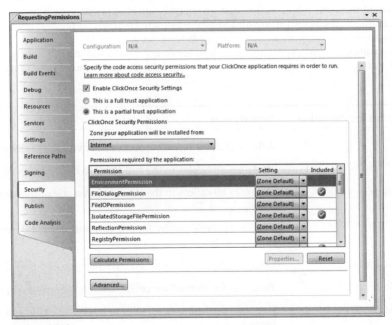

Figure 20-4

Instead of using Visual Studio, you can use the command-line tool `permcalc.exe` to calculate the required permissions of an assembly.

The command line

```
permcalc.exe -show -stacks -cleancache DemandingPermissions.exe
```

creates an XML file that contains all required permissions. With the option -show, the XML file is opened immediately. The option -stacks adds the stack information to the XML file for you to see where the permissions demand originated from.

The required permissions can be added as attributes to the assembly. Following are three examples that demonstrate using attributes to request permissions. If you are following this with the code download, you can find these examples in the RequestingPermissions project. The first attribute requests that the assembly have UIPermission granted, which will allow the application access to the user interface. The request is for the minimum permissions, so if this permission is not granted, the assembly will fail to start:

```
using System.Security.Permissions;
[assembly:UIPermission(SecurityAction.RequestMinimum, Unrestricted=true)]
```

Next, there is a request that the assembly be refused access to the C:\ drive. This attribute's setting means that the entire assembly will be blocked from accessing this drive:

```
[assembly:FileIOPermission(SecurityAction.RequestRefuse, Read="C:/")]
```

Finally, here is an attribute that requests that the assembly be optionally granted the permission to access unmanaged code:

```
[assembly:SecurityPermission(SecurityAction.RequestOptional,
    Flags = SecurityPermissionFlag.UnmanagedCode)]
```

In this scenario, you want to add this attribute to an application that accesses unmanaged code in at least one place. In this case, it is specified that this permission is optional, which means that the application can run without the permission to access unmanaged code. If the assembly is not granted permission to access unmanaged code and attempts to do so, a SecurityException will be raised, which the application should expect and handle accordingly. The following table shows the full list of available SecurityAction enumeration values; some of these values are covered in more detail later in this chapter.

SecurityAction Enumeration	Description
Assert	Allows code to access resources not available to the caller.
Demand	Requires all callers in the call stack to have the specified permission.
DemandChoice	Requires all callers in the stack to have one of the specified permissions.
Deny	Denies a permission by forcing any subsequent demand for the permission to fail.
InheritanceDemand	Requires derived classes to have the specified permission granted.
LinkDemand	Requires the immediate caller to have the specified permission.
LinkDemandChoice	Requires the immediate caller to have one of the specified permissions.
PermitOnly	Similar to Deny; subsequent demands for resources not explicitly listed by PermitOnly are refused.

SecurityAction Enumeration	Description
RequestMinimum	Applied at assembly scope; this contains a permission required for an assembly to operate correctly.
RequestOptional	Applied at assembly scope; this asks for permissions the assembly can use, if available, to provide additional features and functionality.
RequestRefuse	Applied at assembly scope when there is a permission you do not want your assembly to have.

When you consider the permission requirements of your application, you need to decide between two options:

❑ Request all the permissions you need at the start of execution, and degrade gracefully or exit if those permissions are not granted.

❑ Avoid requesting permissions at the start of execution, but be prepared to handle security exceptions throughout your application.

After an assembly has been configured using permission attributes in this way, you can use the permcalc.exe utility to show the required permissions by aiming at the assembly file that contains the assembly manifest using the –assembly option of the permcalc.exe utility:

```
>permcalc.exe -show -assembly RequestingPermissions.exe
```

The output for an application using the three previously discussed attributes looks like this:

```
Microsoft (R) .NET Framework Permissions Calculator.
Copyright (C) Microsoft Corporation 2005. All rights reserved.

Analyzing...
|--------------------------------|
. . . . . . . . . . . . . . . . . . . . . . . . . . . . . . . . . . . . . . . . . . . . . . . . . . . . . . . . . . . . . . . .

RequestingPermissions.exe
Minimal permission set:
<PermissionSet class="System.Security.PermissionSet"
version="1">
<IPermission class="System.Security.Permissions.UIPermission, mscorlib,
Version=2.0.0.0, Culture=neutral, PublicKeyToken=b77a5c561934e089" version="1"
Unrestricted="true"/>
</PermissionSet>

Optional permission set:
<PermissionSet class="System.Security.PermissionSet"
version="1">
<IPermission class="System.Security.Permissions.SecurityPermission, mscorlib,
Version=2.0.0.0, Culture=neutral, PublicKeyToken=b77a5c561934e089" version="1" Flag
s="SecurityPermissionFlag.UnmanagedCode" />
</PermissionSet>
```

(continued)

609

(continued)

```
Refused permission set:
<PermissionSet class="System.Security.PermissionSet"
version="1">
<IPermission class="System.Security.Permissions.FileIOPermission, mscorlib,
Version=2.0.0.0, Culture=neutral, PublicKeyToken=b77a5c561934e089" version="1"
Read="C:"/>
</PermissionSet>

Generating output...
Writing file: RequestingPermissions.exe.PermCalc.xml...
```

In addition to requesting permissions, you can also request a complete permissions set; the advantage is that you don't have to deal with every single permission. However, you can only request permission sets that cannot be altered. The Everything permission set can be altered through the security policy while an assembly is running, so it cannot be requested.

Here is an example of how to request a built-in permission set:

```
[assembly:PermissionSet(SecurityAction.RequestMinimum,
                        Name = "FullTrust")]
```

In this example, the assembly requests that as a minimum it needs the FullTrust built-in permission set granted. If this set of permissions is not granted, the assembly will throw a security exception at runtime.

Implicit Permissions

When permissions are granted, there is often an implicit statement that you are also granted other permissions. For example, if you assign the FileIOPermission for C:\, there is an implicit assumption that there is also access to its subdirectories.

To check whether a granted permission implicitly brings another permission as a subset, you can do this:

```
class Program
{
    static void Main()
    {
        CodeAccessPermission permissionA =
            new FileIOPermission(FileIOPermissionAccess.AllAccess, @"C:\");
        CodeAccessPermission permissionB =
            new FileIOPermission(FileIOPermissionAccess.Read, @"C:\temp");
        if (permissionB.IsSubsetOf(permissionA))
        {
            Console.WriteLine("PermissionB is a subset of PermissionA");
        }
    }
}
```

The output looks like this:

```
PermissionB is a subset of PermissionA
```

Denying Permissions

Under certain circumstances, you might want to perform an action and be absolutely sure that the method that is called is acting within a protected environment. An assembly shouldn't be allowed to do anything unexpected. For example, say that you want to make a call to an add-in component in a way that it will not access the local disk. Create an instance of the permission you want to ensure that the method is not granted, and then call its `Deny()` method before making the call to the class:

```
using System;
using System.IO;
using System.Security;
using System.Security.Permissions;

namespace Wrox.ProCSharp.Security
{
    class Program
    {
        static void Main()
        {
            CodeAccessPermission permission =
                new FileIOPermission(FileIOPermissionAccess.AllAccess,@"C:\");
            permission.Deny();
            UntrustworthyClass.Method();
            CodeAccessPermission.RevertDeny();
        }
    }

    class UntrustworthyClass
    {
        public static void Method()
        {
            try
            {
                using (StreamReader reader = File.OpenText(@"C:\textfile.txt"))
                {
                }
            }
            catch
            {
                Console.WriteLine("Failed to open file");
            }
        }
    }
}
```

If you build this code, the output will state *Failed to open file*, because the untrustworthy class does not have access to the local disk.

Note that the `Deny()` call is made on an instance of the `permission` object, whereas the `RevertDeny()` call is made statically. The reason for this is that the `RevertDeny()` call reverts all deny requests within the current stack frame; if you have made several calls to `Deny()`, you need to make only one follow-up call to `RevertDeny()`.

Asserting Permissions

Imagine that an assembly has been installed with full trust on a user's system. Within that assembly there is a method that saves auditing information to a text file on the local disk. If, later, an application is installed that wants to make use of the auditing feature, it will be necessary for the application to have the relevant `FileIOPermission` permissions to save the data to disk.

This seems excessive, however, because all you really want to do is perform a highly restricted action on the local disk. In these situations, it would be useful if assemblies with limiting permissions could make calls to more trusted assemblies that can temporarily increase the scope of the permissions on the stack, and perform operations on behalf of the caller. The caller, itself, doesn't need to have the permissions.

Another example in which asserts become important is when you create assemblies that invoke native code using platform invoke. The assembly invoking native methods requires full trust. But is it really necessary that all callers of this assembly require full trust as well? Take a look at how this is done with the .NET Framework assemblies. The `File` class invokes the native Windows API `CreateFile()` and thus needs full trust. The `File` class itself asserts the permission it requires by itself so that the caller does not require having this permission itself, but demands the `FileIOPermission`. (Platform invoke is discussed in Chapter 24, "Interoperability.")

Assemblies with a high enough level of trust can assert permissions that they require. If the assembly has the permissions it needs to assert additional permissions, it removes the need for callers up the stack to have such wide-ranging permissions.

The code that follows contains a class called `AuditClass` that implements a method called `Save()`, which takes a string and saves audit data to `C:\audit.txt`. The `AuditClass` method asserts the permissions it needs to add the audit lines to the file. For testing it, the `Main()` method for the application explicitly denies the file permission that the `Audit` method needs:

```csharp
using System;
using System.IO;
using System.Security;
using System.Security.Permissions;

namespace Wrox.ProCSharp.Security
{
    class Program
    {
        static void Main()
        {
            CodeAccessPermission permission =
                new FileIOPermission(FileIOPermissionAccess.Append,
                                     @"C:\audit.txt");
            permission.Deny();
            AuditClass.Save("some data to audit");
            CodeAccessPermission.RevertDeny();
        }
    }
    class AuditClass
    {
        public static void Save(string value)
        {
            try
            {
                FileIOPermission permission =
                    new FileIOPermission(FileIOPermissionAccess.Append,
                                         @"C:\audit.txt");
                permission.Assert();
                FileStream stream = new FileStream(@"C:\audit.txt",
                    FileMode.Append, FileAccess.Write);

                // code to write to audit file here...
```

```
            CodeAccessPermission.RevertAssert();
            Console.WriteLine("Data written to audit file");
        }
        catch
        {
            Console.WriteLine("Failed to write data to audit file");
        }
    }
    }
}
```

When this code is executed, you will find that the call to the AuditClass method does not cause a security exception, even though when it was called it did not have the required permissions to carry out the disk access.

Like RevertDeny(), RevertAssert() is a static method, and it reverts all assertions within the current frame.

It is important to be very careful when using assertions. You are explicitly assigning permissions to a method that has been called by code that might not have those permissions, and this could open a security hole. For example, in the auditing example, even if the security policy dictated that an installed application cannot write to the local disk, your assembly would be able to write to the disk when the auditing assembly asserts FileIOPermissions for writing.

However, to perform the assertion, the auditing assembly must have been installed with permission for FileIOAccess and SecurityPermission. The SecurityPermission allows an assembly to perform an assert, and the assembly will need both the SecurityPermission and the permission being asserted to complete successfully.

Code Groups

This section gets into management of assemblies and their permissions. Instead of managing every assembly on its own, code groups are defined. Code groups have an entry requirement called *membership condition*. For an assembly to be filed in a code group, it must match the group's membership condition. Membership conditions include "the assembly is from the site www.microsoft.com" or "the publisher of this software is Microsoft Corporation."

Each code group has one, and only one, membership condition. Assemblies can be within multiple code groups. The following list provides the types of code group membership conditions available in .NET:

- ❑ **Zone** — The region from which the code originated.
- ❑ **Site** — The Web site from which the code originated.
- ❑ **Strong name** — A unique, verifiable name for the code. Strong names are discussed in Chapter 17, "Assemblies."
- ❑ **Publisher** — The publisher of the code.
- ❑ **URL** — The specific location from which the code originated.
- ❑ **Hash value** — The hash value for the assembly.
- ❑ **Skip verification** — This condition requests that it bypass code verification checks. Code verification ensures that the code accesses types in a well-defined and acceptable way. The runtime cannot enforce security on code that is not type-safe.
- ❑ **Application directory** — The location of the assembly within the application.
- ❑ **All code** — All code fulfills this condition.
- ❑ **Custom** — A user-specified condition.

The first, and most commonly used, type of membership condition is the *Zone* condition. A zone is the region of origin of a piece of code and refers to one of the following: MyComputer, Internet, Intranet, Trusted, or Untrusted. These zones can be managed by using the Internet Options in Windows Security Center.

Code groups are arranged hierarchically with the All Code membership condition at the root (see Figure 20-5). You can see that each code group has a single membership condition and specifies the permissions that the code group has been granted. Note that if an assembly does not match the membership condition in a code group, the CLR does not attempt to match code groups below it.

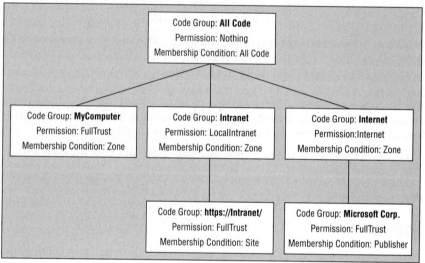

Figure 20-5

caspol.exe — The Code Access Security Policy Tool

This section spends a good deal of time looking at the command-line Code Access Security Policy tool. To get a list of options for the tool, just type the following at the command prompt:

```
caspol.exe -?
```

To send the output to a text file, use:

```
caspol.exe > output.txt
```

Take a look at the code groups on a machine using `caspol.exe`. The output of the command lists the hierarchical structure of the code groups on the machine, and next to each group there is a description of the code group. Type this command:

```
caspol.exe -listdescription
```

Alternatively, the `-listdescription` parameter has a shortcut: `-ld`. A part of the output is shown here:

```
Microsoft (R) .NET Framework CasPol 2.0.50727.1426
Copyright (c) Microsoft Corporation. All rights reserved.

Security is ON
```

```
Execution checking is ON
Policy change prompt is ON

Level = Machine

Full Trust Assemblies:

1. All_Code: Code group grants no permissions and forms the root of the code
group tree.
     1.1. My_Computer_Zone: Code group grants full trust to all code originating
          on the local computer
        1.1.1. Microsoft_Strong_Name: Code group grants full trust to code
               signed with the Microsoft strong name.
        1.1.2. ECMA_Strong_Name: Code group grants full trust to code signed
               with the ECMA strong name.
     1.2. LocalIntranet_Zone: Code group grants the intranet permission set to
          code from the intranet zone. This permission set grants intranet code
          the right to use isolated storage, full UI access, some capability to
          do reflection, and limited access to environment variables.
        1.2.1. Intranet_Same_Site_Access: All intranet code gets the right to
               connect back to the site of its origin.
        1.2.2. Intranet_Same_Directory_Access: All intranet code gets the right
               to read from its install directory.
     1.3. Internet_Zone: Code group grants code from the Internet zone the
          Internet permission set. This permission set grants Internet code the
          right to use isolated storage and limited UI access.
```

The .NET security subsystem ensures that code from each code group is allowed to do only certain things. For example, code from the Internet zone will, by default, have much stricter limits than code from the local drive. Code from the local drive is normally granted access to data stored on the local drive, but assemblies from the Internet are not granted this permission by default.

Using caspol and its equivalent in the Microsoft Management Console, you can specify what level of trust you have for each code access group, as well as managing code groups and permissions in a more granular fashion.

Take another look at the code access groups, but this time in a slightly more compact view. Make sure that you are logged in as a local administrator, go to a command prompt, and type this command:

```
caspol.exe -listgroups
```

You will see something like this:

```
Microsoft (R) .NET Framework CasPol 2.0.50727.1426
Copyright (c) Microsoft Corporation. All rights reserved.

Security is ON
Execution checking is ON
Policy change prompt is ON

Level = Machine

Code Groups:
```

(continued)

(continued)

```
1.  All code: Nothing
    1.1.  Zone - MyComputer: FullTrust
        1.1.1.  StrongName -
0024000004800000940000000602000000240000525341310004 0
0000100010007D1FA57C4AED9F0A32E84AA0FAEFD0DE9E8FD6AEC8F87FB03766C834C99921EB23
BE79AD9D5DCC1DD9AD236132102900B723CF980957FC4E177108FC607774F29E8320E92EA05ECE
4E821C0A5EFE8F1645C4C0C93C1AB99285D622CAA652C1DFAD63D745D6F2DE5F17E5EAF0FC4963
D261C8A12436518206DC093344D5AD293: FullTrust
        1.1.2.  StrongName - 00000000000000000400000000000000: FullTrust
    1.2.  Zone - Intranet: LocalIntranet
        1.2.1.  All code: Same site Web.
        1.2.2.  All code: Same directory FileIO - 'Read, PathDiscovery'
    1.3.  Zone - Internet: Internet
        1.3.1.  All code: Same site Web.
    1.4.  Zone - Untrusted: Nothing
    1.5.  Zone - Trusted: Internet
        1.5.1.  All code: Same site Web.
Success
```

You will notice that near the start of the output it says Security is ON. Later in the chapter you will see that it can be turned off and then turned on again.

The Execution Checking setting is on by default, which means that all assemblies must be granted the permission to execute before they can run. If execution checking is turned off using caspol (caspol.exe -execution on|off), assemblies that do not have the permission to run can execute, although they might cause security exceptions if they attempt to act contrary to the security policy later in their execution.

The Policy Change Prompt option specifies whether you see an "Are you sure" warning message when you attempt to alter the security policy.

As code is broken down into these groups, you can manage security at a more granular level, and apply full trust to a much smaller percentage of code. Note that each group has a label (for example, 1.2). These labels are auto-generated by .NET, and can differ between machines. Generally, security is not managed for each assembly, but for a code group instead.

When a machine has several side-by-side installations of CLR, the copy of caspol.exe that you run will alter the security policy only for the installation of .NET with which it is associated.

Viewing an Assembly's Code Groups

Assemblies are matched to code groups according to the membership conditions they match. If you were to go back to the code groups example and load an assembly from the https://intranet/ Web site, it would match the code groups shown in Figure 20-6. The assembly is a member of the root code group (All Code); because it came from the local network, it is also a member of the Intranet code group. However, because it was loaded from the specific site https://intranet, it is also granted *FullTrust*, which means that it can run unrestricted.

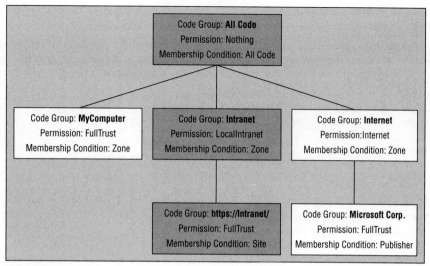

Figure 20-6

You can easily view the code groups that an assembly is a member of using this command:

```
caspol.exe -resolvegroup assembly.dll
```

Running this command on an assembly on the local drive produces the following output:

```
Microsoft (R) .NET Framework CasPol 2.0.50727.1426
Copyright (c) Microsoft Corporation. All rights reserved.

Level = Enterprise

Code Groups:

1.  All code: FullTrust

Level = Machine

Code Groups:

1.  All code: Nothing
    1.1.  Zone - MyComputer: FullTrust

Level = User

Code Groups:

1.  All code: FullTrust

Success
```

You will notice that code groups are listed on three levels — Enterprise, Machine, and User. For now, stay focused on the machine level. In case you are curious about the relationship among the three, the effective permission given to an assembly is the intersection of the permissions from the three levels. For example, if you remove the FullTrust permission from the Internet zone at the enterprise-level policy, all permissions are revoked for code from the Internet zone, and the settings of the other two levels become irrelevant.

Now use this command once more with the same assembly to read the code groups. However, this time, the assembly is accessed from a Web server using the HTTP protocol. You can see that the assembly is a member of different groups that have much more restrictive permissions:

```
caspol.exe -resolvegroup http://server/assembly.dll
Microsoft (R) .NET Framework CasPol 2.0.50727.1426
Copyright (c) Microsoft Corporation. All rights reserved.


Level = Enterprise

Code Groups:

1.  All code: FullTrust
Level = Machine

Code Groups:

1.  All code: Nothing
      1.1.   Zone - Internet: Internet
          1.1.1.   All code: Same site Web.


Level = User

Code Groups:

1.  All code: FullTrust

Success
```

The assembly grants the Internet and the Same Site Web permissions. The intersection of the permissions allows the code limited UI access. It also permits the code to establish connections to the site it originated from.

Code Access Permissions and Permissions Sets

Imagine yourself administering security policy on a network of desktop machines in a large enterprise scenario. In this environment, it is immensely useful for the CLR to collect evidence information on code before the code is allowed to execute. Likewise, you, as the administrator, must have the opportunity to control what code is allowed on the several hundred machines you manage once the CLR has identified its origin. This is where permissions start to act.

After an assembly has been matched to code groups, the CLR looks at the security policy to calculate the permissions it grants to an assembly. When managing permissions in Windows, you generally don't want to apply permissions to users, but you apply permissions to user groups instead. This is also true with assemblies; permissions are applied to code groups rather than to individual assemblies, which makes the management of security policy in .NET a much easier task.

Look more closely at viewing an assembly's permissions. Imagine using a Microsoft application in which you use a feature that you have not used before. The application does not have a copy of the code stored locally, so the code is requested from the Internet and downloaded into the Download Assembly Cache. Figure 20-7 illustrates what an assembly's code group membership might look like with code from the Internet published by a named organization that has signed the assembly with a certificate.

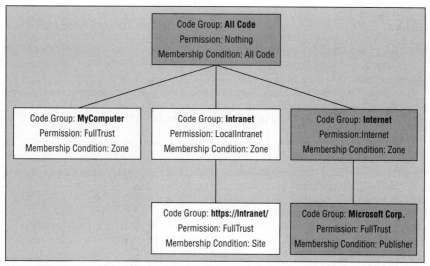

Figure 20-7

Although the All Code and Internet code groups have only limited permissions according to the policy in this example, membership of the code group in the bottom right-hand corner grants the assembly the FullTrust permission. The overall effective permission is the *union* of permissions across the matching code groups. When the permissions are merged this way, the effective permission is that of all permissions granted, that is, each code group to which an assembly belongs brings additional permissions.

Just as you can check what code groups an assembly belongs to, it is also possible to look at the permissions assigned to the code groups. By doing this you will see not only the code access permissions (what the code is allowed to do), but also the code identity permissions that will give you access to the evidence the code presented to the runtime. To see the permissions for an assembly's code groups, use a command like this:

```
caspol.exe -resolveperm assembly.dll
```

Try this on an assembly and look at the granted code access and identity permissions when the assembly is accessed over a local intranet. When you type the following command, you will see the code access permissions and then the three identity permissions at the end:

```
caspol.exe -resolveperm http://somehost/assembly.dll
Microsoft (R) .NET Framework CasPol 2.0.50727.1426
Copyright (c) Microsoft Corporation. All rights reserved.

Resolving permissions for level = Enterprise
Resolving permissions for level = Machine
Resolving permissions for level = User

Grant =
<PermissionSet class="System.Security.PermissionSet"
      version="1">
   <IPermission class="System.Security.Permissions.EnvironmentPermission,
       mscorlib, Version=2.0.0.0, Culture=neutral,
       PublicKeyToken=b77a5c561934e089" Version="1" Read="USERNAME"/>
```

(continued)

(continued)

```
<IPermission class="System.Security.Permissions.FileDialogPermission,
        mscorlib, Version=2.0.0.0, Culture=neutral,
        PublicKeyToken=b77a5c561934e089"
        version="1" Unrestricted="true"/>
<IPermission
        class="System.Security.Permissions.IsolatedStorageFilePermission,
        mscorlib, Version=2.0.0.0, Culture=neutral,
        PublicKeyToken=b77a5c561934e089" version="1"
        Allowed="AssemblyIsolationByUser"
        UserQuota="9223372036854775807" Expiry="9223372036854775807"
        Permanent="True"/>
<IPermission class="System.Security.Permissions.ReflectionPermission,
        mscorlib, Version="2.0.0.0, Culture=neutral,
        PublicKeyToken= b77a5c561934e089" Version="1"
        Flags="ReflectionEmit" />
<IPermission class="System.Security.Permissions.SecurityPermission,
        mscorlib, Version=2.0.0.0, Culture=neutral,
        PublicKeyToken=b77a5c561934e089" version="1"
        Flags="Assertion, Execution, BindingRedirects"/>
<IPermission class="System.Security.Permissions.UIPermission,
        mscorlib, Version=2.0.0.0, Culture=neutral,
        PublicKeyToken=b77a5c561934e089" version="1"
        Unrestricted="true" />
<IPermission class="System.Security.Permissions.SiteIdentityPermission,
        mscorlib, Version=2.0.0.0, Culture=neutral,
        PublicKeyToken=b77a5c561934e089" version="1"
        Site="somehost" />
<IPermission class="System.Security.Permissions.UrlIdentityPermission,
        mscorlib, Version=2.0.0.0, Culture=neutral,
        PublicKeyToken=b77a5c561934e089" version="1"
        Url="http://somehost/assembly.dll" />
<IPermission class="System.Security.Permissions.ZoneIdentityPermission,
        mscorlib, Version=2.0.0.0, Culture=neutral,
        PublicKeyToken=b77a5c561934e089" version="1"
        Zone="Intranet" />
<IPermission class="System.Net.DnsPermission,
        System, Version=2.0.0.0, Culture=neutral,
        PublicKeyToken=b77a5c561934e089" version="1"
        Unrestricted="true" />
<IPermission class="System.Drawing.Printing.PrintingPermission,
        System.Drawing, Version=2.0.0.0, Culture=neutral,
        PublicKeyToken=b03f5f7f11d50a3a" version="1"
        Level="DefaultPrinting" />
<IPermission class="System.Net.WebPermission,
        System, Version=2.0.0.0, Culture=neutral,
        PublicKeyToken=b77a5c561934e089" version="1">
    <ConnectAccess>
        <URI uri="(https|http)://somehost/.*"/>
    </ConnectAccess>
</IPermission>
</PermissionSet>

Success
```

The output shows each of the permissions in XML, including the class defining the permission, the assembly containing the class, the permission version, and an encryption token. The output suggests that it is possible for you to create your own permissions. You can also see that each of the identity permissions includes more detailed information on, for example, the UrlIdentityPermission class, which provides access to the URL from which the code originated.

Note how at the start of the output, caspol.exe resolved the permissions at the enterprise, machine, and user levels and then listed the effective granted permissions, which is worth a closer look.

Policy Levels: Machine, User, and Enterprise

Up to now, you have dealt with security in the context of a single machine. It's often necessary to specify security policies for specific users or for an entire organization, and that is why .NET provides not one but three policy levels:

- ❑ Machine
- ❑ Enterprise
- ❑ User

The code group levels are independently managed and exist in parallel, as shown in Figure 20-8.

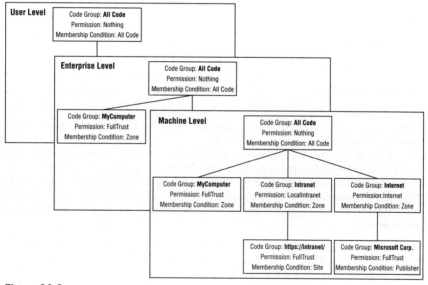

Figure 20-8

If there are three security policies, how do you know which one applies? The effective permission is the *intersection* of the permissions from these three levels. Each of the three levels has the ability to veto the permissions allowed by another — this is really good news for administrators because their settings will override user settings.

To work with code groups and permissions on the user or enterprise levels using caspol.exe, add either the -enterprise or -user argument to change the command's mode. caspol.exe works at the machine level by default and that's how you've been using it until now. Use the following command to see the code groups listing at the user level:

```
caspol.exe -user -listgroups
```

The output of the command on a default installation looks like this:

```
Security is ON
Execution checking is ON
Policy change prompt is ON

Level = User

Code Groups:

1.  All code: FullTrust
Success
```

Now run the same command, but this time with the code groups at the enterprise level:

```
caspol.exe -enterprise -listgroups
```

The output of the command looks like this:

```
Security is ON
Execution checking is ON
Policy change prompt is ON

Level = Enterprise

Code Groups:

1.  All code: FullTrust
Success
```

As you can see, by default, both the user level and the enterprise level are configured to allow FullTrust for the single code group All Code. The result of this is that the default setting for .NET security places no restrictions at the enterprise or user levels, and the enforced policy is dictated solely by the machine-level policy. For example, if you were to assign a more restrictive permission or permission set than FullTrust to either the enterprise or user levels, those restrictions would restrict the overall permissions, and probably override permissions at the machine level. The effective permissions are intersected. If you want to apply FullTrust to a code group, this permission must be assigned to the code group on each of the three policy levels.

When you run caspol.exe as an administrator, it defaults to the machine level, but if you log out and log back in as a user who is not in the Administrator user group, caspol.exe will default to the user level instead. In addition, caspol.exe will not allow you to alter the security policy in a way that renders the caspol.exe utility itself inoperable.

Managing Security Policies

As you have already seen, the glue that connects code groups, permissions, and permission sets consists of three levels of security policy (enterprise, machine, and user). Security configuration information in .NET is stored in XML configuration files that are protected by Windows security. For example, the machine-level security policy is writable only by users in the Administrators and SYSTEM Windows groups.

The files that store the security policy are located in the following paths:

- **Enterprise policy configuration** — `<windows>\Microsoft.NET\Framework\<version>\Config\enterprise.config`

- **Machine policy configuration** — `<windows>\Microsoft.NET\Framework\<version>\Config\security.config`

- **User policy configuration** — `%USERPROFILE%\application data\Microsoft\CLR Security Config\<version>\security.config`

The subdirectory `<version>` varies, depending on the version of the CLR you have on your machine. Because .NET 2.0, 3.0, and .NET 3.5 are based on the same version of the runtime, you find just one configuration for all these Framework versions. If necessary, it's possible to edit these configuration files manually, for example, if an administrator needs to configure policy for a user without logging in to his account. However, in general it's recommended to use `caspol.exe` or other administrator tools.

Given everything you have read so far, you are ready for a simple application that accesses the local drive — the kind of behavior you are likely to want to manage carefully. The application is a C# Windows Forms application with a list box and a button (see Figure 20-9). When you click the button, the list box is populated from a file called `animals.txt` from your local user folder. Before starting the application, you need to copy the file to this folder. In Windows Vista, the file is `c:\users\<username>\Documents\animals.txt`.

Figure 20-9

The application was created by using Visual Studio, and the only changes were to add the list box and Load Data button to the form and to add an event to the button that looks like this:

```
// Example from SimpleExample

private void OnLoadData(object sender, System.EventArgs e)
{
    string filename = Path.Combine(Environment.GetFolderPath(
        Environment.SpecialFolder.MyDocuments), "animals.txt");
    using (StreamReader stream = File.OpenText(filename))
    {
        string str;
        while ((str=stream.ReadLine()) != null)
        {
            listAnimals.Items.Add(str);
        }
    }
}
```

It opens a simple text file `animals.txt` from the user folder, which contains a list of animals on separate lines, and loads each line into a string, which it then uses to create each item in the list box.

If you run the application from your local machine and click the button, you will see the data loaded and displayed in the list box (see Figure 20-10). Behind the scenes the runtime has granted the assembly the permission it needs to execute, access the user interface, and read data from the local disk.

Figure 20-10

As mentioned earlier, the permissions on the Intranet zone code group are more restrictive than on the local machine; in particular, they do not allow access to the local disk. If you run the application again, but this time from a network share, it will run just as before because it is granted the permissions to execute and access the user interface; however, if you now click the Load Data button on the form, a security exception is thrown (see Figure 20-11). You'll see in the exception message text that it mentions the `System.Security.Permissions.FileIOPermission` object; this is the permission that the application was not granted and that was demanded by the class in the Framework that was used to load the data from the file on the local disk.

By default, the Intranet code group is granted the LocalIntranet permission set; change the permission set to FullTrust so that any code from the Intranet zone can run completely unrestricted.

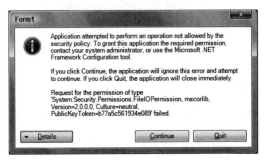

Figure 20-11

First, you need to get the numeric label of the LocalIntranet code group. You can do this with the following command:

```
>caspol.exe -listgroups
```

This will output something like this:

```
Code Groups:

1.  All code: Nothing
    1.1.   Zone - MyComputer: FullTrust
        1.1.1.   StrongName -
00240000004800000940000000060200000024000052534131000040000010001000 7D1FA57C4AED9
F0A32E84AA0FAEFD0DE9E8FD6AEC8F87FB03766C834C99921EB23BE79AD9D5DCC1DD9AD2361321
02900B723CF980957FC4E177108FC607774F29E8320E92EA05ECE4E821C0A5EFE8F1645C4C0C93
C1AB99285D622CAA652C1DFAD63D745D6F2DE5F17E5EAF0FC4963D261C8A12436518206DC09334
4D5AD293: FullTrust
        1.1.2.   StrongName - 0000000000000000400000000000000: FullTrust
    1.2.   Zone - Intranet: LocalIntranet
        1.2.1.   All code: Same site Web.
        1.2.2.   All code: Same directory FileIO - 'Read, PathDiscovery'
    1.3.   Zone - Internet: Internet
        1.3.1.   All code: Same site Web.
    1.4.   Zone - Untrusted: Nothing
    1.5.   Zone - Trusted: Internet
        1.5.1.   All code: Same site Web.
```

Notice that the LocalIntranet group is listed as 1.2. You can use the following command to apply full trust:

```
>caspol.exe -chggroup 1.2 FullTrust
```

If you run the application from the network share again and click the button, you will see that the list box is populated with the content of the file in the root of the c:\ drive and no exception occurs.

In scenarios like these, in which you are making use of resources governed by permissions, it is advisable to extend the code so that security exceptions are caught and the application can degrade gracefully. For example, in the sample application, you can add a try/catch block around the file access code, and if a SecurityException is thrown, you can display a line in the list box saying "Permission denied accessing file":

```csharp
private void OnLoadData(object sender, System.EventArgs e)
{
    try
    {
        string filename = Environment.GetFolderPath(
            Environment.SpecialFolder.MyDocuments) + @"\animals.txt";
        StreamReader din = File.OpenText(filename);
        string str;
        while ((str=din.ReadLine()) != null)
        {
            listAnimals.Items.Add(str);
        }
    }
    catch (SecurityException ex)
    {
        MessageBox.Show(ex.Message);
    }
}
```

In reality, if you wanted to run a specific application from a network share, you would most likely opt for a solution that didn't open up the client machine to all code on the intranet. Instead, code groups and membership conditions can be used to tightly control the requirements of the application — perhaps using its location on the intranet, a strong name, or a certificate proving the identity of the publisher.

Managing Code Groups and Permissions

In managing security on .NET, if you find that an assembly is failing with a security exception, you usually have three choices:

- ❑ **Ease the policy permissions** — You can change the permissions for the Machine policy to allow more permissions for specific code groups. However, it is not a good practice to give more permissions to the assemblies from an intranet or the Internet, because this can lead to Trojan horses gaining access to your system. Instead, you can add new code groups that have specific permissions as required.

- ❑ **Move the assembly** — Assemblies from a network share are not trusted as much as assemblies installed on the local system. Instead of creating a new code group, you can move the assembly to the local system so that it gets more permissions.

- ❑ **Apply a strong name to the assembly** — A good practice is to apply a strong name to the assembly and create a code group that trusts the strong name.

To make these kinds of decisions, you must take into account your level of trust of the assembly.

Turning Security On and Off

By default, .NET security is enabled. If, for any reason, you need to turn it off, you can do so like this:

```
>caspol.exe -security off
```

As a new security feature, running this command from the command prompt turns security off only temporarily. As soon as you press the Enter key, security is turned on again. You can keep this command prompt open as long as required and continue working with another command prompt. When you are finished doing the security related tasks, press the Enter key and security is turned on again. You can also explicitly turn it on again:

```
>caspol.exe -security on
```

To return the security configuration to its original state, you can type this command:

```
>caspol.exe -reset
```

This command resets the security policy to the installation's default.

Creating a Code Group

You can create your own code groups and then apply specific permissions to them. For example, you could specify that you want to trust all code from the Web site www.wrox.com and to give it full access to the system (without trusting code from any other Web site).

Earlier, the tool caspol was used to display a list with the available group and number assignments. The zone Internet is labeled 1.3, so now type this command:

```
>caspol.exe -addgroup 1.3 -site www.wrox.com FullTrust
```

Note that this command will ask for confirmation because this is an attempt to alter the security policy on the machine. If the command caspol.exe -listgroups is now run again, you will see that the new code group has been added and assigned FullTrust:

```
...
1.2.   Zone - Intranet: LocalIntranet
    1.2.1.   All code: Same site Web.
    1.2.2.   All code: Same directory FileIO - Read, PathDiscovery
  1.3.   Zone - Internet: Internet
    1.3.1.   All code: Same site Web.
    1.3.2.   Site - www.wrox.com: FullTrust
  1.4.   Zone - Untrusted: Nothing
  1.5.   Zone - Trusted: Internet
    1.5.1.   All code: Same site Web.
```

Here's another example. Say that you want to create a code group under the Intranet code group (1.2) that grants FullTrust to all applications running from a specific network share. To do so, you run the following command:

```
>caspol.exe -addgroup 1.2 -url file:\\intranetserver/sharename/* FullTrust
```

Deleting a Code Group

To remove a code group that has been created, you can type a command like this:

```
>caspol.exe -remgroup 1.3.2
```

It will ask for confirmation that you want to alter the security policy, and if you give it positive confirmation, it will state that the group has been removed.

> Be aware that although you cannot delete the code group All Code, you can delete code groups at the level below it, including the Internet, MyComputer, and LocalIntranet groups.

Changing a Code Group's Permissions

To ease or restrict the permissions assigned to a code group, you use caspol.exe again. Suppose that you want to apply FullTrust to the Intranet zone; first, you need to get the label that represents the Intranet code group:

```
>caspol.exe -listgroups
```

The output shows the Intranet code group:

```
Code Groups:

1.   All code: Nothing
    1.1.   Zone - MyComputer: FullTrust
        1.1.1.   StrongName -
0024000004800000940000000602000000240000525341310004000001000100007D1FA57C4AED9
F0A32E84AA0FAEFD0DE9E8FD6AEC8F87FB03766C834C99921EB23BE79AD9D5DCC1DD9AD2361321
02900B72
3CF980957FC4E177108FC607774F29E8320E92EA05ECE4E821C0A5EFE8F1645C4C0C93C1AB9928
5D622CAA652C1DFAD63D745D6F2DE5F17E5EAF0FC4963D261C8A12436518206DC093344D5AD293
: FullTrust
        1.1.2.   StrongName - 00000000000000000400000000000000: FullTrust
    1.2.   Zone - Intranet: LocalIntranet
        1.2.1.   All code: Same site Web.
        1.2.2.   All code: Same directory FileIO - Read, PathDiscovery
```

(continued)

(continued)

```
      1.3.  Zone - Internet: Internet
         1.3.1.  All code: Same site Web.
      1.4.  Zone - Untrusted: Nothing
      1.5.  Zone - Trusted: Internet
         1.5.1.  All code: Same site Web.
```

Once you have the Intranet code group's label, 1.2, you can enter a second command to alter the code group's permissions:

```
>caspol.exe -chggroup 1.2 FullTrust
```

The command asks you to confirm the change to the security policy, and if you run the `caspol.exe -listgroups` command again, you can see that the permission on the end of the Intranet line has changed to FullTrust:

```
Code Groups:

1.  All code: Nothing
      1.1.  Zone - MyComputer: FullTrust
         1.1.1.  StrongName -
00240000048000009400000006020000002400005253413100040000010001007D1FA57C4AED9
F0A32E84AA0FAEFD0DE9E8FD6AEC8F87FB03766C834C99921EB23BE79AD9D5DCC1DD9AD2361321
02900B723CF980957FC4E177108FC607774F29E8320E92EA05ECE4E821C0A5EFE8F1645C4C0C93
C1AB99285D622CAA652C1DFAD63D745D6F2DE5F17E5EAF0FC4963D261C8A12436518206DC09334
4D5AD293: FullTrust
         1.1.2.  StrongName - 0000000000000000400000000000000: FullTrust
      1.2.  Zone - Intranet: FullTrust
         1.2.1.  All code: Same site Web.
         1.2.2.  All code: Same directory FileIO - Read, PathDiscovery
      1.3.  Zone - Internet: Internet
         1.3.1.  All code: Same site Web.
      1.4.  Zone - Untrusted: Nothing
      1.5.  Zone - Trusted: Internet
         1.5.1.  All code: Same site Web.
```

Creating and Applying Permissions Sets

You can create new permission sets using a command like this:

```
>caspol.exe -addpset MyCustomPermissionSet permissionset.xml
```

This command specifies that you are creating a new permission set called MyCustomPermissionSet, which is configured with the contents of the specified XML file. The XML file must contain a standard format that specifies a `PermissionSet`. For reference, here is the permission set file for the Everything permission set, which you can trim down to the permission set you want to create:

```xml
<PermissionSet class="System.Security.NamedPermissionSet" version="1"
   Name="Everything"
   Description="Allows unrestricted access to all resources covered by
         built-in permissions">
  <IPermission class="System.Security.Permissions.EnvironmentPermission,
     mscorlib, Version=2.0.0.0, Culture=neutral,
     PublicKeyToken=b77a5c561934e089" version="1" Unrestricted="true" />
  <IPermission class="System.Security.Permissions.FileDialogPermission,
     mscorlib, Version=2.0.0.0, Culture=neutral,
     PublicKeyToken=b77a5c561934e089" version="1" Unrestricted="true" />
```

```
    <IPermission class="System.Security.Permissions.FileIOPermission,
        mscorlib, Version=2.0.0.0, Culture=neutral,
        PublicKeyToken=b77a5c561934e089" version="1" Unrestricted="true" />
    <IPermission class="System.Security.Permissions.IsolatedStorageFilePermission,
        mscorlib, Version=2.0.0.0, Culture=neutral,
        PublicKeyToken=b77a5c561934e089" version="1" Unrestricted="true" />
    <IPermission class="System.Security.Permissions.ReflectionPermission,
        mscorlib, Version=2.0.0.0, Culture=neutral,
        PublicKeyToken=b77a5c561934e089" version="1" Unrestricted="true" />
    <IPermission class="System.Security.Permissions.RegistryPermission,
        mscorlib, Version=2.0.0.0, Culture=neutral,
        PublicKeyToken=b77a5c561934e089" version="1" Unrestricted="true" />
    <IPermission class="System.Security.Permissions.SecurityPermission,
        mscorlib, Version=2.0.0.0, Culture=neutral,
        PublicKeyToken=b77a5c561934e089" version="1"
        Flags="Assertion, UnmanagedCode, Execution, ControlThread,
            ControlEvidence, ControlPolicy, SerializationFormatter,
            ControlDomainPolicy, ControlPrincipal, ControlAppDomain,
            RemotingConfiguration, Infrastructure, BindingRedirects" />
    <IPermission class="System.Security.Permissions.UIPermission,
        mscorlib, Version=2.0.0.0, Culture=neutral,
        PublicKeyToken=b77a5c561934e089" version="1" Unrestricted="true" />
    <IPermission class="System.Security.Permissions.KeyContainerPermission,
        mscorlib, Version=2.0.0.0, Culture=neutral,
        PublicKeyToken=b77a5c561934e089" version="1" Unrestricted="true" />
    <IPermission class="System.Net.DnsPermission, System, Version=2.0.3600.0,
        Culture=neutral, PublicKeyToken=b77a5c561934e089" version="1"
        Unrestricted="true" />
    <IPermission class="System.Net.SocketPermission, System,
        Version=2.0.0.0, Culture=neutral,
        PublicKeyToken=b77a5c561934e089" version="1" Unrestricted="true" />
    <IPermission class="System.Net.WebPermission, System,
        Version=2.0.0.0, Culture=neutral, PublicKeyToken=b77a5c561934e089"
        version="1" Unrestricted="true" />
    <IPermission class="System.Security.Permissions.StorePermission, System,
        Version=2.0.0.0, Culture=neutral,
        PublicKeyToken=b77a5c561934e089" version="1" Unrestricted="true" />
    <IPermission class="System.Diagnostics.PerformanceCounterPermission,
        System, Version=2.0.0.0, Culture=neutral,
        PublicKeyToken=b77a5c561934e089" version="1" Unrestricted="true" />
    <IPermission class="System.Data.OleDb.OleDbPermission,
        System.Data, Version=2.0.0.0, Culture=neutral,
        PublicKeyToken=b77a5c561934e089" version="1" Unrestricted="true" />
    <IPermission class="System.Data.SqlClient.SqlClientPermission,
        System.Data, Version=2.0.0.0, Culture=neutral,
        PublicKeyToken=b77a5c561934e089" version="1" Unrestricted="true" />
    <IPermission class="System.Security.Permissions.DataProtectionPermission,
        System.Security, Version=2.0.0.0, Culture=neutral,
        PublicKeyToken=b03f5f7f11d50a3a" version="1" Unrestricted="true" />
</PermissionSet>
```

To view all permission sets in XML format, you can use this command:

```
>caspol.exe -listpset
```

To give a new definition to an existing permission set by applying an XML `PermissionSet` configuration file, you can use this command:

```
>caspol.exe -chgpset permissionset.xml MyCustomPermissionSet
```

Distributing Code Using a Strong Name

.NET provides the ability to match an assembly to a code group when the assembly's identity and integrity have been confirmed using a strong name. This scenario is very common when assemblies are being deployed across networks (for example, when distributing software over the Internet).

If you are a software company and you want to provide code to your customers via the Internet, you build an assembly and give it a strong name. The strong name ensures that the assembly can be uniquely identified, and also provides protection against tampering. Your customers can incorporate this strong name into their code access security policy; an assembly that matches this unique strong name can then be assigned permissions explicitly. As discussed in Chapter 17, "Assemblies," the strong name includes checksums for hashes of all the files within an assembly, so you have strong evidence that the assembly has not been altered since the publisher created the strong name.

Note that if your application uses an installer, the installer will install assemblies that have already been given a strong name. The strong name is generated once for each distribution before being sent to customers; the installer does not run these commands. The reason for this is that the strong name provides an assurance that the assembly has not been modified since it left your company. A common way to achieve this is to give your customer not only the application code but also, separately, a copy of the strong name for the assembly. You might find it beneficial to pass the strong name to your customer using a secure form (perhaps a fax or an encrypted email) to guard against the assembly being tampered with in the process.

Consider an example in which an assembly with a strong name is created to distribute it in such a way that the recipient of the assembly can use the strong name to grant the `FullTrust` permission to the assembly.

First, a key pair is needed. Creating strong names has already been discussed in Chapter 17, so there is no need to repeat it here. Rebuilding the assembly with the key ensures that the hash is recalculated and the assembly is protected against malicious modifications. Also, the assembly can be uniquely identified with the strong name. This identification can be used with membership conditions of code groups. A membership condition can be based on the requirement to match a specific strong name.

The following command states that a new code group is created using the strong name from the specified assembly manifest file, that the code group is independent of the version number of the assembly, and that the code group has granted the FullTrust permissions:

```
>caspol.exe -addgroup 1 -strong -file SimpleExample.exe -noname -noversion
FullTrust
```

In this example, the application will now run from any zone, even the Internet zone, because the strong name provides powerful evidence that the assembly can be trusted. Look at your code groups using `caspol.exe -listgroups`, and you will see the new code group (1.6 and its associated public key in hexadecimal):

```
Code Groups:

1.  All code: Nothing
    1.1.  Zone - MyComputer: FullTrust
        1.1.1.  StrongName -
0024000004800000940000000602000000240000525341310004000001000100007D1FA57C4AED9
F0A32E84AA0FAEFD0DE9E8FD6AEC8F87FB03766C834C99921EB23BE79AD9D5DCC1DD9AD2361321
```

```
02900B723CF980957FC4E177108FC607774F29E8320E92EA05ECE4E821C0A5EFE8F1645C4C0C93
C1AB99285D622CAA652C1DFAD63D745D6F2DE5F17E5EAF0FC4963D261C8A12436518206DC09334
4D5AD293: FullTrust
     1.1.2.  StrongName - 0000000000000000000400000000000000: FullTrust
   1.2.  Zone - Intranet: LocalIntranet
     1.2.1.  All code: Same site Web
     1.2.2.  All code: Same directory FileIO - 'Read, PathDiscovery'
   1.3.  Zone - Internet: Internet
     1.3.1.  All code: Same site Web
   1.4.  Zone - Untrusted: Nothing
   1.5.  Zone - Trusted: Internet
     1.5.1.  All code: Same site Web
   1.6.  StrongName -
0024000004800000940000000602000000240000525341310004000001000100047008BB48DA2FA
B8C17E6277D76D0E8867273B5BB7962C155A03F118D8C6289CA3F05C08174EE2A933ABF8D3E9E4
24D2635399B9A7B0C7CD45742A3770694456776087AABB92041CB0783CDD9E4AAD04AA8D43488A
C599469ABD2E891DB2B5BDAD5C62EB5AFF23CEEA3EFED03539AC9FFEA8D3165EEBD67B246AB4C3
D6B31EB3: FullTrust
Success
```

To access the strong name in an assembly, you can use the secutil.exe tool against the assembly manifest file. Using the -hex option, the public key is shown in hexadecimal (like caspol.exe); the argument -strongname specifies that the strong name should be shown. Type this command, and you will see a listing containing the strong name public key, the assembly name, and the assembly version:

```
>secutil.exe -hex -strongname SimpleExample.exe
Microsoft (R) .NET Framework SecUtil 3.5.21004.1
Copyright (c) Microsoft Corporation. All rights reserved.

Public Key =
0x0024000004800000940000000602000000240000525341310004000001000100047008BB48DA2
FAB8C17E6277D76D0E8867273B5BB7962C155A03F118D8C6289CA3F05C08174EE2A933ABF8D3E9
E424D2635399B9A7B0C7CD45742A3770694456776087AABB92041CB0783CDD9E4AAD04AA8D4348
8AC599469ABD2E891DB2B5BDAD5C62EB5AFF23CEEA3EFED03539AC9FFEA8D3165EEBD67B246AB4
C3D6B31EB3
Name =
SimpleExample
Version =
1.0.0.0
Success
```

You may be surprised about the two strong name code groups that are installed by default and what they refer to. One is a strong name key for Microsoft code; the other strong name key is for the parts of .NET that have been submitted to the ECMA for standardization, which will give Microsoft much less control.

Distributing Code Using Certificates

The preceding section discussed how a strong name can be applied to an assembly so that system administrators can explicitly grant permissions to assemblies that match that strong name, using a code access group. Although this method of security policy management can be very effective, it is sometimes necessary to work at a higher level, where the administrator of the security policy grants permissions on the basis of the publisher of the software, rather than to each individual software component. You probably have seen a similar method used before when you have downloaded executables from the Internet that have been Authenticode signed.

To provide information about the software publisher, you can make use of digital certificates and sign assemblies so that consumers of the software can verify the identity of the software publisher. In a commercial environment, you would obtain a certificate from a company such as Verisign or Thawte.

The advantage of buying a certificate from a supplier instead of creating your own is that it provides a high level of trust in its authenticity; the supplier acts as a trusted third party. For test purposes, however, .NET includes a command-line utility you can use to create a test certificate. The process of creating certificates and using them for publishing software is complex, but we walk through a simple example in this section.

The example code will be made for the fictitious company called ABC Corporation. In this company, the software product ABC Suite should be trusted. First, create a test certificate by typing the following command:

```
>makecert -sv abckey.pvk -r -n "CN=ABC Corporation" abccorptest.cer
```

The command creates a test certificate under the name ABC Corporation and saves it to a file called `abccorptest.cer`. The `-sv abckey.pvk` argument creates a key file to store the private key. When creating the key file, you are asked for a password that you should remember.

After creating the certificate, you can create a software publisher test certificate with the Software Publisher Certificate Test tool (`Cert2spc.exe`):

```
>cert2spc abccorptest.cer abccorptest.spc
```

To sign the assembly with the certificate, use the `signcode.exe` utility on the assembly file containing the assembly manifest. Often, the easiest way to sign an assembly is to use the `signtool.exe` in its wizard mode; to start the wizard, just type `signtool.exe` with the parameter `signwizard`.

When you click Next, the program asks you to specify where the file is that should be signed. For an assembly, select the file containing the manifest, for example `SimpleExample.exe`, and click the Next button. On the Signing Options page, you must select the Custom option to define the previously created certificate file.

In the next dialog box, you are asked to specify the certificate that should be used to sign the assembly. Click Select from File and browse to the file `abccorptest.spc`. You will now see the screen shown in Figure 20-12.

The next screen that appears asks for your private key. The key file `abckey.pvk` was created by the `makecert` utility, so you can select the options as shown in Figure 20-13. The cryptographic service provider is an application that implements the cryptographic standards.

Next you are asked a series of questions about the encryption algorithm that should be used for signing the assembly (`md5` or `sha1`) and the name and URL of the application, and you are shown a final confirmation dialog.

Because the executable is now signed with the certificate, a recipient of the assembly has access to strong evidence as to who published the software. The runtime can examine the certificate and match the publisher of the assembly to a code group with high levels of confidence about the identity of the code because the trusted third-party certifies the publisher's identity.

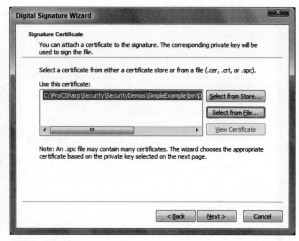

Figure 20-12

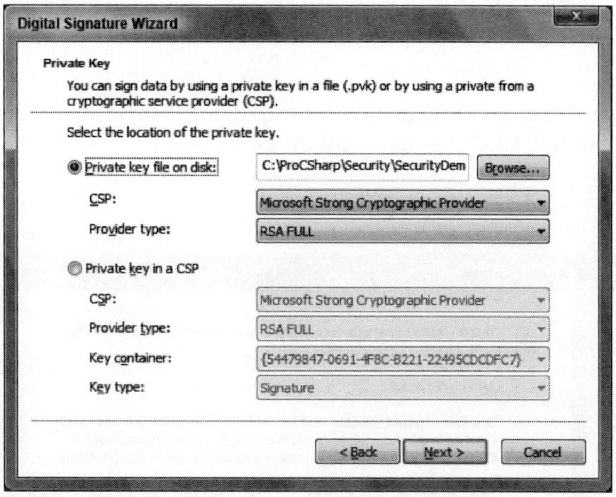

Figure 20-13

The test certificate must now be installed with the trusted certificates. Start the Certificate Manager certmgr:

```
>certmgr
```

Select the Trusted Root Certification Authorities tab and Certificates below in the tree. Select Action ⇨ All Task ⇨ Import . . . to import the certificate file. With the Certificate Import, select the certificate file abccorptest.cer.

After clicking the Next button, verify that the certificate store listed is Trusted Root Certification Authorities, which is the case when you have chosen this selection in the tree view (see Figure 20-14).

Figure 20-14

Before the import is completed, you will get a warning dialog, as shown in Figure 20-15, because the test certificate cannot be validated. Click Yes to install the certificate.

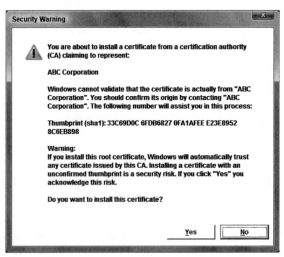

Figure 20-15

After the certificate is installed as a trusted root authority, you can see it in the certificates list, as shown in Figure 20-16.

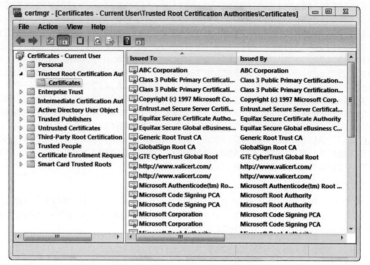

Figure 20-16

Now turn your attention to a machine that you want to configure to trust software from the ABC Corporation. You can create a new code access group that matches this software from ABC Corporation. You just have to grab a hexadecimal representation of the certificate from the assembly using the `secutil.exe` tool:

```
>secutil.exe -hex -x SimpleExample.exe
```

This command results in the following output:

```
Microsoft (R) .NET Framework SecUtil 2.0.50727.42
Copyright (c) Microsoft Corp. All rights reserved.

X.509 Certificate =
0x3082020830820171A0030201020210229DECFA1C01E89D46E23F35B6284691300D06092A8648
86F70D0101040500301A3118301606035504031030F41424320436F72706F726174696F6E301E17
0D303730313232313030323334395A170D3339313233313233353935395A301A3118301606035504
03130F41424320436F72706F726174696F6E30819F300D06092A864886F70D010101050003818D
0030818902818100B7AE9EC301F76CC661EBF7F9C23E2B4A92F6B4BE318F50B7CB0DA36D4BFECC
69E390384AC33717779A0EAD683536A18B98FC8CA67D10CA05B9FF5AEAA42BCA01D85F95E79442
7915B9AAA8CC5C55E9855F5F5D7A5FEEBDF788E2B574E9CBB11B30BC424260415B28A73509048A
DDC9BEF28C07E9C8CE166CB92074D07D17798F0203010001A34F304D304B0603551D0104443042
80101BA15BEAA3E3B66F2497401512C79799A11C301A3118301606035504031030F41424320436F
72706F726174696F6E8210229DECFA1C01E89D46E23F35B6284691300D06092A864886F70D0101
04050003818100746FFF169DE478C34684FAABDBF326A8CEB4588B96C0948BA14D5C73ACF174E5
608CBAE8C7BB77B2A38622E7662BA75F9D0E2A328C8A7E3A28790DC05A7E32557150F8F549E2B3
F36F8A609248AF094387784048A7A4B0FFA505A7105A4DDDAAF12DC622B4E7956247BEF3D95F18
7DAEF1A92A34DE83880174ADCFF93A97BBA8
Success
```

Now create the new code group and apply the FullTrust permission to assemblies published by the ABC Corporation using this (rather long) command:

```
>caspol -addgroup 1 -pub -hex
"0x3082020830820171A0030201020210229DECFA1C01E89D46E23F35B6284691300D06092A864
886F70D0101040500301A31183016060355040313 0F41424320436F72706F726174696F6E301E1
70D30373031323231303233334395A170D33393132333133233353935395A301A3118301606035 50
403130F41424320436F72706F726174696F6E30819F300D06092A864886F70D0101010500038 18
D0030818902818100B7AE9EC301F76CC661EBF7F9C23E2B4A92F6B4BE318F50B7CB0DA36D4BFEC
C69E390384AC33717779A0EAD683536A18B98FC8CA67D10CA05B9FF5AEAA42BCA01D85F95E7944
27915B9AAA8CC5C55E9855F5F5D7A5FEEBDF788E2B574E9CBB11B30BC424260415B28A73509048
ADDC9BEF28C07E9C8CE166CB92074D07D17798F0203010001A34F304D304B0603551D010444304
280101BA15BEAA3E3B66F2497401512C79799A11C301A31183016060355040313 0F41424320436
F72706F726174696F6E8210229DECFA1C01E89D46E23F35B6284691300D06092A864886F70D010
104050003818100746FFF169DE478C34684FAABDBF326A8CEB4588B96C0948BA14D5C73ACF174E
5608CBAE8C7BB77B2A38622E7662BA75F9D0E2A328C8A7E3A28790DC05A7E32557150F8F549E2B
3F36F8A609248AF094387784048A7A4B0FFA505A7105A4DDDAAF12DC622B4E7956247BEF3D95F1
87DAEF1A92A34DE83880174ADCFF93A97BBA8"
FullTrust
```

The parameters specify that the code group should be added at the top level (1) and that the code group membership condition is of the type `Publisher`; the last parameter specifies the permission set to grant (FullTrust). The command will ask for confirmation:

```
Microsoft (R) .NET Framework CasPol 2.0.50727.1426
Copyright (c) Microsoft Corporation. All rights reserved.

The operation you are performing will alter security policy.
Are you sure you want to perform this operation? (yes/no)
y
Added union code group with "-pub" membership condition to the Machine level.
Success
```

The machine is now configured to fully trust all assemblies that have been signed with the certificate from ABC Corporation. To confirm that, you can run a `caspol.exe -lg` command, which lists the new code access group.

As another check, ask `caspol.exe` to tell you what code groups your assembly matches:

```
>caspol.exe -resolvegroup SimpleExample.exe
Level = Enterprise

Code Groups:

1.  All code: FullTrust

Level = Machine

Code Groups:
1.  All code: Nothing
    1.1.  Zone - MyComputer: FullTrust
    1.7.  Publisher -
30818902818100B7AE9EC301F76CC661EBF7F9C23E2B4A92F6B4BE318F50B7CB0DA36D4BFECC69
E390384AC33717779A0EAD683536A18B98FC8CA67D10CA05B9FF5AEAA42BCA01D85F95E7944279
15B9AAA8CC5C55E9855F5F5D7A5FEEBDF788E2B574E9CBB11B30BC424260415B28A73509048ADD
C9BEF28C07E9C8CE166CB92074D07D17798F0203010001: FullTrust
```

```
Level = User

Code Groups:

1.  All code: FullTrust

Success
```

In the center of the results, you can see that the assembly has been successfully matched to your new code group and granted the FullTrust permission set.

Summary

This chapter covered several security aspects with .NET applications. Code-access security adds a security layer to an application in that it gives different permissions to applications based on the evidence of the application. How much can you trust the application? It depends on what .NET permissions apply. Permissions are grouped in permission sets and managed with using user, machine, and enterprise policies.

Authentication and authorization with role-based security allow you to decide in the application which users are allowed to access application features. Users are represented by identities and principals, classes that implement the interface `IIdentity` and `IPrincipal`. Role verification can be done within the code but also in a simple way using attributes.

Cryptography was shown to demonstrate signing and encrypting of data, to exchange keys in a secure way. .NET offers several cryptography algorithms offering both symmetric and asymmetric algorithms. .NET 3.5 also supports Cryptography Next Generation, which is available with Windows Vista and Windows Server 2008.

With access control lists, you have also seen how to read and modify access to operating system resources such as files. Programming ACLs is done in ways similar to the programming of secure pipes, registry keys, Active Directory entries, and many other operating system resources.

You've seen how to use tools to manage security policies such as caspol, and how to distribute code with a certificate.

If your applications are used in different regions and with different languages, in the next chapter you can read about globalization and localization features of .NET.

21

Localization

NASA's Mars Climate Orbiter was lost on September 23, 1999, at a cost of $125 million, because one engineering team used metric units, while another one used inches for a key spacecraft operation. When writing applications for international distribution, different cultures and regions must be kept in mind.

Different cultures have diverging calendars and use different number and date formats. Also, sorting strings may lead to various results because the order of A–Z is defined differently based on the culture. To make applications fit for global markets, you have to globalize and localize them.

Globalization is about internationalizing applications: preparing applications for international markets. With globalization, the application supports number and date formats that vary depending on the culture, different calendars, and so on. *Localization* is about translating applications for specific cultures. For translations of strings, you can use resources.

.NET supports globalization and localization of Windows and Web applications. To globalize an application, you can use classes from the namespace System.Globalization; to localize an application, you can use resources that are supported by the namespace System.Resources.

This chapter covers the globalization and localization of .NET applications; more specifically, it discusses the following:

- ❑ Using classes that represent cultures and regions
- ❑ Globalization of applications
- ❑ Localization of applications

Namespace System.Globalization

The System.Globalization namespace holds all culture and region classes to support different date formats, different number formats, and even different calendars that are represented in classes such as GregorianCalendar, HebrewCalendar, JapaneseCalendar, and so on. By using these classes, you can display different representations depending on the user's locale.

This section looks at the following issues and considerations with using the System.Globalization namespace:

- ❑ Unicode issues
- ❑ Cultures and regions
- ❑ An example showing all cultures and their characteristics
- ❑ Sorting

Unicode Issues

A Unicode character has 16 bits, so there is room for 65,536 characters. Is this enough for all languages currently used in information technology? In the case of the Chinese language, for example, more than 80,000 characters are needed. However, Unicode has been designed to deal with this issue. With Unicode you have to differentiate between base characters and combining characters. You can add multiple combining characters to a base character to build up a single display character or a text element.

Take, for example, the Icelandic character Ogonek. Ogonek can be combined by using the base character 0x006F (Latin small letter o) and the combining characters 0x0328 (combining Ogonek) and 0x0304 (combining Macron) as shown in Figure 21-1. Combining characters are defined within ranges from 0x0300 to 0x0345. For American and European markets, predefined characters exist to facilitate dealing with special characters. The character Ogonek is also defined with the predefined character 0x01ED.

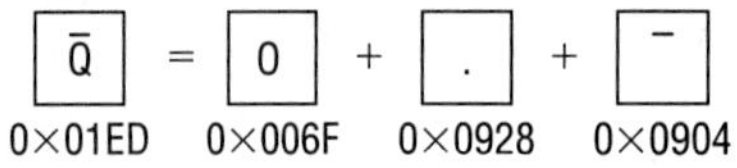

Figure 21-1

For Asian markets, where more than 80,000 characters are necessary for Chinese alone, such predefined characters do not exist. In Asian languages, you always have to deal with combining characters. The problem is getting the right number of display characters or text elements, and getting to the base characters instead of the combined characters. The namespace System.Globalization offers the class StringInfo, which you can use to deal with this issue.

The following table lists the static methods of the class StringInfo that help in dealing with combined characters.

Method	Description
GetNextTextElement	Returns the first text element (base character and all combining characters) of a specified string.
GetTextElementEnumerator	Returns a TextElementEnumerator object that allows iterating all text elements of a string.
ParseCombiningCharacters	Returns an integer array referencing all base characters of a string.

> A single display character can contain multiple Unicode characters. To address this issue, when you write applications that support international markets, don't use the data type `char`; use `string` instead. A string can hold a text element that contains both base characters and combining characters, whereas a `char` cannot.

Cultures and Regions

The world is divided into multiple cultures and regions, and applications have to be aware of these cultural and regional differences. A culture is a set of preferences based on a user's language and cultural habits. RFC 1766 (`www.ietf.org/rfc/rfc1766.txt`) defines culture names that are used worldwide depending on a language and a country or region. Some examples are en-AU, en-CA, en-GB, and en-US for the English language in Australia, Canada, the United Kingdom, and the United States, respectively.

Possibly the most important class in the `System.Globalization` namespace is `CultureInfo`. `CultureInfo` represents a culture and defines calendars, formatting of numbers and dates, and sorting strings used with the culture.

The class `RegionInfo` represents regional settings (such as the currency) and shows whether the region is using the metric system. Some regions can use multiple languages. One example is the region of Spain, which has Basque (eu-ES), Catalan (ca-ES), Spanish (es-ES), and Galician (gl-ES) cultures. Similar to one region having multiple languages, one language can be spoken in different regions; for example, Spanish is spoken in Mexico, Spain, Guatemala, Argentina, and Peru, to name only a few countries.

Later in this chapter, you see a sample application that demonstrates these characteristics of cultures and regions.

Specific, Neutral, and Invariant Cultures

With the use of cultures in the .NET Framework, you have to differentiate between three types: *specific*, *neutral*, and *invariant* cultures.

A specific culture is associated with a real, existing culture defined with RFC 1766, as you saw in the preceding section. A specific culture can be mapped to a neutral culture. For example, de is the neutral culture of the specific cultures de-AT, de-DE, de-CH, and others. de is shorthand for the German language; AT, DE, and CH are shorthand for the countries Austria, Germany, and Switzerland, respectively.

When translating applications, it is typically not necessary to do translations for every region; not much difference exists between the German language in the countries Austria and Germany. Instead of using specific cultures, you can use a neutral culture for localizing applications.

The invariant culture is independent of a real culture. When storing formatted numbers or dates in files, or sending them across a network to a server, using a culture that is independent of any user settings is the best option.

Figure 21-2 shows how the culture types relate to each other.

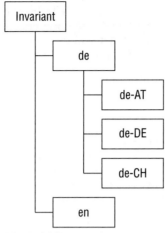

Figure 21-2

CurrentCulture and CurrentUICulture

When you set cultures, you need to differentiate between a culture for the user interface and a culture for the number and date formats. Cultures are associated with a thread, and with these two culture types, two culture settings can be applied to a thread. The Thread class has the properties CurrentCulture and CurrentUICulture. The property CurrentCulture is for setting the culture that is used with formatting and sort options, whereas the property CurrentUICulture is used for the language of the user interface.

Users can change the default setting of the CurrentCulture by using the Regional and Language options in the Windows Control Panel (see Figure 21-3). With this configuration, it is also possible to change the default number, the time, and the date format for the culture.

The CurrentUICulture does not depend on this configuration. The CurrentUICulture setting depends on the language of the operating system. There is one exception, though: If a multi-language user interface (MUI) is installed with Windows Vista or Windows XP, it is possible to change the language of the user interface with the regional configuration, and this influences the property CurrentUICulture.

These settings make a very good default, and in many cases, there is no need to change the default behavior. If the culture should be changed, you can easily do this by changing both cultures of the thread to, say, the Spanish culture, as shown in this code snippet:

```
System.Globalization.CultureInfo ci = new
    System.Globalization.CultureInfo("es-ES");
System.Threading.Thread.CurrentThread.CurrentCulture = ci;
System.Threading.Thread.CurrentThread.CurrentUICulture = ci;
```

Now that you know about setting the culture, the following sections discuss number and date formatting, which are influenced by the CurrentCulture setting.

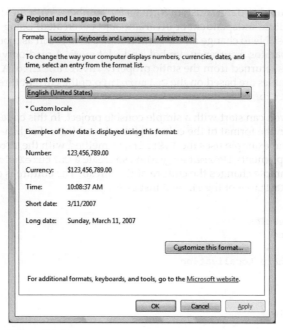

Figure 21-3

Number Formatting

The number structures Int16, Int32, Int64, and so on in the System namespace have an overloaded ToString() method. This method can be used to create a different representation of the number depending on the locale. For the Int32 structure, ToString() is overloaded with these four versions:

```
public string ToString();
public string ToString(IFormatProvider);
public string ToString(string);
public string ToString(string, IFormatProvider);
```

ToString() without arguments returns a string without format options. You can also pass a string and a class that implements IFormatProvider.

The string specifies the format of the representation. The format can be a standard numeric formatting string or a picture numeric formatting string. For standard numeric formatting, strings are predefined, where C specifies the currency notation, D creates a decimal output, E creates scientific output, F creates fixed-point output, G creates general output, N creates number output, and X creates hexadecimal output. With a picture numeric format string, it is possible to specify the number of digits, section and group separators, percent notation, and so on. The picture numeric format string ###,### means two three-digit blocks separated by a group separator.

The IFormatProvider interface is implemented by the NumberFormatInfo, DateTimeFormatInfo, and CultureInfo classes. This interface defines a single method, GetFormat(), that returns a format object.

NumberFormatInfo can be used to define custom formats for numbers. With the default constructor of NumberFormatInfo, a culture-independent or invariant object is created. Using the properties of NumberFormatInfo, it is possible to change all the formatting options, such as a positive sign, a percent symbol, a number group separator, a currency symbol, and a lot more. A read-only culture-independent NumberFormatInfo object is returned from the static property InvariantInfo. A NumberFormatInfo object in which the format values are based on the CultureInfo of the current thread is returned from the static property CurrentInfo.

To create the next example, you can start with a simple console project. In this code, the first example shows a number displayed in the format of the culture of the thread (here: English-US, the setting of the operating system). The second example uses the ToString() method with the IFormatProvider argument. CultureInfo implements IFormatProvider, so create a CultureInfo object using the French culture. The third example changes the culture of the thread. The culture is changed to German using the property CurrentCulture of the Thread instance:

```
using System;
using System.Globalization;
using System.Threading;

namespace Wrox.ProCSharp.Localization
{
    class Program
    {
        static void Main()
        {
            int val = 1234567890;

            // culture of the current thread
            Console.WriteLine(val.ToString("N"));

            // use IFormatProvider
            Console.WriteLine(val.ToString("N",
                            new CultureInfo("fr-FR")));

            // change the culture of the thread
            Thread.CurrentThread.CurrentCulture =
                            new CultureInfo("de-DE");
            Console.WriteLine(val.ToString("N"));
        }
    }
}
```

The output is shown here. You can compare the outputs with the previously listed differences for U.S. English, French, and German.

```
1,234,567,890.00
1 234 567 890,00
1.234.567.890,00
```

Date Formatting

The same support for numbers is available for dates. The DateTime structure has some methods for date-to-string conversions. The public instance methods ToLongDateString(), ToLongTimeString(), ToShortDateString(), and ToShortTimeString() create string representations using the current culture. You can use the ToString() method to assign a different culture:

```
public string ToString();
public string ToString(IFormatProvider);
public string ToString(string);
public string ToString(string, IFormatProvider);
```

With the string argument of the ToString() method, you can specify a predefined format character or a custom format string for converting the date to a string. The class DateTimeFormatInfo specifies the possible values. With DateTimeFormatInfo, the case of the format strings has a different meaning. D defines a long date format, d a short date format. Other examples of possible formats are ddd for the abbreviated day of the week, dddd for the full day of the week, yyyy for the year, T for a long time, and t for a short time format. With the IFormatProvider argument, you can specify the culture. Using an overloaded method without the IFormatProvider argument implies that the culture of the current thread is used:

```
DateTime d = new DateTime(2008, 02, 14);

// current culture
Console.WriteLine(d.ToLongDateString());

// use IFormatProvider
Console.WriteLine(d.ToString("D", new CultureInfo("fr-FR")));

// use culture of thread
CultureInfo ci = Thread.CurrentThread.CurrentCulture;
Console.WriteLine("{0}: {1}", ci.ToString(), d.ToString("D"));

ci = new CultureInfo("es-ES");
Thread.CurrentThread.CurrentCulture = ci;
Console.WriteLine("{0}: {1}", ci.ToString(), d.ToString("D"));
```

The output of this example program shows ToLongDateString() with the current culture of the thread, a French version where a CultureInfo instance is passed to the ToString() method, and a Spanish version where the CurrentCulture property of the thread is changed to es-ES:

```
Thursday, February 14, 2008
jeudi 14 février 2008
en-US: Thursday, February 14, 2008
es-ES: jeuves, 14 de febrero de 2008
```

Cultures in Action

To see all cultures in action, you can use a sample WPF application that lists all cultures and demonstrates different characteristics of culture properties. Figure 21-4 shows the user interface of the application in the Visual Studio 2008 WPF Designer.

During initialization of the application, all available cultures are added to the tree view control that is placed on the left side of the application. This initialization happens in the method AddCulturesToTree() that is called in the constructor of the Window class CultureDemoWindow:

```
public CultureDemoWindow()
{
    InitializeComponent();

    AddCulturesToTree();
}
```

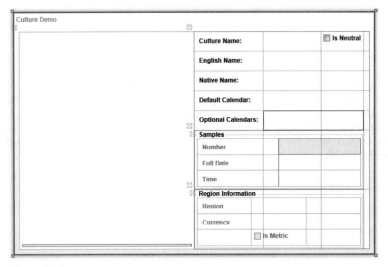

Figure 21-4

In the method `AddCulturesToTree()`, you get all cultures from the static method `CultureInfo.GetCultures()`. Passing `CultureTypes.AllCultures` to this method returns an unsorted array of all available cultures. The array is sorted using a Lambda expression that is passed to the `Comparison` delegate of the second argument of the `Array.Sort()` method. Next, in the `foreach` loop, every single culture is added to the tree view. A `TreeViewItem` object is created for every single culture because the WPF `TreeView` class uses `TreeViewItem` objects for display. The `Tag` property of the `TreeViewItem` object is set to the `CultureInfo` object, so that you can access the `CultureInfo` object at a later time from within the tree.

Where the `TreeViewItem` is added inside the tree depends on the culture type. If the culture does not have a parent culture, it is added to the root nodes of the tree. To find parent cultures, all cultures are remembered inside a dictionary. Recall Chapter 10, "Collections," for more information about dictionaries and Chapter 7, "Delegates and Events" for Lambda expressions.

```
// add all cultures to the tree view
public void AddCulturesToTree()
{
    Dictionary<string, TreeViewItem> culturesByName =
            new Dictionary<string, TreeViewItem>();

    // get all cultures
    var cultures =
        CultureInfo.GetCultures(CultureTypes.AllCultures);
    Array.Sort(cultures, (c1, c2) => c1.Name.CompareTo(c2.Name));

    TreeViewItem[] nodes = new TreeViewItem[cultures.Length];

    int i = 0;
    foreach (var ci in cultures)
    {
        nodes[i] = new TreeViewItem();
        nodes[i].Header = ci.DisplayName;
```

```
            nodes[i].Tag = ci;
            culturesByName.Add(ci.Name, nodes[i]);

            TreeViewItem parent;
            if (String.IsNullOrEmpty(ci.Parent.Name) &&
                    culturesByName.TryGetValue(ci.Parent.Name, out parent)
            {
                parent.Items.Add(nodes[i]);
            }
            else
            {
                treeCultures.Items.Add(nodes[i]);
            }
            i++;
        }
    }
```

When the user selects a node inside the tree, the handler of the `SelectedItemChanged` event of the `TreeView` will be called. Here the handler is implemented in the method `TreeCultures_SelectedItemChanged()`. Within this method, all fields are cleared by calling the method `ClearTextFields()` before you get the `CultureInfo` object from the tree by selecting the `Tag` property of the `TreeViewItem`. Then some text fields are set using the properties `Name`, `NativeName`, and `EnglishName` of the `CultureInfo` object. If the `CultureInfo` is a neutral culture that can be queried with the `IsNeutralCulture` property, the corresponding check box will be set:

```
        private void TreeCultures_SelectedItemChanged(object sender,
                    RoutedPropertyChangedEventArgs<object> e)
    {
        ClearTextFields();

        // get CultureInfo object from tree
        CultureInfo ci = (CultureInfo)((TreeViewItem)e.NewValue).Tag;

        textCultureName.Text = ci.Name;
        textNativeName.Text = ci.NativeName;
        textEnglishName.Text = ci.EnglishName;

        checkIsNeutral.IsChecked = ci.IsNeutralCulture;
```

Then you get the calendar information about the culture. The `Calendar` property of the `CultureInfo` class returns the default `Calendar` object for the specific culture. Because the `Calendar` class doesn't have a property to tell its name, you use the `ToString()` method of the base class to get the name of the class, and remove the namespace of this string to be displayed in the text field `textCalendar`.

Because a single culture might support multiple calendars, the `OptionalCalendars` property returns an array of additional supported `Calendar` objects. These optional calendars are displayed in the list box `listCalendars`. The `GregorianCalendar` class that derives from `Calendar` has an additional property called `CalendarType` that lists the type of the Gregorian calendar. This type can be a value of the enumeration `GregorianCalendarTypes`: `Arabic`, `MiddleEastFrench`, `TransliteratedFrench`, `USEnglish`, or `Localized` depending on the culture. With Gregorian calendars, the type is also displayed in the list box:

```
            // default calendar
            textCalendar.Text = ci.Calendar.ToString().
                Remove(0, 21).Replace("Calendar", "");
```

(continued)

647

(continued)

```
                // fill optional calendars
                listCalendars.Items.Clear();
                foreach (Calendar optCal in ci.OptionalCalendars)
                {
                    StringBuilder calName = new StringBuilder(50);
                    calName.Append(optCal.ToString());
                    calName.Remove(0, 21);
                    calName.Replace("Calendar", "");

                    // for GregorianCalendar add type information
                    GregorianCalendar gregCal = optCal as GregorianCalendar;
                    if (gregCal != null)
                    {
                        calName.AppendFormat(" {0}", gregCal.CalendarType.ToString());
                    }
                    listCalendars.Items.Add(calName.ToString());
                }
```

Next, you check whether the culture is a specific culture (not a neutral culture) by using
`!ci.IsNeutralCulture` in an `if` statement. The method `ShowSamples()` displays number
and date samples. This method is implemented in the next code section. The method
`ShowRegionInformation()` is used to display some information about the region. With the invariant
culture, you can display only number and date samples, but no region information. The invariant culture
is not related to any real language, and therefore it is not associated with a region:

```
                // display number and date samples
                if (!ci.IsNeutralCulture)
                {
                    groupSamples.IsEnabled = true;
                    ShowSamples(ci);

                    // invariant culture doesn't have a region
                    if (ci.ThreeLetterISOLanguageName == "IVL")
                    {
                        groupRegion.IsEnabled = false;
                    }
                    else
                    {
                        groupRegion.IsEnabled = true;
                        ShowRegionInformation(ci.Name);
                    }
                }
                else // neutral culture: no region, no number/date formatting
                {
                    groupSamples.IsEnabled = false;
                    groupRegion.IsEnabled = false;
                }
            }
```

To show some localized sample numbers and dates, the selected object of type `CultureInfo` is passed
with the `IFormatProvider` argument of the `ToString()` method:

```
private void ShowSamples(CultureInfo ci)
{
    double number = 9876543.21;
    textSampleNumber.Text = number.ToString("N", ci);

    DateTime today = DateTime.Today;
    textSampleDate.Text = today.ToString("D", ci);

    DateTime now = DateTime.Now;
    textSampleTime.Text = now.ToString("T", ci);
}
```

To display the information associated with a `RegionInfo` object, in the method `ShowRegionInformation()` a `RegionInfo` object is constructed passing the selected culture identifier. Then you access the properties `DisplayName`, `CurrencySymbol`, `ISOCurrencySymbol`, and `IsMetric` properties to display this information:

```
private void ShowRegionInformation(string culture)
{
    RegionInfo ri = new RegionInfo(culture);
    textRegion.Text = ri.DisplayName;
    textCurrency.Text = ri.CurrencySymbol;
    textCurrencyISO.Text = ri.ISOCurrencySymbol;
    checkIsMetric.IsChecked = ri.IsMetric;
}
```

When you start the application, you can see all available cultures in the tree view, and selecting a culture lists the cultural characteristics, as shown in Figure 21-5.

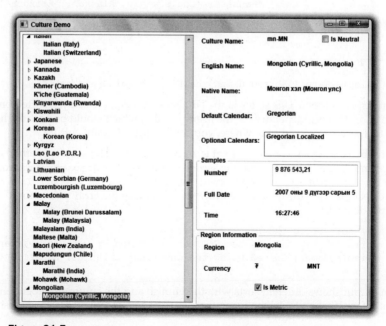

Figure 21-5

Sorting

Sorting strings is dependent on the culture. Some cultures have different sorting orders. One example is Finnish, where the characters V and W are treated the same. The algorithms that compare strings for sorting by default use a culture-sensitive sort, in which the sort is dependent on the culture.

To demonstrate this behavior with a Finnish sort, the following code creates a small sample console application where some U.S. states are stored unsorted inside an array. You are going to use classes from the namespaces `System.Collections.Generic`, `System.Threading`, and `System.Globalization`, so these namespaces must be declared. The method `DisplayNames()` shown here is used to display all elements of an array or of a collection on the console:

```
static void DisplayNames(string title, IEnumerable<string> e)
{
    Console.WriteLine(title);
    foreach (string s in e)
        Console.Write(s + " - ");
    Console.WriteLine();
    Console.WriteLine();
}
```

In the `Main()` method, after creating the array with some of the U.S. states, the thread property `CurrentCulture` is set to the Finnish culture, so that the following `Array.Sort()` uses the Finnish sort order. Calling the method `DisplayNames()` displays all the states on the console:

```
static void Main()
{
    string[] names = {"Alabama", "Texas", "Washington",
                      "Virginia", "Wisconsin", "Wyoming",
                      "Kentucky", "Missouri", "Utah", "Hawaii",
                      "Kansas", "Louisiana", "Alaska", "Arizona"};

    Thread.CurrentThread.CurrentCulture =
        new CultureInfo("fi-FI");

    Array.Sort(names);
    DisplayNames("Sorted using the Finnish culture", names);
```

After the first display of some U.S. states in the Finnish sort order, the array is sorted once again. If you want to have a sort that is independent of the users' culture, which would be useful when the sorted array is sent to a server or stored somewhere, you can use the invariant culture.

You can do this by passing a second argument to `Array.Sort()`. The `Sort()` method expects an object implementing `IComparer` with the second argument. The `Comparer` class from the `System.Collections` namespace implements `IComparer`. `Comparer.DefaultInvariant` returns a `Comparer` object that uses the invariant culture for comparing the array values for a culture-independent sort:

```
    // sort using the invariant culture
    Array.Sort(names, System.Collections.Comparer.DefaultInvariant);
    DisplayNames("Sorted using the invariant culture", names);
}
```

The program output shows different sorts with the Finnish and the culture-independent cultures: Virginia goes before Washington when using the invariant sort order and vice versa using Finnish.

```
Sorted using the Finnish culture
Alabama - Alaska - Arizona - Hawaii - Kansas - Kentucky - Louisiana - Missouri
- Texas - Utah - Washington - Virginia - Wisconsin - Wyoming -

Sorted using the invariant culture
Alabama - Alaska - Arizona - Hawaii - Kansas - Kentucky - Louisiana - Missouri
- Texas - Utah - Virginia - Washington - Wisconsin - Wyoming -
```

> **If sorting a collection should be independent of a culture, the collection must be sorted with the invariant culture. This can be particularly useful when sending the sort result to a server or storing it inside a file.**

In addition to a locale-dependent formatting and measurement system, text and pictures may differ depending on the culture. This is where resources come into play.

Resources

Resources such as pictures or string tables can be put into resource files or satellite assemblies. Such resources can be very helpful when localizing applications, and .NET has built-in support to search for localized resources.

Before you see how to use resources to localize applications, the next sections discuss how resources can be created and read without looking at language aspects.

Creating Resource Files

Resource files can contain such things as pictures and string tables. A resource file is created by using either a normal text file or a .resX file that uses XML. This section starts with a simple text file.

A resource that embeds a string table can be created by using a normal text file. The text file just assigns strings to keys. The key is the name that can be used from a program to get the value. Spaces are allowed in both keys and values.

This example shows a simple string table in the file strings.txt:

```
Title = Professional C#
Chapter = Localization
Author = Christian Nagel
Publisher = Wrox Press
```

When saving text files with Unicode characters, you must save the file with the proper encoding. Select the Unicode encoding with the Save dialog.

Resource File Generator

The Resource File Generator (Resgen.exe) utility can be used to create a resource file out of strings.txt. Typing

```
resgen strings.txt
```

creates the file `strings.resources`. The resulting resource file can either be added to an assembly as an external file or embedded into the DLL or EXE. Resgen also supports the creation of XML-based `.resX` resource files. One easy way to build an XML file is by using Resgen itself:

```
resgen strings.txt strings.resX
```

This command creates the XML resource file `strings.resX`. You see how to work with XML resource files in the section "Windows Forms Localization Using Visual Studio" later in this chapter.

Since .NET 2.0, Resgen supports strongly typed resources. A strongly typed resource is represented by a class that accesses the resource. The class can be created with the `/str` option of the Resgen utility:

```
resgen /str:C#,DemoNamespace,DemoResource,DemoResource.cs strings.resX
```

With the option `/str`, the language, namespace, class name, and the file name for the source code are defined in that order.

The Resgen utility does not support adding pictures. With the .NET Framework SDK samples, you get a ResXGen sample with the tutorials. With ResXGen it is possible to reference pictures in a `.resX` file. Adding pictures can also be done programmatically by using the `ResourceWriter` or `ResXResourceWriter` classes, as you see next.

ResourceWriter

Instead of using the Resgen utility to build resource files, it's a simple task to write a program to create resources. The class `ResourceWriter` from the namespace `System.Resources` can be used to write binary resource files; `ResXResourceWriter` writes XML-based resource files. Both of these classes support pictures and any other object that is serializable. When you use the class `ResXResourceWriter`, the assembly `System.Windows.Forms` must be referenced.

In the following code example, you create a `ResXResourceWriter` object, rw, using a constructor with the file name `Demo.resx`. After creating an instance, you can add a number of resources of up to 2GB in total size using the `AddResource()` method of the `ResXResourceWriter` class. The first argument of `AddResource()` specifies the name of the resource and the second argument specifies the value. A picture resource can be added using an instance of the `Image` class. To use the `Image` class, you have to reference the assembly `System.Drawing`. You also add the `using` directive to open the namespace `System.Drawing`.

Create an `Image` object by opening the file `logo.gif`. You will have to copy the picture to the directory of the executable or specify the full path to the picture in the method argument of `Image.ToFile()`. The `using` statement specifies that the image resource should automatically be disposed at the end of the using block. Additional simple string resources are added to the `ResXResourceWriter` object. The `Close()` method of the `ResXResourceWriter` class automatically calls `ResXResourceWriter.Generate()` to finally write the resources to the file `Demo.resx`:

```
using System;
using System.Resources;
using System.Drawing;

class Program
{
    static void Main()
    {
        ResXResourceWriter rw = new ResXResourceWriter("Demo.resx");
        using (Image image = Image.FromFile("logo.gif"))
        {
            rw.AddResource("WroxLogo", image);
```

```
        rw.AddResource("Title", "Professional C#");
        rw.AddResource("Chapter", "Localization");
        rw.AddResource("Author", "Christian Nagel");
        rw.AddResource("Publisher", "Wrox Press");
        rw.Close();
    }
  }
}
```

Starting this small program creates the resource file `Demo.resx` that embeds the image `logo.gif`. The resources will now be used in the next example with a Windows application.

Using Resource Files

You can add resource files to assemblies with the command-line C# compiler `csc.exe` using the `/resource` option, or directly with Visual Studio 2008. To see how resource files can be used with Visual Studio 2008, create a C# Windows application and name it `ResourceDemo`.

Use the context menu of the Solution Explorer (Add ⇨ Add Existing Item) to add the previously created resource file `Demo.resx` to this project. By default, Build Action of this resource is set to Embedded Resource so that this resource is embedded into the output assembly (see Figure 21-6).

Figure 21-6

Set the Neutral Language setting of the application to the main language, for example, English (United States), as shown in Figure 21-7.

Changing this setting adds the attribute `[NeutralResourceLanguageAttribute]` to the file `assemblyinfo.cs` as you can see here:

```
[assembly: NeutralResourcesLanguageAttribute("en-US")]
```

Figure 21-7

Setting this option gives a performance improvement with the ResourceManager because it more quickly finds the resources for en-US that are also used as a default fallback. With this attribute you can also specify the location of the default resource using the second parameter with the constructor. With the enumeration UltimateResourceFallbackLocation you can specify the default resource to be stored in the main assembly or in a satellite assembly (values MainAssembly and Satellite).

After building the project, you can check the generated assembly with ildasm to see the attribute .mresource in the manifest (see Figure 21-8). .mresource declares the name for the resource in the assembly. If .mresource is declared as public (as in the example), the resource is exported from the assembly and can be used from classes in other assemblies. .mresource private means that the resource is not exported and is available only within the assembly.

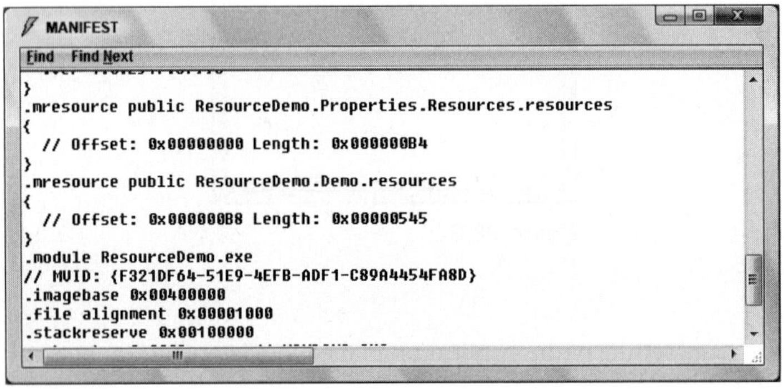

Figure 21-8

When you add resources to the assembly using Visual Studio 2008, the resource is always public, as shown in Figure 21-8. If the assembly generation tool is used to create assemblies, you can use command-line options to differentiate between adding public and private resources. The option /embed:demo.resources,Y adds the resource as public, whereas /embed:demo.resources,N adds the resource as private.

> If the assembly was generated using Visual Studio 2008, you can change the
> visibility of the resources later. Use `ilasm` and select File ⇨ Dump to open the
> assembly and generate an MSIL source file. You can change the MSIL code with
> a text editor. Using the text editor, you can change `.mresource public` to
> `.mresource private`. Using the tool `ilasm`, you can then regenerate the
> assembly with the MSIL source code: `ilasm /exe ResourceDemo.il`.

In your Windows application, you add some text boxes and a picture by dropping Windows Forms
elements from the toolbox into the Designer. The values from the resources will be displayed in these
Windows Forms elements. Change the `Text` and `Name` properties of the text boxes and the labels to the
values that you can see in the following code. The name property of the `PictureBox` control is changed
to logo. Figure 21-9 shows the final form in the Forms Designer. The `PictureBox` control is shown as a
rectangle without a grid in the upper-left corner.

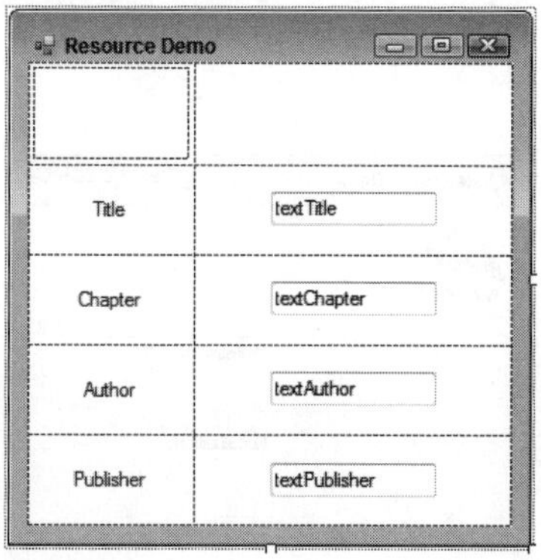

Figure 21-9

To access the embedded resource, use the `ResourceManager` class from the `System.Resources`
namespace. You can pass the assembly that has the resources as an argument to the constructor of the
`ResourceManager` class. In this example, the resources are embedded in the executing assembly, so
pass the result of `Assembly.GetExecutingAssembly()` as the second argument. The first argument
is the root name of the resources. The root name consists of the namespace, with the name of the
resource file but without the resources extension. As you saw earlier, `ildasm` shows the name. All you
have to do is remove the file extension `resources` from the name shown. You can also get the name
programmatically using the `GetManifestResourceNames()` method of the
`System.Reflection.Assembly` class:

```
using System.Reflection;
using System.Resources;

//...

    partial class ResourceDemoForm : Form
    {
        private System.Resources.ResourceManager rm;
```

(continued)

(continued)

```
public ResourceDemoForm()
{
    InitializeComponent();

    Assembly assembly = Assembly.GetExecutingAssembly();

    rm = new ResourceManager("ResourceDemo.Demo", assembly);
```

Using the `ResourceManager` instance rm, you can get all the resources by specifying the key to the methods `GetObject()` and `GetString()`:

```
    logo.Image = (Image)rm.GetObject("WroxLogo");
    textTitle.Text = rm.GetString("Title");
    textChapter.Text = rm.GetString("Chapter");
    textAuthor.Text = rm.GetString("Author");
    textPublisher.Text = rm.GetString("Publisher");
}
```

When you run the code, you can see the string and picture resources (see Figure 21-10).

Figure 21-10

With strongly typed resources, the code written earlier in the constructor of the class `ResourceDemoForm` can be simplified; there is no need to instantiate the `ResourceManager` and access the resources using indexers. Instead, the names of the resources are accessed with properties:

```
public ResourceDemoForm()
{
    InitializeComponent();

    pictureLogo.Image = Demo.WroxLogo;
    textTitle.Text = Demo.Title;
    textChapter.Text = Demo.Chapter;
    textAuthor.Text = Demo.Author;
    textPublisher.Text = Demo.Publisher;
}
```

To create a strongly typed resource, the `Custom Tool` property of the XML-based resource file must be set to `ResXFileCodeGenerator`. By setting this option, the class `Demo` (it has the same name as the resource) is created. This class has static properties for all the resources to offer a strongly typed resource name. With the implementation of the static properties, a `ResourceManager` object is used that is instantiated on first access and then cached:

```
/// <summary>
///     A strongly-typed resource class, for looking up localized strings,
///     etc.
/// </summary>
// This class was auto-generated by the StronglyTypedResourceBuilder
// class via a tool like ResGen or Visual Studio.
// To add or remove a member, edit your .ResX file then rerun ResGen
// with the /str option, or rebuild your VS project.
[global::System.CodeDom.Compiler.GeneratedCodeAttribute(
        "System.Resources.Tools.StronglyTypedResourceBuilder",
        "2.0.0.0")]
[global::System.Diagnostics.DebuggerNonUserCodeAttribute()]
[global::System.Runtime.CompilerServices.CompilerGeneratedAttribute()]
internal class Demo {

    private static global::System.Resources.ResourceManager resourceMan;

    private static global::System.Globalization.CultureInfo resourceCulture;

    [global::System.Diagnostics.CodeAnalysis.SuppressMessageAttribute(
            "Microsoft.Performance", "CA1811:AvoidUncalledPrivateCode")]
    internal Demo() {
    }

    /// <summary>
    ///     Returns the cached ResourceManager instance used by this class.
    /// </summary>
    [global::System.ComponentModel.EditorBrowsableAttribute(
            global::System.ComponentModel.EditorBrowsableState.Advanced)]
    internal static global::System.Resources.ResourceManager
            ResourceManager {
        get {
            if (object.ReferenceEquals(resourceMan, null)) {
                global::System.Resources.ResourceManager temp =
                        new global::System.Resources.ResourceManager(
                        "ResourceDemo.Demo", typeof(Demo).Assembly);
                resourceMan = temp;
            }
            return resourceMan;
        }
    }

    /// <summary>
    ///     Overrides the current thread's CurrentUICulture property for all
    ///     resource lookups using this strongly typed resource class.
```

(continued)

(continued)

```csharp
            /// </summary>
            [global::System.ComponentModel.EditorBrowsableAttribute(
                global::System.ComponentModel.EditorBrowsableState.Advanced)]
            internal static System.Globalization.CultureInfo Culture {
                get {
                    return resourceCulture;
                }
                set {
                    resourceCulture = value;
                }
            }

            /// <summary>
            ///    Looks up a localized string similar to "Christian Nagel".
            /// </summary>
            internal static string Author {
                get {
                    return ResourceManager.GetString("Author", resourceCulture);
                }
            }

            /// <summary>
            ///    Looks up a localized string similar to "Localization".
            /// </summary>
            internal static string Chapter {
                get {
                    return ResourceManager.GetString("Chapter", resourceCulture);
                }
            }

            /// <summary>
            ///    Looks up a localized string similar to "Wrox Press".
            /// </summary>
            internal static string Publisher {
                get {
                    return ResourceManager.GetString("Publisher", resourceCulture);
                }
            }

            /// <summary>
            ///    Looks up a localized string similar to "Professional C#".
            /// </summary>
            internal static string Title {
                get {
                    return ResourceManager.GetString("Title", resourceCulture);
                }
            }

            internal static System.Drawing.Bitmap WroxLogo {
                get {
                    return ((System.Drawing.Bitmap)(ResourceManager.GetObject(
                        "WroxLogo", resourceCulture)));
                }
            }
        }
```

The System.Resources Namespace

Before moving on to the next example, this section concludes with a review of the classes contained in the System.Resources namespace that deal with resources:

❑ The ResourceManager class can be used to get resources for the current culture from assemblies or resource files. Using the ResourceManager, you can also get a ResourceSet for a particular culture.

❑ A ResourceSet represents the resources for a particular culture. When a ResourceSet instance is created, it enumerates over a class, implementing the interface IResourceReader, and it stores all resources in a Hashtable.

❑ The interface IResourceReader is used from the ResourceSet to enumerate resources. The class ResourceReader implements this interface.

❑ The class ResourceWriter is used to create a resource file. ResourceWriter implements the interface IResourceWriter.

❑ ResXResourceSet, ResXResourceReader, and ResXResourceWriter are similar to ResourceSet, ResourceReader, and ResourceWriter; however, they are used to create an XML-based resource file .resX instead of a binary file. You can use ResXFileRef to make a link to a resource instead of embedding it inside an XML file.

Windows Forms Localization Using Visual Studio

In this section, you create a simple Windows application that shows how to use Visual Studio 2008 for localization. This application does not use complex Windows Forms and does not have any real inner functionality because the key feature it is intended to demonstrate here is localization. In the automatically generated source code, change the namespace to Wrox.ProCSharp.Localization and the class name to BookOfTheDayForm. The namespace is not only changed in the source file BookOfTheDayForm.cs but also in the project settings, so that all generated resource files will get this namespace, too. You can change the namespace for all new items that are created by selecting Common Properties from the Project ⇨ Properties menu.

Windows Forms applications are covered in more detail in Chapter 31, "Windows Forms," Chapter 32, "Data Binding," and Chapter 33, "Graphics with GDI+."

Figure 21-11

To show some issues with localization, this program has a picture, some text, a date, and a number. The picture shows a flag that is also localized. Figure 21-11 shows this form of the application as seen in the Windows Forms Designer.

The following table lists the values for the Name and Text properties of the Windows Forms elements.

Name	Text
labelBookOfTheDay	Book of the day
labelItemsSold	Books sold
textDate	Date
textTitle	Professional C#
textItemsSold	30000
pictureFlag	

In addition to this form, you might want a message box that displays a welcome message; this message might change depending on the current time of day. This example demonstrates that the localization for dynamically created dialogs must be done differently. In the method WelcomeMessage(), display a message box using MessageBox.Show(). Call the method WelcomeMessage() in the constructor of the form class BookOfTheDayForm, before the call to InitializeComponent().

Here is the code for the method WelcomeMessage():

```
public void WelcomeMessage()
{
    DateTime now = DateTime.Now;
    string message;
    if (now.Hour <= 12)
    {
        message = "Good Morning";
    }
    else if (now.Hour <= 19)
    {
        message = "Good Afternoon";
    }
    else
    {
        message = "Good Evening";
    }
    MessageBox.Show(String.Format("{0}\nThis is a localization sample",
            message);
}
```

The number and date in the form should be set by using formatting options. Add a new method, SetDateAndNumber(), to set the values with the format option. In a real application, these values could be received from a Web service or a database, but this example is just concentrating on localization. The date is formatted using the D option (to display the long date name). The number is displayed using the picture number format string ###,###,###, where # represents a digit and "," is the group separator.

```
public void SetDateAndNumber()
{
    DateTime today = DateTime.Today;
    textDate.Text = today.ToString("D");
    int itemsSold = 327444;
    textItemsSold.Text = itemsSold.ToString("###,###,###");
}
```

In the constructor of the `BookOfTheDayForm` class, both the `WelcomeMessage()` and `SetDateAndNumber()` methods are called:

```
public BookOfTheDayForm()
{
    WelcomeMessage();

    InitializeComponent();

    SetDateAndNumber();
}
```

A magic feature of the Windows Forms Designer is started when you set the `Localizable` property of the form from `false` to `true`. This results in the creation of an XML-based resource file for the dialog box that stores all resource strings, properties (including the location and size of Windows Forms elements), embedded pictures, and so on. In addition, the implementation of the `InitializeComponent()` method is changed; an instance of the class `System.Resources.ResourceManager` is created, and to get to the values and positions of the text fields and pictures, the `GetObject()` method is used instead of writing the values directly into the code. `GetObject()` uses the `CurrentUICulture` property of the current thread for finding the correct localization of the resources.

Here is part of `InitializeComponent()` from the file `BookOfTheDayForm.Designer.cs` before the `Localizable` property is set to `true`, where all properties of `textboxTitle` are set:

```
private void InitializeComponent()
{
    //...
    this.textTitle = new System.Windows.Forms.TextBox();
    //...
    //
    // textTitle
    //
    this.textTitle.Location = new System.Drawing.Point(24, 152);
    this.textTitle.Name = "textTitle";
    this.textTitle.Size = new System.Drawing.Size(256, 20);
    this.textTitle.TabIndex = 2;
    this.textTitle.Text = "Professional C#";
```

The code for the `IntializeComponent()` method is automatically changed by setting the `Localizable` property to `true`:

```
private void InitializeComponent()
{
    System.ComponentModel.ComponentResourceManager resources =
        new System.ComponentModel.ComponentResourceManager(
        typeof(BookOfTheDayForm));
    //...
    this.textTitle = new System.Windows.Forms.TextBox();
    //...
    resources.ApplyResources(this.textTitle, "textTitle");
```

Where does the resource manager get the data from? When the `Localizable` property is set to `true`, the resource file `BookOfTheDay.resX` is generated. In this file, you can find the scheme of the XML resource, followed by all elements in the form: `Type`, `Text`, `Location`, `TabIndex`, and so on.

The class `ComponentResourceManager` is derived from `ResourceManager` and offers the method `ApplyResources()`. With `ApplyResources()`, the resources that are defined with the second argument are applied to the object in the first argument.

The following XML segment shows a few of the properties of `textBoxTitle`: the `Location` property has a value of `13, 133`; the `TabIndex` property has a value of `2`; the `Text` property is set to `Professional C#`; and so on. For every value, the type of the value is stored as well. For example, the `Location` property is of type `System.Drawing.Point`, and this class can be found in the assembly `System.Drawing`.

Why are the locations and sizes stored in this XML file? With translations, many strings have completely different sizes and no longer fit into the original positions. When the locations and sizes are all stored inside the resource file, everything that is needed for localizations is stored in these files, separate from the C# code:

```
<data name="textTitle.Anchor" type="System.Windows.Forms.AnchorStyles,
    System.Windows.Forms">
    <value>Bottom, Left, Right</value>
</data>
<data name="textTitle.Location" type="System.Drawing.Point, System.Drawing>
    <value>13, 133</value>
</data>
<data name="textTitle.Size" type="System.Drawing.Size, System.Drawing>
    <value>196, 20</value>
</data>
<data name="textTitle.TabIndex" type="System.Int32, mscorlib>
    <value>2</value>
</data>
<data name="textTitle.Text">
    <value xml:space="preserve">Professional C#</value>
</data>
```

When changing some of these resource values, it is not necessary to work directly with the XML code. You can change these resources directly in the Visual Studio 2008 Designer. Whenever you change the `Language` property of the form and the properties of some form elements, a new resource file is generated for the specified language. Create a German version of the form by setting the `Language` property to German, and a French version by setting the `Language` property to French. For every language, you get a resource file with the changed properties: in this case, `BookOfTheDayForm.de.resX` and `BookOfTheDayForm.fr.resX`.

The following table shows the changes needed for the German version.

German Name	Value
`$this.Text` (title of the form)	Buch des Tages
`labelItemsSold.Text`	Bücher verkauft:
`labelBookOfTheDay.Text`	Buch des Tages:

The following table lists the changes for the French version.

French Name	Value
$this.Text (title of the form)	Le livre du jour
labelItemsSold.Text	Des livres vendus:
labelBookOfTheDay.Text	Le livre du jour:

By default, images are not moved to satellite assemblies. However, in the sample application, the flag should be different depending on the country. To do this, you have to add the image of the American flag to the file Resources.resx. You can find this file in the Properties section of the Visual Studio Solution Explorer. With the resource editor, select the Images categories as shown in Figure 21-12, and add the file americanflag.bmp. To make localization with images possible, the image must have the same name in all languages. Here the image in the file Resources.resx has the name Flag. You can rename the image in the properties editor. Within the properties editor, you can also change whether the image should be linked or embedded. For best performance with resources, images are linked by default. With linked images, the image file must be delivered together with the application. If you want to embed the image within the assembly, you can change the Persistence property to Embedded.

Figure 21-12

The localized versions of the flags can be added by copying the file Resource.resx to Resource.de.resx and Resource.fr.resx and replacing the flags with GermanFlag.bmp and FranceFlag.bmp. Because a strongly typed resource class is needed only with the neutral resource, the property CustomTool can be cleared with the resource files of all specific languages.

Compiling the project now creates a *satellite assembly* for each language. Inside the debug directory (or the release, depending on your active configuration), language subdirectories like de and fr are created. In such a subdirectory, you will find the file BookOfTheDay.resources.dll. Such a file is a satellite assembly that includes only localized resources. Opening this assembly with ildasm, you see a manifest with the embedded resources and a defined locale. The assembly has the locale de in the assembly attributes, so it can be found in the de subdirectory. You can also see the name of the resource with .mresource; it is prefixed with the namespace name Wrox.ProCSharp.Localization, followed by the class name BookOfTheDayForm and the language code de.

Changing the Culture Programmatically

After translating the resources and building the satellite assemblies, you will get the correct translations depending on the configured culture for the user. The welcome message is not translated at this time. This needs to be done in a different way, as you'll see shortly.

In addition to the system configuration, it should be possible to send the language code as a command-line argument to your application for testing purposes. The BookOfTheDayForm constructor is changed to allow passing a culture string, and setting the culture depending on this string. A CultureInfo instance is created to pass it to the CurrentCulture and CurrentUICulture properties of the current thread. Remember that the CurrentCulture is used for formatting, and the CurrentUICulture is used for loading of resources.

```
public BookOfTheDayForm(string culture)
{
    if (!String.IsNullOrEmpty(culture))
    {
        CultureInfo ci = new CultureInfo(culture);
        // set culture for formatting
        Thread.CurrentThread.CurrentCulture = ci;
        // set culture for resources
        Thread.CurrentThread.CurrentUICulture = ci;
    }

    WelcomeMessage();

    InitializeComponent();
    SetDateAndNumber();
}
```

The BookOfTheDayForm is instantiated in the Main() method, which can be found in the file Program.cs. In this method, you pass the culture string to the BookOfTheDayForm constructor:

```
[STAThread]
static void Main(string[] args)
{
    string culture = "";
    if (args.Length == 1)
    {
        culture = args[0];
    }

    Application.EnableVisualStyles();
    Application.SetCompatibleTextRenderingDefault(false);
    Application.Run(new BookOfTheDayForm(culture));
}
```

Now you can start the application by using command-line options. With the running application, you can see that the formatting options and the resources that were generated from the Windows Forms Designer show up. Figures 21-13 and 21-14 show two localizations in which the application is started with the command-line options de-DE and fr-FR.

There is still a problem with the welcome message box: the strings are hard-coded inside the program. Because these strings are not properties of elements inside the form, the Forms Designer does not extract XML resources as it does from the properties for Windows controls when changing the Localizable property of the form. You have to change this code yourself.

Figure 21-13

Figure 21-14

Using Custom Resource Messages

For the welcome message, you have to translate the hard-coded strings. The following table shows the translations for German and French. You can write custom resource messages directly in the file `Resources.resx` and the language-specific derivations. Of course, you can also create a new resource file.

Name	English	German	French
GoodMorning	Good Morning	Guten Morgen	Bonjour
GoodAfternoon	Good Afternoon	Guten Tag	Bonjour
GoodEvening	Good Evening	Guten Abend	Bonsoir
Message1	This is a localization sample.	Das ist ein Beispiel mit Lokalisierung.	C'est un exemple avec la localisation.

The source code of the method `WelcomeMessage()` must also be changed to use the resources. With strongly typed resources, there is no need to instantiate the `ResourceManager` class. Instead, the properties of the strongly typed resource can be used:

```
public static void WelcomeMessage()
{
    DateTime now = DateTime.Now;
    string message;
    if (now.Hour <= 12)
    {
        message = Properties.Resources.GoodMorning;
    }
    else if (now.Hour <= 19)
    {
        message = Properties.Resources.GoodAfternoon;
    }
    else
```

(continued)

(continued)

```
                    {
                        message = Properties.Resources.GoodEvening;
                    }
                    MessageBox.Show(message + "\n" +
                        Properties.Resources.Message1);
                }
```

When the program is started using English, German, or French, you will get the message boxes shown in Figures 21-15, 21-16, and 21-17, respectively.

Figure 21-15

Figure 21-16

Figure 21-17

Automatic Fallback for Resources

For the French and German versions in the example, all the resources are inside the satellite assemblies. If not, then all the values of labels or text boxes are changed; this is not a problem at all. You must have only the values that will change in the satellite assembly; the other values will be taken from the parent assembly. For example, for de-at (Austria), you could change the value for the *Good Afternoon* resource to *Grüß Gott* while leaving the other values intact. During runtime, when looking for the value of the resource *Good Morning*, which is not located in the de-at satellite assembly, the parent assembly would be searched. The parent for de-at is de. In cases where the de assembly does not have this resource either, the value would be searched for in the parent assembly of de, the neutral assembly. The neutral assembly does not have a culture code.

> **Keep in mind that with the culture code of the main assembly, you shouldn't define any culture!**

Outsourcing Translations

It is an easy task to outsource translations using resource files. It is not necessary to install Visual Studio for translating resource files; a simple XML editor will suffice. The disadvantage of using an XML editor is that there is no real chance to rearrange Windows Forms elements and change the sizes if the translated text does not fit into the original borders of a label or button. Using a Windows Forms Designer to do translations is a natural choice.

Microsoft provides a tool as part of the .NET Framework SDK that fulfills all these requirements: the Windows Resource Localization Editor `winres.exe` (see Figure 21-18). Users working with this tool do not need access to the C# source files; only binary or XML-based resource files are needed for translations. After these translations are completed, you can import the resource files to the Visual Studio project to build satellite assemblies.

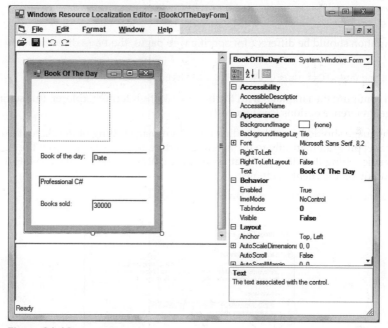

Figure 21-18

If you don't want your translation bureau to change the sizes and locations of labels and buttons, and they cannot deal with XML files, you can send a simple text-based file. With the command-line utility `resgen.exe`, you can create a text file from an XML file:

```
resgen myresource.resX myresource.txt
```

And after you have received the translation from the translation bureau, you can create an XML file from the returned text file. Remember to add the culture name to the file name:

```
resgen myresource.es.txt myresource.es.resX
```

Localization with ASP.NET

With ASP.NET applications, localization happens in a similar way to Windows applications. Chapter 37, "ASP.NET Pages," discusses the functionality of ASP.NET applications; this section discusses the localization issues of ASP.NET applications. ASP.NET 2.0 and Visual Studio 2008 have many new features to support localization. The basic concepts of localization and globalization are the same as discussed before. However, some specific issues are associated with ASP.NET.

As you have already learned, with ASP.NET you have to differentiate between the user interface culture and the culture used for formatting. Both of these cultures can be defined on a web and page level, as well as programmatically.

To be independent of the web server's operating system, the culture and user interface culture can be defined with the `<globalization>` element in the configuration file `web.config`:

```
<configuration>
   <system.web>
      <globalization culture="en-US" uiCulture="en-US" />
   </system.web>
</configuration>
```

If the configuration should be different for specific web pages, the `Page` directive allows assigning the culture:

```
<%Page Language="C#" Culture="en-US" UICulture="en-US" %>
```

The user can configure the language with the browser. With Internet Explorer, this setting is defined with the Language Preference options (see Figure 21-19).

If the page language should be set depending on the language setting of the client, the culture of the thread can be set programmatically to the language setting that is received from the client. ASP.NET 2.0 has an automatic setting that does just that. Setting the culture to the value `Auto` sets the culture of the thread depending on the client's settings.

```
<%Page Language="C#" Culture="Auto" UICulture="Auto" %>
```

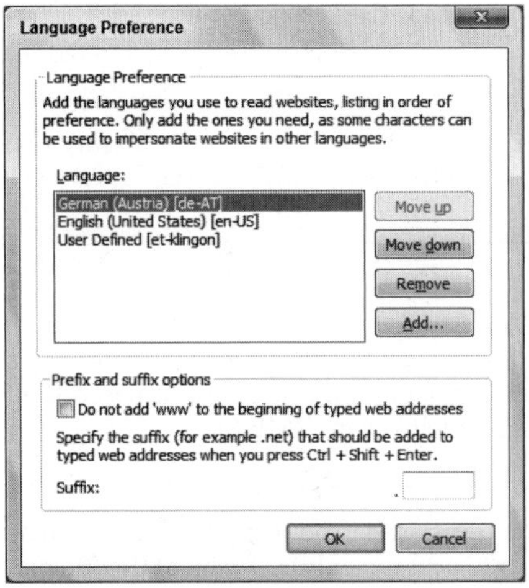

Figure 21-19

In dealing with resources, ASP.NET differentiates resources that are used for the complete web site and resources that are needed only within a page.

If a resource is used within a page, you can create resources for the page by selecting the Visual Studio 2008 menu Tools ⇨ Generate Local Resource in the design view. This way, the subdirectory `App_LocalResources` is created where a resource file for every page is stored. These resources can be localized similarly to Windows applications. The association between the web controls and the local resource files happens with a `meta:resourcekey` attribute as shown here with the ASP.NET `Label` control. `LabelResource1` is the name of the resource that can be changed in the local resource file:

```
<asp:Label ID="Label1" Runat="server" Text="Label"
    meta:resourcekey="LabelResource1"></asp:Label>
```

For the resources that should be shared between multiple pages, you have to create a subdirectory, `App1_GlobalResources`. In this directory, you can add resource files, for example, `Messages.resx` with its resources. To associate the web controls with these resources, you can use Expressions in the property editor. Clicking the Expressions button opens the Expressions dialog (see Figure 21-20). Here, you can select the expression type Resources, set the name of the `ClassKey` (which is the name of the resource file — here, a strongly typed resource file is generated), and the name of the `ResourceKey`, which is the name of the resource.

In the ASPX file, you can see the association to the resource with the binding expressions syntax `<%$:`

```
<asp:Label ID="Label1" Runat="server"
    Text="<%$ Resources:Messages, String1 %>">
</asp:Label>
```

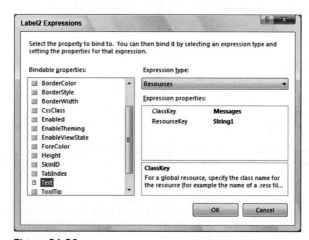

Figure 21-20

Localization with WPF

Visual Studio 2008 does not have great support for localization of WPF (Windows Presentation Foundation) applications. However, you do not have to wait until the next version to localize your WPF application. WPF has localization support built-in from the beginning, and you have several options to localize your applications. You can use .NET resources similar to what you've done with Windows Forms and ASP.NET applications, but you can also use an XAML (XML for Applications Markup Language) resource dictionary.

These options are discussed next. You can read more about WPF and XAML in Chapters 34, "Windows Presentation Foundation," and 35, "Advanced WPF."

WPF Application

To demonstrate the use of resources with a WPF application, create a simple WPF application containing just one button, as shown in Figure 21-21.

Figure 21-21

The XAML code for this application is shown here:

```
<Window x:Class="Wrox.ProCSharp.Localization.Window1"
      xmlns="http://schemas.microsoft.com/winfx/2006/xaml/presentation"
      xmlns:x="http://schemas.microsoft.com/winfx/2006/xaml"
      Title="WPF Sample" Height="300" Width="300">
   <Grid>
      <Button Name="button1" Margin="30,20,30,20" Click="Button_Click"
            Content="English Button" />
   </Grid>
</Window>
```

With the handler code for the click event of the button, just a message box containing a sample message pops up:

```
private void Button_Click(object sender, RoutedEventArgs e)
{
    MessageBox.Show("English Message");
}
```

.NET Resources

You can add .NET resources to a WPF application similar to the way you have with other applications. Define the resources named `Button1Text` and `Button1Message` in the file `Resources.resx`.

To use the generated resource class, you need to change the XAML code. Add an XML namespace alias to reference the .NET namespace `Wrox.ProCSharp.Localization.Properties` as shown. Here, the alias is set to the value `props`. From XAML elements, properties of this class can be used with the `x:Static` markup extension. The `Content` property of the `Button` is set to the `Button1Text` property of the `Resources` class.

```
<Window x:Class="Wrox.ProCSharp.Localization.Window1"
      xmlns="http://schemas.microsoft.com/winfx/2006/xaml/presentation"
      xmlns:x="http://schemas.microsoft.com/winfx/2006/xaml"
```

```
        xmlns:props="clr-namespace:Wrox.ProCSharp.Localization.Properties"
        Title="WPF Sample" Height="300" Width="300">
    <Grid>
        <Button Name="button1" Margin="30,20,30,20" Click="Button_Click"
             Content="{x:Static props:Resources.Button1Text}" />
    </Grid>
</Window>
```

Because resources added in a Visual Studio Solution have the internal *access modifier with the resource class and its members, and there is not an option to change this, you should add a custom build step to use the Resgen utility with the* /publicClass *option and add the generated class to the project. Otherwise, the WPF project won't compile.*

To use the .NET resource from code-behind, you can just access the Button1Message property directly in the same way you did with Windows Forms applications:

```
        private void Button_Click(object sender, RoutedEventArgs e)
        {
            MessageBox.Show(Properties.Resources.Button1Message);
        }
```

Localization with XAML

Instead of using .NET resources for localization of WPF applications, you can work directly with XAML to create localized content. The steps for a localization process can be described by these actions:

❑ Create a satellite assembly from the main content

❑ Use resource dictionaries for localizable content

❑ Add x:Uid attributes to elements that should be localized

❑ Extract localization content from an assembly

❑ Translate the content

❑ Create satellite assemblies for every language

When compiling a WPF application, the XAML code is compiled to a binary format BAML that is stored into an assembly. To move the BAML code from the main assembly to a separate satellite assembly, you can change the .csproj build file and add a <UICulture> element as shown as a child to the <PropertyGroup> element. The culture, here en-US, defines the default culture of the project. Building the project with this build-setting creates a subdirectory en-US and creates a satellite assembly containing BAML code for the default language.

```
        <UICulture>en-US</UICulture>
```

Separating the BAML into a satellite assembly, you should also apply the NeutralResourcesLanguage attribute and supply the resource fallback location to a satellite assembly. If you decide to keep BAML in the main assembly (by not defining the <UICulture> to the .csproj file), the UltimateResourceFallbackLocation should be set to MainAssembly.

```
    [assembly: NeutralResourcesLanguage("en-US",
        UltimateResourceFallbackLocation.Satellite)]
```

For code-behind content that needs to be localized, a resource dictionary can be added. Using XAML, you can define resources within the <ResourceDictionary> element as shown. With Visual Studio, you can create a new resource dictionary by adding a new resource dictionary item and defining the file name. In the example here, the resource dictionary contains one string item. To get access to the String type from the System namespace, an XML namespace alias needs to be defined. Here, the alias system

671

is set to the clr-namespace `System` in the assembly `mscorlib`. The string that is defined can be accessed with the key `message1`. This resource dictionary is defined in the file `LocalizedStrings.xaml`.

```
<ResourceDictionary
        xmlns="http://schemas.microsoft.com/winfx/2006/xaml/presentation"
        xmlns:x="http://schemas.microsoft.com/winfx/2006/xaml"
        xmlns:system="clr-namespace:System;assembly=mscorlib"
        >
    <system:String x:Key="message1">English Message</system:String>
</ResourceDictionary>
```

To have the resource dictionary available with the application, it must be added to the resources. If the resource dictionary would be required only within a window or just within a specific WPF element, it can be added to the resources collection of the specific window or WPF element. Here, the resource dictionary is added to the file `App.xaml` within the `<Application>` element, and thus is available to the complete application.

```
<Application x:Class="Wrox.ProCSharp.Localization.App"
        xmlns="http://schemas.microsoft.com/winfx/2006/xaml/presentation"
        xmlns:x="http://schemas.microsoft.com/winfx/2006/xaml"
        StartupUri="Window1.xaml">
    <Application.Resources>
        <ResourceDictionary>
            <ResourceDictionary.MergedDictionaries>
                <ResourceDictionary Source="LocalizationStrings.xaml" />
            </ResourceDictionary.MergedDictionaries>
        </ResourceDictionary>
    </Application.Resources>
</Application>
```

To use the XAML resource dictionary from code behind, you can use the `FindResource()` method. Because the resource is defined with the application, here an object of the `Application` class is used to find the resource. You can also use the `FindResource()` method from a WPF element, because the resources are searched in a hierarchical way. With the simple application here, if you use the `FindResource()` method of the `Button`, and if it is not found with the `Button` resources, then resources are searched in the `Grid`. If the resource is not there, a lookup to the `Window` resources is done before the `Application` resources are consulted.

```
private void Button_Click(object sender, RoutedEventArgs e)
{
    string message1 =
        (string)Application.Current.FindResource("message1");
    MessageBox.Show(message1);
}
```

With WPF elements, the `x:Uid` attribute is used as a unique identifier for elements that need localization. You don't have to apply this attribute manually to the XAML content; instead you can use the `msbuild` command with this option:

```
msbuild /t:updateuid
```

When you call this command in the directory where the project file is located, the XAML files of the project are modified to add an `x:Uid` attribute with a unique identifier to every element. The same XAML as shown before now has the new attributes applied:

```
<Window x:Uid="Window_1" x:Class="Wrox.ProCSharp.Localization.Window1"
        xmlns="http://schemas.microsoft.com/winfx/2006/xaml/presentation"
        xmlns:x="http://schemas.microsoft.com/winfx/2006/xaml"
```

```
        Title="WPF Sample" Height="300" Width="300">
    <Grid x:Uid="Grid_1">
        <Button x:Uid="button1" Name="button1" Margin="30,20,30,20"
            Click="Button_Click" Content="English Button" />
    </Grid>
</Window>
```

If you change the XAML file after `x:Uid` attributes have been added, you can verify correctness of the `x:Uid` attributes with the option `/t:checkuid`.

Compiling the project creates a satellite assembly containing the BAML code. From this satellite assembly, you can extract the content that needs to be localized with classes from the `System.Windows.Markup.Localizer` namespace. With the Windows SDK you will find the sample program LocBaml. This program can be used to extract localization content from BAML. You need to copy the executable, the satellite assembly with the default content, and `LocBaml.exe` to one directory and start the sample program to produce a `.csv` file with the localization content:

```
LocBaml /parse WPFandXAMLresources.resources.dll /out: trans.csv
```

You can use Microsoft Excel to open the `.csv` file and translate its content. An extract from the `.csv` file that lists the content of the button and the message from the resource dictionary is shown here:

```
WPFandXAMLResources.g.en-US.resources:localizationstrings.baml,
system:String_1:System.String.$Content,None,True,True,,English Message
WPFandXAMLResources.g.en-US.resources:window1.baml,
button1:System.Windows.Controls.ContentControl.Content,Button,True,True,,
English Button
```

This file contains these fields:

❑ Name of the BAML

❑ The identifier of the resource

❑ The category of the resource that gives the type of the content

❑ A Boolean value if the resource is visible for translation (readable)

❑ A Boolean value if the resource can be modified for the translation (modifiable)

❑ Localization comments

❑ The value of the resource

After localization of the resource, you can create a new directory for the new language (for example, de for German). The directory structure follows the same convention as shown earlier in this chapter with satellite assemblies. With the LocBaml tool, you can create satellite assemblies with the translated content:

```
LocBaml /generate WPFandXAMLResources.resources.dll /trans:trans_de.csv /out: ../de
/cul:de-DE
```

Now the same rules for setting the culture of the thread and finding satellite assemblies as shown with Windows Forms applications apply here.

A Custom Resource Reader

With the resource readers that are part of .NET Framework 3.5, you can read resources from resource files and satellite assemblies. If you want to put the resources into a different store (such as a database), you can use a custom resource reader to read these resources.

To use a custom resource reader, you also need to create a custom resource set and a custom resource manager. Doing this is not a difficult task, however, because you can derive the custom classes from existing classes.

For the sample application, you need to create a simple database with just one table for storing messages that has one column for every supported language. The following table lists the columns and their corresponding values.

Key	Default	de	es	fr	it
Welcome	Welcome	Willkommen	Recepción	Bienvenue	Benvenuto
GoodMorning	Good morning	Guten Morgen	Buonas díaz	Bonjour	Buona mattina
GoodEvening	Good evening	Guten Abend	Buonas noches	Bonsoir	Buona sera
ThankYou	Thank you	Danke	Gracias	Merçi	Grazie
Goodbye	Goodbye	Auf Wiedersehen	Adiós	Au revoir	Arrivederci

For the custom resource reader, you create a component library with three classes. The classes are `DatabaseResourceReader`, `DatabaseResourceSet`, and `DatabaseResourceManager`.

Creating a DatabaseResourceReader

With the class `DatabaseResourceReader`, you define two fields: the connection string that is needed to access the database and the language that should be returned by the reader. These fields are filled inside the constructor of this class. The field `language` is set to the name of the culture that is passed with the `CultureInfo` object to the constructor:

```
public class DatabaseResourceReader : IResourceReader
{
    private string connectionString;
    private string language;

    public DatabaseResourceReader(string connectionString,
        CultureInfo culture)
    {
        this.connectionString = connectionString;
        this.language = culture.Name;
    }
```

A resource reader has to implement the interface `IResourceReader`. This interface defines the methods `Close()` and `GetEnumerator()` to return an `IDictionaryEnumerator` that returns keys and values for the resources. In the implementation of `GetEnumerator()`, create a `Hashtable` where all keys and values for a specific language are stored. Next, you can use the `SqlConnection` class in the namespace `System.Data.SqlClient` to access the database in SQL Server. `Connection.CreateCommand()` creates a `SqlCommand()` object that you use to specify the SQL `SELECT` statement to access the data in the database. If the language is set to `de`, the `SELECT` statement is `SELECT [key], [de] FROM Messages`. Then you use a `SqlDataReader` object to read all values from the database, and put it into a `Hashtable`. Finally, the enumerator of the `Hashtable` is returned.

For more information about accessing data with ADO.NET, see Chapter 26, "Data Access."

```csharp
public System.Collections.IDictionaryEnumerator GetEnumerator()
{
    Dictionary<string, string> dict = new Dictionary<string, string>();

    SqlConnection connection = new SqlConnection(connectionString);
    SqlCommand command = connection.CreateCommand();
    if (String.IsNullOrEmpty(language))
        language = "Default";

    command.CommandText = "SELECT [key], [" + language + "] " +
                          "FROM Messages";

    try
    {
        connection.Open();

        SqlDataReader reader = command.ExecuteReader();
        while (reader.Read())
        {
            if (reader.GetValue(1) != System.DBNull.Value)
            {
                dict.Add(reader.GetString(0).Trim(), reader.GetString(1));
            }
        }

        reader.Close();
    }
    catch (SqlException ex)
    {
        if (ex.Number != 207)   // ignore missing columns in the database
            throw;              // rethrow all other exceptions
    }
    finally
    {
        connection.Close();
    }
    return dict.GetEnumerator();
}

public void Close()
{
}
```

Because the interface `IResourceReader` is derived from `IEnumerable` and `IDisposable`, the methods `GetEnumerator()`, which returns an `IEnumerator` interface, and `Dispose()` must be implemented, too:

```csharp
IEnumerator IEnumerable.GetEnumerator()
{
    return this.GetEnumerator();
}

void IDisposable.Dispose()
{
}
}
```

Creating a DatabaseResourceSet

The class `DatabaseResourceSet` can use nearly all implementations of the base class `ResourceSet`.
You just need a different constructor that initializes the base class with your own resource reader,
`DatabaseResourceReader`. The constructor of `ResourceSet` allows passing an object by implementing
`IResourceReader`; this requirement is fulfilled by `DatabaseResourceReader`:

```
public class DatabaseResourceSet : ResourceSet
{
    internal DatabaseResourceSet(string connectionString,
            CultureInfo culture)
        : base(new DatabaseResourceReader(connectionString, culture))
    {
    }

    public override Type GetDefaultReader()
    {
        return typeof(DatabaseResourceReader);
    }
}
```

Creating a DatabaseResourceManager

The third class you have to create is the custom resource manager. `DatabaseResourceManager` is
derived from the class `ResourceManager`, and you only have to implement a new constructor and
override the method `InternalGetResourceSet()`.

In the constructor, create a new `Hashtable` to store all queried resource sets and set it into the field
`ResourceSets` defined by the base class:

```
public class DatabaseResourceManager : ResourceManager
{
    private string connectionString;

    public DatabaseResourceManager(string connectionString)
    {
        this.connectionString = connectionString;
        ResourceSets = new Hashtable();
    }
```

The methods of the `ResourceManager` class that you can use to access resources (such as `GetString()`
and `GetObject()`) invoke the method `InternalGetResourceSet()` to access a resource set where the
appropriate values can be returned.

In the implementation of `InternalGetResourceSet()`, check first if the resource set for the culture
queried for a resource is already in the hash table; if it already exists, return it to the caller. If the resource
set is not available, create a new `DatabaseResourceSet` object with the queried culture, add it to the
hash table, and return it to the caller:

```
protected override ResourceSet InternalGetResourceSet(
        CultureInfo culture, bool createIfNotExists, bool tryParents)
{
    DatabaseResourceSet rs = null;

    if (ResourceSets.Contains(culture.Name))
    {
        rs = ResourceSets[culture.Name] as DatabaseResourceSet;
    }
```

```
        else
        {
            rs = new DatabaseResourceSet(connectionString, culture);
            ResourceSets.Add(culture.Name, rs);
        }
        return rs;
    }
}
```

Client Application for DatabaseResourceReader

How the class `ResourceManager` is used from the client application here does not differ much from the previous use of the `ResourceManager` class. The only difference is that the custom class `DatabaseResourceManager` is used instead of the class `ResourceManager`. The following code snippet demonstrates how you can use your own resource manager.

A new `DatabaseResourceManager` object is created by passing the database connection string to the constructor. Then, you can invoke the `GetString()` method that is implemented in the base class as you did earlier, passing the key and an optional object of type `CultureInfo` to specify a culture. In turn, you get a resource value from the database because this resource manager is using the classes `DatabaseResourceSet` and `DatabaseResourceReader`.

```
DatabaseResourceManager rm = new DatabaseResourceManager(
        "server=(local);database=LocalizationDemo;trusted_connection=true");

string spanishWelcome = rm.GetString("Welcome",
                                    new CultureInfo("es-ES"));
string italianThankyou = rm.GetString("ThankYou",
                                    new CultureInfo("it"));
string threadDefaultGoodMorning = rm.GetString("GoodMorning");
```

Creating Custom Cultures

Over time, more and more languages are supported with the .NET Framework. However, not all languages of the world are available with .NET. You can create a custom culture. Some examples of when creating custom cultures can be useful are to support a minority within a region or to create subcultures for different dialects.

Custom cultures and regions can be created with the class `CultureAndRegionInfoBuilder` in the namespace `System.Globalization`. This class is located in the assembly sysglobl in the file sysglobl.dll.

With the constructor of the class `CultureAndRegionInfoBuilder`, you can pass the culture's name. The second argument of the constructor requires an enumeration of type `CultureAndRegionModifiers`. This enumeration allows one of three values: `Neutral` for a neutral culture, `Replacement` if an existing Framework-culture should be replaced, or `None`.

After the `CultureAndRegionInfoBuilder` object is instantiated, you can configure the culture by setting properties. With the properties of this class, you can define all the cultural and regional information such as name, calendar, number format, metric information, and so on. If the culture should be based on existing cultures and regions, you can set the properties of the instance using the methods `LoadDataFromCultureInfo()` and `LoadDataFromRegionInfo()`, and change the values that are different by setting the properties afterward.

Calling the method `Register()` registers the new culture with the operating system. Indeed, you can find the file that describes the culture in the directory `<windows>\Globalization`. Look for files with the extension `.nlp`.

```
// Create a Styria culture
CultureAndRegionInfoBuilder styria = new CultureAndRegionInfoBuilder(
        "de-AT-ST", CultureAndRegionModifiers.None);
CultureInfo parent = new CultureInfo("de-AT");
styria.LoadDataFromCultureInfo(parent);
styria.LoadDataFromRegionInfo(new RegionInfo("AT"));
styria.Parent = parent;
styria.RegionNativeName = "Steiermark";
styria.RegionEnglishName = "Styria";
styria.CultureEnglishName = "Styria (Austria)";
styria.CultureNativeName = "Steirisch";

styria.Register();
```

The newly created culture can now be used like other cultures:

```
CultureInfo ci = new CultureInfo("de-AT-ST");
Thread.CurrentThread.CurrentCulture = ci;
Thread.CurrentThread.CurrentUICulture = ci;
```

You can use the culture for formatting and also for resources. If you start the Cultures in Action application that was written earlier in this chapter again, you can see the custom culture as well.

Summary

This chapter discussed the globalization and localization of .NET applications.

In the context of globalization of applications, you learned about using the namespace `System.Globalization` to format culture-dependent numbers and dates. Furthermore, you learned that sorting strings by default depends on the culture, and you used the invariant culture for a culture-independent sort. Using the `CultureAndRegionInfoBuilder` class, you've learned how to create a custom culture.

Localization of applications is accomplished by using resources. Resources can be packed into files, satellite assemblies, or a custom store such as a database. The classes used with localization are in the namespace `System.Resources`. For reading resources from other places such as satellite assemblies or resource files, you can create a custom resource reader.

You have seen how to localize Windows Forms, WPF, and ASP.NET applications.

The next chapter provides information about a completely different topic — transactions. Don't expect that transactions are only useful with databases. In addition to database transactions, the chapter also gives you information on memory-based transactional resources and a transactional file system.

22

Transactions

All or nothing — this is the main characteristic of a transaction. When writing a few records, either all are written, or everything will be undone. If there is even one failure when writing one record, all the other things that are done within the transaction will be rolled back.

Transactions are commonly used with databases, but with classes from the namespace `System.Transactions`, you can also perform transactions on volatile or in-memory-based objects such as a list of objects. With a list that supports transactions, if an object is added or removed and the transaction fails, the list action is automatically undone. Writing to a memory-based list can be done in the same transaction as writing to a database.

In Windows Vista, the file system and registry also get transactional support. Writing a file and making changes within the registry supports transactions.

In this chapter, the following topics are covered:

- ❑ Overview of transaction phases and ACID properties
- ❑ Traditional transactions
- ❑ Committable transactions
- ❑ Transaction promotions
- ❑ Dependent transactions
- ❑ Ambient transactions
- ❑ Transaction isolation level
- ❑ Custom resource managers
- ❑ Transactions with Windows Vista and Windows Server 2008

Overview

What are transactions? Think about ordering a book from a web site. The book-ordering process removes the book you want to buy from stock and puts it in your order box, and the cost of your book is charged to your credit card. With these two actions, either both actions should complete successfully or neither of these actions should happen. If there is a failure when getting the book from stock, the credit card should not be charged. Transactions address such scenarios.

The most common use of transactions is writing or updating data within the database. Transactions can also be performed when writing a message to a message queue, or writing data to a file or the registry. Multiple actions can be part of a single transaction.

> `System.Messaging` *is discussed in Chapter 45, "Message Queuing."*

Figure 22-1 shows the main actors in a transaction. Transactions are managed and coordinated by the transaction manager, and a resource manager manages every resource that influences the outcome of the transaction. The transaction manager communicates with resource managers to define the outcome of the transaction.

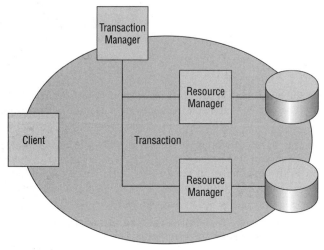

Figure 22-1

Transaction Phases

The timely phases of a transaction are the *active, preparing,* and *committing* phases:

- ❑ **Active phase** — During the active phase, the transaction is created. Resource managers that manage the transaction for resources can enlist with the transaction.

- ❑ **Preparing phase** — During the preparing phase, every resource manager can define the outcome of the transaction. This phase starts when the creator of the transaction sends a commit to end the transaction. The transaction manager sends a *Prepare* message to all resource managers. If the resource manager can produce the transaction outcome successfully, it sends a *Prepared* message to the transaction manager. Resource managers can abort the transaction if they fail to prepare by forcing a rollback with the transaction manager by sending a *Rollback* message. After the Prepared message is sent, the resource managers must guarantee to finish the work successfully in the committing phase. To make this possible, durable resource managers must write a log with the information from the prepared state, so that they can continue from there in case of, for example, a power failure between prepared and committing.

- ❑ **Committing phase** — The committing phase begins when all resource managers have prepared successfully. This is when the *Prepared* message is received from all resource managers. Then the transaction manager can complete the work by sending a *Commit* message to all participants. The resource managers can now finish the work on the transaction and return a *Committed* message.

ACID Properties

A transaction has specific requirements; for example, a transaction must result in a valid state, even if the server has a power failure. The characteristics of transactions can be defined by the term ACID. ACID is a four-letter acronym for *atomicity, consistency, isolation,* and *durability*:

❑ **Atomicity** — Atomicity represents one unit of work. With a transaction, either the complete unit of work succeeds or nothing is changed.

❑ **Consistency** — The state before the transaction was started and after the transaction is completed must be valid. During the transaction, the state may have interim values.

❑ **Isolation** — Isolation means that transactions that happen concurrently are isolated from the state, which is changed during a transaction. Transaction A cannot see the interim state of transaction B until the transaction is completed.

❑ **Durability** — After the transaction is completed, it must be stored in a durable way. This means that if the power goes down or the server crashes, the state must be recovered at reboot.

Not every transaction requires all four ACID properties. For example, a memory-based transaction (for example, writing an entry into a list) does not need to be durable. Also, a complete isolation from the outside is not always required, as we discuss later with transaction isolation levels.

Database and Entity Classes

The sample database `CourseManagement` that is used with the transactions in this chapter is defined by the structure from Figure 22-2. The table `Courses` contains information about courses: course numbers and titles; for example, the course number 2124 with the title Programming C#. The table `CourseDates` contains the date of specific courses and is linked to the `Courses` table. The table `Students` contains information about persons attending a course. The table `CourseAttendees` is the link between `Students` and `CourseDates`. It defines which student is attending what course.

You can download the database along with the source code for this chapter from the Wrox web site.

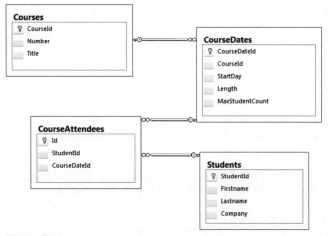

Figure 22-2

The sample applications in this chapter use a library with entity and data access classes. The class `Student` contains properties to define a student; for example, `FirstName`, `LastName`, and `Company`:

```
using System;

namespace Wrox.ProCSharp.Transactions
{
    [Serializable]
    public class Student
    {
        public Student() { }

        public Student(string firstName, string lastName)
        {
            this.FirstName = firstName;
            this.LastName = lastName;
        }

        public string FirstName { get; set; }
        public string LastName { get; set; }
        public string Company { get; set; }
        public int Id { get; set; }

        public override string ToString()
        {
            return String.Format("{0} {1}", FirstName, LastName);
        }
    }
}
```

Adding student information to the database is done in the method `AddStudent()` of the class `StudentData`. Here, an ADO.NET connection is created to connect to the SQL Server database, the `SqlCommand` object defines the SQL statement, and the command is executed by invoking `ExecuteNonQuery()`:

```
using System;
using System.Collections.Generic;
using System.Data;
using System.Data.SqlClient;
using System.Transactions;

namespace Wrox.ProCSharp.Transactions
{
    public class StudentData
    {
        public void AddStudent(Student student)
        {
            SqlConnection connection = new SqlConnection(
                Properties.Settings.Default.CourseManagementConnectionString);
            connection.Open();
            try
            {
                SqlCommand command = connection.CreateCommand();

                command.CommandText = "INSERT INTO Students " +
                    "(FirstName, LastName, Company) VALUES " +
```

```
                "(@FirstName, @LastName, @Company)";
            command.Parameters.AddWithValue("@FirstName", student.FirstName);
            command.Parameters.AddWithValue("@LastName", student.LastName);
            command.Parameters.AddWithValue("@Company", student.Company);

            command.ExecuteNonQuery();
        }
        finally
        {
            connection.Close();
        }
    }
  }
}
```

ADO.NET is covered in detail in Chapter 26, "Data Access"

Traditional Transactions

Before System.Transaction was released, you could create transactions directly with ADO.NET, or you could do transactions with the help of components, attributes, and the COM+ runtime, which is covered in the namespace System.EnterpriseServices. To show you how the new transaction model compares to the traditional ways of working with transactions, we present a short look at how ADO.NET transactions and transactions with Enterprise Services are done.

ADO.NET Transactions

Let's start with traditional ADO.NET transactions. If you don't create transactions manually, there is a single transaction with every SQL statement. If multiple statements need to participate with the same transaction, however, you must create a transaction manually to achieve this.

The following code segment shows how to work with ADO.NET transactions. The SqlConnection class defines the method BeginTransaction(), which returns an object of type SqlTransaction. This transaction object must then be associated with every command that participates with the transaction. To associate a command with a transaction, set the Transaction property of the SqlCommand class to the SqlTransaction instance. For the transaction to be successful, you must invoke the Commit() method of the SqlTransaction object. If there is an error, you have to invoke the Rollback() method, and every change is undone. You can check for an error with the help of a try/catch and do the rollback inside the catch.

```
using System;
using System.Data.SqlClient;
using System.Diagnostics;

namespace Wrox.ProCSharp.Transactions
{
    public class CourseData
    {
        public void AddCourse(Course course)
        {
            SqlConnection connection = new SqlConnection(
                    Properties.Settings.Default.CourseManagementConnectionString);
            SqlCommand courseCommand = connection.CreateCommand();
```

(continued)

(continued)

```
        courseCommand.CommandText =
            "INSERT INTO Courses (Number, Title) VALUES (@Number, @Title)";
        connection.Open();
        SqlTransaction tx = connection.BeginTransaction();

        try
        {
            courseCommand.Transaction = tx;

            courseCommand.Parameters.AddWithValue("@Number", course.Number);
            courseCommand.Parameters.AddWithValue("@Title", course.Title);
            courseCommand.ExecuteNonQuery();

            tx.Commit();
        }
        catch (Exception ex)
        {
            Trace.WriteLine("Error: " + ex.Message);
            tx.Rollback();
        }
        finally
        {
            connection.Close();
        }
    }
  }
}
```

If you have multiple commands that should run in the same transaction, every command must be associated with the transaction. Because the transaction is associated with a connection, every one of these commands must also be associated with the same connection instance. ADO.NET transactions do not support transactions across multiple connections; it is always a local transaction associated with one connection.

When you create an object persistence model using multiple objects, for example, classes `Course` and `CourseDate`, which should be persisted inside one transaction, it gets very difficult using ADO.NET transactions. Here, it is necessary to pass the transaction to all of the objects participating in the same transaction.

> **ADO.NET transactions are not distributed transactions. In ADO.NET transactions, it is difficult to have multiple objects working on the same transaction.**

System.EnterpriseServices

With Enterprise Services you get a lot of services for free. One of them is automatic transactions. Using transactions with `System.EnterpriseServices` has the advantage that it is not necessary to deal with transactions explicitly; transactions are automatically created by the runtime. You just have to add the attribute `[Transaction]` with the transactional requirements to the class. The `[AutoComplete]` attribute marks the method to automatically set the status bit for the transaction: if the method succeeds, the success bit is set, so the transaction can commit. If an exception happens, the transaction is aborted.

```csharp
using System;
using System.Data.SqlClient;
using System.EnterpriseServices;
using System.Diagnostics;

namespace Wrox.ProCSharp.Transactions
{
    [Transaction(TransactionOption.Required)]
    public class CourseData : ServicedComponent
    {
        [AutoComplete]
        public void AddCourse(Course course)
        {
            SqlConnection connection = new SqlConnection(
                    Properties.Settings.Default.CourseManagementConnectionString);
            SqlCommand courseCommand = connection.CreateCommand();
            courseCommand.CommandText =
                    "INSERT INTO Courses (Number, Title) VALUES (@Number, @Title)";
            connection.Open();
            try
            {
                courseCommand.Parameters.AddWithValue("@Number", course.Number);
                courseCommand.Parameters.AddWithValue("@Title", course.Title);
                courseCommand.ExecuteNonQuery();
            }
            finally
            {
                connection.Close();
            }
        }
    }
}
```

A big advantage of creating transactions with `System.EnterpriseServices` is that multiple objects can easily run within the same transaction, and transactions are automatically enlisted. The disadvantages are that it requires the COM+ hosting model, and the class using the features of this technology must be derived from the base class `ServicedComponent`.

Enterprise Services and using COM+ transactional services are covered in Chapter 44, "Enterprise Services."

System.Transactions

The namespace `System.Transactions` has been available since .NET 2.0 and brings a new transaction programming model to .NET applications. Figure 22-3 shows a Visual Studio class diagram with the transaction classes, and their relationships, from the `System.Transactions` namespace: `Transaction`, `CommittableTransaction`, `DependentTransaction`, and `SubordinateTransaction`.

`Transaction` is the base class of all transaction classes and defines properties, methods, and events available with all transaction classes. `CommittableTransaction` is the only transaction class that supports committing. This class has a `Commit()` method; all other transaction classes can do only a rollback. The class `DependentTransaction` is used with transactions that are dependent on another transaction. A dependent transaction can depend on a transaction created from the committable transaction. Then the dependent transaction adds to the outcome of the committable transaction whether or not it is successful.

The class SubordinateTransaction is used in conjunction with the Distributed Transaction Coordinator (DTC). This class represents a transaction that is not a root transaction but can be managed by the DTC.

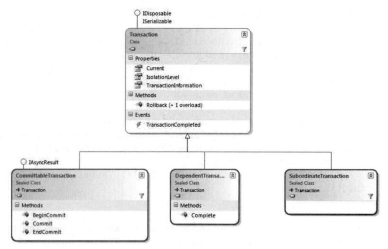

Figure 22-3

The following table describes the properties and methods of the Transaction class.

Transaction Class Members	Description
Current	The property Current is a static property without the need to have an instance. Transaction.Current returns an ambient transaction if one exists. Ambient transactions are discussed later in this chapter.
IsolationLevel	The IsolationLevel property returns an object of type IsolationLevel. IsolationLevel is an enumeration that defines what access other transactions have to the interim results of the transaction. This affects the I of ACID; not all transactions are isolated.
TransactionInformation	The TransactionInformation property returns a TransactionInformation object. TransactionInformation gives you information about the current state of the transaction, the time when the transaction was created, and transaction identifiers.
EnlistVolatile() EnlistDurable() EnlistPromotableSinglePhase()	With the enlist methods EnlistVolatile(), EnlistDurable(), and EnlistPromotableSinglePhase(), you can enlist custom resource managers that participate with the transaction.

Transaction Class Members	Description
Rollback()	With the Rollback() method, you can abort a transaction and undo everything to set all results to the state before the transaction.
DependentClone()	With the DependentClone() method, you can create a transaction that depends on the current transaction.
TransactionCompleted	TransactionCompleted is an event that is fired when the transaction is completed — either successfully or unsuccessfully. With an event handler object of type Transaction CompletedEventHandler, you get access to the Transaction object and can read its status.

For demonstrating the features of System.Transaction, the class Utilities inside a separate assembly offers some static methods. The method AbortTx() returns true or false depending on the input from the user. The method DisplayTransactionInformation() gets a TransactionInformation object as parameter and displays all the information from the transaction: creation time, status, local, and distributed identifiers:

```
public static class Utilities
{
    public static bool AbortTx()
    {
        Console.Write("Abort the Transaction (y/n)?");
        return Console.ReadLine() == "y";
    }

    public static void DisplayTransactionInformation(string title,
            TransactionInformation ti)
    {
        if (ti != null)
        {
            Console.WriteLine(title);

            Console.WriteLine("Creation Time: {0:T}", ti.CreationTime);
            Console.WriteLine("Status: {0}", ti.Status);
            Console.WriteLine("Local ID: {0}", ti.LocalIdentifier);
            Console.WriteLine("Distributed ID: {0}",
                            ti.DistributedIdentifier);
            Console.WriteLine();
        }
    }
}
```

Committable Transactions

The Transaction class cannot be committed programmatically; it does not have a method to commit the transaction. The base class Transaction just supports aborting the transaction. The only transaction class that supports a commit is the class CommittableTransaction.

With ADO.NET, a transaction can be enlisted with the connection. To make this possible, an
AddStudent() method is added to the class StudentData that accepts a System.Transactions.
Transaction object as second parameter. The object tx is enlisted with the connection by calling the
method EnlistTransaction of the SqlConnection class. This way, the ADO.NET connection is
associated with the transaction.

```
public void AddStudent(Student student, Transaction tx)
{
    SqlConnection connection = new SqlConnection(
            Properties.Settings.Default.CourseManagementConnectionString);
    connection.Open();
    try
    {
        if (tx != null)
            connection.EnlistTransaction(tx);
        SqlCommand command = connection.CreateCommand();

        command.CommandText = "INSERT INTO Students (FirstName, " +
                "LastName, Company)" +
                "VALUES (@FirstName, @LastName, @Company)";
        command.Parameters.AddWithValue("@FirstName", student.FirstName);
        command.Parameters.AddWithValue("@LastName", student.LastName);
        command.Parameters.AddWithValue("@Company", student.Company);

        command.ExecuteNonQuery();
    }
    finally
    {
        connection.Close();
    }
}
```

In the Main() method of the console application CommittableTransaction, first a transaction of type
CommittableTransaction is created, and information is shown on the console. Then a Student object
is created, and this object is written to the database from the AddStudent() method. If you verify the
record in the database from outside of the transaction, you cannot see the student added until the
transaction is completed. In case the transaction fails, there is a rollback, and the student is not written
to the database.

After the AddStudent() method is invoked, the helper method Utilities.AbortTx() is called to ask
if the transaction should be aborted. If the user aborts, an exception of type ApplicationException is
thrown and, in the catch block, a rollback with the transaction is done by calling the method
Rollback() of the Transaction class. The record is not written to the database. If the user does not
abort, the Commit() method commits the transaction, and the final state of the transaction is committed.

```
static void Main()
{
    CommittableTransaction tx = new CommittableTransaction();
    Utilities.DisplayTransactionInformation("TX created",
            tx.TransactionInformation);

    try
    {
        Student s1 = new Student();
```

```
            s1.FirstName = "Neno";
            s1.LastName = "Loye";
            s1.Company = "thinktecture";
            StudentData db = new StudentData();
            db.AddStudent(s1, tx);

            if (Utilities.AbortTx())
            {
                throw new ApplicationException("transaction abort");
            }

            tx.Commit();
        }
        catch (Exception ex)
        {
            Console.WriteLine(ex.Message);
            Console.WriteLine();
            tx.Rollback();
        }

        Utilities.DisplayTransactionInformation("TX completed",
            tx.TransactionInformation);

    }
```

Here, you can see the output of the application where the transaction is active and has a local identifier. The output of the application that follows shows the result with the user choice to abort the transaction. After the transaction is finished, you can see the aborted state.

```
TX created
Creation Time: 7:30:49 PM
Status: Active
Local ID: bdcf1cdc-a67e-4ccc-9a5c-cbdfe0fe9177:1
Distributed ID: 00000000-0000-0000-0000-000000000000

Abort the Transaction (y/n)? y
Transaction abort

TX completed
Creation Time: 7:30:49 PM
Status: Aborted
Local ID: bdcf1cdc-a67e-4ccc-9a5c-cbdfe0fe9177:1
Distributed ID: 00000000-0000-0000-0000-000000000000
Press any key to continue ...
```

With the second output of the application that you can see here, the transaction is not aborted by the user. The transaction has the status committed, and the data is written to the database.

```
TX Created
Creation Time: 7:33:04 PM
Status: Active
Local ID: 708bda71-fa24-46a9-86b4-18b83120f6af:1
```

(continued)

(continued)

```
Distributed ID: 00000000-0000-0000-0000-000000000000

Abort the Transaction (y/n)? n

TX completed
Creation Time: 7:33:04 PM
Status: Committed
Local ID: 708bda71-fa24-46a9-86b4-18b83120f6af:1
Distributed ID: 00000000-0000-0000-0000-000000000000

Press any key to continue ...
```

Transaction Promotion

`System.Transactions` supports promotable transactions. Depending on the resources that participate with the transaction, either a local or a distributed transaction is created. SQL Server 2005 and 2008 support promotable transactions. So far you have seen only local transactions. With the samples until now, the distributed transaction ID was always set to 0, and only the local ID was assigned. With a resource that does not support promotable transactions, a distributed transaction is created. If multiple resources are added to the transaction, the transaction may start with a local transaction and promote to a distributed transaction as required. Such a promotion happens when multiple SQL Server database connections are added to the transaction. The transaction starts as a local transaction and then is promoted to a distributed transaction.

The console application is now changed in that a second student is added by using the same transaction object `tx`. Because every `AddStudent()` method opens a new connection, two connections are associated with the transaction after the second student is added.

```
static void Main()
{
    CommittableTransaction tx = new CommittableTransaction();
    Utilities.DisplayTransactionInformation("TX created",
        tx.TransactionInformation);

    try
    {
        Student s1 = new Student();
        s1.FirstName = "Neno";
        s1.LastName = "Loye";
        s1.Company = "thinktecture";
        StudentData db = new StudentData();
        db.AddStudent(s1, tx);

        Student s2 = new Student();
        s2.FirstName = "Dominick";
        s2.LastName = "Baier";
        s2.Company = "thinktecture";
        db.AddStudent(s2, tx);

        Utilities.DisplayTransactionInformation("2nd connection enlisted",
            tx.TransactionInformation);

        if (Utilities.AbortTx())
```

```
        {
            throw new ApplicationException("transaction abort");
        }

        tx.Commit();
    }
    catch (Exception ex)
    {
        Console.WriteLine(ex.Message);
        Console.WriteLine();
        tx.Rollback();
    }

    Utilities.DisplayTransactionInformation("TX finished",
            tx.TransactionInformation);


}
```

Running the application now, you can see that with the first student added the distributed identifier is 0, but with the second student added the transaction was promoted, so a distributed identifier is associated with the transaction.

```
TX created
Creation Time: 7:56:24 PM
Status: Active
Local ID: 0d2f5ada-32aa-40eb-b9d7-cc6aa9a2a554:1
Distributed ID: 00000000-0000-0000-0000-0000000000

2nd connection enlisted
Creation Time: 7:56:24 PM
Status: Active
Local ID: 0d2f5ada-32aa-40eb-b9d7-cc6aa9a2a554:1
Distributed ID: 70762617-2ee8-4d23-aa87-6ac8c1418bdfd

Abort the Transaction (y/n)?
```

Transaction promotion requires the Distributed Transaction Coordinator (DTC) to be started. If promoting transactions fails with your system, verify that the DTC service is started. Starting the Component Services MMC snap-in, you can see the actual status of all DTC transactions running on your system. By selecting Transaction List on the tree view, you can see all active transactions. In Figure 22-4, you can see that there is a transaction active with the same distributed identifier as was shown with the console output earlier. If you verify the output on your system, make sure that the transaction has a timeout and aborts in case the timeout is reached. After the timeout, you cannot see the transaction in the transaction list anymore. You can also verify the transaction statistics with the same tool. Transaction Statistics shows the number of committed and aborted transactions.

Figure 22-4

You can start the Component Services MMC snap-in by starting the Microsoft Management Console (mmc.exe) application, selecting the menu File ⇨ Add/Remove Snap-In, and selecting Component Services from the list of snap-ins.

Dependent Transactions

With dependent transactions, you can influence one transaction from multiple threads. A dependent transaction depends on another transaction and influences the outcome of the transaction.

The sample application DependentTransactions creates a dependent transaction for a new thread. The method TxThread() is the method of the new thread where a DependentTransaction object is passed as a parameter. Information about the dependent transaction is shown with the helper method DisplayTransactionInformation(). Before the thread exits, the Complete() method of the dependent transaction is invoked to define the outcome of the transaction. A dependent transaction can define the outcome of the transaction by calling either the Complete() or Rollback() method. The Complete() method sets the success bit. If the root transaction finishes, and if all dependent transactions have set the success bit to true, the transaction commits. If any of the dependent transactions set the abort bit by invoking the Rollback() method, the complete transaction aborts.

```
static void TxThread(object obj)
{
    DependentTransaction tx = obj as DependentTransaction;
    Utilities.DisplayTransactionInformation("Dependent Transaction",
        tx.TransactionInformation);

    Thread.Sleep(3000);

    tx.Complete();

    Utilities.DisplayTransactionInformation("Dependent TX Complete",
        tx.TransactionInformation);
}
```

With the Main() method, first a root transaction is created by instantiating the class CommittableTransaction, and the transaction information is shown. Next, the method tx.DependentClone() creates a dependent transaction. This dependent transaction is passed to the method TxThread() that is defined as the entry point of a new thread.

The method DependentClone() requires an argument of type DependentCloneOption, which is an enumeration with the values BlockCommitUntilComplete and RollbackIfNotComplete. This option is important if the root transaction completes before the dependent transaction. Setting the option to RollbackIfNotComplete, the transaction aborts if the dependent transaction didn't invoke the Complete() method before the Commit() method of the root transaction. Setting the option to BlockCommitUntilComplete, the method Commit() waits until the outcome is defined by all dependent transactions.

Next, the Commit() method of the CommittableTransaction class is invoked if the user does not abort the transaction.

Chapter 19, "Threading and Synchronization," covers threading.

```
static void Main()
{
    CommittableTransaction tx = new CommittableTransaction();
    Utilities.DisplayTransactionInformation("Root TX created",
        tx.TransactionInformation);
```

```
try
{
    new Thread(TxThread).Start(
            tx.DependentClone(
            DependentCloneOption.BlockCommitUntilComplete));

    if (Utilities.AbortTx())
    {
        throw new ApplicationException("transaction abort");
    }

    tx.Commit();
}
catch (Exception ex)
{
    Console.WriteLine(ex.Message);
    tx.Rollback();
}

Utilities.DisplayTransactionInformation("TX finished",
        tx.TransactionInformation);
}
```

With the output of the application, you can see the root transaction with its identifier. Because of the option `DependentCloneOption.BlockCommitUntilComplete`, the root transaction waits in the `Commit()` method until the outcome of the dependent transaction is defined. As soon as the dependent transaction is finished, the transaction is committed.

```
Root TX created
Creation Time: 8:35:25 PM
Status: Active
Local ID: 50126e07-cd28-4e0f-a21f-a81a8e14a1a8:1
Distributed ID: 00000000-0000-0000-0000-0000000000

Abort the Transaction (y/n)? n

Dependent Transaction
Creation Time: 8:35:25 PM
Status: Active
Local ID: 50126e07-cd28-4e0f-a21f-a81a8e14a1a8:1
Distributed ID: 00000000-0000-0000-0000-0000000000

Dependent TX Complete
Root TX finished
Creation Time: 8:35:25 PM
Status: Committed
Local ID: 50126e07-cd28-4e0f-a21f-a81a8e14a1a8:1
Distributed ID: 00000000-0000-0000-0000-0000000000

Creation Time: 8:35:25 PM
Status: Committed
Local ID: 50126e07-cd28-4e0f-a21f-a81a8e14a1a8:1
Distributed ID: 00000000-0000-0000-0000-0000000000

Press any key to continue ...
```

Ambient Transactions

The really big advantage of System.Transactions is the ambient transactions feature. With ambient transactions, there is no need to manually enlist a connection with a transaction; this is done automatically from the resources supporting ambient transactions.

An ambient transaction is associated with the current thread. You can get and set the ambient transaction with the static property Transaction.Current. APIs supporting ambient transactions check this property to get an ambient transaction, and enlist with the transaction. ADO.NET connections support ambient transactions.

You can create a CommittableTransaction object and assign it to the property Transaction.Current to initialize the ambient transaction. Another way to create ambient transactions is with the TransactionScope class. The constructor of the TransactionScope creates an ambient transaction. Because of the implemented interface IDisposable, you can use a transaction scope easily with the using statement.

The members of TransactionScope are listed in the following table.

TransactionScope Members	Description
Constructor	With the constructor of TransactionScope, you can define the transactional requirements. You can also pass an existing transaction and define the transaction timeout.
Complete()	Invoking the Complete() method, you set the success bit of the transaction scope.
Dispose()	The Dispose() method completes the scope and commits or aborts the transaction if the scope is associated with the root transaction. If the success bit is set with all dependent transactions, the Dispose() method commits; otherwise, a rollback is done.

Because the TransactionScope class implements the IDisposable interface, you can define the scope with the using statement. The default constructor creates a new transaction. Immediately after creating the TransactionScope instance, the transaction is accessed with the get accessor of the property Transaction.Current to display the transaction information on the console.

To get the information when the transaction is completed, the method OnTransactionCompleted() is set to the TransactionCompleted event of the ambient transaction.

Then a new Student object is created and written to the database by calling the StudentData.AddStudent() method. With ambient transactions, it is no longer necessary to pass a Transaction object to this method because the SqlConnection class supports ambient transactions and automatically enlists it with the connection. Then the Complete() method of the TransactionScope class sets the success bit. With the end of the using statement, the TransactionScope is disposed, and a commit is done. If the Complete() method is not invoked, the Dispose() method aborts the transaction.

If an ADO.NET connection should not enlist with an ambient transaction, you can set the value Enlist=false with the connection string.

```
static void Main()
{
    using (TransactionScope scope = new TransactionScope())
    {
        Transaction.Current.TransactionCompleted +=
            OnTransactionCompleted;

        Utilities.DisplayTransactionInformation("Ambient TX created",
            Transaction.Current.TransactionInformation);

        Student s1 = new Student();
        s1.FirstName = "Ingo";
        s1.LastName = "Rammer";
        s1.Company = "thinktecture";
        StudentData db = new StudentData();
        db.AddStudent(s1);

        if (!Utilities.AbortTx())
            scope.Complete();
        else
            Console.WriteLine("transaction will be aborted");

    } // scope.Dispose()
}

static void OnTransactionCompleted(object sender,
                                    TransactionEventArgs e)
{
    Utilities.DisplayTransactionInformation("TX completed",
        e.Transaction.TransactionInformation);
}
```

Running the application, you can see an active ambient transaction after an instance of the TransactionScope class is created. The last output of the application is the output from the TransactionCompleted event handler to display the finished transaction state.

```
Ambient TX created
Creation Time: 9:55:40 PM
Status: Active
Local ID: a06df6fb-7266-435e-b90e-f024f1d6966e:1
Distributed ID: 00000000-0000-0000-0000-0000000000

Abort the Transaction (y/n)? n

TX completed
Creation Time: 9:55:40 PM
Status: Committed
Local ID: a06df6fb-7266-435e-b90e-f024f1d6966e:1
Distributed ID: 00000000-0000-0000-0000-0000000000

Press any key to continue ...
```

Nested Scopes with Ambient Transactions

With the TransactionScope class you can also nest scopes. The nested scope can be directly inside the scope or within a method that is invoked from a scope. A nested scope can use the same transaction as the outer scope, suppress the transaction, or create a new transaction that is independent from the outer scope. The requirement for the scope is defined with a `TransactionScopeOption` enumeration that is passed to the constructor of the `TransactionScope` class.

The values available with the `TransactionScopeOption` enumeration and their functionality are described in the following table.

TransactionScopeOption Member	Description
Required	Required defines that the scope requires a transaction. If the outer scope already contains an ambient transaction, the inner scope uses the existing transaction. If an ambient transaction does not exist, a new transaction is created. If both scopes share the same transaction, every scope influences the outcome of the transaction. Only if all scopes set the success bit can the transaction commit. If one scope does not invoke the `Complete()` method before the root scope is disposed of, the transaction is aborted.
RequiresNew	RequiresNew always creates a new transaction. If the outer scope already defines a transaction, the transaction from the inner scope is completely independent. Both transactions can commit or abort independently.
Suppress	With Suppress, the scope does not contain an ambient transaction, whether or not the outer scope contains a transaction.

The next sample defines two scopes, in which the inner scope is configured to require a new transaction with the option `TransactionScopeOption.RequiresNew`:

```
using (TransactionScope scope = new TransactionScope())
{
    Transaction.Current.TransactionCompleted +=
        OnTransactionCompleted;

    Utilities.DisplayTransactionInformation("Ambient TX created",
        Transaction.Current.TransactionInformation);

    using (TransactionScope scope2 =
        new TransactionScope(TransactionScopeOption.RequiresNew))
    {
        Transaction.Current.TransactionCompleted +=
            OnTransactionCompleted;

        Utilities.DisplayTransactionInformation(
            "Inner Transaction Scope",
            Transaction.Current.TransactionInformation);

        scope2.Complete();
    }
    scope.Complete();
}
```

Running the application, you can see that both scopes have different transaction identifiers, although the same thread is used. Having one thread with different ambient transactions because of different scopes, the transaction identifier differs in the last number following the GUID.

A GUID is a globally unique identifier consisting of a 128-bit unique value.

```
Ambient TX created
Creation Time: 11:01:09 PM
Status: Active
Local ID: 54ac1276-5c2d-4159-84ab-36b0217c9c84:1
Distributed ID: 00000000-0000-0000-0000-0000000000

Inner Transaction Scope
Creation Time: 11:01:09 PM
Status: Active
Local ID: 54ac1276-5c2d-4159-84ab-36b0217c9c84:2
Distributed ID: 00000000-0000-0000-0000-0000000000

TX completed
Creation Time: 11:01:09 PM
Status: Committed
Local ID: 54ac1276-5c2d-4159-84ab-36b0217c9c84:2
Distributed ID: 00000000-0000-0000-0000-0000000000

TX completed
Creation Time: 11:01:09 PM
Status: Committed
Local ID: 54ac1276-5c2d-4159-84ab-36b0217c9c84:1
Distributed ID: 00000000-0000-0000-0000-0000000000
```

If you change the inner scope to the setting `TransactionScopeOption.Required`, you will find that both scopes are using the same transaction, and both scopes influence the outcome of the transaction.

Multithreading with Ambient Transactions

If multiple threads should use the same ambient transaction, you need to do some extra work. An ambient transaction is bound to a thread, so if a new thread is created, it does not have the ambient transaction from the starter thread.

This behavior is demonstrated in the next example. In the `Main()` method, a `TransactionScope` is created. Within this transaction scope, a new thread is started. The main method of the new thread `ThreadMethod()` creates a new transaction scope. With the creation of the scope, no parameters are passed, and therefore, the default option `TransactionScopeOption.Required` gets into play. If an ambient transaction exists, the existing transaction is used. If there is no ambient transaction, a new transaction is created.

```
using System;
using System.Threading;
using System.Transactions;

namespace Wrox.ProCSharp.Transactions
{
    class Program
    {
        static void Main()
```

(continued)

(continued)

```
        {
            try
            {
                using (TransactionScope scope = new TransactionScope())
                {
                    Transaction.Current.TransactionCompleted +=
                        TransactionCompleted;

                    Utilities.DisplayTransactionInformation("Main thread TX",
                        Transaction.Current.TransactionInformation);

                    new Thread(ThreadMethod).Start(null);

                    scope.Complete();
                }
            }
            catch (TransactionAbortedException ex)
            {
                Console.WriteLine("Main - Transaction was aborted, {0}",
                            ex.Message);
            }
        }

        static void TransactionCompleted(object sender, TransactionEventArgs e)
        {
            Utilities.DisplayTransactionInformation("TX completed",
                e.Transaction.TransactionInformation);
        }

        static void ThreadMethod(object dependentTx)
        {
            try
            {
                using (TransactionScope scope = new TransactionScope())
                {
                    Transaction.Current.TransactionCompleted +=
                        Current_TransactionCompleted;

                    Utilities.DisplayTransactionInformation("Thread TX",
                        Transaction.Current.TransactionInformation);
                    scope.Complete();
                }
            }
            catch (TransactionAbortedException ex)
            {
                Console.WriteLine("ThreadMethod - Transaction was aborted, {0}",
                    ex.Message);
            }
        }
    }
}
```

As you start the application, you can see that the transactions from the two threads are completely independent. The transaction from the new thread has a different transaction ID. The transaction ID differs by the last number after the GUID in the same way as you have seen with nested scopes when the nested scope required a new transaction.

```
Main thread TX
Creation Time: 21:41:25
Status: Active
Local ID: f1e736ae-84ab-4540-b71e-3de272ffc476:1
Distributed ID: 00000000-0000-0000-0000-000000000000

TX completed
Creation Time: 21:41:25
Status: Committed
Local ID: f1e736ae-84ab-4540-b71e-3de272ffc476:1
Distributed ID: 00000000-0000-0000-0000-000000000000

Thread TX
Creation Time: 21:41:25
Status: Active
Local ID: f1e736ae-84ab-4540-b71e-3de272ffc476:2
Distributed ID: 00000000-0000-0000-0000-000000000000

TX completed
Creation Time: 21:41:25
Status: Committed
Local ID: f1e736ae-84ab-4540-b71e-3de272ffc476:2
Distributed ID: 00000000-0000-0000-0000-000000000000
```

To use the same ambient transaction in another thread, you need the help of dependent transactions. Now the sample is changed to pass a dependent transaction to the new thread. The dependent transaction is created from the ambient transaction by calling the `DependentClone()` method on the ambient transaction. With this method, the setting `DependentCloneOption.BlockCommitUntilComplete` is set so that the calling thread waits until the new thread is completed before committing the transaction.

```
class Program
{
    static void Main()
    {
        try
        {
            using (TransactionScope scope = new TransactionScope())
            {
                Transaction.Current.TransactionCompleted +=
                    TransactionCompleted;

                Utilities.DisplayTransactionInformation("Main thread TX",
                    Transaction.Current.TransactionInformation);

                new Thread(ThreadMethod).Start(
                    Transaction.Current.DependentClone(
                    DependentCloneOption.BlockCommitUntilComplete));

                scope.Complete();
            }
```

(continued)

(continued)

```
        }
        catch (TransactionAbortedException ex)
        {
            Console.WriteLine("Main - Transaction was aborted, {0}",
                            ex.Message);
        }
    }
```

In the method of the thread, the dependent transaction that is passed is assigned to the ambient transaction by using the set accessor of the `Transaction.Current` property. Now the transaction scope is using the same transaction by using the dependent transaction. When you are finished using the dependent transaction, you need to invoke the `Complete()` method of the `DependentTransaction` object.

```
    static void ThreadMethod(object dependentTx)
    {
        DependentTransaction dTx = dependentTx as DependentTransaction;

        try
        {
            Transaction.Current = dTx;

            using (TransactionScope scope = new TransactionScope())
            {
                Transaction.Current.TransactionCompleted +=
                    Current_TransactionCompleted;

                Utilities.DisplayTransactionInformation("Thread TX",
                    Transaction.Current.TransactionInformation);
                scope.Complete();
            }
        }
        catch (TransactionAbortedException ex)
        {
            Console.WriteLine("ThreadMethod - Transaction was aborted, {0}",
                ex.Message);
        }
        finally
        {
            if (dTx != null)
            {
                dTx.Complete();
            }
        }
    }
}
```

Running the application now, you can see that the main thread and the newly created thread are using, and influencing, the same transaction. The transaction listed by the threads has the same identifier. If with one thread the success bit is not set by calling the `Complete()` method, the complete transaction aborts.

```
Main thread TX
Creation Time: 23:00:57
Status: Active
Local ID: 2fb1b54d-61f5-4d4e-a55e-f4a9e04778be:1
Distributed ID: 00000000-0000-0000-0000-000000000000

Thread TX
Creation Time: 23:00:57
Status: Active
Local ID: 2fb1b54d-61f5-4d4e-a55e-f4a9e04778be:1
Distributed ID: 00000000-0000-0000-0000-000000000000

TX completed
Creation Time: 23:00:57
Status: Committed
Local ID: 2fb1b54d-61f5-4d4e-a55e-f4a9e04778be:1
Distributed ID: 00000000-0000-0000-0000-000000000000

TX completed
Creation Time: 23:00:57
Status: Committed
Local ID: 2fb1b54d-61f5-4d4e-a55e-f4a9e04778be:1
Distributed ID: 00000000-0000-0000-0000-000000000000
```

Isolation Level

At the beginning of this chapter, you saw the ACID properties used to describe transactions. The letter *I* (Isolation) of *ACID* is not always fully required. For performance reasons, you might reduce isolation requirements, but you must be aware of the issues that you will encounter if you change the isolation level.

The problems that you can encounter if you don't completely isolate the scope outside the transaction can be divided into three categories:

❑ **Dirty reads** — With a *dirty read*, another transaction can read records that are changed within the transaction. Because the data that is changed within the transaction might roll back to its original state, reading this intermediate state from another transaction is considered "dirty" — the data has not been committed. You can avoid this by locking the records to be changed.

❑ **Nonrepeatable reads** — *Nonrepeatable reads* occur when data is read inside a transaction, and while the transaction is running, another transaction changes the same records. If the record is read once more inside the transaction, the result is different — nonrepeatable. You can avoid this by locking the read records.

❑ **Phantom reads** — *Phantom reads* happen when a range of data is read, for example, with a WHERE clause. Another transaction can add a new record that belongs to the range that is read within the transaction. A new read with the same WHERE clause returns a different number of rows. Phantom reads can be a specific problem when doing an UPDATE of a range of rows. For example, UPDATE Addresses SET Zip=4711 WHERE (Zip=2315) updates the ZIP code of all records from 2315 to 4711. After doing the update, there may still be records with a ZIP code of 2315 if another user added a new record with ZIP 2315 while the update was running. You can avoid this by doing a range lock.

When defining the isolation requirements, you can set the isolation level. This is set with an `IsolationLevel` enumeration that is configured when the transaction is created (either with the constructor of the `CommittableTransaction` class or with the constructor of the `TransactionScope` class). The `IsolationLevel` defines the locking behavior. The next table lists the values of the `IsolationLevel` enumeration.

Isolation Level	Description
ReadUncommitted	With `ReadUncommitted`, transactions are not isolated from each other. With this level, there is no wait for locked records from other transactions. This way, uncommitted data can be read from other transactions — dirty reads. This level is usually used just for reading records where it does not matter if you read interim changes (for example, reports).
ReadCommitted	`ReadCommitted` waits for records with a write-lock from other transactions. This way, a dirty read cannot happen. This level sets a read-lock for the current record read and a write-lock for the records being written until the transaction is completed. Reading a sequence of records, with every new record that is read, the prior record is unlocked. That's why nonrepeatable reads can happen.
RepeatableRead	`RepeatableRead` holds the lock for the records read until the transaction is completed. This way, the problem of nonrepeatable reads is avoided. Phantom reads can still occur.
Serializable	`Serializable` holds a range lock. While the transaction is running, it is not possible to add a new record that belongs to the same range from which the data is being read.
Snapshot	The isolation level `Snapshot` is possible only with SQL Server 2005 and later versions. This level reduces the locks as modified rows are copied. This way, other transactions can still read the old data without the need to wait for an unlock.
Unspecified	The level `Unspecified` indicates that the provider is using an isolation level value that is different from the values defined by the `IsolationLevel` enumeration.
Chaos	The level `Chaos` is similar to `ReadUncommitted`, but in addition to performing the actions of the `ReadUncommitted` value, `Chaos` does not lock updated records.

The next table gives you a summary of the problems that can occur as a result of setting the most commonly used transaction isolation levels.

Isolation Level	Dirty Reads	Nonrepeatable Reads	Phantom Reads
Read Uncommitted	Y	Y	Y
Read Committed	N	Y	Y
Repeatable Read	N	N	Y
Serializable	N	N	N

The following code segment shows how the isolation level can be set with the `TransactionScope` class. With the constructor of `TransactionScope`, you can set the `TransactionScopeOption` that was discussed earlier and the `TransactionOptions`. The `TransactionOptions` class allows you to define the `IsolationLevel` and the `Timeout`.

```
TransactionOptions options = new TransactionOptions();
options.IsolationLevel = IsolationLevel.ReadUncommitted;
options.Timeout = TimeSpan.FromSeconds(90);
using (TransactionScope scope =
       new TransactionScope(TransactionScopeOption.Required,
       options))
{
   // Read data without waiting for locks from other transactions,
   // dirty reads are possible.
}
```

Custom Resource Managers

One of the biggest advantages of the new transaction model is that it is relatively easy to create custom resource managers that participate in the transaction. A resource manager does not manage only durable resources but can also manage volatile or in-memory resources — for example, a simple int and a generic list.

Figure 22-5 shows the relationship between a resource manager and transaction classes. The resource manager implements the interface `IEnlistmentNotification` that defines the methods `Prepare()`, `InDoubt()`, `Commit()`, and `Rollback()`. The resource manager implements this interface to manage transactions for a resource. To be part of a transaction, the resource manager must enlist with the `Transaction` class. Volatile resource managers invoke the method `EnlistVolatile()`; durable resource managers invoke `EnlistDurable()`. Depending on the transaction's outcome, the transaction manager invokes the methods from the interface `IEnlistmentNotification` with the resource manager.

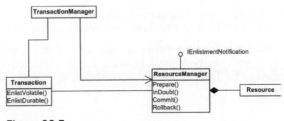

Figure 22-5

The next table explains the methods of the IEnlistmentNotification interface that you must implement with resource managers. As you review the table, recall the active, prepared, and committing phases explained earlier in this chapter.

IEnlistmentNotification Members	Description
Prepare()	The transaction manager invokes the Prepare() method for preparation of the transaction. The resource manager completes the preparation by invoking the Prepared() method of the PreparingEnlistment parameter, which is passed to the Prepare() method. If the work cannot be done successfully, the resource manager informs the transaction manager by invoking the method ForceRollback(). A durable resource manager must write a log so that it can finish the transaction successfully after the prepare phase.
Commit()	When all resource managers have successfully prepared for the transaction, the transaction manager invokes the Commit() method. The resource manager can now complete the work to make it visible outside the transaction and invoke the Done() method of the Enlistment parameter.
Rollback()	If one of the resources could not successfully prepare for the transaction, the transaction manager invokes the Rollback() method with all resource managers. After the state is returned to the state prior to the transaction, the resource manager invokes the Done() method of the Enlistment parameter.
InDoubt()	If there is a problem after the transaction manager invokes the Commit() method (and the resources don't return completion information with the Done() method), the transaction manager invokes the InDoubt() method.

Transactional Resources

A transactional resource must keep the live value and a temporary value. The live value is read from outside the transaction and defines the valid state when the transaction rolls back. The temporary value defines the valid state of the transaction when the transaction commits.

To make non-transactional types transactional, the generic sample class Transactional<T> wraps a non-generic type, so you can use it like this:

```
Transactional<int> txInt = new Transactional<int>();
Transactional<string> txString = new Transactional<string>();
```

Let's look at the implementation of the class Transactional<T>. The live value of the managed resource has the variable liveValue; the temporary value that is associated with a transaction is stored within the ResourceManager<T>. The variable enlistedTransaction is associated with the ambient transaction if there is one.

```
using System.Diagnostics;
using System.Transactions;

namespace Wrox.ProCSharp.Transactions
{

    public partial class Transactional<T>
    {
        private T liveValue;
        private ResourceManager<T> enlistment;
        private Transaction enlistedTransaction;
```

With the `Transactional` constructor, the live value is set to the variable `liveValue`. If the constructor is invoked from within an ambient transaction, the `GetEnlistment()` helper method is invoked. `GetEnlistment()` first checks if there is an ambient transaction and asserts if there is none. If the transaction is not already enlisted, the `ResourceManager<T>` helper class is instantiated, and the resource manager is enlisted with the transaction by invoking the method `EnlistVolatile()`. Also, the variable `enlistedTransaction` is set to the ambient transaction.

If the ambient transaction is different from the enlisted transaction, an exception is thrown. The implementation does not support changing the same value from within two different transactions. If you have this requirement, you can create a lock and wait for the lock to be released from one transaction before changing it within another transaction.

```
        public Transactional(T value)
        {
            if (Transaction.Current == null)
            {
                this.liveValue = value;
            }
            else
            {
                this.liveValue = default(T);
                GetEnlistment().Value = value;
            }
        }

        public Transactional()
                : this(default(T)) {}

        private ResourceManager<T> GetEnlistment()
        {
            Transaction tx = Transaction.Current;
            Trace.Assert(tx != null, "Must be invoked with ambient transaction");

            if (enlistedTransaction == null)
            {
                enlistment = new ResourceManager<T>(this, tx);
                tx.EnlistVolatile(enlistment, EnlistmentOptions.None);
                enlistedTransaction = tx;
                return enlistment;
            }
            else if (enlistedTransaction == Transaction.Current)
```

(continued)

(continued)

```
    {
        return enlistment;
    }
    else
    {
        throw new TransactionException(
                "This class only supports enlisting with one transaction");
    }
}
```

The property `Value` returns the value of the contained class and sets it. However, with transactions, you cannot just set and return the `liveValue` variable. This would be the case only if the object were outside a transaction. To make the code more readable, the property `Value` uses the methods `GetValue()` and `SetValue()` in the implementation:

```
public T Value
{
    get { return GetValue(); }
    set { SetValue(value); }
}
```

The method `GetValue()` checks if an ambient transaction exists. If one doesn't exist, the `liveValue` is returned. If there is an ambient transaction, the `GetEnlistment()` method shown earlier returns the resource manager, and with the `Value` property, the temporary value for the contained object within the transaction is returned.

The method `SetValue()` is very similar to `GetValue()`; the difference is that it changes the live or temporary value.

```
protected virtual T GetValue()
{
    if (Transaction.Current == null)
    {
        return liveValue;
    }
    else
    {
        return GetEnlistment().Value;
    }
}

protected virtual void SetValue(T value)
{
    if (Transaction.Current == null)
    {
        liveValue = value;
    }
    else
    {
        GetEnlistment().Value = value;
    }
}
```

The `Commit()` and `Rollback()` methods that are implemented in the class `Transactional<T>` are invoked from the resource manager. The `Commit()` method sets the live value from the temporary value received with the first argument and nullifies the variable `enlistedTransaction` as the transaction is completed. With the `Rollback()` method, the transaction is completed as well, but here the temporary value is ignored, and the live value is kept in use.

```
internal void Commit(T value, Transaction tx)
{
    liveValue = value;
    enlistedTransaction = null;
}

internal void Rollback(Transaction tx)
{
    enlistedTransaction = null;
}
}
```

Because the resource manager that is used by the class `Transactional<T>` is used only within the `Transactional<T>` class itself, it is implemented as an inner class. With the constructor, the parent variable is set to have an association with the transactional wrapper class. The temporary value used within the transaction is copied from the live value. Remember the isolation requirements with transactions.

```
using System;
using System.Diagnostics;
using System.IO;
using System.Runtime.Serialization.Formatters.Binary;
using System.Transactions;

namespace Wrox.ProCSharp.Transactions
{
    public partial class Transactional<T>
    {
        internal class ResourceManager<T1> : IEnlistmentNotification
        {
            private Transactional<T1> parent;
            private Transaction currentTransaction;

            internal ResourceManager(Transactional<T1> parent, Transaction tx)
            {
                this.parent = parent;
                Value = DeepCopy(parent.liveValue);
                currentTransaction = tx;
            }

            public T1 Value { get; set; }
```

Because the temporary value may change within the transaction, the live value of the wrapper class may not be changed within the transaction. When creating a copy with some classes, it is possible to invoke the `Clone()` method that is defined with the `ICloneable` interface. However, as the `Clone()` method is defined, it allows implementations to create either a shallow or a deep copy. If type `T` contains reference types and implements a shallow copy, changing the temporary value would also change the original value. This would be in conflict with the isolation and consistency features of transactions. Here, a deep copy is required.

To do a deep copy, the method `DeepCopy()` serializes and deserializes the object to and from a stream. Because in C# 3.0 it is not possible to define a constraint to the type `T` indicating that serialization is required, the static constructor of the class `Transactional<T>` checks if the type is serializable by checking the property `IsSerializable` of the `Type` object.

```
        static ResourceManager()
        {
            Type t = typeof(T1);
            Trace.Assert(t.IsSerializable, "Type " + t.Name +
                " is not serializable");
        }

        private T1 DeepCopy(T1 value)
        {
            using (MemoryStream stream = new MemoryStream())
            {
                BinaryFormatter formatter = new BinaryFormatter();
                formatter.Serialize(stream, value);
                stream.Flush();
                stream.Seek(0, SeekOrigin.Begin);

                return (T1)formatter.Deserialize(stream);
            }
        }
```

The interface `IEnlistmentNotification` is implemented by the class `ResourceManager<T>`. This is the requirement for enlisting with transactions.

The implementation of the `Prepare()` method just answers by invoking `Prepared()` with `preparingEnlistment`. There should not be a problem assigning the temporary value to the live value, so the `Prepare()` method succeeds. With the implementation of the `Commit()` method, the `Commit()` method of the parent is invoked, where the variable `liveValue` is set to the value of the `ResourceManager` that is used within the transaction. The `Rollback()` method just completes the work and leaves the live value where it was. With a volatile resource, there is not a lot you can do in the `InDoubt()` method. Writing a log entry could be useful.

```
        public void Prepare(PreparingEnlistment preparingEnlistment)
        {
            preparingEnlistment.Prepared();
        }

        public void Commit(Enlistment enlistment)
        {
            parent.Commit(Value, currentTransaction);
            enlistment.Done();
        }

        public void Rollback(Enlistment enlistment)
        {
            parent.Rollback(currentTransaction);
            enlistment.Done();
        }

        public void InDoubt(Enlistment enlistment)
        {
            enlistment.Done();
        }
    }
}
```

The class `Transactional<T>` can now be used to make non-transactional classes transactional — for example, `int` and `string` but also more complex classes such as `Student` — as long as the type is serializable:

```csharp
using System;
using System.Transactions;

namespace Wrox.ProCSharp.Transactions
{
    class Program
    {
        static void Main()
        {
            Transactional<int> intVal = new Transactional<int>(1);
            Transactional<Student> student1 = new Transactional<Student>(
                new Student());
            student1.Value.FirstName = "Andrew";
            student1.Value.LastName = "Wilson";

            Console.WriteLine("before the transaction, value: {0}",
                intVal.Value);
            Console.WriteLine("before the transaction, student: {0}",
                student1.Value);

            using (TransactionScope scope = new TransactionScope())
            {
                intVal.Value = 2;
                Console.WriteLine("inside transaction, value: {0}", intVal.Value);

                student1.Value.FirstName = "Ten";
                student1.Value.LastName = "Sixty-Nine";

                if (!Utilities.AbortTx())
                    scope.Complete();
            }
            Console.WriteLine("outside of transaction, value: {0}",
                intVal.Value);
            Console.WriteLine("outside of transaction, student: {0}",
                student1.Value);
        }
    }
}
```

The following console output shows a run of the application with a committed transaction:

```
before the transaction, value: 1
before the transaction: student: Andrew Wilson
inside transaction, value: 2

Abort the Transaction (y/n)? n

outside of transaction, value: 2
outside of transaction, student: Ten Sixty-Nine

Press any key to continue . . .
```

Transactions with Windows Vista and Windows Server 2008

You can write a custom durable resource manager that works with the `File` and `Registry` classes. A file-based durable resource manager can copy the original file and write changes to the temporary file inside a temporary directory to make the changes persistent. When committing the transaction, the original file is replaced by the temporary file. Writing custom durable resource managers for files and the registry is no longer necessary with Windows Vista and Windows Server 2008. With these operating systems, native transactions with the file system and with the registry are supported. For this, there are new API calls such as `CreateFileTransacted()`, `CreateHardLinkTransacted()`, `CreateSymbolicLinkTransacted()`, `CopyFileTransacted()`, and so on. What these API calls have in common is that they require a handle to a transaction passed as an argument; they do not support ambient transactions. The transactional API calls are not available from .NET 3.5, but you can create a custom wrapper by using `Platform Invoke`.

`Platform Invoke` *is discussed in more detail in Chapter 24, "Interoperability."*

The sample application wraps the native method `CreateFileTransacted()` for creating transactional file streams from .NET applications.

When invoking native methods, the parameters of the native methods must be mapped to .NET data types. Because of security issues, .NET 2.0 introduced the class `SafeHandle` to map a native `HANDLE` type. `SafeHandle` is an abstract type that wraps operating system handles and supports critical finalization of handle resources. Depending on the allowed values of a handle, the derived classes `SafeHandleMinusOneIsInvalid` and `SafeHandleZeroOrMinusOneIsInvalid` can be used to wrap native handles. `SafeFileHandle` itself derives from `SafeHandleZeroOrMinusOneIsInvalid`. To map a handle to a transaction, the class `SafeTransactionHandle` is defined.

```
using System;
using System.Runtime.Versioning;
using System.Security.Permissions;
using Microsoft.Win32.SafeHandles;

namespace Wrox.ProCSharp.Transactions
{
    [SecurityPermission(SecurityAction.LinkDemand, UnmanagedCode = true)]
    public sealed class SafeTransactionHandle :
            SafeHandleZeroOrMinusOneIsInvalid
    {
        private SafeTransactionHandle()
            : base(true) { }

        public SafeTransactionHandle(IntPtr preexistingHandle, bool ownsHandle)
            : base(ownsHandle)
        {
            SetHandle(preexistingHandle);
        }

        [ResourceExposure(ResourceScope.Machine)]
        [ResourceConsumption(ResourceScope.Machine)]
        protected override bool ReleaseHandle()
        {
            return NativeMethods.CloseHandle(handle);
        }
    }
}
```

All native methods used from .NET are defined with the class NativeMethods shown here. With the sample, the native APIs needed are CreateFileTransacted() and CloseHandle(), which are defined as static members of the class. The methods are declared extern because there is no C# implementation. Instead, the implementation is found in the native DLL as defined by the attribute DllImport. Both of these methods can be found in the native DLL Kernel32.dll. With the method declaration, the parameters defined with the Windows API call are mapped to .NET data types. The parameter txHandle represents a handle to a transaction and is of the previously defined type SafeTransactionHandle.

```csharp
using System;
using System.Runtime.ConstrainedExecution;
using System.Runtime.InteropServices;
using System.Runtime.Versioning;
using Microsoft.Win32.SafeHandles;

namespace Wrox.ProCSharp.Transactions
{
    internal static class NativeMethods
    {
        [DllImport("Kernel32.dll",
                   CallingConvention = CallingConvention.StdCall,
                   CharSet = CharSet.Unicode)]
        internal static extern SafeFileHandle CreateFileTransacted(
            String lpFileName,
            uint dwDesiredAccess,
            uint dwShareMode,
            IntPtr lpSecurityAttributes,
            uint dwCreationDisposition,
            int dwFlagsAndAttributes,
            IntPtr hTemplateFile,
            SafeTransactionHandle txHandle,
            IntPtr miniVersion,
            IntPtr extendedParameter);

        [DllImport("Kernel32.dll", SetLastError = true)]
        [ResourceExposure(ResourceScope.Machine)]
        [ReliabilityContract(Consistency.WillNotCorruptState, Cer.Success)]
        [return: MarshalAs(UnmanagedType.Bool)]
        internal static extern bool CloseHandle(IntPtr handle);

    }
}
```

The interface IKernelTransaction is used to get a transaction handle and pass it to the transacted Windows API calls. This is a COM interface and must be wrapped to .NET by using COM Interop attributes as shown. The attribute GUID must have exactly the identifier as it is used here with the interface definition, because this is the identifier used with the definition of the COM interface.

```csharp
using System;
using System.Runtime.InteropServices;

namespace Wrox.ProCSharp.Transactions
{
    [ComImport]
    [Guid("79427A2B-F895-40e0-BE79-B57DC82ED231")]
    [InterfaceType(ComInterfaceType.InterfaceIsIUnknown)]
    public interface IKernelTransaction
```

(continued)

(continued)

```
    {
        void GetHandle(out SafeTransactionHandle ktmHandle);
    }
}
```

Finally, the class `TransactedFile` is the class that will be used by .NET applications. This class defines the method `GetTransactedFileStream()` that requires a file name as parameter and returns a `System.IO.FileStream`. The returned stream is a normal .NET stream; it just references a transacted file.

With the implementation, `TransactionInterop.GetDtcTransaction()` creates an interface pointer of the `IKernelTransaction` to the ambient transaction that is passed as an argument to `GetDtcTransaction()`. Using the interface `IKernelTransaction`, the handle of type `SafeTransactionHandle` is created. This handle is then passed to the wrapped API call `NativeMethods.CreateFileTransacted()`. With the returned file handle, a new `FileStream` instance is created and returned to the caller.

```csharp
using System;
using System.IO;
using System.Transactions;
using Microsoft.Win32.SafeHandles;
using System.Runtime.InteropServices;

namespace Wrox.ProCSharp.Transactions
{
    public static class TransactedFile
    {
        internal const short FILE_ATTRIBUTE_NORMAL = 0x80;
        internal const short INVALID_HANDLE_VALUE = -1;
        internal const uint GENERIC_READ = 0x80000000;
        internal const uint GENERIC_WRITE = 0x40000000;
        internal const uint CREATE_NEW = 1;
        internal const uint CREATE_ALWAYS = 2;
        internal const uint OPEN_EXISTING = 3;

        [FileIOPermission(SecurityAction.Demand, Unrestricted=true)]
        public static FileStream GetTransactedFileStream(string fileName)
        {
            IKernelTransaction ktx = (IKernelTransaction)
                TransactionInterop.GetDtcTransaction(Transaction.Current);

            SafeTransactionHandle txHandle;
            ktx.GetHandle(out txHandle);

            SafeFileHandle fileHandle = NativeMethods.CreateFileTransacted(
                fileName, GENERIC_WRITE, 0,
                IntPtr.Zero, CREATE_ALWAYS, FILE_ATTRIBUTE_NORMAL,
                null,
                txHandle, IntPtr.Zero, IntPtr.Zero);

            return new FileStream(fileHandle, FileAccess.Write);
        }
    }
}
```

Now it is very easy to use the transactional API from .NET code. You can create an ambient transaction with the `TransactionScope` class and use the `TransactedFile` class within the context of the ambient transaction scope. If the transaction is aborted, the file is not written. If the transaction is committed, you can find the file in the temp directory.

```
using System;
using System.IO;
using System.Transactions;

namespace Wrox.ProCSharp.Transactions
{
    class Program
    {
        static void Main()
        {
            using (TransactionScope scope = new TransactionScope())
            {
                FileStream stream =
                    TransactedFile.GetTransactedFileStream(
                    "c:/temp/sample.txt");

                StreamWriter writer = new StreamWriter(stream);
                writer.WriteLine("Write a transactional file");
                writer.Close();

                if (!Utilities.AbortTx())
                    scope.Complete();
            }
        }
    }
}
```

Now you can use databases, volatile resources, and files within the same transaction.

Summary

In this chapter, you learned the attributes of transactions and how you can create and manage transactions with the classes from the System.Transactions namespace.

Transactions are described with ACID properties: atomicity, consistency, isolation, and durability. Not all of these properties are always required, as you have seen with volatile resources that don't support durability and with isolation options.

The easiest way to deal with transactions is by creating ambient transactions and using the TransactionScope class. Ambient transactions are very useful working with the ADO.NET data adapter and LINQ to SQL where usually you do not open and close database connections explicitly. ADO.NET is covered in Chapter 26. LINQ to SQL is explained in Chapter 27.

Using the same transaction across multiple threads, you can use the DependentTransaction class to create a dependency on another transaction. By enlisting a resource manager that implements the interface IEnlistmentNotification, you can create custom resources that participate with transactions.

Finally, you have seen how to use Windows Vista and Windows Server 2008 transactions with the .NET Framework and C#.

With .NET Enterprise Services, you can create automatic transactions that make use of System.Transactions. You can read about this technology in Chapter 44, "Enterprise Services."

In the next chapter, you can read how to create a Windows service that can be automatically started when the operating system boots. Transactions can be useful within a service as well.

23

Windows Services

Windows Services are programs that can be started automatically at boot time without the need for anyone to log on to the machine.

In this chapter, you learn:

❑ The architecture of Windows Services, including the functionality of a service program, a service control program, and a service configuration program

❑ How to implement a Windows Service with the classes found in the `System.ServiceProcess` namespace

❑ Installation programs to configure the Windows Service in the registry

❑ How to write a program to control the Windows Service using the `ServiceController` class

❑ How to troubleshoot Windows Service programs

❑ How to react to power events from the operating system

The first section explains the architecture of Windows Services. You can download the code for this chapter from the Wrox Web site at `www.wrox.com`.

What Is a Windows Service?

Windows Services are applications that can be automatically started when the operating system boots. They can run without having an interactive user logged on to the system and do some processing in the background. For example, on a Windows Server, system networking services should be accessible from the client without a user logging on to the server. On the client system, services are useful as well; for example, to get a new software version from the Internet or to do some file cleanup on the local disk. You can configure a Windows Service to be run from a specially configured user account or from the system user account — a user account that has even more privileges than that of the system administrator.

Unless otherwise noted, when we refer to a service, we are referring to a Windows Service.

Here are a few examples of services:

❑ Simple TCP/IP Services is a service program that hosts some small TCP/IP servers: echo, daytime, quote, and others.

❑ World Wide Publishing Service is the service of the Internet Information Server (IIS).

❑ Event Log is a service to log messages to the event log system.

❑ Windows Search is a service that creates indexes of data on the disk.

You can use the Services administration tool, shown in Figure 23-1, to see all of the services on a system. On a Windows 2003 server, this program can be accessed by selecting Start ➪ Programs ➪ Administrative Tools ➪ Services; on Windows Vista and Windows XP, the program is accessible through Settings ➪ Control Panel ➪ Administrative Tools ➪ Services.

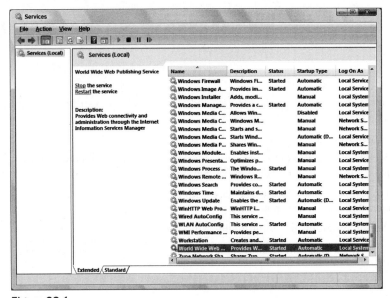

Figure 23-1

Windows Services Architecture

Three program types are necessary to operate a Windows Service:

❑ A service program

❑ A service control program

❑ A service configuration program

The *service program* itself provides the actual functionality you are looking for. With a *service control* program, it is possible to send control requests to a service, such as start, stop, pause, and continue. With a *service configuration* program, a service can be installed; it is copied to the file system, written into the registry, and configured as a service. Although .NET components can be installed simply with an xcopy, because they don't need to write information to the registry, installation for services requires registry configuration. A service configuration program can also be used to change the configuration of that service at a later point.

These three ingredients of a Windows Service are discussed in the following subsections.

Service Program

Before looking at the .NET implementation of a service, let's explore, from an independent point of view, what the Windows architecture of services looks like and what the inner functionality of a service is.

The service program implements the functionality of the service. It needs three parts:

- ❑ A main function
- ❑ A service-main function
- ❑ A handler

Before discussing these parts, we need to quickly introduce you to the *Service Control Manager* (SCM). The SCM plays an important role for services — sending requests to your service to start and to stop it.

Service Control Manager

The SCM is the part of the operating system that communicates with the service. Figure 23-2 illustrates how this communication works with a Unified Modeling Language (UML) sequence diagram.

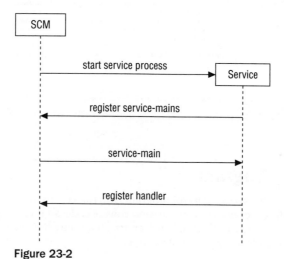

Figure 23-2

At boot time, each process for which a service is set to start automatically is started, and so the main function of this process is called. The service has the responsibility of registering the service-main function for each of its services. The main function is the entry point of the service program, and in this function the entry points for the service-main functions must be registered with the SCM.

Main Function, Service-Main, and Handlers

The main function of the service is the normal entry point of a program, the `Main()` method. The main function of the service might register more than one service-main function. The *service-main* function contains the actual functionality of the service. The service must register a service-main function for each service it provides. A service program can provide a lot of services in a single program; for example, `<windows>\system32\services.exe` is the service program that includes Alerter, Application Management, Computer Browser, and DHCP Client, among other items.

The SCM now calls the service-main function for each service that should be started. One important task of the service-main function is to register a handler with the SCM.

The *handler* function is the third part of a service program. The handler must respond to events from the SCM. Services can be stopped, suspended, and resumed, and the handler must react to these events.

Once a handler has been registered with the SCM, the service control program can post requests to the SCM to stop, suspend, and resume the service. The service control program is independent of the SCM and the service itself. The operating system contains many service control programs, for example, the MMC Services snap-in that you saw earlier. You can also write your own service control program; a good example of this is the SQL Server Configuration Manager shown in Figure 23-3.

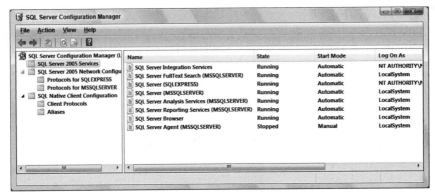

Figure 23-3

Service Control Program

As the name suggests, with a service control program, you can control the service. For stopping, suspending, and resuming the service, you can send control codes to the service, and the handler should react to these events. It is also possible to ask the service about the actual status and to implement a custom handler that responds to custom control codes.

Service Configuration Program

Because services must be configured in the registry, you can't use Xcopy installation with services. The registry contains the startup type of the service which can be set to automatic, manual, or disabled. You also need to configure the user of the service program and dependencies of the service — for example, the services that must be started before this one can start. All of these configurations are made within a service configuration program. The installation program can use the service configuration program to configure the service, but this program can also be used at a later time to change service configuration parameters.

System.ServiceProcess Namespace

In the .NET Framework, you can find service classes in the `System.ServiceProcess` namespace that implement the three parts of a service:

❑ You must inherit from the ServiceBase class to implement a service. The ServiceBase class is used to register the service and to answer start and stop requests.

❑ The ServiceController class is used to implement a service control program. With this class, you can send requests to services.

❑ The ServiceProcessInstaller and ServiceInstaller classes are, as their names suggest, classes to install and configure service programs.

Now you are ready to create a new service.

Creating a Windows Service

The service that you create will host a quote server. With every request that is made from a client, the quote server returns a random quote from a quote file. The first part of the solution uses three assemblies, one for the client and two for the server. Figure 23-4 gives an overview of the solution. The assembly QuoteServer holds the actual functionality. The service reads the quote file in a memory cache, and answers requests for quotes with the help of a socket server. The QuoteClient is a Windows Forms rich-client application. This application creates a client socket to communicate with the QuoteServer. The third assembly is the actual service. The QuoteService starts and stops the QuoteServer; the service controls the server:

Before creating the service part of your program, create a simple socket server in an extra C# class library that will be used from your service process.

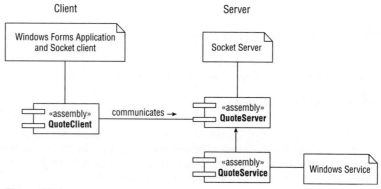

Figure 23-4

A Class Library Using Sockets

You can build any functionality in the service, for example, scanning for files to do a backup or a virus check, or starting a WCF server. However, all service programs share some similarities. The program must be able to start (and to return to the caller), stop, and suspend. This section looks at such an implementation using a socket server.

With Windows Vista, the Simple TCP/IP Services can be installed as part of the Windows components. Part of the Simple TCP/IP Services is a "quote of the day," or qotd, TCP/IP server. This simple service listens to port 17 and answers every request with a random message from the file <windir>\system32\ drivers\etc\quotes. With the sample service, a similar server will be built. The sample server returns a Unicode string, in contrast to the good-old qotd server that returns an ASCII string.

First, create a Class Library called `QuoteServer` and implement the code for the server. The following walks through the source code of your `QuoteServer` class in the file `QuoteServer.cs`:

```
using System;
using System.Collections.Generic;
using System.IO;
using System.Net;
using System.Net.Sockets;
using System.Text;
using System.Threading;

namespace Wrox.ProCSharp.WinServices
{
    public class QuoteServer
    {
        private TcpListener listener;
        private int port;
        private string filename;
        private List<string> quotes;
        private Random random;
        private Thread listenerThread;
```

The constructor `QuoteServer()` is overloaded so that a file name and a port can be passed to the call. The constructor where just the file name is passed uses the default port 7890 for the server. The default constructor defines the default file name for the quotes as `quotes.txt`:

```
        public QuoteServer() : this ("quotes.txt"")
        {
        }
        public QuoteServer(string filename) : this(filename, 7890)
        {
        }
        public QuoteServer(string filename, int port)
        {
            this.filename = filename;
            this.port = port;
        }
```

`ReadQuotes()` is a helper method that reads all the quotes from a file that was specified in the constructor. All the quotes are added to the `StringCollection` quotes. In addition, you are creating an instance of the `Random` class that will be used to return random quotes:

```
        protected void ReadQuotes()
        {
            quotes = new List<string>();
            Stream stream = File.OpenRead(filename);
            StreamReader streamReader = new StreamReader(stream);
            string quote;
            while ((quote = streamReader.ReadLine()) != null)
            {
                quotes.Add(quote);
            }
            streamReader.Close();
            stream.Close();
            random = new Random();
        }
```

Another helper method is GetRandomQuoteOfTheDay(). This method returns a random quote from the StringCollection quotes:

```
protected string GetRandomQuoteOfTheDay()
{
    int index = random.Next(0, quotes.Count);
    return quotes[index];
}
```

In the Start() method, the complete file containing the quotes is read in the StringCollection quotes by using the helper method ReadQuotes(). After this, a new thread is started, which immediately calls the Listener() method — similarly to the TcpReceive example in Chapter 41, "Accessing the Internet."

Here a thread is used because the Start() method cannot block and wait for a client; it must return immediately to the caller (SCM). The SCM would assume that the start failed if the method didn't return to the caller in a timely fashion (30 seconds). The listener thread is set as a background thread so that the application can exit without stopping this thread. The Name property of the thread is set because this helps with debugging, as the name will show up in the debugger:

```
public void Start()
{
    ReadQuotes();
    listenerThread = new Thread(ListenerThread);
    listenerThread.IsBackground = true;
    listenerThread.Name = "Listener";
    listenerThread.Start();
}
```

The thread function ListenerThread() creates a TcpListener instance. The AcceptSocket() method waits for a client to connect. As soon as a client connects, AcceptSocket() returns with a socket associated with the client. Next, GetRandomQuoteOfTheDay() is called to send the returned random quote to the client using socket.Send():

```
protected void ListenerThread()
{
    try
    {
        IPAddress ipAddress = IPAddress.Parse("127.0.0.1");
        listener = new TcpListener(ipAddress, port);
        listener.Start();
        while (true)
        {
            Socket clientSocket = listener.AcceptSocket();
            string message = GetRandomQuoteOfTheDay();
            UnicodeEncoding encoder = new UnicodeEncoding();
            byte[] buffer = encoder.GetBytes(message);
            clientSocket.Send(buffer, buffer.Length, 0);
            clientSocket.Close();
        }
    }
    catch (SocketException ex)
    {
        Console.WriteLine(ex.Message);
    }
}
```

In addition to the `Start()` method, the following methods are needed to control the service: `Stop()`, `Suspend()`, and `Resume()`:

```
public void Stop()
{
    listener.Stop();
}
public void Suspend()
{
    listener.Stop();
}
public void Resume()
{
    Start();
}
```

Another method that will be publicly available is `RefreshQuotes()`. If the file containing the quotes changes, the file is re-read with this method:

```
public void RefreshQuotes()
{
    ReadQuotes();
}
    }
}
```

Before building a service around the server, it is useful to build a test program that creates just an instance of the `QuoteServer` and calls `Start()`. This way, you can test the functionality without the need to handle service-specific issues. This test server must be started manually, and you can easily walk through the code with a debugger.

The test program is a C# console application, `TestQuoteServer`. You need to reference the assembly of the `QuoteServer` class. The file containing the quotes must be copied to the directory `c:\ProCSharp\Services` (or you must change the argument in the constructor to specify where you have copied the file). After calling the constructor, the `Start()` method of the `QuoteServer` instance is called. `Start()` returns immediately after having created a thread, so the console application keeps running until `Return` is pressed:

```
static void Main()
{
    QuoteServer qs = new QuoteServer(
        @"c:\ProCSharp\WindowsServices\quotes.txt", 4567);
    qs.Start();
    Console.WriteLine("Hit return to exit");
    Console.ReadLine();
    qs.Stop();
}
```

Note that `QuoteServer` will be running on port 4567 on localhost using this program — you will have to use these settings in the client later.

TcpClient Example

The client is a simple WPF Windows application in which you can request quotes from the server. This application uses the `TcpClient` class to connect to the running server, and receives the returned message, displaying it in a text box (see Figure 23-5).

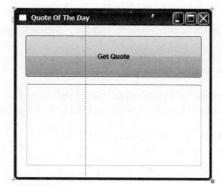

Figure 23-5

Server and port information to connect to the server is configured with settings of the application. You can add settings with the Settings tab inside the properties of the project (see Figure 23-6). Here, you can define the `ServerName` and `PortNumber` settings, and define some default values. From here, with the Scope set to User, the settings go into a user-specific configuration file, and every user of the application can have different settings. This Settings feature of Visual Studio also creates a `Settings` class so that the settings can be read and written with a strongly typed class.

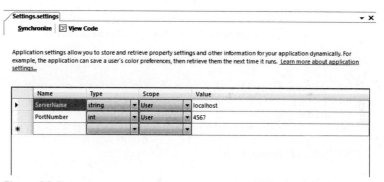

Figure 23-6

You need to add the following `using` directives to your code:

```
using System;
using System.Net.Sockets;
using System.Text;
using System.Windows;
using System.Windows.Input;
```

Within the constructor of the class `QuoteOfTheDayWindow`, you can define a handler method to the `Click` event of the button `buttonGetQuote`:

```
public QuoteOfTheDayWindow()
{
    InitializeComponent();
    this.buttonGetQuote.Click += new RoutedEventHandler(OnGetQuote);
}
```

The major functionality of the client lies in the handler for the click event of the Get Quote button:

```
protected void OnGetQuote(object sender, RoutedEventArgs e)
{
    Cursor currentCursor = this.Cursor;
    this.Cursor = Cursors.Wait;

    string serverName = Properties.Settings.Default.ServerName;
    int port = Properties.Settings.Default.PortNumber;

    TcpClient client = new TcpClient();
    NetworkStream stream = null;
    try
    {
        client.Connect(serverName, port);
        stream = client.GetStream();
        byte[] buffer = new Byte[1024];
        int received = stream.Read(buffer, 0, 1024);
        if (received <= 0)
        {
            return;
        }
        textQuote.Text = Encoding.Unicode.GetString(buffer).Trim('\0');
    }
    catch (SocketException ex)
    {
        MessageBox.Show(ex.Message, "Error Quote of the day"",
            MessageBoxButton.OK, MessageBoxImage.Error);
    }
    finally
    {
        if (stream != null)
        {
            stream.Close();
        }

        if (client.Connected)
        {
            client.Close();
        }
    }
    this.Cursor = currentCursor;
}
```

After starting the test server and this Windows application client, you can test the functionality. Figure 23-7 shows a successful run of this application.

Next, you implement the service functionality in the server. The program is already running, so what else do you need? Well, the server program should be automatically started at boot time without anyone logged on to the system. You want to control this by using service control programs.

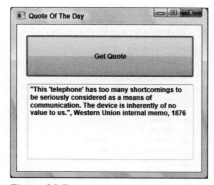

Figure 23-7

Windows Service Project

Using the new project wizard for C# Windows Services, you can now start to create a Windows Service. For the new service, use the name QuoteService (see Figure 23-8).

After you click the OK button to create the Windows Service application, you will see the Designer surface (just as with Windows Forms applications). However, you can't insert any Windows Forms components because the application cannot directly display anything on the screen. The Designer surface is used later in this chapter to add other components, such as performance counters and event logging.

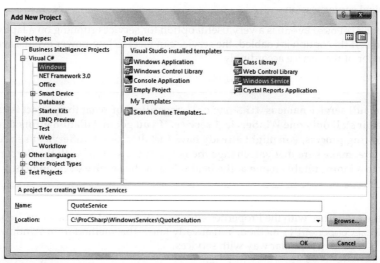

Figure 23-8

Selecting the properties of this service opens up the Properties editor window (see Figure 23-9).

Figure 23-9

With the service properties, you can configure the following values:

❑ AutoLog specifies that events are automatically written to the event log for starting and stopping the service.

❑ CanPauseAndContinue, CanShutdown, and CanStop specify pause, continue, shut down, and stop requests.

❑ ServiceName is the name of the service written to the registry and is used to control the service.

❑ CanHandleSessionChangeEvent defines if the service can handle change events from a terminal server session.

❑ CanHandlePowerEvent is a very useful option for services running on a laptop or mobile devices. If this option is enabled, the service can react to low-power events, and change the behavior of the service accordingly.

> The default service name is WinService1, regardless of what the project is called. You can install only one WinService1 service. If you get installation errors during your testing process, you might already have installed one WinService1 service. Therefore, make sure that you change the name of the service with the Properties editor to a more suitable name at the beginning of the service development.

Changing these properties with the Properties editor sets the values of your ServiceBase-derived class in the InitalizeComponent() method. You already know this method from Windows Forms applications. It is used in a similar way with services.

A wizard generates the code, but change the file name to QuoteService.cs, the name of the namespace to Wrox.ProCSharp.WinServices, and the class name to QuoteService. The code of the service is discussed in detail shortly.

The ServiceBase Class

The ServiceBase class is the base class for all Windows Services developed with the .NET Framework. The class QuoteService is derived from ServiceBase; this class communicates with the SCM using an undocumented helper class, System.ServiceProcess.NativeMethods, which is just a wrapper class to the Win32 API calls. The class is private, so it cannot be used in your code.

The sequence diagram in Figure 23-10 shows the interaction of the SCM, the class QuoteService, and the classes from the System.ServiceProcess namespace. In the sequence diagram, you can see the lifelines of objects vertically and the communication going on horizontally. The communication is time-ordered from top to bottom.

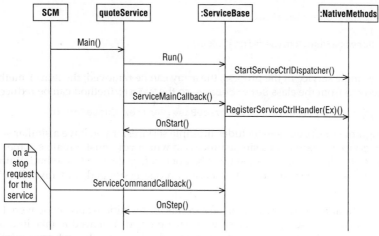

Figure 23-10

The SCM starts the process of a service that should be started. At startup, the Main() method is called. In the Main() method of the sample service, the Run() method of the base class ServiceBase is called. Run() registers the method ServiceMainCallback() using NativeMethods.StartServiceCtrlDispatcher() in the SCM and writes an entry to the event log.

Next, the SCM calls the registered method ServiceMainCallback() in the service program. ServiceMainCallback() itself registers the handler in the SCM using NativeMethods.RegisterServiceCtrlHandler[Ex]() and sets the status of the service in the SCM. Then the OnStart() method is called. In OnStart(), you need to implement the startup code. If OnStart() is successful, the string "Service started successfully" is written to the event log.

The handler is implemented in the ServiceCommandCallback() method. The SCM calls this method when changes are requested from the service. The ServiceCommandCallback() method routes the requests further to OnPause(), OnContinue(), OnStop(), OnCustomCommand(), and OnPowerEvent().

Main Function

This section looks into the application wizard–generated main function of the service process. In the main function, an array of ServiceBase classes, ServicesToRun, is declared. One instance of the QuoteService class is created and passed as the first element to the ServicesToRun array. If more than one service should run inside this service process, it is necessary to add more instances of the specific service classes to the array. This array is then passed to the static Run() method of the ServiceBase class. With the Run() method of ServiceBase, you are giving the SCM references to the entry points of your services. The main thread of your service process is now blocked and waits for the service to terminate.

Here is the automatically generated code:

```
/// <summary>
/// The main entry point for the process
/// </summary>
static void Main()
{
    ServiceBase[] ServicesToRun;
    ServicesToRun = new ServiceBase[]
    {
        new QuoteService()
    };
    ServiceBase.Run(ServicesToRun);
}
```

If there is only a single service in the process, the array can be removed; the Run() method accepts a single object derived from the class ServiceBase, so the Main() method can be reduced to this:

```
System.ServiceProcess.ServiceBase.Run(new QuoteService());
```

The service program Services.exe includes multiple services. If you have a similar service, where more than one service is running in a single process in which you must initialize some shared state for multiple services, the shared initialization must be done before the Run() method. With the Run() method, the main thread is blocked until the service process is stopped, and any following instructions would not be reached before the end of the service.

The initialization shouldn't take longer than 30 seconds. If the initialization code were to take longer than this, the SCM would assume that the service startup failed. You need to take into account the slowest machines where this service should run within the 30-second limit. If the initialization takes longer, you could start the initialization in a different thread so that the main thread calls Run() in time. An event object can then be used to signal that the thread has completed its work.

Service Start

At service start, the OnStart() method is called. In this method, you can start the previously created socket server. You must reference the QuoteServer assembly for the use of the QuoteService. The thread calling OnStart() cannot be blocked; this method must return to the caller, which is the ServiceMainCallback() method of the ServiceBase class. The ServiceBase class registers the handler and informs the SCM that the service started successfully after calling OnStart():

```
protected override void OnStart(string[] args)
{
    quoteServer = new QuoteServer(
        @"c:\ProCSharp\WindowsServices\quotes.txt", 5678);
    quoteServer.Start();
}
```

The quoteServer variable is declared as a private member in the class:

```
namespace Wrox.ProCSharp.WinServices
{
    public partial class QuoteService : ServiceBase
    {
        private QuoteServer quoteServer;
```

Handler Methods

When the service is stopped, the OnStop() method is called. You should stop the service functionality in this method:

```
protected override void OnStop()
{
    quoteServer.Stop();
}
```

In addition to OnStart() and OnStop(), you can override the following handlers in the service class:

❑ OnPause() is called when the service should be paused.

❑ OnContinue() is called when the service should return to normal operation after being paused. To make it possible for the overridden methods OnPause() and OnContinue() to be called, the CanPauseAndContinue property must be set to true.

❑ OnShutdown() is called when Windows is undergoing system shutdown. Normally, the behavior of this method should be similar to the OnStop() implementation; if more time is needed for a shutdown, you can request additional time. Similarly to OnPause() and OnContinue(), a property must be set to enable this behavior: CanShutdown must be set to true.

❑ OnPowerEvent() is called when the power status of the system changes. The information about the change of the power status is in the argument of type PowerBroadcastStatus. PowerBroadcastStatus is an enumeration with values such as Battery Low and PowerStatusChange. Here, you will also get information if the system would like to suspend (QuerySuspend), where you can approve or deny the suspend. You can read more about power events later in this chapter.

❑ OnCustomCommand() is a handler that can serve custom commands that are sent by a service control program. The method signature of OnCustomCommand() has an int argument where you get the custom command number. The value can be in the range from 128 to 256; values below 128 are system-reserved values. In your service, you are re-reading the quotes file with the custom command 128:

```
protected override void OnPause()
{
    quoteServer.Suspend();
}

protected override void OnContinue()
{
    quoteServer.Resume();
}

protected override void OnShutdown()
{
    OnStop();
}

public const int commandRefresh = 128;
protected override void OnCustomCommand(int command)
{
    switch (command)
    {
        case commandRefresh:
            quoteServer.RefreshQuotes();
            break;

        default:
            break;
    }
}
```

Threading and Services

As stated earlier, the SCM will assume that the service failed if the initialization takes too long. To deal with this, you need to create a thread.

The `OnStart()` method in your service class must return in time. If you call a blocking method like `AcceptSocket()` from the `TcpListener` class, you need to start a thread for doing this. With a networking server that deals with multiple clients, a thread pool is also very useful. `AcceptSocket()` should receive the call and hand the processing off to another thread from the pool. This way, no one waits for the execution of code and the system seems responsive.

Service Installation

A service must be configured in the registry. All services can be found in `HKEY_LOCAL_MACHINE\System\CurrentControlSet\Services`. You can view the registry entries by using `regedit`. The type of the service, display name, path to the executable, startup configuration, and so on are all found here. Figure 23-11 shows the registry configuration of the W3SVC service.

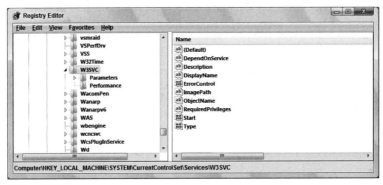

Figure 23-11

This configuration can be done by using the installer classes from the `System.ServiceProcess` namespace, as discussed in the following section.

Installation Program

You can add an installation program to the service by switching to the design view with Visual Studio and then selecting the Add Installer option from the context menu. With this option, a new `ProjectInstaller` class is created, and a `ServiceInstaller` and a `ServiceProcessInstaller` instance are created.

Figure 23-12 shows the class diagram of the installer classes for services.

With this diagram in mind, let's go through the source code in the file `ProjectInstaller.cs` that was created with the Add Installer option.

The Installer Class

The class `ProjectInstaller` is derived from `System.Configuration.Install.Installer`. This is the base class for all custom installers. With the `Installer` class, it is possible to build transaction-based installations. With a transaction-based installation, it is possible to roll back to the previous state if the installation fails, and any changes made by this installation up to that point will be undone. As you can see in Figure 23-12, the `Installer` class has `Install()`, `Uninstall()`, `Commit()`, and `Rollback()` methods, and they are called from installation programs.

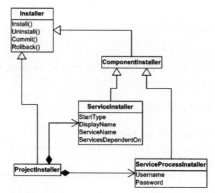

Figure 23-12

The attribute [RunInstaller(true)] means that the class ProjectInstaller should be invoked when installing an assembly. Custom action installers, as well as installutil.exe (which is used later in this chapter), check for this attribute.

Similarly to Windows Forms applications, InitializeComponent() is called inside the constructor of the ProjectInstaller class:

```
using System.ComponentModel;
using System.Configuration.Install;

namespace Wrox.ProCSharp.WinServices
{
    [RunInstaller(true)]
    public partial class ProjectInstaller : Installer
    {
        public ProjectInstaller()
        {
            InitializeComponent();
        }
    }
}
```

The ServiceProcessInstaller and ServiceInstaller Classes

Within the implementation of InitializeComponent(), instances of the ServiceProcessInstaller class and the ServiceInstaller class are created. Both of these classes derive from the ComponentInstaller class, which itself derives from Installer.

Classes derived from ComponentInstaller can be used with an installation process. Remember that a service process can include more than one service. The ServiceProcessInstaller class is used for the configuration of the process that defines values for all services in this process, and the ServiceInstaller class is for the configuration of the service, so one instance of ServiceInstaller is required for each service. If three services are inside the process, you need to add ServiceInstaller objects — three ServiceInstaller instances are needed in that case:

```
partial class ProjectInstaller
{
    /// <summary>
    /// Required designer variable.
    /// </summary>
```

(continued)

(continued)

```
            private System.ComponentModel.Container components = null;

            /// <summary>
            /// Required method for Designer support - do not modify
            /// the contents of this method with the code editor.
            /// </summary>
            private void InitializeComponent()
            {
                this.serviceProcessInstaller1 =
                            new System.ServiceProcess.ServiceProcessInstaller();
                this.serviceInstaller1 =
                            new System.ServiceProcess.ServiceInstaller();
                //
                // serviceProcessInstaller1
                //
                this.serviceProcessInstaller1.Password = null;
                this.serviceProcessInstaller1.Username = null;
                //
                // serviceInstaller1
                //
                this.serviceInstaller1.ServiceName = "QuoteService";
                //
                // ProjectInstaller
                //
                this.Installers.AddRange(
                    new System.Configuration.Install.Installer[]
                        {this.serviceProcessInstaller1,
                         this.serviceInstaller1});
            }

            private System.ServiceProcess.ServiceProcessInstaller
                        serviceProcessInstaller1;
            private System.ServiceProcess.ServiceInstaller serviceInstaller1;

        }
```

`ServiceProcessInstaller` installs an executable that implements the class `ServiceBase`. `ServiceProcessInstaller` has properties for the complete process. The following table explains the properties shared by all the services inside the process.

Property	Description
Username, Password	Indicates the user account under which the service runs if the `Account` property is set to `ServiceAccount.User`.
Account	With this property, you can specify the account type of the service.
HelpText	`HelpText` is a read-only property that returns the help text for setting the username and password.

The process that is used to run the service can be specified with the `Account` property of the `ServiceProcessInstaller` class using the `ServiceAccount` enumeration. The following table explains the different values of the `Account` property.

Value	Meaning
LocalSystem	Setting this value specifies that the service uses a highly privileged user account on the local system, but this account presents an anonymous user to the network. Thus, it doesn't have rights on the network.
LocalService	This account type presents the computer's credentials to any remote server.
NetworkService	Similarly to LocalService, this value specifies that the computer's credentials are passed to remote servers, but unlike LocalService, such a service acts as a nonprivileged user on the local system. As the name implies, this account should be used only for services that need resources from the network.
User	Setting the Account property to ServiceAccount.User means that you can define the account that should be used from the service.

ServiceInstaller is the class needed for every service; it has the following properties for each service inside a process: StartType, DisplayName, ServiceName, and ServicesDependentOn, as described in the following table.

Property	Description
StartType	The StartType property indicates whether the service is manually or automatically started. Possible values are ServiceStartMode. Automatic, ServiceStartMode.Manual, and ServiceStartMode.Disabled. With ServiceStartMode.Disabled, the service cannot be started. This option is useful for services that shouldn't be started on a system. You might want to set the option to Disabled if, for example, a required hardware controller is not available.
DisplayName	DisplayName is the friendly name of the service that is displayed to the user. This name is also used by management tools that control and monitor the service.
ServiceName	ServiceName is the name of the service. This value must be identical to the ServiceName property of the ServiceBase class in the service program. This name associates the configuration of the ServiceInstaller to the required service program.
ServicesDependentOn	Specifies an array of services that must be started before this service can be started. When the service is started, all these dependent services are started automatically, and then your service will start.

> If you change the name of the service in the ServiceBase-derived class, be sure to also change the ServiceName property in the ServiceInstaller object!

In the testing phases, set StartType *to* Manual. *This way, if you can't stop the service (for example, when it has a bug), you still have the possibility to reboot the system. But if you have* StartType *set to* Automatic, *the service would be started automatically with the reboot! You can change this configuration at a later time when you are sure that it works.*

The ServiceInstallerDialog Class

Another installer class in the System.ServiceProcess.Design namespace is ServiceInstallerDialog. This class can be used if you want the System Administrator to enter the username and password during the installation.

If you set the Account property of the class ServiceProcessInstaller to ServiceAccount.User and the Username and Password properties to null, you will see the Set Service Login dialog box at installation time (see Figure 23-13). You can also cancel the installation at this point.

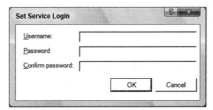

Figure 23-13

installutil

After adding the installer classes to the project, you can use the installutil.exe utility to install and uninstall the service. This utility can be used to install any assembly that has an Installer class. The installutil.exe utility calls the method Install() of the class that derives from the Installer class for installation, and Uninstall() for the *uninstallation*.

The command-line inputs for the installation and uninstallation of our service are:

```
installutil quoteservice.exe
installutil /u quoteservice.exe
```

> If the installation fails, be sure to check the installation log files, InstallUtil. InstallLog and <servicename>.InstallLog. Often, you can find very useful information, such as "The specified service already exists."

Client

After the service has been successfully installed, you can start the service manually from the Services MMC (see the next section for further details), and then you can start the client application. Figure 23-14 shows the client accessing the service.

Monitoring and Controlling the Service

To monitor and control services, you can use the Services MMC snap-in that is part of the Computer Management administration tool. Every Windows system also has a command-line utility, net.exe, which allows you to control services. Another command-line utility is sc.exe. This utility has much

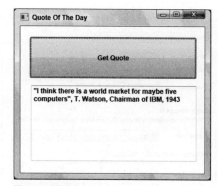

Figure 23-14

more functionality than `net.exe`, which is part of the Platform SDK. In this section, you create a small Windows application that makes use of the `System.ServiceProcess.ServiceController` class to monitor and control services.

MMC Computer Management

Using the Services snap-in to the Microsoft Management Console (MMC), you can view the status of all services (see Figure 23-15). It is also possible to send control requests to services to stop, enable, or disable them, as well as to change their configuration. The Services snap-in is a service control program as well as a service configuration program.

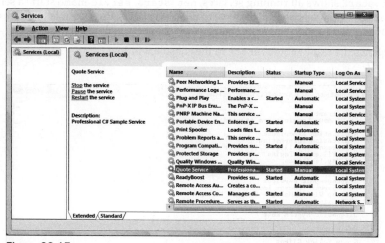

Figure 23-15

When you double-click QuoteService, you will get the Properties dialog box shown in Figure 23-16. This dialog box enables you to view the service name, the description, the path to the executable, the startup type, and the status. The service is currently started. The account for the service process can be changed with the Log On tab in this dialog.

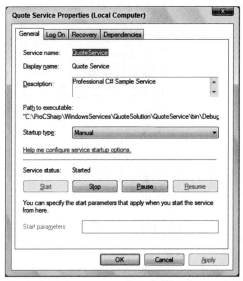

Figure 23-16

net.exe

The Services snap-in is easy to use, but the system administrator cannot automate it because it is not usable within an administrative script. To control services, you can use the command-line utility net.exe: net start shows all running services, net start servicename starts a service, and net stop servicename sends a stop request to the service. It is also possible to pause and to continue a service with net pause and net continue (only if the service allows it, of course).

Figure 23-17 shows the result of net start in the console window.

Figure 23-17

sc.exe

There is a little-known utility delivered as part of the operating system: sc.exe.

sc.exe is a great tool to play with services. Much more can be done with sc.exe than with the net.exe utility. With sc.exe, it is possible to check the actual status of a service, or configure, remove, and add services, as Figure 23-18 shows. This tool also facilitates the deinstallation of the service, if it fails to function correctly.

Figure 23-18

Visual Studio Server Explorer

It is also possible to control services using the Server Explorer within Visual Studio; Services is below Servers and the name of your computer. By selecting a service and opening the context menu, a service can be started and stopped. This context menu can also be used to add a ServiceController class to the project. To control a specific service in your application, drag and drop a service from the Server Explorer to the Designer: a ServiceController instance is added to the application. The properties of this object are automatically set to access the selected service, and the assembly System.ServiceProcess is referenced. You can use this instance to control a service in the same way you can with the application that you develop in the next section.

ServiceController Class

In this section, you create a small Windows application that uses the ServiceController class to monitor and control Windows Services.

Create a WPF application with a user interface as shown in Figure 23-19. The main window of this application has a list box to show all services, four text boxes to display the display name, status, type, and name of the service, and six buttons. Four buttons are used to send control events, one button for a refresh of the list, and one button to exit the application.

You can read more about WPF in Chapter 34, "Windows Presentation Foundation."

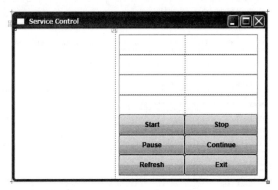

Figure 23-19

Monitoring the Service

With the `ServiceController` class, you can get the information about each service. The following table shows the properties of the `ServiceController` class.

Property	Description
CanPauseAndContinue	Returns true if pause and continue requests can be sent to the service.
CanShutdown	Returns true if the service has a handler for a system shutdown.
CanStop	Returns true if the service is stoppable.
DependentServices	Returns a collection of dependent services. If the service is stopped, then all dependent services are stopped beforehand.
ServicesDependentOn	Returns a collection of the services that this service depends on.
DisplayName	Specifies the name that should be displayed for this service.
MachineName	Specifies the name of the machine that the service runs on.
ServiceName	Specifies the name of the service.
ServiceType	Specifies the type of the service. The service can be run inside a shared process where more than one service uses the same process (Win32ShareProcess), or run in such a way that there is just one service in a process (Win32OwnProcess). If the service can interact with the desktop, the type is InteractiveProcess.
Status	Specifies the status of the service. The status can be running, stopped, paused, or in some intermediate mode like start pending, stop pending, and so on. The status values are defined in the enumeration ServiceControllerStatus.

In the sample application, the properties `DisplayName`, `ServiceName`, `ServiceType`, and `Status` are used to display the service information. Also, `CanPauseAndContinue` and `CanStop` are used to enable or disable the Pause, Continue, and Stop buttons.

To get all the needed information for the user interface, the class `ServiceControllerInfo` is created. This class can be used for data binding and offers status information, the name of the service, the service type, and the information about which buttons to control the service should be enabled or disabled.

> *Because the class* `System.ServiceProcess.ServiceController` *is used, you must reference the assembly* `System.ServiceProcess`.

`ServiceControllerInfo` contains an embedded `ServiceController` that is set with the constructor of the `ServiceControllerInfo` class. There is also a read-only property `Controller` to access the embedded `ServiceController`.

```
public class ServiceControllerInfo
{
    private ServiceController controller;

    public ServiceControllerInfo(ServiceController controller)
    {
        this.controller = controller;
    }

    public ServiceController Controller
    {
        get { return controller; }
    }
```

To display current information about the service, the `ServiceControllerInfo` class has the read-only properties `DisplayName`, `ServiceName`, `ServiceTypeName`, and `ServiceStatusName`. The implementation of the properties `DisplayName` and `ServiceName` just accesses the properties `DisplayName` and `ServiceName` of the underlying `ServiceController` class. With the implementation of the properties `ServiceTypeName` and `ServiceStatusName`, more work is done: The status and type of the service cannot be returned that easily because a string should be displayed instead of a number, which is what the `ServiceController` class returns. The property `ServiceTypeName` returns a string that represents the type of the service. The `ServiceType` you get from the property `ServiceController.ServiceType` represents a set of flags that can be combined by using the bitwise OR operator. The `InteractiveProcess` bit can be set together with `Win32OwnProcess` and `Win32ShareProcess`. So, first it is checked if the `InteractiveProcess` bit is set before continuing to check for the other values. With services, the string returned will be "Win32 Service Process" or "Win32 Shared Process":

```
public string ServiceTypeName
{
    get
    {
        ServiceType type = controller.ServiceType;
        string serviceTypeName = "";
        if ((type & ServiceType.InteractiveProcess) != 0)
        {
            serviceTypeName = "Interactive ";
            type -= ServiceType.InteractiveProcess;
        }
        switch (type)
```

(continued)

739

(continued)

```
            {
                case ServiceType.Adapter:
                    serviceTypeName += "Adapter";
                    break;

                case ServiceType.FileSystemDriver:
                case ServiceType.KernelDriver:
                case ServiceType.RecognizerDriver:
                    serviceTypeName += "Driver";
                    break;

                case ServiceType.Win32OwnProcess:
                    serviceTypeName += "Win32 Service Process";
                    break;

                case ServiceType.Win32ShareProcess:
                    serviceTypeName += "Win32 Shared Process";
                    break;

                default:
                    serviceTypeName += "unknown type " + type.ToString();
                    break;
            }
            return serviceTypeName;
        }
    }

    public string ServiceStatusName
    {
        get
        {
            switch (controller.Status)
            {
                case ServiceControllerStatus.ContinuePending:
                    return "Continue Pending";
                case ServiceControllerStatus.Paused:
                    return "Paused";
                case ServiceControllerStatus.PausePending:
                    return "Pause Pending";
                case ServiceControllerStatus.StartPending:
                    return "Start Pending";
                case ServiceControllerStatus.Running:
                    return "Running";
                case ServiceControllerStatus.Stopped:
                    return "Stopped";
                case ServiceControllerStatus.StopPending:
                    return "Stop Pending";
                default:
                    return "Unknown status";
            }
        }
    }

    public string DisplayName
```

```
{
    get { return controller.DisplayName; }
}

public string ServiceName
{
    get { return controller.ServiceName; }
}
```

The `ServiceControllerInfo` class has some more properties to enable the Start, Stop, Pause, and Continue buttons: `EnableStart`, `EnableStop`, `EnablePause`, and `EnableContinue`. These properties return a Boolean value according to the current status of the service:

```
public bool EnableStart
{
    get
    {
        return controller.Status == ServiceControllerStatus.Stopped;
    }
}

public bool EnableStop
{
    get
    {
        return controller.Status == ServiceControllerStatus.Running;
    }
}

public bool EnablePause
{
    get
    {
        return controller.Status == ServiceControllerStatus.Running &&
                controller.CanPauseAndContinue;
    }
}

public bool EnableContinue
{
    get
    {
        return controller.Status == ServiceControllerStatus.Paused;
    }
}
}
```

In the `ServiceControlWindow` class, the method `RefreshServiceList()` gets all the services using `ServiceController.GetServices()` for display in the list box. The `GetServices()` method returns an array of `ServiceController` instances representing all Windows Services installed on the operating system. The `ServiceController` class also has the static method `GetDevices()` that returns a `ServiceController` array representing all device drivers. The returned array is sorted with the help of the generic `Array.Sort()` method. The sort is done by the `DisplayName` as is defined with the anonymous method that is passed to the `Sort()` method. Using `Array.ConvertAll()`, the `ServiceController` instances are converted to the type `ServiceControllerInfo`. Here, an anonymous method is passed that invokes the `ServiceControllerInfo` constructor for every `ServiceController` object. Last, the `ServiceControllerInfo` array is assigned to the `DataContext` property of the window for data binding.

```
protected void RefreshServiceList()
{
    ServiceController[] services = ServiceController.GetServices();

    Array.Sort<ServiceController>(services,
        delegate(ServiceController s1, ServiceController s2)
        {
            return s1.DisplayName.CompareTo(s2.DisplayName);
        });
    ServiceControllerInfo[] serviceInfo =
        Array.ConvertAll<ServiceController, ServiceControllerInfo>(
        services,
        delegate(ServiceController controller)
        {
            return new ServiceControllerInfo(controller);
        });

    this.DataContext = serviceInfo;
}
```

The method `RefreshServiceList()` to get all the services in the list box is called within the constructor of the class `ServiceControlWindow`. The constructor also defines the event handler for the `Click` event of the buttons:

```
public ServiceControlWindow()
{
    InitializeComponent();

    buttonStart.Click += OnServiceCommand;
    buttonStop.Click += OnServiceCommand;
    buttonPause.Click += OnServiceCommand;
    buttonContinue.Click += OnServiceCommand;
    buttonRefresh.Click += OnRefresh;
    buttonExit.Click += OnExit;

    RefreshServiceList();
}
```

Now, you can define the XAML code to bind the information to the controls.

First, a `DataTemplate` is defined for the information that is shown inside the `ListBox`. The `ListBox` will contain a `Label` where the `Content` is bound to the `DisplayName` property of the data source. As you bind an array of `ServiceControllerInfo` objects, the property `DisplayName` is defined with the `ServiceControllerInfo` class:

```
<Window.Resources>
    <DataTemplate x:Key="listTemplate">
        <Label Content="{Binding Path=DisplayName}"/>
    </DataTemplate>
</Window.Resources>
```

The `ListBox` that is placed in the left side of the Window sets the `ItemsSource` property to `{Binding}`. This way, the data that is shown in the list is received from the `DataContext` property that was set in the `RefreshServiceList()` method. The `ItemTemplate` property references the resource `listTemplate` that is defined with the `DataTemplate` shown earlier. The property `IsSynchronizedWithCurrentItem` is set to `True` so that the `TextBox` and `Button` controls that are inside the same Window are bound to the current item that is selected with the `ListBox`.

```
<ListBox Grid.Row="0" Grid.Column="0" HorizontalAlignment="Left"
    Name="listBoxServices" VerticalAlignment="Top"
    ItemsSource="{Binding}"
    ItemTemplate="{StaticResource listTemplate}"
    IsSynchronizedWithCurrentItem="True">
</ListBox>
```

With the `TextBox` controls, the `Text` property is bound to the corresponding property of the `ServiceControllerInfo` instance. Whether the `Button` controls are enabled or disabled is also defined from the data binding by binding the `IsEnabled` property to the corresponding properties of the `ServiceControllerInfo` instance that return a Boolean value:

```
<TextBox Grid.Row="0" Grid.ColumnSpan="2" Name="textDisplayName"
    Text="{Binding Path=DisplayName, Mode=OneTime}" />
<TextBox Grid.Row="1" Grid.ColumnSpan="2" Name="textStatus"
    Text="{Binding Path=ServiceStatusName, Mode=OneTime}" />
<TextBox Grid.Row="2" Grid.ColumnSpan="2" Name="textType"
    Text="{Binding Path=ServiceTypeName, Mode=OneTime}" />
<TextBox Grid.Row="3" Grid.ColumnSpan="2" Name="textName"
    Text="{Binding Path=ServiceName, Mode=OneTime}" />
<Button Grid.Row="4" Grid.Column="0" Name="buttonStart" Content="Start"
    IsEnabled="{Binding Path=EnableStart, Mode=OneTime}" />
<Button Grid.Row="4" Grid.Column="1" Name="buttonStop" Content="Stop"
    IsEnabled="{Binding Path=EnableStop, Mode=OneTime}" />
<Button Grid.Row="5" Grid.Column="0" Name="buttonPause" Content="Pause"
    IsEnabled="{Binding Path=EnablePause, Mode=OneTime}" />
<Button Grid.Row="5" Grid.Column="1" Name="buttonContinue"
    Content="Continue" IsEnabled="{Binding Path=EnableContinue,
    Mode=OneTime}" />
```

Controlling the Service

With the `ServiceController` class, you can also send control requests to the service. The following table explains the methods that can be applied.

Method	Description
Start()	Start() tells the SCM that the service should be started. In the example service program, OnStart() is called.
Stop()	Stop() calls OnStop() in the example service program with the help of the SCM if the property CanStop is true in the service class.
Pause()	Pause() calls OnPause() if the property CanPauseAndContinue is true.
Continue()	Continue() calls OnContinue() if the property CanPauseAndContinue is true.
ExecuteCommand()	With ExecuteCommand(), it is possible to send a custom command to the service.

The following code controls the services. Because the code for starting, stopping, suspending, and pausing is similar, only one handler is used for the four buttons:

```
protected void OnServiceCommand(object sender, RoutedEventArgs e)
{
    Cursor oldCursor = Cursor.Current;
    Cursor.Current = Cursors.Wait;
    ServiceControllerInfo si =
            (ServiceControllerInfo)listBoxServices.SelectedItem;
    if (sender == this.buttonStart)
    {
        si.Controller.Start();
        si.Controller.WaitForStatus(ServiceControllerStatus.Running);
    }
    else if (sender == this.buttonStop)
    {
        si.Controller.Stop();
        si.Controller.WaitForStatus(ServiceControllerStatus.Stopped);
    }
    else if (sender == this.buttonPause)
    {
        si.Controller.Pause();
        si.Controller.WaitForStatus(ServiceControllerStatus.Paused);
    }
    else if (sender == this.buttonContinue)
    {
        si.Controller.Continue();
        si.Controller.WaitForStatus(ServiceControllerStatus.Running);
    }
    int index =listBoxServices.SelectedIndex;
    RefreshServiceList();
    listBoxServices.SelectedIndex = index;
    Cursor.Current = oldCursor;
}

protected void OnExit(object sender, RoutedEventArgs e)
{
    Application.Current.Shutdown();
}

protected void OnRefresh_Click(object sender, RoutedEventArgs e)
{
    RefreshServiceList();
}
```

Because the action of controlling the services can take some time, the cursor is switched to the wait cursor in the first statement. Then a `ServiceController` method is called depending on the pressed button. With the `WaitForStatus()` method, you are waiting to check that the service changes the status to the requested value, but you only wait 10 seconds maximum. After this time, the information in the `ListBox` is refreshed, and the same service as before is selected, and the new status of this service is displayed. Figure 23-20 shows the completed, running application.

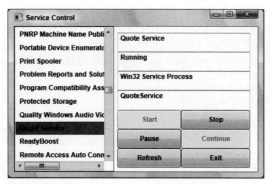

Figure 23-20

Troubleshooting

Troubleshooting services is different from troubleshooting normal applications. This section touches on some service issues, problems specific to interactive services, and event logging.

The best way to start building a service is to create an assembly with the functionality you want and a test client, before the service is actually created. Here, you can do normal debugging and error handling. As soon as the application is running, you can build a service by using this assembly. Of course, there might still be problems with the service:

❑   Don't display errors in a message box from the service (except for interactive services that are running on the client system). Instead, use the event logging service to write errors to the event log. Of course, in the client application that uses the service, you can display a message box to inform the user about errors.

❑   The service cannot be started from within a debugger, but a debugger can be attached to the running service process. Open the solution with the source code of the service and set breakpoints. From the Visual Studio Debug menu, select Processes and attach the running process of the service.

❑   The Performance Monitor can be used to monitor the activity of services. You can add your own performance objects to the service. This can add some useful information for debugging. For example, with the Quote service, you could set up an object to give the total number of quotes returned, the time it takes to initialize, and so on.

Interactive Services

When an interactive service runs with a logged-on user, it can be helpful to display message boxes to the user. If the service should run on a server that is locked inside a computer room, the service should never display a message box. When you open a message box to wait for some user input, the user input probably won't happen for some days because nobody is looking at the server in the computer room. Even worse, if the service isn't configured as an interactive service, the message box opens up on a different, hidden, window station. In this case, no one can respond to that message box because it is hidden, and the service is blocked.

> **Never open dialog boxes for services running on a server system. Nobody will respond to them.**

In cases when you really want to interact with the user, an interactive service can be configured. Some examples of such interactive services are the Print Spooler, which displays paper-out messages to the user, and the NetMeeting Remote Desktop Sharing service.

To configure an interactive service, you must set the option "Allow service to interact with desktop" in the Services configuration tool (see Figure 23-21). This changes the type of the service by adding the SERVICE_INTERACTIVE_PROCESS flag to the type.

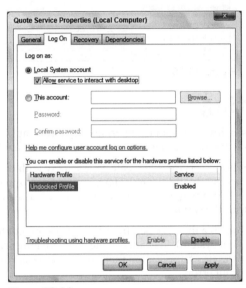

Figure 23-21

Event Logging

Services can report errors and other information by adding events to the event log. A service class derived from ServiceBase automatically logs events when the AutoLog property is set to true. The ServiceBase class checks this property and writes a log entry at start, stop, pause, and continue requests.

Figure 23-22 shows an example of a log entry from a service.

You can read more about event logging and how to write custom events in Chapter 18, "Tracing and Events."

Power Events

The Windows Service can react when the power status changes. One example of a power event is when the system hibernates — all the memory content is written to the disk, so a faster boot is possible. It is also possible to suspend the system to reduce the power consumption, but it can be awakened automatically on demand.

For all power events, the service can receive the control code SERVICE_CONTROL_POWEREVENT with additional parameters. The reason for the event is passed through these parameters. The reason could be

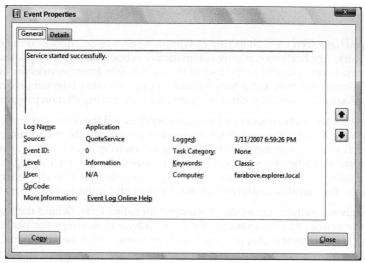

Figure 23-22

low battery power, a power status change, or the system is going to a suspended state. Depending on the circumstances, the service should slow down, suspend background threads, close network connections, close files, and so on.

The classes in the System.ServiceProcess namespace have support for power events. In the same way that you can configure a service so that it reacts to pause and continue events with the CanPauseAndContinue property, you can also set a property for power management: CanHandlePowerEvent. Windows Services that handle power events are registered in the SCM with the Win32 API method RegisterServiceCtrlHandlerEx().

If you set the property CanHandlePowerEvent to true, the method OnPowerEvent() of the class ServiceBase is called. You can override this method to receive power events and to react with your service implementation accordingly. The reason for the power event is passed in an argument of type PowerBroadcastStatus. The possible values of this enumeration are listed in the following table.

Value	Description
BatteryLow	The battery power is low. You should reduce the functionality of the service to a minimum.
PowerStatusChange	A switch from battery power to A/C happened, or the battery power slipped below a threshold, and so on.
QuerySuspend	The system requests permission to go into a suspended mode. You could deny the permission, or prepare to go into the suspended mode by closing files, disconnecting network connections, and so on.
QuerySuspendFailed	The change into the suspended mode was denied for the system. You can go on with the functionality as before.
Suspend	Nobody denied the request to go into the suspended mode. The system will be suspended soon.

Summary

In this chapter, you have seen the architecture of Windows Services and how you can create them with the .NET Framework. Applications can start automatically at boot time with Windows Services, and you can use a privileged system account as the user of the service. Windows Services are built from a main function, a service-main function, and a handler, and you've seen other relevant programs in regard to Windows Services, such as a service control program and a service installation program.

The .NET Framework has great support for Windows Services. All the plumbing code that is necessary for building, controlling, and installing services is built into the .NET Framework classes in the System.ServiceProcess namespace. By deriving a class from ServiceBase, you can override methods that are invoked when the service is paused, resumed, or stopped. For installation of services, the classes ServiceProcessInstaller and ServiceInstaller deal with all registry configurations needed for services. You can also control and monitor services by using ServiceController.

The next chapter gives you information about interop with native code. Behind the scenes, many .NET classes make use of native code. For example, the ServiceBase class wraps the Windows API CreateService(). With the next chapter, you learn how to use native methods and COM objects from your own classes.

24

Interoperability

If you have Windows programs written prior to .NET, you probably don't have the time and resources to rewrite everything for .NET. Sometimes rewriting code is useful for refactoring or rethinking the application architecture. A rewrite can also help with productivity in the long-term, when adding new features is easier to do with the new technology. However, there should not be a reason to rewrite old code just because a new technology is available. You might have thousands of lines of existing, running code, which would require too much effort to rewrite just to move it into the managed environment.

The same applies to Microsoft. With the namespace `System.DirectoryServices`, Microsoft hasn't rewritten the COM objects accessing the hierarchical data store; the classes inside this namespace are wrappers accessing the ADSI COM objects instead. The same thing happens with `System.Data.OleDb`, where the OLE DB providers that are used by classes from this namespace do have quite complex COM interfaces.

The same issue may apply for your own solutions. If you have existing COM objects that should be used from .NET applications, or the other way around, if you want to write .NET components that should be used in old COM clients, this chapter will be a starter for using COM interoperability.

If you don't have existing COM components you want to integrate with your application, or old COM clients that should use some .NET components, you can skip this chapter.

This chapter discusses the following:

- ❑ COM and .NET technologies
- ❑ Using COM objects from within .NET applications
- ❑ Using .NET components from within COM clients
- ❑ Platform invoke for invoking native methods

Like all other chapters, you can download the sample code for this chapter from the Wrox web site at www.wrox.com.

.NET and COM

COM is the predecessor technology to .NET. COM defines a component model where components can be written in different programming languages. A component written with C++ can be used from a Visual Basic client. Components can also be used locally inside a process, across processes, or across the network. Does this sound familiar? Of course, .NET has similar goals. However, the way in which these goals are achieved is different. The COM concepts became more and more complex to use and turned out not to be extensible enough. .NET fulfills goals similar to those of COM, but introduces new concepts to make your job easier.

Even today, when using COM interop the prerequisite is to know COM. It doesn't matter if .NET components are used by COM clients or COM components are used by .NET applications, you must know COM. So, this section compares COM and .NET functionality.

If you already have a good grasp of COM technologies, this section may be a refresher to your COM knowledge. Otherwise, it introduces you to the concepts of COM — now using .NET — that you can be happy not to deal with anymore in your daily business. However, all the problems that came with COM still apply when COM technology is integrated in .NET applications.

COM and .NET do have many similar concepts with very different solutions, including the following:

- ❑ Metadata
- ❑ Freeing memory
- ❑ Interfaces
- ❑ Method binding
- ❑ Data types
- ❑ Registration
- ❑ Threading
- ❑ Error handling
- ❑ Event handling

Metadata

With COM, all information about the component is stored inside the type library. The type library includes information such as names and IDs of interfaces, methods, and arguments. With .NET, all this information can be found inside the assembly itself, as you saw in Chapter 13, "Reflection," and Chapter 17, "Assemblies." The problem with COM is that the type library is not extensible. With C++, IDL (interface definition language) files have been used to describe the interfaces and methods. Some of the IDL modifiers cannot be found inside the type library, because Visual Basic (and the Visual Basic team was responsible for the type library) couldn't use these IDL modifiers. With .NET, this problem doesn't exist because the .NET metadata is extensible using custom attributes.

As a result of this behavior, some COM components have a type library and others don't. Where no type library is available, a C++ header file can be used that describes the interfaces and methods. With .NET, it is easier using COM components that do have a type library, but it is also possible to use COM components without a type library. In that case, it is necessary to redefine the COM interface by using C# code.

Freeing Memory

With .NET, memory is released by the garbage collector. This is completely different with COM. COM relies on reference counts.

The interface IUnknown, which is the interface that is required to be implemented by every COM object, offers three methods. Two of these methods are related to reference counts. The method AddRef() must be called by the client if another interface pointer is needed; this method increments the reference count. The method Release() decrements the reference count, and if the resulting reference count is 0, the object destroys itself to free memory.

Interfaces

Interfaces are the heart of COM. They distinguish between a contract used between the client and the object, and the implementation. The interface (the contract) defines the methods that are offered by the component and that can be used by the client. With .NET, interfaces play an important part, too.

COM distinguishes among three interface types: *custom*, *dispatch*, and *dual* interfaces.

Custom Interfaces

Custom interfaces derive from the interface IUnknown. A custom interface defines the order of the methods in a *virtual table* (*vtable*), so that the client can access the methods of the interface directly. This also means that the client needs to know the vtable during development time, because binding to the methods happens by using memory addresses. As a conclusion, custom interfaces cannot be used by scripting clients. Figure 24-1 shows the vtable of the custom interface IMath that offers the methods Add() and Sub() in addition to the methods of the IUnknown interface.

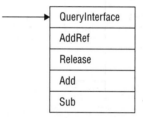

Figure 24-1

Dispatch Interfaces

Because a scripting client (and earlier Visual Basic clients) doesn't support custom interfaces, a different interface type is needed. With dispatch interfaces, the interface available for the client is always the IDispatch interface. IDispatch derives from IUnknown and offers four methods in addition to the IUnknown methods. The two most important methods are GetIDsOfNames() and Invoke(). As shown in Figure 24-2, with a dispatch interface two tables are needed. The first one maps the method or property name to a dispatch ID; the second one maps the dispatch ID to the implementation of the method or property.

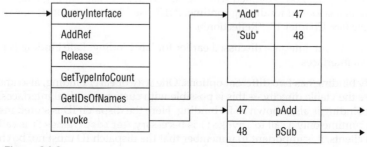

Figure 24-2

When the client invokes a method in the component, at first it calls the method `GetIDsOfNames()`, passing the name of the method it wants to call. `GetIDsOfNames()` makes a lookup into the name-to-ID table to return the dispatch ID. This ID is used by the client to call the `Invoke()` method.

Usually, the two tables for the `IDispatch` interface are stored inside the type library, but this is not a requirement, and some components have the tables in other places.

Dual Interfaces

As you can imagine, dispatch interfaces are a lot slower than custom interfaces. On the other hand, custom interfaces cannot be used by scripting clients. A dual interface can solve this dilemma. As you can see in Figure 24-3, a dual interface is derived from `IDispatch` but offers the additional methods of the interface directly in the vtable. Scripting clients can use the `IDispatch` interface to invoke the methods, whereas clients aware of the vtable can call the methods directly.

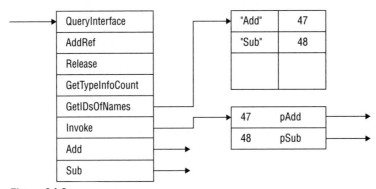

Figure 24-3

Casting and QueryInterface

If a .NET class implements multiple interfaces, casts can be done to get one interface or another. With COM, the interface `IUnknown` offers a similar mechanism with the method `QueryInterface()`. As discussed in the previous section, the interface `IUnknown` is the base interface of every interface, so `QueryInterface()` is available anyway.

Method Binding

How a client maps to a method is defined with the terms *early* and *late binding*. Late binding means that the method to invoke is looked for during runtime. .NET uses the `System.Reflection` namespace to make this possible (see Chapter 13, "Reflection").

COM uses the `IDispatch` interface discussed earlier for late binding. Late binding is possible with dispatch and dual interfaces.

With COM, early binding has two different options. One way of early binding, also known as vtable binding, is to use the vtable directly — this is possible with custom and dual interfaces. The second option for early binding is also known as ID binding. Here the dispatch ID is stored inside the client code, so during runtime only a call to `Invoke()` is necessary. `GetIdsOfNames()` is called during design time. With such clients, it is important to remember that the dispatch ID must not be changed.

Data Types

For dual and dispatch interfaces, the data types that can be used with COM are restricted to a list of automation-compatible data types. The `Invoke()` method of the `IDispatch` interface accepts an array of `VARIANT` data types. The `VARIANT` is a union of many different data types, such as `BYTE`, `SHORT`, `LONG`, `FLOAT`, `DOUBLE`, `BSTR`, `IUnknown*`, `IDispatch*`, and so on. `VARIANT`s have been easy to use from Visual Basic, but it was complex to use them from C++. .NET has the `Object` class instead of `VARIANT`s.

With custom interfaces, all data types available with C++ can be used with COM. However, this also restricts the clients that can use this component to certain programming languages.

Registration

.NET distinguishes between private and shared assemblies, as discussed in Chapter 17, "Assemblies." With COM, all components are globally available by a registry configuration.

All COM objects have a unique identifier that consists of a 128-bit number and is also known as class ID (CLSID). The COM API call to create COM objects, `CoCreateInstance()`, just looks into the registry to find the CLSID and the path to the DLL or EXE to load the DLL or launch the EXE and instantiate the component.

Because such a 128-bit number cannot be easily remembered, many COM objects also have a ProgID. The ProgID is an easy-to-remember name, such as `Excel.Application`, that just maps to the CLSID.

In addition to the CLSID, COM objects also have a unique identifier for each interface (IID) and for the type library (typelib ID).

Information in the registry is discussed in more detail later in the chapter.

Threading

COM uses apartment models to relieve the programmer of having to deal with threading issues. However, this also adds some more complexity. Different apartment types have been added with different releases of the operating system. This section discusses the single-threaded apartment and the multithreaded apartment.

Threading with .NET is discussed in Chapter 19, "Threading and Synchronization."

Single-threaded Apartment

The single-threaded apartment (STA) was introduced with Windows NT 3.51. With an STA, only one thread (the thread that created the instance) is allowed to access the component. However, it is legal to have multiple STAs inside one process, as shown in Figure 24-4.

In this figure, the inner rectangles with the lollipop represent COM components. Components and threads (curved arrows) are surrounded by apartments. The outer rectangle represents a process.

With STAs, there's no need to protect instance variables from multiple thread access, because this protection is provided by a COM facility, and only one thread accesses the component.

A COM object that is not programmed with thread safety marks the requirements for an STA in the registry with the registry key `ThreadingModel` set to `Apartment`.

Multithreaded Apartment

Windows NT 4.0 introduced the concept of a *multithreaded apartment* (MTA). With an MTA, multiple threads can access the component simultaneously. Figure 24-5 shows a process with one MTA and two STAs.

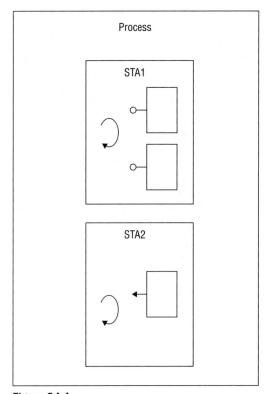

Figure 24-4

A COM object programmed with thread safety in mind marks the requirement for an MTA in the registry with the key `ThreadingModel` set to `Free`. The value `Both` is used for thread-safe COM objects that don't mind the apartment type.

Visual Basic 6.0 didn't offer support for multithreaded apartments. If you're using COM objects that have been developed with VB6 that's an important issue to know.

Error Handling

With .NET, errors are generated by throwing exceptions. With the older COM technology, errors are defined by returning `HRESULT` values with the methods. An `HRESULT` value of `S_OK` means that the method was successful.

If a more detailed error message is offered by the COM component, the COM component implements the interface `ISupportErrorInfo`, where not only an error message but also a link to a help file and the source of the error is returned with an error information object on the return of the method. Objects that implement `ISupportErrorInfo` are automatically mapped to more detailed error information with an exception in .NET.

How to trace and log errors is discussed in Chapter 18, "Tracing and Events."

Event Handling

.NET offers an event-handling mechanism with the C# keywords `event` and `delegate` (see Chapter 7, "Delegates and Events").

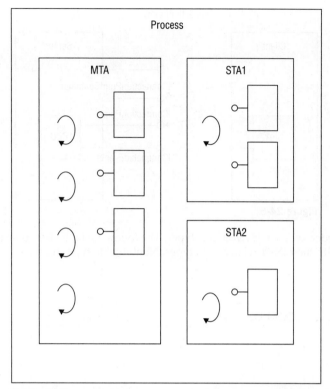

Process

MTA

STA1

STA2

Figure 24-5

Figure 24-6 shows the COM event-handling architecture. With COM events, the component has to implement the interface IConnectionPointContainer and one or more connection point objects (CPOs) that implement the interface IConnectionPoint. The component also defines an outgoing interface — ICompletedEvents in Figure 24-6 — that is invoked by the CPO. The client must implement this out-going interface in the sink object, which itself is a COM object. During runtime, the client queries the server for the interface IConnectionPointContainer. With the help of this interface, the client asks for a CPO with the method FindConnectionPoint() to get a pointer to IConnectionPoint returned. This interface pointer is used by the client to call the Advise() method, where a pointer to the sink object is passed to the server. In turn, the component can invoke methods inside the sink object of the client.

Later in this chapter, you learn how the .NET events and the COM events can be mapped so that COM events can be handled by a .NET client and vice versa.

Marshaling

Data passed from .NET to the COM component and the other way around must be converted to the corresponding representation. This mechanism is also known as *marshaling*. What happens here depends on the data type of the data that is passed: You have to differentiate between blittable and nonblittable data types.

Blittable data types have a common representation with both .NET and COM, and no conversion is needed. Simple data types such as byte, short, int, long, and classes and arrays that only contain these simple data types belong to the blittable data types. Arrays must be one-dimensional to be blittable.

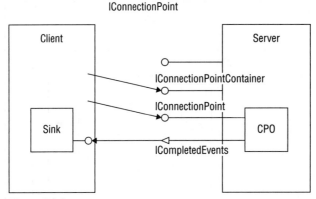

Figure 24-6

A conversion is needed with *nonblittable* data types. The following table lists some of the nonblittable COM data types with their .NET-related data types. Nonblittable types have a higher overhead because of the conversion.

COM Data Type	.NET Data Type
SAFEARRAY	Array
VARIANT	Object
BSTR	String
IUnknown*, IDispatch*	Object

Using a COM Component from a .NET Client

To see how a .NET application can use a COM component, you first have to create a COM component. Creating COM components is not possible with C# or Visual Basic 2005; you need either Visual Basic 6.0 or C++ (or any other language that supports COM). This chapter uses the Active Template Library (ATL) and C++.

A short note about building COM components with Visual Basic 9.0 and C#: With Visual Basic 9.0 and C# it is possible to build .NET components that can be used as COM objects by using a wrapper that is the real COM component. It would make no sense for a .NET component that is wrapped from a COM component to be used by a .NET client with a COM interop.

Because this is not a COM book, it does not discuss all aspects of the code but only what you need to build the sample.

Creating a COM Component

To create a COM component with ATL and C++, create a new ATL Project. You can find the ATL Project Wizard within the Visual C++ Projects group when you select File ⇨ New ⇨ Project. Set the name to COMServer. With the Application Settings, select Dynamic Link Library and click Finish.

The ATL Project Wizard just creates the foundation for the server. A COM object is still needed. Add a class in Solution Explorer and select ATL Simple Object. In the dialog that starts up, enter **COMDemo** in the field for the Short name. The other fields will be filled automatically, but change the interface name to **IWelcome** (see Figure 24-7). Click Finish to create the stub code for the class and the interface.

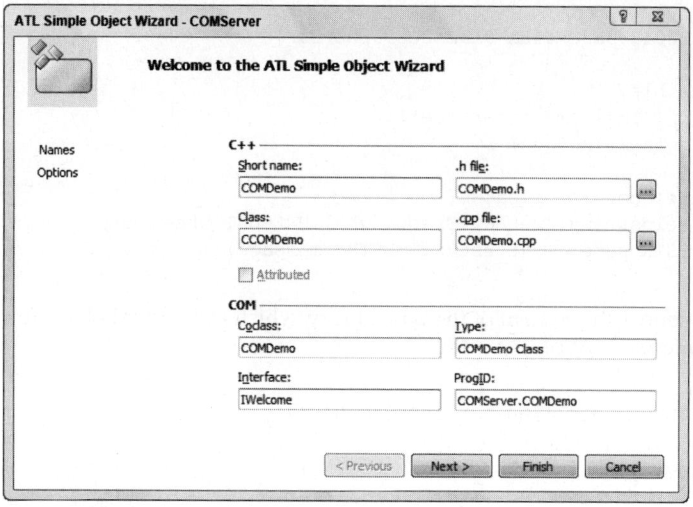

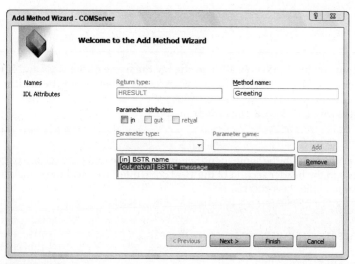

Figure 24-7

The COM component offers two interfaces, so that you can see how QueryInterface() is mapped from .NET, and just three simple methods, so that you can see how the interaction takes place. In class view, select the interface IWelcome and add the method Greeting() (see Figure 24-8) with these parameters:

```
HRESULT Greeting([in] BSTR name, [out, retval] BSTR* message);
```

Figure 24-8

The IDL file COMDemo.idl defines the interface for COM. Your wizard-generated code from the file COMDemo.idl should look similar to the following code. The unique identifiers (uuids) will differ. The interface IWelcome defines the Greeting() method. The brackets before the keyword _interface define some attributes for the interface. uuid defines the interface ID and dual marks the type of the interface:

```
[
    object,
    uuid(615B801E-3A5C-44EA-913B-8C8F53BBFB3F),
    dual,
    nonextensible,
    helpstring("IWelcome Interface"),
    pointer_default(unique)
]
interface IWelcome : IDispatch{
    [id(1), helpstring("method Greeting")] HRESULT Greeting(
        [in] BSTR name, [out,retval] BSTR* message);
};
```

The IDL file also defines the content of the type library, which is the COM object (coclass) that implements the interface IWelcome:

```
[
    uuid(1CE0DFFF-ADA8-47DD-BA06-DDD89C584242),
    version(1.0),
    helpstring("COMServer 1.0 Type Library")
]
library COMServerLib
{
    importlib("stdole2.tlb");
    [
        uuid(AB13E0B8-F8E1-497E-985F-FA30C5F449AA),
        helpstring("COMDemo Class")
    ]
    coclass COMDemo
    {
        [default] interface IWelcome;
    };
};
```

> With custom attributes, it is possible to change the name of the class and interfaces that are generated by a .NET wrapper class. You just have to add the attribute custom with the identifier 0F21F359-AB84-41e8-9A78-36D110E6D2F9, and the name under which it should appear within .NET.

Add the custom attribute with the same identifier and the name Wrox.ProCSharp.COMInterop. Server.IWelcome to the header section of the IWelcome interface. Add the same attribute with a corresponding name to the class CCOMDemo:

```
[
    object,
    uuid(615B801E-3A5C-44EA-913B-8C8F53BBFB3F),
    dual,
    nonextensible,
    helpstring("IWelcome Interface"),
```

```
        pointer_default(unique),
        custom(0F21F359-AB84-41e8-9A78-36D110E6D2F9,
            "Wrox.ProCSharp.COMInterop.Server.IWelcome")
    ]
    interface IWelcome : IDispatch{
        [id(1), helpstring("method Greeting")] HRESULT Greeting([in] BSTR name,
    [out,retval] BSTR* message);
    };

    library COMServerLib
    {
        importlib("stdole2.tlb");
        [
            uuid(AB13E0B8-F8E1-497E-985F-FA30C5F449AA),
            helpstring("COMDemo Class")
            custom(0F21F359-AB84-41e8-9A78-36D110E6D2F9,
                "Wrox.ProCSharp.COMInterop.Server.COMDemo"),
        ]
        coclass COMDemo
        {
            [default] interface IWelcome;
        };
```

Now add a second interface to the file COMDemo.idl. You can copy the header section of the IWelcome interface to the header section of the new IMath interface, but be sure to change the unique identifier that is defined with the uuid keyword. You can generate such an ID with the guidgen utility. The interface IMath offers the methods Add() and Sub():

```
    // IMath
    [
        object,
        uuid("2158751B-896E-461d-9012-EF1680BE0628"),
        dual,
        nonextensible,
        helpstring("IMath Interface"),
        pointer_default(unique),
        custom(0F21F359-AB84-41e8-9A78-36D110E6D2F9,
            "Wrox.ProCSharp.COMInterop.Server.IMath")
    ]
    interface IMath : IDispatch
    {
        [id(1)] HRESULT Add([in] LONG val1, [in] LONG val2,
                            [out, retval] LONG* result);
        [id(2)] HRESULT Sub([in] LONG val1, [in] LONG val2,
                            [out, retval] LONG* result);
    };
```

The coclass COMDemo must also be changed so that it implements both the interfaces IWelcome and IMath. The IWelcome interface is the default interface:

```
    [
        uuid(AB13E0B8-F8E1-497E-985F-FA30C5F449AA),
        helpstring("COMDemo Class"),
        custom(0F21F359-AB84-41e8-9A78-36D110E6D2F9,
            "Wrox.ProCSharp.COMInterop.Server.COMDemo")
    ]
```

(continued)

(continued)

```
coclass COMDemo
{
    [default] interface IWelcome;
    interface IMath;
};
```

Now, you can set the focus away from the IDL file toward the C++ code. In the file COMDemo.h, you can find the class definition of the COM object. The class CCOMDemo uses multiple inheritances to derive from the template classes CComObjectRootEx, CComCoClass, and IDisplatchImpl. CComObjectRootEx offers an implementation of the IUnknown interface functionality such as AddRef and Release, CComCoClass creates a factory that instantiates objects of the template argument, which here is CComDemo, and IDispatchImpl offers an implementation of the methods from the IDispatch interface.

With the macros that are surrounded by BEGIN_COM_MAP and END_COM_MAP, a map is created to define all the COM interfaces that are implemented by the COM class. This map is used by the implementation of the QueryInterface method.

```
class ATL_NO_VTABLE CCOMDemo :
    public CComObjectRootEx<CComSingleThreadModel>,
    public CComCoClass<CCOMDemo, &CLSID_COMDemo>,
    public IDispatchImpl<IWelcome, &IID_IWelcome, &LIBID_COMServerLib,
        /*wMajor =*/ 1, /*wMinor =*/ 0>
{
public:
    CCOMDemo()
    {
    }

DECLARE_REGISTRY_RESOURCEID(IDR_COMDEMO)


BEGIN_COM_MAP(CCOMDemo)
    COM_INTERFACE_ENTRY(IWelcome)
    COM_INTERFACE_ENTRY(IDispatch)
END_COM_MAP()


    DECLARE_PROTECT_FINAL_CONSTRUCT()

    HRESULT FinalConstruct()
    {
        return S_OK;
    }

    void FinalRelease()
    {
    }

public:
    STDMETHOD(Greeting)(BSTR name, BSTR* message);
};

OBJECT_ENTRY_AUTO(__uuidof(COMDemo), CCOMDemo)
```

With this class definition, you have to add the second interface, IMath, as well as the methods that are defined with the IMath interface:

```
class ATL_NO_VTABLE CCOMDemo :
    public CComObjectRootEx<CComSingleThreadModel>,
    public CComCoClass<CCOMDemo, &CLSID_COMDemo>,
    public IDispatchImpl<IWelcome, &IID_IWelcome, &LIBID_COMServerLib,
        /*wMajor =*/ 1, /*wMinor =*/ 0>
    public IDispatchImpl<IMath, &IID_IMath, &LIBID_COMServerLib, 1, 0>
{
public:
    CCOMDemo()
    {
    }

DECLARE_REGISTRY_RESOURCEID(IDR_COMDEMO)

BEGIN_COM_MAP(CCOMDemo)
    COM_INTERFACE_ENTRY(IWelcome)
    COM_INTERFACE_ENTRY(IMath)
    COM_INTERFACE_ENTRY2(IDispatch, IWelcome)
END_COM_MAP()


    DECLARE_PROTECT_FINAL_CONSTRUCT()

    HRESULT FinalConstruct()
    {
        return S_OK;
    }

    void FinalRelease()
    {
    }

public:
    STDMETHOD(Greeting)(BSTR name, BSTR* message);
    STDMETHOD(Add)(long val1, long val2, long* result);
    STDMETHOD(Sub)(long val1, long val2, long* result);
};

OBJECT_ENTRY_AUTO(__uuidof(COMDemo), CCOMDemo)
```

Now, you can implement the three methods in the file COMDemo.cpp with the following code. The CComBSTR is an ATL class that makes it easier to deal with BSTRs. In the Greeting() method, only a welcome message is returned, which adds the name passed in the first argument to the message that is returned. The Add() method just does a simple addition of two values, and the Sub() method does a subtraction and returns the result:

```
STDMETHODIMP CCOMDemo::Greeting(BSTR name, BSTR* message)
{
    CComBSTR tmp("Welcome, ");
    tmp.Append(name);
    *message = tmp;
    return S_OK;
}
```

(continued)

(continued)

```
STDMETHODIMP CCOMDemo::Add(LONG val1, LONG val2, LONG* result)
{
    *result = val1 + val2;
    return S_OK;
}

STDMETHODIMP CCOMDemo::Sub(LONG val1, LONG val2, LONG* result)
{
    *result = val1 - val2;
    return S_OK;
}
```

Now, you can build the component. The build process also configures the component in the registry.

Creating a Runtime Callable Wrapper

You can now use the COM component from within .NET. To make this possible, you must create a runtime callable wrapper (RCW). Using the RCW, the .NET client sees a .NET object instead of the COM component; there is no need to deal with the COM characteristics because this is done by the wrapper. An RCW hides the `IUnknown` and `IDispatch` interfaces (see Figure 24-9) and deals itself with the reference counts of the COM object.

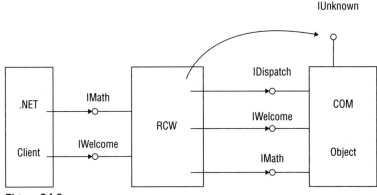

Figure 24-9

The RCW can be created by using the command-line utility `tlbimp` or by using Visual Studio. Starting the command

```
tlbimp COMServer.dll /out:Interop.COMServer.dll
```

creates the file `Interop.COMServer.dll` that contains a .NET assembly with the wrapper class. In this generated assembly, you can find the namespace `COMWrapper` with the class `CCOMDemoClass` and the interfaces `CCOMDemo`, `IMath`, and `IWelcome`. The name of the namespace can be changed by using options of the `tlbimp` utility. The option `/namespace` allows you to specify a different namespace, and with `/asmversion` you can define the version number of the assembly.

> *Another important option of this command-line utility is `/keyfile`, which is used for assigning a strong name to the generated assembly. Strong names are discussed in Chapter 17, "Assemblies."*

An RCW can also be created by using Visual Studio. To create a simple sample application, create a C# console project. In Solution Explorer, add a reference to the COM server by selecting the COM tab in the Add Reference dialog, and scroll down to the entry `COMServer 1.0 Type Library` (see Figure 24-10).

Here, all COM objects are listed that are configured in the registry. Selecting a COM component from the list creates an assembly with an RCW class.

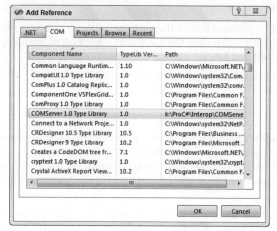

Figure 24-10

Using the RCW

After creating the wrapper class, you can write the code for the application to instantiate and access the component. Because of the custom attributes in the C++ file, the generated namespace of the RCW class is `Wrox.ProCSharp.COMInterop.Server`. Add this namespace as well as the namespace `System.Runtime.InteropServices` to the declarations. From the namespace `System.Runtime.InteropServices`, the `Marshal` class will be used to release the COM object:

```
using System;
using System.Runtime.InteropServices;
using Wrox.ProCSharp.COMInteorp.Server

namespace Wrox.ProCSharp.COMInterop.Client
{
    class Program
    {
        [STAThread]
        static void Main()
        {
```

Now, the COM component can be used similarly to a .NET class. `obj` is a variable of type `COMDemo`. `COMDemo` is a .NET interface that offers the methods of both the `IWelcome` and `IMath` interfaces. However, it is also possible to cast to a specific interface such as `IWelcome`. With a variable that is declared as type `IWelcome`, the method `Greeting()` can be called.

```
COMDemo obj = new COMDemo();
IWelcome welcome = obj;
Console.WriteLine(welcome.Greeting("Christian"));
```

Although `COMDemo` *is an interface, you can instantiate new objects of type* `COMDemo`. *Contrary to normal interfaces, you can do this with wrapped COM interfaces.*

If the object — as in this case — offers multiple interfaces, a variable of the other interface can be declared, and by using a simple assignment with the cast operator, the wrapper class does a `QueryInterface()` with the COM object to return the second interface pointer. With the `math` variable, the methods of the `IMath` interface can be called.

```
IMath math;
math = (IMath)welcome;
int x = math.Add(4, 5);
Console.WriteLine(x);
```

If the COM object should be released before the garbage collector cleans up the object, the static method `Marshal.ReleaseComObject()` invokes the `Release()` method of the component, so that the component can destroy itself and free up memory:

```
        Marshal.ReleaseComObject(math);
    }
  }
}
```

Earlier you learned that the COM object is released as soon as the reference count is 0. `Marshal.ReleaseComObject()` decrements the reference count by 1 by invoking the `Release()` method. Because the RCW does just one call to `AddRef()` to increment the reference count, a single call to `Marshal.ReleaseComObject()` is enough to release the object no matter how many references to the RCW you keep.

After releasing the COM object using `Marshal.ReleaseComObject()`, you may not use any variable that references the object. In the example, the COM object is released by using the variable `math`. The variable `welcome`, which references the same object, cannot be used after releasing the object. Otherwise, you will get an exception of type `InvalidComObjectException`.

> **Releasing COM objects when they are no longer needed is extremely important. COM objects make use of the native memory heap, whereas .NET objects make use of the managed memory heap. The garbage collector only deals with managed memory.**

As you can see, with a runtime callable wrapper, a COM component can be used similarly to a .NET object.

A special case of a runtime callable wrapper is a primary interop assembly, which is discussed next.

Primary Interop Assemblies

A *primary interop assembly* is an assembly that is already prepared by the vendor of the COM component. This makes it easier to use the COM component. A primary interop assembly is a runtime-callable wrapper that might differ from an automatically generated RCW.

You can find primary interop assemblies in the directory `<program files>\Microsoft.NET\Primary Interop Assemblies`. A primary interop assembly already exists for the use of ADO from within .NET. If you add a reference to the COM library Microsoft ActiveX Data Objects 2.7 Library, no wrapper class is created because a primary interop assembly already exists; the primary interop assembly is referenced instead.

Threading Issues

As discussed earlier in this chapter, a COM component marks the apartment (STA or MTA) it wants to live in, based on whether or not it is implemented as thread-safe. However, the thread has to join an apartment. What apartment the thread should join can be defined with the `[STAThread]` and `[MTAThread]` attributes, which can be applied to the `Main()` method of an application. The attribute `[STAThread]` means that the thread joins an STA, whereas the attribute `[MTAThread]` means that the thread joins an MTA. Joining an MTA is the default if no attribute is applied.

It is also possible to set the apartment state programmatically with the ApartmentState property of the Thread class. The ApartmentState property allows you to set a value from the ApartmentState enumeration. ApartmentState has the possible values STA and MTA (and Unknown if it wasn't set). Be aware that the apartment state of a thread can be set only once. If it is set a second time, the second setting is ignored.

> **What happens if the thread chooses a different apartment from the apartments supported by the component? The correct apartment for the COM component is created automatically by the COM runtime. However, the performance decreases if the apartment boundaries are crossed while calling the methods of a component.**

Adding Connection Points

To see how COM events can be handled in a .NET application, first the COM component must be extended. Implementing a COM event in an ATL class using attributes looks very similar to the events in .NET, although the functionality is different.

First, you have to add another interface to the interface definition file COMDemo.idl. The interface _ICompletedEvents is implemented by the client, which is the .NET application, and called by the component. In this example, the method Completed() is called by the component when the calculation is ready. Such an interface is also known as an outgoing interface. An outgoing interface must either be a dispatch or a custom interface. Dispatch interfaces are supported by all clients. The custom attribute with the ID 0F21F359-AB84-41e8-9A78-36D110E6D2F9 defines the name of this interface that will be created in the RCW. The outgoing interface must also be written to the interfaces supported by the component inside the coclass section, and marked as a source interface:

```
library COMServerLib
{
    importlib("stdole2.tlb");

    [
        uuid(5CFF102B-0961-4EC6-8BB4-759A3AB6EF48),
        helpstring("_ICompletedEvents Interface"),
        custom(0F21F359-AB84-41e8-9A78-36D110E6D2F9,
          "Wrox.ProCSharp.COMInterop.Server.ICompletedEvents"),
    ]
    dispinterface _ICompletedEvents
    {
        properties:
        methods:
            [id(1)] void Completed(void);
    };

    [
        uuid(AB13E0B8-F8E1-497E-985F-FA30C5F449AA),
        helpstring("COMDemo Class")
        custom(0F21F359-AB84-41e8-9A78-36D110E6D2F9,
          "Wrox.ProCSharp.COMInterop.Server.COMDemo"),
    ]
    coclass COMDemo
```

(continued)

(continued)

```
    {
        [default] interface IWelcome;
        interface IMath;
        [default, source] dispinterface _ICompletedEvents;
    };
```

You can use a wizard to create an implementation that fires the event back to the client. Open the class view, select the class `CComDemo`, open the context menu, and start the Implement Connection Point Wizard (see Figure 24-11). Select the source interface `ICompletedEvents` for implementation with the connection point.

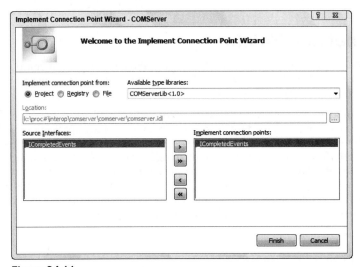

Figure 24-11

The wizard creates the proxy class `CProxy_ICompletedEvents` to fire the events to the client. Also, the class `CCOMDemo` is changed. The class now inherits from `IConnectionPointContainerImpl` and the proxy class. The interface `IConnectionPointContainer` is added to the interface map, and a connection point map is added to the source interface `_ICompletedEvents`.

```
class ATL_NO_VTABLE CCOMDemo :
    public CComObjectRootEx<CComSingleThreadModel>,
    public CComCoClass<CCOMDemo, &CLSID_COMDemo>,
    public IDispatchImpl<IWelcome, &IID_IWelcome, &LIBID_COMServerLib,
        /*wMajor =*/ 1, /*wMinor =*/ 0>,
    public IDispatchImpl<IMath, &IID_IMath, &LIBID_COMServerLib, 1, 0>,
    public IConnectionPointContainerImpl<CCOMDemo>,
    public CProxy_ICompletedEvents<CCOMDemo>
{
public:

//...

BEGIN_COM_MAP(CCOMDemo)
    COM_INTERFACE_ENTRY(IWelcome)
    COM_INTERFACE_ENTRY(IMath)
```

```
    COM_INTERFACE_ENTRY2(IDispatch, IWelcome)
    COM_INTERFACE_ENTRY(IConnectionPointContainer)
END_COM_MAP()

//...

public:
    BEGIN_CONNECTION_POINT_MAP(CCOMDemo)
        CONNECTION_POINT_ENTRY(__uuidof(_ICompletedEvents))
    END_CONNECTION_POINT_MAP()
};
```

Finally, the method `Fire_Completed()` from the proxy class can be called inside the methods `Add()` and `Sub()` in the file `COMDemo.cpp`:

```
STDMETHODIMP CCOMDemo::Add(LONG val1, LONG val2, LONG* result)
{
    *result = val1 + val2;
    Fire_Completed();
    return S_OK;
}

STDMETHODIMP CCOMDemo::Sub(LONG val1, LONG val2, LONG* result)
{
    *result = val1 - val2;
    Fire_Completed();
    return S_OK;
}
```

After rebuilding the COM DLL, you can change the .NET client to use these COM events just like a normal .NET event:

```
static void Main()
{
    COMDemo obj = new COMDemo();

    IWelcome welcome = obj;
    Console.WriteLine(welcome.Greeting("Christian"));

    obj.Completed +=
        delegate
        {
            Console.WriteLine("Calculation completed");
        });

    IMath math = (IMath)welcome;
    int result = math.Add(3, 5);
    Console.WriteLine(result);

    Marshal.ReleaseComObject(math);
}
```

As you can see, the RCW offers automatic mapping from COM events to .NET events. COM events can be used similarly to .NET events in a .NET client.

Using ActiveX Controls in Windows Forms

ActiveX controls are COM objects with a user interface and many optional COM interfaces to deal with the user interface and the interaction with the container. ActiveX controls can be used by many different containers, such as Internet Explorer, Word, Excel, and applications written using Visual Basic 6.0, MFC (Microsoft Foundation Classes), or ATL (Active Template Library). A Windows Forms application is another container that can manage ActiveX controls. ActiveX controls can be used similarly to Windows Forms controls as you'll see shortly.

ActiveX Control Importer

Similar to runtime callable wrappers, you can also create a wrapper for ActiveX controls. A wrapper for an ActiveX control is created by using the command-line utility *Windows Forms ActiveX Control Importer*, `aximp.exe`. This utility creates a class that derives from the base class `System.Windows.Forms.AxHost` that acts as a wrapper to use the ActiveX control.

You can enter this command to create a wrapper class from the Web Forms control:

```
aximp c:\windows\system32\shdocvw.dll
```

ActiveX controls can also be imported directly using Visual Studio. If the ActiveX control is configured within the toolbox, it can be dragged and dropped onto a Windows Forms control that creates the wrapper.

Creating a Windows Forms Application

To see ActiveX controls running inside a Windows Forms application, create a simple Windows Forms application project. With this application, you will build a simple Internet browser that uses the Web Browser control, which comes as part of the operating system.

Create a form as shown in Figure 24-12. The form should include a toolstrip with a text box and three buttons. The text box with the name `toolStripTextUrl` is used to enter a URL, three buttons with the names `toolStripButtonNavigate`, `toolStripButtonBack`, and `toolStripButtonForward` to navigate web pages, and a status strip with the name `statusStrip`. The status strip also needs a label to display status messages.

Figure 24-12

Using Visual Studio, you can add ActiveX controls to the toolbar to use it in the same way as a Windows Forms control. On the Customize Toolbox context menu, select the Add/Remove Items menu entry and select the Microsoft Web Browser control in the COM Components category (see Figure 24-13).

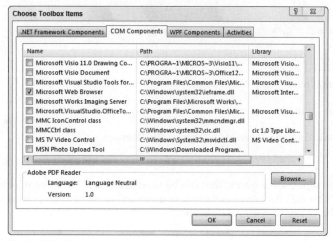

Figure 24-13

This way, an icon will show up in the toolbox. Similarly to other Windows controls, you can drag and drop this icon to the Windows Forms designer to create (with the `aximp` utility) a wrapper assembly hosting the ActiveX control. You can see the wrapper assemblies with the references in the project: `AxSHDocVw` and `SHDocVw`. Now you can invoke methods of the control by using the generated variable `axWebBrowser1`, as shown in the following code. Add a `Click` event handler to the button `toolStripButtonNavigate` in order to navigate the browser to a web page. The method `Navigate()` used for this purpose requires a URL string with the first argument that you get by accessing the `Text` property of the text box control `toolStripTextUrl`:

```
private void OnNavigate(object sender, System.EventArgs e)
{
    try
    {
        axWebBrowser1.Navigate(toolStripTextUrl.Text);
    }
    catch (COMException ex)
    {
        statusStrip.Items[0].Text = ex.Message;
    }
}
```

With the `Click` event handler of the `Back` and `Forward` buttons, call the `GoBack()` and `GoForward()` methods of the browser control:

```
private void OnGoBack(object sender, System.EventArgs e)
{
    try
    {
        axWebBrowser1.GoBack();
    }
    catch (COMException ex)
```

(continued)

(continued)

```
        {
            statusStrip.Items[0].Text = ex.Message;
        }
    }

    private void OnGoForward(object sender, System.EventArgs e)
    {
        try
        {
            axWebBrowser1.GoForward();
        }
        catch (COMException ex)
        {
            statusStrip.Items[0].Text = ex.Message;
        }
    }
```

The web control also offers some events that can be used just like a .NET event. Add the event handler `OnStatusChange()` to the event `StatusTextChange` to set the status that is returned by the control to the status strip in the Windows Forms application:

```
    private void OnStatusChange(object sender,
                        AxSHDocVw.DWebBrowserEvents2_StatusTextChangeEvent e)
    {
        statusStrip.Items[0].Text = e.text;
    }
```

Now, you have a simple browser that you can use to navigate to web pages (see Figure 24-14).

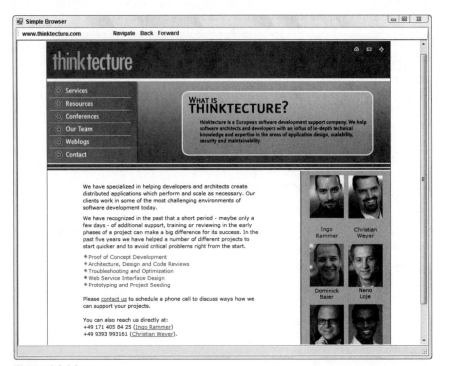

Figure 24-14

Using COM Objects from Within ASP.NET

COM objects can be used in a similar way to what you have seen before from within ASP.NET. However, there is one important distinction. The ASP.NET runtime by default runs in an MTA. If the COM object is configured with the threading model value `Apartment` (as all COM objects that have been written with Visual Basic 6.0 are), an exception is thrown. For performance and scalability reasons, it is best to avoid STA objects within ASP.NET. If you really want to use an STA object with ASP.NET, you can set the `AspCompat` attribute with the `Page` directive as shown in the following snippet. Be aware that the web site performance might suffer when you are using this option:

```
<%@ Page AspCompat="true" Language="C#" %>
```

> Using STA COM objects with ASP.NET can lead to scalability problems. It's best to avoid using STA COM objects with ASP.NET.

Using a .NET Component from a COM Client

So far, you have seen how to access a COM component from a .NET client. Equally interesting is to find a solution for accessing .NET components in an old COM client that is using Visual Basic 6.0, or C++ with MFC, or ATL.

COM Callable Wrapper

If you want to access a COM component with a .NET client, you have to work with an RCW. To access a .NET component from a COM client application, you must use a COM callable wrapper (CCW). Figure 24-15 shows a CCW that wraps a .NET class, and offers COM interfaces that a COM client expects to use. The CCW offers interfaces such as `IUnknown`, `IDispatch`, `ISupportErrorInfo`, and others. It also offers interfaces such as `IConnectionPointContainer` and `IConnectionPoint` for events. A COM client gets what it expects from a COM object — although a .NET component is behind the scenes. The wrapper deals with methods such as `AddRef()`, `Release()`, and `QueryInterface()` from the `IUnknown` interface, whereas in the .NET object you can count on the garbage collector without the need to deal with reference counts.

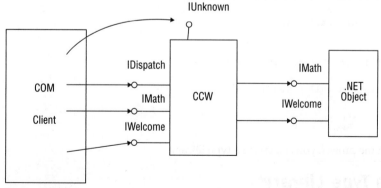

Figure 24-15

Creating a .NET Component

In the following example, you build the same functionality into a .NET class that you have previously built into a COM component. Start by creating a C# class library, and name it `DotNetComponent`. Then add the interfaces `IWelcome` and `IMath`, and the class `DotNetComponent` that implements these interfaces. The attribute `[ComVisible(true)]` makes the class and interfaces available for COM:

```csharp
using System;
using System.Runtime.InteropServices;

namespace Wrox.ProCSharp.COMInterop.Server
{
    [ComVisible(true)]
    public interface IWelcome
    {
        string Greeting(string name);
    }

    [ComVisible(true)]
    public interface IMath
    {
        int Add(int val1, int val2);
        int Sub(int val1, int val2);
    }

    [ComVisible(true)]
    public class DotnetComponent : IWelcome, IMath
    {
        public DotnetComponent()
        {
        }

        public string Greeting(string name)
        {
            return "Hello " + name;
        }

        public int Add(int val1, int val2)
        {
            return val1 + val2;
        }

        public int Sub(int val1, int val2)
        {
            return val1 - val2;
        }
    }
}
```

After building the project, you can create a type library.

Creating a Type Library

A type library can be created by using the command-line utility `tlbexp`. The command

```
tlbexp DotnetComponent.dll
```

creates the type library `DotnetComponent.tlb`. You can view the type library with the utility *OLE/COM Object Viewer*`oleview32.exe`. This tool is part of the Microsoft SDK, and you can start it from the Visual Studio 2008 Command Prompt. Select File ⇨ View TypeLib to open the type library. Now you can see the interface definition shown in the following code. The unique IDs will differ.

The name of the type library is created from the name of the assembly. The header of the type library also defines the full name of the assembly in a custom attribute, and all the interfaces are forward-declared before they are defined:

```
// Generated .IDL file (by the OLE/COM Object Viewer)
//
// typelib filename: dotnetcomponent.dll

[
  uuid(0AA0953A-B2A0-32CB-A5AC-5DA0DF698EB8),
  version(1.0),
  custom(90883F05-3D28-11D2-8F17-00A0C9A6186D, DotNetComponent,
         Version=1.0.0.0., Culture=neutral, PublicKeyToken=null)
]
library DotnetComponent
{
    // TLib : Common Language Runtime Library :
    // {BED7F4EA-1A96-11D2-8F08-00A0C9A6186D}
    importlib("mscorlib.tlb");
    // TLib : OLE Automation : {00020430-0000-0000-c000-000000000046}
    importlib("stdole2.tlb");

    // Forward declare all types defined in this typelib
    interface IWelcome;
    interface IMath;
    interface _DotnetComponent;
```

In the following generated code, you can see that the interfaces `IWelcome` and `IMath` are defined as COM dual interfaces. You can see all methods that have been declared in the C# code are listed here in the type library definition. The parameters changed; the .NET types are mapped to COM types (for example, from the `String` class to the `BSTR` type), and the signature is changed, so that a `HRESULT` is returned. Because the interfaces are dual, dispatch IDs are also generated:

```
    [
      odl,
      uuid(F39A4143-F88D-321E-9A33-8208E256A2DF),
      version(1.0),
      dual,
      oleautomation,
      custom(0F21F359-AB84-41E8-9A78-36D110E6D2F9,
             Wrox.ProCSharp.COMInterop.Server.IWelcome)
    ]
    interface IWelcome : IDispatch {
      [id(0x60020000)]
      HRESULT Greeting([in] BSTR name, [out, retval] BSTR* pRetVal);
    };

    [
      odl,
      uuid(EF596F3F-B69B-3657-9D48-C906CBF12565),
      version(1.0),
      dual,
```

(continued)

(continued)

```
            oleautomation,
            custom(0F21F359-AB84-41E8-9A78-36D110E6D2F9,
                    Wrox.ProCSharp.COMInterop.Server.IMath)
        ]
        interface IMath : IDispatch {
            [id(0x60020000)] HRESULT Add([in] long val1, [in] long val2,
                                        [out, retval] long* pRetVal);
            [id(0x60020001)] HRESULT Sub([in] long val1, [in] long val2,
                                        [out, retval] long* pRetVal);
        };
```

The `coclass` section marks the COM object itself. The `uuid` in the header is the CLSID used to instantiate the object. The class `DotnetComponent` supports the interfaces `_DotnetComponent`, `_Object`, `IWelcome`, and `IMath`. `_Object` is defined in the file `mscorlib.tlb` included in an earlier code section and offers the methods of the base class `Object`. The default interface of the component is `_DotnetComponent`, which is defined after the `coclass` section as a dispatch interface. In the interface declaration it is marked as dual, but because no methods are included, it is a dispatch interface. With this interface, it is possible to access all methods of the component using late binding:

```
        [
          uuid(5BCD9C26-D68D-38C2-92E3-DA0C1741A8CD),
          version(1.0),
          custom(0F21F359-AB84-41E8-9A78-36D110E6D2F9,
                  Wrox.ProCSharp.COMInterop.Server.DotnetComponent)
        ]
        coclass DotnetComponent {
            [default] interface _DotnetComponent;
            interface _Object;
            interface IWelcome;
            interface IMath;
        };

        [
          odl,
          uuid(884C59C6-B3C2-3455-BB74-52753C409097),
          hidden,
          dual,
          oleautomation,
          custom(0F21F359-AB84-41E8-9A78-36D110E6D2F9,
                  Wrox.ProCSharp.COMInterop.Server.DotnetComponent)
        ]
        interface _DotnetComponent : IDispatch {
        };
    };
```

There are quite a few defaults for generating the type library. However, often it is advantageous to change some of the default .NET to COM mappings. This can be done with several attributes in the `System.Runtime.InteropServices` namespaces.

COM Interop Attributes

Applying attributes from the namespace `System.Runtime.InteropServices` to classes, interfaces, or methods allows you to change the implementation of the CCW. The following table lists these attributes and a description.

Attribute	Description
Guid	This attribute can be assigned to the assembly, interfaces, and classes. Using the Guid as an assembly attribute defines the type-library ID, applying it to interfaces defines the interface ID (IID), and setting the attribute to a class defines the class ID (CLSID).
	The unique IDs needed to be defined with this attribute can be created with the utility guidgen.
	The CLSID and type-library IDs are changed automatically with every build. If you don't want to change it with every build, you can fix it by using this attribute. The IID is only changed if the signature of the interface changes; for example, a method is added or removed, or some parameters changed. Because with COM the IID should change with every new version of this interface, this is a very good default behavior, and usually there's no need to apply the IID with the Guid attribute. The only time you want to apply a fixed IID for an interface is when the .NET interface is an exact representation of an existing COM interface, and the COM client already expects this identifier.
ProgId	This attribute can be applied to a class to specify what name should be used when the object is configured in the registry.
ComVisible	This attribute enables you to hide classes, interfaces, and delegates from COM when set to false. This prevents a COM representation from being created.
InterfaceType	This attribute, if set to a ComInterfaceType enumeration value, enables you to modify the default dual interface type that is created for .NET interfaces. ComInterfaceType has the values InterfaceIsDual, InterfaceIsIDispatch, and InterfaceIsIUnknown. If you want to apply a custom interface type to a .NET interface, set the attribute like this: [InterfaceType(ComInterfaceType.InterfaceIsIUnknown)]
ClassInterface	This attribute enables you to modify the default dispatch interface that is created for a class. ClassInterface accepts an argument of a ClassInterfaceType enumeration. The possible values are AutoDispatch, AutoDual, and None. In the previous example, you have seen that the default is AutoDispatch, because a dispatch interface is created. If the class should only be accessible by the defined interfaces, apply the attribute [ClassInterface(ClassInterfaceType.None)] to the class.
DispId	This attribute can be used with dual and dispatch interfaces to define the DispId of methods and properties.
InOut	COM allows specifying attributes to parameter types if the parameter should be sent to the component [In], from the component to the client [Out], or in both directions [In, Out].
Optional	Parameters of COM methods may be optional. Parameters that should be optional can be marked with the Optional attribute.

Now, you can change the C# code to specify a dual interface type for the IWelcome interface and a custom interface type for the IMath interface. With the class DotnetComponent, the attribute ClassInterface with the argument ClassInterfaceType.None specifies that no separate COM interface will be generated. The attributes ProgId and Guid specify a ProgID and a GUID:

```
[InterfaceType(ComInterfaceType.InterfaceIsDual)]
[ComVisible(true)]
public interface IWelcome
{
    [DispId(60040)] string Greeting(string name);
}

[InterfaceType(ComInterfaceType.InterfaceIsIUnknown)]
[ComVisible(true)]
public interface IMath
{
  int Add(int val1, int val2);
  int Sub(int val1, int val2);
}

[ClassInterface(ClassInterfaceType.None)]
[ProgId("Wrox.DotnetComponent")]
[Guid("77839717-40DD-4876-8297-35B98A8402C7")]
[ComVisible(true)]
public class DotnetComponent : IWelcome, IMath
{
    public DotnetComponent()
    {
    }
```

Rebuilding the class library and the type library changes the interface definition. You can verify this with OleView.exe. As you can see in the following IDL code, the interface IWelcome is still a dual interface, whereas the IMath interface now is a custom interface that is derived from IUnknown instead of IDispatch. In the coclass section, the interface _DotnetComponent is removed, and now IWelcome is the new default interface, because it was the first interface in the inheritance list of the class DotnetComponent:

```
// Generated .IDL file (by the OLE/COM Object Viewer)
//
// typelib filename: <could not determine filename>

[
  uuid(11E86506-EA54-3611-A55C-6830C48A554B),
  version(1.0),
  custom(90883F05-3D28-11D2-8F17-00A0C9A6186D, DotNetComponent,
         Version=1.0.1321.28677, Culture=neutral, PublicKeyToken=null)
]
library DotnetComponent
{
    // TLib : Common Language Runtime Library :
    // {BED7F4EA-1A96-11D2-8F08-00A0C9A6186D}
    importlib("mscorlib.tlb");
    // TLib : OLE Automation : {00020430-0000-0000-c000-000000000046}
    importlib("stdole2.tlb");

    // Forward declare all types defined in this typelib
```

```
interface IWelcome;
interface IMath;

[
  odl,
  uuid(F39A4143-F88D-321E-9A33-8208E256A2DF),
  version(1.0),
  dual,
  oleautomation,
  custom(0F21F359-AB84-41E8-9A78-36D110E6D2F9,
         Wrox.ProCSharp.COMInterop.Server.IWelcome)
]
interface IWelcome : IDispatch {
    [id(0x0000ea88)]
    HRESULT Greeting([in] BSTR name, [out, retval] BSTR* pRetVal);
};

[
  odl,
  uuid(EF596F3F-B69B-3657-9D48-C906CBF12565),
  version(1.0),
  oleautomation,
  custom(0F21F359-AB84-41E8-9A78-36D110E6D2F9,
         Wrox.ProCSharp.COMInterop.Server.IMath)
]
interface IMath : IUnknown {
    HRESULT _stdcall Add([in] long val1, [in] long val2,
                         [out, retval] long* pRetVal);
    HRESULT _stdcall Sub([in] long val1, [in] long val2,
                         [out, retval] long* pRetVal);
};

[
  uuid(77839717-40DD-4876-8297-35B98A8402C7),
  version(1.0),
  custom(0F21F359-AB84-41E8-9A78-36D110E6D2F9,
         Wrox.ProCSharp.COMInterop.Server.DotnetComponent)
]
coclass DotnetComponent {
    interface _Object;
    [default] interface IWelcome;
    interface IMath;
};
};
```

COM Registration

Before the .NET component can be used as a COM object, it is necessary to configure it in the registry. Also, if you don't want to copy the assembly into the same directory as the client application, it is necessary to install the assembly in the global assembly cache. The global assembly cache itself is discussed in Chapter 17, "Assemblies."

To install the assembly in the global assembly cache, you must sign it with a strong name (using Visual Studio 2008, you can define a strong name in properties of the solution). Then you can register the assembly in the global assembly cache:

```
gacutil -i dotnetcomponent.dll
```

Now, you can use the `regasm` utility to configure the component inside the registry. The option `/tlb` extracts the type library and also configures the type library in the registry:

```
regasm dotnetcomponent.dll /tlb
```

The information for the .NET component that is written to the registry is as follows. The `All COM` configuration is in the hive `HKEY_CLASSES_ROOT (HKCR)`. The key of the ProgID (in this example, it is `Wrox.DotnetComponent`) is written directly to this hive, along with the CLSID.

The key `HKCR\CLSID\{CLSID}\InProcServer32` has the following entries:

❑   mscoree.dll — `mscoree.dll` represents the CCW. This is a real COM object that is responsible for hosting the .NET component. This COM object accesses the .NET component to offer COM behavior for the client. The file `mscoree.dll` is loaded and instantiated from the client via the normal COM instantiation mechanism.

❑   ThreadingModel=Both — This is an attribute of the `mscoree.dll` COM object. This component is programmed in a way to offer support both for STA and MTA.

❑   Assembly=DotnetComponent, Version=1.0.0.0, Culture=neutral, PublicKeyToken= 5cd57c93b4d9c41a — The value of the `Assembly` stores the assembly full name, including the version number and the public key token, so that the assembly can be uniquely identified. The assembly registered here will be loaded by `mscoree.dll`.

❑   Class=Wrox.ProCSharp.COMInterop.Server.DotnetComponent — The name of the class will also be used by `mscoree.dll`. This is the class that will be instantiated.

❑   RuntimeVersion=v2.0.50727 — The registry entry `RuntimeVersion` specifies the version of the .NET runtime that will be used to host the .NET assembly.

In addition to the configurations shown here, all the interfaces and the type library are configured with their identifiers, too.

Creating a COM Client

Now, it's time to create a COM client. Start by creating a simple C++ Win32 Console application project, and name it `COMClient`. You can leave the default options selected, and click Finish in the project wizard.

At the beginning of the file `COMClient.cpp`, add a preprocessor command to include the `<iostream>` header file and to import the type library that you created for the .NET component. The import statement creates a "smart pointer" class that makes it easier to deal with COM objects. During a build process, the import statement creates `.tlh` and `.tli` files that you can find in the debug directory of your project, which includes the smart pointer class. Then add `using namespace` directives to open the namespace `std` that will be used for writing output messages to the console, and the namespace `DotnetComponent` that is created inside the smart pointer class:

```
// COMClient.cpp : Defines the entry point for the console application.
//

#include "stdafx.h"
#include <iostream>
#import "../DotNetComponent/bin/debug/DotnetComponent.tlb" named_guids

using namespace std;
using namespace DotnetComponent;
```

In the `_tmain()` method, the first thing to do before any other COM call is the initialization of COM with the API call `CoInitialize()`. `CoInitialize()` creates and enters an STA for the thread. The variable `spWelcome` is of type `IWelcomePtr`, which is a smart pointer. The smart pointer method

`CreateInstance()` accepts the ProgID as an argument to create the COM object by using the COM API `CoCreateInstance()`. The operator `->` is overridden with the smart pointer, so that you can invoke the methods of the COM object such as `Greeting()`:

```
int _tmain(int argc, _TCHAR* argv[])
{
  HRESULT hr;
  hr = CoInitialize(NULL);

  try
  {
    IWelcomePtr spWelcome;

    // CoCreateInstance()
    hr = spWelcome.CreateInstance("Wrox.DotnetComponent");

    cout << spWelcome->Greeting("Bill") << endl;
```

The second interface supported by your .NET component is `IMath`, and there is also a smart pointer that wraps the COM interface: `IMathPtr`. You can directly assign one smart pointer to another as in `spMath = spWelcome;`. In the implementation of the smart pointer (the = operator is overridden), the `QueryInterface()` method is called. With a reference to the `IMath` interface, you can call the `Add()` method.

```
    IMathPtr spMath;
    spMath = spWelcome;     // QueryInterface()

    long result = spMath->Add(4, 5);
    cout << "result:" << result << endl;
  }
```

If an `HRESULT` error value is returned by the COM object (this is done by the CCW that returns `HRESULT` errors if the .NET component generates exceptions), the smart pointer wraps the `HRESULT` errors and generates `_com_error` exceptions instead. Errors are handled in the `catch` block. At the end of the program, the COM DLLs are closed and unloaded using `CoUninitialize()`:

```
  catch (_com_error& e)
  {
    cout << e.ErrorMessage() << endl;
  }

  CoUninitialize();
  return 0;
}
```

Now you can run the application, and you will get outputs from the `Greeting()` and the `Add()` methods to the console. You can also try to debug into the smart pointer class, where you can see the COM API calls directly.

> **If you get an exception that the component cannot be found, check if the same version of the assembly that is configured in the registry is installed in the global assembly cache.**

Adding Connection Points

Adding support for COM events to the .NET components requires some changes to the implementation of your .NET class. Offering COM events is not a simple matter of using the `event` and `delegate` keywords; it is necessary to add some more COM interop attributes.

First, you have to add an interface to the .NET project: `IMathEvents`. This interface is the source or outgoing interface for the component, and will be implemented by the `sink` object in the client. A source interface must be either a dispatch or a custom interface. A scripting client supports only dispatch interfaces. Dispatch interfaces are usually preferred as source interfaces:

```
[InterfaceType(ComInterfaceType.InterfaceIsIDispatch)]
[ComVisible(true)]
public interface IMathEvents
{
    [DispId(46200)] void CalculationCompleted();
}
```

Next, you have to add a delegate. The delegate must have the same signature and return type as the method in the outgoing interface. If you have multiple methods in your source interface, for each one that differs in its arguments, you have to specify a separate delegate. Because the COM client does not have to access this delegate directly, the delegate can be marked with the attribute `[ComVisible(false)]`:

```
[ComVisible(false)]
public delegate void CalculationCompletedEventHandler();
```

With the class `DotnetComponent`, a source interface must be specified. This can be done with the attribute `[ComSourceInterfaces]`. Add the attribute `[ComSourceInterfaces]`, and specify the outgoing interface declared earlier. You can add more than one source interface with different constructors of the attribute class; however, the only client language that supports more than one source interface is C++. Visual Basic 6.0 clients support only one source interface.

```
[ClassInterface(ClassInterfaceType.None)]
[ProgId("Wrox.DotnetComponent")]
[Guid("77839717-40DD-4876-8297-35B98A8402C7")]
[ComSourceInterfaces(typeof(IMathEvents))]
[ComVisible(true)]
public class DotnetComponent : IWelcome, IMath
{
    public DotnetComponent()
    {
    }
```

Inside the class `DotnetComponent`, you have to declare an event for every method of the source interface. The type of the method must be the name of the delegate, and the name of the event must be exactly the same as the name of the method inside the source interface. You can add the event calls to the `Add()` and `Sub()` methods. This step is the normal .NET way to invoke events, as discussed in Chapter 7, "Delegates and Events."

```
public event CalculationCompletedEventHandler CalculationCompleted;

public int Add(int val1, int val2)
{
    int result = val1 + val2;
    if (CalculationCompleted != null)
        CalculationCompleted();
    return result;
}
```

```
    public int Sub(int val1, int val2)
    {
        int result = val1 - val2;
        if (CalculationCompleted != null)
            CalculationCompleted();
        return result;
    }
}
```

> The name of the event must be the same as the name of the method inside the source interface. Otherwise, the events cannot be mapped for COM clients.

Creating a Client with a Sink Object

After you've built and registered the .NET assembly, and installed it into the global assembly cache, you can build a client application by using the event sources. Implementing a callback or sink object that implements the IDispatch interface was — using Visual Basic 6.0 — just a matter of adding the With Events keyword, very similar to how Visual Basic deals with .NET events today. It's more work with C++, but here the Active Template Library helps.

Open the C++ Console application created previously and add the following includes to the file stdafx.h:

```
#include <atlbase.h>
extern CComModule _Module;
#include <atlcom.h>
```

The file stdafx.cpp requires an include of the ATL implementation file atlimpl.cpp:

```
#include <atlimpl.cpp>
```

Add the new class CEventHandler to the file COMClient.cpp. This class contains the implementation of the IDispatch interface to be called by the component. The implementation of the IDispatch interface is done by the base class IDispEventImpl. This class reads the type library to match the dispatch IDs of the methods and the parameters to the methods of the class. The template parameters of the class IDispatchEventImpl requires an ID of the sink object (here the ID 4 is used), the class that implements the callback methods (CEventHandler), the interface ID of the callback interface (DIID_IMathEvents), the ID of the type library (LIBID_DotnetComponent), and the version number of the type library. You can find the named IDs DIID_IMathEvents and LIBID_DotnetComponent in the file dotnetcomponent.tlh that was created from the #import statement.

The sink map that is surrounded by BEGIN_SINK_MAP and END_SINK_MAP defines the methods that are implemented by the sink object. SINK_ENTRY_EX maps the method OnCalcCompleted to the dispatch ID 46200. This dispatch ID was defined with the method CalculationCompleted of the IMathEvents interface in the .NET component.

```
class CEventHandler : public IDispEventImpl<4, CEventHandler,
    &DIID_IMathEvents, &LIBID_DotnetComponent, 1, 0>
{
public:
    BEGIN_SINK_MAP(CEventHandler)
        SINK_ENTRY_EX(4, DIID_IMathEvents, 46200, OnCalcCompleted)
    END_SINK_MAP()
```

(continued)

(continued)

```
HRESULT __stdcall OnCalcCompleted()
{
    cout << "calculation completed" << endl;
    return S_OK;
}
};
```

The main method now needs a change to advise the event sink object to the component, so that the component can call back into the sink. This can be done with the method `DispEventAdvise()` of the `CEventHandler` class by passing an `IUnknown` interface pointer. The method `DispEventUnadvise()` unregisters the sink object again.

```
int _tmain(int argc, _TCHAR* argv[])
{
    HRESULT hr;
    hr = CoInitialize(NULL);

    try
    {
        IWelcomePtr spWelcome;
        hr = spWelcome.CreateInstance("Wrox.DotnetComponent");

        IUnknownPtr spUnknown = spWelcome;


        cout << spWelcome->Greeting("Isabella") << endl;

        CEventHandler* eventHandler = new CEventHandler();
        hr = eventHandler->DispEventAdvise(spUnknown);


        IMathPtr spMath;
        spMath = spWelcome;    // QueryInterface()

        long result = spMath->Add(4, 5);
        cout << "result:" << result << endl;

        eventHandler->DispEventUnadvise(spWelcome.GetInterfacePtr());
        delete eventHandler;
    }
    catch (_com_error& e)
    {
        cout << e.ErrorMessage() << endl;
    }

    CoUninitialize();
    return 0;
}
```

Running Windows Forms Controls in Internet Explorer

Windows Forms controls can be hosted in Internet Explorer as ActiveX controls. Because there are many different ActiveX control containers, and all these containers do have different requirements on the ActiveX controls, hosting Windows Forms controls in any container is not supported by Microsoft.

Supported containers are Internet Explorer and MFC containers (MFC containers were supported first in Visual Studio .NET 2003). With MFC containers, however, you have to manually change the code to host ActiveX controls from an MFC application.

To host a Windows Forms control inside Internet Explorer, you have to copy the assembly file to your web server and add some information about the control inside the HTML page. For the support of Windows Forms controls, the syntax of the `<object>` tag has been extended. With the attribute `classid`, you can add the assembly file and the name of the class separated by a # sign: `classid="<assembly file>#class name"`.

With the assembly file `ControlDemo.dll` and the class `UserControl1` in the namespace `Wrox.ProCSharp.COMInterop`, the syntax looks like this:

```
<object id="myControl"
  classid="ControlDemo.dll#Wrox.ProCSharp.COMInterop.UserControl1"
  height="400" width="400">
</object>
```

As soon as a user opens the HTML page, the assembly is downloaded to the client system. The assembly is stored in the download assembly cache, and every time the user accesses the page, the version numbers are rechecked. If the version numbers haven't changed, the assembly will be used from the local cache.

> A requirement for using a Windows Forms control in a web page is that the client must have the .NET runtime installed. Internet Explorer 5.5 or higher must be used, and the security setting must allow the downloading of assemblies.

Platform Invoke

Not all the features of Windows API calls are available from the .NET Framework. This is not only true for old Windows API calls but also for very new features from Windows Vista or Windows Server 2008. Maybe you've written some DLLs that export unmanaged methods, and you would like to use them from C# as well.

You can read about some Windows Vista — and Windows Server 2008–specific features in Appendix C, "Windows Vista and Windows Server 2008."

To reuse an unmanaged library that doesn't contain COM objects but just exported functions, platform invoke can be used. With platform invoke services, the CLR loads the DLL that includes the function that should be called and marshals the parameters.

To use the unmanaged function, first you have to find out the name of the function as it is exported. You can do this by using the `dumpbin` tool with the `/exports` option.

For example, the command

```
dumpbin /exports c:\windows\system32\kernel32.dll | more
```

lists all exported functions from the DLL `kernel32.dll`. In the example, you use the `CreateHardLink()` Windows API function to create a hard link to an existing file. With this API call, you can have several file names that reference the same file as long as the file names are on just one hard disk. This API call is not available from .NET Framework 3.5, so platform invoke must be used.

To call a native function, you have to define a C# external method with the same number of arguments, and the argument types that are defined with the unmanaged method must have mapped types with managed code.

The Windows API call `CreateHardLink()` has this definition in C++:

```
BOOL CreateHardLink(
    LPCTSTR lpFileName,
    LPCTSTR lpExistingFileName,
    LPSECURITY_ATTRIBUTES lpSecurityAttributes);
```

Now, this definition must be mapped to .NET data types. The return type is a `BOOL` with unmanaged code; this simply maps to the `bool` data type. `LPCTSTR` defines a `long` pointer to a `const` string. The Windows API uses the Hungarian naming convention for the data type. `LP` is a `long` pointer, `C` a `const`, and `STR` is a null-terminated string. The `T` marks the type as a generic type, and the type is either resolved to `LPCSTR` (an ANSI string) or `LPWSTR` (a wide Unicode string), depending on compiler settings. C strings map to the .NET type `String`. `LPSECURITY_ATTRIBUTES`, which is a long pointer to a struct of type `SECURITY_ATTRIBUTES`. Because you can pass `NULL` to this argument, mapping this type to `IntPtr` is okay. The C# declaration of this method must be marked with the `extern` modifier, because there's no implementation of this method within the C# code. Instead, the implementation of this method is found in the DLL `kernel32.dll`, which is referenced with the attribute `[DllImport]`. Because the return type of the .NET declaration `CreateHardLink()` is of type `bool`, and the native method `CreateHardLink()` returns a `BOOL`, some additional clarification is useful. Because there are different Boolean data types with C++, for example the native `bool` and the Windows-defined `BOOL`, which have different values, the attribute `[MarshalAs]` specifies to what native type the .NET type `bool` should map.

```
[DllImport("kernel32.dll", SetLastError="true",
    EntryPoint="CreateHardLink", CharSet=CharSet.Unicode)]
[return: MarshalAs(UnmanagedType.Bool)]
public static extern bool CreateHardLink(string newFileName,
    string existingFilename, IntPtr securityAttributes);
```

The settings that you can specify with the attribute `[DllImport]` are listed in the following table.

DllImport Property or Field	Description
EntryPoint	You can give the C# declaration of the function a different name than it has with the unmanaged library. The name of the method in the unmanaged library is defined in the field `EntryPoint`.
CallingConvention	Depending on the compiler or compiler settings that were used to compile the unmanaged function, different calling conventions can be used. The calling convention defines how the parameters are dealt with and where to put them on the stack. You can define the calling convention by setting an enumerable value. The Windows API usually uses the `StdCall` calling convention on the Windows operating system, and it uses the `Cdecl` calling convention on Windows CE. Setting the value to `CallingConvention.Winapi` works for the Windows API both in the Windows and the Windows CE environments.

DllImport Property or Field	Description
CharSet	String parameters can be either ANSI or Unicode. With the CharSet setting, you can define how strings are managed. Possible values that are defined with the CharSet enumeration are Ansi, Unicode, and Auto. CharSet.Auto uses Unicode on the Windows NT platform, and ANSI on Windows 98 and Windows ME.
SetLastError	If the unmanaged function sets an error by using the Windows API SetLastError, you can set the SetLastError field to true. This way, you can read the error number afterward by using Marshal.GetLastWin32Error().

To make the CreateHardLink() method easier to use from a .NET environment, you should follow these guidelines:

❏ Create an internal class named NativeMethods that wraps the platform invoke method calls

❏ Create a public class to offer the native method functionality to .NET applications

❏ Use security attributes to mark the required security

In the sample code, the public method CreateHardLink() in the class FileUtility is the method that can be used by .NET applications. This method has the file name arguments reversed compared to the native Windows API method CreateHardLink(). The first argument is the name of the existing file, and the second argument is the name of the new file. This is similar to other classes in the Framework; for example, File.Copy(). Because the third argument to pass the security attributes for the new file name is not used with this implementation, the public method has just two parameters. The return type is changed as well. Instead of returning an error by returning the value false, an exception is thrown. In case of an error, the unmanaged method CreateHardLink() sets the error number with the unmanaged API SetLastError(). To read this value from .NET, the [DllImport] field SetLastError is set to true. Within the managed method CreateHardLink(), the error number is read by calling Marshal.GetLastWin32Error(). To create an error message from this number, the Win32Exception class from the namespace System.ComponentModel is used. This class accepts an error number with the constructor, and returns a localized error message. In case of an error, an exception of type IOException is thrown, which has an inner exception of type Win32Exception. The public method CreateHardLink() has the FileIOPermission attribute applied to check if the caller has the necessary permission. You can read more information about .NET security in Chapter 20.

```
using System;
using System.Runtime.InteropServices;
using System.ComponentModel;
using System.IO;

namespace Wrox.ProCSharp.Interop
{
    internal static class NativeMethods
    {
        [DllImport("kernel32.dll", SetLastError=true,
            EntryPoint="CreateHardLink", CharSet=CharSet.Unicode)]
        [return: MarshalAs(UnmanagedType.Bool)]
```

(continued)

(continued)

```
        private static extern bool CreateHardLink(
            string newFileName, string existingFileName,
            IntPtr securityAttributes);

        internal static void CreateHardLink(string oldFileName,
                                            string newFileName)
        {
            if (!CreateHardLink(newFileName, oldFileName, IntPtr.Zero))
            {
                Win32Exception ex = new Win32Exception(
                    Marshal.GetLastWin32Error());
                throw new IOException(ex.Message, ex);
            }
        }
    }

    public static class FileUtility
    {
        [FileIOPermission(SecurityAction.LinkDemand, Unrestricted=true)]
        public static void CreateHardLink(string oldFileName,
                                          string newFileName)
        {
            NativeMethods.CreateHardLink(oldFileName, newFileName);
        }
    }
}
```

This class can now be used to create hard links very easily. If the file file1.txt does not exist, you will get an exception with the message "The system cannot find the file specified." If the file exists, you get a new file name referencing the original file. You can easily verify this by changing text in one file; it will show up in the other file as well.

```
        static void Main()
        {
            try
            {
                FileUtility.CreateHardLink("file1.txt", "file2.txt");
            }
            catch (IOException ex)
            {
                Console.WriteLine(ex.Message);
            }
        }
```

With native method calls, often you have to use Window handles. A Window handle is a 32-bit value where depending on the handle types some values are not allowed. With .NET 1.0 for handles, usually the IntPtr structure was used because you can set every possible 32-bit value with this structure. However, with some handle types, this led to security problems and possible threading race conditions and leaked handles with the finalization phase. That's why .NET 2.0 introduced the SafeHandle class. The class SafeHandle is an abstract base class for every Windows handle. Derived classes inside the Microsoft.Win32.SafeHandles namespace are SafeHandleZeroOrMinusOneIsInvalid and SafeHandleMinusOneIsInvalid. As the name tells, these classes do not accept invalid 0 or –1 values. Further derived handle types are SafeFileHandle, SafeWaitHandle, SafeNCryptHandle, and SafePipeHandle that can be used by the specific Windows API calls.

For example, to map the Windows API `CreateFile()`, you can use this declaration to return a `SafeFileHandle`. Of course, usually you could use the .NET classes `File` and `FileInfo` instead.

```
[DllImport("Kernel32.dll", SetLastError = true,
           CharSet = CharSet.Unicode)]
internal static extern SafeFileHandle CreateFile(
    string fileName,
    [MarshalAs(UnmanagedType.U4)] FileAccess fileAccess,
    [MarshalAs(UnmanagedType.U4)] FileShare fileShare,
    IntPtr securityAttributes,
    [MarshalAs(UnmanagedType.U4)] FileMode creationDisposition,
    int flags,
    SafeFileHandle template);
```

In Chapter 22, "Transactions," you see how to create a custom `SafeHandle` class to work with the transacted file API from Windows Vista.

Summary

In this chapter, you have seen how the different generations of COM and .NET applications can interact. Instead of rewriting applications and components, a COM component can be used from a .NET application just like a .NET class. The tool that makes this possible is `tlbimp`, which creates a runtime callable wrapper (RCW) that hides the COM object behind a .NET façade.

Likewise, `tlbexp` creates a type library from a .NET component that is used by the COM callable wrapper (CCW). The CCW hides the .NET component behind a COM façade. Using .NET classes as COM components makes it necessary to use some attributes from the namespace `System.Runtime.InteropServices` to define specific COM characteristics that are needed by the COM client.

With platform invoke, you've seen how native methods can be invoked using C#. Platform invoke requires redefining the native method with C# and .NET data types. After defining the mapping, you can invoke the native method as if it would be a C# method. Another option for doing interop would be to use the technology It Just Works (IJW) with C++/CLI. You can read information about C++/CLI in Appendix B.

The next part of this book is all about data. The next chapter gives information on how to access the file system, followed by chapters on how to read and write from the database and manipulate XML.

Part IV
Data

25

Manipulating Files and the Registry

This chapter examines how to perform tasks involving reading from and writing to files and the system registry in C#. In particular, it covers the following:

- ❏ Exploring the directory structure, finding out what files and folders are present, and checking their properties

- ❏ Moving, copying, and deleting files and folders

- ❏ Reading and writing text in files

- ❏ Reading and writing keys in the registry

- ❏ Reading and writing to isolated storage

Microsoft has provided very intuitive object models covering these areas, and in this chapter, you learn how to use .NET base classes to perform the listed tasks. In the case of file system operations, the relevant classes are almost all found in the `System.IO` namespace, whereas registry operations are dealt with by classes in the `Microsoft.Win32` namespace.

> *The .NET base classes also include a number of classes and interfaces in the `System.Runtime` `.Serialization` namespace concerned with serialization — that is, the process of converting data (for example, the contents of a document) into a stream of bytes for storage. This chapter does not focus on these classes; it focuses on the classes that give you direct access to files.*

Note that security is particularly important when modifying files or registry entries. The whole area of security is covered separately in Chapter 20, "Security." In this chapter, however, we assume that you have sufficient access rights to run all of the examples that modify files or registry entries, which should be the case if you are running from an account with administrator privileges.

Managing the File System

The classes that are used to browse around the file system and perform operations such as moving, copying, and deleting files are shown in Figure 25-1.

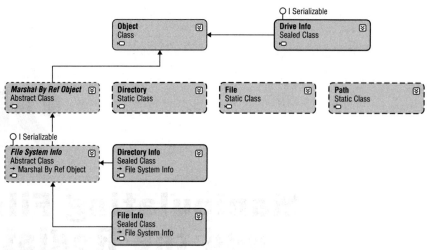

Figure 25-1

The following list explains the function of these classes:

- ❑ System.MarshalByRefObject — This is the base object class for .NET classes that are remotable; permits marshaling of data between application domains.
- ❑ FileSystemInfo — This is the base class that represents any file system object.
- ❑ FileInfo and File — These classes represent a file on the file system.
- ❑ DirectoryInfo and Directory — These classes represent a folder on the file system.
- ❑ Path — This class contains static members that you can use to manipulate path names.
- ❑ DriveInfo — This class provides properties and methods that provide information on a selected drive.

On Windows, the objects that contain files and that are used to organize the file system are termed fold-ers. For example, in the path C:\My Documents\ReadMe.txt, ReadMe.txt *is a file and* My Documents *is a folder. Folder is a very Windows-specific term: on virtually every other operating system the term directory is used in place of folder, and in accordance with Microsoft's goal to design .NET as a platform-independent technology, the corresponding .NET base classes are called* Directory *and* DirectoryInfo. *However, due to the potential for confusion with LDAP directories (as discussed in Chapter 46, "Directory Services"), and because this is a Windows book, we'll stick to the term folder in this discussion.*

.NET Classes That Represent Files and Folders

You will notice from the previous list that two classes are used to represent a folder and two classes are used to represent a file. Which one of these classes you use depends largely on how many times you need to access that folder or file:

❑ `Directory` and `File` contain only static methods and are never instantiated. You use these classes by supplying the path to the appropriate file system object whenever you call a member method. If you want to do only one operation on a folder or file, using these classes is more efficient because it saves the overhead of instantiating a .NET class.

❑ `DirectoryInfo` and `FileInfo` implement roughly the same public methods as `Directory` and `File`, as well as some public properties and constructors, but they are stateful and the members of these classes are not static. You need to instantiate these classes before each instance is associated with a particular folder or file. This means that these classes are more efficient if you are performing multiple operations using the same object. That's because they read in the authentication and other information for the appropriate file system object on construction, and then do not need to read that information again, no matter how many methods and so on you call against each object (class instance). In comparison, the corresponding stateless classes need to check the details of the file or folder again with every method you call.

In this section, you will be mostly using the `FileInfo` and `DirectoryInfo` classes, but it so happens that many (though not all) of the methods called are also implemented by `File` and `Directory` (although in those cases these methods require an extra parameter — the path name of the file system object; also, a couple of the methods have slightly different names). For example:

```
FileInfo myFile = new FileInfo(@"C:\Program Files\My Program\ReadMe.txt");
myFile.CopyTo(@"D:\Copies\ReadMe.txt");
```

has the same effect as:

```
File.Copy(@"C:\Program Files\My Program\ReadMe.txt", @"D:\Copies\ReadMe.txt");
```

The first code snippet will take slightly longer to execute because of the need to instantiate a `FileInfo` object, `myFile`, but it leaves `myFile` ready for you to perform further actions on the same file. By using the second example, there is no need to instantiate an object to copy the file.

You can instantiate a `FileInfo` or `DirectoryInfo` class by passing to the constructor a string containing the path to the corresponding file system object. You have just seen the process for a file. For a folder, the code looks similar:

```
DirectoryInfo myFolder = new DirectoryInfo(@"C:\Program Files");
```

If the path represents an object that does not exist, an exception will not be thrown at construction, but will instead be thrown the first time that you call a method that actually requires the corresponding file system object to be there. You can find out whether the object exists and is of the appropriate type by checking the `Exists` property, which is implemented by both of these classes:

```
FileInfo test = new FileInfo(@"C:\Windows");
Console.WriteLine(test.Exists.ToString());
```

Note that for this property to return `true`, the corresponding file system object must be of the appropriate type. In other words, if you instantiate a `FileInfo` object supplying the path of a folder, or you instantiate a `DirectoryInfo` object, giving it the path of a file, `Exists` will have the value `false`. Most of the properties and methods of these objects will return a value if possible — they won't necessarily throw an exception just because the wrong type of object has been called, unless they are asked to do something that really is impossible. For example, the preceding code snippet might first display `false` (because `C:\Windows` is a folder). However, it still displays the time the folder was created because a folder still has that information. But if you tried to open the folder as if it were a file, using the `FileInfo.Open()` method, you'd get an exception.

After you have established whether the corresponding file system object exists, you can (if you are using the `FileInfo` or `DirectoryInfo` class) find out information about it using the properties in the following table.

Name	Description
CreationTime	Time file or folder was created
DirectoryName (FileInfo only)	Full path name of the containing folder
Parent (DirectoryInfo only)	The parent directory of a specified subdirectory
Exists	Whether file or folder exists
Extension	Extension of the file; returns blank for folders
FullName	Full path name of the file or folder
LastAccessTime	Time file or folder was last accessed
LastWriteTime	Time file or folder was last modified
Name	Name of the file or folder
Root (DirectoryInfo only)	The root portion of the path
Length (FileInfo only)	The size of the file in bytes

You can also perform actions on the file system object using the methods in the following table.

Name	Purpose
Create()	Creates a folder or empty file of the given name. For a FileInfo this also returns a stream object to let you write to the file. (Streams are covered later in the chapter.)
Delete()	Deletes the file or folder. For folders, there is an option for the Delete to be recursive.
MoveTo()	Moves and/or renames the file or folder.
CopyTo()	(FileInfo only) Copies the file. Note that there is no copy method for folders. If you are copying complete directory trees you will need to individually copy each file and create new folders corresponding to the old folders.
GetDirectories()	(DirectoryInfo only) Returns an array of DirectoryInfo objects representing all folders contained in this folder.
GetFiles()	(DirectoryInfo only) Returns an array of FileInfo objects representing all files contained in this folder.
GetFileSystemInfos()	(DirectoryInfo only) Returns FileInfo and DirectoryInfo objects representing all objects contained in this folder, as an array of FileSystemInfo references.

Note that these tables list the main properties and methods and are not intended to be exhaustive.

> The preceding tables do not list most of the properties or methods that allow you to write to or read the data in files. This is actually done using stream objects, which are covered later in this chapter. FileInfo *also implements a number of methods,* Open(), OpenRead(), OpenText(), OpenWrite(), Create(), *and* CreateText(), *that return stream objects for this purpose.*

Interestingly, the creation time, last access time, and last write time are all writable:

```
// displays the creation time of a file,
// then changes it and displays it again
FileInfo test = new FileInfo(@"C:\MyFile.txt");
Console.WriteLine(test.Exists.ToString());
Console.WriteLine(test.CreationTime.ToString());
test.CreationTime = new DateTime(2008, 1, 1, 7, 30, 0);
Console.WriteLine(test.CreationTime.ToString());
```

Running this application produces results similar to the following:

```
True
2/5/2007 2:59:32 PM
1/1/2008 7:30:00 AM
```

Being able to manually modify these properties might seem strange at first, but it can be quite useful. For example, if you have a program that effectively modifies a file by simply reading it in, deleting it, and creating a new file with the new contents, you would probably want to modify the creation date to match the original creation date of the old file.

The Path Class

The Path class is not a class that you would instantiate. Rather, it exposes some static methods that make operations on path names easier. For example, suppose that you want to display the full path name for a file, ReadMe.txt in the folder C:\My Documents. You could find the path to the file using the following code:

```
Console.WriteLine(Path.Combine(@"C:\My Documents", "ReadMe.txt"));
```

Using the Path class is a lot easier than using separation symbols manually, especially because the Path class is aware of different formats for path names on different operating systems. At the time of writing, Windows is the only operating system supported by .NET. However, if .NET were later ported to Unix, Path would be able to cope with Unix paths, in which /, rather than \, is used as a separator in path names. Path.Combine() is the method of this class that you are likely to use most often, but Path also implements other methods that supply information about the path or the required format for it.

Some of the properties available to the Path class include the following:

Property	Description
AltDirectorySeparatorChar	Provides a platform-agnostic way to specify an alternative character to separate directory levels. On Windows, a / symbol is used, whereas on UNIX, a \ symbol is used.
DirectorySeparatorChar	Provides a platform-agnostic way to specify a character to separate directory levels. On Windows, a / symbol is used, whereas on UNIX, a \ symbol is used.
PathSeparator	Provides a platform-agnostic way to specify path strings which divide environmental variables. The default value of this setting is a semicolon.
VolumeSeparatorChar	Provides a platform-agnostic way to specify a volume separator. The default value of this setting is a colon.

The following example illustrates how to browse directories and view the properties of files.

Example: A File Browser

This section presents a sample C# application called `FileProperties`. This application presents a simple user interface that allows you to browse the file system and view the creation time, last access time, last write time, and size of files. (You can download the sample code for this application from the Wrox web site at `www.wrox.com`.)

The `FileProperties` application works like this. You type in the name of a folder or file in the main text box at the top of the window and click the Display button. If you type in the path to a folder, its contents are listed in the list boxes. If you type in the path to a file, its details are displayed in the text boxes at the bottom of the form and the contents of its parent folder are displayed in the list boxes. Figure 25-2 shows the `FileProperties` sample application in action.

The user can very easily navigate around the file system by clicking any folder in the right-hand list box to move down to that folder or by clicking the Up button to move up to the parent folder. Figure 25-2 shows the contents of the My Documents folder. The user can also select a file by clicking its name in the list box. This displays the file's properties in the text boxes at the bottom of the application (see Figure 25-3).

Note that if you wanted to, you could also display the creation time, last access time, and last modification time for folders using the `DirectoryInfo` property. You are going to display these properties only for a selected file to keep things simple.

You create the project as a standard C# Windows application in Visual Studio 2008, and add the various text boxes and the list box from the Windows Forms area of the toolbox. You have also renamed the controls with the more intuitive names of `textBoxInput`, `textBoxFolder`, `buttonDisplay`, `buttonUp`, `listBoxFiles`, `listBoxFolders`, `textBoxFileName`, `textBoxCreationTime`, `textBoxLastAccessTime`, `textBoxLastWriteTime`, and `textBoxFileSize`.

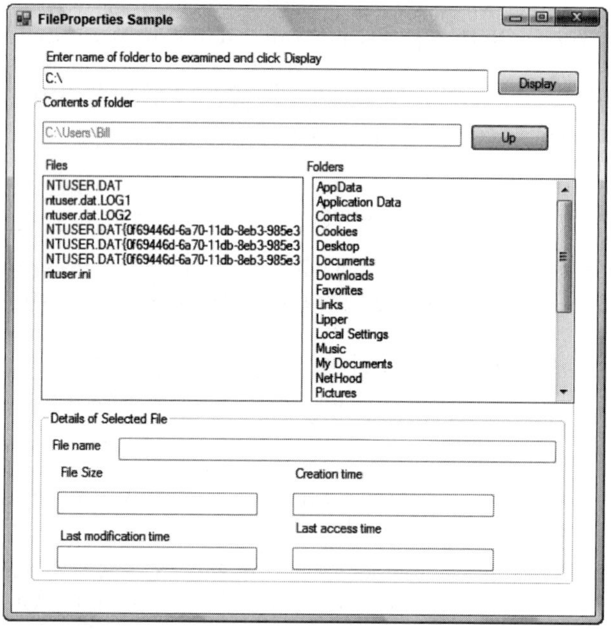

Figure 25-2

Figure 25-3

Next, you need to indicate that you will be using the `System.IO` namespace:

```
using System;
using System.IO;
using System.Windows.Forms;
```

You need to do this for all of the file-system–related examples in this chapter, but this part of the code will not be explicitly shown in the remaining examples. You then add a member field to the main form:

```
public partial class Form1 : Form
{
    private string currentFolderPath;
```

`currentFolderPath` stores the path of the folder whose contents are displayed in the list boxes.

Next, you need to add event handlers for the user-generated events. The possible user inputs are:

❑ User clicks the Display button — In this case, you need to determine whether what the user has typed in the main text box is the path to a file or folder. If it is a folder, you list the files and subfolders of this folder in the list boxes. If it is a file, you still do this for the folder containing that file, but you also display the file properties in the lower text boxes.

❑ User clicks a file name in the Files list box — In this case, you display the properties of this file in the lower text boxes.

❑ User clicks a folder name in the Folders list box — In this case, you clear all the controls and then display the contents of this subfolder in the list boxes.

❑ User clicks the Up button — In this case, you clear all the controls and then display the contents of the parent of the currently selected folder.

Before you see the code for the event handlers, here is the code for the methods that do all the work. First, you need to clear the contents of all the controls. This method is fairly self-explanatory:

```
protected void ClearAllFields()
{
    listBoxFolders.Items.Clear();
    listBoxFiles.Items.Clear();
    textBoxFolder.Text = "";
    textBoxFileName.Text = "";
    textBoxCreationTime.Text = "";
    textBoxLastAccessTime.Text = "";
    textBoxLastWriteTime.Text = "";
    textBoxFileSize.Text = "";
}
```

Next, you define a method, `DisplayFileInfo()`, that handles the process of displaying the information for a given file in the text boxes. This method takes one parameter, the full path name of the file as a `String`, and works by creating a `FileInfo` object based on this path:

```
protected void DisplayFileInfo(string fileFullName)
{
    FileInfo theFile = new FileInfo(fileFullName);

    if (!theFile.Exists)
    {
        throw new FileNotFoundException("File not found: " + fileFullName);
    }

    textBoxFileName.Text = theFile.Name;
    textBoxCreationTime.Text = theFile.CreationTime.ToLongTimeString();
    textBoxLastAccessTime.Text = theFile.LastAccessTime.ToLongDateString();
    textBoxLastWriteTime.Text = theFile.LastWriteTime.ToLongDateString();
    textBoxFileSize.Text = theFile.Length.ToString() + " bytes";
}
```

Note that you take the precaution of throwing an exception if there are any problems locating a file at the specified location. The exception itself will be handled in the calling routine (one of the event handlers). Finally, you define a method, `DisplayFolderList()`, which displays the contents of a given folder in the two list boxes. The full path name of the folder is passed in as a parameter to this method:

```
protected void DisplayFolderList(string folderFullName)
{
    DirectoryInfo theFolder = new DirectoryInfo(folderFullName);

    if (!theFolder.Exists)
    {
        throw new DirectoryNotFoundException("Folder not found: " + folderFullName);
    }

    ClearAllFields();
    textBoxFolder.Text = theFolder.FullName;
    currentFolderPath = theFolder.FullName;
```

```
        // list all subfolders in folder
        foreach(DirectoryInfo nextFolder in theFolder.GetDirectories())
            listBoxFolders.Items.Add(nextFolder.Name);

        // list all files in folder
        foreach(FileInfo nextFile in theFolder.GetFiles())
            listBoxFiles.Items.Add(nextFile.Name);
    }
```

Next, you examine the event handlers. The event handler that manages the event that is triggered when the user clicks the Display button is the most complex because it needs to handle three different possibilities for the text the user enters in the text box. For instance, it could be the path name of a folder, the path name of a file, or neither of these:

```
        protected void OnDisplayButtonClick(object sender, EventArgs e)
        {
            try
            {
                string folderPath = textBoxInput.Text;
                DirectoryInfo theFolder = new DirectoryInfo(folderPath);
                if (theFolder.Exists)
                {
                    DisplayFolderList(theFolder.FullName);
                    return;
                }
                FileInfo theFile = new FileInfo(folderPath);
                if (theFile.Exists)
                {
                    DisplayFolderList(theFile.Directory.FullName);
                    int index = listBoxFiles.Items.IndexOf(theFile.Name);
                    listBoxFiles.SetSelected(index, true);
                    return;
                }
                throw new FileNotFoundException("There is no file or folder with "
                                        + "this name: " + textBoxInput.Text);
            }
            catch(Exception ex)
            {
                MessageBox.Show(ex.Message);
            }
        }
```

In this code, you establish if the supplied text represents a folder or file by instantiating DirectoryInfo and FileInfo instances and examining the Exists property of each object. If neither exists, you throw an exception. If it's a folder, you call DisplayFolderList() to populate the list boxes. If it's a file, you need to populate the list boxes and sort out the text boxes that display the file properties. You handle this case by first populating the list boxes. You then programmatically select the appropriate file name in the Files list box. This has exactly the same effect as if the user had selected that item — it raises the item-selected event. You can then simply exit the current event handler, knowing that the selected item event handler will immediately be called to display the file properties.

The following code is the event handler that is called when an item in the Files list box is selected, either by the user or, as indicated previously, programmatically. It simply constructs the full path name of the selected file, and passes this to the `DisplayFileInfo()` method presented earlier:

```
protected void OnListBoxFilesSelected(object sender, EventArgs e)
{
    try
    {
        string selectedString = listBoxFiles.SelectedItem.ToString();
        string fullFileName = Path.Combine(currentFolderPath, selectedString);
        DisplayFileInfo(fullFileName);
    }
    catch(Exception ex)
    {
        MessageBox.Show(ex.Message);
    }
}
```

The event handler for the selection of a folder in the Folders list box is implemented in a very similar way, except that in this case you call `DisplayFolderList()` to update the contents of the list boxes:

```
protected void OnListBoxFoldersSelected(object sender, EventArgs e)
{
    try
    {
        string selectedString = listBoxFolders.SelectedItem.ToString();
        string fullPathName = Path.Combine(currentFolderPath, selectedString);
        DisplayFolderList(fullPathName);
    }
    catch(Exception ex)
    {
        MessageBox.Show(ex.Message);
    }
}
```

Finally, when the Up button is clicked, `DisplayFolderList()` must also be called, except that this time you need to obtain the path of the parent of the folder currently being displayed. This is done with the `FileInfo.DirectoryName` property, which returns the parent folder path:

```
protected void OnUpButtonClick(object sender, EventArgs e)
{
    try
    {
        string folderPath = new FileInfo(currentFolderPath).DirectoryName;
        DisplayFolderList(folderPath);
    }
    catch(Exception ex)
    {
        MessageBox.Show(ex.Message);
    }
}
```

Moving, Copying, and Deleting Files

As mentioned, moving and deleting files or folders is done by the `MoveTo()` and `Delete()` methods of the `FileInfo` and `DirectoryInfo` classes. The equivalent methods on the `File` and `Directory` classes are `Move()` and `Delete()`. The `FileInfo` and `File` classes also implement the methods `CopyTo()` and

Copy(), respectively. However, no methods exist to copy complete folders — you need to do that by copying each file in the folder.

Using all of these methods is quite intuitive — you can find detailed descriptions in the SDK documentation. This section illustrates their use for the particular cases of calling the static Move(), Copy(), and Delete() methods on the File class. To do this, you will build on the previous FileProperties example and call its iteration FilePropertiesAndMovement. This example will have the extra feature that whenever the properties of a file are displayed, the application gives you the option of deleting that file or moving or copying the file to another location.

Example: FilePropertiesAndMovement

Figure 25-4 shows the user interface of the new sample application.

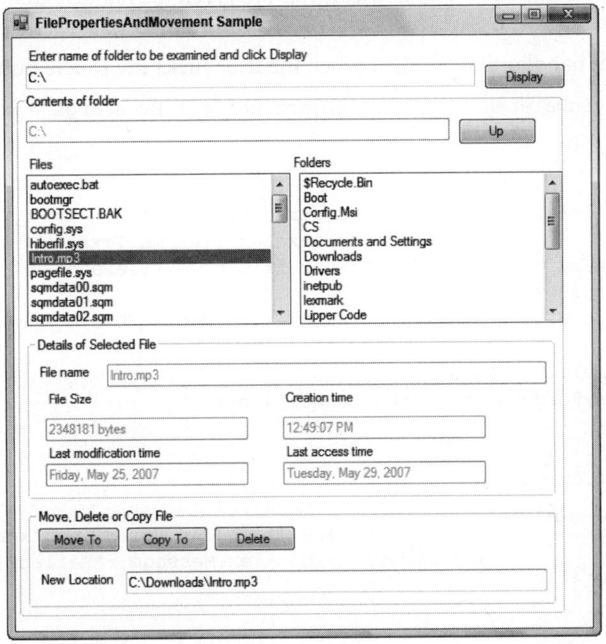

Figure 25-4

As you can see, FilePropertiesAndMovement is similar in appearance to FileProperties, except for the group of three buttons and a text box at the bottom of the window. These controls are enabled only when the example is actually displaying the properties of a file; at all other times, they are disabled. The existing controls are also squashed up a bit to stop the main form from getting too big. When the properties of a selected file are displayed, FilePropertiesAndMovement automatically places the full path name of that file in the bottom text box for the user to edit. Users can then click any of the buttons to perform the appropriate operation. When they do, a message box is displayed that confirms the action taken by the user (see Figure 25-5).

When the user clicks the Yes button, the action will be initiated. There are some actions in the form that the user can take that will then cause the display to be incorrect. For instance, if the user moves or deletes a file, you obviously cannot continue to display the contents of that file in the same location. In addition, if you change the name of a file in the same folder, your display will also be out of date. In these cases, FilePropertiesAndMovement resets its controls to display only the folder where the file resides after the file operation.

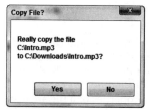

Figure 25-5

Looking at the Code for FilePropertiesAndMovement

To code this process, you need to add the relevant controls, as well as their event handlers, to the code for the `FileProperties` example. The new controls are given the names `buttonDelete`, `buttonCopyTo`, `buttonMoveTo`, and `textBoxNewPath`.

First, look at the event handler that is called when the user clicks the Delete button:

```
protected void OnDeleteButtonClick(object sender, EventArgs e)
{
    try
    {
        string filePath = Path.Combine(currentFolderPath,
                                    textBoxFileName.Text);
        string query = "Really delete the file\n" + filePath + "?";
        if (MessageBox.Show(query,
            "Delete File?", MessageBoxButtons.YesNo) == DialogResult.Yes)
        {
            File.Delete(filePath);
            DisplayFolderList(currentFolderPath);
        }
    }
    catch(Exception ex)
    {
        MessageBox.Show("Unable to delete file. The following exception"
                        + " occurred:\n" + ex.Message, "Failed");
    }
}
```

The code for this method is contained in a `try` block because of the obvious risk of an exception being thrown if, for example, you don't have permission to delete the file, or the file is moved by another process after it has been displayed but before the user presses the Delete button. You construct the path of the file to be deleted from the `CurrentParentPath` field, which contains the path of the parent folder, and the text in the `textBoxFileName` text box, which contains the name of the file.

The methods to move and copy the file are structured in a very similar manner:

```
protected void OnMoveButtonClick(object sender, EventArgs e)
{
    try
    {
        string filePath = Path.Combine(currentFolderPath,
                                    textBoxFileName.Text);
        string query = "Really move the file\n" + filePath + "\nto "
                        + textBoxNewPath.Text + "?";
```

```
        if (MessageBox.Show(query,
            "Move File?", MessageBoxButtons.YesNo) == DialogResult.Yes)
        {
            File.Move(filePath, textBoxNewPath.Text);
            DisplayFolderList(currentFolderPath);
        }
    }
    catch(Exception ex)
    {
        MessageBox.Show("Unable to move file. The following exception"
                        + " occurred:\n" + ex.Message, "Failed");
    }
}

protected void OnCopyButtonClick(object sender, EventArgs e)
{
    try
    {
        string filePath = Path.Combine(currentFolderPath,
                                    textBoxFileName.Text);
        string query = "Really copy the file\n" + filePath + "\nto "
                        + textBoxNewPath.Text + "?";
        if (MessageBox.Show(query,
            "Copy File?", MessageBoxButtons.YesNo) == DialogResult.Yes)
        {
            File.Copy(filePath, textBoxNewPath.Text);
            DisplayFolderList(currentFolderPath);
        }
    }
    catch(Exception ex)
    {
        MessageBox.Show("Unable to copy file. The following exception"
                        + " occurred:\n" + ex.Message, "Failed");
    }
}
```

You are not quite done yet. You also need to make sure that the new buttons and text box are enabled and disabled at the appropriate times. To enable them when you are displaying the contents of a file, you add the following code to DisplayFileInfo():

```
protected void DisplayFileInfo(string fileFullName)
{
    FileInfo theFile = new FileInfo(fileFullName);

    if (!theFile.Exists)
    {
        throw new FileNotFoundException("File not found: " + fileFullName);
    }

    textBoxFileName.Text = theFile.Name;
    textBoxCreationTime.Text = theFile.CreationTime.ToLongTimeString();
    textBoxLastAccessTime.Text = theFile.LastAccessTime.ToLongDateString();
    textBoxLastWriteTime.Text = theFile.LastWriteTime.ToLongDateString();
    textBoxFileSize.Text = theFile.Length.ToString() + " bytes";
```

(continued)

(continued)

```
        // enable move, copy, delete buttons
        textBoxNewPath.Text = theFile.FullName;
        textBoxNewPath.Enabled = true;
        buttonCopyTo.Enabled = true;
        buttonDelete.Enabled = true;
        buttonMoveTo.Enabled = true;
    }
```

You also need to make one change to `DisplayFolderList`:

```
    protected void DisplayFolderList(string folderFullName)
    {
        DirectoryInfo theFolder = new DirectoryInfo(folderFullName);

        if (!theFolder.Exists)
        {
            throw new DirectoryNotFoundException("Folder not found: " + folderFullName);
        }

        ClearAllFields();
        DisableMoveFeatures();
        textBoxFolder.Text = theFolder.FullName;
        currentFolderPath = theFolder.FullName;

        // list all subfolders in folder
        foreach(DirectoryInfo nextFolder in theFolder.GetDirectories())
            listBoxFolders.Items.Add(NextFolder.Name);

        // list all files in folder
        foreach(FileInfo nextFile in theFolder.GetFiles())
            listBoxFiles.Items.Add(NextFile.Name);
    }
```

`DisableMoveFeatures` is a small utility function that disables the new controls:

```
        void DisableMoveFeatures()
        {
            textBoxNewPath.Text = "";
            textBoxNewPath.Enabled = false;
            buttonCopyTo.Enabled = false;
            buttonDelete.Enabled = false;
            buttonMoveTo.Enabled = false;
        }
```

You also need to add extra code to `ClearAllFields()` to clear the extra text box:

```
        protected void ClearAllFields()
        {
            listBoxFolders.Items.Clear();
            listBoxFiles.Items.Clear();
            textBoxFolder.Text = "";
            textBoxFileName.Text = "";
            textBoxCreationTime.Text = "";
```

```
        textBoxLastAccessTime.Text = "";
        textBoxLastWriteTime.Text = "";
        textBoxFileSize.Text = "";
        textBoxNewPath.Text = "";
    }
```

The next section takes a look at reading and writing to files.

Reading and Writing to Files

Reading and writing to files is in principle very simple; however, it is not done through the `DirectoryInfo` or `FileInfo` objects. Instead, using the .NET Framework 3.5, you can do it through the `File` object. Later in this chapter, you see how to accomplish this using a number of other classes that represent a generic concept called a *stream*.

Before the .NET Framework 2.0, it took a bit of wrangling to read and write to files. It was possible using the available classes from the framework, but it was not that straightforward. The .NET Framework 2.0 has expanded the `File` class to make it as simple as just one line of code to read or write to a file. This same functionality is also available in version 3.5 of the .NET Framework.

Reading a File

For an example of reading a file, create a Windows Form application that contains a regular text box, a button, and a multiline text box. In the end, your form should appear something like Figure 25-6.

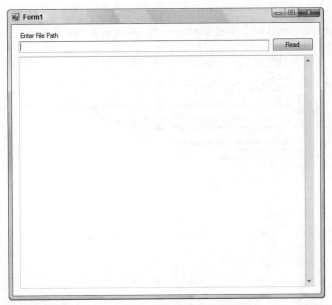

Figure 25-6

The idea of this form is that the end user will enter in the path of a specific file in the first text box and click the Read button. From here, the application will read the specified file and display the file's contents in the multiline text box. This is illustrated in the following code example:

```csharp
using System;
using System.IO;
using System.Windows.Forms;

namespace ReadingFiles
{
    public partial class Form1 : Form
    {
        public Form1()
        {
            InitializeComponent();
        }

        private void button1_Click(object sender, EventArgs e)
        {
            textBox2.Text = File.ReadAllText(textBox1.Text);
        }
    }
}
```

In building this example, the first step is to add the using statement to bring in the System.IO namespace. From there, simply use the button1_Click event for the Send button on the form to populate the text box with what comes back from the file. You can now access the file's contents by using the File.ReadAllText() method. As you can see, you can read files with a single statement. The ReadAllText() method opens the specified file, reads the contents, and then closes the file. The return value of the ReadAllText() method is a string array containing the entire contents of the file specified. The result would be something similar to what is shown in Figure 25-7.

Figure 25-7

The `File.ReadAllText()` signature shown in the preceding example is of the following construction:

```
File.ReadAllText(FilePath);
```

The other option is to also specify the encoding of the file being read:

```
File.ReadAllText(FilePath, Encoding);
```

Using this signature allows you to specify the encoding to use when opening and reading the contents of the file. Therefore, this means that you could do something like the following:

```
File.ReadAllText(textBox1.Text, Encoding.ASCII);
```

Some of the other options for opening and working with files include using the `ReadAllBytes()` and the `ReadAllLines()` methods. The `ReadAllBytes()` method allows you to open a binary file and read the contents into a byte array. The `ReadAllText()` method shown earlier gives you the entire contents of the specified file in a single string array instance. This might not be something that you are interested in. You might instead be interested in working with what comes back from the file in a line-by-line fashion. In this case, you will want to use the `ReadAllLines()` method because it will allow for this kind of functionality.

Writing to a File

Besides making reading from files an extremely simple process under the .NET Framework umbrella, the base class library has made writing to files just as easy. Just as the base class library (BCL) gives you the `ReadAllText()`, `ReadAllLines()`, and `ReadAllBytes()` methods to read files in a few different ways, it gives you the `WriteAllText()`, `WriteAllBytes()`, and `WriteAllLines()` methods to write files.

For an example of how to write to a file, use the same Windows Form application, but use the multiline text box in the form to input data into a file. The code for the `button1_Click` event handler should appear as shown here:

```
private void button1_Click(object sender, EventArgs e)
{
    File.WriteAllText(textBox1.Text, textBox2.Text);
}
```

Build and start the form, type `C:\Testing.txt` in the first text box, type some random content in the second text box, and then click the button. Nothing will happen visually, but if you look in your root C drive, you will see the `Testing.txt` file with the content you specified.

The `WriteAllText()` method went to the specified location, created a new text file, and provided the specified contents to the file before saving and closing the file. Not bad for just one line of code!

If you run the application again, and specify the same file (`Testing.txt`) but with some new content, pressing the button again will cause the application to perform the same task. This time though, the new content is not added to the previous content you specified — instead, the new content completely overrides the previous content. In fact, `WriteAllText()`, `WriteAllBytes()`, and `WriteAllLines()` all override any previous files, so you must be careful when using these methods.

The `WriteAllText()` method in the previous example uses the following signature:

```
File.WriteAllText(FilePath, Contents)
```

You can also specify the encoding of the new file:

```
File.WriteAllText(FilePath, Contents, Encoding)
```

The `WriteAllBytes()` method allows you to write content to a file using a byte array, and the `WriteAllLines()` method allows you to write a string array to a file. An example of this is illustrated in the following event handler:

```
private void button1_Click(object sender, EventArgs e)
{
    string[] movies =
        {"Grease",
         "Close Encounters of the Third Kind",
         "The Day After Tomorrow"};

    File.WriteAllLines(@"C:\Testing.txt", movies);
}
```

Now clicking the button for such an application will give you a `Testing.txt` file with the following contents:

```
Grease
Close Encounters of the Third Kind
The Day After Tomorrow
```

The `WriteAllLines()` method writes out the string array with each array item taking its own line in the file.

Because data may be written not only to disk but to other places as well (such as to named pipes or to memory), it is also important to understand how to deal with file I/O in .NET using streams as a means of moving file contents around. This is shown in the following section.

Streams

The idea of a stream has been around for a very long time. A stream is an object used to transfer data. The data can be transferred in one of two directions:

❑ If the data is being transferred from some outside source into your program, it is called *reading* from the stream.

❑ If the data is being transferred from your program to some outside source, it is called *writing* to the stream.

Very often, the outside source will be a file, but that is not always the case. Other possibilities include:

❑ Reading or writing data on the network using some network protocol, where the intention is for this data to be picked up by or sent from another computer

❑ Reading or writing to a named pipe

❑ Reading or writing to an area of memory

Of these examples, Microsoft has supplied a .NET base class for writing to or reading from memory, the `System.IO.MemoryStream` object. The `System.Net.Sockets.NetworkStream` object handles network data. There are no base stream classes for writing to or reading from pipes, but there is a generic stream class, `System.IO.Stream`, from which you would inherit if you wanted to write such a class. `Stream` does not make any assumptions about the nature of the external data source.

The outside source might even be a variable within your own code. This might sound paradoxical, but the technique of using streams to transmit data between variables can be a useful trick for converting data between data types. The C language used something similar — the function, `sprintf` — to convert between integer data types and strings or to format strings.

The advantage of having a separate object for the transfer of data, rather than using the `FileInfo` or `DirectoryInfo` classes to do this, is that separating the concept of transferring data from the particular data source makes it easier to swap data sources. Stream objects themselves contain a lot of generic code that concerns the movement of data between outside sources and variables in your code. By keeping this code separate from any concept of a particular data source, you make it easier for this code to be reused (through inheritance) in different circumstances. For example, the `StringReader` and `StringWriter` classes are part of the same inheritance tree as two classes that you will be using later on to read and write text files. The classes will almost certainly share a substantial amount of code behind the scenes.

Figure 25-8 illustrates the actual hierarchy of stream-related classes in the `System.IO` namespace.

As far as reading and writing files, the classes that concern us most are:

❑   `FileStream` — This class is intended for reading and writing binary data in a binary file. However, you can also use it to read from or write to any file.

❑   `StreamReader` and `StreamWriter` — These classes are designed specifically for reading from and writing to text files.

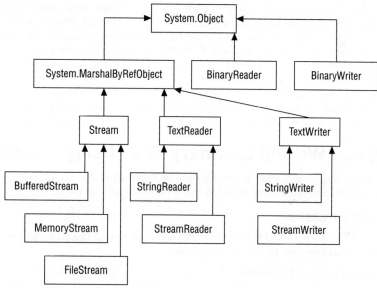

Figure 25-8

You might also find the `BinaryReader` and `BinaryWriter` classes useful, although they are not used in the examples here. These classes do not actually implement streams themselves, but they are able to provide wrappers around other stream objects. `BinaryReader` and `BinaryWriter` provide extra formatting of binary data, which allows you to directly read or write the contents of C# variables to or from the relevant stream. Think of the `BinaryReader` and `BinaryWriter` as sitting between the stream and your code, providing extra formatting (see Figure 25-9).

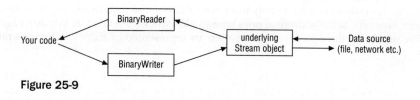

Figure 25-9

The difference between using these classes and directly using the underlying stream objects is that a basic stream works in bytes. For example, suppose that as part of the process of saving some document you want to write the contents of a variable of type `long` to a binary file. Each `long` occupies 8 bytes, and if you used an ordinary binary stream, you would have to explicitly write each of those 8 bytes of memory. In C# code, that would mean you would have to perform some bitwise operations to extract each of those 8 bytes from the `long` value. Using a `BinaryWriter` instance, you can encapsulate the entire operation in an overload of the `BinaryWriter.Write()` method, which takes a `long` as a parameter, and which will place those 8 bytes into the stream (and if the stream is directed to a file, into the file). A corresponding `BinaryReader.Read()` method will extract 8 bytes from the stream and recover the value of the `long`. For more information on the `BinaryReader` and `BinaryWriter` classes, refer to the SDK documentation.

Buffered Streams

For performance reasons, when you read or write to or from a file, the output is buffered. This means that if your program asks for the next 2 bytes of a file stream, and the stream passes the request on to Windows, then Windows will not go through the trouble of connecting to the file system and then locating and reading the file off the disk, just to get 2 bytes. Instead, Windows will retrieve a large block of the file at one time and store this block in an area of memory known as a *buffer*. Subsequent requests for data from the stream are satisfied from the buffer until the buffer runs out, at which point, Windows grabs another block of data from the file. Writing to files works in the same way. For files, this is done automatically by the operating system, but you might have to write a stream class to read from some other device that is not buffered. If so, you can derive your class from `BufferedStream`, which implements a buffer itself. (Note, however, that `BufferedStream` is not designed for the situation in which an application frequently alternates between reading and writing data.)

Reading and Writing to Binary Files Using FileStream

Reading and writing to and from binary files can be done using the `FileStream` class. (Note that if you are working with the .NET Framework 1.x, this will most likely be the case.)

The FileStream Class

A `FileStream` instance is used to read or write data to or from a file. In order to construct a `FileStream`, you need four pieces of information:

1. The **file** you want to access.

2. The **mode**, which indicates how you want to open the file. For example, are you intending to create a new file or open an existing file? And if you are opening an existing file, should any write operations be interpreted as overwriting the contents of the file or appending to the file?

3. The **access**, which indicates how you want to access the file. For example, do you want to read from or write to the file or do both?

4. The **share** access, which specifies whether you want exclusive access to the file. Or, are you willing to have other streams access the file simultaneously? If so, should other streams have access to read the file, to write to it, or to do both?

The first of these pieces of information is usually represented by a string that contains the full path name of the file, and this chapter considers only those constructors that require a string here. Besides those constructors, however, some additional ones take an old Windows-API–style Windows handle to a file instead. The remaining three pieces of information are represented by three .NET enumerations called

`FileMode`, `FileAccess`, and `FileShare`. The values of these enumerations are listed in the following table; they should be self-explanatory.

Enumeration	Values
FileMode	Append, Create, CreateNew, Open, OpenOrCreate, or Truncate
FileAccess	Read, ReadWrite, or Write
FileShare	Delete, Inheritable, None, Read, ReadWrite, or Write

Note that in the case of `FileMode`, exceptions can be thrown if you request a mode that is inconsistent with the existing status of the file. `Append`, `Open`, and `Truncate` will throw an exception if the file does not already exist, and `CreateNew` will throw an exception if it does. `Create` and `OpenOrCreate` will cope with either scenario, but `Create` will delete any existing file to replace it with a new, initially empty, one. The `FileAccess` and `FileShare` enumerations are bitwise flags, so values can be combined with the C# bitwise OR operator, |.

There are a large number of constructors for the `FileStream`. The three simplest ones work as follows:

```
// creates file with read-write access and allows other streams read access
FileStream fs = new FileStream(@"C:\C# Projects\Project.doc",
                  FileMode.Create);
// as above, but we only get write access to the file
FileStream fs2 = new FileStream(@"C:\C# Projects\Project2.doc",
                  FileMode.Create, FileAccess.Write);
// as above but other streams don't get access to the file while
// fs3 is open
FileStream fs3 = new FileStream(@"C:\C# Projects\Project3.doc",
                  FileMode.Create, FileAccess.Write, FileShare.None);
```

As this code reveals, the overloads of these constructors have the effect of providing default values of `FileAccess.ReadWrite` and `FileShare.Read` to the third and fourth parameters. It is also possible to create a file stream from a `FileInfo` instance in various ways:

```
FileInfo myFile4 = new FileInfo(@"C:\C# Projects\Project4.doc");
FileStream fs4 = myFile4.OpenRead();
FileInfo myFile5= new FileInfo(@"C:\C# Projects\Project5doc");
FileStream fs5 = myFile5.OpenWrite();
FileInfo myFile6= new FileInfo(@"C:\C# Projects\Project6doc");
FileStream fs6 = myFile6.Open(FileMode.Append, FileAccess.Write,
                  FileShare.None);
FileInfo myFile7 = new FileInfo(@"C:\C# Projects\Project7.doc");
FileStream fs7 = myFile7.Create();
```

`FileInfo.OpenRead()` supplies a stream that gives you read-only access to an existing file, whereas `FileInfo.OpenWrite()` gives you read-write access. `FileInfo.Open()` allows you to specify the mode, access, and file share parameters explicitly.

Of course, after you have finished with a stream, you should close it:

```
fs.Close();
```

Closing the stream frees up the resources associated with it and allows other applications to set up streams to the same file. This action also flushes the buffer. In between opening and closing the stream, you will want to read data from it and/or write data to it. FileStream implements a number of methods to do this.

ReadByte() is the simplest way of reading data. It grabs 1 byte from the stream and casts the result to an int that has a value between 0 and 255. If you have reached the end of the stream, it returns –1:

```
int NextByte = fs.ReadByte();
```

If you prefer to read a number of bytes at a time, you can call the Read() method, which reads a specified number of bytes into an array. Read() returns the number of bytes actually read — if this value is zero, you know that you are at the end of the stream. Here is an example where you read into a byte array called ByteArray:

```
int nBytesRead = fs.Read(ByteArray, 0, nBytes);
```

The second parameter to Read() is an offset, which you can use to request that the Read operation start populating the array at some element other than the first. The third parameter is the number of bytes to read into the array.

If you want to write data to a file, two parallel methods are available, WriteByte() and Write(). WriteByte() writes a single byte to the stream:

```
byte NextByte = 100;
fs.WriteByte(NextByte);
```

Write(), however, writes out an array of bytes. For instance, if you initialized the ByteArray mentioned before with some values, you could use the following code to write out the first nBytes of the array:

```
fs.Write(ByteArray, 0, nBytes);
```

As with Read(), the second parameter allows you to start writing from some point other than the beginning of the array. Both WriteByte() and Write() return void.

In addition to these methods, FileStream implements various other methods and properties related to bookkeeping tasks such as determining how many bytes are in the stream, locking the stream, or flushing the buffer. These other methods are not usually required for basic reading and writing, but if you need them, full details are in the SDK documentation.

Example: BinaryFileReader

The use of the FileStream class is illustrated by writing an example, BinaryFileReader, which reads in and displays any file. Create the project in Visual Studio 2008 as a Windows application. It has one menu item, which brings up a standard OpenFileDialog asking what file to read in and then displays the file as binary code. As you are reading in binary files, you need to be able to display nonprintable characters. You will do this by displaying each byte of the file individually, showing 16 bytes on each line of a multiline text box. If the byte represents a printable ASCII character, you will display that character; otherwise, you will display the value of the byte in a hexadecimal format. In either case, you pad out the displayed text with spaces so that each byte displayed occupies four columns; this way, the bytes line up nicely under each other.

Figure 25-10 shows what the BinaryFileReader application looks like when viewing a text file. (Because BinaryFileReader can view any file, it is quite possible to use it on text files as well as binary ones.) In this case, the application has read in a basic ASP.NET page (.aspx).

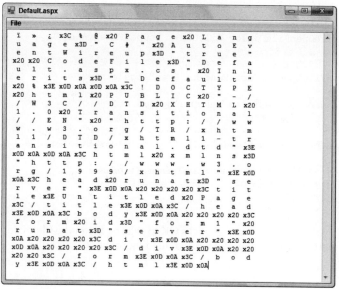

Figure 25-10

Clearly, this format is more suited to looking at the values of individual bytes than to displaying text! Later in this chapter, when you develop an example that is specifically designed to read text files, you will be able to see what this file really says. The advantage of this example is that you can look at the contents of any file.

This example will not demonstrate writing to files because you don't want to get bogged down in the complexities of trying to translate the contents of a text box like the one shown in Figure 25-10 into a binary stream! You see how to write to files later when you develop an example that can read or write, but only to and from text files.

Here is the code used to get these results. First, you need to make sure that you have brought in the System.IO namespace through the use of the using statement:

```
using System.IO;
```

Next, you add a couple of fields to the main form class — one representing the file dialog and a string that gives the path of the file currently being viewed:

```
partial class Form1 : Form
{
    private readonly OpenFileDialog chooseOpenFileDialog =
        new OpenFileDialog();
    private string chosenFile;
```

You also need to add some standard Windows Forms code to deal with the handlers for the menu and the file dialog:

```
public Form1()
{
    InitializeComponent();
```

(continued)

(continued)

```
        menuFileOpen.Click += OnFileOpen;
        chooseOpenFileDialog.FileOk += OnOpenFileDialogOK;
    }

    void OnFileOpen(object Sender, EventArgs e)
    {
        chooseOpenFileDialog.ShowDialog();
    }

    void OnOpenFileDialogOK(object Sender, CancelEventArgs e)
    {
        chosenFile = chooseOpenFileDialog.FileName;
        this.Text = Path.GetFileName(chosenFile);
        DisplayFile();
    }
```

As this code demonstrates, when the user clicks OK to select a file in the file dialog, you call the `DisplayFile()` method, which does the work of reading in the selected file:

```
    void DisplayFile()
    {
        int nCols = 16;
        FileStream inStream = new FileStream(chosenFile, FileMode.Open,
                                                       FileAccess.Read);
        long nBytesToRead = inStream.Length;
        if (nBytesToRead > 65536/4)
            nBytesToRead = 65536/4;

        int nLines = (int)(nBytesToRead/nCols) + 1;
        string [] lines = new string[nLines];
        int nBytesRead = 0;

        for (int i=0 ; i<nLines ; i++)
        {
            StringBuilder nextLine = new StringBuilder();
            nextLine.Capacity = 4*nCols;

            for (int j = 0 ; j<nCols ; j++)
            {
                int nextByte = inStream.ReadByte();
                nBytesRead++;
                if (nextByte < 0 || nBytesRead > 65536)
                    break;
                char nextChar = (char)nextByte;
                if (nextChar < 16)
                    nextLine.Append(" x0" + string.Format("{0,1:X}",
                                                       (int)nextChar));
                else if
                    (char.IsLetterOrDigit(nextChar) ||
                                        char.IsPunctuation(nextChar))
                    nextLine.Append("  " + nextChar + " ");
                else
                    nextLine.Append(" x" + string.Format("{0,2:X}",
                                                  (int)nextChar));
            }
```

```
            lines[i] = nextLine.ToString();
        }
        inStream.Close();
        this.textBoxContents.Lines = lines;
    }
```

There is quite a lot going on in this method, so here is a breakdown. You instantiate a `FileStream` object for the selected file, which specifies that you want to open an existing file for reading. You then work out how many bytes there are to read in and how many lines should be displayed. The number of bytes will normally be the number of bytes in the file. However, text boxes can display a maximum of only 65,536 characters and with the chosen display format, you are displaying four characters for every byte in the file. Therefore, you will need to cap the number of bytes shown in the text box if the selected file is longer than 65,536/4 = 16,384 bytes.

> *If you want to display longer files in this sort of environment, you might want to look up the* `RichTextBox` *class in the* `System.Windows.Forms` *namespace.* `RichTextBox` *is similar to a text box, but has many more advanced formatting facilities and does not have a limit on how much text it can display.* `TextBox` *is used here to keep the example simple and focused on the process of reading in files.*

The bulk of the method is given over to two nested `for` loops that construct each line of text to be displayed. You use a `StringBuilder` class to construct each line for performance reasons: you are appending suitable text for each byte to the string that represents each line 16 times. If on each occasion you allocate a new string and take a copy of the half-constructed line, you are not only going to be spending a lot of time allocating strings but will also be wasting a lot of memory on the heap. Notice that the definition of *printable* characters is anything that is a letter, digit, or punctuation, as indicated by the relevant static `System.Char` methods. You exclude any character with a value less than 16 from the printable list, however; this means that you will trap the carriage return (13) and line feed (10) as binary characters (a multiline text box isn't able to display these characters properly if they occur individually within a line).

Furthermore, using the Properties window, you change the Font property for the text box to a fixed-width font. In this case, you choose `Courier New 9pt regular`, and set the text box to have vertical and horizontal scroll bars.

Upon completion, you close the stream and set the contents of the text box to the array of strings that you have built up.

Reading and Writing to Text Files

Theoretically, it is perfectly possible to use the `FileStream` class to read in and display text files. You have, after all, just done that. The format in which the `Default.aspx` file is displayed in the preceding example is not particularly user-friendly, but that has nothing to do with any intrinsic problem with the `FileStream` class, only with how you chose to display the results in the text box.

Having said that, if you know that a particular file contains text, you will usually find it more convenient to read and write it using the `StreamReader` and `StreamWriter` classes instead of the `FileStream` class. That is because these classes work at a slightly higher level and are specifically geared to reading and writing text. The methods that they implement are able to automatically detect convenient points to stop reading text, based on the contents of the stream. In particular:

❑   These classes implement methods to read or write one line of text at a time, `StreamReader` `.ReadLine()` and `StreamWriter.WriteLine()`. In the case of reading, this means that the stream will automatically determine for you where the next carriage return is and stop reading at that point. In the case of writing, it means that the stream will automatically append the carriage return–line feed combination to the text that it writes out.

❑ By using the StreamReader and StreamWriter classes, you don't need to worry about the encoding (the text format) used in the file. Possible encodings include ASCII (1 byte for each character), or any of the Unicode-based formats, Unicode, UTF7, UTF8, and UTF32. Text files on Windows 9x systems are always in ASCII because Windows 9x does not support Unicode; however, because Windows NT, 2000, XP, 2003, Vista, and Windows Server 2008 all do support Unicode, text files might theoretically contain Unicode, UTF7, UTF8, or UTF32 data instead of ASCII data. The convention is that if the file is in ASCII format, it will simply contain the text. If it is in any Unicode format, this will be indicated by the first 2 or 3 bytes of the file, which are set to particular combinations of values to indicate the format used in the file.

These bytes are known as the *byte code markers*. When you open a file using any of the standard Windows applications, such as Notepad or WordPad, you do not need to worry about this because these applications are aware of the different encoding methods and will automatically read the file correctly. This is also true for the StreamReader class, which will correctly read in a file in any of these formats, and the StreamWriter class is capable of formatting the text it writes out using whatever encoding technique you request. If you wanted to read in and display a text file using the FileStream class, however, you would have to handle all of this yourself.

The StreamReader Class

StreamReader is used to read text files. Constructing a StreamReader is in some ways easier than constructing a FileStream instance because some of the FileStream options are not required when using StreamReader. In particular, the mode and access types are not relevant to StreamReader because the only thing you can do with a StreamReader is read! Furthermore, there is no direct option to specify the sharing permissions. However, there are a couple of new options:

❑ You need to specify what to do about the different encoding methods. You can instruct the StreamReader to examine the byte code markers in the beginning of the file to determine the encoding method, or you can simply tell the StreamReader to assume that the file uses a specified encoding method.

❑ Instead of supplying a file name to be read from, you can supply a reference to another stream.

This last option deserves a bit more discussion because it illustrates another advantage of basing the model for reading and writing data on the concept of streams. Because the StreamReader works at a relatively high level, you might find it useful if you have another stream that is there to read data from some other source, but you would like to use the facilities provided by StreamReader to process that other stream as if it contained text. You can do so by simply passing the output from this stream to a StreamReader. In this way, StreamReader can be used to read and process data from any data source — not only files. This is essentially the situation discussed earlier with regard to the BinaryReader class. However, in this book you will only use StreamReader to connect directly to files.

The result of these possibilities is that StreamReader has a large number of constructors. Not only that, but there are a couple of FileInfo methods that return StreamReader references, too: OpenText() and CreateText(). The following just illustrates some of the constructors.

The simplest constructor takes just a file name. This StreamReader will examine the byte order marks to determine the encoding:

```
StreamReader sr = new StreamReader(@"C:\My Documents\ReadMe.txt");
```

Alternatively, if you prefer to specify that UTF8 encoding should be assumed:

```
StreamReader sr = new StreamReader(@"C:\My Documents\ReadMe.txt",
                                   Encoding.UTF8);
```

You specify the encoding by using one of several properties on a class, `System.Text.Encoding`. This class is an abstract base class, from which a number of classes are derived and which implements methods that actually perform the text encoding. Each property returns an instance of the appropriate class, and the possible properties you can use here are:

- ❏ `ASCII`
- ❏ `Unicode`
- ❏ `UTF7`
- ❏ `UTF8`
- ❏ `UTF32`
- ❏ `BigEndianUnicode`

The following example demonstrates hooking up a `StreamReader` to a `FileStream`. The advantage of this is that you can specify whether to create the file and the share permissions, which you cannot do if you directly attach a `StreamReader` to the file:

```
FileStream fs = new FileStream(@"C:\My Documents\ReadMe.txt",
                  FileMode.Open, FileAccess.Read, FileShare.None);
StreamReader sr = new StreamReader(fs);
```

For this example, you specify that the `StreamReader` will look for byte code markers to determine the encoding method used, as it will do in the following examples, in which the `StreamReader` is obtained from a `FileInfo` instance:

```
FileInfo myFile = new FileInfo(@"C:\My Documents\ReadMe.txt");
StreamReader sr = myFile.OpenText();
```

Just as with a `FileStream`, you should always close a `StreamReader` after use. Failure to do so will result in the file remaining locked to other processes (unless you used a `FileStream` to construct the `StreamReader` and specified `FileShare.ShareReadWrite`):

```
sr.Close();
```

Now that you have gone to the trouble of instantiating a `StreamReader`, you can do something with it. As with the `FileStream`, you will simply see the various ways to read data, and the other, less commonly used `StreamReader` methods are left to the SDK documentation.

Possibly the easiest method to use is `ReadLine()`, which keeps reading until it gets to the end of a line. It does not include the carriage return–line feed combination that marks the end of the line in the returned string:

```
string nextLine = sr.ReadLine();
```

Alternatively, you can grab the entire remainder of the file (or strictly, the remainder of the stream) in one string:

```
string restOfStream = sr.ReadToEnd();
```

You can read a single character:

```
int nextChar = sr.Read();
```

This overload of `Read()` casts the returned character to an `int`. This is so that it has the option of returning a value of `-1` if the end of the stream has been reached.

Finally, you can read a given number of characters into an array, with an offset:

```
// to read 100 characters in.

int nChars = 100;
char [] charArray = new char[nChars];
int nCharsRead = sr.Read(charArray, 0, nChars);
```

nCharsRead will be less than nChars if you have requested to read more characters than are left in the file.

The StreamWriter Class

This works in the same way as the StreamReader, except that you can use StreamWriter only to write to a file (or to another stream). Possibilities for constructing a StreamWriter include:

```
StreamWriter sw = new StreamWriter(@"C:\My Documents\ReadMe.txt");
```

This will use UTF8 encoding, which is regarded by .NET as the default encoding method. If you want, you can specify an alternative encoding:

```
StreamWriter sw = new StreamWriter(@"C:\My Documents\ReadMe.txt", true,
    Encoding.ASCII);
```

In this constructor, the second parameter is a Boolean that indicates whether the file should be opened for appending. There is, oddly, no constructor that takes only a file name and an encoding class.

Of course, you may want to hook up StreamWriter to a file stream to give you more control over the options for opening the file:

```
FileStream fs = new FileStream(@"C:\My Documents\ReadMe.txt",
    FileMode.CreateNew, FileAccess.Write, FileShare.Read);
StreamWriter sw = new StreamWriter(fs);
```

FileStream does not implement any methods that return a StreamWriter class.

Alternatively, if you want to create a new file and start writing data to it, you will find this sequence useful:

```
FileInfo myFile = new FileInfo(@"C:\My Documents\NewFile.txt");
StreamWriter sw = myFile.CreateText();
```

Just as with all other stream classes, it is important to close a StreamWriter class when you have finished with it:

```
sw.Close();
```

Writing to the stream is done using any of four overloads of StreamWriter.Write(). The simplest writes out a string and appends it with a carriage return–line feed combination:

```
string nextLine = "Groovy Line";
sw.Write(nextLine);
```

It is also possible to write out a single character:

```
char nextChar = 'a';
sw.Write(nextChar);
```

And an array of characters:

```
char [] charArray = new char[100];

// initialize these characters

sw.Write(charArray);
```

It is even possible to write out a portion of an array of characters:

```
int nCharsToWrite = 50;
int startAtLocation = 25;
char [] charArray = new char[100];

// initialize these characters

sw.Write(charArray, startAtLocation, nCharsToWrite);
```

Example: ReadWriteText

The ReadWriteText example displays the use of the StreamReader and StreamWriter classes. It is similar to the earlier ReadBinaryFile example, but it assumes that the file to be read in is a text file and displays it as such. It is also capable of saving the file (with any modifications you have made to the text in the text box). It will save any file in Unicode format.

The screenshot in Figure 25-11 shows ReadWriteText displaying the same Default.aspx file that you used earlier. This time, however, you are able to read the contents a bit more easily!

Figure 25-11

We won't cover the details of adding the event handlers for the Open File dialog box, because they are basically the same as in the earlier BinaryFileReader example. As with that example, opening a new file causes the DisplayFile() method to be called. The only real difference between this example and the previous one is the implementation of DisplayFile as well as that you now have the option to save a file. This is represented by another menu option, Save. The handler for this option calls another method you have added to the code, SaveFile(). (Note that the new file always overwrites the original file; this example does not have an option to write to a different file.)

You will look at SaveFile() first because that is the simplest function. You simply write each line of the text box, in turn, to a StreamWriter stream, relying on the StreamReader.WriteLine() method to append the trailing carriage return and line feed to the end of each line:

```
void SaveFile()
{
    StreamWriter sw = new StreamWriter(chosenFile, false, Encoding.Unicode);

    foreach (string line in textBoxContents.Lines)
        sw.WriteLine(line);
    sw.Close();
}
```

chosenFile is a string field of the main form, which contains the name of the file you have read in (just as for the previous example). Notice that you specify Unicode encoding when you open the stream. If you wanted to write files in some other format, you would simply need to change the value of this parameter. The second parameter to this constructor would be set to true if you wanted to append to a file, but you do not in this case. The encoding must be set at construction time for a StreamWriter. It is subsequently available as a read-only property, Encoding.

Now you examine how files are read in. The process of reading in is complicated by the fact that you don't know how many lines it is going to contain until you have read in the file. For example, you don't know how many (char)13(char)10 sequences are in the file because char(13)char(10) is the carriage return–line feed combination that occurs at the end of a line. You solve this problem by initially reading the file into an instance of the StringCollection class, which is in the System.Collections. Specialized namespace. This class is designed to hold a set of strings that can be dynamically expanded. It implements two methods that you will be interested in: Add(), which adds a string to the collection, and CopyTo(), which copies the string collection into a normal array (a System.Array instance). Each element of the StringCollection object will hold one line of the file.

The DisplayFile() method calls another method, ReadFileIntoStringCollection(), which actually reads in the file. After doing this, you now know how many lines there are, so you are in a position to copy the StringCollection into a normal, fixed-size array and feed this array into the text box. Because only the references to the strings, not the strings themselves, are copied when you actually make the copy, the process is reasonably efficient:

```
void DisplayFile()
{
    StringCollection linesCollection = ReadFileIntoStringCollection();
    string [] linesArray = new string[linesCollection.Count];
    linesCollection.CopyTo(linesArray, 0);
    this.textBoxContents.Lines = linesArray;
}
```

The second parameter of StringCollection.CopyTo() indicates the index within the destination array of where you want the collection to start.

Now you examine the ReadFileIntoStringCollection() method. You use a StreamReader to read in each line. The main complication here is the need to count the characters read in to make sure that you do not exceed the capacity of the text box:

```
StringCollection ReadFileIntoStringCollection()
{
    const int MaxBytes = 65536;
    StreamReader sr = new StreamReader(chosenFile);
    StringCollection result = new StringCollection();
```

```
        int nBytesRead = 0;
        string nextLine;
        while ( (nextLine = sr.ReadLine()) != null)
        {
            nBytesRead += nextLine.Length;
            if (nBytesRead > MaxBytes)
                break;
            result.Add(nextLine);
        }
        sr.Close();
        return result;
    }
```

That completes the code for this example.

If you run `ReadWriteText`, read in the `Default.aspx` file, and then save it, the file will be in Unicode format. You would not be able to tell this from any of the usual Windows applications. Notepad, WordPad, and even the `ReadWriteText` example will still read the file in and display it correctly under Windows NT/2000/XP/2003/Vista/2008, although, because Windows 9x doesn't support Unicode, applications like Notepad won't be able to understand the Unicode file on those platforms. (If you download the example from the Wrox Press web site at `www.wrox.com`, you can try this!) However, if you try to display the file again using the earlier `BinaryFileReader` example, you can see the difference immediately, as shown in Figure 25-12. The two initial bytes that indicate the file is in Unicode format are visible, and thereafter you see that every character is represented by 2 bytes. This last fact is obvious because the high-order byte of every character in this particular file is zero, so every second byte in this file now displays `x00`.

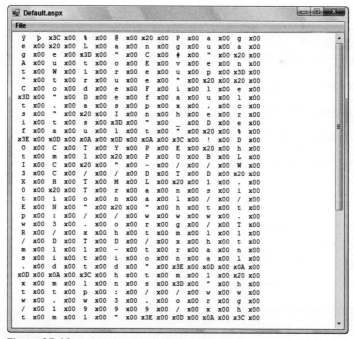

Figure 25-12

Reading Drive Information

In addition to working with files and directories, the .NET Framework includes the ability to read information from a specified drive. This is done using the DriveInfo class. The DriveInfo class can perform a scan of a system to provide a list of available drives and then can dig in deeper, providing you with tons of details about any of the drives.

For an example of using the DriveInfo class, create a simple Windows Form that will list out all the available drives on a computer and then will provide details on a user-selected drive. Your Windows Form will consist of a simple ListBox and should look as illustrated in Figure 25-13.

Figure 25-13

Once you have the form all set, the code will consist of two events — one for when the form loads and another for when the end user makes a drive selection in the list box. The code for this form is shown here:

```
using System;
using System.IO;
using System.Windows.Forms;

namespace DriveInfo
{
    public partial class Form1 : Form
    {
        public Form1()
        {
            InitializeComponent();
        }

        private void Form1_Load(object sender, EventArgs e)
        {
            DriveInfo[] di = DriveInfo.GetDrives();

            foreach (DriveInfo itemDrive in di)
            {
                listBox1.Items.Add(itemDrive.Name);
            }
        }

        private void listBox1_SelectedIndexChanged(object sender, EventArgs e)
        {
            DriveInfo di = new DriveInfo(listBox1.SelectedItem.ToString());
```

```
MessageBox.Show("Available Free Space: "
    + di.AvailableFreeSpace + "\n" +
    "Drive Format: " + di.DriveFormat + "\n" +
    "Drive Type: " + di.DriveType + "\n" +
    "Is Ready: " + di.IsReady + "\n" +
    "Name: " + di.Name + "\n" +
    "Root Directory: " + di.RootDirectory + "\n" +
    "ToString() Value: " + di + "\n" +
    "Total Free Space: " + di.TotalFreeSpace + "\n" +
    "Total Size: " + di.TotalSize + "\n" +
    "Volume Label: " + di.VolumeLabel, di.Name +
    " DRIVE INFO");
        }
    }
}
```

The first step is to bring in the System.IO namespace with the using keyword. Within the Form1_Load event, you use the DriveInfo class to get a list of all the available drives on the system. This is done using an array of DriveInfo objects and populating this array with the DriveInfo.GetDrives() method. Then using a foreach loop, you are able to iterate through each drive found and populate the list box with the results. This produces something similar to what is shown in Figure 25-14.

Figure 25-14

This form allows the end user to select one of the drives in the list. Once a drive is selected, a message box appears that contains details about that drive. As you can see in Figure 25-14, I have six drives on my current computer. Selecting a couple of these drives produces the message boxes collectively shown in Figure 25-15.

Figure 25-15

From here, you can see that these message boxes provide details about three entirely different drives. The first, drive C:\, is my hard drive, as the message box shows its drive type as Fixed. The second drive, drive D:\, is my CD/DVD drive. The third drive, drive F:\, is my USB pen and is labeled with a drive type of Removable.

File Security

When the .NET Framework 1.0/1.1 was first introduced, it didn't come with a way to easily access and work access control lists (ACLs) for files, directories, and registry keys. To do such things at that time usually meant some work with COM interop, thus also requiring a more advanced programming knowledge of working with ACLs.

This has considerably changed since the release of the .NET Framework 2.0, which made the process of working with ACLs considerably easier with a namespace — System.Security.AccessControl. With this namespace, it is now possible to manipulate security settings for files, registry keys, network shares, Active Directory objects, and more.

Reading ACLs from a File

For an example of working with System.Security.AccessControl, this section looks at working with the ACLs for both files and directories. It starts by looking at how you would review the ACLs for a particular file. This example is accomplished in a console application and illustrated here:

```
using System;
using System.IO;
using System.Security.AccessControl;
using System.Security.Principal;

namespace ConsoleApplication1
{
    internal class Program
    {
        private static string myFilePath;

        private static void Main()
        {
            Console.Write("Provide full file path: ");
            myFilePath = Console.ReadLine();

            try
            {
                using (FileStream myFile =
                    new FileStream(myFilePath, FileMode.Open, FileAccess.Read))
                {
                    FileSecurity fileSec = myFile.GetAccessControl();

                    foreach (FileSystemAccessRule fileRule in
                        fileSec.GetAccessRules(true, true,
                            typeof (NTAccount)))
                    {
                        Console.WriteLine("{0} {1} {2} access for {3}",
                            myFilePath,
                            fileRule.AccessControlType ==
```

```
                                  AccessControlType.Allow
                                    ? "provides" : "denies",
                                  fileRule.FileSystemRights,
                                  fileRule.IdentityReference);
                            }
                        }
                    }
                    catch
                    {
                        Console.WriteLine("Incorrect file path given!");
                    }

                    Console.ReadLine();
                }
            }
        }
```

For this example to work, the first step is to refer to the System.Security.AccessControl namespace. This will give you access to the FileSecurity and the FileSystemAccessRule classes later in the program.

After the specified file is retrieved and placed in a FileStream object, the ACLs of the file are grabbed using the GetAccessControl() method now found on the File object. This information from the GetAccessControl() method is then placed in a FileSecurity class. This class has access rights to the referenced item. Each individual access right is then in turn represented by a FileSystemAccessRule object. That is why a foreach loop is used to iterate through all the access rights found in the created FileSecurity object.

Running this example with a simple text file in the root directory produces something similar to the following results:

```
Provide full file path: C:\Sample.txt
C:\Sample.txt provides FullControl access for BUILTIN\Administrators
C:\Sample.txt provides FullControl access for NT AUTHORITY\SYSTEM
C:\Sample.txt provides FullControl access for PUSHKIN\Bill
C:\Sample.txt provides ReadAndExecute, Synchronize access for BUILTIN\Users
```

The next section presents reading ACLs from a directory instead of a file.

Reading ACLs from a Directory

Reading ACL information about a directory instead of an actual file is not much different from the preceding example. The code for this is illustrated in the following sample:

```
using System;
using System.IO;
using System.Security.AccessControl;
using System.Security.Principal;

namespace ConsoleApplication1
{
    internal class Program
    {
        private static string mentionedDir;

        private static void Main()
```

(continued)

(continued)

```
        {
            Console.Write("Provide full directory path: ");
            mentionedDir = Console.ReadLine();

            try
            {
                DirectoryInfo myDir = new DirectoryInfo(mentionedDir);

                if (myDir.Exists)
                {
                    DirectorySecurity myDirSec = myDir.GetAccessControl();

                    foreach (FileSystemAccessRule fileRule in
                        myDirSec.GetAccessRules(true, true,
                                            typeof (NTAccount)))
                    {
                        Console.WriteLine("{0} {1} {2} access for {3}",
                            mentionedDir, fileRule.AccessControlType ==
                            AccessControlType.Allow
                            ? "provides" : "denies",
                            fileRule.FileSystemRights,
                            fileRule.IdentityReference);
                    }
                }
            }
            catch
            {
                Console.WriteLine("Incorrect directory provided!");
            }

            Console.ReadLine();
        }
    }
}
```

The big difference with this example is that it uses the `DirectoryInfo` class, which now also includes the `GetAccessControl()` method to pull information about the directory's ACLs. Running this example produces the following results:

```
Provide full directory path: C:\Test
C:\Test provides FullControl access for BUILTIN\Administrators
C:\Test provides FullControl access for NT AUTHORITY\SYSTEM
C:\Test provides FullControl access for PUSHKIN\Bill
C:\Test provides 268435456 access for CREATOR OWNER
C:\Test provides ReadAndExecute, Synchronize access for BUILTIN\Users
C:\Test provides AppendData access for BUILTIN\Users
C:\Test provides CreateFiles access for BUILTIN\Users
```

The final thing you will look at in working with ACLs is using the new `System.Security.AccessControl` namespace to add and remove items to and from a file's ACL.

Adding and Removing ACLs from a File

It is also possible to manipulate the ACLs of a resource using the same objects that were used in the previous examples. The following code example changes a previous code example where a file's ACL information was read. Here, the ACLs are read for a specified file, changed, and then read again:

```
try
{
    using (FileStream myFile = new FileStream(myFilePath,
        FileMode.Open, FileAccess.ReadWrite))
    {
        FileSecurity fileSec = myFile.GetAccessControl();

        Console.WriteLine("ACL list before modification:");

        foreach (FileSystemAccessRule fileRule in
            fileSec.GetAccessRules(true, true,
             typeof(System.Security.Principal.NTAccount)))
        {
            Console.WriteLine("{0} {1} {2} access for {3}", myFilePath,
                fileRule.AccessControlType == AccessControlType.Allow ?
                "provides" : "denies",
                fileRule.FileSystemRights,
                fileRule.IdentityReference);
        }

        Console.WriteLine();
        Console.WriteLine("ACL list after modification:");

        FileSystemAccessRule newRule = new FileSystemAccessRule(
            new System.Security.Principal.NTAccount(@"PUSHKIN\Tuija"),
            FileSystemRights.FullControl,
            AccessControlType.Allow);

        fileSec.AddAccessRule(newRule);
        File.SetAccessControl(myFilePath, fileSec);

        foreach (FileSystemAccessRule fileRule in
            fileSec.GetAccessRules(true, true,
            typeof(System.Security.Principal.NTAccount)))
        {
            Console.WriteLine("{0} {1} {2} access for {3}", myFilePath,
                fileRule.AccessControlType == AccessControlType.Allow ?
                "provides" : "denies",
                fileRule.FileSystemRights,
                fileRule.IdentityReference);
        }
    }
}
```

In this case, a new access rule is added to the file's ACL. This is done by using the `FileSystemAccessRule` object. The `FileSystemAccessRule` class is an abstraction access control entry (ACE) instance. The ACE defines the user account to use, the type of access that this user account can deal with, and whether or not to allow or deny this access. In creating a new instance of this object, a new `NTAccount` is created and given `Full Control` to the file. Even though a new `NTAccount` is created, it must still reference an existing user. Then the `AddAccessRule` method of the `FileSecurity` class is used to assign the new rule. From there, the `FileSecurity` object reference is used to set the access control to the file in question using the `SetAccessControl()` method of the `File` class.

Next, the file's ACL is listed again. The following is an example of what the preceding code could produce:

```
Provide full file path: C:\Sample.txt
ACL list before modification:
C:\Sample.txt provides FullControl access for BUILTIN\Administrators
C:\Sample.txt provides FullControl access for NT AUTHORITY\SYSTEM
C:\Sample.txt provides FullControl access for PUSHKIN\Bill
C:\Sample.txt provides ReadAndExecute, Synchronize access for BUILTIN\Users

ACL list after modification:
C:\Sample.txt provides FullControl access for PUSHKIN\Tuija
C:\Sample.txt provides FullControl access for BUILTIN\Administrators
C:\Sample.txt provides FullControl access for NT AUTHORITY\SYSTEM
C:\Sample.txt provides FullControl access for PUSHKIN\Bill
C:\Sample.txt provides ReadAndExecute, Synchronize access for BUILTIN\Users
```

To remove a rule from the ACL list, there is really not much that needs to be done to the code. From the previous code example, you simply need to change the line

```
fileSec.AddAccessRule(newRule);
```

to the following to remove the rule that was just added:

```
fileSec.RemoveAccessRule(newRule);
```

Reading and Writing to the Registry

In all versions of Windows since Windows 95, the registry has been the central repository for all configuration information relating to Windows setup, user preferences, and installed software and devices. Almost all commercial software these days uses the registry to store information about itself, and COM components must place information about themselves in the registry in order to be called by clients. The .NET Framework and its accompanying concept of zero-impact installation has slightly reduced the significance of the registry for applications in the sense that assemblies are entirely self-contained; no information about particular assemblies needs to be placed in the registry, even for shared assemblies. In addition, the .NET Framework has brought the concept of isolated storage, by which applications can store information that is particular to each user in files; the .NET Framework ensures that data is stored separately for each user registered on a machine.

The fact that applications can now be installed using the Windows Installer also frees developers from some of the direct manipulation of the registry that used to be involved in installing applications. However, despite this, the possibility exists that if you distribute any complete application, your application will use the registry to store information about its configuration. For instance, if you want your application to show up in the Add/Remove Programs dialog box in the Control Panel, this will involve appropriate registry entries. You may also need to use the registry for backward compatibility with legacy code.

As you would expect from a library as comprehensive as the .NET library, it includes classes that give you access to the registry. Two classes are concerned with the registry, and both are in the `Microsoft.Win32` namespace. The classes are `Registry` and `RegistryKey`. Before you examine these classes, the following section briefly reviews the structure of the registry itself.

The Registry

The registry has a hierarchical structure much like that of the file system. The usual way to view or modify the contents of the registry is with one of two utilities: `regedit` or `regedt32`. Of these, `regedit` comes standard with all versions of Windows since Windows 95. `regedt32` comes with Windows NT and Windows 2000; it is less user-friendly than `regedit`, but allows access to security information that `regedit` is unable to view. Windows Server 2003 has merged `regedit` and `regedt32` into a single new editor simply called `regedit`. For the discussion here, you will use `regedit` from Windows XP Professional, which you can launch by typing in **regedit** in the Run dialog or at the command prompt.

Figure 25-16 shows what you get when you launch `regedit` for the first time.

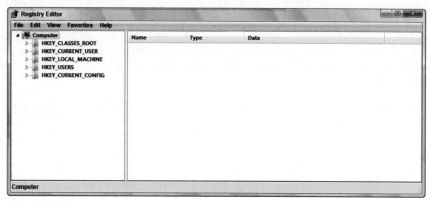

Figure 25-16

`regedit` has a tree view/list view–style user interface similar to Windows Explorer, which matches the hierarchical structure of the registry itself. However, you will see some key differences shortly.

In a file system, the topmost-level nodes can be thought of as being the partitions on your disks, `C:\`, `D:\`, and so on. In the registry, the equivalent to a partition is the *registry hive*. It is not possible to change the existing hives — they are fixed, and there are seven of them, although only five are actually visible through `regedit`:

❑ HKEY_CLASSES_ROOT (HKCR) contains details of types of files on the system (`.txt`, `.doc`, and so on) and which applications are able to open files of each type. It also contains registration information for all COM components (this latter area is usually the largest single area of the registry because Windows, these days, comes with a huge number of COM components).

❑ HKEY_CURRENT_USER (HKCU) contains details of user preferences for the user currently logged on to the machine locally. These settings include desktop settings, environment variables, network and printer connections, and other settings that define the user operating environment of the user.

❑ HKEY_LOCAL_MACHINE (HKLM) is a huge hive that contains details of all software and hardware installed on the machine. These settings are not user-specific but are for all users that log on to the machine. This hive also includes the HKCR hive; HKCR is actually not really an independent hive in its own right but is simply a convenient mapping onto the registry key HKLM/SOFTWARE/Classes.

❑ HKEY_USERS (HKUSR) contains details of user preferences for all users. As you might guess, it also contains the HKCU hive, which is simply a mapping onto one of the keys in HKEY_USERS.

❑ HKEY_CURRENT_CONFIG (HKCF) contains details of hardware on the machine.

The remaining two keys contain information that is temporary and that changes frequently

❑   HKEY_DYN_DATA is a general container for any volatile data that needs to be stored somewhere in the registry.

❑   HKEY_PERFORMANCE_DATA contains information concerning the performance of running applications.

Within the hives is a tree structure of registry *keys*. Each key is in many ways analogous to a folder or file on the file system. However, there is one very important difference. The file system distinguishes between files (which are there to contain data) and folders (which are primarily there to contain other files or folders), but in the registry there are only keys. A key may contain both data and other keys.

If a key contains data, it will be presented as a series of values. Each value will have an associated name, data type, and data. In addition, a key can have a default value, which is unnamed.

You can see this structure by using regedit to examine registry keys. Figure 25-17 shows the contents of the key HKCU\Control Panel\Appearance, which contains the details of the chosen color scheme of the currently logged-in user. regedit shows which key is being examined by displaying it with an open folder icon in the tree view.

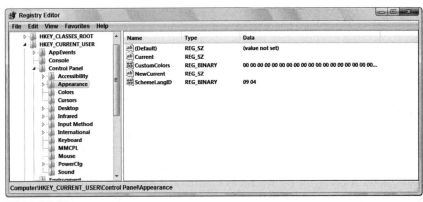

Figure 25-17

The HKCU\Control Panel\Appearance key has three named values set, although the default value does not contain any data. The column in the screenshot marked Type details the data type of each value. Registry entries can be formatted as one of three data types:

❑   REG_SZ (which roughly corresponds to a .NET string instance; the matching is not exact because the registry data types are not .NET data types)

❑   REG_DWORD (corresponds roughly to uint)

❑   REG_BINARY (array of bytes)

An application that stores data in the registry will do so by creating a number of registry keys, usually under the key HKLM\Software\<CompanyName>. Note that it is not necessary for these keys to contain any data. Sometimes the very fact that a key exists provides the data that an application needs.

The .NET Registry Classes

Access to the registry is available through two classes in the Microsoft.Win32 namespace: Registry and RegistryKey. A RegistryKey instance represents a registry key. This class implements methods to browse child keys, to create new keys, or to read or modify the values in the key — in other words, to do everything you would normally want to do with a registry key, including setting the security levels for the key. RegistryKey will be the class you use for much of your work with the registry. Registry, by contrast, is a class that allows for singular access to registry keys for simple operations. Another role of the Registry class is simply to provide you with RegistryKey instances that represent the top-level keys, the different hives, in order to enable you to navigate the registry. Registry provides these instances through static properties, and there are seven of them called, respectively, ClassesRoot, CurrentConfig, CurrentUser, DynData, LocalMachine, PerformanceData, and Users. It should be obvious which property corresponds to which hive.

So, for example, to obtain a RegistryKey instance that represents the HKLM key, you would write:

```
RegistryKey hklm = Registry.LocalMachine;
```

The process of obtaining a reference to a RegistryKey object is known as opening the key.

Although you might expect that the methods exposed by RegistryKey would be similar to those implemented by DirectoryInfo, given that the registry has a similar hierarchical structure to the file system, this actually isn't the case. Often, the way that you access the registry is different from the way that you would use files and folders, and RegistryKey implements methods that reflect this.

The most obvious difference is in how you open a registry key at a given location in the registry. The Registry class does not have any public constructor that you can use, nor does it have any methods that let you go directly to a key, given its name. Instead, you are expected to browse down to that key from the top of the relevant hive. If you want to instantiate a RegistryKey object, the only way is to start off with the appropriate static property of Registry, and work down from there. So, for example, if you want to read some data in the HKLM/Software/Microsoft key, you would get a reference to it like this:

```
RegistryKey hklm = Registry.LocalMachine;
RegistryKey hkSoftware = hklm.OpenSubKey("Software");
RegistryKey hkMicrosoft = hkSoftware.OpenSubKey("Microsoft");
```

A registry key accessed in this way will give you read-only access. If you want to be able to write to the key (that includes writing to its values or creating or deleting direct children of it), you need to use another override to OpenSubKey, which takes a second parameter, of type bool, that indicates whether you want read-write access to the key. For example, if you want to be able to modify the Microsoft key (and assuming that you are a system administrator with permission to do this), you would write this:

```
RegistryKey hklm = Registry.LocalMachine;
RegistryKey hkSoftware = hklm.OpenSubKey("Software");
RegistryKey hkMicrosoft = hkSoftware.OpenSubKey("Microsoft", true);
```

Incidentally, because this key contains information used by Microsoft's applications, in most cases you probably shouldn't be modifying this particular key.

The OpenSubKey() method is the one you will call if you are expecting the key to be present. If the key isn't there, it will return a null reference. If you want to create a key, you should use the CreateSubKey() method (which automatically gives you read-write access to the key through the reference returned):

```
RegistryKey hklm = Registry.LocalMachine;
RegistryKey hkSoftware = hklm.OpenSubKey("Software");
RegistryKey hkMine = hkSoftware.CreateSubKey("MyOwnSoftware");
```

The way that CreateSubKey() works is quite interesting. It will create the key if it does not already exist, but if it does already exist, it will quietly return a RegistryKey instance that represents the existing key. The reason for the method behaving in this manner has to do with how you will normally use the registry. The registry, overall, contains long-term data such as configuration information for

Windows and for various applications. It is not very common, therefore, that you find yourself in a situation where you need to explicitly create a key.

What is much more common is that your application needs to make sure that some data is present in the registry — in other words, create the relevant keys if they do not already exist, but do nothing if they do. `CreateSubKey()` fills that need perfectly. Unlike the situation with `FileInfo.Open()`, for example, there is no chance with `CreateSubKey()` of accidentally removing any data. If deleting registry keys is your intention, you will need to call the `RegistryKey.DeleteSubKey()` method. This makes sense given the importance of the registry to Windows. The last thing you want is to completely break Windows accidentally by deleting a couple of important keys while you are debugging your C# registry calls!

Once you have located the registry key you want to read or modify, you can use the `SetValue()` or `GetValue()` methods to set or get at the data in it. Both of these methods take a string giving the name of the value as a parameter, and `SetValue()` requires an additional object reference containing details of the value. Because the parameter is defined as an object reference, it can actually be a reference to any class you want. `SetValue()` will decide from the type of class actually supplied whether to set the value as a REG_SZ, REG_DWORD, or REG_BINARY value. For example:

```
RegistryKey hkMine = HkSoftware.CreateSubKey("MyOwnSoftware");
hkMine.SetValue("MyStringValue", "Hello World");
hkMine.SetValue("MyIntValue", 20);
```

This code will set the key to have two values: `MyStringValue` will be of type REG_SZ, and `MyIntValue` will be of type REG_DWORD. These are the only two types you will consider here, and use in the example presented later.

`RegistryKey.GetValue()` works in much the same way. It is defined to return an object reference, which means that it is free to actually return a `string` reference if it detects the value is of type REG_SZ, and an `int` if that value is of type REG_DWORD:

```
string stringValue = (string)hkMine.GetValue("MyStringValue");
int intValue = (int)hkMine.GetValue("MyIntValue");
```

Finally, after you have finished reading or modifying the data, close the key:

```
hkMine.Close();
```

`RegistryKey` implements a large number of methods and properties. The following table lists the most useful properties.

Property Name	Description
Name	Name of the key (read-only)
SubKeyCount	The number of children of this key
ValueCount	How many values the key contains

The following table lists the most useful methods.

Method Name	Purpose
Close()	Closes the key.
CreateSubKey()	Creates a subkey of a given name (or opens it if it already exists).
DeleteSubKey()	Deletes a given subkey.
DeleteSubKeyTree()	Recursively deletes a subkey and all its children.
DeleteValue()	Removes a named value from a key.
GetAccessControl()	Returns the access control list (ACL) for a specified registry key. This method is new to the .NET Framework 2.0.
GetSubKeyNames()	Returns an array of strings containing the names of the subkeys.
GetValue()	Returns a named value.
GetValueKind()	Returns a named value whose registry data type is to be retrieved. This method is new to the .NET Framework 2.0.
GetValueNames()	Returns an array of strings containing the names of all the values of the key.
OpenSubKey()	Returns a reference to a RegistryKey instance that represents a given subkey.
SetAccessControl()	Allows you to apply an access control list (ACL) to a specified registry key.
SetValue()	Sets a named value.

Example: SelfPlacingWindow

The use of the registry classes is illustrated with an application called SelfPlacingWindow. This example is a simple C# Windows application that has almost no features. The only thing you can do with it is click a button, which brings up a standard Windows color dialog box (represented by the System.Windows.Forms.ColorDialog class) to let you choose a color, which will become the background color of the form.

Despite its lack of features, the self-placing window scores higher than just about every other application that you have developed in this book in one important and very user-friendly way. If you drag the window around the screen, change its size, or maximize or minimize it before you exit the application, it will remember the new position, as well as the background color, so that the next time it is launched it automatically reappears the way you chose last time. It remembers this information because it writes it to the registry whenever it shuts down. In this way, it demonstrates not only the .NET registry classes themselves but also a very typical use for them, which you will almost certainly want to replicate in any serious commercial Windows Forms application that you write.

The location in which `SelfPlacingWindow` stores its information in the registry is the key `HKLM\`
`Software\WroxPress\SelfPlacingWindow`. HKLM is the usual place for application configuration
information, but note that it is not user-specific. If you wanted to be more sophisticated in a real
application, you would probably want to replicate the information inside the `HK_Users` hive as well, so
that each user can have his or her own profile.

*It is also worth noting that, if you are implementing this in a real .NET application, you may want to
consider using isolated storage instead of the registry to store this information. However, because
isolated storage is available only in .NET, you will need to use the registry if you need any
interoperability with non-.NET apps.*

The very first time that you run the example, it will look for this key and not find it (obviously). Therefore,
it is forced to use a default size, color, and position that you set in the developer environment. The example
also features a list box in which it displays any information read in from the registry. On its first run, it will
look similar to Figure 25-18.

Figure 25-18

If you now modify the background color and resize `SelfPlacingWindow` or move it around on the
screen a bit before exiting, it will create the `HKLM\Software\WroxPress\SelfPlacingWindow` key and
write its new configuration information into it. You can examine the information using `regedit`. The
details are shown in Figure 25-19.

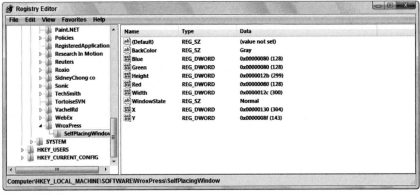

Figure 25-19

As this figure shows, SelfPlacingWindow has placed a number of values in the registry key.

The values Red, Green, and Blue give the color components that make up the selected background color (see Chapter 33, "Graphics with GDI+"). For now, just know that any color display on the system can be completely described by these three components, which are each represented by a number between 0 and 255 (or 0x00 and 0xff in hexadecimal). The values given here make up a bright green color. There are also four more REG_DWORD values, which represent the position and size of the window: X and Y are the coordinates of the top left of the window on the desktop — that is to say the numbers of pixels across from the top left of the screen and the numbers of pixels down. And, Width and Height give the size of the window. WindowsState is the only value for which you have used a string data type (REG_SZ), and it can contain one of the strings Normal, Maximized, or Minimized, depending on the final state of the window when you exited the application.

When you launch SelfPlacingWindow again, it will read this registry key and automatically position itself accordingly (see Figure 25-20).

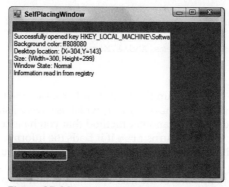

Figure 25-20

This time when you exit SelfPlacingWindow, it will overwrite the previous registry settings with whatever new values are relevant at the time that you exit it. To code the example, you create the usual Windows Forms project in Visual Studio .NET and add the list box and button, using the developer environment's toolbox. You will change the names of these controls, respectively, to listBoxMessages and buttonChooseColor. You also need to ensure that you use the Microsoft.Win32 namespace:

```
using System;
using System.Drawing;
using System.Windows.Forms;
using Microsoft.Win32;
```

You need to add one field (chooseColorDialog) to the main Form1 class, which will represent the color dialog box:

```
public partial class Form1 : Form
{
    private readonly ColorDialog chooseColorDialog = new ColorDialog();
```

Quite a lot of action takes place in the Form1 constructor:

```
public Form1()
{
    InitializeComponent();

    buttonChooseColor.Click += OnClickChooseColor;
```

(continued)

(continued)

```
try
{
    if (ReadSettings() == false)
    {
        listBoxMessages.Items.Add("No information in registry");
    }
    else
    {
        listBoxMessages.Items.Add("Information read in from registry");
    }

    StartPosition = FormStartPosition.Manual;
}
catch (Exception e)
{
    listBoxMessages.Items.Add("A problem occurred reading in data
                              from registry:");
    listBoxMessages.Items.Add(e.Message);
}
}
```

In this constructor, you begin by setting up the event handler for when the user clicks the button. The handler is a method called `OnClickChooseColor()`, which is covered shortly. Reading in the configuration information is done using another method that you have to write, called `ReadSettings()`. `ReadSettings()` returns `true` if it finds the information in the registry, and `false` if it does not (which it should be because this is the first time you have run the application). You place this part of the constructor in a `try` block, just in case any exceptions are generated while reading in the registry values (this might happen if some user has come in and played around with the registry using `regedit`).

The `StartPosition = FormStartPosition.Manual;` statement tells the form to take its initial starting position from the `DeskTopLocation` property instead of using the Windows default location (the default behavior). Possible values are taken from the `FormStartPosition` enumeration.

`SelfPlacingWindow` is also one of the few applications in this book in which you have a serious use for adding code to the `Dispose()` method. Remember that `Dispose()` is called whenever the application terminates normally, so this is the ideal place from which to save the configuration information to the registry. You will find the `Dispose()` method in the `Form1.Designer.cs` file. Within this method, you will place another method that you have to write, `SaveSettings()`:

```
protected override void Dispose(bool disposing)
{
    if (disposing && (components != null))
    {
        components.Dispose();
    }
    SaveSettings();
    base.Dispose(disposing);
}
```

The `SaveSettings()` and `ReadSettings()` methods are the ones that contain the registry code you are interested in, but before you examine them, you have one more piece of housekeeping to do: handle the event of the user clicking that button. This involves displaying the color dialog and setting the background color to whatever color the user chose:

```
void OnClickChooseColor(object Sender, EventArgs e)
{
    if(chooseColorDialog.ShowDialog() == DialogResult.OK)
        BackColor = chooseColorDialog.Color;
}
```

Now, look at how you save the settings:

```
void SaveSettings()
{
    RegistryKey softwareKey =
                Registry.LocalMachine.OpenSubKey("Software", true);
    RegistryKey wroxKey = softwareKey.CreateSubKey("WroxPress");
    RegistryKey selfPlacingWindowKey =
                wroxKey.CreateSubKey("SelfPlacingWindow");
    selfPlacingWindowKey.SetValue("BackColor",
                BackColor.ToKnownColor());
    selfPlacingWindowKey.SetValue("Red", (int)BackColor.R);
    selfPlacingWindowKey.SetValue("Green", (int)BackColor.G);
    selfPlacingWindowKey.SetValue("Blue", (int)BackColor.B);
    selfPlacingWindowKey.SetValue("Width", Width);
    selfPlacingWindowKey.SetValue("Height", Height);
    selfPlacingWindowKey.SetValue("X", DesktopLocation.X);
    selfPlacingWindowKey.SetValue("Y", DesktopLocation.Y);
    selfPlacingWindowKey.SetValue("WindowState",
                WindowState.ToString());
}
```

There is a lot going on here. You start by navigating through the registry to get to the HKLM\Software\ WroxPress\SelfPlacingWindow registry key using the technique demonstrated earlier, starting with the Registry.LocalMachine static property that represents the HKLM hive.

Then you use the RegistryKey.OpenSubKey() method, rather than RegistryKey.CreateSubKey(), to get to the HKLM/Software key. That is because you can be very confident that this key already exists. If it does not, then there is something seriously wrong with your computer, because this key contains settings for a lot of system software! You also indicate that you need write access to this key. That is because if the WroxPress key does not already exist, you will need to create it, which involves writing to the parent key.

The next key to navigate to is HKLM\Software\WroxPress — and here you are not certain whether the key already exists, so you use CreateSubKey() to automatically create it if it does not. Note that CreateSubKey() automatically gives you write access to the key in question. Once you have reached HKLM\Software\WroxPress\SelfPlacingWindow, it is simply a matter of calling the RegistryKey.SetValue() method a number of times to either create or set the appropriate values. There are, however, a couple of complications.

First, you might notice that you are using a couple of classes that you have not encountered before. The DeskTopLocation property of the Form class indicates the position of the top-left corner of the screen and is of type Point. (The Point is discussed in Chapter 33, "Graphics with GDI+".) What you need to know here is that it contains two int values, X and Y, which represent the horizontal and vertical position on the screen. You also look up three member properties of the Form.BackColor property, which is an instance of the Color class: R, G, and B: Color, which represents a color. These properties on it give the red, green, and blue components that make up the color, and they are all of type byte. You also use the Form.WindowState property, which contains an enumeration that gives the current state of the window: Minimized, Maximized, or Normal.

The other complication here is that you need to be a little careful about your casts. SetValue() takes two parameters: a string that gives the name of the key and a System.Object instance, which contains the value. SetValue() has a choice of format for storing the value — it can store it as REG_SZ, REG_BINARY, or REG_DWORD — and it is actually pretty intelligent about making a sensible choice depending on the data type that has been given. Hence for the WindowState, you pass it a string, and SetValue() determines that this should be translated to REG_SZ. Similarly, for the various positions and dimensions, you supply ints, which will be converted into REG_DWORD. However, the color components are more complicated, as you want these to be stored as REG_DWORD too because they are numeric types. However, if SetValue() sees that the data is of type byte, it will store it as a string — as REG_SZ in the registry. To prevent this, you cast the color components to ints.

You have also explicitly cast all the values to the type object. You don't really need to do this because the cast from any other data type to object is implicit, but you are doing this to make it clear what is going on and to remind yourself that SetValue() is defined to take just an object reference as its second parameter.

The ReadSettings() method is a little longer because for each value read in, you also need to interpret it, display the value in the list box, and make the appropriate adjustments to the relevant property of the main form. ReadSettings() looks like this:

```
bool ReadSettings()
{
    RegistryKey softwareKey =
        Registry.LocalMachine.OpenSubKey("Software");
    RegistryKey wroxKey = softwareKey.OpenSubKey("WroxPress");

    if (wroxKey == null)
    {
        return false;
    }

    RegistryKey selfPlacingWindowKey =
        wroxKey.OpenSubKey("SelfPlacingWindow");

    if (selfPlacingWindowKey == null)
    {
        return false;
    }
    else
    {
        listBoxMessages.Items.Add("Successfully opened key " +
                                    selfPlacingWindowKey);
    }

    int redComponent = (int) selfPlacingWindowKey.GetValue("Red");
    int greenComponent = (int) selfPlacingWindowKey.GetValue("Green");
    int blueComponent = (int) selfPlacingWindowKey.GetValue("Blue");
    BackColor = Color.FromArgb(redComponent, greenComponent,
                                blueComponent);
    listBoxMessages.Items.Add("Background color: " + BackColor.Name);
    int X = (int) selfPlacingWindowKey.GetValue("X");
    int Y = (int) selfPlacingWindowKey.GetValue("Y");
```

```
        DesktopLocation = new Point(X, Y);
        listBoxMessages.Items.Add("Desktop location: " +
           DesktopLocation);
        Height = (int) selfPlacingWindowKey.GetValue("Height");
        Width = (int) selfPlacingWindowKey.GetValue("Width");
        listBoxMessages.Items.Add("Size: " + new Size(Width, Height));
        string initialWindowState =
           (string) selfPlacingWindowKey.GetValue("WindowState");
        listBoxMessages.Items.Add("Window State: " + initialWindowState);
        WindowState = (FormWindowState) FormWindowState.Parse
           (WindowState.GetType(), initialWindowState);
           return true;
   }
```

In `ReadSettings()` you first have to navigate to the `HKLM/Software/WroxPress/`
`SelfPlacingWindow` registry key. In this case, however, you are hoping to find the key there so that
you can read it. If it is not there, it is probably the first time you have run the example. In this case, you
just want to abort reading the keys, and you certainly don't want to create any keys. Now you use the
`RegistryKey.OpenSubKey()` method all the way down. If at any stage `OpenSubkey()` returns a `null`
reference, then you know that the registry key is not there, and you can simply return the value `false` to
the calling code.

When it comes to actually reading the keys, you use the `RegistryKey.GetValue()` method, which is
defined as returning an object reference (meaning that this method can actually return an instance of
literally any class it chooses). Like `SetValue()`, it will return a class of object appropriate to the type of
data it found in the key. Therefore, you can usually assume that the `REG_SZ` keys will give you a string,
and the other keys will give you an `int`. You also cast the return reference from `SetValue()`
accordingly. If there is an exception, say someone has fiddled with the registry and mangled the value
types, your cast will cause an exception to be thrown — which will be caught by the handler in the
`Form1` constructor.

The rest of this code uses one more data type, the `Size` structure. This is similar to a `Point` structure but
is used to represent sizes rather than coordinates. It has two member properties, `Width` and `Height`, and
you use the `Size` structure here simply as a convenient way of packaging the size of the form for
displaying in the list box.

Reading and Writing to Isolated Storage

In addition to being able to read and write to and from the registry, another option is reading and
writing values to and from what is called *isolated storage*. If you are having issues writing to the registry
or to disk in general, then isolated storage is where you should turn. You can use isolated storage to store
application state or user settings quite easily.

Think of isolated storage as a virtual disk where you can save items that can be shared only by the
application that created them, or with other application instances. There are two types of access types for
isolated storage. The first is user and assembly.

When accessing isolated storage by user and assembly, there is a single storage location on the machine,
which is accessible via multiple application instances. Access is guaranteed through the user identity and
the application (or assembly) identity. Figure 25-21 shows this in a diagram.

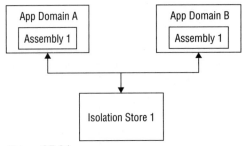

Figure 25-21

This means that you can have multiple instances of the same application all working from the same store.

The second type of access for isolated storage is user, assembly, and domain. In this case, each application instance will work off its own isolation store. This is detailed in Figure 25-22.

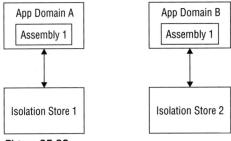

Figure 25-22

In this case, each application instance works off its own store, and the settings that each application instance records are related only to itself. This is a more fine-grained approach to isolated storage.

For an example of using isolated storage from a Windows Forms application (although you can use this from an ASP.NET application just as well), change the SelfPlacingWindow example that was previously used in this chapter to illustrate how to record information to the registry. Through a new ReadSettings() and SaveSettings() method, you read and write values to isolated storage as opposed to doing the same to the registry.

> *It is important to note that the only code shown here is for the* ReadSettings() *and* SaveSettings() *methods. There is more code to the application, and you can see the rest of the code in the previous example titled "Example: SelfPlacingWindow."*

To start, you need to rework the SaveSettings() method. For this next bit of code to work, you need to add the following using directives:

```
using System.IO;
using System.IO.IsolatedStorage;
using System.Text;
```

The `SaveSettings()` method is detailed in the following code example:

```
void SaveSettings()
{
    IsolatedStorageFile storFile = IsolatedStorageFile.GetUserStoreForDomain();
    IsolatedStorageFileStream storStream = new
        IsolatedStorageFileStream("SelfPlacingWindow.xml",

        FileMode.Create, FileAccess.Write);

    System.Xml.XmlTextWriter writer = new
        System.Xml.XmlTextWriter(storStream, Encoding.UTF8);
    writer.Formatting = System.Xml.Formatting.Indented;

    writer.WriteStartDocument();
    writer.WriteStartElement("Settings");

    writer.WriteStartElement("BackColor");
    writer.WriteValue(BackColor.ToKnownColor().ToString());
    writer.WriteEndElement();

    writer.WriteStartElement("Red");
    writer.WriteValue(BackColor.R);
    writer.WriteEndElement();

    writer.WriteStartElement("Green");
    writer.WriteValue(BackColor.G);
    writer.WriteEndElement();

    writer.WriteStartElement("Blue");
    writer.WriteValue(BackColor.B);
    writer.WriteEndElement();

    writer.WriteStartElement("Width");
    writer.WriteValue(Width);
    writer.WriteEndElement();

    writer.WriteStartElement("Height");
    writer.WriteValue(Height);
    writer.WriteEndElement();

    writer.WriteStartElement("X");
    writer.WriteValue(DesktopLocation.X);
    writer.WriteEndElement();

    writer.WriteStartElement("Y");
    writer.WriteValue(DesktopLocation.Y);
    writer.WriteEndElement();

    writer.WriteStartElement("WindowState");
    writer.WriteValue(WindowState.ToString());
    writer.WriteEndElement();

    writer.WriteEndElement();
```

(continued)

```
        writer.Flush();
        writer.Close();

        storStream.Close();
        storFile.Close();
    }
```

It is a bit more code than working with the registry example, but that is mainly due to the code required to build the XML document placed in isolated storage. The first important thing happening with this code is presented here:

```
        IsolatedStorageFile storFile = IsolatedStorageFile.GetUserStoreForDomain();
        IsolatedStorageFileStream storStream = new
            IsolatedStorageFileStream("SelfPlacingWindow.xml",
            FileMode.Create, FileAccess.Write);
```

Here, an instance of an `IsolatedStorageFile` is created using a user, assembly, and domain type of access. A stream is created using the `IsolatedStorageFileStream` object, which will create the virtual `SelfPlacingWindow.xml` file.

From there, an `XmlTextWriter` object is created to build the XML document and the XML contents are written to the `IsolatedStorageFileStream` object instance:

```
        System.Xml.XmlTextWriter writer = new
            System.Xml.XmlTextWriter(storStream, Encoding.UTF8);
```

After the `XmlTextWriter` object is created, all the values are written to the XML document node by node. Once everything is written to the XML document, everything is closed and will now be stored in the isolated storage.

Reading from the storage is done through the `ReadSettings()` method. This method is presented in the following code sample:

```
    bool ReadSettings()
    {
        IsolatedStorageFile storFile = IsolatedStorageFile.GetUserStoreForDomain();
        string[] userFiles = storFile.GetFileNames("SelfPlacingWindow.xml");

        foreach (string userFile in userFiles)
        {
            if(userFile == "SelfPlacingWindow.xml")
            {
                listBoxMessages.Items.Add("Successfully opened file " +
                                        userFile.ToString());

                StreamReader storStream =
                    new StreamReader(new IsolatedStorageFileStream("SelfPlacingWindow.xml",
                    FileMode.Open, storFile));
                System.Xml.XmlTextReader reader = new
                    System.Xml.XmlTextReader(storStream);

                int redComponent = 0;
                int greenComponent = 0;
                int blueComponent = 0;
```

```
            int X = 0;
            int Y = 0;

        while (reader.Read())
        {
            switch (reader.Name)
            {
                case "Red":
                    redComponent = int.Parse(reader.ReadString());
                    break;
                case "Green":
                    greenComponent = int.Parse(reader.ReadString());
                    break;
                case "Blue":
                    blueComponent = int.Parse(reader.ReadString());
                    break;
                case "X":
                    X = int.Parse(reader.ReadString());
                    break;
                case "Y":
                    Y = int.Parse(reader.ReadString());
                    break;
                case "Width":
                    this.Width = int.Parse(reader.ReadString());
                    break;
                case "Height":
                    this.Height = int.Parse(reader.ReadString());
                    break;
                case "WindowState":
                    this.WindowState = (FormWindowState)FormWindowState.Parse
                        (WindowState.GetType(), reader.ReadString());
                    break;
                default:
                    break;
            }
        }

        this.BackColor =
            Color.FromArgb(redComponent, greenComponent, blueComponent);
        this.DesktopLocation = new Point(X, Y);

        listBoxMessages.Items.Add("Background color: " + BackColor.Name);
        listBoxMessages.Items.Add("Desktop location: " +
            DesktopLocation.ToString());
        listBoxMessages.Items.Add("Size: " + new Size(Width, Height).ToString());
        listBoxMessages.Items.Add("Window State: " + WindowState.ToString());

        storStream.Close();
        storFile.Close();
    }
}
return true;
}
```

Using the `GetFileNames()` method, the `SelfPlacingWindow.xml` document is pulled from the isolated storage and then placed into a stream and parsed using the `XmlTextReader` object:

```
IsolatedStorageFile storFile = IsolatedStorageFile.GetUserStoreForDomain();
string[] userFiles = storFile.GetFileNames("SelfPlacingWindow.xml");

foreach (string userFile in userFiles)
{
    if(userFile == "SelfPlacingWindow.xml")
    {
        listBoxMessages.Items.Add("Successfully opened file " +
                                    userFile.ToString());

        StreamReader storStream =
            new StreamReader(new IsolatedStorageFileStream("SelfPlacingWindow.xml",
            FileMode.Open, storFile));
```

Once the XML document is contained within the `IsolatedStorageFileStream` object, it is parsed using the `XmlTextReader` object:

```
System.Xml.XmlTextReader reader = new
    System.Xml.XmlTextReader(storStream);
```

After, it is pulled from the stream via the `XmlTextReader`. The element values are then pushed back into the application. You will now find — just as was accomplished in the `SelfPlacingWindow` example that used the registry to record and retrieve application state values — using isolated storage is just as effective as working with the registry. The application will remember the color, size, and position just as before.

Summary

In this chapter, you have examined how to use the .NET base classes to access the file system and registry from your C# code. You have seen that in both cases the base classes expose simple, but powerful, object models that make it very simple to perform almost any kind of action in these areas. For the file system, these actions are copying files; moving, creating, and deleting files and folders; and reading and writing both binary and text files. For the registry, these are creating, modifying, or reading keys.

This chapter also reviewed isolated storage and how to use this from your applications to store them in the application state.

This chapter assumed that you are running your code from an account that has sufficient access rights to do whatever the code needs to do. Obviously, the question of security is an important one, and it is discussed in Chapter 20, "Security."

The next chapter walks you through data access and ADO.NET, XML, and XML Schemas.

Data Access

This chapter discusses how to access data from your C# programs using ADO.NET. The following details are covered:

- **Connecting to the database** — You learn how to use the `SqlConnection` and `OleDbConnection` classes to connect to and disconnect from the database.

- **Executing commands** — ADO.NET has command objects that can execute SQL commands or issue a call to a stored procedure with optional return values. You learn the various command object options and see how commands can be used for each of the options presented by the `Sql` and `OleDB` classes.

- **Stored procedures** — You learn how to call stored procedures with command objects and how the results of those stored procedures can be integrated into the data cached on the client.

- **The ADO.NET object model** — This is significantly different from the objects available with ADO. The `DataSet`, `DataTable`, `DataRow`, and `DataColumn` classes are discussed as well as the relationships between tables and constraints that are part of `DataSet`. The class hierarchy has changed significantly with version 2 of the .NET Framework, and some of these changes are also described.

- **Using XML and XML schemas** — You examine the XML framework on which ADO.NET is built.

Microsoft has also added support for Language Integrated Query (LINQ) in C# for the 3.0 release. Although this topic largely supersedes the information in this chapter, it is included here for completeness. See Chapters 28, "Manipulating XML,"29, "LINQ to XML," and 31, "Windows Forms," for some details on new data access capabilities in .NET.

As is the case with the other chapters, you can download the code for the examples used in this chapter from the Wrox Web site at `www.wrox.com`. The chapter begins with a brief tour of ADO.NET.

ADO.NET Overview

ADO.NET is more than just a thin veneer over some existing API. The similarity to ADO is fairly minimal — the classes and methods of accessing data are completely different.

ADO (ActiveX Data Objects) is a library of COM components that has had many incarnations over the past few years. Currently at version 2.8, ADO consists primarily of the `Connection`, `Command`, `Recordset`, and `Field` objects. Using ADO, a connection is opened to the database, some data is selected into a record set consisting of fields, that data is then manipulated and updated on the server, and the connection is closed. ADO also introduced a so-called disconnected record set, which is used when keeping the connection open for long periods of time is not desirable.

There were several problems that ADO did not address satisfactorily, most notably the unwieldiness (in physical size) of a disconnected record set. This support was more necessary than ever with the evolution of Web-centric computing, so a fresh approach was required. Upgrading to ADO.NET from ADO shouldn't be too difficult because there are some similarities between the two. What's more, if you are using SQL Server, there is a fantastic new set of managed classes that are tuned to squeeze maximum performance out of the database. This alone should be reason enough to migrate to ADO.NET.

ADO.NET ships with four database client namespaces: one for SQL Server, another for Oracle, the third for ODBC data sources, and the fourth for any database exposed through OLE DB. If your database of choice is not SQL Server or Oracle, use the OLE DB route unless you have no other choice than to use ODBC.

Namespaces

All of the examples in this chapter access data in one way or another. The following namespaces expose the classes and interfaces used in .NET data access.

Namespace	Brief Description
System.Data	All generic data access classes
System.Data.Common	Classes shared (or overridden) by individual data providers
System.Data.Odbc	ODBC provider classes
System.Data.OleDb	OLE DB provider classes
System.Data.ProviderBase	New base classes and connection factory classes
System.Data.Oracle	Oracle provider classes
System.Data.Sql	New generic interfaces and classes for SQL Server data access
System.Data.SqlClient	SQL Server provider classes
System.Data.SqlTypes	SQL Server data types

The main classes in ADO.NET are listed in the following subsections.

Shared Classes

ADO.NET contains a number of classes that are used regardless of whether you are using the SQL Server classes or the OLE DB classes.

The following classes are contained in the System.Data namespace.

Class	Description
DataSet	This object is designed for disconnected use and can contain a set of DataTables and relationships between these tables.
DataTable	A container of data that consists of one or more DataColumns and, when populated, will have one or more DataRows containing data.
DataRow	A number of values, akin to a row from a database table or a row from a spreadsheet.
DataColumn	This object contains the definition of a column, such as the name and data type.
DataRelation	A link between two DataTable classes within a DataSet class; used for foreign key and master/detail relationships.
Constraint	This class defines a rule for a DataColumn class (or set of data columns), such as unique values.

The following classes are found in the System.Data.Common namespace:

Class	Description
DataColumnMapping	Maps the name of a column from the database with the name of a column within a DataTable.
DataTableMapping	Maps a table name from the database to a DataTable within a DataSet.

Database-Specific Classes

In addition to the shared classes introduced in the previous section, ADO.NET contains a number of database-specific classes. These classes implement a set of standard interfaces defined within the System.Data namespace, allowing the classes to be used in a generic manner if necessary.
For example, both the SqlConnection and OleDbConnection classes derive from the DbConnection class, which implements the IDbConnection interface.

Classes	Description
SqlCommand, OleDbCommand, OracleCommand, and ODBCCommand	Used as wrappers for SQL statements or stored procedure calls. Examples for the SqlCommand class are shown later in the chapter.
SqlCommandBuilder, OleDbCommandBuilder, OracleCommandBuilder, and ODBCCommandBuilder	Used to generate SQL commands (such as INSERT, UPDATE, and DELETE statements) from a SELECT statement.
SqlConnection, OleDbConnection, OracleConnection, and ODBCConnection	Used to connect to the database and is similar to an ADO connection. Examples are shown later in the chapter.
SqlDataAdapter, OleDbDataAdapter, OracleDataAdapter, and ODBCDataAdapter	Used to hold select, insert, update, and delete commands, which are then used to populate a DataSet and update the database. Examples of the SqlDataAdapter are presented in this chapter.
SqlDataReader, OleDbDataReader, OracleDataReader, and ODBCDataReader	Used as a forward only, connected data reader. Some examples of the SqlDataReader are shown in this chapter.
SqlParameter, OleDbParameter, OracleParameter, and ODBCParameter	Used to define a parameter to a stored procedure. Examples of how to use the SqlParameter class are shown in this chapter.
SqlTransaction, OleDbTransaction, OracleTransaction, and ODBCTransaction	Used for a database transaction, wrapped in an object.

As you can see from the previous list, there are four classes for each type of object — one for each of the providers that are part of .NET version 1.1. In the rest of this chapter, unless otherwise stated, the prefix <provider> is used to indicate that the particular class used is dependent on the database provider in use. With version 2.0 of .NET, the designers have updated the class hierarchy for these classes significantly. In 1.1, all that was common between the various connection classes was the implementation of the IConnection interface. This has changed in .NET 2.0 because now both share a common base class. Similarly the other classes such as Commands, DataAdapters, DataReaders, and so on also share common base classes.

The most important feature of the ADO.NET classes is that they are designed to work in a disconnected manner, which is important in today's highly Web-centric world. It is now common practice to architect a service (such as an online bookshop) to connect to a server, retrieve some data, and then work on that data on the client before reconnecting and passing the data back for processing. The disconnected nature of ADO.NET enables this type of behavior.

ADO 2.1 introduced the disconnected record set, which would permit data to be retrieved from a database, passed to the client for processing, and then reattached to the server. This used to be cumbersome to use because disconnected behavior was not part of the original design. The ADO.NET classes are different — in all but one case (the `<provider>DataReader`) they are designed for use offline from the database.

The classes and interfaces used for data access in the .NET Framework are introduced in the course of this chapter. The focus is mainly on the SQL classes used when connecting to the database because the Framework SDK samples install an MSDE database (SQL Server). In most cases, the OLE DB, Oracle, and ODBC classes mimic the SQL code exactly.

Using Database Connections

To access the database, you need to provide connection parameters, such as the machine that the database is running on and possibly your login credentials. Anyone who has worked with ADO will be familiar with the .NET connection classes: `OleDbConnection` and `SqlConnection`. Figure 26-1 shows two of the connection classes and includes the class hierarchy.

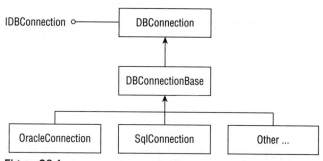

Figure 26-1

This is a significant change from .NET versions 1.0 and 1.1; however, in practice, using the connection class (and other classes in ADO.NET) is backward compatible.

The examples in this chapter use the Northwind database, which is installed with the .NET Framework SDK samples. The following code snippet illustrates how to create, open, and close a connection to the Northwind database:

```
using System.Data.SqlClient;

string source = "server=(local);" +
                "integrated security=SSPI;" +
                "database=Northwind";
SqlConnection conn = new SqlConnection(source);
conn.Open();

// Do something useful

conn.Close();
```

The connection string should be very familiar to you if you have used ADO or OLE DB before — indeed, you should be able to cut and paste from your old code if you use the `OleDb` provider. In the example connection string, the parameters used are as follows (the parameters are delimited by a semicolon in the connection string):

- ❑ `server=(local)` — This denotes the database server to connect to. SQL Server permits a number of separate database server instances to be running on the same machine, and here you are connecting to the default SQL Server instance. If you are using SQL Express, change the server part to `server=./sqlexpress`.

- ❑ `integrated security=SSPI` — This uses Windows Authentication to connect to the database, which is highly recommended over using a username and password within the source code.

- ❑ `database=Northwind` — This describes the database instance to connect to; each SQL Server process can expose several database instances.

> **In case you forget the format of database connection strings (as many of us do now and then), the following URL is very handy:** `www.connectionstrings.com`.

The example opens a database connection using the defined connection string and then closes that connection. Once the connection has been opened, you can issue commands against the data source, and when you are finished, the connection can be closed.

SQL Server has another mode of authentication — it can use Windows-integrated security, so that the credentials supplied at logon are passed to SQL Server. This is accomplished by removing the `uid` and `pwd` portions of the connection string, and adding in `Integrated Security=SSPI`.

In the download code available for this chapter, you will find the file `Login.cs`, which simplifies the examples in this chapter. It is linked to all the example code and includes database connection information used for the examples; you can alter this to supply your own server name, user, and password as appropriate. This by default uses Windows-integrated security; however, you can change the username and password as appropriate.

Managing Connection Strings

In the initial release of .NET, it was up to the developer to manage the database connection strings, often done by storing a connection string in the application configuration file or, more commonly, hard-coded somewhere within the application itself.

With .NET 2.0, you now have a predefined way to store connection strings, and even use database connections in a type-agnostic manner — for example, it would now be possible to write an application and then plug in various database providers, all without altering the main application.

To define a database connection string, you should use the `<connectionStrings>` section of the configuration file. Here, you can specify a name for the connection and the actual database connection string parameters; in addition, you can also specify the provider for this connection type. Here is an example:

```
<configuration>
  ...
  <connectionStrings>
    <add name="Northwind"
         providerName="System.Data.SqlClient"
         connectionString="server=(local);integrated security=SSPI;
                           database=Northwind" />
  </connectionStrings>
</configuration>
```

You use this same connection string in the other examples in this chapter.

Once the database connection information has been defined within the configuration file, you then need to utilize this within the application. You will most likely want to create a method such as the following to retrieve a database connection based on the name of the connection:

```
private DbConnection GetDatabaseConnection ( string name )
{
  ConnectionStringSettings settings =
    ConfigurationManager.ConnectionStrings[name];

  DbProviderFactory factory = DbProviderFactories.GetFactory
    ( settings.ProviderName ) ;

  DbConnection conn = factory.CreateConnection ( ) ;
  conn.ConnectionString = settings.ConnectionString ;

  return conn ;
}
```

This code reads the named connection string section (using the `ConnectionStringSettings` class), and then requests a provider factory from the base `DbProviderFactories` class. This uses the `ProviderName` property, which was set to `"System.Data.SqlClient"` in the application configuration file. You might be wondering how this maps to the actual factory class used to generate a database connection for SQL Server — in this case, it should utilize the `SqlClientFactory` class from `System.Data.SqlClient`. You will need to add a reference to the `System.Configuration` assembly in order to resolve the `ConfigurationManager` class used in the preceding code.

If you look into the `machine.config` file for .NET 2.0, you may notice the `DbProviderFactories` section — this maps the alias names (such as `'System.Data.SqlClient'`) to the factory object for that type of database. The following shows an abridged copy of the information within that file:

```
<system.data>
  <DbProviderFactories>
    . . .
    <add name="SqlClient Data Provider"
         invariant="System.Data.SqlClient" support="FF"
         description=".Net Framework Data Provider for SqlServer"
         type="System.Data.SqlClient.SqlClientFactory, System.Data,
           Version=2.0.0.0, Culture=neutral,
           PublicKeyToken=b77a5c561934e089" />
    . . .
  </DbProviderFactories>
</system.data>
```

This just shows the entry for the `SqlClient` provider — there are other entries for `Odbc`, `OleDb`, `Oracle`, and also `SqlCE`.

So, in the example, the `DbProviderFactory` class just looks up the factory class from the machine configuration settings, and uses that concrete factory class to instantiate the connection object. In the case of the `SqlClientFactory` class, all this does is construct an instance of `SqlConnection` and return this to the caller.

This may seem like a lot of unnecessary work to obtain a database connection, and indeed it is if your application is never going to run on any other database than the one it was designed for. If, however, you use the preceding factory method and also use the generic Db* classes (such as DbConnection, DbCommand, and DbDataReader), you will future-proof the application, and any move in the future to another database system will be fairly simple.

Using Connections Efficiently

In general, when using *scarce* resources in .NET, such as database connections, windows, or graphics objects, it is good practice to ensure that each resource is closed after use. Although the designers of .NET have implemented automatic garbage collection, which will tidy up eventually, it is necessary to release resources as early as possible to avoid starvation of resources.

This is all too apparent when writing code that accesses a database because keeping a connection open for slightly longer than necessary can affect other sessions. In extreme circumstances, not closing a connection can lock other users out of an entire set of tables, hurting application performance considerably. Closing database connections should be considered mandatory, so this section shows how to structure your code to minimize the risk of leaving a resource open.

You have two main ways to ensure that database connections and the like are released after use.

Option One: try . . . catch . . . finally

The first option to ensure that resources are cleaned up is to use try...catch...finally blocks, and ensure that you close any open connections within the finally block. Here is a short example:

```
try
{
    // Open the connection
    conn.Open();
    // Do something useful
}
catch ( SqlException ex )
{
    // Log the exception
}
finally
{
    // Ensure that the connection is freed
    conn.Close ( ) ;
}
```

Within the finally block, you can release any resources you have used. The only trouble with this method is that you have to ensure that you close the connection — it is all too easy to forget to add the finally clause, so something less prone to vagaries in coding style might be worthwhile.

Also, you might find that you open a number of resources (say two database connections and a file) within a given method, so the cascading of try . . . catch . . . finally blocks can sometimes become less easy to read. There is, however, another way to guarantee resource cleanup — the using statement.

Option Two: The using Block Statement

During development of C#, the debate on how .NET uses nondeterministic destruction became very heated.

In C++, as soon as an object went out of scope, its destructor would be automatically called. This was great news for designers of resource-based classes because the destructor was the ideal place to close the resource if the user had forgotten to do so. A C++ destructor is called whenever an object goes out of scope — so, for instance, if an exception was raised and not caught, all destructors would be called.

With C# and the other managed languages, there is no concept of automatic, deterministic destruction. Instead, there is the garbage collector, which disposes of resources at some point in the future. What makes this nondeterministic is that you have little say over when this process actually happens. Forgetting to close a database connection could cause all sorts of problems for a .NET executable. Luckily, help is at hand. The following code demonstrates how to use the using clause to ensure that objects that implement the IDisposable interface (see Chapter 12, "Memory Management and Pointers") are cleared up immediately after the block exits:

```
string source = "server=(local);" +
                "integrated security=SSPI;" +
                "database=Northwind";

using ( SqlConnection conn = new SqlConnection ( source ) )
{
    // Open the connection
    conn.Open ( ) ;

    // Do something useful
}
```

In this instance, the using clause ensures that the database connection is closed, regardless of how the block is exited.

Looking at the IL code for the Dispose() method of the connection classes, all of them check the current state of the connection object, and if open will call the Close() method. A great tool for browsing .NET assemblies is Reflector (available at www.aisto.com/roeder/dotnet). This tool permits you to view the IL code for any .NET method and will also reverse-engineer the IL into C# source code, so you can easily see what a given method is doing.

When programming, you should use at least one of these methods, and probably both. Wherever you acquire resources, it is good practice to use the using statement; even though we all mean to write the Close() statement, sometimes we forget, and in the face of exceptions the using clause does the right thing. There is no substitute for good exception handling either, so in most instances, it is best to use both methods together, as in the following example:

```
try
{
    using (SqlConnection conn = new SqlConnection ( source ))
    {
        // Open the connection
        conn.Open ( ) ;

        // Do something useful

        // Close it myself
        conn.Close ( ) ;
    }
}
catch (SqlException e)
{
    // Log the exception
}
```

Note that this example called `Close()`, which isn't strictly necessary, because the `using` clause will ensure that this is done anyway. However, you should ensure that any resources such as this are released as soon as possible — you might have more code in the rest of the block, and there is no point locking a resource unnecessarily.

In addition, if an exception is raised within the `using` block, the `IDisposable.Dispose` method will be called on the resource guarded by the `using` clause, which in this example ensures that the database connection is always closed. This produces easier-to-read code than having to ensure you close a connection within an exception clause. You might also note that the exception is defined as a `SqlException` rather than the catch-all `Exception` type — always try to catch as specific an exception as possible and let all others that are not explicitly handled rise up the execution stack.

In conclusion, if you are writing a class that wraps a resource, whatever that resource may be, always implement the `IDisposable` interface to close the resource. That way anyone coding with your class can use the `using()` statement and guarantee that the resource will be cleared up.

Transactions

Often when there is more than one update to be made to the database, these updates must be performed within the scope of a transaction. It is common in code to find a transaction object being passed around to many methods that update the database, however in .NET 2.0 and above the `TransactionScope` class has been added which is defined within the `System.Transactions` assembly. This can vastly simplify writing transactional code because you can compose several transactional methods within a transaction scope, and the transaction will be flowed to each of these methods as necessary.

The following sequence of code initiates a transaction on a SQL Server connection:

```
string source = "server=(local);" +
                "integrated security=SSPI;" +
                "database=Northwind";

using (TransactionScope scope = new TransactionScope(TransactionScopeOption
.Required))
{
    using (SqlConnection conn = new SqlConnection(source))
    {
        // Do something in SQL
        ...

        // Then mark complete
        scope.Complete();
    }
}
```

Here the transaction is explicitly marked as complete by using the `scope.Complete()` method. In the absence of this call, the transaction will be rolled back so that no changes are made to the database.

When you use a transaction scope you can optionally choose the isolation level for commands executed within that transaction. The level determines how changes made in one database session are viewed by another. Not all database engines support all of the four levels presented in the following table.

Isolation Level	Description
ReadCommitted	The default for SQL Server. This level ensures that data written by one transaction will be accessible in a second transaction only after the first transaction is committed.
ReadUncommitted	This permits your transaction to read data within the database, even data that has not yet been committed by another transaction. For example, if two users were accessing the same database, and the first inserted some data without concluding the transaction (by means of a Commit or Rollback), the second user with his or her isolation level set to ReadUncommitted could read the data.
RepeatableRead	This level, which extends the ReadCommitted level, ensures that if the same statement is issued within the transaction, regardless of other potential updates made to the database, the same data will always be returned. This level does require extra locks to be held on the data, which could adversely affect performance. This level guarantees that, for each row in the initial query, no changes can be made to that data. It does, however, permit "phantom" rows to show up — these are completely new rows that another transaction might have inserted while your transaction was running.
Serializable	This is the most "exclusive" transaction level, which in effect serializes access to data within the database. With this isolation level, phantom rows can never show up, so a SQL statement issued within a serializable transaction will always retrieve the same data. The negative performance impact of a Serializable transaction should not be underestimated — if you don't absolutely need to use this level of isolation, stay away from it.

The SQL Server default isolation level, ReadCommitted, is a good compromise between data coherence and data availability because fewer locks are required on data than in RepeatableRead or Serializable modes. However, situations exist where the isolation level should be increased, and so within .NET you can simply begin a transaction with a different level from the default. There are no hard-and-fast rules as to which levels to pick — that comes with experience.

> If you are currently using a database that does not support transactions, it is well worth changing to a database that does. Once I was working as a trusted employee and had been given complete access to the bug database. I typed what I thought was delete from bug where id=99999, but in fact had typed a < rather than an =. I deleted the entire database of bugs (except the one I wanted to!). Luckily for me, our IS team backed up the database on a nightly basis and we could restore this, but a rollback command would have been much easier.

Commands

The "Using Database Connections" section briefly touched on the idea of issuing commands against a database. A command is, in its simplest form, a string of text containing SQL statements that is to be issued to the database. A command could also be a stored procedure, or the name of a table that will return all columns and all rows from that table (in other words, a SELECT *-style clause).

A command can be constructed by passing the SQL clause as a parameter to the constructor of the `Command` class, as shown in this example:

```
string source = "server=(local);" +
                "integrated security=SSPI;" +
                "database=Northwind";
string select = "SELECT ContactName,CompanyName FROM Customers";
SqlConnection conn = new SqlConnection(source);
conn.Open();
SqlCommand cmd = new SqlCommand(select, conn);
```

The `<provider>Command` classes have a property called `CommandType`, which is used to define whether the command is a SQL clause, a call to a stored procedure, or a full table statement (which simply selects all columns and rows from a given table). The following table summarizes the `CommandType` enumeration.

CommandType	Example

`Text` (default)	`String select = "SELECT`
	`ContactName FROM Customers";`
	`SqlCommand cmd = new SqlCommand(select , conn);`

`StoredProcedure`	`SqlCommand cmd = new`
	`SqlCommand("CustOrderHist", conn);`
	`cmd.CommandType =`
	`CommandType.StoredProcedure;`
	`cmd.Parameters.AddWithValue("@CustomerID", "QUICK");`

`TableDirect`	`OleDbCommand cmd = new`
	`OleDbCommand("Categories", conn);`
	`cmd.CommandType =`
	`CommandType.TableDirect;`

When executing a stored procedure, it might be necessary to pass parameters to that procedure. The previous example sets the `@CustomerID` parameter directly, although there are other ways of setting the parameter value, which you look at later in this chapter. Note that in .NET 2.0, the `AddWithValue()` method was added to the command parameters collection — and the `Add ( name, value)` member was attributed as `Obsolete`. If you have used this original method of constructing parameters for calling a stored procedure, you will receive compiler warnings when you recompile your code. We suggest altering your code now because Microsoft will most likely remove the older method in a subsequent release of .NET.

> The `TableDirect` command type is valid only for the `OleDb` provider; other providers will throw an exception if you attempt to use this command type with them.

Executing Commands

After you have defined the command, you need to execute it. A number of ways exist to issue the statement, depending on what you expect to be returned (if anything) from that command. The `<provider>Command` classes provide the following execute methods:

❑   `ExecuteNonQuery()` — Executes the command but does not return any output

❑   `ExecuteReader()` — Executes the command and returns a typed `IDataReader`

❑   `ExecuteScalar()` — Executes the command and returns a single value

In addition to these methods, the `SqlCommand` class exposes the following method:

❑ `ExecuteXmlReader()` — Executes the command and returns an `XmlReader` object, which can be used to traverse the XML fragment returned from the database

As with the other chapters, you can download the sample code from the Wrox Web site at www.wrox.com.

ExecuteNonQuery()

This method is commonly used for UPDATE, INSERT, or DELETE statements, where the only returned value is the number of records affected. This method can, however, return results if you call a stored procedure that has output parameters:

```
using System;
using System.Data.SqlClient;
public class ExecuteNonQueryExample
{
    public static void Main(string[] args)
    {
        string source = "server=(local);" +
                        "integrated security=SSPI;" +
                        "database=Northwind";
        string select = "UPDATE Customers " +
                        "SET ContactName = 'Bob' " +
                        "WHERE ContactName = 'Bill'";
        SqlConnection  conn = new SqlConnection(source);
        conn.Open();
        SqlCommand cmd = new SqlCommand(select, conn);
        int rowsReturned = cmd.ExecuteNonQuery();
        Console.WriteLine("{0} rows returned.", rowsReturned);
        conn.Close();
    }
}
```

`ExecuteNonQuery()` returns the number of rows affected by the command as an `int`.

ExecuteReader()

This method executes the command and returns a typed data reader object, depending on the provider in use. The object returned can be used to iterate through the record(s) returned, as shown in the following code:

```
using System;
using System.Data.SqlClient;
public class ExecuteReaderExample
{
    public static void Main(string[] args)
    {
        string source = "server=(local);" +
                        "integrated security=SSPI;" +
                        "database=Northwind";
        string select = "SELECT ContactName,CompanyName FROM Customers";
        SqlConnection conn = new SqlConnection(source);
        conn.Open();
        SqlCommand cmd = new SqlCommand(select, conn);
```

(continued)

(continued)

```
        SqlDataReader reader = cmd.ExecuteReader();
        while(reader.Read())
        {
            Console.WriteLine("Contact : {0,-20} Company : {1}" ,
                              reader[0] , reader[1]);
        }
    }
}
```

Figure 26-2 shows the output of this code.

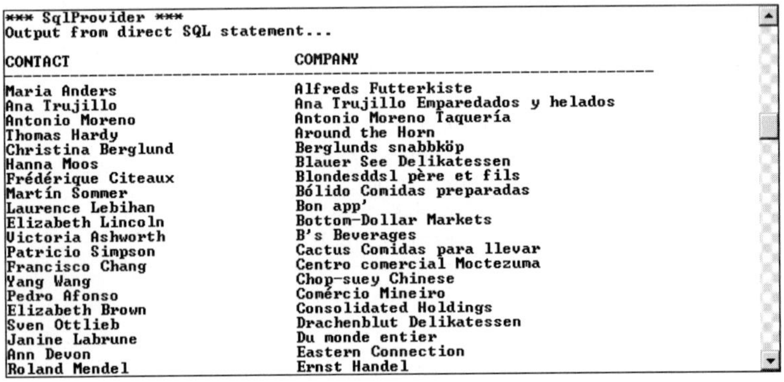

Figure 26-2

The `<provider>DataReader` objects are discussed later in this chapter.

ExecuteScalar()

On many occasions, it is necessary to return a single result from a SQL statement, such as the count of records in a given table, or the current date/time on the server. The ExecuteScalar method can be used in such situations:

```
using System;
using System.Data.SqlClient;
public class ExecuteScalarExample
{
    public static void Main(string[] args)
    {
        string source = "server=(local);" +
                        "integrated security=SSPI;" +
                        "database=Northwind";
        string select = "SELECT COUNT(*) FROM Customers";
        SqlConnection conn = new SqlConnection(source);
        conn.Open();
        SqlCommand cmd = new SqlCommand(select, conn);
        object o = cmd.ExecuteScalar();
        Console.WriteLine ( o ) ;
    }
}
```

The method returns an object, which you can cast to the appropriate type if required. If the SQL you are calling returns only one column, it is preferable to use ExecuteScalar over any other method of retrieving that column. That also applies to stored procedures that return a single value.

ExecuteXmlReader() (SqlClient Provider Only)

As its name implies, this method executes the command and returns an XmlReader object to the caller. SQL Server permits a SQL SELECT statement to be extended with a FOR XML clause. This clause can take one of three options:

❑　FOR XML AUTO — Builds a tree based on the tables in the FROM clause

❑　FOR XML RAW — Maps result set rows to elements, with columns mapped to attributes

❑　FOR XML EXPLICIT — Requires that you specify the shape of the XML tree to be returned

Professional SQL Server 2000 XML (Wrox Press, ISBN 1-861005-46-6) includes a complete description of these options. For this example, use AUTO:

```
using System;
using System.Data.SqlClient;
using System.Xml;
public class ExecuteXmlReaderExample
{
    public static void Main(string[] args)
    {
        string source = "server=(local);" +
                        "integrated security=SSPI;" +
                        "database=Northwind";
        string select = "SELECT ContactName,CompanyName " +
                        "FROM Customers FOR XML AUTO";
        SqlConnection conn = new SqlConnection(source);
        conn.Open();
        SqlCommand cmd = new SqlCommand(select, conn);
        XmlReader xr = cmd.ExecuteXmlReader();
        xr.Read();
        string data;
        do
        {
            data = xr.ReadOuterXml();
            if (!string.IsNullOrEmpty(data))
                Console.WriteLine(data);
        } while (!string.IsNullOrEmpty(data));
        conn.Close();
    }
}
```

Note that you have to import the System.Xml namespace in order to output the returned XML. This namespace and further XML capabilities of .NET Framework are explored in more detail in Chapter 28, "Manipulating XML." Here, you include the FOR XML AUTO clause in the SQL statement, then call the ExecuteXmlReader() method. Figure 26-3 shows the output of this code.

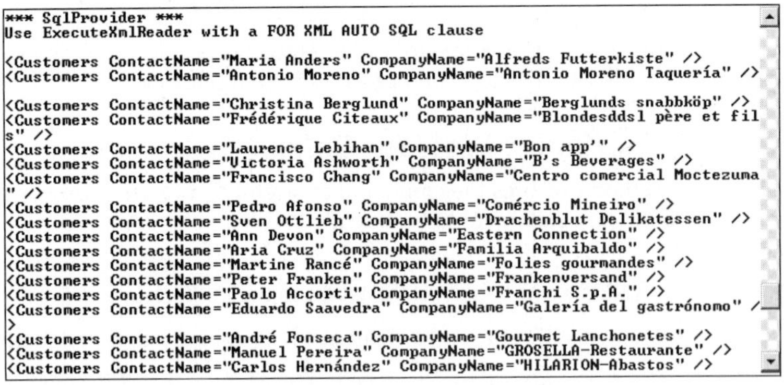

```
*** SqlProvider ***
Use ExecuteXmlReader with a FOR XML AUTO SQL clause

<Customers ContactName="Maria Anders" CompanyName="Alfreds Futterkiste" />
<Customers ContactName="Antonio Moreno" CompanyName="Antonio Moreno Taquería" />

<Customers ContactName="Christina Berglund" CompanyName="Berglunds snabbköp" />
<Customers ContactName="Frédérique Citeaux" CompanyName="Blondesddsl père et fil
s" />
<Customers ContactName="Laurence Lebihan" CompanyName="Bon app'" />
<Customers ContactName="Victoria Ashworth" CompanyName="B's Beverages" />
<Customers ContactName="Francisco Chang" CompanyName="Centro comercial Moctezuma
" />
<Customers ContactName="Pedro Afonso" CompanyName="Comércio Mineiro" />
<Customers ContactName="Sven Ottlieb" CompanyName="Drachenblut Delikatessen" />
<Customers ContactName="Ann Devon" CompanyName="Eastern Connection" />
<Customers ContactName="Aria Cruz" CompanyName="Familia Arquibaldo" />
<Customers ContactName="Martine Rancé" CompanyName="Folies gourmandes" />
<Customers ContactName="Peter Franken" CompanyName="Frankenversand" />
<Customers ContactName="Paolo Accorti" CompanyName="Franchi S.p.A." />
<Customers ContactName="Eduardo Saavedra" CompanyName="Galería del gastrónomo" /
>
<Customers ContactName="André Fonseca" CompanyName="Gourmet Lanchonetes" />
<Customers ContactName="Manuel Pereira" CompanyName="GROSELLA-Restaurante" />
<Customers ContactName="Carlos Hernández" CompanyName="HILARION-Abastos" />
```

Figure 26-3

In the SQL clause, you specified FROM Customers, so an element of type Customers is shown in the output. To this are added attributes, one for each column selected from the database. This builds up an XML fragment for each row selected from the database.

Calling Stored Procedures

Calling a stored procedure with a command object is just a matter of defining the name of the stored procedure, adding a definition for each parameter of the procedure, and then executing the command with one of the methods presented in the previous section.

To make the examples in this section more useful, a set of stored procedures has been defined that can be used to insert, update, and delete records from the Region table in the Northwind sample database. Despite its small size, this is a good candidate to choose for the example because it can be used to define examples for each of the types of stored procedures you will commonly write.

Calling a Stored Procedure That Returns Nothing

The simplest example of calling a stored procedure is one that returns nothing to the caller. Two such procedures are defined in the following two subsections: one for updating a preexisting Region record and one for deleting a given Region record.

Record Update

Updating a Region record is fairly trivial because there is only one column that can be modified (assuming primary keys cannot be updated). You can type these examples directly into the SQL Server Query Analyzer, or run the StoredProcs.sql file that is part of the downloadable code for this chapter. This file installs each of the stored procedures in this section:

```
CREATE PROCEDURE RegionUpdate (@RegionID INTEGER,
                               @RegionDescription NCHAR(50)) AS

    SET NOCOUNT OFF
    UPDATE Region
        SET RegionDescription = @RegionDescription
        WHERE RegionID = @RegionID
    GO
```

An update command on a more real-world table might need to reselect and return the updated record in its entirety. This stored procedure takes two input parameters (@RegionID and @RegionDescription), and issues an UPDATE statement against the database.

To run this stored procedure from within .NET code, you need to define a SQL command and execute it:

```
SqlCommand cmd = new SqlCommand("RegionUpdate", conn);

cmd.CommandType = CommandType.StoredProcedure;
cmd.Parameters.AddWithValue ( "@RegionID", 23 );
cmd.Parameters.AddWithValue ( "@RegionDescription", "Something" );
```

This code creates a new `SqlCommand` object named aCommand, and defines it as a stored procedure. You then add each parameter in turn using the `AddWithValue` method. This constructs a parameter and also sets its value — you can also manually construct `SqlParameter` instances and add these to the `Parameters` collection if appropriate.

The stored procedure takes two parameters: the unique primary key of the `Region` record being updated and the new description to be given to this record. After the command has been created, it can be executed by issuing the following command:

```
cmd.ExecuteNonQuery();
```

Because the procedure returns nothing, `ExecuteNonQuery()` will suffice. Command parameters can be set directly using the `AddWithValue` method, or by constructing `SqlParameter` instances. Note that the parameter collection is indexable by position or parameter name.

Record Deletion

The next stored procedure required is one that can be used to delete a `Region` record from the database:

```
CREATE PROCEDURE RegionDelete (@RegionID INTEGER) AS
    SET NOCOUNT OFF
    DELETE FROM Region
    WHERE       RegionID = @RegionID
GO
```

This procedure requires only the primary key value of the record. The code uses a `SqlCommand` object to call this stored procedure as follows:

```
SqlCommand cmd = new SqlCommand("RegionDelete" , conn);
cmd.CommandType = CommandType.StoredProcedure;
cmd.Parameters.Add(new SqlParameter("@RegionID" , SqlDbType.Int , 0 ,
                                    "RegionID"));
cmd.UpdatedRowSource = UpdateRowSource.None;
```

This command accepts only a single parameter, as shown in the following code, which will execute the `RegionDelete` stored procedure; here, you see an example of setting the parameter by name. If you have many similar calls to make to the same stored procedure, then constructing `SqlParameter` instances and setting the values as in the following may lead to better performance than re-constructing the entire `SqlCommand` for each call.

```
cmd.Parameters["@RegionID"].Value= 999;
cmd.ExecuteNonQuery();
```

Calling a Stored Procedure That Returns Output Parameters

Both of the previous examples execute stored procedures that return nothing. If a stored procedure includes output parameters, these need to be defined within the .NET client so that they can be filled when the procedure returns. The following example shows how to insert a record into the database and return the primary key of that record to the caller.

Record Insertion

The Region table consists of only a primary key (RegionID) and description field
(RegionDescription). To insert a record, this numeric primary key must be generated, and then a new
row needs to be inserted into the database. The primary key generation in this example has been
simplified by creating one within the stored procedure. The method used is exceedingly crude, which is
why there is a section on key generation later in this chapter. For now, this primitive example suffices:

```
CREATE PROCEDURE RegionInsert(@RegionDescription NCHAR(50),
                             @RegionID INTEGER OUTPUT)AS
    SET NOCOUNT OFF
    SELECT @RegionID = MAX(RegionID)+ 1
    FROM Region
    INSERT INTO Region(RegionID, RegionDescription)
    VALUES(@RegionID, @RegionDescription)
GO
```

The insert procedure creates a new Region record. Because the primary key value is generated by the
database itself, this value is returned as an output parameter from the procedure (@RegionID). This is
sufficient for this simple example, but for a more complex table (especially one with default values),
it is more common not to use output parameters, and instead select the entire inserted row and return
this to the caller. The .NET classes can cope with either scenario.

```
SqlCommand  cmd = new SqlCommand("RegionInsert" , conn);
cmd.CommandType = CommandType.StoredProcedure;
cmd.Parameters.Add(new SqlParameter("@RegionDescription" ,
                                    SqlDbType.NChar ,
                                    50 ,
                                    "RegionDescription"));
cmd.Parameters.Add(new SqlParameter("@RegionID" ,
                                    SqlDbType.Int,
                                    0 ,
                                    ParameterDirection.Output ,
                                    false ,
                                    0 ,
                                    0 ,
                                    "RegionID" ,
                                    DataRowVersion.Default ,
                                    null));
cmd.UpdatedRowSource = UpdateRowSource.OutputParameters;
```

Here, the definition of the parameters is much more complex. The second parameter, @RegionID, is
defined to include its parameter direction, which in this example is Output. In addition to this flag, on
the last line of the code, the UpdateRowSource enumeration is used to indicate that data will be
returned from this stored procedure via output parameters. This flag is mainly used when issuing stored
procedure calls from a DataTable (which is discussed later in this chapter).

Calling this stored procedure is similar to the previous examples, except in this instance the output
parameter is read after executing the procedure:

```
cmd.Parameters["@RegionDescription"].Value = "South West";
cmd.ExecuteNonQuery();
int newRegionID = (int) cmd.Parameters["@RegionID"].Value;
```

After executing the command, the value of the @RegionID parameter is read and cast to an integer.
A shorthand version of the preceding is the ExecuteScalar() method, which will return (as an object)
the first value returned from the stored procedure.

You might be wondering what to do if the stored procedure you call returns output parameters and a set of rows. In this instance, define the parameters as appropriate, and rather than calling `ExecuteNonQuery()`, call one of the other methods (such as `ExecuteReader()`) that will permit you to traverse any record(s) returned.

Fast Data Access: The Data Reader

A data reader is the simplest and fastest way of selecting some data from a data source, but it is also the least capable. You cannot directly instantiate a data reader object — an instance is returned from the appropriate database's command object (such as `SqlCommand`) after having called the `ExecuteReader()` method.

The following code demonstrates how to select data from the `Customers` table in the Northwind database. The example connects to the database, selects a number of records, loops through these selected records, and outputs them to the console.

This example uses the OLE DB provider as a brief respite from the SQL provider. In most cases, the classes have a one-to-one correspondence with their `SqlClient` cousins; for example, there is the `OleDbConnection` object, which is similar to the `SqlConnection` object used in the previous examples.

To execute commands against an OLE DB data source, the `OleDbCommand` class is used. The following code shows an example of executing a simple SQL statement and reading the records by returning an `OleDbDataReader` object.

Note the second `using` directive that makes available the `OleDb` classes:

```
using System;
using System.Data.OleDb;
```

Most of the data providers currently available are shipped within the same assembly, so it is only necessary to reference the `System.Data.dll` assembly to import all classes used in this section. The only exceptions are the Oracle classes, which reside in `System.Data.Oracle.dll`.

```
public class DataReaderExample
{
    public static void Main(string[] args)
    {
        string source = "Provider=SQLOLEDB;" +
                        "server=(local);" +
                        "integrated security=SSPI;" +
                        "database=northwind";
        string select = "SELECT ContactName,CompanyName FROM Customers";
        OleDbConnection conn = new OleDbConnection(source);
        conn.Open();
        OleDbCommand cmd = new OleDbCommand(select , conn);
        OleDbDataReader aReader = cmd.ExecuteReader();
        while(aReader.Read())
            Console.WriteLine("'{0}' from {1}" ,
                              aReader.GetString(0) , aReader.GetString(1));
        aReader.Close();
        conn.Close();
    }
}
```

The preceding code includes many familiar aspects of C# already covered in this chapter. To compile the example, issue the following command:

```
csc /t:exe /debug+ DataReaderExample.cs /r:System.Data.dll
```

The following code from the previous example creates a new OLE DB .NET database connection, based on the source connection string:

```
OleDbConnection conn = new OleDbConnection(source);
    conn.Open();
    OleDbCommand cmd = new OleDbCommand(select, conn);
```

The third line creates a new `OleDbCommand` object, based on a particular SELECT statement, and the database connection to be used when the command is executed. When you have a valid command, you need to execute it, which returns an initialized `OleDbDataReader`:

```
OleDbDataReader aReader = cmd.ExecuteReader();
```

An `OleDbDataReader` is a forward-only "connected" cursor. In other words, you can only traverse the records returned in one direction, and the database connection used is kept open until the data reader has been closed.

> An `OleDbDataReader` **keeps the database connection open until it is explicitly closed.**

The `OleDbDataReader` class cannot be instantiated directly — it is always returned by a call to the `ExecuteReader()` method of the `OleDbCommand` class. Once you have an open data reader, there are various ways to access the data contained within the reader.

When the `OleDbDataReader` object is closed (via an explicit call to `Close()`, or the object being garbage collected), the underlying connection may also be closed, depending on which of the `ExecuteReader()` methods is called. If you call `ExecuteReader()` and pass `CommandBehavior.CloseConnection`, you can force the connection to be closed when the reader is closed.

The `OleDbDataReader` class has an indexer that permits access (although not type-safe access) to any field using the familiar array style syntax:

```
    object o = aReader[0];
or
    object o = aReader["CategoryID"];
```

Assuming that the `CategoryID` field was the first in the SELECT statement used to populate the reader, these two lines are functionally equivalent, although the second is slower than the first; to verify this, a test application was written that performed a million iterations of accessing the same column from an open data reader, just to get some numbers that were big enough to read. You probably don't read the same column a million times in a tight loop, but every (micro) second counts, so you should write code that is as optimal as possible.

As an aside, the numeric indexer took on average 0.09 seconds for the million accesses, and the textual one 0.63 seconds. The reason for this difference is that the textual method looks up the column number internally from the schema and then accesses it using its ordinal. If you know this information beforehand you can do a better job of accessing the data.

So, should you use the numeric indexer? Maybe, but there is a better way.

In addition to the indexers just presented, `OleDbDataReader` has a set of type-safe methods that can be used to read columns. These are fairly self-explanatory, and all begin with `Get`. There are methods to read most types of data, such as `GetInt32`, `GetFloat`, `GetGuid`, and so on.

The million iterations using `GetInt32` took 0.06 seconds. The overhead in the numeric indexer is incurred while getting the data type, calling the same code as `GetInt32`, then boxing (and in this instance unboxing) an integer. So, if you know the schema beforehand, are willing to use cryptic numbers instead of column names, and can be bothered to use a type-safe function for each and every column access, you stand to gain somewhere in the region of a tenfold speed increase over using a textual column name (when selecting those million copies of the same column).

Needless to say, there is a tradeoff between maintainability and speed. If you must use numeric indexers, define constants within class scope for each of the columns that you will be accessing. The preceding code can be used to select data from any OLE DB database; however, there are a number of SQL Server–specific classes that can be used with the obvious portability tradeoff.

The following example is the same as the previous one, except that in this instance the OLE DB provider and all references to OLE DB classes have been replaced with their SQL counterparts. The example is in the `04_DataReaderSql` directory:

```
using System;
using System.Data.SqlClient;
public class DataReaderSql
{
    public static int Main(string[] args)
    {
        string source = "server=(local);" +
                        "integrated security=SSPI;" +
                        "database=northwind";
        string select = "SELECT ContactName,CompanyName FROM Customers";
        SqlConnection conn = new SqlConnection(source);
        conn.Open();
        SqlCommand cmd = new SqlCommand(select , conn);
        SqlDataReader aReader = cmd.ExecuteReader();
        while(aReader.Read())
           Console.WriteLine("'{0}' from {1}" , aReader.GetString(0) ,
                             aReader.GetString(1));
        aReader.Close();
        conn.Close();
        return 0;
    }
}
```

Notice the difference? If you're typing this, do a global replace on `OleDb` with `Sql`, change the data source string, and recompile. It's that easy!

The same performance tests were run on the indexers for the SQL provider, and this time the numeric indexers were both exactly the same at 0.13 seconds for the million accesses, and the string-based indexer ran at about 0.65 seconds.

Managing Data and Relationships: The DataSet Class

The `DataSet` class has been designed as an offline container of data. It has no notion of database connections. In fact, the data held within a `DataSet` does not necessarily need to have come from a database — it could just as easily be records from a CSV file, or points read from a measuring device.

A `DataSet` class consists of a set of data tables, each of which will have a set of data columns and data rows (see Figure 26-4). In addition to defining the data, you can also define *links* between tables within the `DataSet` class. One common scenario would be when defining a parent-child relationship (commonly known as master/detail). One record in a table (say `Order`) links to many records in another table (say `Order_Details`). This relationship can be defined and navigated within the `DataSet`.

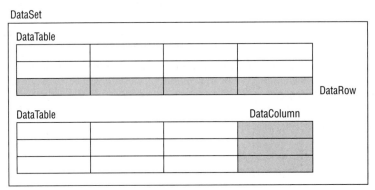

Figure 26-4

The following sections describe the classes that are used with a `DataSet` class.

Data Tables

A data table is very similar to a physical database table — it consists of a set of columns with particular properties and might have zero or more rows of data. A data table might also define a primary key, which can be one or more columns, and might also contain constraints on columns. The generic term for this information used throughout the rest of the chapter is *schema*.

Several ways exist to define the schema for a particular data table (and indeed the `DataSet` class as a whole). These are discussed after introducing data columns and data rows. Figure 26-5 shows some of the objects that are accessible through the data table.

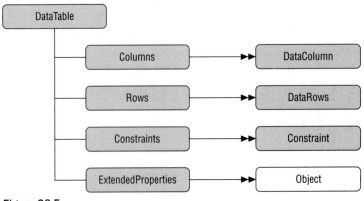

Figure 26-5

A `DataTable` object (and also a `DataColumn`) can have an arbitrary number of extended properties associated with it. This collection can be populated with any user-defined information pertaining to the object. For example, a given column might have an input mask used to validate the contents of that column — a typical example is the U.S. Social Security number. Extended properties are especially useful when the data is constructed within a middle tier and returned to the client for some processing. You could, for example, store validation criteria (such as `min` and `max`) for numeric columns in extended properties and use this in the UI tier when validating user input.

When a data table has been populated — by selecting data from a database, reading data from a file, or manually populating within code — the `Rows` collection will contain this retrieved data.

The `Columns` collection contains `DataColumn` instances that have been added to this table. These define the schema of the data, such as the data type, nullability, default values, and so on. The `Constraints` collection can be populated with either unique or primary key constraints.

One example of where the schema information for a data table is used is when displaying that data in a `DataGrid` (which is discussed in Chapter 32, "Data Binding"). The `DataGrid` control uses properties such as the data type of the column to decide what control to use for that column. A bit field within the database will be displayed as a check box within the `DataGrid`. If a column is defined within the database schema as `NOT NULL`, this fact will be stored within the `DataColumn` so that it can be tested when the user attempts to move off a row.

Data Columns

A `DataColumn` object defines properties of a column within the `DataTable`, such as the data type of that column, whether the column is read-only, and various other facts. A column can be created in code, or it can be automatically generated by the runtime.

When creating a column, it is also useful to give it a name; otherwise, the runtime will generate a name for you in the form `Column` where n is an incrementing number.

The data type of the column can be set either by supplying it in the constructor or by setting the `DataType` property. Once you have loaded data into a data table you cannot alter the type of a column — you will just receive an `ArgumentException`.

Data columns can be created to hold the following .NET Framework data types:

Boolean	Decimal
Int64	TimeSpan
Byte	Double
Sbyte	UInt16
Char	Int16
Single	UInt32
DateTime	Int32
String	UInt64

Once created, the next thing to do with a DataColumn object is to set up other properties, such as the nullability of the column or the default value. The following code fragment shows a few of the more common options to set on a DataColumn object:

```
DataColumn customerID = new DataColumn("CustomerID" , typeof(int));
customerID.AllowDBNull = false;
customerID.ReadOnly = false;
customerID.AutoIncrement = true;
customerID.AutoIncrementSeed = 1000;
DataColumn name = new DataColumn("Name" , typeof(string));
name.AllowDBNull = false;
name.Unique = true;
```

The following table shows the properties that can be set on a DataColumn object.

Property	Description
AllowDBNull	If true, permits the column to be set to DBNull.
AutoIncrement	Defines that this column value is automatically generated as an incrementing number.
AutoIncrementSeed	Defines the initial seed value for an AutoIncrement column.
AutoIncrementStep	Defines the step between automatically generated column values, with a default of one.
Caption	Can be used for displaying the name of the column onscreen.
ColumnMapping	Defines how a column is mapped into XML when a DataSet class is saved by calling DataSet.WriteXml.
ColumnName	The name of the column; this is auto-generated by the runtime if not set in the constructor.
DataType	Defines the System.Type value of the column.
DefaultValue	Can define a default value for a column.
Expression	Defines the expression to be used in a computed column.

Data Rows

This class makes up the other part of the DataTable class. The columns within a data table are defined in terms of the DataColumn class. The actual data within the table is accessed using the DataRow object. The following example shows how to access rows within a data table. First, the connection details:

```
string source = "server=(local);" +
                " integrated security=SSPI;" +
                "database=northwind";
string select = "SELECT ContactName,CompanyName FROM Customers";
SqlConnection  conn = new SqlConnection(source);
```

The following code introduces the SqlDataAdapter class, which is used to place data into a DataSet class. SqlDataAdapter issues the SQL clause and fills a table in the DataSet class called Customers with the output of the following query. (For more details on the `SqlDataAdapter` class, see the section "Populating a DataSet" later in this chapter.)

```
SqlDataAdapter da = new SqlDataAdapter(select, conn);
DataSet ds = new DataSet();
da.Fill(ds , "Customers");
```

In the following code, you might notice the use of the `DataRow` indexer to access values from within that row. The value for a given column can be retrieved using one of the several overloaded indexers. These permit you to retrieve a value knowing the column number, name, or `DataColumn`:

```
foreach(DataRow row in ds.Tables["Customers"].Rows)
    Console.WriteLine("'{0}' from {1}" , row[0] ,row[1]);
```

One of the most appealing aspects of `DataRow` is that it is versioned. This permits you to receive various values for a given column in a particular row. The versions are described in the following table.

DataRow Version Value	Description
Current	The value existing at present within the column. If no edit has occurred, this will be the same as the original value. If an edit (or edits) has occurred, the value will be the last valid value entered.
Default	The default value (in other words, any default set up for the column).
Original	The value of the column when originally selected from the database. If the `DataRow`'s `AcceptChanges()` method is called, this value will update to the `Current` value.
Proposed	When changes are in progress for a row, it is possible to retrieve this modified value. If you call `BeginEdit()` on the row and make changes, each column will have a proposed value until either `EndEdit()` or `CancelEdit()` is called.

The version of a given column could be used in many ways. One example is when updating rows within the database, in which instance it is common to issue a SQL statement such as the following:

```
UPDATE Products
SET     Name = Column.Current
WHERE   ProductID = xxx
AND     Name = Column.Original;
```

Obviously, this code would never compile, but it shows one use for original and current values of a column within a row.

To retrieve a versioned value from the `DataRow` indexer, use one of the indexer methods that accepts a `DataRowVersion` value as a parameter. The following snippet shows how to obtain all values of each column in a `DataTable` object:

```
foreach (DataRow row in ds.Tables["Customers"].Rows )
{
    foreach ( DataColumn dc in ds.Tables["Customers"].Columns )
    {
```

(continued)

(continued)

```
        Console.WriteLine ("{0} Current  = {1}" , dc.ColumnName ,
                                            row[dc,DataRowVersion.Current]);
        Console.WriteLine ("    Default  = {0}" , row[dc,DataRowVersion.Default]);
        Console.WriteLine ("    Original = {0}" ,
                        row[dc,DataRowVersion.Original]);
    }
}
```

The whole row has a state flag called `RowState`, which can be used to determine what operation is needed on the row when it is persisted back to the database. The `RowState` property is set to keep track of all the changes made to the `DataTable`, such as adding new rows, deleting existing rows, and changing columns within the table. When the data is reconciled with the database, the row state flag is used to determine what SQL operations should occur. The following table provides an overview of the flags that are defined by the `DataRowState` enumeration.

DataRowState Value	Description
Added	Indicates that the row has been newly added to a `DataTable`'s `Rows` collection. All rows created on the client are set to this value and will ultimately issue SQL `INSERT` statements when reconciled with the database.
Deleted	Indicates that the row has been marked as deleted from the `DataTable` by means of the `DataRow.Delete()` method. The row still exists within the `DataTable` but will not normally be viewable onscreen (unless a `DataView` has been explicitly set up). `DataViews` are discussed in the next chapter. Rows marked as deleted in the `DataTable` will be deleted from the database when reconciled.
Detached	Indicates that a row is in this state immediately after it is created, and can also be returned to this state by calling `DataRow.Remove()`. A detached row is not considered to be part of any data table, and, as such, no SQL for rows in this state will be issued.
Modified	Indicates that a row will be `Modified` if the value in any column has been changed.
Unchanged	Indicates that the row has not been changed since the last call to `AcceptChanges()`.

The state of the row depends also on what methods have been called on the row. The `AcceptChanges()` method is generally called after successfully updating the data source (that is, after persisting changes to the database).

The most common way to alter data in a `DataRow` is to use the indexer; however, if you have a number of changes to make, you also need to consider the `BeginEdit()` and `EndEdit()` methods.

When an alteration is made to a column within a DataRow, the ColumnChanging event is raised on the row's DataTable. This permits you to override the ProposedValue property of the DataColumnChangeEventArgs class, and change it as required. This is one way of performing some data validation on column values. If you call BeginEdit() before making changes, the ColumnChanging event will not be raised. This permits you to make multiple changes and then call EndEdit() to persist these changes. If you want to revert to the original values, call CancelEdit().

A DataRow can be linked in some way to other rows of data. This permits the creation of navigable links between rows, which is common in master/detail scenarios. The DataRow contains a GetChildRows() method that will return an array of associated rows from another table in the same DataSet as the current row. These are discussed in the "Data Relationships" section later in this chapter.

Schema Generation

You can create the schema for a DataTable in three ways:

❑ Let the runtime do it for you.

❑ Write code to create the table(s).

❑ Use the XML schema generator.

Runtime Schema Generation

The DataRow example shown earlier presented the following code for selecting data from a database and populating a DataSet class:

```
SqlDataAdapter da = new SqlDataAdapter(select , conn);
DataSet ds = new DataSet();
da.Fill(ds , "Customers");
```

This is obviously easy to use, but it has a few drawbacks as well. For example, you have to make do with the default column names, which might work for you, but in certain instances, you might want to rename a physical database column (say PKID) to something more user-friendly.

You could naturally alias columns within your SQL clause, as in SELECT PID AS PersonID FROM PersonTable; it's best to not rename columns within SQL, though, because a column only really needs to have a "pretty" name onscreen.

Another potential problem with automated DataTable/DataColumn generation is that you have no control over the column types that the runtime chooses for your data. It does a fairly good job of deciding the correct data type for you, but as usual there are instances where you need more control. For example, you might have defined an enumerated type for a given column to simplify user code written against your class. If you accept the default column types that the runtime generates, the column will likely be an integer with a 32-bit range, as opposed to an enum with your predefined options.

Last, and probably most problematic, is that when using automated table generation, you have no type-safe access to the data within the DataTable — you are at the mercy of indexers, which return instances of object rather than derived data types. If you like sprinkling your code with typecast expressions, skip the following sections.

Hand-Coded Schema

Generating the code to create a DataTable, replete with associated DataColumns, is fairly easy. The examples within this section access the Products table from the Northwind database shown in Figure 26-6.

Column Name	Data Type	Allow Nulls
ProductID	int	☐
ProductName	nvarchar(40)	☐
SupplierID	int	☑
CategoryID	int	☑
QuantityPerUnit	nvarchar(20)	☑
UnitPrice	money	☑
UnitsInStock	smallint	☑
UnitsOnOrder	smallint	☑
ReorderLevel	smallint	☑
Discontinued	bit	☐

Figure 26-6

The following code manufactures a `DataTable`, which corresponds to the schema shown in Figure 26-6 (but does not cover the nullability of columns):

```
public static void ManufactureProductDataTable(DataSet ds)
{
   DataTable   products = new DataTable("Products");
   products.Columns.Add(new DataColumn("ProductID", typeof(int)));
   products.Columns.Add(new DataColumn("ProductName", typeof(string)));
   products.Columns.Add(new DataColumn("SupplierID", typeof(int)));
   products.Columns.Add(new DataColumn("CategoryID", typeof(int)));
   products.Columns.Add(new DataColumn("QuantityPerUnit", typeof(string)));
   products.Columns.Add(new DataColumn("UnitPrice", typeof(decimal)));
   products.Columns.Add(new DataColumn("UnitsInStock", typeof(short)));
   products.Columns.Add(new DataColumn("UnitsOnOrder", typeof(short)));
   products.Columns.Add(new DataColumn("ReorderLevel", typeof(short)));
   products.Columns.Add(new DataColumn("Discontinued", typeof(bool)));
   ds.Tables.Add(products);
}
```

You can alter the code in the `DataRow` example to use this newly generated table definition as follows:

```
string source = "server=(local);" +
                "integrated security=sspi;" +
                "database=Northwind";
string select = "SELECT * FROM Products";
SqlConnection conn = new SqlConnection(source);
SqlDataAdapter cmd = new SqlDataAdapter(select, conn);
DataSet ds = new DataSet();
ManufactureProductDataTable(ds);
cmd.Fill(ds, "Products");
foreach(DataRow row in ds.Tables["Products"].Rows)
   Console.WriteLine("'{0}' from {1}", row[0], row[1]);
```

The `ManufactureProductDataTable()` method creates a new `DataTable`, adds each column in turn, and finally appends this to the list of tables within the `DataSet`. The `DataSet` has an indexer that takes the name of the table and returns that `DataTable` to the caller.

The previous example is still not really type-safe because indexers are being used on columns to retrieve the data. What would be better is a class (or set of classes) derived from `DataSet`, `DataTable`, and `DataRow` that defines type-safe accessors for tables, rows, and columns. You can generate this code yourself; it is not particularly tedious and you end up with truly type-safe data access classes.

If you don't like generating these type-safe classes yourself, help is at hand. The .NET Framework includes support for the third method listed at the start of this section: using XML schemas to define a `DataSet` class, a `DataTable` class, and the other classes that we have described here. (For more details on this method, see the section "XML Schemas: Generating Code with XSD" later in this chapter.)

Data Relationships

When writing an application, it is often necessary to obtain and cache various tables of information. The `DataSet` class is the container for this information. With regular OLE DB, it was necessary to provide a strange SQL dialect to enforce hierarchical data relationships, and the provider itself was not without its own subtle quirks.

The `DataSet` class, however, has been designed from the start to establish relationships between data tables with ease. The code in this section shows how to generate manually and populate two tables with data. So, if you don't have access to SQL Server or the Northwind database, you can run this example anyway:

```
DataSet ds = new DataSet("Relationships");
ds.Tables.Add(CreateBuildingTable());
ds.Tables.Add(CreateRoomTable());
ds.Relations.Add("Rooms",
                 ds.Tables["Building"].Columns["BuildingID"],
                 ds.Tables["Room"].Columns["BuildingID"]);
```

The tables used in this example are shown in Figure 26-7. They contain a primary key and name field, with the Room table having `BuildingID` as a foreign key.

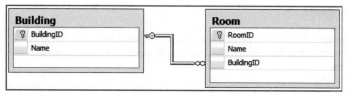

Figure 26-7

These tables have been kept deliberately simple. The following code shows how to iterate through the rows in the `Building` table and traverse the relationship to list all of the child rows from the `Room` table:

```
foreach(DataRow theBuilding in ds.Tables["Building"].Rows)
{
    DataRow[] children = theBuilding.GetChildRows("Rooms");
    int roomCount = children.Length;
    Console.WriteLine("Building {0} contains {1} room{2}",
                      theBuilding["Name"],
                      roomCount,
                      roomCount > 1 ? "s" : "");
    // Loop through the rooms
    foreach(DataRow theRoom in children)
        Console.WriteLine("Room: {0}", theRoom["Name"]);
}
```

The key difference between the `DataSet` class and the old-style hierarchical `Recordset` object is in the way the relationship is presented. In a hierarchical `Recordset` object, the relationship was presented as a pseudo-column within the row. This column itself was a `Recordset` object that could be iterated through. Under ADO.NET, however, a relationship is traversed simply by calling the `GetChildRows()` method:

```
DataRow[] children = theBuilding.GetChildRows("Rooms");
```

This method has a number of forms, but the preceding simple example uses just the name of the relationship to traverse between parent and child rows. It returns an array of rows that can be updated as appropriate by using the indexers, as shown in earlier examples.

What's more interesting with data relationships is that they can be traversed both ways. Not only can you go from a parent to the child rows, but you can also find a parent row (or rows) from a child record simply by using the `ParentRelations` property on the `DataTable` class. This property returns a `DataRelationCollection`, which can be indexed using the `[]` array syntax (for example, `ParentRelations["Rooms"]`), or as an alternative, the `GetParentRows()` method can be called, as shown here:

```
foreach(DataRow theRoom in ds.Tables["Room"].Rows)
{
    DataRow[] parents = theRoom.GetParentRows("Rooms");
    foreach(DataRow theBuilding in parents)
        Console.WriteLine("Room {0} is contained in building {1}",
                          theRoom["Name"],
                          theBuilding["Name"]);
}
```

Two methods with various overrides are available for retrieving the parent row(s): `GetParentRows()` (which returns an array of zero or more rows) and `GetParentRow()` (which retrieves a single parent row given a relationship).

Data Constraints

Changing the data type of columns created on the client is not the only thing a `DataTable` is good for. ADO.NET permits you to create a set of constraints on a column (or columns), which are then used to enforce rules within the data.

The following table lists the constraint types that are currently supported by the runtime, embodied as classes in the `System.Data` namespace.

Constraint	Description
ForeignKeyConstraint	Enforces a link between two `DataTables` within a `DataSet`.
UniqueConstraint	Ensures that entries in a given column are unique.

Setting a Primary Key

As is common with a table in a relational database, you can supply a primary key, which can be based on one or more columns from the `DataTable`.

The following code creates a primary key for the `Products` table, whose schema was constructed by hand earlier.

Note that a primary key on a table is just one form of constraint. When a primary key is added to a `DataTable`, the runtime also generates a unique constraint over the key column(s). This is because there isn't actually a constraint type of `PrimaryKey` — a primary key is simply a unique constraint over one or more columns.

```
public static void ManufacturePrimaryKey(DataTable dt)
{
    DataColumn[] pk = new DataColumn[1];
    pk[0] = dt.Columns["ProductID"];
    dt.PrimaryKey = pk;
}
```

Because a primary key can contain several columns, it is typed as an array of `DataColumns`. A table's primary key can be set to those columns simply by assigning an array of columns to the property.

To check the constraints for a table, you can iterate through the `ConstraintCollection`. For the auto-generated constraint produced by the preceding code, the name of the constraint is `Constraint1`. That's not a very useful name, so to avoid this problem it is always best to create the constraint in code first, then define which column(s) make up the primary key.

The following code names the constraint before creating the primary key:

```
DataColumn[] pk = new DataColumn[1];
pk[0] = dt.Columns["ProductID"];
dt.Constraints.Add(new UniqueConstraint("PK_Products", pk[0]));
dt.PrimaryKey = pk;
```

Unique constraints can be applied to as many columns as you want.

Setting a Foreign Key

In addition to unique constraints, a `DataTable` class can also contain foreign key constraints. These are primarily used to enforce master/detail relationships but can also be used to replicate columns between tables if you set up the constraint correctly. A master/detail relationship is one where there is commonly one parent record (say an order) and many child records (order lines), linked by the primary key of the parent record.

A foreign key constraint can operate only over tables within the same `DataSet`, so the following example uses the `Categories` table from the Northwind database (shown in Figure 26-8), and assigns a constraint between it and the `Products` table.

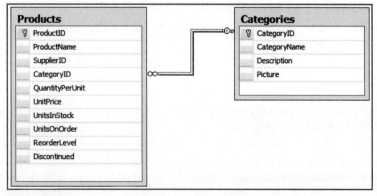

Figure 26-8

The first step is to generate a new data table for the `Categories` table:

```
DataTable categories = new DataTable("Categories");
categories.Columns.Add(new DataColumn("CategoryID", typeof(int)));
categories.Columns.Add(new DataColumn("CategoryName", typeof(string)));
categories.Columns.Add(new DataColumn("Description", typeof(string)));
categories.Constraints.Add(new UniqueConstraint("PK_Categories",
                           categories.Columns["CategoryID"]));
categories.PrimaryKey = new DataColumn[1]
                           {categories.Columns["CategoryID"]};
```

The last line of this code creates the primary key for the `Categories` table. The primary key in this instance is a single column; however, it is possible to generate a key over multiple columns using the array syntax shown.

Then the constraint can be created between the two tables:

```
DataColumn parent = ds.Tables["Categories"].Columns["CategoryID"];
DataColumn child = ds.Tables["Products"].Columns["CategoryID"];
ForeignKeyConstraint fk =
    new ForeignKeyConstraint("FK_Product_CategoryID", parent, child);
fk.UpdateRule = Rule.Cascade;
fk.DeleteRule = Rule.SetNull;
ds.Tables["Products"].Constraints.Add(fk);
```

This constraint applies to the link between `Categories.CategoryID` and `Products.CategoryID`. There are four different `ForeignKeyConstraints` — use those that permit you to name the constraint.

Setting Update and Delete Constraints

In addition to defining that there is some type of constraint between parent and child tables, you can define what should happen when a column in the constraint is updated.

The previous example sets the update rule and the delete rule. These rules are used when an action occurs to a column (or row) within the parent table, and the rule is used to decide what should happen to the row(s) within the child table that could be affected. Four different rules can be applied through the `Rule` enumeration:

❏ `Cascade` — If the parent key has been updated, copy the new key value to all child records. If the parent record has been deleted, delete the child records also. This is the default option.

❏ `None` — No action whatsoever. This option leaves orphaned rows within the child data table.

❏ `SetDefault` — Each child record affected has the foreign key column(s) set to its default value, if one has been defined.

❏ `SetNull` — All child rows have the key column(s) set to `DBNull`. (Following the naming convention that Microsoft uses, this should really be `SetDBNull`.)

> **Constraints are enforced only within a** `DataSet` **class if the** `EnforceConstraints` **property of the** `DataSet` **is** `true`**.**

This section has covered the main classes that make up the constituent parts of the `DataSet` class and has shown how to manually generate each of these classes in code. You can also define a `DataTable`, `DataRow`, `DataColumn`, `DataRelation`, and `Constraint` using the XML schema file(s) and the XSD tool that ships with .NET. The following section describes how to set up a simple schema and generate type-safe classes to access your data.

XML Schemas: Generating Code with XSD

XML is firmly entrenched in ADO.NET — indeed, the remoting format for passing data between objects is now XML. With the .NET runtime, it is possible to describe a `DataTable` class within an XML schema definition file (XSD). What's more, you can define an entire `DataSet` class, with a number of `DataTable` classes, and a set of relationships between these tables, and you can include various other details to fully describe the data.

When you have defined an XSD file, there is a tool in the runtime that will convert this schema to the corresponding data access class(es), such as the type-safe product `DataTable` class shown earlier. Let's start with a simple XSD file (`Products.xsd`) that describes the same information as the `Products` sample discussed earlier and then extend it to include some extra functionality:

```xml
<?xml version="1.0" encoding="utf-8" ?>
<xs:schema id="Products" targetNamespace="http://tempuri.org/XMLSchema1.xsd"
  xmlns:mstns="http://tempuri.org/XMLSchema1.xsd"
   xmlns:xs="http://www.w3.org/2001/XMLSchema"
   xmlns:msdata="urn:schemas-microsoft-com:xml-msdata">
   <xs:element name="Product">
     <xs:complexType>
       <xs:sequence>
         <xs:element name="ProductID" msdata:ReadOnly="true"
           msdata:AutoIncrement="true" type="xs:int" />
         <xs:element name="ProductName" type="xs:string" />
         <xs:element name="SupplierID" type="xs:int" minOccurs="0" />
         <xs:element name="CategoryID" type="xs:int" minOccurs="0" />
         <xs:element name="QuantityPerUnit" type="xs:string" minOccurs="0" />
         <xs:element name="UnitPrice" type="xs:decimal" minOccurs="0" />
         <xs:element name="UnitsInStock" type="xs:short" minOccurs="0" />
         <xs:element name="UnitsOnOrder" type="xs:short" minOccurs="0" />
         <xs:element name="ReorderLevel" type="xs:short" minOccurs="0" />
         <xs:element name="Discontinued" type="xs:boolean" />
       </xs:sequence>
     </xs:complexType>
   </xs:element>
</xs:schema>
```

These options are covered in detail in Chapter 28, "Manipulating XML"; for now, this file basically defines a schema with the id attribute set to `Products`. A complex type called `Product` is defined, which contains a number of elements, one for each of the fields within the `Products` table.

These items map to data classes as follows. The `Products` schema maps to a class derived from `DataSet`. The `Product` complex type maps to a class derived from `DataTable`. Each sub-element maps to a class derived from `DataColumn`. The collection of all columns maps to a class derived from `DataRow`.

Thankfully, there is a tool within the .NET Framework that produces the code for these classes with the help of the input XSD file. Because its sole job is to perform various functions on XSD files, the tool itself is called `XSD.EXE`.

Assuming that you saved the preceding file as `Product.xsd`, you would convert the file into code by issuing the following command in a command prompt:

```
xsd Product.xsd /d
```

This creates the file `Product.cs`.

Various switches can be used with XSD to alter the output generated. Some of the more commonly used switches are shown in the following table.

Switch	Description
/dataset (/d)	Enables you to generate classes derived from `DataSet`, `DataTable`, and `DataRow`.
/language:<language>	Permits you to choose which language the output file will be written in. C# is the default, but you can choose VB for a Visual Basic .NET file.
/namespace:<namespace>	Enables you to define the namespace that the generated code should reside within. The default is no namespace.

The following is an abridged version of the output from XSD for the `Products` schema. The output has been altered slightly to fit into a format appropriate for this book. To see the complete output, run XSD .EXE on the `Products` schema (or one of your own making) and take a look at the .cs file generated. The example includes the entire source code plus the `Product.xsd` file (note that this output is part of the downloadable code file available at www.wrox.com):

```
//------------------------------------------------------------------------------
// <autogenerated>
//      This code was generated by a tool.
//      Runtime Version:2.0.50727.312
//
//      Changes to this file may cause incorrect behavior and will be lost if
//      the code is regenerated.
// </autogenerated>
//------------------------------------------------------------------------------

using System;

//
// This source code was auto-generated by xsd, Version=2.0.40426.16.
//


[Serializable()]
[System.ComponentModel.DesignerCategoryAttribute("code")]
[System.Diagnostics.DebuggerStepThrough()]
[System.ComponentModel.ToolboxItem(true)]
[System.Xml.Serialization.XmlSchemaProviderAttribute("GetTypedDataSetSchema")]
[System.Xml.Serialization.XmlRootAttribute("Products")]
public partial class Products : System.Data.DataSet {
{
    private ProductDataTable tableProduct;
    public Products()
    public ProductDataTable Product
```

```
        public override DataSet Clone()
        public delegate void ProductRowChangeEventHandler ( object sender,
                                                ProductRowChangeEvent e);

        [System.Diagnostics.DebuggerStepThrough()]
        public partial class ProductDataTable : DataTable, IEnumerable

        [System.Diagnostics.DebuggerStepThrough()]
        public class ProductRow : DataRow
    }
```

All private and protected members have been removed to concentrate on the public interface. The ProductDataTable and ProductRow definitions show the positions of two nested classes, which will be implemented next. You review the code for these classes after a brief explanation of the DataSet-derived class.

The Products() constructor calls a private method, InitClass(), which constructs an instance of the DataTable-derived class ProductDataTable, and adds the table to the Tables collection of the DataSet class. The Products data table can be accessed by the following code:

```
DataSet ds = new Products();
DataTable products = ds.Tables["Products"];
```

Or, more simply by using the property Product, available on the derived DataSet object:

```
DataTable products = ds.Product;
```

Because the Product property is strongly typed, you could naturally use ProductDataTable rather than the DataTable reference shown in the previous code.

The ProductDataTable class includes far more code (note this is an abridged version of the code):

```
 [System.Serializable()]
[System.Diagnostics.DebuggerStepThrough()]
[System.Xml.Serialization.XmlSchemaProviderAttribute("GetTypedTableSchema")]
public partial class ProductDataTable : DataTable, System.Collections.IEnumerable
{
    private DataColumn columnProductID;
    private DataColumn columnProductName;
    private DataColumn columnSupplierID;
    private DataColumn columnCategoryID;
    private DataColumn columnQuantityPerUnit;
    private DataColumn columnUnitPrice;
    private DataColumn columnUnitsInStock;
    private DataColumn columnUnitsOnOrder;
    private DataColumn columnReorderLevel;
    private DataColumn columnDiscontinued;

    public ProductDataTable()    {
        this.TableName = "Product";
        this.BeginInit();
        this.InitClass();
        this.EndInit();    }
```

The `ProductDataTable` class, derived from `DataTable` and implementing the `IEnumerable` interface, defines a private `DataColumn` instance for each of the columns within the table. These are initialized again from the constructor by calling the private `InitClass()` member. Each column is given an internal accessor, which is used by the `DataRow` class (which is described shortly):

```
[System.ComponentModel.Browsable(false)]
public int Count
{
    get { return this.Rows.Count; }
}
internal DataColumn ProductIDColumn
{
    get { return this.columnProductID; }
}
// Other row accessors removed for clarity -- there is one for each  column
```

Adding rows to the table is taken care of by the two overloaded (and significantly different) `AddProductRow()` methods. The first takes an already constructed `DataRow` and returns a void. The second takes a set of values, one for each of the columns in the `DataTable`, constructs a new row, sets the values within this new row, adds the row to the `DataTable` object, and returns the row to the caller. Such widely different functions shouldn't really have the same name!

```
public void AddProductRow(ProductRow row)
{
    this.Rows.Add(row);
}

public ProductRow AddProductRow ( string ProductName , int SupplierID ,
                                  int CategoryID , string QuantityPerUnit ,
                                  System.Decimal UnitPrice , short UnitsInStock ,
                                  short UnitsOnOrder , short ReorderLevel ,
                                  bool Discontinued )
{
    ProductRow rowProductRow = ((ProductRow)(this.NewRow()));
    rowProductRow.ItemArray = new object[]
    {
        null,
        ProductName,
        SupplierID,
        CategoryID,
        QuantityPerUnit,
        UnitPrice,
        UnitsInStock,
        UnitsOnOrder,
        ReorderLevel,
        Discontinued
    };
    this.Rows.Add(rowProductRow);
    return rowProductRow;
}
```

Just like the `InitClass()` member in the `DataSet`-derived class, which added the table into the `DataSet` class, the `InitClass()` member in `ProductDataTable` adds columns to the `DataTable` class.

Each column's properties are set as appropriate, and the column is then appended to the columns collection:

```
private void InitClass()
{
    this.columnProductID = new DataColumn ( "ProductID",
                                            typeof(int),
                                            null,
                                            System.Data.MappingType.Element);
    this.columnProductID.ExtendedProperties.Add
        ("Generator_ChangedEventName", "ProductIDChanged");
    this.columnProductID.ExtendedProperties.Add
        ("Generator_ChangingEventName", "ProductIDChanging");
    this.columnProductID.ExtendedProperties.Add
        ("Generator_ColumnPropNameInRow", "ProductID");
    this.columnProductID.ExtendedProperties.Add
        ("Generator_ColumnPropNameInTable", "ProductIDColumn");
    this.columnProductID.ExtendedProperties.Add
        ("Generator_ColumnVarNameInTable", "columnProductID");
    this.columnProductID.ExtendedProperties.Add
        ("Generator_DelegateName", "ProductIDChangeEventHandler");
    this.columnProductID.ExtendedProperties.Add
        ("Generator_EventArgName", "ProductIDChangeEventArg");
    this.Columns.Add(this.columnProductID);
    // Other columns removed for clarity

    this.columnProductID.AutoIncrement = true;
    this.columnProductID.AllowDBNull = false;
    this.columnProductID.ReadOnly = true;
    this.columnProductName.AllowDBNull = false;
    this.columnDiscontinued.AllowDBNull = false;
}

public ProductRow NewProductRow()
{
    return ((ProductRow)(this.NewRow()));
}
```

NewRowFromBuilder() is called internally from the DataTable class's NewRow() method. Here, it creates a new strongly typed row. The DataRowBuilder instance is created by the DataTable class, and its members are accessible only within the System.Data assembly:

```
protected override DataRow NewRowFromBuilder(DataRowBuilder builder)
{
    return new ProductRow(builder);
}
```

The last class to discuss is the ProductRow class, derived from DataRow. This class is used to provide type-safe access to all fields in the data table. It wraps the storage for a particular row, and provides members to read (and write) each of the fields in the table.

In addition, for each nullable field, there are functions to set the field to `null`, and to check if the field is `null`. The following example shows the functions for the `SupplierID` column:

```
[System.Diagnostics.DebuggerStepThrough()]
public class ProductRow : DataRow
{
    private ProductDataTable tableProduct;

    internal ProductRow(DataRowBuilder rb) : base(rb)
    {
        this.tableProduct = ((ProductDataTable)(this.Table));
    }

    public int ProductID
    {
        get { return ((int)(this[this.tableProduct.ProductIDColumn])); }
        set { this[this.tableProduct.ProductIDColumn] = value; }
    }
    // Other column accessors/mutators removed for clarity

    public bool IsSupplierIDNull()
    {
        return this.IsNull(this.tableProduct.SupplierIDColumn);
    }

    public void SetSupplierIDNull()
    {
        this[this.tableProduct.SupplierIDColumn] = System.Convert.DBNull;
    }
}
```

The following code uses the classes ouptut from the XSD tool to retrieve data from the `Products` table and display that data to the console:

```
using System;
using System.Data;
using System.Data.SqlClient;

public class XSD_DataSet
{
    public static void Main()
    {
        string source = "server=(local);" +
                        " integrated security=SSPI;" +
                        "database=northwind";
        string select = "SELECT * FROM Products";
        SqlConnection conn = new SqlConnection(source);
        SqlDataAdapter da = new SqlDataAdapter(select , conn);
        Products ds = new Products();
        da.Fill(ds , "Product");
        foreach(Products.ProductRow row in ds.Product )
        Console.WriteLine("'{0}' from {1}" ,
                            row.ProductID ,
                            row.ProductName);
    }
}
```

The output of the XSD file contains a class derived from DataSet, Products, which is created and then filled by the use of the data adapter. The foreach statement uses the strongly typed ProductRow and also the Product property, which returns the Product data table.

To compile this example, issue the following commands:

```
xsd product.xsd /d
```

and

```
csc /recurse:*.cs
```

The first generates the Products.cs file from the Products.XSD schema, and then the csc command uses the /recurse:*.cs parameter to go through all files with the extension .cs and add these to the resulting assembly.

Populating a DataSet

After you have defined the schema of your data set, replete with DataTable, DataColumn, and Constraint classes, and whatever else is necessary, you need to be able to populate the DataSet class with some information. You have two main ways to read data from an external source and insert it into the DataSet class:

❑ Use a data adapter.

❑ Read XML into the DataSet class.

Populating a DataSet Class with a Data Adapter

The section on data rows briefly introduced the SqlDataAdapter class, as shown in the following code:

```
string select = "SELECT ContactName,CompanyName FROM Customers";
SqlConnection conn = new SqlConnection(source);
SqlDataAdapter da = new SqlDataAdapter(select , conn);
DataSet ds = new DataSet();
da.Fill(ds , "Customers");
```

The bold line shows the SqlDataAdapter class in use; the other data adapter classes are again virtually identical in functionality to the Sql equivalent.

To retrieve data into a DataSet, it is necessary to have some form of command that is executed to select that data. The command in question could be a SQL SELECT statement, a call to a stored procedure, or for the OLE DB provider, a TableDirect command. The preceding example uses one of the constructors available on SqlDataAdapter that converts the passed SQL SELECT statement into a SqlCommand, and issues this when the Fill() method is called on the adapter.

In the stored procedures example earlier in this chapter, the INSERT, UPDATE, and DELETE procedures were defined but the SELECT procedure was not. That gap is filled in the next section, which also shows how to call a stored procedure from a SqlDataAdapter class to populate data in a DataSet class.

Using a Stored Procedure in a Data Adapter

The first step in this example is to define the stored procedure. The stored procedure to SELECT data is:

```
CREATE PROCEDURE RegionSelect AS
    SET NOCOUNT OFF
    SELECT * FROM Region
GO
```

You can type this stored procedure directly into the SQL Server Query Analyzer, or you can run the `StoredProc.sql` file that is provided for use by this example.

Next, you need to define the `SqlCommand` that executes this stored procedure. Again the code is very simple, and most of it was already presented in the earlier section on issuing commands:

```
private static SqlCommand GenerateSelectCommand(SqlConnection conn )
{
    SqlCommand   aCommand = new SqlCommand("RegionSelect" , conn);
    aCommand.CommandType = CommandType.StoredProcedure;
    aCommand.UpdatedRowSource = UpdateRowSource.None;
    return aCommand;
}
```

This method generates the `SqlCommand` that calls the `RegionSelect` procedure when executed. All that remains is to hook up this command to a `SqlDataAdapter` class, and call the `Fill()` method:

```
DataSet ds = new DataSet();
// Create a data adapter to fill the DataSet
SqlDataAdapter da = new SqlDataAdapter();
// Set the data adapter's select command
da.SelectCommand = GenerateSelectCommand (conn);
da.Fill(ds , "Region");
```

Here, the `SqlDataAdapter` class is created, and the generated `SqlCommand` is then assigned to the `SelectCommand` property of the data adapter. Subsequently, `Fill()` is called, which will execute the stored procedure and insert all rows returned into the `Region DataTable` (which in this instance is generated by the runtime).

There's more to a data adapter than just selecting data by issuing a command, as discussed shortly in the "Persisting DataSet Changes" section.

Populating a DataSet from XML

In addition to generating the schema for a given `DataSet`, associated tables, and so on, a `DataSet` class can read and write data in native XML, such as a file on disk, a stream, or a text reader.

To load XML into a `DataSet` class, simply call one of the `ReadXML()` methods to read data from a disk file, as shown in this example:

```
DataSet ds = new DataSet();
ds.ReadXml(".\\MyData.xml");
```

The `ReadXml()` method attempts to load any inline schema information from the input XML, and if found, uses this schema in the validation of any data loaded from that file. If no inline schema is found, the `DataSet` will extend its internal structure as data is loaded. This is similar to the behavior of `Fill()` in the previous example, which retrieves the data and constructs a `DataTable` based on the data selected.

Persisting DataSet Changes

After editing data within a `DataSet`, it is usually necessary to persist these changes. The most common example is selecting data from a database, displaying it to the user, and returning those updates to the database.

In a less "connected" application, changes might be persisted to an XML file, transported to a middle-tier application server, and then processed to update several data sources.

A `DataSet` class can be used for either of these examples; what's more, it's really easy to do.

Updating with Data Adapters

In addition to the `SelectCommand` that a `SqlDataAdapter` most likely includes, you can also define an `InsertCommand`, `UpdateCommand`, and `DeleteCommand`. As these names imply, these objects are instances of the command object appropriate for your provider such as `SqlCommand` and `OleDbCommand`.

With this level of flexibility, you are free to tune the application by judicious use of stored procedures for frequently used commands (say SELECT and INSERT), and use straight SQL for less commonly used commands such as DELETE. In general, it is recommended to provide stored procedures for all database interaction because it is faster and easier to tune.

This example uses the stored procedure code from the "Calling Stored Procedures" section for inserting, updating, and deleting `Region` records, coupled with the `RegionSelect` procedure written previously, which produces an example that uses each of these commands to retrieve and update data in a `DataSet` class. The main body of code is shown in the following section.

Inserting a New Row

You can add a new row to a `DataTable` in two ways. The first way is to call the `NewRow()` method, which returns a blank row that you then populate and add to the `Rows` collection, as follows:

```
DataRow r = ds.Tables["Region"].NewRow();
r["RegionID"]=999;
r["RegionDescription"]="North West";
ds.Tables["Region"].Rows.Add(r);
```

The second way to add a new row would be to pass an array of data to the `Rows.Add()` method as shown in the following code:

```
DataRow r = ds.Tables["Region"].Rows.Add
              (new object [] { 999 , "North West" });
```

Each new row within the `DataTable` will have its `RowState` set to `Added`. The example dumps out the records before each change is made to the database, so after adding a row (either way) to the `DataTable`, the rows will look something like the following. Note that the right-hand column shows the row state:

```
New row pending inserting into database
    1    Eastern                                    Unchanged
    2    Western                                    Unchanged
    3    Northern                                   Unchanged
    4    Southern                                   Unchanged
    999 North West                                  Added
```

To update the database from the `DataAdapter`, call one of the `Update()` methods as shown here:

```
da.Update(ds , "Region");
```

For the new row within the `DataTable`, this executes the stored procedure (in this instance `RegionInsert`). The example then dumps the state of the data so you can see that changes have been made to the database.

```
New row updated and new RegionID assigned by database
    1    Eastern                                    Unchanged
    2    Western                                    Unchanged
    3    Northern                                   Unchanged
    4    Southern                                   Unchanged
    5    North West                                 Unchanged
```

Look at the last row in the `DataTable`. The `RegionID` had been set in code to `999`, but after executing the `RegionInsert` stored procedure the value has been changed to `5`. This is intentional — the database will often generate primary keys for you, and the updated data in the `DataTable` is due to the fact that the `SqlCommand` definition within the source code has the `UpdatedRowSource` property set to `UpdateRowSource.OutputParameters`:

```
SqlCommand aCommand = new SqlCommand("RegionInsert" , conn);

aCommand.CommandType = CommandType.StoredProcedure;
aCommand.Parameters.Add(new SqlParameter("@RegionDescription" ,
                        SqlDbType.NChar ,
                        50 ,
                        "RegionDescription"));
aCommand.Parameters.Add(new SqlParameter("@RegionID" ,
                        SqlDbType.Int,
                        0 ,
                        ParameterDirection.Output ,
                        false ,
                        0 ,
                        0 ,
                        "RegionID" ,    // Defines the SOURCE column
                        DataRowVersion.Default ,
                        null));
aCommand.UpdatedRowSource = UpdateRowSource.OutputParameters;
```

What this means is that whenever a data adapter issues this command, the output parameters should be mapped to the source of the row, which in this instance was a row in a `DataTable`. The flag states what data should be updated — the stored procedure has an output parameter that is mapped to the `DataRow`. The column it applies to is `RegionID` because this is defined within the command definition.

The following table shows the values for `UpdateRowSource`.

UpdateRowSource Value	Description
Both	A stored procedure might return output parameters and also a complete database record. Both of these data sources are used to update the source row.
FirstReturnedRecord	This infers that the command returns a single record, and that the contents of that record should be merged into the original source `DataRow`. This is useful where a given table has a number of default (or computed) columns because after an `INSERT` statement these need to be synchronized with the `DataRow` on the client. An example might be `'INSERT (columns) INTO (table) WITH (primarykey)'`, then `'SELECT (columns) FROM (table) WHERE (primarykey)'`. The returned record would then be merged into the original row.
None	All data returned from the command is discarded.
OutputParameters	Any output parameters from the command are mapped onto the appropriate column(s) in the `DataRow`.

Updating an Existing Row

Updating an existing row within the `DataTable` is just a case of using the `DataRow` class's indexer with either a column name or column number, as shown in the following code:

```
r["RegionDescription"]="North West England";
r[1] = "North Wast England";
```

Both of these statements are equivalent (in this example):

```
Changed RegionID 5 description
    1    Eastern                                 Unchanged
    2    Western                                 Unchanged
    3    Northern                                Unchanged
    4    Southern                                Unchanged
    5    North West England                      Modified
```

Prior to updating the database, the row updated has its state set to `Modified` as shown.

Deleting a Row

Deleting a row is a matter of calling the `Delete()` method:

```
r.Delete();
```

A deleted row has its row state set to `Deleted`, but you cannot read columns from the deleted `DataRow` because they are no longer valid. When the adaptor's `Update()` method is called, all deleted rows will use the `DeleteCommand`, which in this instance executes the `RegionDelete` stored procedure.

Writing XML Output

As you have seen already, the `DataSet` class has great support for defining its schema in XML, and just as you can read data from an XML document, you can also write data to an XML document.

The `DataSet.WriteXml()` method enables you to output various parts of the data stored within the `DataSet`. You can elect to output just the data, or the data and the schema. The following code shows an example of both for the `Region` example shown earlier:

```
ds.WriteXml(".\\WithoutSchema.xml");
ds.WriteXml(".\\WithSchema.xml" , XmlWriteMode.WriteSchema);
```

The first file, `WithoutSchema.xml`, is shown here:

```
<?xml version="1.0" standalone="yes"?>
<NewDataSet>
   <Region>
      <RegionID>1</RegionID>
      <RegionDescription>Eastern                </RegionDescription>
   </Region>
   <Region>
      <RegionID>2</RegionID>
      <RegionDescription>Western                </RegionDescription>
   </Region>
   <Region>
      <RegionID>3</RegionID>
      <RegionDescription>Northern               </RegionDescription>
```

(continued)

(continued)

```
      </Region>
      <Region>
         <RegionID>4</RegionID>
         <RegionDescription>Southern                          </RegionDescription>
      </Region>
   </NewDataSet>
```

The closing tag on `RegionDescription` is over to the right of the page because the database column is defined as `NCHAR(50)`, which is a 50-character string padded with spaces.

The output produced in the `WithSchema.xml` file includes the XML schema for the `DataSet` as well as the data itself:

```
<?xml version="1.0" standalone="yes"?>
<NewDataSet>
   <xs:schema id="NewDataSet" xmlns=""
              xmlns:xs="http://www.w3.org/2001/XMLSchema"
              xmlns:msdata="urn:schemas-microsoft-com:xml-msdata">
      <xs:element name="NewDataSet" msdata:IsDataSet="true">
         <xs:complexType>
            <xs:choice maxOccurs="unbounded">
               <xs:element name="Region">
                  <xs:complexType>
                     <xs:sequence>
                        <xs:element name="RegionID"
                                    msdata:AutoIncrement="true"
                                    msdata:AutoIncrementSeed="1"
                                    type="xs:int" />
                        <xs:element name="RegionDescription"
                                    type="xs:string" />
                     </xs:sequence>
                  </xs:complexType>
               </xs:element>
            </xs:choice>
         </xs:complexType>
      </xs:element>
   </xs:schema>
   <Region>
      <RegionID>1</RegionID>
      <RegionDescription>Eastern                           </RegionDescription>
   </Region>
   <Region>
      <RegionID>2</RegionID>
      <RegionDescription>Western                           </RegionDescription>
   </Region>
   <Region>
      <RegionID>3</RegionID>
      <RegionDescription>Northern                          </RegionDescription>
   </Region>
   <Region>
      <RegionID>4</RegionID>
      <RegionDescription>Southern                          </RegionDescription>
   </Region>
</NewDataSet>
```

Note the use in this file of the `msdata` schema, which defines extra attributes for columns within a `DataSet`, such as `AutoIncrement` and `AutoIncrementSeed` — these attributes correspond directly with the properties definable on a `DataColumn` class.

Working with ADO.NET

This section addresses some common scenarios when developing data access applications with ADO.NET.

Tiered Development

Producing an application that interacts with data is often done by splitting up the application into tiers. A common model is to have an application tier (the front end), a data services tier, and the database itself.

One of the difficulties with this model is deciding what data to transport between tiers, and the format that it should be transported in. With ADO.NET you will be pleased to learn that these wrinkles have been ironed out, and support for this style of architecture is part of the design.

One of the things that is much better in ADO.NET than OLE DB is the support for copying an entire record set. In .NET it is easy to copy a `DataSet`:

```
DataSet source = {some dataset};
DataSet dest = source.Copy();
```

This creates an exact copy of the source `DataSet` — each `DataTable`, `DataColumn`, `DataRow`, and `Relation` will be copied, and all data will be in exactly the same state as it was in the source. If all you want to copy is the schema of the `DataSet`, you can use the following code:

```
DataSet source = {some dataset};
DataSet dest = source.Clone();
```

This again copies all tables, relations, and so on. However, each copied `DataTable` will be empty. This process really couldn't be more straightforward.

A common requirement when writing a tiered system, whether based on a Windows client application or the Web, is to be able to ship as little data as possible between tiers. This reduces the amount of resources consumed.

To cope with this requirement, the `DataSet` class has the `GetChanges()` method. This simple method performs a huge amount of work, and returns a `DataSet` with only the changed rows from the source data set. This is ideal for passing data between tiers because only a minimal set of data has to be passed along.

The following example shows how to generate a "changes" `DataSet`:

```
DataSet source = {some dataset};
DataSet dest = source.GetChanges();
```

Again, this is trivial. Under the hood, things are a little more interesting. There are two overloads of the `GetChanges()` method. One overload takes a value of the `DataRowState` enumeration, and returns only rows that correspond to that state (or states). `GetChanges()` simply calls `GetChanges(Deleted | Modified | Added)`, and first checks to ensure that there are some changes by calling `HasChanges()`. If no changes have been made, `null` is returned to the caller immediately.

The next operation is to clone the current `DataSet`. Once done, the new `DataSet` is set up to ignore constraint violations (`EnforceConstraints = false`), and then each changed row for every table is copied into the new `DataSet`.

When you have a `DataSet` that just contains changes, you can then move these off to the data services tier for processing. After the data has been updated in the database, the "changes" `DataSet` can be returned to the caller (for example, there might be some output parameters from the stored procedures that have updated values in the columns). These changes can then be merged into the original `DataSet` using the `Merge()` method. Figure 26-9 depicts this sequence of operations.

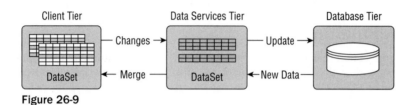

Figure 26-9

Key Generation with SQL Server

The `RegionInsert` stored procedure presented earlier in this chapter is one example of generating a primary key value on insertion into the database. The method for generating the key in this particular example is fairly crude and wouldn't scale well, so for a real application you should use some other strategy for generating keys.

Your first instinct might be to define an identity column, and return the `@@IDENTITY` value from the stored procedure. The following stored procedure shows how this might be defined for the `Categories` table in the Northwind example database. Type this stored procedure into SQL Query Analyzer, or run the `StoredProcs.sql` file that is part of the code download:

```
CREATE PROCEDURE CategoryInsert(@CategoryName NVARCHAR(15),
                                @Description NTEXT,
                                @CategoryID INTEGER OUTPUT) AS

   SET NOCOUNT OFF
   INSERT INTO Categories (CategoryName, Description)
      VALUES(@CategoryName, @Description)
   SELECT @CategoryID = @@IDENTITY
GO
```

This inserts a new row into the `Category` table and returns the generated primary key to the caller (the value of the `CategoryID` column). You can test the procedure by typing the following in SQL Query Analyzer:

```
DECLARE @CatID int;
EXECUTE CategoryInsert 'Pasties' , 'Heaven Sent Food' , @CatID OUTPUT;
PRINT @CatID;
```

When executed as a batch of commands, this inserts a new row into the `Categories` table, and returns the identity of the new record, which is then displayed to the user.

Suppose that some months down the line, someone decides to add a simple audit trail, which will record all insertions and modifications made to the category name. In that case, you define a table similar to the one shown in Figure 26-10, which will record the old and new value of the category.

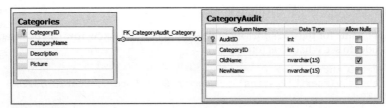

Figure 26-10

The script for this table is included in the `StoredProcs.sql` file. The `AuditID` column is defined as an `IDENTITY` column. You then construct a couple of database triggers that will record changes to the `CategoryName` field:

```
CREATE TRIGGER CategoryInsertTrigger
    ON Categories
    AFTER UPDATE
AS
    INSERT INTO CategoryAudit(CategoryID , OldName , NewName )
        SELECT old.CategoryID, old.CategoryName, new.CategoryName
        FROM Deleted AS old,
            Categories AS new
        WHERE old.CategoryID = new.CategoryID;
GO
```

If you are used to Oracle stored procedures, SQL Server doesn't exactly have the concept of OLD and NEW rows; instead, for an insert trigger there is an in-memory table called `Inserted`, and for deletes and updates the old rows are available within the `Deleted` table.

This trigger retrieves the `CategoryID` of the record(s) affected and stores this together with the old and new value of the `CategoryName` column.

Now, when you call your original stored procedure to insert a new `CategoryID`, you receive an identity value; however, this is no longer the identity value from the row inserted into the `Categories` table — it is now the new value generated for the row in the `CategoryAudit` table. Ouch!

To view the problem first-hand, open a copy of SQL Server Enterprise Manager, and view the contents of the `Categories` table (see Figure 26-11).

CategoryID	CategoryName	Description	Picture
1	Beverages	Soft drinks, coffees, teas, beers, and ales	<Binary data>
2	Condiments	Sweet and savory sauces, relishes, spreads, and seasonings	<Binary data>
3	Confections	Desserts, candies, and sweet breads	<Binary data>
4	Dairy Products	Cheeses	<Binary data>
5	Grains/Cereals	Breads, crackers, pasta, and cereal	<Binary data>
6	Meat/Poultry	Prepared meats	<Binary data>
7	Produce	Dried fruit and bean curd	<Binary data>
8	Seafood	Seaweed and fish	<Binary data>
NULL	NULL	NULL	NULL

Figure 26-11

This lists all the categories in the Northwind database.

The next identity value for the `Categories` table should be 9, so a new row can be inserted by executing the following code, to see what `ID` is returned:

```
DECLARE @CatID int;
EXECUTE CategoryInsert 'Pasties' , 'Heaven Sent Food' , @CatID OUTPUT;
PRINT @CatID;
```

The output value of this on a test PC was 1. If you look at the `CategoryAudit` table shown in Figure 26-12, you will find that this is the identity of the newly inserted audit record, not the identity of the category record created.

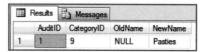

Figure 26-12

The problem lies in the way that `@@IDENTITY` actually works. It returns the LAST identity value created by your session, so as shown in Figure 26-12, it isn't completely reliable.

Two other identity functions can be used instead of `@@IDENTITY`, but neither is free from possible problems. The first, `SCOPE_IDENTITY()`, returns the last identity value created within the current *scope*. SQL Server defines scope as a stored procedure, trigger, or function. This may work most of the time, but if for some reason someone adds another `INSERT` statement into the stored procedure, you can receive this value rather than the one you expected.

The other identity function, `IDENT_CURRENT()`, returns the last identity value generated for a given table in any scope. For example, if two users were accessing SQL Server at exactly the same time, it might be possible to receive the other user's generated identity value.

As you might imagine, tracking down a problem of this nature isn't easy. The moral of the story is to beware when using `IDENTITY` columns in SQL Server.

Naming Conventions

The following tips and conventions are not directly .NET-related. However, they are worth sharing and following, especially when naming constraints. Feel free to skip this section if you already have your own views on this subject.

Conventions for Database Tables

❑ Always use singular names — `Product` rather than `Products`. This one is largely due to having to explain a database schema to customers; it is much better grammatically to say "The `Product` table contains products" than "The `Products` table contains products." Check out the Northwind database to see an example of how not to do this.

❑ Adopt some form of naming convention for the fields that go into a table — Ours is `<Table>_Id` for the primary key of a table (assuming that the primary key is a single column), `Name` for the field considered to be the user-friendly name of the record, and `Description` for any textual information about the record itself. Having a good table convention means you can look at virtually any table in the database and instinctively know what the fields are used for.

Conventions for Database Columns

❑ Use singular rather than plural names.

❑ Any columns that link to another table should be named the same as the primary key of that table. For example, a link to the `Product` table would be `Product_Id`, and to the `Sample` table `Sample_Id`. This isn't always possible, especially if one table has multiple references to another. In that case, use your own judgment.

❑ Date fields should have a suffix of `_On`, as in `Modified_On` and `Created_On`. Then it is easy to read some SQL output and infer what a column means just by its name.

❑ Fields that record the user should be suffixed with `_By`, as in `Modified_By` and `Created_By`. Again, this aids legibility.

Conventions for Constraints

❑ If possible, include in the name of the constraint the table and column name, as in `CK_<Table>_<Field>`. For example, `CK_Person_Sex` for a check constraint on the `Sex` column of the `Person` table. A foreign key example would be `FK_Product_Supplier_Id`, for the foreign key relationship between product and supplier.

❑ Show the type of constraint with a prefix, such as `CK` for a check constraint and `FK` for a foreign key constraint. Feel free to be more specific, as in `CK_Person_Age_GT0` for a constraint on the age column indicating that the age should be greater than zero.

❑ If you have to trim the length of the constraint, do it on the table name part rather than the column name. When you get a constraint violation, it is usually easy to infer which table was in error, but sometimes not so easy to check which column caused the problem. Oracle has a 30-character limit on names, which is easy to surpass.

Stored Procedures

Just like the obsession many have fallen into over the past few years of putting a C in front of each and every class they declare (you know you have!), many SQL Server developers feel compelled to prefix every stored procedure with `sp_` or something similar. This is not a good idea.

SQL Server uses the `sp_` prefix for all (well, most) system stored procedures. So, you risk confusing your users into thinking that `sp_widget` is something that comes as standard with SQL Server. In addition, when looking for a stored procedure, SQL Server treats procedures with the `sp_` prefix differently from those without it.

If you use this prefix and do not qualify the database/owner of the stored procedure, SQL Server will look in the current scope and then jump into the master database and look up the stored procedure there. Without the `sp_` prefix, your users would get an error a little earlier. What's worse, and also possible to do, is to create a local stored procedure (one within your database) that has the same name and parameters as a system stored procedure. Avoid this at all costs — if in doubt, don't prefix.

When calling stored procedures, always prefix them with the owner of the procedure, as in `dbo.selectWidgets`. This is slightly faster than not using the prefix, because SQL Server has less work to do to find the stored procedure. Something like this is not likely to have a huge impact on the execution speed of your application, but it is a tuning trick that is essentially available for free.

Above all, when naming entities, whether within the database or within code, *be consistent*.

Summary

The subject of data access is a large one, especially in .NET, because there is an abundance of new material to cover. This chapter has provided an outline of the main classes in the ADO.NET namespaces and has shown how to use the classes when manipulating data from a data source.

First, the `Connection` object was explored, through the use of both `SqlConnection` (SQL Server–specific) and `OleDbConnection` (for any OLE DB data sources). The programming model for these two classes is so similar that one can normally be substituted for the other, and the code will continue to run. With the advent of .NET version 1.1, you can use an Oracle provider and also an ODBC provider.

This chapter also discussed how to use connections properly, so that these scarce resources could be closed as early as possible. All of the connection classes implement the `IDisposable` interface, called when the object is placed within a `using` clause. If there is one thing you should take away from this chapter, it is the importance of closing database connections as early as possible.

In addition, this chapter discussed database commands by way of examples that executed with no returned data to calling stored procedures with input and output parameters. It described various execute methods, including the `ExecuteXmlReader` method available only on the SQL Server provider. This vastly simplifies the selection and manipulation of XML-based data.

The generic classes within the `System.Data` namespace were all described in detail, from the `DataSet` class through `DataTable`, `DataColumn`, `DataRow`, and on to relationships and constraints. The `DataSet` class is an excellent container of data, and various methods make it ideal for cross-tier data flow. The data within a `DataSet` is represented in XML for transport, and in addition, methods are available that pass a minimal amount of data between tiers. The ability to have many tables of data within a single `DataSet` can greatly increase its usability; being able to maintain relationships automatically between master/details rows is explored further in the next chapter, "LINQ to SQL."

Having the schema stored within a `DataSet` is one thing, but .NET also includes the data adapter that, next to various `Command` objects, can be used to select data for a `DataSet` and subsequently update data in the data store. One of the beneficial aspects of a data adapter is that a distinct command can be defined for each of the four actions: `SELECT`, `INSERT`, `UPDATE`, and `DELETE`. The system can create a default set of commands based on database schema information and a `SELECT` statement, but for the best performance, a set of stored procedures can be used, with the `DataAdapter`'s commands defined appropriately to pass only the necessary information to these stored procedures.

The XSD tool (`XSD.EXE`) was described, using an example that shows how to work with classes based on an XML schema from within .NET. The classes produced are ready to be used within an application, and their automatic generation can save many hours of laborious typing.

Finally, this chapter discussed some best practices and naming conventions for database development.

Further information about accessing SQL Server databases is provided in Chapter 30, ".NET Programming with SQL Server."

27

LINQ to SQL

Probably the biggest and most exciting addition to the .NET Framework 3.5 is the addition of the .NET Language Integrated Query Framework (LINQ) into C# 2008. Basically, what LINQ provides is a lightweight façade over programmatic data integration. This is such a big deal because *data is king*.

Pretty much every application deals with data in some manner, whether that data comes from memory (in-memory data), databases, XML files, text files, or something else. Many developers find it very difficult to move from the strongly typed object-oriented world of C# to the data tier where objects are second-class citizens. The transition from the one world to the next was a kludge at best and was full of error-prone actions.

In C#, programming with objects means a wonderful strongly typed ability to work with code. You can navigate very easily through the namespaces, work with a debugger in the Visual Studio IDE, and more. However, when you have to access data, you will notice that things are dramatically different.

You end up in a world that is not strongly typed, where debugging is a pain or even non-existent, and you end up spending most of the time sending strings to the database as commands. As a developer, you also have to be aware of the underlying data and how it is structured or how all the data points relate.

Microsoft has provided LINQ as a lightweight façade that provides a strongly typed interface to the underlying data stores. LINQ provides the means for developers to stay within the coding environment they are used to and access the underlying data as objects that work with the IDE, IntelliSense, and even debugging.

With LINQ, the queries that you create now become first-class citizens within the .NET Framework alongside everything else you are used to. When you work with queries for the data store you are working with, you will quickly realize that they now work and behave as if they are types in the system. This means that you can now use any .NET-compliant language and query the underlying data store as you never have before.

   Chapter 11, "Language Integrated Query," provides an introduction to LINQ.

Figure 27-1 shows LINQ's place in querying data.

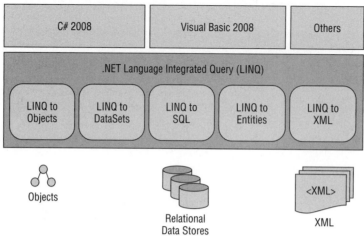

Figure 27-1

Looking at the figure, you can see that there are different types of LINQ capabilities depending on the underlying data that you are going to be working with in your application. From the list, you will find the following LINQ technologies:

- ❑ LINQ to Objects
- ❑ LINQ to DataSets
- ❑ LINQ to SQL
- ❑ LINQ to Entities
- ❑ LINQ to XML

As a developer, you are given class libraries that provide objects that, using LINQ, can be queried as any other data store can. Objects are really nothing more than data that is stored in memory. In fact, your objects themselves might be querying data. This is where LINQ to Objects comes into play.

LINQ to SQL (the focus of this chapter), LINQ to Entities, and LINQ to DataSets provide the means to query relational data. Using LINQ, you can query directly against your database and even against the stored procedures that your database exposes. The last item from the diagram is the ability to query against your XML using LINQ to XML (this topic is covered in Chapter 29). The big thing that makes LINQ exciting is that it matters very little what you are querying against, because your queries will be quite similar.

This chapter looks at the following:

- ❑ Working with LINQ to SQL along with Visual Studio 2008
- ❑ Looking at how LINQ to SQL objects map to database entities
- ❑ Building LINQ to SQL operations without the O/R Designer
- ❑ Using the O/R Designer with custom objects
- ❑ Querying the SQL Server database using LINQ
- ❑ Stored procedures and LINQ to SQL

LINQ to SQL and Visual Studio 2008

LINQ to SQL in particular is a means to have a strongly typed interface against a SQL Server database. You will find the approach that LINQ to SQL provides is by far the easiest approach to querying SQL Server available at the moment. It is not just simply about querying single tables within the database, but, for instance, if you call the `Customers` table of the Northwind database and want to pull a customer's specific orders from the `Orders` table in the same database, LINQ will use the relations of the tables and make the query on your behalf. LINQ will query the database and load up the data for you to work with from your code (again, strongly typed).

It is important to remember that LINQ to SQL is not only about querying data, but you also are able to perform the Insert/Update/Delete statements that you need to perform.

You can also interact with the entire process and customize the operations performed to add your own business logic to any of the CRUD operations (Create/Read/Update/Delete).

Visual Studio 2008 comes into strong play with LINQ to SQL in that you will find an extensive user interface that allows you to design the LINQ to SQL classes you will work with.

The next section of the chapter focuses on showing you how to set up your first LINQ to SQL instance and pull items from the `Products` table of the Northwind database.

Calling the Products Table Using LINQ to SQL — Creating the Console Application

For an example of using LINQ to SQL, this chapter starts by calling a single table from the Northwind database and using this table to populate some results to the screen.

To start off, create a console application (using the .NET Framework 3.5) and add the Northwind database file to this project (`Northwind.MDF`).

> *The following example makes use of the* `Northwind.mdf` *SQL Server Express Database file. To get this database, please search for "Northwind and pubs Sample Databases for SQL Server 2000." You can find this link at* http://www.microsoft.com/downloads/details.aspx?familyid=06616212-0356-46a0-8da2-eebc53a68034&displaylang=en. *Once installed, you will find the* `Northwind.mdf` *file in the* `C:\SQL Server 2000 Sample Databases` *directory. To add this database to your application, right-click the solution you are working with and select Add Existing Item. From the provided dialog, you are then able to browse to the location of the* `Northwind.mdf` *file that you just installed. If you are having trouble getting permissions to work with the database, make a data connection to the file from the Visual Studio Server Explorer and you will be asked to be made the appropriate user of the database. VS will make the appropriate changes on your behalf for this to occur.*

By default now, when creating many of the application types provided in the .NET Framework 3.5 within Visual Studio 2008, you will notice that you already have the proper references in place to work with LINQ. When creating a console application, you will get the following `using` statements in your code:

```
using System;
using System.Collections.Generic;
using System.Linq;
using System.Net;
using System.Net.Sockets;
using System.Runtime.Remoting.Messaging;
using System.Text;
```

From this, you can see that the LINQ reference that will be required is already in place. The next step is to add a LINQ to SQL class.

Adding a LINQ to SQL Class

When working with LINQ to SQL, one of the big advantages you will find is that Visual Studio 2008 does an outstanding job of making it as easy as possible. VS2008 provides an object-relational mapping designer, called the O/R Designer, which allows you to visually design the object to database mapping.

To start this task, right-click your solution and select Add New Item from the provided menu. From the items in the Add New Item dialog, you will find LINQ to SQL Classes as an option. This is presented in Figure 27-2.

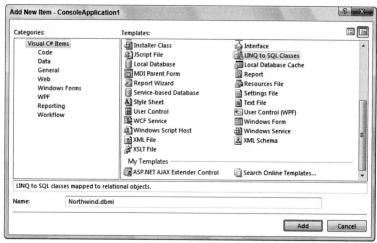

Figure 27-2

Because this example is using the Northwind database, name the file Northwind.dbml. Click the Add button, and you will see that this operation creates a couple of files for you. Figure 27-3 presents the Solution Explorer after adding the Northwind.dbml file.

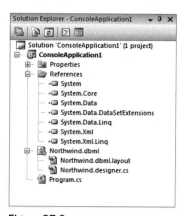

Figure 27-3

A number of things were added to your project with this action. The Northwind.dbml file was added and it contains two components. Because the LINQ to SQL class that was added works with LINQ, the following references were also added on your behalf: System.Core, System.Data .DataSetExtensions, System.Data.Linq, and System.Xml.Linq.

Introducing the O/R Designer

Another big addition to the IDE that appeared when you added the LINQ to SQL class to your project (the Northwind.dbml file), was a visual representation of the .dbml file. The new O/R Designer will appear as a tab within the document window directly in the IDE. Figure 27-4 shows a view of the O/R Designer when it is first initiated.

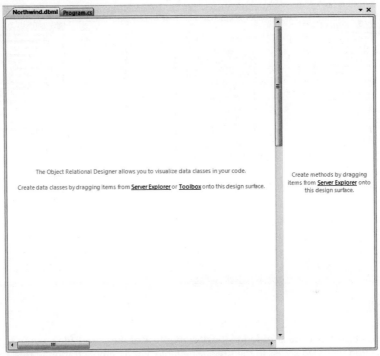

Figure 27-4

The O/R Designer is made up of two parts. The first part is for data classes, which can be tables, classes, associations, and inheritances. Dragging such items on this design surface will give you a visual representation of the object that can be worked with. The second part (on the right) is for methods, which map to the stored procedures within a database.

When viewing your .dbml file within the O/R Designer, you will also have an Object Relational Designer set of controls in the Visual Studio toolbox. The toolbox is presented in Figure 27-5.

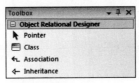

Figure 27-5

Creating the Product Object

For this example, you want to work with the `Products` table from the Northwind database, which means that you are going to have to create a `Products` table that will use LINQ to SQL to map to this table. Accomplishing this task is simply a matter of opening up a view of the tables contained within the database from the Server Explorer dialog within Visual Studio and dragging and dropping the `Products` table onto the design surface of the O/R Designer. This action's results are illustrated in Figure 27-6.

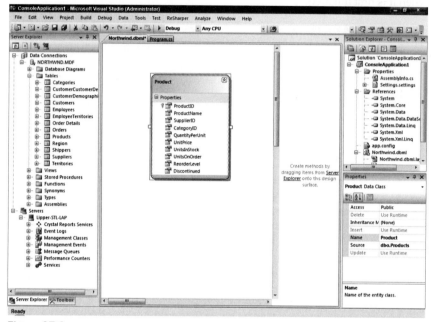

Figure 27-6

With this action, a bunch of code is added to the designer files of the `.dbml` file on your behalf. These classes will give you a strongly typed access to the `Products` table. For a demonstration of this, turn your attention to the console application's `Program.cs` file. The following shows the code that is required for this example:

```
using System;
using System.Linq;

namespace ConsoleApplication1
{
    class Class1
    {
        static void Main(string[] args)
        {
            NorthwindDataContext dc = new NorthwindDataContext();

            var query = dc.Products;

            foreach (Product item in query)
```

```
            {
                Console.WriteLine("{0} | {1} | {2}",
                    item.ProductID, item.ProductName, item.UnitsInStock);
            }

            Console.ReadLine();
        }
    }
}
```

This bit of code does not have many lines to it, but it is querying the `Products` table within the Northwind database and pulling out the data to display. It is important to step through this code starting with the first line in the `Main()` method:

```
NorthwindDataContext dc = new NorthwindDataContext();
```

The `NorthwindDataContext` object is an object of type `DataContext`. Basically, you can view this as something that maps to a `Connection` type object. This object works with the connection string and connects to the database for any required operations.

The next line is quite interesting:

```
var query = dc.Products;
```

Here, you are using the new `var` keyword, which is an implicitly typed variable. If you are unsure of the output type, you can use `var` instead of defining a type and the type will be set into place at compile time. Actually, the code `dc.Products;` returns a `System.Data.Linq.Table<ConsoleApplication1.Product>` object and this is what `var` is set as when the application is compiled. Therefore, this means that you could have also just as easily written the statement as such:

```
Table<Product> query = dc.Products;
```

This approach is actually better because programmers coming to look at the code of the application will find it easier to understand what is happening. Using the `var` keyword has so much of a hidden aspect to it that programmers might find it problematic. To use `Table<Product>`, which is basically a generic list of `Product` objects, you should make a reference to the `System.Data.Linq` namespace.

The value assigned to the `query` object is the value of the `Products` property, which is of type `Table<Product>`. From there, the next bit of code iterates through the collection of `Product` objects found in `Table<Product>`:

```
foreach (Product item in query)
{
    Console.WriteLine("{0} | {1} | {2}",
        item.ProductID, item.ProductName, item.UnitsInStock);
}
```

The iteration, in this case, pulls out the `ProductID`, `ProductName`, and `UnitsInStock` properties from the `Product` object and writes them out to the program. Because you are using only a few of the items from the table, you also have the option from the O/R Designer to delete the columns that you are not interested in pulling from the database. The results coming out from the program are presented here:

```
1 | Chai | 39
2 | Chang | 17
3 | Aniseed Syrup | 13
4 | Chef Anton's Cajun Seasoning | 53
5 | Chef Anton's Gumbo Mix | 0

** Results removed for space reasons **

73 | Röd Kaviar | 101
74 | Longlife Tofu | 4
75 | Rhönbräu Klosterbier | 125
76 | Lakkalikööri | 57
77 | Original Frankfurter grüne Soße | 32
```

From this example, you can see just how easy it is to query a SQL Server database using LINQ to SQL.

How Objects Map to LINQ Objects

The great thing about LINQ is that it gives you strongly typed objects to use in your code (with IntelliSense) and these objects map to existing database objects. Again, LINQ is nothing more than a thin façade over these pre-existing database objects. The following table shows the mappings that are between the database objects and the LINQ objects.

Database Object	LINQ Object
Database	DataContext
Table	Class and Collection
View	Class and Collection
Column	Property
Relationship	Nested Collection
Stored Procedure	Method

On the left side, you are dealing with your database. The database is the entire entity — the tables, views, triggers, stored procedures — everything that makes up the database. On the LINQ side of this, you have an object called the DataContext object. A DataContext object is bound to the database. For the required interaction with the database, it contains a connection string, it will manage all of the transactions that occur, it will take care of any logging, and it will manage the output of the data. The DataContext object completely manages the transactions with the database on your behalf.

Tables, as you saw in the example, are converted to classes. This means that if you have a `Products` table, you will have a `Product` class. You will notice that LINQ is name-friendly in that it changes plural tables to singular to give the proper name to the class that you are using in your code. In addition to database tables being treated as classes, you will find that database views are also treated as the same. Columns, on the other hand, are treated as properties. This gives you the ability to manage the attributes (names and type definitions) of the column directly.

Relationships are nested collections that map between these various objects. This gives you the ability to define relationships that are mapped to multiple items.

It is also important to understand the mapping of stored procedures. These actually map to methods within your code from the `DataContext` instance. The next section takes a closer look at the `DataContext` and the table objects within LINQ.

When dealing with the architecture of LINQ to SQL, you will notice that there are really three layers to this — your application, the LINQ to SQL layer, and the SQL Server database. As you saw from the previous examples, you can create a strongly typed query in your application's code:

```
dc.Products;
```

This in turn gets translated to a SQL query by the LINQ to SQL layer, which is then supplied to the database on your behalf:

```
SELECT [t0].[ProductID], [t0].[ProductName], [t0].[SupplierID],
[t0].[CategoryID], [t0].[QuantityPerUnit], [t0].[UnitPrice],
[t0].[UnitsInStock], [t0].[UnitsOnOrder], [t0].[ReorderLevel],
[t0].[Discontinued]
FROM [dbo].[Products] AS [t0]
```

In return, the LINQ to SQL layer takes the rows coming out of the database from this query and turns the returned data into a collection of strongly typed objects that you can easily work with.

The DataContext Object

Again, the `DataContext` object manages the transactions that occur with the database that you are working with when working with LINQ to SQL. There is actually a lot that you can do with the `DataContext` object.

In instantiating one of these objects, you will notice that it takes a couple of optional parameters. These options include:

- ❑ A string that represents the location of the SQL Server Express database file or the name of the SQL Server that is used
- ❑ A connection string
- ❑ Another `DataContext` object

The first two string options also have the option of including your own database mapping file. Once you have instantiated this object, you are then able to programmatically use it for many types of operations.

Using ExecuteQuery

One of the simpler things that you can accomplish with the `DataContext` object is to run quick commands that you write yourself using the `ExecuteQuery<T>()` method. For instance, if you are going to pull all the products from the `Products` table using the `ExecuteQuery<T>()` method, your code would be similar to the following:

```
using System;
using System.Collections.Generic;
using System.Data.Linq;

namespace ConsoleApplication1
{
    class Class1
    {
        static void Main(string[] args)
        {
            DataContext dc = new DataContext(@"Data Source=.\SQLEXPRESS;
                AttachDbFilename=|DataDirectory|\NORTHWND.MDF;
                Integrated Security=True;User Instance=True");

            IEnumerable<Product> myProducts =
                dc.ExecuteQuery<Product>("SELECT * FROM PRODUCTS", "");

            foreach (Product item in myProducts)
            {
              Console.WriteLine(item.ProductID + " | " + item.ProductName);
            }

            Console.ReadLine();
        }
    }
}
```

In this case, the `ExecuteQuery<T>()` method is called passing in a query string and returning a collection of `Product` objects. The query utilized in the method call is a simple `Select` statement that doesn't require any additional parameters to be passed in. Because there are no parameters passed in with the query, you will instead need to use the double quotes as the second required parameter to the method call. If you were going to optionally substitute any values in the query, you would construct your `ExecuteQuery<T>()` call as such:

```
IEnumerable<Product> myProducts =
    dc.ExecuteQuery<Product>("SELECT * FROM PRODUCTS WHERE UnitsInStock > {0}",
    50);
```

In this case, the `{0}` is a placeholder for the substituted parameter value that you are going to pass in, and the second parameter of the `ExecuteQuery<T>()` method is the parameter that will be used in the substitution.

Using Connection

The `Connection` property actually returns an instance of the `System.Data.SqlClient.SqlConnection` that is used by the `DataContext` object. This is ideal if you need to share this connection with other ADO.NET code that you might be using in your application, or if you need to get at any of the `SqlConnection` properties or methods that it exposes. For instance, getting at the connection string is a simple affair:

```
NorthwindDataContext dc = new NorthwindDataContext();

Console.WriteLine(dc.Connection.ConnectionString);
```

Using Transaction

If you have an ADO.NET transaction that you can use, you are able to assign that transaction to the DataContext object instance using the Transaction property. You can also make use of transactions using the TransactionScope object that is from the .NET 2.0 Framework:

```
using System;
using System.Collections.Generic;
using System.Data.Linq;
using System.Transactions;

namespace ConsoleApplication1
{
    class Class1
    {
        static void Main(string[] args)
        {
            NorthwindDataContext dc = new NorthwindDataContext();

            using (TransactionScope myScope = new TransactionScope())
            {
                Product p1 = new Product() { ProductName = "Bill's Product" };
                dc.Products.InsertOnSubmit(p1);

                Product p2 = new Product() { ProductName = "Another Product" };
                dc.Products.InsertOnSubmit(p2);

                try
                {
                    dc.SubmitChanges();

                    Console.WriteLine(p1.ProductID);
                    Console.WriteLine(p2.ProductID);
                }
                catch (Exception ex)
                {
                    Console.WriteLine(ex.ToString());
                }

                myScope.Complete();
            }

            Console.ReadLine();
        }
    }
}
```

In this case, the TransactionScope object is used and if one of the operations on the database fails, everything will be rolled back to the original state.

Other Methods and Properties of the DataContext Object

In addition to the items just described, a number of other methods and properties are available from the DataContext object. The following table shows some of the available methods from DataContext.

Method	Description
CreateDatabase	Allows you to create a database on the server.
DatabaseExists	Allows you to determine whether a database exists and can be opened.
DeleteDatabase	Deletes the associated database.
ExecuteCommand	Allows you to pass in a command to the database to be executed.
ExecuteQuery	Allows you to pass queries directly to the database.
GetChangeSet	The DataContext object keeps track of changes occurring in the database on your behalf and this method allows you access to these changes.
GetCommand	Gives you access to the commands that are performed.
GetTable	Provides access to a collection of tables from the database.
Refresh	Allows you to refresh your objects from the data that is stored within the database.
SubmitChanges	Executes your CRUD commands in the database that have been established in your code.
Translate	Converts an IDataReader to objects.

In addition to these methods, the DataContext object exposes some of the properties shown in the following table.

Property	Description
ChangeConflicts	Provides a collection of objects that cause concurrency conflicts when the SubmitChanges() method is called.
CommandTimeout	Allows you to set the timeout period in which a command against the database is allowed to run. You should set this to a higher value if your query needs more time to execute.
Connection	Allows you to work with the System.Data.SqlClient.SqlConnection object used by the client.
DeferredLoadingEnabled	Allows you to specify whether or not to delay the loading of one-to-many or one-to-one relationships.
LoadOptions	Allows you to specify or retrieve the value of the DataLoadOptions object.
Log	Allows you to specify the location of the output of the command that was used in the query.
Mapping	Provides the MetaModel on which the mapping is based.
ObjectTrackingEnabled	Specifies whether or not to track changes to the objects within the database for transactional purposes. If you are dealing with a read-only database, you should set this property to false.
Transaction	Allows you to specify the local transaction used with the database.

The Table<TEntity> Object

The Table<TEntity> object is a representation of the tables that you are working with from the database. For instance, you saw the use of the Product class, which is a Table<Product> instance. As you will see throughout this chapter, a number of methods are available from the Table<TEntity> object. Some of these methods are defined in the following table.

Method	Description
Attach	Allows you to attach an entity to the DataContext instance.
AttachAll	Allows you to attach a collection of entities to the DataContext instance.
DeleteAllOnSubmit<TSubEntity>	Allows you to put all the pending actions into a state of being ready for deletion. Everything here is enacted when the SubmitChanges() method is called from the DataContext object.
DeleteOnSubmit	Allows you to put a pending action into a state of being ready for deletion. Everything here is enacted when the SubmitChanges() method is called from the DataContext object.
GetModifiedMembers	Provides an array of modified objects. You will be able to access their current and changed values.
GetNewBindingList	Provides a new list for binding to the data store.
GetOriginalEntityState	Provides you an instance of the object as it appeared in its original state.
InsertAllOnSubmit<TSubEntity>	Allows you to put all the pending actions into a state of being ready for insertion. Everything here is enacted with the SubmitChanges() method called off of the DataContext object.
InsertOnSubmit	Allows you to put a pending action into a state of being ready for insertion. Everything here is enacted when the SubmitChanges() method is called from the DataContext object.

Working Without the O/R Designer

Although the new O/R Designer in Visual Studio 2008 makes the creation of everything you need for LINQ to SQL quite easy, it is important to note that the underlying framework upon which this all rests allows you to do everything from the ground up yourself. This provides the most control over the situation and what is actually happening.

Creating Your Own Custom Object

To accomplish the same task as was accomplished earlier with the Customer table, you will need to expose the Customer table yourself via a class. The first step is to create a new class in your project called Customer.cs. The code for this class is presented here:

```
using System.Data.Linq.Mapping;

namespace ConsoleApplication1
{
    [Table(Name = "Customers")]
    public class Customer
    {
        [Column(IsPrimaryKey = true)]
        public string CustomerID { get; set; }
        [Column]
        public string CompanyName { get; set; }
        [Column]
        public string ContactName { get; set; }
        [Column]
        public string ContactTitle { get; set; }
        [Column]
        public string Address { get; set; }
        [Column]
        public string City { get; set; }
        [Column]
        public string Region { get; set; }
        [Column]
        public string PostalCode { get; set; }
        [Column]
        public string Country { get; set; }
        [Column]
        public string Phone { get; set; }
        [Column]
        public string Fax { get; set; }
    }
}
```

Here, the Customer.cs file defines the Customer object that you want to use with LINQ to SQL. The class has the Table attribute assigned to it in order to signify the table class. The Table class attribute includes a property called Name, which defines the name of the table to use within the database that is referenced with the connection string. Using the Table attribute also means that you need to make a reference to the System.Data.Linq.Mapping namespace in your code.

In addition to the Table attribute, each of the defined properties in the class makes use of the Column attribute. As stated earlier, columns from the SQL Server database will map to properties in your code.

Querying with Your Custom Object and LINQ

With only the Customer class in place, you are then able to query the Northwind database for the Customers table. The code to accomplish this task is illustrated in the following example:

```
using System;
using System.Data.Linq;
```

```
namespace ConsoleApplication1
{
    class Program
    {
        static void Main()
        {
            DataContext dc = new DataContext(@"Data Source=.\SQLEXPRESS;
                AttachDbFilename=|DataDirectory|\NORTHWND.MDF;
                Integrated Security=True;User Instance=True");

            dc.Log = Console.Out; // Used for outputting the SQL used

            Table<Customer> myCustomers = dc.GetTable<Customer>();

            foreach (Customer item in myCustomers)
            {
                Console.WriteLine("{0} | {1}",
                    item.CompanyName, item.Country);
            }

            Console.ReadLine();
        }
    }
}
```

In this case, the default `DataContext` object is used and the connection string to the Northwind SQL Server Express database is passed in as a parameter. A `Table` class of type `Customer` is then populated using the `GetTable<TEntity>()` method. For this example, the `GetTable<TEntity>()` operation uses your custom-defined `Customer` class:

```
dc.GetTable<Customer>();
```

What happens is that LINQ to SQL will use the `DataContext` object to make the query to the SQL Server database on your behalf and will get the returned rows as strongly typed `Customer` objects. This will allow you to then iterate through each of the `Customer` objects in the `Table` object's collection and get at the information that you need, as is done with the `Console.WriteLine()` statements here:

```
foreach (Customer item in myCustomers)
{
    Console.WriteLine("{0} | {1}",
        item.CompanyName, item.Country);
}
```

Running this code produces the following results in your console application:

```
SELECT [t0].[CustomerID], [t0].[CompanyName], [t0].[ContactName],
[t0].[ContactTitle], [t0].[Address], [t0].[City], [t0].[Region],
[t0].[PostalCode], [t0].[Country], [t0].[Phone], [t0].[Fax]
FROM [Customers] AS [t0]
-- Context: SqlProvider(Sql2005) Model: AttributedMetaModel Build: 3.5.21022.8

Alfreds Futterkiste | Germany
Ana Trujillo Emparedados y helados | Mexico
Antonio Moreno Taquería | Mexico
```

(continued)

(continued)
```
Around the Horn | UK
Berglunds snabbköp | Sweden

// Output removed for clarity

Wartian Herkku | Finland
Wellington Importadora | Brazil
White Clover Markets | USA
Wilman Kala | Finland
Wolski  Zajazd | Poland
```

Limiting the Columns Called with the Query

You will notice that the query retrieved every single column that was specified in your `Customer` class file. If you remove the columns that you are not going to need, you can then have a new `Customer` class file as shown here:

```
using System.Data.Linq.Mapping;

namespace ConsoleApplication1
{
    [Table(Name = "Customers")]
    public class Customer
    {
        [Column(IsPrimaryKey = true)]
        public string CustomerID { get; set; }
        [Column]
        public string CompanyName { get; set; }
        [Column]
        public string Country { get; set; }
    }
}
```

In this case, I removed all the columns that are not utilized by the application. Now if you run the console application and look at the SQL query that is produced, you will see the following results:

```
SELECT [t0].[CustomerID], [t0].[CompanyName], [t0].[Country]
FROM [Customers] AS [t0]
```

You can see that only the three columns that are defined within the `Customer` class are utilized in the query to the `Customers` table.

The property `CustomerID` is interesting in that you are able to signify that this column is a primary key for the table through the use of the `IsPrimaryKey` setting in the `Column` attribute. This setting takes a `Boolean` value and in this case, it is set to `true`.

Working with Column Names

The other important point of the columns is that the name of the property that you define in the `Customer` class needs to be the same name as what is used in the database. For instance, if you change the name of the `CustomerID` property to `MyCustomerID`, you will get the following exception when you try to run your console application:

```
System.Data.SqlClient.SqlException was unhandled
    Message="Invalid column name 'MyCustomerID'."
    Source=".Net SqlClient Data Provider"
    ErrorCode=-2146232060
    Class=16
    LineNumber=1
    Number=207
    Procedure=""
    Server="\\\\.\\pipe\\F5E22E37-1AF9-44\\tsql\\query"
```

To get around this, you need to define the name of the column in the custom `Customer` class that you have created. You can do this by using the `Column` attribute as illustrated here:

```
[Column(IsPrimaryKey = true, Name = "CustomerID")]
public string MyCustomerID { get; set; }
```

Like the `Table` attribute, the `Column` attribute includes a `Name` property that allows you to specify the name of the column as it appears in the `Customers` table.

Doing this will generate a query as shown here:

```
SELECT [t0].[CustomerID] AS [MyCustomerID], [t0].[CompanyName], [t0].[Country]
FROM [Customers] AS [t0]
```

This also means that you will need to now reference the column using the new name of `MyCustomerID` (for example, `item.MyCustomerID`).

Creating Your Own DataContext Object

Now it is probably not the best approach to use the plain-vanilla `DataContext` object, but instead, you will find that you have more control by creating your own `DataContext` class. To accomplish this task, create a new class called `MyNorthwindDataContext.cs` and have the class inherit from `DataContext`. Your class in its simplest form is illustrated here:

```
using System.Data.Linq;

namespace ConsoleApplication1
{
    public class MyNorthwindDataContext : DataContext
    {
        public Table<Customer> Customers;

        public MyNorthwindDataContext()
            : base(@"Data Source=.\SQLEXPRESS;
                    AttachDbFilename=|DataDirectory|\NORTHWND.MDF;
                    Integrated Security=True;User Instance=True")
        {
        }
    }
}
```

Here, the class `MyNorthwindDataContext` inherits from `DataContext` and provides an instance of the `Table<Customer>` object from the `Customer` class that you created earlier. The constructor is the other requirement of this class. This constructor uses a base to initialize a new instance of the object referencing a file (in this case a connection to a SQL database file).

Using your own `DataContext` object now allows you to change the code in your application to the following:

```
using System;
using System.Data.Linq;

namespace ConsoleApplication1
{
    class Program
    {
        static void Main()
        {
            MyNorthwindDataContext dc = new MyNorthwindDataContext();
            Table<Customer> myCustomers = dc.Customers;

            foreach (Customer item in myCustomers)
            {
                Console.WriteLine("{0} | {1}",
                    item.CompanyName, item.Country);
            }

            Console.ReadLine();
        }
    }
}
```

By creating an instance of the `MyNorthwindDataContext` object, you are now allowing the class to manage the connection to the database. You will also notice that now you have direct access to the `Customer` class through the `dc.Customers` statement.

Note that the examples provided in this chapter are considered bare-bones examples in that they don't include all the error handling and logging that would generally go into building your applications. This is done to illustrate the points being discussed in the chapter and nothing more.

Custom Objects and the O/R Designer

In addition to building your custom object in your own `.cs` file and then tying that class to the `DataContext` that you have built, you can also use the O/R Designer in Visual Studio 2008 to build your class files. When you use Visual Studio in this manner, it will create the appropriate `.cs` file on your behalf, but by using the O/R Designer, you will also have a visual representation of the class file and any possible relationships that you have established.

When viewing the Designer view of your `.dbml` file, you will notice that there are three items present in the toolbox. These items are Class, Association, and Inheritance.

For an example of this, take the Class object from the toolbox and drop it onto the design surface. You will be presented with an image of the generic class as shown in Figure 27-7.

Figure 27-7

From here, you can now click the Class1 name and rename this class to Customer. Right-clicking next to the name enables you to add properties to the class file by selecting Add ⇨ Property from the provided menu. For this example, give the Customer class three properties — CustomerID, CompanyName, and Country. If you highlight the CustomerID property, you will be able to configure the property from the Properties dialog in Visual Studio and change the Primary Key setting from False to True. You also want to highlight the entire class and go to the Properties dialog and change the Source property to Customers because this is the name of the table from which this Customer object needs to work. After this is all done, you will have a visual representation of the class as shown in Figure 27-8.

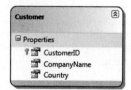

Figure 27-8

As you can see from this image, the CustomerID property is properly represented with a primary key icon next to the name. With this in place, you can expand the plus sign next to the Northwind.dbml file and you will find two files here — Northwind.dbml.layout and Northwind.designer.cs. The Northwind.dbml.layout file is an XML file that helps Visual Studio with the visual representation shown in the O/R Designer. The file that is the most important is the Northwind.designer.cs file. This is the Customer class file that was created on your behalf. When you open this file, you are able to see what Visual Studio created for you.

First, you will find the Customer class file within the code of the page:

```
[Table(Name="Customers")]
public partial class Customer : INotifyPropertyChanging,
                               INotifyPropertyChanged
{

    // Code removed for clarity

}
```

The Customer class is the name of the class according to what you provided in the designer. The class comes with the Table attribute and provides a name value of Customers because this is the name of the database that this object will need to work with when connecting to the Northwind database.

Within the Customer class, you will find the three properties that you defined. Presented here is just one of the properties — CustomerID:

```
[Column(Storage="_CustomerID", CanBeNull=false, IsPrimaryKey=true)]
public string CustomerID
{
    get
    {
        return this._CustomerID;
    }
    set
```

(continued)

(continued)

```
    {
        if ((this._CustomerID != value))
        {
            this.OnCustomerIDChanging(value);
            this.SendPropertyChanging();
            this._CustomerID = value;
            this.SendPropertyChanged("CustomerID");
            this.OnCustomerIDChanged();
        }
    }
}
```

Similar to when you built a class for yourself from the earlier example, the properties defined use the `Column` attribute and some of the properties available to this attribute. You can see that the primary key setting is set using the `IsPrimaryKey` item.

In addition to the `Customer` class, you will find that a class inheriting from the `DataContext` object is also within the created file:

```
[System.Data.Linq.Mapping.DatabaseAttribute(Name="NORTHWND")]
public partial class NorthwindDataContext : System.Data.Linq.DataContext
{

    // Code removed for clarity

}
```

This `DataContext` object, `NorthwindDataContext`, allows you to connect to the Northwind database and class the `Customers` table as was accomplished in the previous examples.

You will find that using the O/R Designer is a process that can make the creation of your database object class files simple and straightforward. However, at the same time, if you want complete control, you can code up everything yourself and get the results you are after.

Querying the Database

As you've seen, there are a number of ways in which you can query the database from the code of your application. In some of the simplest forms, your queries looked like the following:

```
Table<Product> query = dc.Products;
```

This command was pulling down the entire `Products` table to your `query` object instance.

Using Query Expressions

In addition to a pulling a table straight out of the database using `dc.Products`, you also can use a query expression directly in your code that is strongly typed. An example of this is shown in the following code:

```
using System;
using System.Linq;
```

```
namespace ConsoleApplication1
{
    class Class1
    {
        static void Main(string[] args)
        {
            NorthwindDataContext dc = new NorthwindDataContext();

            var query = from p in dc.Products
                        select p;

            foreach (Product item in query)
            {
                Console.WriteLine(item.ProductID + " | " + item.ProductName);
            }

            Console.ReadLine();
        }
    }
}
```

In this case, a `query` object (again, a `Table<Product>` object) is populated with the query value of `from p in dc.Products select p;`. This command, though shown on two lines for readability purposes, can also be presented on a single line if you wish.

Query Expressions in Detail

You will find that there are a number of query expressions that you can use from your code. The previous example is a simple select statement that returns the entire table. The following list of items are some of the other query expressions that you have at your disposal.

Segmentation	Syntax
Project	select <expression>
Filter	where <expression>, distinct
Test	any(<expression>), all(<expression>)
Join	<expression> join <expression> on <expression> equals <expression>
Group	group by <expression>, into <expression>, <expression> group join <decision> on <expression> equals <expression> into <expression>
Aggregate	count([<expression>]), sum(<expression>), min(<expression>), max(<expression>), avg(<expression>)
Partition	skip [while] <expression>, take [while] <expression>
Set	union, intersect, except
Order	order by <expression>, <expression> [ascending | descending]

Filtering Using Expressions

In addition to straight queries for the entire table, you can filter items using the `where` and `distinct` options. The following provides an example of querying the `Products` table for a specific type of record:

```
var query = from p in dc.Products
            where p.ProductName.StartsWith("L")
            select p;
```

In this case, this query is selecting all the records from the `Products` table that start with the letter `L`. This is done via the `where p.ProductName.StartsWith("L")` expression. You will find a large selection of methods available from the `ProductName` property that allows you to fine-tune the filtering you need. This operation produces the following results:

```
65 | Louisiana Fiery Hot Pepper Sauce
66 | Louisiana Hot Spiced Okra
67 | Laughing Lumberjack Lager
74 | Longlife Tofu
76 | Lakkalikööri
```

You can also add as many of these expressions to the list as you need. For instance, here is an example of adding two `where` statements to your query:

```
var query = from p in dc.Products
            where p.ProductName.StartsWith("L")
            where p.ProductName.EndsWith("i")
            select p;
```

In this case, there is a filter expression that looks for items with a product name starting with the letter `L` and then a second expression is done to make sure that the second criteria is also applied, which states that the items must also end with the letter `i`. This would give you the following results:

```
76 | Lakkalikööri
```

Performing Joins

In addition to working with one table, you can work with multiple tables and perform joins with your queries. If you drag and drop both the `Customers` table and the `Orders` table onto the `Northwind.dbml` design surface, you will get the result presented in Figure 27-9.

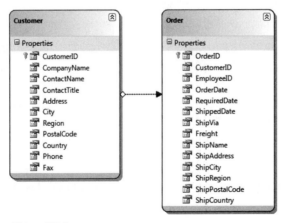

Figure 27-9

From this figure, you can see that after you drag and drop both of these elements onto the design surface, Visual Studio will know that there is a relationship between these items and will create this relationship for you in the code and represent it with the black arrow.

From here, you can use a `join` statement in your query to work with both of the tables as presented in the following example:

```
using System;
using System.Linq;

namespace ConsoleApplication1
{
    class Class1
    {
        static void Main(string[] args)
        {
            NorthwindDataContext dc = new NorthwindDataContext();
            dc.Log = Console.Out;

            var query = from c in dc.Customers
                    join o in dc.Orders on c.CustomerID equals o.CustomerID
                    orderby c.CustomerID
                    select new { c.CustomerID, c.CompanyName,
                        c.Country, o.OrderID, o.OrderDate };

            foreach (var item in query)
            {
                Console.WriteLine(item.CustomerID + " | " + item.CompanyName
                    + " | " + item.Country  + " | " + item.OrderID
                    + " | " + item.OrderDate);
            }

            Console.ReadLine();
        }
    }
}
```

This example is pulling from the `Customers` table and joining on the `Orders` table where the `CustomerID` columns match. This is done through the `join` statement:

```
join o in dc.Orders on c.CustomerID equals o.CustomerID
```

From here, a new object is created with the `select new` statement and this new object comprises of the `CustomerID`, `CompanyName`, and `Country` columns from the `Customer` table as well as the `OrderID` and `OrderDate` columns from the `Orders` table.

When it comes to iterating through the collection of this new object, the interesting part is that the `foreach` statement also uses the `var` keyword because the type is not known at this point in time:

```
foreach (var item in query)
{
    Console.WriteLine(item.CustomerID + " | " + item.CompanyName
        + " | " + item.Country  + " | " + item.OrderID
        + " | " + item.OrderDate);
}
```

Regardless, the `item` object here has access to all the properties that you specified. When you run this example, you will get results similar to what is presented in this partial result:

```
WILMK | Wilman Kala | Finland | 10695 | 10/7/1997 12:00:00 AM
WILMK | Wilman Kala | Finland | 10615 | 7/30/1997 12:00:00 AM
WILMK | Wilman Kala | Finland | 10673 | 9/18/1997 12:00:00 AM
WILMK | Wilman Kala | Finland | 11005 | 4/7/1998 12:00:00 AM
WILMK | Wilman Kala | Finland | 10879 | 2/10/1998 12:00:00 AM
WILMK | Wilman Kala | Finland | 10873 | 2/6/1998 12:00:00 AM
WILMK | Wilman Kala | Finland | 10910 | 2/26/1998 12:00:00 AM
```

Grouping Items

You are also easily able to group items with your queries. In the `Northwind.dbml` example that you are working with, drag and drop the `Categories` table onto the design surface and you will see that there is a relation with this table and the `Products` table from earlier. The following example shows you how to group products by categories:

```csharp
using System;
using System.Linq;

namespace ConsoleApplication1
{
    class Class1
    {
        static void Main(string[] args)
        {
            NorthwindDataContext dc = new NorthwindDataContext();

            var query = from p in dc.Products
                        orderby p.Category.CategoryName ascending
                        group p by p.Category.CategoryName into g
                        select new { Category = g.Key, Products = g};

            foreach (var item in query)
            {
                Console.WriteLine(item.Category);

                foreach (var innerItem in item.Products)
                {
                    Console.WriteLine("      " + innerItem.ProductName);
                }

                Console.WriteLine();
            }

            Console.ReadLine();
        }
    }
}
```

This example creates a new object, which is a group of categories, and packages the entire `Product` table into this new table called `g`. Before that, the categories are ordered by name using the `orderby` statement because the order provided is an `ascending` order (the other option being `descending`). The output is the `Category` (passed in through the `Key` property) and the `Product` instance. The iteration with the `foreach` statements is done once for the categories and another for each of the products that are found in the category.

A partial output of this program is presented here:

```
Beverages
        Chai
        Chang
        Guaraná Fantástica
        Sasquatch Ale
        Steeleye Stout
        Côte de Blaye
        Chartreuse verte
        Ipoh Coffee
        Laughing Lumberjack Lager
        Outback Lager
        Rhönbräu Klosterbier
        Lakkalikööri

Condiments
        Aniseed Syrup
        Chef Anton's Cajun Seasoning
        Chef Anton's Gumbo Mix
        Grandma's Boysenberry Spread
        Northwoods Cranberry Sauce
        Genen Shouyu
        Gula Malacca
        Sirop d'érable
        Vegie-spread
        Louisiana Fiery Hot Pepper Sauce
        Louisiana Hot Spiced Okra
        Original Frankfurter grüne Sobe
```

You will find that there a lot more commands and expressions available to you beyond what are presented in this short chapter.

Stored Procedures

So far, you have been querying the tables directly and leaving it up to LINQ to create the appropriate SQL statement for the operation. When working with pre-existing databases that make heavy use of stored procedures and for those that want to follow the best practice of using stored procedures within a database, you will find that LINQ is still a viable option.

LINQ to SQL treats working with stored procedures as a method call. As you saw in Figure 27-4, there is a design surface called the O/R Designer that allows you to drag and drop tables onto it so that you can then programmatically work with the table. On the right side of the O/R Designer, you will find a spot where you are able to drag and drop stored procedures.

Any stored procedures that you drag and drop onto this part of the O/R Designer will now become available methods to you from `DataContext` object. For this example, drag and drop the `TenMostExpensiveProducts` stored procedure onto this part of the O/R Designer.

The following example shows how you would call this stored procedure within the Northwind database:

```
using System;
using System.Collections.Generic;
using System.Data.Linq;
using System.Linq;

namespace ConsoleApplication1
{
    class Class1
    {
        static void Main(string[] args)
        {
            NorthwindDataContext dc = new NorthwindDataContext();

            ISingleResult<Ten_Most_Expensive_ProductsResult> result =
                dc.Ten_Most_Expensive_Products();

            foreach (Ten_Most_Expensive_ProductsResult item in result)
            {
                Console.WriteLine(item.TenMostExpensiveProducts + " | " +
                    item.UnitPrice);
            }

            Console.ReadLine();
        }
    }
}
```

From this example, you can see that the rows coming out of the stored procedure are collected into an `ISingleResult<Ten_Most_Expensive_ProductsResult>` object. From here, iteration through this object is as simple as all the rest.

As you can see from this example, calling your stored procedures is a simple process.

Summary

One of the more exciting features of the .NET Framework 3.5 release is the LINQ capabilities that the platform provides. This chapter focused on using LINQ to SQL and some of the options available to you in querying your SQL Server databases.

Using LINQ to SQL enables to have a strongly typed set of operations for performing CRUD operations against your database. With that said, though, you are still able to use pre-existing access capabilities whether that is interacting with ADO.NET or working with your stored procedures.

The next chapter takes a look manipulating XML, in preparation for Chapter 29, "LINQ to XML."

28

Manipulating XML

XML plays a significant role in the .NET Framework. Not only does the .NET Framework allow you to use XML in your application, but the .NET Framework itself uses XML for configuration files and source code documentation, as do SOAP, Web services, and ADO.NET, to name just a few.

To accommodate this extensive use of XML, the .NET Framework includes the `System.Xml` namespace. This namespace is loaded with classes that can be used for the processing of XML, and many of these classes are discussed in this chapter.

This chapter discusses how to use the `XmlDocument` class, which is the implementation of the Document Object Model (DOM), as well as what .NET offers as a replacement for SAX (the `XmlReader` and `XmlWriter` classes). It also discusses the class implementations of XPath and XSLT and demonstrates how XML and ADO.NET work together, as well as how easy it is to transform one to the other. You also learn how you can serialize your objects to XML and create an object from (or deserialize) an XML document using classes in the `System.Xml.Serialization` namespace. More to the point, you learn how you can incorporate XML into your C# applications.

You should note that the XML namespace allows you to get similar results in a number of different ways. It is impossible to include all these variations in one chapter, so while exploring one possible way of doing things we'll try our best to mention alternative routes that will yield the same or similar results.

Because it's beyond the scope of this book to teach you XML from scratch, we assume that you are already somewhat familiar with XML technology. For example, you should be familiar with elements, attributes, and nodes, and you should also know what we mean when we refer to a well-formed document. You should also be familiar with SAX and DOM. If you want to find out more about XML, Wrox's *Beginning XML* (Wiley Publishing, Inc., ISBN 0-7645-7077-3) is a great place to start.

This chapter covers the following:

- ❏ XML standards
- ❏ `XmlReader` and `XmlWriter`
- ❏ `XmlDocument`

❑ XPathDocument

❑ XmlNavigator

The discussion begins with a brief overview of the current status of XML standards.

XML Standards Support in .NET

The World Wide Web Consortium (W3C) has developed a set of standards that give XML its power and potential. Without these standards, XML would not have the impact on the development world that it does. The W3C Web site (www.w3.org) is a valuable source for all things XML.

The .NET Framework supports the following W3C standards:

❑ XML 1.0 (www.w3.org/TR/1998/REC-xml-19980210), including DTD support

❑ XML namespaces (www.w3.org/TR/REC-xml-names), both stream level and DOM

❑ XML schemas (www.w3.org/2001/XMLSchema)

❑ XPath expressions (www.w3.org/TR/xpath)

❑ XSLT transformations (www.w3.org/TR/xslt)

❑ DOM Level 1 Core (www.w3.org/TR/REC-DOM-Level-1)

❑ DOM Level 2 Core (www.w3.org/TR/DOM-Level-2-Core)

❑ SOAP 1.1 (www.w3.org/TR/SOAP)

The level of standards support will change as the framework matures and the W3C updates the recommended standards. Because of this, you need to make sure you stay up-to-date with the standards and the level of support provided by Microsoft.

Introducing the System.Xml Namespace

Support for processing XML is provided by the classes in the System.Xml namespace in .NET. This section looks (in no particular order) at some of the more important classes that the System.Xml namespace provides. The following table lists the main XML reader and writer classes.

Class Name	Description
XmlReader	An abstract reader class that provides fast, non-cached XML data. XmlReader is forward-only, like the SAX parser.
XmlWriter	An abstract writer class that provides fast, non-cached XML data in stream or file format.
XmlTextReader	Extends XmlReader. Provides fast forward-only stream access to XML data.
XmlTextWriter	Extends XmlWriter. Fast forward-only generation of XML streams.

The following table lists some other useful classes for handling XML.

Class Name	Description
XmlNode	An abstract class that represents a single node in an XML document. Base class for several classes in the XML namespace.
XmlDocument	Extends XmlNode. This is the W3C DOM implementation. It provides a tree representation in memory of an XML document, enabling navigation and editing.
XmlDataDocument	Extends XmlDocument. This is a document that can be loaded from XML data or from relational data in an ADO.NET DataSet. Allows the mixing of XML and relational data in the same view.
XmlResolver	An abstract class that resolves external XML-based resources such as DTD and schema references. Also used to process `<xsl:include>` and `<xsl:import>` elements.
XmlNodeList	A list of XmlNodes that can be iterated through.
XmlUrlResolver	Extends XmlResolver. Resolves external resources named by a uniform resource identifier (URI).

Many of the classes in the System.Xml namespace provide a means to manage XML documents and streams, whereas others (such as the XmlDataDocument class) provide a bridge between XML data stores and the relational data stored in DataSets.

It is worth noting that the XML namespace is available to any language that is part of the .NET family. This means that all of the examples in this chapter could also be written in Visual Basic .NET, managed C++, and so on.

Using System.Xml Classes

The following examples use books.xml as the source of data. You can download this file from the Wrox Web site (www.wrox.com), but it is also included in several examples in the .NET SDK. The books.xml file is a book catalog for an imaginary bookstore. It includes book information such as genre, author name, price, and ISBN number. As with the other chapters, you can download all code examples in this chapter from the Wrox Web site (www.wrox.com).

This is what the books.xml file looks like:

```
<?xml version='1.0'?>
<!-- This file represents a fragment of a book store inventory database -->
<bookstore>
    <book genre="autobiography" publicationdate="1991" ISBN="1-861003-11-0">
        <title>The Autobiography of Benjamin Franklin</title>
        <author>
            <first-name>Benjamin</first-name>
            <last-name>Franklin</last-name>
        </author>
```

(continued)

(continued)

```
        <price>8.99</price>
    </book>
    <book genre="novel" publicationdate="1967" ISBN="0-201-63361-2">
        <title>The Confidence Man</title>
        <author>
            <first-name>Herman</first-name>
            <last-name>Melville</last-name>
        </author>
        <price>11.99</price>
    </book>
    <book genre="philosophy" publicationdate="1991" ISBN="1-861001-57-6">
        <title>The Gorgias</title>
        <author>
            <name>Plato</name>
        </author>
        <price>9.99</price>
    </book></bookstore>
```

Reading and Writing Streamed XML

The `XmlReader` and `XmlWriter` classes will feel familiar if you have ever used SAX. `XmlReader`-based classes provide a very fast, forward-only, read-only cursor that streams the XML data for processing. Because it is a streaming model, the memory requirements are not very demanding. However, you don't have the navigation flexibility and the read or write capabilities that would be available from a DOM-based model. `XmlWriter`-based classes produce an XML document that conforms to the W3C's XML 1.0 Namespace Recommendations.

`XmlReader` and `XmlWriter` are both abstract classes. The following classes are derived from `XmlReader`:

- ❑ `XmlNodeReader`
- ❑ `XmlTextReader`
- ❑ `XmlValidatingReader`

The following classes are derived from `XmlWriter`:

- ❑ `XmlTextWriter`
- ❑ `XmlQueryOutput`

`XmlTextReader` and `XmlTextWriter` work with either a stream-based object from the `System.IO` namespace or `TextReader`/`TextWriter` objects. `XmlNodeReader` uses an `XmlNode` as its source instead of a stream. The `XmlValidatingReader` adds DTD and schema validation and therefore offers data validation. You look at these a bit more closely later in this chapter.

Using the XmlReader Class

`XmlReader` is a lot like SAX in the MSXML SDK. One of the biggest differences, however, is that whereas SAX is a *push* type of model (that is, it pushes data out to the application, and the developer has to be ready to accept it), the `XmlReader` has a *pull* model, where data is pulled into an application requesting it. This provides an easier and more intuitive programming model. Another advantage to this is that a pull model can be selective about the data that is sent to the application: if you don't want all of the data, you don't need to process it. In a push model, all of the XML data has to be processed by the application, whether it is needed or not.

The following is a very simple example of reading XML data, and later you take a closer look at the XmlReader class. You'll find the code in the XmlReaderSample folder. Here is the code for reading in the books.xml document. As each node is read, the NodeType property is checked. If the node is a text node, the value is appended to the text box:

```
using System.Xml;
private void button3_Click(object sender, EventArgs e)
{
    richTextBox1.Clear();
    XmlReader rdr = XmlReader.Create("books.xml");
    while (rdr.Read())
    {
        if (rdr.NodeType == XmlNodeType.Text)
            richTextBox1.AppendText(rdr.Value + "\r\n");
    }
}
```

As previously discussed, XmlReader is an abstract class. So in order to use the XmlReader class directly, a Create static method has been added. The create method returns an XmlReader object. The overload list for the Create method contains nine entries. In the preceding example, a string that represents the file name of the XmlDocument is passed in as a parameter. Stream-based objects and TextReader-based objects can also be passed in.

An XmlReaderSettings object can also be used. XmlReaderSettings specifies the features of the reader. For example, a schema can be used to validate the stream. Set the Schemas property to a valid XmlSchemaSet object, which is a cache of XSD schemas. Then the XsdValidate property on the XmlReaderSettings object can be set to true.

Several Ignore properties exist that can be used to control the way the reader processes certain nodes and values. These properties include IgnoreComments, IgnoreIdentityConstraints, IgnoreInlineSchema, IgnoreProcessingInstructions, IgnoreSchemaLocation, and IgnoreWhitespace. These properties can be used to strip certain items from the document.

Read Methods

Several ways exist to move through the document. As shown in the previous example, Read() takes you to the next node. You can then verify whether the node has a value (HasValue()) or, as you see shortly, whether the node has any attributes (HasAttributes()). You can also use the ReadStartElement() method, which verifies whether the current node is the start element and then positions you on to the next node. If you are not on the start element, an XmlException is raised. Calling this method is the same as calling the IsStartElement() method followed by a Read() method.

ReadElementString() is similar to ReadString(), except that you can optionally pass in the name of an element. If the next content node is not a start tag, or if the Name parameter does not match the current node Name, an exception is raised.

Here is an example of how ReadElementString() can be used. Notice that this example uses FileStreams, so you will need to make sure that you include the System.IO namespace via a using statement:

```
private void button6_Click(object sender, EventArgs e)
{
    richTextBox1.Clear();
        XmlReader rdr = XmlReader.Create("books.xml");
    while (!rdr.EOF)
```

(continued)

(continued)

```
    {
      //if we hit an element type, try and load it in the listbox
      if (rdr.MoveToContent() == XmlNodeType.Element && rdr.Name == "title")
      {
        richTextBox1.AppendText(rdr.ReadElementString() + "\r\n");
      }
      else
      {
        //otherwise move on
        rdr.Read();
      }
    }
  }
}
```

In the `while` loop, you use `MoveToContent()` to find each node of type `XmlNodeType.Element` with the name `title`. You use the `EOF` property of the `XmlTextReader` as the loop condition. If the node is not of type `Element` or not named `title`, the `else` clause will issue a `Read()` method to move to the next node. When you find a node that matches the criteria, you add the result of a `ReadElementString()` to the list box. This should leave you with just the book titles in the list box. Note that you don't have to issue a `Read()` call after a successful `ReadElementString()` because `ReadElementString()` consumes the entire `Element` and positions you on the next node.

If you remove `&& rdr.Name=="title"` from the `if` clause, you will have to catch the `XmlException` when it is thrown. If you look at the data file, you will see that the first element that `MoveToContent()` will find is the `<bookstore>` element. Because it is an element, it will pass the check in the `if` statement. However, because it does not contain a simple text type, it will cause `ReadElementString()` to raise an `XmlException`. One way to work around this is to put the `ReadElementString()` call in a function of its own. Then, if the call to `ReadElementString()` fails inside this function, you can deal with the error and return to the calling function.

Go ahead and do this; call this new method `LoadTextBox()` and pass in the `XmlTextReader` as a parameter. This is what the `LoadTextBox()` method looks like with these changes:

```
private void LoadTextBox(XmlReader reader)
{
    try
    {
        richTextBox1.AppendText (reader.ReadElementString() + "\r\n");
    }
    // if an XmlException is raised, ignore it.
    catch(XmlException er){}
}
```

This section from the previous example:

```
if (tr.MoveToContent() == XmlNodeType.Element && tr.Name == "title")
{
    richTextBox1.AppendText(tr.ReadElementString() + "\r\n");
}
else
{
    //otherwise move on
    tr.Read();
}
```

will have to change to the following:

```
if (tr.MoveToContent() == XmlNodeType.Element)
{
  LoadTextBox(tr);
}
else
{
  //otherwise move on
  tr.Read();
}
```

After running this example, the results should be the same as before. What you are seeing is that there is more than one way to accomplish the same goal. This is where the flexibility of the classes in the `System.Xml` namespace starts to become apparent.

The `XmlReader` can also read strongly typed data. There are several `ReadElementContentAs` methods, such as `ReadElementContentAsDouble`, `ReadElementContentAsBoolean`, and so on. The following example shows how to read in the values as a decimal and do some math on the value. In this case, the value from the price element is increased by 25 percent:

```
private void button5_Click(object sender, EventArgs e)
{
  richTextBox1.Clear();
  XmlReader rdr = XmlReader.Create("books.xml");
  while (rdr.Read())
  {
    if (rdr.NodeType == XmlNodeType.Element)
    {
      if (rdr.Name == "price")
      {
        decimal price = rdr.ReadElementContentAsDecimal();
        richTextBox1.AppendText("Current Price = " + price + "\r\n");
        price += price * (decimal).25;
        richTextBox1.AppendText("New Price = " + price + "\r\n\r\n");
      }
      else if(rdr.Name== "title")
        richTextBox1.AppendText(rdr.ReadElementContentAsString() + "\r\n");
    }
  }
}
```

If the value cannot be converted to a decimal value, a `FormatException` is raised. This is a much more efficient method than reading the value as a string and casting it to the proper data type.

Retrieving Attribute Data

As you play with the sample code, you might notice that when the nodes are read in, you don't see any attributes. This is because attributes are not considered part of a document's structure. When you are on an element node, you can check for the existence of attributes and optionally retrieve the attribute values.

For example, the `HasAttributes` property returns `true` if there are any attributes; otherwise, it returns `false`. The `AttributeCount` property tells you how many attributes there are, and the `GetAttribute()` method gets an attribute by name or by index. If you want to iterate through the attributes one at a time, you can use the `MoveToFirstAttribute()` and `MoveToNextAttribute()` methods.

The following is an example of iterating through the attributes of the books.xml document:

```
private void button7_Click(object sender, EventArgs e)
{
  richTextBox1.Clear();
  XmlReader tr = XmlReader.Create("books.xml");
  //Read in node at a time
  while (tr.Read())
  {
    //check to see if it's a NodeType element
    if (tr.NodeType == XmlNodeType.Element)
    {
      //if it's an element, then let's look at the attributes.
      for (int i = 0; i < tr.AttributeCount; i++)
      {
        richTextBox1.AppendText(tr.GetAttribute(i) + "\r\n");
      }
    }
  }
}
```

This time you are looking for element nodes. When you find one, you loop through all of the attributes and, using the GetAttribute() method, you load the value of the attribute into the list box. In this example, those attributes would be genre, publicationdate, and ISBN.

Validating with XmlReader

Sometimes it's important to know not only that the document is well formed but also that the document is valid. An XmlReader can validate the XML according to an XSD schema by using the XmlReaderSettings class. The XSD schema is added to the XmlSchemaSet that is exposed through the Schemas property. The XsdValidate property must also be set to true; the default for this property is false.

The following example demonstrates the use of the XmlReaderSettings class. The following is the XSD schema that will be used to validate the books.xml document:

```
<?xml version="1.0" encoding="utf-8"?>
<xs:schema attributeFormDefault="unqualified"
        elementFormDefault="qualified" xmlns:xs="http://www.w3.org/2001/XMLSchema">
  <xs:element name="bookstore">
    <xs:complexType>
      <xs:sequence>
        <xs:element maxOccurs="unbounded" name="book">
          <xs:complexType>
            <xs:sequence>
              <xs:element name="title" type="xs:string" />
              <xs:element name="author">
                <xs:complexType>
                  <xs:sequence>
                    <xs:element minOccurs="0" name="name"
                                               type="xs:string" />
                    <xs:element minOccurs="0" name="first-name"
                                               type="xs:string" />
                    <xs:element minOccurs="0" name="last-name"
                                               type="xs:string" />
                  </xs:sequence>
```

```
          </xs:complexType>
        </xs:element>
        <xs:element name="price" type="xs:decimal" />
      </xs:sequence>
      <xs:attribute name="genre" type="xs:string" use="required" />
      <!-- <xs:attribute name="publicationdate"
                         type="xs:unsignedShort" use="required" /> -->
      <xs:attribute name="ISBN" type="xs:string" use="required" />
    </xs:complexType>
  </xs:element>
</xs:sequence>
</xs:complexType>
</xs:element>
</xs:schema>
```

This schema was generated from the books.xml in Visual Studio. Notice that the publicationdate attribute has been commented out. This will cause the validation to fail.

The following is the code that uses the schema to validate the books.xml document:

```
private void button8_Click(object sender, EventArgs e)
{

 richTextBox1.Clear();
  XmlReaderSettings settings = new XmlReaderSettings();
  settings.Schemas.Add(null, "books.xsd");
  settings.ValidationType = ValidationType.Schema;
  settings.ValidationEventHandler +=
new System.Xml.Schema.ValidationEventHandler(settings_ValidationEventHandler);
  XmlReader rdr = XmlReader.Create("books.xml", settings);
  while (rdr.Read())
  {
    if (rdr.NodeType == XmlNodeType.Text)
      richTextBox1.AppendText(rdr.Value + "\r\n");
  }
}
```

After the XmlReaderSettings object setting is created, the schema books.xsd is added to the XmlSchemaSet object. The Add method for XmlSchemaSet has four overloads. One takes an XmlSchema object. The XmlSchema object can be used to create a schema on-the-fly without having to create the schema file on disk. Another overload takes another XmlSchemaSet object as a parameter. Another takes two string values: the first is the target namespace and the other is the URL for the XSD document. If the target namespace parameter is null, the targetNamespace of the schema will be used. The last overload takes the targetNamespace as the first parameter as well, but it used an XmlReader-based object to read in the schema. The XmlSchemaSet preprocesses the schema before the document to be validated is processed.

After the schema is referenced, the XsdValidate property is set to one of the ValidationType enumeration values. These valid values are DTD, Schema, or None. If the value selected is set to None, then no validation will occur.

Because the XmlReader object is being used, if there is a validation problem with the document, it will not be found until that attribute or element is read by the reader. When the validation failure does occur, an XmlSchemaValidationException is raised. This exception can be handled in a catch block; however, handling exceptions can make controlling the flow of the data difficult. To help with this, a `ValidationEvent` is available in the `XmlReaderSettings` class. This way, the validation failure can be handled without your having to use exception handling. The event is also raised by validation warnings, which do not raise an exception. The `ValidationEvent` passes in a `ValidationEventArgs` object that contains a `Severity` property. This property determines whether the event was raised by an error or a warning. If the event was raised by an error, the exception that caused the event to be raised is passed in as well. There is also a message property. In the example, the message is displayed in a `MessageBox`.

Using the XmlWriter Class

The `XmlWriter` class allows you write XML to a stream, a file, a `StringBuilder`, a `TextWriter`, or another `XmlWriter` object. Like `XmlTextReader`, it does so in a forward-only, non-cached manner. `XmlWriter` is highly configurable, allowing you to specify such things as whether or not to indent content, the amount to indent, what quote character to use in attribute values, and whether namespaces are supported. Like the `XmlReader`, this configuration is done using an `XmlWriterSettings` object.

Here's a simple example that shows how the `XmlTextWriter` class can be used:

```
private void button9_Click(object sender, EventArgs e)
{
    XmlWriterSettings settings = new XmlWriterSettings();
    settings.Indent = true;
    settings.NewLineOnAttributes = true;
    XmlWriter writer = XmlWriter.Create("newbook.xml", settings);
    writer.WriteStartDocument();
    //Start creating elements and attributes
    writer.WriteStartElement("book");
    writer.WriteAttributeString("genre", "Mystery");
    writer.WriteAttributeString("publicationdate", "2001");
    writer.WriteAttributeString("ISBN", "123456789");
    writer.WriteElementString("title", "Case of the Missing Cookie");
    writer.WriteStartElement("author");
    writer.WriteElementString("name", "Cookie Monster");
    writer.WriteEndElement();
    writer.WriteElementString("price", "9.99");
    writer.WriteEndElement();
    writer.WriteEndDocument();
    //clean up
    writer.Flush();
    writer.Close();
}
```

Here, you are writing to a new XML file called `newbook.xml`, adding the data for a new book. Note that `XmlWriter` will overwrite an existing file with a new one. You look at inserting a new element or node into an existing document later in this chapter. You are instantiating the `XmlWriter` object using the `Create` static method. In this example, a string representing a file name is passed as a parameter along with an instance of an `XmlWriterSetting` class.

The `XmlWriterSettings` class has properties that control the way that the XML is generated. The `CheckedCharacters` property is a Boolean that will raise an exception if a character in the XML does not conform to the W3C XML 1.0 recommendation. The `Encoding` class sets the encoding used for the XML being generated; the default is Encoding.UTF8. The `Indent` property is a Boolean value that determines if elements should be indented. The `IndentChars` property is set to the character string that it is used to indent. The default is two spaces. The NewLine property is used to determine the characters for line breaks. In the preceding example, the NewLineOnAttribute is set to true. This will put each attribute in a separate line, which can make the XML generated a little easier to read.

WriteStartDocument() adds the document declaration. Now you start writing data. First comes the book element; then you add the genre, publicationdate, and ISBN attributes. Then you write the title, author, and price elements. Note that the author element has a child element name.

When you click the button, you produce the booknew.xml file, which looks like this:

```
<?xml version="1.0" encoding="utf-8"?>
<book
  genre="Mystery"
  publicationdate="2001"
  ISBN="123456789">
  <title>Case of the Missing Cookie</title>
  <author>
    <name>Cookie Monster</name>
  </author>
  <price>9.99</price>
</book>
```

The nesting of elements is controlled by paying attention to when you start and finish writing elements and attributes. You can see this when you add the name child element to the authors element. Note how the WriteStartElement() and WriteEndElement() method calls are arranged and how that arrangement produces the nested elements in the output file.

To go along with the WriteElementString() and WriteAttributeString() methods, there are several other specialized write methods. WriteCData() outputs a CData section (<!CDATA[...]]>), writing out the text it takes as a parameter. WriteComment() writes out a comment in proper XML format. WriteChars() writes out the contents of a char buffer. This works in a similar fashion to the ReadChars() method that you looked at earlier; they both use the same type of parameters. WriteChars() needs a buffer (an array of characters), the starting position for writing (an integer), and the number of characters to write (an integer).

Reading and writing XML using the XmlReader- and XmlWriter-based classes are surprisingly flexible and simple to do. Next you'll learn how the DOM is implemented in the System.Xml namespace through the XmlDocument and XmlNode classes.

Using the DOM in .NET

The DOM implementation in .NET supports the W3C DOM Level 1 and Core DOM Level 2 specifications. The DOM is implemented through the XmlNode class, which is an abstract class that represents a node of an XML document.

There is also an XmlNodeList class, which is an ordered list of nodes. This is a live list of nodes, and any changes to any node are immediately reflected in the list. XmlNodeList supports indexed access or iterative access.

The XmlNode and XmlNodeList classes make up the core of the DOM implementation in the .NET Framework. The following table lists some of the classes that are based on XmlNode.

Class Name	Description
XmlLinkedNode	Returns the node immediately before or after the current node. Adds NextSibling and PreviousSibling properties to XmlNode.
XmlDocument	Represents the entire document. Implements the DOM Level 1 and Level 2 specifications.
XmlDocumentFragment	Represents a fragment of the document tree.
XmlAttribute	Represents an attribute object of an XmlElement object.
XmlEntity	Represents a parsed or unparsed entity node.
XmlNotation	Contains a notation declared in a DTD or schema.

The following table lists classes that extend XmlCharacterData.

Class Name	Description
XmlCDataSection	Represents a CData section of a document.
XmlComment	Represents an XML comment object.
XmlSignificantWhitespace	Represents a node with whitespace. Nodes are created only if the PreserveWhiteSpace flag is true.
XmlWhitespace	Represents whitespace in element content. Nodes are created only if the PreserveWhiteSpace flag is true.
XmlText	Represents the textual content of an element or attribute.

The following table lists classes that extend the XmlLinkedNode.

Class Name	Description
XmlDeclaration	Represents the declaration node (<?xml version='1.0'...>).
XmlDocumentType	Represents data relating to the document type declaration.
XmlElement	Represents an XML element object.
XmlEntityReferenceNode	Represents an entity reference node.
XmlProcessingInstruction	Contains an XML processing instruction.

As you can see, .NET makes available a class to fit just about any XML type that you might encounter. Because of this, you end up with a very flexible and powerful tool set. This section won't look at every class in detail, but you will see several examples to give you an idea of what you can accomplish.

Using the XmlDocument Class

`XmlDocument` and its derived class `XmlDataDocument` (discussed later in this chapter) are the classes that you will be using to represent the DOM in .NET. Unlike `XmlReader` and `XmlWriter`, `XmlDocument` gives you read and write capabilities as well as random access to the DOM tree. `XmlDocument` resembles the DOM implementation in MSXML. If you have experience programming with MSXML, you will feel comfortable using `XmlDocument`.

This section introduces an example that creates an `XmlDocument` object, loads a document from disk, and loads a text box with data from the title elements. This is similar to one of the examples that you constructed in the "Using the XmlReader Class" section. The difference here is that you will be selecting the nodes you want to work with, instead of going through the entire document as in the `XmlReader`-based example.

Here is the code to create an `XmlDocument` object. Notice how simple it looks in comparison to the `XmlReader` example:

```
private void button1_Click(object sender, System.EventArgs e)
{
//doc is declared at the module level
        //change path to match your path structure
        _doc.Load("books.xml");
        //get only the nodes that we want.
        XmlNodeList nodeLst = _doc.GetElementsByTagName("title");
        //iterate through the XmlNodeList
        textBox1.Text = "";
        foreach (XmlNode node in nodeLst)
        {
            textBox1.Text += node.OuterXml + "\r\n";
        }
}
```

Note that you also add the following declaration at the module level for the examples in this section:

```
private XmlDocument doc=new XmlDocument();
```

If this is all that you wanted to do, using the `XmlReader` would have been a much more efficient way to load the text box, because you just go through the document once and then you are finished with it. This is exactly the type of work that `XmlReader` was designed for. However, if you wanted to revisit a node, using `XmlDocument` is a better way.

Here is an example of using the XPath syntax to retrieve a set of nodes from the document.

```
private void button2_Click(object sender, EventArgs e)
{
  //doc is declared at the module level
  //change path to match your path structure
  doc.Load("books.xml");
  //get only the nodes that we want.
  XmlNodeList nodeLst = _doc.SelectNodes("/bookstore/book/title");
  textBox1.Text = "";
  //iterate through the XmlNodeList
  foreach (XmlNode node in nodeLst)
  {
      textBox1.Text += node.OuterXml + "\r\n";
  }
}
```

SelectNodes() returns a NodeList, or a collection of XmlNodes. The list contains only nodes that match the XPath statement passed in as the parameter SelectNodes. In this example, all you want to see are the title nodes. If you would have made the call to SelectSingleNode, then you would have received a single node object that contained the first node in the XmlDocument that matched the XPath criteria.

A quick comment regarding the SelectSingleNode() method: This is an XPath implementation in the XmlDocument class. Both the SelectSingleNode() and SelectNodes() methods are defined in XmlNode, which XmlDocument is based on. SelectSingleNode() returns an XmlNode and SelectNodes() returns an XmlNodeList. However, the System.Xml.XPath namespace contains a richer XPath implementation, and you look at that in a later section.

Inserting Nodes

Earlier, you looked at an example using XmlTextWriter that created a new document. The limitation was that it would not insert a node into a current document. With the XmlDocument class, you can do just that. Change the button1_Click() event handler from the last example to the following (DOMSample3 in the download code):

```
private void button4_Click(object sender, System.EventArgs e)
{
//change path to match your structure
    _doc.Load("books.xml");
    //create a new 'book' element
    XmlElement newBook = _doc.CreateElement("book");
    //set some attributes
    newBook.SetAttribute("genre", "Mystery");
    newBook.SetAttribute("publicationdate", "2001");
    newBook.SetAttribute("ISBN", "123456789");
    //create a new 'title' element
    XmlElement newTitle = _doc.CreateElement("title");
    newTitle.InnerText = "Case of the Missing Cookie";
    newBook.AppendChild(newTitle);
    //create new author element
    XmlElement newAuthor = _doc.CreateElement("author");
    newBook.AppendChild(newAuthor);
    //create new name element
    XmlElement newName = _doc.CreateElement("name");
    newName.InnerText = "Cookie Monster";
    newAuthor.AppendChild(newName);
    //create new price element
    XmlElement newPrice = _doc.CreateElement("price");
    newPrice.InnerText = "9.95";
    newBook.AppendChild(newPrice);
    //add to the current document
    _doc.DocumentElement.AppendChild(newBook);
    //write out the doc to disk
    XmlTextWriter tr = new XmlTextWriter("booksEdit.xml", null);
    tr.Formatting = Formatting.Indented;
    _doc.WriteContentTo(tr);
    tr.Close();
    //load listBox1 with all of the titles, including new one
    XmlNodeList nodeLst = _doc.GetElementsByTagName("title");
```

```
        textBox1.Text = "";
        foreach (XmlNode node in nodeLst)
        {
            textBox1.Text += node.OuterXml + "\r\n";
        }
    }
```

After executing this code, you end up with the same functionality as in the previous example, but there is one additional book in the text box, *The Case of the Missing Cookie* (a soon-to-be classic). If you look closely at the code, you can see that this is actually a fairly simple process. The first thing that you do is create a new `book` element:

```
XmlElement newBook = doc.CreateElement("book");
```

`CreateElement()` has three overloads that allow you to specify the following:

❑   The element name

❑   The name and namespace URI

❑   The prefix, localname, and namespace

Once the element is created you need to add attributes:

```
newBook.SetAttribute("genre","Mystery");
newBook.SetAttribute("publicationdate","2001");
newBook.SetAttribute("ISBN","123456789");
```

Now that you have the attributes created, you need to add the other elements of a book:

```
XmlElement newTitle = doc.CreateElement("title");
newTitle.InnerText = "The Case of the Missing Cookie";
newBook.AppendChild(newTitle);
```

Once again, you create a new `XmlElement`-based object (`newTitle`). Then you set the `InnerText` property to the title of our new classic, and append the element as a child to the `book` element. You repeat this for the rest of the elements in this `book` element. Note that you add the `name` element as a child to the `author` element. This will give you the proper nesting relationship, as in the other `book` elements.

Finally, you append the `newBook` element to the `doc.DocumentElement` node. This is the same level as all of the other `book` elements. You have now updated an existing document with a new element.

The last thing to do is to write the new XML document to disk. In this example, you create a new `XmlTextWriter` and pass it to the `WriteContentTo()` method. `WriteContentTo()` and `WriteTo()` both take an `XmlTextWriter` as a parameter. `WriteContentTo()` saves the current node and all of its children to the `XmlTextWriter`, whereas `WriteTo()` just saves the current node. Because `doc` is an `XmlDocument`-based object, it represents the entire document and so that is what is saved. You could also use the `Save()` method. It will always save the entire document. `Save()` has four overloads. You can specify a string with the file name and path, a `Stream`-based object, a `TextWriter`-based object, or an `XmlWriter`-based object.

You also call the `Close()` method on `XmlTextWriter` to flush the internal buffers and close the file.

Figure 28-1 shows what you get when you run this example. Notice the new entry at the bottom of the list.

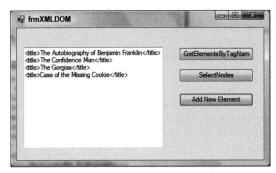

Figure 28-1

Earlier in the chapter, you saw how to create a document using the XmlTextWriter class. You can also use XmlDocument. Why would you use one in preference to the other? If the data that you want streamed to XML is available and ready to write, then the XmlTextWriter class is the best choice. However, if you need to build the XML document a little at a time, inserting nodes into various places, then creating the document with XmlDocument might be the better choice. You can accomplish this by changing the following line:

```
doc.Load("books.xml");
```

to this:

```
//create the declaration section
XmlDeclaration newDec = doc.CreateXmlDeclaration("1.0",null,null);
doc.AppendChild(newDec);
//create the new root element
XmlElement newRoot = doc.CreateElement("newBookstore");
doc.AppendChild(newRoot);
```

First, you create a new XmlDeclaration. The parameters are the version (always 1.0 for now), the encoding, and the standalone flag. The encoding parameter should be set to a string that is part of the System.Text.Encoding class if null isn't used (null defaults to UTF-8). The standalone flag can be either yes, no, or null. If it is null, the attribute is not used and will not be included in the document.

The next element that is created will become the DocumentElement. In this case, it is called newBookstore so that you can see the difference. The rest of the code is the same as in the previous example and works in the same way. This is booksEdit.xml, which is generated from the following code:

```
<?xml version="1.0"?>
<newBookstore>
    <book genre="Mystery" publicationdate="2001" ISBN="123456789">
        <title>The Case of the Missing Cookie</title>
        <author>
            <name>C. Monster</name>
        </author>
        <price>9.95</price>
    </book>
</newBookstore>
```

You will want to use the XmlDocument class when you want to have random access to the document, or the XmlReader-based classes when you want a streaming-type model instead. Remember that there is a cost for the flexibility of the XmlNode-based XmlDocument class — memory requirements are higher and the performance of reading the document is not as good as when using XmlReader. There is another way to traverse an XML document: the XPathNavigator.

Using XPathNavigators

An XPathNavigator is used to select, iterate, and sometimes edit data from an XML document. An XPathNavigator can be created from an XmlDocument to allow editing capabilities or from an XPathDocument for read-only use. Because the XPathDocument is read-only, it performs very well. Unlike the XmlReader, the XPathNavigator isn't a streaming model, so the same document can be used without having to re-read and parse.

The XPathNavigaor is part of the System.Xml.XPath namespace. XPath is a query language used to select specific nodes or elements from an XML document for processing.

The System.Xml.XPath Namespace

The System.Xml.XPath namespace is built for speed. It provides a read-only view of your XML documents, so there are no editing capabilities. Classes in this namespace are built to do fast iteration and selections on the XML document in a cursory fashion.

The following table lists the key classes in System.Xml.XPath and gives a short description of the purpose of each class.

Class Name	Description
XPathDocument	Provides a view of the entire XML document. Read-only.
XPathNavigator	Provides the navigational capabilities to an XPathDocument.
XPathNodeIterator	Provides iteration capabilities to a node set.
XPathExpression	Represents a compiled XPath expression. Used by SelectNodes, SelectSingleNodes, Evaluate, and Matches.
XPathException	An XPath exception class.

XPathDocument

XPathDocument doesn't offer any of the functionality of the XmlDocument class. Its sole purpose is to create XPathNavigators. As a matter of fact, that is the only method available on the XPathDocument class (other then those provided by Object).

An XPathDocument can be created in a number of different ways. You can pass in an XmlReader, a file name of an XML document or a Stream-based object to the constructor. This allows a great deal of flexibility. For example, you can use the XmlValidatingReader to validate the XML and then use that same object to create the XPathDocument.

XPathNavigator

XPathNavigator contains all of the methods for moving and selecting elements that you need. The following table lists some of the "move" methods defined in this class.

Method Name	Description
MoveTo()	Takes XPathNavigator as a parameter. Moves the current position to be the same as that passed in to XPathNavigator.
MoveToAttribute()	Moves to the named attribute. Takes the attribute name and namespace as parameters.
MoveToFirstAttribute()	Moves to the first attribute in the current element. Returns true if successful.
MoveToNextAttribute()	Moves to the next attribute in the current element. Returns true if successful.
MoveToFirst()	Moves to the first sibling in the current node. Returns true if successful; otherwise it returns false.
MoveToLast()	Moves to the last sibling in the current node. Returns true if successful.
MoveToNext()	Moves to the next sibling in the current node. Returns true if successful.
MoveToPrevious()	Moves to the previous sibling in the current node. Returns true if successful.
MoveToFirstChild()	Moves to the first child of the current element. Returns true if successful.
MoveToId()	Moves to the element with the ID supplied as a parameter. There needs to be a schema for the document, and the data type for the element must be of type ID.
MoveToParent()	Moves to the parent of the current node. Returns true if successful.
MoveToRoot()	Moves to the root node of the document.

In order to select a subset of the document you can use one of the Select methods listed in the following table.

Method Name	Description
Select()	Selects a node set using an XPath expression.
SelectAncestors()	Selects all of the ancestors of the current node based on an XPath expression.
SelectChildren()	Selects all of the children of the current node based on an XPath expression.
SelectDescendants()	Selects all of the descendants of the current node based on an XPath expression.
SelectSingleNode()	Selects one node based on an XPath expression.

If the XPathNavigator was created from an XPathDocument, it is read-only. If it is created from an XmlDocument, the XPathNavigator can be used to edit the document. This can be verified by checking the CanEdit property. If it is true, you can use one of the Insert methods. InsertBefore and InsertAfter will create a new node either before or after the current node. The source of the new node can be from an XmlReader or a string. Optionally, an XmlWriter can be returned and used to write the new node information.

Strongly typed values can be read from the nodes using the ValueAs properties. Notice that this is different from XmlReader, which used ReadValue methods.

XPathNodeIterator

XPathNodeIterator can be thought of as the equivalent of a NodeList or a NodeSet in XPath. This object has three properties and two methods:

- ❑ Clone — Creates a new copy of itself
- ❑ Count — Number of nodes in the XPathNodeIterator object
- ❑ Current — Returns an XPathNavigator pointing to the current node
- ❑ CurrentPosition() — Returns an integer with the current position
- ❑ MoveNext() — Moves to the next node that matches the XPath expression that created the XPathNodeIterator

The XPathNodeIterator is returned by the XPathNavigator Select methods. You use it to iterate over the set of nodes returned by a Select method of the XPathNavigator. Using the MoveNext method of the XPathNodeIterator does not change the location of the XPathNavigator that created it.

Using Classes from the XPath Namespace

The best way to see how these classes are used is to look at some code that iterates through the books.xml document. This will allow you to see how the navigation works. In order to use the examples, you first add a reference to the System.Xml.Xsl and System.Xml.XPath namespaces:

```
using System.Xml.XPath;
using System.Xml.Xsl;
```

For this example, you use the file booksxpath.xml. It is similar to the books.xml file that you have been using, except that there are a couple of extra books added. Here's the form code, which is part of the XmlSample project:

```
private void button1_Click(object sender, EventArgs e)
{
  //modify to match your path structure
  XPathDocument doc = new XPathDocument("books.xml");
  //create the XPath navigator
  XPathNavigator nav = ((IXPathNavigable)doc).CreateNavigator();
  //create the XPathNodeIterator of book nodes
  // that have genre attribute value of novel
  XPathNodeIterator iter = nav.Select("/bookstore/book[@genre='novel']");
  textBox1.Text = "";
  while (iter.MoveNext())
  {
    XPathNodeIterator newIter =
  iter.Current.SelectDescendants(XPathNodeType.Element, false);
```

(continued)

(continued)

```
        while (newIter.MoveNext())
        {
          textBox1.Text += newIter.Current.Name + ": " +
              newIter.Current.Value + "\r\n";
        }
      }
    }
```

The first thing you do in the button1_Click() method is create the XPathDocument (called doc), passing in the file and path string of the document you want opened. The next line is where the XPathNavigator is created:

```
    XPathNavigator nav = doc.CreateNavigator();
```

In the example, you can see that you use the Select() method to retrieve a set of nodes that all have novel as the value of the genre attribute. You then use the MoveNext() method to iterate through all of the novels in the book list.

To load the data into the list box, you use the XPathNodeIterator.Current property. This creates a new XPathNavigator object based on just the node that the XPathNodeIterator is pointing to. In this case, you are creating an XPathNavigator for one book node in the document.

The next loop takes this XPathNavigator and creates another XPathNodeIterator by issuing another type of select method, the SelectDescendants() method. This gives you an XPathNodeIterator of all of the child nodes and children of the child nodes of the book node.

Then you do another MoveNext() loop on the XPathNodeIterator and load the text box with the element names and element values.

Figure 28-2 shows what the screen looks like after running the code. Note that novels are the only books listed now.

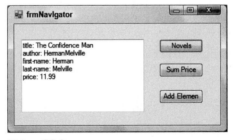

Figure 28-2

What if you wanted to add up the cost of these books? XPathNavigator includes the Evaluate() method for just this reason. Evaluate() has three overloads. The first one contains a string that is the XPath function call. The second overload uses the XPathExpression object as a parameter, and the third uses XPathExpression and an XPathNodeIterator as parameters. The following code is similar to the previous example, except this time all of the nodes in the document are iterated. The Evaluate method call at the end totals up the cost of all of the books:

```
    private void button2_Click(object sender, EventArgs e)
    {
      //modify to match your path structure
      XPathDocument doc = new XPathDocument("books.xml");
      //create the XPath navigator
      XPathNavigator nav = ((IXPathNavigable)doc).CreateNavigator();
```

```
//create the XPathNodeIterator of book nodes
XPathNodeIterator iter = nav.Select("/bookstore/book");
textBox1.Text = "";
while (iter.MoveNext())
{
   XPathNodeIterator newIter =
iter.Current.SelectDescendants(XPathNodeType.Element, false);
   while (newIter.MoveNext())
   {
      textBox1.Text += newIter.Current.Name + ": " + newIter.Current.Value +
"\r\n";
   }
}
textBox1.Text += "=========================" + "\r\n";
textBox1.Text += "Total Cost = " + nav.Evaluate("sum(/bookstore/book/price)");
}
```

This time, you see the total cost of the books evaluated in the text box (see Figure 28-3).

Figure 28-3

Now let's say that you need to add a node for discount. You can use the `InsertAfter` method to get this done fairly easily. Here is the code:

```
private void button3_Click(object sender, EventArgs e)
{
   XmlDocument doc = new XmlDocument();
   doc.Load("books.xml");
   XPathNavigator nav = doc.CreateNavigator();

   if (nav.CanEdit)
   {
      XPathNodeIterator iter = nav.Select("/bookstore/book/price");
      while (iter.MoveNext())
      {
         iter.Current.InsertAfter("<disc>5</disc>");
      }
   }
   doc.Save("newbooks.xml");
}
```

Here, you add the `<disc>5</disc>` element after the price elements. First, all of the price nodes are selected. The XPathNodeIterator is used to iterate over the nodes and the new node is inserted. The modified document is saved with a new name, newbooks.xml. The new version looks like the following:

```
<?xml version="1.0"?>
<!-- This file represents a fragment of a book store inventory database -->
<bookstore>
    <book genre="autobiography" publicationdate="1991" ISBN="1-861003-11-0">
        <title>The Autobiography of Benjamin Franklin</title>
        <author>
            <first-name>Benjamin</first-name>
            <last-name>Franklin</last-name>
        </author>
        <price>8.99</price>
        <disc>5</disc>
    </book>
    <book genre="novel" publicationdate="1967" ISBN="0-201-63361-2">
        <title>The Confidence Man</title>
        <author>
            <first-name>Herman</first-name>
            <last-name>Melville</last-name>
        </author>
        <price>11.99</price>
        <disc>5</disc>
    </book>
    <book genre="philosophy" publicationdate="1991" ISBN="1-861001-57-6">
        <title>The Gorgias</title>
        <author>
            <name>Plato</name>
        </author>
        <price>9.99</price>
        <disc>5</disc>
    </book>
</bookstore>
```

Nodes can be inserted before or after a selected node. The nodes can also be changed, and they can be deleted. If you have changes that have to be done to large numbers of nodes, using the XPathNavigator created from an XmlDocument may be your best choice.

The System.Xml.Xsl Namespace

The System.Xml.Xsl namespace contains the classes that the .NET Framework uses to support XSL transforms. The contents of this namespace are available to any store whose classes implement the IXPathNavigable interface. In the .NET Framework, that would currently include XmlDocument, XmlDataDocument, and XPathDocument. Again, just as with XPath, use the store that makes the most sense. If you plan to create a custom store, such as one using the file system and you want to be able to do transforms, be sure to implement the IXPathNavigable interface in your class.

XSLT is based on a streaming pull model. Because of this, you can chain several transforms together. You could even apply a custom reader between transforms if needed. This allows a great deal of flexibility in design.

Transforming XML

The first example you look at takes the `books.xml` document and transforms it into a simple HTML document for display using the XSLT file `books.xsl`. (This code is in the `XSLSample` folder.) You will need to add the following `using` statements:

```
using System.IO;
using System.Xml.Xsl;
using System.Xml.XPath;
```

The following is the code to perform the transform:

```
private void button1_Click(object sender, EventArgs e)
{
    XslCompiledTransform trans = new XslCompiledTransform();
    trans.Load("books.xsl");
    trans.Transform("books.xml", "out.html");
    webBrowser1.Navigate(AppDomain.CurrentDomain.BaseDirectory + "out.html");
}
```

A transform doesn't get any simpler than this. First, a new `XmlCompiledTransform` object is created. It loads the `books.xsl` transform document and then performs the transform. In this example, a string with the file name is used as the input. The output is `out.html`. This file is then loaded into the Web browser control used on the form. Instead of the file name `books.xml` as the input document, you can also use an `IXPathNavigable`-based object. This would be any object that can create an `XPathNavigator`.

After the `XmlCompiledTransform` object is created and the stylesheet is loaded, the transform is performed. The `Transform` method can take just about any combination of `IXPathNavigable` objects, `Streams`, `TextWriters`, `XmlWriters`, and URIs as parameters. This allows a great deal of flexibility on transform flow. You can pass the output of one transform in as the input to the next transform.

`XsltArgumentLists` and `XmlResolver` objects are also included in the parameter options. We look at the `XsltArgumentList` object in the next section. `XmlResolver`-based objects are used to resolve items that are external to the current document. This could be things such as schemas, credentials and, of course, stylesheets.

The `books.xsl` document is a fairly straightforward stylesheet. The document looks like this:

```
<xsl:stylesheet version="1.0"
                xmlns:xsl="http://www.w3.org/1999/XSL/Transform">
<xsl:template match="/">
   <html>
      <head>
         <title>Price List</title>
      </head>
      <body>
         <table>
            <xsl:apply-templates/>
         </table>
      </body>
   </html>
    </xsl:template>
   <xsl:template match="bookstore">
      <xsl:apply-templates select="book"/>
```

(continued)

(continued)

```
        </xsl:template>
        <xsl:template match="book">
          <tr><td>
            <xsl:value-of select="title"/>
          </td><td>
            <xsl:value-of select="price"/>
          </td></tr>
        </xsl:template>
    </xsl:stylesheet>
```

Using XsltArgumentList

`XsltArgumentList` is a way that you can bind an object with methods to a namespace. Once this is done, you can invoke the methods during the transform. Here's an example:

```
private void button3_Click(object sender, EventArgs e)
{
  //new XPathDocument
  XPathDocument doc = new XPathDocument("books.xml");
  //new XslTransform
  XslCompiledTransform trans = new XslCompiledTransform();
  trans.Load("booksarg.xsl");
  //new XmlTextWriter since we are creating a new xml document
  XmlWriter xw = new XmlTextWriter("argSample.xml", null);
  //create the XslArgumentList and new BookUtils object
  XsltArgumentList argBook = new XsltArgumentList();
  BookUtils bu = new BookUtils();
  //this tells the argumentlist about BookUtils
  argBook.AddExtensionObject("urn:XslSample", bu);
  //new XPathNavigator
  XPathNavigator nav = doc.CreateNavigator();
  //do the transform
  trans.Transform(nav, argBook, xw);
  xw.Close();
  webBrowser1.Navigate(AppDomain.CurrentDomain.BaseDirectory + "argSample.xml");
}
```

The following is the code for the `BooksUtil` class. This is the class that will be called from the transform:

```
class BookUtils
{
  public BookUtils() { }

  public string ShowText()
  {
    return "This came from the ShowText method!";
  }
}
```

The following is what the output of the transform looks like; the output has been formatted for easier viewing (`argSample.xml`):

```
<books>
  <discbook>
    <booktitle>The Autobiography of Benjamin Franklin</booktitle>
    <showtext>This came from the ShowText method!</showtext>
```

```
      </discbook>
      <discbook>
         <booktitle>The Confidence Man</booktitle>
         <showtext>This came from the ShowText method!</showtext>
      </discbook>
      <discbook>
         <booktitle>The Gorgias</booktitle>
         <showtext>This came from the ShowText method!</showtext>
      </discbook>
      <discbook>
         <booktitle>The Great Cookie Caper</booktitle>
         <showtext>This came from the ShowText method!</showtext>
      </discbook>
      <discbook>
         <booktitle>A Really Great Book</booktitle>
         <showtext>This came from the ShowText method!</showtext>
      </discbook>
   </books>
```

In this example, you define a new class, `BookUtils`. In this class, you have one rather useless method that returns the string `This came from the ShowText method!` In the `button3_Click()` event, you create the `XPathDocument` and `XslTransform` objects. In a previous example, you loaded the XML document and the transform document directly into the `XslCompiledTransform` object. This time, you will use the `XPathNavigator` to load the documents.

Next, you need to do the following:

```
XsltArgumentList argBook=new XsltArgumentList();
BookUtils bu=new BookUtils();
argBook.AddExtensionObject("urn:XslSample",bu);
```

This is where you create the `XsltArgumentList` object. You create an instance of the `BookUtils` object, and when you call the `AddExtensionObject()` method, you pass in a namespace for your extension and the object that you want to be able to call methods from. When you make the `Transform()` call, you pass in the `XsltArgumentList` (argBook) along with the `XPathNavigator` and the `XmlWriter` object you made.

The following is the `booksarg.xsl` document (based on `books.xsl`):

```
<xsl:stylesheet version="1.0" xmlns:xsl="http://www.w3.org/1999/XSL/Transform"
    xmlns:bookUtil="urn:XslSample">
<xsl:output method="xml" indent="yes"/>

<xsl:template match="/">
   <xsl:element name="books">
      <xsl:apply-templates/>
   </xsl:element>
</xsl:template>
<xsl:template match="bookstore">
   <xsl:apply-templates select="book"/>
</xsl:template>
<xsl:template match="book">
   <xsl:element name="discbook">
      <xsl:element name="booktitle">
```

(continued)

(continued)

```
                <xsl:value-of select="title"/>
            </xsl:element>
            <xsl:element name="showtext">
                <xsl:value-of select="bookUtil:ShowText()"/>
            </xsl:element>
        </xsl:element>
    </xsl:template>
</xsl:stylesheet>
```

The two important new lines are highlighted. First, you add the namespace that you created when you added the object to XsltArgumentList. Then when you want to make the method call, you use standard XSLT namespace prefixing syntax and make the method call.

Another way you could have accomplished this is with XSLT scripting. You can include C#, Visual Basic, and JavaScript code in the stylesheet. The great thing about this is that unlike current non-.NET implementations, the script is compiled at the XslTransform.Load() call; this way, you are executing already compiled scripts.

Go ahead and modify the previous XSLT file in this way. First, you add the script to the stylesheet. You can see the following changes in booksscript.xsl:

```
<xsl:stylesheet version="1.0" xmlns:xsl="http://www.w3.org/1999/XSL/Transform"
                            xmlns:msxsl="urn:schemas-microsoft-com:xslt"
                            xmlns:user="http://wrox.com">

    <msxsl:script language="C#" implements-prefix="user">

        string ShowText()
        {
            return "This came from the ShowText method!";

        }
    </msxsl:script>
    <xsl:output method="xml" indent="yes"/>
        <xsl:template match="/">
    <xsl:element name="books">
        <xsl:apply-templates/>
    </xsl:element>
        </xsl:template>
    <xsl:template match="bookstore">
        <xsl:apply-templates select="book"/>
    </xsl:template>
        <xsl:template match="book">
        <xsl:element name="discbook">
        <xsl:element name="booktitle">
            <xsl:value-of select="title"/>
        </xsl:element>
        <xsl:element name="showtext">
            <xsl:value-of select="user:ShowText()"/>
        </xsl:element>
    </xsl:element>
    </xsl:template>
</xsl:stylesheet>
```

Once again, the changes are highlighted. You set the scripting namespace, add the code (which was copied and pasted in from the Visual Studio .NET IDE), and make the call in the stylesheet. The output looks the same as that of the previous example.

Debugging XSLT

Visual Studio 2008 has the capability to debug transforms. You can actually step through a transform line by line, inspect variables, access the call stack, and set break points just like you were debugging C# source code. You can debug a transform in two ways: by just using the stylesheet and input XML file or by running the application that the transform belongs to.

Debugging Without the Application

When you first start creating the transforms, sometimes you don't really want to run through the entire application. You just want to get a stylesheet working. Visual Studio 2008 allows you to do this using the XSLT editor.

Load the `books.xsl` stylesheet into the Visual Studio 2008 XSLT editor. Set a break point on the following line:

```
<xsl:value-of select="title"/>
```

Now select the XML menu and then Debug XSLT. You will be asked for the input XML document. This is the XML that you will want transformed. Now under the default configuration the next thing you will see is in Figure 28-4.

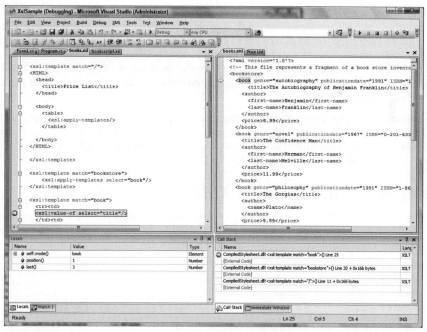

Figure 28-4

Now that the transform has been paused, you can explore almost all of the same debug information you can when debugging source code. Notice that the debugger is showing you the XSLT, the input document with the current element highlighted and the output of the transform. Now you can step through the transform line by line. If your XSLT had any scripting, you could also set breakpoints in the scripts and have the same debugging experience.

Debugging with the Application

If you want to debug a transform and the application at the same time, then you will have to make one small change when you create the `XslCompiledTransform` object. The constructor has an overload that takes a Boolean as a parameter. This parameter is `enableDebug`. The default is false, which means that even if you have a breakpoint set in the transform, if you run the application code that calls the transform, it will not break. If you set the parameter to true, the debug information for the CSLT is generated and the break point will be hit. So in the previous example, the line of code that created the `XlsCompiledTransform` would change to this:

```
XslCompiledTransform trans = new XslCompiledTransform(true);
```

Now when the application is run in debug mode, even the XSLT will have debug information and you will again have the full Visual Studio debugging experience in your stylesheets.

To summarize, the key thing to keep in mind when performing transforms is to remember to use the proper XML data store. Use `XPathDocument` if you don't need editing capabilities, `XmlDataDocument` if you're getting your data from ADO.NET, and `XmlDocument` if you need to be able to edit the data. In each case, you are dealing with the same process.

XML and ADO.NET

XML is the glue that binds ADO.NET to the rest of the world. ADO.NET was designed from the ground up to work within the XML environment. XML is used to transfer the data to and from the data store and the application or Web page. Because ADO.NET uses XML as the transport in remoting scenarios, data can be exchanged with applications and systems that are not even aware of ADO.NET. Because of the importance of XML in ADO.NET, there are some powerful features in ADO.NET that allow the reading and writing of XML documents. The `System.Xml` namespace also contains classes that can consume or utilize ADO.NET relational data.

The database that is used for the examples is from the AdventureWorksLT sample application. The sample database can be downloaded from `codeplex.com/SqlServerSamples`. Note that there are several versions of the AdventureWorks database. Most will work, but the LT version is the simplified version and is more than adequate for the purposes of this chapter.

Converting ADO.NET Data to XML

The first example uses ADO.NET, streams, and XML to pull some data from the database into a `DataSet`, load an `XmlDocument` object with the XML from the `DataSet`, and load the XML into a text box. To run the next few examples, you need to add the following `using` statements:

```
using System.Data;
using System.Xml;
using System.Data.SqlClient;
using System.IO;
```

The connection string is defined as a module-level variable.

```
string _connectString = "Server=.\\SQLExpress;
                         Database=adventureworkslt;Trusted_Connection=Yes";
```

The ADO.NET samples have a `DataGrid` object added to the forms. This will allow you to see the data in the ADO.NET `DataSet` because it is bound to the grid, as well as the data from the generated XML documents that you load in the text box. Here is the code for the first example. The first step in the examples is to create the standard ADO.NET objects to create a dataset. After the dataset has been created, it is bound to the grid.

```
private void button1_Click(object sender, EventArgs e)
{
  XmlDocument doc = new XmlDocument();
  DataSet ds = new DataSet("XMLProducts");
  SqlConnection conn = new SqlConnection(_connectString);
  SqlDataAdapter da = new SqlDataAdapter
                    ("SELECT Name, StandardCost FROM SalesLT.Product", conn);
  //fill the dataset
  da.Fill(ds, "Products");
  //load data into grid
  dataGridView1.DataSource = ds.Tables["Products"];
```

After you create the ADO.Net objects and bind to the grid, you instantiate a MemoryStream object, a StreamReader object, and a StreamWriter object. The StreamReader and StreamWriter objects will use the MemoryStream to move the XML around:

```
MemoryStream memStrm=new MemoryStream();
StreamReader strmRead=new StreamReader(memStrm);
StreamWriter strmWrite=new StreamWriter(memStrm);
```

You use a MemoryStream so that you don't have to write anything to disk; however, you could have used any object that was based on the Stream class, such as FileStream.

This next step is where the XML is generated. You call the WriteXml() method from the DataSet class. This method generates an XML document. WriteXml() has two overloads: one takes a string with the file path and name, and the other adds a mode parameter. This mode is an XmlWriteMode enumeration, with the following possible values:

❑   IgnoreSchema

❑   WriteSchema

❑   DiffGram

IgnoreSchema is used if you don't want WriteXml() to write an inline schema at the start of your XML file; use the WriteSchema parameter if you do want one. A DiffGram shows the data before and after an edit in a DataSet.

```
    //write the xml from the dataset to the memory stream
  ds.WriteXml(strmWrite, XmlWriteMode.IgnoreSchema);
  memStrm.Seek(0, SeekOrigin.Begin);
  //read from the memory stream to a XmlDocument object
  doc.Load(strmRead);
  //get all of the products elements
  XmlNodeList nodeLst = doc.SelectNodes("//XMLProducts/Products");
  textBox1.Text = "";

  foreach (XmlNode node in nodeLst)
  {
    textBox1.Text += node.InnerXml + "\r\n";
  }
```

Figure 28-5 shows the data in the list as well as the bound data grid.

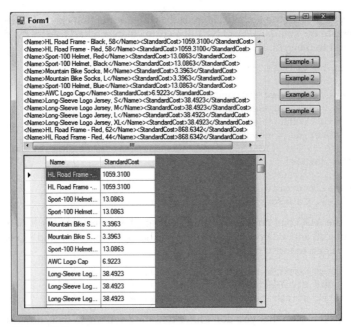

Figure 28-5

If you had wanted only the schema, you could have called `WriteXmlSchema()` instead of `WriteXml()`. This method has four overloads. One takes a string, which is the path and file name of where to write the XML document. The second overload uses an object that is based on the `XmlWriter` class. The third overload uses an object based on the `TextWriter` class. The fourth overload is derived from the `Stream` class.

Also, if you wanted to persist the XML document to disk, you would have used something like this:

```
string file = "c:\\test\\product.xml";
ds.WriteXml(file);
```

This would give you a well-formed XML document on disk that could be read in by another stream, or by `DataSet`, or used by another application or Web site. Because no `XmlMode` parameter is specified, this `XmlDocument` would have the schema included. In this example, you use the stream as a parameter to the `XmlDocument.Load()` method.

You now have two views of the data, but more important, you can manipulate the data using two different models. You can use the `System.Data` namespace to use the data, or you can use the `System.Xml` namespace on the data. This can lead to some very flexible designs in your applications, because now you are not tied to just one object model to program with. This is the real power to the ADO.NET and `System.Xml` combination. You have multiple views of the same data and multiple ways to access the data.

The following example simplifies the process by eliminating the three streams and by using some of the ADO capabilities built into the `System.Xml` namespace. You will need to change the module-level line of code:

```
private XmlDocument doc = new XmlDocument();
```

to:

```
private XmlDataDocument doc;
```

You need this because you are now using the `XmlDataDocument`. Here is the code (which you can find in the `ADOSample2` folder):

```
private void button3_Click(object sender, EventArgs e)
{
  XmlDataDocument doc;
  //create a dataset
  DataSet ds = new DataSet("XMLProducts");
  //connect to the northwind database and
  //select all of the rows from products table
  SqlConnection conn = new SqlConnection(_connectString);
  SqlDataAdapter da = new SqlDataAdapter
                      ("SELECT Name, StandardCost FROM SalesLT.Product", conn);
  //fill the dataset
  da.Fill(ds, "Products");
  ds.WriteXml("sample.xml", XmlWriteMode.WriteSchema);
  //load data into grid
  dataGridView1.DataSource = ds.Tables[0];
  doc = new XmlDataDocument(ds);
  //get all of the products elements
  XmlNodeList nodeLst = doc.GetElementsByTagName("Products");
  textBox1.Text = "";
  foreach (XmlNode node in nodeLst)
  {
    textBox1.Text += node.InnerXml + "\r\n";
  }
}
```

As you can see, the code to load the `DataSet` object into the XML document has been simplified. Instead of using the `XmlDocument` class, you are using the `XmlDataDocument` class. This class was built specifically for using data with a `DataSet` object.

The `XmlDataDocument` is based on the `XmlDocument` class, so it has all of the functionality that the `XmlDocument` class has. One of the main differences is the overloaded constructor that the `XmlDataDocument` has. Note the line of code that instantiates `XmlDataDocument` (`doc`):

```
doc = new XmlDataDocument(ds);
```

It passes in the `DataSet` object that you created, `ds`, as a parameter. This creates the XML document from the `DataSet`, and you don't have to use the `Load()` method. In fact, if you instantiate a new `XmlDataDocument` object without passing in a `DataSet` as the parameter, it will contain a `DataSet` with the name `NewDataSet` that has no `DataTables` in the `tables` collection. There is also a `DataSet` property, which you can set after an `XmlDataDocument`-based object is created.

Suppose that you add the following line of code after the `DataSet.Fill()` call:

```
ds.WriteXml("c:\\test\\sample.xml", XmlWriteMode.WriteSchema);
```

In this case, the following XML file, `sample.xml`, is produced in the folder `c:\test`:

```
<?xml version="1.0" standalone="yes"?>
<XMLProducts>
  <xs:schema id="XMLProducts" xmlns="" xmlns:xs="http://www.w3.org/2001/XMLSchema"
xmlns:msdata="urn:schemas-microsoft-com:xml-msdata">
    <xs:element name="XMLProducts" msdata:IsDataSet="true" msdata:
UseCurrentLocale="true">
      <xs:complexType>
```

(continued)

(continued)

```
            <xs:choice minOccurs="0" maxOccurs="unbounded">
              <xs:element name="Products">
                <xs:complexType>
                  <xs:sequence>
                    <xs:element name="Name" type="xs:string" minOccurs="0" />
                    <xs:element name="StandardCost" type="xs:decimal" minOccurs="0" />
                  </xs:sequence>
                </xs:complexType>
              </xs:element>
            </xs:choice>
          </xs:complexType>
        </xs:element>
      </xs:schema>
      <Products>
        <Name>HL Road Frame - Black, 58</Name>
        <StandardCost>1059.3100</StandardCost>
      </Products>
      <Products>
        <Name>HL Road Frame - Red, 58</Name>
        <StandardCost>1059.3100</StandardCost>
      </Products>
      <Products>
        <Name>Sport-100 Helmet, Red</Name>
        <StandardCost>13.0863</StandardCost>
      </Products>
    </XMLProducts>
```

Only the first couple of Products elements are shown. The actual XML file would contain all of the products in the Products table of Northwind database.

Converting Relational Data

This looks simple enough for a single table, but what about relational data, such as multiple DataTables and Relations in the DataSet? It all still works the same way. Here is an example using two related tables:

```
private void button5_Click(object sender, EventArgs e)
{
    XmlDocument doc = new XmlDocument();
    DataSet ds = new DataSet("XMLProducts");
    SqlConnection conn = new SqlConnection(_connectString);
    SqlDataAdapter daProduct = new SqlDataAdapter
    ("SELECT Name, StandardCost, ProductCategoryID FROM SalesLT.Product", conn);
    SqlDataAdapter daCategory = new SqlDataAdapter
        ("SELECT ProductCategoryID, Name from SalesLT.ProductCategory", conn);
    //Fill DataSet from both SqlAdapters
    daProduct.Fill(ds, "Products");
    daCategory.Fill(ds, "Categories");
    //Add the relation
    ds.Relations.Add(ds.Tables["Categories"].Columns["ProductCategoryID"],
    ds.Tables["Products"].Columns["ProductCategoryID"]);
    //Write the Xml to a file so we can look at it later
    ds.WriteXml("Products.xml", XmlWriteMode.WriteSchema);
    //load data into grid
    dataGridView1.DataSource = ds.Tables[0];
```

```
        //create the XmlDataDocument
        doc = new XmlDataDocument(ds);
        //Select the productname elements and load them in the grid
        XmlNodeList nodeLst = doc.SelectNodes("//XMLProducts/Products");
        textBox1.Text = "";
        foreach (XmlNode node in nodeLst)
        {
            textBox1.Text += node.InnerXml + "\r\n";
        }
    }
```

In this sample you are creating, two `DataTables` in the `XMLProducts` `DataSet`: `Products` and `Categories`. You create a new relation on the `ProductCategoryID` column in both tables.

By making the same `WriteXml()` method call that you did in the previous example, you will get the following XML file (`SuppProd.xml`):

```
<?xml version="1.0" standalone="yes"?>
<XMLProducts>
  <xs:schema id="XMLProducts" xmlns="" xmlns:xs="http://www.w3.org/2001/XMLSchema"
xmlns:msdata="urn:schemas-microsoft-com:xml-msdata">
    <xs:element name="XMLProducts" msdata:IsDataSet="true"
msdata:UseCurrentLocale="true">
      <xs:complexType>
        <xs:choice minOccurs="0" maxOccurs="unbounded">
          <xs:element name="Products">
            <xs:complexType>
              <xs:sequence>
                <xs:element name="Name" type="xs:string" minOccurs="0" />
                <xs:element name="StandardCost" type="xs:decimal" minOccurs="0" />
                <xs:element name="ProductCategoryID" type="xs:int" minOccurs="0" />
              </xs:sequence>
            </xs:complexType>
          </xs:element>
          <xs:element name="Categories">
            <xs:complexType>
              <xs:sequence>
                <xs:element name="ProductCategoryID" type="xs:int" minOccurs="0" />
                <xs:element name="Name" type="xs:string" minOccurs="0" />
              </xs:sequence>
            </xs:complexType>
          </xs:element>
        </xs:choice>
      </xs:complexType>
      <xs:unique name="Constraint1">
        <xs:selector xpath=".//Categories" />
        <xs:field xpath="ProductCategoryID" />
      </xs:unique>
      <xs:keyref name="Relation1" refer="Constraint1">
        <xs:selector xpath=".//Products" />
        <xs:field xpath="ProductCategoryID" />
      </xs:keyref>
    </xs:element>
```

(continued)

(continued)

```
    </xs:schema>
    <Products>
      <Name>HL Road Frame - Black, 58</Name>
      <StandardCost>1059.3100</StandardCost>
      <ProductCategoryID>18</ProductCategoryID>
    </Products>
    <Products>
      <Name>HL Road Frame - Red, 58</Name>
      <StandardCost>1059.3100</StandardCost>
      <ProductCategoryID>18</ProductCategoryID>
    </Products>
  </XMLProducts>
```

The schema includes both DataTables that were in the DataSet. In addition, the data includes all of the data from both tables. For the sake of brevity, only the first Products and ProductCategory records are shown here. As before, you could have saved just the schema or just the data by passing in the correct XmlWriteMode parameter.

Converting XML to ADO.NET Data

Suppose that you have an XML document that you would like to get into an ADO.NET DataSet. You would want to do this so that you could load the XML into a database, or perhaps bind the data to a .NET data control such as a DataGrid. This way, you could actually use the XML document as your data store and eliminate the overhead of the database altogether. If your data is reasonably small in size, this is an attractive possibility. Here is some code to get you started (ADOSample5):

```
private void button7_Click(object sender, EventArgs e)
{
//create the DataSet
DataSet ds = new DataSet("XMLProducts");
//read in the xml document
ds.ReadXml("Products.xml");
//load data into grid
dataGridView1.DataSource = ds.Tables[0];
        textBox1.Text = "";
foreach (DataTable dt in ds.Tables)
{
            textBox1.Text += dt.TableName + "\r\n";
foreach (DataColumn col in dt.Columns)
{
textBox1.Text += "\t" + col.ColumnName + " - " + col.DataType.FullName + "\r\n";
}
}
}
```

It is that easy. You instantiate a new DataSet object. Then you call the ReadXml() method, and you have XML in a DataTable in your DataSet. As with the WriteXml() methods, ReadXml() has an XmlReadMode parameter. ReadXml() has a few more options in the XmlReadMode, as shown in the following table.

Value	Description
Auto	Sets the `XmlReadMode` to the most appropriate setting. If the data is in `DiffGram` format, `DiffGram` is selected. If a schema has already been read, or an inline schema is detected, then `ReadSchema` is selected. If no schema has been assigned to the `DataSet`, and none is detected inline, then `IgnoreSchema` is selected.
DiffGram	Reads in the `DiffGram` and applies the changes to the `DataSet`.
Fragment	Reads documents that contain XDR schema fragments, such as the type created by SQL Server.
IgnoreSchema	Ignores any inline schema that may be found. Reads data into the current `DataSet` schema. If data does not match `DataSet` schema, it is discarded.
InferSchema	Ignores any inline schema. Creates the schema based on data in the XML document. If a schema exists in the `DataSet`, that schema is used, and extended with additional columns and tables if needed. An exception is thrown if a column exists but is of a different data type.
ReadSchema	Reads the inline schema and loads the data. Will not overwrite a schema in the `DataSet` but will throw an exception if a table in the inline schema already exists in the `DataSet`.

There is also the `ReadXmlSchema()` method. This reads in a standalone schema and creates the tables, columns, and relations. You use this if your schema is not inline with your data. `ReadXmlSchema()` has the same four overloads: a string with file and path name, a `Stream`-based object, a `TextReader`-based object, and an `XmlReader`-based object.

To show that the data tables are getting created properly we iterate through the tables and columns and display the names in the text box. You can compare this to the database and see that all is well. The last foreach loops perform this task.

Figure 28-6 shows the output.

Looking at the list box, you can check that the data tables were created with the columns all having the correct names and data types.

Something else you might want to note is that because the previous two examples didn't transfer any data to or from a database, no `SqlDataAdapter` or `SqlConnection` was defined. This shows the real flexibility of both the `System.Xml` namespace and ADO.NET: You can look at the same data in multiple formats. If you need to do a transform and show the data in HTML format, or if you need to bind the data to a grid, you can take the same data and, with just a method call, have it in the required format.

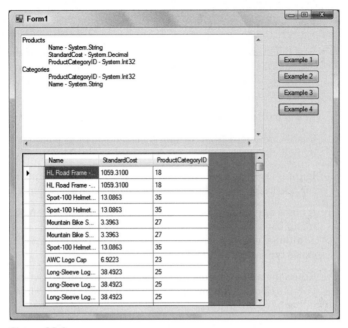

Figure 28-6

Serializing Objects in XML

Serializing is the process of persisting an object to disk. Another part of your application, or even a separate application, can deserialize the object and it will be in the same state it was in prior to serialization. The .NET Framework includes a couple of ways to do this.

This section looks at the `System.Xml.Serialization` namespace, which contains classes used to serialize objects into XML documents or streams. This means that an object's public properties and public fields are converted into XML elements or attributes or both.

The most important class in the `System.Xml.Serialization` namespace is `XmlSerializer`. To serialize an object, you first need to instantiate an `XmlSerializer` object, specifying the type of the object to serialize. Then you need to instantiate a stream/writer object to write the file to a stream/document. The final step is to call the `Serialize()` method on the `XMLSerializer`, passing it the stream/writer object and the object to serialize.

Data that can be serialized can be primitive types, fields, arrays, and embedded XML in the form of `XmlElement` and `XmlAttribute` objects.

To deserialize an object from an XML document, you reverse the process in the previous example. You create a stream/reader and an `XmlSerializer` object and then pass the stream/reader to the `Deserialize()` method. This method returns the deserialized object, although it needs to be cast to the correct type.

The XML serializer cannot convert private data, only public data, and it cannot serialize object graphs.

However, these should not be serious limitations; by carefully designing your classes, they should be easily avoided. If you do need to be able to serialize public and private data as well as an object graph containing many nested objects, you will want to use the `System.Runtime.Serialization.Formatters.Binary` namespace.

Some of the other tasks that you can accomplish with System.Xml.Serialization classes are:

❑ Determine if the data should be an attribute or element

❑ Specify the namespace

❑ Change the attribute or element name

The links between your object and the XML document are the custom C# attributes that annotate your classes. These attributes are what are used to inform the serializer how to write out the data. The xsd .exe tool, which is included with the .NET Framework, can help create these attributes for you. xsd.exe can do the following:

❑ Generate an XML schema from an XDR schema file

❑ Generate an XML schema from an XML file

❑ Generate DataSet classes from an XSD schema file

❑ Generate runtime classes that have the custom attributes for XmlSerialization

❑ Generate an XSD file from classes that you have already developed

❑ Limit which elements are created in code

❑ Determine which programming language the generated code should be in (C#, Visual Basic .NET, or JScript .NET)

❑ Create schemas from types in compiled assemblies

You should refer to the framework documentation for details of command-line options for xsd.exe.

Despite these capabilities, you don't *have* to use xsd.exe to create the classes for serialization. The process is quite simple. The following is a simple application that serializes a class. At the beginning of the example, you have very simple code that creates a new Product object, pd, and fills it with some data:

```
private void button1_Click(object sender, EventArgs e)
{
  //new products object
  Product pd = new Product();
  //set some properties
  pd.ProductID = 200;
  pd.CategoryID = 100;
  pd.Discontinued = false;
  pd.ProductName = "Serialize Objects";
  pd.QuantityPerUnit = "6";
  pd.ReorderLevel = 1;
  pd.SupplierID = 1;
  pd.UnitPrice = 1000;
  pd.UnitsInStock = 10;
  pd.UnitsOnOrder = 0;


}
```

The Serialize() method of the XmlSerializer class actually performs the serialization, and it has nine overloads. One of the parameters required is a stream to write the data to. It can be a Stream, TextWriter, or an XmlWriter parameter. In the example, you create a TextWriter-based object, tr. The next thing to do is to create the XmlSerializer-based object, sr. The XmlSerializer needs to know type information for the object that it is serializing, so you use the typeof keyword with the type that is to be serialized. After the sr object is created, you call the Serialize() method, passing in the `tr` (`Stream`-based object) and the object that you want serialized, in this case `pd`. Be sure to close the stream when you are finished with it:

```
//new TextWriter and XmlSerializer
TextWriter tr = new StreamWriter("serialprod.xml");
XmlSerializer sr = new XmlSerializer(typeof(Product));
//serialize object
sr.Serialize(tr, pd);
tr.Close();
webBrowser1.Navigate(AppDomain.CurrentDomain.BaseDirectory + "serialprod.xml");
```

Next is the `Product` class, the class to be serialized. The only differences between this and any other class that you may write are the C# attributes that have been added. The `XmlRootAttribute` and `XmlElementAttribute` classes in the attributes inherit from the `System.Attribute` class. Don't confuse these attributes with the attributes in an XML document. A C# attribute is simply some declarative information that can be retrieved at runtime by the CLR (see Chapter 7, "Delegates and Events," for more details). In this case, the attributes describe how the object should be serialized:

```
//class that will be serialized.
//attributes determine how object is serialized
[System.Xml.Serialization.XmlRootAttribute()]
  public class Product {
     private int prodId;
     private string prodName;
     private int suppId;
     private int catId;
     private string qtyPerUnit;
     private Decimal unitPrice;
     private short unitsInStock;
     private short unitsOnOrder;
     private short reorderLvl;
     private bool discont;
     private int disc;
     //added the Discount attribute
     [XmlAttributeAttribute(AttributeName="Discount")]
     public int Discount {
       get {return disc;}
       set {disc=value;}
     }
     [XmlElementAttribute()]
     public int   ProductID {
       get {return prodId;}
       set {prodId=value;}
     }
     [XmlElementAttribute()]
     public string ProductName {
       get {return prodName;}
       set {prodName=value;}
     }
     [XmlElementAttribute()]
     public int SupplierID {
       get {return suppId;}
       set {suppId=value;}
     }
     [XmlElementAttribute()]
```

```
        public int CategoryID {
          get {return catId;}
          set {catId=value;}
        }
        [XmlElementAttribute()]
        public string QuantityPerUnit {
          get {return qtyPerUnit;}
          set {qtyPerUnit=value;}
        }
        [XmlElementAttribute()]
        public Decimal UnitPrice {
          get {return unitPrice;}
          set {unitPrice=value;}
        }
        [XmlElementAttribute()]
        public short UnitsInStock {
          get {return unitsInStock;}
          set {unitsInStock=value;}
        }
        [XmlElementAttribute()]
        public short UnitsOnOrder {
          get {return unitsOnOrder;}
          set {unitsOnOrder=value;}
        }
        [XmlElementAttribute()]
        public short ReorderLevel {
          get {return reorderLvl;}
          set {reorderLvl=value;}
        }
        [XmlElementAttribute()]
        public bool Discontinued {
          get {return discont;}
          set {discont=value;}
        }
        public override string ToString()
        {
          StringBuilder outText = new StringBuilder();
          outText.Append(prodId);
          outText.Append(" ");
          outText.Append(prodName);
          outText.Append(" ");
          outText.Append(unitPrice);
          return outText.ToString();
        }
    }
```

The XmlRootAttribute() invocation in the attribute above the Products class definition identifies this class as a root element (in the XML file produced upon serialization). The attribute containing XmlElementAttribute() identifies that the member below the attribute represents an XML element.

You will also notice that the ToString() method has been overridden. This provides the string that the message box will show when you run the deserialize example.

If you take a look at the XML document created during serialization, you will see that it looks like any other XML document that you might have created, which is the point of the exercise:

```
<?xml version="1.0" encoding="utf-8"?>
<Products xmlns:xsi=http://www.w3.org/2001/XMLSchema-instance
                    xmlns:xsd="http://www.w3.org/2001/XMLSchema"
Discount="0">
  <ProductID>200</ProductID>
  <ProductName>Serialize Objects</ProductName>
  <SupplierID>1</SupplierID>
  <CategoryID>100</CategoryID>
  <QuantityPerUnit>6</QuantityPerUnit>
  <UnitPrice>1000</UnitPrice>
  <UnitsInStock>10</UnitsInStock>
  <UnitsOnOrder>0</UnitsOnOrder>
  <ReorderLevel>1</ReorderLevel>
  <Discontinued>false</Discontinued>
</Products>
```

There is nothing out of the ordinary here. You could use this any way that you would use an XML document. You could transform it and display it as HTML, load it into a `DataSet` using ADO.NET, load an `XmlDocument` with it, or, as you can see in the example, deserialize it and create an object in the same state that pd was in prior to serializing it (which is exactly what you're doing with the second button).

Next, you add another button event handler to deserialize a new `Products`-based object, `newPd`. This time you use a `FileStream` object to read in the XML:

```
private void button2_Click(object sender, EventArgs e)
    {
        //create a reference to producst type
        Product newPd;
        //new filestream to open serialized object
        FileStream f = new FileStream("serialprod.xml", FileMode.Open);
```

Once again, you create a new `XmlSerializer`, passing in the type information of `Product`. You can then make the call to the `Deserialize()` method. Note that you still need to do an explicit cast when you create the `newPd` object. At this point, `newPd` is in exactly the same state that pd was:

```
        //new serializer
        XmlSerializer newSr = new XmlSerializer(typeof(Product));
        //deserialize the object
        newPd = (Product)newSr.Deserialize(f);
        f.Close();
        MessageBox.Show(newPd.ToString());
    }
```

The message box should show you the product ID, product name, and the unit price of the object you just deserialized. This comes from the `ToString()` override that you implemented in the `Product` class.

What about situations where you have derived classes and possibly properties that return an array? `XmlSerializer` has that covered as well. Here's a slightly more complex example that deals with these issues.

First, you define three new classes, `Product`, `BookProduct` (derived from `Product`), and `Inventory` (which contains both of the other classes). Notice that once again you have overridden the `ToString()` method. This time you're just going to list the items in the `Inventory` class:

```
public class BookProduct : Product
{
    private string isbnNum;
```

```
      public BookProduct() {}
      public string ISBN
      {
         get {return isbnNum;}
         set {isbnNum=value;}
      }
   }
public class Inventory
{
      private Product[] stuff;
      public Inventory() {}
      //need to have an attribute entry for each data type
      [XmlArrayItem("Prod",typeof(Product)),
      XmlArrayItem("Book",typeof(BookProduct))]
      public Product[] InventoryItems
      {
         get {return stuff;}
         set {stuff=value;}
      }
      public override string ToString()
      {
        StringBuilder outText = new StringBuilder();
        foreach (Product prod in stuff)
        {
          outText.Append(prod.ProductName);
          outText.Append("\r\n");
        }
        return outText.ToString();
      }
}
```

The `Inventory` class is the one of interest here. If you are to serialize this class, you need to insert an attribute containing `XmlArrayItem` constructors for each type that can be added to the array. You should note that `XmlArrayItem` is the name of the .NET attribute represented by the `XmlArrayItemAttribute` class.

The first parameter supplied to these constructors is what you would like the element name to be in the XML document that is created during serialization. If you leave off the `ElementName` parameter, the elements will be given the same name as the object type (`Product` and `BookProduct` in this case). The second parameter that must be specified is the type of the object.

There is also an `XmlArrayAttribute` class that you would use if the property were returning an array of objects or primitive types. Because you are returning different types in the array, you use `XmlArrayItemAttribute`, which allows the higher level of control.

In the `button4_Click()` event handler, you create a new `Product` object and a new `BookProduct` object (`newProd` and `newBook`). You add data to the various properties of each object, and add the objects to a `Product` array. You then create a new `Inventory` object and pass in the array as a parameter. You can then serialize the `Inventory` object to recreate it at a later time:

```
   private void button4_Click(object sender, EventArgs e)
   {
     //create the XmlAttributes boject
     XmlAttributes attrs = new XmlAttributes();
     //add the types of the objects that will be serialized
     attrs.XmlElements.Add(new XmlElementAttribute("Book", typeof(BookProduct)));
```

(continued)

961

(continued)

```
        attrs.XmlElements.Add(new XmlElementAttribute("Product", typeof(Product)));
        XmlAttributeOverrides attrOver = new XmlAttributeOverrides();
        //add to the attributes collection
        attrOver.Add(typeof(Inventory), "InventoryItems", attrs);
        //create the Product and Book objects
        Product newProd = new Product();
        BookProduct newBook = new BookProduct();
        newProd.ProductID = 100;
        newProd.ProductName = "Product Thing";
        newProd.SupplierID = 10;
        newBook.ProductID = 101;
        newBook.ProductName = "How to Use Your New Product Thing";
        newBook.SupplierID = 10;
        newBook.ISBN = "123456789";
        Product[] addProd ={ newProd, newBook };
        Inventory inv = new Inventory();
        inv.InventoryItems = addProd;
        TextWriter tr = new StreamWriter("inventory.xml");
        XmlSerializer sr = new XmlSerializer(typeof(Inventory), attrOver);
        sr.Serialize(tr, inv);
        tr.Close();
        webBrowser1.Navigate(AppDomain.CurrentDomain.BaseDirectory + "inventory.xml");
    }
    }
```

The XML document looks like this:

```
<?xml version="1.0" encoding="utf-8"?>
<Inventory xmlns:xsi="http://www.w3.org/2001/XMLSchema-instance"
xmlns:xsd="http://www.w3.org/2001/XMLSchema">
  <Product Discount="0">
    <ProductID>100</ProductID>
    <ProductName>Product Thing</ProductName>
    <SupplierID>10</SupplierID>
    <CategoryID>0</CategoryID>
    <UnitPrice>0</UnitPrice>
    <UnitsInStock>0</UnitsInStock>
    <UnitsOnOrder>0</UnitsOnOrder>
    <ReorderLevel>0</ReorderLevel>
    <Discontinued>false</Discontinued>
  </Product>
  <Book Discount="0">
    <ProductID>101</ProductID>
    <ProductName>How to Use Your New Product Thing</ProductName>
    <SupplierID>10</SupplierID>
    <CategoryID>0</CategoryID>
    <UnitPrice>0</UnitPrice>
    <UnitsInStock>0</UnitsInStock>
    <UnitsOnOrder>0</UnitsOnOrder>
    <ReorderLevel>0</ReorderLevel>
    <Discontinued>false</Discontinued>
    <ISBN>123456789</ISBN>
  </Book>
</Inventory>
```

The `button2_Click()` event handler implements deserialization of the `Inventory` object. Note that you iterate through the array in the newly created `newInv` object to show that it is the same data:

```
private void button2_Click(object sender, System.EventArgs e)
{
    Inventory newInv;
    FileStream f=new FileStream("order.xml",FileMode.Open);
    XmlSerializer newSr=new XmlSerializer(typeof(Inventory));
    newInv=(Inventory)newSr.Deserialize(f);
    foreach(Product prod in newInv.InventoryItems)
        listBox1.Items.Add(prod.ProductName);
    f.Close();
}
```

Serialization Without Source Code Access

Well, this all works great, but what if you don't have access to the source code for the types that are being serialized? You can't add the attribute if you don't have the source. There is another way. You can use the `XmlAttributes` class and the `XmlAttributeOverrides` class. Together these classes enable you to accomplish exactly what you have just done, but without adding the attributes. This section looks at an example of how this works.

For this example, imagine that the `Inventory`, `Product`, and derived `BookProduct` classes are in a separate DLL and that you don't have the source. The `Product` and `BookProduct` classes are the same as in the previous example, but you should note that there are now no attributes added to the `Inventory` class:

```
public class Inventory
{
    private Product[] stuff;
    public Inventory() {}
    public Product[] InventoryItems
    {
        get {return stuff;}
        set {stuff=value;}
    }
}
```

Next, you deal with the serialization in the `button1_Click()` event handler:

```
private void button1_Click(object sender, System.EventArgs e)
{
```

The first step in the serialization process is to create an `XmlAttributes` object and an `XmlElementAttribute` object for each data type that you will be overriding:

```
XmlAttributes attrs=new XmlAttributes();
attrs.XmlElements.Add(new XmlElementAttribute("Book",typeof(BookProduct)));
attrs.XmlElements.Add(new XmlElementAttribute("Product",typeof(Product)));
```

Here you can see that you are adding new `XmlElementAttribute` objects to the `XmlElements` collection of the `XmlAttributes` class. The `XmlAttributes` class has properties that correspond to the attributes that can be applied; `XmlArray` and `XmlArrayItems`, which you looked at in the previous example, are just a couple of these. You now have an `XmlAttributes` object with two `XmlElementAttribute`-based objects added to the `XmlElements` collection.

The next thing you have to do is create an `XmlAttributeOverrides` object:

```
XmlAttributeOverrides attrOver=new XmlAttributeOverrides();
attrOver.Add(typeof(Inventory),"InventoryItems",attrs);
```

The `Add()` method of this class has two overloads. The first one takes the type information of the object to override and the `XmlAttributes` object that you created earlier. The other overload, which is the one you are using, also takes a string value that is the member in the overridden object. In this case, you want to override the `InventoryItems` member in the `Inventory` class.

When you create the `XmlSerializer` object, you add the `XmlAttributeOverrides` object as a parameter. Now the `XmlSerializer` knows which types you want to override and what you need to return for those types:

```
//create the Product and Book objects
Product newProd=new Product();
BookProduct newBook=new BookProduct();
newProd.ProductID=100;
newProd.ProductName="Product Thing";
newProd.SupplierID=10;
newBook.ProductID=101;
newBook.ProductName="How to Use Your New Product Thing";
newBook.SupplierID=10;
newBook.ISBN="123456789";
Product[] addProd={newProd,newBook};

Inventory inv=new Inventory();
inv.InventoryItems=addProd;
TextWriter tr=new StreamWriter("inventory.xml");
XmlSerializer sr=new XmlSerializer(typeof(Inventory),attrOver);
sr.Serialize(tr,inv);
tr.Close();
}
```

If you execute the `Serialize()` method, you get this XML output:

```
<?xml version="1.0" encoding="utf-8"?>
<Inventory xmlns:xsi="http://www.w3.org/2001/XMLSchema-instance"
xmlns:xsd="http://www.w3.org/2001/XMLSchema">
  <Product Discount="0">
    <ProductID>100</ProductID>
    <ProductName>Product Thing</ProductName>
    <SupplierID>10</SupplierID>
    <CategoryID>0</CategoryID>
    <UnitPrice>0</UnitPrice>
    <UnitsInStock>0</UnitsInStock>
    <UnitsOnOrder>0</UnitsOnOrder>
    <ReorderLevel>0</ReorderLevel>
    <Discontinued>false</Discontinued>
  </Product>
  <Book Discount="0">
    <ProductID>101</ProductID>
    <ProductName>How to Use Your New Product Thing</ProductName>
    <SupplierID>10</SupplierID>
    <CategoryID>0</CategoryID>
    <UnitPrice>0</UnitPrice>
    <UnitsInStock>0</UnitsInStock>
```

```
            <UnitsOnOrder>0</UnitsOnOrder>
            <ReorderLevel>0</ReorderLevel>
            <Discontinued>false</Discontinued>
            <ISBN>123456789</ISBN>
        </Book>
    </Inventory>
```

As you can see, you get the same XML as you did with the earlier example. To deserialize this object and recreate the `Inventory`-based object that you started out with, you need to create all of the same `XmlAttributes`, `XmlElementAttribute`, and `XmlAttributeOverrides` objects that you created when you serialized the object. Once you do that, you can read in the XML and recreate the `Inventory` object just as you did before. Here is the code to deserialize the `Inventory` object:

```
private void button2_Click(object sender, System.EventArgs e)
{
    //create the new XmlAttributes collection
    XmlAttributes attrs=new XmlAttributes();
    //add the type information to the elements collection
    attrs.XmlElements.Add(new XmlElementAttribute("Book",typeof(BookProduct)));
    attrs.XmlElements.Add(new XmlElementAttribute("Product",typeof(Product)));

    XmlAttributeOverrides attrOver=new XmlAttributeOverrides();
    //add to the Attributes collection
    attrOver.Add(typeof(Inventory),"InventoryItems",attrs);

    //need a new Inventory object to deserialize to
    Inventory newInv;

    //deserialize and load data into the listbox from deserialized object
    FileStream f=new FileStream("..\\..\\..\\inventory.xml",FileMode.Open);
    XmlSerializer newSr=new XmlSerializer(typeof(Inventory),attrOver);

    newInv=(Inventory)newSr.Deserialize(f);
    if(newInv!=null)
    {
        foreach(Product prod in newInv.InventoryItems)
        {
            listBox1.Items.Add(prod.ProductName);
        }
    }
    f.Close();
}
```

Note that the first few lines of code are identical to the code you used to serialize the object.

The `System.Xml.XmlSerialization` namespace provides a very powerful tool set for serializing objects to XML. By serializing and deserializing objects to XML instead of to binary format, you are given the option of doing something else with this XML, greatly adding to the flexibility of your designs.

Summary

In this chapter, you explored many aspects of the `System.Xml` namespace of the .NET Framework. You looked at how to read and write XML documents using the very fast `XmlReader`- and `XmlWriter`-based classes. You looked at how the DOM is implemented in .NET and how to use the power of DOM. You saw that XML and ADO.NET are indeed very closely related. A `DataSet` and an XML document are just two different views of the same underlying architecture. And, of course, you visited XPath and XSL transforms and the debugging features added to Visual Studio.

Finally, you serialized objects to XML and were able to bring them back with just a couple of method calls.

XML will be an important part of your application development for years to come. The .NET Framework has made available a very rich and powerful toolset for working with XML. The next chapter will delve into using LINQ with XML.

29

LINQ to XML

As stated in Chapter 27, "LINQ to SQL," probably the biggest and most exciting addition to the .NET Framework 3.5 is the addition of the .NET Language Integrated Query framework (LINQ) into C# 2008. LINQ comes in many flavors depending on the final data store that you are working with in querying your data. Chapter 27 took a look at using LINQ to SQL to query SQL Server databases; this chapter takes a quick look at using LINQ to query your XML data sources instead.

You read about the following in this chapter:

❑   What LINQ to XML brings to the table

❑   The new objects available in the `System.Xml.Linq` namespace

❑   How to query your XML documents using LINQ

❑   Moving around your XML documents using LINQ

❑   Using LINQ to SQL and LINQ to XML together

Extensible Markup Language (XML) is now in widespread use. Many applications on the Internet or residing on individual computers use some form of XML to run or manage the processes of an application. Earlier books about XML commented that XML was to be the "next big thing." Now, it *is* "the big thing." In fact, there really isn't anything bigger.

Microsoft has been working for years to make using XML in the .NET world as easy as possible. You can't help but notice the additional capability and the enhancements to XML usage introduced in each new version of the .NET Framework. In fact, Bill Gates highlighted Microsoft's faith in XML in his keynote address at the Microsoft Professional Developers Conference in 2005 in Los Angeles. He stated that XML is being pushed deeper and deeper into the Windows core each year. If you look around the .NET Framework, you will probably agree.

For this reason, this chapter focuses on using LINQ to XML to query your XML documents. Figure 29-1 shows LINQ's place in querying XML data.

Much of what you learned in the chapter on using LINQ to SQL can be applied here when working with LINQ to XML.

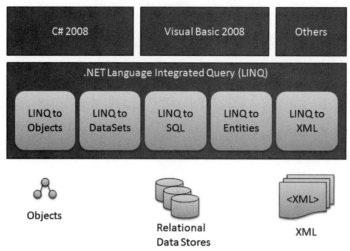

Figure 29-1

LINQ to XML and .NET 3.5

With the introduction of LINQ to the .NET Framework 3.5, the focus was on easy access to the data that you want to work with in your applications. One of the main data stores in the application space is XML and, therefore, it really was considered a no-brainer to create the LINQ to XML implementation.

Prior to the LINQ to XML release, working with XML using System.Xml was really not the easiest thing in the world to achieve. With the inclusion of System.Xml.Linq, you now find a series of capabilities that make the process of working with XML in your code that much easier.

New Objects for Creating XML Documents

In creating XML within application code, many developers turned to the XmlDocument object to do this job. This object allows you to create XML documents that enable you to append elements, attributes, and other items in a hierarchical fashion. With LINQ to XML and the inclusion of the new System.Xml.Linq namespace, you will now find some new objects that make the creation of XML documents a much simpler process.

Visual Basic 2008 Ventures Down Another Path

An interesting side note to the LINQ to XML feature set is that the Visual Basic 2008 team at Microsoft actually took the LINQ to XML capabilities a little further in some areas. For instance, something you are unable to accomplish in C# 2008 that you can do in Visual Basic 2008 is include XML as a core part of the language. XML literals are now a true part of the Visual Basic language and you are able to paste XML fragments directly in your code for inclusion, and the XML included is not treated as a string.

Namespaces and Prefixes

One issue that was somewhat ignored in parts of the .NET Framework 2.0 was how the items in the framework dealt with the inclusion of XML namespaces and prefixes in documents. LINQ to XML makes this an important part of the XML story, and you will find the capabilities to work with these types of objects to be quite simple.

New XML Objects from the .NET Framework 3.5

Even if the LINQ querying ability wasn't available in this release of the .NET Framework, the new XML objects provided by the .NET Framework 3.5 to work with the XML that are available in place of working directly with the DOM in this release are so good, that they even can stand on their own outside of LINQ. Within the new `System.Xml.Linq` namespace you will find a series of new LINQ to XML helper objects that make working with an XML document in memory that much easier.

The following sections work through the new objects that are available to you within this new namespace.

Many of the examples in this chapter use a file called `Hamlet.xml`. *This is a file you can find at* `http://metalab.unc.edu/bosak/xml/eg/shaks200.zip` *that includes all of Shakespeare's plays as XML files.*

XDocument

The `XDocument` is a replacement of the `XmlDocument` object from the pre-.NET 3.5 world. You will find the `XDocument` object easier to work with in dealing with XML documents. The `XDocument` object works with the other new objects in this space, such as the `XNamespace`, `XComment`, `XElement`, and `XAttribute` objects.

One of the more important members of the `XDocument` object is the `Load()` method:

```
XDocument xdoc = XDocument.Load(@"C:\Hamlet.xml");
```

This operation will load up the `Hamlet.xml` contents as an in-memory `XDocument` object. You are also able to pass a `TextReader` or `XmlReader` object into the `Load()` method. From here, you are able to programmatically work with the XML:

```
XDocument xdoc = XDocument.Load(@"C:\Hamlet.xml");
Console.WriteLine(xdoc.Root.Name.ToString());
Console.WriteLine(xdoc.Root.HasAttributes.ToString());
```

This produces the following results:

```
PLAY
False
```

Another important member to be aware of is the `Save()` method, which, similar to the `Load()` method, allows you to save to a physical disk location or to a `TextWriter` or `XmlWriter` object:

```
XDocument xdoc = XDocument.Load(@"C:\Hamlet.xml");

xdoc.Save(@"C:\CopyOfHamlet.xml");
```

XElement

One of the more common objects that you will work with is the `XElement` object. With these objects, you are easily able to create just single-element objects that are XML documents themselves and even just fragments of XML. For instance, here is an example of writing an XML element with a corresponding value:

```
XElement xe = new XElement("Company", "Lipper");
Console.WriteLine(xe.ToString());
```

In the creation of a new XElement object, you are able to define the name of the element as well as the value used in the element. In this case, the name of the element will be <Company>, and the value of the <Company> element will be Lipper. Running this in a console application with a System.Xml.Linq reference produces the following result:

```
<Company>Lipper</Company>
```

You are able to create an even more complete XML document using multiple XElement objects, as illustrated in the following example:

```
using System;
using System.Linq;
using System.Xml.Linq;

namespace ConsoleApplication1
{
    class Class1
    {
        static void Main()
        {
            XElement xe = new XElement("Company",
                new XElement("CompanyName", "Lipper"),
                new XElement("CompanyAddress",
                    new XElement("Address", "123 Main Street"),
                    new XElement("City", "St. Louis"),
                    new XElement("State", "MO"),
                    new XElement("Country", "USA")));

            Console.WriteLine(xe.ToString());

            Console.ReadLine();
        }
    }
}
```

Running this application produces the results illustrated in Figure 29-2.

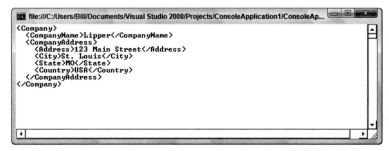

Figure 29-2

XNamespace

The XNamespace is an object that represents an XML namespace and is easily applied to elements within your document. For example, you can take the previous example and easily apply a namespace to the root element:

```
using System;
using System.Linq;
using System.Xml.Linq;

namespace ConsoleApplication1
{
    class Class1
    {
        static void Main()
        {
            XNamespace ns = "http://www.lipperweb.com/ns/1";

            XElement xe = new XElement(ns + "Company",
                new XElement("CompanyName", "Lipper"),
                new XElement("CompanyAddress",
                    new XElement("Address", "123 Main Street"),
                    new XElement("City", "St. Louis"),
                    new XElement("State", "MO"),
                    new XElement("Country", "USA")));

            Console.WriteLine(xe.ToString());

            Console.ReadLine();
        }
    }
}
```

In this case, an XNamespace object is created by assigning it a value of http://www.lipperweb.com/ns/1. From there, it is actually used in the root element <Company> with the instantiation of the XElement object:

```
XElement xe = new XElement(ns + "Company", // ...
```

This produces the results illustrated in Figure 29-3.

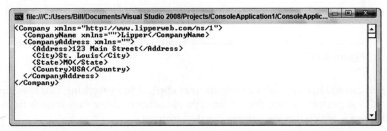

Figure 29-3

In addition to dealing with only the root element, you can also apply namespaces to all your elements as shown in the following example:

```
using System;
using System.Linq;
using System.Xml.Linq;

namespace ConsoleApplication1
{
    class Class1
    {
        static void Main()
        {
            XNamespace ns1 = "http://www.lipperweb.com/ns/root";
            XNamespace ns2 = "http://www.lipperweb.com/ns/sub";

            XElement xe = new XElement(ns1 + "Company",
                new XElement(ns2 + "CompanyName", "Lipper"),
                new XElement(ns2 + "CompanyAddress",
                    new XElement(ns2 + "Address", "123 Main Street"),
                    new XElement(ns2 + "City", "St. Louis"),
                    new XElement(ns2 + "State", "MO"),
                    new XElement(ns2 + "Country", "USA")));

            Console.WriteLine(xe.ToString());

            Console.ReadLine();
        }
    }
}
```

This produces the results shown in Figure 29-4.

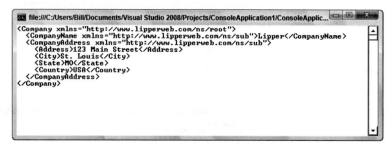

Figure 29-4

In this case, you can see that the sub-namespace was applied to everything you specified except for the <Address>, <City>, <State>, and the <Country> elements because they inherit from their parent, <CompanyAddress>, which has the namespace declaration.

XComment

The XComment object allows you to easily add XML comments to your XML documents. The following example shows adding a comment to the top of the document:

```
using System;
using System.Linq;
using System.Xml.Linq;

namespace ConsoleApplication1
{
    class Class1
    {
        static void Main(string[] args)
        {
            XDocument xdoc = new XDocument();

            XComment xc = new XComment("Here is a comment.");
            xdoc.Add(xc);

            XElement xe = new XElement("Company",
                new XElement("CompanyName", "Lipper"),
                new XElement("CompanyAddress",
                    new XComment("Here is another comment."),
                    new XElement("Address", "123 Main Street"),
                    new XElement("City", "St. Louis"),
                    new XElement("State", "MO"),
                    new XElement("Country", "USA")));
            xdoc.Add(xe);

            Console.WriteLine(xdoc.ToString());

            Console.ReadLine();
        }
    }
}
```

Here, an XDocument object that contains two XML comments is written to the console, one at the top of the document and another within the <CompanyAddress> element. The output of this is presented in Figure 29-5.

Figure 29-5

XAttribute

In addition to elements, another important factor of XML is attributes. Adding and working with attributes is done through the use of the XAttribute object. The following example shows adding an attribute to the root <Customers> node:

```
using System;
using System.Linq;
using System.Xml.Linq;

namespace ConsoleApplication1
{
    class Class1
    {
        static void Main()
        {
            XElement xe = new XElement("Company",
                new XAttribute("MyAttribute", "MyAttributeValue"),
                new XElement("CompanyName", "Lipper"),
                new XElement("CompanyAddress",
                    new XElement("Address", "123 Main Street"),
                    new XElement("City", "St. Louis"),
                    new XElement("State", "MO"),
                    new XElement("Country", "USA")));

            Console.WriteLine(xe.ToString());

            Console.ReadLine();
        }
    }
}
```

Here, the attribute MyAttribute with a value of MyAttributeValue is added to the root element of the XML document, producing the results shown in Figure 29-6.

Figure 29-6

Using LINQ to Query XML Documents

Now that you can get your XML documents into an XDocument object and work with the various parts of this document, you can also use LINQ to XML to query your XML documents and work with the results.

Querying Static XML Documents

You will notice that querying a static XML document using LINQ to XML takes almost no work at all. The following example makes use of the hamlet.xml file and queries to get all the players (actors) that appear in the play. Each one of these players is defined in the XML document with the <PERSONA> element:

```
using System;
using System.Linq;
using System.Xml.Linq;

namespace ConsoleApplication1
{
    class Class1
    {
        static void Main(string[] args)
        {
            XDocument xdoc = XDocument.Load(@"C:\hamlet.xml");

            var query = from people in xdoc.Descendants("PERSONA")
                        select people.Value;

            Console.WriteLine("{0} Players Found", query.Count());
            Console.WriteLine();

            foreach (var item in query)
            {
                Console.WriteLine(item);
            }

            Console.ReadLine();
        }
    }
}
```

In this case, an XDocument object loads up a physical XML file (hamlet.xml) and then performs a LINQ query over the contents of the document:

```
var query = from people in xdoc.Descendants("PERSONA")
            select people.Value;
```

The people object is an object that is a representation of all the <PERSONA> elements found in the document. Then the select statement gets at the values of these elements. From there, a Console .WriteLine() method is used to write out a count of all the players found using query.Count(). Then, each of the items is written to the screen in a foreach loop. The results you should see are presented here:

```
26 Players Found

CLAUDIUS, king of Denmark.
HAMLET, son to the late king, and nephew to the present king.
POLONIUS, lord chamberlain.
HORATIO, friend to Hamlet.
LAERTES, son to Polonius.
LUCIANUS, nephew to the king.
```

(continued)

(continued)

```
VOLTIMAND
CORNELIUS
ROSENCRANTZ
GUILDENSTERN
OSRIC
A Gentleman
A Priest.
MARCELLUS
BERNARDO
FRANCISCO, a soldier.
REYNALDO, servant to Polonius.
Players.
Two Clowns, grave-diggers.
FORTINBRAS, prince of Norway.
A Captain.
English Ambassadors.
GERTRUDE, queen of Denmark, and mother to Hamlet.
OPHELIA, daughter to Polonius.
Lords, Ladies, Officers, Soldiers, Sailors, Messengers, and other Attendants.
Ghost of Hamlet's Father.
```

Querying Dynamic XML Documents

A lot of dynamic XML documents are available on the Internet these days. You will find blog feeds, podcast feeds, and more that provide an XML document by sending a request to a specific URL endpoint. These feeds can be viewed either in the browser, through an RSS-aggregator, or as pure XML.

```csharp
using System;
using System.Linq;
using System.Xml.Linq;

namespace ConsoleApplication1
{
    class Class1
    {
        static void Main()
        {
            XDocument xdoc =
                XDocument.Load(@"http://geekswithblogs.net/evjen/Rss.aspx");

            var query = from rssFeed in xdoc.Descendants("channel")
                        select new
                        {
                          Title = rssFeed.Element("title").Value,
                          Description = rssFeed.Element("description").Value,
                          Link = rssFeed.Element("link").Value,
                        };

            foreach (var item in query)
            {
                Console.WriteLine("TITLE: " + item.Title);
                Console.WriteLine("DESCRIPTION: " + item.Description);
                Console.WriteLine("LINK: " + item.Link);
            }
```

```
        Console.WriteLine();

        var queryPosts = from myPosts in xdoc.Descendants("item")
                         select new
                         {
                             Title = myPosts.Element("title").Value,
                             Published =
                                 DateTime.Parse(
                                     myPosts.Element("pubDate").Value),
                             Description =
                                 myPosts.Element("description").Value,
                             Url = myPosts.Element("link").Value,
                             Comments = myPosts.Element("comments").Value
                         };

        foreach (var item in queryPosts)
        {
            Console.WriteLine(item.Title);
        }

        Console.ReadLine();
    }
  }
}
```

Looking at this code, you can see that the Load() method off of the XDocument object points to a URL where the XML is retrieved. The first query pulls out all the main sub-elements of the <channel> element in the feed and creates new objects called Title, Description, and Link to get at the values of these sub-elements.

From there, a foreach statement is run to iterate through all the items found in this query. The results are as follows:

```
TITLE: Bill Evjen's Blog
DESCRIPTION: Code, Life and Community
LINK: http://geekswithblogs.net/evjen/Default.aspx
```

The second query works through all the <item> elements and the various sub-elements it has (these are all the blog entries found in the blog). Though a lot of the items found are rolled up into properties, in the foreach loop, only the Title property is used. You will see something similar to the following results from this query:

```
AJAX Control Toolkit Controls Grayed Out - HOW TO FIX
Welcome .NET 3.5!
Visual Studio 2008 Released
IIS 7.0 Rocks the House!
Word Issue - Couldn't Select Text
Microsoft Releases XML Schema Designer CTP1
Silverlight Book
Microsoft Tafiti as a beta
ReSharper on Visual Studio 2008
Windows Vista Updates for Performance and Reliability Issues
New Version of ODP.NET for .NET 2.0 Released as Beta Today
First Review of Professional XML
Go to MIX07 for free!
```

(continued)

(continued)

```
Microsoft Surface and the Future of Home Computing?
Alas my friends - I'm *not* TechEd bound
New Book - Professional VB 2005 with .NET 3.0!
An article showing Oracle and .NET working together
My Latest Book - Professional XML
CISCO VPN Client Software on Windows Vista
Server-Side Excel Generation
Scott Guthrie Gives Short Review of Professional ASP.NET 2.0 SE
Windows Forms Additions in the Next Version of .NET
Tag, I'm It
```

Working Around the XML Document

If you have been working with the XML document, hamlet.xml, you will notice that it is quite large. Querying into the XML document was shown in a couple of ways throughout this chapter, but this next section takes a look at reading and writing to the XML document.

Reading from an XML Document

Earlier you saw just how easy it was to query into an XML document using the LINQ query statements as shown here:

```
var query = from people in xdoc.Descendants("PERSONA")
            select people.Value;
```

This query returned all the players that were found in the document. Using the Element() method of the XDocument object, you can also get at specific values of the XML document that you are working with. For instance, continuing to work with the hamlet.xml document, the following XML fragment shows you how the title is represented in the XML document:

```
<?xml version="1.0"?>

<PLAY>
    <TITLE>The Tragedy of Hamlet, Prince of Denmark</TITLE>

    <!-- XML removed for clarity -->

</PLAY>
```

As you can see, the <TITLE> element is a nested element of the <PLAY> element. You can easily get at the title by using the following bit of code in your console application:

```
XDocument xdoc = XDocument.Load(@"C:\hamlet.xml");

Console.WriteLine(xdoc.Element("PLAY").Element("TITLE").Value);
```

This bit of code will write out the title, The Tragedy of Hamlet, Prince of Denmark, to the console screen. In the code, you were able to work down the hierarchy of the XML document by using two Element() method calls — first calling the <PLAY> element and then the <TITLE> element found nested within the <PLAY> element.

Looking more at the `hamlet.xml` document, you will see a large list of players that are defined with the use of the `<PERSONA>` element:

```xml
<?xml version="1.0"?>

<PLAY>
    <TITLE>The Tragedy of Hamlet, Prince of Denmark</TITLE>

    <!-- XML removed for clarity -->

    <PERSONAE>
        <TITLE>Dramatis Personae</TITLE>

        <PERSONA>CLAUDIUS, king of Denmark. </PERSONA>
        <PERSONA>HAMLET, son to the late king,
         and nephew to the present king.</PERSONA>
        <PERSONA>POLONIUS, lord chamberlain. </PERSONA>
        <PERSONA>HORATIO, friend to Hamlet.</PERSONA>
        <PERSONA>LAERTES, son to Polonius.</PERSONA>
        <PERSONA>LUCIANUS, nephew to the king.</PERSONA>

        <!-- XML removed for clarity -->

    </PERSONAE>

</PLAY>
```

Using this XML document, review the following bit of C# code's use of this XML:

```csharp
XDocument xdoc = XDocument.Load(@"C:\hamlet.xml");

Console.WriteLine(
    xdoc.Element("PLAY").Element("PERSONAE").Element("PERSONA").Value);
```

This bit of code starts at `<PLAY>`, works down to the `<PERSONAE>` element, and then makes use of the `<PERSONA>` element. However, using this will produce the following results:

```
CLAUDIUS, king of Denmark
```

The reason for this is that, although there is a collection of `<PERSONA>` elements, you are dealing only with the first one that is encountered using the `Element().Value` call.

Writing to an XML Document

In addition to reading from an XML document, you can also write to the document just as easily. For instance, if you wanted to change the name of the first player of the Hamlet play file, you could make use of the following code to accomplish this task:

```csharp
using System;
using System.Linq;
using System.Xml.Linq;

namespace ConsoleApplication1
{
    class Class1
    {
        static void Main()
```

(continued)

(continued)

```
            {
                XDocument xdoc = XDocument.Load(@"C:\hamlet.xml");

                xdoc.Element("PLAY").Element("PERSONAE").
                    Element("PERSONA").SetValue("Bill Evjen, king of Denmark");

                Console.WriteLine(xdoc.Element("PLAY").
                    Element("PERSONAE").Element("PERSONA").Value);

                Console.ReadLine();
            }
        }
    }
```

In this case, the first instance of the <PERSONA> element is overwritten with the value of Bill Evjen, king of Denmark using the SetValue() method of the Element() object. After the SetValue() is called and the value is applied to the XML document, the value is then retrieved using the same approach as before. When you run this bit of code, you can indeed see that the value of the first <PERSONA> element has been changed.

Another way to change the document (by adding items to it in this example) is to create the element you want as XElement objects and then add them to the document:

```
using System;
using System.Linq;
using System.Xml.Linq;

namespace ConsoleApplication1
{
    class Class1
    {
        static void Main()
        {
            XDocument xdoc = XDocument.Load(@"C:\hamlet.xml");

            XElement xe = new XElement("PERSONA",
                "Bill Evjen, king of Denmark");

            xdoc.Element("PLAY").Element("PERSONAE").Add(xe);

            var query = from people in xdoc.Descendants("PERSONA")
                        select people.Value;

            Console.WriteLine("{0} Players Found", query.Count());
            Console.WriteLine();

            foreach (var item in query)
            {
                Console.WriteLine(item);
            }

            Console.ReadLine();
        }
    }
}
```

In this case, an `XElement` document is created called `xe`. The construction of `xe` will give you the following XML output:

```
<PERSONA>Bill Evjen, king of Denmark</PERSONA>
```

Then using the `Element().Add()` method from the `XDocument` object, you are able to add the created element:

```
xdoc.Element("PLAY").Element("PERSONAE").Add(xe);
```

Now when you query all the players, you will find that instead of 26 as before, you now have 27 with the new one at the bottom of the list. In addition to `Add()`, you can also use `AddFirst()`, which will do what it says — add it to the beginning of the list instead of the end as is the default.

Using LINQ to SQL with LINQ to XML

When working with LINQ to SQL or LINQ to XML, you are limited to working with the specific data source for which it was designed. In fact, you are able to mix multiple data sources together when working with LINQ. For an example of this, this section uses LINQ to SQL to query the customers in the Northwind database and turn the results pulled into an XML document.

You can find instructions on how to get the Northwind sample database file as well as information on working with LINQ to SQL in Chapter 27.

Setting up the LINQ to SQL Components

The first step for this to work is to add the Northwind SQL Server Express Edition database file to your project. From there, right-click the project to add a new LINQ to SQL class file to your project. Name the file `Northwind.dbml`.

This operation will give you a design surface that you are able to work with. From the Server Explorer, drag and drop tables from the database onto this design surface. You want to drag and drop both the `Customers` and the `Orders` tables onto the design surface. By doing this, you will notice that there is then a relationship established between these two tables. Once to this point, your view in the IDE should look as is illustrated in Figure 29-7.

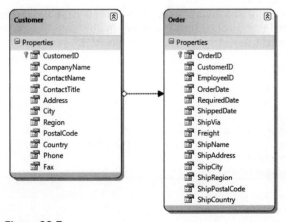

Figure 29-7

Now that you have your `Northwind.dbml` in place, you are ready to query this database structure and output the results as an XML file.

Querying the Database and Outputting XML

The next step in your console application is to put the following code in your `Program.cs` file:

```
using System;
using System.Linq;
using System.Xml.Linq;

namespace ConsoleApplication1
{
    class Class1
    {
        static void Main()
        {
            NorthwindDataContext dc = new NorthwindDataContext();

            XElement xe = new XElement("Customer",
                from c in dc.Customers
                select new XElement("Customer",
                    new XElement("CustomerId", c.CustomerID),
                    new XElement("CompanyName", c.CompanyName),
                    new XElement("Country", c.Country),
                    new XElement("OrderNum", c.Orders.Count)));

            xe.Save(@"C:\myCustomers.xml");
            Console.WriteLine("File created");
            Console.ReadLine();
        }
    }
}
```

This example creates a new instance of the `NorthwindDataContext` object that is created for you automatically with the LINQ to SQL class you created. Then instead of doing the normal

```
var query = [query]
```

you populate the query performed in an `XElement` object called `xe`. Within the select statement of the query, you also create an iteration of `Customers` objects with the nested elements of `<Customer>`, `<CustomerId>`, `<CompanyName>`, `<Country>`, and `<OrderNum>`. Once queried, the `xe` instance is then saved to disk using `xe.Save()`. When you go to disk and look at the `myCustomers.xml` file, you will see the following results (shown only partially here):

```
<?xml version="1.0" encoding="utf-8"?>
<Customer>
  <Customer>
    <CustomerId>ALFKI</CustomerId>
    <CompanyName>Alfreds Futterkiste</CompanyName>
    <Country>Germany</Country>
    <OrderNum>6</OrderNum>
  </Customer>
  <Customer>
    <CustomerId>ANATR</CustomerId>
    <CompanyName>Ana Trujillo Emparedados y helados</CompanyName>
```

```
      <Country>Mexico</Country>
      <OrderNum>4</OrderNum>
    </Customer>

    <!-- XML removed for clarity -->

    <Customer>
      <CustomerId>WILMK</CustomerId>
      <CompanyName>Wilman Kala</CompanyName>
      <Country>Finland</Country>
      <OrderNum>7</OrderNum>
    </Customer>
    <Customer>
      <CustomerId>WOLZA</CustomerId>
      <CompanyName>Wolski  Zajazd</CompanyName>
      <Country>Poland</Country>
      <OrderNum>7</OrderNum>
    </Customer>
  </Customer>
```

From this, you can see just how easy it is to mix the two data sources using LINQ. Using LINQ to SQL, the customers were pulled from the database, and then using LINQ to XML, an XML file was created and output to disk.

Summary

This chapter focused on using LINQ to XML and some of the options available to you in reading and writing from XML files and XML sources, whether the source is static or dynamic.

Using LINQ to XML, you are able to have a strongly typed set of operations for performing CRUD operations against your XML files and sources. However, with that said, you can still use your `XmlReader` and `XmlWriter` code along with the new LINQ to XML capabilities.

This chapter also introduced the new LINQ to XML helper objects of `XDocument`, `XElement`, `XNamespace`, `XAttribute`, and `XComment`. You will find these are outstanding new objects that make working with XML easier than ever before.

The next chapter looks at programming with Microsoft's SQL Server.

Summary

30

.NET Programming with SQL Server

SQL Server 2005 was the first version of this database product to host the .NET runtime. In fact, it was the first new version of Microsoft's SQL Server product in nearly six years. It allows running .NET assemblies in the SQL Server process. Furthermore, it enables you to create stored procedures, functions, and data types with .NET programming languages such as C# and Visual Basic.

In this chapter, you learn about the following:

❑   Hosting the .NET runtime with SQL Server

❑   Classes from the namespace `System.Data.SqlServer`

❑   Creating user-defined types

❑   Creating user-defined aggregates

❑   Stored procedures

❑   User-defined functions

❑   Triggers

❑   XML data types

This chapter requires SQL Server 2005 or a later version of this database product.

SQL Server has many features that are not directly associated with the CLR, such as many T-SQL improvements, but they are not covered in this book. To get more information about these features you can read Wrox's SQL Server 2005 Express Edition Starter Kit *(Wiley Publishing, Inc., ISBN 0-7645-8923-7).*

The samples in this chapter make use of a ProCSharp database that you can download with the code samples, and the AdventureWorks database. The AdventureWorks database is a sample data-base from Microsoft that you can install as an optional component with SQL Server.

.NET Runtime Host

SQL Server is a host of the .NET runtime. In versions prior to CLR 2.0, multiple hosts already existed to run .NET applications; for example, a host for Windows Forms and a host for ASP.NET. Internet Explorer is another runtime host that allows running Windows Forms controls.

SQL Server allows running a .NET assembly inside the SQL Server process, where it is possible to create stored procedures, functions, data types, and triggers with CLR code.

Every database that makes use of CLR code creates its own *application domain*. This guarantees that CLR code from one database doesn't have any influence on any other database.

> *You can read more about application domains in Chapter 17, "Assemblies."*

.NET 1.0 already had a well-thought-out security environment with evidence-based security. However, this security environment was not enough for mission-critical databases — .NET needed some extensions. SQL Server as a .NET runtime host defines additional permission levels: *safe*, *external*, and *unsafe*.

> *You can read more about evidence-based security in Chapter 20, "Security."*

❑ **Safe** — With the safety level *safe*, only computational CLR classes can be used. The assembly is able to perform only local data access. The functionality of these classes is similar to a T-SQL stored procedure. The code access security defines that the only .NET permission is execution of CLR code.

❑ **External** — With the safety level *external* it is possible to access the network, file system, registry, or other databases with client-side ADO.NET.

❑ **Unsafe** — The safety level *unsafe* means that everything can happen, because this safety level allows you to invoke native code. Assemblies with the unsafe permission level can be installed only by a database administrator.

To enable custom .NET code to be run within SQL Server, the CLR must be enabled with the `sp_configure` stored procedure:

```
sp_configure [clr enabled], 1
reconfigure
```

With .NET 2.0, the attribute class `HostProtectionAttribute` in the namespace `System.Security.Permissions` was invented for better protection of the hosting environment. With this attribute, it is possible to define if a method uses shared state, exposes synchronization, or controls the hosting environment. Because such behavior is usually not needed within SQL Server code (and could influence the performance of the SQL Server), assemblies that have these settings applied are not allowed to be loaded in SQL Server with safe and external safety levels.

For using assemblies with SQL Server, the assembly can be installed with the `CREATE ASSEMBLY` command. With this command, the name of the assembly used in SQL Server, the path to the assembly, and the safety level can be applied:

```
CREATE ASSEMBLY mylibrary FROM c:/ProCSharp/SqlServer/Demo.dll
    WITH PERMISSION SET = SAFE
```

With Visual Studio 2008, the permission level of the generated assembly can be defined with the Database properties of the project, as shown in Figure 30-1.

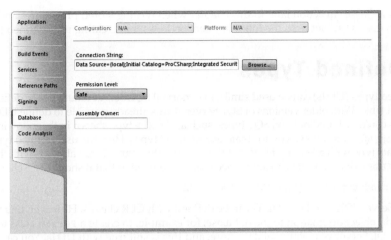

Figure 30-1

Microsoft.SqlServer.Server

Chapter 26, "Data Access," discussed classes from the namespace System.Data.SqlClient. This section discusses another namespace, the Microsoft.SqlServer.Server namespace. The Microsoft.SqlServer.Server namespace includes classes, interfaces, and enumerations specific to the .NET Framework. However, many of the System.Data.SqlClient classes are also needed within server-side code as you will see.

The following table lists the major classes from the Microsoft.SqlServer.Server namespace and their functionality.

Class	Description
SqlContext	Like an HTTP context, the SQL context is associated with the request of a client. With static members of the SqlContext class, SqlPipe, SqlTriggerContext, and WindowsIdentity can be accessed.
SqlPipe	With the SqlPipe class results or information can be sent to the client. This class offers the methods ExecuteAndSend(), Send(), and SendResultsRow(). The Send() method has different overloads to either send a SqlDataReader, SqlDataRecord, or string.
SqlDataRecord	The SqlDataRecord represents a single row of data. This class is used in conjunction with SqlPipe to send or receive information from the client.
SqlTriggerContext	The SqlTriggerContext class is used within triggers. This class provides information about the trigger that was fired.

This namespace also includes several attribute classes: SqlProcedureAttribute, SqlFunctionAttribute, SqlUserDefinedAttribute, and SqlTriggerAttribute. These classes are used for deployment of stored procedures, functions, user-defined types, and triggers in SQL Server. When deploying from Visual Studio, it is required that you apply these attributes. When deploying the database objects using SQL statements, these attributes are not needed but they help, because some properties of these attributes influence the characteristics of the database objects.

You see these classes in action later in this chapter when writing stored procedures and user-defined functions is discussed, but first, the following section looks into creating user-defined types with C#.

User-Defined Types

User-defined types (UDTs) can be used similarly to normal SQL Server data types to define the type of a column in a table. With older versions of SQL Server, it was already possible to define UDTs. Of course, these UDTs could be based only on SQL types, such as the ZIP type shown in the following code. The stored procedure sp_addtype allows you to create user-defined types. Here the user-defined type ZIP is based on the CHAR data type with a length of 5. NOT NULL specifies that NULL is not allowed with the ZIP data type. By using ZIP as a data type, it is no longer necessary to remember that it should be 5 char long and not null:

```
EXEC sp_addtype ZIP 'CHAR(5)', 'NOT NULL'
```

With SQL Server 2005 and later, UDTs can be defined with CLR classes. However, this feature is not meant to add object orientation to the database; for example, to create a Person class to have a Person data type. SQL Server is a relational data store, and this is still true with UDTs. You cannot create a class hierarchy of UDTs, and it is not possible to reference fields or properties of a UDT type with a SELECT statement. If properties of a person (for example, Firstname or Lastname) must be accessed or a list of Person objects must be sorted (for example, by Firstname or Lastname), it is still better to define columns for first name or last name inside a Persons table or to use the XML data type.

UDTs are meant for very simple data types. Before .NET, it was also possible to create custom data types; for example, the ZIP data type. With UDTs it is not possible to create a class hierarchy, and they are not meant to get complex data types to the database. One requirement of a UDT is that it must be convertible to a string, because the string representation is used to display the value.

How the data is stored within SQL Server can be defined: either an automatic mechanism can be used to store the data in a native format, or you can convert the data to a byte stream to define how the data should be stored.

Creating UDTs

Next, you look at how to create a user-defined type. You create a SqlCoordinate type representing the world coordinates longitude and latitude for easily defining the location of places, cities, and the like. To create CLR objects with Visual Studio you can use the Visual Studio 2008 SQL Server Project (in the category Visual C# ➪ Database). Select the Solution Explorer and add a UDT by using the User-Defined Type template. Name the type SqlCoordinate. With the template, the base functionality of a custom type is already defined:

```
using System;
using System.Data;
using System.Data.Sql;
using System.Data.SqlTypes;
using Microsoft.SqlServer.Server;

[Serializable]
[Microsoft.SqlServer.Server.SqlUserDefinedType(Format.Native)]
public struct SqlCoordinate : INullable
{
    public override string ToString()
    {
        // Replace the following code with your code
        return "";
    }

    public bool IsNull
```

```
    {
        get
        {
            // Put your code here
            return m_Null;
        }
    }

    public static SqlCoordinate Null
    {
        get
        {
            SqlCoordinate h = new SqlCoordinate();
            h.m_Null = true;
            return h;
        }
    }

    public static SqlCoordinate Parse(SqlString s)
    {
        if (s.IsNull)
            return Null;
        SqlCoordinate u = new SqlCoordinate();
        // Put your code here
        return u;
    }

    // This is a place-holder method
    public string Method1()
    {
        //Insert method code here
        return "Hello";
    }

    // This is a place-holder static method
    public static SqlString Method2()
    {
        // Insert method code here
        return new SqlString("Hello");
    }

    // This is a placeholder field member
    public int var1;
    // Private member
    private bool m_Null;
}
```

Because this type can also be used directly from client code, it is a good idea to add a namespace, which is not done automatically.

The struct SqlCoordinate implements the interface INullable. The interface INullable is required for UDTs because database types can also be null. The attribute [SqlUserDefinedType] is used for automatic deployment with Visual Studio for UDTs. The argument Format.Native defines the serialization format to be used. Two serialization formats are possible: `Format.Native` and `Format.UserDefined`. `Format.Native` is the simple serialization format where the engine performs serialization and deserialization of instances. This serialization allows only blittable data types (*blittable data types* have the same memory representation in managed and native code). With the `Coordinate` class, the data types to serialize are of type `int` and `bool`, which are blittable data types. A `string` is not a blittable data type. Using `Format.UserDefined` requires the interface `IBinarySerialize` to be implemented. The `IBinarySerialize` interface provides custom implementation for user-defined types. `Read()` and `Write()` methods must be implemented for serialization of the data to a `BinaryReader` and a `BinaryWriter`.

> *Blittable data types have the same memory representation in both managed and unmanaged memory. Conversion is not needed with blittable data types. Blittable data types are* `byte`, `sbyte`, `short`, `ushort`, `int`, `uint`, `long`, `ulong`, *and combinations of these data types such as arrays and structs that contain only these data types.*

```
namespace Wrox.ProCSharp.SqlServer
{

    [Serializable]
    [SqlUserDefinedType(Format.Native)]
    public struct SqlCoordinate : INullable
    {
        private int longitude;
        private int latitude;
        private bool isNull;
```

The attribute `[SqlUserDefinedType]` allows setting several properties, which are shown in the following table.

SqlUserDefinedTypeAttribute Property	Description
Format	The property `Format` defines how the data type is stored within SQL Server. Currently supported formats are `Format.Native` and `Format.UserDefined`.
IsByteOrdered	If the property `IsByteOrdered` is set to `true`, it is possible to create an index for the data type, and it can be used with GROUP BY and ORDER BY SQL statements. The disk representation will be used for binary comparisons. Each instance can have only one serialized representation, so binary comparisons can succeed. The default is `false`.
IsFixedLength	If the disk representation of all instances is of the same size, `IsFixedLength` can be set to true.
MaxByteSize	The maximum number of bytes needed to store the data is set with `MaxByteSize`. This property is specified only with a user-defined serialization.
Name	With the `Name` property, a different name of the type can be set. By default the name of the class is used.
ValidationMethodName	With the `ValidationMethodName` property a method name can be defined to validate instances when the deserialization takes place.

To represent the direction of the coordinate, the enumeration `Orientation` is defined:

```
public enum Orientation
{
    NorthEast,
    NorthWest,
    SouthEast,
    SouthWest
}
```

This enumeration can be used only within methods of the struct `Coordinate`, not as a member field because enumerations are not blittable. Future versions may support enums with the native format in SQL Server.

The struct `Coordinate` specifies some constructors to initialize the `longitude`, `latitude`, and `isNull` variables. The variable `isNull` is set to `true` if no values are assigned to `longitude` and `latitude`, which is the case in the default constructor. A default constructor is needed with UDTs.

With the worldwide coordination system, longitude and latitude are defined with degrees, minutes, and seconds. Vienna, Austria has the coordinates 48° 14' longitude and 16° 20' latitude. The symbols °, ', and " represent degrees, minutes, and seconds, respectively.

With the variables `longitude` and `latitude`, the longitude and latitude values are stored using seconds. The constructor with seven integer parameters converts degrees, minutes, and seconds to seconds, and sets the longitude and latitude to negative values if the coordinate is based in the South or West:

```
public SqlCoordinate(int longitude, int latitude)
{
    isNull = false;
    this.longitude = longitude;
    this.latitude = latitude;
}


public SqlCoordinate(int longitudeDegrees, int longitudeMinutes,
        int longitudeSeconds, int latitudeDegrees, int latitudeMinutes,
        int latitudeSeconds, Orientation orientation)
{
    isNull = false;
    this.longitude = longitudeSeconds + 60 * longitudeMinutes + 3600 *
        longitudeDegrees;
    this.latitude = latitudeSeconds + 60 * latitudeMinutes + 3600 *
        latitudeDegrees;
    switch (orientation)
    {
        case Orientation.SouthWest:
            longitude = -longitude;
            latitude = -latitude;
            break;
        case Orientation.SouthEast:
            longitude = -longitude;
            break;
        case Orientation.NorthWest:
            latitude = -latitude;
            break;
    }
}
```

The `INullable` interface defines the property `IsNull`, which must be implemented to support nullability. The static property `Null` is used to create an object that represents a null value. In the `get` accessor a `Coordinate` object is created, and the `isNull` field is set to `true`:

```
public bool IsNull
{
    get
    {
        return isNull;
    }
}

public static SqlCoordinate Null
{
    get
    {
        SqlCoordinate c = new SqlCoordinate();
        c.isNull = true;
        return c;
    }
}
```

A UDT must be converted from and to a string. For conversion to a string, the `ToString()` method of the `Object` class must be overridden. The variables `longitude` and `latitude` are converted in the following code for a string representation to show the degrees, minutes, and seconds notation:

```
public override string ToString()
{
    if (this.isNull)
        return null;

    char northSouth = longitude > 0 ? 'N' : 'S';
    char eastWest = latitude > 0 ? 'E' : 'W';

    int longitudeDegrees = Math.Abs(longitude) / 3600;
    int remainingSeconds = Math.Abs(longitude) % 3600;
    int longitudeMinutes = remainingSeconds / 60;
    int longitudeSeconds = remainingSeconds % 60;

    int latitudeDegrees = Math.Abs(latitude) / 3600;
    remainingSeconds = Math.Abs(latitude) % 3600;
    int latitudeMinutes = remainingSeconds / 60;
    int latitudeSeconds = remainingSeconds % 60;

    return String.Format("{0}°{1}'{2}\"{3},{4}°{5}'{6}\"{7}",
        longitudeDegrees, longitudeMinutes, longitudeSeconds,
        northSouth, latitudeDegrees, latitudeMinutes,
        latitudeSeconds, eastWest);
}
```

The string that is entered from the user is represented in the `SqlString` parameter of the static method `Parse()`. First, the `Parse()` method checks if the string represents a null value, in which case the `Null` property is invoked to return an empty `Coordinate` object. If the `SqlString` `s` does not represent a null value, the text of the string is converted to pass the longitude and latitude values to the `Coordinate` constructor:

```
public static SqlCoordinate Parse(SqlString s)
{
    if (s.IsNull)
        return SqlCoordinate.Null;

    try
    {
        string[] coordinates = s.Value.Split(',');
        char[] separators = { '°', '\'', '\"' };
        string[] longitudeVals = coordinates[0].Split(separators);
        string[] latitudeVals = coordinates[1].Split(separators);

        Orientation orientation;
        if (longitudeVals[3] == "N" && latitudeVals[3] == "E")
            orientation = Orientation.NorthEast;
        else if (longitudeVals[3] == "S" && latitudeVals[3] == "W")
            orientation = Orientation.SouthWest;
        else if (longitudeVals[3] == "S" && latitudeVals[3] == "E")
            orientation = Orientation.SouthEast;
        else
            orientation = Orientation.NorthWest;

        return new SqlCoordinate(
                int.Parse(longitudeVals[0]), int.Parse(longitudeVals[1]),
                int.Parse(longitudeVals[2]),
                int.Parse(latitudeVals[0]), int.Parse(latitudeVals[1]),
                int.Parse(latitudeVals[2]), orientation);
    }
    catch (Exception ex)
    {
        throw new ArgumentException(
                "Argument has a wrong syntax. " +
                "This syntax is required: 37°47\'0\"N,122°26\'0\"W",
                ex.Message);
    }
}
}
```

Using UDTs

After building the assembly, it can be deployed with SQL Server. Configuration of the UDT in SQL Server can either be done with Visual Studio 2008 using the Build ⇨ Deploy Project menu or using these SQL commands:

```
CREATE ASSEMBLY SampleTypes FROM
'c:\ProCSharp\SqlServer\PropCSharp.SqlTypes.dll'
CREATE TYPE Coordinate EXTERNAL NAME
[ProCSharp.SqlTypes].[ProCSharp.SqlTypes.SqlCoordinate]
```

With EXTERNAL NAME, the name of the assembly as well as the name of the class, including the namespace, must be set.

Now, it is possible to create a table called Cities that contains the data type SqlCoordinate, as shown in Figure 30-2. Fill the table with data as shown in Figure 30-3.

Figure 30-2

	Id	Name	Location
	1	Vienna	50°10'0"N,16°20'0"E
	2	Paris	48°52'0"N,2°20'0"E
	3	Seattle	47°36'0"N,122°20'0"W
	4	London	51°30'0"N,0°10'0"W
	5	Oslo	59°55'0"N,10°45'0"E
	6	Moscow	55°46'0"N,37°40'0"E
	7	Ulan Bator	47°55'0"N,106°55'0"E
▶*	NULL	NULL	NULL

Cities: Query(farabove.ProCSharp)

Figure 30-3

Using UDTs from Client-Side Code

The assembly of the UDT must be referenced to use the UDT from client-side code. Then it can be used like any other type on the client.

> Because the assembly containing the UDTs is used both from the client and from the SQL Server, it is a good idea to put UDTs in a separate assembly from the other SQL Server extensions such as stored procedures and functions.

In the sample code, the SELECT statement of the SqlCommand object references the columns of the Cities table that contains the Location column, which is of type SqlCoordinate. Calling the method ToString() invokes the ToString() method of the SqlCoordinate class to display the coordinate value in a string format:

```
// UDTClient
using System;
using System.Data;
using System.Data.SqlClient;
using Wrox.ProCSharp.SqlServer;

class Program
{
    static void Main()
    {
        string connectionString =
            @"server=(local);database=ProCSharp;trusted_connection=true";
        SqlConnection connection = new SqlConnection(connectionString);
        SqlCommand command = connection.CreateCommand();
```

```
command.CommandText = "SELECT Id, Name, Location FROM Cities";
connection.Open();

SqlDataReader reader =
        command.ExecuteReader(CommandBehavior.CloseConnection);
while (reader.Read())
{

   Console.WriteLine("{0,-10}: {1}", reader[1].ToString(),
         reader[2].ToString());
}
reader.Close();
   }
}
```

Of course, it is also possible to cast the returned object from the SqlDataReader to a SqlCoordinate
type for using any other implemented methods of the Coordinate type:

```
SqlCoordinate coordinate = (SqlCoordinate)reader[2];
```

Running the application produces the following output:

```
Vienna      50°10'0"N,16°20'0"E
Paris       48°52'0"N,2°20'0"E
Seattle     47°36'0"N,122°20'0"W
London      51°30'0"N,0°10'0"W
Oslo        59°55'0"N,10°45'0"E
Moscow      55°46'0"N,37°40'0"E
Ulan Bator  47°55'0"N,106°55'0"E
```

With all the great functionality of UDTs, you have to be aware of an important restriction. Before deploying a new version of a UDT, the existing version must be dropped. This is possible only if all columns using the type are removed. Don't plan on using UDTs for types that you change frequently.

User-Defined Aggregates

An aggregate is a function that returns a single value based on multiple rows. Examples of built-in
aggregates are COUNT, AVG, and SUM. COUNT returns the record count of all selected records, AVG returns
the average of values from a column of selected rows, and SUM returns the sum of all values of a column.
All built-in aggregates work only with built-in value types.

A simple usage of the built-in aggregate AVG is shown here to return the average unit price of all
products from the AdventureWorks sample database by passing the ListPrice column to the AVG
aggregate in the SELECT statement:

```
SELECT AVG(ListPrice) AS 'average list price'
FROM Production.Product
```

The result from the SELECT gives the average list price of all products:

```
average list price
438,6662
```

The SELECT statement returns just a single value that represents the average of all ListPrice column
values. Aggregates can also work with groups. In the next example, the AVG aggregate is combined with
the GROUP BY clause to return the average list price of every product line:

```
SELECT ProductLine, AVG(ListPrice) AS 'average list price'
FROM Production.Product
GROUP BY ProductLine
```

The average list price is now grouped by the product line:

```
ProductLine      average list price
NULL             16,8429
M                827,0639
R                965,3488
S                50,3988
T                840,7621
```

For custom value types, and if you want to do a specific calculation based on a selection of rows, you can create a user-defined aggregate.

Creating User-Defined Aggregates

To write a user-defined aggregate with CLR code, a simple class with the methods `Init()`, `Accumulate()`, `Merge()`, and `Terminate()` must be implemented. The functionality of these methods is shown in the following table.

UDT Method	Description
Init()	The Init() method is invoked for every group of rows to be processed. In this method, initialization can be done for calculation of every row group.
Accumulate()	The Accumulate() method is invoked for every value in all groups. The parameter of this method must be of the correct type that is accumulated; this can also be the class of a user-defined type.
Merge()	The Merge() method is invoked when the result of one aggregation must be combined with another aggregation.
Terminate()	After the last row of every group is processed, the Terminate() method is invoked. Here, the result of the aggregate must be returned with the correct data type.

The code sample shows how to implement a simple user-defined aggregate to calculate the sum of all rows in every group. For deployment with Visual Studio, the attribute [SqlUserDefinedAggregate] is applied to the class SampleSum. As with the user-defined type, with user-defined aggregates the format for storing the aggregate must be defined with a value from the Format enumeration. Again, Format .Native is for using automatic serialization with blittable data types.

In the code sample the variable sum is used for accumulation of all values of a group. In the Init() method, the variable sum is initialized for every new group to accumulate. The method Accumulate(), which is invoked for every value, adds the value of the parameter to the sum variable. With the Merge() method, one aggregated group is added to the current group. Finally, the method Terminate() returns the result of a group:

```
[Serializable]
[SqlUserDefinedAggregate(Format.Native)]
public struct SampleSum
{
    private int sum;

    public void Init()
    {
        sum = 0;
    }
```

```
public void Accumulate(SqlInt32 Value)
{
    sum += Value.Value;
}

public void Merge(SampleSum Group)
{
    sum += Group.sum;
}

public SqlInt32 Terminate()
{
    return new SqlInt32(sum);
}
}
```

You can use the Aggregate template from Visual Studio to create the core code for building the user-defined aggregate. The template from Visual Studio creates a struct that uses the SqlString *type as a parameter and return type with the* Accumulate *and* Terminate *methods. You can change the type to a type that represents the requirement of your aggregate. In the example, the* SqlInt32 *type is used.*

Using User-Defined Aggregates

The user-defined aggregate can be deployed either with Visual Studio or with the CREATE AGGREGATE statement. Following the CREATE AGGREGATE is the name of the aggregate, the parameter (@value int), and the return type. EXTERNAL NAME requires the name of the assembly and the .NET type including the namespace.

```
CREATE AGGREGATE [SampleSum] (@value int) RETURNS [int] EXTERNAL NAME
[Demo].[SampleSum]
```

After the user-defined aggregate has been installed, it can be used as shown in the following SELECT statement, where the number of ordered products is returned by joining the Product and PurchaseOrderDetail tables. For the user-defined aggregate, the OrderQty column of the Order PurchaseOrderDetail table is defined as an argument:

```
SELECT Purchasing.PurchaseOrderDetail.ProductID AS Id,
    Production.Product.Name AS Product,
    dbo.SampleSum(Purchasing.PurchaseOrderDetail.OrderQty) AS Sum
FROM Production.Product INNER JOIN
    Purchasing.PurchaseOrderDetail ON
    Purchasing.PurchaseOrderDetail.ProductID = Production.Product.ProductID
GROUP BY Purchasing.PurchaseOrderDetail.ProductID, Production.Product.Name
ORDER BY Id
```

An extract of the returned result that shows the number of orders for products by using the aggregate function SampleSum is presented here:

```
Id      Product                 Sum
1       Adjustable Race         154
2       Bearing Ball            150
4       Headset Ball Bearings   153
317     LL Crankarm             44000
318     ML Crankarm             44000
319     HL Crankarm             71500
320     Chainring Bolts         375
321     Chainring Nut           375
322     Chainring               7440
```

Stored Procedures

SQL Server allows the creation of stored procedures with C#. A stored procedure is a subroutine, and they are physically stored in the database. They definitely are not to be considered a replacement for T-SQL. T-SQL still has an advantage when the procedure is mainly data-driven.

Take a look at the T-SQL stored procedure GetCustomerOrders, which returns information from customer orders from the AdventureWorks database. This stored procedure returns orders from the customer that is specified with the parameter CustomerID:

```
CREATE PROCEDURE GetCustomerOrders
    (
    @CustomerID int
    )
AS
SELECT SalesOrderID, OrderDate, DueDate, ShipDate FROM Sales.SalesOrderHeader
    WHERE (CustomerID = @CustomerID)
    ORDER BY SalesOrderID
```

Creating Stored Procedures

As you can see in the following code listing, implementing the same stored procedure with C# has more complexity. The attribute [SqlProcedure] is used to mark a stored procedure for deployment. With the implementation, a SqlCommand object is created. With the constructor of the SqlConnection object, the string "Context Connection=true" is passed to use the connection that was already opened by the client calling the stored procedure. Very similarly to the code you saw in Chapter 26, the SQL SELECT statement is set and one parameter is added. The ExecuteReader() method returns a SqlDataReader object. This reader object is returned to the client by invoking the Send() method of the SqlPipe:

```
using System.Data;
using System.Data.SqlClient;
using Microsoft.SqlServer.Server;

public partial class StoredProcedures
{
    [SqlProcedure]
    public static void GetCustomerOrdersCLR(int customerId)
    {
        SqlConnection connection = new SqlConnection("Context Connection=true");
        connection.Open();
        SqlCommand command = new SqlCommand();
        command.Connection = connection;
        command.CommandText = "SELECT SalesOrderID, OrderDate, DueDate, " +
                "ShipDate " +
                "FROM Sales.SalesOrderHeader " +
                "WHERE (CustomerID = @CustomerID)" +
                "ORDER BY SalesOrderID";

        command.Parameters.Add("@CustomerID", SqlDbType.Int);
        command.Parameters["@CustomerID"].Value = customerId;
```

```
        SqlDataReader reader = command.ExecuteReader();
        SqlPipe pipe = SqlContext.Pipe;
        pipe.Send(reader);
        connection.Close();
    }
};
```

CLR stored procedures are deployed to SQL Server either using Visual Studio or with the CREATE
PROCEDURE statement. With this SQL statement the parameters of the stored procedure are defined, as
well as the name of the assembly, class, and method:

```
CREATE PROCEDURE GetCustomerOrdersCLR
(
    @CustomerID nchar(5)
)
AS EXTERNAL NAME Demo.StoredProcedures.GetCustomerOrdersCLR
```

Using Stored Procedures

The CLR stored procedure can be invoked just like a T-SQL stored procedure by using classes
from the namespace System.Data.SqlClient. First, a SqlConnection object is created. The
CreateCommand() method returns a SqlCommand object. With the command object, the name of the
stored procedure GetCustomerOrdersCLR is set to the CommandText property. As with all stored
procedures, the CommandType property must be set to CommandType.StoredProcedure. The method
ExecuteReader() returns a SqlDataReader object to read record by record:

```
using System;
using System.Data;
using System.Data.SqlClient;

//...

        string connectionString =
            @"server=(local);database=AdventureWorks;trusted_connection=true";
        SqlConnection connection = new SqlConnection(connectionString);
        SqlCommand command = connection.CreateCommand();
        command.CommandText = "GetCustomerOrdersCLR";
        command.CommandType = CommandType.StoredProcedure;
        SqlParameter param = new SqlParameter("@customerId", 3);
        command.Parameters.Add(param);
        connection.Open();
        SqlDataReader reader =
                command.ExecuteReader(CommandBehavior.CloseConnection);
        while (reader.Read())
        {
            Console.WriteLine("{0} {1:d}", reader["SalesOrderID"],
                reader["OrderDate"]);
        }
        reader.Close();
```

The classes from the namespace System.Data.SqlClient *are discussed in Chapter 26,
"Data Access."*

Invoking the stored procedure written with T-SQL or with C# is not different at all. The code for calling stored procedures is completely identical; from the caller code you don't know if the stored procedure is implemented with T-SQL or the CLR. An extract of the result shows the order dates for the customer with ID 3:

```
44124 9/1/2001
44791 12/1/2001
45568 3/1/2002
46377 6/1/2002
47439 9/1/2002
48378 12/1/2002
```

As you have seen, mainly data-driven stored procedures are better done with T-SQL. The code is a lot shorter. Writing stored procedures with the CLR has the advantage if you need some specific data-processing, for example, by using the .NET cryptography classes.

User-Defined Functions

User-defined functions are somewhat similar to stored procedures. The big difference is that user-defined functions can be invoked within SQL statements.

Creating User-Defined Functions

A CLR user-defined function can be defined with the attribute [SqlFunction]. The sample function CalcHash() converts the string that is passed to a hashed string. The MD5 algorithm that is used for hashing the string is implemented with the class MD5CryptoServiceProvider from the namespace System.Security.Cryptography. The ComputeHash() method computes the hash from the byte array input and returns a computed hash byte array. The hashed byte array is converted back to a string by using the StringBuilder class:

```csharp
using System.Data.SqlTypes;
using System.Security.Cryptography;
using System.Text;
using Microsoft.SqlServer.Server;

public partial class UserDefinedFunctions
{
    [SqlFunction]
    public static SqlString CalcHash(SqlString value)
    {
        byte[] source;
        byte[] hash;

        source = ASCIIEncoding.ASCII.GetBytes(value.ToString());
        hash = new MD5CryptoServiceProvider().ComputeHash(source);

        StringBuilder output = new StringBuilder(hash.Length);

        for (int i = 0; i < hash.Length - 1; i++)
        {
            output.Append(hash[i].ToString("X2"));
        }

        return new SqlString(output.ToString());
    }
}
```

Using User-Defined Functions

A user-defined function can be deployed with SQL Server very similarly to the other .NET extensions: either with Visual Studio 2008 or with the CREATE FUNCTION statement:

```
CREATE FUNCTION CalcHash
(
    @value nvarchar
)
RETURNS nvarchar
AS EXTERNAL NAME Demo.UserDefinedFunctions.CalcHash
```

A sample usage of the CalcHash() function is shown with this SELECT statement where the credit card number is accessed from the CreditCard table in the AdventureWorks database by returning just the hash code from the credit card number:

```
SELECT Sales.CreditCard.CardType AS [Card Type],
    dbo.CalcHash(Sales.CreditCard.CardNumber) AS [Hashed Card]
FROM Sales.CreditCard INNER JOIN Sales.ContactCreditCard ON
    Sales.CreditCard.CreditCardID = Sales.ContactCreditCard.CreditCardID
WHERE Sales.ContactCreditCard.ContactID = 11
```

The result returned shows the hashed credit card number for contact ID 11:

```
Card Type       Hashed Card
ColonialVoice   7482F7B4E613F71144A9B336A3B9F6
```

Triggers

A *trigger* is a special kind of stored procedure invoked when a table is modified (for example, when a row is inserted, updated, or deleted). Triggers are associated with tables and the action that should activate them (for example, on insert/update/delete of rows).

With triggers, changes of rows can be cascaded through related tables or more complex data integrity can be enforced.

Within a trigger you have access to the current data of a row and the original data, so it is possible to reset the change to the earlier state. Triggers are automatically associated with the same transaction as the command that fires the trigger, so you get a correct transactional behavior.

The trigger uCreditCard that follows is part of the AdventureWorks sample database. This trigger is fired when a row in the CreditCard table is updated. With this trigger the ModifiedDate column of the CreditCard table is updated to the current date. For accessing the data that is changed, the temporary table inserted is used.

```
CREATE TRIGGER [Sales].[uCreditCard] ON [Sales].[CreditCard]
AFTER UPDATE NOT FOR REPLICATION AS
BEGIN
    SET NOCOUNT ON;

    UPDATE [Sales].[CreditCard]
    SET [Sales].[CreditCard].[ModifiedDate] = GETDATE()
    FROM inserted
    WHERE inserted.[CreditCardID] = [Sales].[CreditCard].[CreditCardID];
END;
```

Creating Triggers

The example shown here demonstrates implementing data integrity with triggers when new records are inserted into the Users table. To create a trigger with the CLR, a simple class must be defined that includes static methods that have the attribute [SqlTrigger] applied. The attribute [SqlTrigger] defines the table that is associated with the trigger and the event when the trigger should occur. In the example, the associated table is Person.Contact, which is indicated by the Target property. The Event property defines when the trigger should occur; here, the event string is set to FOR INSERT, which means the trigger is started when a new row is inserted in the Users table.

The property SqlContext.TriggerContext returns the trigger context in an object of type SqlTriggerContext. The SqlTriggerContext class offers three properties: ColumnsUpdated returns a Boolean array to flag every column that was changed, EventData contains the new and the original data of an update in XML format, and TriggerAction returns an enumeration of type TriggerAction to mark the reason for the trigger. The example compares whether the TriggerAction of the trigger context is set to TriggerAction.Insert before continuing.

Triggers can access temporary tables; for example, in the following code listing the INSERTED table is accessed. With INSERT, UPDATE, and DELETE SQL statements, temporary tables are created. The INSERT statement creates an INSERTED table; the DELETE statement creates a DELETED table. With the UPDATE statement both INSERTED and DELETED tables are used. The temporary tables have the same columns as the table that is associated with the trigger. The SQL statement SELECT Username, Email FROM INSERTED is used to access username and email, and to check the email address for correct syntax. SqlCommand.ExecuteRow() returns a row represented in a SqlDataRecord. Username and email are read from the data record. Using the regular expression class, RegEx, the expression used with the IsMatch() method checks if the email address conforms to valid email syntax. If it does not conform, an exception is thrown and the record is not inserted, because a rollback occurs with the transaction:

```
using System;
using System.Data.SqlClient;
using System.Text.RegularExpressions;
using Microsoft.SqlServer.Server;

public partial class Triggers
{
    [SqlTrigger(Name ="InsertContact", Target="Person.Contact",
            Event="FOR INSERT")]
    public static void InsertContact()
    {
        SqlTriggerContext triggerContext = SqlContext.TriggerContext;

        if (triggerContext.TriggerAction == TriggerAction.Insert)
        {
            SqlConnection connection = new SqlConnection(
                    "Context Connection=true");
            SqlCommand command = new SqlCommand();
            command.Connection = connection;
            command.CommandText = "SELECT EmailAddress FROM INSERTED";
            connection.Open();
            string email = (string)command.ExecuteScalar();
            connection.Close();

            if (!Regex.IsMatch(email,
                    @"([\w-]+\.)*?[\w-]+@[\w-]+\.([\w-]+\.)*?[\w]+$"))
```

```
        {
            throw new FormatException("Invalid email");
        }
    }
  }
}
```

Using Triggers

Using deployment of Visual Studio 2008, the trigger can be deployed to the database. You can use the CREATE TRIGGER command to create the trigger manually:

```
CREATE TRIGGER InsertContact ON Person.Contact
FOR INSERT
AS EXTERNAL NAME Demo.Triggers.InsertContact
```

Trying to insert rows into the Users table with an incorrect email throws an exception, and the insert is not done.

XML Data Type

One of the major programming features of SQL Server is the XML data type. With older versions of SQL Server, XML data is stored inside a string or a blob. Now XML is a supported data type that allows you to combine SQL queries with XQuery expressions to search within XML data. An XML data type can be used as a variable, a parameter, a column, or a return value from a UDF.

With Office 2007, it is possible to store Word and Excel documents as XML. Word and Excel also support using custom XML schemas, where only the content (and not the presentation) is stored with XML. The output of Office applications can be stored directly in SQL Server, where it is possible to search within this data. Of course, custom XML data can also be stored in SQL Server.

> Don't use XML types for relational data. If you do a search for some of the elements and if the schema is clearly defined for the data, storing these elements in a relational fashion allows the data to be accessed faster. If the data is hierarchical and some elements are optional and may change over time, storing XML data has many advantages.

Tables with XML Data

Creating tables with XML data is as simple as selecting the Xml data type with a column. The following CREATE TABLE SQL command creates the Exams table with a column ID that is also the primary key, the column Number, and the column Info, which is of type xml:

```
CREATE TABLE [dbo].[Exams](
    [Id] [int] IDENTITY(1,1) NOT NULL,
    [Number] [nchar] (10) NOT NULL,
    [Info] [xml] NOT NULL,
    CONSTRAINT [PK_Exams] PRIMARY KEY CLUSTERED
    (
        [Id] ASC
    ) ON [PRIMARY]
) ON [PRIMARY]
```

For a simple test, the table is filled with this data:

```
INSERT INTO Exams values('70-536',
  '<Exam Number="70-536">
    <Title>TS: Microsoft .NET Framework 2.0 - Application Development Foundation
    </Title>
    <Certification Name="MCTS Windows Applications" Status="Core" />
    <Certification Name="MCTS Web Applications" Status="Core" />
    <Certification Name="MCTS Distributed Applications" Status="Core" />
    <Course>2956</Course>
    <Course>2957</Course>
    <Topic>Developing applications that use system types and collections
    </Topic>
    <Topic>Implementing service processes, threading, and application domains
    </Topic>
    <Topic>Embedding configuration, diagnostics, management, and installation
features
    </Topic>
    <Topic>Implementing serialization and input/output functionality</Topic>
    <Topic>Improving the security</Topic>
    <Topic>Implementing interoperability, reflection, and mailing functionality
    </Topic>
    <Topic>Implementing globalization, drawing, and text manipulation functionality
    </Topic>
  </Exam>')

INSERT INTO Exams values('70-528',
  '<Exam Number="70-528">
    <Title>TS: Microsoft .NET Framework - Web-Based Client Development</Title>
    <Certification Name="MCTS Web Applications" Status="Core" />
    <Course>2541</Course>
    <Course>2542</Course>
    <Course>2543</Course>
    <Course>2544</Course>
    <Topic>Creating and Programming a Web Application</Topic>
    <Topic>Integrating Data in a Web Application by using ADO.NET, XML, and
    Data-Bound Controls</Topic>
    <Topic>Creating Custom Web Controls</Topic>
    <Topic>Tracing, Configuring, and Deploying Applications</Topic>
    <Topic>Customizing and Personalizing a Web Application</Topic>
    <Topic>Implementing Authentication and Authorization</Topic>
    <Topic>Creating ASP.NET Mobile Web Applications</Topic>
  </Exam>')

INSERT INTO Exams values('70-526',
  '<Exam Number="70-526">
    <Title>TS: Microsoft .NET Framework 2.0 - Windows-Based Client Development
    </Title>
    <Certification Name="MCTS Windows Applications" Status="Core" />
    <Course>2541</Course>
    <Course>2542</Course>
    <Course>2546</Course>
    <Course>2547</Course>
    <Topic>Creating a UI for a Windows Forms Application by Using Standard Controls
    </Topic>
    <Topic>Integrating Data in a Windows Forms Application</Topic>
```

```
    <Topic>Implementing Printing and Reporting Functionality</Topic>
    <Topic>Enhancing Usability</Topic>
    <Topic>Implementing Asynchronous Programming Techniques to Improve the User
    Experience</Topic>
    <Topic>Developing Windows Forms Controls</Topic>
    <Topic>Configuring and Deploying Applications</Topic>
</Exam>')
```

Reading XML Values

You can read the XML data with ADO.NET using a SqlDataReader object. The SqlDataReader method GetSqlXml() returns a SqlXml object. The SqlXml class has a property Value that returns the complete XML representation and a CreateReader() method that returns an XmlReader object.

The Read() method of the XmlReader is repeated in a while loop to read node by node. With the output there's interest only in information about the value of the attribute Number, and the values of the elements Title and Course. The node to which the reader is positioned is compared with the corresponding XML element names, and the corresponding values are written to the console.

```
using System;
using System.Data;
using System.Data.SqlClient;
using System.Data.SqlTypes;
using System.Text;
using System.Xml;

class Program
{
    static void Main()
    {
        string connectionString =
            @"server=(local);database=ProCSharp;trusted_connection=true";
        SqlConnection connection = new SqlConnection(connectionString);
        SqlCommand command = connection.CreateCommand();
        command.CommandText = "SELECT Id, Number, Info FROM Exams";
        connection.Open();
        SqlDataReader reader = command.ExecuteReader(
                CommandBehavior.CloseConnection);
        while (reader.Read())
        {
            SqlXml xml = reader.GetSqlXml(2);

            XmlReader xmlReader = xml.CreateReader();

            StringBuilder courses = new StringBuilder("Course(s): ", 40);
            while (xmlReader.Read())
            {
                if (xmlReader.Name == "Exam" && xmlReaderIsStartElement)
                {
                    Console.WriteLine("Exam: {0}",
                        xmlReader.GetAttribute("Number"));
                }
                else if (xmlReader.Name == "Title" && xmlReader.IsStartElement)
```

(continued)

1005

```
            {
                Console.WriteLine("Title: {0}", xmlReader.ReadString());
            }
            else if (xmlReader.Name == "Course" &&
                    xmlReader.IsStartElement)
            {
                courses.AppendFormat("{0} ", xmlReader.ReadString());
            }
        }
        xmlReader.Close();
        Console.WriteLine(courses.ToString());
        Console.WriteLine();
    }
    reader.Close();
}
}
```

Running the application you will get the output as shown:

```
Exam: 70-536
Title: TS: Microsoft .NET Framework 2.0 - Application Development Foundation
Course(s): 2956 2957

Exam: 70-528
Title: TS: Microsoft .NET Framework 2.0 - Web-Based Client Development
Course(s): 2541 2542 2543 2544

Exam: 70-526
Title: TS: Microsoft .NET Framework 2.0 - Windows-Based Client Development
Course(s): 2541 2542 2546 2547
```

Instead of using the XmlReader class you can read the complete XML content into the XmlDocument class and parse the elements by using the DOM model. The method SelectSingleNode() requires an XPath expression and returns an XmlNode object. The XPath expression //Exam looks for the Exam XML element inside the complete XML tree. The XmlNode object returned can be used to read the children of the represented element. The value of the Number attribute is accessed to write the exam number to the console, then the Title element is accessed and the content of the Title element is written to the console, and the content of all Course elements is written to the console as well.

```
string connectionString =
        @"server=(local);database=ProCSharp;trusted_connection=true";
SqlConnection connection = new SqlConnection(connectionString);
SqlCommand command = connection.CreateCommand();
command.CommandText = "SELECT Id, Number, Info FROM Exams";
connection.Open();
SqlDataReader reader = command.ExecuteReader(
        CommandBehavior.CloseConnection);
while (reader.Read())
{
    SqlXml xml = reader.GetSqlXml(2);
    XmlDocument doc = new XmlDocument();
    doc.LoadXml(xml.Value);

    XmlNode examNode = doc.SelectSingleNode("//Exam");
    Console.WriteLine("Exam: {0}",
            examNode.Attributes["Number"].Value);
```

```
        XmlNode titleNode = examNode.SelectSingleNode("./Title");
        Console.WriteLine("Title: {0}", titleNode.InnerText);
        Console.Write("Course(s): ");
        foreach (XmlNode courseNode in examNode.SelectNodes("./Course"))
        {
            Console.Write("{0} ", courseNode.InnerText);
        }
        Console.WriteLine();

    }
    reader.Close();
```

The XmlReader *and* XmlDocument *classes are discussed in Chapter 28, "Manipulating XML."*

With .NET 3.5 there's another option to access the XML column from the database. You can combine LINQ to SQL and LINQ to XML, which makes the programming code smaller.

You can use the LINQ to SQL designer by selecting the LINQ to SQL Classes template from the Data templates category. Name the file ProCSharp.dbml to create a mapping for the database ProCSharp. Create the mapping by dragging and dropping the Exams table from the Solution Explorer to the design surface as shown in Figure 30-4.

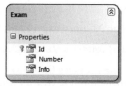

Figure 30-4

The mapping class that is created by the designer has the name ProCSharpDataContext and defines a property Exams to return all exam rows. Here a foreach statement is used to iterate through all records. Of course you can also define a LINQ query with a where expression if not all records are required. The Exam class defines the properties Id, Number, and Info accordingly to the columns in the database table. The Info property is of type XDocument and thus can be accessed by using the new LINQ to XML classes from the namespace System.Xml.Linq. Invoking the method Element() passing the name of the XML element Exam returns an XElement object that is then used to access the values of the attribute Number and the elements Title and Course in a much simpler way, as was done earlier with the XmlDocument class.

```
using System;
using System.Xml.Linq;

namespace Wrox.ProCSharp.SqlServer
{
    class Program
    {
        static void Main()
        {
            ProCSharpDataContext db = new ProCSharpDataContext();

            foreach (Exam item in db.Exams)
```

(continued)

(continued)

```
        {
            XElement exam = item.Info.Element("Exam");
            Console.WriteLine("Exam: {0}", exam.Attribute("Number").Value);
            Console.WriteLine("Title: {0}", exam.Element("Title").Value);
            Console.Write("Course(s): ");
            foreach (var course in exam.Elements("Course"))
            {
                Console.Write("{0} ", course.Value);
            }
            Console.WriteLine();
        }
    }
  }
}
```

LINQ to SQL and LINQ to XML are explained in Chapters 27 and 29, respectively.

Query of Data

Up until now, you haven't seen the really great features of the XML data type. SQL SELECT statements can be combined with XML XQuery.

A SELECT statement combined with an XQuery expression to read into the XML value is shown here:

```
SELECT [Id], [Number], [Info].query('/Exam/Course') AS Course FROM [Exams]
```

The XQuery expression /Exam/Course accesses the Course elements that are children of the Exam element. The result of this query returns the IDs, exam numbers, and courses:

```
1 70-536 <Course>2956</Course><Course>2957</Course>
2 70-528 <Course>2541</Course><Course>2542</Course><Course>2543</Course>
           <Course>2544</Course>
3 70-526 <Course>2541</Course><Course>2542</Course><Course>2546</Course>
           <Course>2547</Course>
```

With an XQuery expression, you can create more complex statements to query data within the XML content of a cell. The next example converts the XML from the exam information to XML that lists information about courses:

```
SELECT [Info].query('
    for $course in /Exam/Course
    return
<Course>
    <Exam>{ data(/Exam[1]/@Number) }</Exam>
    <Number>{ data($course) }</Number>
</Course>')
AS Course
FROM [Exams]
WHERE Id=2
```

Here, just a single row is selected with SELECT [Info]... FROM Exams WHERE Id = 2. With the result of this SQL query, the for and return statements of an XQuery expression are used. for $course in /Exam/Course iterates through all Course elements. $course declares a variable that is set with every iteration (similar to a C# foreach statement). Following the return statement, the result of the query for every row is defined. The result for every course element is surrounded by the <Course> element. Embedded inside the <Course> element are <Exam> and <Number>. The text within the <Exam> element is defined with data(/Exam[1]/@Number). data() is an XQuery function that returns the value of the node specified with the argument. The node /Exam[1] is used to access the first <Exam> element; @Number specifies the XML attribute Number. The text within the element <Number> is defined from the variable $course.

Contrary to C#, where the first element in a collection is accessed with an index of 0, with XPath the first element in a collection is accessed with an index of 1.

The result of this query is shown here:

```
<Course>
   <Exam>70-528</Exam>
   <Number>2541</Number>
</Course>
<Course>
   <Exam>70-528</Exam>
   <Number>2542</Number>
</Course>
<Course
   <Exam>70-528</Exam>
   <Number>2543</Number>
</Course>
<Course>
   <Exam>70-528</Exam>
   <Number>2544</Number>
</Course>
```

You can change the XQuery statement to also include a where clause for filtering XML elements. The following example only returns courses from the XML column if the course number has a value higher than 2542:

```
SELECT [Info].query('
   for $course in /Exam/Course
   where ($course > 2542)
   return
<Course>
   <Exam>{ data(/Exam[1]/@Number) }</Exam>
   <Number>{ data($course) }</Number>
</Course>')
AS Course
FROM [Exams]
WHERE Id=2
```

The result is reduced to just two course numbers:

```
<Course>
   <Exam>70-528</Exam>
   <Number>2543</Number>
</Course>
<Course>
   <Exam>70-528</Exam>
   <Number>2544</Number>
</Course>
```

XQuery in SQL Server allows using several other XQuery functions for getting minimum, maximum, or summary values, working with strings, numbers, checking for positions within collections, and so on.

The next example shows the use of the `count()` function to get the number of `/Exam/Course` elements:

```
SELECT [Id], [Number], [Info].query('
    count(/Exam/Course)')
    AS "Course Count"
FROM [Exams]
```

The data returned displays the number of courses for the exams:

```
Id          Number          Course Count
1           70-536          2
2           70-528          4
3           70-526          4
```

XML Data Modification Language (XML DML)

XQuery as it is defined by the W3C (`http://www.w3c.org`) allows only querying of data. Because of this XQuery restriction, Microsoft defined an extension to XQuery that has the name XML Data Modification Language (XML DML). XML DML makes it possible to modify XML data with the following XQuery extensions: `insert`, `delete`, and `replace value of`.

This section looks at some examples to insert, delete, and modify XML contents within a cell.

You can use the `insert` keyword to insert some XML content within an XML column without replacing the complete XML cell. Here, `<Course>2555</Course>` is inserted as the last child element of the first `Exam` element:

```
UPDATE [Exams]
SET [Info].modify('
    insert <Course>2555</Course> as last into Exam[1]')
WHERE [Id]=3
```

XML content can be deleted with the `delete` keyword. Within the first `Exam` element, the last `Course` element is deleted. The last element is selected by using the `last()` function.

```
UPDATE [Exams]
SET [Info].modify('
    delete /Exam[1]/Course[last()]')
FROM [Exams] WHERE [Id]=3
```

It is also possible to change XML content. Here, the keyword `replace value of` is used. The expression `/Exam/Course[text() = 2543]` accesses only the child elements `Course` where the text content contains the string `2543`. From these elements, only the text content is accessed for replacement with the `text()` function. If only a single element is returned from the query, it is still required that you specify just one element for replacement. This is why explicitly the first text element returned is specified with `[1]`. `2599` specifies that the new course number is `2599`:

```
UPDATE [Exams]
SET [Info].modify('
    replace value of (/Exam/Course[text() = 2543]/text())[1] with 2599')
FROM [Exams]
```

XML Indexes

If some specific elements are often searched within the XML data, you can specify indexes within the XML data type. XML indexes must be distinguished as being a primary or a secondary XML index type. A primary XML index is created for the complete persisted representation of the XML value.

The following SQL command, CREATE PRIMARY XML INDEX, creates the index idx_exams on the Info column:

```
CREATE PRIMARY XML INDEX idx_exams on Exams (Info)
```

Primary indexes don't help if the query contains an XPath expression to directly access XML elements of the XML type. For XPath and XQuery expressions, XML secondary indexes can be used. If an XML secondary index is created, the primary index must already exist. With secondary indexes, these index types must be distinguished:

❑   PATH index

❑   VALUE index

❑   PROPERTY index

A PATH index is used if exists() or query() functions are used and XML elements are accessed with an XPath expression. Using the XPath expression /Exam/Course, it might be useful to do a PATH index:

```
CREATE XML INDEX idx_examNumbers on [Exams] (Info)
    USING XML INDEX idx_exams FOR PATH
```

The PROPERTY index is used if properties are fetched from elements with the value() function. The FOR PROPERTY statement with the index creation defines a PROPERTY index:

```
CREATE XML INDEX idx_examNumbers on [Exams] (Info)
    USING XML INDEX idx_exams FOR PROPERTY
```

If elements are searched through the tree with an XPath descendant-or-self axis expression, the best performance might be achieved with a VALUE index. The XPath expression //Certification searches all Certification elements with the descendant-or-self axis. The expression [@Name="MCTS Web Applications"] returns only the elements where the attribute Name has the value MCTS Web Applications:

```
SELECT [Info].query('/Exam/Title/text()') FROM [Exams]
    WHERE [Info].exist('//Certification[@Name="MCTS Web Applications"]') = 1
```

The result returned lists the titles of the exams that contain the requested certification:

```
TS: Microsoft .NET Framework 2.0 - Application Development Foundation
TS: Microsoft .NET Framework - Web-Based Client Development
```

The VALUE index is created with the FOR VALUE statement:

```
CREATE XML INDEX idx_examNumbers on [Exams] (Info)
    USING XML INDEX idx_exams FOR VALUE
```

Strongly Typed XML

The XML data type in SQL Server can also be strongly typed with XML schemas. With a strongly typed XML column, it is verified if the data conforms to the schema when XML data is inserted.

A XML schema can be created with the CREATE XML SCHEMA COLLECTION statement. The statement shown here creates a simple XML schema, CourseSchema. The schema defines the type CourseElt that contains a sequence of Number and Title, which are both of type string, and an element Any, which can be any type. Number and Title may occur only once. Because Any has the minOccurs attribute set to 0, and the maxOccurs attribute set to unbounded, this element is optional. This allows you to add any additional information to the CourseElt type in future versions, while the schema still remains valid. Finally, the element name Course is of type CourseElt.

```
CREATE XML SCHEMA COLLECTION CourseSchema AS
'<?xml version="1.0" encoding="UTF-8"?>
<xs:schema id="Courses" targetNamespace="http://thinktecture.com/Courses.xsd"
  elementFormDefault="qualified" xmlns="http://thinktecture.com/Courses.xsd"
  xmlns:mstns="http://thinktecture.com/Courses.xsd"
  xmlns:xs="http://www.w3.org/2001/XMLSchema">
    <xs:complexType name="CourseElt">
      <xs:sequence>
        <xs:element name="Number" type="xs:string" maxOccurs="1"
              minOccurs="1" />
        <xs:element name="Title" type="xs:string" maxOccurs="1"
              minOccurs="1" />
        <xs:element name="Any" type="xs:anyType"
            maxOccurs="unbounded" minOccurs="0" />
      </xs:sequence>
    </xs:complexType>
    <xs:element name="Course" type="CourseElt">
    </xs:element>
</xs:schema>'
```

With this schema, a valid XML looks like this:

```
<Course xmlns="http://thinktecture.com/Courses.xsd">
  <Number>2549</Number>
  <Title>Advanced Distributed Application Development with Visual Studio 2008</
Title>
</Course>
```

With the Visual Studio Database project type, there's no support to add a schema to the database. This feature is not available from the GUI by Visual Studio 2008 but must be created manually. To create an XML schema with Visual Studio 2008, create a new Visual Studio project by using the Empty Project template. Add a new XML schema to the project. Then copy the XML syntax of the schema into the CREATE XML SCHEMA statement.

Besides using Visual Studio, you can copy the XML syntax into SQL Server Management Studio to create and view the XML schemas (see Figure 30-5). The Object Explorer lists the XML schemas under the Types entry.

The XML schema can be assigned to a column by setting it with the xml data type:

```
CREATE TABLE [Courses]
(
    [Id] [int] IDENTITY(1,1) NOT NULL,
    [Course] [xml]([dbo].[CourseSchema]) NOT NULL
)
```

By creating the table with Visual Studio 2008 or with SQL Server Management Studio, the XML schema can be assigned to a column by setting the property XML schema namespace.

Now as you add data to the XML column, the schema is verified. If the XML does not satisfy the schema definition, a SqlException is thrown with an XML Validation error.

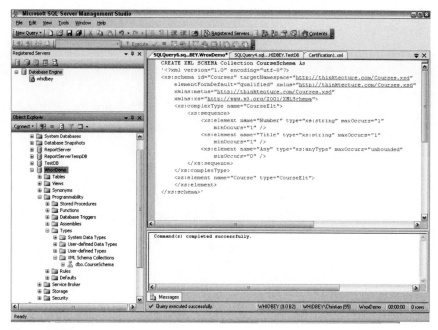

Figure 30-5

Summary

This chapter discussed the new features of SQL Server as they relate to CLR functionality. The CLR is hosted by SQL Server, so it is possible to create user-defined types, aggregates, stored procedures, functions, and triggers with C#.

User-defined types have some strict requirements in the .NET class for conversion to and from a string. How the data is stored internally in SQL Server depends on the format that is defined in the type. User-defined aggregates make it possible to do a custom accumulation using .NET classes. With stored procedures and functions, it is possible to make use of CLR classes for server-side code.

Using CLR with SQL Server doesn't mean that T-SQL is obsolete. You've seen that T-SQL has advantages because it requires less code if only data-intensive queries are done. CLR classes can have advantages in data-processing if .NET features such as cryptography come into play.

You've also had a glance into the XML data type of SQL Server to combine XQuery expressions with T-SQL statements.

This chapter concludes Part IV, "Data." Part V, "Presentation," gives details about defining the user interface of applications. With the user interface you have the options of working with Windows Forms, WPF, and ASP.NET.

Part V
Presentation

31

Windows Forms

Web-based applications have become very popular over the past several years. The ability to have all of your application logic reside on a centralized server is very appealing from an administrator's viewpoint. Deploying client-based software can be very difficult, especially COM-based client software. The downside of Web-based applications is that they cannot provide that rich user experience. The .NET Framework has given developers the ability to create rich, smart client applications and eliminate the deployment problems and "DLL Hell" that existed before. Whether Windows Forms or Windows Presentation Foundation (see Chapter 34, "Windows Presentation Foundation") is chosen, client applications are no longer difficult to develop or deploy.

Windows Forms had quite an impact on Windows development. Now when an application is in the initial design phase, the decision between building a Web-based application or a client application has become a little more difficult. Windows client applications can be developed quickly and efficiently, and they can provide users with the rich experience that they expect.

Windows Forms will seem somewhat familiar if you are a Visual Basic developer. You create new forms (also known as windows or dialogs) in much the same way that you drag and drop controls from a toolbox onto the Form Designer. However, if your background is in the classic C style of Windows programming where you create the message pump and monitor messages, or if you're an MFC programmer, you will find that you're able to get to the lower-level internals if you need to. You can override the wndproc and catch those messages, but you might be surprised that you really won't need to very often.

This chapter looks at the following aspects of Windows Forms:

- ❑ The Form class
- ❑ The class hierarchy of Windows Forms
- ❑ The controls and components that are part of the System.Windows.Forms namespace
- ❑ Menus and toolbars
- ❑ Creating controls
- ❑ Creating user controls

Creating a Windows Form Application

First, you need to create a Windows Forms application. For the following example, create a blank form and show it on the screen. This example does not use Visual Studio .NET. It has been entered in a text editor and compiled using the command-line compiler.

```
using System;
using System.Windows.Forms;
namespace NotepadForms
{
  public class MyForm : System.Windows.Forms.Form
  {
    public MyForm()
    {
    }
    [STAThread]
    static void Main()
    {
      Application.Run(new MyForm());
    }
  }
}
```

When you compile and run this example, you will get a small blank form without a caption. Not real functional, but it is a Windows Form.

As you look at the code, two items deserve attention. The first is the fact that you have used inheritance to create the `MyForm` class. The following line declares that `MyForm` is derived from `System.Windows.Forms`:

```
public class MyForm : System.Windows.Forms.Form
```

The `Form` class is one of the main classes in the `System.Windows.Forms` namespace. The other section of code that you want to look at is:

```
[STAThread]
static void Main()
{
  Application.Run(new MyForm());
}
```

`Main` is the default entry point into any C# client application. Typically in larger applications, the `Main()` method would not be in a form, but in a class that is responsible for any startup processing that needs to be done. In this case, you would set the startup class name in the project properties dialog box. Notice the attribute `[STAThread]`. This sets the COM threading model to single-threaded apartment (STA). The STA threading model is required for COM interop and is added by default to a Windows Form project.

The `Application.Run()` method is responsible for starting the standard application message loop. `ApplicationRun()` has three overloads: the first takes no parameter, the second takes an `ApplicationContext` object as a parameter, and the one you see in the example takes a form object as a parameter. In the example, the `MyForm` object will become the main form of the application. This means that when this form is closed, the application ends. By using the `ApplicationContext` class, you can gain a little more control over when the main message loop ends and the application exits.

The `Application` class contains some very useful functionality. It provides a handful of static methods and properties for controlling the application's starting and stopping process and to gain access to the Windows messages that are being processed by the application. The following table lists some of the more useful of these methods and properties.

Method/Property	Description
CommonAppDataPath	The path for the data that is common for all users of the application. Typically this is BasePath\Company Name\Product Name\Version, where BasePath is C:\Documents and Settings\username\ ApplicationData. If it does not exist, the path will be created.
ExecutablePath	This is the path and file name of the executable file that starts the application.
LocalUserAppDataPath	Similar to CommonAppDataPath with the exception that this property supports roaming.
MessageLoop	True or false if a message loop exists on the current thread.
StartupPath	Similar to ExecutablePath, except that the file name is not returned.
AddMessageFilter	Used to preprocess messages. By implementing an IMessageFilter-based object, the messages can be filtered from the message loop, or special processing can take place prior to the message being passed to the loop.
DoEvents	Similar to the Visual Basic DoEvents statement. Allows messages in the queue to be processed.
EnableVisualStyles	Enables XP visual styles for the various visual elements of the application. There are two overloads that will accept manifest information. One is a stream of the manifest, and the other is the full name and path of where the manifest exists.
Exit and ExitThread	Exit ends all currently running message loops and exits the application. ExitThread ends the message loop and closes all windows on the current thread.

Now, what does this sample application look like when it is generated in Visual Studio 2005? The first thing to notice is that two files are created because Visual Studio 2008 takes advantage of the partial class feature of the framework and separates all of the Designer-generated code into a separate file. Using the default name of Form1, the two files are Form1.cs and Form1.Designer.cs. Unless you have the Show All Files option checked on the Project menu you won't see Form1.Designer.cs in Solution Explorer. Following is the code that Visual Studio generates for the two files. First is Form1.cs:

```
using System;
using System.Collections.Generic;
using System.ComponentModel;
using System.Data;
using System.Drawing;
using System.Linq;
using System.Text;
using System.Windows.Forms;
namespace VisualStudioForm
{
public partial class Form1 : Form
{
public Form1()
```

(continued)

(continued)

```
{
InitializeComponent();
}
}
}
```

This is pretty simple, a handful of using statements and a simple constructor. Here is the code in Form1.Designer.cs:

```
namespace VisualStudioForm
{
partial class Form1
{
/// <summary>
/// Required designer variable.
/// </summary>
private System.ComponentModel.IContainer components = null;
/// <summary>
/// Clean up any resources being used.
/// </summary>
/// <param name="disposing">true if managed resources should be disposed;
otherwise, false.</param>
protected override void Dispose(bool disposing)
{
if (disposing && (components != null))
{
  components.Dispose();
}
base.Dispose(disposing);
}
#region Windows Form Designer generated code
/// <summary>
/// Required method for Designer support - do not modify
/// the contents of this method with the code editor.
/// </summary>
private void InitializeComponent()
{
this.components = new System.ComponentModel.Container();
this.AutoScaleMode = System.Windows.Forms.AutoScaleMode.Font;
this.Text = "Form1";
}
#endregion
}
}
```

The Designer file of a form should rarely be edited directly. The only exception would be if there is any special processing that needs to take place in the Dispose method. The InitializeComponent method is discussed later in this chapter.

Looking at the code as a whole for this sample application, you can see it is much longer than the simple command-line example. There are several using statements at the start of the class; most are not necessary for this example. There is no penalty for keeping them there. The class Form1 is derived from System.Windows.Forms just like the earlier Notepad example, but things start to get different at this point. First, there is this line in the Form1.Designer file:

```
private System.ComponentModel.IContainer components = null;
```

In the example, this line of code doesn't really do anything. When you add a component to a form, you can also add it to the components object, which is a container. The reason for adding to this container has to do with disposing of the form. The form class supports the IDisposable interface because it is implemented in the Component class. When a component is added to the components container, the container will make sure that the components are tracked properly and disposed of when the form is disposed of. You can see this if you look at the Dispose method in the code:

```
protected override void Dispose(bool disposing)
{
   if (disposing && (components != null))
   {
     components.Dispose();
   }
   base.Dispose(disposing);
}
```

Here you can see that when the Dispose method is called, the Dispose method of the components object is also called, and because the component object contains the other components, they are also disposed of.

The constructor of the Form1 class, which is in the Form1.cs file, looks like this:

```
public Form1()
{
   InitializeComponent();
}
```

Notice the call to InitializeComponent(). InitializeComponent() is located in Form1.Designer. cs and does pretty much what it describes, and that is to initialize any controls that might have been added to the form. It also initializes the form properties. For this example, InitializeComponent() looks like the following:

```
private void InitializeComponent()
{
this.components = new System.ComponentModel.Container();
this.AutoScaleMode = System.Windows.Forms.AutoScaleMode.Font;
this.Text = "Form1";
}
```

As you can see, it is basic initialization code. This method is tied to the Designer in Visual Studio. When you make changes to the form by using the Designer, the changes are reflected in InitializeComponent(). If you make any type of code change in InitializeComponent(), the next time you make a change in the Designer, your changes will be lost. InitializeComponent() gets regenerated after each change in the Designer. If you need to add additional initialization code for the form or controls and components on the form, be sure to add it after InitializeComponent() is called. InitializeComponent() is also responsible for instantiating the controls so any call that references a control prior to InitializeComponent() will fail with a null reference exception.

To add a control or component to the form, press Ctrl+Alt+X or select Toolbox from the View menu in Visual Studio .NET. Form1 should be in design mode. Right-click Form1.cs in Solution Explorer and select View Designer from the context menu. Select the Button control and drag it to the form in the Designer. You can also double-click the control, and it will be added to the form. Do the same with the TextBox control.

Now that you have added a `TextBox` control and a `Button` control to the form, `InitializeComponent()` expands to include the following code:

```
private void InitializeComponent()
{
    this.button1 = new System.Windows.Forms.Button();
    this.textBox1 = new System.Windows.Forms.TextBox();
    this.SuspendLayout();
    //
    // button1
    //
    this.button1.Location = new System.Drawing.Point(77, 137);
    this.button1.Name = "button1";
    this.button1.Size = new System.Drawing.Size(75, 23);
    this.button1.TabIndex = 0;
    this.button1.Text = "button1";
    this.button1.UseVisualStyleBackColor = true;
    //
    // textBox1
    //
    this.textBox1.Location = new System.Drawing.Point(67, 75);
    this.textBox1.Name = "textBox1";
    this.textBox1.Size = new System.Drawing.Size(100, 20);
    this.textBox1.TabIndex = 1;
    //
    // Form1
    //
    this.AutoScaleDimensions = new System.Drawing.SizeF(6F, 13F);
    this.AutoScaleMode = System.Windows.Forms.AutoScaleMode.Font;
    this.ClientSize = new System.Drawing.Size(284, 264);
    this.Controls.Add(this.textBox1);
    this.Controls.Add(this.button1);
    this.Name = "Form1";
    this.Text = "Form1";
    this.ResumeLayout(false);
    this.PerformLayout();
}
```

If you look at the first three lines of code in the method, you can see the `Button` and `TextBox` controls are instantiated. Notice the names given to the controls, `textBox1` and `button1`. By default, the Designer uses the name of the control and adds an integer value to the name. When you add another button, the Designer adds the name `button2`, and so on. The next line is part of the `SuspendLayout` and `ResumeLayout` pair. `SuspendLayout()` temporarily suspends the layout events that take place when a control is first initialized. At the end of the method the `ResumeLayout()` method is called to set things back to normal. In a complex form with many controls, the `InitializeComponent()` method can get quite large.

To change a property value of a control, either press F4 or select Properties Window from the View menu. The properties window enables you to modify most of the properties for a control or component. When a change is made in the properties window, the `InitializeComponent()` method is rewritten to reflect the new property value. For example, if the `Text` property is changed to `My Button` in the properties window, `InitializeComponent()` will contain this code:

```
//
// button1
//
this.button1.Location = new System.Drawing.Point(77, 137);
this.button1.Name = "button1";
```

```
    this.button1.Size = new System.Drawing.Size(75, 23);
    this.button1.TabIndex = 0;
    this.button1.Text = "My Button";
    this.button1.UseVisualStyleBackColor = true;
```

If you are using an editor other than Visual Studio .NET, you will want to include an `InitializeComponent()` type function in your designs. Keeping all of this initialization code in one spot will help keep the constructor cleaner, not to mention that if you have multiple constructors you can make sure that the initialization code is called from each constructor.

Class Hierarchy

The importance of understanding the hierarchy becomes apparent during the design and construction of custom controls. If your custom control is a derivative of a current control — for example, a text box with some added properties and methods — you will want to inherit from the text box control and then override and add the properties and methods to suit your needs. However, if you are creating a control that doesn't match up to any of the controls included with the .NET Framework, you will have to inherit from one of the three base control classes — `Control` or `ScrollableControl` if you need autoscrolling capabilities, and `ContainerControl` if your control needs to be a container of other controls.

The rest of this chapter is devoted to looking at many of these classes — how they work together and how they can be used to build professional-looking client applications.

Control Class

The `System.Windows.Forms` namespace has one particular class that is the base class for virtually every control and form that is created. This class is the `System.Windows.Forms.Control` class. The `Control` class implements the core functionality to create the display that the user sees. The `Control` class is derived from the `System.ComponentModel.Component` class. The `Component` class provides the `Control` class with the necessary infrastructure that is required to be dropped on a design surface and to be contained by another object. The `Control` class provides a large list of functionality to the classes that are derived from it. The list is too long to itemize here, so this section looks at the more important items that are provided by the `Control` class. Later in the chapter, when you look at the specific controls based on the `Control` class, you will see the properties and methods in some example code. The following subsections group the methods and properties by functionality, so related items can be looked at together.

Size and Location

The size and location of a control are determined by the properties `Height`, `Width`, `Top`, `Bottom`, `Left`, and `Right` along with the complementary properties `Size` and `Location`. The difference is that `Height`, `Width`, `Top`, `Bottom`, `Left`, and `Right` all take single integers as their value. `Size` takes a `Size` structure and `Location` takes a `Point` structure as their values. The `Size` and `Point` structures are a contained version of X,Y coordinates. `Point` generally relates to a location and `Size` is the height and width of an object. `Size` and `Point` are in the `System.Drawing` namespace. Both are very similar in that they provide an X,Y coordinate pair but also have overridden operators for easy comparison and conversion. You can, for example, add two `Size` structures together. In the case of the `Point` structure, the `Addition` operator is overridden so that you can add a `Size` structure to a `Point` and get a new `Point` in return. This has the effect of adding distance to a location and getting a new location. This is very handy if you have to dynamically create forms or controls.

The `Bounds` property returns a `Rectangle` object that represents the area of a control. This area includes scroll bars and title bars. `Rectangle` is also part of the `System.Drawing` namespace. The `ClientSize` property is a `Size` structure that represents the client area of the control, minus the scroll bars and title bar.

The `PointToClient` and `PointToScreen` methods are handy conversion methods that take a `Point` and return a `Point`. `PointToClient` takes a `Point` that represents screen coordinates and translates it to coordinates based on the current client object. This is handy for drag-and-drop actions. `PointToScreen` does just the opposite — it takes coordinates of a client object and translates them to screen coordinates. The `RectangleToScreen` and `ScreenToRectangle` methods perform the same functionality with `Rectangle` structures instead of `Points`.

The `Dock` property determines which edge of the parent control the control will be docked to. A `DockStyle` enumeration value is used as the property's value. This value can be `Top`, `Bottom`, `Right`, `Left`, `Fill`, or `None`. `Fill` sets the control's size to match the client area of the parent control.

The `Anchor` property anchors an edge of the control to the edge of the parent control. This is different from docking in that it does not set the edge to the parent control, but sets the current distance from the edge to be constant. For example, if you anchor the right edge of the control to the right edge of the parent and the parent is resized, the right edge of the control will maintain the same distance from the parent's right edge. The `Anchor` property takes a value of the `AnchorStyles` enumeration. The values are `Top`, `Bottom`, `Left`, `Right`, and `None`. By setting the values, you can make the control resize dynamically with the parent as the parent is resized. This way, buttons and text boxes will not be cut off or hidden as the form is resized by the user.

The `Dock` and `Anchor` properties used in conjunction with the `Flow` and `Table` layout controls (discussed later in this chapter) enable you to create very sophisticated user windows. Window resizing can be difficult with complex forms with many controls. These tools help make that process much easier.

Appearance

Properties that relate to the appearance of the control are `BackColor` and `ForeColor`, which take a `System.Drawing.Color` object as a value. The `BackGroundImage` property takes an `Image`-based object as a value. The `System.Drawing.Image` class is an abstract class that is used as the base for the `Bitmap` and `Metafile` classes. The `BackgroundImageLayout` property uses the `ImageLayout` enumeration to set how the image is displayed on the control. Valid values are `Center`, `Tile`, `Stretch`, `Zoom`, and `None`.

The `Font` and `Text` properties deal with displaying the written word. In order to change the `Font` you will need to create a `Font` object. When you create the `Font` object, you specify the font name, size, and style.

User Interaction

User interaction is best described as the various events that a control creates and responds to. Some of the more common events are `Click`, `DoubleClick`, `KeyDown`, `KeyPress`, `Validating`, and `Paint`.

The Mouse events — `Click`, `DoubleClick`, `MouseDown`, `MouseUp`, `MouseEnter`, `MouseLeave`, and `MouseHover` — deal with the interaction of the mouse and the control. If you are handling both the `Click` and the `DoubleClick` events, every time you catch a `DoubleClick` event, the `Click` event is raised as well. This can result in undesired results if not handled properly. Also, `Click` and `DoubleClick` receive `EventArgs` as an argument, whereas the `MouseDown` and `MouseUp` events receive `MouseEventArgs`. The `MouseEventArgs` contain several pieces of useful information such as the button that was clicked, the number of times the button was clicked, the number of mouse wheel detents (notches in the mouse wheel), and the current X and Y coordinates of the mouse. If you have access to any of this information, you will have to handle either the `MouseDown` or `MouseUp` events, not the `Click` or `DoubleClick` events.

The keyboard events work in a similar fashion: the amount of information needed determines the event that is handled. For simple situations, the `KeyPress` event receives `KeyPressEventArgs`. This contains `KeyChar`, which is a char value that represents the key pressed. The `Handled` property is used to determine whether or not the event was handled. If you set the `Handled` property to `true`, the event is not passed on for default handling by the operating system. If you need more information about the key that was pressed, the `KeyDown` or `KeyUp` event is more appropriate to handle this. They both receive `KeyEventArgs`. Properties in `KeyEventArgs` include whether the Ctrl, Alt, or Shift key was pressed. The `KeyCode` property returns a `Keys` enumeration value that identifies the key that was pressed. Unlike the `KeyPressEventArgs.KeyChar` property, the `KeyCode` property tells you about every key on the keyboard, not just the alphanumeric keys. The `KeyData` property returns a `Keys` value and will also set the modifier. The modifiers are OR'd with the value. This tells you that the Shift key or the Ctrl key was pressed as well. The `KeyValue` property is the `int` value of the `Keys` enumeration. The `Modifiers` property contains a `Keys` value that represents the modifier keys that were pressed. If more than one has been selected, the values are OR'd together. The key events are raised in the following order:

1. `KeyDown`
2. `KeyPress`
3. `KeyUp`

The `Validating`, `Validated`, `Enter`, `Leave`, `GotFocus`, and `LostFocus` events all deal with a control gaining focus (or becoming active) or losing focus. This happens when the user tabs into a control or selects the control with the mouse. `Enter`, `Leave`, `GotFocus`, and `LostFocus` seem to be very similar in what they do. The `GotFocus` and `LostFocus` events are lower-level events that are tied to the `WM_SETFOCUS` and the `WM_KILLFOCUS` Windows messages. Generally, you should use the `Enter` and `Leave` events if possible. The `Validating` and `Validated` events are raised when the control is validating. These events receive `CancelEventArgs`. With this, you can cancel the following events by setting the `Cancel` property to `true`. If you have custom validation code, and validation fails, you can set `Cancel` to `true` and the control will not lose focus. `Validating` occurs during validation; `Validated` occurs after validation. The order in which these events are raised is:

1. `Enter`
2. `GotFocus`
3. `Leave`
4. `Validating`
5. `Validated`
6. `LostFocus`

Understanding the order of these events is important so that you don't inadvertently create a recursive situation. For example, trying to set the focus of a control from the control's `LostFocus` event creates a message deadlock and the application stops responding.

Windows Functionality

The `System.Windows.Forms` namespace is one of the few namespaces that relies on Windows functionality. The `Control` class is a good example of that. If you were to do a disassembly of the `System.Windows.Forms.dll`, you would see a list of references to the `UnsafeNativeMethods` class. The .NET Framework uses this class to wrap all of the standard Win32 API calls. By using interop to the Win32 API, the look and feel of a standard Windows application can still be achieved with the `System.Windows.Forms` namespace.

Functionality that supports the interaction with Windows includes the `Handle` and `IsHandleCreated` properties. `Handle` returns an `IntPtr` that contains the HWND (windows handle) for the control. The window handle is an HWND that uniquely identifies the window. A control can be considered a window, so it has a corresponding HWND. You can use the `Handle` property to call any number of Win32 API calls.

To gain access to the Windows messages, you can override the WndProc method. The WndProc method takes a Message object as a parameter. The Message object is a simple wrapper for a windows message. It contains the HWnd, LParam, WParam, Msg, and Result properties. If you want to have the message processed by the system, you must make sure that you pass the message to the base.WndProc(msg) method. If you want to handle the message, you don't want to pass the message on.

Miscellaneous Functionality

Some items that are a little more difficult to classify are the data-binding capabilities. The BindingContext property returns a BindingManagerBase object. The DataBindings collection maintains a ControlBindingsCollection, which is a collection of binding objects for the control. Data binding is discussed in Chapter 32, "Data Binding."

The CompanyName, ProductName, and Product versions provide data on the origination of the control and its current version.

The Invalidate method allows you to invalidate a region of the control for repainting. You can invalidate the entire control or specify a region or rectangle to invalidate. This causes a paint message to be sent to the control's WndProc. You also have the option to invalidate any child controls at the same time.

Dozens of other properties, methods, and events make up the Control class. This list represents some of the more commonly used ones and is meant to give you an idea of the functionality available.

Standard Controls and Components

The previous section covered some of the common methods and properties for controls. This section looks at the various controls that ship with the .NET Framework, and explains what each of them offers in added functionality. The sample download (www.wrox.com) includes a sample application called FormExample. This sample application is an MDI application (discussed later in the chapter) and includes a form named frmControls that contains many controls with basic functionality enabled. Figure 31-1 shows what frmControls looks like.

Button

The Button class represents the simple command button and is derived from the ButtonBase class. The most common thing to do is to write code to handle the Click event of the button. The following code snippet implements an event handler for the Click event. When the button is clicked, a message box pops up that displays the button's name:

```
private void btnTest_Click(object sender, System.EventArgs e)
{
    MessageBox.Show(((Button)sender).Name + " was clicked.");
}
```

With the PerformClick method, you can simulate the Click event on a button without the user actually clicking the button. The NotifyDefault method takes a Boolean value as a parameter and tells the button to draw itself as the default button. Typically, the default button on a form has a slightly thicker border. To identify the button as default, you set the AcceptButton property on the form to the button. Then, when the user presses the Enter key, the button Click event for the default button is raised. Figure 31-2 shows that the button with the caption Default is the default button (notice the dark border).

Buttons can have images as well as text. Images are supplied by way of an ImageList object or the Image property. ImageList objects are exactly what they sound like: a list of images managed by a component placed on a form. They are explained in detail later in this chapter.

Both `Text` and `Image` have an `Align` property to align the text or image on the `Button`. The `Align` property takes a `ContentAlignment` enumeration value. The text or image can be aligned in combinations of left and right and top and bottom.

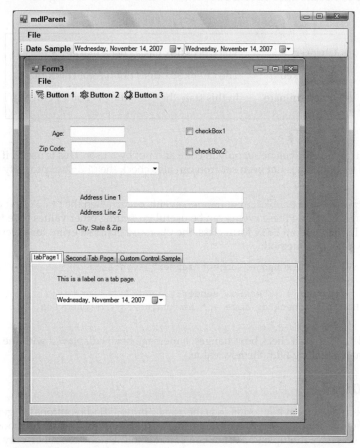

Figure 31-1

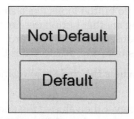

Figure 31-2

CheckBox

The CheckBox control is also derived from ButtonBase and is used to accept a two-state or three-state response from the user. If you set the ThreeState property to true, the CheckBox's CheckState property can be one of the three CheckState enum values in the following table.

Checked	The CheckBox has a check mark.
Unchecked	The CheckBox does not have a check mark.
Indeterminate	In this state the CheckBox becomes gray.

The Indeterminate value can be set only in code and not by a user. This is useful if you need to convey to the user that an option has not been set. You can also check the Checked property if you want a Boolean value.

The CheckedChanged and CheckStateChanged events occur when the CheckState or Checked properties change. Catching these events can be useful for setting other values based on the new state of the CheckBox. In the frmControls form class, the CheckedChanged event for several CheckBoxes is handled by the following method:

```
private void checkBoxChanged(object sender, EventArgs e)
{
   CheckBox checkBox = (CheckBox)sender;
   MessageBox.Show(checkBox.Name + " new value is " + checkBox.Checked.ToString());
}
```

As the checked state of each check box changes, a message box is displayed with the name of the check box that was changed along with the new value.

RadioButton

The last control derived from ButtonBase is the radio button. Radio buttons are generally used as a group. Sometimes referred to as option buttons, radio buttons allow the user to choose one of several options. When you have multiple RadioButton controls in the same container, only one at a time may be selected. So, if you have three options — for example, Red, Green, and Blue — if the Red option is selected and the user clicks the Blue option, the Red is automatically deselected.

The Appearance property takes an Appearance enumeration value. This can be either Button or Normal. When you choose Normal, the radio button looks like a small circle with a label beside it. Selecting the button fills the circle; selecting another button deselects the currently selected button and makes the circle look empty. When you choose Button, the control looks like a standard button, but it works like a toggle — selected is the in position, and deselected is the normal, or out, position.

The CheckedAlign property determines where the circle is in relation to the label text. It could be on top of the label, on either side, or below.

The CheckedChanged event is raised whenever the value of the Checked property changes. This way, you can perform other actions based on the new value of the control.

ComboBox, ListBox, and CheckedListBox

ComboBox, ListBox, and CheckedListBox are all derived from the ListControl class. This class provides some of the basic list management functionality. The most important aspects of using list controls are adding data to and selecting data from the list. Which list is used is generally determined by how the list is used and the type of data that is going to be in the list. If there is a need to have multiple selections or if the user needs to be able to see several items in the list at any time, the ListBox or CheckedListBox is going to be the best choice. If only a single item is ever selected in the list at any time, a ComboBox may be a good choice.

Data must be added to a list box before it can be useful. This is done by adding objects to the ListBox. ObjectCollection. This collection is exposed by the list's Items property. Because the collection stores objects, any valid .NET type can be added to the list. In order to identify the items, two important properties need to be set. The first is the DisplayMember property. This setting tells the ListControl what property of your object should be displayed in the list. The other is ValueMember, which is the property of your object that you want to return as the value. If strings have been added to the list, by default the string value is used for both of these properties. The frmLists form in the sample application shows how both objects and strings (which are of course objects) can be loaded into a list box. The example uses Vendor objects for the list data. The Vendor object contains just two properties: Name and PhoneNo. The DisplayMember property is set to the Name property. This tells the list control to display the value from the Name property in the list to the user.

You can access the data in the list control in a couple of ways, as shown in the following code example. The list is loaded with the Vendor objects. The DisplayMember and ValueMember properties are set. You can find this code in the frmLists form class in the sample application.

First is the LoadList method. This method loads the list with either Vendor objects or a simple string containing the vendor name. An option button is checked to see which values should be loaded in the list:

```
private void LoadList(Control ctrlToLoad)
    {
      ListBox tmpCtrl = null;
      if (ctrlToLoad is ListBox)
        tmpCtrl = (ListBox)ctrlToLoad;
      tmpCtrl.Items.Clear();
      tmpCtrl.DataSource = null;
      if (radioButton1.Checked)
      {
        //load objects
        tmpCtrl.Items.Add(new Vendor("XYZ Company", "555-555-1234"));
        tmpCtrl.Items.Add(new Vendor("ABC Company", "555-555-2345"));
        tmpCtrl.Items.Add(new Vendor("Other Company", "555-555-3456"));
        tmpCtrl.Items.Add(new Vendor("Another Company", "555-555-4567"));
        tmpCtrl.Items.Add(new Vendor("More Company", "555-555-6789"));
        tmpCtrl.Items.Add(new Vendor("Last Company", "555-555-7890"));
        tmpCtrl.DisplayMember = "Name";
      }
      else
      {
        tmpCtrl.Items.Clear();
        tmpCtrl.Items.Add("XYZ Company");
        tmpCtrl.Items.Add("ABC Company");
        tmpCtrl.Items.Add("Other Company");
        tmpCtrl.Items.Add("Another Company");
        tmpCtrl.Items.Add("More Company");
        tmpCtrl.Items.Add("Last Company");
      }
    }
```

Once the data is loaded in the list the `SelectedItem` and `SelectedIndex` properties can be used to get at the data. The `SelectedItem` property returns the object that is currently selected. If the list is set to allow multiple selections, there is no guarantee which of the selected items will be returned. In this case, the `SelectObject` collection should be used. This contains a list of all of the currently selected items in the list.

If the item at a specific index is needed, the `Items` property can be used to access the `ListBox.ObjectCollection`. Because this is a standard .NET collection class, the items in the collection can be accessed in the same way as any other collection class.

If `DataBinding` is used to populate the list, the `SelectedValue` property will return the property value of the selected object that was set to the `ValueMember` property. If `Phone` is set to `ValueMember`, the `SelectedValue` will return the `Phone` value from the selected item. In order to use `ValueMember` and `SelectValue` the list must be loaded by way of the `DataSource` property. An `ArrayList` or any other `IList`-based collection must be loaded with the objects first, then the list can be assigned to the `DataSource` property. This short example demonstrates this:

```
listBox1.DataSource = null;
System.Collections.ArrayList lst = new System.Collections.ArrayList();
lst.Add(new Vendor("XYZ Company", "555-555-1234"));
lst.Add(new Vendor("ABC Company", "555-555-2345"));
lst.Add(new Vendor("Other Company", "555-555-3456"));
lst.Add(new Vendor("Another Company", "555-555-4567"));
lst.Add(new Vendor("More Company", "555-555-6789"));
lst.Add(new Vendor("Last Company", "555-555-7890"));
listBox1.Items.Clear();
listBox1.DataSource = lst;
listBox1.DisplayMember = "Name";
listBox1.ValueMember = "Phone";
```

Using `SelectedValue` without using `DataBinding` will result in a `NullException` error.

The following lines of code show the syntax of accessing the data in the list:

```
//obj is set to the selected Vendor object
obj = listBox1.SelectedItem;
//obj is set to the Vendor object with index of 3 (4th object).
//obj is set to the values of the Phone property of the selected vendor object.
//This example assumes that databinding was used to populate the list.
listBox1.ValuesMember = "Phone";
obj = listBox1.SelectValue;
```

The thing to remember is that all of these methods return `object` as the type. A cast to the proper data type will need to be done in order to use the value of `obj`.

The `Items` property of the `ComboBox` returns `ComboBox.ObjectCollection`. A `ComboBox` is a combination of an edit control and a list box. You set the style of the `ComboBox` by passing a `DropDownStyle` enumeration value to the `DropDownStyle` property. The following table lists the various `DropDownStyle` values.

value	Description
DropDown	The text portion of the combo box is editable, and users can enter a value. They also must click the arrow button to show the list.
DropDownList	The text portion is not editable. Users must make a selection from the list.
Simple	This is similar to DropDown except that the list is always visible.

If the values in the list are wide, you can change the width of the drop-down portion of the control with the `DropDownWidth` property. The `MaxDropDownItems` property sets the number of items to show when the drop-down portion of the list is displayed.

The `FindString` and `FindStringExact` methods are two other useful methods of the list controls. `FindString` finds the first string in the list that starts with the passed-in string. `FindStringExact` finds the first string that matches the passed-in string. Both return the index of the value that is found or `-1` if the value is not found. They can also take an integer that is the starting index to search from.

DateTimePicker

The `DateTimePicker` allows users to select a date or time value (or both) in a number of different formats. You can display the `DateTime`-based value in any of the standard time and date formats. The Format property takes a `DateTimePickerFormat` enumeration that sets the format to `Long`, `Short`, `Time`, or `Custom`. If the Format property is set to `DateTiemePickerFormat.Custom`, you can set the `CustomFormat` property to a string that represents the format.

There is both a `Text` property and a `Value` property. The `Text` property returns a text representation of the `DateTime` value, whereas the `Value` property returns the `DateTime` object. You can also set the maximum and minimum allowable date values with the `MinDate` and `MaxDate` properties.

When users click the down arrow, a calendar is displayed allowing the users to select a date in the calendar. Properties are available that allow you to change the appearance of the calendar by setting the title and month background colors as well as the foreground colors.

The `ShowUpDown` property determines whether an `UpDown` arrow is displayed on the control. The currently highlighted value can be changed by clicking the up or down arrow.

ErrorProvider

`ErrorProvider` is actually not a control but a component. When you drag a component to the Designer, it shows in the component tray under the Designer. The `ErrorProvider` flashes an icon next to a control when an error condition or validation failure exists. Suppose that you have a `TextBox` entry for an age. Your business rules say that the age value cannot be greater than 65. If users try to enter an age greater than that, you must inform them that the age is greater than the allowable value and that they need to change the entered value. The check for a valid value takes place in the `Validated` event of the text box. If the validation fails, you call the `SetError` method, passing in the control that caused the error and a string that informs the user what the error is. An icon starts flashing, indicating that an error has occurred, and when the user hovers over the icon the error text is displayed. Figure 31-3 shows the icon that is displayed when an invalid entry is made in the text box.

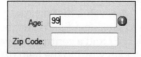

Figure 31-3

You can create an `ErrorProvider` for each control that produces errors on a form, but if you have a large number of controls this can become unwieldy. Another option is to use one error provider and, in the validate event, to call the `IconLocation` method with the control that is causing the validation and one of the `ErrorIconAlignment` enumeration values. This value sets where the icon is aligned near the control. Then you call the `SetError` method. If no error condition exists, you can clear the `ErrorProvider` by calling `SetError` with an empty string as the error string. The following example shows how this works:

```
private void txtAge_Validating(object sender,
System.ComponentModel.CancelEventArgs e)
{
   if(txtAge.TextLength > 0 && Convert.ToInt32(txtAge.Text) > 65)
   {
      errMain.SetIconAlignment((Control)sender,
                                 ErrorIconAlignment.MiddleRight);
      errMain.SetError((Control)sender, "Value must be less then 65.");
      e.Cancel = true;
   }
   else
   {
      errMain.SetError((Control)sender, "");
   }
}
private void txtZipCode_Validating(object sender, CancelEventArgs e)
   {
      if(txtZipCode.Text.Length != 5)
      {
         errMain.SetIconAlignment((Control)sender,
                     ErrorIconAlignment.MiddleRight);
         errMain.SetError((Control)sender, "Must be 5 charactors..");
         e.Cancel = true;
      }
      else
      {
         errMain.SetError((Control)sender, "");
      }
   }
```

If the validation fails (the age is over 65 in `txtAge`, for example), then the `SetIcon` method of the `ErrorProvider errMain` is called. It will set the icon next to the control that failed validation. The error is set next so that when users hover over the icon, the message informs them of what is responsible for the failed validation.

HelpProvider

`HelpProvider`, like `ErrorProvider`, is a component and not a control. `HelpProvider` allows you to hook up controls to help topics. To associate a control with the help provider, you call the `SetShowHelp` method, passing the control and a `Boolean` value that determines whether help will be shown. The `HelpNamespace` property allows you to set a help file. When the `HelpNamespace` property is set, the help file is displayed any time you select F1 and a control that you have registered with the `HelpProvider` is in focus. You can set a keyword to the help file with the `SetHelpKeyword` method. `SetHelpNavigator` takes a `HelpNavigator` enumeration value to determine which element in the help file should be displayed. You can set it for a specific topic, the index, the table of contents, or the search page. `SetHelpString` associates a string value of help-related text to a control. If the `HelpNamespace` property has not been set, pressing F1 will show this text in a pop-up window. Go ahead and add a `HelpProvider` to the previous example:

```
helpProvider1.SetHelpString(txtAge,"Enter an age that is less than 65."
helpProvider1.SetHelpString(txtZipCode,"Enter a 5-digit zip code."
```

ImageList

An `ImageList` component is exactly what the name implies — a list of images. Typically, this component is used for holding a collection of images that are used as toolbar icons or icons in a `TreeView` control. Many controls have an `ImageList` property. The `ImageList` property typically comes with an `ImageIndex` property. The `ImageList` property is set to an instance of the `ImageList` component, and the `ImageIndex` property is set to the index in the `ImageList` that represents the image that should be displayed on the control. You add images to the `ImageList` component by using the `Add` method of the `ImageList.Images` property. The `Images` property returns an `ImageCollection`.

The two most commonly used properties are `ImageSize` and `ColorDepth`. `ImageSize` uses a `Size` structure as its value. The default value is 16 × 16 but it can be any value from 1 to 256. The `ColorDepth` uses a `ColorDepth` enumeration as its value. The color depth values go from 4-bit to 32-bit. For .NET Framework 1.1, the default is `ColorDepth.Depth8Bit`.

Label

`Label`s are generally used to provide descriptive text to the user. The text might be related to other controls or the current system state. You usually see a label together with a text box. The label provides the user with a description of the type of data to be entered in the text box. The `Label` control is always read-only — the user cannot change the string value of the `Text` property. However, you can change the `Text` property in your code. The `UseMnemonic` property allows you to enable the access key functionality. When you precede a character in the `Text` property with the ampersand (`&`), that letter will appear underlined in the label control. Pressing the Alt key in combination with the underlined letter puts the focus on the next control in the tab order. If the `Text` property contains an ampersand in the text, add a second one and it will not underline the next letter. For example, if the label text is "Nuts & Bolts," set the property to "Nuts && Bolts." Because the `Label` control is read-only, it cannot gain focus; that's why focus is sent to the next control. Because of this, it is important to remember that if you enable mnemonics, you must be certain to set the tab order properly on your form.

The `AutoSize` property is a `Boolean` value that specifies whether the `Label` will resize itself based on the contents of the `Label`. This can be useful for multi-language applications where the length of the `Text` property can change based on the current language.

ListView

The `ListView` control enables you to display items in one of four different ways. You can display text with an optional large icon, text with an optional small icon, or text and small icons in a vertical list or in detail view, which allows you to display the item text plus any subitems in columns. If this sounds familiar, it should, because this is what the right side of File Explorer uses to display the contents of folders. `ListView` contains a collection of `ListViewItems`. `ListViewItems` allow you to set a `Text` property used for the display. `ListViewItem` has a property called `SubItems` that contains the text that appears in detail view.

The following example demonstrates how you might use `ListView`. This example includes a short list of countries. Each `CountryList` object contains a property for the country name, country abbreviation, and currency. Here is the code for the `CountryList` class:

```
using System;
namespace FormsSample
{

    public class CountryItem   : System.Windows.Forms.ListViewItem
    {
```

(continued)

1033

(continued)

```
        string _cntryName = "";
        string _cntryAbbrev = "";
        public CountryItem(string countryName,
                              string countryAbbreviation, string currency)
        {
          _cntryName = countryName;
          _cntryAbbrev = countryAbbreviation;
          base.Text = _cntryName;
          base.SubItems.Add(currency);
        }
        public string CountryName
        {
          get {return _cntryName;}
        }
        public string CountryAbbreviation
        {
          get {return _cntryAbbrev;}
        }
    }
}
```

Notice that you are deriving the CountryList class from ListViewItem. This is because you can add only ListViewItem-based objects to the ListView control. In the constructor, you pass the country name to the base.Text property and add the currency value to the base.SubItems property. This displays the country name in the list and the currency in a separate column when in details view.

Next, you need to add a couple of the CountryItem objects to the ListView control in the code of the form:

```
    lvCountries.Items.Add(new CountryItem("United States","US","Dollar"));
    lvCountries.Items[0].ImageIndex = 0;
    lvCountries.Items.Add(new CountryItem("Great Britain", "GB", "Pound"));
    lvCountries.Items[1].ImageIndex = 1;
    lvCountries.Items.Add(new CountryItem("Canada", "CA", "Dollar"));
    lvCountries.Items[2].ImageIndex = 2;
    lvCountries.Items.Add(new CountryItem("Japan", "JP", "Yen"));
    lvCountries.Items[3].ImageIndex = 3;
    lvCountries.Items.Add(new CountryItem("Germany", "GM"", "Deutch Mark"));
    lvCountries.Items[4].ImageIndex = 4;
```

Here you add a new CountryItem to the Items collection of the ListView control (lvCountries). Notice that you set the ImageIndex property of the item after you add it to the control. There are two ImageIndex objects, one for large icons and one for small icons (SmallImageList and LargeImageList properties). The trick to having two ImageLists with differing image sizes is to make sure you add the items to the ImageList in the same order. This way, the index of each ImageList represents the same image, just different sizes. In the example, the ImageLists contain icons of the flags for each country added.

On top of the form, there is a ComboBox (cbView) that lists the four different View enumeration values. You add the items to the cbView like this:

```
    cbView.Items.Add(View.LargeIcon);
    cbView.Items.Add(View.SmallIcon);
    cbView.Items.Add(View.List);
    cbView.Items.Add(View.Details);
    cbView.SelectedIndex = 0;
```

In the SelectedIndexChanged event of cbView, you add the single line of code:

```
lvCountries.View = (View)cbView.SelectedItem;
```

This sets the `View` property of `lvCountries` to the new value selected in the `ComboBox` control. Notice that you need to cast to the `View` type because `object` is returned from the `SelectedItem` property of the `cbView`.

Last, but hardly least, you have to add columns to the `Columns` collection. The columns are for details view. In this case, you are adding two columns: Country Name and Currency. The order of the columns is as follows: the `Text` of the `ListViewItem`, then each item in the `ListViewItem.SubItem` collection, in the order it appears in the collection. You can add columns either by creating a `ColumnHeader` object and setting the `Text` property and optionally the `Width` and `Alignment` properties. After creating the `ColumnHeader` object, you can add it to the `Columns` property. The other way to add columns is to use an override of the `Columns.Add` method. It allows you to pass in the `Text`, `Width`, and `Alignment` values. Here is an example:

```
lvCountries.Columns.Add("Country",100, HorizontalAlignment.Left);
lvCountries.Columns.Add("Currency"",100, HorizontalAlignment.Left);
```

If you set the `AllowColumnReorder` property to `true`, the user can drag the column headers around and rearrange the column order.

The `CheckBoxes` property on the `ListView` shows check boxes next to the items in the `ListView`. This allows the user to easily select multiple items in the `ListView` control. You can check which items are selected by checking the `CheckedItems` collection.

The `Alignment` property sets the alignment of icons in Large and Small icon view. The value can be any of the `ListViewAlignment` enumeration values. They are `Default`, `Left`, `Top`, and `SnapToGrid`. The `Default` value allows users to arrange the icons in any position that they want. When choosing `Left` or `Top`, the items are aligned with the left or top of the `ListView` control. When choosing `SnapToGrid`, the items snap to an invisible grid on the `ListView` control. The `AutoArrange` property can be set to a `Boolean` value and will automatically align the icons based on the `Alignment` property.

PictureBox

The `PictureBox` control is used to display an image. The image can be a BMP, JPEG, GIF, PNG, metafile, or icon. The `SizeMode` property uses the `PictureBoxSizeMode` enumeration to determine how the image is sized and positioned in the control. The `SizeMode` property can be `AutoSize`, `CenterImage`, `Normal`, and `StretchImage`.

You can change the size of the display of the `PictureBox` by setting the `ClientSize` property. You load the `PictureBox` by first creating an `Image`-based object. For example, to load a JPEG file into a `PictureBox` you would do the following:

```
Bitmap myJpeg = new Bitmap("mypic.jpg");
pictureBox1.Image = (Image)myJpeg;
```

Notice that you will need to cast back to an `Image` type because that is what the `Image` property expects.

ProgressBar

The `ProgressBar` control is a visual clue to the status of a lengthy operation. It indicates to users that there is something going on and that they should wait. The `ProgressBar` control works by setting the `Minimum` and `Maximum` properties, which correspond to the progress indicator being all the way to the left (`Minimum`) or all the way to the right (`Maximum`). You set the `Step` property to determine the number that the value is incremented each time the `PerformStep` method is called. You can also use the `Increment` method and increment the value by the value passed in the method call. The `Value` property returns the current value of the `ProgressBar`.

You can use the Text property to inform the user of the percentage of the operation that has been completed or the number of items left to process. There is also a BackgroundImage property to customize the look of the progress bar.

TextBox, RichTextBox, and MaskedTextBox

The TextBox control is one of the most used controls in the toolbox. The TextBox, RichTextBox, and MaskedTextBox controls are all derived from TextBoxBase. TextBoxBase provides properties such as MultiLine and Lines. MultiLine is a Boolean value that allows the TextBox control to display text in more than one line. Each line in a text box is a part of an array of strings. This array is exposed through the Lines property. The Text property returns the entire text box contents as a single string. TextLength is the total length of the string that text would return. The MaxLength property will limit the length of the text to the specified amount.

SelectedText, SelectionLength, and SelectionStart all deal with the currently selected text in the text box. The selected text is highlighted when the control has focus.

The TextBox control adds a couple of interesting properties. AcceptsReturn is a Boolean value that will allow the TextBox to accept the Enter key as a new line or whether it activates the default button on the form. When set to true, pressing the Enter key creates a new line in the TextBox. CharacterCasing determines the casing of the text in the text box. The CharacterCasing enumeration contains three values, Lower, Normal, and Upper. Lower lowercases all text regardless of how it is entered, Upper renders all text in uppercase letters, and Normal displays the text as it is entered. The PasswordChar property takes a char that represents what is displayed to the users when they type text in the text box. This is typically used for entering passwords and PINs. The text property will return the actual text that was entered; only the display is affected by this property.

The RichTextBox is a text editing control that can handle special formatting features. As the name implies, the RichTextBox control uses Rich Text Format (RTF) to handle the special formatting. You can make formatting changes by using the Selection properties: SelectionFont, SelectionColor, and SelectionBullet, and paragraph formatting with SelectionIndent, SelectionRightIndent, and SelectionHangingIndent. All of the Selection properties work in the same way. If a section of text is highlighted, a change to a Selection property affects the selected text. If no text is selected, the change takes effect with any text that is inserted to the right of the current insertion point.

The text of the control can be retrieved by using the Text property or the Rtf property. The Text property returns just the text of the control, whereas the Rtf property returns the formatted text.

The LoadFile method can load text from a file in a couple of different ways. It can use either a string that represents the path and file name or it can use a stream object. You can also specify the RichTextBoxStreamType. The following table lists the values of RichTextBoxStreamType.

Value	Description
PlainText	No formatting information. In places that contained OLE objects, spaces are used.
RichNoOleObjs	Rich text formatting, but spaces where the OLE objects would have been.
RichText	Formatted RTF with OLE objects in place.
TextTextOleObjs	Plain text with text replacing the OLE objects.
UnicodePlainText	Same as PlainText but Unicode encoded.

The `SaveFile` method works with the same parameters, saving the data from the control to a specified file. If a file by that name already exists, it will be overwritten.

The `MaskedTextBox` supplies the ability to limit what the user may input into the control. It also allows for automatic formatting of the data entered. Several properties are used in order to validate or format the user's input. `Mask` is the property that contains the mask string, which is similar to a format string. The number of characters allowed, the data type of allowed characters, and the format of the data are all set using the `Mask` string. A `MaskedTextProvider`-based class can also provide the formatting and validation information needed. The `MaskedTextProvider` can only be set by passing it in on one of the constrictors.

Three different properties will return the text of the `MaskedTextControl`. The `Text` property returns the text of the control at the current moment. This could be different depending on whether or not the control has focus, which depends on the value of the `HidePromptOnLeave` property. The prompt is a string that users see to guide them on what should be entered. The `InputText` property always returns just the text that the user entered. The `OutputText` property returns the text-formatted based on the `IncludeLiterals` and `IncludePrompt` properties. If, for example, the mask is for a phone number, the `Mask` string would possibly include parentheses and a couple of dashes. These would be the literal characters and would be included in the `OutputText` property if the `IncludeLiteral` property were set to `true`.

A couple of extra events also exist for the `MaskedTextBox` control. `OutputTextChanged` and `InputTextChanged` are raised when `InputText` or `OutputText` changes.

Panel

A `Panel` is simply a control that contains other controls. By grouping controls together and placing them in a panel, it is a little easier to manage the controls. For example, you can disable all of the controls in the panel by disabling the panel. Because the `Panel` control is derived from `ScrollableControl`, you also can get the advantage of the `AutoScroll` property. If you have too many controls to display in the available area, place them in a `Panel` and set `AutoScroll` to `true` — now you can scroll through all of the controls.

Panels do not show a border by default, but by setting the `BorderStyle` property to something other than none, you can use the `Panel` to visually group related controls using borders. This makes the user interface more user-friendly.

`Panel` is the base class for the `FlowLayoutPanel`, `TableLayoutPanel`, `TabPage`, and `SplitterPanel`. By using these controls, a very sophisticated and professional-looking form or window can be created. The `FlowLayoutPanel` and `TableLayoutPanel` are especially useful for creating forms that resize properly.

FlowLayoutPanel and TableLayoutPanel

`FlowLayoutPanel` and `TableLayoutPanel` are new additions to the .NET Framework. As the names might suggest, the panels offer the capability to lay out a form using the same paradigm as a Web Form. `FlowLayoutPanel` is a container that allows the contained controls to flow in either the horizontal or vertical directions. Instead of flowing, it allows for the clipping of the controls. Flow direction is set using the `FlowDirection` property and the `FlowDirection` enumeration. The `WrapContents` property determines if controls flow to the next row or column when the form is resized or if the control is clipped.

`TableLayoutPanel` uses a grid structure to control the layout of controls. Any Windows Forms control can be a child of the `TableLayoutPanel`, including another `TableLayoutPanel`. This allows for a very flexible and dynamic window design. When a control is added to a `TableLayoutPanel`, four additional properties are added to the Layout category of the property page. They are Column, ColumnSpan, Row, and RowSpan. Much like an HTML table on a Web page, column and row spans can be set for each control. By default, the control will be centered in the cell of the table, but this can be changed by using the Anchor and Dock properties.

The default style of the rows and columns can be changed using RowStyles and ColumnsStyles collections. These collections contain RowStyle and ColumnsStyle objects, respectively. The Style objects have a common property, SizeType. SizeType uses the SizeType enumeration to determine how the column width or row height should be sized. Values include AutoSize, Absolute, and Percent. AutoSize shares the space with other peer controls. Absolute allows a set number of pixels for the size and Percent tells the control to size the column or width as a percentage of the parent control.

Rows, columns, and child controls can be added or removed at runtime. The GrowStyle property takes a TableLayoutPanelGrowStyle enumeration value that sets the table to add a column or a row, or stay a fixed size when a new control is added to a full table. If the value is FixedSized, an ArgumentException is thrown when there is an attempt to add another control. If a cell in the table is empty, the control will be placed in the empty cell. This property has an effect only when the table is full and a control is added.

The formPanel form in the sample application has FlowLayoutPanels and TableLayoutPanels with a variety of controls set in them. Experimenting with the controls, especially the Dock and Anchor properties of the controls placed in the layout panels, is the best way to understand how they work.

SplitContainer

The SplitContainer control is really three controls in one. It has two panel controls with a bar or splitter between them. The user is able to move the bar and resize the panels. As the panels resize, the controls in the panels also can be resized. The best example of a SplitContainer is File Explorer. The left panel contains a TreeView of folders and the right side contains a ListView of folder contents. When the user moves the mouse over the splitter bar, the cursor changes, showing that the bar can be moved. The SplitContainer can contain any control, including layout panels and other SplitContainers. This allows the creation of very complex and sophisticated forms.

The movement and position of the splitter bar can be controlled with the SplitterDistance and SplitterIncrement properties. The SplitterDistance property determines where the splitter starts in relation to the left or top of the control. The SplitterIncrement determines the number of pixels the splitter moves when being dragged. The panels can have their minimum size set with the Panel1MinSize and Panel2MinSize properties. These properties are also in pixels.

The Splitter control raises two events that relate to moving: the SplitterMoving event and the SplitterMoved event. One takes place during the move and the other takes place after the move has happened. They both receive SplitterEventArgs. SplitterEventArgs contains properties for the X and Y coordinates of the upper-left corner of the Splitter (SplitX and SplitY) and the X and Y coordinates of the mouse pointer (X and Y).

TabControl and TabPages

TabControl allows you to group related controls onto a series of tab pages. TabControl manages the collection of TabPages. Several properties control the appearance of TabControl. The Appearance property uses the TabAppearance enumeration to determine what the tabs look like. The values are FlatButtons, Buttons, or Normal. The Multiline property is a Boolean that determines if more than one row of tabs is shown. If the Multiline property is set to false and there are more tabs than can fit in the display, arrows appear that allow the user to scroll and see the rest of the tabs.

The TabPage Text property is what is displayed on the tab. The Text property is a parameter in a constructor override as well.

Once you create a `TabPage` control, it is basically a container control for you to place other controls. The Designer in Visual Studio .NET makes it easy to add `TabPage` controls to a `TabControl` control by using the collection editor. You can set the various properties as you add each page. Then you can drag the other child controls to each `TabPage` control.

You can determine the current tab by looking at the `SelectedTab` property. The `SelectedIndex` event is raised each time a new tab is selected. By listening to the `SelectedIndex` property and then confirming the current tab with `SelectedTab`, you can do special processing based on each tab. You could, for example, manage the data displayed for each tab.

ToolStrip

The `ToolStrip` control is a container control used to create toolbars, menu structures, and status bars. The `ToolStrip` is used directly for toolbars, and serves as the base class for the `MenuStrip` and `StatusStrip` controls.

When used as a toolbar, the `ToolStrip` control uses a set of controls based on the abstract `ToolStripItem` class. `ToolStripItem` adds the common display and layout functionality as well as managing most of the events used by the controls. `ToolStripItem` is derived from the `System .ComponentModel.Component` class and not from the `Control` class. `ToolStripItem`-based classes must be contained in a `ToolStrip`-based container.

`Image` and `Text` are probably the most common properties that will be set. Images can be set with either the `Image` property or by using the `ImageList` control and setting it to the `ImageList` property of the `ToolStrip` control. The `ImageIndex` property of the individual controls can then be set.

Formatting of the text on a `ToolStripItem` is handled with the `Font`, `TextAlign`, and `TextDirection` properties. `TextAlign` sets the alignment of the text in relation to the control. This can be any of the `ControlAlignment` enumeration values. The default is `MiddleRight`. The `TextDirection` property sets the orientation of the text. Values can be any of the `ToolStripTextDirection` enumeration values, which include `Horizontal`, `Inherit`, `Vertical270`, and `Vertical90`. `Vertical270` rotates the text 270 degrees and `Vertical90` rotates the text 90 degrees.

The `DisplayStyle` property controls whether text, image, text and image, or nothing is displayed on the control. When `AutoSize` is set to `true`, the `ToolStripItem` will resize itself so only the minimum amount of space is used.

The controls that are derived directly from `ToolStripItem` are listed in the following table.

Tool Strip Items	Description
`ToolStripButton`	Represents a button that the user can select.
`ToolStripLabel`	Displays nonselectable text or images on the `ToolStrip`. The `ToolStripLabel` can also display one or more hyperlinks.
`ToolStripSeparator`	Used to separate and group other `ToolStripItems`. Items can be grouped according to functionality.
`ToolStripDropDownItem`	Displays drop-down items. Base class for `ToolStripDropDownButton`, `ToolStripMenuItem`, and `ToolStripSplitButton`.
`ToolStripControlHost`	Hosts other non–`ToolStripItem`-derived controls on a `ToolStrip`. Base class for `ToolStripComboBox`, `ToolStripProgressBar`, and `ToolStripTextBox`.

The first two items in the list, `ToolStripDropDownItem` and `ToolStripControlHost`, deserve a little more discussion. `ToolStripDropDownItem` is the base class for `ToolStripMenuItems`, which are used to build the menu structure. `ToolStripMenuItems` are added to `MenuStrip` controls. As mentioned earlier, `MenuStrips` are derived from `ToolStrip` controls. This is important when it comes time to manipulate or extend menu items. Because toolbars and menus are derived from the same classes, creating a framework for managing and executing commands becomes much easier.

`ToolStripControlHost` can be used to host other controls that do not derive from `ToolStripItem`. Remember that the only controls that can be directly hosted by a `ToolStrip` are those that derive from `ToolStripItem`. The following example shows how to host a `DateTimePicker` control on a `ToolStrip`:

```
public mdiParent()
{
    InitializeComponent();
    ToolStripControlHost _dateTimeCtl;
    _dateTimeCtl = new ToolStripControlHost(new DateTimePicker());
    ((DateTimePicker)_dateTimeCtl.Control).ValueChanged +=
            delegate {
                        toolStripLabel1.Text =
    ((DateTimePicker)_dateTimeCtl.Control).Value.Subtract(DateTime.Now).ToString();
                     };

    _dateTimeCtl.Width = 200;
    _dateTimeCtl.DisplayStyle = ToolStripItemDisplayStyle.Text;
    toolStrip1.Items.Add(_dateTimeCtl);
}
```

This is the constructor from the `frmMain` form in the code sample. First, a `ToolStripControlHost` is declared and instantiated. Notice that when the control is instantiated, the control that is to be hosted is passed in on the constructor. The next line sets up the `ValueChanged` event of the `DateTimePicker` control. The control can be accessed through the `Control` property of the `ToolStripHostControl`. This returns a `Control` object, so it will need to be cast back to the proper type of control. Once that is done, the properties and methods of the hosted control are available to use.

Another way to do this that would perhaps enforce encapsulation a little better is to create a new class derived from `ToolStripControlHost`. The following code is another version of the toolstrip version of the `DateTimePicker` called `ToolStripDateTimePicker`:

```
namespace FormsSample.SampleControls
{
  public class DTPickerToolStrip   : System.Windows.Forms.ToolStripControlHost
  {
    public event EventHandler ValueChanged;
    public DTPickerToolStrip()   : base(new DateTimePicker())
    {
    }
    public new DateTimePicker Control
    {
       get{return (DateTimePicker)base.Control;}
    }
    public DateTime Value
    {
       get { return Control.Value; }
    }

    protected override void OnSubscribeControlEvents(Control control)
```

```
    {
      base.OnSubscribeControlEvents(control);
      ((DateTimePicker)control).ValueChanged +=
new EventHandler(ValueChangedHandler);
    }

    protected override void OnUnsubscribeControlEvents(Control control)
    {
      base.OnSubscribeControlEvents(control);
      ((DateTimePicker)control).ValueChanged -=
new EventHandler(ValueChanged);
    }

    private void ValueChangedHandler(object sender, EventArgs e)
    {
      if (ValueChanged != null)
        ValueChanged(this, e);
    }
  }
}
```

Most of what this class is doing is exposing selected properties, methods, and events of the
DateTimePicker. This way, a reference to the underlying control doesn't have to be maintained by the
hosting application. The process of exposing events is a bit involved. The OnSubscribeControlEvents
method is used to synchronize the events of the hosted control, in this case DateTimePicker, to the
ToolStripControlHost-based class, which is DTPickerToolStrip in the example. In this example,
the ValueChanged event is being passed up to the DTPickerToolStrip. What this effectively does is
allow the user of the control to set up the event in the host application as if DTPickerToolStrip were
derived from DateTimePicker instead of ToolStripControlHost. The following code example shows
this. This is the code to use DTPickerToolStrip:

```
public mdiParent()
{
  DTPickerToolStrip otherDateTimePicker = new DTPickerToolStrip();
  otherDateTimePicker.Width = 200;
  otherDateTimePicker.ValueChanged +=
new EventHandler(otherDateTimePicker_ValueChanged);
  toolStrip1.Items.Add(otherDateTimePicker);
}
```

Notice that when the ValueChanged event handler is set up that the reference is to the
DTPickerToolStrip class and not to the DateTimePicker control as in the previous example. Also
notice how much cleaner the code in this example looks as compared to the first example. In addition,
because the DateTimePicker is wrapped in another class, encapsulation has improved dramatically
and DTPickerToolStrip is now much easier to use in other parts of the application or in other projects.

MenuStrip

The MenuStrip control is the container for the menu structure of an application. As mentioned earlier,
MenuStrip is derived from the ToolStrip class. The menu system is built by adding ToolStripMenu
objects to the MenuStrip. You can do this in code or in the Designer of Visual Studio. Drag a MenuStrip
control onto a form in the Designer and the MenuStrip will allow the entry of the menu text directly on
the menu items.

The MenuStrip control has only a couple of additional properties. GripStyle uses the
ToolStripGripStyle enumeration to set the grip as visible or hidden. The MdiWindowListItem

property takes or returns a `ToolStripMenuItem`. This `ToolStripMenuItem` is the menu that shows all open windows in an MDI application.

ContextMenuStrip

To show a context menu, or a menu displayed when the user right-clicks the mouse, the `ContextMenuStrip` class is used. Like `MenuStrip`, `ContextMenuStrip` is a container for `ToolStripMenuItems` objects. However, it is derived from `ToolStripDropDownMenu`. A `ContextMenu` is created the same way as a `MenuStrip`. `ToolStripMenuItems` are added, and the `Click` event of each item is defined to perform a specific task. Context menus are assigned to specific controls. This is done by setting the `ContextMenuStrip` property of the control. When the user right-clicks the control, the menu is displayed.

ToolStripMenuItem

`ToolStripMenuItem` is the class that builds the menu structures. Each `ToolStripMenuItem` object represents a single menu choice on the menu system. Each `ToolStripMenuItem` has a `ToolStripItemCollection` that maintains the child menus. This functionality is inherited from `ToolStripDropDownItem`.

Because `ToolStripMenuItem` is derived from `ToolStripItem`, all of the same formatting properties apply. Images appear as small icons to the right of the menu text. Menu items can have check marks show up next to them with the `Checked` and `CheckState` properties.

Shortcut keys can be assigned to each menu item. They are generally two key chords such as Ctrl+C (common shortcut for Copy). When a shortcut key is assigned, it can optionally be displayed on the menu by setting the `ShowShortCutKey` property to `true`.

To be useful, the menu item has to do something when the user clicks it or uses the defined shortcut keys. The most common way is to handle the `Click` event. If the `Checked` property is being used, the `CheckStateChanged` and `CheckedChanged` events can be used to determine a change in the checked state.

ToolStripManager

Menu and toolbar structures can become large and cumbersome to manage. The `ToolStripManager` class provides the ability to create smaller, more manageable pieces of a menu or toolbar structure and then combine them when needed. An example of this is a form that has several different controls on it. Each control must display a context menu. Several menu choices will be available for all of the controls, but each control will also have a couple of unique menu choices. The common choices can be defined on one `ContextMenuStrip`. Each of the unique menu items can be predefined or created at runtime. For each control that needs a context menu assigned to it, the common menu is cloned and the unique choices are merged with the common menu using the `ToolStripManager.Merge` method. The resulting menu is assigned to the `ContextMenuStrip` property of the control.

ToolStripContainer

The `ToolStripContainer` control is used for docking of `ToolStrip`-based controls. When you add a `ToolStripContainer` and set the `Docked` property to `Fill`, a `ToolStripPanel` is added to each side of the form, and a `ToolStripContainerPanel` is added to middle of the form. Any `ToolStrip` (`ToolStrip`, `MenuStrip`, or `StatusStrip`) can be added to any of the `ToolStripPanels`. The user can move the `ToolStrips` by grabbing the `ToolStrip` and dragging it to either side or bottom of the form. If you set the `Visible` property to false on any of the `ToolStripPanels`, a `ToolStrip` can no longer be placed in the panel. The `ToolStripContainerPanel` in the center of the form can be used to place the other controls the form may need.

Forms

Earlier in this chapter, you learned how to create a simple Windows application. The example contained one class derived from the `System.Windows.Forms.Form` class. According to the .NET Framework documentation, "a Form is a representation of any window in your application." If you come from a Visual Basic background, the term "form" will seem familiar. If your background is C++ using MFC, you're probably used to calling a form a window, dialog box, or maybe a frame. Regardless, the form is the basic means of interacting with the user. Earlier, the chapter covered some of the more common and useful properties, methods, and events of the `Control` class, and because the `Form` class is a descendant of the `Control` class, all of the same properties, methods, and events exist in the `Form` class. The `Form` class adds considerable functionality to what the `Control` class provides, and that's what this section discusses.

Form Class

A Windows client application can contain one form or hundreds of forms. The forms can be an SDI-based (Single Document Interface) or MDI-based (Multiple Document Interface) application. Regardless, the `System.Windows.Forms.Form` class is the heart of the Windows client. The `Form` class is derived from `ContainerControl`, which is derived from `ScrollableControl`, which is derived from `Control`. Because of this, you can assume that a form is capable of being a container for other controls, capable of scrolling when the contained controls do not fit the client area, and has many of the same properties, methods, and events that other controls have. This also makes the `Form` class rather complex. This section looks at much of that functionality.

Form Instantiation and Destruction

The process of form creation is important to understand. What you want to do depends on where you write the initialization code. For instantiation, the events occur in the following order:

- ❑   Constructor
- ❑   Load
- ❑   Activated
- ❑   Closing
- ❑   Closed
- ❑   Deactivate

The first three events are of concern during initialization. The type of initialization you want to do could determine which event you hook into. The constructor of a class occurs during the object instantiation. The `Load` event occurs after object instantiation, but just before the form becomes visible. The difference between this and the constructor is the viability of the form. When the `Load` event is raised, the form exists but isn't visible. During constructor execution, the form is in the process of coming into existence. The `Activated` event occurs when the form becomes visible and current.

This order can be altered slightly in one particular situation. If during the constructor execution of the form, the `Visible` property is set to `true` or the `Show` method is called (which sets the `Visible` property to `true`), the `Load` event fires immediately. Because this also makes the form visible and current, the `Activate` event is also raised. If there is code after the `Visible` property has been set, it will execute. So, the startup event might look something like this:

- ❑   Constructor, up to `Visible = true`
- ❑   Load
- ❑   Activate
- ❑   Constructor, after `Visible = true`

This could potentially lead to some unexpected results. From a best practices standpoint, it would seem that doing as much initialization as possible in the constructor might be a good idea.

Now what happens when the form is closed? The `Closing` event gives you the opportunity to cancel the process. The `Closing` event receives `CancelEventArgs` as a parameter. This has a `Cancel` property that, if set to `true`, cancels the event and the form remains open. The `Closing` event happens as the form is being closed, whereas the `Closed` event happens after the form has been closed. Both allow you to do any cleanup that might have to be done. Notice that the `Deactivate` event occurs after the form has been closed. This is another potential source of difficult-to-find bugs. Be sure that you don't have anything in `Deactivate` that could keep the form from being properly garbage collected. For example, setting a reference to another object would cause the form to remain alive.

If you call the `Application.Exit()` method and you have one or more forms currently open, the `Closing` and `Closed` events will not be raised. This is an important consideration if you have open files or database connections that you were going to clean up. The `Dispose` method is called, so perhaps another best practice would be to put most of your cleanup code in the `Dispose` method.

Some properties that relate to the startup of a form are `StartPosition`, `ShowInTaskbar`, and `TopMost`. `StartPosition` can be any of the `FormStartPosition` enumeration values. They are:

- ❑   `CenterParent` — The form is centered in the client area of the parent form.
- ❑   `CenterScreen` — The form is centered in the current display.
- ❑   `Manual` — The form's location is based on the values in the `Location` property.
- ❑   `WindowsDefaultBounds` — The form is located at the default Windows position and uses the default size.
- ❑   `WindowsDefaultLocation` — The Windows default location is used, but the size is based on the `Size` property.

The `ShowInTaskbar` property determines if the form should be available in the taskbar. This is relevant only if the form is a child form and you only want the parent form to show in the taskbar. The `TopMost` property tells the form to start in the topmost position in the Z-order of the application. This is true even if the form does not immediately have focus.

In order for users to interact with the application, they must be able to see the form. The `Show` and `ShowDialog` methods accomplish this. The `Show` method just makes the form visible to the user. The following code segment demonstrates how to create a form and show it to the user. Assume that the form you want to display is called `MyFormClass`.

```
MyFormClass myForm = new MyFormClass();
myForm.Show();
```

That's the simple way. The one drawback to this is that there isn't any notification back to the calling code that `myForm` is finished and has been exited. Sometimes this isn't a big deal, and the `Show` method will work fine. If you do need some type of notification, `ShowDialog` is a better option.

When the `Show` method is called, the code that follows the `Show` method is executed immediately. When `ShowDialog` is called, the calling code is blocked and will wait until the form that `ShowDialog` called is closed. Not only will the calling code be blocked, but the form will optionally return a `DialogResult` value. The `DialogResult` enumeration is a list of identifiers that describe the reason the dialog is closed. These include `OK`, `Cancel`, `Yes`, `No`, and several others. In order for the form to return a `DialogResult`, the form's `DialogResult` property must be set or the `DialogResult` property on one of the form's buttons must be set.

For example, suppose that part of application asks for the phone number of a client. The form has a text box for the phone number and two buttons; one is labeled `OK` and the other is labeled `Cancel`. If you set the `DialogResult` of the `OK` button to `DialogResult.OK` and the `DialogResult` property on the `Cancel` button to `DialogResult.Cancel`, then when either of these buttons is selected, the form becomes invisible and returns to the calling form the appropriate `DialogResult` value. Now notice that the form is not destroyed; the `Visible` property is just set to `false`. That's because you still must get values from the form. For this example, you need to get a phone number. By creating a property on the form for the phone number, the parent form can now get the value and call the `Close` method on the form. This is what the code for the child form looks like:

```
namespace FormsSample.DialogSample
{
  partial class Phone : Form
  {
    public Phone()
    {
      InitializeComponent();
      btnOK.DialogResult = DialogResult.OK;
      btnCancel.DialogResult = DialogResult.Cancel;
    }

    public string PhoneNumber
    {
      get { return textBox1.Text; }
      set { textBox1.Text = value; }
    }
  }
}
```

The first thing to notice is that there is no code to handle the `click` events of the buttons. Because the `DialogResult` property is set for each of the buttons, the form disappears after either the `OK` or `Cancel` button is clicked. The only property added is the `PhoneNumber` property. The following code shows the method in the parent form that calls the `Phone` dialog:

```
Phone frm = new Phone();
frm.ShowDialog();
if (frm.DialogResult == DialogResult.OK)
{
  label1.Text = "Phone number is " + frm.PhoneNumber;
}
else if (frm.DialogResult == DialogResult.Cancel)
{
  label1.Text = "Form was canceled. ";
}
frm.Close();
```

This looks simple enough. Create the new `Phone` object (`frm`). When the `frm.ShowDialog()` method is called, the code in this method will stop and wait for the `Phone` form to return. You can then check the `DialogResult` property of the `Phone` form. Because it has not been destroyed yet, just made invisible, you can still access the public properties, one of them being the `PhoneNumber` property. Once you get the data you need, you can call the `Close` method on the form.

This works well, but what if the returned phone number is not formatted correctly? If you put the `ShowDialog` inside of the loop, you can just recall it and have the user reenter the value. This way, you get a proper value. Remember that you must also handle the `DialogResult.Cancel` if the user clicks the `Cancel` button.

```
Phone frm = new Phone();
while (true)
{
  frm.ShowDialog();
```

(continued)

(continued)

```
    if (frm.DialogResult == DialogResult.OK)
    {
        label1.Text = "Phone number is " + frm.PhoneNumber;
        if (frm.PhoneNumber.Length == 8 || frm.PhoneNumber.Length == 12)
        {
            break;
        }
        else
        {
            MessageBox.Show("Phone number was not formatted correctly.
                                            Please correct entry. ");
        }
    }
    else if (frm.DialogResult == DialogResult.Cancel)
    {
        label1.Text = "Form was canceled. ";
        break;
    }
}
frm.Close();
```

Now if the phone number does not pass a simple test for length, the Phone form appears so the user can correct the error. The ShowDialog box does not create a new instance of the form. Any text entered on the form will still be there, so if the form has to be reset, it will be up to you to do that.

Appearance

The first thing that the user sees is the form for the application. It should be first and foremost functional. If the application doesn't solve a business problem, it really doesn't matter how it looks. This is not to say that the form and application's overall GUI design should not be pleasing to the eye. Simple things like color combinations, font sizing, and window sizing can make an application much easier for the user.

Sometimes you don't want the user to have access to the system menu. This is the menu that appears when you click the icon on the top-left corner of a window. Generally, it has such items as Restore, Minimize, Maximize, and Close. The ControlBox property allows you to set the visibility of the system menu. You can also set the visibility of the Maximize and Minimize buttons with the MaximizeBox and MinimizeBox properties. If you remove all of the buttons and then set the Text property to an empty string (""), the title bar disappears completely.

If you set the Icon property of a form and you don't set the ControlBox property to false, the icon will appear in the top-left corner of the form. It's common to set this to the app.ico. This makes each form's icon the same as the application icon.

The FormBorderStyle property sets the type of border that appears around the form. This uses the FormBorderStyle enumeration. The values can be as follows:

- ❑ Fixed3D
- ❑ FixedDialog
- ❑ FixedSingle
- ❑ FixedToolWindow
- ❑ None
- ❑ Sizable
- ❑ SizableToolWindow

Most of these are self-explanatory, with the exception of the two tool window borders. A `Tool` window will not appear in the taskbar, regardless of how `ShowInTaskBar` is set. Also a `Tool` window will not show in the list of windows when the user presses Alt+Tab. The default setting is `Sizable`.

Unless a requirement dictates otherwise, colors for most GUI elements should be set to system colors and not to specific colors. This way, if some users like to have all of their buttons green with purple text, the application will follow along with the same colors. To set a control to use a specific system color, you must call the `FromKnownColor` method of the `System.Drawing.Color` class. The `FromKnownColor` method takes a `KnownColor` enumeration value. Many colors are defined in the enumeration, as well as the various GUI element colors, such as `Control`, `ActiveBorder`, and `Desktop`. So, for example, if the `Background` color of the form should always match the `Desktop` color, the code would look like this:

```
myForm.BackColor = Color.FromKnownColor(KnownColor.Desktop);
```

Now if users change the color of their desktops, the background of the form changes as well. This is a nice, friendly touch to add to an application. Users might pick out some strange color combinations for their desktops, but it is their choice.

Windows XP introduced a feature called visual styles. Visual styles change the way buttons, text boxes, menus, and other controls look and react when the mouse pointer is either hovering or clicking. You can enable visual styles for your application by calling the `Application.EnableVisualStyles` method. This method has to be called before any type of GUI is instantiated. Because of this, it is generally called in the `Main` method, as demonstrated in this example:

```
[STAThread]
static void Main()
{
  Application.EnableVisualStyles();
  Application.Run(new Form1());
}
```

This code allows the various controls that support visual styles to take advantage of them. Because of an issue with the `EnableVisualStyles` method, you might have to add an `Application.DoEvents()` method right after the call to `EnableVisualStyles`. This should resolve the problem if icons on toolbars begin to disappear at runtime. Also, `EnableVisualStyles` is available in .NET Framework 1.1 only.

You have to accomplish one more task pertaining to the controls. Most controls expose the `FlatStyle` property, which takes a `FlatStyle` enumeration as its value. This property can take one of four different values:

❑ `Flat` — Similar to flat, except that when the mouse pointer hovers over the control, it appears in 3D.

❑ `Standard` — The control appears in 3D.

❑ `System` — The look of the control is controlled by the operating system.

To enable visual styles, the control's `FlatStyle` property should be set to `FlatStyle.System`. The application will now take on the XP look and feel and will support XP themes.

Multiple Document Interface

MDI-type applications are used when you have an application that can show either multiple instances of the same type of form or different forms that must be contained in some way — for example, a text editor that can show multiple edit windows at the same time or Microsoft Access, respectively. You can have query windows, design windows, and table windows all open at the same time. The windows never leave the boundaries of the main Access application.

The project that contains the examples for this chapter is an MDI application. The form mdiParent in the project is the MDI parent form. Setting the IsMdiContainer to true will make any form an MDI parent form. If you have the form in the Designer you'll notice that the background turns a dark gray color. This is to let you know that this is an MDI parent form. You can still add controls to the form, but it is generally not recommended.

For the child forms to behave like MDI children, the child form needs to know what form the parent is. This is done by setting the MdiParent property to the parent form. In the example, all children forms are created using the ShowMdiChild method. It takes a reference to the child form that is to be shown. After setting the MdiParent property to this, which is referencing the mdiParent form, the form is shown. Here is the code for the ShowMdiParent method:

```
private void ShowMdiChild(Form childForm)
{
  childForm.MdiParent = this;
  childForm.Show();
}
```

One of the issues with MDI applications is that there may be several child forms open at any given time. A reference to the current active child can be retrieved by using the ActiveMdiChild property on the parent form. This is demonstrated on the Current Active menu choice on the Window menu. This choice will show a message box with the form's name and text value.

The child forms can be arranged by calling the LayoutMdi method. The LayoutMdi method takes an MdiLayout enumeration value as a parameter. The possible values include Cascade, TileHorizontal, and TileVertical.

Custom Controls

Using controls and components is a big part of what makes developing with a forms package such as Windows Forms so productive. The ability to create your own controls, components, and user controls makes it even more productive. By creating controls, functionality can be encapsulated into packages that can be reused over and over.

You can create a control in a number of ways. You can start from scratch, deriving your class from either Control, ScrollableControl, or ContainerControl. You will have to override the Paint event and do all of your drawing, not to mention adding the functionality that your control is supposed to provide. If the control is supposed to be an enhanced version of a current control, the thing to do is to derive from the control that is being enhanced. For example, if a TextBox control is needed that changes background color if the ReadOnly property is set, creating a completely new TextBox control would be a waste of time. Derive from the TextBox control and override the ReadOnly property. Because the ReadOnly property of the TextBox control is not marked override, you have to use the new clause. The following code shows the new ReadOnly property:

```
public new bool ReadOnly
{
  get  { return base.ReadOnly;}
  set  {
    if(value)
      this.BackgroundColor = Color.Red;
    else
      this.BackgroundColor = Color.FromKnowColor(KnownColor.Window);

    base.ReadOnly = value;
  }
}
```

For the property get, you return what the base object is set to. The way that the property handles the process of making a text box read-only is not relevant here, so you just pass that functionality to the base object. In the property set, check to see if the passed-in value is true or false. If it is true, change the color to the read-only color (Red in this case); if it is false, set the BackgroundColor to the default. Finally, pass the value down to the base object so that the text box actually does become read-only. As you can see, you can add new functionality to a control by overriding one simple property.

Control Attributes

You can add attributes to the custom control that will enhance the design-time capabilities of the control. The following table describes some of the more useful attributes.

Attribute Name	Description
BindableAttribute	Used at design time to determine if the property supports two-way data binding.
BrowsableAttribute	Determines if the property is shown in the visual Designer.
CategoryAttribute	Determines under what category the property is displayed in the Property window. Use on predefined categories or create new ones. Default is Misc.
DefaultEventAttribute	Specifies the default event for a class.
DefaultPropertyAttribute	Specifies the default property for a class.
DefaultValueAttribute	Specifies the default value for a property. Typically, this is the initial value.
DecriptionAttribute	This is the text that appears at the bottom of the Designer window when the property is selected.
DesignOnlyAttribute	This marks the property as being editable in design mode only.

Other attributes are available that relate to the editor that the property uses in design time and other advanced design-time capabilities. The Category and Description attributes should almost always be added. This helps other developers who use the control to better understand the property's purpose. To add IntelliSense support, you should add XML comments for each property, method, and event. When the control is compiled with the /doc option, the XML file of comments that is generated will provide IntelliSense for the control.

TreeView-Based Custom Control

This section shows you how to develop a custom control based on the TreeView control. This control displays the file structure of a drive. You'll add properties that set the base or root folder and determine whether files and folders will be displayed. You also use the various attributes discussed in the previous section.

As with any new project, requirements for the control have to be defined. Here is a list of basic requirements that have to be implemented:

❑ Read folders and files and display to user.

❑ Display folder structure in a treelike hierarchical view.

❑ Optionally hide files from view.

❑ Define what folder should be the base or root folder.

❑ Return the currently selected folder.

❑ Provide the ability to delay loading of the file structure.

This should be a good starting point. One requirement has been satisfied by the fact that the `TreeView` control will be the base of the new control.

The `TreeView` control displays data in a hierarchical format. It displays text describing the object in the list and optionally an icon. This list can be expanded and contracted by clicking an object or using the arrow keys.

Create a new Windows Control Library project in Visual Studio .NET named `FolderTree`, and delete the class `UserControl1`. Add a new class and call it `FolderTree`. Because `FolderTree` will be derived from `TreeView`, change the class declaration from:

```
public class FolderTree
```

to:

```
public class FolderTree  :  System.Windows.Forms.TreeView
```

At this point, you actually have a fully functional and working `FolderTree` control. It will do everything that the `TreeView` can do, and nothing more.

The `TreeView` control maintains a collection of `TreeNode` objects. You can't load files and folders directly into the control. You have a couple of ways to map the `TreeNode` that is loaded into the `Nodes` collection of the `TreeView` and the file or folder that it represents.

For example, when each folder is processed, a new `TreeNode` object is created, and the text property is set to the name of the file or folder. If at some point additional information about the file or folder is needed, you have to make another trip to the disk to gather that information or store additional data regarding the file or folder in the `Tag` property.

Another method is to create a new class that is derived from `TreeNode`. New properties and methods can be added and the base functionality of the `TreeNode` is still there. This is the path that you use in this example. It allows for a more flexible design. If you need new properties, you can add them easily without breaking the existing code.

You must load two types of objects into the control: folders and files. Each has its own characteristics. For example, folders have a `DirectoryInfo` object that contains additional information, and files have a `FileInfo` object. Because of these differences, you use two separate classes to load the `TreeView` control: `FileNode` and `FolderNode`. You add these two classes to the project; each is derived from `TreeNode`. This is the listing for `FileNode`:

```
namespace FormsSample.SampleControls
{
  public class FileNode : System.Windows.Forms.TreeNode
  {
    string _fileName = "";
    FileInfo _info;
    public FileNode(string fileName)
    {
      _fileName = fileName;
      _info = new FileInfo(_fileName);
      base.Text = _info.Name;
      if (_info.Extension.ToLower() == ".exe")
        this.ForeColor = System.Drawing.Color.Red;
    }
    public string FileName
```

```
      {
        get { return _fileName; }
        set { _fileName = value; }
      }

      public FileInfo FileNodeInfo
      {
        get { return _info; }
      }
    }
  }
```

The name of the file being processed is passed into the constructor of `FileNode`. In the constructor, the `FileInfo` object for the file is created and set to the member variable `_info`. The `base.Text` property is set to the name of the file. Because you are deriving from `TreeNode`, this sets the `TreeNode`'s `Text` property. This is the text displayed in the `TreeView` control.

Two properties are added to retrieve the data. `FileName` returns the name of the file and `FileNodeInfo` returns the `FileInfo` object for the file.

The following is the code for the `FolderNode` class. It is very similar in structure to the `FileNode` class, but you have a `DirectoryInfo` property instead of `FileInfo`, and instead of `FileName` you have `FolderPath`:

```
namespace FormsSample.SampleControls
{
  public class FolderNode : System.Windows.Forms.TreeNode
  {
    string _folderPath = "";
    DirectoryInfo _info;
    public FolderNode(string folderPath)
    {
      _folderPath = folderPath;
      _info = new DirectoryInfo(folderPath);
      this.Text = _info.Name;
    }
    public string FolderPath
    {
      get { return _folderPath; }
      set { _folderPath = value; }
    }
    public DirectoryInfo FolderNodeInfo
    {
      get { return _info; }
    }
  }
}
```

Now you can construct the `FolderTree` control. Based on the requirements, you need a property to read and set the `RootFolder`. You also need a `ShowFiles` property for determining if files should be shown in the tree. A `SelectedFolder` property returns the currently highlighted folder in the tree. This is what the code looks like so far for the `FolderTree` control:

```
using System;
using System.Windows.Forms;
using System.IO;
using System.ComponentModel;
```

(continued)

(continued)

```
namespace FolderTree
{
  /// <summary>
  /// Summary description for FolderTreeCtrl.
  /// </summary>
  public class FolderTree :   System.Windows.Forms.TreeView
  {
    string _rootFolder = "";
    bool _showFiles = true;
    bool _inInit = false;
    public FolderTree()
    {

    }

    [Category("Behavior"),
        Description("Gets or sets the base or root folder of the tree"),
        DefaultValue("C:\\ ")]
    public string RootFolder
    {
      get {return _rootFolder;}
      set
      {
        _rootFolder = value;
        if(!_inInit)
          InitializeTree();

      }
    }

    [Category("Behavior"),
        Description("Indicates whether files will be seen in the list. "),
        DefaultValue(true)]
    public bool ShowFiles
    {
      get {return _showFiles;}
      set {_showFiles = value;}
    }

    [Browsable(false)]
    public string SelectedFolder
    {
      get
      {
        if(this.SelectedNode is FolderNode)
          return ((FolderNode)this.SelectedNode).FolderPath;

        return "";
      }
    }
  }
}
```

Three properties were added: `ShowFiles`, `SelectedFolder`, and `RootFolder`. Notice the attributes that have been added. You set `Category`, `Description`, and `DefaultValues` for the `ShowFiles` and

RootFolder. These two properties will appear in the property browser in design mode. The SelectedFolder really has no meaning at design time, so you select the Browsable=false attribute. SelectedFolder does not appear in the property browser. However, because it is a public property, it will appear in IntelliSense and is accessible in code.

Next, you have to initialize the loading of the file system. Initializing a control can be tricky. Both design-time and runtime initializing must be well thought out. When a control is sitting on a Designer, it is actually running. If there is a call to a database in the constructor, for example, this call will execute when you drop the control on the Designer. In the case of the FolderTree control, this can be an issue.

Here's a look at the method that is actually going to load the files:

```
private void LoadTree(FolderNode folder)
{
  string[] dirs = Directory.GetDirectories(folder.FolderPath);
  foreach(string dir in dirs)
  {
    FolderNode tmpfolder = new FolderNode(dir);
    folder.Nodes.Add(tmpfolder);
    LoadTree(tmpfolder);
  }
  if(_showFiles)
  {
    string[] files = Directory.GetFiles(folder.FolderPath);
    foreach(string file in files)
    {
      FileNode fnode = new FileNode(file);
      folder.Nodes.Add(fnode);
    }
  }
}
```

showFiles is a Boolean member variable that is set from the ShowFiles property. If true, files are also shown in the tree. The only question now is when LoadTree should be called. You have several options. It can be called when the RootFolder property is set. That is desirable in some situations, but not at design time. Remember that the control is "live" on the Designer, so when the RootNode property is set, the control will attempt to load the file system.

To solve this, check the DesignMode property, which returns true if the control is in the Designer. Now you can write the code to initialize the control:

```
private void InitializeTree()
{
  if (!this.DesignMode)
  {
    FolderNode rootNode = new FolderNode(_rootFolder);
    LoadTree(rootNode);
    this.Nodes.Clear();
    this.Nodes.Add(rootNode);
  }
}
```

If the control is not in design mode and _rootFolder is not an empty string, the loading of the tree will begin. The Root node is created first and this is passed into the LoadTree method.

Another option is to implement a public Init method. In the Init method, the call to LoadTree can happen. The problem with this option is that the developer who uses your control is required to make the Init call. Depending on the situation, this might be an acceptable solution.

For added flexibility, implement the ISupportInitialize interface. ISupportInitialize has two methods, BeginInit and EndInit. When a control implements ISupportInitialize, the BeginInit and EndInit methods are called automatically in the generated code in InitializeComponent. This allows the initialization process to be delayed until all of the properties are set. ISupportInitialize allows the code in the parent form to delay initialization as well. If the RootNode property is being set in code, a call to BeginInit first will allow the RootNode property as well as other properties to be set or actions to be performed before the control loads the file system. When EndInit is called, the control initializes. This is what BeginInit and EndInit code looks like:

```
#region ISupportInitialize Members
public void ISupportInitialize.BeginInit()
{
  _inInit = true;
}
public void ISupportInitialize.EndInit()
{

  if(_rootFolder != "")
  {
    InitializeTree();
  }

  _inInit = false;
}
#endregion
```

In the BeginInit method, all that is done is that a member variable _inInit is set to true. This flag is used to determine if the control is in the initialization process and is used in the RootFolder property. If the RootFolder property is set outside of the InitializeComponent class, the tree will need to be reinitialized. In the RootFolder property you check to see if _inInit is true or false. If it is true, then you don't want to go through the initialization process. If inInit is false, you call InitializeTree. You can also have a public Init method and accomplish the same task.

In the EndInit method, you check to see if the control is in design mode and if _rootFolder has a valid path assigned to it. Only then is InitializeTree called.

To add a final professional-looking touch, you have to add a bitmap image. This is the icon that shows up in the Toolbox when the control is added to a project. The bitmap image should be 16 × 6 pixels and 16 colors. You can create this image file with any graphics editor as long as the size and color depth are set properly. You can even create this file in Visual Studio .NET: Right-click the project and select Add New Item. From the list, select Bitmap File to open the graphics editor. After you have created the bitmap file, add it to the project, making sure that it is in the same namespace and has the same name as the control. Finally, set the Build Action of the bitmap to Embedded Resource: Right-click the bitmap file in the Solution Explorer and select Properties. Select Embedded Resource from the Build Action property.

To test the control, create a TestHarness project in the same solution. The TestHarness is a simple Windows Forms application with a single form. In the references section, add a reference to the FolderTreeCtl project. In the Toolbox window, add a reference to the FolderTreeCtl.DLL .FolderTreeCtl should now show up in the toolbox with the bitmap added as the icon. Click the icon and drag it to the TestHarness form. Set the RootFolder to an available folder and run the solution.

This is by no means a complete control. Several things could be enhanced to make this a full-featured, production-ready control. For example, you could add the following:

❑   **Exceptions** — If the control tries to load a folder that the user does not have access to, an exception is raised.

❑   **Background loading** — Loading a large folder tree can take a long time. Enhancing the initialization process to take advantage of a background thread for loading is a good idea.

❑   **Color codes** — You can make the text of certain file types a different color.

❑   **Icons** — You can add an `ImageList` control and add an icon to each file or folder as it is loaded.

User Control

User controls are one of the more powerful features of Windows Forms. They enable you to encapsulate user interface designs into nice reusable packages that can be plugged into project after project. It is not uncommon for an organization to have a couple of libraries of frequently used user controls. Not only can user interface functionality be contained in user controls, but common data validation can be incorporated in them as well, such as formatting phone numbers or ID numbers. A predefined list of items can be in the user control for fast loading of a list box or combo box. State codes or country codes fit into this category. Incorporating as much functionality that does not depend on the current application as possible into a user control makes the control that much more useful in the organization.

In this section, you create a simple address user control. You also will add the various events that make the control ready for data binding. The address control will have text entry for two address lines: city, state, and zip code.

To create a user control in a current project, just right-click the project in Solution Explorer and select Add; then select Add New User Control. You can also create a new Control Library project and add user controls to it. After a new user control has been started, you will see a form without any borders on the Designer. This is where you drop the controls that make up the user control. Remember that a user control is actually one or more controls added to a container control, so it is somewhat like creating a form. For the address control there are five `TextBox` controls and three `Label` controls. The controls can be arranged any way that seems appropriate (see Figure 31-4).

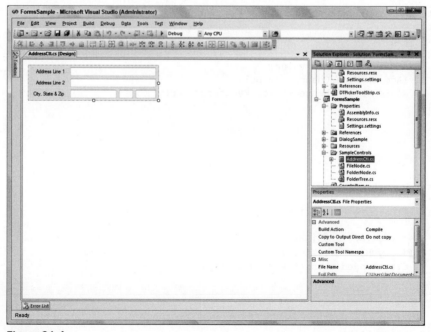

Figure 31-4

The TextBox controls in this example are named as follows:

- ❏ txtAddress1
- ❏ txtAddress2
- ❏ txtCity
- ❏ txtState
- ❏ txtZip

After the TextBox controls are in place and have valid names, add the public properties. You might be tempted to set the visibility of the TextBox controls to public instead of private. However, this is not a good idea because it defeats the purpose of encapsulating the functionality that you might want to add to the properties. The following is a listing of the properties that must be added:

```
public string AddressLine1
{
  get{return txtAddress1.Text;}
  set{
    if(txtAddress1.Text != value)
    {
      txtAddress1.Text = value;
      if(AddressLine1Changed != null)
        AddressLine1Changed(this, EventArgs.Empty);
    }
  }
}

public string AddressLine2
{
  get{return txtAddress2.Text;}
  set{
    if(txtAddress2.Text != value)
    {
      txtAddress2.Text = value;
      if(AddressLine2Changed != null)
        AddressLine2Changed(this, EventArgs.Empty);
    }
  }
}

public string City
{
  get{return txtCity.Text;}
  set{
    if(txtCity.Text != value)
    {
      txtCity.Text = value;
      if(CityChanged != null)
        CityChanged(this, EventArgs.Empty);
    }
  }
}

public string State
```

```
  {
    get{return txtState.Text;}
    set{
      if(txtState.Text != value)
      {
        txtState.Text = value;
        if(StateChanged != null)
          StateChanged(this, EventArgs.Empty);
      }
    }
  }

  public string Zip
  {
    get{return txtZip.Text;}
    set{
      if(txtZip.Text != value)
      {
        txtZip.Text = value;
        if(ZipChanged != null)
          ZipChanged(this, EventArgs.Empty);
      }
    }
  }
```

The instances of the `get` property are fairly straightforward. They return the value of the corresponding `TextBox` control's text property. The instances of the `set` property, however, are doing a bit more work. All of the `set`s work the same way. A check is made to see whether or not the value of the property is actually changing. If the new value is the same as the current value, then a quick escape can be made. If there is a new value sent in, set the text property of the `TextBox` to the new value and test to see if an event has been instantiated. The event to look for is the changed event for the property. It has a specific naming format, `propertynameChanged`, where `propertyname` is the name of the property. In the case of the `AddressLine1` property, this event is called `AddressLine1Changed`. The properties are declared as follows:

```
public event EventHandler AddressLine1Changed;
public event EventHandler AddressLine2Changed;
public event EventHandler CityChanged;
public event EventHandler StateChanged;
public event EventHandler ZipChanged;
```

The purpose of the events is to notify binding that the property has changed. Once validation occurs, binding will make sure that the new value makes its way back to the object that the control is bound to. One other step should be done to support binding. A change to the text box by the user will not set the property directly. So, the `propertynameChanged` event must be raised when the text box changes as well. The easiest way to do this is to monitor the `TextChanged` event of the `TextBox` control. This example has only one `TextChanged` event handler and all of the text boxes use it. The control name is checked to see which control raised the event and the appropriate `propertynameChanged` event is raised. The following is the code for the event handler:

```
private void controls_TextChanged (object sender, System.EventArgs e)
{
  switch(((TextBox)sender).Name)
  {
    case "txtAddress1" :
      if(AddressLine1Changed != null)
```

(continued)

(continued)

```
              AddressLine1Changed(this, EventArgs.Empty);
          break;

      case "txtAddress2" :
        if(AddressLine2Changed != null)
          AddressLine2Changed(this, EventArgs.Empty);
        break;
      case "txtCity" :
        if(CityChanged != null)
          CityChanged(this, EventArgs.Empty);
        break;
      case "txtState" :
          if(StateChanged != null)
            StateChanged(this, EventArgs.Empty);
          break;
      case "txtZip" :
          if(ZipChanged != null)
            ZipChanged(this, EventArgs.Empty);
          break;
    }
  }
```

This example uses a simple `switch` statement to determine which text box raised the `TextChanged` event. Then a check is made to verify that the event is valid and not equal to null. Then the `Changed` event is raised. One thing to note is that an empty `EventArgs` is sent (`EventArgs.Empty`). The fact that these events have been added to the properties to support data binding does not mean that the only way to use the control is with data binding. The properties can be set in and read from code without using data binding. They have been added so that the user control is able to use binding if it is available. This is just one way of making the user control as flexible as possible so that it might be used in as many situations as possible.

Because a user control is essentially a control with some added features, all of the design-time issues discussed in the previous section apply here as well. Initializing user controls can bring on the same issues that you saw in the `FolderTree` example. Care must be taken in the design of user controls so that you avoid giving access to data stores that might not be available to other developers using your control.

Also similar to the control creation are the attributes that can be applied to user controls. The public properties and methods of the user control are displayed in the properties window when the control is placed on the Designer. In the example of the address user control it is a good idea to add `Category`, `Description`, and `DefaultValue` attributes to the address properties. A new `AddressData` category can be created and the default values would all be `""`. The following is an example of these attributes applied to the `AddressLine1` property:

```
    [Category("AddressData"),
        Description("Gets or sets the AddressLine1 value"),
        DefaultValue("")]
    public string AddressLine1
    {
      get{return txtAddress1.Text;}
      set{
        if(txtAddress1.Text != value)
        {
```

```
            txtAddress1.Text = value;
            if(AddressLine1Changed != null)
              AddressLine1Changed(this, EventArgs.Empty);
        }
      }
   }
```

As you can see, all that needs to be done to add a new category is to set the text in the Category attribute. The new category is automatically added.

There is still a lot of room for improvement. For example, you could include a list of state names and abbreviations in the control. Instead of just the state property, the user control could expose both the state name and state abbreviation properties. Exception handling should also be added. You could also add validation for the address lines. Making sure that the casing is correct, you might ask yourself whether AddressLine1 could be optional or whether apartment and suite numbers should be entered on AddressLine2 and not on AddressLine1.

Summary

This chapter has given you the basics for building Windows client-based applications. It explained each of the basic controls by discussing the hierarchy of the Windows.Forms namespace and examining the various properties and methods of the controls.

The chapter also showed you how to create a basic custom control as well as a basic user control. The power and flexibility of creating your own controls cannot be emphasized enough. By creating your own toolbox of custom controls, Windows-based client applications will become easier to develop and to test because you will be reusing the same tested components over and over again.

The next chapter, "Data Binding," covers how to link a data source to controls on a form. This will allow you to create forms that automatically update the data and keep the data on the form in sync.

32

Data Binding

This chapter builds on the content of Chapter 26, "Data Access," which covered various ways of selecting and changing data, by showing you how to present data to the user by binding to various Windows controls. More specifically, this chapter discusses:

❑ Displaying data using the `DataGridView` control

❑ The .NET data-binding capabilities and how they work

❑ How to use the Server Explorer to create a connection and generate a `DataSet` class (all without writing a line of code)

❑ How to use hit testing and reflection on rows in the `DataGrid`

You can download the source code for the examples in this chapter from the Wrox Web site at `www.wrox.com`.

The DataGridView Control

The `DataGrid` control that has been available from the initial release of .NET was functional, but had many areas that made it unsuitable for use in a commercial application — such as an inability to display images, drop-down controls, or lock columns, to name but a few. The control always felt half-completed, so many control vendors provided custom grid controls that overcame these deficiencies and also provided much more functionality.

.NET 2.0 introduced an additional `Grid` control — the `DataGridView`. This addresses many of the deficiencies of the original control, and adds significant functionality that previously was available only with add-on products.

The `DataGridView` control has binding capabilities similar to the old `DataGrid`, so it can bind to an `Array`, `DataTable`, `DataView`, or `DataSet` class, or a component that implements either the `IListSource` or `IList` interface. It gives you a variety of views of the same data. In its simplest guise, data can be displayed (as in a `DataSet` class) by setting the `DataSource` and `DataMember` properties — note that this control is not a plugin replacement for the `DataGrid`, so the programmatic interface to it is entirely different from that of the `DataGrid`. This control also provides more complex capabilities, which are discussed in the course of this chapter.

Displaying Tabular Data

Chapter 19, "Threading and Synchronization," introduced numerous ways of selecting data and reading it into a data table, although the data was displayed in a very basic fashion using `Console.WriteLine()`.

The following example demonstrates how to retrieve some data and display it in a `DataGridView` control. For this purpose, you will build a new application, `DisplayTabularData`, shown in Figure 32-1.

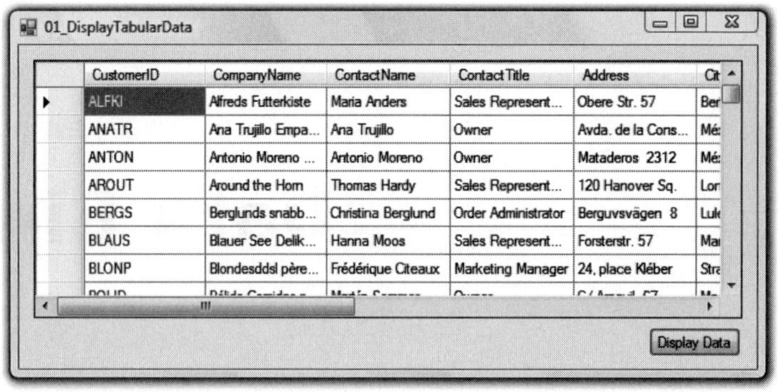

Figure 32-1

This simple application selects every record from the `Customer` table in the Northwind database and displays these records to the user in the `DataGridView` control. The following snippet shows the code for this example (excluding the form and control definition code):

```
using System;
using System.Configuration;
using System.Data;
using System.Data.Common;
using System.Data.SqlClient;
using System.Windows.Forms;

namespace DisplayTabularData
{
   partial class Form1: Form
   {
      public Form1()
      {
         InitializeComponent();
      }

      private void getData_Click(object sender, EventArgs e)
      {
         string customers = "SELECT * FROM Customers";

         using (SqlConnection con =
                new SqlConnection (ConfigurationManager.
                   ConnectionStrings["northwind"].ConnectionString))
         {
            DataSet ds = new DataSet();

            SqlDataAdapter da = new SqlDataAdapter(customers, con);
```

```
                da.Fill(ds, "Customers");

                dataGridView.AutoGenerateColumns = true;
                dataGridView.DataSource = ds;
                dataGridView.DataMember = "Customers";
            }
        }
    }
}
```

The form consists of the `getData` button, which when clicked calls the `getData_Click()` method shown in the example code.

This constructs a `SqlConnection` object, using the `ConnectionStrings` property of the `ConfigurationManager` class. Subsequently a data set is constructed and filled from the database table, using a `DataAdapter` object. The data is then displayed by the `DataGridView` control by setting the `DataSource` and `DataMember` properties. Note that the `AutoGenerateColumns` property is also set to `true` because this ensures that something is displayed to the user. If this flag is not specified, you need to create all columns yourself.

Data Sources

The `DataGridView` control provides a flexible way to display data; in addition to setting the `DataSource` to a `DataSet` and the `DataMember` to the name of the table to display, the `DataSource` property can be set to any of the following sources:

❑ An array (the grid can bind to any one-dimensional array)

❑ `DataTable`

❑ `DataView`

❑ `DataSet` or `DataViewManager`

❑ Components that implement the `IListSource` interface

❑ Components that implement the `IList` interface

❑ Any generic collection class or object derived from a generic collection class

The following sections give an example of each of these data sources.

Displaying Data from an Array

At first glance this seems to be easy. Create an array, fill it with some data, and set the `DataSource` property on the `DataGridView` control. Here's some example code:

```
string[] stuff = new string[] {"One", "Two", "Three"};
dataGridView.DataSource = stuff;
```

If the data source contains multiple possible candidate tables (such as when using a `DataSet` or `DataViewManager`), you need to also set the `DataMember` property.

You could replace the code in the previous example's `getData_Click` event handler with the preceding array code. The problem with this code is the resulting display (see Figure 32-2).

Instead of displaying the strings defined within the array, the grid displays the length of those strings. That's because when using an array as the source of data for a `DataGridView` control, the grid looks for the first public property of the object within the array and displays this value rather than the string value. The first (and only) public property of a string is its length, so that is what is displayed. The list of properties for any class can be obtained by using the `GetProperties` method of the `TypeDescriptor` class. This returns a collection of `PropertyDescriptor` objects, which can then be used when displaying data. The .NET `PropertyGrid` control uses this method when displaying arbitrary objects.

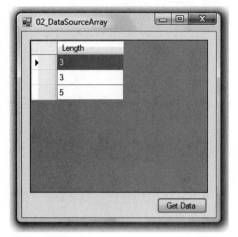

Figure 32-2

One way to rectify the problem with displaying strings in the `DataGridView` is to create a wrapper class:

```
protected class Item
{
    public Item(string text)
    {
        _text = text;
    }
    public string Text
    {
        get{return _text;}
    }
    private string _text;
}
```

Figure 32-3 shows the output when an array of this `Item` class (which could just as well be a `struct` for all the processing that it does) is added to your data source array code.

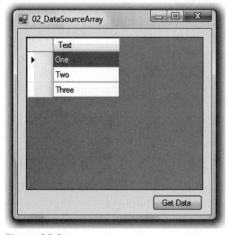

Figure 32-3

DataTable

You can display a `DataTable` within a `DataGridView` control in two ways:

❑ If you have a standalone `DataTable`, simply set the `DataSource` property of the control to the table.

❑ If your `DataTable` is contained within a `DataSet`, you need to set the `DataSource` to the data set and the `DataMember` property should be set to the name of the `DataTable` within the data set.

Figure 32-4 shows the result of running the `DataSourceDataTable` sample code.

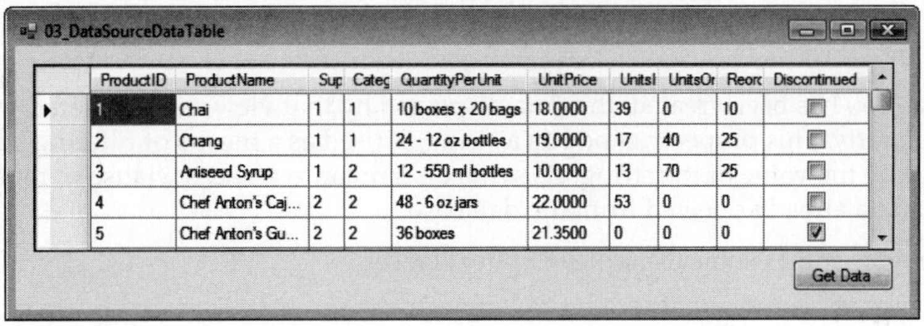

Figure 32-4

Note the display of the last column; it shows a check box instead of the more common edit control. The `DataGridView` control, in the absence of any other information, will read the schema from the data source (which in this case is the `Products` table), and infer from the column types what control is to be displayed. Unlike the original `DataGrid` control, the `DataGridView` control has built-in support for image columns, buttons, and combo boxes.

The data in the database does not change when fields are altered in the data grid because the data is stored only locally on the client computer — there is no active connection to the database. Updating data in the database is discussed later in this chapter.

Displaying Data from a DataView

A `DataView` provides a means to filter and sort data within a `DataTable`. When data has been selected from the database, it is common to permit the user to sort that data, for example, by clicking on column headings. In addition, the user might want to filter the data to show only certain rows, such as all those that have been altered. A `DataView` can be filtered so that only selected rows are shown to the user; however, you cannot filter the columns from the `DataTable`.

> A `DataView` **does not permit the filtering of columns, only rows.**

To create a `DataView` based on an existing `DataTable`, use the following code:

```
DataView dv = new DataView(dataTable);
```

Once created, further settings can be altered on the `DataView`, which affect the data and operations permitted on that data when it is displayed within the data grid. For example:

- ❑ Setting `AllowEdit = false` disables all column edit functionality for rows.
- ❑ Setting `AllowNew = false` disables the new row functionality.
- ❑ Setting `AllowDelete = false` disables the delete row capability.
- ❑ Setting the `RowStateFilter` displays only rows of a given state.
- ❑ Setting the `RowFilter` enables you to filter rows.

The next section explains how to use the `RowStateFilter` setting; the other options are fairly self-explanatory.

Filtering Rows by Data

After the `DataView` has been created, the data displayed by that view can be altered by setting the `RowFilter` property. This property, typed as a string, is used as a means of filtering based on certain criteria defined by the value of the string. Its syntax is similar to a WHERE clause in regular SQL, but it is issued against data already selected from the database.

The following table shows some examples of filter clauses.

Clause	Description
`UnitsInStock > 50`	Shows only those rows where the `UnitsInStock` column is greater than 50.
`Client = 'Smith'`	Returns only the records for a given client.
`County LIKE 'C*'`	Returns all records where the `County` field begins with a C — in this example, the rows for Cornwall, Cumbria, Cheshire, and Cambridgeshire would be returned. The % character can be used as a single-character wildcard, whereas the * denotes a general wildcard that will match zero or more characters.

The runtime will do its best to coerce the data types used within the filter expression into the appropriate types for the source columns. For instance, it is perfectly legal to write `"UnitsInStock > '50'"` in the earlier example, even though the column is an integer. If an invalid filter string is provided, an `EvaluateException` will be thrown.

Filtering Rows on State

Each row within a `DataView` has a defined row state, which has one of the values shown in the following table. This state can also be used to filter the rows viewed by the user.

DataViewRowState	Description
`Added`	Lists all rows that have been newly created.
`CurrentRows`	Lists all rows except those that have been deleted.
`Deleted`	Lists all rows that were originally selected and have been deleted; does not show newly created rows that have been deleted.

DataViewRowState	Description
ModifiedCurrent	Lists all rows that have been modified and shows the current value of each column.
ModifiedOriginal	Lists all rows that have been modified but shows the original value of the column and not the current value.
OriginalRows	Lists all rows that were originally selected from a data source. Does not include new rows. Shows the original values of the columns (that is, not the current values if changes have been made).
Unchanged	Lists all rows that have not changed in any way.

Figure 32-5 shows a grid that can have rows added, deleted, or amended, and a second grid that lists rows in one of the preceding states.

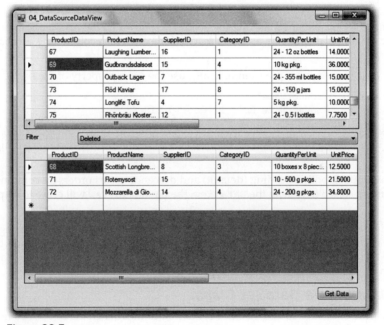

Figure 32-5

The filter not only applies to the visible rows but also to the state of the columns within those rows. This is evident when choosing the ModifiedOriginal or ModifiedCurrent selections. These states are described in Chapter 20, "Security," and are based on the DataRowVersion enumeration. For example, when the user has updated a column in the row, the row will be displayed when either ModifiedOriginal or ModifiedCurrent is chosen; however, the actual value will be either the Original value selected from the database (if ModifiedOriginal is chosen) or the current value in the DataColumn (if ModifiedCurrent is chosen).

Sorting Rows

Apart from filtering data, you might also have to sort the data within a `DataView`. To sort data in ascending or descending order, simply click the column header in the `DataGridView` control (see Figure 32-6). The only trouble is that the control can sort by only one column, whereas the underlying `DataView` control can sort by multiple columns.

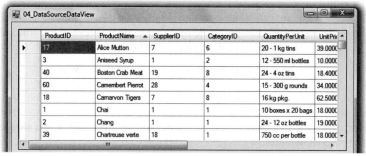

Figure 32-6

When a column is sorted, either by clicking the header (as shown on the `ProductName` column) or in code, the `DataGrid` displays an arrow bitmap to indicate which column the sort has been applied to.

To set the sort order on a column programmatically, use the `Sort` property of the `DataView`:

```
dataView.Sort = "ProductName";
dataView.Sort = "ProductName ASC, ProductID DESC";
```

The first line sorts the data based on the `ProductName` column, as shown in Figure 32-6. The second line sorts the data in ascending order, based on the `ProductName` column, then in descending order of `ProductID`.

The `DataView` supports both ascending (default) and descending sort orders on columns. If more than one column is sorted in code in the `DataView`, the `DataGridView` will cease to display any sort arrows.

Each column in the grid can be strongly typed, so its sort order is not based on the string representation of the column but instead is based on the data within that column. The upshot is that if there is a date column in the `DataGrid`, the user can sort numerically on the date rather than on the date string representation.

Displaying Data from a DataSet Class

There is one feature of `DataSets` that the `DataGridView` cannot match the `DataGrid` in — this is when a `DataSet` is defined that includes relationships between tables. As with the preceding `DataGridView` examples, the `DataGrid` can display only a single `DataTable` at a time. However, as shown in the following example, `DataSourceDataSet`, it is possible to navigate relationships within the `DataSet` onscreen. The following code can be used to generate such a `DataSet` based on the `Customers` and `Orders` tables in the Northwind database. This example loads data from these two `DataTables` and then creates a relationship between these tables called `CustomerOrders`:

```
string orders = "SELECT * FROM Orders";
string customers = "SELECT * FROM Customers";
SqlConnection conn = new SqlConnection(source);
SqlDataAdapter da = new SqlDataAdapter(orders, conn);
DataSet ds = new DataSet();
da.Fill(ds, "Orders");
da = new SqlDataAdapter(customers , conn);
da.Fill(ds, "Customers");
ds.Relations.Add("CustomerOrders",
                 ds.Tables["Customers"].Columns["CustomerID"],
                 ds.Tables["Orders"].Columns["CustomerID"]);
```

Once created, the data in the DataSet is bound to the DataGrid simply by calling SetDataBinding():

```
dataGrid1.SetDataBinding(ds, "Customers");
```

This produces the output shown in Figure 32-7.

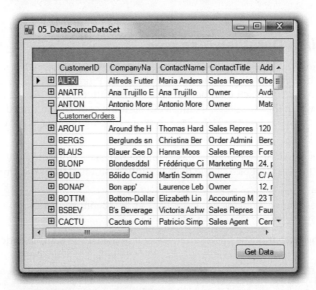

Figure 32-7

Unlike the DataGridView examples shown in this chapter, there is now a + sign to the left of each record. This reflects the fact that the DataSet has a navigable relationship between customers and orders. Any number of such relationships can be defined in code.

When the user clicks the + sign, the list of relationships is shown (or hidden if already visible). Clicking the name of the relationship enables you to navigate to the linked records (see Figure 32-8), in this example, listing all orders placed by the selected customer.

The DataGrid control also includes a couple of new icons in the top-right corner. The arrow permits the user to navigate to the parent row, and will change the display to that on the previous page. The header row showing details of the parent record can be shown or hidden by clicking the other button.

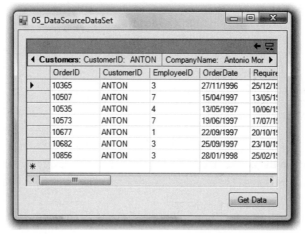

Figure 32-8

Displaying Data in a DataViewManager

The display of data in a `DataViewManager` is the same as that for the `DataSet` shown in the previous section. However, when a `DataViewManager` is created for a `DataSet`, an individual `DataView` is created for each `DataTable`, which then permits the code to alter the displayed rows based on a filter or the row state, as shown in the `DataView` example. Even if the code doesn't need to filter data, it is good practice to wrap the `DataSet` in a `DataViewManager` for display because it provides more options when revising the source code.

The following creates a `DataViewManager` based on the `DataSet` from the previous example and then alters the `DataView` for the `Customer` table to show only customers from the United Kingdom:

```
DataViewManager dvm = new DataViewManager(ds);
dvm.DataViewSettings["Customers"].RowFilter = "Country='UK'";
dataGrid.SetDataBinding(dvm, "Customers");
```

Figure 32-9 shows the output of the `DataSourceDataViewManager` sample code.

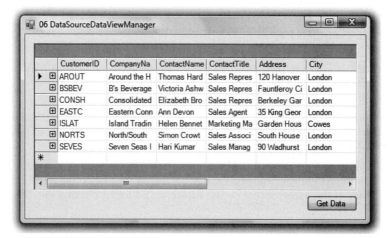

Figure 32-9

IListSource and IList Interfaces

The `DataGridView` also supports any object that exposes one of the interfaces `IListSource` or `IList`. `IListSource` has only one method, `GetList()`, which returns an `IList` interface. `IList`, however, is somewhat more interesting and is implemented by a large number of classes in the runtime. Some of the classes that implement this interface are `Array`, `ArrayList`, and `StringCollection`.

When using `IList`, the same caveat for the object within the collection holds true as for the `Array` implementation shown earlier — if a `StringCollection` is used as the data source for the `DataGrid`, the length of the strings is displayed within the grid, not within the text of the item as expected.

Displaying Generic Collections

In addition to the types already described, the `DataGridView` also supports binding to generic collections. The syntax is just as in the other examples already provided in this chapter — simply set the `DataSource` property to the collection, and the control will generate an appropriate display.

Once again, the columns displayed are based on the properties of the object — all public readable fields are displayed in the `DataGridView`. The following example shows the display for a list class defined as follows:

```csharp
class PersonList : List < Person >
{
}

class Person
{
    public Person( string name, Sex sex, DateTime dob )
    {
        _name = name;
        _sex = sex;
        _dateOfBirth = dob;
    }

    public string Name
    {
        get { return _name; }
        set { _name = value; }
    }

    public Sex Sex
    {
        get { return _sex; }
        set { _sex = value; }
    }

    public DateTime DateOfBirth
    {
        get { return _dateOfBirth; }
        set { _dateOfBirth = value; }
    }

    private string _name;
    private Sex _sex;
    private DateTime _dateOfBirth;
}

enum Sex
```

(continued)

(continued)

```
    {
        Male,
        Female
    }
```

The display shows several instances of the `Person` class that were constructed within the `PersonList` class. See Figure 32-10.

In some circumstances, it might be necessary to hide certain properties from the grid display — for this you can use the `Browsable` attribute as shown in the following code snippet. Any properties marked as non-browsable are not displayed in the property grid.

```
    [Browsable(false)]
    public bool IsEmployed
    {
        ...
    }
```

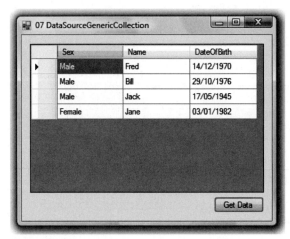

Figure 32-10

The `DataGridView` uses this property to determine whether to display the property or hide it. In the absence of the attribute, the default is to display the property. If a property is read-only, the grid control will display the values from the object, but it will be read-only within the grid.

Any changes made in the grid view are reflected in the underlying objects — so, for example, if in the previous code the name of a person was changed within the user interface, the setter method for that property would be called.

DataGridView Class Hierarchy

The class hierarchy for the main parts of the `DataGridView` control is shown in Figure 32-11.

The control uses objects derived from `DataGridViewColumn` when displaying data. As you can see from Figure 32-11, there are now far more options for displaying data than there were with the original `DataGrid`. One major omission was the display of drop-down columns within the `DataGrid` — this functionality is now provided for the `DataGridView` in the form of the `DataGridViewComboBoxColumn`.

When you specify a data source for the DataGridView, by default it will construct columns for you automatically. These will be created based on the data types in the data source, so, for example, any Boolean field will be mapped to the DataGridViewCheckBoxColumn. If you would rather handle the creation of columns yourself, you can set the AutoGenerateColumns property to false and construct the columns yourself.

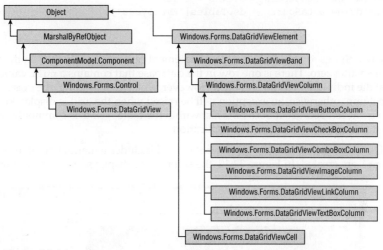

Figure 32-11

The following example shows how to construct columns and includes an image and a ComboBox column. The code uses a DataSet and retrieves data into two data tables. The first DataTable contains the employee information from the Northwind database. The second table consists of the EmployeeID column and a generated Name column, which is used when rendering the ComboBox:

```
using (SqlConnection con =
  new SqlConnection (
    ConfigurationSettings.ConnectionStrings["northwind"].ConnectionString ) )
{
    string select = "SELECT EmployeeID, FirstName, LastName, Photo,
                      IsNull(ReportsTo,0) as ReportsTo FROM Employees";

    SqlDataAdapter da = new SqlDataAdapter(select, con);

    DataSet ds = new DataSet();

    da.Fill(ds, "Employees");

    select = "SELECT EmployeeID, FirstName + ' ' + LastName as Name
             FROM Employees UNION SELECT 0,'(None)'";

    da = new SqlDataAdapter(select, con);
    da.Fill(ds, "Managers");

    // Construct the columns in the grid view
    SetupColumns(ds);
```

(continued)

(continued)

```
        // Set the default height for a row
        dataGridView.RowTemplate.Height = 100 ;

        // Then set up the datasource
        dataGridView.AutoGenerateColumns = false;
        dataGridView.DataSource = ds.Tables["Employees"];


}
```

Here there are two things to note. The first select statement replaces null values in the ReportsTo column with the value zero. There is one row in the database that contains a null value in this field, indicating that the individual has no manager. However, when data binding, the ComboBox needs a value in this column; otherwise, an exception will be raised when the grid is displayed. In the example, the value zero is chosen because it does not exist within the table — this is commonly termed a *sentinel value* because it has special meaning to the application.

The second SQL clause selects data for the ComboBox and includes a manufactured row where the values Zero and (None) are created. In Figure 32-12, the second row displays the (None) entry.

Figure 32-12

The custom columns are created by the following function:

```
    private void SetupColumns(DataSet ds)
    {
        DataGridViewTextBoxColumn forenameColumn = new DataGridViewTextBoxColumn();
        forenameColumn.DataPropertyName = "FirstName";
        forenameColumn.HeaderText = "Forename";
        forenameColumn.ValueType = typeof(string);
        forenameColumn.Frozen = true;
        dataGridView.Columns.Add(forenameColumn);

        DataGridViewTextBoxColumn surnameColumn = new DataGridViewTextBoxColumn();
        surnameColumn.DataPropertyName = "LastName";
        surnameColumn.HeaderText = "Surname";
```

```
            surnameColumn.Frozen = true;
            surnameColumn.ValueType = typeof(string);
            dataGridView.Columns.Add(surnameColumn);

            DataGridViewImageColumn photoColumn = new DataGridViewImageColumn();
            photoColumn.DataPropertyName = "Photo";
            photoColumn.Width = 100;
            photoColumn.HeaderText = "Image";
            photoColumn.ReadOnly = true;
            photoColumn.ImageLayout = DataGridViewImageCellLayout.Normal;
            dataGridView.Columns.Add(photoColumn);

            DataGridViewComboBoxColumn reportsToColumn = new DataGridViewComboBoxColumn();
            reportsToColumn.HeaderText = "Reports To";
            reportsToColumn.DataSource = ds.Tables["Managers"];
            reportsToColumn.DisplayMember = "Name";
            reportsToColumn.ValueMember = "EmployeeID";
            reportsToColumn.DataPropertyName = "ReportsTo";
            dataGridView.Columns.Add(reportsToColumn);
        }
```

The `ComboBox` is created last in this example — and uses the `Managers` table in the passed data set as its data source. This contains `Name` and `EmployeeID` columns, and these are assigned to the `DisplayMember` and `ValueMember` properties, respectively. These properties define where the data is coming from for the `ComboBox`.

The `DataPropertyName` is set to the column in the main data table that the combo box links to — this provides the initial value for the column, and if the user chooses another entry from the combo box, this value is updated.

The only other thing this example needs to do is handle `null` values correctly when updating the database. At present, it will attempt to write the value zero into any row if you choose the (None) item onscreen. This will cause an exception from SQL Server because this violates the foreign key constraint on the `ReportsTo` column. To overcome this, you need to preprocess the data before sending it back to SQL Server, and set to `null` the `ReportsTo` column for any rows where this value was zero.

Data Binding

The previous examples have used the `DataGrid` and `DataGridView` controls, which form only a small part of the controls in the .NET runtime that can be used to display data. The process of linking a control to a data source is called *data binding*.

In the Microsoft Foundation Class library, the process of linking data from class variables to a set of controls was termed *Dialog Data Exchange* (DDX). The facilities available within .NET for binding data to controls are substantially easier to use and also more capable. For example, in .NET you can bind data to most properties of a control, not just the text property. You can also bind data in a similar manner to ASP.NET controls (see Chapter 37, "ASP.NET Pages").

Simple Binding

A control that supports single binding typically displays only a single value at once, such as a text box or radio button. The following example shows how to bind a column from a `DataTable` to a `TextBox`:

```
DataSet ds = CreateDataSet();
textBox.DataBindings.Add("Text", ds , "Products.ProductName");
```

After retrieving some data from the `Products` table and storing it in the returned `DataSet` with the `CreateDataSet()` method as shown here, the second line binds the `Text` property of the control (`textBox1`) to the `Products.ProductName` column. Figure 32-13 shows the result of this type of data binding.

Figure 32-13

The text box displays a string from the database. Figure 32-14 shows how the SQL Server Management Studio tool could be used to verify the contents of the `Products` table to check that it is the right column and value.

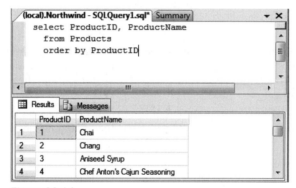

Figure 32-14

Having a single text box onscreen with no way to scroll to the next or the previous record and no way to update the database is not very useful. The following section shows a more realistic example and introduces the other objects that are necessary for data binding to work.

Data-Binding Objects

Figure 32-15 shows a class hierarchy for the objects that are used in data binding. This section discusses the `BindingContext`, `CurrencyManager`, and `PropertyManager` classes of the `System.Windows .Forms` namespace and shows how they interact when data is bound to one or more controls on a form. The shaded objects are those used in binding.

In the previous example, the `DataBindings` property of the `TextBox` control was used to bind a column from a `DataSet` to the `Text` property of the control. The `DataBindings` property is an instance of the `ControlBindingsCollection` shown in Figure 32-15:

```
textBox1.DataBindings.Add("Text", ds, "Products.ProductName");
```

This line adds a `Binding` object to the `ControlBindingsCollection`.

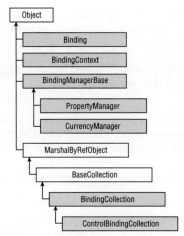

Figure 32-15

BindingContext

Each Windows Form has a `BindingContext` property. Incidentally, `Form` is derived from `Control`, which is where this property is actually defined, so most controls have this property. A `BindingContext` object has a collection of `BindingManagerBase` instances (see Figure 32-16). These instances are created and added to the binding manager object when a control is data-bound.

The `BindingContext` might contain several data sources, wrapped in either a `CurrencyManager` or a `PropertyManager`. The decision of which class is used is based on the data source itself.

If the data source contains a list of items, such as a `DataTable`, `DataView`, or any object that implements the `IList` interface, a `CurrencyManager` will be used. A `CurrencyManager` can maintain the current position within that data source. If the data source returns only a single value, a `PropertyManager` will be stored within the `BindingContext`.

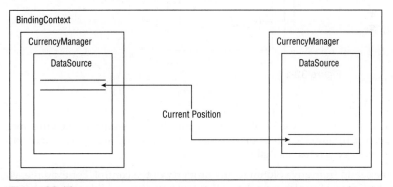

Figure 32-16

A `CurrencyManager` or `PropertyManager` is created only once for a given data source. If two text boxes are bound to a row from a `DataTable`, only one `CurrencyManager` will be created within the binding context.

Each control added to a form is linked to the form's binding manager, so all controls share the same instance. When a control is initially created, its `BindingContext` property is null. When the control is added to the `Controls` collection of the form, the `BindingContext` is set to that of the form.

To bind a control to a form, an entry needs to be added to its `DataBindings` property, which is an instance of `ControlBindingsCollection`. The following code creates a new binding:

```
textBox.DataBindings.Add("Text", ds, "Products.ProductName");
```

Internally, the `Add()` method of `ControlBindingsCollection` creates a new instance of a `Binding` object from the parameters passed to this method and adds this to the bindings collection represented in Figure 32-17.

Figure 32-17 illustrates roughly what is going on when a `Binding` object is added to a `Control`. The binding links the control to a data source, which is maintained within the `BindingContext` of the `Form` (or control itself). Changes within the data source are reflected into the control, as are changes in the control.

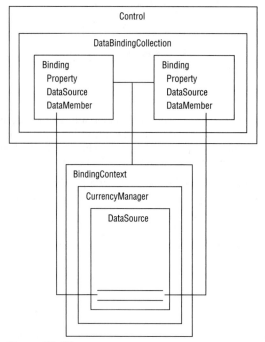

Figure 32-17

Binding

This class links a property of the control to a member of the data source. When that member changes, the control's property is updated to reflect this change. The opposite is also true — if the text in the text box is updated, this change is reflected in the data source.

Bindings can be set up from any column to any property of the control. For example, you can bind not only the text of a text box but also the color of that text box. It is possible to bind properties of a control to completely different data sources; for example, the color of the cell might be defined in a colors table, and the actual data might be defined in another table.

CurrencyManager and PropertyManager

When a `Binding` object is created, a corresponding `CurrencyManager` or `PropertyManager` object is also created, provided that this is the first time that data from the given source has been bound. The purpose of this class is to define the position of the current record within the data source and to coordinate all list bindings when the current record is changed. Figure 32-18 displays two fields from the `Products` table and includes a way to move between records by means of a `TrackBar` control.

Figure 32-18

The following example shows the main `ScrollingDataBinding` code:

```
namespace ScrollingDataBinding
{
  partial class Form1: Form
  {
    public Form1()
    {
      InitializeComponent();
    }

    private DataSet CreateDataSet()
    {
      string customers = "SELECT * FROM Products";
      DataSet ds = new DataSet();

      using (SqlConnection con = new SqlConnection (
              ConfigurationSettings.
              ConnectionStrings["northwind"].ConnectionString))
      {
        SqlDataAdapter da = new SqlDataAdapter(customers, con);

        da.Fill(ds, "Products");
      }

      return ds;
    }

    private void trackBar_Scroll(object sender, EventArgs e)
    {
        this.BindingContext[ds, "Products"].Position = trackBar.Value;
    }

    private void retrieveButton_Click(object sender, EventArgs e)
    {
```

(continued)

(continued)

```
        retrieveButton.Enabled = false;

        ds = CreateDataSet();

        textName.DataBindings.Add("Text", ds, "Products.ProductName");
        textQuan.DataBindings.Add("Text", ds, "Products.QuantityPerUnit");

        trackBar.Minimum = 0;
        trackBar.Maximum = this.BindingContext[ds, "Products"].Count - 1;

        textName.Enabled = true;
        textQuan.Enabled = true;
        trackBar.Enabled = true;

    }

    private DataSet ds;
  }
}
```

The scrolling mechanism is provided by the `trackBar_Scroll` event handler, which sets the position of the `BindingContext` to the current position of the track bar thumb. Altering the binding context here updates the data displayed on the screen.

Data is bound to the two text boxes in the `retrieveButton_Click` event by adding a data binding expression. Here the `Text` properties of the controls are set to fields from the data source. It is possible to bind any simple property of a control to an item from the data source; for example, you could bind the text color, enabled, or other properties as appropriate.

When the data is originally retrieved, the maximum position on the track bar is set to be the number of records. Then, in the scroll method, the position of the `BindingContext` for the products `DataTable` is set to the position of the scroll bar thumb. This changes the current record from the `DataTable`, so all controls bound to the current row (in this example, the two text boxes) are updated.

Now that you know how to bind to various data sources, such as arrays, data tables, data views, and various other containers of data, and how to sort and filter that data, the next section discusses how Visual Studio has been extended to permit data access to be better integrated with the application.

Visual Studio .NET and Data Access

This section discusses some of the ways that Visual Studio allows data to be integrated into the GUI, including how to create a connection, select some data, generate a `DataSet`, and use all of the generated objects to produce a simple application. The available tools enable you to create a database connection with the `OleDbConnection` or `SqlConnection` classes. The class you use depends on the type of database you are using. After a connection has been defined, you can create a `DataSet` and populate it from within Visual Studio .NET. This generates an XSD file for the `DataSet` and the `.cs` code. The result is a type-safe `DataSet`.

Creating a Connection

First, create a new Windows application, and then create a new database connection. Using the Server Explorer (see Figure 32-19), you can manage various aspects of data access.

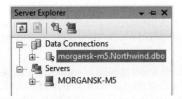

Figure 32-19

For this example, create a connection to the Northwind database. Select the Add Connection option from the context menu available on the Data Connections item to launch a wizard that enables you to choose a database provider. Select the .NET Framework Provider for SQL Server. Figure 32-20 shows the Add Connection dialog box.

Figure 32-20

Depending on your .NET Framework installation, the sample databases might be located in SQL Server, MSDE (Microsoft SQL Server Data Engine), or both.

To connect to the local MSDE database, if it exists, type **(local)\\sqlexpress** for the name of the server. To connect to a regular SQL Server instance, type **(local)** or '**.**' to select a database on the current machine, or the name of the desired server on the network. You may need to enter a user name and password to access the database.

Select the Northwind database from the drop-down list of databases, and to ensure that everything is set up correctly, click the Test Connection button. If everything is set up properly, you should see a message box with a confirmation message.

Visual Studio 2005 had numerous changes when accessing data, and these are available from several places in the user interface. The Data menu is a good choice because it permits you to view any data sources already added to the project, add a new data source, and preview data from the underlying database (or other data source).

The following example uses the Northwind database connection to generate a user interface for selecting data from the `Employees` table. The first step is to choose Add New Data Source from the Data menu, which begins a wizard that walks you through the process. The dialog shown in Figure 32-21 shows part of the Data Source Configuration Wizard, in this case where you can select appropriate tables for the data source.

As you progress through the wizard, you can choose the data source, which can be a database, local database file (such as an `.mdb` file), a Web service, or an object. You will then be prompted for further information based on the type of data source you choose. For a database connection, this includes the name of the connection (which is subsequently stored in the application configuration file shown in the following code), and you can then select the table, view, or stored procedure that supplies the data. Ultimately, this generates a strongly typed `DataSet` within your application.

```xml
<?xml version="1.0" encoding="utf-8"?>
<configuration>
  <connectionStrings>
    <add name="SimpleApp.Properties.Settings.NorthwindConnection"
        connectionString="Data Source=.;Integrated Security=True;Initial
Catalog=Northwind"
        providerName="System.Data.SqlClient" />
  </connectionStrings>
</configuration>
```

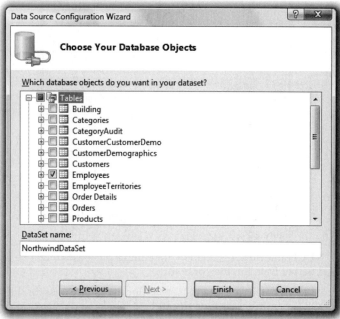

Figure 32-21

This includes the name of the connection, the connection string itself, and a provider name, which is used when generating the connection object. You can manually edit this information as necessary. To display a user interface for the employee data, you can simply drag the chosen data from the Data Sources window onto your form. This will generate one of two styles of user interface for you — a grid-style UI that utilizes the `DataGridView` control described earlier or a details view that presents just the data for a single record at a time. Figure 32-22 shows the details view.

Figure 32-22

Dragging the data source onto the form generates a number of objects, both visual and nonvisual. The nonvisual objects are created within the tray area of the form and comprise a `DataConnector`, a strongly typed `DataSet`, and a `TableAdapter`, which contains the SQL used to select/update the data. The visual objects created depend on whether you have chosen the `DataGridView` or the details view. Both include a `DataNavigator` control that can be used to page through the data. Figure 32-23 shows the user interface generated using the `DataGridView` control — one of the goals of Visual Studio 2005 was to simplify data access to the point where you could generate functional forms without writing a single line of code.

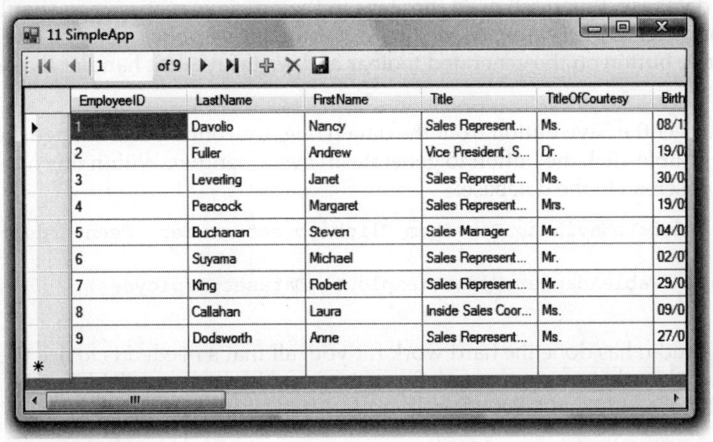

EmployeeID	LastName	FirstName	Title	TitleOfCourtesy	Birth
1	Davolio	Nancy	Sales Represent...	Ms.	08/1
2	Fuller	Andrew	Vice President, S...	Dr.	19/0
3	Leverling	Janet	Sales Represent...	Ms.	30/0
4	Peacock	Margaret	Sales Represent...	Mrs.	19/0
5	Buchanan	Steven	Sales Manager	Mr.	04/0
6	Suyama	Michael	Sales Represent...	Mr.	02/0
7	King	Robert	Sales Represent...	Mr.	29/0
8	Callahan	Laura	Inside Sales Coor...	Ms.	09/0
9	Dodsworth	Anne	Sales Represent...	Ms.	27/0

Figure 32-23

When the data source is created, it adds a number of files to your solution. To view these, click the Show All Files button in the Solution Explorer. You will then be able to expand the data set node and view the extra files added. The main one of interest is the `.Designer.cs` file, which includes the C# source code used to populate the data set.

You will find several classes defined within the `.Designer.cs` file. The classes represent the strongly typed data set, which acts in a similar way to the standard `DataAdapter` class. This class internally uses the `DataAdapter` to fill the `DataSet`.

Selecting Data

The table adapter generated contains commands for SELECT, INSERT, UPDATE, and DELETE. Needless to say, these can (and probably should) be tailored to call stored procedures rather than using straight SQL. The wizard-generated code will do for now, however. Visual Studio .NET adds the following code to the `.Designer` file:

```
private System.Data.SqlClient.SqlCommand m_DeleteCommand;
private System.Data.SqlClient.SqlCommand m_InsertCommand;
private System.Data.SqlClient.SqlCommand m_UpdateCommand;
private System.Data.SqlClient.SqlDataAdapter m_adapter;
```

An object is defined for each of the SQL commands, with the exception of the `Select` command, and also a `SqlDataAdapter`. Further down the file, in the `InitializeComponent()` method, the wizard has generated code to create each one of these commands as well as the data adapter.

In previous versions of Visual Studio .NET, the commands generated for `Insert` and `Update` also included a select clause — this was used as a way to resynchronize the data with that on the server, just in case any fields within the database were calculated (such as identity columns and/or computed fields).

The wizard-generated code works but is less than optimal. For a production system, all the generated SQL should probably be replaced with calls to stored procedures. If the INSERT or UPDATE clauses didn't have to resynchronize the data, the removal of the redundant SQL clause would speed up the application a little.

Updating the Data Source

So far, the applications have selected data from the database. This section discusses how to persist changes to the database. If you followed the steps in the previous section, you should have an application that contains everything needed for a rudimentary application. The one change necessary is to enable the Save button on the generated toolbar and write an event handler that will update the database.

From the IDE, select the Save button from the data navigator control, and change the `Enabled` property to `true`. Then, double-click the button to generate an event handler. Within this handler, save the changes made onscreen to the database:

```
private void dataNavigatorSaveItem_Click(object sender, EventArgs e)
{
    employeesTableAdapter.Update(employeesDataset.Employees);
}
```

Because Visual Studio has done the hard work for you, all that's needed is to use the `Update` method of the table adapter class that was generated. Six `Update` methods are available on the table adapter — this example uses the override that takes a `DataTable` as the parameter.

Other Common Requirements

A common requirement when displaying data is to provide a pop-up menu for a given row. You can do this in numerous ways. The example in this section focuses on one approach that can simplify the code required, especially if the display context is a `DataGrid`, where a `DataSet` with some relations is displayed. The problem here is that the context menu depends on the row that is selected, and that row could be part of any source `DataTable` in the `DataSet`.

Because the context menu functionality is likely to be general-purpose in nature, the implementation here uses a base class (`ContextDataRow`) that supports the menu-building code, and each data row class that supports a pop-up menu derives from this base class.

When the user right-clicks any part of a row in the `DataGrid`, the row is looked up to check if it derives from `ContextDataRow`, and if so, `PopupMenu()` can be called. This could be implemented using an interface; however, in this instance, a base class provides a simpler solution.

This example demonstrates how to generate `DataRow` and `DataTable` classes that can be used to provide type-safe access to data in much the same way as the previous XSD sample. However, this time you write the code yourself to show how to use custom attributes and reflection in this context.

Figure 32-24 illustrates the class hierarchy for this example.

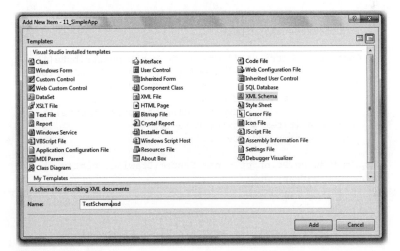

Figure 32-24

Here is the code for this example:

```
using System;
using System.Windows.Forms;
using System.Data;
using System.Data.SqlClient;
using System.Reflection;

public class ContextDataRow : DataRow
{
    public ContextDataRow(DataRowBuilder builder) : base(builder)
    {
    }
```

(continued)

(continued)

```
public void PopupMenu(System.Windows.Forms.Control parent, int x, int y)
{

    // Use reflection to get the list of popup menu commands.
    MemberInfo[] members = this.GetType().FindMembers (MemberTypes.Method,
                        BindingFlags.Public | BindingFlags.Instance ,
                        new System.Reflection.MemberFilter(Filter),
                        null);
    if (members.Length > 0)
    {

        // Create a context menu

        ContextMenu menu = new ContextMenu();

        // Now loop through those members and generate the popup menu.
        // Note the cast to MethodInfo in the foreach
        foreach (MethodInfo meth in members)
        {

            // Get the caption for the operation from the
            // ContextMenuAttribute

            ContextMenuAttribute[] ctx = (ContextMenuAttribute[])
                meth.GetCustomAttributes(typeof(ContextMenuAttribute), true);
            MenuCommand callback = new MenuCommand(this, meth);
            MenuItem item = new MenuItem(ctx[0].Caption, new
                                EventHandler(callback.Execute));
            item.DefaultItem = ctx[0].Default;
            menu.MenuItems.Add(item);
        }
        System.Drawing.Point pt = new System.Drawing.Point(x,y);
        menu.Show(parent, pt);
    }
}

private bool Filter(MemberInfo member, object criteria)
{
    bool bInclude = false;

    // Cast MemberInfo to MethodInfo

    MethodInfo meth = member as MethodInfo;
    if (meth != null)
    {
        if (meth.ReturnType == typeof(void))
        {
            ParameterInfo[] parms = meth.GetParameters();
            if (parms.Length == 0)
            {

                // Lastly check if there is a ContextMenuAttribute on the
```

```
            // method...

            object[] atts = meth.GetCustomAttributes
                    (typeof(ContextMenuAttribute), true);
            bInclude = (atts.Length == 1);
        }
    }
}
    return bInclude;
}
}
```

The ContextDataRow class is derived from DataRow and contains just two member functions: PopupMenu and Filter(). PopupMenu uses reflection to look for methods that correspond to a particular signature, and it displays a pop-up menu of these options to the user. Filter() is used as a delegate by PopupMenu when enumerating methods. It simply returns true if the member function does correspond to the appropriate calling convention:

```
MemberInfo[] members = this.GetType().FindMembers(MemberTypes.Method,
            BindingFlags.Public | BindingFlags.Instance,
            new System.Reflection.MemberFilter(Filter),
            null);
```

This single statement is used to filter all methods on the current object and return only those that match the following criteria:

- ❑ The member must be a method.

- ❑ The member must be a public instance method.

- ❑ The member must return void.

- ❑ The member must accept zero parameters.

- ❑ The member must include the ContextMenuAttribute.

The last of these criteria refers to a custom attribute, written specifically for this example. (It's discussed after discussing the PopupMenu method.)

```
ContextMenu menu = new ContextMenu();
foreach (MethodInfo meth in members)
{
    // ... Add the menu item
}
System.Drawing.Point pt = new System.Drawing.Point(x,y);
menu.Show(parent, pt);
```

A context menu instance is created, and a pop-up menu item is added for each method that matches the preceding criteria. The menu is subsequently displayed as shown in Figure 32-25.

The main area of difficulty with this example is the following section of code, repeated once for each member function to be displayed on the pop-up menu:

```
System.Type ctxtype = typeof(ContextMenuAttribute);
ContextMenuAttribute[] ctx = (ContextMenuAttribute[])
                    meth.GetCustomAttributes(ctxtype, true);
MenuCommand callback = new MenuCommand(this, meth);
MenuItem item = new MenuItem(ctx[0].Caption,
            new EventHandler(callback.Execute));
item.DefaultItem = ctx[0].Default;
menu.MenuItems.Add(item);
```

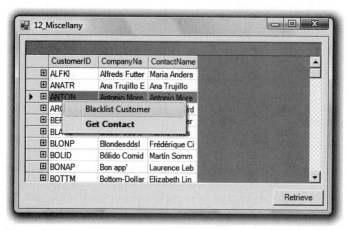

Figure 32-25

Each method that should be displayed on the context menu is attributed with the `ContextMenuAttribute`. This defines a user-friendly name for the menu option because a C# method name cannot include spaces, and it's wise to use real English on pop-up menus rather than some internal code. The attribute is retrieved from the method, and a new menu item is created and added to the menu items collection of the pop-up menu.

This sample code also shows the use of a simplified `Command` class (a common design pattern). The `MenuCommand` class used in this instance is triggered by the user choosing an item on the context menu, and it forwards the call to the receiver of the method — in this case, the object and method that was attributed. This also helps keep the code in the receiver object more isolated from the user interface code. This code is explained in the following sections.

Manufactured Tables and Rows

The XSD example earlier in the chapter showed the code produced when the Visual Studio .NET editor is used to generate a set of data access classes. The following class shows the required methods for a `DataTable`, which are fairly minimal (and they all have been generated manually):

```
public class CustomerTable : DataTable
{
    public CustomerTable() : base("Customers")
    {
        this.Columns.Add("CustomerID", typeof(string));
        this.Columns.Add("CompanyName", typeof(string));
        this.Columns.Add("ContactName", typeof(string));
    }
    protected override System.Type GetRowType()
    {
        return typeof(CustomerRow);
    }
    protected override DataRow NewRowFromBuilder(DataRowBuilder builder)
    {
        return(DataRow) new CustomerRow(builder);
    }
}
```

The first prerequisite of a `DataTable` is to override the `GetRowType()` method. This is used by the .NET internals when generating new rows for the table. The type used to represent each row should be returned from this method.

The next prerequisite is to implement `NewRowFromBuilder()`, which is called by the runtime when creating new rows for the table. That's enough for a minimal implementation. The corresponding `CustomerRow` class is fairly simple. It implements properties for each of the columns within the row and then implements the methods that ultimately are displayed on the context menu:

```
public class CustomerRow : ContextDataRow
{
    public CustomerRow(DataRowBuilder builder) : base(builder)
    {
    }
    public string CustomerID
    {
        get { return (string)this["CustomerID"];}
        set { this["CustomerID"] = value;}
    }

    // Other properties omitted for clarity

    [ContextMenu("Blacklist Customer")]
    public void Blacklist()
    {
        // Do something
    }
    [ContextMenu("Get Contact",Default=true)]
    public void GetContact()
    {
        // Do something else
    }
}
```

The class simply derives from `ContextDataRow`, including the appropriate getter/setter methods on properties that are named the same as each field, and then a set of methods may be added that are used when reflecting on the class:

```
[ContextMenu("Blacklist Customer")]
public void Blacklist()
{

    // Do something
}
```

Each method that is to be displayed on the context menu has the same signature and includes the custom ContextMenu attribute.

Using an Attribute

The idea behind writing the `ContextMenu` attribute is to be able to supply a free text name for a given menu option. The following example also adds a `Default` flag, which is used to indicate the default menu choice. The entire attribute class is presented here:

```
[AttributeUsage(AttributeTargets.Method,AllowMultiple=false,Inherited=true)]
public class ContextMenuAttribute : System.Attribute
{
    public ContextMenuAttribute(string caption)
    {
        Caption = caption;
```

(continued)

(continued)

```
        Default = false;
    }
    public readonly string Caption;
}
```

The `AttributeUsage` attribute on the class marks `ContextMenuAttribute` as being usable on only a method, and it also defines that there can only be one instance of this object on any given method. The `Inherited=true` clause defines whether the attribute can be placed on a superclass method and still reflected on by a subclass.

A number of other members could be added to this attribute, including the following:

- ❑ A hotkey for the menu option
- ❑ An image to be displayed
- ❑ Some text to be displayed in the toolbar as the mouse pointer rolls over the menu option
- ❑ A help context ID

Dispatching Methods

When a menu is displayed in .NET, each menu option is linked to the processing code for that option by means of a delegate. In implementing the mechanism for connecting menu choices to code, you have two options:

- ❑ Implement a method with the same signature as the `System.EventHandler`. This is defined as shown in this snippet:

```
public delegate void EventHandler(object sender, EventArgs e);
```

- ❑ Define a proxy class, which implements the preceding delegate and forwards calls to the received class. This is known as the Command pattern and is what has been chosen for this example.

The Command pattern separates the sender and the receiver of the call by means of a simple intermediate class. This may be overkill for such an example, but it makes the methods on each `DataRow` simpler (because they don't need the parameters passed to the delegate), and it is more extensible:

```
public class MenuCommand
{
    public MenuCommand(object receiver, MethodInfo method)
    {
        Receiver = receiver;
        Method = method;
    }
    public void Execute(object sender, EventArgs e)
    {
        Method.Invoke(Receiver, new object[] {} );
    }
    public readonly object Receiver;
    public readonly MethodInfo Method;
}
```

The class simply provides an `EventHandler` delegate (the `Execute` method), which invokes the desired method on the receiver object. This example handles two different types of row: rows from the `Customers` table and rows from the `Orders` table. Naturally, the processing options for each of these types of data are likely to differ. Figure 32-25 showed the operations available for a `Customer` row, whereas Figure 32-26 shows the options available for an `Order` row.

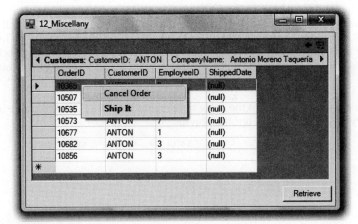

Figure 32-26

Getting the Selected Row

The last piece of the puzzle for this example is how to work out which row within the DataSet the user has selected. You might think that it must be a property on the DataGrid. However, this control is not available in this context. The hit test information obtained from within the MouseUp() event handler might also be a likely candidate to look at, but that only helps if the data displayed is from a single DataTable.

Remember how the grid is filled:

```
dataGrid.SetDataBinding(ds,"Customers");
```

This method adds a new CurrencyManager to the BindingContext, which represents the current DataTable and the DataSet. Now, the DataGrid has two properties, DataSource and DataMember, which are set when the SetDataBinding() is called. DataSource in this instance refers to a DataSet and the DataMember property refers to Customers.

Given the data source, a data member, and the binding context of the form, the current row can be located with the following code:

```
protected void dataGrid_MouseUp(object sender, MouseEventArgs e)
{
    // Perform a hit test
    if(e.Button == MouseButtons.Right)
    {
        // Find which row the user clicked on, if any
        DataGrid.HitTestInfo hti = dataGrid.HitTest(e.X, e.Y);

        // Check if the user hit a cell
        if(hti.Type == DataGrid.HitTestType.Cell)
        {
            // Find the DataRow that corresponds to the cell
            //the user has clicked upon
```

After calling dataGrid.HitTest() to calculate where the user has clicked the mouse, the BindingManagerBase instance for the data grid is retrieved:

```
BindingManagerBase bmb = this.BindingContext[ dataGrid.DataSource,
                                              dataGrid.DataMember];
```

This uses the DataGrid's DataSource and DataMember to name the object to be returned. All that is left now is to find the row the user clicked and display the context menu. With a right-click on a row, the current row indicator doesn't normally move, but that's not good enough. The row indicator should be moved and then the pop-up menu should be displayed. The HitTestInfo object includes the row number, so the BindingManagerBase object's current position can be changed as follows:

```
bmb.Position = hti.Row;
```

This changes the cell indicator, and at the same time means that when a call is made into the class to get the Row, the current row is returned, not the previous one selected:

```
DataRowView drv = bmb.Current as DataRowView;
if(drv != null)
{
    ContextDataRow ctx = drv.Row as ContextDataRow;
    if(ctx != null) ctx.PopupMenu(dataGrid,e.X,e.Y);
}
        }
    }
}
```

Because the DataGrid is displaying items from a DataSet, the Current object within the BindingManagerBase collection is a DataRowView, which is tested by an explicit cast in the previous code. If this succeeds, the actual row that the DataRowView wraps can be retrieved by performing another cast to check if it is indeed a ContextDataRow, and finally pop up a menu.

In this example, you will notice that two data tables, Customers and Orders, have been created, and a relationship has been defined between these tables, so that when users click CustomerOrders they see a filtered list of orders. When the user clicks, the DataGrid changes the DataMember from Customers to Customers.CustomerOrders, which just so happens to be the correct object that the BindingContext indexer uses to retrieve the data being shown.

Summary

This chapter introduced some of the methods of displaying data under .NET. System.Windows.Forms includes a large number of classes to be explored, and this chapter used the DataGridView and DataGrid controls to display data from many different data sources, such as an Array, DataTable, or DataSet.

Because it is not always appropriate to display data in a grid, this chapter also discussed how to link a column of data to a single control in the user interface. The binding capabilities of .NET make this type of user interface very easy to support because it's generally just a case of binding a control to a column and letting .NET do the rest of the work.

Moving on, the next chapter covers presentation in the form of Graphics with GDI+.

33

Graphics with GDI+

This is the third of the eight chapters that deal with user interaction and the .NET Framework. Chapter 31, "Windows Forms," focused on how to display a dialog box or SDI or MDI window, and how to place various controls such as buttons, text boxes, and list boxes. Chapter 32, "Data Binding," looked at how to work with data in Windows Forms using a number of the Windows Forms controls that work with the disparate data sources that you might encounter.

Although these standard controls are powerful and, by themselves, quite adequate for the complete user interface for many applications, some situations require more flexibility. For example, you might want to draw text in a given font in a precise position in a window, or display images without using a picture box control, or draw simple shapes or other graphics. None of this can be done with the controls discussed in Chapter 31. To display that kind of output, the application must instruct the operating system what to display and where in its window to display it.

Therefore, this chapter shows you how to draw a variety of items including:

- ❑ Principles of drawing
- ❑ Lines and simple shapes
- ❑ BMP images and other image files
- ❑ Text
- ❑ Dealing with printing

In the process, you will need to use a variety of helper objects, including pens (to define the characteristics of lines), brushes (to define how areas are filled in), and fonts (to define the shape of the characters of text). This chapter also goes into some detail on how devices interpret and display different colors.

The chapter starts, however, by discussing a technology called *GDI+*. GDI+ consists of the set of .NET base classes that are available to control custom drawing on the screen. These classes arrange for the appropriate instructions to be sent to graphics device drivers to ensure the correct output is placed on the screen (or printed to a hard copy).

Understanding Drawing Principles

This section examines the basic principles that you need to understand to start drawing to the screen. It starts by giving an overview of GDI and the underlying technology on which GDI+ is based. It also shows how GDI and GDI+ are related. Then, we will move on to a couple of simple examples.

GDI and GDI+

In general, one of the strengths of Windows — and indeed of modern operating systems in general — lies in its ability to abstract the details of particular devices without input from the developer. For example, you do not need to understand anything about your hard drive device driver to programmatically read and write files to and from disk. You simply call the appropriate methods in the relevant .NET classes (or in pre-.NET days, the equivalent Windows API functions). This principle is also true when it comes to drawing. When the computer draws anything to the screen, it does so by sending instructions to the video card. However, many hundreds of different video cards are on the market, most of which have different instruction sets and capabilities. If you had to take that into account and write specific code for each video driver, writing any such application would be an almost impossible task. The Windows graphical device interface (GDI) has been around since the earliest versions of Windows because of these reasons.

GDI provides a layer of abstraction, hiding the differences between the different video cards. You simply call the Windows API function to do the specific task, and internally the GDI figures out how to get the client's particular video card to do whatever it is you want when the client runs your particular piece of code. Not only does GDI accomplish this, but if the client has several display devices — for example, monitors and printers — GDI achieves the remarkable feat of making the printer look the same as the screen, as far as the application is concerned. If the client wants to print something instead of displaying it, your application will simply inform the system that the output device is the printer, and then call the same API functions in exactly the same way.

As you can see, the device-context (DC) object (covered shortly) is a very powerful object, and you won't be surprised to learn that under GDI *all* drawing had to be done through a device context. The DC was even used for operations that do not involve drawing to the screen or to any hardware device, such as modifying images in memory.

Although GDI exposes a relatively high-level API to developers, it is still an API that is based on the old Windows API, with C-style functions. GDI+, to a large extent, sits as a layer between GDI and your application, providing a more intuitive, inheritance-based object model. Although GDI+ is basically a wrapper around GDI, Microsoft has been able, through GDI+, to provide new features and performance improvements to some of the older features of GDI as well.

The GDI+ part of the .NET base class library is huge, and this chapter barely scratches the surface of its features because trying to cover more than a tiny fraction of the library would have turned this chapter into a huge reference guide that simply listed classes and methods. It is more important to understand the fundamental principles involved in drawing so that you are in a good position to explore the available classes. Full lists of all the classes and methods available in GDI+ are, of course, available in the SDK documentation.

Visual Basic 6 developers are likely to find the concepts involved in drawing quite unfamiliar because Visual Basic 6 focuses on controls that handle their own painting. C++/MFC developers are likely to be in more familiar territory because MFC does require developers to take control of more of the drawing process, using GDI. However, even if you have a strong background in the classic GDI, you will find that a lot of the material presented in this chapter is new.

GDI+ Namespaces

The following table provides an overview of the main namespaces you will need to explore to find the GDI+ base classes.

You should note that almost all of the classes and structs used in this chapter are taken from the `System.Drawing` namespace.

Namespace	Description
`System.Drawing`	Contains most of the classes, structs, enums, and delegates concerned with the basic functionality of drawing
`System.Drawing.Drawing2D`	Provides most of the support for advanced 2D and vector drawing, including anti-aliasing, geometric transformations, and graphics paths
`System.Drawing.Imaging`	Contains various classes that assist in the manipulation of images (bitmaps, GIF files, and so on)
`System.Drawing.Printing`	Contains classes to assist when specifically targeting a printer or print preview window as the "output device"
`System.Drawing.Design`	Contains some predefined dialog boxes, property sheets, and other user interface elements concerned with extending the design-time user interface
`System.Drawing.Text`	Contains classes to perform more advanced manipulation of fonts and font families

Device Contexts and the Graphics Object

In GDI, you identify which device you want your output to go to through an object known as the *device context* (DC). The DC stores information about a particular device and is able to translate calls to the GDI API functions into whatever instructions need to be sent to that device. You can also query the device context to find out what the capabilities of the corresponding device are (for example, whether a printer prints in color or only in black and white), so the output can be adjusted accordingly. If you ask the device to do something it is not capable of, the DC will normally detect this and take appropriate action (which, depending on the situation, might mean throwing an exception or modifying the request to get the closest match that the device is actually capable of using).

However, the DC does not deal only with the hardware device. It acts as a bridge to Windows and is able to take account of any requirements or restrictions placed on the drawing by Windows. For example, if Windows knows that only a portion of your application's window needs to be redrawn, the DC can trap and nullify attempts to draw outside that area. Because of the DC's relationship with Windows, working through the device context can simplify your code in other ways.

For example, hardware devices need to be told where to draw objects, and they usually want coordinates relative to the top-left corner of the screen (or output device). Usually, however, your application will be thinking of drawing something at a certain position within the client area (the area reserved for drawing) of its own window, possibly using its own coordinate system. Because the window might be positioned anywhere on the screen, and a user might move it at any time, translating between the two coordinate systems is potentially a difficult task. However, the DC always knows where your window is and is able to perform this translation automatically.

With GDI+, the device context is wrapped up in the .NET base class `System.Drawing.Graphics`. Most drawing is done by calling methods on an instance of `Graphics`. In fact, because the `Graphics` class is the class that is responsible for handling most drawing operations, very little gets done in GDI+ that does not involve a `Graphics` instance somewhere, so understanding how to manipulate this object is the key to understanding how to draw to display devices with GDI+.

Drawing Shapes

This section starts with a short example, `DisplayAtStartup`, to illustrate drawing to an application's main window. The examples in this chapter are all created in Visual Studio 2008 as C# Windows Applications. Recall that for this type of project the code wizard gives you a class called `Form1`, derived from `System.Windows.Form`, which represents the application's main window. Also generated for you is a class called `Program` (found in the `Program.cs` file), which represents the application's main starting point. Unless otherwise stated, in all code samples, new or modified code means code that you have added to the wizard-generated code. (You can download the sample code from the Wrox Web site at www.wrox.com.)

> *In .NET usage, when we are talking about applications that display various controls, the terminology "form" has largely replaced "window" to represent the rectangular object that occupies an area of the screen on behalf of an application. In this chapter, we have tended to stick to the term window because in the context of manually drawing items it is more meaningful. We will also talk about the form when we are referring to the .NET class used to instantiate the form/window. Finally, we will use the terms "drawing" and "painting" interchangeably to describe the process of displaying some item on the screen or other display device.*

The first example simply creates a form and draws to it in the constructor when the form starts up. Note that this is not actually the best or the correct way to draw to the screen — you will quickly find that this example has a problem because it is unable to redraw anything after starting up. However, this example illustrates quite a few points about drawing without your having to do very much work.

For this example, start Visual Studio 2008 and create a Windows Application. First, set the background color of the form to white. In the example, this line comes after the `InitializeComponent()` method so that Visual Studio 2008 recognizes the line and is able to alter the design view appearance of the form. You can find the `InitializeComponent()` method by first clicking the Show All Files button in the Visual Studio Solution Explorer and then clicking the plus sign next to the `Form1.cs` file. Here, you will find the `Form1.Designer.cs` file. It is in this file that you will find the `InitializeComponent()` method. You could have used the design view to set the background color, but this would have resulted in pretty much the same line being added automatically:

```
private void InitializeComponent()
{
    this.components = new System.ComponentModel.Container();
    this.AutoScaleMode = System.Windows.Forms.AutoScaleMode.Font;
    this.Text = "Form1";
    this.BackColor = System.Drawing.Color.White;
}
```

Then you add code to the `Form1` constructor. You create a `Graphics` object using the form's `CreateGraphics()` method. This `Graphics` object contains the Windows DC that you need to draw with. The device context created is associated with the display device and also with this window:

```
public Form1()
{
    InitializeComponent();
    Graphics dc = CreateGraphics();
    Show();
    Pen bluePen = new Pen(Color.Blue, 3);
    dc.DrawRectangle(bluePen, 0,0,50,50);
    Pen redPen = new Pen(Color.Red, 2);
    dc.DrawEllipse(redPen, 0, 50, 80, 60);
}
```

As you can see, you then call the `Show()` method to display the window. This is really done to force the window to display immediately because you cannot actually do any drawing until the window has been displayed. If the window is not displayed, there's nothing for you to draw onto.

Finally, you display a rectangle at coordinates (0,0) and with width and height 50, and an ellipse with coordinates (0,50) and with width 80 and height 50. Note that coordinates (x,y) translate to x pixels to the right and y pixels down from the top-left corner of the client area of the window — and these coordinates start from the top-left corner of the shape to be displayed.

The overloads that you are using of the `DrawRectangle()` and `DrawEllipse()` methods each take five parameters. The first parameter of each is an instance of the class `System.Drawing.Pen`. A `Pen` is one of a number of supporting objects to help with drawing — it contains information about how lines are to be drawn. Your first pen instructs the system that lines should be the color blue with a width of 3 pixels; the second pen instructs the system that the lines should be red and have a width of 2 pixels. The final four parameters are coordinates and size. For the rectangle, they represent the (x,y) coordinates of the top-left corner of the rectangle in addition to its width and height. For the ellipse, these numbers represent the same thing, except that you are talking about a hypothetical rectangle that the ellipse just fits into, rather than the ellipse itself. Figure 33-1 shows the result of running this code. Of course, because this book is not in color, you cannot see the colors.

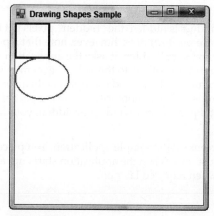

Figure 33-1

Figure 33-1 demonstrates a couple of points. First, you can see clearly where the client area of the window is located. It's the white area — the area that has been affected by setting the BackColor property. Notice that the rectangle nestles up in the corner of this area, as you would expect when you specify the coordinates of (0,0) for it. Second, notice that the top of the ellipse overlaps the rectangle slightly, which you would not expect from the coordinates given in the code. The culprit here is Windows itself and where it places the lines that border the rectangle and ellipse. By default, Windows will try to center the line on the border of the shape — that is not always possible to do exactly because the line has to be drawn on pixels (obviously). Normally, the border of each shape theoretically lies between two pixels. The result is that lines that are 1 pixel thick will get drawn just *inside* the top and left sides of a shape, but just *outside* the bottom and right sides — which means that shapes that are next to each other have their borders overlapping by one pixel. You have specified wider lines; therefore, the overlap is greater. It is possible to change the default behavior by setting the Pen. Alignment property, as detailed in the SDK documentation, but for these purposes, the default behavior is adequate.

Unfortunately, if you actually run the sample, you will notice that the form behaves a bit strangely. It is fine if you just leave it there. It is also fine if you drag it around the screen with the mouse. However, if you try minimizing the window and then restoring it, then your carefully drawn shapes just vanish! The same thing happens if you drag another window across the sample so that it only obscures a portion of your shapes. When you drag the other window away again, you will find that the temporarily obscured portion has disappeared and you are left with half an ellipse or half a rectangle!

So what's going on? The problem arises when part of a window is hidden because Windows usually discards immediately all the information concerning exactly what has been displayed. This is something Windows has to do or else the memory usage for storing screen data would be astronomical. A typical computer might be running with the video card set to display 1024 × 768 pixels, perhaps in a 24-bit color mode, which implies that each pixel on the screen occupies 3 bytes — 2.25MB to display the screen. (24-bit color is covered later in this chapter.) However, it is not uncommon for a user to work with 10 or 20 minimized windows in the taskbar. In a worst-case scenario, you might have 20 windows, each of which would occupy the whole screen if it was not minimized. If Windows actually stored the visual information those windows contained, ready for when the user restored them, then that would amount to some 45MB! These days, a good graphics card might have 64MB of memory and be able to cope with that, but it was only a few years ago that 4MB was considered generous in a graphics card — and the excess would need to be stored in the computer's main memory. Many people still have old machines, some of them with only 4MB graphic cards. Clearly, it would not be practical for Windows to manage its user interface like that.

The moment any part of a window is hidden, the "hidden" pixels get lost because Windows frees the memory that was holding those pixels. It does, however, note that a portion of the window is hidden, and when it detects that it is no longer hidden, it asks the application that owns the window to redraw its contents. There are a couple of exceptions to this rule — generally for cases in which a small portion of a window is hidden very temporarily (a good example is when you select an item from the main menu and that menu item drops down, temporarily obscuring part of the window below). In general, however, you can expect that if part of your window is hidden, your application will need to redraw it later.

That is the source of the problem for the sample application. You placed your drawing code in the Form1 constructor, which is called just once when the application starts up, and you cannot call the constructor again to redraw the shapes when required later on.

When working with Windows Forms server controls, there is no need to know anything about how to accomplish this task. This is because the standard controls are pretty sophisticated, and they are able to redraw themselves correctly whenever Windows asks them to. That is one reason why, when programming controls, you do not need to worry about the actual drawing process at all. If you are taking responsibility for drawing to the screen in your application, you also need to make sure that your application will respond correctly whenever Windows asks it to redraw all or part of its window. In the next section, you modify the sample to do just that.

Painting Shapes Using OnPaint()

If the preceding explanation has made you worried that drawing your own user interface is going to be terribly complicated, do not worry. Getting your application to redraw itself when necessary is actually quite easy.

Windows notifies an application that some repainting needs to be done by raising a Paint event. Interestingly, the Form class has already implemented a handler for this event, so you do not need to add one yourself. The Form1 handler for the Paint event will at some point in its processing call up a virtual method, OnPaint(), passing to it a single PaintEventArgs parameter. This means that all you need to do is override OnPaint() to perform your painting.

Although for this example you work by overriding OnPaint(), it is equally possible to achieve the same results by simply adding your own event handler for the Paint event (a Form1_Paint() method, say) — in much the same way as you would for any other Windows Forms event. This other approach is arguably more convenient because you can add a new event handler through the Visual Studio 2008 properties window, saving yourself from typing some code. However, the approach of overriding OnPaint() is slightly more flexible in terms of letting you control when the call to the base class window processing occurs, and it is the approach recommended in the documentation.

In this section, you create a new Windows Application called DrawShapes to do this. As before, you set the background color to white, using the properties window. You will also change the form's text to DrawShapes Sample. Then you add the following code to the generated code for the Form1 class:

```
protected override void OnPaint( PaintEventArgs e )
{
    base.OnPaint(e);
    Graphics dc = e.Graphics;
    Pen bluePen = new Pen(Color.Blue, 3);
    dc.DrawRectangle(bluePen, 0,0,50,50);
    Pen redPen = new Pen(Color.Red, 2);
    dc.DrawEllipse(redPen, 0, 50, 80, 60);
}
```

Notice that OnPaint() is declared as protected, because it is normally used internally within the class, so there is no reason for any other code outside the class to know about its existence.

PaintEventArgs is a class that is derived from the EventArgs class normally used to pass in information about events. PaintEventArgs has two additional properties, of which the more important one is a `Graphics` instance, already primed and optimized to paint the required portion of the window. This means that you do not have to call `CreateGraphics()` to get a DC in the `OnPaint()` method — you have already been provided with one. You will look at the other additional property soon. This property contains more detailed information about which area of the window actually needs repainting.

In your implementation of `OnPaint()`, you first get a reference to the `Graphics` object from `PaintEventArgs`, and then you draw your shapes exactly as you did before. When you start this, you call the base class's `OnPaint()` method. This step is important. You have overridden `OnPaint()` to do your own painting, but it is possible that Windows may have some additional work of its own to do in the painting process — any such work will be dealt with in an `OnPaint()` method in one of the .NET base classes.

For this example, you will find that removing the call to `base.OnPaint()` does not seem to have any effect. Do not, however, be tempted to leave this call out. You might be stopping Windows from doing its work properly, and the results could be unpredictable.

`OnPaint()` will also be called when the application first starts up and your window is displayed for the first time. Thus, there is no need to duplicate the drawing code in the constructor.

Running this code gives the same results initially as in the previous example, except that now your application behaves properly when you minimize it or hide parts of the window.

Using the Clipping Region

The `DrawShapes` sample from the previous section illustrates the main principles involved with drawing to a window, although the sample is not very efficient. The reason is that it attempts to draw everything in the window, regardless of how much needs to be drawn. Figure 33-2 shows the result of running the `DrawShapes` example and opening another window and moving it over the `DrawShapes` form so part of it is hidden.

However, when you move the overlapping window so that the `DrawShapes` window is fully visible again, Windows will, as usual, send a `Paint` event to the form, asking it to repaint itself. The rectangle and ellipse both lie in the top-left corner of the client area, and so were visible all the time. Therefore, there is actually nothing that needs to be done in this case apart from repainting the white background area. However, Windows does not know that, so it thinks it should raise the `Paint` event, resulting in your `OnPaint()` implementation being called. `OnPaint()` will then unnecessarily attempt to redraw the rectangle and ellipse.

Actually, in this case, the shapes will not be repainted because of the device context. Windows has preinitialized the device context with information concerning what area actually needed repainting. In the days of GDI, the region marked for repainting was known as the *invalidated region*, but with GDI+ the terminology has largely changed to *clipping region*. The device context recognizes this region. Therefore, it will intercept any attempts to draw outside this region and not pass the relevant drawing commands on to the graphics card. That sounds good, but there is still a potential performance hit here. You do not know how much processing the device context had to do before it figured out that the drawing was outside the invalidated region. In some cases, it might be quite a lot because calculating which pixels need to be changed to what color can be very processor-intensive (although a good graphics card will provide hardware acceleration to help with some of this).

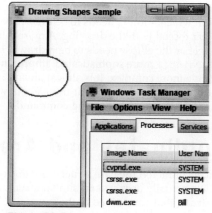

Figure 33-2

The bottom line to this is that asking the Graphics instance to do some drawing outside the invalidated region is almost certainly wasting processor time and slowing your application down. In a well-designed application, your code will help the device context by carrying out a few simple checks to see if the proposed drawing work is likely to be needed before it calls the relevant Graphics instance methods. In this section, you code a new example, DrawShapesWithClipping, by modifying the DisplayShapes example to do just that. In your OnPaint() code, you will do a simple test to see whether the invalidated region intersects the area you need to draw in, and you will call the drawing methods only if it does.

First, you need to obtain the details of the clipping region. This is where an extra property, ClipRectangle, on PaintEventArgs comes in. ClipRectangle contains the coordinates of the region to be repainted, wrapped up in an instance of a struct, System.Drawing.Rectangle. Rectangle is quite a simple struct — it contains four properties of interest: Top, Bottom, Left, and Right. These respectively contain the vertical coordinates of the top and bottom of the rectangle and the horizontal coordinates of the left and right edges.

Next, you need to decide what test you will use to determine whether drawing should take place. You will go for a simple test here. Notice that in your drawing, the rectangle and ellipse are both entirely contained within the rectangle that stretches from point (0,0) to point (80,130) of the client area. Actually, use point (82,132) to be on the safe side because you know that the lines might stray a pixel or so outside this area. So, you will check whether the top-left corner of the clipping region is inside this rectangle. If it is, then you will go ahead and redraw. If it is not, then you won't bother.

The following is the code to do this:

```
protected override void OnPaint( PaintEventArgs e )
{
    base.OnPaint(e);
    Graphics dc = e.Graphics;
    if (e.ClipRectangle.Top < 132 && e.ClipRectangle.Left < 82)
    {
        Pen bluePen = new Pen(Color.Blue, 3);
        dc.DrawRectangle(bluePen, 0,0,50,50);
        Pen redPen = new Pen(Color.Red, 2);
        dc.DrawEllipse(redPen, 0, 50, 80, 60);
    }
}
```

Note that what is displayed is exactly the same as before. However, performance is improved now by the early detection of some cases in which nothing needs to be drawn. Notice also that the example uses a fairly crude test for whether to proceed with the drawing. A more refined test might be to check separately whether the rectangle or the ellipse needs to be redrawn. However, there is a balance here. You can make your tests in `OnPaint()` more sophisticated, improving performance, but you will also make your own `OnPaint()` code more complex. It is almost always worth putting some test in — because you have written the code, you understand far more about what is being drawn than the `Graphics` instance, which just blindly follows drawing commands.

Measuring Coordinates and Areas

In the previous example, you encountered the base struct, `Rectangle`, which is used to represent the coordinates of a rectangle. GDI+ actually uses several similar structures to represent coordinates or areas. The following table lists the structs that are defined in the `System.Drawing` namespace.

Struct	Main Public Properties
`Point` and `PointF`	`X, Y`
`Size` and `SizeF`	`Width, Height`
`Rectangle` and `RectangleF`	`Left, Right, Top, Bottom, Width, Height, X, Y, Location, Size`

Note that many of these objects have a number of other properties, methods, or operator overloads not listed here. This section just discusses some of the most important ones.

Point and PointF

`Point` is conceptually the simplest of these structs. Mathematically, it is equivalent to a 2D vector. It contains two public integer properties, which represent how far you move horizontally and vertically from a particular location (perhaps on the screen), as shown in Figure 33-3.

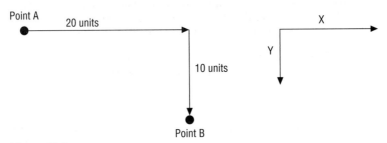

Figure 33-3

To get from point A to point B, you move 20 units across and 10 units down, marked as x and y on the diagram because this is how they are commonly referred to. The following `Point` struct represents that line:

```
Point ab = new Point(20, 10);
Console.WriteLine("Moved {0} across, {1} down", ab.X, ab.Y);
```

X and Y are read-write properties, which means that you can also set the values in a Point, like this:

```
Point ab = new Point();
ab.X = 20;
ab.Y = 10;
Console.WriteLine("Moved {0} across, {1} down", ab.X, ab.Y);
```

Note that although conventionally horizontal and vertical coordinates are referred to as x and y coordinates (lowercase), the corresponding Point properties are X and Y (uppercase) because the usual convention in C# is for public properties to have names that start with an uppercase letter.

PointF is essentially identical to Point, except that X and Y are of type float instead of int. PointF is used when the coordinates are not necessarily integer values. A cast has been defined so that you can implicitly convert from Point to PointF. (Note that because Point and PointF are structs, this cast involves actually making a copy of the data.) There is no corresponding reverse case — to convert from PointF to Point you have to copy the values across, or use one of three conversion methods, Round(), Truncate(), and Ceiling():

```
PointF abFloat = new PointF(20.5F, 10.9F);
// converting to Point
Point ab = new Point();
ab.X = (int)abFloat.X;
ab.Y = (int)abFloat.Y;
Point ab1 = Point.Round(abFloat);
Point ab2 = Point.Truncate(abFloat);
Point ab3 = Point.Ceiling(abFloat);
// but conversion back to PointF is implicit
PointF abFloat2 = ab;
```

You might be wondering what a unit is measured in. By default, GDI+ interprets units as pixels along the screen (or printer, whatever the graphics device is); that is how the Graphics object methods will view any coordinates that they are passed as parameters. For example, the point new Point(20,10) represents 20 pixels across the screen and 10 pixels down. Usually these pixels are measured from the top-left corner of the client area of the window, as has been the case in the previous examples. However, that will not always be the case. For example, on some occasions you might want to draw relative to the top-left corner of the whole window (including its border), or even to the top-left corner of the screen. In most cases, however, unless the documentation tells you otherwise, you can assume that you are talking about pixels relative to the top-left corner of the client area.

You will learn more on this subject later, after scrolling is examined, when we discuss the three different coordinate systems in use — world, page, and device coordinates.

Size and SizeF

As with Point and PointF, sizes come in two varieties. The Size struct is for int types. SizeF is available if you need to use float types. Otherwise, Size and SizeF are identical. This section focuses on the Size struct.

In many ways, the Size struct is identical to the Point struct. It has two integer properties that represent a distance horizontally and a distance vertically. The main difference is that instead of X and Y, these properties are named Width and Height. You can represent the earlier diagram using this code:

```
Size ab = new Size(20,10);
Console.WriteLine("Moved {0} across, {1} down", ab.Width, ab.Height);
```

Although Size mathematically represents exactly the same thing as Point, conceptually, it is intended to be used in a slightly different way. Point is used when you are talking about where something is, and

Size is used when you are talking about how big it is. However, because Size and Point are so closely related, there are even supported conversions between these two:

```
Point point = new Point(20, 10);
Size size = (Size) point;
Point anotherPoint = (Point) size;
```

As an example, think about the rectangle you drew earlier, with top-left coordinate (0,0) and size (50,50). The size of this rectangle is (50,50) and might be represented by a Size instance. The bottom-right corner is also at (50,50), but that would be represented by a Point instance. To see the difference, suppose that you draw the rectangle in a different location, so that its top-left coordinate is at (10,10):

```
dc.DrawRectangle(bluePen, 10,10,50,50);
```

Now the bottom-right corner is at coordinate (60,60), but the size is unchanged at (50,50).

The addition operator has been overloaded for Point and Size structs so that it is possible to add a Size to a Point struct, resulting in another Point struct:

```
static void Main(string[] args)
{
    Point topLeft = new Point(10,10);
    Size rectangleSize = new Size(50,50);
    Point bottomRight = topLeft + rectangleSize;
    Console.WriteLine("topLeft = " + topLeft);
    Console.WriteLine("bottomRight = " + bottomRight);
    Console.WriteLine("Size = " + rectangleSize);
}
```

This code, running as a simple console application called PointsAndSizes, produces the output shown in Figure 33-4.

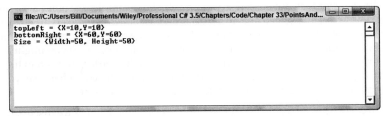

Figure 33-4

Note that this output also shows how the ToString() method has been overridden in both Point and Size to display the value in {X,Y} format.

It is also possible to subtract a Size from a Point struct to produce a Point struct, and you can add two Size structs together, producing another Size. It is not possible, however, to add a Point struct to another Point. Microsoft decided that adding Point structs does not conceptually make sense, and so it chose not to supply any overload to the + operator that would have allowed that.

You can also explicitly cast a Point to a Size struct and vice versa:

```
Point topLeft = new Point(10,10);
Size s1 = (Size)topLeft;
Point p1 = (Point)s1;
```

With this cast, s1.Width is assigned the value of topLeft.X, and s1.Height is assigned the value of topLeft.Y. Hence, s1 contains (10,10). p1 will end up storing the same values as topLeft.

Rectangle and RectangleF

These structures represent a rectangular region (usually of the screen). Just as with `Point` and `Size`, only the `Rectangle` struct is considered here. `RectangleF` is basically identical except that its properties that represent dimensions all use `float`, whereas those of `Rectangle` use `int`.

A `Rectangle` struct can be thought of as composed of a point, representing the top-left corner of the rectangle, and a `Size` struct, representing how large it is. One of its constructors actually takes a `Point` struct and a `Size` struct as its parameters. You can see this by rewriting the earlier code from the `DrawShapes` sample that draws a rectangle:

```
Graphics dc = e.Graphics;
Pen bluePen = new Pen(Color.Blue, 3);
Point topLeft = new Point(0,0);
Size howBig = new Size(50,50);
Rectangle rectangleArea = new Rectangle(topLeft, howBig);
dc.DrawRectangle(bluePen, rectangleArea);
```

This code also uses an alternative override of `Graphics.DrawRectangle()`, which takes a `Pen` and a `Rectangle` struct as its parameters.

You can also construct a `Rectangle` struct by supplying the top-left horizontal coordinate, top-left vertical coordinate, width, and height separately, and in that order, as individual numbers:

```
Rectangle rectangleArea = new Rectangle(0, 0, 50, 50)
```

`Rectangle` makes quite a few read-write properties available to set or extract its dimensions in different combinations. See the following table for details.

Property	Description
int Left	x-coordinate of left-hand edge
int Right	x-coordinate of right-hand edge
int Top	y-coordinate of top
int Bottom	y-coordinate of bottom
int X	Same as Left
int Y	Same as Top
int Width	Width of rectangle
int Height	Height of rectangle
Point Location	Top-left corner
Size Size	Size of rectangle

Note that these properties are not all independent. For example, setting `Width` also affects the value of `Right`.

Region

`Region` represents an area of the screen that has some complex shape. For example, the shaded area in Figure 33-5 could be represented by `Region`.

Figure 33-5

As you can imagine, the process of initializing a `Region` instance is itself quite complex. Broadly speaking, you can do it by indicating either what component simple shapes make up the region or what path you take as you trace around the edge of the region. If you do need to start working with areas like this, it is worth looking up the `Region` class in the SDK documentation.

A Note About Debugging

You are just about ready to do some more advanced types of drawing now. First, however, we just want to say a few things about debugging. If you have tried setting break points in the examples of this chapter, then you have noticed that debugging drawing routines is not quite as simple as debugging other parts of your program because entering and leaving the debugger often causes `Paint` messages to be sent to your application. As a result, setting a break point in your `OnPaint()` override can simply cause your application to keep painting itself over and over again, so it is basically unable to do anything else.

A typical scenario is as follows: You want to find out why your application is displaying something incorrectly, so you set a break point within the `OnPaint()` event. As expected, the application hits your break point and the debugger comes in, at which point your developer environment MDI window comes to the foreground. You more than likely have the developer environments set to full-screen display so that you can more easily view all the debugging information, which means it always completely hides the application you are debugging.

Moving on, you examine the values of some variables and hopefully discover something useful. Then you press F5 to tell the application to continue, so that you can go on to see what happens when the application displays something else after some processing. Unfortunately, the first thing that happens is that the application comes to the foreground, and Windows efficiently detects that the form is visible again and promptly sends it a `Paint` event. This means, of course, that your break point is hit again. If that is what you want, fine. More commonly, what you really want is to hit the break point *later*, when the application is drawing something more interesting, perhaps after you have selected some menu option to read in a file or in some other way changed what gets displayed. It looks like you are stuck. Either you do not have a break point in `OnPaint()` at all, or your application can never get beyond the point where it is displaying its initial startup window.

There is a workaround to this problem.

With a big screen, the easiest way is simply to keep your developer environment window tiled rather than maximized. Also, you want to keep it well away from your application window, so that your application is never hidden in the first place. Unfortunately, in most cases that is not a practical solution because that would make your developer environment window too small (you can also get a second monitor). An alternative that uses the same principle is to have your application declare itself as the topmost application while you are debugging. You do this by setting a property in the Form class, TopMost, which you can easily do in the InitializeComponent() method:

```
private void InitializeComponent()
{
    this.TopMost = true;
```

You can also set this property through the properties window in Visual Studio 2008.

Being a TopMost window means your application can never be hidden by other windows (except other topmost windows). It always remains above other windows even when another application has the focus. This is how the Task Manager behaves.

Even with this technique, you have to be careful because you can never be certain when Windows might decide for some reason to raise a Paint event. If you really want to trap some problem that occurs in OnPaint() in some specific circumstance (for example, the application draws something after you select a certain menu option, and something goes wrong at that point), then the best way to do this is to place some dummy code in OnPaint() that tests some condition, which will only be true in the specified circumstances. Then place the break point inside the if block, like this:

```
protected override void OnPaint( PaintEventArgs e )
{
    // Condition() evaluates to true when we want to break
    if (Condition())
    {
        int ii = 0;   // <-- SET BREAKPOINT HERE!!!
    }
}
```

This is a quick-and-easy way of setting a conditional break point.

Drawing Scrollable Windows

The earlier DrawShapes example worked very well because everything you needed to draw fit into the initial window size. This section covers what you need to do if that is not the case.

For this example, you expand the DrawShapes sample to demonstrate scrolling. To make things a bit more realistic, you start by creating an example, BigShapes, in which you make the rectangle and ellipse a bit bigger. Also, while you are at it, you will see how to use the Point, Size, and Rectangle structs by using them to assist in defining the drawing areas. With these changes, the relevant part of the Form1 class looks like this:

```
// member fields
private readonly Point rectangleTopLeft = new Point(0, 0);
private readonly Size rectangleSize = new Size(200,200);
private readonly Point ellipseTopLeft = new Point(50, 200);
private readonly Size ellipseSize = new Size(200, 150);
private readonly Pen bluePen = new Pen(Color.Blue, 3);
private readonly Pen redPen = new Pen(Color.Red, 2);
```

(continued)

(continued)

```
protected override void OnPaint( PaintEventArgs e )
{
    base.OnPaint(e);
    Graphics dc = e.Graphics;
    if (e.ClipRectangle.Top < 350 || e.ClipRectangle.Left < 250)
    {
        Rectangle rectangleArea =
            new Rectangle (rectangleTopLeft, rectangleSize);
        Rectangle ellipseArea =
            new Rectangle (ellipseTopLeft, ellipseSize);
        dc.DrawRectangle(bluePen, rectangleArea);
        dc.DrawEllipse(redPen, ellipseArea);
    }
}
```

Note that you have also turned the `Pen`, `Size`, and `Point` objects into member fields. This is more efficient than creating a new `Pen` every time you need to draw anything, as you have been doing so far.

The result of running this example looks like Figure 33-6.

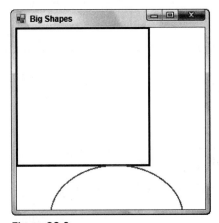

Figure 33-6

You can see a problem instantly. The shapes do not fit in your 300 × 300 pixel drawing area.

Normally, if a document is too large to display, an application will add scroll bars to let you scroll the window and look at a chosen part of it. This is another area in which if you were building Windows Forms using standard controls, you would simply allow the .NET runtime and the base classes to handle everything for you. If your form has various controls attached to it, then the `Form` instance will normally know where these controls are, and it will therefore know if its window becomes so small that scroll bars are necessary. The `Form` instance automatically adds the scroll bars for you. It is also able to draw correctly the portion of the screen you have scrolled to. In that case, there is nothing you need to do in your code. In this chapter, however, you are taking responsibility for drawing to the screen. Therefore, you need to help the Form instance out when it comes to scrolling.

Adding the scroll bars is actually very easy. The Form can still handle all that for you because the Form does not know how big an area you will want to draw in. (The reason it didn't do so in the earlier BigShapes example is that Windows does not know they are needed.) You need to determine whether the size of a rectangle that stretches from the top-left corner of the document (or equivalently, the top-left corner of the client area before you have done any scrolling) is big enough to contain the entire document. In this chapter, this area is called the document area. As shown in Figure 33-7, the document area for this example is (250 × 350) pixels.

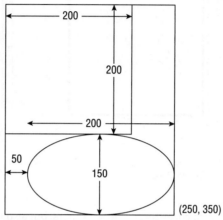

Figure 33-7

It is easy to tell the form how big the document is. You use the relevant property, Form .AutoScrollMinSize. Therefore, you can add this code to either the InitializeComponent() method or the Form1 constructor:

```
private void InitializeComponent()
{
    this.components = new System.ComponentModel.Container();
    this.AutoScaleMode = System.Windows.Forms.AutoScaleMode.Font;
    this.Text = "Form1";
    this.BackColor = System.Drawing.Color.White;
    this.AutoScrollMinSize = new Size(250, 350);
}
```

Alternatively, the AutoScrollMinSize property can be set using the Visual Studio 2008 properties window. Note that to gain access to the Size class, you need to add the following using statement:

```
using System.Drawing;
```

Setting the minimum size at application startup and leaving it thereafter is fine in this particular example because you know that is how big the screen area will always be. Your document never changes size while this particular application is running. Keep in mind, however, that if your application does things like display contents of files or something else for which the area of the screen might change, you will need to set this property at other times (and in that case you will have to sort out the code manually — the Visual Studio 2008 properties window can help you only with the initial value that a property has when the form is constructed).

Setting `AutoScrollMinSize` is a start, but it is not yet quite enough. Figure 33-8 shows what the sample application looks like now — initially you get the screen that correctly displays the shapes.

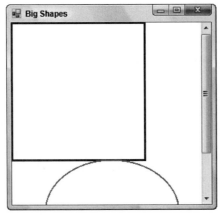

Figure 33-8

Notice that not only has the form correctly set the scroll bars, but also it has correctly sized them to indicate what proportion of the document is currently displayed. You can try resizing the window while the sample is running — you will find the scroll bars respond properly, and even disappear if you make the window big enough so that they are no longer needed.

However, look at what happens when you actually use one of the scroll bars to scroll down a bit (see Figure 33-9). Clearly, something has gone wrong!

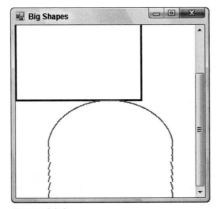

Figure 33-9

What's wrong is that you haven't taken into account the position of the scroll bars in the code in your `OnPaint()` override. You can see this very clearly if you force the window to repaint itself completely by minimizing and restoring it (see Figure 33-10).

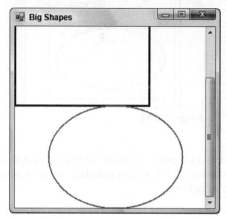

Figure 33-10

The shapes have been painted, just as before, with the top-left corner of the rectangle nestled into the top-left corner of the client area — as if you hadn't moved the scroll bars at all.

Before you see how to correct this problem, take a closer look at precisely what is happening in these screenshots.

Start with the BigShapes sample, shown in Figure 33-8. In this example, the entire window has just been repainted. Reviewing your code, you learn that it instructs the graphics instance to draw a rectangle with top-left coordinates (0,0) — relative to the top-left corner of the client area of the window — which is what has been drawn. The problem is that the graphics instance by default interprets coordinates as relative to the client window and is unaware of the scroll bars. Your code, as yet, does not attempt to adjust the coordinates for the scroll bar positions. The same goes for the ellipse.

Now, you can tackle the screenshot in Figure 33-9. After you scroll down, you notice that the top half of the window looks fine because it was drawn when the application first started up. When you scroll windows, Windows does not ask the application to redraw what was already on the screen. Windows is smart enough to determine which currently displayed bits can be smoothly moved around to match where the scroll bars now are located. This is a much more efficient process because it may be able to use some hardware acceleration to do that, too. The bit in this screenshot that is wrong is the bottom third of the window. This part of the window was not drawn when the application first appeared because before you started scrolling, it was outside the client area. This means that Windows asks your BigShapes application to draw this area. It will raise a Paint event passing in just this area as the clipping rectangle. And that is exactly what your OnPaint() override has done.

One way to look at the problem is that you are, at the moment, expressing your coordinates relative to the top-left corner of the start of the document — you need to convert them to express them relative to the top-left corner of the client area instead (see Figure 33-11).

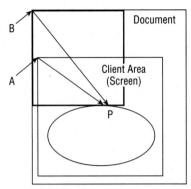

Figure 33-11

To make the diagram clearer, the document is actually extended further downward and to the right, beyond the boundaries of the screen, but this does not change our reasoning. It also assumes a small horizontal scroll as well as a vertical one.

In Figure 33-11, the thin rectangles mark the borders of the screen area and of the entire document. The thick lines mark the rectangle and ellipse that you are trying to draw. P marks some arbitrary point that you are drawing and that is being used as an example. When calling the drawing methods, the graphics instance was supplied with the vector from point B to (say) point P, expressed as a `Point` instance. You actually need to give it the vector from point A to point P.

The problem is that you do not know what the vector from A to P is. You know what B to P is; that is just the coordinates of P relative to the top-left corner of the document — the position where you want to draw point P in the document. You also know that the vector from B to A is just the amount you have scrolled by. This is stored in a property of the `Form` class called `AutoScrollPosition`. However, you do not know the vector from A to P.

To solve this problem, you subtract the one vector from the other. Say, for example, to get from B to P you move 150 pixels across and 200 pixels down, whereas to get from B to A you move 10 pixels across and 57 pixels down. That means to get from A to P you have to move 140 (150 minus 10) pixels across and 143 (200 minus 57) pixels down. To make it even simpler, the `Graphics` class actually implements a method that will do these calculations for you. It is called `TranslateTransform()`. You pass it the horizontal and vertical coordinates that say where the top left of the client area is relative to the top-left corner of the document (your `AutoScrollPosition` property, that is, the vector from B to A in the diagram). The `Graphics` device will now work out all its coordinates, taking into account where the client area is relative to the document.

If we translate this long explanation into code, all you typically need to do is add the following line to your drawing code:

```
dc.TranslateTransform(this.AutoScrollPosition.X, this.AutoScrollPosition.Y);
```

However, in this example, it is a little more complicated because you are also separately testing whether you need to do any drawing by looking at the clipping region. You need to adjust this test to take the scroll position into account, too. When you have done that, the full drawing code for the sample looks like this:

```
protected override void OnPaint( PaintEventArgs e )
{
    base.OnPaint(e);
```

```
Graphics dc = e.Graphics;
Size scrollOffset = new Size(this.AutoScrollPosition);
if (e.ClipRectangle.Top+scrollOffset.Width < 350 ||
    e.ClipRectangle.Left+scrollOffset.Height < 250)
{
    Rectangle rectangleArea = new Rectangle
        (rectangleTopLeft+scrollOffset, rectangleSize);
    Rectangle ellipseArea = new Rectangle
        (ellipseTopLeft+scrollOffset, ellipseSize);
    dc.DrawRectangle(bluePen, rectangleArea);
    dc.DrawEllipse(redPen, ellipseArea);
}
}
```

Now you have your scroll code working perfectly. You can at last obtain a correctly scrolled screenshot (see Figure 33-12).

Figure 33-12

World, Page, and Device Coordinates

The distinction between measuring position relative to the top-left corner of the document and measuring it relative to the top-left corner of the screen (desktop) is so important that GDI+ has special names for these coordinate systems:

❑ **World coordinates** specify the position of a point measured in pixels from the top-left corner of the document.

❑ **Page coordinates** specify the position of a point measured in pixels from the top-left corner of the client area.

Developers familiar with GDI will note that world coordinates correspond to what in GDI were known as logical coordinates. Page coordinates correspond to what were known as device coordinates. As a developer familiar with GDI, you should also note that the way you code conversion between logical and device coordinates has changed in GDI+. In GDI, conversions took place via the device context, using the LPtoDP() and DPtoLP() Windows API functions. In GDI+, it is the Control class, from which both Form and all the various Windows Forms controls derive, that maintains the information needed to carry out the conversion.

GDI+ also distinguishes a third coordinate system, which is now known as *device coordinates*. Device coordinates are similar to page coordinates, except that you do not use pixels as the unit of measurement. Instead, you use some other unit that can be specified by the user by calling the `Graphics.PageUnit` property. Possible units, besides the default of pixels, include inches and millimeters. Although you will not use the `PageUnit` property in this chapter, you might find it useful as a way of getting around the different pixel densities of devices. For example, 100 pixels on most monitors will occupy approximately an inch. However, laser printers can have 1,200 or more dpi (dots per inch), which means that a shape specified to be 100 pixels wide will look a lot smaller when printed. By setting the units to, say, inches and specifying that the shape should be 1 inch wide, you can ensure that the shape will look the same size on the different devices. This is illustrated in the following:

```
Graphics dc = this.CreateGraphics();
dc.PageUnit = GraphicsUnit.Inch;
```

Possible units available via the `GraphicsUnit` enumeration include the following:

❑ **Display** — Defines the display's unit measure

❑ **Document** — Defines the document unit (1/300 inch) as the unit of measure

❑ **Inch** — Defines the inch measurement as the unit of measure

❑ **Millimeter** — Defines the millimeter measurement as the unit of measure

❑ **Pixel** — Defines the pixel measurement as the unit of measure

❑ **Point** — Defines the printer point (1/72 inch) as the unit of measure

❑ **World** — Defines the world coordinate system as the unit of measure

Colors

This section discusses the ways that you can specify what color you want something to be drawn in.

Colors in GDI+ are represented by instances of the `System.Drawing.Color` struct. Generally, once you have instantiated this struct, you won't do much with the corresponding `Color` instance — you just pass it to whatever other method you are calling that requires a `Color`. You have encountered this struct before, when you set the background color of the client area of the window in each of the examples, as well as when you set the colors of the various shapes you were displaying. The `Form.BackColor` property actually returns a `Color` instance. This section looks at this struct in more detail. In particular, it examines several different ways that you can construct a `Color`.

Red-Green-Blue Values

The total number of colors that can be displayed by a monitor is huge — more than 16 million. To be exact, the number is 2 to the power 24, which works out to 16,777,216. Obviously, you need some way of indexing those colors so that you can indicate which one is the color you want to display at any given pixel.

The most common way of indexing colors is by dividing them into the red, green, and blue components. This idea is based on the theory that any color that the human eye can distinguish can be constructed from a certain amount of red light, a certain amount of green light, and a certain amount of blue light. These colors are known as *components*. In practice, dividing the amount of each component light into 256 possible intensities yields a sufficiently fine gradation to be able to display images that are perceived by the human eye to be of photographic quality. You, therefore, specify colors by giving the amounts of these components on a scale of 0 to 255 where 0 means that the component is not present and 255 means that it is at its maximum intensity.

This gives you your first way of telling GDI+ about a color. You can indicate a color's red, green, and blue values by calling the static function `Color.FromArgb()`. Microsoft has chosen not to supply a constructor to do this task. The reason is that there are other ways, besides the usual RGB components, to indicate a color. Because of this, Microsoft felt that the meaning of parameters passed to any constructor they defined would be open to misinterpretation:

```
Color redColor = Color.FromArgb(255,0,0);
Color funnyOrangyBrownColor = Color.FromArgb(255,155,100);
Color blackColor = Color.FromArgb(0,0,0);
Color whiteColor = Color.FromArgb(255,255,255);
```

The three parameters are, respectively, the quantities of red, green, and blue. This function has a number of other overloads, some of which also allow you to specify something called an alpha-blend (that is the `A` in the name of the method, `FromArgb()`). Alpha blending is beyond the scope of this chapter, but it allows you to paint a color semitransparently by combining it with whatever color was already on the screen. This can give some beautiful effects and is often used in games.

The Named Colors

Constructing a `Color` using `FromArgb()` is the most flexible technique because it literally means you can specify any color that the human eye can see. However, if you want a simple, standard, well-known color such as red or blue, it is a lot easier to just be able to name the color you want. Hence, Microsoft has also provided a large number of static properties in `Color`, each of which returns a named color. It was one of these properties that you used when you set the background color of your windows to white in the examples:

```
this.BackColor = Color.White;
// has the same effect as:
// this.BackColor = Color.FromArgb(255, 255 , 255);
```

Several hundred such colors exist. The full list is given in the SDK documentation. They include all the simple colors: `Red`, `White`, `Blue`, `Green`, `Black`, and so on, as well as such delights as `MediumAquamarine`, `LightCoral`, and `DarkOrchid`. There is also a `KnownColor` enumeration, which lists the named colors.

> Each of these named colors represents a precise set of RGB values. They were originally chosen many years ago for use on the Internet. The idea was to provide a useful set of colors right across the spectrum whose names would be recognized by Web browsers, thus saving you from having to write explicit RGB values in your HTML code. A few years ago, these colors were also important because early browsers could not necessarily display very many colors accurately, and the named colors were supposed to provide a set of colors that would be displayed correctly by most browsers. These days, that aspect is less important because modern Web browsers are quite capable of displaying any RGB value correctly. Web-safe color palettes are also available that provide developers with a comprehensive list of colors that work with most browsers.

Graphics Display Modes and the Safety Palette

Although in principle monitors can display any of the more than 16 million RGB colors, in practice this depends on how you have set the display properties on your computer. In Windows, there are traditionally three main color options (although some machines might provide other options depending on the hardware): true color (24 bit), high color (16 bit), and 256 colors. (On some graphics cards these days, true color is actually marked as 32 bit. This has to do with optimizing the hardware, though in that case only 24 bits of the 32 bits are used for the color itself.)

Only true color mode allows you to display all of the RGB colors simultaneously. This sounds like the best option, but it comes at a cost: 3 bytes are needed to hold a full RGB value, which means that 3 bytes of graphics card memory are needed to hold each pixel that is displayed. If graphics card memory is at a premium (a restriction that is less common now than it used to be), then you might want to choose one of the other modes. High color mode gives you 2 bytes per pixel, which is enough to give 5 bits for each RGB component. Therefore, instead of 256 gradations of red intensity, you get just 32 gradations. The same applies to blue and green,which produce a total of 65,536 colors. That is just about enough to give apparent photographic quality on a casual inspection, although areas of subtle shading tend to be broken up a bit.

The 256-color mode gives you even fewer colors. However, in this mode, you get to choose the colors. The system sets up something known as a *palette*. This is a list of 256 colors chosen from the 16 million RGB colors. Once you have specified the colors in the palette, the graphics device will be able to display just those colors. The palette can be changed at any time, but the graphics device can only display 256 different colors on the screen at any one time. The 256-color mode is used only when high performance is necessary and video memory is at a premium. Most computer games use this mode. They can still achieve decent-looking graphics because of a very careful choice of palette.

In general, if a display device is in high-color or 256-color mode and a particular RGB color is requested, then it will pick the nearest mathematical match from the pool of colors that it is able to display. It is for this reason that it is important to be aware of the color modes. If you are drawing something that involves subtle shading or photographic-quality images, and the user does not have 24-bit color mode selected, she might not see the image the same way you intended it. So if you are doing that kind of work with GDI+, then you should test your application in different color modes. (It is also possible for your application to programmatically set a given color mode, although that is not discussed in this chapter for lack of space.)

The Safety Palette

For reference, this section quickly mentions the safety palette, which is a very commonly used default palette. To use the safety palette, you set six equally spaced possible values for each color component: 0, 51, 102, 153, 204, and 255. In other words, the red component can have any of these values. The green component can have any of these values and so can the blue component. Possible colors from the safety palette include (0,0,0), black; (153,0,0), a fairly dark shade of red; (0, 255,102), green with a smattering of blue added; and so on. This gives you a total of 6 cubed = 216 colors. The idea is that this provides an easy way of creating a palette that contains colors from right across the spectrum and of all degrees of brightness. In practice, however, this does not actually work that well because equal mathematical spacing of color components does not mean equal perception of color differences by the human eye.

If you set Windows to 256-color mode, you will find that the default palette is the safety palette, with 20 Windows-standard colors added to it, and 20 spare colors.

Pens and Brushes

This section reviews two helper classes that are needed to draw shapes. You have already encountered the Pen class, which you used to instruct the graphics instance how to draw lines. A related class is System.Drawing.Brush, which instructs the graphics instance how to fill regions. For example, the Pen is needed to draw the outlines of the rectangle and ellipse in the previous examples. If you had needed to draw these shapes as solid, you would have used a brush to specify how to fill them. One aspect of both of these classes is that you will hardly ever call any methods on them. You simply construct a Pen or Brush instance with the required color and other properties, and then pass it to drawing methods that require a Pen or Brush.

If you have programmed using GDI before, you may have noticed from the first few examples that pens are used in a different way in GDI+. In GDI, the normal practice was to call a Windows API function, SelectObject(), which actually associated a pen with the device context. That pen was then used in all drawing operations that required a pen until you informed the device context otherwise, by calling `SelectObject()` *again. The same principle held for brushes and other objects such as fonts or bitmaps. With GDI+, Microsoft has opted for a stateless model in which there is no default pen or other helper object. Rather, you simply specify with each method call the appropriate helper object to be used for that particular method.*

Brushes

GDI+ has several different kinds of brushes — more than there is space to go into in this chapter, so this section just explains the simpler ones to give you an idea of the principles. Each type of brush is represented by an instance of a class derived from the abstract class `System.Drawing.Brush`. The simplest brush, `System.Drawing.SolidBrush`, indicates that a region is to be filled with solid color:

```
Brush solidBeigeBrush = new SolidBrush(Color.Beige);
Brush solidFunnyOrangyBrownBrush = new SolidBrush(Color.FromArgb(255,155,100));
```

Alternatively, if the brush is one of the Web-safe colors, then you can construct the brush using another class, `System.Drawing.Brushes`. Brushes is one of those classes that you never actually instantiate (it has a private constructor to stop you from doing that). It simply has a large number of static properties, each of which returns a brush of a specified color. You can use `Brushes` like this:

```
Brush solidAzureBrush = Brushes.Azure;
Brush solidChocolateBrush = Brushes.Chocolate;
```

The next level of complexity is a hatch brush, which fills a region by drawing a pattern. This type of brush is considered more advanced, so it is in the `Drawing2D` namespace, represented by the class `System.Drawing.Drawing2D.HatchBrush`. The `Brushes` class cannot help you with hatch brushes; you will need to construct one explicitly by supplying the hatch style and two colors — the foreground color followed by the background color. (Note, you can omit the background color, in which case it defaults to black). The hatch style comes from an enumeration, `System.Drawing.Drawing2D` `.HatchStyle`. You can choose from a large number of `HatchStyle` values (see the SDK documentation for the full list). To give you an idea, typical styles include `ForwardDiagonal`, `Cross`, `DiagonalCross`, `SmallConfetti`, and `ZigZag`. Examples of constructing a hatch brush include:

```
Brush crossBrush = new HatchBrush(HatchStyle.Cross, Color.Azure);
// background color of CrossBrush is black
Brush brickBrush = new HatchBrush(HatchStyle.DiagonalBrick,
                                  Color.DarkGoldenrod, Color.Cyan);
```

Solid and hatch brushes are the only brushes available under GDI. GDI+ has added a couple of new styles of brushes:

❑   `System.Drawing.Drawing2D.LinearGradientBrush` fills in an area with a color that varies across the screen.

❑   `System.Drawing.Drawing2D.PathGradientBrush` is similar, but in this case, the color varies along a path around the region to be filled.

Note that both brushes can render some spectacular effects if used carefully.

Pens

Unlike brushes, pens are represented by just one class: `System.Drawing.Pen`. However, the pen is slightly more complex than the brush because it needs to indicate how thick lines should be (how many pixels wide) and, for a wide line, how to fill the area inside the line. Pens can also specify a number of other properties, which are beyond the scope of this chapter, but which include the `Alignment` property mentioned earlier. This property indicates where in relation to the border of a shape a line should be drawn, as well as what shape to draw at the end of a line (whether to round off the shape).

The area inside a thick line can be filled with solid color or by using a brush. Hence, a `Pen` instance might contain a reference to a `Brush` instance. This is quite powerful because it means that you can draw lines that are colored in by using, say, hatching or linear shading. There are four different ways to construct a `Pen` instance that you have designed yourself. One is by passing a color; a second is by passing in a brush. Both of these constructors will produce a pen with a width of one pixel. Alternatively, a third way is to pass in a color or a brush, and additionally a `float`, which represents the width of the pen. (It needs to be a `float` in case you are using non-default units such as millimeters or inches for the `Graphics` object that will do the drawing, so you can, for example, specify fractions of an inch.) For example, you can construct pens like this:

```
Brush brickBrush = new HatchBrush(HatchStyle.DiagonalBrick,
                                   Color.DarkGoldenrod, Color.Cyan);
Pen solidBluePen = new Pen(Color.FromArgb(0,0,255));
Pen solidWideBluePen = new Pen(Color.Blue, 4);
Pen brickPen = new Pen(brickBrush);
Pen brickWidePen = new Pen(brickBrush, 10);
```

Additionally, a fourth way offers the quick construction of pens by using the class `System.Drawing.Pens`, which, like the `Brushes` class, contains a number of stock pens. These pens all have a 1-pixel width and come in the usual sets of Web-safe colors. This allows you to construct pens in this way:

```
Pen solidYellowPen = Pens.Yellow;
```

Drawing Shapes and Lines

You have almost finished the first part of the chapter, and you have seen all the basic classes and objects required to draw specified shapes and so on to the screen. This section starts by reviewing some of the drawing methods the `Graphics` class makes available and presents a short example that illustrates the use of several brushes and pens.

`System.Drawing.Graphics` has a large number of methods that allow you to draw various lines, outline shapes, and solid shapes. Once again, there are too many to provide a comprehensive list here, but the following table lists the main ones and should give you some idea of the variety of shapes you can draw.

Method	Typical Parameters	What It Draws
DrawLine	Pen, start and end points	A single straight line
DrawRectangle	Pen, position, and size	Outline of a rectangle
DrawEllipse	Pen, position, and size	Outline of an ellipse
FillRectangle	Brush, position, and size	Solid rectangle
FillEllipse	Brush, position, and size	Solid ellipse
DrawLines	Pen, array of points	Series of lines, connecting each point to the next one in the array
DrawBezier	Pen, four points	A smooth curve through the two end points, with the remaining two points used to control the shape of the curve

Method	Typical Parameters	What It Draws
DrawCurve	Pen, array of points	A smooth curve through the points
DrawArc	Pen, rectangle, two angles	Portion of circle within the rectangle defined by the angles
DrawClosedCurve	Pen, array of points	Like DrawCurve but also draws a straight line to close the curve
DrawPie	Pen, rectangle, two angles	Wedge-shaped outline within the rectangle
FillPie	Brush, rectangle, two angles	Solid wedge-shaped area within the rectangle
DrawPolygon	Pen, array of points	Like DrawLines but also connects first and last points to close the figure drawn

Before we leave the subject of drawing simple objects, this section rounds off with a simple example that demonstrates the kinds of visual effects you can achieve using brushes. The example is called ScrollMoreShapes, and it is essentially a revision of ScrollShapes. Besides the rectangle and ellipse, you will add a thick line and fill in the shapes with various custom brushes. You have already learned the principles of drawing, so the code speaks for itself. First, because of your new brushes, you need to indicate that you are using the System.Drawing.Drawing2D namespace:

```
using System;
using System.Collections.Generic;
using System.ComponentModel;
using System.Data;
using System.Drawing;
using System.Drawing.Drawing2D;
using System.Text;
using System.Windows.Forms;
```

Next are some extra fields in your Form1 class, which contain details of the locations where the shapes are to be drawn, as well as various pens and brushes you will use:

```
private Rectangle rectangleBounds = new Rectangle(new Point(0,0),
                                                  new Size(200,200));
private Rectangle ellipseBounds = new Rectangle(new Point(50,200),
                                                new Size(200,150));
private readonly Pen bluePen = new Pen(Color.Blue, 3);
private readonly Pen redPen = new Pen(Color.Red, 2);
private readonly Brush solidAzureBrush = Brushes.Azure;
private readonly Brush solidYellowBrush = new SolidBrush(Color.Yellow);
private static readonly Brush brickBrush = new
    HatchBrush(HatchStyle.DiagonalBrick, Color.DarkGoldenrod, Color.Cyan);
private readonly Pen brickWidePen = new Pen(brickBrush, 10);
```

The brickBrush field has been declared as static so that you can use its value to initialize the brickWidePen field. C# will not let you use one instance field to initialize another instance field because it has not defined which one will be initialized first. However, declaring the field as static solves the problem. Because only one instance of the Form1 class will be instantiated, it is immaterial whether the fields are static or instance fields.

The following is the OnPaint() override:

```
protected override void OnPaint( PaintEventArgs e )
{
    base.OnPaint(e);
    Graphics dc = e.Graphics;
    Point scrollOffset = AutoScrollPosition;
    dc.TranslateTransform(scrollOffset.X, scrollOffset.Y);
    if (e.ClipRectangle.Top+scrollOffset.X < 350 ||
        e.ClipRectangle.Left+scrollOffset.Y < 250)
    {
        dc.DrawRectangle(bluePen, rectangleBounds);
        dc.FillRectangle(solidYellowBrush, rectangleBounds);
        dc.DrawEllipse(redPen, ellipseBounds);
        dc.FillEllipse(solidAzureBrush, ellipseBounds);
        dc.DrawLine(brickWidePen, rectangleBounds.Location,
                            ellipseBounds.Location+ellipseBounds.Size);
    }
}
```

As before, you also set the AutoScrollMinSize to (250,350). Figure 33-13 shows the new results.

Notice that the thick diagonal line has been drawn on top of the rectangle and ellipse because it was the last item to be painted.

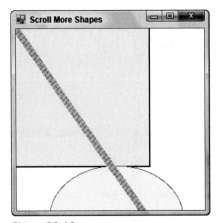

Figure 33-13

Displaying Images

One of the most common things you might want to do with GDI+ is display an image that already exists in a file. This is actually a lot simpler than drawing your own user interface because the image is already pre-drawn. Effectively, all you have to do is load the file and instruct GDI+ to display it. The image can be a simple line drawing, an icon, or a complex image such as a photograph. You can also manipulate the image by stretching or rotating it, or simply displaying only a portion of it.

This section, just for a change, presents the sample first. Then it discusses some of the issues you need to be aware of when displaying images. Presenting it this way is possible because the code needed to display an image is so simple.

The class you need is the .NET base class, `System.Drawing.Image`. An instance of `Image` represents one image. Reading in an image simply takes one line of code:

```
Image myImage = Image.FromFile("FileName");
```

`FromFile()` is a static member of `Image` and is the usual way of instantiating an image. The file can be any of the commonly supported graphics file formats, including `.bmp`, `.jpg`, `.gif`, and `.png`.

Displaying an image is also very simple, assuming that you have a suitable `Graphics` instance at hand — a call to either `Graphics.DrawImageUnscaled()` or `Graphics.DrawImage()` suffices. There are quite a few overloads of these methods, allowing you a lot of flexibility in the information you supply in terms of where the image is located and how big it is to be drawn. But this example uses `DrawImage()`, like this:

```
dc.DrawImage(myImage, points);
```

In this line of code, `dc` is assumed to be a `Graphics` instance, and `myImage` is the `Image` to be displayed. `points` is an array of `Point` structs, where `points[0]`, `points[1]`, and `points[2]` are the coordinates of the top-left, top-right, and bottom-left corner of the image.

> *Images are probably the area in which developers familiar with GDI will notice the biggest difference between GDI and GDI+. In GDI, displaying an image involved several nontrivial steps. If the image was a bitmap, then loading it was reasonably simple. Nevertheless, if it was any other file type, then loading it would involve a sequence of calls to OLE objects. Actually, getting a loaded image onto the screen required getting a handle to it, selecting it into a memory device context, and then performing a block transfer between device contexts. Although the device contexts and handles are still there behind the scenes and will be needed if you want to start doing sophisticated editing of the images from your code, simple tasks have now been extremely well wrapped up in the GDI+ object model.*

The process of displaying an image is illustrated with an example called `DisplayImage`. The example simply displays a `.jpg` file in the application's main window. To keep things simple, the path of the `.jpg` file is hard-coded into the application (so if you run the example, then you will need to change it to reflect the location of the file in your system). The `.jpg` file you will display is a sunset picture in St. Petersburg.

As with the other examples, the `DisplayImage` project is a standard C# Visual Studio 2008–generated Windows application. You add the following fields to your `Form1` class:

```
readonly Image piccy;
private readonly Point [] piccyBounds;
```

You then load the file in the `Form1()` constructor:

```
public Form1()
{
    InitializeComponent();
    piccy =
        Image.FromFile(@"C:\ProCSharp\GdiPlus\Images\London.jpg");
    AutoScrollMinSize = piccy.Size;
    piccyBounds = new Point[3];
    piccyBounds[0] = new Point(0,0);              // top left
    piccyBounds[1] = new Point(piccy.Width,0);    // top right
    piccyBounds[2] = new Point(0,piccy.Height);   // bottom left
}
```

Note that the size in pixels of the image is obtained as its `Size` property, which you use to set the document area. You also set up the `piccyBounds` array, which is used to identify the position of the image on the screen. You have chosen the coordinates of the three corners to draw the image in its actual size and shape here, but if you had wanted the image to be resized, stretched, or even sheared into a nonrectangular parallelogram, then you could do so simply by changing the values of the Points in the piccyBounds array.

The image is displayed in the OnPaint() override:

```
protected override void OnPaint(PaintEventArgs e)
{
    base.OnPaint(e);
    Graphics dc = e.Graphics;
    dc.ScaleTransform(1.0f, 1.0f);
    dc.TranslateTransform(AutoScrollPosition.X, AutoScrollPosition.Y);
    dc.DrawImage(piccy, piccyBounds);
}
```

Finally, note the modification made to the IDE-generated Form1.Dispose() method:

```
protected override void Dispose(bool disposing)
{
    piccy.Dispose();
    if (disposing && (components != null))
    {
        components.Dispose();
    }
    base.Dispose(disposing);
}
```

Disposing of the image as soon as possible when it is no longer needed is important because images generally take up a lot of memory while in use. After Image.Dispose() has been called, the Image instance no longer refers to any actual image, and so it can no longer be displayed (unless you load a new image).

Figure 33-14 shows the result of running this code.

Figure 33-14

Issues When Manipulating Images

Although displaying images is very simple, it still pays to have some understanding of what is going on behind the scenes.

The most important point to understand about images is that they are always rectangular. That is not just a convenience; it is because of the underlying technology. All modern graphics cards have hardware built in that can efficiently copy blocks of pixels from one area of memory to another area of memory, provided that the block of pixels represents a rectangular region. This hardware-accelerated operation can occur virtually as one single operation, and as such, is extremely fast. Indeed, it is the key to modern high-performance graphics. This operation is known as a *bitmap block transfer* (or *BitBlt*). `Graphics.DrawImageUnscaled()` internally uses a `BitBlt`, which is why you can see a huge image, perhaps containing as many as a million pixels, appearing almost instantly. If the computer had to copy the image to the screen pixel by pixel, you would see the image gradually being drawn over a period of up to several seconds.

`BitBlts` are very efficient; therefore, almost all drawing and manipulation of images is carried out using them. Even some editing of images will be done by manipulating portions of images with `BitBlts` between DCs that represent areas of memory. In the days of GDI, the Windows 32 API function `BitBlt()` was arguably the most important and widely used function for image manipulation, although with GDI+, the `BitBlt` operations are largely hidden by the GDI+ object model.

It's not possible to `BitBlt` areas of images that are not rectangular, although similar effects can be easily simulated. One way is to mark a certain color as transparent for the purposes of a `BitBlt`, so that areas of that color in the source image will not overwrite the existing color of the corresponding pixel in the destination device. It is also possible to specify that in the process of a `BitBlt`, each pixel of the resultant image will be formed by some logical operation (such as a bitwise AND) on the colors of that pixel in the source image and in the destination device before the `BitBlt`. Such operations are supported by hardware acceleration and can be used to give a variety of subtle effects. Note that the `Graphics` object implements another method, `DrawImage()`. This is similar to `DrawImageUnscaled()` but comes in a large number of overloads that allow you to specify more complex forms of `BitBlt` to be used in the drawing process. `DrawImage()` also allows you to draw (using `BitBlt`) only a specified part of the image, or to perform certain other operations on it such as scaling it (expanding or reducing it in size) as it is drawn.

Drawing Text

We have chosen to cover the very important topic of displaying text late in this chapter because drawing text to the screen is (in general) more complex than drawing simple graphics. Although displaying a line or two of text when you don't care about the appearance is extremely easy (it takes one single call to the `Graphics.DrawString()` method), if you are trying to display a document that has a fair amount of text in it, then you will rapidly find that things become a lot more complex. This is for two reasons:

❏ If you are concerned about getting the appearance just right, then you must understand fonts. Whereas shape drawing requires brushes and pens as helper objects, the process of drawing text requires fonts as helper objects. Moreover, understanding fonts is not a trivial undertaking.

❏ Text needs to be very carefully laid out in the window. Users generally expect words to follow naturally from one word to another and to be lined up with clear spaces in between. Doing that is harder than you might think. For starters, you do not usually know in advance how much space on the screen a word is going to take up. That has to be calculated (using the `Graphics.MeasureString()` method). In addition, the space a word occupies on the screen affects where in the document every subsequent word is placed. If your application does any line wrapping, then it will need to assess word sizes carefully before deciding where to place the line break. The next time you run Microsoft Word, look carefully at the way Word is continually repositioning text as you do your work; there is a lot of complex processing going on there. Chances are that any GDI+ application you work on will not be nearly as complex as Word. However, if you need to display any text, many of the same considerations apply.

In short, high-quality text processing is tricky to get right. However, putting a line of text on the screen, assuming that you know the font and where you want it to go, is actually very simple. Therefore, the next section presents a quick example that shows you how to display some text, followed by a short review of the principles of fonts and font families and a more realistic (and involved) text-processing example, CapsEditor.

Simple Text Example

This example, DisplayText, is your usual Windows Forms effort. This time you override OnPaint() and add member fields as follows:

```
private readonly Brush blackBrush = Brushes.Black;
private readonly Brush blueBrush = Brushes.Blue;
private readonly Font haettenschweilerFont = new Font("Haettenschweiler", 12);
private readonly Font boldTimesFont = new Font("Times New Roman", 10,
    FontStyle.Bold);
private readonly Font italicCourierFont = new Font("Courier", 11,
    FontStyle.Italic | FontStyle.Underline);
protected override void OnPaint(PaintEventArgs e)
{
    base.OnPaint(e);
    Graphics dc = e.Graphics;
    dc.DrawString("This is a groovy string", haettenschweilerFont, blackBrush,
                10, 10);
    dc.DrawString("This is a groovy string " +
                "with some very long text that will never fit in the box",
                boldTimesFont, blueBrush,
                new Rectangle(new Point(10, 40), new Size(100, 40)));
    dc.DrawString("This is a groovy string", italicCourierFont, blackBrush,
                new Point(10, 100));
}
```

Figure 33-15 shows the result of running this example.

Figure 33-15

The example demonstrates the use of the `Graphics.DrawString()` method to draw items of text. The method `DrawString()` comes in a number of overloads, three of which are demonstrated here. The different overloads require parameters that indicate the text to be displayed, the font that the string should be drawn in, and the brush that should be used to construct the various lines and curves that make up each character of text. A few alternatives exist for the remaining parameters. In general, however, it is possible to specify either a `Point` (or equivalently, two numbers) or a `Rectangle`.

If you specify a `Point`, then the text will start with its top-left corner at that `Point` and simply stretch out to the right. If you specify a `Rectangle`, then the `Graphics` instance will lay out the string inside that rectangle. If the text does not fit within the boundaries of the rectangle, it will be cut off (see the fourth line of text in Figure 33-15). Passing a rectangle to `DrawString()` means that the drawing process will take longer because `DrawString()` will need to figure out where to put line breaks, but the result may look nicer — provided the string fits in the rectangle!

This example also shows a few ways to construct fonts. You always need to include the name of the font and its size (height). You can also optionally pass in various styles that modify how the text is to be drawn (bold, underline, and so on).

Fonts and Font Families

A font describes exactly how each letter should be displayed. Selection of the appropriate font and providing a reasonable variety of fonts within a document are important factors in improving readability.

Most people, if asked to name a font, might mention Arial or Times New Roman (if they are Windows users) or Times or Helvetica (if they are Mac OS users). In fact, these are not fonts at all — they are *font families*. The font family tells you, in generic terms, the visual style of the text and is a key factor in the overall appearance of your application. Most of us recognize the styles of the most common font families, even if we are not consciously aware of it.

An actual *font* would be something like Arial 9-point italic. In other words, the size and other modifications to the text are specified as well as the font family. These modifications might include whether text is **bold**, *italic*, underlined, or displayed in SMALL CAPS or as a subscript; this is technically referred to as the *style*, although in some ways, the term is misleading because the visual appearance is determined as much by the font family.

The size of the text is measured by specifying its height. The height is measured in *points* — a traditional unit that represents ½₂ of an inch (0.351 mm). So letters in a 10-point font are roughly ⅐", or 3.5 mm high. However, you will not get seven lines of 10-point text into one inch of vertical screen or paper space, as you need to allow for the spacing between the lines as well.

Strictly speaking, measuring the height is not quite as simple as that because there are several different heights that you must consider. For example, there is the height of tall letters such as the A or F (this is the measurement that we are referring to when we talk about the height), the additional height occupied by any accents on letters such as Å or Ñ (the internal leading), and the extra height below the baseline needed for the tails of letters such as y and g (the descent). However, for this chapter we will not worry about that. Once you specify the font family and the main height, these subsidiary heights are determined automatically.

When you are dealing with fonts, you might also encounter some other terms commonly used to describe certain font families:

❑ **Serif** font families have feet at the ends of many of the lines that make up the characters (these ticks are known as serifs). Times New Roman is a classic example of this.

❑ **Sans serif** font families, by contrast, do not have these feet. Good examples of sans serif fonts are Arial and Verdana. The lack of feet often gives text a blunt, in-your-face appearance, so sans serif fonts are often used for important text.

❑ A **True Type** font family is one that is defined by expressing the shapes of the curves that make up the characters in a precise mathematical manner. This means that the same definition can be used to calculate how to draw fonts of any size within the family. These days, virtually all the fonts you might use are TrueType fonts. Some older font families from the days of Windows 3.1 were defined by individually specifying the bitmap for each character separately for each font size, but the use of these fonts is now discouraged.

Microsoft has provided two main classes that you need to deal with when selecting or manipulating fonts:

❑ `System.Drawing.Font`

❑ `System.Drawing.FontFamily`

You have already seen the main use of the `Font` class. When you want to draw text, you instantiate an instance of `Font` and pass it to the `DrawString()` method to indicate how the text should be drawn. A `FontFamily` instance is used to represent a family of fonts.

You can use the `FontFamily` class, for example, if you know you want a font of a particular type (serif, sans serif, or true type), but do not have a preference for which font. The static properties `GenericSerif`, `GenericSansSerif`, and `GenericMonospace` return default fonts that satisfy these criteria:

```
FontFamily sansSerifFont = FontFamily.GenericSansSerif;
```

However, if you are writing a professional application, then you will want to choose your font in a more sophisticated way. Most likely, you will implement your drawing code so that it checks the font families available and selects the appropriate one, perhaps by taking the first available one on a list of preferred fonts. Moreover, if you want your application to be very user-friendly, then the first choice on the list will probably be the one that users selected the last time they ran your software. Usually, if you are dealing with the most popular font families, such as Arial and Times New Roman, you will be safe. However, if you do try to display text using a font that does not exist, the results aren't always predictable. You are quite likely to find that Windows just substitutes the standard system font, which is very easy for the system to draw, but that it does not look very pleasant — and if it does appear in your document, then it is likely to give the impression of software that is of poor quality.

You can find out what fonts are available on your system using a class called `InstalledFontCollection`, which is in the `System.Drawing.Text` namespace. This class implements a property, `Families`, which is an array of all the fonts that are available to use on your system:

```
InstalledFontCollection insFont = new InstalledFontCollection();
FontFamily [] families = insFont.Families;
foreach (FontFamily family in families)
{
    // do processing with this font family
}
```

Example: Enumerating Font Families

In this section, you work through a quick example, `EnumFontFamilies`, which lists all the font families available on the system and illustrates them by displaying the name of each family using an appropriate font (the 12-point regular version of that font family). Figure 33-16 shows the result of running `EnumFontFamilies`.

Of course, the results that you get will depend on the fonts you have installed on your computer.

Figure 33-16

For this example, you create a standard C# Windows application, EnumFontFamilies. You start by adding an extra namespace to be searched. You will be using the InstalledFontCollection class, which is defined in System.Drawing.Text.

```
using System.Drawing;
using System.Drawing.Text;
using System.Windows.Forms;
```

You then add the following constant to the Form1 class:

```
private const int margin = 10;
```

margin is the size of the left and top margin between the text and the edge of the document — it stops the text from appearing right at the edge of the client area.

This is designed as a quick-and-easy way of showing off font families; therefore, the code is crude and in many instances does not do things the way you ought to in a real application. For example, here you hard-code an estimated value for the document size of (200, 1500) and set the AutoScrollMinSize property to this value using the Visual Studio 2008 properties window. Typically, you would have to examine the text to be displayed to work out the document size. You do that in the next section.

Here is the OnPaint() method:

```
protected override void OnPaint(PaintEventArgs e)
{
    base.OnPaint(e);
    int verticalCoordinate = margin;
    InstalledFontCollection insFont = new InstalledFontCollection();
    FontFamily [] families = insFont.Families;
    e.Graphics.TranslateTransform(AutoScrollPosition.X,
                                  AutoScrollPosition.Y);
    foreach (FontFamily family in families)
    {
        if (family.IsStyleAvailable(FontStyle.Regular))
        {
            Font f = new Font(family.Name, 12);
            Point topLeftCorner = new Point(margin, verticalCoordinate);
            verticalCoordinate += f.Height;
            e.Graphics.DrawString (family.Name, f,
                                   Brushes.Black,topLeftCorner);
            f.Dispose();
        }
    }
}
```

In this code, you start by using an `InstalledFontCollection` object to obtain an array that contains details of all the available font families. For each family, you instantiate a 12-point `Font`. You use a simple constructor for `Font` — there are many more that allow additional options to be specified. The constructor takes two parameters, the name of the family and the size of the font:

```
Font f = new Font(family.Name, 12);
```

This constructor builds a font that has the regular style. To be on the safe side, however, you first check that this style is available for each font family before attempting to display anything using that font. This is done using the `FontFamily.IsStyleAvailable()` method. This check is important because not all fonts are available in all styles:

```
if (family.IsStyleAvailable(FontStyle.Regular))
```

`FontFamily.IsStyleAvailable()` takes one parameter, a `FontStyle` enumeration. This enumeration contains a number of flags that might be combined with the bitwise OR operator. The possible flags are `Bold`, `Italic`, `Regular`, `Strikeout`, and `Underline`.

Finally, note that you use a property of the `Font` class, `Height`, which returns the height needed to display text of that font, to work out the line spacing:

```
Font f =  new Font(family.Name, 12);
Point topLeftCorner = new Point(margin, verticalCoordinate);
verticalCoordinate += f.Height;
```

Again, to keep things simple, this version of `OnPaint()` reveals some bad programming practices. For example, you have not bothered to check what area of the document actually needs drawing — you just tried to display everything. Also, instantiating a `Font` is, as remarked earlier, a computationally intensive process, so you really ought to save the fonts rather than instantiating new copies every time `OnPaint()` is called. Because of the way the code has been designed, you might note that this example actually takes a noticeable amount of time to paint itself. To try to conserve memory and help the garbage collector you do, however, call `Dispose()` on each font instance after you have finished with it. If you did not, after 10 or 20 paint operations, there would be a lot of wasted memory storing fonts that are no longer needed.

Editing a Text Document: The CapsEditor Sample

You now come to the extended example in this chapter. The CapsEditor example is designed to demonstrate how the principles of drawing that you have learned so far have to be applied in a more realistic context. The CapsEditor example does not require any new material, apart from responding to user input via the mouse, but it shows how to manage the drawing of text so that the application maintains performance while ensuring that the contents of the client area of the main window are always kept up-to-date.

The CapsEditor program allows the user to read in a text file, which is then displayed line by line in the client area. If the user double-clicks any line, then that line will be changed to all uppercase. That is literally all the example does. Even with this limited set of features, you will find that the work involved in making sure everything is displayed in the right place while considering performance issues is quite complex. In particular, you have a new element here: The contents of the document can change — either when the user selects the menu option to read a new file, or when she double-clicks to capitalize a line. In the first case, you need to update the document size so the scroll bars still work correctly, and you have to redisplay everything. In the second case, you need to check carefully whether the document size has changed, and what text needs to be redisplayed.

This section starts by reviewing the appearance of CapsEditor. When the application is first run, it has no document loaded and resembles Figure 33-17.

Figure 33-17

The File menu has two options: Open, which evokes OpenFileDialog when selected and reads in whatever file the user clicks, and Exit, which closes the application when clicked. Figure 33-18 shows CapsEditor displaying its own source file, Form1.cs. (A few lines have been double-clicked in this image to convert them to uppercase.)

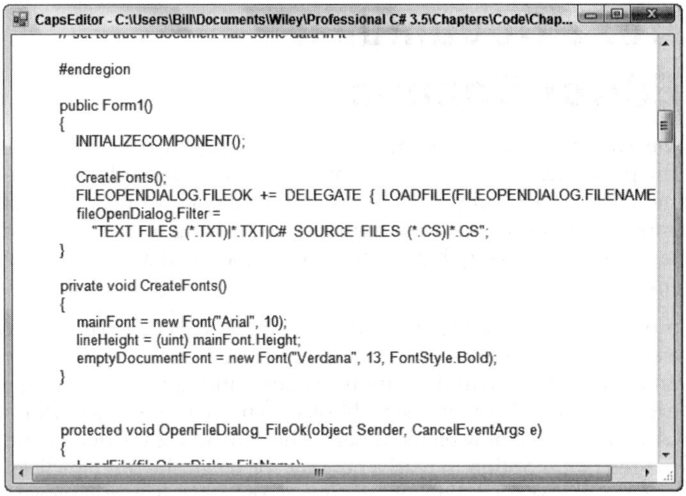

Figure 33-18

The sizes of the horizontal and vertical scroll bars are correct. The client area will scroll just enough to view the entire document. `CapsEditor` does not try to wrap lines of text — the example is already complicated enough as is. It just displays each line of the file exactly as it is read in. There are no limits to the size of the file, but you are assuming that it is a text file and does not contain any nonprintable characters.

Begin by adding a `using` command:

```
using System;
using System.Collections;
using System.ComponentModel;
using System.Drawing;
using System.IO;
using System.Windows.Forms;
```

You will be using the `StreamReader` class, which is in the `System.IO` namespace. Next, you add some fields to the `Form1` class:

```
#region Constant fields
private const string standardTitle = "CapsEditor";
                                         // default text in titlebar
private const uint margin = 10;
                         // horizontal and vertical margin in client area
#endregion
#region Member fields
// The 'document'
private readonly List<TextLineInformation> documentLines =
    new List<TextLineInformation>();
private uint lineHeight;         // height in pixels of one line
private Size documentSize;       // how big a client area is needed to
                                 // display document
private uint nLines;            // number of lines in document
private Font mainFont;          // font used to display all lines
private Font emptyDocumentFont;  // font used to display empty message
```

```
private readonly Brush mainBrush = Brushes.Blue;
                                   // brush used to display document text
private readonly Brush emptyDocumentBrush = Brushes.Red;
                           // brush used to display empty document message
private Point mouseDoubleClickPosition;
        // location mouse is pointing to when double-clicked
private readonly OpenFileDialog fileOpenDialog = new OpenFileDialog();
        // standard open file dialog
private bool documentHasData = false;
        // set to true if document has some data in it
#endregion
```

Most of these fields should be self-explanatory. The `documentLines` field is a `List<TextLineInformation>` that contains the actual text of the file that has been read in. Actually, this is the field that contains the data in the document. Each element of `documentLines` contains information for one line of text that has been read in. Because it is a `List<TextLineInformation>` rather than a plain array, you can dynamically add elements to it as you read in a file.

As previously mentioned, each `documentLines` element contains information about a line of text. This information is actually an instance of another class, `TextLineInformation`:

```
class TextLineInformation
{
    public string Text;
    public uint Width;
}
```

`TextLineInformation` looks like a classic case where you would normally use a struct rather than a class because it is just there to group a couple of fields. However, its instances are always accessed as elements of a `List<TextLineInformation>`, which expects its elements to be stored as reference types.

Each `TextLineInformation` instance stores a line of text — and that can be thought of as the smallest item that is displayed as a single item. In general, for each similar item in a GDI+ application, you would probably want to store the text of the item, as well as the world coordinates of where it should be displayed and its size. (The page coordinates will change frequently, whenever the user scrolls, whereas world coordinates will normally change only when other parts of the document are modified in some way.) In this case, you have stored only the `Width` of the item because the height in this case is just the height of whatever your selected font is. It is the same for all lines of text so there is no point storing the height separately for each one; you store it once, in the `Form1.lineHeight` field. As for the position, well, in this case, the x coordinate is just equal to the margin, and the y coordinate is easily calculated as:

```
margin + lineHeight*(however many lines are above this one)
```

If you had been trying to display and manipulate, say, individual words instead of complete lines, then the x position of each word would have to be calculated using the widths of all the previous words on that line of text, but the intent is to keep it simple here, which is why you are treating each line of text as one single item.

Let's turn to the main menu now. This part of the application is more the realm of Windows Forms (see Chapter 31, "Windows Forms") than of GDI+. Add the menu options using the design view in Visual Studio 2008, but rename them `menuFile`, `menuFileOpen`, and `menuFileExit`. Next, add event handlers for the File Open and File Exit menu options using the Visual Studio 2008 properties window. The event handlers have their Visual Studio 2008–generated names of `menuFileOpen_Click()` and `menuFileExit_Click()`.

Add some extra initialization code in the `Form1()` constructor:

```
public Form1()
{
    InitializeComponent();
    CreateFonts();
    fileOpenDialog.FileOk += delegate { LoadFile(fileOpenDialog.FileName); };
    fileOpenDialog.Filter =
        "Text files (*.txt)|*.txt|C# source files (*.cs)|*.cs";

}
```

You add the event handler here for instances when the user clicks OK in the File Open dialog box. You have also set the filter for the Open File dialog box, so that you can load text files only. The example in this case only uses .txt files, in addition to the C# source files, so you can use the application to examine the source code for the samples.

`CreateFonts()` is a helper method that sorts out the fonts you intend to use:

```
private void CreateFonts()
{
    mainFont = new Font("Arial", 10);
    lineHeight = (uint)mainFont.Height;
    emptyDocumentFont = new Font("Verdana", 13, FontStyle.Bold);
}
```

The actual definitions of the handlers are pretty standard:

```
protected void OpenFileDialog_FileOk(object Sender, CancelEventArgs e)
{
    LoadFile(fileOpenDialog.FileName);
}
protected void menuFileOpen_Click(object sender, EventArgs e)
{
    fileOpenDialog.ShowDialog();
}
protected void menuFileExit_Click(object sender, EventArgs e)
{
    Close();
}
```

Next, take a look at the `LoadFile()` method. It handles the opening and reading of a file (as well as ensuring a `Paint` event is raised to force a repaint with the new file):

```
private void LoadFile(string FileName)
{
    StreamReader sr = new StreamReader(FileName);
    string nextLine;
    documentLines.Clear();
    nLines = 0;
    TextLineInformation nextLineInfo;
    while ( (nextLine = sr.ReadLine()) != null)
    {
        nextLineInfo = new TextLineInformation();
        nextLineInfo.Text = nextLine;
        documentLines.Add(nextLineInfo);
        ++nLines;
    }
```

```
            sr.Close();
            documentHasData = (nLines>0) ? true : false;
            CalculateLineWidths();
            CalculateDocumentSize();
            Text = standardTitle + " - " + FileName;
            Invalidate();
        }
```

Most of this function is just standard file-reading (see Chapter 25, "Manipulating Files and the Registry"). Note that as the file is read, you progressively add lines to `documentLines ArrayList`, so this array ends up containing information for each of the lines in order. After you have read in the file, you set the `documentHasData` flag, which indicates whether there is actually anything to display. Your next task is to work out where everything is to be displayed, and, having done that, how much client area you need to display the file as well as the document size that will be used to set the scroll bars. Finally, you set the title bar text and call `Invalidate()`. `Invalidate()` is an important method supplied by Microsoft, so the next section discusses its use first, before examining the code for the `CalculateLineWidths()` and `CalculateDocumentSize()` methods.

The Invalidate() Method

`Invalidate()` is a member of `System.Windows.Forms.Form`. It marks an area of the client window as invalid and, therefore, in need of repainting, and then makes sure a `Paint` event is raised. `Invalidate()` has a couple of overrides: You can pass it a rectangle that specifies (in page coordinates) precisely which area of the window needs repainting. If you do not pass any parameters, it will just mark the entire client area as invalid.

If you know that something needs painting, why don't you just call `OnPaint()` or some other method to do the painting directly? The answer is that, in general, calling painting routines directly is regarded as bad programming practice — if your code decides it wants some painting done, you should call `Invalidate()`. Here is why:

❑ Drawing is almost always the most processor-intensive task a GDI+ application will carry out, so doing it in the middle of other work holds up the other work. With the example, if you had directly called a method to do the drawing from the `LoadFile()` method, then the `LoadFile()` method would not return until that drawing task was complete. During that time, your application cannot respond to any other events. However, by calling `Invalidate()`, you are simply getting Windows to raise a `Paint` event before immediately returning from `LoadFile()`. Windows is then free to examine the events that are in line to be handled. How this works internally is that the events sit as what are known as *messages* in a *message queue*. Windows periodically examines the queue, and if there are events in it, then it picks one and calls the corresponding event handler. Although the `Paint` event might be the only one sitting in the queue (so `OnPaint()` is called immediately anyway), in a more complex application there might be other events that ought to get priority over your `Paint` event. In particular, when the user has decided to quit the application, this will be marked by a message known as `WM_QUIT`.

❑ If you have a more complicated, multithreaded application, then you will probably want just one thread to handle all the drawing. Using `Invalidate()` to route all drawing through the message queue provides a good way of ensuring that the same thread does all the drawing, no matter what other thread requested the drawing operation. (Whatever thread is responsible for the message queue will be the thread that called `Application.Run()`.)

❑ There is an additional performance-related reason. Suppose that a couple of different requests to draw part of the screen come in at about the same time. Maybe your code has just modified the document and wants to ensure the updated document is displayed, while at the same time the user has just moved another window that was covering part of the client area out of the way.

By calling `Invalidate()`, you are giving Windows a chance to notice that this has occurred. Windows can then merge the `Paint` events if appropriate, combining the invalidated areas, so that the painting is only done once.

❑ The code to do the painting is probably going to be one of the most complex parts of the code in your application, especially if you have a very sophisticated user interface. The people who have to maintain your code in a couple of years time will thank you for having kept your painting code all in one place and as simple as you reasonably can — something that is easier to do if you do not have too many pathways into it from other parts of the program.

The bottom line from all of this is that it is good practice to keep all of your painting in the `OnPaint()` routine, or in other methods called from that method. However, you have to strike a balance; if you want to replace just one character on the screen and you know perfectly well that it won't affect anything else that you have drawn, then you might decide that it's not worth the overhead of going through `Invalidate()` and just write a separate drawing routine.

In a very complicated application, you might even write a full class that takes responsibility for drawing to the screen. A few years ago when MFC was the standard technology for GDI-intensive applications, MFC followed this model, with a C++ class, C<ApplicationName>View, that was responsible for painting. However, even in this case, this class had one member function, OnDraw(), which was designed to be the entry point for most drawing requests.

Calculating Item Sizes and Document Size

This section returns to the `CapsEditor` example and examines the `CalculateLineWidths()` and `CalculateDocumentSize()` methods called from `LoadFile()`:

```
private void CalculateLineWidths()
{
    Graphics dc = this.CreateGraphics();
    foreach (TextLineInformation nextLine in documentLines)
    {
        nextLine.Width = (uint)dc.MeasureString(nextLine.Text,
            mainFont).Width;
    }
}
```

This method simply runs through each line that has been read in and uses the `Graphics` `.MeasureString()` method to work out and store how much horizontal screen space the string requires. You store the value because `MeasureString()` is computationally intensive. If the `CapsEditor` sample had not been simple enough to easily work out the height and location of each item, then this method would almost certainly have needed to be implemented in such a way as to compute all those quantities, too.

Now that you know how big each item on the screen is and you can calculate where each item goes, you are in a position to work out the actual document size. The height is the number of lines multiplied by the height of each line. The width will need to be worked out by iterating through the lines to find the longest. For both height and width, you will also want to make an allowance for a small margin around the displayed document to make the application look more attractive.

The following is the method that calculates the document size:

```
private void CalculateDocumentSize()
{
    if (!documentHasData)
```

```
                     {
                         documentSize = new Size(100, 200);
                     }
                     else
                     {
                         documentSize.Height = (int)(nLines*lineHeight) + 2*(int)margin;
                         uint maxLineLength = 0;
                         foreach (TextLineInformation nextWord in documentLines)
                         {
                             uint tempLineLength = nextWord.Width;
                             if (tempLineLength > maxLineLength)
                             {
                                 maxLineLength = tempLineLength;
                             }
                         }
                         maxLineLength += 2*margin;
                         documentSize.Width = (int)maxLineLength;
                     }
                     AutoScrollMinSize = documentSize;
                 }
```

This method first checks whether there is any data to be displayed. If there is not, then you cheat a bit and use a hard-coded document size, which is big enough to display the big red <Empty Document> warning. If you had wanted to really do it properly, you would have used MeasureString() to check how big that warning actually is.

Once you have worked out the document size, you tell the Form instance what the size is by setting the Form.AutoScrollMinSize property. When you do this, something interesting happens behind the scenes. In the process of setting this property, the client area is invalidated and a Paint event is raised, for the very sensible reason that changing the size of the document means scroll bars will need to be added or modified and the entire client area will almost certainly be repainted. Why is that interesting? If you look back at the code for LoadFile(), you will realize that the call to Invalidate() in that method is actually redundant. The client area will be invalidated anyway when you set the document size. The explicit call to Invalidate() was left in the LoadFile() implementation to illustrate how you should normally do things. In fact, in this case, calling Invalidate() again will only needlessly request a duplicate Paint event. However, this in turn illustrates how Invalidate() gives Windows the chance to optimize performance. The second Paint event will not, in fact, get raised: Windows will see that there is a Paint event already sitting in the queue and will compare the requested invalidated regions to see if it needs to do anything to merge them. In this case, both Paint events will specify the entire client area, so nothing needs to be done, and Windows will quietly drop the second Paint request. Of course, going through that process will take up a little bit of processor time, but it will be a negligible amount of time compared to how long it takes to actually do some painting.

OnPaint()

Now that you have seen how CapsEditor loads the file, it's time to look at how the painting is done:

```
                 protected override void OnPaint(PaintEventArgs e)
                 {
                     base.OnPaint(e);
                     Graphics dc = e.Graphics;
                     int scrollPositionX = AutoScrollPosition.X;
                     int scrollPositionY = AutoScrollPosition.Y;
                     dc.TranslateTransform(scrollPositionX, scrollPositionY);
```

(continued)

(continued)

```
        if (!documentHasData)
        {
            dc.DrawString("<Empty document>", emptyDocumentFont,
                emptyDocumentBrush, new Point(20,20));
            base.OnPaint(e);
            return;
        }
        // work out which lines are in clipping rectangle
        int minLineInClipRegion =
                    WorldYCoordinateToLineIndex(e.ClipRectangle.Top -
                                        scrollPositionY);
        if (minLineInClipRegion == -1)
        {
            minLineInClipRegion = 0;
        }
        int maxLineInClipRegion =
                    WorldYCoordinateToLineIndex(e.ClipRectangle.Bottom -
                                        scrollPositionY);
        if (maxLineInClipRegion >= documentLines.Count ||
            maxLineInClipRegion == -1)
        {
            maxLineInClipRegion = documentLines.Count-1;
        }
        TextLineInformation nextLine;
        for (int i=minLineInClipRegion; i<=maxLineInClipRegion ; i++)
        {
            nextLine = (TextLineInformation)documentLines[i];
            dc.DrawString(nextLine.Text, mainFont, mainBrush,
                        LineIndexToWorldCoordinates(i));
        }
    }
}
```

At the heart of this `OnPaint()` override is a loop that goes through each line of the document, calling `Graphics.DrawString()` to paint each one. The rest of this code is mostly concerned with optimizing the painting — figuring out what exactly needs painting instead of rushing in and telling the graphics instance to redraw everything.

You begin by checking if there is any data in the document. If there is not, then you draw a quick message saying so, call the base class's `OnPaint()` implementation, and exit. If there is data, then you start looking at the clipping rectangle by calling another method, `WorldYCoordinateToLineIndex()`. This method is examined next, but essentially it takes a given y position relative to the top of the document, and works out what line of the document is being displayed at that point.

The first time you call the `WorldYCoordinateToLineIndex()` method, you pass it the coordinate value (`e.ClipRectangle.Top - scrollPositionY`). This is just the top of the clipping region, converted to world coordinates. If the return value is –1, you play it safe and assume that you need to start at the beginning of the document (this is the case if the top of the clipping region is within the top margin).

Once you have done all that, you essentially repeat the same process for the bottom of the clipping rectangle to find the last line of the document that is inside the clipping region. The indices of the first and last lines are respectively stored in `minLineInClipRegion` and `maxLineInClipRegion`, so then you can just run a `for` loop between these values to do your painting. Inside the painting loop, you actually need to do roughly the reverse transformation to the one performed by `WorldYCoordinateToLineIndex()`. You are given the index of a line of text, and you need to check where it should be drawn. This calculation is actually quite simple, but you have wrapped it up in another method, LineIndexToWorldCoordinates(), which returns the required coordinates of the top-left corner of the item. The returned coordinates are world coordinates, but that is fine because you have already called TranslateTransform() on the Graphics object so that you need to pass it world, rather than page, coordinates when asking it to display items.

Coordinate Transforms

This section examines the implementation of the helper methods that are written in the CapsEditor sample to help you with coordinate transforms. These are the WorldYCoordinateToLineIndex() and LineIndexToWorldCoordinates() methods referred to in the previous section, as well as a couple of other methods.

First, LineIndexToWorldCoordinates() takes a given line index, and works out the world coordinates of the top-left corner of that line, using the known margin and line height:

```
private Point LineIndexToWorldCoordinates(int index)
{
    Point TopLeftCorner = new Point(
        (int)margin, (int)(lineHeight*index + margin));
    return TopLeftCorner;
}
```

You also use a method that roughly does the reverse transform in OnPaint().
WorldYCoordinateToLineIndex() works out the line index, but it takes into account only a vertical world coordinate because it is used to work out the line index corresponding to the top and bottom of the clip region:

```
private int WorldYCoordinateToLineIndex(int y)
{
    if (y < margin)
    {
        return -1;
    }
    return (int)((y-margin)/lineHeight);
}
```

There are three more methods, which will be called from the handler routine that responds to the user double-clicking the mouse. First, you have a method that works out the index of the line being displayed at given world coordinates. Unlike WorldYCoordinateToLineIndex(), this method takes into account the x and y positions of the coordinates. It returns –1 if there is no line of text covering the coordinates passed in:

```
private int WorldCoordinatesToLineIndex(Point position)
{
    if (!documentHasData)
    {
        return -1;
    }
    if (position.Y < margin || position.X < margin)
    {
        return -1;
    }
    int index = (int)(position.Y-margin)/(int)this.lineHeight;
    // check position is not below document
```

(continued)

(continued)

```
            if (index >= documentLines.Count)
            {
                return -1;
            }
            // now check that horizontal position is within this line
            TextLineInformation theLine =
                                (TextLineInformation)documentLines[index];
            if (position.X > margin + theLine.Width)
            {
                return -1;
            }
            // all is OK. We can return answer
            return index;
        }
```

Finally, on occasion, you also need to convert between line index and page, rather than world, coordinates. The following methods achieve this:

```
        private Point LineIndexToPageCoordinates(int index)
        {
            return LineIndexToWorldCoordinates(index) +
                                new Size(AutoScrollPosition);
        }
        private int PageCoordinatesToLineIndex(Point position)
        {
            return WorldCoordinatesToLineIndex(position - new
                                Size(AutoScrollPosition));
        }
```

Note that when converting *to* page coordinates, you add the `AutoScrollPosition`, which is negative.

Although these methods by themselves do not look particularly interesting, they do illustrate a general technique that you will probably need to use often. With GDI+, you will often find yourself in a situation where you have been given specific coordinates (for example the coordinates of where the user has clicked the mouse), and you will need to figure out what item is being displayed at that point. Or it could happen the other way around — given a particular display item, where should it be displayed? Hence, if you are writing a GDI+ application, you will probably find it useful to write methods that do the equivalent of the coordinate transformation methods illustrated here.

Responding to User Input

So far, with the exception of the File menu in the `CapsEditor` sample, everything you have done in this chapter has been one way: The application has talked to the user by displaying information on the screen. Almost all software of course works both ways: the user can talk to the software as well. You are now going to add that functionality to `CapsEditor`.

Getting a GDI+ application to respond to user input is actually a lot simpler than writing the code to draw to the screen. (Chapter 31, "Windows Forms," covers how to handle user input.) Essentially, you override methods from the `Form` class that are called from the relevant event handler, in much the same way that `OnPaint()` is called when a `Paint` event is raised.

The following table lists the methods you might want to override when the user clicks or moves the mouse.

Method	Called When . . .
OnClick(EventArgs e)	Mouse is clicked.
OnDoubleClick(EventArgs e)	Mouse is double-clicked.
OnMouseDown(MouseEventArgs e)	Left mouse button is pressed.
OnMouseHover(MouseEventArgs e)	Mouse stays still somewhere after moving.
OnMouseMove(MouseEventArgs e)	Mouse is moved.
OnMouseUp(MouseEventArgs e)	Left mouse button is released.

If you want to detect when the user types in any text, then you will probably want to override the methods listed in the following table.

Method	Called When . . .
OnKeyDown(KeyEventArgs e)	A key is pressed.
OnKeyPress(KeyPressEventArgs e)	A key is pressed and released.
OnKeyUp(KeyEventArgs e)	A pressed key is released.

Note that some of these events overlap. For example, when the user presses a mouse button, the MouseDown event is raised. If the button is immediately released again, then this will raise the MouseUp event and the Click event. In addition, some of these methods take an argument that is derived from EventArgs rather than an instance of EventArgs itself. These instances of derived classes can be used to give more information about a particular event. MouseEventArgs has two properties, X and Y, which give the device coordinates of the mouse at the time it was pressed. Both KeyEventArgs and KeyPressEventArgs have properties that indicate which key or keys the event concerns.

That is all there is to it. It is up to you to think about the logic of precisely what you want to do. The only point to note is that you will probably find yourself doing a bit more logic work with a GDI+ application than you would have with a Windows.Forms application. That is because in a Windows.Forms application you are typically responding to high-level events (TextChanged for a text box, for example). By contrast, with GDI+, the events tend to be more elementary — user clicks the mouse or presses the H key. The action your application takes is likely to depend on a sequence of events rather than on a single event. For example, say your application works like Microsoft Word for Windows: to select some text, the user clicks the left mouse button, and then moves the mouse and releases the left mouse button. Your application receives the MouseDown event, but there is not much you can do with this event except record that the mouse was clicked with the cursor in a certain position. Then, when the MouseMove event is received, you will want to check from the record whether the left button is currently down, and if so, highlight text as the user selects it. When the user releases the left mouse button, your corresponding action (in the OnMouseUp() method) will need to check whether any dragging took place while the mouse button was down and act accordingly within the method. Only at this point is the sequence complete.

Another point to consider is that, because certain events overlap, you will often have a choice of which event you want your code to respond to.

The golden rule is to think carefully about the logic of every combination of mouse movement or click and keyboard event that the user might initiate, and ensure that your application responds in a way that is intuitive and in accordance with the expected behavior of applications in *every* case. Most of your work here will be in thinking rather than in coding, although the coding you do will be tricky because you might need to take into account many combinations of user input. For example, what should your application do if the user starts typing in text while one of the mouse buttons is held down? It might sound like an improbable combination, but eventually some user is going to try it!

The CapsEditor example keeps things very simple, so you do not really have any combinations to think about. The only thing you are going to respond to in the example is when the user double-clicks, in which case you capitalize whatever line of text the mouse pointer is hovering over.

This should be a simple task, but there is one snag. You need to trap the DoubleClick event, but the previous table shows that this event takes an EventArgs parameter, not a MouseEventArgs parameter. The trouble is that you need to know where the mouse is when the user double-clicks if you are to identify correctly the line of text to be capitalized — and you need a MouseEventArgs parameter to do that. There are two workarounds. One is to use a static method implemented by the Form1 object Control.MousePosition to find the mouse position:

```
protected override void OnDoubleClick(EventArgs e)
{
    Point MouseLocation = Control.MousePosition;
    // handle double click
}
```

In most cases, this will work. However, there could be a problem if your application (or even some other application with a high priority) is doing some computationally intensive work at the moment the user double-clicks. It just might happen in that case that the OnDoubleClick() event handler does not get called until perhaps half a second or so *after* the user has double-clicked. You do not want such delays because they usually annoy users intensely, but even so, occasionally it does happen and sometimes for reasons beyond the control of your application (a slow computer, for instance). The trouble is that half a second is easily enough time for the mouse to be moved halfway across the screen, in which case your call to Control.MousePosition will return the completely wrong location!

A better approach here is to rely on one of the many overlaps between mouse event meanings. The first part of double-clicking a mouse involves pressing the left button down. This means that if OnDoubleClick() is called, you know that OnMouseDown() has also just been called, with the mouse at the same location. You can use the OnMouseDown() override to record the position of the mouse, ready for OnDoubleClick(). This is the approach taken in CapsEditor:

```
protected override void OnMouseDown(MouseEventArgs e)
{
    base.OnMouseDown(e);
    mouseDoubleClickPosition = new Point(e.X, e.Y);
}
```

Now look at the OnDoubleClick() override. There is quite a bit more work to do here:

```
protected override void OnDoubleClick(EventArgs e)
{
    int i = PageCoordinatesToLineIndex(mouseDoubleClickPosition);
    if (i >= 0)
    {
        TextLineInformation lineToBeChanged =
                        (TextLineInformation)documentLines[i];
        lineToBeChanged.Text = lineToBeChanged.Text.ToUpper();
        Graphics dc = this.CreateGraphics();
        uint newWidth =(uint)dc.MeasureString(lineToBeChanged.Text,
                                    mainFont).Width;
```

```
        if (newWidth > lineToBeChanged.Width)
            lineToBeChanged.Width = newWidth;
        if (newWidth+2*margin > this.documentSize.Width)
        {
            documentSize.Width = (int)newWidth;
            AutoScrollMinSize = this.documentSize;
        }
        Rectangle changedRectangle = new Rectangle(
                                    LineIndexToPageCoordinates(i),
                                    new Size((int)newWidth,
                                    (int)this.lineHeight));
        Invalidate(changedRectangle);
    }
    base.OnDoubleClick(e);
}
```

You start off by calling `PageCoordinatesToLineIndex()` to work out which line of text the mouse pointer was hovering over when the user double-clicked. If this call returns –1, then you weren't over any text, so there is nothing to do — except, of course, call the base class version of `OnDoubleClick()` to let Windows do any default processing.

Assuming that you have identified a line of text, you can use the `string.ToUpper()` method to convert it to uppercase. That was the easy part. The hard part is figuring out what needs to be redrawn where. Fortunately, because this example is simple, there are not too many combinations. You can assume that converting to uppercase will always either leave the width of the line on the screen unchanged or increase it. Capital letters are bigger than lowercase letters; therefore, the width will never go down. You also know that because you are not wrapping lines, your line of text will not overflow to the next line and push out other text below. Your action of converting the line to uppercase will not, therefore, actually change the locations of any of the other items being displayed. That is a big simplification!

The next thing the code does is use `Graphics.MeasureString()` to work out the new width of the text. There are now just two possibilities:

❑   The new width might make your line the longest line and cause the width of the entire document to increase. If that is the case, then you will need to set `AutoScrollMinSize` to the new size so that the scroll bars are correctly placed.

❑   The size of the document might be unchanged.

In either case, you need to get the screen redrawn by calling `Invalidate()`. Only one line has changed; therefore, you do not want to have the entire document repainted. Rather, you need to work out the bounds of a rectangle that contains just the modified line, so that you can pass this rectangle to `Invalidate()`, ensuring that just that line of text will be repainted. That is precisely what the previous code does. Your call to `Invalidate()` initiates a call to `OnPaint()` when the mouse event handler finally returns. Keeping in mind the earlier comments about the difficulty in setting a break point in `OnPaint()`, if you run the sample and set a break point in `OnPaint()` to trap the resultant painting action, then you will find that the `PaintEventArgs` parameter to `OnPaint()` does indeed contain a clipping region that matches the specified rectangle. And because you have overloaded `OnPaint()` to take careful account of the clipping region, only the one required line of text will be repainted.

Printing

So far, the chapter has focused exclusively on drawing to the screen. However, at some point you will probably also want to be able to produce a hard copy of the data. That is the topic of this section. You are going to extend the `CapsEditor` sample so that it is able to print preview and print the document that is being edited.

Unfortunately, there is not enough space to go into too much detail about printing here, so the printing functionality you will implement is very basic. Typically, when you are implementing the ability for an application to print data, you will need to add three items to the application's main File menu:

❑ **Page Setup**, which allows the user to choose options such as which pages to print, which printer to use, and so on.

❑ **Print Preview**, which opens a new Form that displays a mock-up of what the printed copy should look like.

❑ **Print**, which prints the document.

In this case, to keep things simple, you will not implement a Page Setup menu option. Printing will only be possible using default settings. Note, however, that if you do want to implement Page Setup, Microsoft has already written a page setup dialog class for you to use `System.Windows.Forms .PrintDialog`. You will normally want to write an event handler that displays this form and saves the settings chosen by the user.

In many ways, printing is just the same as displaying to a screen. You will be supplied with a device context (`Graphics` instance) and call all the usual display commands against that instance. Microsoft has written a number of classes to assist you in doing this; the two main ones that you need to use are `System .Drawing.Printing.PrintDocument` and `System.Drawing.Printing.PrintPreviewDialog`. These two classes handle the process of making sure that drawing instructions passed to a device context are handled appropriately for printing, leaving you to think about the logic of what to print where.

Some important differences exist between printing or print previewing on the one hand, and displaying to the screen on the other hand. Printers cannot scroll; instead, they turn out pages. Therefore, you will need to make sure that you find a sensible way of dividing your document into pages and draw each page as requested. Among other things, that means calculating how much of your document will fit onto a single page and, therefore, how many pages you will need and which page each part of the document needs to be written to.

Despite these complications, the process of printing is quite simple. Programmatically, the steps you need to go through look roughly like this:

❑ **Printing** — You instantiate a `PrintDocument` object and call its `Print()` method. This method signals the `PrintPage` event to print the first page. `PrintPage` takes a `PrintPageEventArgs` parameter, which supplies information concerning paper size and setup, as well as a `Graphics` object used for the drawing commands. You should therefore have written an event handler for this event, and have implemented this handler to print a page. This event handler should also set a Boolean property of the `PrintPageEventArgs` called `HasMorePages` to either `true` or `false` to indicate whether there are more pages to be printed. The `PrintDocument.Print()` method will repeatedly raise the `PrintPage` event until it sees that `HasMorePages` has been set to `false`.

❑ **Print Previewing** — In this case, you instantiate both a `PrintDocument` object and a `PrintPreviewDialog` object. You attach the `PrintDocument` to the `PrintPreviewDialog` (using the property `PrintPreviewDialog.Document`) and then call the dialog's `ShowDialog()` method. This method modally displays the dialog, which turns out to be a standard Windows print preview form and which displays pages of the document. Internally, the pages are displayed once again by repeatedly raising the `PrintPage` event until the `HasMorePages` property is `false`. There is no need to write a separate event handler for this; you can use the same event handler as used for printing each page because the drawing code ought to be identical in both cases. (After all, whatever is print previewed ought to look identical to the printed version!)

Implementing Print and Print Preview

Now that this process has been outlined in broad strokes, in this section you see how this works in code terms. You can download the code as the `PrintingCapsEdit` project at www.wrox.com; it consists of the `CapsEditor` project with the changes displayed in the following snippet.

You begin by using the Visual Studio 2008 design view to add two new items to the File menu: Print and Print Preview. You also use the properties window to name these items `menuFilePrint` and `menuFilePrintPreview`, and to set them to be disabled when the application starts up (you cannot print anything until a document has been opened!). You arrange for these menu items to be enabled by adding the following code to the main form's `LoadFile()` method, which is responsible for loading a file into the `CapsEditor` application:

```
private void LoadFile(string FileName)
{
    StreamReader sr = new StreamReader(FileName);
    string nextLine;
    documentLines.Clear();
    nLines = 0;
    TextLineInformation nextLineInfo;
    while ( (nextLine = sr.ReadLine()) != null)
    {
        nextLineInfo = new TextLineInformation();
        nextLineInfo.Text = nextLine;
        documentLines.Add(nextLineInfo);
        ++nLines;
    }
    sr.Close();
    if (nLines > 0)
    {
        documentHasData = true;
        menuFilePrint.Enabled = true;
        menuFilePrintPreview.Enabled = true;
    }
    else
    {
        documentHasData = false;
        menuFilePrint.Enabled = false;
        menuFilePrintPreview.Enabled = false;
    }
    CalculateLineWidths();
    CalculateDocumentSize();
    Text = standardTitle + " - " + FileName;
    Invalidate();
}
```

The above code is the new code added to this method. Next, you add a member field to the `Form1` class:

```
public partial class Form1 : Form
{
    private int pagesPrinted = 0;
```

This field will be used to indicate which page you are currently printing. You are making it a member field because you will need to remember this information between calls to the `PrintPage` event handler.

Next, you will find the event handlers that handle the selection of the Print or Print Preview menu options:

```
private void menuFilePrintPreview_Click(object sender, System.EventArgs e)
{
    this.pagesPrinted = 0;
    PrintPreviewDialog ppd = new PrintPreviewDialog();
    PrintDocument pd = new PrintDocument();
    pd.PrintPage += this.pd_PrintPage;
    ppd.Document = pd;
    ppd.ShowDialog();
}
private void menuFilePrint_Click(object sender, System.EventArgs e)
{
    this.pagesPrinted = 0;
    PrintDocument pd = new PrintDocument();
    pd.PrintPage += new PrintPageEventHandler
        (this.pd_PrintPage);
    pd.Print();
}
```

You have already seen the steps involved in printing, and you can see that these event handlers are simply implementing that procedure. In both cases, you are instantiating a `PrintDocument` object and attaching an event handler to its `PrintPage` event. In the case of printing, you call `PrintDocument.Print()`, whereas for print previewing, you attach the `PrintDocument` object to a `PrintPreviewDialog` and call the preview dialog box object's `ShowDialog()` method. The real work to the `PrintPage` event is done in the event handler. Here is what this handler looks like:

```
private void pd_PrintPage(object sender, PrintPageEventArgs e)
{
    float yPos = 0;
    float leftMargin = e.MarginBounds.Left;
    float topMargin = e.MarginBounds.Top;
    string line = null;
    // Calculate the number of lines per page.
    int linesPerPage = (int)(e.MarginBounds.Height /
        mainFont.GetHeight(e.Graphics));
    int lineNo = pagesPrinted * linesPerPage;
    // Print each line of the file.
    int count = 0;
    while(count < linesPerPage && lineNo < this.nLines)
    {
        line = ((TextLineInformation)this.documentLines[lineNo]).Text;
        yPos = topMargin + (count * mainFont.GetHeight(e.Graphics));
        e.Graphics.DrawString(line, mainFont, Brushes.Blue,
            leftMargin, yPos, new StringFormat());
        lineNo++;
        count++;
    }
    // If more lines exist, print another page.
    if(this.nLines > lineNo)
        e.HasMorePages = true;
    else
        e.HasMorePages = false;
    pagesPrinted++;
}
```

After declaring a couple of local variables, the first thing you do is work out how many lines of text can be displayed on one page, which will be the height of a page divided by the height of a line and rounded down. The height of the page can be obtained from the `PrintPageEventArgs.MarginBounds` property. This property is a `RectangleF` struct that has been initialized to give the bounds of the page. The height of a line is obtained from the `Form1.mainFont` field, which is the font used for displaying the text. There is no reason here for not using the same font for printing too. Note that for the `PrintingCapsEditor` sample, the number of lines per page is always the same, so you arguably could have cached the value the first time you calculated it. However, the calculation is not too hard, and in a more sophisticated application the value might change, so it is not bad practice to recalculate it every time you print a page.

You also initialize a variable called `lineNo`. This gives the zero-based index of the line of the document that will be the first line of this page. This information is important because, in principle, the `pd_PrintPage()` method could have been called to print any page, not just the first page. `lineNo` is computed as the number of lines per page times the number of pages that have so far been printed.

Next, you run through a loop, printing each line. This loop will terminate either when you find that you have printed all the lines of text in the document, or when you find that you have printed all the lines that will fit on this page, whichever condition occurs first. Finally, you check whether there is any more of the document to be printed, and set the `HasMorePages` property of your `PrintPageEventArgs` accordingly. You also increment the `pagesPrinted` field so that you know to print the correct page the next time the `PrintPage` event handler is invoked.

One point to note about this event handler is that you do not worry about where the drawing commands are being sent. You simply use the `Graphics` object that was supplied with the `PrintPageEventArgs`. The `PrintDocument` class that Microsoft has written will internally take care of making sure that, if you are printing, the `Graphics` object has been hooked up to the printer; if you are print previewing, then the `Graphics` object has been hooked up to the print preview form on the screen.

Finally, you need to ensure that the `System.Drawing.Printing` namespace is searched for type definitions:

```
using System;
using System.Collections.Generic;
using System.ComponentModel;
using System.Data;
using System.Drawing;
using System.Drawing.Printing;
using System.Text;
using System.Windows.Forms;
using System.IO;
```

All that remains is to compile the project and check that the code works. Figure 33-19 shows what happens when you run `CapsEdit`, load a text document (as before, you have picked the C# source file for the project), and select Print Preview.

In Figure 33-19, the document is scrolled to page 5 and the preview is set to display normal size. The `PrintPreviewDialog` has supplied quite a lot of features, as you can see by looking at the toolbar at the top of the form. The options available include printing the document, zooming in or out, and displaying two, three, four, or six pages together. These options are all fully functional, without your having to do any work. Figure 33-20 shows the result of changing the zoom to auto and clicking to display four pages (third toolbar button from the right).

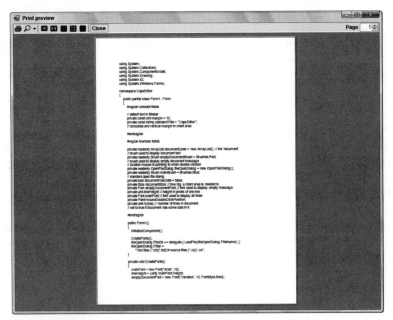

Figure 33-19

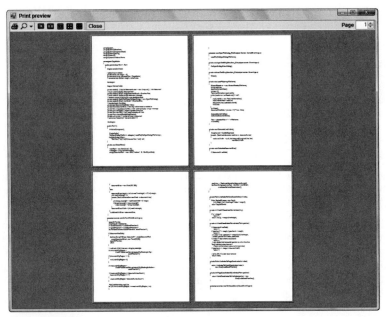

Figure 33-20

Part V: Presentation

1146

Summary

This chapter covered the realm of GDI+ — the area of drawing to a display device, where the drawing is done by your code rather than by some predefined control or dialog box. GDI+ is a powerful tool, and there are many .NET base classes available to help you draw to a device. You have seen that the process of drawing is actually relatively simple. In most cases you can draw text or sophisticated figures or display images with just a couple of C# statements. However, managing your drawing — the behind-the-scenes work involving working out what to draw, where to draw it, and what does or does not need repainting in any given situation — is far more complex and requires careful algorithm design. For this reason, it is also important to have a good understanding of how GDI+ works and what actions Windows takes to get something drawn. In particular, because of the architecture of Windows, it is important that, where possible, drawing should be done by invalidating areas of the window and relying on Windows to respond by issuing a `Paint` event.

Many more .NET classes can be used for drawing than there is space to cover in this chapter. However, if you have worked through it and understood the principles involved in drawing, then you will be in an excellent position to explore these classes by looking at their lists of methods in the SDK documentation and instantiating instances of them to see what they do. In the end, drawing, as with almost any other aspect of programming, requires logic, careful thought, and clear algorithms if you want to go beyond the standard controls. Your software will benefit in both user-friendliness and visual appearance if it is well thought out. Many applications out there rely entirely on controls for their user interface. Although this can be effective, such applications very quickly end up resembling each other. By adding some GDI+ code to do some custom drawing you can mark out your software as distinct and make it appear more original, which can only help increase your sales!

The next chapter takes a look at the latest thick-client presentation technology — Windows Presentation Foundation (WPF).

34

Windows Presentation Foundation

Windows Presentation Foundation (WPF) is one of the major extensions of .NET Framework 3.0. WPF is a new library to create the UI for smart client applications. While the Windows Forms controls are native Windows controls that use Window handles that are based on screen pixels, WPF is based on DirectX. The application does not use Window handles. It is easy to resize the UI, and it supports sound and video.

The main topics of this chapter are, as follows:

- ❑ An overview of WPF
- ❑ Shapes as the base drawing elements
- ❑ Scaling, rotating, and skewing with transformations
- ❑ Different kind of brushes to fill elements
- ❑ WPF controls and their features
- ❑ How to define a layout with WPF panels
- ❑ The WPF event-handling mechanism
- ❑ Styles, templates, and resources

Overview

One of the big features of WPF is that work can be easily separated between designers and developers. The outcome from the designer's work can directly be used by the developer. To make this possible, you need to understand XAML. The first topic of this chapter gives you an overview of WPF, including enough information to understand the principles of XAML. It also covers information on how designers and developers can cooperate. WPF consists of several assemblies containing thousands of classes. So that you can navigate within this vast number of classes and find what you need, the overview explains the class hierarchy and namespaces in WPF.

XAML

XML for Applications Markup Language (XAML) is an XML syntax used to define the hierarchical structure of the user interface. In the following line, you can see the declaration of a button named button1 with the content Click Me!. The <Button> element specifies the use of the Button class:

```
<Button Name="button1">Click Me!</Button>
```

There's always a .NET class behind an XAML element. With attributes and child elements, you set the value of properties and define handler methods for events.

To test simple XAML code, you can start the utility XAMLPad.exe (see Figure 34-1) and enter the XAML code in the edit field. You can write the <Button> element within the <Page> and <Grid> elements that are already prepared from XAMLPad. With XAMLPad, you can see the XAML outcome immediately.

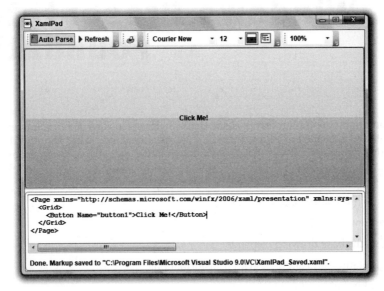

Figure 34-1

XAML code can be interpreted by the WPF runtime, but it can also be compiled to BAML (Binary Application Markup Language), which is done by default by Visual Studio WPF projects. BAML is added as a resource to the executable.

Instead of writing XAML, you can also create a button with C# code. You can create a normal C# console application, add references to the assemblies WindowsBase, PresentationCore, and PresentationFramework, and write the following code. In the Main() method, a Window object from the namespace System.Windows is created, and the property Title is set. Then a Button object from the namespace System.Windows.Controls is created, the Content is set, and the Content of the window is set to the button. The Run() method of the Application class is responsible for processing Windows messages:

```
using System;
using System.Windows;
using System.Windows.Controls;
namespace Wrox.ProCSharp.WPF
```

```
{
    class Program
    {
        [STAThread]
        static void Main()
        {
            Window mainWindow = new Window();
            mainWindow.Title = "WPF Application";
            Button button1 = new Button();
            button1.Content = "Click Me!";
            mainWindow.Content = button1;
            button1.Click +=
                (sender, e) => MessageBox.Show("Button clicked");
            Application app = new Application();
            app.Run(mainWindow);
        }
    }
}
```

The Application *class can also be defined by using XAML. With a Visual Studio WPF project, open the file* App.xaml *that includes the properties and* StartupUri *of the* Application *class.*

Running the application, you get a Window containing the button, as shown in Figure 34-2.

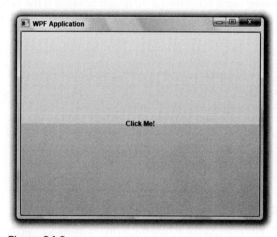

Figure 34-2

As you can see, programming WPF is very similar to Windows Forms programming — with the small difference that the Button has a Content instead of a Text property. However, compared to creating the UI forms with code, XAML has some great advantages. With XAML, the designer and developer can cooperate much better. The designer can work on the XAML code and design a stylish UI, while the developer adds functionality from the code behind using C#. It's much easier to separate the UI from the functionality by using XAML.

You can directly interact with the elements that are defined with XAML from the C# code using code behind and XAML. You just need to define a name for the element and use the same name as a variable to change properties and invoke methods.

The button has a `Content` property instead of a `Text` property because the button can show anything. You can add text to the content, but also a graphic, a list box, a video — whatever you can think of.

Properties as Attributes

Before working with XAML, you need to know important characteristics of the XAML syntax. You can use XML attributes to specify the properties of classes. The example shows the setting of the `Content` and `Background` properties of the `Button` class:

```
<Button Content="Click Me!" Background="LightGreen" />
```

Properties as Elements

Instead of using XML attributes, the properties can also be specified as child elements. The value for the content can be directly set by specifying the child elements of the `Button` element. For all other properties of the `Button`, the name of the child element is defined by the name of the outer element, followed by the property name:

```
<Button>
  <Button.Background>
    LightGreen
  </Button.Background>
  Click Me!
</Button>
```

In the previous example, it is not necessary to use child elements. By using XML attributes, the same result was achieved. However, using attributes is no longer possible if the value is more complex than a string. For example, the background can be set to not only a simple color but also to a brush. For example, you can define the following linear gradient brush:

```
<Button>
  <Button.Background>
    <LinearGradientBrush StartPoint="0,0" EndPoint="1,1">
      <GradientStop Color="Yellow" Offset="0.0" />
      <GradientStop Color="Orange" Offset="0.25" />
      <GradientStop Color="Red" Offset="0.75" />
      <GradientStop Color="Violet" Offset="1.0" />
    </LinearGradientBrush>
  </Button.Background>
  Click Me!
</Button>
```

Dependency Property

When programming WPF, you often come across the term *dependency property*. WPF elements are classes with methods, properties, and events. Nearly every property of a WPF element is a dependency property. What does this mean? A dependency property can be dependent on other inputs; for example, themes and user preferences. Dependency properties are used with data binding, animation, resources, and styles.

From the programmatic viewpoint, a dependency property can be read and written not only by invoking the strongly typed property but also by methods passing a dependency property object.

Only a class that derives from the base class `DependencyObject` can include dependency properties. The following class, `MyDependencyObject`, defines the dependency property `SomeState`. `SomeStateProperty` is a static field of type `DependencyProperty` that backs the dependency property. The dependency property is registered with the WPF dependency property system using the `Register()` method. The `Register()` method gets the name of the dependency property, the type of the dependency property, and the owner type. You can set the value of the dependency property by using the SetValue() method of the DependencyObject base class, and get the value by using the method GetValue(). Dependency properties usually have a strongly typed access as well. Instead of using the methods of the DependencyObject base class, the class MyDependencyObject includes the property SomeState, which invokes the methods of the base class from the implementation of the set and get accessors. You shouldn't do something else in the implementation of the set and get accessors as these property accessors might not be invoked.

```
public class MyDependencyObject : DependencyObject
{
    public static readonly DependencyProperty SomeStateProperty =
        DependencyProperty.Register("SomeState", typeof(String),
            typeof(MyDependencyObject));

    public string SomeState
    {
        get { return (string)this.GetValue(SomeStateProperty); }
        set { this.SetValue(SomeStateProperty, value); }
    }
}
```

With WPF, the class DependencyObject *is very high in the hierarchy. Every WPF element is derived from this base class.*

Attached Property

A WPF element can also get features from the parent element. For example, if the Button element is located inside a Canvas element, the button has Top and Left properties that are prefixed with the parent element's name. Such a property is known as *attached property:*

```
<Canvas>
  <Button Canvas.Top="30" Canvas.Left="40">
    Click Me!
  </Button>
</Canvas>
```

Writing the same functionality from the code behind is a bit different because the Button class doesn't have a Canvas.Top and Canvas.Left property, even if it is contained within the Canvas class. There is a naming pattern for setting attached properties that is common with all classes. The class supporting attached properties has static methods with the names Set<Property> and Get<Property>, where the first parameter is the object that the property value is applied to. The Canvas class defines the static methods SetLeft() and SetTop() to get the same result as in the XAML code shown earlier.

```
[STAThread]
static void Main()
{
    Window mainWindow = new Window();
    Canvas canvas = new Canvas();
    mainWindow.Content = canvas;
    Button button1 = new Button();
    canvas.Children.Add(button1);
    button1.Content = "Click Me!";
    Canvas.SetLeft(button1, 40);
    Canvas.SetTop(button1, 30);
    Application app = new Application();
    app.Run(mainWindow);
}
```

An attached property can be implemented as a dependency object. The method `DependencyProperty` *.RegisterAttached() registers an attached property.*

Markup Extensions

When setting values for elements, you can set the value directly. However, sometimes markup extensions are very helpful. Markup extensions consist of curly brackets followed by a string token that defines the type of the markup extension. Here is an example of a `StaticResource` markup extension:

```
<Button Name="button1" Style="{StaticResource key}" Content="Click Me" />
```

Instead of using the markup extension, you can write the same thing using child elements:

```
<Button Name="button1">
  <Button.Style>
    <StaticResource ResourceKey="key" />
  </Button.Style>
  Click Me!
</Button>
```

Markup extensions are mainly used for accessing resources and for data binding. Both of these topics are discussed later in this chapter.

Cooperation of Designers and Developers

Very often, developers not only implement Windows applications, but are also responsible for the design. This is especially true if the application was built just for in-house use. If someone with UI design skills was hired to design the UI, usually the developer is given a JPG file of the designer's vision of how the UI should look. The developer then has the problem of trying to match the designer's plans. Even simple changes by the designer, such as a different look for list boxes or buttons, can lead to a huge investment using owner-drawn controls. As a result, the UI done by the developer looks very different from the UI that was originally designed.

With WPF, this changes. The designer and developer can work on the same XAML code. The designer can use a tool such as Expression Blend, while the developer uses Visual Studio 2008. Both can work using the same project files. In the typical progression of this cooperative process, the designer starts a project with Expression Blend, using the same project files as in Visual Studio. Then the developer takes over to work on the code behind, while the designer enhances the UI. As the developer enhances the functionality, the designer can also add new UI features that take advantage of the functionality provided by the developer.

Of course, it is also possible to start the application with Visual Studio and enhance the UI later with Expression Blend. You just need to be careful not to do a UI as you used to do with Windows Forms because this doesn't take full advantage of WPF.

Figure 34-3 shows Expression Blend that was created by using WPF.

Comparing Expression Blend to Visual Studio extensions, the Expression Blend has great features for defining styles, creating animations, using graphics, and the like. To work cooperatively, the Expression Blend can use code-behind classes done by the developer, and the designer can specify the data binding from the WPF elements to the .NET classes. The designer can also test the complete application by starting it from Expression Blend. Because Expression Blend uses the same MS-Build files as Visual Studio does, the code-behind C# code is compiled to run the application.

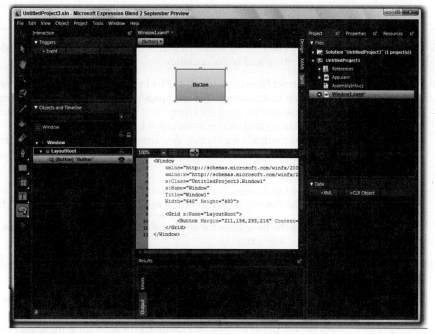

Figure 34-3

Class Hierarchy

WPF consists of thousands of classes with a deep hierarchy. To help in understanding the relationship among the classes, Figure 34-4 shows some of the WPF classes in a class diagram. Some classes and their functionality are described in the following table.

Class	Description
DispatcherObject	DispatcherObject is an abstract base class for classes that are bound to one thread. Similar to Windows Forms, WPF requires that methods and properties be invoked only from the creator thread. Classes that are derived from DispatcherObject have an associated Dispatcher object that can be used to switch the thread.
Application	In a WPF application, one instance of the Application class is created. This class implements a Singleton pattern for access to the windows of the application, resources, and properties.
DependencyObject	DependencyObject is the base class for all classes that support dependency properties. Dependency properties were discussed earlier.

Class	Description
Visual	The base class for all visual elements is Visual. This class includes features for hit testing and transformation.
UIElement	The abstract base class for all WPF elements that need basic presentation features is UIElement. This class provides tunneling and bubbling events for mouse moves, drag and drop, and key clicks. It exposes virtual methods for rendering that can be overridden by derived classes, and it provides methods for layout. You already know that WPF no longer uses Window handles. You can consider this class equivalent to a Windows handle.
FrameworkElement	FrameworkElement is derived from the base class UIElement and implements the default behavior of the methods defined by the base class.
Shape	Shape is the base class for all shape elements, for example, Line, Ellipse, Polygon, Rectangle.
Control	Control derives from FrameworkElement and is the base class for all user-interactive elements.
Panel	The class Panel derives from FrameworkElement and is the abstract base class for all panels. This class has a Children property for all UI elements within the panel and defines methods for arranging the child controls. Classes that are derived from Panel define different behavior for how the children are organized, for example, WrapPanel, StackPanel, Canvas, Grid.
ContentControl	ContentControl is the base class for all controls that have a single content (for example, Label, Button). The default style of a content control may be limited, but it is possible to change the look by using templates.

As you can see, WPF classes have a really deep hierarchy. In this and the next chapter, you will see classes of the core functionality, but it is not possible to cover all the features of WPF with two chapters.

Namespaces

Classes from Windows Forms and WPF can easily be confused. The Windows Forms classes are located in the namespace System.Windows.Forms, while the WPF classes are located inside the namespace System.Windows and subnamespaces thereof, with the exception of System.Windows.Forms. The Button class for Windows Forms has the full name System.Windows.Forms.Button, and the Button class for WPF has the full name System.Windows.Controls.Button. Windows Forms is covered in Chapters 31 and 32.

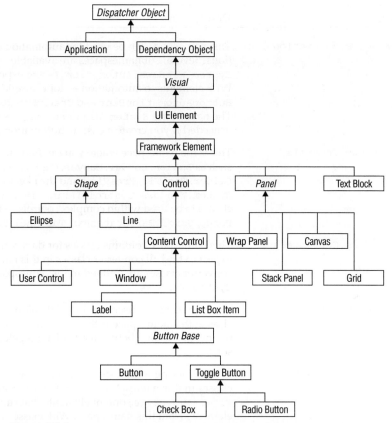

Figure 34-4

Namespaces and their functionality with WPF are described in the following table.

Namespace	Description
System.Windows	This is the core namespace of WPF. Here you can find core classes from WPF such as the Application class; classes for dependency objects, DependencyObject and DependencyProperty; and the base class for all WPF elements, FrameworkElement.
System.Windows.Annotations	The classes from this namespace are used for user-created annotations and notes on application data that are stored separately from the document. The namespace System.Windows.Annotations.Storage contains classes for storing annotations.

Namespace	Description
System.Windows.Automation	This namespace can be used for automation of WPF applications. Several subnamespaces are available. System.Windows.Automation.Peers exposes WPF elements to automation — for example, ButtonAutomationPeer and CheckBoxAutomationPeer. The namespace System.Windows.Automation.Provider is needed if you create a custom automation provider.
System.Windows.Controls	This is the namespace where you can find all the WPF controls, such as Button, Border, Canvas, ComboBox, Expander, Slider, ToolTip, TreeView, and the like. In the namespace System.Windows.Controls.Primitives, you can find classes to be used within complex controls — for example, Popup, ScrollBar, StatusBar, TabPanel, and so on.
System.Windows.Converters	This namespace contains classes for data conversion. Don't expect to find all converter classes in this namespace; core converter classes are defined in the namespace System.Windows.
System.Windows.Data	This namespace is used by WPF data binding. An important class in this namespace is the Binding class, which is used to define the binding between a WPF target element and a CLR source.
System.Windows.Documents	When working with documents, you can find many helpful classes in this namespace. FixedDocument and FlowDocument are content elements that can contain other elements from this namespace. With classes from the namespace System.Windows.Documents.Serialization you can write documents to disk.
System.Windows.Ink	The Windows Tablet PC and Ultra Mobile PCs are being used more and more. With these PCs, ink can be used for user input. The namespace System.Windows.Ink contains classes to deal with ink input.
System.Windows.Input	This namespace contains several classes for command handling, keyboard inputs, working with a stylus, and so on.
System.Windows.Interop	For integration with Win32 and WPF, you can find classes in this namespace.
System.Windows.Markup	Helper classes for XAML markup code are located in this namespace.
System.Windows.Media	To work with images, audio, and video content, you can use classes in this namespace.
System.Windows.Navigation	This namespace contains classes for navigation between windows.
System.Windows.Resources	This namespace contains supporting classes for resources.

Namespace	Description
System.Windows.Shapes	The core classes for the UI are located in the namespace System.Windows.Shapes: Line, Ellipse, Rectangle, and the like.
System.Windows.Threading	WPF elements are similar to Windows Forms controls bound to a single thread. In the namespace System.Windows.Threading, you can find classes to deal with multiple threads — for example, the Dispatcher class belongs to this namespace.
System.Windows.Xps	XML Paper Specification (XPS) is a new document specification that is also supported by Microsoft Word. In the namespaces System.Windows.Xps, System.Windows.Xps.Packaging, and System.Windows.Xps.Serialization, you can find classes to create and stream XPS documents.

Shapes

Shapes are the core elements of WPF. With shapes you can draw 2D graphics using rectangles, lines, ellipses, paths, polygons, and polylines that are represented by classes derived from the abstract base class Shape. Shapes are defined in the namespace System.Windows.Shapes.

The following XAML example draws a yellow face with blue legs, consisting of an ellipse for the face, two ellipses for the eyes, a path for the mouth, and four lines for the legs:

```
<Window x:Class="ProCSharp.WPF.Window1"
xmlns="http://schemas.microsoft.com/winfx/2006/xaml/presentation"
    xmlns:x="http://schemas.microsoft.com/winfx/2006/xaml"
    Title="WPF Samples" Height="260" Width="230">
  <Canvas>
    <Ellipse Canvas.Left="50" Canvas.Top="50" Width="100" Height="100"
        Stroke="Blue" StrokeThickness="4" Fill="Yellow" />
    <Ellipse Canvas.Left="60" Canvas.Top="65" Width="25" Height="25"
        Stroke="Blue" StrokeThickness="3" Fill="White" />
    <Ellipse Canvas.Left="70" Canvas.Top="75" Width="5" Height="5"
        Fill="Black" />
    <Path Stroke="Blue" StrokeThickness="4"
        Data="M 62,125 Q 95,122 102,108" />
    <Line X1="124" X2="132" Y1="144" Y2="166" Stroke="Blue"
        StrokeThickness="4" />
    <Line X1="114" X2="133" Y1="169" Y2="166" Stroke="Blue"
        StrokeThickness="4" />
    <Line X1="92" X2="82" Y1="146" Y2="168" Stroke="Blue"
        StrokeThickness="4" />
    <Line X1="68" X2="83" Y1="160" Y2="168" Stroke="Blue"
        StrokeThickness="4" />
  </Canvas>
</Window>
```

Figure 34-5 shows the result from the XAML code.

Figure 34-5

All of these WPF elements can be accessed programmatically, even if they are buttons or shapes such as lines or rectangles. Setting the Name property with the Path element to mouth allows you to access this element programmatically with the variable name mouth:

```
<Path Name="mouth" Stroke="Blue" StrokeThickness="4"
    Data="M 62,125 Q 95,122 102,108" />
```

In the code-behind Data property of the Path element, mouth is set to a new geometry. For setting the path, the Path class supports PathGeometry with path markup syntax. The letter M defines the starting point for the path; the letter Q specifies a control point and an endpoint for a quadratic Bézier curve. Running the application, you see the window shown in Figure 34-6.

```
public Window1()
{
    InitializeComponent();
    mouth.Data = Geometry.Parse(
        "M 62,125 Q 95,122 102,128");
}
```

Figure 34-6

Earlier in this chapter, you learned that a button can have content. Making a small change to the XAML code and adding the Button element as content to the window causes the graphic to be displayed inside a button (see Figure 34-7).

```
<Window x:Class="ShapesDemo.Window1"
xmlns="http://schemas.microsoft.com/winfx/2006/xaml/presentation"
    xmlns:x="http://schemas.microsoft.com/winfx/2006/xaml"
    Title="ShapesDemo" Height="260" Width="230">
  <Button Margin="5">
    <Canvas Height="250" Width="220">
      <Ellipse Canvas.Left="50" Canvas.Top="50" Width="100"
          Height="100" Stroke="Blue" StrokeThickness="4"
          Fill="Yellow" />
      <Ellipse Canvas.Left="60" Canvas.Top="65" Width="25"
          Height="25" Stroke="Blue" StrokeThickness="3"
          Fill="White" />
      <Ellipse Canvas.Left="70" Canvas.Top="75" Width="5"
          Height="5" Fill="Black" />
      <Path Name="mouth" Stroke="Blue" StrokeThickness="4"
          Data="M 62,125 Q 95,122 102,108" />
      <Line X1="124" X2="132" Y1="144" Y2="166" Stroke="Blue"
          StrokeThickness="4" />
      <Line X1="114" X2="133" Y1="169" Y2="166" Stroke="Blue"
          StrokeThickness="4" />
      <Line X1="92" X2="82" Y1="146" Y2="168" Stroke="Blue"
          StrokeThickness="4" />
      <Line X1="68" X2="83" Y1="160" Y2="168" Stroke="Blue"
          StrokeThickness="4" />
    </Canvas>
  </Button>
</Window>
```

Figure 34-7

Following are the shapes available in the namespace System.Windows.Shapes.

Shape Class	Description
Line	You can draw a line from the coordinates X1.Y1 to X2.Y2.
Rectangle	With the Rectangle class, you can draw a rectangle by specifying Width and Height.
Ellipse	With the Ellipse class, you can draw an ellipse.
Path	You can use the Path class to draw a series of lines and curves. The Data property is of type Geometry. You can do the drawing by using classes that derive from the base class Geometry, or you can use the path markup syntax to define geometry.
Polygon	You can draw a closed shape formed by connected lines with the Polygon class. The polygon is defined by a series of Point objects assigned to the Points property.
Polyline	Similarly to the Polygon class, you can draw connected lines with the Polyline. The difference is that the poly-line does not need to be a closed shape.

Transformation

Because WPF is based on DirectX, which is vector-based, you can resize every element. The vector-based graphics are now scaled, rotated, and skewed. Hit testing (for example with mouse moves and mouse clicks) is still working without the need for manual position calculation.

Adding the ScaleTransform element to the LayoutTransform property of the Canvas element, as shown, resizes the content of the complete canvas by 2 in X and Y direction.

```
<Canvas.LayoutTransform>
  <ScaleTransform ScaleX="2" ScaleY="2" />
</Canvas.LayoutTransform>
```

Rotation can be done in a similar way as scaling. Using the RotateTransform element you can define the Angle for the rotation.

```
<Canvas.LayoutTransform>
   <RotateTransform Angle="40" />
</Canvas.LayoutTransform>
```

For skewing, you can use the SkewTransform element. With skewing you can assign angles for the X and the Y direction.

```
<Canvas.LayoutTransform>
   <SkewTransform AngleX="20" AngleY="25" />
</Canvas.LayoutTransform>
```

Figure 34-8 shows the results of all the transformations. The figures are placed inside a StackPanel. Starting from the left side, the first figure is resized, the second figure rotated, and the third figure skewed. To more easily see the difference, the Background property of the Canvas elements are set to different colors.

Figure 34-8

Brushes

This section illustrates how to use the brushes that WPF offers for drawing backgrounds and foregrounds. Throughout this section, we will reference Figure 34-9, which shows the effects of using various brushes within the Background of Button elements.

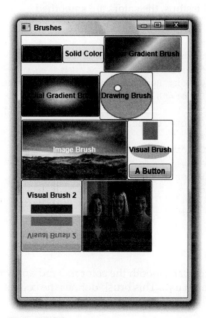

Figure 34-9

SolidColorBrush

The first button in Figure 34-9 uses the SolidColorBrush, which, by name, uses a solid color. The complete area is drawn with the same color.

You can define a solid color just by setting the `Background` attribute to a string that defines a solid color. The string is converted to a `SolidColorBrush` element.

```
<Button Height="30" Background="Purple">Solid Color</Button>
```

Of course, you will get the same effect by setting the `Background` child element and adding a `SolidColorBrush` element as its content. The second button in the application is using the solid color `Yellow` for the background.

```
<Button Height="30" >
    <Button.Background>
        <SolidColorBrush>Yellow</SolidColorBrush>
    </Button.Background>
    Solid Color
</Button>
```

LinearGradientBrush

For a smooth color change, you can use the `LinearGradientBrush`, as shown with the third button. This brush defines the `StartPoint` and `EndPoint` properties. With this, you can assign two-dimensional coordinates for the linear gradient. The default gradient is diagonal linear from $0, 0$ to $1, 1$. By defining different values, the gradient can take different directions. For example, with a `StartPoint` of $0, 0$ and an `EndPoint` of $0, 1$ you get a vertical gradient. The same `StartPoint` and an `EndPoint` value of $1, 0$ creates a horizontal gradient.

With the content of this brush, you can define the color values at the specified offsets with the `GradientStop` element. Between the stops, the colors are smoothed.

```
<Button Height="60">
    <Button.Background>
        <LinearGradientBrush StartPoint="0,0"
            EndPoint="0.5,1.2">
            <GradientStop Color="Red" Offset="0"></GradientStop>
            <GradientStop Color="Blue" Offset="0.2">
            </GradientStop>
            <GradientStop Color="BlanchedAlmond" Offset="0.7">
            </GradientStop>
            <GradientStop Color="DarkOrange" Offset="1">
            </GradientStop>
        </LinearGradientBrush>
    </Button.Background>
    Linear Gradient Brush
</Button>
```

RadialGradientBrush

With the `RadialGradientBrush` you can smooth the color in a radiant way. In Figure 34-9, the fourth button is using the `RadialGradientBrush`. This brush defines the color start with the `GradientOrigin` point.

```
<Button Height="70" >
    <Button.Background>
        <RadialGradientBrush Center="0.5,0.5"
            GradientOrigin="0.5,0.5"
            RadiusX="0.5" RadiusY="0.5" SpreadMethod="Pad">
```

```
        <GradientStop Color="White" Offset="0" />
        <GradientStop Color="LightBlue" Offset="0.4" />
        <GradientStop Color="DarkBlue" Offset="1" />
      </RadialGradientBrush>
    </Button.Background>
    Radial Gradient Brush
  </Button>
```

DrawingBrush

The DrawingBrush allows you to define a drawing that is painted with the brush. The drawing that is shown with the brush is defined within a GeometryDrawing element. The GeometryGroup, which you can see within the Geometry property, consists of Geometry elements such as EllipseGeometry, LineGeometry, RectangleGeometry, and CombinedGeometry.

```
      <Button Height="80">
        <Button.Background>
          <DrawingBrush>
            <DrawingBrush.Drawing>
              <GeometryDrawing Brush="LightBlue">
                <GeometryDrawing.Geometry>
                  <GeometryGroup>
                    <EllipseGeometry RadiusX="30" RadiusY="30"
                        Center="20,20" />
                    <EllipseGeometry RadiusX="4" RadiusY="4"
                        Center="10,10" />
                  </GeometryGroup>
                </GeometryDrawing.Geometry>
                <GeometryDrawing.Pen>
                  <Pen>
                    <Pen.Brush>Red
                    </Pen.Brush>
                  </Pen>
                </GeometryDrawing.Pen>
              </GeometryDrawing>
            </DrawingBrush.Drawing>
          </DrawingBrush>
        </Button.Background>
        Drawing Brush
      </Button>
```

ImageBrush

To load an image into a brush, you can use the ImageBrush element. With this element, the image defined by the ImageSource property is displayed.

```
      <Button Height="100">
        <Button.Background>
          <ImageBrush
              ImageSource=" C:\Windows\Web\Wallpaper\img21.bmp"
          />
        </Button.Background>
        <Button.Foreground>White</Button.Foreground>
        Image Brush
      </Button>
```

VisualBrush

The `VisualBrush` allows you to use other WPF elements in a brush. Here, you can add a WPF element to the `Visual` property. The seventh button in Figure 34-9 contains a `Rectangle`, an `Ellipse`, and a `Button`.

```
<Button Height="100">
    <Button.Background>
        <VisualBrush >
            <VisualBrush.Visual>
                <StackPanel Background="White">
                    <Rectangle Width="25" Height="25"
                        Fill="LightCoral" Margin="2" />
                    <Ellipse Width="65" Height="20"
                        Fill="Aqua" Margin="5" />
                    <Button Margin="2">A Button</Button>
                </StackPanel>
            </VisualBrush.Visual>
        </VisualBrush>
    </Button.Background>
    Visual Brush
</Button>
```

With the `VisualBrush`, you can also create effects such as reflection. The button shown here contains a `StackPanel` that itself contains a `Border` and a `Rectangle`. The `Border` contains a `StackPanel` with a `Label` and a `Rectangle`. But that's not the real point here. The second `Rectangle` is filled with a `VisualBrush`. This brush defines an opacity value and a transformation. The `Visual` property is bound to the `Border` element. The transformation is done by setting the `RelativeTransform` property of the `VisualBrush`. This transformation is using relative coordinates. By setting `ScaleY` to -1, a reflection in Y direction is done. `TranslateTransform` moves the transformation in Y direction so that the reflection is below the original object. You can see the result in the eighth button ("Visual Brush 2") in Figure 34-9.

Data Binding and the Binding element that is used here are explained in detail in the next chapter, "Advanced WPF."

```
<Button Height="120">
    <StackPanel>
        <Border x:Name="reflected">
            <Border.Background>Yellow</Border.Background>
            <StackPanel>
                <Label>Visual Brush 2</Label>
                <Rectangle Width="70" Height="15" Margin="2"
                    Fill="BlueViolet" />
            </StackPanel>
        </Border>
        <Rectangle Height="30">
            <Rectangle.Fill>
                <VisualBrush Opacity="0.35" Stretch="None"
                        Visual="{Binding ElementName=reflected}">
                    <VisualBrush.RelativeTransform>
                        <TransformGroup>
                            <ScaleTransform ScaleX="1" ScaleY="-1"
                            />
                            <TranslateTransform Y="1" />
                        </TransformGroup>
                    </VisualBrush.RelativeTransform>
                </VisualBrush>
            </Rectangle.Fill>
```

```
        </Rectangle>
      </StackPanel>
    </Button>
```

You can also use the `VisualBrush` to display a video, simply by setting the `Visual` property to a `MediaElement`. With the `MediaControl`, the `Source` property is set to a WMV file. In Figure 34-9, the ninth button showing the three women meant to serve as an example of displaying a video. However, in a print media it is difficult to show a video. You can try that on your own — and if you've the Ultimate edition of Windows Vista you will find the same video on your hard disk. Otherwise just select a different video file.

```
<Button Height="120">
    <Button.Background>
        <VisualBrush>
            <VisualBrush.Visual>
                <MediaElement x:Name="video"
                    Source="C:\Windows\ehome\ColorTint.wmv" />
            </VisualBrush.Visual>
        </VisualBrush>
    </Button.Background>
</Button>
```

Controls

You can use hundreds of controls with WPF. For a better understanding, the controls are categorized into these groups:

❑ Simple controls

❑ Content controls

❑ Headered content controls

❑ Items controls

❑ Headered items controls

Simple Controls

Simple controls are controls that don't have a `Content` property. With the `Button` class, you have seen that the `Button` can contain any shape, or any element you like. This is not possible with simple controls. The following table shows simple controls and their functionality.

Simple Control	Description
PasswordBox	This control is used to enter a password and has specific properties for password input, for example, `PasswordChar` to define the character that should show up as the user enters the password, or `Password` to access the password entered. The `PasswordChanged` event is invoked as soon as the password is changed.
ScrollBar	This control contains a `Thumb` where the user can select a value. A scroll bar can be used, for example, if a document doesn't fit on the screen. Some controls contain scroll bars that show up if the content is too big.

Simple Control	Description
ProgressBar	With this control, you can indicate the progress of a lengthy operation.
Slider	With this control, the user can select a range of values by moving a Thumb. ScrollBar, ProgressBar, and Slider are derived from the same base class, RangeBase.
TextBox	Used to display simple unformatted text.
RichTextBox	Supports rich text with the help of the FlowDocument class. RichTextBox and TextBox are derived from the same base class, TextBoxBase.

Although simple controls do not have a Content property, you can completely customize the look of the control by defining a template. Templates are discussed later in this chapter.

Content Controls

A ContentControl has a Content property, with which you can add any content to the control. The Button class derives from the base class ContentControl, so you can add any content to this control. In a previous example, you saw a Canvas control within the Button. Content controls are described in the following table.

ContentControl Controls	Description
Button RepeatButton ToggleButton CheckBox RadioButton	The classes Button, RepeatButton, ToggleButton, and GridViewColumnHeader are derived from the same base class, ButtonBase. All buttons react to the Click event. The RepeatButton raises the Click event repeatedly until the button is released. ToggleButton is the base class for CheckBox and RadioButton. These buttons have an on and off state. The CheckBox can be selected and cleared by the user; the RadioButton can be selected by the user. Clearing the RadioButton must be done programmatically.
Label	The Label class represents the text label for a control. This class also has support for access keys, for example, a menu command.
Frame	The Frame control supports navigation. You can navigate to a page content with the Navigate() method. If the content is a Web page, then a browser control is used for display.
ListBoxItem	ListBoxItem is an item inside a ListBox control.
StatusBarItem	StatusBarItem is an item inside a StatusBar control.
ScrollViewer	The ScrollViewer control is a content control that includes scroll bars. You can put any content in this control; the scroll bars will show up as needed.
ToolTip	ToolTip creates a pop-up Window to display additional information for a control.

ContentControl Controls	Description
UserControl	Using the class UserControl as a base class provides a simple way to create custom controls. However, the base class UserControl does not support templates.
Window	The Window class allows you to create windows and dialog boxes. With the Window class, you get a frame with minimize/maximize/close buttons and a system menu. When showing a dialog box, you can use the method ShowDialog(); the method Show() opens a window.
NavigationWindow	The class NavigationWindow derives from the Window class and supports content navigation.

Only a Frame control is contained within the Window of the following XAML code. The Source property is set to http://www.wrox.com, so the Frame control navigates to this Web site, as you can see in Figure 34-10.

```
<Window x:Class="FrameSample.Window1"
xmlns="http://schemas.microsoft.com/winfx/2006/xaml/presentation"
    xmlns:x="http://schemas.microsoft.com/winfx/2006/xaml"
    Title="Frame Sample" Height="400" Width="400">
  <Frame Source="http://www.wrox.com" />
</Window>
```

Figure 34-10

Headered Content Controls

Content controls with a header are derived from the base class `HeaderedContentControl`, which itself is derived from the base class `ContentControl`. The class `HeaderedContentControl` has a property `Header` to define the content of the header and `HeaderTemplate` for complete customization of the header. The controls that are derived from the base class `HeaderedContentControl` are listed in the following table.

HeaderedContentControl	Description
Expander	With the `Expander` control, you can create an "advanced" mode with a dialog box that, by default, does not show all information but that can be expanded by the user to show more information. In the unexpanded mode, header information is shown. In expanded mode, the content is visible.
GroupBox	The `GroupBox` control provides a border and a header to group controls.
TabItem	`TabItem` controls are items within the class `TabControl`. The `Header` property of the `TabItem` defines the content of the header shown with the tabs of the `TabControl`.

A simple use of the `Expander` control is shown in the next example. The `Expander` control has the property `Header` set to `Click for more`. This text is displayed for expansion. The content of this control is shown only if the control is expanded. Figure 34-11 shows the sample application with a collapsed `Expander` control. Figure 34-12 shows the same application with an expanded `Expander` control.

```
<Window x:Class="ExpanderSample.Window1"
        xmlns="http://schemas.microsoft.com/winfx/2006/xaml/presentation"
    xmlns:x="http://schemas.microsoft.com/winfx/2006/xaml"
    Title="Expander Sample" Height="300" Width="300">
    <StackPanel>
      <TextBlock>Short information</TextBlock>
      <Expander Header="Click for more">
          <Border Height="200" Width="200" Background="Yellow">
              <TextBlock HorizontalAlignment="Center"
                  VerticalAlignment="Center">
                  More information here!
              </TextBlock>
          </Border>
      </Expander>
    </StackPanel>
</Window>
```

To make the header text of the `Expander` *control change when the control is expanded, you can create a trigger. Triggers are explained later in this chapter.*

Figure 34-11

Figure 34-12

Items Controls

The class ItemsControl contains a list of items that can be accessed with the Items property. Classes that are derived from ItemsControl are shown in the following table.

ItemsControl	Description
Menu ContextMenu	The classes Menu and ContextMenu are derived from the abstract base class MenuBase. You can offer menus to the user by placing MenuItem elements in the items list and associating commands.
StatusBar	The StatusBar control is usually shown at the bottom of an application to give status information to the user. You can put StatusBarItem elements inside a StatusBar list.
TreeView	For a hierarchical display of items, you can use the TreeView control.
ListBox ComboBox TabControl	ListBox, ComboBox, and TabControl have the same abstract base class, Selector. This base class makes it possible to select items from a list. The ListBox displays the items from a list. The ComboBox has an additional Button control to display the items only if the button is clicked. With the TabControl, content can be arranged in tabular form.

Headered Items Controls

HeaderedItemsControl is the base class of controls that include items but also has a header. The class HeaderedItemsControl is derived from ItemsControl.

Classes that are derived from HeaderedItemsControl are listed in the following table.

HeaderedItemsControl	Description
MenuItem	The menu classes Menu and ContextMenu include items of type MenuItem. Menu items can be connected to commands, as the MenuItem class implements the interface ICommandSource.
TreeViewItem	The TreeView class can include items of type TreeViewItem.
ToolBar	The ToolBar control is a container for a group of controls, usually Button and Separator elements. You can place the ToolBar inside a ToolBarTray that handles rearranging of ToolBar controls.

Layout

To define the layout of the application, you can use a class that derives from the Panel base class. Several layout containers are available that are discussed here. A layout container needs to do two main tasks: measure and arrange. With measuring, the container asks its children for the preferred sizes. Because the complete size answered by the controls might not be available, the container next decides and arranges the size and positions of its children.

StackPanel

The Window can contain just a single element as content. If you want to have more than one element inside there, then you can use a StackPanel as a child of the Window, and add elements to the content of the StackPanel. The StackPanel is a simple container control that just shows one element after the other. The orientation of the StackPanel can be horizontal or vertical. The class ToolBarPanel is derived from StackPanel.

```
<Window x:Class="LayoutSamples.Window1"
xmlns="http://schemas.microsoft.com/winfx/2006/xaml/presentation"
    xmlns:x="http://schemas.microsoft.com/winfx/2006/xaml"
    Title="Layout Samples" Height="300" Width="283">
  <StackPanel Orientation="Vertical">
    <Label>Label</Label>
    <TextBox>TextBox</TextBox>
    <CheckBox>Checkbox</CheckBox>
    <CheckBox>Checkbox</CheckBox>
    <ListBox>
      <ListBoxItem>ListBoxItem One</ListBoxItem>
      <ListBoxItem>ListBoxItem Two</ListBoxItem>
    </ListBox>
    <Button>Button</Button>
  </StackPanel>
</Window>
```

You can see the child controls of the StackPanel organized vertically in Figure 34-13.

> For data-binding items to a StackPanel, if there is not enough space for all items to display, then you can use the VirtualizingStackPanel instead. With this panel, only the items shown are generated.

Figure 34-13

WrapPanel

The Wrap Panel positions the children from left to right, one after the other, as long as they fit into the line, and then continues with the next line. The orientation of the panel can be horizontal or vertical.

```
<Window x:Class="LayoutSamples.WrapPanelDemo"
xmlns="http://schemas.microsoft.com/winfx/2006/xaml/presentation"
    xmlns:x="http://schemas.microsoft.com/winfx/2006/xaml"
    Title="Layout Samples" Height="160" Width="250">
  <WrapPanel>
    <Button Width="100">Button</Button>
    <Button Width="100">Button</Button>
    <Button Width="100">Button</Button>
    <Button Width="100">Button</Button>
    <Button Width="100">Button</Button>
    <Button Width="100">Button</Button>
    <Button Width="100">Button</Button>
    <Button Width="100">Button</Button>
  </WrapPanel>
</Window>
```

Figure 34-14 shows the output of the panel. If you resize the application, then the buttons will be rearranged so that they fit into a line.

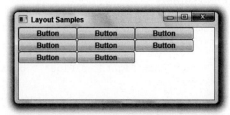

Figure 34-14

Canvas

Canvas is a panel that allows you to explicitly position controls. Canvas defines the attached properties Left, Right, Top, and Bottom that can be used by the children for positioning within the panel.

```
<Window x:Class="LayoutSamples.CanvasDemo"
xmlns="http://schemas.microsoft.com/winfx/2006/xaml/presentation"
    xmlns:x="http://schemas.microsoft.com/winfx/2006/xaml"
    Title="Layout Samples" Height="300" Width="300">
  <Canvas Background="LightBlue">
    <Label Canvas.Top="30" Canvas.Left="20">Enter here:</Label>
    <TextBox Canvas.Top="30" Canvas.Left="130" Width="100"></TextBox>
    <Button Canvas.Top="70" Canvas.Left="130">Click Me!</Button>
  </Canvas>
</Window>
```

Figure 34-15 shows the output of the Canvas panel with the positioned children Label, TextBox, and Button.

Figure 34-15

DockPanel

The DockPanel is very similar to the Windows Forms docking functionality. Here, you can specify the area where child controls should be arranged. DockPanel defines the attached property Dock, which you can set in the children of the controls to the values Left, Right, Top, and Bottom. Figure 34-16 shows the outcome of text blocks with borders that are arranged in the dock panel. For easier differentiation, different colors are specified for the various areas.

```
<Window x:Class="LayoutSamples.DockPanelDemo"
xmlns="http://schemas.microsoft.com/winfx/2006/xaml/presentation"
    xmlns:x="http://schemas.microsoft.com/winfx/2006/xaml"
    Title="Layout Samples" Height="300" Width="300">
  <DockPanel Background="LightBlue">
    <Border Height="25" Background="AliceBlue" DockPanel.Dock="Top">
      <TextBlock>Menu</TextBlock>
    </Border>
    <Border Height="25" Background="Aqua" DockPanel.Dock="Top">
      <TextBlock>Toolbar</TextBlock>
    </Border>
    <Border Height="30" Background="LightSteelBlue" DockPanel.Dock="Bottom">
      <TextBlock>Status</TextBlock>
    </Border>
    <Border Width="80" Background="Azure" DockPanel.Dock="Left">
      <TextBlock>Left Side</TextBlock>
    </Border>
    <Border Background="HotPink">
      <TextBlock>Remaining Part</TextBlock>
    </Border>
  </DockPanel>
</Window>
```

Figure 34-16

Grid

Using the Grid, you can arrange your controls with rows and columns. For every column, you can specify a ColumnDefinition. For every row, you can specify a RowDefinition. The sample code lists two columns and three rows. With each column and row, you can specify the width or height. ColumnDefinition has a Width dependency property; RowDefinition has a Height dependency property. You can define the height and width in pixels, centimeters, inches, or points, or by setting it to Auto to determine the size depending on the content. The grid also allows star sizing, whereby the space for the rows and columns is calculated according to the available space and relative to other rows and columns. When providing the available space for a column, you can set the Width property to *. To have the size doubled for another column, you specify 2*. The sample code, which defines two columns and three rows, doesn't define additional settings with the column and row definitions; the default is the star setting.

The grid contains several Label and TextBox controls. Because the parent of these controls is a grid, you can set the attached properties Column, ColumnSpan, Row, and RowSpan.

```
<Window x:Class="LayoutSamples.GridDemo"
xmlns="http://schemas.microsoft.com/winfx/2006/xaml/presentation"
    xmlns:x="http://schemas.microsoft.com/winfx/2006/xaml"
    Title="Layout Samples" Height="300" Width="283">
  <Grid ShowGridLines="True">
    <Grid.ColumnDefinitions>
      <ColumnDefinition />
      <ColumnDefinition />
    </Grid.ColumnDefinitions>
    <Grid.RowDefinitions>
      <RowDefinition />
      <RowDefinition />
      <RowDefinition />
    </Grid.RowDefinitions>
    <Label Grid.Column="0" Grid.ColumnSpan="2" Grid.Row="0"
        VerticalAlignment="Center" HorizontalAlignment="Center">Title</Label>
    <Label Grid.Column="0" Grid.Row ="1" VerticalAlignment="Center">
        Firstname:</Label>
    <TextBox Grid.Column="1" Grid.Row="1" Width="100" Height="30"></TextBox>
```

(continued)

1175

(continued)

```
    <Label Grid.Column="0" Grid.Row ="2" VerticalAlignment="Center">
        Lastname:</Label>
    <TextBox Grid.Column="1" Grid.Row="2" Width="100" Height="30"></TextBox>
</Grid>
</Window>
```

The outcome arranging controls in a grid is shown in Figure 34-17. For easier viewing of the columns and rows, the property ShowGridLines is set to true.

Figure 34-17

For a grid where every cell has the same size, you can use the UniformGrid *class.*

Event Handling

WPF classes define events where you can add your handlers. For example, you can add MouseEnter, MouseLeave, MouseMove, Click, and the like. This is based on the events and delegates mechanism on .NET. Chapter 7, "Delegates and Events," covers the event and delegate architecture of .NET.

With WPF, you can assign the event handler either with XAML or in the code behind. With button1, the XML attribute Click is used to assign the method button_Click to the click event. button2 has no event handler assigned in XAML:

```
    <Button Name="button1" Click="button_Click">Button 1</Button>
    <Button Name="button2"> Button 2</Button>
```

The Click event for button2 is assigned in the code behind by creating an instance of the delegate RoutedEventHandler and passing the method button_Click to the delegate. The method button_Click() that is invoked from both buttons has arguments as defined by the RoutedEventHandler delegate:

```
    public Window1()
    {
        InitializeComponent();
        button2.Click += button_Click;
    }
    void button_Click(object sender, RoutedEventArgs e)
    {
        MessageBox.Show("Click Event");
    }
```

The event-handling mechanism for WPF is based on .NET events but extended with bubbling and tunneling features. As you have already learned, a Button can contain graphics, list boxes, another button, and so on. What happens if a CheckBox is contained inside a Button and you click the CheckBox? Where should the event arrive? The answer is that the event is bubbled. First, the Click event arrives with the CheckBox, and then it bubbles up to the Button. This way, you can handle the Click event for all elements that are inside the Button with the Button.

Some events are tunneling events; others are bubbling events. A tunneling event first arrives with the outer element and tunnels to the inner elements. Bubbling events start with the inner element and bubble to the outer elements. Tunneling and bubbling events are usually paired. Tunneling events are prefixed with Preview, for example, PreviewMouseMove. This event tunnels from the outer controls to the inner controls. After the PreviewMouseMove event, the MouseMove event occurs. This event is a bubbling event that goes from the inner to the outer controls.

You can stop tunneling and bubbling by setting the Handled property of the event argument to true. The Handled property is a member of the RoutedEventArgs class. All event handlers that participate with the tunneling and bubbling facility have an event argument of type RoutedEventArgs or a type that derives from RoutedEventArgs.

If you stop the tunneling of an event by setting the Handled property to true, then the bubbling event that follows the tunneling event will not happen anymore.

Styles, Templates, and Resources

You can define the look and feel of the WPF elements by setting properties, such as FontSize and Background, with the Button element as shown:

```
<StackPanel>
   <Button Name="button1" Width="150" FontSize="12" Background="AliceBlue">
      Click Me!
   </Button>
</StackPanel>
```

Instead of defining the look and feel with every element, you can define styles that are stored with resources. To completely customize the look for controls, you can use templates and store them into resources.

Styles

To define styles, you can use a Style element containing Setter elements. With the Setter, you specify the Property and the Value of the style, for example, the property Button.Background and the value AliceBlue.

To assign the styles to specific elements, you can assign a style to all elements of a type or use a key for the style. To assign a style to all elements of a type, use the TargetType property of the Style and assign it to a Button by specifying the x:Type markup extension {x:Type Button}.

```
<Window.Resources>
  <Style TargetType="{x:Type Button}">
    <Setter Property="Button.Background" Value="LemonChiffon"
    />
    <Setter Property="Button.FontSize" Value="18" />
  </Style>
  <Style x:Key="ButtonStyle">
    <Setter Property="Button.Background" Value="AliceBlue" />
```

(continued)

(continued)

```
            <Setter Property="Button.FontSize" Value="18" />
        </Style>
    </Window.Resources>
```

In the following XAML code, `button2`, which doesn't have a style defined with the element properties, gets the style that is defined for the `Button` type. For `button3`, the `Style` property is set with the `StaticResource` markup extension to `{StaticResource ButtonStyle}`, whereas `ButtonStyle` specifies the key value of the style resource defined earlier, so `button3` has an aliceblue background.

```
<Button Name="button2" Width="150">Click Me!</Button>
<Button Name="button3" Width="150" Style="{StaticResource ButtonStyle}">
  Click Me, Too!
</Button>
```

Instead of setting the `Background` of a button to just a single value, you can also do more. You can set the `Background` property to a `LinearGradientBrush` with a gradient color definition as shown:

```
    <Style x:Key="FancyButtonStyle">
        <Setter Property="Button.FontSize" Value="22" />
        <Setter Property="Button.Foreground" Value="White" />
        <Setter Property="Button.Background">
          <Setter.Value>
            <LinearGradientBrush StartPoint="0.5,0"
                EndPoint="0.5,1">
              <GradientStop Offset="0.0" Color="LightCyan" />
              <GradientStop Offset="0.14" Color="Cyan" />
              <GradientStop Offset="0.7" Color="DarkCyan" />
            </LinearGradientBrush>
          </Setter.Value>
        </Setter>
    </Style>
```

`button4` has the fancy style with the linear gradient cyan color applied:

```
<Button Name="button4" Width="200" Style="{StaticResource FancyButtonStyle}">
  Fancy!
</Button>
```

You can see the results of all these buttons styled in Figure 34-18.

Figure 34-18

Resources

As you have seen with the styles sample, usually styles are stored within resources. You can define any element within a resource. For example, the brush created earlier for the background style of the button can itself be defined as a resource, so you can use it everywhere a brush is required.

The following example defines a LinearGradientBrush with the key name MyGradientBrush inside the StackPanel resources. button1 assigns the Background property by using a StaticResource markup extension to the resource MyGradientBrush. Figure 34-19 shows the output from this XAML code:

```xml
<Window x:Class="ResourcesSample.Window1"
            xmlns="http://schemas.microsoft.com/winfx/2006/xaml/presentation"
    xmlns:x="http://schemas.microsoft.com/winfx/2006/xaml"
    Title="Resources" Height="100" Width="300">
  <Window.Resources>
  </Window.Resources>
  <StackPanel>
    <StackPanel.Resources>
      <LinearGradientBrush x:Key="MyGradientBrush"
          StartPoint="0.5,0" EndPoint="0.5,1">
        <GradientStop Offset="0.0" Color="LightCyan" />
        <GradientStop Offset="0.14" Color="Cyan" />
        <GradientStop Offset="0.7" Color="DarkCyan" />
      </LinearGradientBrush>
    </StackPanel.Resources>
    <Button Name="button1" Width="200" Height="50"
      Foreground="White"
      Background="{StaticResource MyGradientBrush}">
      Click Me!
    </Button>
  </StackPanel>
</Window>
```

Figure 34-19

Here, the resources have been defined with the StackPanel. In the previous example, the resources were defined with the Window element. The base class FrameworkElement defines the property Resources of type ResourceDictionary. That's why resources can be defined with every class that is derived from the FrameworkElement—any WPF element.

Resources are searched hierarchically. If you define the resource with the window, it applies to every child element of the window. If the Window contains a Grid, and the Grid contains a StackPanel, and if you define the resource with the StackPanel, then the resource applies to every control within the StackPanel. If the StackPanel contains a Button, and you define the resource just with the Button, then this style is valid just for the button.

In regard to hierarchies, you need to pay attention if you use the TargetType without a Key for styles. If you define a resource with the Canvas element and set the TargetType for the style to apply to TextBox elements, then the style applies to all TextBox elements within the Canvas. The style even applies to TextBox elements that are contained in a ListBox when the ListBox is in the Canvas.

If you need the same style for more than one Window, then you can define the style with the application. In a Visual Studio WPF project, the file App.xaml is created for defining global resources of the application. The application styles are valid for every window of the application. Every element can access resources that are defined with the application. If resources are not found with the parent window, then the search for resources continues with the Application.

```
<Application x:Class="ResourcesSample.App"
xmlns="http://schemas.microsoft.com/winfx/2006/xaml/presentation"
    xmlns:x="http://schemas.microsoft.com/winfx/2006/xaml"
    StartupUri="Window1.xaml">
    <Application.Resources>

    </Application.Resources>
</Application>
```

System Resources

There are also some system-wide resources for colors and fonts that are available for all applications. These resources are defined with the classes `SystemColors`, `SystemFonts`, and `SystemParameters`:

❑ With `SystemColors` you get the color settings for borders, controls, the desktop, and windows, such as `ActiveBorderColor`, `ControlBrush`, `DesktopColor`, `WindowColor`, `WindowBrush`, and so on.

❑ The class `SystemFonts` returns the settings for the fonts of the menu, status bar, and message box. These include `CaptionFont`, `DialogFont`, `MenuFont`, `MessageBoxFont`, `StatusFont`, and so on.

❑ The class `SystemParameters` gives you settings for sizes of menu buttons, cursors, icons, borders, captions, timing information, and keyboard settings, such as `BorderWidth`, `CaptionHeight`, `CaptionWidth`, `MenuButtonWidth`, `MenuPopupAnimation`, `MenuShowDelay`, `SmallIcon-Height`, `SmallIconWidth`, and so on.

Figure 34-20 shows the dialog box where the user can configure these settings. You can find the Appearance dialog box with the Personalization settings in the Control Panel.

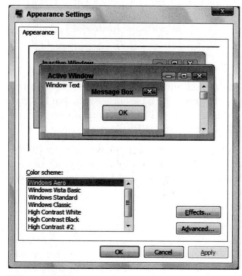

Figure 34-20

Accessing Resources from Code

To access resources from code behind, the base class `FrameworkElement` implements the method `FindResource()`, so you can invoke the `FindResource()` method with every WPF object.

To do this, button1 doesn't have a background specified, but the Click event is assigned to the method button1_Click.

```
<StackPanel Name="myContainer">
  <StackPanel.Resources>
    <LinearGradientBrush x:Key="MyGradientBrush"
        StartPoint="0.5,0" EndPoint="0.5,1">
      <GradientStop Offset="0.0" Color="LightCyan" />
      <GradientStop Offset="0.14" Color="Cyan" />
      <GradientStop Offset="0.7" Color="DarkCyan" />
    </LinearGradientBrush>
  </StackPanel.Resources>
  <Button Name="button1" Width="200" Height="50"
      Click="button1_Click">
    Apply Resource Programmatically
  </Button>
</StackPanel>
```

With the implementation of button1_Click(), the FindResource() method is used on the Button that was clicked. Then a search for the resource MyGradientBrush happens hierarchically, and the brush is applied to the Background property of the control.

```
public void button1_Click(object sender, RoutedEventArgs e)
{
    Control ctrl = sender as Control;
    ctrl.Background =
        ctrl.FindResource("MyGradientBrush") as Brush;
}
```

> If FindResource() **does not find the resource key, then an exception is thrown. If you don't know for sure if the resource is available, then you can use the method** TryFindResource() **instead.** TryFindResource() **returns** null **if the resource is not found.**

Dynamic Resources

With the StaticResource markup extension, resources are searched at load time. If the resource changes while the program is running, then you should use the DynamicResource markup extension instead.

The next example is using the same resource as defined previously. button1 uses the resource as a StaticResource, and button3 uses the resource as a DynamicResource with the DynamicResource markup extension. button2 is used to change the resource programmatically. It has the Click event handler method button2_Click assigned.

```
<Button Name="button1" Width="200" Height="50"
    Background="{StaticResource MyGradientBrush}">
    Static Resource
</Button>
<Button Name="button2" Width="200" Height="50"
    Click="button2_Click">
    Change Resource
</Button>
<Button Name="button3" Width="200" Height="50"
    Background="{DynamicResource MyGradientBrush}">
    Dynamic Resource
</Button>
```

The implementation of button2_Click() clears the resources of the StackPanel and adds a new resource with the same name, MyGradientBrush. This new resource is very similar to the resource that is defined in XAML code; it just defines different colors.

```
public void button2_Click(object sender, RoutedEventArgs e)
{
    myContainer.Resources.Clear();
    LinearGradientBrush brush = new LinearGradientBrush();
    brush.StartPoint = new Point(0.5, 0);
    brush.EndPoint = new Point(0.5, 1);
    GradientStopCollection stops =
        new GradientStopCollection();
    stops.Add(new GradientStop(Colors.White, 0.0));
    stops.Add(new GradientStop(Colors.Yellow, 0.14));
    stops.Add(new GradientStop(Colors.YellowGreen, 0.7));
    brush.GradientStops = stops;
    myContainer.Resources.Add("MyGradientBrush", brush);
}
```

If you run the application and change the resource dynamically by clicking the third button, then button4 immediately gets the new resource. button1, which was defined with the StaticResource, keeps the old resource that was loaded.

> The DynamicResource **requires more performance than the** StaticResource
> **because the resource is always loaded when needed. Use** DynamicResource **only with resources where you expect changes during runtime.**

Triggers

With triggers you can change the look and feel of your controls dynamically because of some events or some property value changes. For example, when the user moves with the mouse over a button, the button can change its look. Usually, you need to do this with the C# code. With WPF, you can also do this with XAML, as long as only the UI is influenced.

The Style class has a Triggers property where you can assign property triggers. The following example includes two TextBox elements inside a Canvas panel. With the Window resources, a style TextBoxStyle is defined that is referenced by the TextBox elements using the Style property. The TextBoxStyle specifies that the Background is set to LightBlue and the FontSize to 17. This is the style of the TextBox elements when the application is started. Using triggers, the style of the controls change. The triggers are defined within the Style.Triggers element, using the Trigger element. One trigger is assigned to the property IsMouseOver; the other trigger is assigned to the property IsKeyboardFocused. Both of these properties are defined with the TextBox class that the style applies to. If IsMouseOver has a value of true, then the trigger fires and sets the Background property to Red and the FontSize property to 22. If the TextBox has a keyboard focus, then the property IsKeyboardFocused is true, and the second trigger fires and sets the Background property of the TextBox to Yellow.

```
<Window x:Class="TriggerSample.Window1"
xmlns="http://schemas.microsoft.com/winfx/2006/xaml/presentation"
    xmlns:x="http://schemas.microsoft.com/winfx/2006/xaml"
    Title="Triggers" Height="200" Width="400">
  <Window.Resources>
    <Style x:Key="TextBoxStyle" TargetType="{x:Type TextBox}">
```

```
          <Setter Property="Background" Value="LightBlue" />
          <Setter Property="FontSize" Value="17" />
          <Style.Triggers>
            <Trigger Property="IsMouseOver" Value="True">
              <Setter Property="Background" Value="Red" />
              <Setter Property="FontSize" Value="22" />
            </Trigger>
            <Trigger Property="IsKeyboardFocused" Value="True">
              <Setter Property="Background" Value="Yellow" />
              <Setter Property="FontSize" Value="22" />
            </Trigger>
          </Style.Triggers>
        </Style>
      </Window.Resources>
      <Canvas>
        <TextBox Canvas.Top="80" Canvas.Left="30" Width="300"
            Style="{StaticResource TextBoxStyle}" />
        <TextBox Canvas.Top="120" Canvas.Left="30" Width="300"
            Style="{StaticResource TextBoxStyle}" />
      </Canvas>
    </Window>
```

You don't need to reset the property values to the original values when the reason for the trigger is not valid anymore. For example, you don't need to define a trigger for IsMouseOver=true and IsMouseOver=false. As soon as the reason for the trigger is no longer valid, the changes made by the trigger action are reset to the original values automatically.

Figure 34-21 shows the trigger sample application, where the first text box has the keyboard input focus, and the second text box has the default values of the style for the background and font size.

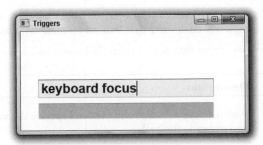

Figure 34-21

> When using property triggers, it is extremely easy to change the look of controls, fonts, colors, opacity, and the like. When the mouse moves over them, the keyboard sets the focus — not a single line of programming code is required.

The Trigger class defines the following properties to specify the trigger action.

Trigger Property	Description
PropertyValue	With property triggers, the Property and Value properties are used to specify when the trigger should fire, for example, Property="IsMouseOver" Value="True".
Setters	As soon as the trigger fires, you can use Setters to define a collection of Setter elements to change values for properties. The Setter class defines the properties Property, TargetName, and Value for the object properties to change.
EnterActions ExitActions	Instead of defining setters, you can define EnterActions and ExitActions. With both of these properties, you can define a collection of TriggerAction elements. EnterActions fires when the trigger starts (with a property trigger, when the Property/Value combination applies); ExitActions fires before it ends (just at the moment when the Property/Value combination no longer applies). Trigger actions that you can specify with these actions are derived from the base class TriggerAction, such as, SoundPlayerAction and BeginStoryboard. With SoundPlayerAction, you can start the playing of sound. BeginStoryboard is used with animation, which will be shown later in this chapter.

Property triggers are just one type of trigger possible in WPF. Another trigger type is event triggers. Event triggers are discussed later in this chapter along with animations.

Templates

In this chapter, you have already seen that a Button control can have any content. The content can be a simple text, but you can also add a Canvas element, which can contain shapes. You can add a Grid, or a video to the button. However, there is even more than that you can do with a button!

In WPF, the functionality of controls is completely separate from their look and feel. A button has a default look, but you can completely customize that look as you like with templates.

WPF gives you several template types that derive from the base class FrameworkTemplate.

Template Type	Description
ControlTemplate	With a ControlTemplate you can specify the visual structure of a control and override the look.
ItemsPanelTemplate	For an ItemsControl you can specify the layout of its items by assigning an ItemsPanelTemplate. Each ItemsControl has a default ItemsPanelTemplate. For the MenuItem, it is a WrapPanel. The StatusBar uses a DockPanel, and the ListBox uses a VirtualizingStackPanel.
DataTemplate	DataTemplates are very useful for graphical representations of objects. Styling a ListBox, you will see that, by default, the items of the ListBox are shown according to the output of the ToString() method. By applying a DataTemplate you can override this behavior and define a custom presentation of the items.
HierarchicalData Template	The HierarchicalDataTemplate is used for arranging a tree of objects. This control supports HeaderedItemsControls, such as TreeViewItem and MenuItem.

The next sample shows several buttons, and later, list boxes are customized step by step, so you can see the intermediate results of the changes. First, start with two very simple buttons, in which the first button doesn't have a style at all. The second button references the style ButtonStyle1 with changes to the Background and the FontSize. You can see this first result in Figure 34-22.

```
<Window x:Class="TemplateSample.Window1"
           xmlns="http://schemas.microsoft.com/winfx/2006/xaml/presentation"
    xmlns:x="http://schemas.microsoft.com/winfx/2006/xaml"
    Title="Template" Height="300" Width="300">
  <Window.Resources>
    <Style x:Key="ButtonStyle1" TargetType="{x:Type Button}">
      <Setter Property="Background" Value="Yellow" />
      <Setter Property="FontSize" Value="18" />
    </Style>
  </Window.Resources>
  <StackPanel>
    <Button Name="button1" Height="50" Width="150">Default Button</Button>
    <Button Name="button2" Height="50" Width="150"
        Style="{StaticResource ButtonStyle1}">Styled Button
    </Button>
  </StackPanel>
</Window>
```

Figure 34-22

Now, add the new style ButtonStyle2 to the resources. This style again sets the TargetType to the Button type. The Setter now specifies the Template property. By specifying the Template property, you can replace the look of the button completely. The value for the Template property is defined by a ControlTemplate element. A ControlTemplate defines the content of a control and allows the accessing of content from the control itself, as you will see soon. Here, the ControlTemplate defines a Grid with two rows. The rows use star sizing where the height of the first row is twice the height of the second row. Then two Rectangle elements are defined. The first rectangle spans both rows, and sets the Stroke property to Green for a green outline, and RadiusX and RadiusY values for rounded corners. The second rectangle, which is only within the first row, has its Fill property set to a linear gradient brush. button3, with the content Template Button, references style ButtonStyle2. Figure 34-23 shows button3 with the new style, but the content is missing.

```
<Window x:Class="TemplateSample.Window1"
xmlns="http://schemas.microsoft.com/winfx/2006/xaml/presentation"
    xmlns:x="http://schemas.microsoft.com/winfx/2006/xaml"
    Title="Template" Height="300" Width="300"
    >
  <Window.Resources>
    <!-- other styles -->
    <Style x:Key="ButtonStyle2" TargetType="{x:Type Button}">
```

(continued)

(continued)

```
          <Setter Property="Template">
            <Setter.Value>
              <ControlTemplate>
                <Grid>
                  <Grid.RowDefinitions>
                    <RowDefinition Height="2*" />
                    <RowDefinition Height="*" />
                  </Grid.RowDefinitions>
                  <Rectangle Grid.RowSpan="2" RadiusX="4" RadiusY="8"
                      Stroke="Green" />
                  <Rectangle RadiusX="4" RadiusY="8" Margin="2">
                    <Rectangle.Fill>
                      <LinearGradientBrush StartPoint="0,0"
                          EndPoint="0,1">
                        <GradientStop Offset="0" Color="LightBlue" />
                        <GradientStop Offset="0.5" Color="#afff" />
                        <GradientStop Offset="1" Color="#6faa" />
                      </LinearGradientBrush>
                    </Rectangle.Fill>
                  </Rectangle>
                </Grid>
              </ControlTemplate>
            </Setter.Value>
          </Setter>
        </Style>
      </Window.Resources>
      <StackPanel>
        <!-- other buttons -->
        <Button Name="button3" Background="Yellow" Height="100"
            Width="220" FontSize="24"
            Style="{StaticResource ButtonStyle2}">
          Template Button
        </Button>
      </StackPanel>
    </Window>
```

Figure 34-23

The button now has a completely different look. However, the content that is defined with the button itself is missing in Figure 34-23. The template created previously must be extended. The first rectangle in the template now has its `Fill` property set to `{TemplateBinding Background}`. The `TemplateBinding` markup extension enables a control template to use content from the templated control. Here, the rectangle is filled with the background that is defined with the button. `button3` defines a yellow background, which is combined with the background from the second rectangle of the control template. After the definition of the second rectangle, the element `ContentPresenter` is used. This element takes the content from the templated control and places it as defined — here on both rows, as `Grid.RowSpan` is set to 2. If a `ContentPresenter` is defined, then the `TargetType` with the `ControlTemplate` must also be set. The content is positioned by setting the `HorizontalAlignment`, `VerticalAlignment`, and `Margin` properties to values defined by the button itself by using `TemplateBinding` markup extensions. With the `ControlTemplate` you can also define triggers, as previously shown within resources. Figure 34-24 shows the new outcome of the button, including the content and the background combined with the template.

```xml
<Style x:Key="ButtonStyle2" TargetType="{x:Type Button}">
  <Setter Property="Template">
    <Setter.Value>
      <ControlTemplate TargetType="{x:Type Button}" >
        <Grid>
          <Grid.RowDefinitions>
            <RowDefinition Height="2*" />
            <RowDefinition Height="*" />
          </Grid.RowDefinitions>
          <Rectangle Grid.RowSpan="2" RadiusX="4" RadiusY="8"
              Stroke="Green"
              Fill="{TemplateBinding Background}" />
          <Rectangle RadiusX="4" RadiusY="8" Margin="2">
            <Rectangle.Fill>
              <LinearGradientBrush StartPoint="0,0"
                  EndPoint="0,1">
                <GradientStop Offset="0" Color="LightBlue" />
                <GradientStop Offset="0.5" Color="#afff" />
                <GradientStop Offset="1" Color="#6faa" />
              </LinearGradientBrush>
            </Rectangle.Fill>
          </Rectangle>
          <ContentPresenter Grid.RowSpan="2"
              HorizontalAlignment="{TemplateBinding
              HorizontalContentAlignment}"
              VerticalAlignment="{TemplateBinding
              VerticalContentAlignment}"
              Margin="{TemplateBinding Padding}" />
        </Grid>
        <ControlTemplate.Triggers>
          <Trigger Property="IsMouseOver" Value="True">
            <Setter Property="Foreground" Value="Aqua" />
          </Trigger>
          <Trigger Property="IsPressed" Value="True">
            <Setter Property="Foreground" Value="Black" />
          </Trigger>
        </ControlTemplate.Triggers>
      </ControlTemplate>
```

(continued)

1187

(continued)

```
                    </Setter.Value>
                </Setter>
            </Style>
        </Window.Resources>
```

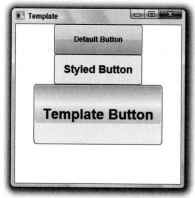

Figure 34-24

Let's make an even fancier button by using transparent features. The style GelButton sets the properties Background, Height, Foreground and Margin, and the Template. The template is the most interesting aspect with this style. The template specifies a Grid with just one row and one column.

Inside this cell, you can find a rectangle with the name GelBackground. This rectangle has rounded corners and a linear gradient brush for the stroke. The rounded corners are defined by the RadiusX and RadiusY settings. The stroke that surrounds the rectangle is very thin because the StrokeThickness is set to 0.35.

The second rectangle, GelShine, is just a small rectangle with a height of 15 pixels, and because of the Margin settings, it is visible within the first rectangle. The stroke is transparent, so there is no line surrounding the rectangle. This rectangle just uses a linear gradient fill brush, which goes from a light, partly transparent color to full transparency. This gives the rectangle a shimmering effect.

After the two rectangles, there is a ContentPresenter element that defines alignment for the content and takes the content from the button to display.

Such a styled button now looks very fancy on the screen. However, there is no action if the mouse is clicked or the mouse moves over the button. With a template-styled button, you must have triggers for the button to appear differently in response to mouse clicks. The property trigger, IsMouseOver, defines a new value for the Rectangle.Fill property with a different color for the radial gradient brush. The rectangle that gets the new fill is referenced with the TargetName property. The property trigger, IsPressed, is very similar; here, simply other radial gradient brush colors are used to fill the rectangle. You can see a button that references the style GelButton in Figure 34-25. Figure 34-26 shows the same button while the mouse moved over it where you can see the effect of the radial gradient brush.

```xml
<Style x:Key="GelButton" TargetType="{x:Type Button}">
  <Setter Property="Background" Value="Black" />
  <Setter Property="Height" Value="40" />
  <Setter Property="Foreground" Value="White" />
  <Setter Property="Margin" Value="3" />
  <Setter Property="Template">
    <Setter.Value>
      <ControlTemplate TargetType="{x:Type Button}">
        <Grid>
          <Rectangle Name="GelBackground" RadiusX="9"
              RadiusY="9"
              Fill="{TemplateBinding Background}"
              StrokeThickness="0.35">
            <Rectangle.Stroke>
              <LinearGradientBrush StartPoint="0,0"
                  EndPoint="0,1">
                <GradientStop Offset="0" Color="White" />
                <GradientStop Offset="1" Color="#666666" />
              </LinearGradientBrush>
            </Rectangle.Stroke>
          </Rectangle>
          <Rectangle Name="GelShine" Margin="2,2,2,0"
              VerticalAlignment="Top" RadiusX="6" RadiusY="6"
              Stroke="Transparent" Height="15px">
            <Rectangle.Fill>
              <LinearGradientBrush StartPoint="0,0"
                  EndPoint="0,1">
                <GradientStop Offset="0" Color="#ccffffff" />
                <GradientStop Offset="1" Color="Transparent"
                />
              </LinearGradientBrush>
            </Rectangle.Fill>
          </Rectangle>
          <ContentPresenter Name="GelButtonContent"
              VerticalAlignment="Center"
              HorizontalAlignment="Center"
              Content="{TemplateBinding Content}" />
        </Grid>
        <ControlTemplate.Triggers>
          <Trigger Property="IsMouseOver" Value="True">
            <Setter Property="Rectangle.Fill"
                TargetName="GelBackground">
              <Setter.Value>
                <RadialGradientBrush>
                  <GradientStop Offset="0" Color="Lime" />
                  <GradientStop Offset="1" Color="DarkGreen"
                  />
                </RadialGradientBrush>
              </Setter.Value>
            </Setter>
            <Setter Property="Foreground" Value="Black" />
          </Trigger>
          <Trigger Property="IsPressed" Value="True">
            <Setter Property="Rectangle.Fill"
```

(continued)

(continued)

```
                        TargetName="GelBackground">
                  <Setter.Value>
                    <RadialGradientBrush>
                      <GradientStop Offset="0" Color="#ffcc34" />
                      <GradientStop Offset="1" Color="#cc9900" />
                    </RadialGradientBrush>
                  </Setter.Value>
                </Setter>
              </Trigger>
            </ControlTemplate.Triggers>
          </ControlTemplate>
        </Setter.Value>
      </Setter>
    </Style>
```

Figure 34-25

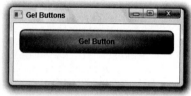

Figure 34-26

Instead of having a rectangular button, an ellipse can be used as a button. In the next example, you can also see how one style can be based on another style.

The style RoundedGelButton can be based on the style GelButton by setting the BasedOn property with the Style element. If one style is based on another style, then the new style gets all settings from the base style unless the settings are redefined. For example, the RoundedGelButtonStyle gets the Foreground and Margin settings from the GelButton because these settings are not redefined. If you change a setting in a base style, then all styles that are based on the style automatically get the new values.

The Height and Template properties are redefined with the new style. Here, the template defines two Ellipse elements instead of rectangles. The outer ellipse GelBackground defines a black ellipse with a gradient stroke around it. The second ellipse is smaller with a small margin (5) at the top and a large margin (50) at the bottom. This ellipse again has a linear gradient brush that goes from a light color to transparent and specifies the shine effect. Again, there are triggers for IsMouseOver and IsPressed that change the value of the Fill property for the first ellipse.

You can see the new button based on the RoundedGelButton style — and it is still a button — in Figure 34-27.

```
<Style x:Key="RoundedGelButton"
    BasedOn="{StaticResource GelButton}"
    TargetType="Button">
  <Setter Property="Width" Value="100" />
  <Setter Property="Height" Value="100" />
  <Setter Property="Grid.Row" Value="2" />
  <Setter Property="Template">
    <Setter.Value>
```

```xml
<ControlTemplate TargetType="{x:Type Button}">
  <Grid>
    <Ellipse Name="GelBackground" StrokeThickness="0.5"
        Fill="Black">
      <Ellipse.Stroke>
        <LinearGradientBrush StartPoint="0,0"
            EndPoint="0,1">
          <GradientStop Offset="0" Color="#ff7e7e7e" />
          <GradientStop Offset="1" Color="Black" />
        </LinearGradientBrush>
      </Ellipse.Stroke>
    </Ellipse>
    <Ellipse Margin="15,5,15,50">
      <Ellipse.Fill>
        <LinearGradientBrush StartPoint="0,0"
            EndPoint="0,1">
          <GradientStop Offset="0" Color="#aaffffff" />
          <GradientStop Offset="1" Color="Transparent"
          />
        </LinearGradientBrush>
      </Ellipse.Fill>
    </Ellipse>
    <ContentPresenter Name="GelButtonContent"
        VerticalAlignment="Center"
        HorizontalAlignment="Center"
        Content="{TemplateBinding Content}" />
  </Grid>
  <ControlTemplate.Triggers>
    <Trigger Property="IsMouseOver" Value="True">
      <Setter Property="Rectangle.Fill"
          TargetName="GelBackground">
        <Setter.Value>
          <RadialGradientBrush>
            <GradientStop Offset="0" Color="Lime" />
            <GradientStop Offset="1" Color="DarkGreen"
            />
          </RadialGradientBrush>
        </Setter.Value>
      </Setter>
      <Setter Property="Foreground" Value="Black" />
    </Trigger>
    <Trigger Property="IsPressed" Value="True">
      <Setter Property="Rectangle.Fill"
          TargetName="GelBackground">
        <Setter.Value>
          <RadialGradientBrush>
            <GradientStop Offset="0" Color="#ffcc34" />
            <GradientStop Offset="1" Color="#cc9900" />
          </RadialGradientBrush>
        </Setter.Value>
      </Setter>
      <Setter Property="Foreground" Value="Black" />
```

(continued)

(continued)

```
            </Trigger>
          </ControlTemplate.Triggers>
        </ControlTemplate>

      </Setter.Value>
    </Setter>
  </Style>
```

Figure 34-27

Styling a ListBox

Changing a style of a button or a label is a simple task. How about changing the style of an element that contains a list of elements. For example, how about changing a `ListBox`? Again, a list box has behavior and a look. It can display a list of elements, and you can select one or more elements from the list. For the behavior, the `ListBox` class defines methods, properties, and events. The look of the `ListBox` is separate from its behavior. The `ListBox` element has a default look, but you can change this look by creating a template.

To display some items in the list, the `Country` class has been created to represent the name and flag with a path to an image. The class `Country` defines the `Name` and `ImagePath` properties, and it has an overridden `ToString()` method for a default string representation:

```
public class Country
{
    public Country(string name)
        : this(name, null)
    {
    }
    public Country(string name, string imagePath)
    {
        this.Name = name;
        this.ImagePath = imagePath;
    }
    public string Name { get; set; }
    public string ImagePath { get; set; }
    public override string ToString()
    {
        return Name;
    }
}
```

The static class `Countries` returns a list of a few countries that will be displayed:

```
public static class Countries
{
    public static IEnumerable<Country> GetCountries()
    {
        List<Country> countries = new List<Country>();
        countries.Add(new Country("Austria",
            "Images/Austria.bmp"));
        countries.Add(new Country("Germany",
            "Images/Germany.bmp"));
        countries.Add(new Country("Norway",
            "Images/Norway.bmp"));
        countries.Add(new Country("USA", "Images/USA.bmp"));
        return countries;
    }
}
```

Inside the code-behind file in the constructor of the `Window1` class, the `DataContext` property of the `Window1` instance is set to the list of countries that is returned from the method `Countries`.`GetCountries()`. (The `DataContext` property is a feature for data binding that we will discuss in the next chapter.)

```
public partial class Window1 : System.Windows.Window
{
    public Window1()
    {
        InitializeComponent();
        this.DataContext = Countries.GetCountries();
    }
}
```

Within the XAML code, the `ListBox` named `countryList1` is defined. `countryList1` doesn't have a different style. It uses the default look from the `ListBox` element. The property `ItemsSource` is set to the `Binding` markup extension, which is used by data binding. From the code behind, you have seen that the binding is done to an array of `Country` objects. Figure 34-28 shows the default look of the `ListBox`. By default, just the names of the countries returned by the `ToString()` method are displayed in a simple list.

```
<Window x:Class="ListboxStyling.Window1"
xmlns="http://schemas.microsoft.com/winfx/2006/xaml/presentation"
    xmlns:x="http://schemas.microsoft.com/winfx/2006/xaml"
    Title="ListBox Styling" Height="300" Width="300">
  <StackPanel>
    <ListBox Name="countryList1" ItemsSource="{Binding}" />
  </StackPanel>
</Window>
```

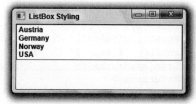

Figure 34-28

The Country objects do have both the name and the flag in the object. Of course, you can also display both values in the list box. To do this, you need to define a template.

The ListBox element contains ListBoxItem elements. You can define the content for an item with the ItemTemplate. The style listBoxStyle1 defines an ItemTemplate with a value of a DataTemplate. A DataTemplate is used to bind data to elements. You can use the Binding markup extension with DataTemplate elements.

The DataTemplate contains a grid with three columns. The first column contains the string Country:. The second column contains the name of the country. The third column contains the flag for the country. Because the country names have different lengths, but the view should be the same size for every country name, the SharedSizeGroup property is set with the second column definition. This shared size information for the column is used only because the property Grid.IsSharedSizeScope is also set.

After the column and row definitions, you can see two TextBlock elements. The first TextBlock element contains the text Country:. The second TextBlock element binds to the Name property that is defined in the Country class.

The content for the third column is a Border element containing a Grid. The Grid contains a Rectangle with a linear gradient brush and an Image element that is bound to the ImagePath property of the Country class. Figure 34-29 shows the countries in a ListBox with completely different output than before.

```
<Window.Resources>
  <Style x:Key="listBoxStyle1" TargetType="{x:Type ListBox}" >
    <Setter Property="ItemTemplate">
      <Setter.Value>
        <DataTemplate>
          <Grid>
            <Grid.ColumnDefinitions>
              <ColumnDefinition Width="Auto" />
              <ColumnDefinition Width="*"
                  SharedSizeGroup="MiddleColumn" />
              <ColumnDefinition Width="Auto" />
            </Grid.ColumnDefinitions>
            <Grid.RowDefinitions>
              <RowDefinition Height="60" />
            </Grid.RowDefinitions>
            <TextBlock FontSize="16" VerticalAlignment="Center"
                Margin="5" FontStyle="Italic"
                Grid.Column="0">Country:</TextBlock>
            <TextBlock FontSize="16" VerticalAlignment="Center"
                Margin="5" Text="{Binding Name}"
                FontWeight="Bold" Grid.Column="1" />
            <Border Margin="4,0" Grid.Column="2"
                BorderThickness="2" CornerRadius="4">
              <Border.BorderBrush>
                <LinearGradientBrush StartPoint="0,0"
                    EndPoint="0,1">
                  <GradientStop Offset="0" Color="#aaa" />
                  <GradientStop Offset="1" Color="#222" />
                </LinearGradientBrush>
              </Border.BorderBrush>
              <Grid>
                <Rectangle>
```

```
            <Rectangle.Fill>
              <LinearGradientBrush StartPoint="0,0"
                  EndPoint="0,1">
                <GradientStop Offset="0" Color="#444" />
                <GradientStop Offset="1" Color="#fff" />
              </LinearGradientBrush>
            </Rectangle.Fill>
          </Rectangle>
          <Image Width="48" Margin="2,2,2,1"
                Source="{Binding ImagePath}" />
        </Grid>
      </Border>
    </Grid>
  </DataTemplate>
</Setter.Value>
</Setter>
<Setter Property="Grid.IsSharedSizeScope" Value="True" />
</Style>
</Window.Resources>
```

Figure 34-29

It is not necessary that a ListBox have items that follow vertically, one after the other. You can give the user a different view with the same functionality. The next style, listBoxStyle2, defines a template in which the items are shown horizontally with a scroll bar.

In the previous example, only an ItemTemplate was created to define how the items should look in the default ListBox. Now, a template is created to define a different ListBox. The template contains a ControlTemplate element to define the elements of the ListBox. The element is now a ScrollViewer — a view with a scroll bar — that contains a StackPanel. As the items should now be listed horizontally, the Orientation of the StackPanel is set to Horizontal. The stack panel will contain the items that are defined with the ItemsTemplate. As a result, the IsItemsHost of the StackPanel element is set to true. IsItemsHost is a property that is available with every Panel element that can contain a list of items.

The ItemTemplate defines the look for the items in the stack panel. Here, a grid with two rows is created. The first row contains Image elements that are bound to the ImagePath property. The second row contains TextBlock elements that are bound to the Name property.

Figure 34-30 shows the `ListBox` styled with `listBoxStyle2` where the scroll bar appears automatically when the view is too small to display all items in the list.

```xml
<Style x:Key="listBoxStyle2" TargetType="{x:Type ListBox}">
  <Setter Property="Template">
    <Setter.Value>
      <ControlTemplate TargetType="{x:Type ListBox}">
        <ScrollViewer HorizontalScrollBarVisibility="Auto">
          <StackPanel Name="StackPanel1" IsItemsHost="True"
              Orientation="Horizontal" />
        </ScrollViewer>
      </ControlTemplate>
    </Setter.Value>
  </Setter>
  <Setter Property="VerticalAlignment" Value="Center" />
  <Setter Property="ItemTemplate">
    <Setter.Value>
      <DataTemplate>
        <Grid>
          <Grid.ColumnDefinitions>
            <ColumnDefinition Width="Auto" />

          </Grid.ColumnDefinitions>
          <Grid.RowDefinitions>
            <RowDefinition Height="60" />
            <RowDefinition Height="30" />
          </Grid.RowDefinitions>
          <Image Grid.Row="0" Width="48" Margin="2,2,2,1"
              Source="{Binding ImagePath}" />
          <TextBlock Grid.Row="1" FontSize="14"
              HorizontalAlignment="Center" Margin="5"
              Text="{Binding Name}" FontWeight="Bold" />
        </Grid>
      </DataTemplate>
    </Setter.Value>
  </Setter>
</Style>
```

Figure 34-30

Certainly you see the advantages of separating the look of the controls from their behavior. You may already have many ideas about how you can display your items in a list that best fits the requirements of your application. Perhaps you just want to display as many items as will fit in the window, position them horizontally, and then continue to the next line vertically. That's where a WrapPanel comes in. And, of course, you can have a WrapPanel inside a template for a ListBox, as shown in listBoxStyle3. Figure 34-31 shows the result of using the WrapPanel.

```xml
<Style x:Key="listBoxStyle3" TargetType="{x:Type ListBox}">
  <Setter Property="Template">
    <Setter.Value>
      <ControlTemplate TargetType="{x:Type ListBox}">
        <ScrollViewer VerticalScrollBarVisibility="Auto"
              HorizontalScrollBarVisibility="Disabled">
          <WrapPanel IsItemsHost="True" />
        </ScrollViewer>
      </ControlTemplate>
    </Setter.Value>
  </Setter>
  <Setter Property="ItemTemplate">
    <Setter.Value>
      <DataTemplate>
        <Grid>
          <Grid.ColumnDefinitions>
            <ColumnDefinition Width="140" />
          </Grid.ColumnDefinitions>
          <Grid.RowDefinitions>
            <RowDefinition Height="60" />
            <RowDefinition Height="30" />
          </Grid.RowDefinitions>
          <Image Grid.Row="0" Width="48" Margin="2,2,2,1"
              Source="{Binding ImagePath}" />
          <TextBlock Grid.Row="1" FontSize="14"
              HorizontalAlignment="Center"
              Margin="5" Text="{Binding Name}" />

        </Grid>
      </DataTemplate>
    </Setter.Value>
  </Setter>
</Style>
```

Figure 34-31

In the next chapter, you can read more about the `DataTemplate` *with data binding functionality.*

Summary

In this chapter, you have taken a first tour through the many features of WPF. WPF makes it easy to separate work between developers and designers. Both Microsoft Expression Blend and Visual Studio make it possible to work with XAML code. Compared to prior Windows Forms applications, XAML code does a better separation of the UI from the functionality behind it. All UI features can be created with XAML, and the functionality by using code behind.

You have seen many controls and containers that are all based on vector-graphics. Because of the vector-graphics, WPF elements can be scaled, sheared, and rotated. Because of the content flexibility of content controls, the event handling mechanism is based on bubbling and tunneling events.

Different kinds of brushes are available to paint background and foreground of elements. You can use solid brushes, linear or radial gradient brushes, but also visual brushes to do reflections or show videos.

Styling and templates allow you to customize the look of controls. Triggers allow you to change properties of WPF elements dynamically. Animations can be done easily by animating a property value from a WPF control.

The next chapter continues with WPF showing animations, 3D, data binding, and several more features.

35

Advanced WPF

In the previous chapter you read about some of the core functionality of WPF. In this chapter programming with WPF continues. Here you read about some important aspects for creating complete applications such as data binding and command handling, and you also get an introduction to animations and 3-D programming.

The main topics of this chapter are:

- ❑ Data binding
- ❑ Commands
- ❑ Animations
- ❑ 3-D
- ❑ Windows Forms integration

Data Binding

In the previous chapter you saw a few features of data binding when styling the ListBox. But of course there is a lot more. WPF data binding takes another huge step forward compared to Windows Forms. This section gives you a good start in data binding with WPF and discusses these topics:

- ❑ Overview
- ❑ Binding with XAML
- ❑ Simple object binding
- ❑ Object data provider
- ❑ List binding
- ❑ Binding to XML

Overview

With WPF data binding, the target can be any dependency property of a WPF element, and every property of a CLR object can be the source. Because a WPF element is implemented as a .NET class, every WPF element can be the source as well. See Figure 35-1 for the connection between the source and the target. The `Binding` object defines the connection.

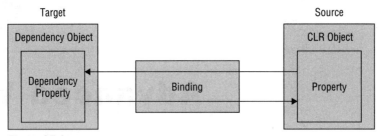

Figure 35-1

Binding supports several binding modes between the target and source. Binding can be *one-way*, where the source information goes to the target, but if the user changes information in the user interface, the source does not get updated. For updates to the source, *two-way* binding is required.

The following table shows the binding modes and their requirements.

Binding Mode	Description
One-time	Binding goes from the source to the target and occurs only once when the application is started or the data context changes. Here, you get a snapshot of the data.
One-way	Binding goes from the source to the target. This is useful for read-only data, because it is not possible to change the data from the user interface. To get updates to the user interface, the source must implement the interface `INotifyPropertyChanged`.
Two-way	With a two-way binding, the user can make changes to the data from the UI. Binding occurs in both directions — from the source to the target and from the target to the source. The source needs to implement read/write properties so that changes can be updated from the UI to the source.
One-way-to-source	With one-way-to-source binding, if the target property changes, the source object gets updated.

Binding with XAML

A WPF element can not only be the target for data binding, it can also be the source. You can bind the source property of one WPF element to the target of another WPF element.

The following code example uses the funny face created earlier, which is built up from WPF shapes and binds it to a slider, so you can move it across the window. The Slider is the source element with the name slider. The property Value gives the actual value of the slider position. The target for data binding is the inner Canvas element. The inner Canvas element with the name FunnyFace contains all the shapes needed to draw the funny face. This canvas is contained within an outer Canvas element, so it is possible to position this canvas within the outer canvas by setting the attached properties. The attached property Canvas.Left is set to the Binding markup extension. In the Binding markup extension, the ElementName is set to slider to reference the WPF slider element, and the Path is set to Value to get the value from the Value property.

```
<Window x:Class="DataBindingSample.Window1"
    xmlns="http://schemas.microsoft.com/winfx/2006/xaml/presentation"
    xmlns:x="http://schemas.microsoft.com/winfx/2006/xaml"
    Title="Data Binding" Height="345" Width="310">
    <StackPanel>
      <Canvas Height="210" Width="280">
        <Canvas Canvas.Top="0"
                Canvas.Left="{Binding Path=Value, ElementName=slider}"
                Name="FunnyFace" Height="210" Width="230">
          <Ellipse Canvas.Left="20" Canvas.Top="50" Width="100" Height="100"
              Stroke="Blue" StrokeThickness="4" Fill="Yellow" />
          <Ellipse Canvas.Left="40" Canvas.Top="65" Width="25" Height="25"
              Stroke="Blue" StrokeThickness="3" Fill="White" />
          <Ellipse Canvas.Left="50" Canvas.Top="75" Width="5" Height="5"
              Fill="Black" />
          <Path Name="mouth" Stroke="Blue" StrokeThickness="4"
              Data="M 32,125 Q 65,122 72,108" />

          <Line X1="94" X2="102" Y1="144" Y2="166" Stroke="Blue"
              StrokeThickness="4" />
          <Line X1="84" X2="103" Y1="169" Y2="166" Stroke="Blue"
              StrokeThickness="4" />

          <Line X1="62" X2="52" Y1="146" Y2="168" Stroke="Blue"
              StrokeThickness="4" />
          <Line X1="38" X2="53" Y1="160" Y2="168" Stroke="Blue"
              StrokeThickness="4" />
        </Canvas>
      </Canvas>

      <Slider Name="slider" Orientation="Horizontal" Value="10"
          Maximum="100" />

    </StackPanel>
</Window>
```

When running the application, you can move the slider and make the funny face move, as you can see in Figures 35-2 and 35-3.

Instead of defining the binding information with XAML code, as was done in the preceding code with the Binding metadata extension, you can do it with code behind. Have one more look at the XAML version of binding:

```
<Canvas Canvas.Top="0"
    Canvas.Left="{Binding Path=Value, ElementName=slider}"
    Name="FunnyFace" Height="210" Width="230">
```

With code behind you have to create a new `Binding` object and set the `Path` and `Source` properties. The `Source` property must be set to the source object; here, it is the WPF object `slider`. The `Path` is set to a `PropertyPath` instance that is initialized with the name of the property of the source object, `Value`.

Figure 35-2

Figure 35-3

With the target, you can invoke the method `SetBinding()` to define the binding. Here, the target is the `Canvas` object with the name `FunnyFace`. The method `SetBinding()` requires two parameters: the first one is a dependency property and the second one is the binding object. The `Canvas.Left` property should be bound, so the dependency property of type `DependencyProperty` can be accessed with the `Canvas.LeftProperty` field:

```
Binding binding = new Binding();
binding.Path = new PropertyPath("Value");
binding.Source = slider;

FunnyFace.SetBinding(Canvas.LeftProperty, binding);
```

You can configure a number of binding options with the `Binding` class, as described in the following table.

Binding Class Members	Description
Source	With the `Source` property, you define the source object for data binding.
RelativeSource	With `RelativeSource`, you can specify the source in relation to the target object. This is useful to display error messages when the source of the error comes from the same control.
ElementName	If the source is a WPF element, you can specify the source with the `ElementName` property.
Path	With the `Path` property, you specify the path to the source object. This can be the property of the source object, but indexers and properties of child elements are also supported.

Binding Class Members	Description
XPath	With an XML data source, you can define an XPath query expression to get the data for binding.
Mode	The mode defines the direction for the binding. The Mode property is of type BindingMode. BindingMode is an enumeration with the following values: Default, OneTime, OneWay, TwoWay, OneWayToSource. The default mode depends on the target: with a TextBox, two-way binding is the default; with a Label that is read-only, the default is one-way. OneTime means that the data is only init loaded from the source; OneWay also does updates from the source to the target. With TwoWay binding changes from the WPF elements are written back to the source. OneWayToSource means that the data is never read but always written from the target to the source.
Converter	With the Converter property, you can specify a converter class that converts the data for the UI and back. The converter class must implement the interface IValueConverter, which defines the methods Convert() and ConvertBack(). You can pass parameters to the converter methods with the ConverterParameter property. The converter can be culture-sensitive; the culture can be set with the ConverterCulture property.
FallbackValue	With the FallbackValue property, you can define a default value that is used if binding doesn't return a value.
ValidationRules	With the ValidationRules property, you can define a collection of ValiationRule objects that are checked before the source is updated from the WPF target elements. The class ExceptionValidationRule is derived from the class ValidationRule and checks for exceptions.

Simple Object Binding

For binding to CLR objects, with the .NET classes you just have to define properties, as shown in this example with the class Book and the properties Title, Publisher, Isbn, and Authors:

```
public class Book
{
    public Book(string title, string publisher, string isbn,
        params string[] authors)
    {
        this.Title = title;
        this.Publisher = publisher;
        this.Isbn = isbn;
        foreach (string author in authors)
        {
            this.authors.Add(author);
        }
    }
```

(continued)

(continued)

```
        public Book()
            : this("unknown", "unknown", "unknown")
        {
        }

        public string Title { get; set; }
        public string Publisher { get; set; }
        public string Isbn { get; set; }

        public override string ToString()
        {
            return Title;
        }

        private readonly List<string> authors = new List<string>();
        public string[] Authors
        {
            get { return authors.ToArray(); }
        }
    }
```

In the user interface, several labels and TextBox controls are defined to display book information. Using Binding markup extensions, the TextBox controls are bound to the properties of the Book class. With the Binding markup extension nothing more than the Path property is defined to bind it to the property of the Book class. There's no need to define a source because the source is defined by assigning the DataContext, as you can see in the code behind that follows. The mode is defined by its default with the TextBox element, and this is two-way binding.

```xml
<Window x:Class="ObjectBindingSample.Window1"
    xmlns="http://schemas.microsoft.com/winfx/2006/xaml/presentation"
    xmlns:x="http://schemas.microsoft.com/winfx/2006/xaml"
    Title="Object Binding Sample" Height="300" Width="340"
    >
    <Grid Name="bookGrid" Margin="5" >
      <Grid.ColumnDefinitions>
        <ColumnDefinition Width="30*" />
        <ColumnDefinition Width="70*" />
      </Grid.ColumnDefinitions>
      <Grid.RowDefinitions>
        <RowDefinition Height="50" />
        <RowDefinition Height="50" />
        <RowDefinition Height="50" />
        <RowDefinition Height="50" />
        <RowDefinition Height="50" />
      </Grid.RowDefinitions>
      <Label Grid.Column="0" Grid.Row="0">Title:</Label>
      <TextBox Margin="5" Height="30" Grid.Column="1" Grid.Row="0"
          Text="{Binding Title}" />

      <Label Grid.Column="0" Grid.Row="1">Publisher:</Label>
      <TextBox Margin="5" Height="30" Grid.Column="1" Grid.Row="1"
          Text="{Binding Publisher}" />

      <Label Grid.Column="0" Grid.Row="2">ISBN:</Label>
```

```
<TextBox Margin="5" Height="30" Grid.Column="1" Grid.Row="2"
    Text="{Binding Isbn}" />

<Button Margin="5" Grid.Column="1" Grid.Row="4"
    Click="bookButton_Click" Name="bookButton">Open Dialog</Button>

    </Grid>
</Window>
```

With the code behind, a new `Book` object is created, and the book is assigned to the `DataContext` property of the `Grid` control. `DataContext` is a dependency property that is defined with the base class `FrameworkElement`. Assigning the `DataContext` with the `Grid` control means that every element in the `Grid` control has a default binding to the same data context.

```
public partial class Window1 : System.Windows.Window
{
    private Book book1 = new Book();

    public Window1()
    {
        InitializeComponent();

        book1.Title = "Professional C# 2005 with .NET 3.0";
        book1.Publisher = "Wrox Press";
        book1.Isbn = "978-0470124727";

        bookGrid.DataContext = book1;
    }
}
```

After starting the application, you can see the bound data, as shown in Figure 35-4.

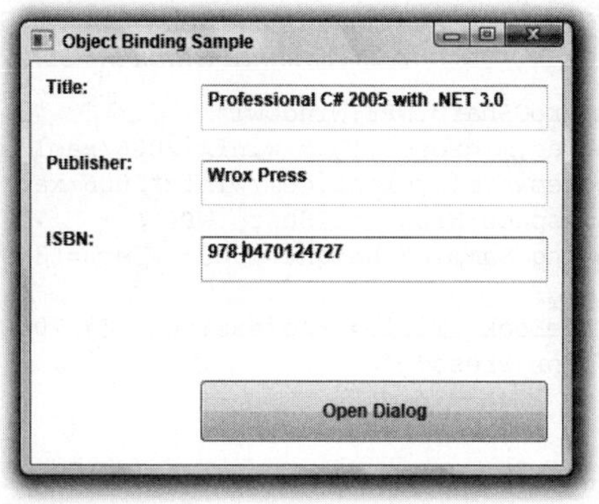

Figure 35-4

To demonstrate the two-way binding (changes to the input of the WPF element are reflected inside the CLR object), the `OnOpenBookDialog()` method is implemented. This method is assigned to the `Click` event of the `bookButton`, as you can see in the XAML code. When implemented a message box pops up to show the current title and ISBN number of the `book1` object. Figure 35-5 shows the output from the message box after a change to the input was made during runtime.

```
void bookButton_Click(object sender, RoutedEventArgs e)
{
    string message = book1.Title;
    string caption = book1.Isbn;
    MessageBox.Show(message, caption);
}
```

Figure 35-5

Object Data Provider

Instead of defining the object in code behind, you can define an object instance with XAML. To make this possible, you have to reference the namespace with the namespace declarations in the XML root element. The XML attribute xmlns:src="clr-namespace:Wrox.ProCsharp.WPF" assigns the .NET namespace Wrox.ProCSharp.WPF to the XML namespace alias src.

One object of the Book class is now defined with the Book element inside the Window resources. By assigning values to the XML attributes Title and Publisher, you set the values of the properties from the Book class. x:Key="theBook" defines the identifier for the resource so that you can reference the book object. In the TextBox element, now the Source is defined with the Binding markup extension to reference the theBook resource.

XAML markup extensions can be combined. In the following sample, the StaticResource markup extension used to reference the book resource is contained within the Binding markup extension.

```
<Window x:Class="Wrox.ProCSharp.WPF.Window1"
    xmlns="http://schemas.microsoft.com/winfx/2006/xaml/presentation"
    xmlns:x="http://schemas.microsoft.com/winfx/2006/xaml"
    xmlns:src="clr-namespace:Wrox.ProCSharp.WPF"
    Title="Object Binding Sample" Height="300" Width="340">
  <Window.Resources>
    <src:Book x:Key="theBook" Title="Professional C# 2008"
         Publisher="Wrox Press" />
  </Window.Resources>

<!-- ... -->
    <TextBox Margin="5" Height="30" Grid.Column="1" Grid.Row="0"
         Text="{Binding Source={StaticResource theBook}, Path=Title}" />
<!-- ... -->
```

If the .NET namespace to reference is in a different assembly, you have to add the assembly as well to the XML declaration:

```
xmlns:system="clr-namespace:System;assembly=mscorlib"
```

Instead of defining the object instance directly within XAML code, you can define an object data provider that references a class to invoke a method. For use by the `ObjectDataProvider`, it's best to create a factory class that returns the object to display, as shown with the `BookFactory` class:

```
public class BookFactory
{
    private List<Book> books = new List<Book>();

    public BookFactory()
    {
        books.Add(new Book("Professional C# 2008",
            "Wrox Press", "978-0470191378"));
    }

    public Book GetTheBook()
    {
        return books[0];
    }
}
```

The `ObjectDataProvider` element can be defined in the resources section. The XML attribute `ObjectType` defines the name of the class; with `MethodName` you specify the name of the method that is invoked to get the book object:

```
<Window.Resources>
    <ObjectDataProvider ObjectType="src:BookFactory" MethodName="GetTheBook"
        x:Key="theBook">
    </ObjectDataProvider>
</Window.Resources>
```

The properties you can specify with the `ObjectDataProvider` class are listed in the following table.

ObjectDataProvider	Description
ObjectType	The ObjectType property defines the type to create an instance of.
ConstructorParameters	Using the ConstructorParameters collection, you can add parameters to the class to create an instance.
MethodName	The MethodName property defines the name of the method that is invoked by the object data provider.
MethodParameters	With the MethodParameters property, you can assign parameters to the method defined with the MethodName property.
ObjectInstance	With the ObjectInstance property, you can get and set the object that is used by the ObjectDataProvider class. For example, you can assign an existing object programmatically instead of defining the ObjectType so that an object is instantiated by the ObjectDataProvider.
Data	With the Data property you can access the underlying object that is used for data binding. If the MethodName is defined, with the Data property you can access the object that is returned from the method defined.

List Binding

Binding to a list is more frequently done than binding to a simple object. Binding to a list is very similar to binding to a simple object. You can assign the complete list to the DataContext from code behind, or you can use an ObjectDataProvider that accesses an object factory that returns a list. With elements that support binding to a list (for example, a ListBox), the complete list is bound. With elements that support binding to just one object (for example, a TextBox), the current item is bound.

With the BookFactory class, now a list of Book objects is returned:

```
public class BookFactory
{
    private List<Book> books = new List<Book>();

    public BookFactory()
    {
        books.Add(new Book("Professional C# 2008", "Wrox Press",
                "978-0470191378", "Christian Nagel", "Bill Evjen",
                "Jay Glynn", "Karli Watson", "Morgan Skinner"));
        books.Add(new Book("Professional C# 2005 with .NET 3.0",
                "Wrox Press", "978-0-470-12472-7", "Christian Nagel",
                "Bill Evjen", "Jay Glynn", "Karli Watson", "Morgan Skinner"));
        books.Add(new Book("Professional C# 2005",
                "Wrox Press", "978-0-7645-7534-1", "Christian Nagel",
                "Bill Evjen","Jay Glynn", "Karli Watson", "Morgan Skinner",
                "Allen Jones"));
        books.Add(new Book("Beginning Visual C#",
                "Wrox Press", "978-0-7645-4382-1", "Karli Watson",
                "David Espinosa", "Zach Greenvoss", "Jacob Hammer Pedersen",
                "Christian Nagel", "John D. Reid", "Matthew Reynolds",
                "Morgan Skinner", "Eric White"));
        books.Add(new Book("ASP.NET Professional Secrets",
                "Wiley", "978-0-7645-2628-2", "Bill Evjen",
                "Thiru Thangarathinam", "Bill Hatfield", "Doug Seven",
                "S. Srinivasa Sivakumar", "Dave Wanta", "Jason T. Roff"));
        books.Add(new Book("Design and Analysis of Distributed Algorithms",
                "Wiley", "978-0-471-71997-7", "Nicolo Santoro"));
    }

    public IEnumerable<Book> GetBooks()
    {
        return books;
    }
}
```

In the WPF code-behind constructor of the class Window1 a BookFactory is instantiated and the method GetBooks() is invoked to assign the Book array with the DataContext of the Window1 instance:

```
public partial class Window1 : System.Windows.Window
{
    private BookFactory factory = new BookFactory();

    public Window1()
```

```
        {
            InitializeComponent();

            this.DataContext = factory.GetBooks();
        }
    }
```

In XAML you just need a control that supports lists, such as the ListBox, and to bind the ItemsSource property as shown:

```
    <Window x:Class=" Wrox.ProCSharp.WPF.Window1"
        xmlns="http://schemas.microsoft.com/winfx/2006/xaml/presentation"
        xmlns:x="http://schemas.microsoft.com/winfx/2006/xaml"
        Title="List Binding Sample" Height="300" Width="518"
        >
    <DockPanel>
      <Grid >
        <Grid.ColumnDefinitions>
          <ColumnDefinition />
        </Grid.ColumnDefinitions>
        <Grid.RowDefinitions>
          <RowDefinition />
          <RowDefinition />
          <RowDefinition />
          <RowDefinition />
        </Grid.RowDefinitions>
        <ListBox HorizontalAlignment="Left" Margin="5" Grid.RowSpan="4"
            Grid.Row="0" Grid.Column="0" Name="booksList"
            ItemsSource="{Binding}" />
      </Grid>
    </DockPanel>
  </Window>
```

Because the Window has the Book array assigned to the DataContext, and the ListBox is placed within the Window, the ListBox shows all books with the default template, as illustrated in Figure 35-6.

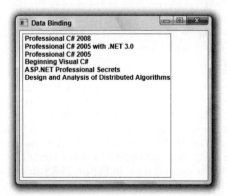

Figure 35-6

For a more flexible layout of the ListBox, you have to define a template, as was discussed in the previous chapter for ListBox styling. The ItemTemplate contained in the style listBoxStyle defines a DataTemplate with a Label element. The content of the label is bound to the Title. The item template is repeated for every item in the list.

The `ListBox` element has the `Style` property assigned. `ItemsSource` is, as before, set to the default binding. Figure 35-7 shows the output of the application with the new `ListBox` style.

```
<Window.Resources>
  <Style x:Key="listBoxStyle" TargetType="{x:Type ListBox}" >
    <Setter Property="ItemTemplate">
      <Setter.Value>
        <DataTemplate>
          <Label Content="{Binding Title}" />
        </DataTemplate>
      </Setter.Value>
    </Setter>
  </Style>
</Window.Resources>

<!-- ... -->

<ListBox HorizontalAlignment="Left" Margin="5"
    Style="{StaticResource listBoxStyle}" Grid.RowSpan="4"
    ItemsSource="{Binding}" />
```

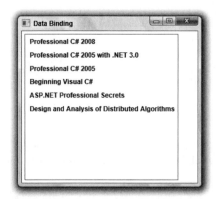

Figure 35-7

Master-Details Binding

Instead of just showing all the elements inside a list, you might want or need to show detail information about the selected item. It doesn't require a lot of work to do this. You just have to define the elements to display the current selection. In the sample application, three `Label` elements are defined with the `Binding` markup extension set to the `Book` properties `Title`, `Publisher`, and `Isbn`. There's one important change you have to make to the `ListBox`. By default, the labels are bound to just the first element of the list. By setting the `ListBox` property `IsSynchronizedWithCurrentItem="True"`, the selection of the list box is set to the current item. In Figure 35-8 you can see the result; the selected item is shown in the detail section labels.

```
<Window x:Class=" Wrox.ProCSharp.WPF.Window1"
    xmlns="http://schemas.microsoft.com/winfx/2006/xaml/presentation"
    xmlns:x="http://schemas.microsoft.com/winfx/2006/xaml"
    Title="List Binding Sample" Height="300" Width="518"
    >
```

```xml
<Window.Resources>
  <Style x:Key="listBoxStyle" TargetType="{x:Type ListBox}" >
    <Setter Property="ItemTemplate">
      <Setter.Value>
        <DataTemplate>
          <Label Content="{Binding Title}" />
        </DataTemplate>
      </Setter.Value>
    </Setter>
  </Style>
  <Style x:Key="labelStyle" TargetType="{x:Type Label}">
    <Setter Property="Width" Value="190" />
    <Setter Property="Height" Value="40" />
    <Setter Property="Margin" Value="5,5,5,5" />
  </Style>
</Window.Resources>
<DockPanel>
  <Grid >
    <Grid.ColumnDefinitions>
      <ColumnDefinition />
      <ColumnDefinition />
    </Grid.ColumnDefinitions>
    <Grid.RowDefinitions>
      <RowDefinition />
      <RowDefinition />
      <RowDefinition />
      <RowDefinition />
    </Grid.RowDefinitions>
    <ListBox IsSynchronizedWithCurrentItem="True" HorizontalAlignment="Left"
        Margin="5" Style="{StaticResource listBoxStyle}"
        Grid.RowSpan="4" ItemsSource="{Binding}" />
    <Label Style="{StaticResource labelStyle}" Content="{Binding Title}"
        Grid.Row="0" Grid.Column="1" />
    <Label Style="{StaticResource labelStyle}" Content="{Binding Publisher}"
        Grid.Row="1" Grid.Column="1" />
    <Label Style="{StaticResource labelStyle}" Content="{Binding Isbn}"
        Grid.Row="2" Grid.Column="1" />

  </Grid>
</DockPanel>
</Window>
```

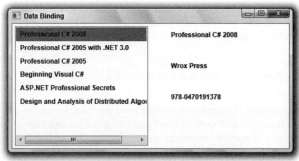

Figure 35-8

Value Conversion

The authors of the book are still missing in the output. If you bind the `Authors` property to a `Label` element, the `ToString()` method of the `Array` class is invoked, which just returns the name of the type. One solution to this is to bind the `Authors` property to a `ListBox`. For the `ListBox`, you can define a template for a specific view. Another solution is to convert the string array returned by the `Authors` property to a string and use the string for binding.

The class `StringArrayConverter` converts a string array to a string. WPF converter classes must implement the interface `IValueConverter` from the namespace `System.Windows.Data`. This interface defines the methods `Convert()` and `ConvertBack()`. With the `StringArrayConverter`, the `Convert()` method converts the string array from the variable `value` to a string by using the `String.Join()` method. The separator parameter of the `Join()` is taken from the variable `parameter` received with the `Convert()` method.

You can read more about the methods of the String classes in Chapter 8, "Strings and Regular Expressions."

```
public class StringArrayConverter : IValueConverter
{
    public object Convert(object value, Type targetType, object parameter,
          System.Globalization.CultureInfo culture)
    {
        string[] stringCollection = (string[])value;
        string separator = (string)parameter;

        return String.Join(separator, stringCollection);
    }

    public object ConvertBack(object value, Type targetType,
          object parameter, System.Globalization.CultureInfo culture)
    {
        string s = (string)value;
        char separator = (char)parameter;

        return s.Split(separator);
    }
}
```

In the XAML code, the `StringArrayConverter` class can be declared as a resource for referencing it from the `Binding` markup extension:

```
<Window x:Class=" Wrox.ProCSharp.WPF.Window1"
    xmlns="http://schemas.microsoft.com/winfx/2006/xaml/presentation"
    xmlns:x="http://schemas.microsoft.com/winfx/2006/xaml"
    xmlns:src="clr-namespace:Wrox.ProCSharp.WPF"
    Title="List Binding Sample" Height="300" Width="518"
    >
  <Window.Resources>
    <src:StringArrayConverter x:Key="stringArrayConverter" />
    <!-- ... -->
```

For multiline output, a `TextBlock` element is declared with the `TextWrapping` property set to `Wrap` to make it possible to display multiple authors. In the `Binding` markup extension the `Path` is set to `Authors`, which is defined as a property returning a string array. The string array is converted from the resource `stringArrayConverter` as defined by the `Converter` property. The `Convert` method of the converter implementation receives the `ConverterParameter', '` as input to separate the authors:

```
<TextBlock Width="190" Height="50" Margin="5" TextWrapping="Wrap"
    Text="{Binding Path=Authors,
    Converter={StaticResource stringArrayConverter},
    ConverterParameter=', ' }"
    Grid.Row="3" Grid.Column="1" />
```

Figure 35-9 shows the book details, including authors.

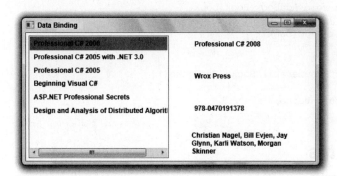

Figure 35-9

Adding List Items Dynamically

What if list items are added dynamically? The WPF element must be notified of elements added to the list.

In the XAML code of the WPF application, a `Button` element is added inside a `StackPanel`. The `Click` event is assigned to the method `OnAddBook()`:

```
<!-- ... -->
<DockPanel>
  <StackPanel Orientation="Horizontal" DockPanel.Dock="Bottom" Height="60">
    <Button Click="addBookButton_Click" Name="addBookButton" Margin="5"
        Width="80" Height="40">Add Book</Button>
  </StackPanel>
  <Grid >
   <!-- ... -->
```

In the method `OnAddBook()`, which implements the event handler code for the `addBookButton`, a new `Book` object is added to the list. If you test the application with the `BookFactory` as it is implemented now, there's no notification to the WPF elements that a new object has been added to the list.

```
void addBookButton_Click(object sender, RoutedEventArgs e)
{
    factory.AddBook(new Book(".NET 2.0 Wrox Box", "Wrox Press",
        "978-0-470-04840-5"));
}
```

The object that is assigned to the `DataContext` must implement the interface `INotifyCollectionChanged`. This interface defines the `CollectionChanged` event that is used by the WPF application. Instead of implementing this interface on your own with a custom collection class, you can use the generic collection class ObservableCollection<T> that is defined with the namespace System.Collections.ObjectModel in the assembly WindowsBase. Now, as a new item is added to the collection, the new item immediately shows up in the ListBox:

```
public class BookFactory
{
    private ObservableCollection<Book> books =
        new ObservableCollection<Book>();

    // ...

    public void AddBook(Book book)
    {
        books.Add(book);
    }

    public IEnumerable<Book> GetBooks()
    {
        return books;
    }
}
```

Data Templates

In the previous chapter, you saw how controls can be customized with templates. You can also define a template for a data type, for example, the Book class. No matter where the Book class is used, the template defines the default look.

In the example, the DataTemplate is defined within the Window resources. The DataType property references the class Book from the namespace Wrox.ProCSharp.WPF. The template defines a border with two label elements contained in a stack panel. With the ListBox element you can see there's no template referenced. The only property that is defined by the ListBox is ItemsSource with a value for the default Binding markup extension. Because the DataTemplate does not define a key, it is used by all lists containing Book objects. Figure 35-10 shows the output of the application with the data template.

```
<Window x:Class=" Wrox.ProCSharp.WPF.DataTemplateDemo"
    xmlns="http://schemas.microsoft.com/winfx/2006/xaml/presentation"
    xmlns:x="http://schemas.microsoft.com/winfx/2006/xaml"
    xmlns:src="clr-namespace:Wrox.ProCSharp.WPF"
    Title="Data Binding" Height="300" Width="300"
    >
  <Window.Resources>
    <DataTemplate DataType="{x:Type src:Book}">
      <Border BorderBrush="Blue" BorderThickness="2" Background="LightBlue"
          Margin="10" Padding="15">
        <StackPanel>
          <Label Content="{Binding Path=Title}" />
          <Label Content="{Binding Path=Publisher}" />
        </StackPanel>
      </Border>
    </DataTemplate>
  </Window.Resources>
    <Grid>
      <ListBox ItemsSource="{Binding}" />
    </Grid>
</Window>
```

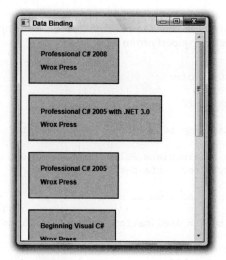

Figure 35-10

In case you want to use a different data template with the same data type, you can create a data template selector. A data template selector is implemented in a class that derives from the base class `DataTemplateSelector`.

Here a data template selector is implemented by selecting a different template based on the publisher. Within the `Window` resources these templates are defined. One template can be accessed by the key name `WroxBookTemplate`; the other template has the key name `WileyBookTemplate`:

```
<DataTemplate x:Key="WroxBookTemplate" DataType="{x:Type src:Book}">
    <Border BorderBrush="Blue" BorderThickness="2" Background="LightBlue"
            Margin="10" Padding="15">
        <StackPanel>
            <Label Content="{Binding Path=Title}" />
            <Label Content="{Binding Path=Publisher}" />
        </StackPanel>
    </Border>
</DataTemplate>

<DataTemplate x:Key="WileyBookTemplate" DataType="{x:Type src:Book}">
    <Border BorderBrush="Yellow" BorderThickness="2"
            Background="LightGreen" Margin="10" Padding="15">
        <StackPanel>
            <Label Content="{Binding Path=Title}" />
            <Label Content="{Binding Path=Publisher}" />
        </StackPanel>
    </Border>
</DataTemplate>
```

For selecting the template the class `BookDataTemplateSelector` overrides the method `SelectTemplate` from the base class `DataTemplateSelector`. The implementation selects the template based on the `Publisher` property from the `Book` class:

```
using System.Windows;
using System.Windows.Controls;

namespace Wrox.ProCSharp.WPF
{
    public class BookDataTemplateSelector : DataTemplateSelector
    {
        public override DataTemplate SelectTemplate(object item,
            DependencyObject container)
        {
            if (item != null && item is Book)
            {
                Window window = Application.Current.MainWindow;

                Book book = item as Book;
                switch (book.Publisher)
                {
                    case "Wrox Press":
                        return window.FindResource("WroxBookTemplate")
                            as DataTemplate;
                    case "Wiley":
                        return window.FindResource("WileyBookTemplate")
                            as DataTemplate;
                    default:
                        return window.FindResource("BookTemplate") as DataTemplate;
                }
            }
            return null;
        }
    }
}
```

For accessing the class `BookDataTemplateSelector` from XAML code, the class is defined within the `Window` resources:

```
<src:BookDataTemplateSelector x:Key="bookTemplateSelector" />
```

Now the selector class can be assigned to the `ItemTemplateSelector` property of the `ListBox`:

```
<ListBox ItemsSource="{Binding}"
        ItemTemplateSelector="{StaticResource bookTemplateSelector}" />
```

When running the application, you can see different data templates based on the publisher, as shown in Figure 35-11.

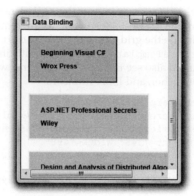

Figure 35-11

Binding to XML

WPF data binding has special support for binding to XML data. You can use XmlDataProvider as a data source and bind the elements by using XPath expressions. For a hierarchical display, you can use the TreeView control and create the view for the items by using the HierarchicalDataTemplate.

The following XML file containing Book elements is used as a source in the next examples:

```xml
<?xml version="1.0" encoding="utf-8" ?>
<Books>
  <Book isbn="978-0-470-12472-7">
    <Title>Professional C# 2008</Title>
    <Publisher>Wrox Press</Publisher>
    <Author>Christian Nagel</Author>
    <Author>Bill Evjen</Author>
    <Author>Jay Glynn</Author>
    <Author>Karli Watson</Author>
    <Author>Morgan Skinner</Author>
  </Book>
  <Book isbn="978-0-7645-4382-1">
    <Title>Beginning Visual C# 2008</Title>
    <Publisher>Wrox Press</Publisher>
    <Author>Karli Watson</Author>
    <Author>David Espinosa</Author>
    <Author>Zach Greenvoss</Author>
    <Author>Jacob Hammer Pedersen</Author>
    <Author>Christian Nagel</Author>
    <Author>John D. Reid</Author>
    <Author>Matthew Reynolds</Author>
    <Author>Morgan Skinner</Author>
    <Author>Eric White</Author>
  </Book>
</Books>
```

Similarly to defining an object data provider, you can define an XML data provider. Both ObjectDataProvider and XmlDataProvider are derived from the same base class, DataSourceProvider. With the XmlDataProvider in the example, the Source property is set to reference the XML file books.xml. The XPath property defines an XPath expression to reference the

XML root element `Books`. The `Grid` element references the XML data source with the `DataContext` property. With the data context for the grid, all `Book` elements are required for a list binding, so the XPath expression is set to `Book`. Inside the grid, you can find the `ListBox` element that binds to the default data context and uses the `DataTemplate` to include the title in `TextBlock` elements as items of the `ListBox`. Inside the grid, you can also see three `Label` elements with data binding set to XPath expressions to display the title, publisher, and ISBN numbers.

```xml
<Window x:Class="Wrox.ProCSharp.WPF.Window1"
    xmlns="http://schemas.microsoft.com/winfx/2006/xaml/presentation"
    xmlns:x="http://schemas.microsoft.com/winfx/2006/xaml"
    Title="XML Binding" Height="348" Width="498"
    >
  <Window.Resources>
    <XmlDataProvider x:Key="books" Source="Books.xml" XPath="Books" />

    <DataTemplate x:Key="listTemplate">
      <TextBlock Text="{Binding XPath=Title}" />
    </DataTemplate>

    <Style x:Key="labelStyle" TargetType="{x:Type Label}">
      <Setter Property="Width" Value="190" />
      <Setter Property="Height" Value="40" />
      <Setter Property="Margin" Value="5" />
    </Style>

  </Window.Resources>
    <Grid DataContext="{Binding Source={StaticResource books}, XPath=Book}">
      <Grid.ColumnDefinitions>
        <ColumnDefinition />
        <ColumnDefinition />
      </Grid.ColumnDefinitions>
      <Grid.RowDefinitions>
        <RowDefinition />
        <RowDefinition />
        <RowDefinition />
        <RowDefinition />
      </Grid.RowDefinitions>
      <ListBox IsSynchronizedWithCurrentItem="True" Margin="5"
          Grid.Column="0" Grid.RowSpan="4" ItemsSource="{Binding}"
          ItemTemplate="{StaticResource listTemplate}" />

      <Label Style="{StaticResource labelStyle}"
          Content="{Binding XPath=Title}"
          Grid.Row="0" Grid.Column="1" />
      <Label Style="{StaticResource labelStyle}"
          Content="{Binding XPath=Publisher}"
          Grid.Row="1" Grid.Column="1" />
      <Label Style="{StaticResource labelStyle}"
          Content="{Binding XPath=@isbn}"
          Grid.Row="2" Grid.Column="1" />
    </Grid>
</Window>
```

Figure 35-12 shows the result of the XML binding.

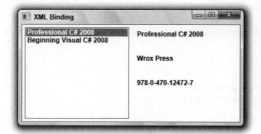

Figure 35-12

If XML data should be shown hierarchically, you can use the `TreeView` control.

Binding Validation

Several options are available to validate data from the user before it is used with the .NET objects. These options are:

❑ Handling exceptions

❑ Data error information

❑ Custom validation rules

Handling Exceptions

One of the options demonstrated here is that the .NET class throws an exception if an invalid value is set as shown in the class `SomeData`. The property `Value1` accepts only values larger or equal to 5 and smaller than 12:

```
public class SomeData
{
    private int value1;
    public int Value1 {
        get
        {
            return value1;
        }
        set
        {
            if (value < 5 || value > 12)
                throw new ArgumentException(
                        "value must not be less than 5 or greater than 12");
            value1 = value;
        }
    }
}
```

In the constructor of the `Window1` class, a new object of the class `SomeData` is initialized and passed to the `DataContext` for data binding:

```
public partial class Window1 : Window
{
    SomeData p1 = new SomeData() { Value1 = 11 };

    public Window1()
    {
        InitializeComponent();
        this.DataContext = p1;
    }

}
```

The event handler method `buttonSubmit_Click` displays a message box to show the actual value of the `SomeData` instance:

```
private void buttonSubmit_Click(object sender, RoutedEventArgs e)
{
    MessageBox.Show(p1.Value1.ToString());
}
```

With simple data binding, here the `Text` property of a `TextBox` is bound to the `Value1` property. If you run the application now and try to change the value to one that is not valid, you can verify that the value never changed by clicking the Submit button. WPF catches and ignores the exception thrown by the set accessor of the property `Value1`.

```
<Label Margin="5" Grid.Row="0" Grid.Column="0" >Value1:</Label>
<TextBox Margin="5" Grid.Row="0" Grid.Column="1"
        Text="{Binding Path=Value1}" />
```

To display an error as soon as the context of the input field changes, you can set the `ValidatesOnException` property of the `Binding` markup extension to `True`. With an invalid value (as soon as the exception is thrown when the value should be set), the `TextBox` is surrounded by a red colored line as shown in Figure 35-13.

```
<Label Margin="5" Grid.Row="0" Grid.Column="0" >Value1:</Label>
<TextBox Margin="5" Grid.Row="0" Grid.Column="1"
        Text="{Binding Path=Value1, ValidatesOnExceptions=True}" />
```

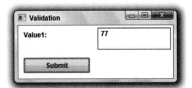

Figure 35-13

To return the error information in a different way to the user, you can assign the attached property `ErrorTemplate` that is defined by the `Validation` class to a template defining the UI for errors. The new template to mark the error is shown here with the key `validationTemplate`. The `ControlTemplate` puts a red exclamation point in front of the existing control content.

```
<ControlTemplate x:Key="validationTemplate">
   <DockPanel>
      <TextBlock Foreground="Red" FontSize="20">!</TextBlock>
      <AdornedElementPlaceholder/>
   </DockPanel>
</ControlTemplate>
```

Setting the `validationTemplate` with the `Validation.ErrorTemplate` attached property activates the template with the `TextBox`:

```
<Label Margin="5" Grid.Row="0" Grid.Column="0" >Value1:</Label>
<TextBox Margin="5" Grid.Row="0" Grid.Column="1"
      Text="{Binding Path=Value1, ValidatesOnExceptions=True}"
      Validation.ErrorTemplate="{StaticResource validationTemplate}" />
```

The new look of the application is shown in Figure 35-14.

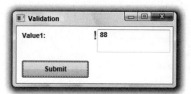

Figure 35-14

Another option for a custom error message is to register to the Error *event of the* Validation *class. Here the property* NotifyOnValidationError *must be set to true.*

The error information itself can be accessed from the `Errors` collection of the `Validation` class. To display the error information in the `ToolTip` of the `TextBox` you can create a property trigger as shown. The trigger is activated as soon as the `HasError` property of the `Validation` class is set to `True`. The trigger sets the `ToolTip` property of the `TextBox`.

```
<Style TargetType="{x:Type TextBox}">
   <Style.Triggers>
      <Trigger Property="Validation.HasError" Value="True">
         <Setter Property="ToolTip"
               Value="{Binding RelativeSource=
                     {x:Static RelativeSource.Self},
                  Path=(Validation.Errors)[0].ErrorContent}" />
      </Trigger>
   </Style.Triggers>
</Style>
```

Data Error Information

Another way to deal with errors is if the .NET object implements the interface IDataErrorInfo.

The class SomeData is now changed to implement the interface IDataErrorInfo. This interface defines the property Error and an indexer with a string argument. With WPF validation during data binding, the indexer is called and the name of the property to validate is passed as the columnName argument. With the implementation the value is verified if it is valid, and an error string is passed otherwise.

Here the validation is done on the property `Value2` that is implemented by using the C# 3.0 simple property notation:

```
public class SomeData : IDataErrorInfo
{
    private int value1;
    public int Value1 {
        get
        {
            return value1;
        }
        set
        {
            if (value < 5 || value > 12)
                throw new ArgumentException(
                        "value must not be less than 5 or greater than 12");
            value1 = value;
        }
    }

    public int Value2 { get; set; }

    string IDataErrorInfo.Error
    {
        get
        {
            return null;
        }
    }

    string IDataErrorInfo.this[string columnName]
    {
        get
        {
            if (columnName == "Value2")
            {
                if (this.Value2 < 0 || this.Value2 > 80)
                    return "age must not be less than 0 or greater than 80";

            }
            return null;
        }
    }
}
```

With a .NET entity class it would not be clear what an indexer would return; for example, what would you expect from an object of type Person *calling an indexer? That's why it is best to do an explicit implementation of the interface* IDataErrorInfo. *This way this indexer can be accessed only by using the interface, and the .NET class could do a different implementation for other purposes.*

If you set the property `ValidatesOnDataErrors` of the `Binding` class to `true`, the interface `IDataErrorInfo` is used during binding. Here, when the `TextBox` is changed, the binding mechanism invokes the indexer of the interface and passes `Value2` to the `columnName` variable:

```
<Label Margin="5" Grid.Row="1" Grid.Column="0" >Value2:</Label>
<TextBox Margin="5" Grid.Row="1" Grid.Column="1"
        Text="{Binding Path=Value2, ValidatesOnDataErrors=True}" />
```

Custom Validation Rules

To get more control of the validation you can implement a custom validation rule. A class implementing a custom validation rule needs to derive from the base class `ValidationRule`. With the previous two examples, validation rules have been used as well. Two classes that derive from the abstract base class `ValidationRule` are `DataErrorValidationRule` and `ExceptionValidationRule`. `DataErrorValidationRule` is activated by setting the property `ValidatesOnDataErrors` and uses the interface `IDataErrorInfo`; `ExceptionValidationRule` deals with exceptions and is activated by setting the property `ValidatesOnException`.

Here a validation rule is implemented to verify for a regular expression. The class `RegularExpressionValidationRule` derives from the base class `ValidationRule` and overrides the abstract method `Validate()` that is defined by the base class. With the implementation, the `RegEx` class from the namespace `System.Text.RegularExpressions` is used to validate the expression defined by the `Expression` property.

```
public class RegularExpressionValidationRule : ValidationRule
{
    public string Expression { get; set; }
    public string ErrorMessage { get; set; }

    public override ValidationResult Validate(object value,
        CultureInfo cultureInfo)
    {
        ValidationResult result = null;
        if (value != null)
        {
            Regex regEx = new Regex(Expression);
            bool isMatch = regEx.IsMatch(value.ToString());
            result = new ValidationResult(isMatch, isMatch ?
                null : ErrorMessage);
        }
        return result;
    }
}
```

Instead of using the `Binding` markup extension, now the binding is done as a child of the `TextBox.Text` element. The bound object now defines an `Email` property that is implemented with the simple property syntax. The `UpdateSourceTrigger` property defines when the source should be updated. Possible options for updating the source are:

❑ When the property value changes, which would be every character that is typed by the user

❑ When the focus is lost

❑ Explicitly

`ValidationRules` is a property of the `Binding` class that contains `ValidationRule` elements. Here the validation rule used is the custom class `RegularExpressionValidationRule`, where the `Expression` property is set to a regular expression that verifies if the input is a valid e-mail, and the `ErrorMessage` property that gives the error message in case the data entered to the `TextBox` is not valid:

```
<Label Margin="5" Grid.Row="2" Grid.Column="0">Email:</Label>
<TextBox Margin="5" Grid.Row="2" Grid.Column="1">
    <TextBox.Text>
        <Binding Path="Email" UpdateSourceTrigger="LostFocus">
            <Binding.ValidationRules>
```

(continued)

(continued)

```
            <src:RegularExpressionValidationRule
                Expression="^([\w-\.]+)@((\[[0-9]{1,3}\.[0-9]{1,3}\.[0-9]{1,3}\.)
|(([\w-]+\.)+))([a-zA-Z]{2,4}|[0-9]{1,3})(\]?)$"
                ErrorMessage="Email is not valid" />
        </Binding.ValidationRules>
      </Binding>
    </TextBox.Text>
  </TextBox>
```

Command Bindings

WPF has `Menu` and `ToolBar` controls that serve the same purpose as the controls you know from Windows Forms: to start commands. With these controls you could add event handlers to fulfill the functionality of the commands. However, you can start commands by selecting menus, clicking toolbar buttons, or by pressing some special keys on the keyboard. To handle all these different input gestures, WPF supplies another feature: commands.

Some of the WPF controls offer an implementation for predefined commands that make it extremely easy to get to some functionality.

WPF offers some predefined commands with the commands classes `ApplicationCommands`, `EditingCommands`, `ComponentCommands`, and `NavigationCommands`. All these commands classes are static classes with static properties that return `RoutedUICommand` objects. For example, some of the `ApplicationCommands` properties are New, Open, Save, SaveAs, Print, and Close — commands you know from many applications.

To get started with commands, create a simple WPF project and add a `Menu` control with items for undo and redo and cut, copy, and paste. The `TextBox` named `textContent` takes the remaining space of the `Window` and allows for multiline user input. Within the window a `DockPanel` is created to define the layout. Docked on top you can find the `Menu` control with `MenuItem` elements. The header is set to define the text of the menu. The _ (underscore) defines the letter that can be accessed directly with the keyboard without using the mouse. When you press the Alt key, the underscore is shown below the letter that follows in the header text. The `Command` property defines the command associated with the menu item.

```
<Window x:Class="Wrox.ProCSharp.WPF.WPFEditorWindow"
    xmlns="http://schemas.microsoft.com/winfx/2006/xaml/presentation"
    xmlns:x="http://schemas.microsoft.com/winfx/2006/xaml"
    Title="WPF Editor" Height="300" Width="300">

  <DockPanel>
    <Menu DockPanel.Dock="Top">
      <MenuItem Header="_Edit">
        <MenuItem Name="editUndoMenu" Header="_Undo"
            Command="ApplicationCommands.Undo" />
        <MenuItem Name="editRedoMenu" Header="_Redo"
            Command="ApplicationCommands.Redo" />
        <Separator />
        <MenuItem Name="editCutMenu" Header="Cu_t"
            Command="ApplicationCommands.Cut" />
        <MenuItem Name="editCopyMenu" Header="_Copy"
```

```
                        Command="ApplicationCommands.Copy" />
            <MenuItem Name="editPasteMenu" Header="_Paste"
                        Command="ApplicationCommands.Paste" />
        </MenuItem>
    </Menu>

    <TextBox Name="textContent" TextWrapping="Wrap" AcceptsReturn="True"
            AcceptsTab="True" />
    </DockPanel>

</Window>
```

That's all you need to do for clipboard functionality. The TextBox class already includes functionality for these predefined command bindings. Starting the application, when you enter text in the text box you can see possible menu items enabled. Selecting text in the text box makes the cut and copy menu items available. Figure 35-15 shows the running application.

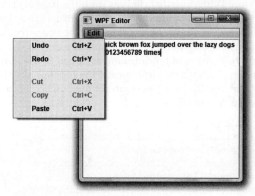

Figure 35-15

Now the application is going to be changed to add command bindings that are not previously defined with the controls. Commands to open and save a file are added to the editor.

To make the commands accessible, more MenuItem elements are added to the Menu element as shown:

```
<MenuItem Header="_File">
    <MenuItem Name="fileNewMenu" Header="_New"
            Command="ApplicationCommands.New" />
    <MenuItem Name="fileOpenMenu" Header="_Open"
            Command="ApplicationCommands.Open" />
    <Separator />
    <MenuItem Name="fileSave" Header="_Save"
            Command="ApplicationCommands.Save" />
    <MenuItem Name="fileSaveAs" Header="Save _As"
            Command="ApplicationCommands.SaveAs" />
</MenuItem>
```

The commands can also be accessed from a toolbar. With the `ToolBar` element the same commands that are available from the menu are defined. For arranging the toolbar, the `ToolBar` element is placed within a `ToolBarTray`:

```
<ToolBarTray DockPanel.Dock="Top">
    <ToolBar>
        <Button Command="ApplicationCommands.New">
            <Image Source="toolbargraphics/New.bmp" />
        </Button>
        <Button Command="ApplicationCommands.Open">
            <Image Source="toolbargraphics/Open.bmp" />
        </Button>
        <Button Command="ApplicationCommands.Save">
            <Image Source="toolbargraphics/Save.bmp" />
        </Button>
    </ToolBar>
</ToolBarTray>
```

Now command bindings must be defined to associate the commands to event handlers. Command bindings can be assigned to any WPF class that derives from the base class `UIElement` that is very high in the hierarchy. Command bindings are added to the `CommandBindings` property by defining `CommandBinding` elements. The `CommandBinding` class has the property `Command` where you can specify an object implementing the `ICommand` interface, and the events `CanExecute` and `Executed` to specify event handlers. Here the command bindings are assigned to the `Window` class. The `Executed` event is set to the event handler methods that implement the functionality behind the commands. If a command should not be available at all times, you can set the `CanExecute` event to a handler that decides if the command should be available.

```
<Window.CommandBindings>
    <CommandBinding Command="ApplicationCommands.New"
        Executed="NewFileExecuted" />
    <CommandBinding Command="ApplicationCommands.Open"
        Executed="OpenFileExecuted" />
    <CommandBinding Command="ApplicationCommands.Save"
        Executed="SaveFileExecuted"
        CanExecute="SaveFileCanExecute" />
    <CommandBinding Command="ApplicationCommands.SaveAs"
        Executed="SaveAsFileExecuted" CanExecute="SaveFileCanExecute" />
</Window.CommandBindings>
```

In the code behind the handler method, `NewFileExecuted()` empties the text box and writes the file name `untitled.txt` to the `Title` property of the `Window` class. In `OpenFileExecuted()` the `Microsoft.Win32.OpenFileDialog` is created and shown as a dialog. With a successful exit of the dialog, the selected file is opened and its content is written to the `TextBox` control.

> A dialog for opening a file is not predefined in WPF. You can either create a custom window for selecting files and folders, or you can use the `OpenFileDialog` class from the `Microsoft.Win32` namespace that is a wrapper around the new Windows dialog.

```csharp
public partial class Window1 : System.Windows.Window
{
    private string fileName;
    private readonly string defaultFileName;
    private const string appName = "WPF Editor";
    private bool isChanged = false;

    public Window1()
    {
        defaultFileName = System.IO.Path.Combine(
            Environment.GetFolderPath(
                Environment.SpecialFolder.MyDocuments),
            @"untitled.txt");
        InitializeComponent();
        NewFile();
    }

    private void NewFileExecuted(object sender, ExecutedRoutedEventArgs e)
    {
        NewFile();
    }

    private void NewFile()
    {
        textContent.Clear();
        filename = defaultFilename;
        SetTitle();
        isChanged = false;
    }

    private void SetTitle()
    {
        Title = String.Format("{0} {1}",
                    System.IO.Path.GetFileName(filename), appName);
    }

    private void OpenFileExecuted(object sender, ExecutedRoutedEventArgs e)
    {
        try
        {
            OpenFileDialog dlg = new OpenFileDialog();
            bool? dialogResult = dlg.ShowDialog();
            if (dialogResult == true)
            {
                filename = dlg.FileName;
                SetTitle();
                textContent.Text = File.ReadAllText(filename);
            }
        }
        catch (IOException ex)
        {
            MessageBox.Show(ex.Message, "Error WPF Editor",
                MessageBoxButton.OK, MessageBoxImage.Error);
        }
    }
```

The handler `SaveFileCanExecute()` returns the decision as to whether the command to save the file should be available depending on if the content has been changed:

```
private void SaveFileCanExecute(object sender,
    CanExecuteRoutedEventArgs e)
{
    if (isChanged)
    {
        e.CanExecute = true;
    }
    else
    {
        e.CanExecute = false;
    }
}
```

The application with the opened file `sample.txt` is shown in Figure 35-16.

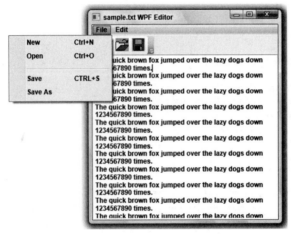

Figure 35-16

Animations

With animations you can make a smooth transition using moving elements, color changes, transforms, and so on. WPF makes it easy to create animations. You can animate the value of any dependency property. Different animation classes exist to animate the values of different properties, depending on their type.

The major elements of animations are as follows:

❑ **Timeline** — The timeline defines how a value changes over time. Different kinds of timelines are available for changing different types of values. The base class for all timelines is `Timeline`. To animate a `double`, the class `DoubleAnimation` can be used. `Int32Animation` is the animation class for `int` values.

❑ **Storyboard** — A storyboard is used to combine animations. The Storyboard class itself is derived from the base class TimelineGroup, which derives from Timeline. With DoubleAnimation you can animate a double value; with a Storyboard you combine all the animations that belong together.

❑ **Triggers** — With triggers you can start and stop animations. You've seen property triggers previously. Property triggers fire when a property value changes. You can also create an event trigger. An event trigger fires when an event occurs.

The namespace for animation classes is System.Windows.Media.Animation.

Timeline

A Timeline defines how a value changes over time. The first sample animates the size of an ellipse. Here a DoubleAnimation that is a timeline that changes a double value is used. The Triggers property of the Ellipse class is set to an EventTrigger. The event trigger is fired when the ellipse is loaded as defined with the RoutedEvent property of the EventTrigger. BeginStoryboard is a trigger action that begins the Storyboard. With the storyboard, a DoubleAnimation element is used to animate the Width property of the Ellipse class. The animation changes the width of the ellipse from 100 to 300 within 3 seconds, and reverses the animation after the 3 seconds.

```xml
<Window x:Class="EllipseAnimation.Window1"
    xmlns="http://schemas.microsoft.com/winfx/2006/xaml/presentation"
    xmlns:x="http://schemas.microsoft.com/winfx/2006/xaml"
    Title="Ellipse Animation" Height="300" Width="300">
  <Grid>
    <Ellipse Height="50" Width="100" Fill="SteelBlue">
      <Ellipse.Triggers>
        <EventTrigger RoutedEvent="Ellipse.Loaded" >
          <EventTrigger.Actions>
            <BeginStoryboard>
              <Storyboard Duration="00:00:06" RepeatBehavior="Forever">
                <DoubleAnimation
                    Storyboard.TargetProperty="(Ellipse.Width)"
                    Duration="0:0:3" AutoReverse="True"
                    FillBehavior="Stop" RepeatBehavior="Forever"
                    AccelerationRatio="0.9" DecelerationRatio="0.1"
                    From="100" To="300" />
              </Storyboard>
            </BeginStoryboard>
          </EventTrigger.Actions>
        </EventTrigger>
      </Ellipse.Triggers>
    </Ellipse>
  </Grid>
</Window>
```

Figures 35-17 and 35-18 show two states from the animated ellipse.

Figure 35-17

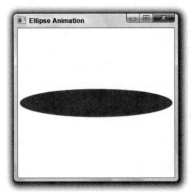

Figure 35-18

Animations are far more than typical window-dressing animation that appears onscreen constantly and immediately. You can add animation to business applications that make the user interface more responsive.

The following example demonstrates a decent animation and also shows how the animation can be defined in a style. Within the Window resources you can see the style AnimatedButtonStyle for buttons. In the template a rectangle named outline is defined. This template has a thin stroke with the thickness set to 0.4.

The template has a property trigger for the IsMouseOver property defined. The EnterActions property of this trigger applies as soon as the mouse is moved over the button. The action to start is BeginStoryboard. BeginStoryboard is a trigger action that can contain and thus start Storyboard elements. The Storyboard element defines a DoubleAnimation to animate a double value. The property value that is changed in this animation is the Rectangle.StrokeThickness of the Rectangle element with the name outline. The value is changed in a smooth way by 1.2, as the By property specifies, for a time length of 0.3 seconds as specified by the Duration property. At the end of the animation, the stroke thickness is reset to its original value because AutoReverse="True". To summarize: as soon as the mouse moves over the button, the thickness of the outline is incremented by 1.2 for 0.3 seconds. Figure 35-19 shows the button without animation, and Figure 35-20 shows the button at the moment 0.3 seconds after the mouse moved over it. It's just not possible to show the smooth animation and intermediate looks in a print medium.

```
<Window x:Class="AnimationSample.ButtonAnimation"
    xmlns="http://schemas.microsoft.com/winfx/2006/xaml/presentation"
    xmlns:x="http://schemas.microsoft.com/winfx/2006/xaml"
    Title="Button Animation" Height="300" Width="300">
  <Window.Resources>
    <Style x:Key="AnimatedButtonStyle" TargetType="{x:Type Button}">
      <Setter Property="Template">
        <Setter.Value>
          <ControlTemplate TargetType="{x:Type Button}">
            <Grid>
                <Rectangle Name="outline" RadiusX="9" RadiusY="9" Stroke="Black"
                    Fill="{TemplateBinding Background}" StrokeThickness="0.4">
                </Rectangle>
```

```
                <ContentPresenter VerticalAlignment="Center"
                        HorizontalAlignment="Center"
                          />
            </Grid>
            <ControlTemplate.Triggers>
                <Trigger Property="IsMouseOver" Value="True">
                    <Trigger.EnterActions>
                        <BeginStoryboard>
                            <Storyboard>
                                <DoubleAnimation Duration="0:0:0.3" AutoReverse="True"
                                    Storyboard.TargetProperty=
                                        "(Rectangle.StrokeThickness)"
                                    Storyboard.TargetName="outline" By="1.2" />
                            </Storyboard>
                        </BeginStoryboard>
                    </Trigger.EnterActions>
                </Trigger>
            </ControlTemplate.Triggers>

        </ControlTemplate>
      </Setter.Value>
    </Setter>
  </Style>
</Window.Resources>
<Grid>

    <Button Style="{StaticResource AnimatedButtonStyle}" Width="200"
            Height="100">
            Click Me!
    </Button>
  </Grid>
</Window>
```

Figure 35-19

Figure 35-20

Things you can do with a Timeline are listed in the following table.

Timeline Properties	Description
AutoReverse	With the AutoReverse property, you can specify if the value that is animated should return to the original value after the animation.
SpeedRatio	With SpeedRatio, you can transform the speed at which an animation moves. With this property, you can define the relation in regard to the parent. The default value is 1; setting the ratio to a smaller value makes the animation move slower; setting the value to a value higher than 1 makes it move faster.
BeginTime	With BeginTime you can specify the time span from the start of the trigger event until the moment the animation should start. You can specify days, hours, minutes, seconds, and fractions of seconds. This might not be the real time, depending on the speed ratio. For example, if the speed ratio is set to 2, and the beginning time is set to 6 seconds, the animation will start after 3 seconds.
AccelerationRatio DecelerationRatio	With an animation the values need not be changed in a linear way. You can specify an AccelerationRatio and DecelerationRatio to define the impact of acceleration and deceleration. The sum of both values set must not be greater than 1.
Duration	With the Duration property, you specify the time length for one iteration of the animation.
RepeatBehavior	Assigning a RepeatBehavior struct to the RepeatBehavior property lets you define how many times or how long the animation should be repeated.
FillBehavior	The FillBehavior property is important if the parent timeline has a different duration. For example, if the parent timeline is shorter than the duration of the actual animation, setting the FillBehavior to Stop means that the actual animation stops. If the parent timeline is longer than the duration of the actual animation, HoldEnd keeps the actual animation active before resetting it to its original value (if AutoReverse is set).

Depending on the type of the Timeline class, some more properties may be available. For example, with DoubleAnimation you can specify the following additional properties.

DoubleAnimation Properties	Description
From To	By setting the From and To properties, you can specify the values to start and end the animation.
By	Instead of defining the start value for the animation, by setting the By property the animation starts with the current value of the bound property and is incremented with the value specified by the By property for the animation's end.

Triggers

Instead of having a property trigger, you can define an event trigger to start the animation. The next example creates an animation for the funny face you know from the previous chapter, where the eye moves as soon as a `Click` event from a button is fired. This example also demonstrates that you can start the animation both from XAML and code behind.

Figure 35-21 shows the running application of the animated face example.

Figure 35-21

Inside the `Window` element a `DockPanel` element is defined to arrange the funny face and the buttons. A `Grid` containing the `Canvas` element is docked on top. Bottom-docking is configured with a `StackPanel` element that contains four buttons. The first two buttons are used to animate the eye from code behind; the last two buttons are used to animate the eye from XAML.

The animation is defined within the `<DockPanel.Triggers>` section. Instead of a property trigger, an event trigger is used. The first event trigger is fired as soon as the `Click` event occurs with the button `startButtonXAML` defined by the `RoutedEvent` and `SourceName` properties. The trigger action is defined by the `BeginStoryboard` element that starts the containing `Storyboard`. `BeginStoryboard` has a name defined, because this is needed to control the storyboard with pause, continue, and stop actions. The `Storyboard` element contains two animations. The first animation changes the `Canvas.Left` position value of the eye; the second animation changes the `Canvas.Top` value. Both animations have different time values that make the eye movement very interesting using the defined repeated behavior.

The second event trigger is fired as soon as the `Click` event of the `stopButtonXAML` button occurs. Here, the storyboard is stopped with the `StopStoryboard` element, which references the started storyboard `beginMoveEye`:

```
<Window x:Class="AnimatedFace.Window1"
    xmlns="http://schemas.microsoft.com/winfx/2006/xaml/presentation"
    xmlns:x="http://schemas.microsoft.com/winfx/2006/xaml"
    Title="Face Animation" Height="300" Width="406">
  <DockPanel>

    <Grid DockPanel.Dock="Top">
      <!-- Funny Face -->
```

(continued)

(continued)

```xml
        <Canvas Width="200" Height="200">
          <Ellipse Canvas.Left="50" Canvas.Top="50" Width="100" Height="100"
              Stroke="Blue" StrokeThickness="4" Fill="Yellow" />
          <Ellipse Canvas.Left="60" Canvas.Top="65" Width="25" Height="25"
              Stroke="Blue" StrokeThickness="3" Fill="White" />
          <Ellipse Name="eye" Canvas.Left="67" Canvas.Top="72" Width="5"
              Height="5" Fill="Black" />
          <Path Name="mouth" Stroke="Blue" StrokeThickness="4"
              Data="M 62,125 Q 95,122 102,108" />

          <Line Name="LeftLeg" X1="92" X2="82" Y1="146" Y2="168" Stroke="Blue"
              StrokeThickness="4" />
          <Line Name="LeftFoot" X1="68" X2="83" Y1="160" Y2="169" Stroke="Blue"
              StrokeThickness="4" />

          <Line Name="RightLeg" X1="124" X2="132" Y1="144" Y2="166"
              Stroke="Blue" StrokeThickness="4" />
          <Line Name="RightFoot" X1="114" X2="133" Y1="169" Y2="166"
              Stroke="Blue" StrokeThickness="4" />
        </Canvas>
      </Grid>

      <StackPanel DockPanel.Dock="Bottom" Orientation="Horizontal">
        <Button Width="80" Height="40" Margin="20,5,5,5"
            Name="startAnimationButton">Start</Button>
        <Button Width="80" Height="40" Margin="5,5,5,5"
            Name="stopAnimationButton">Stop</Button>
        <Button Width="80" Height="40" Margin="5,5,5,5"
            Name="startButtonXAML">Start</Button>
        <Button Width="80" Height="40" Margin="5,5,5,5"
            Name="stopButtonXAML">Stop
        </Button>
      </StackPanel>

      <DockPanel.Triggers>

        <EventTrigger RoutedEvent="Button.Click" SourceName="startButtonXAML">
          <BeginStoryboard Name="beginMoveEye">
            <Storyboard Name="moveEye">
              <DoubleAnimation RepeatBehavior="Forever" DecelerationRatio=".8"
                  AutoReverse="True" By="8" Duration="0:0:1"
                  Storyboard.TargetName="eye"
                  Storyboard.TargetProperty="(Canvas.Left)" />
              <DoubleAnimation RepeatBehavior="Forever" AutoReverse="True"
                  By="8" Duration="0:0:5" Storyboard.TargetName="eye"
                  Storyboard.TargetProperty="(Canvas.Top)" />
            </Storyboard>
          </BeginStoryboard>
        </EventTrigger>

        <EventTrigger RoutedEvent="Button.Click" SourceName="stopButtonXAML">
```

```
        <StopStoryboard BeginStoryboardName="beginMoveEye" />
    </EventTrigger>

  </DockPanel.Triggers>
 </DockPanel>

</Window>
```

Instead of starting and stopping the animation directly from event triggers in XAML, you can easily control the animation from code behind. The buttons `startAnimationButton` and `stopAnimationButton` have the event handlers `OnStartAnimation` and `OnStopAnimation` associated with them. Within the event handlers, the animation is started with the `Begin()` method and stopped with the `Stop()` method. With the `Begin()` method the second parameter is set to `true` to allow you to control the animation with a stop request.

```
public partial class Window1 : System.Windows.Window
{
    public Window1()
    {
        InitializeComponent();
        startAnimationButton.Click += OnStartAnimation;
        stopAnimationButton.Click += OnStopAnimation;
    }

    void OnStartAnimation(object sender, RoutedEventArgs e)
    {
        moveEye.Begin(eye, true);
    }
    void OnStopAnimation(object sender, RoutedEventArgs e)
    {
        moveEye.Stop(eye);
    }
}
```

Now, you can start the application and watch the eye move as soon as one of the Start buttons is clicked.

Storyboard

The `Storyboard` class inherits from the base class `Timeline` but can contain multiple timelines. The `Storyboard` class can be used to control timelines. The following table describes the methods of the `Storyboard` class.

Storyboard Methods	Description
Begin()	The Begin() method starts the animations associated with the storyboard.
BeginAnimation()	With BeginAnimation(), you can start a single animation for a dependency property.
CreateClock()	The CreateClock() method returns a Clock object that you can use to control the animations.

Storyboard Methods	Description
Pause() Resume()	With Pause() and Resume(), you can pause and resume animations.
Seek()	With the Seek() method, you can jump in time and move the animation to a specified time interval.
Stop()	The Stop() method halts the clock and stops the animation.

The EventTrigger class makes it possible to define actions when events occur. The following table describes the properties of this class.

EventTrigger Properties	Description
RoutedEvent	With the RoutedEvent property, you can define the event when the trigger should start; for example, a Click event of a Button.
SourceName	The SourceName property defines to what WPF element the event should connect.

Trigger actions that you can put within an EventTrigger are listed in the following table. You've seen the BeginStoryboard and StopStoryboard actions in the example, but the following table shows some others.

TriggerAction Classes	Description
SoundPlayerAction	With SoundPlayerAction, you can play a .wav file.
BeginStoryboard	BeginStoryboard starts an animation defined by a Storyboard.
PauseStoryboard	PauseStoryboard pauses an animation.
ResumeStoryboard	ResumeStoryboard resumes an animation that was paused.
StopStoryboard	StopStoryboard stops a running animation.
SeekStoryboard	With SeekStoryboard, you can change the current time of an animation.
SkipStoryboardToFill	SkipStoryboardToFill advances an animation to the fill period at the end.
SetStoryboardSpeedRatio	With SetStoryboardSpeedRatio, you can change the speed of an animation.

Adding 3-D Features in WPF

This section gives you an introduction to the 3-D features of WPF. Here you'll find the information to get started.

The namespace for 3-D with WPF is System.Windows.Media.Media3D.

To understand 3-D with WPF it is important to know the difference of the coordination system. Figure 35-22 shows the coordination system of WPF 3-D. The origin is placed in the center. The x-axis has positive values to the right and negative values to the left. The y-axis is vertical with positive values up and negative values down. The z-axis defines positive values in direction to the viewer.

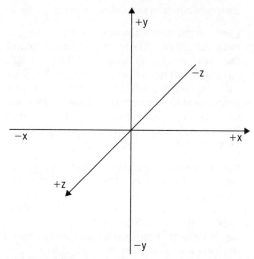

Figure 35-22

The most important classes and their functionality are described in the following table.

Class	Description
ViewPort3D	ViewPort3D defines the rendering surface for 3-D objects. This element contains all the visual elements for 3-D drawing.
ModelVisual3D	ModelVisual3D is contained in a ViewPort3D and contains all the visual elements. You can assign a transformation to a complete model.
GeometryModel3D	GeometryModel3D is contained within a ModelVisual3D and consists of a mesh and a material.
Geometry3D	Geometry3D is an abstract base class to define geometric shapes. The concrete class that derives from Geometry3D is MeshGeometry3D. With MeshGeometry3D you can define positions of triangles to build a 3-D model.

Class	Description
Material	Material is an abstract base class to define the front and back side from the triangles defined with the MeshGeometry3D. Material is contained within a GeometryModel3D. .NET 3.5 defines several material classes, such as DiffuseMaterial, EmissiveMaterial, and SpecularMaterial. Depending on the material type, the light calculates differently. EmissiveMaterial behaves with lighting calculations that the material emits the light equal to the color of the brush. DiffuseMaterial lights with a diffuse light, and SpecularMaterial defines a specularly lit model. With the MaterialGroup class you can create a combination consisting of other materials.
Light	Light is the abstract base class for lighting. Concrete implementations are AmbientLight, DirectionalLight, PointLight and SpotLight. AmbientLight is an unnatural light that lights the complete scene similarly. You will not see edges using that light. DirectionalLight defines a directed light. Sunlight is a example of directed light. The light comes from one side and here you can see edges and shadows. PointLight is a light with a specified position and lights in all directions. SpotLight lights in a specified direction. This light defines a cone so you can get a very intensive illuminated area.
Camera	Camera is the abstract base class for the camera that is used to map the 3-D scene to a 2-D display. Concrete implementations are PerspectiveCamera, OrthographicCamera, and MatrixCamera. With the PerspectiveCamera the 3-D objects are smaller the further away they are. This is different with the OrthographicCamera. Here the distance of the camera doesn't influence the size. With the MatrixCamera you can define the view and transformation in a matrix.
Transform3D	Transform3D is the abstract base class for 3-D transformations. Concrete implementations are RotateTransform3D, ScaleTransform3D, TranslateTransform3D, MatrixTransform3D, and Transform3DGroup. TranslateTransform3D allows transforming an object in the x, y, and z direction. ScaleTransform3D allows for an object resize. With the RotateTransform3D class you can rotate the object defined by an angle in the x, y, and z direction. With Transform3DGroup you can combine other transformations.

Triangle

This section starts with a simple 3-D sample. A 3-D model is made up of triangles, so a simple model is just one triangle. The triangle is defined by the Positions property of the MeshGeometry3D. The three points all use the same z coordinate, –4, and x/y coordinates –1 –1, 1 –1, and 0 1. The property TriangleIndices indicates the order of the positions in a counterclockwise way. With this property you define which side of the triangle is visible. One side of the triangle shows the color defined with the Material property of the GeometryModel3D class, and the other side shows the BackMaterial property.

The camera that is used to show the scenario is positioned at the coordinates 0, 0, 0, and looks into the direction 0, 0, –8. Changing the camera position to the left side, the rectangle moves to the right and vice versa. Changing the y position of the camera, the rectangle appears larger or smaller.

The light that is used in this scene is an AmbientLight to light up the complete scene with a white light. Figure 35-23 shows the result of the triangle.

```xml
<Window x:Class="Triangle3D.Window1"
    xmlns="http://schemas.microsoft.com/winfx/2006/xaml/presentation"
    xmlns:x="http://schemas.microsoft.com/winfx/2006/xaml"
    Title="3D" Height="300" Width="300">
  <Grid>
    <Viewport3D>
      <Viewport3D.Camera>
        <PerspectiveCamera Position="0 0 0" LookDirection="0 0 -8" />
      </Viewport3D.Camera>

      <ModelVisual3D>
        <ModelVisual3D.Content>
          <AmbientLight Color="White" />
        </ModelVisual3D.Content>
      </ModelVisual3D>

      <ModelVisual3D>
        <ModelVisual3D.Content>
          <GeometryModel3D>
            <GeometryModel3D.Geometry>
              <MeshGeometry3D
                  Positions="-1 -1 -4, 1 -1 -4, 0 1 -4"
                  TriangleIndices="0, 1, 2" />
            </GeometryModel3D.Geometry>
            <GeometryModel3D.Material>
              <MaterialGroup>
                <DiffuseMaterial>
                  <DiffuseMaterial.Brush>
                    <SolidColorBrush Color="Red" />
                  </DiffuseMaterial.Brush>
                </DiffuseMaterial>
              </MaterialGroup>
            </GeometryModel3D.Material>
          </GeometryModel3D>
        </ModelVisual3D.Content>
      </ModelVisual3D>
    </Viewport3D>
  </Grid>
</Window>
```

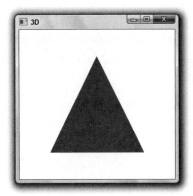

Figure 35-23

Changing Lights

Figure 35-23 just shows a simple triangle where you can get the same result with less effort using 2-D. However, from here you can continue getting into 3-D features. For example, by changing the light from an ambient light to a spotlight with the element SpotLight you can immediately see a different appearance of the triangle. With the spotlight you define a position where the light is placed, and the position to which the light is directed. Specifying -1 1 2 for the position, the light is placed at the left corner of the triangle and the y coordinate to the height of the triangle. From there the light is directed down and to the left. You can see the new appearance of the triangle in Figure 35-24.

```
<ModelVisual3D>
    <ModelVisual3D.Content>
        <SpotLight Position="-1 1 -2" Color="White"
                Direction="-1.5, -1, -5" />
    </ModelVisual3D.Content>
</ModelVisual3D>
```

Figure 35-24

Adding Textures

Instead of using a solid color brush with the materials of the triangle, you can use a different brush such as the `LinearGradientBrush` as shown with the following XAML code. The `LinearGradientBrush` element defined with `DiffuseMaterial` defines gradient stops with the colors yellow, orange, red, blue, and violet. To map a 2-D surface from an object such as the brush to a 3-D geometry, the `TextCoordinates` property must be set. `TextCoordinates` defines a collection of 2-D points that map to the 3-D positions. Figure 35-25 shows the 2-D coordinates of the brush from the sample application. The first position in the triangle, –1 –1, maps to the brush coordinates 0 1; the position 1 –1, which is the lower corner on the right, maps to 1 1 of the brush, which is violet; and 0 1 maps to 0.5 0. Figure 35-26 shows the triangle with the material of the gradient brush, again with the ambient light.

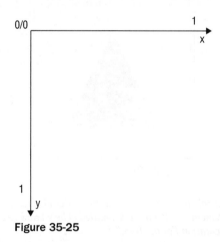

Figure 35-25

```
<ModelVisual3D>
    <ModelVisual3D.Content>
        <GeometryModel3D>
            <GeometryModel3D.Geometry>
                <MeshGeometry3D
                Positions="-1 -1 -4, 1 -1 -4, 0 1 -4"
                TriangleIndices="0, 1, 2"
                TextureCoordinates="0 1, 1 1, 0.5 0" />
            </GeometryModel3D.Geometry>

            <GeometryModel3D.Material>
                <MaterialGroup>
                    <DiffuseMaterial>
                        <DiffuseMaterial.Brush>
                            <LinearGradientBrush StartPoint="0,0"
                                EndPoint="1,1">
                                <GradientStop Color="Yellow" Offset="0" />
                                <GradientStop Color="Orange" Offset="0.25" />
                                <GradientStop Color="Red" Offset="0.50" />
                                <GradientStop Color="Blue" Offset="0.75" />
```

(continued)

(continued)

```
                                <GradientStop Color="Violet" Offset="1" />
                            </LinearGradientBrush>
                        </DiffuseMaterial.Brush>
                    </DiffuseMaterial>
                </MaterialGroup>
            </GeometryModel3D.Material>
        </GeometryModel3D>
    </ModelVisual3D.Content>
</ModelVisual3D>
```

Figure 35-26

You can add text or other controls in a similar way to the materials. To do this you just need to create a VisualBrush *with the elements that should be painted. The* VisualBrush *is discussed in Chapter 34, "Windows Presentation Foundation."*

3-Dimensional Object

Now let's get into a real three-dimensional object: a box. The box is made up of five rectangles: the back, front, left, right, and bottom sides. Each rectangle is made up of two triangles because this is the core of a mesh. With WPF and 3-D the term *mesh* is used to describe the triangle primitive for building 3-D shapes.

Here is the code of the rectangle for the front side of the box that consists of two triangles. The positions of the triangles are set in a counterclockwise order as defined by the TriangleIndices. The front side of the rectangle is done with a red brush; the back side with a gray brush. Both of these brushes are of type SolidColorBrush and defined with the resources of the Window.

```
                <!-- Front -->
                <GeometryModel3D>
                    <GeometryModel3D.Geometry>
                        <MeshGeometry3D
                            Positions="-1 -1 1, 1 -1 1, 1 1 1, 1 1 1,
                                       -1 1 1, -1 -1 1"
                            TriangleIndices="0 1 2, 3 4 5" />
                    </GeometryModel3D.Geometry>
                    <GeometryModel3D.Material>
                        <DiffuseMaterial Brush="{StaticResource redBrush}" />
```

```
    </GeometryModel3D.Material>
    <GeometryModel3D.BackMaterial>
        <DiffuseMaterial Brush="{StaticResource grayBrush}" />
    </GeometryModel3D.BackMaterial>
</GeometryModel3D>
```

The other rectangles look very similar, just with different positions. Here you can see the XAML code of the left side of the box:

```
<!-- Left side -->
<GeometryModel3D>
    <GeometryModel3D.Geometry>
        <MeshGeometry3D
        Positions="-1 -1 1, -1 1 1, -1 -1 -1, -1 -1 -1, -1 1 1,
                   -1 1 -1"
        TriangleIndices="0 1 2, 3 4 5" />
    </GeometryModel3D.Geometry>
    <GeometryModel3D.Material>
        <DiffuseMaterial Brush="{StaticResource redBrush}" />
    </GeometryModel3D.Material>
    <GeometryModel3D.BackMaterial>
        <DiffuseMaterial Brush="{StaticResource grayBrush}" />
    </GeometryModel3D.BackMaterial>
</GeometryModel3D>
```

The sample code defines a separate GeometryModel3D *with every side of the box. This is just for better understanding of the code. As long as the same material is used with every side, it's also possible to define a mesh containing all 10 triangles from all sides of the box.*

All the rectangles are combined within a Model3DGroup, so one transformation can be done with all the sides of the box:

```
<!-- the model -->
<ModelVisual3D>
    <ModelVisual3D.Content>
        <Model3DGroup>

        <!--GeometryModel3D elements for every side of the box -->

        </Model3DGroup>
```

With the Transform property of the Model3DGroup element, all the geometries inside this group can be transformed. Here a RotateTransform3D is used that defines an AxisAngleRotation3D. To rotate the box during runtime, the Angle property is bound to the value of a Slider control.

```
<!-- Transformation of the complete model -->
<Model3DGroup.Transform>
    <RotateTransform3D CenterX="0" CenterY="0" CenterZ="0">
        <RotateTransform3D.Rotation>
            <AxisAngleRotation3D x:Name="axisRotation"
                    Axis="0, 0, 0"
                    Angle="{Binding Path=Value,
                                ElementName=axisAngle}" />
        </RotateTransform3D.Rotation>
    </RotateTransform3D>
</Model3DGroup.Transform>
```

To see the box, a camera is needed. Here the `PerspectiveCamera` is used so that the box gets smaller the further the camera is. The position and direction of the camera can be set during runtime.

```
<!-- Camera -->
<Viewport3D.Camera>
    <PerspectiveCamera x:Name="camera"
            Position="{Binding Path=Text,
                    ElementName=textCameraPosition}"
            LookDirection="{Binding Path=Text,
                    ElementName=textCameraDirection}" />
</Viewport3D.Camera>
```

The application uses two different light sources. One light source is a `DirectionalLight`:

```
<!-- directional light -->
<ModelVisual3D>
    <ModelVisual3D.Content>
        <DirectionalLight Color="White" x:Name="directionalLight">
            <DirectionalLight.Direction>
                <Vector3D X="1" Y="2" Z="3" />
            </DirectionalLight.Direction>
        </DirectionalLight>
    </ModelVisual3D.Content>
</ModelVisual3D>
```

The other light source is a `SpotLight`. With this light source it is possible to highlight a specific area on the box. The `SpotLight` defines the properties `InnerConeAngle` and `OuterConeAngle` to define the area of the full illumination:

```
<!-- spot light -->
<ModelVisual3D>
    <ModelVisual3D.Content>
        <SpotLight x:Name="spotLight"
        InnerConeAngle="{Binding Path=Value,
                        ElementName=spotInnerCone}"
        OuterConeAngle="{Binding Path=Value,
                        ElementName=spotOuterCone}"
        Color="#FFFFFF"
        Direction="{Binding Path=Text, ElementName=spotDirection}"
        Position="{Binding Path=Text, ElementName=spotPosition}"
        Range="{Binding Path=Value, ElementName=spotRange}" />
    </ModelVisual3D.Content>
</ModelVisual3D>
```

When running the application you can change the rotation of the box, the camera, and lights as shown in Figure 35-27.

> *Creating a 3-D model that consists of just rectangles or triangles is easy to do. You would not manually create more complex models; instead you would use one of several tools. You can find 3-D tools for WPF at* `www.codeplex/3DTools`.

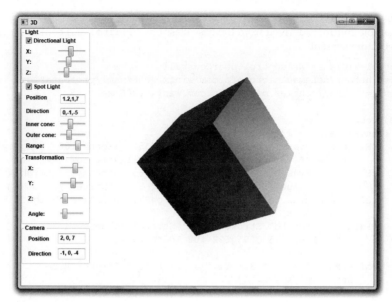

Figure 35-27

Windows Forms Integration

Instead of rewriting your user interface completely from scratch for WPF, you can use existing Windows Forms controls within WPF applications, and create new WPF controls to be used within Windows Forms applications. The best way of integrating Windows Forms and WPF is by creating controls and integrating the controls in the application types of the other technology.

The integration of Windows Forms and WPF has a big drawback. If you integrate Windows Forms with WPF, the Windows Forms controls still look like they looked in the old days. Windows Forms controls and applications don't get the new look of WPF. From a user interface standpoint, it would be better to rewrite the UI completely.

> To integrate Windows Forms and WPF, you need classes from the namespace System. Windows.Forms.Integration in the assembly WindowsFormsIntegration.

WPF Controls Within Windows Forms

You can use WPF controls within a Windows Forms application. A WPF element is a normal .NET class. However, you cannot use it directly from the Windows Forms code; a WPF control is not a Windows Forms control. The integration can be done by the wrapper class ElementHost from the namespace System.Windows.Forms.Integration. ElementHost is a Windows Forms control, because it derives from System.Windows.Forms.Control, and can be used like any other Windows Forms control in a Windows Forms application. ElementHost hosts and manages WPF controls.

Let's start with a simple WPF control. With Visual Studio 2008, you can create a WPF User Control Library. The sample control is derived from the base class `UserControl` and contains a grid and a button with a custom content:

```xml
<UserControl x:Class="WPFControl.UserControl1"
    xmlns="http://schemas.microsoft.com/winfx/2006/xaml/presentation"
    xmlns:x="http://schemas.microsoft.com/winfx/2006/xaml" >
  <Grid>
    <Button>
      <Canvas Height="230" Width="230">
        <Ellipse Canvas.Left="50" Canvas.Top="50" Width="100" Height="100"
            Stroke="Blue" StrokeThickness="4" Fill="Yellow" />
        <Ellipse Canvas.Left="60" Canvas.Top="65" Width="25" Height="25"
            Stroke="Blue" StrokeThickness="3" Fill="White" />
        <Ellipse Canvas.Left="70" Canvas.Top="75" Width="5" Height="5"
            Fill="Black" />
        <Path Name="mouth" Stroke="Blue" StrokeThickness="4"
            Data="M 62,125 Q 95,122 102,108" />

        <Line X1="124" X2="132" Y1="144" Y2="166" Stroke="Blue"
            StrokeThickness="4" />
        <Line X1="114" X2="133" Y1="169" Y2="166" Stroke="Blue"
            StrokeThickness="4" />

        <Line X1="92" X2="82" Y1="146" Y2="168" Stroke="Blue"
            StrokeThickness="4" />
        <Line X1="68" X2="83" Y1="160" Y2="168" Stroke="Blue"
            StrokeThickness="4" />
      </Canvas>
    </Button>
  </Grid>
</UserControl>
```

You can create a Windows Forms application by selecting the Windows Forms Application template. Because the WPF user control project is in the same solution as the Windows Forms application, you can drag and drop the WPF user control from the toolbox to the designer surface of the Windows Forms application. This adds references to the assemblies `PresentationCore`, `PresentationFramework`, `WindowsBase`, `WindowsFormsIntegration`, and of course, the assembly containing the WPF control.

Within the designer-generated code you will find a variable referencing the WPF user control and an object of type `ElementHost` that wraps the control:

```csharp
private System.Windows.Forms.Integration.ElementHost elementHost1;
private WPFControl.UserControl1 userControl11;
```

In the method `InitializeComponent` you can see object initializations and the assigning of the WPF control instance to the `Child` property of the `ElementHost` class:

```csharp
private void InitializeComponent()
{
    this.elementHost1 = new
            System.Windows.Forms.Integration.ElementHost();
    this.userControl11 = new WPFControl.UserControl1();
    this.SuspendLayout();
    //
    // elementHost1
    //
```

```
this.elementHost1.Location = new System.Drawing.Point(39, 44);
this.elementHost1.Name = "elementHost1";
this.elementHost1.Size = new System.Drawing.Size(259, 229);
this.elementHost1.TabIndex = 0;
this.elementHost1.Text = "elementHost1";
this.elementHost1.Child = this.userControl11;

//...
}
```

Starting the Windows Forms application, you can see both the WPF control as well the Windows Forms control inside one form, as shown in Figure 35-28.

Of course, you can add methods, properties, and events to the WPF control and use them the same way as other controls.

Figure 35-28

Windows Forms Controls Within WPF Applications

You can integrate Windows Forms and WPF in the other direction as well by placing a Windows Forms control within a WPF application. As with the ElementHost class used to host a WPF control inside Windows Forms, now you need a wrapper that is a WPF control to host a Windows Forms control. This class has the name WindowsFormsHost and is in the same assembly, WindowsFormsIntegration. The class WindowsFormsHost is derived from the base classes HwndHost and FrameworkElement, and thus can be used as a WPF element.

For this integration, a Windows Control Library is created first. Add a TextBox and Button control to the form by using the Designer. To change the Text property of the button, the property ButtonText is added to the code behind:

```
public partial class UserControl1 : UserControl
{
    public UserControl1()
    {
        InitializeComponent();
    }
```

(continued)

(continued)

```
        public string ButtonText
        {
            get { return button1.Text; }
            set { button1.Text = value; }
        }
    }
```

In the WPF application, you can add a `WindowsFormsHost` object from the toolbox to the Designer. This adds a reference to the assemblies `WindowsFormsIntegration`, `System.Windows.Forms`, and the assembly of the Windows Forms control. To use the Windows Forms control from XAML, you must add an XML namespace alias to reference the .NET namespace. Because the assembly containing the Windows Forms control is in a different assembly than the WPF application, you also must add the assembly name to the namespace alias. The Windows Forms control can now be contained within the `WindowsFormsHost` element as shown. You can assign a value for the property `ButtonText` directly from XAML similarly to .NET Framework elements.

```
    <Window x:Class="WPFApplication.Window1"
        xmlns="http://schemas.microsoft.com/winfx/2006/xaml/presentation"
        xmlns:x="http://schemas.microsoft.com/winfx/2006/xaml"
        xmlns:winforms=
            "clr-namespace:Wrox.ProCSharp.WPF;assembly=WindowsFormsControl"
        Title="WPF Interop Application" Height="300" Width="300"
        >
        <Grid>
          <Grid.RowDefinitions>
            <RowDefinition />
            <RowDefinition />
          </Grid.RowDefinitions>
          <WindowsFormsHost Grid.Row="0" Height="180">
            <winforms:UserControl1 x:Name="myControl" ButtonText="Click Me!" />
          </WindowsFormsHost>
          <StackPanel Grid.Row="1">
            <TextBox Margin="5,5,5,5" Width="140" Height="30"></TextBox>
            <Button Margin="5,5,5,5" Width="80" Height="40">WPF Button</Button>
          </StackPanel>
        </Grid>
    </Window>
```

You can see a view of the WPF application in Figure 35-29. Of course, the Windows Forms control still looks like a Windows Forms control and does not have all the resizing and styling features you get with WPF.

Figure 35-29

WPF Browser Application

Visual Studio 2008 has another WPF project template: a WPF Browser Application. Such an application can run within Internet Explorer, but still the .NET Framework version that you use must be installed with the client system. Here you get the features of the rich client to the browser. However, with WPF Browser Applications, the .NET Framework is required to be available on the client system, and only Internet Explorer is supported.

Creating such a project type, an XBAP (XAML Browser Application) file is created. XBAP is an XML file that defines the application and the assemblies it consists of for ClickOnce deployment.

An XBAP application is a partial-trust application. You can use only .NET code that is available with the Internet permissions.

ClickOnce is explained in Chapter 16, "Deployment."

WPF Browser Applications are different from Silverlight. Silverlight defines a subset of WPF that does not require the .NET Framework to be installed with the client system. Silverlight requires an add-in with the browser but supports different browsers and different operating systems. Silverlight 1.0 cannot be programmed using .NET; you can use only JavaScript for accessing the XAML elements programmatically. Silverlight 1.1 will support the .NET Microframework.

Summary

This chapter covered some more features of WPF.

WPF data binding gives a leap forward compared to Windows Forms. You can bind any property of a .NET class to a property of a WPF element. The binding mode defines the direction of the binding. You can bind .NET objects and lists, and define a data template to create a default look for a .NET class with a data template.

Command binding makes it possible to map handler code to menus and toolbars. You've also seen how easy it is to do copy and paste with WPF because a command handler for this technology is already included in the `TextBox` control.

Animation allows the user to dynamically change every property of a WPF element. Animations can be very decent and not annoying and make the UI more responsive and attractive for the user.

WPF also allows for an easy 3-D mapping to the 2-D surface of a screen. You've seen how to create a 3-D model and view it with the help of different light sources and cameras.

This and the previous chapter gave you an overview of WPF and enough information to get started with this technology. For more information on WPF, you should read a book that focuses on WPF; for example, Professional WPF Programming: .NET Development with the Windows Presentation Foundation *by Chris Andrade et al. (Wiley Publishing, 2007).*

36

Add-Ins

Add-ins allow you to add functionality to an application at a later time. You can create a hosting application that gains more and more functionality over time — functionality that might be written by your developer team but also different vendors can extend your application by creating add-ins.

Today, add-ins are used with many different applications, such as Internet Explorer and Visual Studio. Internet Explorer is a hosting application that offers an add-in framework that is used by many companies to offer extensions when viewing Web pages. The Shockwave Flash Object allows you to view Web pages with Flash content. The Google toolbar offers specific Google features that can be accessed quickly from Internet Explorer. Visual Studio also has an add-in model that allows you to extend Visual Studio with different levels of extensions.

For your custom applications it has always been possible to create an add-in model to dynamically load and use functionality from assemblies. With an add-in model many issues need to be thought about. How can new assemblies be detected? How can versioning issues be resolved? Can the add-in change the stability of the hosting application?

The .NET Framework 3.5 offers a framework for hosting and creating add-ins with the assembly System.AddIn. This framework is also known by the name Managed AddIn Framework (MAF).

Add-ins are also known by different terms such as "add-on" or "plug-in."

Topics covered in this chapter are

❑ System.AddIn architecture

❑ Creating a simple add-in

System.AddIn Architecture

When you create an application that allows you to add add-ins during runtime, you will need to deal with certain issues — for example, how to find the add-ins, and how to solve versioning issues so that the hosting application and the add-in can progress independently. There are several ways to resolve these issues. In this section, you read about the issues of add-ins and how the architecture of MAF solves them:

❑ Issues with add-ins

❑ Pipeline architecture

❑ Discovery

❑ Activation

❑ Isolation

❑ Lifetime

❑ Versioning

Issues with Add-ins

Creating a hosted application that dynamically loads assemblies that are added at a later time has several issues that must be dealt with, as shown in the table that follows.

Add-Ins Issues	Description
Discovery	How can new add-ins be found for the hosting application? There are several different options. One way is to add information about add-ins to a configuration file. This has the disadvantage that the installation of new add-ins needs to change an existing configuration file. Another option is to just copy the assembly containing the add-in to a predefined directory and read information about the assembly with reflection. You can read more about reflection in Chapter 13, "Reflection."
Activation	With assemblies that are dynamically loaded it is not possible to just use the new operator to create an instance. You can create such assemblies with the Activator class. Also, different activation options might apply if the add-in is loaded within a different application domain or a new process. Assemblies and application domains are described in Chapter 17, "Assemblies."
Isolation	An add-in can break the hosting application as you've probably already seen with Internet Explorer crashes caused by various add-ins. Depending on the type of the hosting application and how the add-ins are integrated, the add-in can be loaded within a different application domain or also within a different process.
Lifetime	Cleaning up objects is a job of the garbage collector. However, the garbage collector cannot help here because add-ins might be active in a different application domain or a different process. Other ways to keep the object in memory are reference count or leasing and sponsoring mechanisms.
Versioning	Versioning is a big issue with add-ins. Usually it should be possible that a new version of the host still can load old add-ins, and an old host should have the option to load newer add-ins.

Now let's look at the architecture of MAF and how this framework solves these issues. The design of MAF was influenced by these goals:

❏ It should be easy to develop add-ins.

❏ Finding add-ins during runtime should be performant.

❏ Developing hosts should be an easy process as well, but not as easy as developing add-ins.

❏ The add-in and the host application should progress independently.

Pipeline Architecture

The MAF architecture is based on a pipeline of seven assemblies. This pipeline solves the versioning issues with add-ins. Because the assemblies from the pipeline have a very light dependency, it is possible that the contract, the hosting, and the add-in applications progress with new versions completely independent of one another.

Figure 36-1 shows the pipeline of the MAF architecture. In the center is the contract assembly. This assembly contains a contract interface that lists methods and properties that must be implemented by the add-in and can be called by the host. Left of the contract is the host side, and on the right, the add-in side. In the figure you can see the dependencies between the assemblies. The host assembly shown leftmost does not have a real dependency to the contract assembly; the same is true of the add-in assembly. Both do not really implement the interface that is defined by the contract. Instead, they just have a reference to a view assembly. The host application references the host view; the add-in references the add-in view. The views contain abstract view classes that define methods and properties as defined by the contract.

Figure 36-1

Figure 36-2 shows the relationship of the classes from the pipeline. The host class has an association with the abstract host view class and invokes its methods. The abstract host view class is implemented by the host adapter. Adapters make the connection between the views and the contract. The add-in adapter implements the methods and properties of the contract. This adapter contains a reference to the add-in view and forwards calls from the host side to the add-in view. The host adapter class defines a concrete class that derives from the abstract base class of the host view to implement the methods and properties. This adapter includes a reference to the contract to forward calls from the view to the contract.

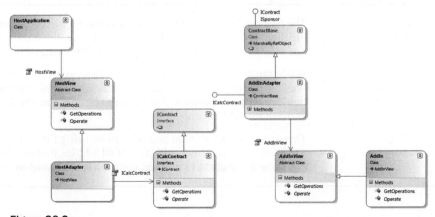

Figure 36-2

With this model it is possible that the add-in side and the host side emerge completely independent. Just the mapping layer needs to adapt. For example, if a new version of the host is done that uses completely new methods and properties, the contract can still stay the same and only the adapter needs to change. It is also possible that a new contract is defined. Adapters can change, or several contracts can be used in parallel.

Discovery

How can new add-ins be found for the hosting application? The MAF architecture uses a predefined directory structure to find add-ins and the other assemblies of the pipeline. The components of the pipeline must be stored in these subdirectories:

- ❑   HostSideAdapters
- ❑   Contracts
- ❑   AddInSideAdapters
- ❑   AddInViews
- ❑   AddIns

All these directories with the exception of the AddIns directory directly contain the assembly of the specific part of the pipeline. The AddIns directory contains subdirectories for every add-in assembly. With add-ins, it is also possible to store them in directories that are completely independent of the other pipeline components.

The assemblies of the pipeline are not just loaded dynamically to get all the information about the add-in using reflection. With many add-ins, this would increase the startup time of the hosting application. Instead, MAF uses a cache with information about the pipeline components. The cache is created by the program installing the add-in or by the hosting application if the hosting application has write access to the directory of the pipeline.

The cache information about the pipeline components is created by invoking methods of the AddInStore class. The method Update() finds new add-ins that are not already listed with the store files. The Rebuild() method rebuilds the complete binary store file with information about the add-ins.

The following table lists the members of the AddInStore class.

AddInStore Members	Description
Rebuild() RebuildAddIns()	The Rebuild() method rebuilds the cache for all components of the pipeline. If the add-ins are stored in a different directory, the method RebuildAddIns() can be used to rebuild the cache of the add-ins.
Update() UpdateAddIns()	While the Rebuild() method rebuilds the complete cache of the pipeline, the Update method just updates the cache with information about new pipeline components. The UpdateAddIns() method updates the cache of the add-ins only.
FindAddIn() FindAddIns()	These methods are used to find add-ins by using the cache. The method FindAddIns() returns a collection of all add-ins that match the host view. The FindAddIn() method returns a specific add-in.

Activation and Isolation

The `FindAddIns()` method of the `AddInStore` class returns a collection of `AddInToken` objects that represent an add-in. With the `AddInToken` class, you can access information about the add-in such as name, description, publisher, and version. You can activate the add-in by using the `Activate()` method. The following table lists properties and methods of the `AddInToken` class.

AddInToken Members	Description
Name Publisher Version Description	The `Name`, `Publisher`, `Version` and `Description` properties of the `AddInToken` class return information about an add-in that was assigned to the add-in with the attribute `AddInAttribute`.
AssemblyName	`AssemblyName` returns the name of the assembly that contains the add-in.
EnableDirectConnect	With the property `EnableDirectConnect` you can set a value that the host should directly connect to the add-in instead of using the components of the pipeline. This is only possible if the add-in and the host are running in the same application domain, and the types of the add-in view and the host view are the same. With this it is still required that all components of the pipeline exist.
QualificationData	The add-in can mark appdomain and security requirements with the attribute `QualificationDataAttribute`. The add-in can list requirements for security and isolation requirements. For example, `[QualificationData("Isolation", "NewAppDomain")]` means that the add-in requires to be hosted in a new process. You can read this information from the `AddInToken` to activate the add-in with the specified requirements. In addition to appdomain and security requirements, you can use this attribute to pass custom information through the pipeline.
Activate()	The add-in is activated with the `Activate()` method. With parameters of this method, you can define if the add-in should be loaded inside a new application domain or a new process. You can also define what permissions the add-in gets.

One add-in can break the complete application. You may have seen Internet Explorer crash because of a failing add-in. Depending on the application type and the add-in type, you can avoid this by letting the add-in run within a different application domain or within a different process. MAF gives you several options here. You can activate the add-in in a new application domain or a new process. The new application domain might also have restricted permissions.

The `Activate()` method of the `AddInToken` class has several overloads where you can pass the environment into which the add-in should be loaded. The different options are listed in the following table.

Parameters of AddInToken.Activate()	Description
AppDomain	You can pass a new application domain into which the add-in should be loaded. This way you can make it independent of the host application, and it can also be unloaded with the application domain.
AddInSecurityLevel	If the add-in should run with different security levels you can pass a value of the AddInSecurityLevel enumeration. Possible values are Internet, Intranet, FullTrust, and Host.
PermissionSet	If the predefined security levels are not specific enough, you can also assign a PermissionSet to the appdomain of the add-in.
AddInProcess	Add-ins can also run within a different process from the hosting application. You can pass a new AddInProcess to the Activate() method. The new process can shut down if all add-ins are unloaded, or it can keep running. This is an option that can be set with the property KeepAlive.
AddInEnvironment	Passing an AddInEnvironment object is another option to define the application domain where the add-in should be loaded. With the constructor of AddInEnvironment, you can pass an AppDomain object. You can also get an existing AddInEnvironment of an add-in with the AddInEnvironment property of the AddInController class.

Application domains are explained in Chapter 17, "Assemblies."

The type of application may restrict the choices you have. WPF add-ins currently do not support crossing processes. With Windows Forms, it is not possible to have Windows controls connected across different application domains.

Let's get into the steps of the pipeline when the Activate() method of an AddInToken is invoked:

1. The application domain is created with the permissions specified.

2. The assembly of the add-in is loaded into the new application domain with the Assembly .LoadFrom() method

3. The default constructor of the add-in is invoked by using reflection. Because the add-in derives from the base class that is defined with the add-in view, the assembly of the view is loaded as well.

4. Next, an instance of the add-in side adapter is constructed. The instance of the add-in is passed to the constructor of the adapter, so the adapter can connect the contract to the add-in. The add-in adapter derives from the base class MarshalByRefObject, so it can be invoked across application domains.

5. The activation code returns a proxy to the add-in side adapter to the application domain of the hosting application. Because the add-in adapter implements the contract interface, the proxy contains methods and properties of the contract interface.

6. An instance of the host side adapter is constructed in the application domain of the hosting application. The proxy of the add-in side adapter is passed to the constructor. The activation finds the type of the host-side adapter from the add-in token.

The host side adapter is returned to the hosting application.

Contracts

Contracts define the boundary between the host side and the add-in side. Contracts are defined with an interface that needs to derive from the base interface IContract. The contract should be well-thought in that it supports flexible add-in scenarios as needed.

Contracts are not versionable and may not be changed so that previous add-in implementations can still run in newer hosts. New versions are created by defining a new contract.

There's some restriction on the types you can use with the contract. The restriction exists because of versioning issues and also because application domains are crossed from the hosting application to the add-in. The types need to be safe and versionable, and able to pass it across the boundaries (application domain or cross-process) to pass it between hosts and add-ins.

Possible types that can be passed with a contract are:

- Primitive types
- Other contracts
- Serializable system types
- Simple serializable custom types that consists of primitive types, contracts, and do not have an implementation

The members of the IContract interface are explained in the following table.

IContract Members	Description
QueryContract()	With QueryContract() it is possible to query a contract to verify if another contract is implemented as well. An add-in can support several contracts.
RemoteToString()	The parameter of QueryContract() requires a string representation of the contract. RemoteToString() returns a string representation of the current contract.
AcquireLifetimeToken() RevokeLifetimeToken()	The client invokes AcquireLifetimeToken() to keep a reference to the contract. AcquireLifetimeToken() increments a reference count. RevokeLifetimeToken() decrements a reference count.
RemoteEquals()	RemoteEquals() can be used to compare two contract references.

Contract interfaces are defined in the namespaces System.AddIn.Contract, System.AddIn .Contract.Collections, and System.AddIn.Contract.Automation. The following table lists contract interfaces that you can use with a contract:

Contract	Description
`IListContract<T>`	The `IListContract<T>` can be used to return a list of contracts.
`IEnumeratorContract<T>`	`IEnumeratorContract<T>` is used to enumerate the elements of a `IListContract<T>`.
`IServiceProviderContract`	An add-in can offer services for other add-ins. Add-ins that offer services are known as service provider and implement the interface `IServiceProviderContract`. With the method `QueryService()` an add-in implementing this interface can be queried for services offered.
`IProfferServiceContract`	`IProfferServiceContract` is the interface offered by a service provider in conjunction with `IServiceProviderContract`. `IProfferServiceContract` defines the methods `ProfferService()` and `RevokeService()`. `ProfferService()` adds an `IServiceProviderContract` to the services offered, `RevokeService()` removes it.
`INativeHandleContract`	This interface provides access to native Window handles with the `GetHandle()` method. This contract is used with WPF hosts to use WPF add-ins.

Lifetime

How long does an add-in need to be loaded? How long is it used? When is it possible to unload the application domain? There are several options to resolve this. One option is to use reference counts. Every use of the add-in increments the reference count. If the reference count decrements to zero, the add-in can be unloaded. Another option is to use the garbage collector. If the garbage collector runs, and there's no more reference to an object, the object is the target of garbage collection. .NET Remoting is using a leasing mechanism and a sponsor to keep objects alive. As soon as the leasing time ends, sponsors are asked if the object should stay alive.

With add-ins, there's a specific issue for unloading add-ins because they can run in different application domains and also in different processes. The garbage collector cannot work across different processes. MAF is using a mixed model for lifetime management. Within a single application domain, garbage collection is used. Within the pipeline an implicit sponsorship is used, but reference counting is available from the outside to control the sponsor.

Let's consider a scenario where the add-in is loaded into a different application domain. Within the host application, the garbage collector cleans up the host view and the host side adapter when the reference is not needed anymore. For the add-in side, the contract defines the methods `AcquireLifetimeToken()` and `RevokeLifetimeToken()` to increment and decrement the reference count of the sponsor. These methods do not just increment and decrement a value which could lead to release an object too early if one party would call the revoke method too often. Instead, `AcquireLifetimeToken()` returns an identifier for the lifetime token, and this identifier must be used to invoke the `RevokeLifetimeToken()` method. So these methods are always called in pairs.

Usually you do not have to deal with invoking the `AcquireLifetimeToken()` and `RevokeLifetimeToken()` methods. Instead you can use the `ContractHandle` class that invokes `AcquireLifetimeToken()` in the constructor and `RevokeLifetimeToken()` in the finalizer.

The finalizer is explained in Chapter 12, "Memory Management and Pointers."

In scenarios where the add-in is loaded in a new application domain, it is possible to get rid of the loaded code when the add-in is not needed anymore. MAF uses a simple model to define one add-in as the owner of the application domain to unload the application domain if this add-in is not needed anymore. An add-in is the owner of the application domain if the application domain is created when the add-in is activated. The application domain is not unloaded automatically if it was created previously.

The class `ContractHandle` is used in the host side adapter to add a reference count to the add-in. The members of this class are explained in the following table.

ContractHandle Members	Description
Contract	In the construction of the `ContractHandle` class, an object implementing `IContract` can be assigned to keep a reference to it. The `Contract` property returns this object.
Dispose()	The `Dispose()` method can be called instead of waiting for the garbage collector to do the finalization to revoke the lifetime token.
AppDomainOwner()	`AppDomainOwner()` is a static method of the `ContractHandle` class that returns the add-in adapter if it owns the application domain that is passed with the method.
ContractOwnsAppDomain()	With the static method `ContractOwnsAppDomain()` you can verify if the specified contract is an owner of the application domain. Thus, the application domain gets unloaded when the contract is disposed.

Versioning

Versioning is a very big issue with add-ins. The host application is developed further as are the add-ins. One requirement for an add-in is that it should be possible that a new version of the host application can still load old versions of add-ins. The other direction should work as well: older hosts should run newer versions of add-ins. But what if the contract changes?

System.AddIn is completely independent from the implementation of the host application and add-ins. This is done with a pipeline concept that consists of seven parts.

Add-In Sample

Let's start a simple sample of a hosting application that can load calculator add-ins. The add-ins can support different calculation operations that are offered by add-ins.

You need to create a solution with six library projects and one console application. The projects of the sample application are listed in the following table. The table lists the assemblies that need to be referenced. With the references to the other projects within the solution you need to set the property

Copy Local to False, so that the assembly does not get copied. One exception is the HostApp console project that needs a reference to the HostView project. This assembly needs to be copied so it can be found from the host application. Also you need to change the output path of the generated assemblies so that the assemblies are copied to the correct directories of the pipeline.

Project	References	Output Path	Description
CalcContract	`System.AddIn.Contract`	`..\Pipeline\` `Contracts\`	This assembly contains the contract for communication with the add-in. The contract is defined with an interface.
CalcView	`System.AddIn`	`..\Pipeline\` `AddInViews\`	The CalcView assembly contains an abstract class that is referenced by the add-in. This is the add-in side of the contract.
CalcAddIn	`System.AddIn` `CalcView`	`..\Pipeline\` `AddIns\CalcAddIn\`	CalcAddIn is the add-in project that references the add-in view assembly. This assembly contains the implementation of the add-in.

CalcAddIn Adapter	`System.AddIn`
	`System.AddIn.Contract`
	`CalcView`
	`CalcContract`
		`..\Pipeline\`
		`AddInSideAdapters\`
			CalcAddInAdapter connects the add-in view and the contract assembly and maps the contract to the add-in view.

HostView			The assembly containing the abstract class of the host view does not need to reference any Add-In assembly and also does not have a reference to another project in the solution.

HostAdapter	`System.AddIn`
	`System.AddIn.Contract`
	`HostView`
	`CalcContract`
		`..\Pipeline\`
		`HostSideAdapters\`
			The host adapter maps the host view to the contract. Thus, it needs to reference both of these projects.

HostApp	`System.AddIn` `HostView`		The hosting application activates the add-in.

Calculator Contract

Let's start by implementing the contract assembly. Contract assemblies contain a contract interface that defines the protocol for communication between the host and the add-in.

With the following code you can see the contract defined for the calculator sample application. The application defines a contract with the methods `GetOperations()` and `Operate()`. `GetOperations()` returns a list of mathematical operations supported by the calculator add-in. An operation is defined by the interface `IOperationContract` that is a contract by itself. `IOperationContract` defines the read-only properties `Name` and `NumberOperands`.

The `Operate()` method invokes the operation within the add-in and requires an operation defined by the `IOperation` interface and the operands with a `double` array.

With this contract it is possible that the add-in supports any operations that require any number of `double` operands and returns one `double`.

The attribute `AddInContract` is used by the `AddInStore` to build the cache. The `AddInContract` attribute marks the class as an add-in contract interface.

```
using System.AddIn.Contract;
using System.AddIn.Pipeline;
namespace Wrox.ProCSharp.AddIns
{
    [AddInContract]
    public interface ICalculatorContract : IContract
    {
        IListContract<IOperationContract> GetOperations();
        double Operate(IOperationContract operation, double[] operands);
    }
    public interface IOperationContract : IContract
    {
        string Name { get; }
        int NumberOperands { get; }
    }
}
```

Calculator Add-In View

The add-in view redefines the contract as it is seen by the add-in. The contract defined the interfaces `ICalculatorContract` and `IOperationContract`. For this, the add-in view defines the abstract class `Calculator` and the concrete class `Operation`.

With `Operation` there's not a specific implementation required by every add-in. Instead, the class is already implemented with the add-in view assembly. This class describes an operation for mathematical calculations with the `Name` and `NumberOperands` properties.

The abstract class `Calculator` defines the methods that need to be implemented by the add-ins. While the contract defines parameters and return types that need to be passed across appdomain- and process-boundaries, that's not the case with the add-in view. Here you can use types, which make it easy to write add-ins for the add-in developer. The `GetOperations()` method returns `IList<Operation>` instead of `IListOperation<IOperationContract>`, as you've seen with the contract assembly.

The `AddInBase` attribute identifies the class as an add-in view for the store.

```
using System.AddIn.Pipeline;
using System.Collections.Generic;
```

(continued)

(continued)

```
namespace Wrox.ProCSharp.AddIns
{
    [AddInBase]
    public abstract class Calculator
    {
        public abstract IList<Operation> GetOperations();
        public abstract double Operate(Operation operation, double[] operand);
    }
    public class Operation
    {
        public string Name { get; set; }
        public int NumberOperands { get; set; }
    }
}
```

Calculator Add-In Adapter

The add-in adapter maps the contract to the add-in view. This assembly has references to both the contract and the add-in view assemblies. The implementation of the adapter needs to map the method `IListContract<IOperationContract> GetOperations()` from the contract to the view method `IList<Operation> GetOperations()`.

The assembly includes the classes `OperationViewToContractAddInAdapter` and `CalculatorViewToContractAddInAdapter`. These classes implement the interfaces `IOperationContract` and `ICalculatorContract`. The methods of the base interface `IContract` can be implemented by deriving from the base class `ContractBase`. This class offers a default implementation. `OperationViewToContractAddInAdapter` implements the other members of the `IOperationContract` interface and just forwards the calls to the `Operation` view that is assigned in the constructor.

The class `OperationViewToContractAddInAdapter` also contains static helper methods `ViewToContractAdapter()` and `ContractToViewAdapter()` that map `Operation` to `IOperationContract` and the other way around.

```
using System.AddIn.Pipeline;
namespace Wrox.ProCSharp.AddIns
{
    internal class OperationViewToContractAddInAdapter : ContractBase,
            IOperationContract
    {
        private Operation view;
        public OperationViewToContractAddInAdapter(Operation view)
        {
            this.view = view;
        }
        public string Name
        {
            get { return view.Name; }
        }
        public int NumberOperands
        {
            get { return view.NumberOperands; }
        }
        public static IOperationContract ViewToContractAdapter(Operation view)
```

```
        {
            return new OperationViewToContractAddInAdapter(view);
        }
        public static Operation ContractToViewAdapter(
            IOperationContract contract)
        {
            return (contract as OperationViewToContractAddInAdapter).view;
        }
    }
}
```

The class CalculatorViewToContractAddInAdapter is very similar to
OperationViewToContractAddInAdapter: It derives from ContractBase to inherit a default
implementation of the IContract interface, and it implements a contract interface. This time the
ICalculatorContract interface is implemented with the GetOperations() and Operate() methods.

The Operate() method of the adapter invokes the Operate() method of the view class
Calculator where IOperationContract needs to be converted to Operation. This is done with the
static helper method ContractToViewAdapter() that is defined with the
OperationViewToContractAddInAdapter class.

The implementation of the GetOperations method needs to convert the collection
IListContract<IOperationContract> to IList<Operation>. For such collection conversions, the
class CollectionAdapters defines conversion methods ToIList() and ToIListContract().
Here, the method ToIListContract() is used for the conversion.

The attribute AddInAdapter identifies the class as an add-in side adapter for the add-in store.

```
using System.AddIn.Contract;
using System.AddIn.Pipeline;
namespace Wrox.ProCSharp.AddIns
{
    [AddInAdapter]
    internal class CalculatorViewToContractAddInAdapter : ContractBase,
        ICalculatorContract
    {
        private Calculator view;
        public CalculatorViewToContractAddInAdapter(Calculator view)
        {
            this.view = view;
        }
        public IListContract<IOperationContract> GetOperations()
        {
            return CollectionAdapters.ToIListContract<Operation,
                IOperationContract>(view.GetOperations(),
                OperationViewToContractAddInAdapter.ViewToContractAdapter,
                OperationViewToContractAddInAdapter.ContractToViewAdapter);
        }
        public double Operate(IOperationContract operation, double[] operands)
        {
            return view.Operate(
                OperationViewToContractAddInAdapter.ContractToViewAdapter(
                    operation), operands);
        }
    }
}
```

> Because the adapter classes are invoked by .NET reflection, it is possible that the
> internal access modifier is used with these classes. As these classes are an
> implementation detail, it's a good idea to use the `internal` access modifier.

Calculator Add-In

The add-in now contains the real implementation of the add-in. The add-in is implemented by the class
`CalculatorV1`. The add-in assembly has a dependency on the add-in view assembly as it needs to
implement the abstract `Calculator` class.

The attribute `AddIn` marks the class as an add-in for the add-in store, and adds publisher, version, and
description information. On the host side, this information can be accessed from the `AddInToken`.

`CalculatorV1` returns a list of supported operations in the method `GetOperations()`. `Operate()`
calculates the operands based on the operation.

```
using System;
using System.AddIn;
using System.Collections.Generic;
namespace Wrox.ProCSharp.AddIns
{
    [AddIn("CalculatorAddIn", Publisher="Wrox Press", Version="1.0.0.0",
            Description="Sample AddIn")]
    public class CalculatorV1 : Calculator
    {
        private List<Operation> operations;
        public CalculatorV1()
        {
            operations = new List<Operation>();
            operations.Add(new Operation() { Name = "+", NumberOperands = 2 });
            operations.Add(new Operation() { Name = "-", NumberOperands = 2 });
            operations.Add(new Operation() { Name = "/", NumberOperands = 2 });
            operations.Add(new Operation() { Name = "*", NumberOperands = 2 });
        }
        public override IList<Operation> GetOperations()
        {
            return operations;
        }
        public override double Operate(Operation operation, double[] operand)
        {
            switch (operation.Name)
            {
                case "+":
                    return operand[0] + operand[1];
                case "-":
                    return operand[0] - operand[1];
                case "/":
                    return operand[0] / operand[1];
                case "*":
                    return operand[0] * operand[1];
```

```
            default:
                throw new InvalidOperationException(
                    String.Format("invalid operation {0}", operation.Name));
            }
        }
    }
}
```

Calculator Host View

Let's continue with the host view of the host side. Similar to the add-in view, the host view defines an abstract class with methods similar to the contract. However, the methods defined here are invoked by the host application.

Both the class `Calculator` and `Operation` are abstract as the members are implemented by the host adapter. The classes here just need to define the interface to be used by the host application.

```
using System.Collections.Generic;
namespace Wrox.ProCSharp.AddIns
{
    public abstract class Calculator
    {
        public abstract IList<Operation> GetOperations();
        public abstract double Operate(Operation operation,
            params double[] operand);
    }
    public abstract class Operation
    {
        public abstract string Name { get; }
        public abstract int NumberOperands { get; }
    }
}
```

Calculator Host Adapter

The host adapter assembly references the host view and the contract to map the view to the contract. The class `OperationContractToViewHostAdapter` implements the members of the abstract `Operation` class. The class `CalculatorContractToViewHostAdapter` implements the members of the abstract `Calculator` class.

With `OperationContractToViewHostAdapter`, the reference to the contract is assigned in the constructor. The adapter class also contains a `ContractHandle` instance that adds a lifetime reference to the `contract`, so that add-in stays loaded as long it is needed by the hosting application.

```
using System.AddIn.Pipeline;
namespace Wrox.ProCSharp.AddIns
{
    internal class OperationContractToViewHostAdapter : Operation
    {
        private ContractHandle handle;
        public IOperationContract Contract { get; private set; }
        public OperationContractToViewHostAdapter(IOperationContract contract)
```

(continued)

(continued)

```
        {
            this.Contract = contract;
            handle = new ContractHandle(contract);
        }
        public override string Name
        {
            get
            {
                return Contract.Name;
            }
        }
        public override int NumberOperands
        {
            get
            {
                return Contract.NumberOperands;
            }
        }
    }
    internal static class OperationHostAdapters
    {
        internal static IOperationContract ViewToContractAdapter(Operation view)
        {
            return ((OperationContractToViewHostAdapter)view).Contract;
        }
        internal static Operation ContractToViewAdapter(
            IOperationContract contract)
        {
            return new OperationContractToViewHostAdapter(contract);
        }
    }
}
```

The class `CalculatorContractToViewHostAdapter` implements the methods of the abstract host view `Calculator` class and forwards the call to the contract. Again, you can see the `ContractHandle` holding the reference to the contract, which is similar to the adapter from the add-in side type conversions. This time the type conversions are just in the other direction from the add-in adapters.

The attribute `HostAdapter` marks the class as an adapter that needs to be installed in the HostSideAdapters directory.

```
using System.Collections.Generic;
using System.AddIn.Pipeline;
namespace Wrox.ProCSharp.AddIns
{
    [HostAdapter]
    internal class CalculatorContractToViewHostAdapter : Calculator
    {
        private ICalculatorContract contract;
        private ContractHandle handle;
        public CalculatorContractToViewHostAdapter(ICalculatorContract contract)
```

```
        {
            this.contract = contract;
            handle = new ContractHandle(contract);
        }
        public override IList<Operation> GetOperations()
        {
            return CollectionAdapters.ToIList<IOperationContract, Operation>(
                contract.GetOperations(),
                OperationHostAdapters.ContractToViewAdapter,
                OperationHostAdapters.ViewToContractAdapter);
        }
        public override double Operate(Operation operation, double[] operands)
        {
            return contract.Operate(OperationHostAdapters.ViewToContractAdapter(
                operation), operands);
        }
    }
}
```

Calculator Host

The sample host application uses the WPF technology. You can see the user interface of this application in Figure 36-3. On top is the list of available add-ins. On the left, the operations of the active add-in are shown. As you select the operation that should be invoked, operands are shown. After entering the values for the operands, the operation of the add-in can be invoked.

The buttons on the bottom row are used to rebuild and update the add-in store, and to exit the application.

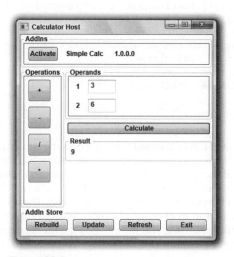

Figure 36-3

The XAML code that follows shows the tree of the user interface. With the ListBox elements, different styles with item templates are used to give a specific representation of the list of add-ins, the list of operations, and the list of operands.

You can read information about item templates in Chapter 35, "Advanced WPF."

```xml
<DockPanel>
    <GroupBox Header="AddIn Store" DockPanel.Dock="Bottom">
        <UniformGrid Columns="4">
            <Button x:Name="rebuildStore" Click="RebuildStore"
                Margin="5">Rebuild</Button>
            <Button x:Name="updateStore" Click="UpdateStore"
                Margin="5">Update</Button>
            <Button x:Name="refresh" Click="RefreshAddIns"
                Margin="5">Refresh</Button>
            <Button x:Name="exit" Click="App_Exit" Margin="5">Exit</Button>
        </UniformGrid>
    </GroupBox>
    <GroupBox Header="AddIns" DockPanel.Dock="Top">
        <ListBox x:Name="listAddIns" ItemsSource="{Binding}"
            Style="{StaticResource listAddInsStyle}" />
    </GroupBox>
    <GroupBox DockPanel.Dock="Left" Header="Operations">
        <ListBox x:Name="listOperations" ItemsSource="{Binding}"
            Style="{StaticResource listOperationsStyle}" />
    </GroupBox>
    <StackPanel DockPanel.Dock="Right" Orientation="Vertical">
        <GroupBox Header="Operands">
            <ListBox x:Name="listOperands" ItemsSource="{Binding}"
                Style="{StaticResource listOperandsStyle}">
            </ListBox>
        </GroupBox>
        <Button x:Name="buttonCalculate" Click="Calculate" IsEnabled="False"
            Margin="5">Calculate</Button>
        <GroupBox DockPanel.Dock="Bottom" Header="Result">
            <Label x:Name="labelResult" />
        </GroupBox>
    </StackPanel>
</DockPanel>
```

In the code behind, the FindAddIns() method is invoked in the constructor of the Window. FindAddIns() uses the AddInStore class to get a collection of AddInToken objects and pass them to the DataContext property of the ListBox listAddIns for display. The first parameter of the AddInStore.FindAddIns() method passes the abstract Calculator class that is defined by the host view to find all add-ins from the store that apply to the contract. The second parameter passes the directory of the pipeline that is read from the application configuration file. When you run the sample application from the Wrox download site you have to change the directory in the application configuration file to match your directory structure.

```csharp
using System;
using System.AddIn.Hosting;
using System.AddIn.Pipeline;
using System.IO;
using System.Linq;
using System.Windows;
```

```
using System.Windows.Controls;
using Wrox.ProCSharp.AddIns.Properties;
namespace Wrox.ProCSharp.AddIns
{
    public partial class CalculatorHostWindow : Window
    {
        private Calculator activeAddIn = null;
        private Operation currentOperation = null;
        public CalculatorHostWindow()
        {
            InitializeComponent();
            FindAddIns();
        }
        void FindAddIns()
        {
            try
            {
                this.listAddIns.DataContext =
                    AddInStore.FindAddIns(typeof(Calculator),
                    Settings.Default.PipelinePath);
            }
            catch (DirectoryNotFoundException ex)
            {
                MessageBox.Show("Verify the pipeline directory in the " +
                    "config file");
                Application.Current.Shutdown();
            }
        }
    //...
```

To update the cache of the Add-In store, the `UpdateStore()` and `RebuildStore()` methods are mapped to the `Click` events of the Update and Rebuild buttons. Within the implementation of these methods, the `Rebuild()` or `Update()` methods of the `AddInStore` class are used. These methods return a string array of warnings if assemblies are stored in the wrong directories. Because of the complexity of the pipeline structure, there's a good chance that the first time you may not get the project configuration completely right for copying the assemblies to the correct directories. Reading the returned information from these methods, you will get a clear explanation about what's wrong. For example, the message "No usable AddInAdapter parts could be found in assembly Pipeline\AddInSideAdapters\CalcView .dll" gives a hint that the assembly CalcView is stored inside the wrong directory.

```
        private void UpdateStore(object sender, RoutedEventArgs e)
        {
            string[] messages = AddInStore.Update(Settings.Default.PipelinePath);
            if (messages.Length != 0)
            {
                MessageBox.Show(string.Join("\n", messages),
                    "AddInStore Warnings", MessageBoxButton.OK,
                    MessageBoxImage.Warning);
            }
        }
        private void RebuildStore(object sender, RoutedEventArgs e)
```

(continued)

1269

(continued)

```
        {
            string[] messages =
                AddInStore.Rebuild(Settings.Default.PipelinePath);
            if (messages.Length != 0)
            {
                MessageBox.Show(string.Join("\n", messages),
                    "AddInStore Warnings", MessageBoxButton.OK,
                    MessageBoxImage.Warning);
            }
        }
    }
```

In Figure 36-2 you can see an Activate button beside the available add-in. Clicking this button invokes the handler method `ActivateAddIn()`. With this implementation, the add-in is activated by using the `Activate()` method of the `AddInToken` class. Here the add-in is loaded inside a new process that is created with the `AddInProcess` class. This class starts the process AddInProcess32.exe. Setting the `KeepAlive` property of the process to `false`, the process is stopped as soon as the last add-in reference is garbage collected. The parameter `AddInSecurityLevel.Internet` leads to an add-in running with restricted permissions. The last statement of `ActivateAddIn()` invokes the `ListOperations()` method, which in turn invokes the `GetOperations()` method of the add-in. `GetOperations()` assigns the returned list to the data context of the `ListBox` `listOperations` for displaying all operations.

```
        private void ActivateAddIn(object sender, RoutedEventArgs e)
        {
            FrameworkElement el = sender as FrameworkElement;
            Trace.Assert(el != null, "ActivateAddIn invoked from the wrong " +
                "control type");

            AddInToken addIn = el.Tag as AddInToken;
            Trace.Assert(el.Tag != null, String.Format(
                "An AddInToken must be assigned to the Tag property " +
                "of the control {0}", el.Name);
            AddInProcess process = new AddInProcess();
            process.KeepAlive = false;

            activeAddIn = addIn.Activate<Calculator>(process,
                AddInSecurityLevel.Internet);
            ListOperations();
        }
        void ListOperations()
        {
            this.listOperations.DataContext = activeAddIn.GetOperations();
        }
```

After the add-in is activated and the list of operations displays in the UI, the user can select an operation. The `Click` event of the `Button` shown in the Operations category is assigned to the handler method `OperationSelected()`. In the implementation, the `Operation` object that is assigned to the `Tag` property of the `Button` is retrieved to get the number of operands needed with the operation. To allow the user adding values to the operands, an array of `OperandUI` objects is bound to the `ListBox` `listOperands`.

```
        private void OperationSelected(object sender, RoutedEventArgs e)
        {
            FrameworkElement el = sender as FrameworkElement;
            Trace.Assert(el != null, "OperationSelected invoked from " +
                "the wrong control type");
```

```
            Operation op = el.Tag as Operation;
            Trace.Assert(el.Tag != null, String.Format(
                    "An AddInToken must be assigned to the Tag property " +
                    "of the control {0}", el.Name);
            currentOperation = op;
            ListOperands(new double[op.NumberOperands]);
        }
        private class OperandUI
        {
            public int Index { get; set; }
            public double Value { get; set; }
        }
        void ListOperands(double[] operands)
        {
            this.listOperands.DataContext =
                operands.Select((operand, index) =>
                        new OperandUI()
                        { Index = index + 1, Value = operand }).ToArray();
        }
```

The `Calculate()` method is invoked with the `Click` event of the Calculate button. Here, the operands are retrieved from the UI, the operation and operands are passed to the `Operate()` method of the add-in, and the result is shown with the content of a label.

```
        private void Calculate(object sender, RoutedEventArgs e)
        {
            OperandUI[] operandsUI = (OperandUI[])this.listOperands.DataContext;
            double[] operands = operandsUI.Select(opui => opui.Value).ToArray();
            labelResult.Content = activeAddIn.Operate(currentOperation,
                    operands);
        }
```

Additional Add-Ins

The hard work is now done. The pipeline components and the host application are created. The pipeline is now working, yet it's an easy task to add other add-ins such as the Advanced Calculator add-in shown in the following code segment into the host application.

```
    [AddIn("Advanced Calc", Publisher = "Wrox Press", Version = "1.1.0.0",
            Description = "Another AddIn Sample")]
    public class AdvancedCalculatorV1 : Calculator
```

Summary

In this chapter you've learned the concepts of a new .NET 3.5 technology: the Managed Add-In Framework.

MAF uses a pipeline concept to create a complete independence between the hosting and add-in assemblies. A clearly defined contract separates the host view from the add-in view. Adapters make it possible for both sides to change independently of each other.

The next chapter starts a sequence of three chapters for developing the UI with ASP.NET.

37

ASP.NET Pages

If you are new to the world of C# and .NET, you might wonder why a chapter on ASP.NET has been included in this book. It's a whole new language, right? Well, not really. In fact, as you will see, you can use C# to create ASP.NET pages.

ASP.NET is part of the .NET Framework and is a technology that allows for the dynamic creation of documents on a Web server when they are requested via HTTP. This mostly means HTML and XHTML documents, although it is equally possible to create XML documents, CSS files, images, PDF documents, or anything else that supports MIME types.

In some ways, ASP.NET is similar to many other technologies — such as PHP, ASP, or ColdFusion. There is, however, one key difference: ASP.NET, as its name suggests, has been designed to be fully integrated with the .NET Framework, part of which includes support for C#.

Perhaps you are familiar with Active Server Pages (ASP) technology, which enables you to create dynamic content. If you are, you will probably know that programming in this technology used scripting languages such as VBScript or JScript. The result was not always perfect, at least not for those of us used to "proper," compiled programming languages, and it certainly resulted in a loss of performance.

One major difference related to the use of more advanced programming languages is the provision of a complete server-side object model for use at runtime. ASP.NET provides access to all of the controls on a page as objects, in a rich environment. On the server side, you also have access to other .NET classes, allowing for the integration of many useful services. Controls used on a page expose a lot of functionality; in fact, you can do almost as much as with Windows Forms classes, which provide plenty of flexibility. For this reason, ASP.NET pages that generate HTML content are often called *Web Forms*.

This chapter takes a more detailed look at ASP.NET, including how it works, what you can do with it, and how C# fits in. The following is a brief outline of what is covered:

- ❑ An introduction to ASP.NET
- ❑ How to create ASP.NET Web Forms with server controls
- ❑ How to bind data to ASP.NET controls with ADO.NET
- ❑ Application configuration

ASP.NET Introduction

ASP.NET works with Internet Information Server (IIS) to deliver content in response to HTTP requests. ASP.NET pages are found in .aspx files. Figure 37-1 illustrates the technology's basic architecture.

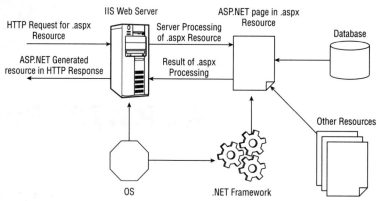

Figure 37-1

During ASP.NET processing, you have access to all .NET classes, custom components created in C# or other languages, databases, and so on. In fact, you have as much power as you would have running a C# application; using C# in ASP.NET is, in effect, running a C# application.

An ASP.NET file can contain any of the following:

❑   Processing instructions for the server

❑   Code in C#, Visual Basic .NET, JScript .NET, or any other language that the .NET Framework supports

❑   Content in whatever form is appropriate for the generated resource, such as HTML

❑   Client-side script code, such as JavaScript

❑   Embedded ASP.NET server controls

So, in fact, you could have an ASP.NET file as simple as this:

```
Hello!
```

This would simply result in an HTML page being returned (as HTML is the default output of ASP.NET pages) containing just this text.

As you will see later in this chapter, it is also possible to split certain portions of the code into other files, which can provide a more logical structure.

State Management in ASP.NET

One of the key properties of ASP.NET pages is that they are effectively stateless. By default, no information is stored on the server between user requests (although there are methods for doing this, as you will see later in this chapter). At first glance, this seems a little strange because state management is something that seems essential for user-friendly interactive sessions. However, ASP.NET provides a workaround to this problem, such that session management becomes almost transparent.

In short, information such as the state of controls on a Web Form (including data entered in text boxes or selections from drop-down lists) is stored in a hidden *viewstate* field that is part of the page generated by the server and passed to the user. Subsequent actions, such as triggering events that require server-side processing, like submitting form data, result in this information being sent back to the server; this is known as a *postback* operation. On the server, this information is used to repopulate the page object model allowing you to operate on it as if the changes had been made locally.

You will see this in action shortly and examine the details.

ASP.NET Web Forms

As mentioned earlier, much of the functionality in ASP.NET is achieved using Web Forms. Before long, you will dive in and create a simple Web Form to give you a starting point to explore this technology. First, however, this section reviews some key points pertinent to Web Form design. Note that some ASP.NET developers simply use a text editor such as Notepad to create files. We wouldn't advocate this ourselves because the benefits you get via an IDE such as Visual Studio or Web Developer Express are substantial, but it's worth mentioning because it is a possibility. If you do take this route, you have a great deal of flexibility as to which parts of a Web application you put where. This enables you, for example, to combine all of your code in one file. You can achieve this by enclosing code in `<script>` elements, using two attributes on the opening `<script>` tag:

```
<script language="c#" runat="server">
   // Server-side code goes here.
</script>
```

The `runat="server"` attribute here is crucial because it instructs the ASP.NET engine to execute this code on the server rather than sending it to the client, thus giving you access to the rich environment hinted at earlier. You can place your functions, event handlers, and so on in server-side script blocks.

If you omit the `runat="server"` attribute, you are effectively providing client-side code, which will fail if it uses any of the server-side style coding that is discussed in this chapter. You can, however, use `<script>` elements to supply client-side script in languages such as JavaScript. For example:

```
<script language="JavaScript" type="text/JavaScript">
   // Client-side code goes here; you can also use "vbscript".
</script>
```

Note that the `type` *attribute here is optional, but necessary if you want XHTML compliance.*

It may seem strange that the facility to add JavaScript code to your pages is included with ASP.NET. However, JavaScript allows you to add dynamic client-side behavior to your Web pages and can be very useful. This is especially true for Ajax programming, as you will see in Chapter 39, "ASP.NET AJAX."

It is possible to create ASP.NET files in Visual Studio, which is great for you, as you are already familiar with this environment for C# programming. However, the default project setup for Web applications in this environment has a slightly more complex structure than a single `.aspx` file. This isn't a problem for you, however, and does make things a bit more logical (more programmer-like and less Web developer–like). For this reason, you will use Visual Studio throughout this chapter for your ASP.NET programming (instead of Notepad).

The `.aspx` files can also include code in blocks enclosed by `<%` and `%>` tags. However, function definitions and variable declarations cannot go here. Instead, you can insert code that is executed as soon as the block is reached, which is useful when outputting simple HTML content. This behavior is similar to that of old-style ASP pages, with one important difference: The code is compiled, not interpreted. This results in far better performance.

Now it's time for an example. In Visual Studio, you create a new Web application by using the File ⇨ New ⇨ Web Site menu option. From the dialog box that appears, select the Visual C# language type and the ASP.NET Web Site template. At this point, you have a choice to make. Visual Studio can create Web sites in a number of different locations:

❑ On your local IIS Web server

❑ On your local disk, configured to use the built-in Visual Web Developer Web server

❑ At any location accessible via FTP

❑ On a remote Web server that supports Front Page Server Extensions

The latter two choices use remote servers so you are left with the first two choices. In general, IIS is the best place to install ASP.NET Web sites because it is likely to be closest to the configuration required when you deploy a Web site. The alternative, using the built-in Web server, is fine for testing but has certain limitations:

❑ Only the local computer can see the Web site.

❑ Access to services such as SMTP is restricted.

❑ The security model is different from IIS — the application runs in the context of the current user rather than in an ASP.NET-specific account.

This last point requires clarification because security is very important when it comes to accessing databases or anything else that requires authentication. By default, Web applications running on IIS do so in an account called ASPNET on Windows XP, 2000, and Vista Web servers, or in an account called NETWORK SERVICES on Windows Server 2003. This is configurable if you are using IIS, but not if you use the built-in Web server.

For the purposes of illustration, however, and because you may not have IIS installed on your computer, you can use the built-in Web server. You aren't worried about security at this stage, so you can go with simplicity.

Create a new ASP.NET Web site called PCSWebApp1 using the File System option, at C:\ProCSharp\ Chapter37, as shown in Figure 37-2.

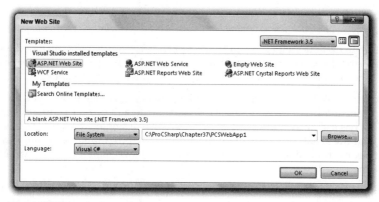

Figure 37-2

After a few moments, Visual Studio .NET should have set up the following:

❑ PCSWebApp1, a new solution containing the C# Web application PCSWebApp1

❑ A reserved folder called App_Data for containing data files, such as XML files or database files

❑ Default.aspx, the first ASP.NET page in the Web application

❑ Default.aspx.cs, a "code-behind" class file for Default.aspx

❑ Web.config, a configuration file for the Web application

You can see all of this in the Solution Explorer, as shown in Figure 37-3.

Figure 37-3

You can view .aspx files in design or source (HTML) view. This is the same as for Windows Forms (as discussed in Chapter 31, "Windows Forms"). The initial view in Visual Studio is either the design or source view for Default.aspx (you can toggle between the views or view them together in a split view using the buttons in the bottom left). The design view is shown in Figure 37-4.

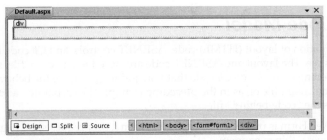

Figure 37-4

Underneath the (currently empty) form, you can see where in the HTML for the form the cursor is currently positioned. Here the cursor is in a `<div>` element inside a `<form>` element inside the `<body>` element of the page. The `<form>` element is displayed as `<form#form1>` to identify the element by its id attribute, which you will see shortly. The `<div>` element is also labeled in the design view.

The source view for the page shows you the code generated inside the .aspx file:

```
<%@ Page Language="C#" AutoEventWireup="true" CodeFile="Default.aspx.cs"
    Inherits="_Default" %>
<!DOCTYPE html PUBLIC "-//W3C//DTD XHTML 1.0 Transitional//EN"
    "http://www.w3.org/TR/xhtml1/DTD/xhtml1-transitional.dtd">
<html xmlns="http://www.w3.org/1999/xhtml">
<head runat="server">
```

(continued)

(continued)

```
    <title>Untitled Page</title>
  </head>
  <body>
    <form id="form1" runat="server">
      <div>
      </div>
    </form>
  </body>
  </html>
```

If you know any HTML syntax, then this will look familiar to you. You are presented with the basic code required for an HTML page following the XHTML schema, with a few extra bits of code. The most important extra is the `<form>` element, which has an `id` attribute of `form1`. This element will contain your ASP.NET code. The most important thing to note here is the `runat` attribute. Just as with the server-side code blocks you saw at the start of this section, this is set to `server`, meaning that the processing of the form will take place on the server. If you don't include this reference, then no server-side processing will be performed, and the form won't do anything. There can be only one server-side `<form>` element in an ASP.NET page.

The other interesting thing about this code is the `<%@ Page %>` tag at the top. This tag defines page characteristics that are important to you as a C# Web application developer. There is a `Language` attribute that specifies that you will use C# throughout your page, as you saw earlier with `<script>` blocks. (The default for Web applications is Visual Basic .NET, although this can be changed using a `Web.config` file, which you will see later in this chapter.) The other three attributes — `AutoEventWireup`, `CodeFile`, and `Inherits` — are used to associate the Web Form with a class in a code-behind code file, in this case the partial class `_Default` in the file `Default.aspx.cs`. This leads straight into a necessary discussion about the ASP.NET code model.

The ASP.NET Code Model

In ASP.NET, a combination of layout (HTML) code, ASP.NET controls, and C# code is used to generate the HTML that users see. The layout and ASP.NET code are stored in an `.aspx` file, such as the one you looked at in the preceding section. The C# code that you add to customize the behavior of the form is contained either in the `.aspx` file or, as in the preceding example, in a separate `.aspx.cs` file, which is usually referred to as the "code-behind" file.

When an ASP.NET Web Form is processed — typically when a user requests the page, although sites can be precompiled — several things happen:

❑ The ASP.NET process examines the page, and determines what objects must be created to instantiate the page object model.

❑ A base class for the page is dynamically created, including members for the controls on the page as well as event handlers for these controls (such as button click events).

❑ Additional code contained in the `.aspx` page is combined with this base class to complete the object model.

❑ The complete code is compiled and cached ready to process subsequent requests.

❑ HTML is generated and returned to the user.

The code-behind file generated for you in the PCSWebApp1 Web site for `Default.aspx` is initially very sparse. First, you see the default set of namespace references that you are likely to use in ASP.NET Web pages:

```
using System;
using System.Data;
using System.Configuration;
using System.Linq;
using System.Web;
using System.Web.Security;
using System.Web.UI;
using System.Web.UI.WebControls;
using System.Web.UI.WebControls.WebParts;
using System.Web.UI.HtmlControls;
using System.Xml.Linq;
```

Below these references, you see an almost completely empty partial class definition for `Default_aspx`:

```
public partial class _Default : System.Web.UI.Page
{
    protected void Page_Load(object sender, EventArgs e)
    {
    }
}
```

Here, the `Page_Load()` event handler can be used to add any code that is required when the page is loaded. As you add more event handlers, and so on, this class file will become increasingly full of code. Note that you don't see the code that wires up this event handler to the page — event handlers are inferred by the ASP.NET runtime, as noted earlier. This is due to the `AutoEventWireUp` attribute — setting this to `false` will mean that you will need to associate the event handlers in your code with events on your own.

This class is a partial class definition because the process outlined earlier requires it. When the page is precompiled, a separate partial class definition is created from the ASP.NET code for your page. This includes all the controls you have added to the page. At design time, the compiler infers this partial class definition, which allows you to use IntelliSense in your code behind to reference controls on your page.

ASP.NET Server Controls

Your generated code doesn't do very much yet, so next you need to add some content. You can do this in Visual Studio using the Web Form designer, which supports drag-and-drop in just the same way as the Windows Forms designer.

You can add three types of controls to your ASP.NET pages:

- ❑ **HTML server controls** — These controls mimic HTML elements, which will be familiar to HTML developers.

- ❑ **Web server controls** — This is a new set of controls, some of which have the same functionality as HTML controls. These controls have a common naming scheme for properties and other elements to ease development, and provide consistency with analogous Windows Forms controls. There are also some completely new and very powerful controls, as you will see later. Several types of Web server controls exist, including the standard ones such as buttons, validation controls for validating user input, login controls to simplify user management, and more complicated controls for dealing with data sources.

- ❑ **Custom and user controls** — These controls are defined by the developer and can be created in a number of ways, as discussed in Chapter 38, "ASP.NET Development."

The next section provides a list of many of the frequently used Web server controls, along with usage notes. Some additional controls are examined in the next chapter. HTML controls will not be covered in this book. These controls don't do anything more than the Web server controls, and the Web server controls provide a richer environment for developers more familiar with programming than with HTML design. If you learn how to use the Web server controls, then you will have all the information you require to use HTML server controls. For more information, check out Professional ASP.NET 2.0 (Wiley Publishing, Inc., ISBN 0-7645-7610-0).

Now you add a couple of Web server controls to the PCSWebApp1 Web site you created in the last section. All Web server controls are used in the following XML element-type form:

```
<asp:controlName runat="server" attribute="value">Contents</asp:controlName>
```

In the preceding code, `controlName` is the name of the ASP.NET server control, `attribute="value"` is one or more attribute specifications, and `Contents` specifies the control content, if any. Some controls allow properties to be set using attributes and control element content, such as `Label` (used for simple text display), where `Text` can be specified in either way. Other controls might use an element containment scheme to define their hierarchy — for example `Table` (which defines a table), which can contain `TableRow` elements in order to specify table rows declaratively.

Because the syntax for controls is based on XML (although the controls may be used embedded in non-XML code such as HTML), it is an error to omit the closing tags and `/>` for empty elements, or to overlap controls.

Finally, you once again see the `runat="server"` attribute on the Web server controls. It is just as essential here as it is elsewhere, and it is a common mistake to skip this attribute. If you do, your Web Forms won't work.

This first example is simple. Change the HTML design view for `Default.aspx` as follows:

```
<%@ Page Language="C#" AutoEventWireup="true" CodeFile="Default.aspx.cs"
Inherits="_Default" %>
<!DOCTYPE html PUBLIC "-//W3C//DTD XHTML 1.1//EN"
"http://www.w3.org/TR/xhtml11/DTD/xhtml11.dtd">
<html xmlns="http://www.w3.org/1999/xhtml">
<head runat="server">
  <title>Untitled Page</title>
</head>
<body>
  <form id="form1" runat="server">
    <div>
      <asp:Label runat="server" ID="resultLabel" /><br />
      <asp:Button runat="server" ID="triggerButton" Text="Click Me" />
    </div>
  </form>
</body>
</html>
```

Here you have added two Web Form controls: a label and a button.

Note that as you do this, Visual Studio .NET IntelliSense predicts your code entry, just as in the C# code editor. Also, if you edit your code in split view and synchronize the views, the element that you are editing in the source pane will be highlighted in the design pane.

Going back to the design screen, you can see that your controls have been added, and named using their ID attributes (the ID attribute is often known as the *identifier* of a control). As with Windows Forms, you have full access to properties, events, and so on through the Properties window and get instant feedback in code or design whenever you make changes.

You can also use the CSS Properties window and other style windows to style your controls. However, unless you are familiar with CSS, you will probably want to leave this technique alone for now and concentrate on the functionality of the controls.

Any server controls you add will automatically become part of the object model for the form that you are building. This is an instant bonus for Windows Forms developers — the similarities are beginning to emerge!

To make this application do something, you can add an event handler for clicking the button. Here you can either enter a method name in the Properties window for the button or just double-click the button to get the default event handler. If you double-click the button, you will automatically add an event-handling method as follows:

```
protected void triggerButton_Click(object sender, EventArgs e)
{
}
```

This is hooked up to the button by some code added to the source of Default.aspx:

```
<div>
  <asp:Label Runat="server" ID="resultLabel" /><br />
  <asp:Button Runat="server" ID="triggerButton" Text="Click Me"
    onclick="triggerButton_Click" />
</div>
```

Here, the onclick attribute lets the ASP.NET runtime know to wire up the click event of the button to the triggerButton_Click() method when it generates the code model for the form.

Modify the code in triggerButton_Click() as follows (note that the label control type is inferred from the ASP.NET code so that you can use it directly from the code behind):

```
void triggerButton_Click(object sender, EventArgs e)
{
    resultLabel.Text = "Button clicked!";
}
```

Now you're ready to make it go. There is no need to build the project; you simply need to make sure everything is saved and then point a Web browser at the location of the Web site. If you had used IIS, this would be simple because you would know the URL to point at. However, because you are using the built-in Web server for this example, you need to start things running. The quickest way to do this is to press Ctrl+F5, which will start the server and open a browser pointing at the required URL.

When the built-in Web server is running, an icon will appear in your system tray. By double-clicking this icon, you can see what the Web server is doing, and stop it if required (see Figure 37-5).

In Figure 37-5, you can see the port that the Web server is running on and the URL required to see the Web site you have created.

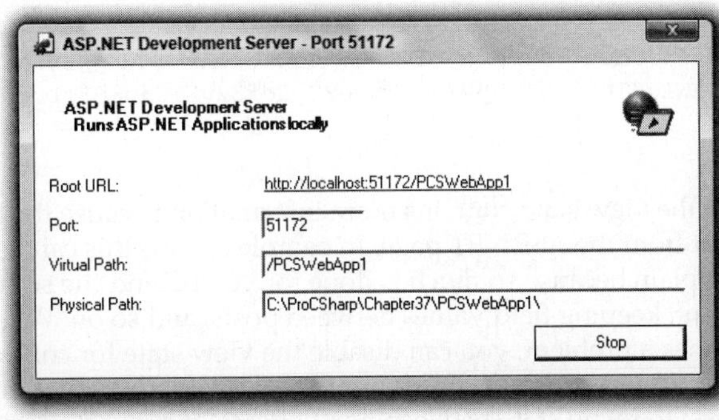

Figure 37-5

The browser that has opened should display the Click Me button on a Web page. Before you press the button, take a quick look at the code received by the browser by selecting Page ⇨ View Source (in IE7). The <form> section should look something like this:

```
<form method="post" action="Default.aspx" id="form1">
  <div>
     <input type="hidden" name="__VIEWSTATE" id="__VIEWSTATE"
        value="/wEPDwUKLTE2MjY5MTY1NWRkzNjRYstd1OK5KcJ9a8/X3pYTHvM=" />
  </div>
  <div>
    <span id="resultLabel"></span><br />
    <input type="submit" name="triggerButton" value="Click Me"
       id="triggerButton" />
  </div>
  <div>
     <input type="hidden" name="__EVENTVALIDATION" id="__EVENTVALIDATION"
        value="/wEWAgK39qTFBwLHpP+yC4rCCl122/GGMaFwD0l7nokvyFZ8Q" />
  </div>
</form>
```

The Web server controls have generated straight HTML: <span> and <input> for <asp:Label> and <asp:Button>, respectively. There is also an <input type="hidden"> field with the name VIEWSTATE. This encapsulates the state of the form, as mentioned earlier. This information is used when the form is posted back to the server to re-create the user interface, so that the server can keep track of changes and so on. Note that the <form> element has been configured for this; it will post data back to Default.aspx (specified in action) via an HTTP POST operation (specified in method). It has also been assigned the name form1.

After clicking the button and seeing the text appear, check out the source HTML again (spacing has been added for clarity):

```
<form method="post" action="Default.aspx" id="form1">
  <div>
     <input type="hidden" name="__VIEWSTATE" id="__VIEWSTATE"
        value="/wEPDwUKLTE2MjY5MTY1NQ9kFgICAw9kFgICAQ8PFgIeBFRleHQFD0J1dHR
               vbiBjbGlja2VkIWRkZExUtMwuSlVTrzMtG7wrmj98tVn7" />
  </div>
  <div>
    <span id="resultLabel">Button clicked!</span><br />
    <input type="submit" name="triggerButton" value="Click Me"
       id="triggerButton" />
  </div>
  <div>
     <input type="hidden" name="__EVENTVALIDATION" id="__EVENTVALIDATION"
        value="/wEWAgKTpL7LBALHpP+yC0Ymqe9SgScfB2yHTGjnlQKtbudV" />
  </div>
</form>
```

This time, the value of the view state contains more information because the HTML result relies on more than the default output from the ASP.NET page. In complex forms this can be a very long string indeed, but you shouldn't complain because so much is done for you behind the scenes. You can almost forget about state management, keeping field values between posts, and so on. Where the length of the view state string becomes a problem, you can disable the view state for controls that do not need to retain state information. You can also do this for entire pages if you want, which can be useful if the page does not ever need to retain state between postbacks to improve performance.

For more on view state, see Chapter 38, "ASP.NET Development."

To convince yourself that you don't need to perform any compilation manually, try changing the text "Button clicked!" in `Default.aspx.cs` to something else, saving the file, and clicking the button again. The text on the Web page should change appropriately.

The Control Palette

This section takes a quick look at some of the available controls before you put more of them together into a full, and more interesting, application. Figure 37-6 shows the toolbox that you see when editing ASP.NET pages.

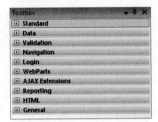

Figure 37-6

Note that the following control descriptions discuss properties — in all cases, the corresponding attribute for use in ASP.NET code is identically named. This section isn't an attempt to provide a complete reference, so instead, we will focus on only the most frequently used controls and properties. The controls you will see in this chapter are in the Standard, Data, and Validation categories. The Navigation and Login and WebParts categories are covered in Chapter 38, "ASP.NET Development," and the AJAX Extensions controls in Chapter 39, "ASP.NET AJAX." The Reporting controls to be presented on Web pages, which enable reporting information, including Crystal Reports, are not covered in this book.

Standard Web Server Controls

Almost all the Web server controls (in this and other categories) inherit from `System.Web.UI` `.WebControls.WebControl`, which in turn inherits from `System.Web.UI.Control`. Those that don't use this inheritance instead derive either directly from `Control` or from a more specialized base class that derives (eventually) from `Control`. As a result, the Web server controls have many common properties and events that you can use as required. There are quite a few of these, so we won't attempt to cover them all, just as with the properties and events of the Web server controls themselves.

Many of the frequently used inherited properties are those that deal with display style. This can be controlled simply, using properties such as `ForeColor`, `BackColor`, `Font`, and so on, but can also be controlled using cascading style sheet (CSS) classes. To use CSS styling you set the string property `CssClass` to the name of a CSS class in a separate file. You can use the CSS Properties window along with the style management windows to assist you with CSS control styling. Other notable properties include `Width` and `Height` to size a control, `AccessKey` and `TabIndex` to ease user interaction, and `Enabled` to set whether the control's functionality is activated in the Web Form.

Some controls can contain other controls, building up a control hierarchy on a page. You can get access to the controls contained by a given control using its `Controls` property, or to the container of a control via the `Parent` property.

You are likely to use the inherited `Load` event most often, to perform initialization on a control, and `PreRender` to perform last-minute modifications before HTML is output by the control.

Plenty more events and properties exist, and you will see many of these in more detail in the next chapter. In particular, the next chapter deals with more advanced styling and skinning techniques. The following table describes the standard Web server controls in more detail.

Control	Description
Label	Simple text display; use the `Text` property to set and programmatically modify displayed text.
TextBox	Provides a text box that users can edit. Use the `Text` property to access the entered data, and the `TextChanged` event to act on selection changes on postback. If automatic postback is required (as opposed to using a button), then set the `AutoPostBack` property to `true`.
Button	Adds a standard button for the user to click. Use the `Text` property for text on the button, and the `Click` event to respond to clicks (server postback is automatic). You can also use the `Command` event to respond to clicks, which gives access to additional `CommandName` and `CommandArgument` properties on receipt.
LinkButton	Is identical to `Button`, but displays button as a hyperlink.
ImageButton	Displays an image that doubles as a clickable button. Properties and events are inherited from `Button` and `Image`.
HyperLink	Adds an HTML hyperlink. Set the destination with `NavigateUrl` and the text to display with `Text`. You can also use `ImageUrl` to specify an image for the link and `Target` to specify the browser window to use. This control has no nonstandard events, so use a `LinkButton` instead if additional processing is required when the link is followed.
DropDownList	Allows the user to select one of a list of choices, either by choosing it directly from a list or by typing the first letter or two. Use the `Items` property to set the item list (this is a `ListItemCollection` class containing `ListItem` objects) and the `SelectedItem` and `SelectedIndex` properties to determine what is selected. The `SelectedIndexChanged` event can be used to determine whether the selection has changed, and this control also has an `AutoPostBack` property so that this selection change will trigger a postback operation.
ListBox	Allows the user to make one or more selections from a list. Set `SelectionMode` to `Multiple` or `Single` to specify if only one, or multiple items can be selected at the same time, and `Rows` to determine how many items to display. Other properties and events are the same as for `DropDownList`.
CheckBox	Displays a box that can be checked or unchecked. The state is stored in the Boolean property `Checked`, and the text associated with the check box in `Text`. The `AutoPostBack` property can be used to initiate automatic postback and the `CheckedChanged` event to act on changes.

Control	Description
CheckBoxList	Creates a group of check boxes. Properties and events are identical to other list controls, such as DropDownList.
RadioButton	Displays a button that can be turned on or off. Generally, these are grouped such that only one in the group is active at any time. Use the GroupName property to link RadioButton controls into a group. Other properties and events are as per CheckBox.
RadioButtonList	Creates a group of radio buttons where only one button in the group can be selected at a time. Properties and events are the same for other list controls, such as DropDownList.
Image	Displays an image. Use ImageUrl for the image reference, and AlternateText to provide text if the image fails to load.
ImageMap	Like Image, but it allows you to specify specific actions to trigger if users click one or more hotspots in the image. The action to take can either be a postback or a redirection to another URL. Hotspots are supplied by embedded controls that derive from HotSpot, such as RectangleHotSpot and CircleHotSpot.
Table	Specifies a table. Use this in conjunction with TableRow and TableCell at design time, or programmatically assign rows using the Rows property of type TableRowCollection. You can also use this property for runtime modifications. This control has several styling properties unique to tables, as do TableRow and TableCell.
BulletedList	Formats a list of items as a bulleted list. Unlike the other list controls, this one has a Click event that you can use to determine what item a user has clicked during a postback. Other properties and events are the same as for DropDownList.
HiddenField	Used to provide a hidden field, to store nondisplayed values for any reason. These can be very useful to store settings that would otherwise need an alternative storage mechanism to function. Use the Value property to access the stored value.
Literal	Performs the same function as Label, but has no styling properties because it derives from Control, not WebControl. You set the text to display for this control with the Text property.
Calendar	Allows the user to select a date from a graphical calendar display. This control has many style-related properties, but essential functionality can be achieved using the SelectedDate and VisibleDate properties (of type System.DateTime) to get access to the date selected by the user and the month to display (which will always contain VisibleDate). The key event to hook up to is SelectionChanged. Postback from this control is automatic.

Control	Description
AdRotator	Displays several images in succession, with a different one displayed after each server round trip. Use the AdvertisementFile property to specify the XML file describing the possible images, and the AdCreated event to perform processing before each image is sent back. You can also use the Target property to name a window to open when an image is clicked.
FileUpload	This control presents the user with a text box and a Browse button, such that a file to be uploaded can be selected. Once the user has done this, you can look at the HasFile property to determine if a file has been selected, and then use the SaveAs() method from code behind to perform the file upload.
Wizard	An advanced control used to simplify the common task of getting several pages of user input in one go. You can add multiple steps to a wizard, which can be presented to a user sequentially or nonsequentially, and rely on this control to maintain state and so on.
Xml	A more complicated text display control, used for displaying XML content, which may be transformed using an XSLT style sheet. The XML content is set using one of the Document, DocumentContent, or DocumentSource properties (depending on the format of the original XML), and the XSLT style sheet (optional) using either Transform or TransformSource.
MultiView	A control that contains one or more View controls, where only one View is rendered at a time. The currently displayed view is specified using ActiveViewIndex, and you can detect if the view changes (perhaps because a Next link on the currently displayed view is clicked) with the ActiveViewChanged event.
Panel	Adds a container for other controls. You can use HorizontalAlign and Wrap to specify how the contents are arranged.
PlaceHolder	This control doesn't render any output but can be handy for grouping other controls together, or for adding controls programmatically to a given location. Contained controls can be accessed using the Controls property.
View	A container for controls, much like PlaceHolder, but designed for use as a child of MultiView. You can tell if a given View is being displayed using Visible, or use the Activate and Deactivate events to detect changes in activation state.
Substitution	Specifies a section of a Web page that isn't cached along with other output. This is an advanced topic related to ASP.NET caching behavior, which you won't be looking at in this book.
Localize	Exactly like Literal, but enables text to be localized by using project resources to specify the text to display for various locales.

Data Web Server Controls

The data Web server controls are divided into two types:

❑ Data source controls (SqlDataSource, AccessDataSource, LinqDataSource, ObjectDataSource, XmlDataSource, and SiteMapDataSource)

❑ Data display controls (GridView, DataList, DetailsView, FormView, ListView, Repeater, and DataPager)

In general, you will place one of the (nonvisual) data source controls on a page to link to a data source; then you will add a data display control that binds to a data source control to display that data. Some of the more advanced data display controls, such as GridView, also allow you to edit data.

All the data source controls derive from either System.Web.UI.DataSource or System.Web.UI.HierarchicalDataSource. These classes expose methods such as GetView() (or GetHierarchicalView()) to give access to internal data views and skinning capabilities.

The following table describes the various data source controls. Note that there is less detail about properties in this section than in others — mainly because configuration of these controls is best done graphically or through wizards. Later in this chapter, you will see some of these controls in action.

Control	Description
SqlDataSource	Acts as a conduit for data stored in an SQL Server database. By placing this control on a page, you can manipulate SQL Server data using a data display control. You will see this control in action later in the chapter.
AccessDataSource	Like SqlDataSource, but it works with data stored in a Microsoft Access database.
LinqDataSource	This control allows you to manipulate objects in a LINQ-enabled data model.
ObjectDataSource	This control allows you to manipulate data stored in objects that you have created, which may be grouped in a collection class. This can be a very quick way to expose custom object models to an ASP.NET page.
XmlDataSource	Enables you to bind to XML data. This works well in binding to, for example, a TreeView control (one of the Navigation controls). You can also transform XML data using an XSL style sheet using this control if desired.
SiteMapDataSource	Allows binding to hierarchical site map data. See the section on navigation Web server controls in Chapter 38 for more information.

Next, you have the data display controls, shown in the following table. Several of these are available to suit various needs. Some are more fully functional than others, but often you can go with simplicity (for example, when you don't need to be able to edit data items).

Control	Description
GridView	Displays multiple data items (such as rows in a database) in the form of rows, where each row has columns reflecting data fields. By manipulating the properties of this control, you can select, sort, and edit data items.
DataList	Displays multiple data items where you can supply templates for each item to display data fields in any way you choose. As with GridView, you can select, sort, and edit data items.
DetailsView	Displays a single data item in tabular form, with each row of the table relating to a data field. This control enables you to add, edit, and delete data items.
FormView	Displays a single data item using a template. As with DetailsView, this control enables you to add, edit, and delete data items.
ListView	Like DataList, but with support for pagination using DataPager and more template capabilities.
Repeater	Like DataList, but without selecting or editing capabilities.
DataPager	Allows pagination of ListView controls.

Validation Web Server Controls

Validation controls provide a method of validating user input without (in most cases) your having to write any code at all. Whenever postback is initiated, each validation control checks the control it is validating and changes its IsValid property accordingly. If this property is false, then the user input for the validated control has failed validation. The page containing all the controls also has an IsValid property — if any of the validation controls has its version of this property set to false, then this will be false also. You can check this property from your server-side code and act on it.

Validation controls also have another function. Not only do they validate controls at runtime; they can also output helpful hints to users. Simply setting the ErrorMessage property to the text you want means users will see it when they attempt to postback invalid data.

The text stored in ErrorMessage may be output at the point where the validation control is located, or at a separate point, along with the messages from all other validation controls on a page. This latter behavior is achieved using the ValidationSummary control, which displays all error messages along with additional text as required.

On browsers that support it, these controls even generate client-side JavaScript functions to streamline their validation behavior. This means that in some cases postback won't even occur, because the validation controls can prevent this under certain circumstances and output error messages without involving the server.

All validation controls inherit from BaseValidator and thus share several important properties. Perhaps the most important is the ErrorMessage property discussed earlier, with the ControlToValidate property coming in a close second. This property specifies the programmatic ID of the control that is being validated. Another important property is Display, which determines whether to place text at the validation summary position (if set to none), or at the validator position. You also have the choice to make space for the error message even when it is not being displayed (set Display to Static) or to dynamically allocate space when required, which might shift page contents around slightly (set Display to Dynamic). The following table describes the validation controls.

Control	Description
RequiredFieldValidator	Used to check if the user has entered data in a control such as TextBox.
CompareValidator	Used to check that data entered fulfills simple requirements, by use of an operator set using the Operator property and a ValueToCompare property to validate against. Operator can be Equal, GreaterThan, GreaterThanEqual, LessThan, LessThanEqual, NotEqual, and DataTypeCheck. DataTypeCheck simply compares the data type of ValueToCompare with the data in the control to be validated. ValueToCompare is a string property but is interpreted as different data types based on its contents. To further control the comparison, you can set the Type property to Currency, Date, Double, Integer, or String.
RangeValidator	Validates that data in the control falls between MaximumValue and MinimumValue property values. Has a Type property like that of CompareValidator.
RegularExpressionValidator	Validates the contents of a field based on a regular expression stored in ValidationExpression. This can be useful for known sequences such as zip codes, phone numbers, IP numbers, and so on.
CustomValidator	Used to validate data in a control using a custom function. ClientValidationFunction is used to specify a client-side function used to validate a control (which means, unfortunately, that you can't use C#). This function should return a Boolean value indicating whether validation was successful. Alternatively, you can use the ServerValidate event to specify a server-side function to use for validation. This function is a bool type event handler that receives a string containing the data to validate, instead of an EventArgs parameter. Returns true if validation succeeds, otherwise false.
ValidationSummary	Displays validation errors for all validation controls that have an ErrorMessage set. The display can be formatted by setting the DisplayMode (BulletList, List, or SingleParagraph) and HeaderText properties. The display can be disabled by setting ShowSummary to false, and displayed in a pop-up message box by setting ShowMessageBox to true.

Server Control Example

In this example, you create the framework for a Web application, a meeting room booking tool. (As with the other examples in this book, you can download the sample application and code from the Wrox Web site at www.wrox.com.) At first, you will include only the front end and simple event processing; later, you will extend this example with ADO.NET and data binding to include server-side business logic.

The Web Form you are going to create contains fields for user name, event name, meeting room, and attendees, along with a calendar to select a date (you are assuming for the purposes of this example that you are dealing with all-day events). You will include validation controls for all fields except the calendar, which you will validate on the server side, and provide a default date in case none has been entered.

For user interface (UI) testing, you will also have a `Label` control on the form that you can use to display submission results.

For starters, create a new Web site in Visual Studio .NET in the `C:\ProCSharp\Chapter37\` directory, and call it PCSWebApp2. Next, modify the code in `Default.aspx` as follows:

```
<%@ Page Language="C#" AutoEventWireup="true" CodeFile="Default.aspx.cs"
  Inherits="_Default" %>
<!DOCTYPE html PUBLIC "-//W3C//DTD XHTML 1.1//EN"
  "http://www.w3.org/TR/xhtml11/DTD/xhtml11.dtd">
<html xmlns="http://www.w3.org/1999/xhtml">
<head runat="server">
  <title>Meeting Room Booker</title>
</head>
<body>
  <form id="form1" runat="server">
    <div>
      <h1 style="text-align: center;">
        Enter details and set a day to initiate an event.
      </h1>
    </div>
```

After the title of the page (which is enclosed in HTML `<h1>` tags to get large, title-style text), the main body of the form is enclosed in an HTML `<table>`. You could use a Web server control table, but this introduces unnecessary complexity because you are using a table purely for formatting the display, not to be a dynamic UI element. This is an important point to bear in mind when designing Web Forms — don't add Web server controls unnecessarily. The table is divided into three columns: the first column holds simple text labels; the second column holds UI fields corresponding to the text labels (along with validation controls for these); and the third column contains a calendar control for date selection, which spans four rows. The fifth row contains a submission button spanning all columns, and the sixth row contains a `ValidationSummary` control to display error messages, when required (all the other validation controls have `Display="None"`, because they will use this summary for display). Beneath the table is a simple label that you can use to display results for now, before you add database access later:

```
<div style="text-align: center;">
  <table style="text-align: left; border-color: #000000;
    border-width: 2px; background-color: #fff99e;" cellspacing="0"
    cellpadding="8" rules="none" width="540">
    <tr>
      <td valign="top">
        Your Name:</td>
      <td valign="top">
        <asp:TextBox ID="nameBox" Runat="server" Width="160px" />
        <asp:RequiredFieldValidator ID="validateName" Runat="server"
          ErrorMessage="You must enter a name."
          ControlToValidate="nameBox" Display="None" />
      </td>
      <td valign="middle" rowspan="4">
        <asp:Calendar ID="calendar" Runat="server" BackColor="White" />
      </td>
    </tr>
```

```
<tr>
  <td valign="top">
    Event Name:</td>
  <td valign="top">
    <asp:TextBox ID="eventBox" Runat="server" Width="160px" />
    <asp:RequiredFieldValidator ID="validateEvent" Runat="server"
      ErrorMessage="You must enter an event name."
      ControlToValidate="eventBox" Display="None" />
  </td>
</tr>
```

Most of the ASP.NET code in this file is remarkably simple, and much can be learned simply by reading through it. Of particular note in this code is the way in which list items are attached to the controls for selecting a meeting room and multiple attendees for the event:

```
<tr>
  <td valign="top">
    Meeting Room:</td>
  <td valign="top">
    <asp:DropDownList ID="roomList" Runat="server" Width="160px">
      <asp:ListItem Value="1">The Happy Room</asp:ListItem>
      <asp:ListItem Value="2">The Angry Room</asp:ListItem>
      <asp:ListItem Value="3">The Depressing
        Room</asp:ListItem>
      <asp:ListItem Value="4">The Funked Out
        Room</asp:ListItem>
    </asp:DropDownList>
    <asp:RequiredFieldValidator ID="validateRoom" Runat="server"
      ErrorMessage="You must select a room."
      ControlToValidate="roomList" Display="None" />
  </td>
</tr>
<tr>
  <td valign="top">
    Attendees:</td>
  <td valign="top">
    <asp:ListBox ID="attendeeList" Runat="server" Width="160px"
      SelectionMode="Multiple" Rows="6">
      <asp:ListItem Value="1">Bill Gates</asp:ListItem>
      <asp:ListItem Value="2">Monica Lewinsky</asp:ListItem>
      <asp:ListItem Value="3">Vincent Price</asp:ListItem>
      <asp:ListItem Value="4">Vlad the Impaler</asp:ListItem>
      <asp:ListItem Value="5">Iggy Pop</asp:ListItem>
      <asp:ListItem Value="6">William
        Shakespeare</asp:ListItem>
    </asp:ListBox>
```

Here you are associating ListItem objects with the two Web server controls. These objects are not Web server controls in their own right (they simply inherit from System.Object), which is why you don't need to use Runat="server" on them. When the page is processed, the <asp:ListItem> entries are used to create ListItem objects, which are added to the Items collection of their parent list control. This makes it easier for you to initialize lists than to write code for this yourself (you would need to create a ListItemCollection object, add ListItem objects, and then pass the collection to the list control). Of course, you can still do all of this programmatically if you want.

```
          <asp:RequiredFieldValidator ID="validateAttendees" Runat="server"
            ErrorMessage="You must have at least one attendee."
            ControlToValidate="attendeeList" Display="None" />
        </td>
      </tr>
      <tr>
        <td align="center" colspan="3">
          <asp:Button ID="submitButton" Runat="server" Width="100%"
            Text="Submit meeting room request" />
        </td>
      </tr>
      <tr>
        <td align="center" colspan="3">
          <asp:ValidationSummary ID="validationSummary" Runat="server"
            HeaderText="Before submitting your request:" />
        </td>
      </tr>
    </table>
  </div>
  <div>
    <p>
      Results:
      <asp:Label Runat="server" ID="resultLabel" Text="None." />
    </p>
  </div>
</form>
</body>
</html>
```

In design view, the form you have created looks like Figure 37-7. This is a fully functioning UI, which maintains its own state between server requests, and validates user input. Considering the brevity of the preceding code, this is quite something. In fact, it leaves you with very little to do, at least for this example; you just need to specify the button click event for the submission button.

Actually, that's not quite true. So far, you have no validation for the calendar control. All you need to do is give it an initial value. You can do this in the `Page_Load()` event handler for your page in the code-behind file:

```
private void Page_Load(object sender, EventArgs e)
{
    if (!this.IsPostBack)
    {
        calendar.SelectedDate = DateTime.Now;
    }
}
```

Here you just select today's date as a starting point. Note that you first check to see if `Page_Load()` is being called as the result of a postback operation, by checking the `IsPostBack` property of the page. If a postback is in progress, this property will be `true` and you leave the selected date alone (you don't want to lose the user's selection, after all).

To add the button click handler, simply double-click the button and add the following code:

```
private void submitButton_Click(object sender, EventArgs e)
{
    if (this.IsValid)
```

```
    {
        resultLabel.Text = roomList.SelectedItem.Text +
            " has been booked on " +
            calendar.SelectedDate.ToLongDateString() +
            " by " + nameBox.Text + " for " +
            eventBox.Text + " event. ";
        foreach (ListItem attendee in attendeeList.Items)
        {
            if (attendee.Selected)
            {
                resultLabel.Text += attendee.Text + ", ";
            }
        }
        resultLabel.Text += " and " + nameBox.Text +
            " will be attending.";
    }
}
```

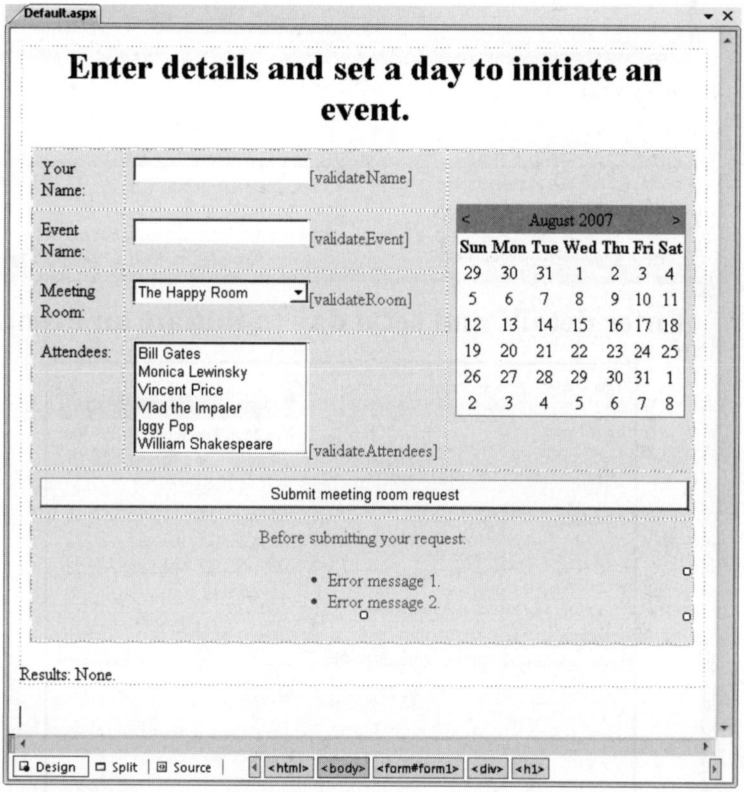

Figure 37-7

Here you just set the resultLabel control Text property to a result string, which will then appear below the main table. In IE, the result of such a submission might look something like Figure 37-8, unless there are errors, in which case the ValidationSummary will activate instead, as shown in Figure 37-9.

Figure 37-8

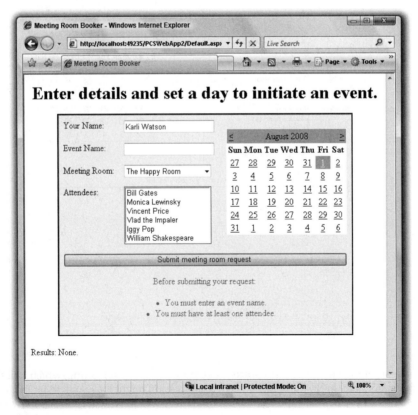

Figure 37-9

ADO.NET and Data Binding

The Web Form application you created in the previous section is perfectly functional, but it contains only static data. In addition, the event-booking process does not include persisting event data. To solve both of these problems, you can make use of ADO.NET to access data stored in a database, so that you can store and retrieve event data along with the lists of rooms and attendees.

Data binding makes the process of retrieving data even easier. Controls such as list boxes (and some of the more specialized controls you'll look at a bit later) come enabled for this technique. They can be bound to any object that exposes an `IEnumerable`, `ICollection`, or `IListSource` interface, as well as any of the data source Web server controls.

In this section, you start by updating your event-booking application to be data-aware, and then move on to take a look at some of the other results you can achieve with data binding, using some of the other data-aware Web controls.

Updating the Event-Booking Application

To keep things separate from the last example, create a new Web site called PCSWebApp3 in the directory C:\ProCSharp\Chapter37\ and copy the code from the PCSWebApp2 application created earlier into the new application. Before you start on your new code, take a look at the database you will be accessing.

The Database

For the purposes of this example, you will use a Microsoft SQL Server Express database called MeetingRoomBooker.mdf, which is part of the downloadable code for this book. For an enterprise-scale application, it makes more sense to use a full SQL Server database, but the techniques involved are practically identical, and SQL Server Express makes life a bit easier for testing. The code will also be identical.

> If you are adding your own version of this database, you will need to add a new database to the App_Data folder in the Solution Explorer. You can do this by right-clicking on the App_Data folder, selecting Add New Item, selecting a database, naming it MeetingRoomBooker, and clicking Add. This will also configure a data connection in the Server Explorer window ready for you to use. Next, you can add the tables required as shown in the next sections and supply your own data. Alternatively, to use the downloadable database with your own code, simply copy it to the App_Data directory for your Web site.

The database provided contains three tables:

❑ Attendees, which contains a list of possible event attendees

❑ Rooms, which contains a list of possible rooms for events

❑ Events, which contains a list of booked events

Attendees

The Attendees table contains the columns shown in the following table.

Column	Type	Notes
ID	Identity, primary key	Attendee identification number
Name	varchar, required, 50 chars	Name of attendee
Email	varchar, optional, 50 chars	E-mail address of attendee

The supplied database includes entries for 20 attendees, all with their own (fictional) e-mail addresses. You can envision that in a more developed application, e-mails could automatically be sent to attendees when a booking is made, but this is left to you as an optional exercise using techniques found elsewhere in this book.

Rooms

The Rooms table contains the columns shown in the following table.

Column	Type	Notes
ID	Identity, primary key	Room identification number
Room	varchar, required, 50 chars	Name of room

Twenty records are supplied in the database.

Events

The Events table contains the columns shown in the following table.

Column	Type	Notes
ID	Identity, primary key	Event identification number
Name	varchar, required, 255 chars	Name of event
Room	int, required	ID of room for event
AttendeeList	text, required	List of attendee names
EventDate	datetime, required	Date of event

A few events are supplied in the downloadable database.

Binding to the Database

The two controls you are going to bind to data are attendeeList and roomList. Before you do this, you need to add SqlDataSource Web server controls that map to the tables you want to access in the MeetingRoomBooker.mdf database. The quickest way to do this is to drag them from the toolbox onto the Default.aspx Web Form and configure them via the Configuration Wizard. Figure 37-10 shows how to access this wizard for a SqlDataSource control.

Figure 37-10

From the first page of the data source Configuration Wizard, you need to select the connection to the database created earlier. Next, choose to save the connection string as MRBConnectionString; then choose to select * (all fields) from the Attendees table in the database.

After completing the wizard, change the ID of the SqlDataSource control to MRBAttendeeData. You also need to add and configure two more SqlDataSource controls to obtain data from the Rooms and Events tables, with ID values of MRBRoomData and MRBEventData respectively. For these subsequent controls, you can use the saved MRBConnectionString for your connection.

Once you've added these data sources, you will see in the code for the form that the syntax is very simple:

```
<asp:SqlDataSource ID="MRBAttendeeData" runat="server"
  ConnectionString="<%$ ConnectionStrings:MRBConnectionString %>"
  SelectCommand="SELECT * FROM [Attendees]"></asp:SqlDataSource>
<asp:SqlDataSource ID="MRBRoomData" runat="server"
  ConnectionString="<%$ ConnectionStrings:MRBConnectionString %>"
  SelectCommand="SELECT * FROM [Rooms]"></asp:SqlDataSource>
<asp:SqlDataSource ID="MRBEventData" runat="server"
  ConnectionString="<%$ ConnectionStrings:MRBConnectionString %>"
  SelectCommand="SELECT * FROM [Events]"></asp:SqlDataSource>
```

The definition of the connection string in use is found in the web.config file, which we will look at in more detail later in this chapter.

Next, you need to set the data-binding properties of the roomList and attendeeList controls. For roomList the settings required are as follows:

❑ DataSourceID — MRBRoomData

❑ DataTextField — Room

❑ DataValueField — ID

And, similarly, for attendeeList:

❑ DataSourceID — MRBAttendeeData

❑ DataTextField — Name

❑ DataValueField — ID

You can also remove the existing hard-coded list items from the code for these controls.

Running the application now will result in the full attendee and room data being available from your data-bound controls. You will use the MRBEventData control shortly.

Customizing the Calendar Control

Before adding events to the database, you need to modify your calendar display. It would be nice to display all days where a booking has previously been made in a different color, and prevent such days from being selectable. This requires that you modify the way you set dates in the calendar and the way day cells are displayed.

You will start with date selection. You need to check three places for dates where events are booked and modify the selection accordingly: when you set the initial date in Page_Load(), when the user attempts to select a date from the calendar, and when an event is booked and you want to set a new date to prevent the user from booking two events on the same day before selecting a new date. Because this is going to be a common feature, you might as well create a private method to perform this calculation. This method should accept a trial date as a parameter and return the date to use, which will either be the same date as the trial date, or the next available day after the trial date.

Before adding this method, you need to give your code access to data in the Events table. You can use the MRBEventData control to do this because this control is capable of populating a DataView. To facilitate this, add the following private member and property:

```
private DataView eventData;
private DataView EventData
{
    get
    {
        if (eventData == null)
        {
            eventData =
                MRBEventData.Select(new DataSourceSelectArguments())
                as DataView;
        }
        return eventData;
    }
    set
    {
        eventData = value;
    }
}
```

The EventData property populated the eventData member with data as it is required, with the results cached for subsequent use. Here you use the SqlDataSource.Select() method to obtain a DataView.

Next, add this method, GetFreeDate(), to the code-behind file:

```
private DateTime GetFreeDate(DateTime trialDate)
{
    if (EventData.Count > 0)
    {
        DateTime testDate;
        bool trialDateOK = false;
        while (!trialDateOK)
        {
            trialDateOK = true;
            foreach (DataRowView testRow in EventData)
            {
                testDate = (DateTime)testRow["EventDate"];
                if (testDate.Date == trialDate.Date)
                {
                    trialDateOK = false;
                    trialDate = trialDate.AddDays(1);
                }
            }
        }
    }
    return trialDate;
}
```

This simple code uses the EventData DataView to extract event data. First, you check for the trivial case where no events have been booked, in which case you can just confirm the trial date by returning it. Next, you iterate through the dates in the Event table, comparing them with the trial date. If you find a match, add one day to the trial date and perform another search.

Extracting the date from the `DataTable` is remarkably simple:

```
testDate = (System.DateTime)testRow["EventDate"];
```

Casting the column data into `System.DateTime` works fine.

The first place you will use `getFreeDate()`, then, is back in `Page_Load()`. This simply means making a minor modification to the code that sets the calendar `SelectedDate` property:

```
if (!this.IsPostBack)
{
    DateTime trialDate = DateTime.Now;
    calendar.SelectedDate = GetFreeDate(trialDate);
}
```

Next, you need to respond to date selection on the calendar. To do this, simply add an event handler for the `SelectionChanged` event of the calendar, and force the date to be checked against existing events. Double-click the calendar in the Designer and add this code:

```
void calendar_SelectionChanged(object sender, EventArgs e)
{
    DateTime trialDate = calendar.SelectedDate;
    calendar.SelectedDate = GetFreeDate(trialDate);
}
```

The code here is practically identical to that in `Page_Load()`.

The third place that you must perform this check is in response to the pressed booking button. We will come back to this shortly, as you have several changes to make here.

Next, you need to color the day cells of the calendar to signify existing events. To do this, you add an event handler for the `DayRender` event of the `calendar` object. This event is raised each time an individual day is rendered, and gives you access to the `cell` object being displayed and the date of this cell through the `Cell` and `Date` properties of the `DayRenderEventArgs` parameter you receive in the handler function. You simply compare the date of the cell being rendered to the dates in the `eventTable` object and color the cell using the `Cell.BackColor` property if there is a match:

```
void calendar_DayRender(object sender, DayRenderEventArgs e)
{
    if (EventData.Count > 0)
    {
        DateTime testDate;
        foreach (DataRowView testRow in EventData)
        {
            testDate = (DateTime)testRow["EventDate"];
            if (testDate.Date == e.Day.Date)
            {
                e.Cell.BackColor = System.Drawing.Color.Red;
            }
        }
    }
}
```

Here you are using red, which will give you a display along the lines of Figure 37-11, in which June 12, 15, and 22 (2008) all contain events, and the user has selected June 24.

With the addition of the date-selection logic, it is now impossible to select a day that is shown in red. If you attempt it, a later date is selected instead (for example, selecting June 15 results in the selection of June 16).

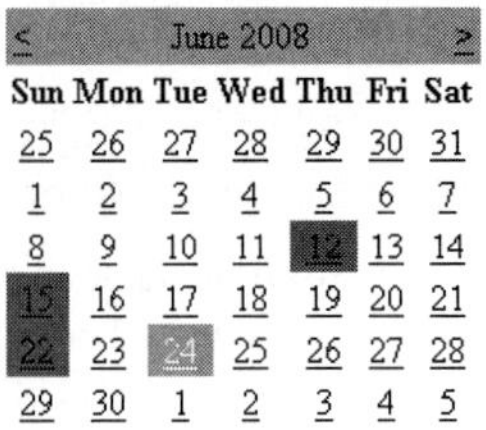

Figure 37-11

Adding Events to the Database

The submitButton_Click() event handler currently assembles a string from the event characteristics and displays it in the resultLabel control. To add an event to the database, you simply reformat the string created into a SQL INSERT query and execute it.

> Note that in the development environment that you are using you don't have to worry too much about security. Adding a SQL Server 2005 Express database via a Web site solution and configuring SqlDataSource controls to use it will automatically give you a connection string that you can use to write to the database. In more advanced situations, you might want to access resources using other accounts — for example, a domain account used to access a SQL Server instance elsewhere on a network. The capability to do this (via impersonation, COM+ Services, or other means) exists in ASP.NET, but is beyond the scope of this chapter. In most cases, configuring the connection string appropriately is as complicated as things need to get.

Much of the following code will therefore look familiar:

```
void submitButton_Click(object sender, EventArgs e)
{
    if (this.IsValid)
    {
        System.Text.StringBuilder sb = new System.Text.StringBuilder();
        foreach (ListItem attendee in attendeeList.Items)
        {
            if (attendee.Selected)
            {
                sb.AppendFormat("{0} ({1}), ", attendee.Text, attendee.Value);
            }
        }
        sb.AppendFormat(" and {0}", nameBox.Text);
        string attendees = sb.ToString();
        try
        {
            System.Data.SqlClient.SqlConnection conn =
                new System.Data.SqlClient.SqlConnection(
                    ConfigurationManager.ConnectionStrings[
                    "MRBConnectionString"].ConnectionString);
            System.Data.SqlClient.SqlCommand insertCommand =
                new System.Data.SqlClient.SqlCommand("INSERT INTO [Events] "
                    + "(Name, Room, AttendeeList, EventDate) VALUES (@Name, "
                    + "@Room, @AttendeeList, @EventDate)", conn);
            insertCommand.Parameters.Add(
                "Name", SqlDbType.VarChar, 255).Value = eventBox.Text;
            insertCommand.Parameters.Add(
```

```
            "Room", SqlDbType.Int, 4).Value = roomList.SelectedValue;
        insertCommand.Parameters.Add(
            "AttendeeList", SqlDbType.Text, 16).Value = attendees;
        insertCommand.Parameters.Add(
            "EventDate", SqlDbType.DateTime, 8).Value =
            calendar.SelectedDate;
```

The most interesting thing here is how you access the connection string you created earlier, using the following syntax:

```
ConfigurationManager.ConnectionStrings["MRBConnectionString"].ConnectionString
```

The `ConfigurationManager` class gives you access to all assorted configuration information, all stored in the `Web.config` configuration file for your Web application. You will look at this in more detail later in this chapter.

After you have created your SQL command, you can use it to insert the new event:

```
                conn.Open();
                int queryResult = insertCommand.ExecuteNonQuery();
                conn.Close();
```

`ExecuteNonQuery()` returns an integer representing how many table rows were affected by the query. If this is equal to 1, your insertion was successful. If so, put a success message in `resultLabel`, clear `EventData` because it is now out of date, and change the calendar selection to a new, free date. Because `GetFreeDate()` involves using `EventData`, and the `EventData` property automatically refreshes itself if it has no data, the stored event data will be refreshed:

```
                if (queryResult == 1)
                {
                    resultLabel.Text = "Event Added.";
                    EventData = null;
                    calendar.SelectedDate =
                        GetFreeDate(calendar.SelectedDate.AddDays(1));
                }
```

If `ExecuteNonQuery()` returns a number other than 1, you know that there has been a problem. The code in this example throws an exception if a number other than 1 is returned. This exception is caught by the general catch block for the database access code.

This catch block simply displays a general failure notification in `resultLabel`:

```
                else
                {
                    throw new System.Data.DataException("Unknown data error.");
                }
            }
            catch
            {
                resultLabel.Text = "Event not added due to DB access "
                                    + "problem.";
            }
        }
    }
```

This completes your data-aware version of the event-booking application.

More on Data Binding

As mentioned earlier in this chapter, the available Web server controls include several that deal with data display (GridView, DataList, DetailsView, FormView, and Repeater). These are all extremely useful when it comes to outputting data to a Web page because they perform many tasks automatically that would otherwise require a fair amount of coding.

First, you will look at how easy using these controls can be, by adding an event list display to the bottom of the display of PCSWebApp3.

Drag a GridView control from the toolbox to the bottom of Default.aspx, and select the MRBEventData data source you added earlier for it, as shown in Figure 37-12.

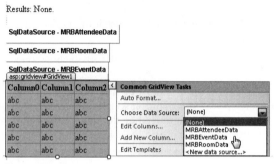

Figure 37-12

Next, click Refresh Schema, and that's all you need to do to display a list of events under the form — try viewing the Web site now and you should see the events, as shown in Figure 37-13.

ID	Name	Room	AttendeeList	EventDate
1	My Birthday	4	Iggy Pop (5), Sean Connery (7), Albert Einstein (10), George Clooney (14), Jules Verne (18), Robin Hood (20), and Karli Watson	9/17/2008 12:00:00 AM
2	Dinner	1	Bill Gates (1), Monika Lewinsky (2), and Bruce Lee	8/5/2008 12:00:00 AM
3	Discussion of darkness	6	Vlad the Impaler (4), Myra Hindley (13), and Beelzebub	10/29/2008 12:00:00 AM
4	Christmas with Pals	9	Dr Frank N Furter (11), Bobby Davro (15), John F Kennedy (16), Stephen King (19), and Karli Watson	12/25/2008 12:00:00 AM
5	Escape	17	Monika Lewinsky (2), Stephen King (19), and Spartacus	5/10/2008 12:00:00 AM
6	Planetary Conquest	14	Bill Gates (1), Albert Einstein (10), Dr Frank N Furter (11), Bobby Davro (15), and Darth Vader	6/15/2008 12:00:00 AM
7	Homecoming Celebration	7	William Shakespeare (6), Christopher Columbus (12), Robin Hood (20), and Ulysses	6/22/2008 12:00:00 AM
8	Dalek Reunion Ball	12	Roger Moore (8), George Clooney (14), Bobby Davro (15), and Davros	6/12/2008 12:00:00 AM
9	Romantic meal for two	13	George Clooney (14), and Donna Watson	3/29/2008 12:00:00 AM

Figure 37-13

You can also make one further modification in `submitButton_Click()` to ensure that this data is updated when new records are added:

```
if (queryResult == 1)
{
    resultLabel.Text = "Event Added.";
    EventData = null;
    calendar.SelectedDate =
        GetFreeDate(calendar.SelectedDate.AddDays(1));
    GridView1.DataBind();
}
```

All data-bindable controls support this method, which is normally called by the form if you call the top-level (`this`) `DataBind()` method.

You probably noticed in Figure 37-13 that the date/time display for the `EventDate` field is a little messy. Because you are looking at dates only, the time is always `12:00:00 AM` — information that it isn't really necessary to display. In the next sections, you will see how this date information can be displayed in a more user-friendly fashion in the context of a `ListView` control. As you might expect, the `DataGrid` control contains many properties that you can use to format the displayed data, but I'll leave these for you to discover.

Data Display with Templates

Many of the data display controls allow you to use templates to format data for display. Templates, in an ASP.NET sense, are parameterized sections of HTML that are used as elements of output in certain controls. They enable you to customize exactly how data is output to the browser, and can result in professional-looking displays without too much effort.

Several templates are available to customize various aspects of list behavior. One of the most important templates is `<ItemTemplate>`, which is used in the display of each data item in a list for `Repeater`, `DataList`, and `ListView` controls. You declare this template (and all the others) inside the control declaration. For example:

```
<asp:DataList Runat="server" ... >
  <ItemTemplate>
    ...
  </ItemTemplate>
</asp:DataList>
```

Within template declarations, you will normally want to output sections of HTML along with parameters from the data that is bound to the control. You can use a special syntax to output such parameters:

```
<%# expression %>
```

The *expression* placeholder might be simply an expression binding the parameter to a page or control property, but is more likely to consist of an `Eval()` or `Bind()` expression. These functions can be used to output data from a table bound to a control simply by specifying the column. The following syntax is used for `Eval()`:

```
<%# Eval("ColumnName") %>
```

An optional second parameter allows you to format the data returned, which has syntax identical to string formatting expressions used elsewhere. This can be used, for example, to format date strings into a more readable format — something that was lacking in the earlier example.

The `Bind()` expression is identical but allows you to insert data into attributes of server controls. For example:

```
<asp:Label RunAt="server" ID="ColumnDisplay" Text='<%# Bind("ColumnName") %>' />
```

Note that because double quotes are used in the `Bind()` parameter, single quotes are required to enclose the attribute value.

The following table provides a list of available templates and when they are used.

Template	Applies To	Description
`<ItemTemplate>`	`DataList`, `Repeater`, `ListView`	Used for list items
`<HeaderTemplate>`	`DataList`, `DetailsView`, `FormView`, `Repeater`	Used for output before item(s)
`<FooterTemplate>`	`DataList`, `DetailsView`, `FormView`, `Repeater`	Used for output after item(s)
`<LayoutTemplate>`	`ListView`	Used to specify output surrounding items
`<SeparatorTemplate>`	`DataList`, `Repeater`	Used between items in list
`<ItemSeparatorTemplate>`	`ListView`	Used between items in list
`<AlternatingItemTemplate>`	`DataList`, `ListView`	Used for alternate items; can aid visibility
`<SelectedItemTemplate>`	`DataList`, `ListView`	Used for selected items in the list
`<EditItemTemplate>`	`DataList`, `FormView`, `ListView`	Used for items being edited
`<InsertItemTemplate>`	`FormView`, `ListView`	Used for items being inserted
`<EmptyDataTemplate>`	`GridView`, `DetailsView`, `FormView`, `ListView`	Used to display empty items — for example, when no records are available in a `GridView`
`<PagerTemplate>`	`GridView`, `DetailsView`, `FormView`	Used to format pagination
`<GroupTemplate>`	`ListView`	Used to specify the output surrounding groups of items
`<GroupSeparatorTemplate>`	`ListView`	Used between groups of items
`<EmptyItemTemplate>`	`ListView`	When using item groups, used to supply output for empty items in a group. This template is used when there are not enough items in a group to fill the group.

The easiest way to understand how to use these is through an example.

Using Templates

You will extend the table at the top of the Default.aspx page of PCSWebApp3 to contain a ListView displaying each of the events stored in the database. You will make these events selectable such that details of any event can be displayed by clicking on its name, in a FormView control.

First, you need to create new data sources for the data-bound controls. It is good practice (and strongly recommended) to have a separate data source for each data-bound control.

The SqlDataSource control required for the ListView control, MRBEventData2, is much like MRBEventData, except that it needs to return only Name and ID data. The required code is as follows:

```
<asp:SqlDataSource ID="MRBEventData2" Runat="server"
  SelectCommand="SELECT [ID], [Name] FROM [Events]"
  ConnectionString="<%$ ConnectionStrings:MRBConnectionString %>">
</asp:SqlDataSource>
```

The data source for the FormView control, MRBEventDetailData, is more complicated, although you can build it easily enough through the data source Configuration Wizard. This data source uses the selected item of the ListView control, which you will call EventList, to get only the selected item data. This is achieved using a parameter in the SQL query, as follows:

```
<asp:SqlDataSource ID="MRBEventDetailData" Runat="server"
  SelectCommand="SELECT dbo.Events.Name, dbo.Rooms.Room,
                 dbo.Events.AttendeeList, dbo.Events.EventDate
                 FROM dbo.Events INNER JOIN dbo.Rooms
                 ON dbo.Events.ID = dbo.Rooms.ID WHERE dbo.Events.ID = @ID"
  ConnectionString="<%$ ConnectionStrings:MRBConnectionString %>">
  <SelectParameters>
    <asp:ControlParameter Name="ID" DefaultValue="-1" ControlID="EventList"
      PropertyName="SelectedValue" />
  </SelectParameters>
</asp:SqlDataSource>
```

Here, the ID parameter results in a value being inserted in place of @ID in the select query. The ControlParameter entry takes this value from the SelectedValue property of EventList, or uses –1 if there is no selected item. At first glance, this syntax seems a little odd, but it is very flexible, and once you've generated a few of these using the wizard, you won't have any trouble assembling your own.

Next, you need to add the ListView and FormView controls. The changes to the code in Default.aspx in the PCSWebApp3 project are shown in the following code:

```
<tr>
  <td align="center" colspan="3">
    <asp:ValidationSummary ID="validationSummary" Runat="server"
      HeaderText="Before submitting your request:" />
  </td>
</tr>
<tr>
  <td align="left" colspan="3" style="width: 40%;">
    <table cellspacing="4" style="width: 100%;">
      <tr>
        <td colspan="2" style="text-align: center;">
          <h2>Event details</h2>
        </td>
```

(continued)

(continued)

```
            </tr>
            <tr>
              <td style="width: 40%; background-color: #ccffcc;"
                valign="top">
                <asp:ListView ID="EventList" runat="server"
                  DataSourceID="MRBEventData2" DataKeyNames="ID"
                  OnSelectedIndexChanged="EventList_SelectedIndexChanged">
                  <LayoutTemplate>
                    <ul>
                      <asp:PlaceHolder ID="itemPlaceholder"
                        runat="server" />
                    </ul>
                  </LayoutTemplate>
                  <ItemTemplate>
                    <li>
                      <asp:LinkButton Text='<%# Bind("Name") %>'
                        runat="server" ID="NameLink" CommandName="Select"
                        CommandArgument='<%# Bind("ID") %>'
                        CausesValidation="false" />
                    </li>
                  </ItemTemplate>
                  <SelectedItemTemplate>
                    <li>
                      <b><%# Eval("Name") %></b>
                    </li>
                  </SelectedItemTemplate>
                </asp:ListView>
              </td>
              <td valign="top">
                <asp:FormView ID="FormView1" Runat="server"
                  DataSourceID="MRBEventDetailData">
                  <ItemTemplate>
                    <h3><%# Eval("Name") %></h3>
                    <b>Date:</b>
                    <%# Eval("EventDate", "{0:D}") %>
                    <br />
                    <b>Room:</b>
                    <%# Eval("Room") %>
                    <br />
                    <b>Attendees:</b>
                    <%# Eval("AttendeeList") %>
                  </ItemTemplate>
                </asp:FormView>
              </td>
            </tr>
          </table>
        </td>
      </tr>
    </table>
```

Here you have added a new table row containing a table with a `ListView` control in one column and a `FormView` control in the other.

The `ListView` uses `<LayoutTemplate>` to output a bulleted list and `<ItemTemplate>` and `<SelectedItemTemplate>` to display event details as list items. In `<LayoutTemplate>`, a container element for items is specified with a `PlaceHolder` control that has the `ID="itemPlaceholder"` attribute. To facilitate selection, you raise a `Select` command from the event name link rendered in `<ItemTemplate>`, which automatically changes the selection. You also use the `OnSelectedIndexChanged` event, triggered when the `Select` command changes the selection, to ensure that the list display updates itself to display the selected item in a different style. The event handler for this is shown in the following code:

```
protected void EventList_SelectedIndexChanged(object sender, EventArgs e)
{
    EventList.DataBind();
}
```

You also need to ensure new events are added to the list:

```
if (queryResult == 1)
{
    resultLabel.Text = "Event Added.";
    EventData = null;
    calendar.SelectedDate =
        GetFreeDate(calendar.SelectedDate.AddDays(1));
    GridView1.DataBind();
    EventList.DataBind();
}
```

Now selectable event details are available in the table, as shown in Figure 37-14.

There is *much* more that you can do with templates and data-bound controls in general, enough in fact to fill a whole book. However, this should be enough to get you started with your experimentation.

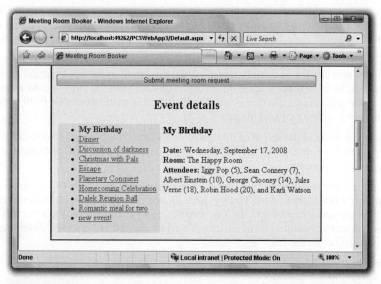

Figure 37-14

Application Configuration

Throughout this chapter, we have alluded to the existence of a conceptual application containing Web pages and configuration settings. This is an important concept to grasp, especially when configuring your Web site for multiple concurrent users.

A few notes on terminology and application lifetime are necessary here. An *application* is defined as all files in your project, and is configured by the `Web.config` file. An `Application` object is created when an application is started for the first time, which will be when the first HTTP request arrives. Also at this time, the `Application_Start` event is triggered and a pool of `HttpApplication` instances is created. Each incoming request receives one of these instances, which performs request processing. Note that this means `HttpApplication` objects do not need to cope with concurrent access, unlike the global `Application` object. When all `HttpApplication` instances finish their work, the `Application_End` event fires and the application terminates, destroying the `Application` object.

The event handlers for the events mentioned earlier (along with handlers for all other events discussed in this chapter) can be defined in a `Global.asax` file, which you can add to any Web site project. The generated file contains blanks for you to fill in; for example:

```
protected void Application_Start(Object sender, EventArgs e)
{
}
```

When an individual user accesses the Web application, a *session* is started. Similar to the application, this involves the creation of a user-specific `Session` object, along with the triggering of a `Session_Start` event. Within a session, individual *requests* trigger `Application_BeginRequest` and `Application_EndRequest` events. These can occur several times over the scope of a session as different resources within the application are accessed. Individual sessions can be terminated manually, or will time out if no further requests are received. Session termination triggers a `Session_End` event and the destruction of the `Session` object.

Against the background of this process, you can do several things to streamline your application. If all instances of your application use a single, resource-heavy object, for example, then you might consider instantiating it at the application level. This can improve performance and reduce memory usage with multiple users because in most requests no such instantiation will be required.

Another technique you can use is to store session-level information for use by individual users across requests. This might include user-specific information that is extracted from a data store when the user first connects (in the `Session_Start()` event handler), and is made available until the session is terminated (through a timeout or user request).

These techniques are beyond the scope of this book — and you might want to consult *Professional ASP. NET 2.0* (Wiley Publishing, Inc., ISBN 0-7645-7610-0) for details — but it helps to have a broad understanding of the processes.

Finally, you need to look at `Web.config` files. A Web site will usually have one of these in its root directory (although it is not created for you by default), and may have additional ones in subdirectories to configure directory-specific settings (such as security). The `PCSWebApp3` Web site developed in this chapter received an auto-generated `Web.config` file when you added a stored database connection string, which you can see in the file:

```
<connectionStrings>
  <add name="MRBConnectionString"
      connectionString="Data Source=.\SQLEXPRESS;
      AttachDbFilename=|DataDirectory|\MeetingRoomBooker.mdf;
      Integrated Security=True;User Instance=True"
      providerName="System.Data.SqlClient" />
</connectionStrings>
```

If you ran the project in debug mode, then you will also see some additional settings in the Web.config file.

You can edit Web.config files manually, but you can also configure Web sites (and their underlying configuration files) using a tool that is accessible on the Web site menu in Visual Studio, under ASP.NET Configuration. The display for this tool is shown in Figure 37-15.

As you can see from the text, this tool lets you configure a number of settings, including security. You will see much more of this tool in the next chapter.

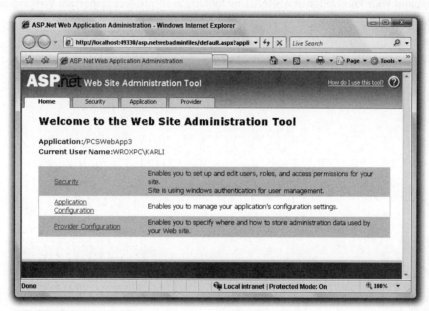

Figure 37-15

Summary

This chapter has provided an overview of Web application creation with ASP.NET. You have seen how you can use C# in combination with Web server controls to provide a truly rich development environment. You have developed an event-booking sample application to which illustrates many of the techniques available, such as the variety of server controls that exist, and data binding with ADO.NET.

Specifically, you have seen the following:

❑ An introduction to ASP.NET and how it fits in with .NET development in general

❑ How the basic syntax of ASP.NET works, how state management is achieved, and how to integrate C# code with ASP.NET pages

❑ How to create an ASP.NET Web application using Visual Studio, and what options exist for hosting and testing of Web sites

❑ A summary of the Web controls available to ASP.NET developers, and how they work together to deliver dynamic and/or data-driven content

❏   How to work with event handlers to both detect and act on user interaction with controls and customize controls via page and rendering events

❏   How to bind data to Web controls, and format the data displayed using templates and data binding expressions

❏   How to put all this together to build a meeting room booker application

With this information, you are already at a point where you could assemble powerful Web applications of your own. However, we've only scratched the surface of what's possible. So, before you put down this book and dive into your own Web development, we recommend that you keep reading. In Chapter 38, you will expand your knowledge of ASP.NET by looking at some more important Web topics, including master pages, skinning, and personalization. And trust us — the results are worth it!

38

ASP.NET Development

Sometimes the tools available for Web development, however powerful, don't quite match up with your requirements for a specific project. Perhaps a given control doesn't quite work as you would like it to, or perhaps one section of code, intended for reuse on several pages, is too complex in the hands of multiple developers. In such cases, there is a strong argument for building your own controls. Such controls can, at their simplest, wrap multiple existing controls together, perhaps with additional properties specifying layout. They can also be completely unlike any existing control. Using a control you have built yourself can be as simple as using any other control in ASP.NET (if you have written it well), which can certainly ease Web site coding.

In the first part of this chapter, you examine the options available to control developers, and assemble some simple user controls of your own. You also look at the basics of more advanced control construction, although you won't see these in any great depth; whole books are devoted to the subject.

Next, you look at master pages, a technique new to ASP.NET 2.0 that enables you to provide templates for your Web sites. Using master pages, you can implement complex layouts on Web pages throughout a Web site with a great deal of code reuse. You also see how you can use the navigation Web server controls in combination with a master page to provide consistent navigation across a Web site.

Site navigation can be made user-specific, such that only certain users (those that are registered with the site, or site administrators, say) can access certain sections. You also look at site security and how to log in to Web sites — something that is made extremely easy via the login Web server controls.

After that, you look at some more advanced styling techniques, namely, providing and choosing themes for Web sites, which separate the presentation of your Web pages from their functionality. You can supply alternative cascading style sheets for your sites, as well as different skins for Web server controls.

Finally, you will see how to use Web Parts to enable your users to dynamically personalize Web pages by positioning and customizing controls on a page.

To summarize, in this chapter you look at:

- ❑ User and custom controls
- ❑ Master pages
- ❑ Site navigation
- ❑ Security
- ❑ Themes
- ❑ Web Parts

Throughout this chapter, you will refer to one large example application that includes all the techniques that you have seen in this and the previous chapter. This application, PCSDemoSite, is available in the downloadable code for this chapter. It is a little too large to include all the code here, but you don't need to have it running in front of you to learn about the techniques it illustrates. The relevant sections of code are examined as and when necessary, and the additional code (mostly dummy content or simple code you have already seen) is left for you to examine at your convenience.

User and Custom Controls

In the past, implementing custom-built controls was tricky, especially on large-scale systems where complex registration procedures might be required to use them. Even on simple systems, the coding required to create a custom control could become a very involved process. The scripting capabilities of older Web languages also suffered by not giving you complete access to your cunningly crafted object models, which resulted in poor performance.

The .NET Framework provides an ideal setting for the creation of custom controls, using simple programming techniques. Every aspect of ASP.NET server controls is exposed for you to customize, including such capabilities as templating and client-side scripting. However, there is no need to write code for all of these eventualities; simpler controls can be a lot easier to create.

In addition, the dynamic discovery of assemblies that is inherent in a .NET system makes installation of Web applications on a new Web server as simple as copying the directory structure containing your code. To make use of the controls you have created, you simply copy the assemblies containing those controls along with the rest of the code. You can even place frequently used controls in an assembly located in the global assembly cache (GAC) on the Web server, so that all Web applications on the server have access to them.

This chapter discusses two different kinds of controls:

- ❑ **User controls** (and how to convert existing ASP.NET pages into controls)
- ❑ **Custom controls** (and how to group the functionality of several controls, extend existing controls, and create new controls from scratch)

User controls are illustrated with a simple control that displays a card suit (club, diamond, heart, or spade), so that you can embed it in other ASP.NET pages with ease. We won't go into too much depth for custom controls, although we will show you the basic principles and direct you to more information beyond this book.

User Controls

User controls are controls that you create using ASP.NET code, just as you use in standard ASP.NET Web pages. The difference is that after you have created a user control you can reuse it in multiple ASP.NET pages.

For example, say that you have created a page that displays some information from a database, perhaps information about an order. Instead of creating a fixed page that does this, it is possible to place the relevant code into a user control, and then insert that control into as many different Web pages as you want.

In addition, it is possible to define properties and methods for user controls. For example, you can specify a property for the background color for displaying your database table in a Web page, or a method to re-run a database query to check for changes.

To start, you create a simple user control. As is the case with the other chapters, you can download the code for the sample projects in this chapter from the Wrox Web site at www.wrox.com.

A Simple User Control

In Visual Studio .NET, create a new Web site called PCSUserCWebApp1 in the directory C:\ProCSharp\ Chapter38. After the standard files have been generated, select the Website ⇨ Add New Item . . . menu option and add a Web User Control called PCSUserC1.ascx, as shown in Figure 38-1.

Figure 38-1

The files added to your project, with the extensions .ascx and .ascx.cs, work in a very similar way to the .aspx files that you have seen already. The .ascx file contains your ASP.NET code and looks very similar to a normal .aspx file. The .ascx.cs file is your code-behind file, which defines custom code for the user control, much in the same way that forms are extended by .aspx.cs files.

The .ascx files can be viewed in Design or Source view, just like .aspx files. Looking at the file in Source view reveals an important difference: there is no HTML code present, and in particular no <form> element. This is because user controls are inserted inside ASP.NET forms in other files and so don't need a <form> tag of their own. The generated code is as follows:

```
<%@ Control Language="C#" AutoEventWireup="true" CodeFile="PCSUserC1.ascx.cs"
    Inherits="PCSUserC1" %>
```

This is very similar to the <%@ Page %> directive generated in .aspx files, except that Control is specified rather than Page. The CodeFile attribute specifies the code-behind file and Inherits specifies the class defined in the code-behind file from which the page inherits. The code in the .ascx.cs file contains, as in auto-generated .aspx.cs files, a class definition that is empty apart from a Page_Load() event handler method.

Your simple control will be one that displays a graphic corresponding to one of the four standard suits in cards (club, diamond, heart, or spade). The graphics required for this were shipped as part of a previous version of Visual Studio .NET; you can find them in the downloadable code for this chapter, in the CardSuitImages directory, with the file names CLUB.BMP, DIAMOND.BMP, HEART.BMP, and SPADE.BMP. Copy these files into a new Images subdirectory of your project's directory, so that you can use them in a moment. If you do not have access to this download, you can use any images you like for this example because they are not important to the functionality of the code.

Note that unlike earlier versions of Visual Studio, changes you make to the Web site structure outside of Visual Studio are automatically reflected in the IDE. You have to hit the refresh button in the Solution Explorer window, but you should see the new Images directory and bitmap files appear automatically.

Now add some code to your new control. In the HTML view of PCSUserC1.ascx, add the following:

```
<%@ Control Language="C#" AutoEventWireup="true" CodeFile="PCSUserC1.ascx.cs"
    Inherits="PCSUserC1" %>
<table cellspacing="4">
  <tr valign="middle">
    <td>
      <asp:Image Runat="server" ID="suitPic" ImageURL="~/Images/club.bmp"/>
    </td>
    <td>
      <asp:Label Runat="server" ID="suitLabel">Club</asp:Label>
    </td>
  </tr>
</table>
```

This defines a default state for your control, which is a picture of a club along with a label. The ~ in the path to the image means "start at the root directory of the Web site." Before you add functionality, you will test this default by adding this control to your project Web page webForm1.aspx.

To use a custom control in an .aspx file, you first need to specify how you will refer to it, that is, the name of the tag that will represent the control in your HTML. To do this, you use the <%@ Register %> directive at the top of the code in Default.aspx, as follows:

```
<%@ Register TagPrefix="pcs" TagName="UserC1" Src="PCSUserC1.ascx" %>
```

The TagPrefix and TagName attributes specify the tag name to use (in the form <TagPrefix: TagName>), and you use the Src attribute to point to the file containing your user control. Now you can use the control by adding the following element:

```
<form id="Form1" method="post" runat="server">
  <div>
    <pcs:UserC1 Runat="server" ID="myUserControl"/>
  </div>
</form>
```

This is all you need to do to test your user control. Figure 38-2 shows the results of running this code.

Figure 38-2

As it stands, this control groups two existing controls, an image and a label, in a table layout. Therefore, it falls into the category of a composite control.

To gain control over the displayed suit, you can use an attribute on the <PCS:UserC1> element. Attributes on user control elements are automatically mapped to properties on user controls, so all you have to do to make this work is add a property to the code behind your control, PCSUserC1.ascx.cs. Call this property Suit, and let it take any suit value. To make it easier for you to represent the state of the control, you define an enumeration to hold the four suit names. The best way to do this is to add an App_Code directory to your Web site, and then add a .cs file called Suit.cs in this directory. App_Code is another "special" directory, like App_Data, whose functionality is defined for you — in this case it holds additional code files for your Web application. You can add this directory by right-clicking the Web site in Solution Explorer and clicking Add ASP.NET Folder ⇨ App_Code. When you have done this, add Suit.cs with code as follows:

```
using System;

public enum suit
{
    club, diamond, heart, spade
}
```

The PCSUserC1 class needs a member variable to hold the suit type, currentSuit:

```
public partial class PCSUserC1 : System.Web.UI.UserControl
{
    protected suit currentSuit;
```

And a property to access this member variable, Suit:

```
public suit Suit
{
    get
    {
        return currentSuit;
    }
    set
    {
        currentSuit = value;
        suitPic.ImageUrl = "~/Images/" + currentSuit.ToString() + ".bmp";
        suitLabel.Text = currentSuit.ToString();
    }
}
```

The set accessor here sets the URL of the image to one of the files you copied earlier, and the text displayed to the suit name.

Next, you must add code to Default.aspx so that you can access this new property. You could simply specify the suit using the property you have just added:

```
<PCS:UserC1 Runat="server" id="myUserControl" Suit="diamond"/>
```

The ASP.NET processor is intelligent enough to get the correct enumeration item from the string provided. To make things a bit more interesting and interactive, though, you will use a radio button list to select a suit:

```
<form id="form1" runat="server">
  <div>
    <pcs:UserC1 id="myUserControl" runat="server" />
    <asp:RadioButtonList Runat="server" ID="suitList" AutoPostBack="True">
```

(continued)

(continued)

```
            <asp:ListItem Value="club" Selected="True">Club</asp:ListItem>
            <asp:ListItem Value="diamond">Diamond</asp:ListItem>
            <asp:ListItem Value="heart">Heart</asp:ListItem>
            <asp:ListItem Value="spade">Spade</asp:ListItem>
        </asp:RadioButtonList>
    </div>
  </form>
```

You also need to add an event handler for the `SelectedIndexChanged` event of the list, which you can do simply by double-clicking the radio button list control in Design view.

> *Note that you have set the `AutoPostBack` property of this list to `True`, because the `suitList_SelectedIndexChanged()` event handler won't be executed on the server unless a postback is in operation, and this control doesn't trigger a postback by default.*

The `suitList_SelectedIndexChanged()` method requires the following code in `Default.aspx.cs`:

```
public partial class Default
{
    protected void suitList_SelectedIndexChanged(object sender, EventArgs e)
    {
        myUserControl.Suit = (suit)Enum.Parse(typeof(suit),
                                          suitList.SelectedItem.Value);
    }
}
```

You know that the `Value` attributes on the `<ListItem>` elements represent valid values for the suit enumeration you defined earlier, so you simply parse these as enumeration types and use them as values of the `Suit` property of your user control. You cast the returned object type to `suit` using simple casing syntax, because this cannot be achieved implicitly.

Now you can change the suit when you run your Web application (see Figure 38-3).

Figure 38-3

Next, you give your control some methods. Again, this is very simple; you just add methods to the `PCSUserC1` class:

```
public void Club()
{
    Suit = suit.club;
}

public void Diamond()
```

```
    {
        Suit = suit.diamond;
    }

    public void Heart()
    {
        Suit = suit.heart;
    }

    public void Spade()
    {
        Suit = suit.spade;
    }
```

These four methods — Club(), Diamond(), Heart(), and Spade() — change the suit displayed on the screen to the respective suit clicked.

You call these functions from four ImageButton controls in your .aspx page:

```
    </asp:RadioButtonList>
    <asp:ImageButton Runat="server" ID="clubButton"
      ImageUrl="~/Images/CLUB.BMP" OnClick="clubButton_Click" />
    <asp:ImageButton Runat="server" ID="diamondButton"
      ImageUrl="~/Images/DIAMOND.BMP" OnClick="diamondButton_Click" />
    <asp:ImageButton Runat="server" ID="heartButton"
      ImageUrl="~/Images/HEART.BMP" OnClick="heartButton_Click" />
    <asp:ImageButton Runat="server" ID="spadeButton"
      ImageUrl="~/Images/SPADE.BMP" OnClick="spadeButton_Click" />
  </div>
</form>
```

You use the following event handlers:

```
    protected void clubButton_Click(object sender, ImageClickEventArgs e)
    {
        myUserControl.Club();
        suitList.SelectedIndex = 0;
    }

    protected void diamondButton_Click(object sender, ImageClickEventArgs e)
    {
        myUserControl.Diamond();
        suitList.SelectedIndex = 1;
    }

    protected void heartButton_Click(object sender, ImageClickEventArgs e)
    {
        myUserControl.Heart();
        suitList.SelectedIndex = 2;
    }

    protected void spadeButton_Click(object sender, ImageClickEventArgs e)
    {
        myUserControl.Spade();
        suitList.SelectedIndex = 3;
    }
```

Note that you could use a single event handler for all four buttons, because they have identical method signatures. You could detect which button has been pressed by the value passed to sender, *and thus determine which method of* myUserControl *to call and which index to set dynamically. In this case, though, there wouldn't be a huge difference in the amount of code required, so, for simplicity, things are kept separate.*

Now you have four new buttons you can use to change the suit, as shown in Figure 38-4.

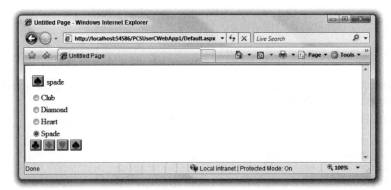

Figure 38-4

Now that you have created your user control, you can use it in any other Web page simply by using the <%@ Register %> directive and the two source code files (PCSUserC1.ascx and PCSUserC1.ascx.cs) you have created for the control.

User Controls in PCSDemoSite

In the PCSDemoSite, the meeting room booker application from the previous chapter has been converted into a user control for ease of reuse. To see the control, you have to log in to the site as User1, with password User1!!, and navigate to the Meeting Room Booker page, as shown in Figure 38-5. (You learn how the logging-in system works later in the chapter.)

Apart from the obvious change in style, which is achieved by themes, as you see later in this chapter, the major modifications are as follows:

❑ The username is automatically taken from user details.

❑ There is no extra data display at the bottom of the page, and corresponding DataBind() calls are removed from the code behind.

❑ There is no result label beneath the control — the user gets enough feedback by seeing events added to the calendar and event list, without being told that event addition was successful.

❑ The page containing the user control uses a master page.

The code modifications to achieve all of this are remarkably simple. You won't look at them here, but you will come back to this control later in the chapter, when you look at logging in.

Custom Controls

Custom controls go a step beyond user controls in that they are entirely self-contained in C# assemblies, requiring no separate ASP.NET code. This means that you don't need to go through the process of assembling a user interface (UI) in an .ascx file. Instead, you have complete control over what is written to the output stream, that is, the exact HTML generated by your control.

Figure 38-5

In general, it will take longer to develop custom controls than user controls because the syntax is more complex, and you often have to write significantly more code to get results. A user control may be as simple as a few other controls grouped together, as you have seen, whereas a custom control can do just about anything short of making you a cup of coffee.

To get the most customizable behavior for your custom controls, you can derive a class from System .Web.UI.WebControls.WebControl. If you do this, you are creating a full custom control. Alternatively, you can extend the functionality of an existing control, creating a derived custom control. Finally, you can group existing controls together, much as you did in the last section but with a more logical structure, to create a composite custom control.

Whatever you create can be used in ASP.NET pages in pretty much the same way. All you need to do is place the generated assembly in a location where the Web application that will use it can find it, and register the element names to use with the <%@ Register %> directive. For this location, you have two options: you can either put the assembly in the bin directory of the Web application, or place it in the GAC if you want all Web applications on the server to have access to it. Alternatively, if you are just using a user control on a single Web site, you can just put the .cs file for the control in the App_Code directory for the site.

The <%@ Register %> directive takes a slightly different syntax for custom controls:

```
<%@ Register TagPrefix="PCS" Namespace="PCSCustomWebControls"
        Assembly="PCSCustomWebControls"%>
```

You use the `TagPrefix` option in the same way as before, but you don't use the `TagName` or `Src` attributes. This is because the custom control assembly you use may contain several custom controls, and each of these will be named by its class, so `TagName` is redundant. In addition, because you can use the dynamic discovery capabilities of the .NET Framework to find your assembly, you simply have to name it and the namespace in it that contains your controls.

In the previous line of code, you are instructing the program to use an assembly called `PCSCustomWebControls.dll` with controls in the `PCSCustomWebControls` namespace, and use the tag prefix `PCS`. If you have a control called `Control1` in this namespace, you could use it with the ASP.NET code:

```
<PCS:Control1 Runat="server" ID="MyControl1"/>
```

The `Assembly` attribute of the `<%@ Register %>` directive is optional — if you have custom controls in the `App_Code` directory of your site, you can omit this, and the Web site will look at code here for controls. One thing though — the `Namespace` attribute is *not* optional. You must include a namespace in code files for custom controls, or the ASP.NET runtime will not be able to find them.

With custom controls, it is also possible to reproduce some of the control nesting behavior that exists in list controls, for example the way that you can nest `<asp:ListItem>` controls inside a list control to populate the list control:

```
<asp:DropDownList ID="roomList" Runat="server" Width="160px">
   <asp:ListItem Value="1">The Happy Room</asp:ListItem>
   <asp:ListItem Value="2">The Angry Room</asp:ListItem>
   <asp:ListItem Value="3">The Depressing Room</asp:ListItem>
   <asp:ListItem Value="4">The Funked Out Room</asp:ListItem>
</asp:DropDownList>
```

You can create controls that should be interpreted as being children of other controls in a very similar way to this. This is one of the more advanced techniques that you won't be looking at in this book.

Custom Control Sample

Now it's time to put some of this theory into practice. You will use a single Web site called `PCSCustomCWebApp1` in the `C:\ProCSharp\Chapter38\` directory, with a custom control in its `App_Code` directory to illustrate a simple custom control. The control here will be a multicolored version of the existing `Label` control, with the ability to cycle through a set of colors for each letter in its text.

The code for the control, `RainbowLabel`, in the file `App_Code\Rainbow.cs`, starts with the following `using` statements:

```
using System;
using System.Data;
using System.Configuration;
using System.Linq;
using System.Web;
using System.Web.Security;
using System.Web.UI;
using System.Web.UI.WebControls;
using System.Web.UI.WebControls.WebParts;
using System.Web.UI.HtmlControls;
using System.Xml.Linq;
using System.Drawing;
```

Apart from `System.Drawing`, these are the default namespaces that are added when you add a class file to a Web site. The `System.Drawing` namespace is required for the `Color` enumeration. The class maintains an array of colors to use for letters in its text in a private `Color` array called `colors`:

```
namespace PCSCustomWebControls
{
    public class RainbowLabel : Label
    {
        private Color[] colors = new Color[] {Color.Red,
                                              Color.Orange,
                                              Color.Yellow,
                                              Color.GreenYellow,
                                              Color.Blue,
                                              Color.Indigo,
                                              Color.Violet};
```

Also notice that the namespace PCSCustomWebControls is used to contain the control. As discussed earlier, this is necessary so that Web pages can reference the control correctly.

To enable color cycling, you also store an integer offset value in a private offset property:

```
private int offset
{
    get
    {
        object rawOffset = ViewState["_offset"];
        if (rawOffset != null)
        {
            return (int)rawOffset;
        }
        else
        {
            ViewState["_offset"] = 0;
            return 0;
        }
    }
    set
    {
        ViewState["_offset"] = value;
    }
}
```

Note that this property isn't as simple as just storing a value in a member field. This is due to the way ASP.NET maintains state, as discussed in the previous chapter. Controls are instantiated on each postback operation, so to store values you must make use of view state. This is easy to access — you simply use the ViewState collection, which can store any object that is serializable. Otherwise, offset would revert to its initial value between each postback.

To modify offset, you use a method called Cycle():

```
public void Cycle()
{
    offset = ++offset;
}
```

This simply increments the value stored in the view state for offset.

Finally, you come to perhaps the most important method override for any custom control — Render(). This is where you output HTML, and as such it can be a very complicated method to implement. If you were to take into account all the browsers that may view your controls, and all the variables that could affect rendering, this method could get very big. Fortunately, for this example, it's quite simple:

```
protected override void Render(HtmlTextWriter output)
{
    string text = Text;
    for (int pos = 0; pos < text.Length; pos++)
    {
        int rgb = colors[(pos + offset) % colors.Length].ToArgb()
                                                    & 0xFFFFFF;
        output.Write(string.Format(
            "<font color=\"#{0:X6}\">{1}</font>", rgb, text[pos]));
    }
}
```

This method gives you access to the output stream to display your control content. There are only two cases where you don't need to implement this method:

❑ When you are designing a control that has no visual representation (usually known as a component)

❑ When you are deriving from an existing control and don't need to change its display characteristics

Custom controls can also expose custom methods, raise custom events, and respond to child controls (if any). In the case of RainbowLabel, you don't have to worry about any of this.

Next, you need to modify Default.aspx to view the control and provide access to Cycle(), as follows:

```
<%@ Page Language="C#" AutoEventWireup="true" CodeFile="Default.aspx.cs"
    Inherits="_Default" %>

<%@ Register TagPrefix="pcs" Namespace="PCSCustomWebControls" %>
<!DOCTYPE html PUBLIC "-//W3C//DTD XHTML 1.1//EN"
    "http://www.w3.org/TR/xhtml11/DTD/xhtml11.dtd">
<html xmlns="http://www.w3.org/1999/xhtml">
<head runat="server">
    <title>Untitled Page</title>
</head>
<body>
    <form id="form1" runat="server">
        <div>
            <pcs:RainbowLabel runat="server" ID="rainbowLabel1"
                Text="Multicolored label!" />
            <asp:Button Runat="server" ID="cycleButton" Text="Cycle colors"
                OnClick="cycleButton_Click" />
        </div>
    </form>
</body>
</html>
```

The required code in Default.aspx.cs is simply:

```
public partial class _Default : System.Web.UI.Page
{
    protected void Page_Load(object sender, EventArgs e)
```

```
        {

        }

    protected void cycleButton_Click(object sender, EventArgs e)
    {
        rainbowLabel1.Cycle();
    }
}
```

Now you can view the sample and cycle the colors in the sample text, as shown in Figure 38-6.

Figure 38-6

You can do a lot more with custom controls; indeed, the possibilities are practically limitless, but you will have to experiment with these possibilities on your own.

Master Pages

Master pages provide an excellent way to make your Web sites easier to design. Putting all (or at least most) of your page layout in a single file allows you to concentrate on the more important things for the individual Web pages of your site.

Master pages are created in files with the extension .master, and can be added via the Web site ➪ Add New Item . . . menu item, like any other site content. At first glance, the code generated for a master page is much like that for a standard .aspx page:

```
<%@ Master Language="C#" AutoEventWireup="true"
   CodeFile="MyMasterPage.master.cs" Inherits="MyMasterPage" %>
<!DOCTYPE html PUBLIC "-//W3C//DTD XHTML 1.0 Transitional//EN"
   "http://www.w3.org/TR/xhtml1/DTD/xhtml1-transitional.dtd">
<html xmlns="http://www.w3.org/1999/xhtml">
<head runat="server">
  <title>Untitled Page</title>
  <asp:ContentPlaceHolder id="head" runat="server">
  </asp:ContentPlaceHolder>
</head>
<body>
  <form id="form1" runat="server">
    <div>
      <asp:ContentPlaceHolder ID="ContentPlaceHolder1" Runat="server">
      </asp:ContentPlaceHolder>
    </div>
  </form>
</body>
</html>
```

The differences are:

❑ A <%@ Master %> directive is used instead of a <%@ Page %> directive, although the attributes are the same.

❑ A ContentPlaceHolder control with an ID of head is placed in the page header.

❑ A ContentPlaceHolder control with an ID of ContentPlaceHolder1 is placed in the page body.

The ContentPlaceHolder controls are what make master pages so useful. You can have any number of these on a page, and they are used by .aspx pages using the master page to "plug in" content. You can put default content inside a ContentPlaceHolder control, but .aspx pages can override this content.

For an .aspx page to use a master page, you need to modify the <%@ Page %> directive as follows:

```
<%@ Page Language="C#" AutoEventWireup="true" CodeFile="Default.aspx.cs"
    Inherits="_Default" MasterPageFile="~/MyMasterPage.master"
    Title="Page Title" %>
```

Here you have added two new attributes: a MasterPageFile attribute saying which master page to use and a Title attribute that sets the content of the <title> element in the master page.

When you add an .aspx page to a Web site, you can choose to select a master page, as shown in Figure 38-7.

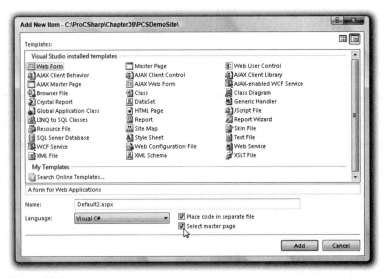

Figure 38-7

If you do this, you can navigate through your site structure to find the master page you want, as shown in Figure 38-8.

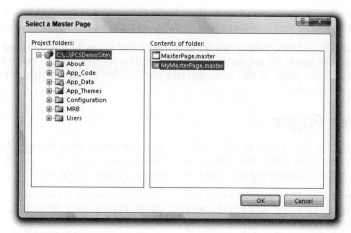

Figure 38-8

The `.aspx` page doesn't have to contain any other code, if you want to use the default master page content. In fact, it is an error to include a `Form` control, because a page may only have one of these and there is one in the master page.

`.aspx` pages that use a master page can contain no root-level content other than directives, script elements, and `Content` controls. You can have as many `Content` controls as you like, where each one inserts content into one of the `ContentPlaceHolder` controls in the master page. The only thing to look out for is to make sure that the `ContentPlaceHolderID` attribute of the `Content` control matches the `ID` of the `ContentPlaceHolder` control where you want to insert content. So, to add content into the master page shown earlier, you would simply need the following in the `.aspx` file:

```
<%@ Page Language="C#" MasterPageFile="~/MyMasterPage.master"
   AutoEventWireup="true" CodeFile="Default2.aspx.cs" Inherits="Default2"
   Title="Untitled Page" %>

<asp:Content ID="Content1" ContentPlaceHolderID="head" Runat="Server">
</asp:Content>
<asp:Content ID="Content2" ContentPlaceHolderID="ContentPlaceHolder1"
   runat="Server">
   Custom content!
</asp:Content>
```

The true power of master pages comes when you surround the `ContentPlaceHolder` controls in your master pages with other content, such as navigation controls, site logos, and HTML. You can supply multiple `ContentPlaceHolder` controls for main content, sidebar content, footer text, and so on.

You can omit `Content` controls on a page if you do not wish to supply content for a specific `ContentPlaceHolder`. For example, you could remove the `Content1` control from the preceding code without affecting the resultant display.

Accessing Master Page Content from Web Pages

When you add a master page to a Web page, you will sometimes need to access the master page from code in your Web page. To do this, you can use the `Page.Master` property, which will return a reference to the master page in the form of a `MasterPage` object. You can cast this to the type of the master page as defined by the master page file (for the example in the previous section, this class would be called `MyMasterPage`). Once you have this reference, you can access any public members of the master page class.

Also, you can use the `MasterPage.FindControl()` method to locate controls on the master page by their identifier. This enables you to manipulate content on the master page that is outside of content placeholders.

One typical use of this might be if you define a master page that is used for a standard form, with a submit button. You can locate the submit button in the child page and add an event handler for the submit button in the master page. In this way, you can provide, for example, custom validation logic in response to a form submission.

Nested Master Pages

The Select master page option is also available when you create a new master page. By using this option, you can create a *nested* master page that is based on a parent master page. For example, you can create a master page called `MyNestedMasterPage` that uses `MyMasterPage` as follows:

```
<%@ Master Language="C#" MasterPageFile="~/MyMasterPage.master"
  AutoEventWireup="false" CodeFile="MyNestedMasterPage.master.cs"
  Inherits="MyNestedMasterPage" %>

<asp:Content ID="Content1" ContentPlaceHolderID="head" Runat="Server">
  <!-- Disabled for child controls. -->
</asp:Content>
<asp:Content ID="Content2" ContentPlaceHolderID="ContentPlaceHolder1"
  Runat="Server">
  First nested place holder:
  <asp:ContentPlaceHolder ID="NestedContentPlaceHolder1" runat="server">

  </asp:ContentPlaceHolder>
  <br />
  <br />
  Second nested place holder:
  <asp:ContentPlaceHolder ID="NestedContentPlaceHolder2" runat="server">

  </asp:ContentPlaceHolder>
</asp:Content>
```

Pages that use this master page would supply content for `NestedContentPlaceHolder1` and `NestedContentPlaceHolder2`, but would not have direct access to the `ContentPlaceHolder` controls specified in `MyMasterPage`. In this example, `MyNestedMasterPage` fixes the content for the `head` control and supplies a template for the `ContentPlaceHolder1` control.

By creating a family of nested master pages, you can provide alternate layouts for pages while leaving some aspects of the base master pages untouched. For example, the root master page might include navigation and basic layout, and nested master pages could provide layouts with different amounts of columns. You could then use the nested master pages in the pages of your site and quickly switch between these alternate layouts on different pages.

Master Pages in PCSDemoSite

In PCSDemoSite, the single master page `MasterPage.master` (the default name for a master page) is used, with code as follows:

```
<%@ Master Language="C#" AutoEventWireup="true"
CodeFile="MasterPage.master.cs"
  Inherits="MasterPage" %>
<!DOCTYPE html PUBLIC "-//W3C//DTD XHTML 1.1//EN"
  "http://www.w3.org/TR/xhtml11/DTD/xhtml11.dtd">
```

```
<html xmlns="http://www.w3.org/1999/xhtml">
<head runat="server">
  <link rel="stylesheet" href="StyleSheet.css" type="text/css" />
  <title></title>
</head>
<body>
  <form id="form1" runat="server">
    <div id="header">
      <h1><asp:literal ID="Literal1" runat="server"
        text="<%$ AppSettings:SiteTitle %>" /></h1>
      <asp:SiteMapPath ID="SiteMapPath1" Runat="server"
        CssClass="breadcrumb" />
    </div>
    <div id="nav">
      <div class="navTree">
        <asp:TreeView ID="TreeView1" runat="server"
          DataSourceID="SiteMapDataSource1" ShowLines="True" />
      </div>
      <br />
      <br />
      <asp:LoginView ID="LoginView1" Runat="server">
        <LoggedInTemplate>
          You are currently logged in as
          <b><asp:LoginName ID="LoginName1" Runat="server" /></b>.
          <asp:LoginStatus ID="LoginStatus1" Runat="server" />
        </LoggedInTemplate>
      </asp:LoginView>
    </div>
    <div id="body">
      <asp:ContentPlaceHolder ID="ContentPlaceHolder1" Runat="server" />
    </div>
  </form>
  <asp:SiteMapDataSource ID="SiteMapDataSource1" Runat="server" />
</body>
</html>
```

Many of the controls here are ones that you haven't looked at yet, and you will come back to those shortly. The important things to note here are the `<div>` elements that hold the various content sections (header, navigation bar, and body), and the use of `<%$ AppSettings:SiteTitle %>` to obtain the site title from the `Web.config` file:

```
<appSettings>
  <add key="SiteTitle" value="Professional C# Demo Site"/>
</appSettings>
```

There is also a style sheet link to `StyleSheet.css`:

```
<link rel="stylesheet" href="StyleSheet.css" type="text/css" />
```

This CSS style sheet contains the basic layout information for the `<div>` elements on this page, as well as for a section of the meeting room booker control:

```
div#header
{
    position: absolute;
    top: 0px;
    left: 0px;
```

(continued)

(continued)

```
            height: 80px;
            width: 780px;
            padding: 10px;
    }

    div#nav
    {
            position: absolute;
            left: 0px;
            top: 100px;
            width: 180px;
            height: 580px;
            padding: 10px;
    }

    div#body
    {
            position: absolute;
            left: 200px;
            top: 100px;
            width: 580px;
            height: 580px;
            padding: 10px;
    }

    .mrbEventList
    {
            width: 40%;
    }
```

Note that none of this style information includes colors, fonts, and so on. This is achieved by style sheets within themes, which you will see later in this chapter. The only information here is layout information, such as `<div>` sizes.

> *Note that Web site best practices have been adhered to in this chapter whenever possible. Using CSS for layout rather than tables is fast becoming the industry standard for Web site layout and is well worth learning about. In the preceding code, # symbols are used to format `<div>` elements with specific `id` attributes, whereas `.mrbEventList` will format an HTML element with a specific `class` attribute.*

Site Navigation

The three navigation Web server controls, `SiteMapPath`, `Menu`, and `TreeView`, can work with an XML site map that you provide for your Web site, or a site map provided in a different format if you implement an alternative site map provider. Once you have created such a data source, these navigation Web server controls are able to automatically generate location and navigation information for users.

> *You see an example XML site map shortly.*

You can also use a `TreeView` control to display other structured data, but it really comes into its own with site maps, and gives you an alternative view of navigation information.

The navigation Web server controls are shown in the following table.

Control	Description
SiteMapPath	Displays breadcrumb-style information, allowing users to see where they are in the structure of a site and navigate to parent areas. You can supply various templates, such as NodeStyle and CurrentNodeStyle to customize the appearance of the breadcrumb trail.
Menu	Links to site map information via a SiteMapDataSource control, and enables a view of the complete site structure. The appearance of this control can be customized by templates.
TreeView	Allows the display of hierarchical data, such as a table of contents, in a tree structure. Tree nodes are stored in a Nodes property, with the selected node stored in SelectedNode. Several events allow for server-side processing of user interaction, including SelectedNodeChanged and TreeNodeCollapsed. This control is typically data-bound.

To provide a site map XML file for your site, you can add a site map file (.sitemap) using the Web site ⇨ Add New Item . . . menu item. You link to site maps via providers. The default XML provider looks for a file called Web.sitemap in the root of your site, so unless you are going to use a different provider, you should accept the default file name supplied.

A site map XML file contains a root <siteMap> element containing a single <siteMapNode> element, which in turn can contain any number of nested <siteMapNode> elements.

Each <siteMapNode> element uses the attributes shown in the following table.

Attribute	Description
Title	Page title, used as the text for links in site map displays
url	Page location, used as the hyperlink location in site map displays
Roles	The user roles that are allowed to see this site map entry in menus and so on
description	Optional text used for tooltip pop-ups for site map displays

Once a site has a Web.sitemap file, adding a breadcrumb trail is as simple as putting the following code on your page:

```
<asp:SiteMapPath ID="SiteMapPath1" Runat="server" />
```

This will use the default provider and the current URL location to format a list of links to parent pages.

Adding a menu or tree view menu requires a SiteMapDataSource control, but again this can be very simple:

```
<asp:SiteMapDataSource ID="SiteMapDataSource1" Runat="server" />
```

When using a custom provider, the only difference is that you can supply the provider ID via a SiteMapProvider attribute. You can also remove upper levels of the menu data (such as the root Home item) using StartingNodeOffset; remove just the top-level link using ShowStartingNode="False";

start from the current location using `StartFromCurrentNode="True"`; and override the root node using `StartingNodeUrl`.

The data from this data source is consumed by `Menu` and `TreeView` controls simply by setting their `DataSourceID` to the ID of the `SiteMapDataSource`. Both controls include numerous styling properties and can be themed, as you see later in this chapter.

Navigation in PCSDemoSite

The site map for PCSDemoSite is as follows:

```xml
<?xml version="1.0" encoding="utf-8" ?>
<siteMap>
  <siteMapNode url="~/Default.aspx" title="Home">
    <siteMapNode url="~/About/Default.aspx" title="About" />
    <siteMapNode url="~/MRB/Default.aspx" title="Meeting Room Booker"
      roles="RegisteredUser,SiteAdministrator" />
    <siteMapNode url="~/Configuration/Default.aspx" title="Configuration"
      roles="RegisteredUser,SiteAdministrator">
      <siteMapNode url="~/Configuration/Themes/Default.aspx" title="Themes"
        roles="RegisteredUser,SiteAdministrator"/>
    </siteMapNode>
    <siteMapNode url="~/Users/Default.aspx" title="User Area"
      roles="SiteAdministrator" />
    <siteMapNode url="~/Login.aspx" title="Login Details" />
  </siteMapNode>
</siteMap>
```

The PCSDemoSite Web site uses a custom provider to obtain information from `Web.sitemap` — which is necessary because the default provider ignores the `roles` attributes. The provider is defined in the `Web.config` file for the Web site as follows:

```xml
<configuration xmlns="http://schemas.microsoft.com/.NetConfiguration/v2.0">
  ...
  <system.Web>
    ...
    <siteMap defaultProvider="CustomProvider">
      <providers>
        <add name="CustomProvider"
          description="SiteMap provider which reads in .sitemap XML files."
          type="System.Web.XmlSiteMapProvider, System.Web, Version=2.0.3600.0,
              Culture=neutral, PublicKeyToken=b03f5f7f11d50a3a"
          siteMapFile="Web.sitemap" securityTrimmingEnabled="true" />
      </providers>
    </siteMap>
    ...
```

The only difference between this and the default provider is the addition of `securityTrimmingEnabled="true"`, which instructs the provider to supply data for just those nodes that this current user is allowed to see. This visibility is determined by the role membership of the user, as you see in the next section.

The `MasterPage.master` page in PCSDemoSite includes `SiteMapPath` and `TreeView` navigation displays along with a data source, as follows:

```html
<div id="header">
  <h1><asp:literal ID="Literal1" runat="server"
    text="<%$ AppSettings:SiteTitle %>" /></h1>
```

```
      <asp:SiteMapPath ID="SiteMapPath1" Runat="server"
        CssClass="breadcrumb" />
    </div>
    <div id="nav">
      <div class="navTree">
        <asp:TreeView ID="TreeView1" runat="server"
          DataSourceID="SiteMapDataSource1" ShowLines="True" />
      </div>
      <br />
      <br />
      <asp:LoginView ID="LoginView1" Runat="server">
        <LoggedInTemplate>
          You are currently logged in as
          <b><asp:LoginName ID="LoginName1" Runat="server" /></b>.
          <asp:LoginStatus ID="LoginStatus1" Runat="server" />
        </LoggedInTemplate>
      </asp:LoginView>
    </div>
    <div id="body">
      <asp:ContentPlaceHolder ID="ContentPlaceHolder1" Runat="server" />
    </div>
  </form>
  <asp:SiteMapDataSource ID="SiteMapDataSource1" Runat="server" />
```

The only point to note here is that CSS classes are supplied for both `SiteMapPath` and `TreeView`, to facilitate theming (discussed later in this chapter).

Security

Security and user management have often been seen as quite complicated to implement in Web sites, and with good reason. You have to consider a number of factors, including:

- ❑ What sort of user management system will I implement? Will users map to Windows user accounts, or will I implement something independent?

- ❑ How do I implement a login system?

- ❑ Do I let users register on the site, and if so, how?

- ❑ How do I let some users see and do only some things, while supplying other users with additional privileges?

- ❑ What happens in the case of forgotten passwords?

With ASP.NET 2.0, you have a whole suite of tools at your disposal for dealing with questions such as these, and it can in fact take only a matter of minutes to implement a user system on your site. You have three types of authentication at your disposal:

- ❑ Windows Authentication, whereby users have Windows accounts, typically used with intranet sites or WAN portals

- ❑ Forms Authentication, whereby the Web site maintains its own list of users and handles its own authentication

- ❑ Passport Authentication, whereby Microsoft provides a centralized authentication service for you to use

A full discussion of security in ASP.NET would take up at least a full chapter, but we provide a brief look in this section to give you an idea of how things work. You will concentrate on Forms Authentication here, because it is the most versatile system and very quick to get up and running.

The quickest way to implement Forms Authentication is via the Website ⇨ ASP.NET Configuration tool, which you saw briefly in the previous chapter. This tool has a Security tab, and on it a security wizard. This wizard lets you choose an authentication type, add roles, add users, and secure areas of your site.

Adding Forms Authentication Using the Security Wizard

For the purposes of this explanation, create a new Web site called PCSAuthenticationDemo in the directory C:\ProCSharp\Chapter38\. Once you create the site, open the Web site ⇨ ASP.NET Configuration tool. Navigate to the Security tab and click the "Use the security Setup Wizard to configure security step by step." link. Click Next on the first step after reading the information there. On the second step, select "From the internet," as shown in Figure 38-9.

Click Next, and then Next again after confirming that you will be using the default "Advanced provider settings" provider to store security information. This provider information is configurable via the Provider tab, where you can choose to store information elsewhere, such as in an SQL Server database, but an Access database is fine for illustrative purposes.

Check the "Enable roles for this Web site." option, as shown in Figure 38-10, and click Next.

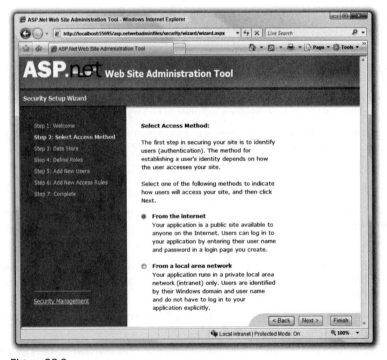

Figure 38-9

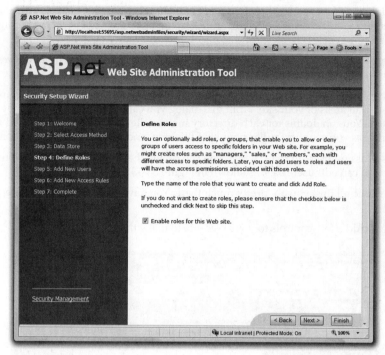

Figure 38-10

Then, add some roles, as shown in Figure 38-11.

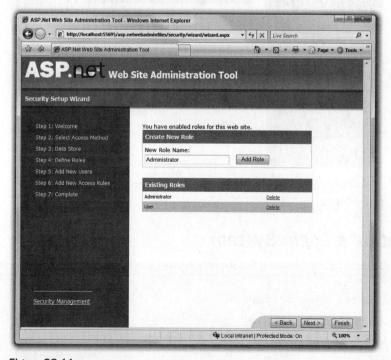

Figure 38-11

Click Next and then add some users, as shown in Figure 38-12. Note that the default security rules for passwords (defined in `machine.config`) are quite strong; there is a seven-character minimum, including at least one symbol character and a mix of uppercase and lowercase.

In the downloadable code for this chapter, two users are added in this example. The usernames are User and Administrator, and the password for both users is Pa$$w0rd.

After clicking Next again, you can define access rules for your site. By default, all users and roles will have access to all areas of your site. From this dialog you can restrict areas by role, by user, or for anonymous users. You can do this for each directory in your site because this is achieved via `Web.config` files in directories, as you see shortly. For now, skip this step, and complete authentication setup.

The last step is to assign users to roles, which you can do via the "Manage users" link on the Security tab. From here you can edit user roles, as shown in Figure 38-13.

Once you have done all this, you are pretty much there. You have a user system in place, as well as roles and users.

Now you have to add a few controls to your Web site to make things work.

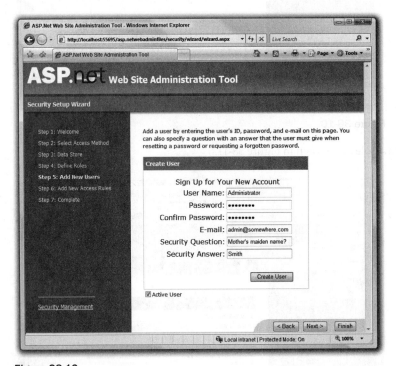

Figure 38-12

Implementing a Login System

If you open `Web.config` after running the security wizard you will see that it has been modified with the following content:

```
<roleManager enabled="true" />
```

and:

```
<authentication mode="Forms" />
```

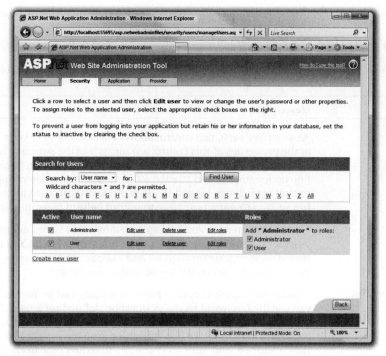

Figure 38-13

This doesn't seem like a lot for the work that you have put in, but remember that a lot of information is stored in an SQL Express database, which you can see in the App_Data directory, called ASPNETDB.MDF. You can inspect the data that has been stored in this file using any standard database management tool, including Visual Studio. You can even add users and roles directly to this database, if you are careful.

By default, logging in is achieved via a page called Login.aspx in the root of your Web site. If users attempt to navigate to a location that they don't have permission to access, they will automatically be redirected to this page and returned to the desired location after successfully logging in.

Add a Web Form called Login.aspx to the PCSAuthenticationDemo site and drag a Login control onto the form from the toolbox.

This is all you need to do to enable users to log in to your Web site. Open the site in a browser, and navigate to Login.aspx; then enter the details for a user you added in the wizard, as shown in Figure 38-14.

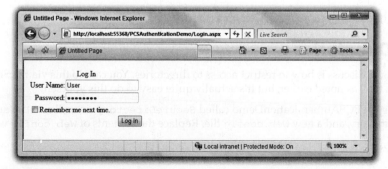

Figure 38-14

Once you have logged in, you will be sent back to `Default.aspx`, currently a blank page.

Login Web Server Controls

The Login section of the toolbox contains several controls, as shown in the following table.

Control	Description
Login	As you have seen, this control allows users to log in to your Web site. Most of the properties of this control are for styling the supplied template. You can also use `DestinationPageUrl` to force redirection to a specific location on logging in, and `VisibleWhenLoggedIn` to determine whether the control is visible to logged-in users. And, you can use various text properties such as `CreateUserText` to output helpful messages to users.
LoginView	This control enables you to display content that varies depending on whether users are logged in, or what roles users are in. You can put content in `<AnonymousTemplate>` and `<LoggedInTemplate>`, as well as `<RoleGroups>` to control the output of this control.
PasswordRecovery	This control enables users to have their password mailed to them, and it can use the password recovery question defined for a user. Again, most properties are for display formatting, but there are properties such as `MailDefinition-Subject` for configuring the email to be sent to the user's address, and `SuccessPageUrl` to redirect the users after they have requested a password.
LoginStatus	This control displays a Login or Logout link, with customizable text and images, to users depending on whether they are logged in.
LoginName	This control outputs the username for the currently logged-in user.
CreateUserWizard	This control displays a form that users can use to register with your site and to be added to the user list. As with other login controls, there are a large number of properties relating to layout formatting, but the default is perfectly serviceable.
ChangePassword	This control enables users to change their passwords. There are three fields, for the old password, the new password, and the confirmation. There are many styling properties.

You see some of these in action in PCSDemoSite shortly.

Securing Directories

One final thing to discuss is how to restrict access to directories. You can do this via the Site Configuration tool, as noted earlier, but it's actually quite easy to do this yourself.

Add a directory to PCSAuthenticationDemo called `SecureDirectory`, as well as a `Default.aspx` Web page in this directory, and a new `Web.config` file. Replace the contents of `Web.config` with the following:

```
<?xml version="1.0" ?>
<configuration>
  <system.web>
    <authorization>
      <deny users="?" />
      <allow roles="Administrator" />
      <deny roles="User" />
    </authorization>
  </system.web>
</configuration>
```

The `<authorization>` element can contain one or more `<deny>` or `<allow>` elements representing permission rules, each of which can have a `users` or `roles` attribute saying what the rule applies to. The rules are applied from top to bottom, so more specific rules should generally be near the top if the membership of rules overlaps. In this example, `?` refers to anonymous users, who will be denied access to this directory, along with users in the `User` role. Note that users in both the `User` and `Administrator` roles will be allowed access only if the `<allow>` rule shown here comes before the `<deny>` rule for the `User` role — all of a user's roles are taken into account, but the rule order still applies.

Now when you log in to the Web site and try to navigate to `SecureDirectory/Default.aspx`, you will be permitted only if you are in the `Admin` role. Other users, or users that are not authenticated, will be redirected to the login page.

Security in PCSDemoSite

The PCSDemoSite site uses the `Login` control that you have already seen, as well as a `LoginView` control, a `LoginStatus` control, a `LoginName` control, a `PasswordRecovery` control, and a `ChangePassword` control.

One difference is that a `Guest` role is included, and one consequence of this is that guest users should not be able to change their password — an ideal use for `LoginView`, as illustrated by `Login.aspx`:

```
<asp:Content ID="Content1" ContentPlaceHolderID="ContentPlaceHolder1"
  Runat="server">
<h2>Login Page</h2>
<asp:LoginView ID="LoginView1" Runat="server">
  <RoleGroups>
    <asp:RoleGroup Roles="Guest">
      <ContentTemplate>
        You are currently logged in as <b>
        <asp:LoginName ID="LoginName1" Runat="server" /></b>.
        <br />
        <br />
        <asp:LoginStatus ID="LoginStatus1" Runat="server" />
      </ContentTemplate>
    </asp:RoleGroup>
    <asp:RoleGroup Roles="RegisteredUser,SiteAdministrator">
      <ContentTemplate>
        You are currently logged in as <b>
        <asp:LoginName ID="LoginName2" Runat="server" /></b>.
        <br />
        <br />
        <asp:ChangePassword ID="ChangePassword1" Runat="server">
        </asp:ChangePassword>
        <br />
```

(continued)

(continued)

```
          <br />
          <asp:LoginStatus ID="LoginStatus2" Runat="server" />
       </ContentTemplate>
     </asp:RoleGroup>
    </RoleGroups>
    <AnonymousTemplate>
      <asp:Login ID="Login1" Runat="server">
      </asp:Login>
      <asp:PasswordRecovery ID="PasswordRecovery1" Runat="Server" />
    </AnonymousTemplate>
  </asp:LoginView>
</asp:Content>
```

The view here displays one of several pages:

- ❑ For anonymous users a `Login` and a `PasswordRecovery` control are shown.
- ❑ For `Guest` users `LoginName` and `LoginStatus` controls are shown, giving the logged-in username and the facility to log out if required.
- ❑ For `RegisteredUser` and `SiteAdministrator` users `LoginName`, `LoginStatus`, and `ChangePassword` controls are shown.

The site also includes various `Web.config` files in various directories to limit access, and the navigation is also restricted by role.

> Note that the configured users for the site are shown on the About page, or you can add your own. The users in the base site (and their passwords) are User1 (User1!!), Admin (Admin!!), and Guest (Guest!!).

One point to note here is that while the root of the site denies anonymous users, the Themes directory (described in the next section) overrides this setting by permitting anonymous users. This is necessary because without this, anonymous users would see a themeless site, because the theme files would not be accessible. In addition, the full security specification in the root `Web.config` file is as follows:

```
<configuration xmlns="http://schemas.microsoft.com/.NetConfiguration/v2.0">
  ...
  <location path="StyleSheet.css">
    <system.web>
      <authorization>
        <allow users="?"/>
      </authorization>
    </system.web>
  </location>
  <system.web>
    <authorization>
      <deny users="?" />
    </authorization>
    ...
  </system.web>
</configuration>
```

Here a `<location>` element is used to override the default setting for a specific file specified using a `path` attribute, in this case for the file `StyleSheet.css`. `<location>` elements can be used to apply any `<system.web>` settings to specific files or directories, and can be used to centralize all directory-specific settings in one place, if desired (as an alternative to multiple `Web.config` files). In the preceding code, permission is given for anonymous users to access the root style sheet for the Web site, which is necessary because this file defines the layout of the `<div>` elements in the master page. Without this, the HTML shown on the login page for anonymous users would be difficult to read.

Another point to note is in the code-behind file for the meeting room booker user control, in the `Page_Load()` event handler:

```
void Page_Load(object sender, EventArgs e)
{
    if (!this.IsPostBack)
    {
        nameBox.Text = Context.User.Identity.Name;
        DateTime trialDate = DateTime.Now;
        calendar.SelectedDate = GetFreeDate(trialDate);
    }
}
```

Here the username is extracted from the current context. Note that in your code-behind files you will probably also use `Context.User.IsInRole()` frequently to check access.

Themes

By combining ASP.NET pages with master pages and CSS style sheets, you can go a long way in separating form and function, whereby the look and feel of your pages are defined separately from their operation. With themes you can take this a step further and dynamically apply this look and feel from one of several themes that you supply yourself.

A theme consists of the following:

❑   A name for the theme

❑   An optional CSS style sheet

❑   Skin (`.skin`) files allowing individual control types to be styled

These can be applied to pages in two different ways — as a `Theme` or as a `StyleSheetTheme`:

❑   **Theme** — All skin properties are applied to controls, overriding any properties that the controls on the page may already have.

❑   **StyleSheetTheme** — Existing control properties take precedence over properties defined in skin files.

CSS style sheets work in the same way whichever method is used because they are applied in the standard CSS way.

Applying Themes to Pages

You can apply a theme to a page in several ways, declaratively or programmatically. The simplest declarative way to apply a theme is via the `<%@ Page %>` directive, using the `Theme` or `StyleSheetTheme` attribute:

```
<%@ Page Theme="myTheme" ... %>
```

or:

```
<%@ Page StyleSheetTheme="myTheme" ... %>
```

Here `myTheme` is the name defined for the theme.

Alternatively, you can specify a theme to use for all pages in a site, using an entry in the `Web.config` file for your Web site:

```
<configuration xmlns="http://schemas.microsoft.com/.NetConfiguration/v2.0">
  <system.web>
    <pages Theme="myTheme" />
  </system.web>
</configuration>
```

Again, you can use `Theme` or `StyleSheetTheme` here. You can also be more specific by using `<location>` elements to override this setting for individual pages or directories, in the same way as this element was used in the previous section for security information.

Programmatically, you can apply themes in the code-behind file for a page. There is only one place where you are allowed to do this — in the `Page_PreInit()` event handler, which is triggered very early on in the life cycle of the page. In this event, you simply have to set the `Page.Theme` or `Page.StyleSheetTheme` property to the name of the theme you want to apply, for example:

```
protected override void OnPreInit(EventArgs e)
{
   Page.Theme = "myTheme";
}
```

Because you are using code to do this, you can dynamically apply a theme file from a selection of themes. This technique is used in PCSDemoSite, as you see shortly.

Defining Themes

Themes are defined in yet another of the "special" directories in ASP.NET — in this case `App_Themes`. The `App_Themes` directory can contain any number of subdirectories, one per theme, where the name of the subdirectory defines the name of the theme.

Defining a theme involves putting the required files for the theme in the theme subdirectory. For CSS style sheets, you don't have to worry about the file name; the theme system simply looks for a file with a `.css` extension. Similarly, `.skin` files can have any file name, although it is recommended that you use multiple `.skin` files, one for each control type you want to skin, and each named after the control it skins.

Skin files contain server control definitions in exactly the same format as you would use in standard ASP.NET pages. The difference is that the controls in skin files are never added to your page; they are simply used to extract properties. A definition for a button skin, typically placed in a file called `Button.skin`, might be as follows:

```
<asp:Button Runat="server" BackColor="#444499" BorderColor="#000000"
   ForeColor="#ccccff" />
```

This skin is actually taken from the `DefaultTheme` theme in PCSDemoSite, and is responsible for the look of the button on the Meeting Room Booker page you saw earlier in this chapter.

When you create a skin for a control type in this way you don't use an `ID` property.

Themes in PCSDemoSite

The PCSDemoSite Web site includes three themes that you can select on the `/Configuration/Themes/Default.aspx` page — as long as you are logged in as a member of the `RegisteredUser` or `SiteAdministrator` role. This page is shown in Figure 38-15.

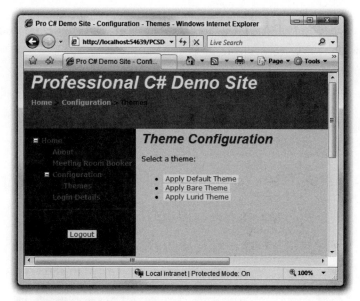

Figure 38-15

The theme in use here is DefaultTheme, but you can select from the other options on this page.
Figure 38-16 shows the BareTheme theme.

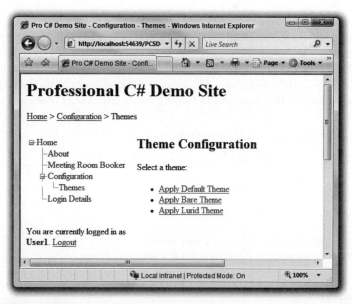

Figure 38-16

This sort of theme is useful in, for example, printable versions of Web pages. The `BareTheme` directory actually consists of no files at all — the only file in use here is the root `StyleSheet.css` style sheet.

Figure 38-17 shows the `LuridTheme` theme.

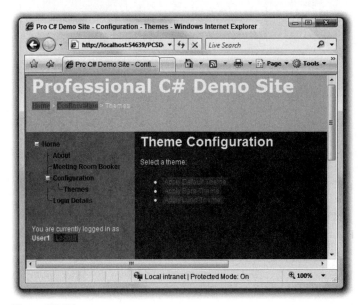

Figure 38-17

This brightly colored and difficult to read theme is just a bit of fun, really, but it does show how the look of a site can be dramatically changed using themes. On a more serious note, themes similar to this can be used to provide high-contrast or large-text versions of Web sites for accessibility purposes.

In PCSDemoSite, the currently selected theme is stored in session state, so the theme is maintained when you navigate around the site. The code-behind file for `/Configuration/Themes/Default.aspx` is as follows:

```
public partial class _Default : MyPageBase
{
    private void ApplyTheme(string themeName)
    {
        if (Session["SessionTheme"] != null)
        {
            Session.Remove("SessionTheme");
        }
        Session.Add("SessionTheme", themeName);
        Response.Redirect("~/Configuration/Themes", true);
    }

    void applyDefaultTheme_Click(object sender, EventArgs e)
```

```
    {
        ApplyTheme("DefaultTheme");
    }

    void applyBareTheme_Click(object sender, EventArgs e)
    {
        ApplyTheme("BareTheme");
    }

    void applyLuridTheme_Click(object sender, EventArgs e)
    {
        ApplyTheme("LuridTheme");
    }
}
```

The key functionality here is in `ApplyTheme()`, which puts the name of the selected theme into session state, using the key `SessionTheme`. It also checks to see if there is already an entry here, and if so, removes it.

As mentioned earlier, themes must be applied in the `Page_PreInit()` event handler. This isn't accessible from the master page that all pages use, so if you want to apply a selected theme to all pages, you are left with two options:

❑ Override the `Page_PreInit()` event handler in all pages where you want themes to be applied.

❑ Provide a common base class for all pages where you want themes to be applied, and override the `Page_PreInit()` event handler in this base class.

PCSDemoSite uses the second option, with a common page base class provided in `Code/MyPageBase.cs`:

```
public class MyPageBase : Page
{
    protected override void OnPreInit(EventArgs e)
    {
        // theming
        if (Session["SessionTheme"] != null)
        {
            Page.Theme = Session["SessionTheme"] as string;
        }
        else
        {
            Page.Theme = "DefaultTheme";
        }

        // base call
        base.OnPreInit(e);
    }
}
```

This event handler checks the session state for an entry in `SessionTheme` and applies the selected theme if there is one; otherwise `DefaultTheme` is used.

Note also that this class inherits from the usual page base class `Page`. This is necessary because, otherwise, the page wouldn't function as an ASP.NET Web page.

For this to work, it is also necessary to specify this base class for all Web pages. There are several ways of doing this, the most obvious being either in the `<@ Page %>` directive for a page or in the code behind a page. The former strategy is fine for simple pages but precludes the use of custom code behind for a page, as the page will no longer use the code in its own code-behind file. The other alternative is to change the class that the page inherits from in the code-behind file. By default, new pages inherit from `Page`, but you can change this. In the code-behind file for the theme selection page shown earlier, you may have noticed the following code:

```
public partial class _Default : MyPageBase
{
    ...
}
```

Here `MyPageBase` is specified as the base of the `Default` class, and thus the method override in `MyPageBase.cs` is used.

Web Parts

ASP.NET contains a group of server controls known as Web Parts, which are designed to enable users to personalize Web pages. You may have seen this in action in, for example, SharePoint-based Web sites and the MSN home page `http://www.msn.com/`. When you use Web Parts, the resultant functionality is as follows:

❑   Users are presented with a default page layout that you supply. This layout consists of a number of component Web Parts, each of which has a title and content.

❑   Users can change the position of the Web Parts on a page.

❑   Users can customize the appearance of Web Parts on a page or remove them from the page completely.

❑   Users can be supplied with a catalog of Web Parts that they can add to the page.

❑   Users can export Web Parts from a page, and then import them on a different page or site.

❑   Connections can exist between Web Parts. For example, the content displayed in a Web Part could be a graphical representation of the content displayed in another Web Part.

❑   Any changes that users make persist between site visits.

ASP.NET supplies a complete framework for implanting Web Parts functionality, including management and editing controls.

The use of Web Parts is a complex topic, and this section does not describe all available functionality or list all of the properties and methods that the Web Part components supply. However, you do see enough to get a flavor of Web Parts and to understand the basic functionality that is possible.

Web Parts Application Components

The Web Parts section of the toolbox contains 13 controls, as shown in Figure 38-18 (note that `Pointer` is not a control).

These controls are described in the following table. The table also introduces some of the key concepts for Web Parts pages.

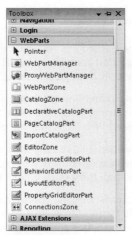

Figure 38-18

Control	Description
WebPartManager	Every page that uses Web Parts must have one (and only one) instance of the WebPartManager control. You can place it on a master page if you wish, although if you do you should use the master page only when you want to use Web Parts on a page. This control is responsible for the majority of Web Parts functionality, which it supplies without much intervention. You may not need to do much more than place it on a Web page, depending on the functionality you require. For more advanced functionality, you can use the large number of properties and events that this control exposes.
ProxyWebPartManager	If you place the WebPartManager control on a master page, it can be difficult to configure it on individual pages — and impossible to do so declaratively. This is particularly relevant for the definition of static connections between Web Parts. The ProxyWebPartManager control enables you to define static connections declaratively on a Web page, which circumvents the problem of not being able to have two WebPartManager controls on the same page.
WebPartZone	The WebPartZone control is used to define a region of a page that can contain Web Parts. You will typically use more than one of these controls on a page. For example, you might use three of them in a three-column layout on a page. Users can move Web Parts between WebPartZone regions or reposition them within a single WebPartZone.
CatalogZone	The CatalogZone control enables users to add Web Parts to a page. This control contains controls that derive from CatalogPart, of which three are supplied for you — the next three entries in this table describe these controls. Whether the CatalogZone control and the controls it contains are visible depends on the current display mode set by WebPartManager.

Control	Description
DeclarativeCatalogPart	The DeclarativeCatalogPart control enables you to define Web Part controls inline. These controls will then be available to the user through the CatalogZone control.
PageCatalogPart	Users can remove (close) Web Parts that are displayed on a page. To retrieve them, the PageCatalogPart control provides a list of closed Web Parts that can be replaced on the page.
ImportCatalogPart	The ImportCatalogPart control enables Web Parts that have been exported from a page to be imported to another page through the CatalogPart interface.
EditorZone	The EditorZone control contains controls that enable users to edit various aspects of Web Part display and behavior, depending on what controls it contains. It can contain controls that derive from EditorPart, including the four that are listed in the next four rows of this table. As with CatalogZone, the display of this control depends on the current display mode.
AppearanceEditorPart	This control enables users to modify the look and size of Web Part controls, as well as to hide them.
BehaviorEditorPart	This control enables users to configure the behavior of Web Parts by using a variety of properties that control, for example, whether a Web Part can be closed or what URL the title of a Web Part links to.
LayoutEditorPart	This control enables users to change layout properties of a Web Part, such as what zone it is contained in and whether it is displayed in a minimized state.
PropertyGridEditorPart	This is the most general Web Part editor control and enables you to define properties that can be edited for custom Web Part controls. Users can then edit these properties.
ConnectionsZone	This control enables users to create connections between Web Parts that expose connection functionality. Unlike CatalogZone and EditorZone, there are no controls to place inside this control. The user interface that this control generates depends on the controls on the page that are available for connections. The visibility of this control is dependant on the display mode.

You may notice that this list of controls does not include any Web Parts. This is because you create these yourself. Any control that you put into a WebPartZone region automatically becomes a Web Part — including (most important) user controls. By using user controls, you can group together other controls to provide the user interface and functionality of a Web Part control.

Web Parts Example

To illustrate the functionality of Web Parts, you can look at the example in the downloadable code for this chapter, PCSWebParts. This example uses the same security database as the PCSAuthenticationDemo example. It has two users with usernames of User and Administrator and a password of Pa$$w0rd for both. You can log in as a user, manipulate the Web Parts on the page, log out, log in as the other user, and manipulate the Web Parts in a completely different way. The personalization for both users is retained between site visits.

Once you have logged in to the site, the initial display (with User logged in) is as shown in Figure 38-19.

Figure 38-19

This page contains the following controls:

❑ A WebPartManager control (which doesn't have a visual component).

❑ Three WebPartZone controls.

❑ Three Web Parts (Date, Events, and User Info), one in each WebPartZone. Two of the Web Parts are connected by a static connection — if you change the date in Date, the date displayed in Events updates.

❑ A drop-down list for changing the display mode. This list doesn't contain all of the possible display modes, just the available ones. The available modes are obtained from the WebPartManager control, as you see shortly. The modes listed are:

   ❑ **Browse** — This mode is the default and allows you to view and use Web Parts. In this mode, each Web Part can be minimized or closed by using the drop-down menu accessible in the top right of each Web Part.

   ❑ **Design** — In this mode, you can reposition Web Parts.

   ❑ **Edit** — In this mode, you can edit Web Part properties. An additional item in the drop-down menu for each Web Part becomes available: Edit.

   ❑ **Catalog** — In this mode, you can add new Web Parts to the page.

❑ A link to reset the Web Part layout to the default (for the current user only).

❑ An EditorZone control (visible only in Edit mode).

❑ A CatalogZone control (visible only in Catalog mode).

❑ One additional Web Part in the catalog that you can add to the page.

Each of the Web Parts is defined in a user control.

To illustrate how layout can be changed, use the drop-down list to change the display mode to Design. You will notice that each WebPartZone is then labeled with an ID value (LeftZone, CenterZone, and RightZone, respectively). You will also be able to move Web Parts simply by dragging their titles — and will even see visual feedback as you drag. This is illustrated in Figure 38-20, which shows the Date Web Part being moved.

Figure 38-20

Next, try adding a new Web Part from the catalog. Change the display mode to Catalog, and you will notice that the CatalogZone control becomes visible at the bottom of the page. Click the Declarative Catalog link, and you will be able to add a Links control to the page, as shown in Figure 38-21.

Notice that there is also a Page Catalog link here. If you close a Web Part by using the drop-down menu for the part, you will find it here — it's not completely deleted, merely hidden.

Next, change the display mode to Edit and select the Edit item from the drop-down list for a Web Part, as shown in Figure 38-22.

When you select this menu option, you will open the EditorZone control. In the example, this control contains an AppearanceEditorPart control, as shown in Figure 38-23.

Figure 38-21

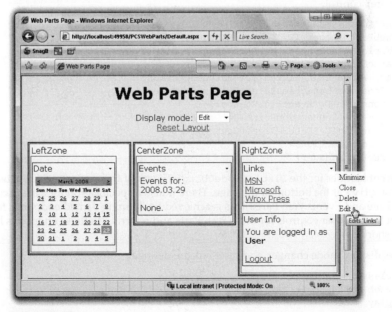

Figure 38-22

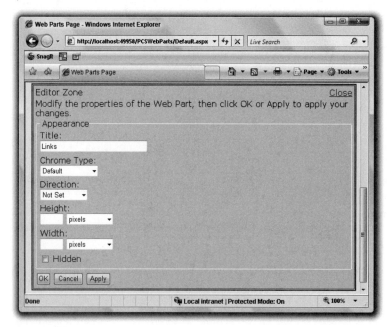

Figure 38-23

You can edit and apply property values for Web Parts by using this interface.

After making changes, confirm that they are stored for the user by logging off and logging in as a different user, and then switching back to the first user.

Now, you might think that this functionality requires quite a lot of code. In fact, the code in this example is remarkably simple. Look at the code for the Web Parts page. The `<form>` element starts with a `WebPartManager` control:

```
<form id="form1" runat="server">
  <asp:WebPartManager ID="WebPartManager1" runat="server"
    OnDisplayModeChanged="WebPartManager1_DisplayModeChanged">
    <StaticConnections>
      <asp:WebPartConnection ID="dateConnection"
        ConsumerConnectionPointID="DateConsumer"
        ConsumerID="EventListControl1"
        ProviderConnectionPointID="DateProvider"
        ProviderID="DateSelectorControl1" />
    </StaticConnections>
  </asp:WebPartManager>
```

There is an event handler for the `DisplayModeChanged` event of this control, which is used to show or hide the editor `<div>` at the bottom of the page. There is also a specification for a static connection between the Date and Events Web Parts. This is achieved by defining named endpoints for the connection in the two user controls for these Web Parts and referring to those endpoints here. You see the code for this shortly.

Next, the title, display mode changer, and reset link are defined:

```
<div class="mainDiv">
  <h1>Web Parts Page</h1>
  Display mode:
```

```
<asp:DropDownList ID="displayMode" runat="server" AutoPostBack="True"
  OnSelectedIndexChanged="displayMode_SelectedIndexChanged" />
<br />
<asp:LinkButton runat="server" ID="resetButton" Text="Reset Layout"
  OnClick="resetButton_Click" />
<br />
<br />
```

The display mode drop-down list is populated in the `Page_Load()` event handler, by using the `WebPartManager1.SupportedDisplayModes` property. The reset button uses the `WebPartManager1.Personalization.ResetPersonalizationState()` method to reset the personalization state for the current user.

Next come the three `WebPartZone` controls, each of which contains a user control that is loaded as a Web Part:

```
<div class="innerDiv">
  <div class="zoneDiv">
    <asp:WebPartZone ID="LeftZone" runat="server">
      <ZoneTemplate>
        <uc1:DateSelectorControl ID="DateSelectorControl1" runat="server"
          title="Date" />
      </ZoneTemplate>
    </asp:WebPartZone>
  </div>
  <div class="zoneDiv">
    <asp:WebPartZone ID="CenterZone" runat="server">
      <ZoneTemplate>
        <uc2:EventListControl ID="EventListControl1" runat="server"
          title="Events" />
      </ZoneTemplate>
    </asp:WebPartZone>
  </div>
  <div class="zoneDiv">
    <asp:WebPartZone ID="RightZone" runat="server">
      <ZoneTemplate>
        <uc4:UserInfo ID="UserInfo1" runat="server" title="User Info" />
      </ZoneTemplate>
    </asp:WebPartZone>
  </div>
```

And, finally you have the `EditorZone` and `CatalogZone` controls, containing an `AppearanceEditor` control and `PageCatalogPart` and `DeclarativeCatalogPart` controls, respectively:

```
<asp:PlaceHolder runat="server" ID="editorPH" Visible="false">
  <div class="footerDiv">
    <asp:EditorZone ID="EditorZone1" runat="server">
      <ZoneTemplate>
        <asp:AppearanceEditorPart ID="AppearanceEditorPart1"
          runat="server" />
      </ZoneTemplate>
    </asp:EditorZone>
    <asp:CatalogZone ID="CatalogZone1" runat="server">
      <ZoneTemplate>
        <asp:PageCatalogPart ID="PageCatalogPart1" runat="server" />
```

(continued)

(continued)

```
                    <asp:DeclarativeCatalogPart ID="DeclarativeCatalogPart1"
                      runat="server">
                      <WebPartsTemplate>
                        <uc3:LinksControl ID="LinksControl1" runat="server"
                          title="Links" />
                      </WebPartsTemplate>
                    </asp:DeclarativeCatalogPart>
                  </ZoneTemplate>
                </asp:CatalogZone>
              </div>
            </asp:PlaceHolder>
          </div>
        </div>
      </form>
```

The `DeclarativeCatalogPart` control contains a fourth user control, which is the `Links` control that users can add to the page.

The code for the Web Parts is equally simple. The Links Web part, for example, simply contains the following code:

```
<%@ Control Language="C#" AutoEventWireup="true"
CodeFile="LinksControl.ascx.cs"
   Inherits="LinksControl" %>
<a href="http://www.msn.com/">MSN</a>
<br />
<a href="http://www.microsoft.com/">Microsoft</a>
<br />
<a href="http://www.wrox.com/">Wrox Press</a>
```

No additional markup is required to make this user control work as a Web Part. The only point to note here is that the `<uc3:LinksControl>` element for the user control has a `title` attribute — even though the user control doesn't have a `Title` property. This attribute is used by the `DeclarativeCatalogPart` control to infer a title to display for the Web Part (which you can edit at runtime with the `AppearanceEditorPart`).

The connection between the Date and Events controls is achieved by passing an interface reference from `DateSelectorControl` to `EventListControl` (the two user control classes used by these Web Parts):

```
public interface IDateProvider
{
   SelectedDatesCollection SelectedDates
   {
      get;
   }
}
```

`DateSelectorControl` supports this interface, and so can pass an instance of `IDateProvider` by using `this`. The reference is passed by an endpoint method in `DateSelectorControl`, which is decorated with the `ConnectionProvider` attribute:

```
[ConnectionProvider("Date Provider", "DateProvider")]
public IDateProvider ProvideDate()
{
   return this;
}
```

This is all that is required to mark a Web Part as a provider control. You can then reference the provider by its endpoint ID, in this case `DateProvider`.

To consume a provider, you use the `ConnectionConsumer` attribute to decorate a consumer method in `EventListControl`:

```
[ConnectionConsumer("Date Consumer", "DateConsumer")]
public void GetDate(IDateProvider provider)
{
    this.provider = provider;
    IsConnected = true;
    SetDateLabel();
}
```

This method stores a reference to the `IDateProvider` interface passed, sets a flag, and changes the label text in the control.

There is not a lot more to look at in this example. There are a few minor cosmetic sections of code, and details for the event handlers in `Page_Load()`, but nothing that you really need to see here. You can investigate further by examining the downloadable code for this chapter.

There is, however, a whole lot more to Web Parts than this. The Web Parts framework is extremely powerful and richly featured. Whole books are devoted to the subject. Hopefully, though, this section has enabled you to get an insight into Web Parts and has demystified some of their functionality.

Summary

In this chapter you looked at several more advanced techniques for creating ASP.NET pages and Web sites, and you saw these techniques in action in a demonstration Web site called PCSDemoSite.

First, you learned how to create reusable ASP.NET server controls by using C#. You saw how to create simple user controls from existing ASP.NET pages, as well as how to create custom controls from scratch. You also saw how the meeting room booker sample from the previous chapter can be reformatted as a user control.

Next, you looked at master pages, and how to provide a template for the pages of your Web site, which is another way to reuse code and simplify development. In PCSDemoSite, in the downloadable code for this chapter, you saw a master page that included navigation Web server controls to enable users to move around the site. The PCSDemoSite sample also laid the framework for themes, which are an excellent way to separate functionality from design and can be a powerful accessibility technique.

You also took a brief look at security and how you can implement forms-based authentication on your Web sites with minimal effort.

Finally, you investigated Web Parts and how to use the Web Parts server controls to put together a basic application that illustrated some of the possibilities that this technology offers.

You have only scratched the surface of what is possible in ASP.NET 2.0. For example, you can do a whole lot more with custom controls. It would have been interesting to discuss templates and data-binding, and how to create controls with this in mind. However, with the information in this chapter, you should be able to start building (and experimenting with) your own custom controls, as well as all the other techniques discussed.

In the next chapter you look at a way to make ASP.NET applications more dynamic by using Ajax techniques.

39

ASP.NET AJAX

Web application programming is subject to continuous change and improvement. In the previous two chapters, you learned how to use ASP.NET to create fully functional Web applications, and you may think that you have seen all the tools that you need to create your own Web applications. However, if you spend much time on the Internet, you may have noticed that more recent Web sites are significantly better, in terms of usability, than older Web sites. Many of today's best Web sites provide rich user interfaces that feel almost as responsive as Windows applications. They achieve this by using client-side processing, primarily through JavaScript code, and increasingly through a technology known as Ajax.

This change of direction is possible because the browsers that clients use to browse Web sites, and the computers that clients use to run browsers, have become more powerful. The current generation of Web browsers, such as Internet Explorer 7 and Firefox, also support a wide variety of standards. These standards, which include JavaScript, enable Web applications to provide functionality far in advance of what was previously possible using plain HTML. You have already seen some of this in previous chapters — for example the use of cascading style sheets (CSS) to style Web applications.

Ajax — as you will discover shortly — is not a new technology. Rather, it is a combination of standards that makes it possible to realize the rich potential functionality of current Web browsers.

Perhaps the key defining feature of Ajax-enabled Web applications is the ability for the Web browser to communicate with the Web server in out-of-band operations; this is known as asynchronous, or partial-page, postbacks. In practice, this means that the user can interact with server-side functionality and data without needing a full-page refresh. For example, when a link is followed to move to the second page of data in a table, Ajax makes it possible to refresh just the table's content rather than the entire Web page. This means that there is less traffic required across the Internet, which leads to a more responsive Web application. You will see this example in practice later in this chapter, as well as many more examples that illustrate the power of Ajax in Web applications.

You will be using Microsoft's implementation of Ajax in the code in this chapter, known as ASP.NET AJAX. This implementation takes the Ajax model and applies it to the ASP.NET framework. ASP.NET AJAX provides a number of server controls and client-side techniques that are specifically targeted at ASP.NET developers and that enable you to add Ajax functionality to your Web applications with surprisingly little effort.

This chapter is organized as follows:

❑ First, you learn more about Ajax and the technologies that make Ajax possible.

❑ Next, you learn about ASP.NET AJAX and its component parts, as well as the functionality that ASP.NET AJAX offers.

❑ Last, you see how to use ASP.NET AJAX in your Web applications, by using both server-side and client-side code. This coverage forms the largest part of this chapter.

What Is Ajax?

Ajax enables you to enhance the user interfaces of Web applications by means of asynchronous postbacks and dynamic client-side Web page manipulation. The term Ajax was invented by Jesse James Garrett and is shorthand for "Asynchronous JavaScript and XML."

> Note that Ajax is not an acronym, which is why it is not capitalized as AJAX. However, it is capitalized in the product name ASP.NET AJAX, which is Microsoft's implementation of Ajax, as you will see in the next section of this chapter.

By definition, Ajax involves both JavaScript and XML. However, the Ajax programming requires the use of other technologies as well, which are described in the following table.

Technology	Description
HTML/XHTML	HTML (Hypertext Markup Language) is the presentation and layout language used by Web browsers to render information in a graphical user interface. In the previous two chapters, you have seen how HTML achieves this functionality and how ASP.NET generates HTML code. Extensible HTML (XHTML) is a stricter definition of HTML that uses XML structure.
CSS	CSS (cascading style sheets) is a means by which HTML elements can be styled according to rules defined in a separate style sheet. This enables you to apply styles simultaneously to multiple HTML elements and to swap styles to change the way a Web page looks without HTML modifications. CSS includes both layout and style information, so you can also use CSS to position HTML elements on a page. You have seen how to do this in the examples in previous chapters.
DOM	The DOM (Document Object Model) is a means of representing and manipulating (X)HTML code in a hierarchical structure. This enables you to access, for example, "the second column of the third row in table x" in a Web page, rather than having to locate this element using more primitive text processing.
JavaScript	JavaScript is a client-side scripting technology that enables you to execute code inside a Web browser. The syntax of JavaScript is similar to other C-based languages, including C#, and provides variables, functions, branching code, looping statements, event handlers, and other familiar programming elements. However, unlike C#, JavaScript is not strongly typed, and debugging JavaScript code can be notoriously difficult. In terms of Ajax programming, JavaScript is a key technology because it allows dynamic modifications to Web pages by way of DOM manipulation — among other functionality.

Technology	Description
XML	XML, as you have seen throughout this book, is a platform-neutral way to mark up data and is crucial to Ajax both as a way to manipulate data and as a language for communication between the client and the server.
XMLHttpRequest	Since Internet Explorer 5, browsers have supported the XMLHttpRequest API as a means of performing asynchronous communication between the client and server. This was originally introduced by Microsoft as a technology to access email stored in an Exchange server over the Internet, in a product known as Outlook Web Access. Since then, it has become the standard way to perform asynchronous communications in Web applications, and is a core technology of Ajax-enabled Web applications. Microsoft's implementation of this API is known as XMLHTTP, which communicates over what is often called the XMLHTTP protocol.

Ajax also requires server-side code to handle partial-page postbacks as well as full-page postbacks. This can include both event handlers for server-control events and Web services. Figure 39-1 shows how these technologies fit together in the Ajax Web browser model, in contrast to the "traditional" Web browser model.

Prior to Ajax, the first four technologies listed in the preceding table (HTML, CSS, the DOM, and JavaScript) were used to create what was known as Dynamic HTML (DHTML) Web applications. These applications were notable for two reasons: they provided a much better user interface, and they generally worked on only one type of Web browser.

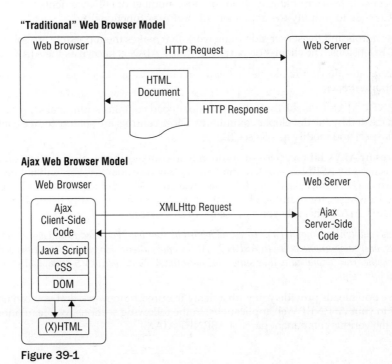

Figure 39-1

Since DHTML, standards have improved, along with the level of adherence to standards in Web browsers. However, there are still differences, and an Ajax solution must take these differences into account. This has meant that most developers have been quite slow to implement Ajax solutions. Only with the advent of more abstracted Ajax frameworks (such as ASP.NET AJAX) has Ajax-enabled Web site creation really become a viable option for enterprise-level development.

What Is ASP.NET AJAX?

ASP.NET AJAX is Microsoft's implementation of the Ajax framework and is specifically targeted at ASP.NET developers. With the latest release of ASP.NET, ASP.NET AJAX is part of the core ASP.NET functionality. It is also available for use with previous versions of ASP.NET from the Web site `http://ajax.asp.net`. This Web site also has documentation, forums, and sample code that you may find useful for whichever version of ASP.NET you are using.

ASP.NET AJAX provides the following functionality:

❑   A server-side framework that enables ASP.NET Web pages to respond to partial-page postback operations

❑   ASP.NET server controls that make the implementation of Ajax functionality easy

❑   An HTTP handler that enables ASP.NET Web services to communicate with client-side code by using JavaScript Object Notation (JSON) serialization in partial-page postback operations

❑   Web services that enable client-side code to gain access to ASP.NET application services, including authentication and personalization services

❑   A Web site template for creating ASP.NET AJAX-enabled Web applications

❑   A client-side JavaScript library that provides a number of enhancements to JavaScript syntax as well as code to simplify the implementation of Ajax functionality

These server controls and the server-side framework that makes them possible are collectively known as the ASP.NET Extensions. The client-side part of ASP.NET AJAX is known as the AJAX Library.

There are several additional downloads that you can obtain from `http://ajax.asp.net`, including the following important ones:

❑   **ASP.NET AJAX Control Toolkit** — This download contains additional server controls that have been created by the developer community. These controls are shared-source controls that you can inspect and modify as you see fit.

❑   **Microsoft AJAX Library 3.5** — This download contains the JavaScript client-side framework that is used by ASP.NET AJAX to implement Ajax functionality. You will not need this if you are developing ASP.NET AJAX applications. Instead, this download is intended to be used with other languages, for example PHP, to implement Ajax functionality using the same codebase as ASP.NET AJAX. This is beyond the scope of this chapter.

There is also a download known as Futures, which in the past has been used to add additional, pre-release, or legacy functionality to ASP.NET AJAX applications. However, at the time of writing it is unclear whether this download will be supported with the RTM release of VS 2008, and so it is not covered in this chapter.

Together these downloads provide you with a richly featured framework that you can use to add Ajax functionality to your ASP.NET Web applications. In the following sections, you learn more about what is contained in the various component parts of ASP.NET AJAX.

Core Functionality

The core functionality of ASP.NET AJAX is divided into two parts, the AJAX Extensions and the AJAX Library.

AJAX Extensions

ASP.NET AJAX functionality is contained in two assemblies that are installed in the GAC:

- ❑ `System.Web.Extensions.dll` — This assembly contains the ASP.NET AJAX functionality, including the AJAX Extensions and the AJAX Library JavaScript files, which are available through the `ScriptManager` component (which is described shortly).

- ❑ `System.Web.Extensions.Design.dll` — This assembly contains ASP.NET Designer components for the AJAX Extensions server controls. This is used by the ASP.NET Designer in Visual Studio or Visual Web developer.

Much of the AJAX Extensions component of ASP.NET AJAX is concerned with enabling partial-page postbacks and JSON serialization for Web services. This includes various HTTP handler components and extensions to the existing ASP.NET framework. All of this functionality can be configured through the `Web.config` file for a Web site. There are also classes and attributes that you can use for additional configuration. However, most of this configuration is transparent, and you will rarely need to change what is supplied in, for example, the ASP.NET Web Site template.

Your main interaction with AJAX Extensions will be using server controls to add Ajax functionality to your Web applications. There are several of these, which you can use to enhance your applications in various ways. The following table shows a selection of the server-side components. You see these components in action later in this chapter.

Control	Description
ScriptManager	This control is central to ASP.NET AJAX functionality and is required on every page that uses partial-page postbacks. Its main purpose is to manage client-side references to the AJAX Library JavaScript files, which are served from the ASP.NET AJAX assembly. The AJAX Library is used extensively by the AJAX Extensions server controls, which all generate their own client-side code.
	This control is also responsible for the configuration of Web services that you intend to access from client-side code. By supplying Web service information to the `ScriptManager` control, you can generate client-side and server-side classes to manage asynchronous communication with Web services transparently.
	You can also use the `ScriptManager` control to maintain references to your own JavaScript files.
UpdatePanel	The `UpdatePanel` control is an extremely useful one and is perhaps the ASP.NET AJAX control that you will use most often. This control acts like a standard ASP.NET placeholder and can contain any other controls. More important, it also marks a section of a page as a region that can be updated independently of the rest of the page, in a partial-page postback.
	Any controls contained by an `UpdatePanel` control that cause a postback (a `Button` control, for example) will not cause full-page postbacks. Instead, they cause partial-page postbacks that will update only the contents of the `UpdatePanel`.

Control	Description
	In many situations, this control is all you need to implement Ajax functionality. For example, you can place a `GridView` control in an `UpdatePanel` control, and any pagination, sorting, and other postback functionality of the control will take place in a partial-page postback.
`UpdateProgress`	This control enables you to provide feedback to users when a partial page postback is in progress. You can supply a template for this control that will be displayed when an `UpdatePanel` is updating. For example, you could use a floating `<div>` control to display a message such as "`Updating...`" so that the user is aware that the application is busy. Note that partial-page postbacks do not interfere with the rest of a Web page, which will remain responsive.
`Timer`	The ASP.NET AJAX `Timer` control is a useful way to cause an `UpdatePanel` to update periodically. You can configure this control to trigger postbacks at regular intervals. If this control is contained in an `UpdatePanel` control, then the `UpdatePanel` will be updated every time the `Timer` control is triggered. This control also has an associated event so that you can carry out periodic server-side processing.
`AsyncPostBackTrigger`	You can use this control to trigger `UpdatePanel` updates from controls that aren't contained in the `UpdatePanel`. For example, you can enable a drop-down list elsewhere on a Web page to cause an `UpdatePanel` containing a `GridView` control to update.

The AJAX Extensions also include the `ExtenderControl` abstract base class for extending existing ASP.NET server controls. This is used, for example, by various classes in the ASP.NET AJAX Control Toolkit, as you will see shortly.

AJAX Library

The AJAX Library consists of JavaScript files that are used by client-side code in ASP.NET AJAX-enabled Web applications. There is a lot of functionality included in these JavaScript files, some of which is general code that enhances the JavaScript language and some of which is specific to Ajax functionality. The AJAX Library contains layers of functionality that are built on top of each other, as shown in the following table.

Layer	Description
Browser compatibility	The lowest-level code in the AJAX Library consists of code that maps various JavaScript functionality according to the client Web browser. This is necessary because there are differences in the implementation of JavaScript in different browsers. By providing this layer, JavaScript code in other layers does not have to worry about browser compatibility, and you can write browser-neutral code that will work in all client environments.
Core services	This layer contains the enhancements to the JavaScript language, in particular OOP functionality. By using the code in this layer you can define namespaces, classes, derived classes, and interfaces using JavaScript script files. This is of particular interest to C# developers, because it makes writing JavaScript code much more like writing .NET code with using C# and encourages reusability.

Layer	Description
Base class library	The client base class library (BCL) includes many JavaScript classes that provide low-level functionality to classes further down the AJAX Library hierarchy. Most of these classes are not intended to be used directly.
Networking	Classes in the networking layer enable client-side code to call server-side code asynchronously. This layer includes the basic framework for making a call to a URL and responding to the result in a callback function. For the most part, this is also functionality that you will not use directly; instead, you will use classes that wrap this functionality. This layer also contains classes for JSON serialization and deserialization. You will find most of the networking classes on the client-side `Sys.Net` namespace.
User interface	This layer contains classes that abstract user interface elements such as HTML elements and DOM events. You can use the properties and methods of this layer to write language-neutral JavaScript code to manipulate Web pages from the client. User interface classes are contained in the `Sys.UI` namespace.
Controls	The final layer of the AJAX Library contains the highest-level code, which provides Ajax behaviors and server control functionality. This includes dynamically generated code that you can use, for example, to call Web services from client-side JavaScript code.

You can use the AJAX Library to extend and customize the behavior of ASP.NET AJAX-enabled Web applications, but it is important to note that you don't have to. You can go a long way without using any additional JavaScript in your applications — it becomes a requirement only when you require more advanced functionality. If you do write additional client-side code, however, you will find that it is much easier with the functionality that the AJAX Library offers.

ASP.NET AJAX Control Toolkit

The AJAX Control Toolkit is a collection of additional server controls, including extender controls, that have been written by the ASP.NET AJAX community. Extender controls are controls that enable you to add functionality to an existing ASP.NET server control, typically by associating a client-side behavior with it. For example, one of the extenders in the AJAX Control Toolkit extends the `TextBox` control by placing "watermark" text in the `TextBox`, which appears when the user hasn't yet added any content to the text box. This extender control is implemented in a server control called `TextBoxWatermark`.

You can use the AJAX Control Toolkit to add quite a lot more functionality to your sites, beyond what is in the core download. These controls are also interesting simply to browse and will probably give you plenty of ideas about enhancing your Web applications. However, because the AJAX Control Toolkit is separate from the core download, you should not expect the same level of support for these controls.

Using ASP.NET AJAX

Now that you have seen the component parts of ASP.NET AJAX, it is time to start looking at how to use them to enhance your Web sites. In this section, you see how Web applications that use ASP.NET AJAX work, and how to use the various aspects of functionality that ASP.NET AJAX includes. You start by examining and dissecting a simple application, and then add additional functionality in subsequent sections.

ASP.NET AJAX Web Site Example

The ASP.NET Web Site template includes all the ASP.NET AJAX core functionality. You can also use the AJAX Control Toolkit Web Site template (once installed) to include controls from the AJAX Control Toolkit. For the purposes of this example, you can create a new Web site that uses the default ASP.NET Web Site template in the `C:\ProCSharp\Chapter39` directory, called `PCSAjaxWebApp1`.

Modify the code in `Default.aspx` as follows:

```
<%@ Page Language="C#" AutoEventWireup="true" CodeFile="Default.aspx.cs"
  Inherits="_Default" %>

<!DOCTYPE html PUBLIC "-//W3C//DTD XHTML 1.0 Transitional//EN"
 "http://www.w3.org/TR/xhtml1/DTD/xhtml1-transitional.dtd">
<html xmlns="http://www.w3.org/1999/xhtml">
<head runat="server">
  <title>Pro C# ASP.NET AJAX Sample</title>
</head>
<body>
  <form id="form1" runat="server">
    <asp:ScriptManager ID="ScriptManager1" runat="server" />
    <div>
      <h1>Pro C# ASP.NET AJAX Sample</h1>
      This sample obtains a list of primes up to a maximum value.
      <br />
      Maximum:
      <asp:TextBox runat="server" id="MaxValue" Text="2500" />
      <br />
      Result:
      <asp:UpdatePanel runat="server" ID="ResultPanel">
        <ContentTemplate>
          <asp:Button runat="server" ID="GoButton" Text="Calculate " />
          <br />
          <asp:Label runat="server" ID="ResultLabel" />
          <br />
          <small>
            Panel render time: <% =DateTime.Now.ToLongTimeString() %>
          </small>
        </ContentTemplate>
      </asp:UpdatePanel>
      <asp:UpdateProgress runat="server" ID="UpdateProgress1">
        <ProgressTemplate>
         <div style="position: absolute; left: 100px; top: 200px;
             padding: 40px 60px 40px 60px; background-color: lightyellow;
             border: black 1px solid; font-weight: bold; font-size: larger;
             filter: alpha(opacity=80);">Updating...</div>
        </ProgressTemplate>
      </asp:UpdateProgress>
      <small>Page render time: <% =DateTime.Now.ToLongTimeString() %></small>
    </div>
  </form>
</body>
</html>
```

Switch to design view (note that the ASP.NET AJAX controls such as `UpdatePanel` and `UpdateProgress` have visual designer components), and double-click the Calculate button to add an event handler. Modify the code as follows:

```
protected void GoButton_Click(object sender, EventArgs e)
{
    int maxValue = 0;
    System.Text.StringBuilder resultText = new System.Text.StringBuilder();
    if (int.TryParse(MaxValue.Text, out maxValue))
    {
        for (int trial = 2; trial <= maxValue; trial++)
        {
            bool isPrime = true;
            for (int divisor = 2; divisor <= Math.Sqrt(trial); divisor++)
            {
                if (trial % divisor == 0)
                {
                    isPrime = false;
                    break;
                }
            }
            if (isPrime)
            {
                resultText.AppendFormat("{0} ", trial);
            }
        }
    }
    else
    {
        resultText.Append("Unable to parse maximum value.");
    }
    ResultLabel.Text = resultText.ToString();
}
```

Save your modifications and press F5 to run the project. If prompted, enable debugging in Web.config.

When the Web page appears as shown in Figure 39-2, note that the two render times shown are the same.

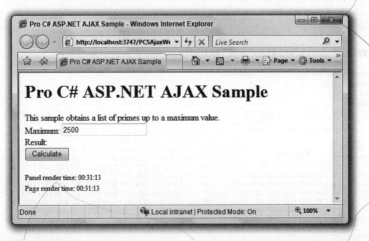

Figure 39-2

Click the Calculate button to display prime numbers less than or equal to 2500. Unless you are running on a slow machine, this should be almost instantaneous. Note that the render times are now different — only the one in the UpdatePanel has changed. This is shown in Figure 39-3.

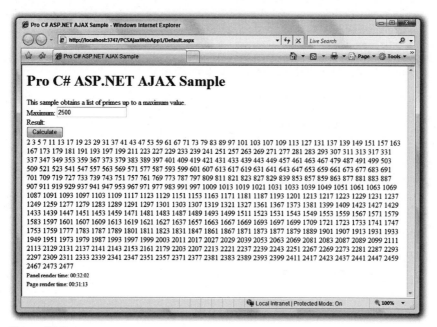

Figure 39-3

Finally, add some zeros to the maximum value to introduce a processing delay (about three more should be enough on a fast PC) and click the Calculate button again. This time, before the result is displayed, note that the UpdateProgress control displays a partially transparent feedback message, as shown in Figure 39-4.

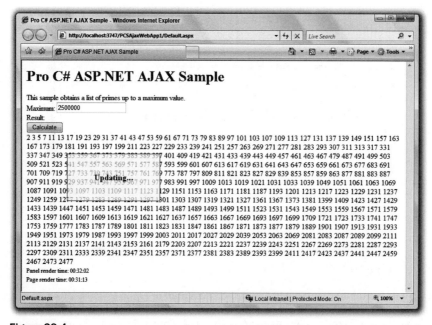

Figure 39-4

While the application updates, the page remains responsive. You can, for example, scroll through the page.

> *Note that when the update completes, the scroll position of the browser is set to the point it was at before you clicked Calculate. In most cases, when partial-page updates are quick to execute, this is great for usability.*

Close the browser to return to Visual Studio.

ASP.NET AJAX-Enabled Web Site Configuration

Now that you have seen a simple ASP.NET AJAX-enabled Web application, you can examine it more closely to see how it works. The first thing to look at is the `Web.config` file for the application, in particular the following two blocks of code in the `<system.web>` configuration section of `<configuration>`:

```
<?xml version="1.0"?>
<configuration>
  ...
  <system.web>
    <compilation debug="true">
      <assemblies>
        <add assembly="System.Core, Version=3.5.0.0, Culture=neutral,
          PublicKeyToken=B77A5C561934E089"/>
        <add assembly="System.Web.Extensions, Version=3.5.0.0,
          Culture=neutral, PublicKeyToken=31BF3856AD364E35"/>
        <add assembly="System.Data.DataSetExtensions, Version=3.5.0.0,
          Culture=neutral, PublicKeyToken=B77A5C561934E089"/>
        <add assembly="System.Xml.Linq, Version=3.5.0.0, Culture=neutral,
          PublicKeyToken=B77A5C561934E089"/>
      </assemblies>
    </compilation>
    ...
    <compilation debug="true">
      <pages>
        <controls>
          <add tagPrefix="asp" namespace="System.Web.UI"
            assembly="System.Web.Extensions, Version=3.5.0.0, Culture=neutral,
            PublicKeyToken=31BF3856AD364E35"/>
          <add tagPrefix="asp" namespace="System.Web.UI.WebControls"
            assembly="System.Web.Extensions, Version=3.5.0.0, Culture=neutral,
            PublicKeyToken=31BF3856AD364E35"/>
        </controls>
      </pages>
    </compilation>
    ...
  </system.web>
  ...
</configuration>
```

The code in the `<assemblies>` configuration section in `<compilation>` ensures that the ASP.NET AJAX `System.Web.Extensions.dll` assembly is loaded from the GAC. The code in the `<controls>` configuration element in `<pages>` references this assembly and associates the controls it contains (in both the `System.Web.UI` and `System.Web.UI.WebControls` namespaces) with the tag prefix `asp`. These two sections are essential for all ASP.NET AJAX-enabled Web applications.

The next two sections, `<httpHandlers>` and `<httpModules>`, are also required for ASP.NET AJAX functionality. The `<httpHandlers>` section defines three things. First, the handler for `.asmx` Web services is replaced with a new class from the `System.Web.Extensions` namespace. This new class is capable of handling requests from client-side calls from the AJAX Library, including JSON serialization and deserialization. Second, a handler is added to enable the use of ASP.NET application services. Third, a new handler is added for the `ScriptResource.axd` resource. This resource serves the AJAX Library JavaScript files from the ASP.NET AJAX assembly, so that these files do not need to be included directly in your applications.

```
<system.web>
  ...
  <httpHandlers>
    <remove verb="*" path="*.asmx"/>
    <add verb="*" path="*.asmx" validate="false"
      type="System.Web.Script.Services.ScriptHandlerFactory,
      System.Web.Extensions, Version=3.5.0.0, Culture=neutral,
      PublicKeyToken=31BF3856AD364E35"/>
    <add verb="*" path="*_AppService.axd" validate="false"
      type="System.Web.Script.Services.ScriptHandlerFactory,
      System.Web.Extensions, Version=3.5.0.0, Culture=neutral,
      PublicKeyToken=31BF3856AD364E35"/>
    <add verb="GET,HEAD" path="ScriptResource.axd"
      type="System.Web.Handlers.ScriptResourceHandler,
      System.Web.Extensions, Version=3.5.0.0, Culture=neutral,
      PublicKeyToken=31BF3856AD364E35" validate="false"/>
  </httpHandlers>
  ...
</system.web>
```

The `<httpModules>` section adds a new HTTP module that adds additional processing for HTTP requests in the Web application. This enables partial-page postbacks.

```
<system.web>
  ...
  <httpModules>
    <add name="ScriptModule" type="System.Web.Handlers.ScriptModule,
      System.Web.Extensions, Version=3.5.0.0, Culture=neutral,
      PublicKeyToken=31BF3856AD364E35"/>
  </httpModules>
</system.web>
```

The remaining configuration settings are configured by the `<configSections>` settings, which are included as the first child element of `<configuration>`. This section, which is not listed here, must be included so that you can use the `<system.web.extensions>` and `<system.webServer>` sections.

The `<system.web.extensions>` section is not included in the default ASP.NET Web Site configuration file; you look at it in the next section.

The next configuration element, `<system.webServer>`, contains settings that relate to the IIS 7 Web server; this element is not required if you are using an earlier version of IIS. This configuration section is not listed here.

Finally, there is a `<runtime>` section as follows:

```
<runtime>
  <assemblyBinding xmlns="urn:schemas-microsoft-com:asm.v1">
    <dependentAssembly>
      <assemblyIdentity name="System.Web.Extensions"
```

```
            publicKeyToken="31bf3856ad364e35"/>
         <bindingRedirect oldVersion="1.0.0.0-1.1.0.0" newVersion="3.5.0.0"/>
      </dependentAssembly>
      <dependentAssembly>
         <assemblyIdentity name="System.Web.Extensions.Design"
            publicKeyToken="31bf3856ad364e35"/>
         <bindingRedirect oldVersion="1.0.0.0-1.1.0.0" newVersion="3.5.0.0"/>
      </dependentAssembly>
   </assemblyBinding>
</runtime>
```

This section is included to ensure backward compatibility with older versions of ASP.NET AJAX and will have no effect unless you have version 1.0 of ASP.NET AJAX installed. If you do have this version installed, this section enables third-party controls to bind to the latest version of ASP.NET AJAX.

Additional Configuration Options

The `<system.web.extensions>` section contains settings that provide additional configuration for ASP.NET AJAX, all of which is optional. This section is not included in the default ASP.NET Web application template, but you can add it if you need its functionality. Most of the configuration that you can add with this section concerns Web services and is contained in an element called `<webServices>`, which in turn is placed in a `<scripting>` element. First, you can add a section to enable access to the ASP.NET authentication service through a Web service (you can choose to enforce SSL here if you wish):

```
<system.web.extensions>
  <scripting>
    <webServices>
      <authenticationService enabled="true" requireSSL = "true|false"/>
```

Next, you can enable and configure access to ASP.NET personalization functionality through the profile Web service:

```
<profileService enabled="true"
  readAccessProperties="propertyname1,propertyname2"
  writeAccessProperties="propertyname1,propertyname2" />
```

The last Web service-related setting is for enabling and configuring access to ASP.NET role functionality through the role Web service:

```
<roleService enabled="true"/>
</webServices>
```

Finally, the `<system.web.extensions>` section can contain an element that enables you to configure compression and caching for asynchronous communications:

```
<scriptResourceHandler enableCompression="true" enableCaching="true" />
  </scripting>
</system.web.extensions>
```

Additional Configuration for the AJAX Control Toolkit

To use the controls in the AJAX Control Toolkit, you can add the following configuration to `Web.config`:

```
<controls>
  ...
  <add namespace="AjaxControlToolkit" assembly="AjaxControlToolkit"
    tagPrefix="ajaxToolkit"/>
</controls>
```

This maps the toolkit controls to the `ajaxToolkit` tag prefix. These controls are contained in the `AjaxControlToolkit.dll` assembly, which should be in the `/bin` directory for the Web application.

Alternatively, you could register the controls individually on Web pages using the `<%@ Register %>` directive:

```
<%@ Register Assembly="AjaxControlToolkit" Namespace="AjaxControlToolkit"
  TagPrefix="ajaxToolkit" %>
```

Adding ASP.NET AJAX Functionality

The first step in adding Ajax functionality to a Web site is to add a `ScriptManager` control to your Web pages. Next, you add server controls such as `UpdatePanel` controls to enable partial-page rendering and dynamic controls such as those supplied in the AJAX Control Toolkit to add usability and glitz to your application. You may also add client-side code, and you can use the AJAX Library for further assistance in customizing and enhancing the functionality of your application.

In this section, you learn about the functionality you can add using server controls. Later in the chapter you look at client-side techniques.

The ScriptManager Control

As mentioned earlier in the chapter, the `ScriptManager` control must be included on all pages that use partial-page postbacks and several other aspects of ASP.NET AJAX functionality.

> A great way to ensure that all the pages in your Web application contain the `ScriptManager` control is to add this control to the master page (or master pages) that your application uses.

As well as enabling ASP.NET AJAX functionality, you can also use properties to configure this control. The simplest of these properties is `EnablePartialRendering`, which is true by default. If you set this property to `false`, you will disable all asynchronous postback processing, such as that provided by `UpdatePanel` controls. This can be useful, for example, if you want to compare your AJAX-enabled Web site with a traditional Web site, perhaps if you are giving a demonstration to a manager.

You can use the `ScriptManager` control for several reasons, such as in the following common situations:

- ❏ To determine whether server-side code is being called as a result of a partial-page postback
- ❏ To add references to additional client-side JavaScript files
- ❏ To reference Web services
- ❏ To return error messages to the client

These configuration options are covered in the following sections.

Detect Partial-Page Postbacks

The `ScriptManager` control includes a Boolean property called `IsInAsyncPostBack`. You can use this property in server-side code to detect whether a partial-page postback is in progress. Note that the `ScriptManager` for a page may actually be on a master page. Rather than accessing this control through the master page, you can obtain a reference to the current `ScriptManager` instance by using the static `GetCurrent()` method, for example:

```
ScriptManager scriptManager = ScriptManager.GetCurrent(this);
if (scriptManager != null && scriptManager.IsInAsyncPostBack)
{
    // Code to execute for partial-page postbacks.
}
```

You must pass a reference to a `Page` control to the `GetCurrent()` method. For example, if you use this method in a `Page_Load()` event handler for an ASP.NET Web page, you can use `this` as your `Page` reference. Also, remember to check for a `null` reference to avoid exceptions.

Client-Side JavaScript References

Rather than adding code to the HTML page header, or in `<script>` elements on the page, you can use the `Scripts` property of the `ScriptManager` class. This centralizes your script references and makes it easier to maintain them. You can do this declaratively by adding a child `<Scripts>` element to the `<UpdatePanel>` control element, and then adding `<asp:ScriptReference>` child control elements to `<Scripts>`. You use the `Path` property of a `ScriptReference` control to reference a custom script.

The following sample shows how to add references to a custom script file called `MyScript.js` in the root folder of the Web application:

```
<asp:ScriptManager runat="server" ID="ScriptManager1">
  <Scripts>
    <asp:ScriptReference Path="~/MyScript.js" />
  </Scripts>
</asp:ScriptManager>
```

Web Service References

To access Web services from client-side JavaScript code, ASP.NET AJAX must generate a proxy class. To control this behavior, you use the `Services` property of the `ScriptManager` class. As with `Scripts`, you can specify this property declaratively, this time with a `<Services>` element. You add `<asp:ServiceReference>` controls to this element. For each `ServiceReference` object in the `Services` property, you specify the path to the Web service by using the `Path` property.

The `ServiceReference` class also has a property called `InlineScript`, which defaults to `false`. When this property is `false`, client-side code obtains a proxy class to call the Web service by requesting it from the server. To enhance performance (particularly if you use a lot of Web services on a page), you can set `InlineScript` to `true`. This causes the proxy class to be defined in the client-script for the page.

ASP.NET Web services use a file extension of `.asmx`. Without wanting to get into too much detail in this chapter, to add a reference to a Web service called `MyService.asmx` in the root folder of a Web application, you would use code as follows:

```
<asp:ScriptManager runat="server" ID="ScriptManager1">
  <Services>
    <asp:ServiceReference Path="~/MyService.asmx" />
  </Services>
</asp:ScriptManager>
```

You can only add references to local Web services (that is, Web services in the same Web application as the calling code) in this way. You can call remote Web services indirectly via local Web methods.

Later in this chapter you see how to make asynchronous Web method calls from client-side JavaScript code that uses proxy classes generated in this way.

Client-Side Error Messages

If an exception is thrown as part of a partial-page postback, the default behavior is to place the error message contained in the exception into a client-side JavaScript alert message box. You can customize the message that is displayed by handling the `AsyncPostBackError` event of the `ScriptManager` instance. In the event handler, you can use the `AsyncPostBackErrorEventArgs.Exception` property to access the exception that is thrown and the `ScriptManager.AsyncPostBackErrorMessage` property to set the message that is displayed to the client. You might do this to hide the exception details from users.

If you want to override the default behavior and display a message in a different way, you must handle the endRequest event of the client-side PageRequestManager object by using JavaScript. This is described later in this chapter.

Using UpdatePanel Controls

The UpdatePanel control is perhaps the control that you will use most often when you write ASP.NET AJAX-enabled Web applications. This control, as you have seen in the simple example earlier in the chapter, enables you to wrap a portion of a Web page so that it is capable of participating in a partial-page postback operation. To do this, you add an UpdatePanel control to the page and fill its child <ContentTemplate> element with the controls that you want it to contain.

```
<asp:UpdatePanel runat="Server" ID="UpdatePanel1">
  <ContentTemplate>
    ...
  </ContentTemplate>
</asp:UpdatePanel>
```

The contents of the <ContentTemplate> template are rendered in either a <div> or <span> element according to the value of the RenderMode property of the UpdatePanel. The default value of this property is Block, which will result in a <div> element. To use a <span> element, set RenderMode to Inline.

Multiple UpdatePanel Controls on a Single Web Page

You can include any number of UpdatePanel controls on a page. If a postback is caused by a control that is contained in the <ContentTemplate> of any UpdatePanel on the page, a partial-page postback will occur instead of a full-page postback. This will cause all the UpdatePanel controls to update according to the value of their UpdateMode property. The default value of this property is Always, which means that the UpdatePanel will update for a partial-page postback operation on the page, even if this operation occurs in a different UpdatePanel control. If you set this property to Conditional, the UpdatePanel updates only when a control that it contains causes a partial-page postback or when a trigger that you have defined occurs. Triggers are covered shortly.

If you have set UpdateMode to Conditional, you can also set the ChildrenAsTriggers property to false to prevent controls that are contained by the UpdatePanel from triggering an update of the panel. Note, though, that in this case these controls still trigger a partial-page update, which may result in other UpdatePanel controls on the page being updated. For example, this will update controls that have an UpdateMode property value of Always. This is illustrated in the following code:

```
<asp:UpdatePanel runat="Server" ID="UpdatePanel1" UpdateMode="Conditional"
  ChildrenAsTriggers="false">
  <ContentTemplate>
    <asp:Button runat="Server" ID="Button1" Text="Click Me" />
    <small>Panel 1 render time: <% =DateTime.Now.ToLongTimeString() %></small>
  </ContentTemplate>
</asp:UpdatePanel>
<asp:UpdatePanel runat="Server" ID="UpdatePanel2">
  <ContentTemplate>
    <small>Panel 2 render time: <% =DateTime.Now.ToLongTimeString() %></small>
  </ContentTemplate>
</asp:UpdatePanel>
<small>Page render time: <% =DateTime.Now.ToLongTimeString() %></small>
```

In this code, the UpdatePanel2 control has an UpdateMode property of Always; the default value. When the button is clicked, it will cause a partial-page postback, but only UpdatePanel2 will be updated. Visually, you will notice that only the "Panel 2 render time" label is updated.

Server-Side UpdatePanel Updates

Sometimes when you have multiple UpdatePanel controls on a page, you might decide not to update one of them unless certain conditions are met. In this case, you would configure the UpdateMode property of the panel to Conditional as shown in the previous section and possibly also set the ChildrenAsTriggers property to false. Then, in your server-side event-handler code for one of the controls on the page that causes a partial-page update, you would (conditionally) call the Update() method of the UpdatePanel. For example:

```
protected void Button1_Click(object sender, EventArgs e)
{
    if (TestSomeCondition())
    {
        UpdatePanel1.Update();
    }
}
```

UpdatePanel Triggers

You can cause an UpdatePanel control to be updated by a control elsewhere on the Web page by adding triggers to the Triggers property of the control. A trigger is an association between an event of a control elsewhere on the page and the UpdatePanel control. All controls have default events (for example, the default event of a Button control is Click), so specifying the name of an event is optional. There are two types of triggers that you can add, represented by the following two classes:

❑ AsyncPostBackTrigger — This class causes the UpdatePanel to update when the specified event of the specified control is triggered.

❑ PostBackTrigger — This class causes a full-page update to be triggered when the specified event of the specified control is triggered.

You will mostly use AsyncPostBackTrigger, but PostBackTrigger can be useful if you want a control inside an UpdatePanel to trigger a full-page postback.

Both of these trigger classes have two properties: ControlID, which specifies the control that causes the trigger by its identifier, and EventName, which specifies the name of the event for the control that is linked to the trigger.

To extend an earlier example, consider the following code:

```
<asp:UpdatePanel runat="Server" ID="UpdatePanel1" UpdateMode="Conditional"
    ChildrenAsTriggers="false">
    <Triggers>
        <asp:AsyncPostBackTrigger ControlID="Button2" />
    </Triggers>
    <ContentTemplate>
        <asp:Button runat="Server" ID="Button1" Text="Click Me" />
        <small>Panel 1 render time: <% =DateTime.Now.ToLongTimeString() %></small>
    </ContentTemplate>
</asp:UpdatePanel>
<asp:UpdatePanel runat="Server" ID="UpdatePanel2">
    <ContentTemplate>
        <asp:Button runat="Server" ID="Button2" Text="Click Me" />
        <small>Panel 2 render time: <% =DateTime.Now.ToLongTimeString() %></small>
    </ContentTemplate>
</asp:UpdatePanel>
<small>Page render time: <% =DateTime.Now.ToLongTimeString() %></small>
```

The new `Button` control, `Button2`, is specified as a trigger in the `UpdatePanel1`. When this button is clicked, both `UpdatePanel1` and `UpdatePanel2` will be updated: `UpdatePanel1` because of the trigger, and `UpdatePanel2` because it uses the default `UpdateMode` value of `Always`.

Using UpdateProgress

The `UpdateProgress` control, as you saw in the earlier example, enables you to display a progress message to the user while a partial-page postback is in operation. You use the `ProgressTemplate` property to supply an `ITemplate` for the progress display. You will typically use the `<ProgressTemplate>` child element of the control to do this.

You can place multiple `UpdateProgress` controls on a page by using the `AssociatedUpdatePanelID` property to associate the control with a specific `UpdatePanel`. If this is not set (the default), the `UpdateProgress` template will be displayed for any partial-page postback, regardless of which `UpdatePanel` causes it.

When a partial-page postback occurs, there is a delay before the `UpdateProgress` template is displayed. This delay is configurable through the `DisplayAfter` property, which is an `int` property that specifies the delay in milliseconds. The default is 500 milliseconds.

Finally, you can use the Boolean `DynamicLayout` property to specify whether space is allocated for the template before it is displayed. For the default value of `true` for this property, space on the page is dynamically allocated, which may result in other controls being moved out of the way for an inline progress template display. If you set this property to `false`, space will be allocated for the template before it is displayed, so the layout of other controls on the page will not change. You will set this property according to the effect you want to achieve when displaying progress. For a progress template that is positioned by using absolute coordinates, as in the earlier example, you should leave this property set to the default value.

Using Extender Controls

The core ASP.NET AJAX download includes a class called `ExtenderControl`. The purpose of this control is to enable you to extend (that is, add functionality to) other ASP.NET server controls. This is used extensively in the AJAX Control Toolkit to great effect, and you can use the ASP.NET AJAX Server Control Extender project template to create your own extended controls. `ExtenderControl` controls all work in a similar way — you place them on a page, associate them with target controls, and add further configuration. The extender then emits client-side code to add functionality.

To see this in action in a simple example, create a new Web site called `PCSExtenderDemo` in the `C:\ ProCSharp\Chapter39` directory, add the AJAX Control Toolkit assembly to the bin directory of the Web Site, and then add the following code to `Default.aspx`:

```
<%@ Page Language="C#" AutoEventWireup="true" CodeFile="Default.aspx.cs"
  Inherits="_Default" %>
<%@ Register Assembly="AjaxControlToolkit" Namespace="AjaxControlToolkit"
  TagPrefix="ajaxToolkit" %>

<!DOCTYPE html PUBLIC "-//W3C//DTD XHTML 1.0 Transitional//EN"
  "http://www.w3.org/TR/xhtml1/DTD/xhtml1-transitional.dtd">
<html xmlns="http://www.w3.org/1999/xhtml">
<head runat="server">
  <title>Color Selector</title>
</head>
<body>
  <form id="form1" runat="server">
    <asp:ScriptManager ID="ScriptManager1" runat="server" />
    <div>
      <asp:UpdatePanel runat="server" ID="updatePanel1">
```

```
            <ContentTemplate>
              <span style="display: inline-block; padding: 2px;">
                My favorite color is:
              </span>
              <asp:Label runat="server" ID="favoriteColorLabel" Text="green"
                style="color: #00dd00; display: inline-block; padding: 2px;
                       width: 70px; font-weight: bold;" />
              <ajaxToolkit:DropDownExtender runat="server" ID="dropDownExtender1"
                TargetControlID="favoriteColorLabel"
                DropDownControlID="colDropDown" />
              <asp:Panel ID="colDropDown" runat="server"
                Style="display: none; visibility: hidden; width: 60px;
                       padding: 8px; border: double 4px black;
                       background-color: #ffffdd; font-weight: bold;">
                <asp:LinkButton runat="server" ID="OptionRed" Text="red"
                  OnClick="OnSelect" style="color: #ff0000;" /><br />
                <asp:LinkButton runat="server" ID="OptionOrange" Text="orange"
                  OnClick="OnSelect" style="color: #dd7700;" /><br />
                <asp:LinkButton runat="server" ID="OptionYellow" Text="yellow"
                  OnClick="OnSelect" style="color: #dddd00;" /><br />
                <asp:LinkButton runat="server" ID="OptionGreen" Text="green"
                  OnClick="OnSelect" style="color: #00dd00;" /><br />
                <asp:LinkButton runat="server" ID="OptionBlue" Text="blue"
                  OnClick="OnSelect" style="color: #0000dd;" /><br />
                <asp:LinkButton runat="server" ID="OptionPurple" Text="purple"
                  OnClick="OnSelect" style="color: #dd00ff;" />
              </asp:Panel>
            </ContentTemplate>
          </asp:UpdatePanel>
        </div>
      </form>
  </body>
</html>
```

You also need to add the following event handler to the code behind this file:

```
protected void OnSelect(object sender, EventArgs e)
{
    favoriteColorLabel.Text = ((LinkButton)sender).Text;
    favoriteColorLabel.Style["color"] = ((LinkButton)sender).Style["color"];
}
```

In the browser, not very much is visible at first, and the extender seems to have no effect. This is shown in Figure 39-5.

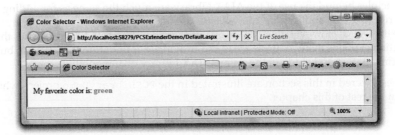

Figure 39-5

However, when you hover over the text that reads "green," a drop-down dynamically appears. If you click this drop-down, a list appears, as shown in Figure 39-6.

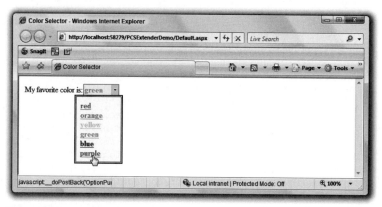

Figure 39-6

When you click one of the links in the drop-down list, the text changes accordingly (after a partial-page postback operation).

There are two important points to note about this simple example. First, it was extremely easy to associate the extender with target controls. Second, the drop-down list was styled using custom code — meaning that you can place whatever content you like in the list. This simple extender is a great way to add functionality to your Web applications, and it is very simple to use.

The extenders that are contained in the AJAX Control Toolkit are continually being added to and updated, so check `http://ajax.asp.net/ajaxtoolkit` regularly. This Web page includes live demonstrations of all the current extenders so that you can see them in action.

In addition to the extender controls that are supplied by the AJAX Control Toolkit, you can create your own. To make this process as simple as possible, you can use the ASP.NET AJAX Control project template. This project includes all the basic functionality that you require for an extender, including the server-side class for the extender and the client-side JavaScript behavior file that the extender uses. To create an effective extender, you must use the AJAX Library.

Using the AJAX Library

There is a great deal of functionality available in the AJAX Library that you can use to further enhance your Web applications. However, to do this you need at least a working knowledge of JavaScript. In this section, you see some of this functionality, although this is not an exhaustive tutorial.

The basic principles behind the use of the AJAX Library are much the same as for adding any type of client-side script to a Web application. You will still use the core JavaScript language, and you will still interact with the DOM. However, there are many areas where the AJAX Library makes things easier for you. This section explains many of these areas and provides a foundation that you can build on with further experimentation and study of the online AJAX Library documentation.

The techniques covered in this section are illustrated in the `PCSLibraryDemo` project, which is referred to throughout the rest of this chapter.

Adding JavaScript to a Web Page

The first thing you need to know is how to add client-side JavaScript to a Web Page. You have three options here:

❑   Add JavaScript inline in ASP.NET Web pages, by using the `<script>` element.

❑   Add JavaScript to separate JavaScript files with the extension `.js` and reference these files from `<script>` elements or (preferably) by using the `<Scripts>` child element of the `ScriptManager` control.

❑   Generate JavaScript from server-side code, such as code behind or custom extender controls.

Each of these techniques has its own benefits. For prototyping code, there is no substitute for inline code because it is so quick and easy to use. You will also find it easy to associate client-side event handlers of HTML elements and server controls with client-side functions, because everything is in the same file.

Having separate files is good for reusability, because you may create your own library of classes much like the existing AJAX Library JavaScript files.

Generating code from code behind can be tricky to implement because you will not usually have access to IntelliSense for JavaScript programming when you use C# code. However, you will be able to generate code dynamically in response to application state, and sometimes this is the only way to do things.

The extenders that you can create with the AJAX Control Toolkit include a separate JavaScript file that you use to define behaviors, which gets around some of the problems of exposing client-side code from the server.

In this chapter, you use the inline code technique, because it is simplest and allows you to concentrate on the JavaScript functionality.

Global Utility Functions

One of the features supplied by the AJAX Library that you will use most often is the set of global functions that wrap other functionality. These include the following:

❑   `$get()` — This function enables you to get a reference to a DOM element by supplying its client-side `id` value as a parameter, with an optional second parameter to specify the parent element to search in.

❑   `$create()` — This function enables you to create objects of a specific JavaScript type and perform initialization at the same time. You can supply between one and five parameters to this function. The first parameter is the type you want to instantiate, which will typically be a type defined by the AJAX Library. The other parameters enable you to specify initial property values, event handlers, references to other components, and the DOM element that the object is attached to, respectively.

❑   `$addHandler()` — This function provides a shorthand for adding an event handler to an object.

There are more global functions, but these are the ones you will use most often. `$create()` in particular is a very useful way to reduce the amount of code required to create and initialize an object.

Using the AJAX Library JavaScript OOP Extensions

The AJAX Library includes an enhanced framework for defining types that uses an OOP-based system that maps closely to .NET Framework techniques. You can create namespaces, add types to namespaces, add constructors, methods, properties, and events to types, and even use inheritance and interfaces in type definitions.

In this section, you see how to implement the basics of this functionality, but you won't look at events and interfaces here. These constructs are beyond the scope of this chapter.

Defining Namespaces

To define a namespace, you use the `Type.registerNamespace()` function, for example:

```
Type.registerNamespace("ProCSharp");
```

Once you have registered a namespace you can add types to it.

Defining Classes

Defining a class is a three-stage process. First, you define the constructor. Next, you add properties and methods. Finally, you register the class.

To define a constructor, you define a function using a namespace and class name, for example:

```
ProCSharp.Shape = function(color, scaleFactor) {
    this._color = color;
    this._scaleFactor = scaleFactor;
}
```

This constructor takes two parameters and uses them to set local fields (note that you do not have to explicitly define these fields — you just have to set their values).

To add properties and methods, you assign them to the `prototype` property of the class as follows:

```
ProCSharp.Shape.prototype = {

    getColor : function() {
       return this._color;
    },

    setColor : function(color) {
       this._color = color;
    },

    getScaleFactor : function() {
       return this._scaleFactor;
    },

    setScaleFactor : function(scaleFactor) {
       this._scaleFactor = scaleFactor;
    }

}
```

This code defines two properties by their get and set accessors.

To resister a class, you call its `registerClass()` function:

```
ProCSharp.Shape.registerClass('ProCSharp.Shape');
```

Inheritance

You derive a class in much the same way as creating a class but with some slight differences. You use the `initializeBase()` function to initialize the base class in the constructor, passing parameters in the form of an array:

```
ProCSharp.Circle = function(color, scaleFactor, diameter) {
    ProCSharp.Circle.initializeBase(this, [color, scaleFactor]);
    this._diameter = diameter;
}
```

You define properties and methods in the same way as before:

```
ProCSharp.Circle.prototype = {

  getDiameter : function() {
    return this._diameter;
  },

  setDiameter : function(diameter) {
    this._diameter = diameter;
  },

  getArea : function() {
    return Math.PI * Math.pow((this._diameter * this._scaleFactor) / 2, 2);
  },

  describe : function() {
    var description = "This is a " + this._color + " circle with an area of "
      + this.getArea();
    alert(description);
  }
}
```

When you register the class, you provide the base class type as a second parameter:

```
ProCSharp.Circle.registerClass('ProCSharp.Circle', ProCSharp.Shape);
```

You can implement interfaces by passing them as additional parameters, although, to keep things simple, you won't see details of that here.

Using User-Defined Types

Once you have defined classes in this way, you can instantiate and use them with simple syntax. For example:

```
var myCircle = new ProCSharp.Circle('red', 1.0, 4.4);
myCircle.describe();
```

This code would result in a JavaScript alert box, as shown in Figure 39-7.

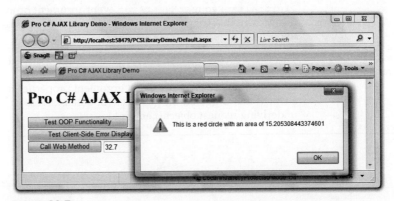

Figure 39-7

If you want to test this, run the PCSLibraryDemo project and click the Test OOP Functionality button.

The PageRequestManager and Application Objects

Among the most useful classes that the AJAX Library provides are the PageRequestManager and Application classes. You will find PageRequestManager in the Sys.WebForms namespace and Application in the Sys namespace. The important thing about these classes is that they expose several events that you can attach JavaScript event handlers to. These events occur at particularly interesting points in the life cycle of a page (for Application) or partial-page postback (for PageRequestManager) and enable you to perform operations at these critical times.

The AJAX Library defines event handlers in a similar way to event handlers in the .NET Framework. Every event handler has a similar signature, with two parameters. The first parameter is a reference to the object that generated the event. The second parameter is an instance of the Sys.EventArgs class or an instance of a class that derives from this class. Many of the events exposed by PageRequestManager and Application include specialized event argument classes that you can use to determine more information about the event. The following table lists these events in the order they will occur in a page that is loaded, triggers a partial-page postback, and is then closed.

Event	Description
Application.init	This event is the first to occur in the life cycle of a page. It is raised after all the JavaScript files have been loaded but before any objects in the application have been created.
Application.load	This event fires after the objects in the application have loaded and been initialized. You will often use an event handler attached to this event to perform actions when the page is first loaded. You can also provide an implementation for a function called pageLoad() on a page, which is automatically defined as an event handler for this event. It sends event arguments by using a Sys.ApplicationLoadEventArgs object, which includes the isPartialLoad property that you can use to determine if a partial-page postback has occurred. Access this property with the get_isPartialLoad() accessor.
PageRequestManager .initializeRequest	This event occurs before a partial-page postback, before the request object is created. You can use the Sys.WebForms .InitializeRequestEventArgs event argument properties to access the element that triggered the postback (postBackElement) and the underlying request object (request).
PageRequestManager .beginRequest	This event occurs before a partial-page postback, after the request object is created. You can use the Sys.WebForms. BeginRequestEventArgs event argument properties to access the element that triggered the postback (postBackElement) and the underlying request object (request).

Event	Description
PageRequestManager .pageLoading	This event is raised after a partial-page postback, before any subsequent processing occurs. This processing can include `<div>` elements that will be deleted or updated, which you can reference through the `Sys.WebForms.PageLoadingEventArgs` object by using the `panelsDeleting` and `panelsUpdating` properties.
PageRequestManager .pageLoaded	This event is raised after a partial-page postback, after `UpdatePanel` controls have been processed. This processing can include `<div>` elements that have been created or updated, which you can reference through the `Sys.WebForms.PageLoadedEventArgs` object by using the `panelsCreated` and `panelsUpdated` properties.
PageRequestManager .endRequest	This event occurs after processing of a partial-page postback has completed. The `Sys.WebForms.EndRequestEventArgs` object passed to the event handler enables you to detect and process server-side errors (by using the `error` and `errorHandled` properties) as well as to access the response object through `response`.
Application.unload	This event is raised just before the objects in the application are disposed, which gives you a chance to perform final actions or cleanup if necessary.

You can add an event handler to an event of the `Application` object by using the static `add_xxx()` functions, for example:

```
Sys.Application.add_load(LoadHandler);

function LoadHandler(sender, args)
{
   // Event handler code.
}
```

The process is similar for `PageRequestManager`, but you must use the `get_instance()` function to obtain an instance of the current object, for example:

```
Sys.WebForms.PageRequestManager.getInstance().add_beginRequest(
   BeginRequestHandler);

function BeginRequestHandler(sender, args)
{
   // Event handler code.
}
```

In the `PCSLibraryDemo` application, an event handler is added to the `PageRequestManager`.`endRequest` event. This event handler responds to server-side processing errors and displays an error message in a `<span>` element with an `id` of `errorDisplay`. To test this method, click the Test Client-Side Error Display button, as shown in Figure 39-8.

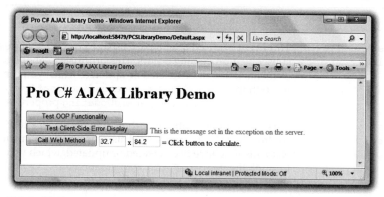

Figure 39-8

The code that achieves this is:

```
Sys.WebForms.PageRequestManager.getInstance().add_endRequest(
  EndRequestHandler);

function EndRequestHandler(sender, args)
{
  if (args.get_error() != undefined)
  {
    var errorMessage = args.get_error().message;
    args.set_errorHandled(true);
    $get('errorDisplay').innerHTML = errorMessage;
  }
}
```

Note that the errorHandled property of the EndRequestEventArgs object is set to true. This prevents the default behavior, which is to display the error message in a dialog box by using the JavaScript alert() function.

The error itself is generated by throwing an exception on the server as follows:

```
protected void testErrorDisplay_Click(object sender, EventArgs e)
{
    throw new ApplicationException(
  "This is the message set in the exception on the server.");
}
```

There are many other situations when you will want to use event handling techniques to act on the Application and PageRequestManager events.

JavaScript Debugging

In the past, JavaScript has had a reputation of being difficult to debug. However, this has been addressed in the latest version of Visual Studio. You can now add breakpoints and step through JavaScript code just like C# code. You can also interrogate object state in break mode, change property values, and so on. The IntelliSense that is available when you write JavaScript code is also vastly improved in the latest version of Visual Studio.

However, there will still be times when you will want to add debug and trace code to report information as code is executed. For example, you might want to use the JavaScript alert() function to show information in dialog boxes.

There are also some third-party tools that you can use to add a client-side UI for debugging. These include:

❑ **Fiddler** — This tool, which you can obtain from www.fiddlertool.com, enables you to log all HTTP traffic between your computer and a Web application — including partial-page postbacks. There are also additional tools that you can use to look at what occurs during the processing of Web pages in more detail.

❑ **Nikhil's Web Development Helper** — This tool, available at http://projects.nikhilk.net/Projects/WebDevHelper.aspx, can also log HTTP traffic. In addition, this tool contains a number of utilities specifically aimed at ASP.NET and ASP.NET AJAX development, for example, the ability to examine view state and to execute immediate JavaScript code. This latter feature is particularly useful to test objects that you may have created on the client. The Web Development Helper also displays extended error information when JavaScript errors occur, which makes it easier to track down bugs in JavaScript code.

The AJAX Library also provides the Sys.Debug class, which you can use to add some extra debugging features to your application. One of the most useful features of this class is the Sys.Debug.traceDump() function, which enables you to analyze objects. One way to use this function is to place a textarea control on your Web page with an id attribute of TraceConsole. Then, all output from Debug will be sent to this control. For example, you can use the traceDump() method to output information about the Application object to the console:

```
Sys.Application.add_load(LoadHandler);

function LoadHandler(sender, args)
{
   Sys.Debug.traceDump(sender);
}
```

This results in output along the lines of the following:

```
traceDump {Sys._Application}
    _updating: false
    _id: null
    _disposing: false
    _creatingComponents: false
    _disposableObjects {Array}
    _components {Object}
    _createdComponents {Array}
    _secondPassComponents {Array}
    _loadHandlerDelegate: null
    _events {Sys.EventHandlerList}
        _list {Object}
            load {Array}
                [0] {Function}
    _initialized: true
    _initializing: true
```

You can see all the properties of this object in this output. This technique can be extremely useful for ASP.NET AJAX development.

Making Asynchronous Web Method Calls

One of the most powerful features of ASP.NET AJAX is the ability to call Web methods from client-side script. This gives you access to data, server-side processing, and all manner of other functionality.

You will not be looking at Web methods in this book until Chapter 42, "Windows Communication Foundation," so we will save the details until then and cover the basics here. Put simply, a Web method is a method that you can expose from a Web service that enables you to access remote resources over the Internet. In ASP.NET AJAX, you can also expose Web methods as static methods of server-side Web page code-behind code. You can use parameters and return values in Web methods just as you do in other method types.

In ASP.NET AJAX, Web methods are called asynchronously. You pass parameters to a Web method and define a callback function, which is called when the Web method call completes. You use this callback function to process the Web method response. You can also provide an alternative callback function to call in the event of a call failure.

In the `PCSLibraryDemo` application, you can see a Web method call being performed by clicking the Call Web Method button, as shown in Figure 39-9.

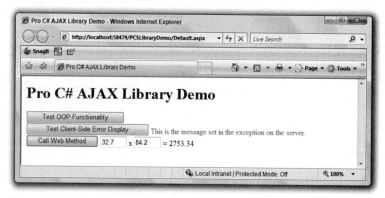

Figure 39-9

Before you can use a Web method from client-side script, you must generate a client-side proxy class to perform the communication. The easiest way to do this is simply to reference the URL of the Web service that contains the Web method in the `ScriptManager` control:

```
<asp:ScriptManager ID="ScriptManager1" runat="server">
  <Services>
    <asp:ServiceReference Path="~/SimpleService.asmx" />
  </Services>
</asp:ScriptManager>
```

ASP.NET Web services use the extension `.asmx`, as shown in this code. To use a client-side proxy to access a Web method in a Web service, you must apply the `System.Web.Script.Services` `.ScriptService` attribute to the Web service.

For Web methods in the code behind for the Web page, you do not need this attribute, or this reference in `ScriptManager`, but you must use static methods and apply the `System.Web.Services.WebMethod` attribute to the methods.

Once you have generated a client-side stub, you can access the Web method by its name, which is defined as a function of a class with the same name as the Web service. In `PCSLibraryDemo`, the `SimpleService.asmx` Web service has a Web method called `Multiply()`, which multiplies two double parameters. When you call this method from client-side code, you pass the two parameters required by the method (obtained from HTML `<input>` elements in the example) and can pass one or two callback function references. If you pass one reference, this is the callback function that is used when the call returns a success result. If you pass two references, the second one is the callback function that is used for Web method failure.

In `PCSLibraryDemo`, a single callback function is used, which takes the result of the Web method call and assigns it to the <span> with the id of `webMethodResult`:

```
function callWebMethod()
{
    SimpleService.Multiply(parseFloat($get('xParam').value),
        parseFloat($get('yParam').value), multiplyCallBack);
}

function multiplyCallBack(result)
{
    $get('webMethodResult').innerHTML = result;
}
```

This method is a very simple one but illustrates the ease with which you can call Web services asynchronously from client-side code.

ASP.NET Application Services

ASP.NET AJAX includes three specialized Web services that you can use to access ASP.NET application services. These services are accessed through the following client-side classes:

❑   `Sys.Services.AuthenticationService` — This service includes methods to log in or log out a user or determine whether a user is logged in.

❑   `Sys.Services.ProfileService` — This service enables you to get and set profile properties for the currently logged-on user. The profile properties are configured in the `Web.config` file for the application.

❑   `Sys.Services.RoleService` — This service enables you to determine role membership for the currently logged-on user.

Used properly, these classes enable you to implement extremely responsive user interfaces that include authorization, profile, and membership functionality.

These services are beyond the scope of this chapter, but you should be aware of them, and they are well worth investigating.

Summary

In this chapter, you have seen how you can use ASP.NET AJAX to enhance ASP.NET Web applications. ASP.NET AJAX contains a wealth of functionality that makes Web applications far more responsive and dynamic and can provide a much better user experience.

First, you learned what Ajax is, and about the separate components of ASP.NET AJAX that are available and what they offer. You saw the difference between AJAX Extensions and the AJAX Library and how these components work together to provide the core ASP.NET AJAX functionality. You also looked at the AJAX Control Toolkit, which adds to this core functionality.

Next, you looked at server-side techniques for creating ASP.NET AJAX-enabled Web applications. You saw how ASP.NET AJAX is configured in the `Web.config` file of your ASP.NET Web applications and how to use the various server controls that are part of the AJAX Extensions. Specifically, you learned about `ScriptManager`, `UpdatePanel` (and triggers), `UpdateProgress`, and extender controls. You saw how easy it is to use these controls to add a great deal of functionality to a Web application very quickly.

You then examined the AJAX Library, which extends and enhances JavaScript and provides you with additional functionality that you can add to applications. It does, however, require at least a working knowledge of JavaScript programming.

You learned about the global functions that the AJAX Library adds to JavaScript and how to define namespaces and classes by using the OOP extensions that the AJAX Library adds to JavaScript. You learned how to interact with events that occur on the client during the life cycle of a page and partial-page postbacks. You saw how to use one of these events, `PageRequestManager.endRequest`, to customize how server errors that occur during a partial-page postback are displayed in the Web browser.

Finally, you looked at client-side Web method calls. You saw how an asynchronous model is used for these and how to write the required code to call a simple Web method. You also learned about accessing the ASP.NET application services (authorization, profile, and membership) through Web services.

We hope that this chapter has given you an appetite for this exciting new technology. Ajax is blossoming across the Web, and ASP.NET AJAX is an excellent way to integrate Ajax functionality with ASP.NET applications. This product is also very well supported, and the community-based releases, such as the AJAX Control Toolkit, provide you with even more great functionality that you are free to use in your applications.

Even though you may find yourself having to learn the JavaScript language you never thought you would need, the end result is well worth the effort. By using ASP.NET AJAX you will make far better, more functional, and more dynamic Web applications than you could with ASP.NET alone. And with the latest release of Visual Studio you have tools that make ASP.NET AJAX much easier to use.

In the next chapter you move away from Web development and look at how you can extend Microsoft Office applications such as Word, Excel, and Outlook with code written in Visual Studio.

40

Visual Studio Tools for Office

Visual Studio Tools for Office (VSTO) is a technology that enables you to customize and extend Microsoft Office applications and documents by using the .NET Framework. It also includes tools that you can use to make this customization easier in Visual Studio — for example, a visual designer for office ribbon controls.

VSTO is the latest in a long line of products that Microsoft has released to allow the customization of Office applications. The object model that you use to access Office applications has evolved over time. If you have used it in the past, then parts of it will be familiar to you. If you have programmed VBA add-ins for Office applications, then you will be well prepared for the techniques discussed in this chapter (and, as you will see, VSTO is capable of interoperability with VBA). However, the classes that VSTO makes available so that you can interact with Office through the Office Primary Interop Assemblies (PIAs) have been extended beyond the Office object model. For example, the VSTO classes include .NET data binding functionality.

Up until Visual Studio 2008, VSTO was a separate download that you could obtain if you wanted to develop Office solutions. With Visual Studio 2008, VSTO is integrated with the VS IDE. This version of VSTO, which is also known as VSTO 3, includes full support for Office 2007 and has many new features. This includes the ability to interact with Word content controls, the visual ribbon designer mentioned previously, VBA integration, and more.

This chapter does not assume any prior knowledge of VSTO or its predecessors. In this chapter, you learn the following:

- ❑ What types of projects you can create with VSTO and what capabilities you can include in these projects
- ❑ Fundamental techniques that apply to all types of VSTO solutions
- ❑ How to build VSTO solutions with a custom UI, VBA interoperability, and ClickOnce deployment

VSTO Overview

VSTO consists of the following components:

- ❑ A selection of project templates that you can use to create various types of Office solutions
- ❑ Designer support for visual layout of ribbons, action panes, and custom task panels
- ❑ Classes built on top of the Office Primary Interop Assemblies (PIAs) that provide extensive capabilities

VSTO supports both 2003 and 2007 versions of Office. The VSTO class library comes in two flavors, one for each of these Office versions, which use different sets of assemblies. For simplicity (and because of its richer feature set), this chapter focuses on the 2007 version.

The general architecture of VSTO solutions is shown in Figure 40-1.

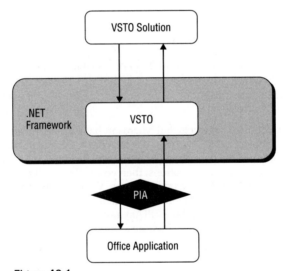

Figure 40-1

Project Types

Figure 40-2 shows the project templates that are available in VS.

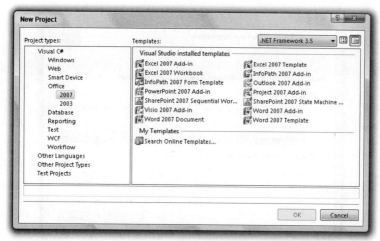

Figure 40-2

Note that when you create a project using one of the VSTO templates you may be asked to enable access to the VBA project system. This is necessary for VBA interoperability.

The VSTO project templates can be divided into the following categories:

❑ Document-level customizations

❑ Application-level add-ins

❑ SharePoint workflow templates

❑ InfoPath form templates

There are 2003 and 2007 versions of some of the project types, but as discussed earlier, you will look at only the 2007 versions here.

This chapter concentrates on the most commonly used project types, which are document-level customizations and application-level add-ins.

Document-Level Customizations

When you create a project of this type, you will generate an assembly that will be linked to an individual document — for example a Word document, Word template, or Excel workbook. When you load the document, the associated Office application will detect the customization, load the assembly, and make the VSTO customization available.

You might use a project of this type to provide additional functionality to a particular line-of-business document, or to a whole class of documents by adding customizations to a document template. You can include code that manipulates the document and the content of the document, including any embedded objects. You can also provide custom menus, including ribbon menus that you can create using the VS Ribbon Designer.

When you create a document-level project, you can choose to create a new document or to copy an existing document as a starting point for your development. You can also choose the type of document to create. For a Word document, for example, you can choose to create .docx (the default), .doc, or .docm documents (.docm is a macro-enabled document). The dialog box for this is shown in Figure 40-3.

Figure 40-3

Application-Level Add-Ins

Application-level add-ins are different from document-level customizations in that they are available throughout their targeted Office application. You can access add-in code, which might include menus, document manipulations and so on, regardless of what documents are loaded.

When you start an Office application such as Word, it will look for associated add-ins that have entries in the registry and will load any assemblies that it needs to.

SharePoint Workflow Templates

These projects provide a template to create SharePoint workflow applications. These are used to manage the flow of documents within SharePoint processes. By creating a project of this type, you can execute custom code at key times during the document lifecycle.

InfoPath Form Templates

These are a form of document-level customization for InfoPath forms, although they use a slightly different methodology for Word and Excel document customizations and, so, are usually classified differently. You can create templates for InfoPath forms that extend the functionality of the InfoPath designer and that provide additional functionality and business logic for designers and end-users of InfoPath forms.

When you create an InfoPath Form template, you are presented with a wizard to specify exactly the sort of project you want to create, as shown in Figure 40-4.

As you can see in Figure 40-4, this wizard gives you quite a lot of flexibility in the source for the form you are creating — you can choose a variety of starting points (including forms on a SharePoint site). You can also create complete forms or template parts and limit functionality to browser-compatible features if desired.

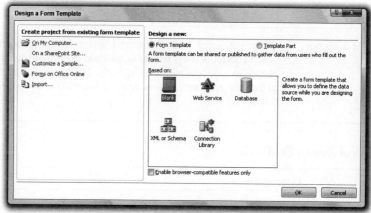

Figure 40-4

Project Features

There are several features that you can use in the various VSTO project types, such as interactive panes and controls. The project type you use determines the features that are available to you. The following tables list these features according to the projects in which they are available.

Document-Level Customization Features

Feature	Description
Actions pane	Actions panes are dialog boxes that are hosted inside the action pane of Word or Excel. You can display whatever controls you like here, which makes this an extremely versatile way of extending documents and applications.
Data cache	Data caching enables you to store data that is used in your documents externally to those documents in cached data islands. These data islands can be updated from data sources or manually, and enable the Office documents to access data when data sources are offline or unavailable.
Endpoints for VBA code	As discussed earlier, VSTO enables VBA interoperability. In document-level customizations, you can provide endpoint methods that can be called from VBA code.
Host controls	Host controls are extended wrappers around existing controls in the Office object model. You can manipulate and data-bind to these objects.
Smart tags	Smart tags are objects that are embedded in Office documents and that have typed content. They are automatically detected within the content of Office documents; for example, a stock quote smart tag is added automatically when the application detects appropriate text. You can create your own smart tag types and define operations that can be performed on them.

Feature	Description
Visual document designer	When you work with document customization projects, the Office object model is used to create a visual design surface that you can use to lay out controls interactively. The toolbars and menus shown in the designer are, as you will see later in this chapter, fully functional.

Application-Level Add-In Features

Feature	Description
Custom task pane	Task panes are typically docked to one edge of an Office application and provide a variety of functionality. For example, Word has a task pane used for manipulating styles. As with action panes, these give you a great deal of flexibility.
Cross-application communication	Once you have created an add-in for one Office application, you can expose that functionality to other add-ins. You could, for example, create a financial calculating service in Excel and then use that service from Word — without creating a separate add-in.
Outlook form regions	You can create form regions that can be used in Outlook.

Features Usable In All Project Types

Feature	Description
ClickOnce deployment	You can distribute any VSTO project that you create to end users through ClickOnce deployment methods. This enables users to stay up-to-date with updates to your document- and application-level solutions by detecting changes to the application manifest.
Ribbon menus	Ribbon menus are used in all Office applications, and VSTO includes two ways to create your own ribbon menus. You can either use XML to define a ribbon or use the Ribbon Designer. Typically, you will use the Ribbon Designer as it is much easier to use, although you may want the XML version for backwards compatibility.

VSTO Fundamentals

Now that you have seen what is included in VSTO, it is time to look at the more practical side of things, and how you can build VSTO projects. The techniques demonstrated in this section are general ones that apply to all types of VSTO projects.

In this section, you will look at the following:

- ❑ Office object model
- ❑ VSTO namespaces
- ❑ Host items and host controls
- ❑ Basic VSTO project structure
- ❑ The Globals class
- ❑ Event handling

Office Object Model

The Office 2007 suite of applications exposes its functionality through a COM object model. You can use this object model directly from VBA to control just about any aspect of Office functionality. The Office object model was introduced in Office 97, and has evolved since then as functionality in Office has changed.

There are a huge number of classes in the Office object model, some of which are used across the suite of Office applications and some of which are specific to individual applications. For example, the Word 2007 object model includes a `Documents` collection representing the currently loaded objects, each of which is represented by a `Document` object. In VBA code, you can access documents by name or index and call methods to perform operations on them. For example, the following VBA code closes the document with the name `My Document` without saving changes:

```
Documents("My Document").Close SaveChanges:=wdDoNotSaveChanges
```

The Office object model includes named constants (such as `wdDoNotSaveChanges` in the preceding code) and enumerations to make it easier to use.

VSTO Namespaces

VSTO contains a collection of namespaces, which contain types that you can use to program against the Office object model. Many of the classes and enumerations in these namespaces map directly to objects and enumerations in the Office object model. These are accessed through Office PIAs. However, VSTO also contains types that do not map directly, or are unrelated to the Office object model. For example, there are a lot of classes that are used for designer support in VS.

The types that do wrap or communicate with objects in the Office object model are divided into namespaces containing types for use with Office 2003 and those for use with Office 2007. The namespaces that you will use for Office 2007 development are summarized in the following table.

Namespace	Description
`Microsoft.Office.Core`, `Microsoft.Office.Interop.*`	These namespaces contain thin wrappers around the PIA classes and, so, provide the base functionality for working with the Office classes. There are several nested namespaces in the `Microsoft.Office.Interop` namespace for each of the Office products.

Namespace	Description
Microsoft.Office.Tools	This namespace contains general types that provide VSTO functionality and base classes for many of the classes in nested namespaces. For example, this namespace includes the classes required to implement action panes in document-level customizations and the base class for application-level add-ins.
Microsoft.Office.Tools.Excel, Microsoft.Office.Tools.Excel.*	These namespaces contain the types required to interact with the Excel application and Excel documents.
Microsoft.Office.Tools.Outlook	These namespaces contain the types required to interact with the Outlook application.
Microsoft.Office.Tools.Ribbon	This namespace includes the types required to work with and create your own ribbon menus.
Microsoft.Office.Tools.Word, Microsoft.Office.Tools.Word.*	These namespaces contain the types required to interact with the Word application and Word documents.
Microsoft.VisualStudio.Tools.*	These namespaces provide the VSTO infrastructure that you work with when you develop VSTO solutions in VS.

Host Items and Host Controls

Host items and host controls are classes that have been extended to make it easier for document-level customizations to interact with Office documents. These classes simplify your code as they expose .NET-style events and are fully managed. The "host" part of the name of host items and host classes references the fact that these classes wrap and extend the native Office objects that are accessed through PIAs.

Often when you use host items and host controls, you will find that it is necessary to use the underlying PIA interop types as well. For example, if you create a new Word document, then you receive a reference to the interop Word document type rather than the Word document host item. You need to be aware of this and write your code accordingly.

There are host items and host controls for both Word and Excel document-level customizations.

Word

There is a single host item for Word, Microsoft.Office.Tools.Word.Document. This represents a Word document. As you might expect, this class has an enormous number of methods and properties that you can use to interact with Word documents.

There are 12 host controls for Word, as shown in the following table, all of which are found in the Microsoft.Office.Tools.Word namespace.

Control	Description
Bookmark	This control represents a location within the Word document. This might be a single location or a range of characters.
XMLNode, XmlNodes	These controls are used when the document has an attached XML schema. They allow you to reference document content by the XML node location of that content. You can also manipulate the XML structure of a document with these controls.
ContentControl	This class is the base class for the remaining eight controls in this table, and enables you to deal with Word content controls. A content control is a control that presents content as a control or that enables functionality above and beyond that offered by plain text in a document.
BuildingBlockGalleryContentControl	This control enables you to add and manipulate document building blocks, such as formatted tables, cover pages, and so on.
ComboBoxContentControl	This control represents content formatted as a combo box.
DatePickerContentControl	This control represents content formatted in a date picker.
DropDownListContentControl	This control represents content formatted as a drop-down list.
GroupContentControl	This control represents content that is a grouped collection of other content items, including text and other content controls.
PictureContentControl	This control represents an image.
RichTextContentControl	This control represents a block of rich text content.
PlainTextContentControl	This control represents a block of plain text content.

Excel

There are three host items and four host controls for Excel, all of which are contained in the `Microsoft.Office.Tools.Excel` namespace.

The Excel host items are shown in the following table.

Host Item	Description
Workbook	This host item represents an entire Excel workbook, which may contain multiple worksheets and chartsheets.
Worksheet	This host item is used for individual worksheets within a workbook.
Chartsheet	This host item is used for individual chartsheets within a workbook.

The Excel host controls are shown in the following table.

Control	Description
Chart	This control represents a chart that is embedded in a worksheet.
ListObject	This control represents a list in a worksheet.
NamedRange	This control represents a named range in a worksheet.
XmlMappedRange	This control is used when an Excel spreadsheet has an attached schema, and is used to manipulate ranges that are mapped to XML schema elements.

Basic VSTO Project Structure

When you first create a VSTO project, the files you start with vary according to the project type, but there are some common features. In this section, you will see what constitutes a VSTO project.

Document-Level Customization Project Structure

When you create a document-level customization project, you will see an entry in Solution Explorer that represents the document type. This may be:

- ❏ A .docx file for a Word document
- ❏ A .dotx file for a Word template
- ❏ A .xlsx file for an Excel workbook
- ❏ A .xltx file for an Excel template

Each of these has a designer view and a code file, which you will see if you expand the item in Solution Explorer. The Excel templates also include sub-items representing the workbook as a whole and each spreadsheet in the workbook. This structure enables you to provide custom functionality on a per-sheet or per-workbook basis.

If you view the hidden files in one of these projects, you will see several designer files that you can look at to see the template-generated code. Each Office document item has an associated class from the VSTO namespaces, and the classes in the code files derive from these classes. These classes are defined as partial class definitions so that your custom code is separated from the code generated by the visual designer, similar to the structure of Windows Forms applications.

For example, the Word document template provides a class that derives from the host item Microsoft.Office.Tools.Word.Document. This code is contained in ThisDocument.cs, as follows:

```
using System;
using System.Collections.Generic;
using System.Data;
using System.Linq;
using System.Text;
using System.Windows.Forms;
using System.Xml.Linq;
using Microsoft.VisualStudio.Tools.Applications.Runtime;
using Office = Microsoft.Office.Core;
using Word = Microsoft.Office.Interop.Word;
namespace WordDocument1
{
    public partial class ThisDocument
    {
        private void ThisDocument_Startup(object sender, System.EventArgs e)
        {
        }
        private void ThisDocument_Shutdown(object sender, System.EventArgs e)
        {
        }
        #region VSTO Designer generated code
        /// <summary>
        /// Required method for Designer support - do not modify
        /// the contents of this method with the code editor.
        /// </summary>
        private void InternalStartup()
        {
            this.Startup += new System.EventHandler(ThisDocument_Startup);
            this.Shutdown += new System.EventHandler(ThisDocument_Shutdown);
        }
        #endregion
    }
}
```

This template-generated code includes aliases for the two main namespaces that you will use when creating a document-level customization for Word, Microsoft.Office.Core for the main VSTO Office classes and Microsoft.Office.Interop.Word for Word-specific classes. Note that if you want to use Word host controls, then you would also add a using statement for the Microsoft.Office.Tools.Word namespace. The template-generated code also defines two event handler hooks that you can use to execute code when the document is loaded or unloaded, ThisDocument_Startup() and ThisDocument_Shutdown().

Every one of the document-level customization project types has a similar structure in its code file (or, in the case of Excel, code files). There are namespace aliases defined for you and handlers for the various Startup and Shutdown events that the VSTO classes define. From this starting point, you add dialog boxes, action panes, ribbon controls, event handlers, and custom code to define the behavior of your customization.

With document-level customizations, you can also customize the document or documents through the document designer. Depending on the type of solution you are creating, this might involve adding boilerplate content to templates, interactive content to documents, or something else. The designers are effectively hosted versions of Office applications, and you can use them to enter content just as you can in the applications themselves. However, you can also add controls such as host controls and Windows Forms controls to documents, and code around these controls.

Application-Level Add-In Project Structure

When you create an application-level add-in, there will be no document or documents in Solution Explorer. Instead, you will see an item representing the application that you are creating an add-in for, and if you expand this item, you will see a file called `ThisAddIn.cs`. This file contains a partial class definition for a class called `ThisAddIn`, which provides the entry point for your add-in. This class derives from `Microsoft.Office.Tools.AddIn`, which provides code add-in functionality, and implements the `Microsoft.VisualStudio.Tools.Office.IOfficeEntryPoint` interface, which is an infrastructure interface.

For example, the code generated by the Word add-in template is as follows:

```
using System;
using System.Collections.Generic;
using System.Linq;
using System.Text;
using System.Xml.Linq;
using Word = Microsoft.Office.Interop.Word;
using Office = Microsoft.Office.Core;
namespace WordAddIn1
{
    public partial class ThisAddIn
    {
        private void ThisAddIn_Startup(object sender, System.EventArgs e)
        {
        }
        private void ThisAddIn_Shutdown(object sender, System.EventArgs e)
        {
        }
        #region VSTO generated code
        /// <summary>
        /// Required method for Designer support - do not modify
        /// the contents of this method with the code editor.
        /// </summary>
        private void InternalStartup()
        {
            this.Startup += new System.EventHandler(ThisAddIn_Startup);
            this.Shutdown += new System.EventHandler(ThisAddIn_Shutdown);
        }

        #endregion
    }
}
```

As you can see, this structure is very similar to the structure used in document-level customizations. It includes aliases for the same `Microsoft.Office.Core` and `Microsoft.Office.Interop.Word` namespaces, and gives you event handlers for `Startup` and `Shutdown` events (`ThisAddIn_Startup()` and `ThisAddIn_Shutdown()`). These events are slightly different from the document ones, as they are raised when the add-in is loaded or unloaded rather than when individual documents are opened or closed.

You proceed to customize application-level add-ins much as you do document-level customizations: by adding ribbon controls, task panes, and additional code.

The Globals Class

All VSTO project types define a class called `Globals` that gives you global access to the following:

- ❏ For document-level customizations, all documents in the solution. These are exposed through members with names that match the document class names — for example, `Globals.ThisWorkbook` and `Globals.Sheet1`.

- ❏ For application-level add-ins, the add-in object. This is exposed through `Globals.ThisAddIn`.

- ❏ For Outlook add-in projects, all Outlook form regions.

- ❏ All ribbons in the solution, through the `Globals.Ribbons` property.

Behind the scenes, the `Globals` class is created through a series of partial definitions in the various designer-maintained code files in your solution. For example, the default `Sheet1` worksheet in an Excel Workbook project includes the following designer-generated code:

```
internal sealed partial class Globals
{
    private static Sheet1 _Sheet1;
    internal static Sheet1 Sheet1
    {
        get
        {
            return _Sheet1;
        }
        set
        {
            if ((_Sheet1 == null))
            {
                _Sheet1 = value;
            }
            else
            {
                throw new System.NotSupportedException();
            }
        }
    }
}
```

This code adds the `Sheet1` member to the `Globals` class.

Event Handling

Earlier in this chapter, you saw how the host item and host control classes expose events that you can handle. Unfortunately, this is not the case for the interop classes. There are a few events that you can use, but for the most part, you will find it difficult to create event-driven solutions by using these events. Most often, to respond to events you should focus on the events exposed by host items and host controls.

The obvious problem here is that there are no host items or host controls for application-level add-in projects. Sadly, this is a problem that you must learn to live with when you use VSTO. However, the most common events that you are likely to listen for in add-ins are those associated with ribbon menu and task pane interaction. You design ribbons with the integrated ribbon designer, and you can respond to any events generated by the ribbon to make the control interactive. Task panes are usually implemented as Windows Forms user controls (although you can use WPF), and you can use Windows Forms events here rather than PIA interop events. This means that you will not often encounter situations in which there is no event available for the functionality you require.

When you do need to use a PIA-exposed event, you will find that events are exposed through interfaces on the PIA objects. Consider a Word Add-In project. The `ThisAddIn` class in this project exposes a property called `Application` through which you can obtain a reference to the Office application. This property is of type `Microsoft.Office.Interop.Word.Application`, and exposes events through the `Microsoft.Office.Interop.Word.ApplicationEvents4_Event` interface. This interface exposes a total of 29 events (which really doesn't seem to be a lot for an application as complex as Word, does it?). You can handle, for example, the `DocumentBeforeClose` event to respond to Word document close requests.

Building VSTO Solutions

The previous sections explained what VSTO projects are, how they are structured, and the features that you can use in the various project types. In this section, you look at implementing VSTO solutions.

Figure 40-5 outlines the structure of document-level customization solutions.

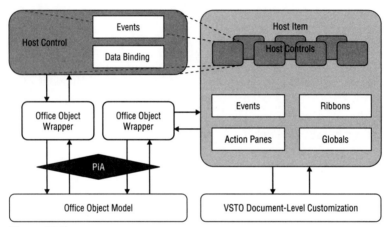

Figure 40-5

For document-level customizations you will interact with at least one host item, which will typically contain multiple host controls. You may use Office object wrappers directly, but for the most part, you will access the Office object model and its functionality through host items and host controls.

You will make use of host item and host control events, data binding, ribbon menus, action panes, and global objects in your code.

Figure 40-6 outlines the structure of application-level add-in solutions.

In this slightly simpler model, you are more likely to use the thinner wrappers around Office objects directly, or at least through the add-in class that encapsulates your solution. You will also use events exposed by the add-in class, ribbon menus, task panes, and global objects in your code.

In this section, you will look at both of these types of applications as appropriate, as well as the following topics:

- ❑ Managing application-level add-ins
- ❑ Interacting with applications and documents
- ❑ UI customization

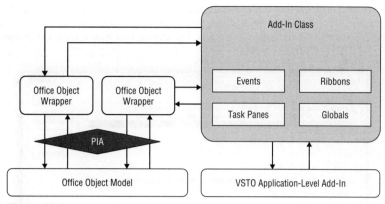

Figure 40-6

Managing Application-Level Add-Ins

One of the first things you will find when you create an application-level add-in is that VS carries out all the steps necessary to register the add-in with the Office application. This means that registry entries are added so that when the Office application starts, it will automatically locate and load your assembly. If you subsequently want to add or remove add-ins, then you must either navigate through Office application settings or manipulate the registry manually.

For example, in Word, you must open the Office Button menu, click Word Options, and select the Add-Ins tab, as shown in Figure 40-7.

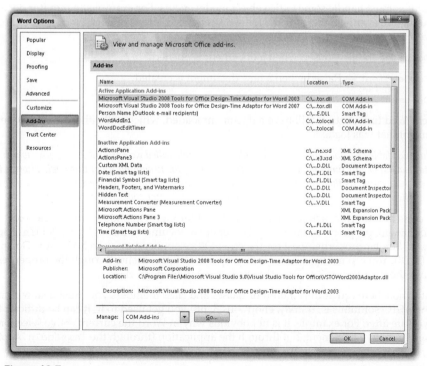

Figure 40-7

Figure 40-7 shows two add-ins that have been created with VSTO: `WordAddIn1` and
`WordDocEditTimer`. To add or remove add-ins, you must select COM Add-Ins in the Manage drop-
down (the default option) and click the Go button. The dialog box that appears is shown in Figure 40-8.

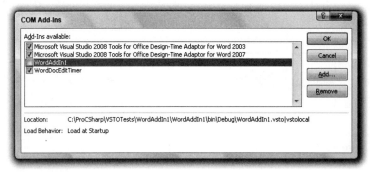

Figure 40-8

You can unload add-ins by deselecting them in the COM Add-Ins dialog box (as shown in Figure 40-8),
and you can add new add-ins or remove old ones with the Add and Remove buttons.

Interacting with Applications and Documents

Whatever type of application you are creating, you will want to interact with the host application and/or
documents in the host operation. In part, this includes using UI customizations, which you learn about
in the next section. However, you may also need to monitor documents within an application, which
means that you must handle some Office object model events. For example, to monitor documents in
Word, you require event handlers for the following events of the `Microsoft.Office.Interop.Word`
`.ApplicationEvents4_Event` interface:

❑ `DocumentOpen` — Raised when a document is opened.

❑ `NewDocument` — Raised when a new document is created.

❑ `DocumentBeforeClose` — Raised when a document is saved.

Also, when Word first starts, it will have a document loaded, which will either be a blank new document
or a document that was loaded.

> *The downloadable code for this chapter includes an example called `WordDocEditTimer`, which
> maintains a list of edit times for Word documents. Part of the functionality of this application is to
> monitor the documents that are loaded, for reasons that are explained later. Because this example also
> uses a custom task pane and ribbon menu, you will look at it after covering those topics.*

You can access the currently active document in Word through `ThisAddIn.Application`
`.ActiveDocument` property, and the collection of open documents through `ThisAddIn.Application`
`.Documents`. Similar properties exist for the other Office applications with a Multiple Document
Interface (MDI). You can manipulate various properties of documents through the properties exposed by,
for example, the `Microsoft.Office.Interop.Word.Document` class.

One point to note here is that the amount of classes and class members you must deal with when
developing VSTO solutions is, frankly, enormous. Until you get used to it, it can be difficult to locate the
features you are after. For example, it is not obvious why in Word the current active selection is available
not through the active document, but through the application (through the `ThisAddIn.Application`
`.Selection` property).

The selection is useful for inserting, reading, or replacing text through the Range property. For example:

```
ThisAddIn.Application.Selection.Range.Text = "Inserted text";
```

Unfortunately, there is not enough space in this chapter to cover the object libraries in great depth. Instead, you will learn about the object libraries as they are relevant to the ongoing discussion.

UI Customization

Perhaps the most important aspect of the latest release of VSTO is the flexibility that is available for customizing the UI of your customizations and add-ins. You can add content to any of the existing ribbon menus, add completely new ribbon menus, customize task panes by adding action panes, add completely new task panes, and integrate Windows Forms and WPF forms and controls.

In this section, we look at each of these subjects.

Ribbon Menus

You can add ribbon menus to any of the VSTO projects that you are looking at in this chapter. When you add a ribbon, you will see the designer window shown in Figure 40-9.

Figure 40-9

The designer allows you to customize this ribbon by adding controls to the Office button menu (shown in the top left of Figure 40-9) and to groups on the ribbon. You can also add additional groups.

The classes used in ribbons are found in the Microsoft.Office.Tools.Ribbon namespace. This includes the ribbon class that you derive from to create a ribbon, OfficeRibbon. This class can contain RibbonTab objects, each of which includes content for a single tab. Tabs contain RibbonGroup objects, like the group1 group in Figure 40-9. These tabs can contain a variety of controls.

It is possible for the groups on a tab to be positioned on a completely new tab, or on one of the existing tabs in the Office application that you are targeting. Where the groups appear is determined by the RibbonTab.ControlId property. This property has a ControlIdType property, which you can set to RibbonControlIdType.Custom or RibbonControlIdType.Office. If you use Custom, then you must also set RibbonTab.ControlId.CustomId to a string value, which is the tab identifier. You can use any identifier you like here. However, if you use Office for ControlIdType, then you must set RibbonTab.ControlId.OfficeId to a string value that matches one of the identifiers used in the Office product you are using. For example, in Excel you could set this property to TabHome to add groups to the Home tab, TabInsert for the Insert tab, and so on. The default for add-ins is TabAddIns, which will be shared by all add-ins.

> Many tabs are available, especially in Outlook; you can download a series of spreadsheets containing the full list from: www.microsoft.com/downloads/details .aspx?FamilyID=4329D9E9-4D11-46A5-898D-23E4F331E9AE&displaylang=en.

Once you have decided where to put your ribbon groups, you can add any of the controls shown in the following table.

Control	Description
RibbonBox	This is a container control that you can use to lay out other controls in a group. You can lay out controls in a RibbonBox horizontally or vertically by changing the BoxStyle property to RibbonBoxStyle .Horizontal or RibbonBoxStyle.Vertical.
RibbonButton	You can use this control to add a small or large button with or without a text label to a group. Set the ControlSize property to RibbonControlSize.RibbonControlSizeLarge or RibbonControlSize.RibbonControlSizeRegular to control the size. The button has a Click event handler that you can use to respond to interaction. You can also set the image to a custom image or to one of the images stored in the Office system (described following this table).
RibbonButtonGroup	This is a container control that represents a group of buttons. It can contain RibbonButton, RibbonGallery, RibbonMenu, RibbonSplitButton, and RibbonToggleButton controls.
RibbonCheckBox	A check box control with a Click event and a Checked property.
RibbonComboBox	A combo box (combined text entry with drop-down list of items). Use the Items property for items, the Text property for the entered text, and the TextChanged event to respond to changed.
RibbonDropDown	A container that can contain RibbonDropDownItem and RibbonButton items, in Items and Buttons properties respectively. The buttons and items are formatted into a drop-down list. You use the SelectionChanged event to respond to interaction.
RibbonEditBox	A text box that users can use to enter or edit text in the Text property. This control has a TextChanged event.
RibbonGallery	As with RibbonDropDown, this control can contain RibbonDropDownItem and RibbonButton items, in Items and Buttons properties respectively. This control uses Click and ButtonClick events rather than the SelectionChanged event that RibbonDropDown has.
RibbonLabel	Simple text display, set with the Label property.
RibbonMenu	A pop-up menu that you can populate with other controls, such as RibbonButton and nested RibbonMenu controls, when it is open in design view. Handle events for the items on the menu.
RibbonSeparator	A simple separator used to customize control layout in groups.

Control	Description
RibbonSplitButton	Control that combines a RibbonButton or RibbonToggleButton with a RibbonMenu. Set the button style with ButtonType, which can be RibbonButtonType.Button or RibbonButtonType.ToggleButton. Use the Click event for the main button or individual button Click events in the menu to respond to interaction.
RibbonToggleButton	A button that can be in a selected or unselected state, as indicated by the Checked property. This control also has a Click event.

You can also set the DialogBoxLauncher property of a group so that an icon appears in the bottom right of the group. You can use this to display a dialog box as its name suggests, or to open a task pane, or to perform any other action you want. You add or remove this icon through the GroupView Tasks menu, as shown in Figure 40-10, which also shows some of the other controls in the previous table as they appear on a ribbon in design view.

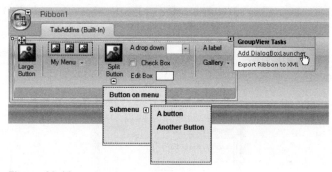

Figure 40-10

To set the image for a control, for example a RibbonButton control, you can either set the Image property to a custom image and ImageName to a name for the image (so that you can optimize image loading in an OfficeRibbon.LoadImage event hander), or you can use one of the built-in Office images. To do this, you set the OfficeImageId property to the ID of the image.

There are many images that you can use; you can download a spreadsheet that lists them from www.microsoft.com/downloads/details.aspx?familyid=12b99325-93e8-4ed4-8385-74d0f7661318&displaylang=en. Figure 40-11 shows a sample.

Figure 40-11 shows the Developer ribbon tab, which you can enable through the Office button, in the Excel Options dialog box, on the Popular tab.

When you click on an image, a dialog box appears to tell you what the image ID is, as shown in Figure 40-12.

The ribbon designer is extremely flexible, and you can provide pretty much any functionality that you would expect to find on an Office ribbon. However, if you want to customize your UI further, then you will want to use action and task panes, as you can create any UI and functionality you like there.

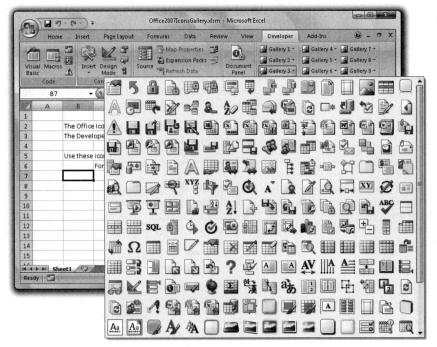

Figure 40-11

Figure 40-12

Action Panes and Custom Task Panes

You can use action and task panes to display content that is docked in the task pane area of the Office application interface. Task panes are used in application-level add-ins, and action panes are used in document-level customizations. Both task and action panes must inherit from UserControl objects, which means that you create a UI by using Windows Forms. You can also use a WPF UI if you host a WPF form in an ElementHost control on the UserControl. One difference between these controls is that you can add action panes to a document-level customization through the Action Pane Template item in the New Item Wizard or with a simple user control. Task panes must be added as plain user controls.

To add an action pane to a document in a document-level customization, you add an instance of the action pane class to the Controls collection of the ActionsPane property of the document. For example:

```
public partial class ThisWorkbook
{
    Private ActionsPaneControl1 actionsPane;
    private void ThisWorkbook_Startup(object sender, System.EventArgs e)
    {
        actionsPane = new ActionsPaneControl1();
        this.ActionsPane.Controls.Add(actionsPane);
    }
    ...
}
```

This code adds the actions pane when the document (in this case an Excel workbook) is loaded. You can also do this in, for example, a ribbon button event handler.

Custom task panes are added through the `ThisAddIn.CustomTaskPanes.Add()` method property in application-level add-in projects. This method also allows you to name the task window. For example:

```
public partial class ThisAddIn
{
    Microsoft.Office.Tools.CustomTaskPane taskPane;
    private void ThisAddIn_Startup(object sender, System.EventArgs e)
    {
        taskPane = this.CustomTaskPanes.Add(new UserControl1(), "My Task Pane");
        taskPane.Visible = true;
    }
    ...
}
```

Note that the `Add()` method returns an object of type `Microsoft.Office.Tools.CustomTaskPane`. You can access the user control itself through the `Control` property of this object. You can also use other properties exposed by this type — for example, the `Visible` property as shown in the previous code — to control the task pane.

At this point, it is worth mentioning a slightly unusual feature of Office applications, and in particular, a difference between Word and Excel. For historical reasons, although both Word and Excel are MDI applications, the way in which these applications host documents is different. In Word, every document has a unique parent window. In Excel, every document shares the same parent window.

When you call the `CustomTaskPanes.Add()` method, the default behavior is to add the task pane to the currently active window. In Excel, this means that every document will display the task pane, as the same parent window is used for all of them. In Word, the situation is different. If you want the task pane to appear for every document, then you must add it to every window that contains a document.

To add the task pane to a specific document, you pass an instance of the `Microsoft.Office.Interop.Word.Window` class to the `Add()` method as a third parameter. You can obtain the window associated with a document through the `Microsoft.Office.Interop.Word.Document.ActiveWindow` property.

In the next section, you will see how to do this in practice.

Example Application

As mentioned in previous sections, the example code for this chapter includes an application called `WordDocEditTimer`, which maintains a list of edit times for Word documents. In this section, we examine the code for this application in detail, as it illustrates everything you've read about so far and includes some useful tips.

The general operation of this application is that whenever a document is created or loaded, a timer is started, linked to the document name. If you close a document, then the timer for that document pauses. If you open a document that has previously been timed, then the timer resumes. Also, if you use Save As to save a document with a different filename, then the timer is updated to use the new filename.

This application is a Word application-level add-in, and uses a custom task pane and a ribbon menu. The ribbon menu contains a button that you can use to turn the task pane on and off and a check box that enables you to pause the timer for the currently active document. The group containing these controls is appended to the Home ribbon tab. The task pane displays a list of active timers.

This user interface is shown in Figure 40-13.

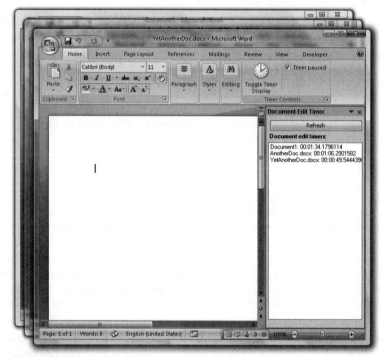

Figure 40-13

Timers are maintained through the DocumentTimer class:

```
public class DocumentTimer
{
    public Word.Document Document { get; set; }
    public DateTime LastActive { get; set; }
    public bool IsActive { get; set; }
    public TimeSpan EditTime { get; set; }
}
```

This keeps a reference to a Microsoft.Office.Interop.Word.Document object as well as the total edit time, whether the timer is active, and the time it last became active. The ThisAddIn class maintains a collection of these objects, associated with document names:

```
public partial class ThisAddIn
{
    private Dictionary<string, DocumentTimer> documentEditTimes;
```

Each timer can therefore be located by document reference or document name. This is necessary because document references allow you to keep track of document name changes (there is no event that you can use to monitor this), and document names allow you to keep track of closed and reopened documents.

The `ThisAddIn` class also maintains a list of `CustomTaskPane` objects (as noted earlier, one is required for each window in Word):

```
    private List<Tools.CustomTaskPane> timerDisplayPanes;
```

When the add-in starts, the `ThisAddIn_Startup()` method performs several tasks. First, it initializes the two collections:

```
    private void ThisAddIn_Startup(object sender, System.EventArgs e)
    {
        // Initialize timers and display panels
        documentEditTimes = new Dictionary<string, DocumentTimer>();
        timerDisplayPanes = new List<Microsoft.Office.Tools.CustomTaskPane>();
```

Next, it adds several event handlers through the `ApplicationEvents4_Event` interface:

```
        // Add event handlers
        Word.ApplicationEvents4_Event eventInterface = this.Application;
        eventInterface.DocumentOpen += new Microsoft.Office.Interop.Word
            .ApplicationEvents4_DocumentOpenEventHandler(
                eventInterface_DocumentOpen);
        eventInterface.NewDocument += new Microsoft.Office.Interop.Word
            .ApplicationEvents4_NewDocumentEventHandler(
                eventInterface_NewDocument);
        eventInterface.DocumentBeforeClose += new Microsoft.Office.Interop.Word
            .ApplicationEvents4_DocumentBeforeCloseEventHandler(
                eventInterface_DocumentBeforeClose);
        eventInterface.WindowActivate += new Microsoft.Office.Interop.Word
            .ApplicationEvents4_WindowActivateEventHandler(
                eventInterface_WindowActivate);
```

These event handlers are used to monitor documents as they are opened, created, and closed, and also to ensure that the Pause check box is kept up-to-date on the ribbon. This latter functionality is achieved by keeping track of window activations with the `WindowActivate` event.

The last task performed in this event handler is to start monitoring the current document and add the custom task panel to the window containing the document:

```
        // Start monitoring active document
        MonitorDocument(this.Application.ActiveDocument);
        AddTaskPaneToWindow(this.Application.ActiveDocument.ActiveWindow);
    }
```

The `MonitorDocument()` utility method adds a timer for a document:

```
    internal void MonitorDocument(Word.Document Doc)
    {
        // Monitor doc
        documentEditTimes.Add(Doc.Name, new DocumentTimer
```

(continued)

(continued)

```
    {
        Document = Doc,
        EditTime = new TimeSpan(0),
        IsActive = true,
        LastActive = DateTime.Now
    });
}
```

This method simply creates a new `DocumentTimer` for the document. The `DocumentTimer` references the document, has zero edit time, is active, and was made active at the current time. It then adds this timer to the `documentEditTimes` collection and associates it with the document name.

The `AddTaskPaneToWindow()` method adds the custom task pane to a window. This method starts by checking the existing task panes to ensure that there isn't one in the window already. Also, one other strange feature of Word is that if you immediately open an old document after loading the application, the default Document1 document vanishes, without raising a close event. This can lead to an exception being raised when the window for the task pane that was in the document is accessed, so the method also checks for the `ArgumentNullException` that indicates this:

```
private void AddTaskPaneToWindow(Word.Window Wn)
{
    // Check for task pane in window
    Tools.CustomTaskPane docPane = null;
    Tools.CustomTaskPane paneToRemove = null;
    foreach (Tools.CustomTaskPane pane in timerDisplayPanes)
    {
        try
        {
            if (pane.Window == Wn)
            {
                docPane = pane;
                break;
            }
        }
        catch (ArgumentNullException)
        {
            // pane.Window is null, so document1 has been unloaded.
            paneToRemove = pane;
        }
    }
```

If an exception is thrown, then the offending task pane is removed from the collection:

```
    // Remove pane if necessary
    timerDisplayPanes.Remove(paneToRemove);
```

If no task pane was found for the window, then the method finishes by adding one:

```
    // Add task pane to doc
    if (docPane == null)
    {
        Tools.CustomTaskPane pane = this.CustomTaskPanes.Add(
            new TimerDisplayPane(documentEditTimes),
            "Document Edit Timer",
            Wn);
```

```
                timerDisplayPanes.Add(pane);
                pane.VisibleChanged +=
                    new EventHandler(timerDisplayPane_VisibleChanged);
            }
        }
```

The added task pane is an instance of the `TimerDisplayPane` class. You will look at this class shortly. It is added with the name "Document Edit Timer." Also, an event handler is added for the `VisibleChanged` event of the `CustomTaskPane` that you obtain after calling the `CustomTaskPanes` `.Add()` method. This enables you to refresh the display when it first appears:

```
        private void timerDisplayPane_VisibleChanged(object sender, EventArgs e)
        {
            // Get task pane and toggle visibility
            Tools.CustomTaskPane taskPane = (Tools.CustomTaskPane)sender;
            if (taskPane.Visible)
            {
                TimerDisplayPane timerControl = (TimerDisplayPane)taskPane.Control;
                timerControl.RefreshDisplay();
            }
        }
```

The `TimerDisplayPane` class exposes a `RefreshDisplay()` method that is called in the preceding code. This method, as its name suggests, refreshes the display of the `timerControl` object.

Next, there is the code that ensures that all documents are monitored. First, when a new document is created, the `eventInterface_NewDocument()` event handler is called, and the document is monitored by calling the `MonitorDocument()` and `AddTaskPaneToWindow()` methods, which you've already seen.

```
        private void eventInterface_NewDocument(Word.Document Doc)
        {
            // Monitor new doc
            MonitorDocument(Doc);
            AddTaskPaneToWindow(Doc.ActiveWindow);
```

This method also clears the Pause check box in the ribbon menu as new documents start with the time running. This is achieved through a utility method, `SetPauseStatus()`, which is defined on the ribbon:

```
            // Set checkbox
            Globals.Ribbons.TimerRibbon.SetPauseStatus(false);
        }
```

Just before a document is closed, the `eventInterface_DocumentBeforeClose()` event handler is called. This method freezes the timer for the document, updates the total edit time, clears the `Document` reference, and removes the task pane from the document window (with `RemoveTaskPaneFromWindow()`, detailed shortly) before the document is closed.

```
        private void eventInterface_DocumentBeforeClose(Word.Document Doc,
            ref bool Cancel)
        {
            // Freeze timer
            documentEditTimes[Doc.Name].EditTime += DateTime.Now
                - documentEditTimes[Doc.Name].LastActive;
            documentEditTimes[Doc.Name].IsActive = false;
            documentEditTimes[Doc.Name].Document = null;
            // Remove task pane
            RemoveTaskPaneFromWindow(Doc.ActiveWindow);
        }
```

When a document is opened, the eventInterface_DocumentOpen() method is called. There is a little more work to be done here, as before monitoring the document, the method must determine whether a timer already exists for the document by looking at its name:

```
private void eventInterface_DocumentOpen(Word.Document Doc)
{
    if (documentEditTimes.ContainsKey(Doc.Name))
    {
        // Monitor old doc
        documentEditTimes[Doc.Name].LastActive = DateTime.Now;
        documentEditTimes[Doc.Name].IsActive = true;
        documentEditTimes[Doc.Name].Document = Doc;
        AddTaskPaneToWindow(Doc.ActiveWindow);
    }
```

If the document isn't already being monitored, then a new monitor is configured as for a new document:

```
    else
    {
        // Monitor new doc
        MonitorDocument(Doc);
        AddTaskPaneToWindow(Doc.ActiveWindow);
    }
}
```

The RemoveTaskPaneFromWindow() method is used to remove the task pane from a window. The code for this method first checks that a task pane exists for the specified window:

```
private void RemoveTaskPaneFromWindow(Word.Window Wn)
{
    // Check for task pane in window
    Tools.CustomTaskPane docPane = null;
    foreach (Tools.CustomTaskPane pane in timerDisplayPanes)
    {
        if (pane.Window == Wn)
        {
            docPane = pane;
            break;
        }
    }
```

If a task window is found, then it is removed by calling the CustomTaskPanes.Remove() method. It is also removed from the local collection of task pane references.

```
    // Remove document task pane
    if (docPane != null)
    {
        this.CustomTaskPanes.Remove(docPane);
        timerDisplayPanes.Remove(docPane);
    }
}
```

The last event handler in this class is eventInterface_WindowActivate(), called when a window is activated. This method gets the timer for the active document and sets the check box on the ribbon menu so that the check box is kept updated for the document:

```
private void eventInterface_WindowActivate(Word.Document Doc,
    Word.Window Wn)
{
    // Ensure pause checkbox in ribbon is accurate, start by getting timer
    DocumentTimer documentTimer =
        documentEditTimes[this.Application.ActiveDocument.Name];
    // Set checkbox
    Globals.Ribbons.TimerRibbon.SetPauseStatus(!documentTimer.IsActive);
}
```

The code for ThisAddIn also includes two utility methods. The first of these, ToggleTaskPaneDisplay(), is used to show or hide the display of the task pane for the currently active document by setting the CustomTaskPane.Visible property.

```
internal void ToggleTaskPaneDisplay()
{
    // Ensure window has task window
    AddTaskPaneToWindow(this.Application.ActiveDocument.ActiveWindow);
    // toggle document task pane
    Tools.CustomTaskPane docPane = null;
    foreach (Tools.CustomTaskPane pane in timerDisplayPanes)
    {
        if (pane.Window == this.Application.ActiveDocument.ActiveWindow)
        {
            docPane = pane;
            break;
        }
    }
    docPane.Visible = !docPane.Visible;
}
```

The ToggleTaskPaneDisplay() method shown in the preceding code is called by event handlers on the ribbon control, as you will see shortly.

Finally, the class has another method that is called from the ribbon menu, which enables ribbon controls to pause or resume the timer for a document:

```
internal void PauseOrResumeTimer(bool pause)
{
    // Get timer
    DocumentTimer documentTimer =
        documentEditTimes[this.Application.ActiveDocument.Name];
    if (pause && documentTimer.IsActive)
    {
        // Freeze timer
        documentTimer.EditTime += DateTime.Now - documentTimer.LastActive;
        documentTimer.IsActive = false;
    }
    else if (!pause && !documentTimer.IsActive)
    {
        // Resume timer
        documentTimer.IsActive = true;
        documentTimer.LastActive = DateTime.Now;
    }
}
}
```

The only other code in this class definition is an empty event handler for Shutdown, and the VSTO-generated code to hook up the Startup and Shutdown event handlers.

Next, the ribbon in the project, TimerRibbon, is laid out, as shown in Figure 40-14.

Figure 40-14

This ribbon contains a RibbonButton, a RibbonSeparator, a RibbonCheckBox, and a DialogBoxLauncher. The button uses the large display style, and has an OfficeImageId of StartAfterPrevious, which displays the clock face shown in Figure 40-13. (These images are not visible at design time.) The ribbon uses the TabHome tab type, which causes its contents to be appended to the Home tab.

The ribbon has three event handlers, each of which calls on one of the utility methods in ThisAddIn described earlier:

```
private void group1_DialogLauncherClick(object sender,
    RibbonControlEventArgs e)
{
    // Show or hide task pane
    Globals.ThisAddIn.ToggleTaskPaneDisplay();
}
private void pauseCheckBox_Click(object sender, RibbonControlEventArgs e)
{
    // Pause timer
    Globals.ThisAddIn.PauseOrResumeTimer(pauseCheckBox.Checked);
}
private void toggleDisplayButton_Click(object sender,
    RibbonControlEventArgs e)
{
    // Show or hide task pane
    Globals.ThisAddIn.ToggleTaskPaneDisplay();
}
```

The ribbon also includes its own utility method, SetPauseStatus(), which as you saw earlier is called by code in ThisAddIn to select or clear the check box:

```
internal void SetPauseStatus(bool isPaused)
{
    // Ensure checkbox is accurate
    pauseCheckBox.Checked = isPaused;
}
```

The other component in this solution is the `TimerDisplayPane` user control that is used in the task pane. The layout of this control is shown in Figure 40-15.

Figure 40-15

This control includes a button, a label, and a list box — not the most exciting of displays, although it would be simple enough to replace it with, for example, a prettier WPF control.

The code for the control keeps a local reference to the document timers, which is set in the constructor:

```
public partial class TimerDisplayPane : UserControl
{
    private Dictionary<string, DocumentTimer> documentEditTimes;
    public TimerDisplayPane()
    {
        InitializeComponent();
    }
    public TimerDisplayPane(Dictionary<string, DocumentTimer>
        documentEditTimes) : this()
    {
        // Store reference to edit times
        this.documentEditTimes = documentEditTimes;
    }
```

The button event handler calls the `RefreshDisplay()` method to refresh the timer display:

```
    private void refreshButton_Click(object sender, EventArgs e)
    {
        RefreshDisplay();
    }
```

The `RefreshDisplay()` method is also called from `ThisAddIn`, as you saw earlier. It is a surprisingly complicated method considering what it does. It also checks the list of monitored documents against the list of loaded documents and corrects any problems. This sort of code is often necessary in VSTO applications, as the interface with the COM Office object model occasionally doesn't work quite as it should. The rule of thumb here is to code defensively.

The method starts by clearing the current list of timers in the `timerList` list box:

```
    internal void RefreshDisplay()
    {
        // Clear existing list
        this.timerList.Items.Clear();
```

Next, the monitors are checked. The method iterates through each document in the `Globals`
`.ThisAddIn.Application.Documents` collection and determines if the document is monitored,
unmonitored, or monitored but has had a name change since the last refresh.

Finding monitored documents simply involves checking the document name against the document
names in the `documentEditTimes` collection of keys:

```
// Ensure all docs are monitored
foreach (Word.Document doc in Globals.ThisAddIn.Application.Documents)
{
    bool isMonitored = false;
    bool requiresNameChange = false;
    DocumentTimer oldNameTimer = null;
    string oldName = null;
    foreach (string documentName in documentEditTimes.Keys)
    {
        if (doc.Name == documentName)
        {
            isMonitored = true;
            break;
        }
```

If the names don't match, then the document references are compared, which enables you to detect name
changes to documents, as shown in the following code:

```
        else
        {
            if (documentEditTimes[documentName].Document == doc)
            {
                // Monitored, but name changed!
                oldName = documentName;
                oldNameTimer = documentEditTimes[documentName];
                isMonitored = true;
                requiresNameChange = true;
                break;
            }
        }
    }
```

For unmonitored documents, a new monitor is created:

```
    // Add monitor if not monitored
    if (!isMonitored)
    {
        Globals.ThisAddIn.MonitorDocument(doc);
    }
```

Whereas documents with name changes are re-associated with the monitor used for the old named
document:

```
    // Rename if necessary
    if (requiresNameChange)
    {
        documentEditTimes.Remove(oldName);
        documentEditTimes.Add(doc.Name, oldNameTimer);
    }
}
```

After reconciling the document edit timers, a list is generated. This code also detects whether referenced documents are still loaded, and pauses the timer for documents that aren't by setting the IsActive property to false. Again, this is defensive programming.

```
// Create new list
foreach (string documentName in documentEditTimes.Keys)
{
    // Check to see if doc is still loaded
    bool isLoaded = false;
    foreach (Word.Document doc in
        Globals.ThisAddIn.Application.Documents)
    {
        if (doc.Name == documentName)
        {
            isLoaded = true;
            break;
        }
    }
    if (!isLoaded)
    {
        documentEditTimes[documentName].IsActive = false;
        documentEditTimes[documentName].Document = null;
    }
```

For each monitor, a list item is added to the list box that includes the document name and its total edit time:

```
    // Add item
    this.timerList.Items.Add(string.Format("{0}: {1}", documentName,
        documentEditTimes[documentName].EditTime +
        (documentEditTimes[documentName].IsActive ?
        (DateTime.Now - documentEditTimes[documentName].LastActive) :
        new TimeSpan(0))));
    }
  }
}
```

This completes the code in this example. This example has shown you how to use ribbon and task pane controls and how to maintain task panes in multiple Word documents. It has also illustrated many of the techniques covered earlier in the chapter.

VBA Interoperability

Because the Office system has existed for some years now, you may well be familiar with VBA code, and you may well have some in your existing applications. It is possible to rewrite VBA code in VSTO solutions, but this isn't always practical. However, having seen what is possible with VSTO you may want to replace existing VBA functionality, or add new functionality, with managed VSTO code.

VSTO makes it possible to expose VSTO functionality to VBA code to achieve just this. To do this, however, there are a few steps that you must perform to provide VBA code with a COM interface. These nine steps are shown here, along with example code and screenshots from the ExcelVBAInterop project in the downloadable code:

1. Before you start to expose VSTO code to VBA, you must have a document that includes a VBA project. For ease of development, it is also a good idea to have macros enabled in the document before you start. Then, when you create a document-level customization in VSTO, you use that document as the starting point for the document in your solution.

2. Once you have this starting point, you can proceed to write code that accesses the application and/or document in the usual way. This code needn't be accessible through the VSTO project, as you will provide a VBA interface later. Instead, create methods that you want VBA to be capable of calling. For example:

```
public partial class ThisWorkbook : ExcelVBAInterop.IThisWorkbook
{
    ...
    public void NameSheet()
    {
        NamingDialog dlg = new NamingDialog();
        if (dlg.ShowDialog() == DialogResult.OK)
        {
            ((Excel.Worksheet)this.ActiveSheet).Name = dlg.SheetName;
        }
    }
}
```

This code uses a simple custom dialog box that you will see shortly. This dialog box enables users to enter a string and select whether to include the current date in the sheet name.

3. You must override the `GetAutomationObject()` method to return the correct object for automation for VBA code as follows:

```
public partial class ThisWorkbook : ExcelVBAInterop.IThisWorkbook
{
    ...
    protected override object GetAutomationObject()
    {
        return this;
    }
}
```

4. Because the COM system works through interfaces, you must expose the method you want to call through an interface. The easiest way to do this is to right-click in your code and select Refactor ⇨ Extract Interface. You then select the method you want to be exposed on the interface, and the wizard (shown in Figure 40-16) does the rest.

Figure 40-16

5. You must also add attributes from the `System.Runtime.InteropServices` namespace to the class to expose the class to COM (see Chapter 24, "Interoperability"):

```
using System.Runtime.InteropServices;
namespace ExcelVBAInterop
{
    [ComVisible(true)]
    [ClassInterface(ClassInterfaceType.None)]
    public partial class ThisWorkbook : ExcelVBAInterop.IThisWorkbook
    {
        ...
    }
}
```

6. The generated interface also needs the `ComVisible` attribute, and the interface must be made public:

```
using System.Runtime.InteropServices;
namespace ExcelVBAInterop
{
    [ComVisible(true)]
    public interface IThisWorkbook
    {
        void NameSheet();
    }
}
```

7. You must change the `ReferenceAssemblyFromVbaProject` property of the document to `true`, as shown in Figure 40-17. If the document doesn't contain VBA code, then you will not be able to change this property. When you change it, you will receive a warning that any VBA code you add to the project when it is running will be lost, so you should keep a copy of any VB code you change.

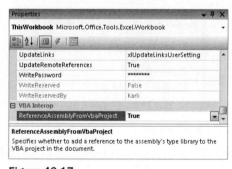

Figure 40-17

8. The remaining changes must be made to the VBA code in the document. You can run the project at this point, and when it is running you can access the VBA code through the Developer tab or by pressing Alt+F11. The first thing you need to add is a property that enables VBA to access your VSTO code, as follows (you reference the class that you have exposed by name, qualified by namespace):

```
Property Get VSTOAssembly() As ExcelVBAInterop.ThisWorkbook
    Set VSTOAssembly = GetManagedClass(Me)
End Property
```

9. You can then call the VSTO method through this property:

```
Public Sub RenameSheet()
    VSTOAssembly.NameSheet
End Sub
```

Once you have performed these steps, you can add code that calls the method on the interface, or just call it manually, as shown in Figure 40-18.

Figure 40-18

If your code includes a UI, as in this example, then it will display and be available to use. The UI in the sample project is shown in Figure 40-19.

Figure 40-19

In this way, you can make any VSTO code you want available to VBA code.

Summary

In this chapter you have learned how to use VSTO to create managed solutions for Office products.

In the first part of this chapter, you learned about the general structure of VSTO projects and the project types that you can create. You also saw the features that you can use to make VSTO programming easier.

In the next section, you looked, in great depth, at some of the features available in VSTO solutions and you saw how communication with the Office object model is achieved. You also looked at the namespaces and types available in VSTO and learned how to use those types to implement a variety of functionality. Then, you explored some of the code features of VSTO projects and how to use these features to get the effect you want.

After this, you moved on to the more practical side of things. You learned how add-ins are managed in Office applications and how to interact with the Office object model. You also saw how to customize the UI of your applications with ribbon menus, task panes, and action panes.

Next, you explored a sample application that illustrated the UI and interaction techniques that you learned earlier. The example contained a lot of code, but it included useful techniques, including how to manage task panes in multiple Word document windows.

Finally, you looked at interoperability with VBA code. You saw how to expose your managed code to VBA through COM interop, and you looked at another example to illustrate the techniques.

This is the last chapter in Part V, "Presentation." In the first chapter in Part VI, "Communication," you will learn how to access the Internet from your applications with classes in the `System.Net` namespace.

Part VI
Communication

41

Accessing the Internet

Chapters 37 through 39 discuss how you can use C# to write powerful, efficient, and dynamic Web pages using ASP.NET. For the most part, the clients accessing ASP.NET pages will be users running Internet Explorer or other Web browsers such as Opera or Firefox. However, you might want to add Web-browsing features to your own application, or you might need your applications to programmatically obtain information from a Web site. In this latter case, it is usually better for the site to implement a Web service. However, when you are accessing public Internet sites, you might not have any control over how the site is implemented.

This chapter covers facilities provided through the .NET base classes for using various network protocols, particularly HTTP and TCP, to access networks and the Internet as a client. In particular, this chapter covers:

❑   Downloading files from the World Wide Web

❑   Using the Web Browser control in a Windows Forms application

❑   Manipulating IP addresses and performing DNS lookups

❑   Socket programming with TCP, UDP, and socket classes

This chapter covers some of the lower-level means of getting at these protocols through the .NET Framework. You will also find other means of communicating via these items using technologies, such as the Windows Communication Foundation (WCF), which is covered in the next chapter.

The two namespaces of most interest for networking are `System.Net` and `System.Net.Sockets`. The `System.Net` namespace is generally concerned with higher-level operations, for example, downloading and uploading files, and making Web requests using HTTP and other protocols, whereas `System.Net.Sockets` contains classes to perform lower-level operations. You will find these classes useful when you want to work directly with sockets or protocols, such as TCP/IP. The methods in these classes closely mimic the Windows socket (Winsock) API functions derived from the Berkeley sockets interface. You will also find that some of the objects that this chapter works with are found in the `System.IO` namespace.

This chapter takes a fairly practical approach, mixing examples with a discussion of the relevant theory and networking concepts as appropriate. This chapter is not a guide to computer networking but an introduction to using the .NET Framework for network communication.

You will learn how to use the WebBrowser control in a Windows Forms environment. You will also learn how the WebBrowser control can make some specific Internet access tasks easier to accomplish.

However, the chapter starts with the simplest case, sending a request to a server and storing the information sent back in the response. (As with other chapters, you can download the sample code for this chapter from the Wrox Web site at www.wrox.com.)

The WebClient Class

If you only want to request a file from a particular URI, then you will find that the easiest .NET class to use is System.Net.WebClient. This is an extremely high-level class designed to perform basic operations with only one or two commands. The .NET Framework currently supports URIs beginning with the http:, https:, and file: identifiers.

> *It is worth noting that the term URL (Uniform Resource Locator) is no longer in use in new technical specifications, and URI (Uniform Resource Identifier) is now preferred. URI has roughly the same meaning as URL, but is a bit more general because URI does not imply you are using one of the familiar protocols, such as HTTP or FTP.*

Downloading Files

Two methods are available for downloading a file using WebClient. The method you choose depends on how you want to process the file's contents. If you simply want to save the file to disk, then you use the DownloadFile() method. This method takes two parameters: the URI of the file and a location (path and file name) to save the requested data:

```
WebClient Client = new WebClient();
Client.DownloadFile("http://www.reuters.com/", "ReutersHomepage.htm");
```

More commonly, your application will want to process the data retrieved from the Web site. To do this, you use the OpenRead() method, which returns a Stream reference that you can then use to retrieve the data into memory:

```
WebClient Client = new WebClient();
Stream strm = Client.OpenRead("http://www.reuters.com/");
```

Basic Web Client Example

The first example demonstrates the WebClient.OpenRead() method. You will display the contents of the downloaded page in a ListBox control. To begin, create a new project as a standard C# Windows Forms application and add a ListBox called listBox1 with the docking property set to DockStyle.Fill. At the beginning of the file, you will need to add the System.Net and System.IO namespaces references to your list of using directives. You then make the following changes to the constructor of the main form:

```
public Form1()
{
    InitializeComponent();
    WebClient Client = new WebClient();
    Stream strm = Client.OpenRead("http://www.reuters.com");
    StreamReader sr = new StreamReader(strm);
    string line;
    while ( (line=sr.ReadLine()) != null )
```

```
    {
        listBox1.Items.Add(line);
    }

    strm.Close();
}
```

In this example, you connect a `StreamReader` class from the `System.IO` namespace to the network stream. This allows you to obtain data from the stream as text through the use of higher-level methods, such as `ReadLine()`. This is an excellent example of the point made in Chapter 25, "Manipulating Files and the Registry," about the benefits of abstracting data movement into the concept of a stream.

Figure 41-1 shows the results of running this sample code.

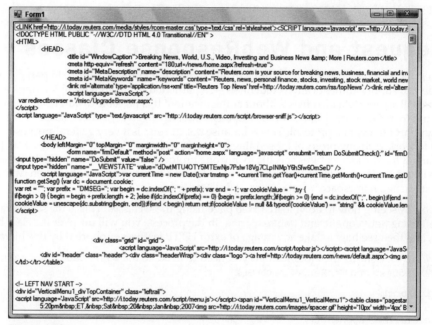

Figure 41-1

The `WebClient` class also has an `OpenWrite()` method. This method returns a writable stream for you to send data to a URI. You can also specify the method used to send the data to the host; the default method is `POST`. The following code snippet assumes a writable directory named `accept` on the local machine. The code will create a file in the directory with the name `newfile.txt` and the contents `Hello World`:

```
WebClient webClient = new WebClient();
Stream stream = webClient.OpenWrite("http://localhost/accept/newfile.txt", "PUT");
StreamWriter streamWriter = new StreamWriter(stream);
streamWriter.WriteLine("Hello World");
streamWriter.Close();
```

Uploading Files

The `WebClient` class also features `UploadFile()` and `UploadData()` methods. You use these methods when you need to post an HTML form or to upload an entire file. `UploadFile()` uploads a file to a specified location given the local file name, whereas `UploadData()` uploads binary data supplied as an array of bytes to the specified URI (there is also a `DownloadData()` method for retrieving an array of bytes from a URI):

```
WebClient client = new WebClient();
client.UploadFile("http://www.ourwebsite.com/NewFile.htm",
                  "C:\\WebSiteFiles\\NewFile.htm");
byte[] image;
// code to initialize image so it contains all the binary data for
// some jpg file
client.UploadData("http://www.ourwebsite.com/NewFile.jpg", image);
```

WebRequest and WebResponse Classes

Although the `WebClient` class is very simple to use, it has very limited features. In particular, you cannot use it to supply authentication credentials — a particular problem with uploading data is that not many sites will accept uploaded files without authentication! It is possible to add header information to requests and to examine any headers in the response, but only in a very generic sense — there is no specific support for any one protocol. This is because `WebClient` is a very general-purpose class designed to work with any protocol for sending a request and receiving a response (such as HTTP or FTP). It cannot handle any features specific to any one protocol, such as cookies, which are specific to HTTP. To take advantage of these features, you need to use a family of classes based on two other classes in the `System.Net` namespace: `WebRequest` and `WebResponse`.

You start off by seeing how to download a Web page using these classes. This is the same example as before, but using `WebRequest` and `WebResponse`. In the process, you will uncover the class hierarchy involved, and then see how to take advantage of extra HTTP features supported by this hierarchy.

The following code shows the modifications you need to make to the `BasicWebClient` sample to use the `WebRequest` and `WebResponse` classes:

```
public Form1()
{
    InitializeComponent();

    WebRequest wrq = WebRequest.Create("http://www.reuters.com");
    WebResponse wrs = wrq.GetResponse();
    Stream strm = wrs.GetResponseStream();
    StreamReader sr = new StreamReader(strm);
    string line;
    while ( (line = sr.ReadLine()) != null)
    {
        listBox1.Items.Add(line);
    }
    strm.Close();
}
```

In the code example, you start by instantiating an object representing a Web request. You don't do this using a constructor, but instead call the static method `WebRequest.Create()`. As you will learn in more detail later in this chapter, the `WebRequest` class is part of a hierarchy of classes supporting different network protocols. In order to receive a reference to the correct object for the request type, a factory mechanism is in place. The WebRequest.Create() method will create the appropriate object for the given protocol.

The WebRequest class represents the request for information to send to a particular URI. The URI is passed as a parameter to the Create() method. A WebResponse represents the data you retrieve from the server. By calling the WebRequest.GetResponse() method, you actually send the request to the Web server and create a WebResponse object to examine the return data. As with the WebClient object, you can obtain a stream to represent the data, but in this case you use the WebResponse .GetResponseStream() method.

Other WebRequest and WebResponse Features

This section briefly discusses a few of the other areas supported by WebRequest, WebResponse, and other related classes.

HTTP Header Information

An important part of the HTTP protocol is the ability to send extensive header information with both request and response streams. This information can include cookies and the details of the particular browser sending the request (the user agent). As you would expect, the .NET Framework provides full support for accessing the most significant data. The WebRequest and WebResponse classes provide some support for reading the header information. However, two derived classes provide additional HTTP-specific information: HttpWebRequest and HttpWebResponse. As you will see in more detail later, creating a WebRequest with an HTTP URI results in an HttpWebRequest object instance. Because HttpWebRequest is derived from WebRequest, you can use the new instance whenever a WebRequest is required. In addition, you can cast the instance to an HttpWebRequest reference and access properties specific to the HTTP protocol. Likewise, the GetResponse() method call will actually return an HttpWebResponse instance as a WebResponse reference when dealing with HTTP. Again, you can perform a simple cast to access the HTTP-specific features.

You can examine a few of the header properties by adding the following code before the GetResponse() method call:

```
WebRequest wrq = WebRequest.Create("http://www.reuters.com");
HttpWebRequest hwrq = (HttpWebRequest)wrq;
listBox1.Items.Add("Request Timeout (ms) = " + wrq.Timeout);
listBox1.Items.Add("Request Keep Alive = " + hwrq.KeepAlive);
listBox1.Items.Add("Request AllowAutoRedirect = " + hwrq.AllowAutoRedirect);
```

The Timeout property is specified in milliseconds, and the default value is 100,000. You can set the Timeout property to control how long the WebRequest object will wait for the response before throwing a WebException. You can check the WebException.Status property to view the reason for an exception. This enumeration includes status codes for timeouts, connection failures, protocol errors, and more.

The KeepAlive property is a specific extension to the HTTP protocol, so you access this property through an HttpWebRequest reference. KeepAlive allows multiple requests to use the same connection, saving time in closing and reopening connections on subsequent requests. The default value for this property is true.

The AllowAutoRedirect property is also specific to the HttpWebRequest class. Use this property to control whether the Web request should automatically follow redirection responses from the Web server. Again, the default value is true. If you want to allow only a limited number of redirections, then set the MaximumAutomaticRedirections property of the HttpWebRequest to the desired number.

Although the request and response classes expose most of the important headers as properties, you can also use the Headers property itself to view the entire collection of headers. Add the following code after the GetResponse() method call to place all of the headers in the ListBox control:

```
WebRequest wrq = WebRequest.Create("http://www.reuters.com");
WebResponse wrs = wrq.GetResponse();
WebHeaderCollection whc = wrs.Headers;
for(int i = 0; i < whc.Count; i++)
{
    listBox1.Items.Add(string.Format("Header {0} : {1}",
        whc.GetKey(i), whc[i]));
}
```

This example code produces the list of headers shown in Figure 41-2.

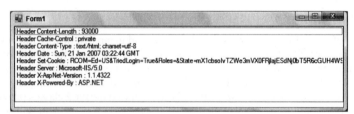

Figure 41-2

Authentication

Another property in the WebRequest class is the Credentials property. If you need authentication credentials to accompany your request, then you can create an instance of the NetworkCredential class (also from the System.Net namespace) with a username and password. You can place the following code *before* the call to GetResponse().

```
NetworkCredential myCred = new NetworkCredential("myusername", "mypassword");
wrq.Credentials = myCred;
```

Working with Proxies

You will find in enterprises that many firms must deal with a proxy server to make any type of HTTP or FTP request. Many times, the proxy server, which routes all of the organization's requests and responses, uses some form of security (usually a username and a password). For your applications that use the WebClient or the WebRequest objects, you might need to take these proxy servers into account. As with the preceding NetworkCredential object, you are going to want to use the WebProxy object *before* you make a call to make the actual request.

```
WebProxy wp = new WebProxy("192.168.1.100", true);
wp.Credentials = new NetworkCredential("user1", "user1Password");
WebRequest wrq = WebRequest.Create("http://www.reuters.com");
wrq.Proxy = wp;
WebResponse wrs = wrq.GetResponse();
```

If you also require a designation of the user's domain in addition to its credentials, then you would use a different signature on the NetworkCredential instantiation:

```
WebProxy wp = new WebProxy("192.168.1.100", true);
wp.Credentials = new NetworkCredential("user1", "user1Password", "myDomain");
WebRequest wrq = WebRequest.Create("http://www.reuters.com");
wrq.Proxy = wp;
WebResponse wrs = wrq.GetResponse();
```

Asynchronous Page Requests

An additional feature of the `WebRequest` class is the ability to request pages asynchronously. This feature is significant because there can be quite a long delay between sending a request to a host and receiving the response. Methods such as `WebClient.DownloadData()` and `WebRequest.GetResponse()` will not return until the response from the server is complete. You might not want your application frozen due to a long period of inactivity, and in such scenarios it is better to use the `BeginGetResponse()` and `EndGetResponse()` methods. `BeginGetResponse()` works asynchronously and returns almost immediately. Under the covers, the runtime will asynchronously manage a background thread to retrieve the response from the server. Instead of returning a `WebResponse` object, `BeginGetResponse()` returns an object implementing the `IAsyncResult` interface. With this interface, you can poll or wait for the response to become available and then invoke `EndGetResponse()` to gather the results.

You can also pass a callback delegate into the `BeginGetResponse()` method. The target of a callback delegate is a method returning `void` and accepting an `IAsyncResult` reference as a parameter. When the worker thread is finished gathering the response, the runtime invokes the callback delegate to inform you of the completed work. As shown in the following code, calling `EndGetResponse()` in the callback method allows you to retrieve the `WebResponse` object:

```
public Form1()
{
    InitializeComponent();
    WebRequest wrq = WebRequest.Create("http://www.reuters.com");
    wrq.BeginGetResponse(new AsyncCallback(OnResponse), wrq);
}
protected static void OnResponse(IAsyncResult ar)
{
    WebRequest wrq = (WebRequest)ar.AsyncState;
    WebResponse wrs = wrq.EndGetResponse(ar);
    // read the response ...
}
```

Notice that you can retrieve the original `WebRequest` object by passing the object as the second parameter to `BeginGetResponse()`. The third parameter is an object reference known as the state parameter. During the callback method, you can retrieve the same state object using the `AsyncState` property of `IAsyncResult`.

Displaying Output as an HTML Page

The examples show how the .NET base classes make it very easy to download and process data from the Internet. However, so far, you have displayed files only as plain text. Quite often, you will want to view an HTML file in an Internet Explorer–style interface in which the rendered HTML allows you to see what the Web document actually looks like. Unfortunately, there is no .NET version of Microsoft's Internet Explorer, but that does not mean that you cannot easily accomplish this task. Before the release of the .NET Framework 2.0, you could make reference to a COM object that was an encapsulation of Internet Explorer and use the .NET-interop capabilities to have aspects of your application work as a browser. Now, in the .NET Framework 2.0, as well as the .NET Framework 3.5, you can use the built-in `WebBrowser` control available for your Windows Forms applications.

The WebBrowser control encapsulates the COM object even further for you making tasks that were once more complicated even easier. In addition to the WebBrowser control, another option is to use the programmatic ability to call up Internet Explorer instances from your code.

When not using the new WebBrowser control, you can programmatically start an Internet Explorer process and navigate to a Web page using the Process class in the System.Diagnostics namespace:

```
Process myProcess = new Process();
myProcess.StartInfo.FileName = "iexplore.exe";
myProcess.StartInfo.Arguments = "http://www.wrox.com";
myProcess.Start();
```

However, the preceding code launches Internet Explorer as a separate window. Your application has no connection to the new window and therefore cannot control the browser.

Using the new WebBrowser control, however, allows you to display and control the browser as an integrated part of your application. The new WebBrowser control is quite sophisticated, featuring a large number of methods, properties, and events.

Allowing Simple Web Browsing from Your Applications

For the sake of simplicity, start by creating a Windows Form application that simply has a TextBox control and a WebBrowser control. You will build the application so that the end user will simply enter a URL into the text box and press Enter, and the WebBrowser control will do all the work of fetching the Web page and displaying the resulting document.

In Visual Studio 2008 Designer, your application should look as shown in Figure 41-3.

With this application, when the end user types a URL and presses Enter, this key press will register with the application. Then the WebBrowser control will go off to retrieve the requested page, subsequently displaying it in the control itself.

Figure 41-3

The code behind this application is illustrated here:

```
using System;
using System.Windows.Forms;
namespace CSharpInternet
{
    partial class Form1 : Form
    {
        public Form1()
        {
            InitializeComponent();
        }
        private void textBox1_KeyPress(object sender, KeyPressEventArgs e)
        {
            if (e.KeyChar == (char)13)
            {
                webBrowser1.Navigate(textBox1.Text);
            }
        }
    }
}
```

From this example, you can see that each key press that the end user makes in the text box is captured by the textBox1_KeyPress event. If the character input is a carriage return (a press of the Enter key, which is (char)13), then you take action with the WebBrowser control. Using the WebBrowser control's Navigate method, you specify the URL (as a string) using the textBox1.Text property. The end result is shown in Figure 41-4.

Figure 41-4

Launching Internet Explorer Instances

It might be that you are not interested in hosting a browser inside of your application, as shown in the previous section, but instead are only interested in allowing the user to find your Web site in a typical browser (for example, by clicking a link inside of your application). For an example of this task, create a Windows Form application that has a `LinkLabel` control on it. For instance, you can have a form that has a `LinkLabel` control on it that states "Visit our company Web site!"

Once you have this control in place, use the following code to launch your company's Web site in an independent browser as opposed to directly being in the form of your application:

```
private void linkLabel1_LinkClicked(object sender, LinkLabelLinkClickedEventArgs e)
{
    WebBrowser wb = new WebBrowser();
    wb.Navigate("http://www.wrox.com", true);
}
```

In this example, when the `LinkLabel` control is clicked by the user, a new instance of the `WebBrowser` class is created. Then, using the `WebBrowser` class's `Navigate()` method, the code specifies the location of the Web page as well as a Boolean value that specifies whether this endpoint should be opened within the Windows Form application (a `false` value) or from within an independent browser (using a `true` value). By default, this is set to `false`. With the preceding construct, when the end user clicks the link found in the Windows application, a browser instance will be instantiated, and the Wrox Web site at www.wrox.com will be immediately launched.

Giving Your Application More IE-Type Features

In the previous example, in which you used the `WebBrowser` control directly in the Windows Form application, you will notice that when you clicked on the links contained in the page, the text within the `TextBox` control was not updated to show the URL of the exact location where you were in the browsing process. You can fix this by listening for events coming from the `WebBrowser` control and adding handlers to the control.

Updating the form's title with the title of the HTML page is easy. You just need to use the `Navigated` event and update the `Text` property of the form:

```
private void webBrowser1_Navigated(object sender, EventArgs e)
{
    this.Text = webBrowser1.DocumentTitle.ToString();
}
```

In this case, when the `WebBrowser` control moves onto another page, the `Navigated` event will fire, and this will cause the form's title to change to the title of the page being viewed. In some instances when working with pages on the Web, even though you have typed in a specific address, you are going to be redirected to another page altogether. You are most likely going to want to reflect this in the textbox (address bar) of the form; to do this, you change the form's text box based on the complete URL of the page being viewed. To accomplish this task, you can use the `WebBrowser` control's `Navigated` event as well:

```
private void webBrowser1_Navigated(object sender, WebBrowserNavigatedEventArgs e)
{
    textBox1.Text = webBrowser1.Url.ToString();
    this.Text = webBrowser1.DocumentTitle.ToString();
}
```

In this case, when the requested page has finished downloading in the `WebBrowser` control, the `Navigated` event is fired. In your case, you simply update the `Text` value of the `textBox1` control to the

URL of the page. This means that once a page is loaded in the `WebBrowser` control's HTML container, and if the URL changes in this process (for instance, if there is a redirect), then the new URL will be shown in the text box. If you employ these steps and navigate to the Wrox Web site (www.wrox.com), then you will notice that the page's URL will immediately change to www.wrox.com/WileyCDA/. This process also means that if the end user clicks one of the links contained within the HTML view, then the URL of the newly requested page will also be shown in the text box.

Now if you run the application with the preceding changes in place, you will find that the form's title and address bar work as they do in Microsoft's Internet Explorer, as demonstrated in Figure 41-5.

Figure 41-5

The next step is to create an IE-like toolbar that will allow the end user to control the `WebBrowser` control a little better. This means that you will incorporate buttons such as Back, Forward, Stop, Refresh, and Home.

Rather than using the `ToolBar` control, you will just add a set of `Button` controls at the top of the form where you currently have the address bar. Add five buttons to the top of the control, as illustrated in Figure 41-6.

In this example, the text on the button face is changed to indicate the function of the button. Of course, you can even go as far as to use a screen capture utility to "borrow" button images from IE and use those. The buttons should be named `buttonBack`, `buttonForward`, `buttonStop`, `buttonRefresh`, and `buttonHome`. To get the resizing to work properly, make sure that you set the `Anchor` property of the three buttons on the right to `Top, Right`.

On startup, `buttonBack`, `buttonForward`, and `buttonStop` should be disabled because there is no point to the buttons if there is no initial page loaded in the `WebBrowser` control. You will later tell the application when to enable and disable the Back and Forward buttons yourself, depending on where the user is in the page stack. In addition, when a page is being loaded, you will need to enable the Stop button — but also, you will need to disable the Stop button once the page has finished being loaded. You will also have a Submit button on the page that will allow for the submission of the URL being requested.

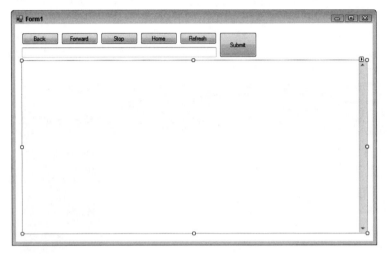

Figure 41-6

First, however, you will add the functionality behind the buttons. The WebBrowser class itself has all of the methods that you need, so this is all very straightforward:

```
using System;
using System.Windows.Forms;
namespace CSharpInternet
{
    partial class Form1 : Form
    {
        public Form1()
        {
            InitializeComponent();
        }
        private void textBox1_KeyPress(object sender, KeyPressEventArgs e)
        {
            if (e.KeyChar == (char)13)
            {
                webBrowser1.Navigate(textBox1.Text);
            }
        }
        private void webBrowser1_Navigated(object sender,
            WebBrowserNavigatedEventArgs e)
        {
            textBox1.Text = webBrowser1.Url.ToString();
            this.Text = webBrowser1.DocumentTitle.ToString();
        }
```

```
private void Form1_Load(object sender, EventArgs e)
{
    buttonBack.Enabled = false;
    buttonForward.Enabled = false;
    buttonStop.Enabled = false;
}
private void buttonBack_Click(object sender, EventArgs e)
{
    webBrowser1.GoBack();
    textBox1.Text = webBrowser1.Url.ToString();
}
private void buttonForward_Click(object sender, EventArgs e)
{
    webBrowser1.GoForward();
    textBox1.Text = webBrowser1.Url.ToString();
}
private void buttonStop_Click(object sender, EventArgs e)
{
    webBrowser1.Stop();
}
private void buttonHome_Click(object sender, EventArgs e)
{
    webBrowser1.GoHome();
    textBox1.Text = webBrowser1.Url.ToString();
}
private void buttonRefresh_Click(object sender, EventArgs e)
{
    webBrowser1.Refresh();
}
private void buttonSubmit_Click(object sender, EventArgs e)
{
    webBrowser1.Navigate(textBox1.Text);
}
private void webBrowser1_Navigating(object sender,
    WebBrowserNavigatingEventArgs e)
{
    buttonStop.Enabled = true;
}
private void webBrowser1_DocumentCompleted(object sender,
    WebBrowserDocumentCompletedEventArgs e)
{
    buttonStop.Enabled = false;
    if (webBrowser1.CanGoBack)
    {
        buttonBack.Enabled = true;
    }
    else
    {
        buttonBack.Enabled = false;
    }
    if (webBrowser1.CanGoForward)
    {
        buttonForward.Enabled = true;
    }
```

(continued)

(continued)

```
            else
            {
                buttonForward.Enabled = false;
            }
        }
    }
}
```

Many different activities are going on in this example because there are so many options for the end user when using this application. For each of the button-click events, there is a specific WebBrowser class method assigned as the action to initiate. For instance, for the Back button on the form, you simply use the WebBrowser control's GoBack() method; for the Forward button you have the GoForward() method; and for the others, you have methods such as Stop(), Refresh(), and GoHome(). This makes it fairly simple and straightforward to create a toolbar that will give you action similar to that of Microsoft's Internet Explorer.

When the form is first loaded, the Form1_Load event disables the appropriate buttons. From there, the end user can enter a URL into the text box and click the Submit button to have the application retrieve the desired page.

To manage the enabling and disabling of the buttons, you must key into a couple of events. As mentioned before, whenever downloading begins, you need to enable the Stop button. For this, you simply added an event handler for the Navigating event to enable the Stop button:

```
private void webBrowser1_Navigating(object sender,
    WebBrowserNavigatingEventArgs e)
{
    buttonStop.Enabled = true;
}
```

Then, the Stop button is again disabled when the document has finished loading:

```
private void webBrowser1_DocumentCompleted(object sender,
    WebBrowserDocumentCompletedEventArgs e)
{
    buttonStop.Enabled = false;
}
```

Enabling and disabling the appropriate Back and Forward buttons really depends on the ability to go backward or forward in the page stack. This is achieved by using both the CanGoForwardChanged() and the CanGoBackChanged() events:

```
private void webBrowser1_CanGoBackChanged(object sender, EventArgs e)
{
    if (webBrowser1.CanGoBack == true)
    {
        buttonBack.Enabled = true;
    }
    else
    {
        buttonBack.Enabled = false;
    }
}
private void webBrowser1_CanGoForwardChanged(object sender, EventArgs e)
{
    if (webBrowser1.CanGoForward == true)
```

```
    {
        buttonForward.Enabled = true;
    }
    else
    {
        buttonForward.Enabled = false;
    }
}
```

Run the project now, visit a Web page, and click through a few links. You should also be able to use the toolbar to enhance your browsing experience. The end product is shown in Figure 41-7.

Figure 41-7

Printing Using the WebBrowser Control

Not only can users use the WebBrowser control to view pages and documents, but they can also use the control to send these pages and documents to the printer for printing. To print the page or document being viewed in the control, simply use the following construct:

```
webBrowser1.Print();
```

As before, you do not need to view the page or document to print it. For instance, you can use the WebBrowser class to load an HTML document and print it without even displaying the loaded document. This can be accomplished as shown here:

```
WebBrowser wb = new WebBrowser();
wb.Navigate("http://www.wrox.com");
wb.Print();
```

Displaying the Code of a Requested Page

In the beginning of this chapter, you used the `WebRequest` and the `Stream` classes to get at a remote page to display the code of the requested page. You used this code to accomplish this task:

```
public Form1()
{
    InitializeComponent();
    System.Net.WebClient Client = new WebClient();
    Stream strm = Client.OpenRead("http://www.reuters.com");
    StreamReader sr = new StreamReader(strm);
    string line;
    while ( (line=sr.ReadLine()) != null )
    {
        listBox1.Items.Add(line);
    }

    strm.Close();
}
```

Now, however, with the introduction of the `WebBrowser` control, it is quite easy to accomplish the same results. To accomplish this, change the browser application that you have been working on thus far in this chapter. To make this change, simply add a single line to the `Document_Completed` event, as illustrated here:

```
private void webBrowser1_DocumentCompleted(object sender,
    WebBrowserDocumentCompletedEventArgs e)
{
    buttonStop.Enabled = false;
    textBox2.Text = webBrowser1.DocumentText.ToString();
}
```

In the application itself, add another `TextBox` control below the `WebBrowser` control. The idea is that when the end user requests a page, you display not only the visual aspect of the page but also the code for the page, in the `TextBox` control. The code of the page is displayed simply by using the `DocumentText` property of the `WebBrowser` control, which will give you the entire page's content as a `String`. The other option is to get the contents of the page as a `Stream` using the `DocumentStream` property. The end result of adding the second `TextBox` to display the contents of the page as a `String` is shown in Figure 41-8.

The Web Request and Web Response Hierarchy

In this section, you will take a closer look at the underlying architecture of the `WebRequest` and `WebResponse` classes.

Figure 41-9 illustrates the inheritance hierarchy of the classes involved.

The hierarchy contains more than just the two classes you have used in your code. You should also know that the `WebRequest` and `WebResponse` classes are both abstract and cannot be instantiated. These base classes provide general functionality for dealing with Web requests and responses independent of the protocol used for a given operation. Requests are made using a particular protocol (HTTP, FTP, SMTP, and so on), and a derived class written for the given protocol will handle the request. Microsoft refers to this scheme as *pluggable protocols*. Remember in the code you examined earlier, your variables are defined as references to the base classes. However, `WebRequest.Create()` actually gives you an `HttpWebRequest` object, and the `GetResponse()` method actually returns an `HttpWebResponse` object. This factory-based mechanism hides many of the details from the client code, allowing support for a wide variety of protocols from the same code base.

1438

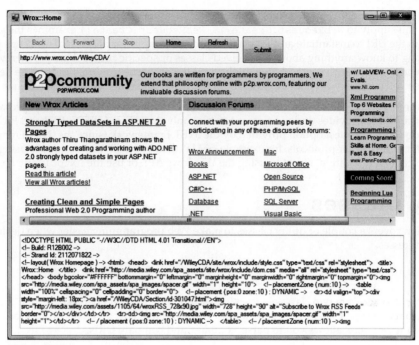

Figure 41-8

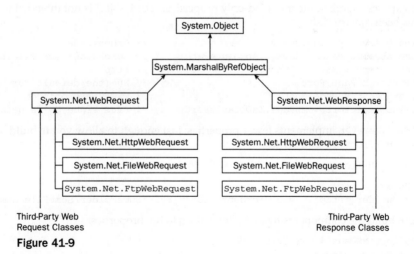

Third-Party Web
Request Classes

Third-Party Web
Response Classes

Figure 41-9

The fact that you need an object specifically capable of dealing with the HTTP protocol is clear from the URI that you supply to `WebRequest.Create()`. `WebRequest.Create()` examines the protocol specifier in the URI to instantiate and return an object of the appropriate class. This keeps your code free from having to know anything about the derived classes or specific protocol used. When you need to access specific features of a protocol, you might need the properties and methods of the derived class, in which case you can cast your `WebRequest` or `WebResponse` reference to the derived class.

With this architecture, you should be able to send requests using any of the common protocols. However, Microsoft currently provides derived classes to cover only the HTTP, HTTPS, FTP, and FILE protocols. The FTP option is the latest option provided by the .NET Framework (since the .NET Framework 2.0). If you want to utilize other protocols, for example, SMTP, then you will need to turn to using the Windows Communication Foundation, revert to using the Windows API, or use the `SmtpClient` object.

Utility Classes

This section covers a couple of utility classes to make Web programming easier when dealing with URIs and IP addresses.

URIs

`Uri` and `UriBuilder` are two classes in the `System` (not `System.Net`) namespace, and they are both intended to represent a URI. `UriBuilder` allows you to build a URI given the strings for the component parts, and the `Uri` class allows you to parse, combine, and compare URIs.

For the `Uri` class, the constructor requires a completed URI string:

```
Uri MSPage = new

Uri("http://www.Microsoft.com/SomeFolder/SomeFile.htm?Order=true");
```

The class exposes a large number of read-only properties. A `Uri` object is not intended to be modified once it has been constructed:

```
string Query = MSPage.Query;                    // Order=true;
string AbsolutePath = MSPage.AbsolutePath;      // SomeFolder/SomeFile.htm
string Scheme = MSPage.Scheme;                  // http
int Port = MSPage.Port;                         // 80 (the default for http)
string Host = MSPage.Host;                      // www.Microsoft.com
bool IsDefaultPort = MSPage.IsDefaultPort;      // true since 80 is default
```

`URIBuilder`, however, implements fewer properties, just enough to allow you to build up a complete URI. These properties are read-write.

You can supply the components to build up a URI to the constructor:

```
Uri MSPage = new
    UriBuilder("http", "www.Microsoft.com", 80, "SomeFolder/SomeFile.htm");
```

Or, you can build the components by assigning values to the properties:

```
UriBuilder MSPage = new UriBuilder();
MSPage.Scheme ="http";
MSPage.Host = "www.Microsoft.com";
MSPage.Port = 80;
MSPage.Path = "SomeFolder/SomeFile.htm";
```

Once you have completed initializing the `UriBuilder`, you can obtain the corresponding `Uri` object with the `Uri` property:

```
Uri CompletedUri = MSPage.Uri;
```

IP Addresses and DNS Names

On the Internet, you identify servers as well as clients by IP address or host name (also referred to as a DNS name). Generally speaking, the host name is the human-friendly name that you type in a Web browser window, such as `www.wrox.com` or `www.microsoft.com`. An IP address is the identifier computers use to identify each other. IP addresses are the identifiers used to ensure that Web requests and responses reach the appropriate machines. It is even possible for a computer to have more than one IP address.

Today, IP addresses are typically a 32-bit value. An example of a 32-bit IP address is 192.168.1.100. This format of IP address is referred to as Internet Protocol version 4. Because there are now so many computers and other devices vying for a spot on the Internet, a newer type of address was developed — Internet Protocol version 6. IPv6 provides a 64-bit IP address. IPv6 can potentially provide a maximum number of about 3×10^{28} unique addresses. You will find that the .NET Framework allows your applications to work with both IPv4 and IPv6.

For host names to work, you must first send a network request to translate the host name into an IP address, a task carried out by one or more DNS servers.

A DNS server stores a table mapping host names to IP addresses for all the computers it knows about, as well as the IP addresses of other DNS servers to look up the host names it does not know about. Your local computer should always know about at least one DNS server. Network administrators configure this information when a computer is set up.

Before sending out a request, your computer will first ask the DNS server to tell it the IP address corresponding to the host name you have typed in. Once armed with the correct IP address, the computer can address the request and send it over the network. All of this work normally happens behind the scenes while the user is browsing the Web.

.NET Classes for IP Addresses

The .NET Framework supplies a number of classes that are able to assist with the process of looking up IP addresses and finding information about host computers.

IPAddress

`IPAddress` represents an IP address. The address itself is available as the `GetAddressBytes` property and may be converted to a dotted decimal format with the `ToString()` method. `IPAddress` also implements a static `Parse()` method, which effectively performs the reverse conversion of `ToString()` — converting from a dotted decimal string to an `IPAddress`:

```
IPAddress ipAddress = IPAddress.Parse("234.56.78.9");
byte[] address = ipAddress.GetAddressBytes();
string ipString = ipAddress.ToString();
```

In this example, the `byte` integer `address` is assigned a binary representation of the IP address, and the string `ipString` is assigned the text `"234.56.78.9"`.

IPAddress also provides a number of constant static fields to return special addresses. For example, the Loopback address allows a machine to send messages to itself, whereas the Broadcast address allows multicasting to the local network:

```
// The following line will set loopback to "127.0.0.1".
// the loopback address indicates the local host.
string loopback = IPAddress.Loopback.ToString();
// The following line will set broadcast address to "255.255.255.255".
// the broadcast address is used to send a message to all machines on
// the local network.
string broadcast = IPAddress.Broadcast.ToString();
```

IPHostEntry

The IPHostEntry class encapsulates information relating to a particular host computer. This class makes the host name available via the HostName property (which returns a string), and the AddressList property returns an array of IPAddress objects. You are going to use the IPHostEntry class in the next example: DNSLookupResolver.

Dns

The Dns class is able to communicate with your default DNS server to retrieve IP addresses. The two important (static) methods are Resolve(), which uses the DNS server to obtain the details of a host with a given host name, and GetHostByAddress(), which also returns details of the host but this time using the IP address. Both methods return an IPHostEntry object:

```
IPHostEntry wroxHost = Dns.Resolve("www.wrox.com");
IPHostEntry wroxHostCopy = Dns.GetHostByAddress("208.215.179.178");
```

In this code, both IPHostEntry objects will contain details of the Wrox.com servers.

The Dns class differs from the IPAddress and IPHostEntry classes because it has the ability to actually communicate with servers to obtain information. In contrast, IPAddress and IPHostEntry are more along the lines of simple data structures with convenient properties to allow access to the underlying data.

The DnsLookup Example

The DNS and IP-related classes are illustrated with an example that looks up DNS names: DnsLookup (see Figure 41-10).

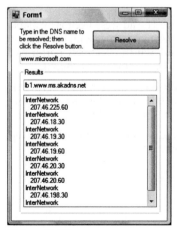

Figure 41-10

This sample application simply invites the user to type in a DNS name using the main text box. When the user clicks the Resolve button, the sample uses the `Dns.Resolve()` method to retrieve an `IPHostEntry` reference and display the host name and IP addresses. Note how the host name displayed may be different from the name typed in. This can occur if one DNS name (`www.microsoft.com`) simply acts as a proxy for another DNS name (`lb1.www.ms.akadns.net`).

The `DnsLookup` application is a standard C# Windows application. The controls are added as shown in Figure 41-10, giving them the names `txtBoxInput`, `btnResolve`, `txtBoxHostName`, and `listBoxIPs`, respectively. Then, you simply add the following method to the `Form1` class as the event handler for the `buttonResolve Click` event:

```csharp
void btnResolve_Click (object sender, EventArgs e)
{
    try
    {
        IPHostEntry iphost = Dns.GetHostEntry(txtBoxInput.Text);
        foreach (IPAddress ip in iphost.AddressList)
        {
            string ipaddress = ip.AddressFamily.ToString();
            listBoxIPs.Items.Add(ipaddress);
            listBoxIPs.Items.Add("   " + ip.ToString());
        }
        txtBoxHostName.Text = iphost.HostName;
    }
    catch(Exception ex)
    {
        MessageBox.Show("Unable to process the request because " +
            "the following problem occurred:\n" +
            ex.Message, "Exception occurred");
    }
}
```

Notice that in this code you are careful to trap any exceptions. An exception might occur if the user types an invalid DNS name or if the network is down.

After retrieving the `IPHostEntry` instance, you use the `AddressList` property to obtain an array containing the IP addresses, which you then iterate through with a `foreach` loop. For each entry, you display the IP address as an integer and as a string, using the `IPAddress.AddressFamily.ToString()` method.

Lower-Level Protocols

This section briefly discusses some of the .NET classes used to communicate at a lower level.

Network communications work on several different levels. The classes you have seen in this chapter so far work at the highest level: the level at which specific commands are processed. It is probably easiest to understand this concept if you think of file transfer using FTP. Although today's GUI applications hide many of the FTP details, it was not so long ago when you executed FTP from a command-line prompt. In this environment, you explicitly typed commands to send to the server for downloading, uploading, and listing files.

FTP is not the only high-level protocol relying on textual commands. HTTP, SMTP, POP, and other protocols are based on a similar type of behavior. Again, many of the modern graphical tools hide the transmission of commands from the user, so you are generally not aware of them. For example, when you type a URL into a Web browser, and the Web request goes off to a server, the browser is actually sending a (plain-text) GET command to the server, which fulfills a similar purpose as the FTP get command. It can also send a POST command, which indicates that the browser has attached other data to the request.

These protocols, however, are not sufficient by themselves to achieve communication between computers. Even if both the client and the server understand, for example, the HTTP protocol, it will still not be possible for them to understand each other unless there is also agreement on exactly how to transmit the characters: What binary format will be used? Moreover, getting down to the lowest level, what voltages will be used to represent 0s and 1s in the binary data? Because there are so many items to configure and agree upon, developers and hardware engineers in the networking field often refer to a *protocol stack*. When you list all of the various protocols and mechanisms required for communication between two hosts, you create a protocol stack with high-level protocols on the top and low-level protocols on the bottom. This approach results in a modular and layered approach to achieving efficient communication.

Luckily, for most development work, you do not need to go far down the stack or work with voltage levels. If you are writing code that requires efficient communication between computers, then it's not unusual to write code that works directly at the level of sending binary data packets between computers. This is the realm of protocols such as TCP, and Microsoft has supplied a number of classes that allow you to conveniently work with binary data at this level.

Lower-Level Classes

The System.Net.Sockets namespace contains the relevant classes. These classes, for example, allow you to directly send out TCP network requests or to listen to TCP network requests on a particular port. The following table explains the main classes.

Class	Purpose
Socket	Deals with managing connections. Classes such as WebRequest, TcpClient, and UdpClient use this class internally.
NetworkStream	Derived from Stream. Represents a stream of data from the network.
SmtpClient	Enables you to send messages (mail) through the Simple Mail Transfer Protocol.
TcpClient	Enables you to create and use TCP connections.
TcpListener	Enables you to listen for incoming TCP connection requests.
UdpClient	Enables you to create connections for UDP clients. (UDP is an alternative protocol to TCP but is much less widely used, mostly on local networks.)

Using SmtpClient

The SmtpClient object allows you to send mail messages through the Simple Mail Transfer Protocol. A simple sample of using the SmtpClient object is illustrated here:

```
SmtpClient sc = new SmtpClient("mail.mySmtpHost.com");
sc.Send("evjen@yahoo.com", "editor@wrox.com",
    "The latest chapter", "Here is the latest.");
```

In its simplest form, you work from an instance of the SmtpClient object. In this case, the instantiation also provided the host of the SMTP server that is used to send the mail messages over the Internet. You could have also achieved the same task by using the Host property.

```
SmtpClient sc = new SmtpClient();
sc.Host = "mail.mySmtpHost.com";
sc.Send("evjen@yahoo.com", "editor@wrox.com",
    "The latest chapter", "Here is the latest.");
```

Once you have the `SmtpClient` in place, it is simply a matter of calling the `Send()` method and providing the From address, the To address, and the Subject, followed by the Body of the mail message.

In many cases, you will have mail messages that are more complex than this. To work with this possibility, you can also pass in a `MailMessage` object into the `Send()` method.

```
SmtpClient sc = new SmtpClient();
sc.Host = "mail.mySmtpHost.com";
MailMessage mm = new MailMessage();
mm.Sender = new MailAddress("evjen@yahoo.com", "Bill Evjen");
mm.To.Add(new MailAddress("editor@wrox.com", "Katie Mohr"));
mm.To.Add(new MailAddress("marketing@wrox.com", "Wrox Marketing"));
mm.CC.Add(new MailAddress("publisher@wrox.com", "Joe Wikert"));
mm.Subject = "The latest chapter";
mm.Body = "<b>Here you can put a long message</b>";
mm.IsBodyHtml = true;
mm.Priority = MailPriority.High;
sc.Send(mm);
```

Using `MailMessage` allows you to really fine-tune how you build your mail messages. You are able to send HTML messages, add as many To and CC recipients as you wish, change the message priority, work with the message encodings, and add attachments. The ability to add attachments is defined here in the following code snippet.

```
SmtpClient sc = new SmtpClient();
sc.Host = "mail.mySmtpHost.com";
MailMessage mm = new MailMessage();
mm.Sender = new MailAddress("evjen@yahoo.com", "Bill Evjen");
mm.To.Add(new MailAddress("editor@wrox.com", "Katie Mohr"));
mm.To.Add(new MailAddress("marketing@wrox.com", "Wrox Marketing"));
mm.CC.Add(new MailAddress("publisher@wrox.com", "Joe Wikert"));
mm.Subject = "The latest chapter";
mm.Body = "<b>Here you can put a long message</b>";
mm.IsBodyHtml = true;
mm.Priority = MailPriority.High;
Attachment att = new Attachment("myExcelResults.zip",
    MediaTypeNames.Application.Zip);
mm.Attachments.Add(att);
sc.Send(mm);
```

In this case, an `Attachment` object is created and added, using the `Add()` method, to the `MailMessage` object before the `Send()` method is called.

Using the TCP Classes

The Transmission Control Protocol (TCP) classes offer simple methods for connecting and sending data between two endpoints. An endpoint is the combination of an IP address and a port number. Existing protocols have well-defined port numbers, for example, HTTP uses port 80, whereas SMTP uses port 25. The Internet Assigned Number Authority, IANA, (www.iana.org) assigns port numbers to these well-known services. Unless you are implementing a well-known service, you will want to select a port number above 1,024.

TCP traffic makes up the majority of traffic on the Internet today. TCP is often the protocol of choice because it offers guaranteed delivery, error correction, and buffering. The `TcpClient` class encapsulates a TCP connection and provides a number of properties to regulate the connection, including buffering, buffer size, and timeouts. Reading and writing is accomplished by requesting a `NetworkStream` object via the `GetStream()` method.

The `TcpListener` class listens for incoming TCP connections with the `Start()` method. When a connection request arrives, you can use the `AcceptSocket()` method to return a socket for communication with the remote machine, or use the `AcceptTcpClient()` method to use a higher-level `TcpClient` object for communication. The easiest way to see how the `TcpListener` and `TcpClient` classes work together is to work through an example.

The TcpSend and TcpReceive Examples

To demonstrate how these classes work, you need to build two applications. Figure 41-11 shows the first application, `TcpSend`. This application opens a TCP connection to a server and sends the C# source code for itself.

Figure 41-11

Once again, you create a C# Windows application. The form consists of two text boxes (`txtHost` and `txtPort`) for the host name and port, respectively, as well as a button (`btnSend`) to click and start a connection. First, you ensure that you include the relevant namespaces:

```
using System;
using System.IO;
using System.Net.Sockets;
using System.Windows.Forms;
```

The following code shows the event handler for the button's `Click` event:

```
private void btnSend_Click(object sender, System.EventArgs e)
{
    TcpClient tcpClient = new TcpClient(txtHost.Text, Int32.Parse(txtPort.Text));
    NetworkStream ns = tcpClient.GetStream();
    FileStream fs = File.Open(Server.MapPath("form1.cs"), FileMode.Open);

    int data = fs.ReadByte();
    while(data != -1)
    {
        ns.WriteByte((byte)data);
        data = fs.ReadByte();
    }
    fs.Close();
    ns.Close();
    tcpClient.Close();
}
```

This example creates the `TcpClient` using a host name and a port number. Alternatively, if you have an instance of the `IPEndPoint` class, then you can pass the instance to the `TcpClient` constructor. After retrieving an instance of the `NetworkStream` class, you open the source code file and begin to read bytes. As with many of the binary streams, you need to check for the end of the stream by comparing the return value of the `ReadByte()` method to -1. After your loop has read all of the bytes and sent them along to the network stream, you must close all of the open files, connections, and streams.

On the other side of the connection, the `TcpReceive` application displays the received file after the transmission is finished (see Figure 41-12).

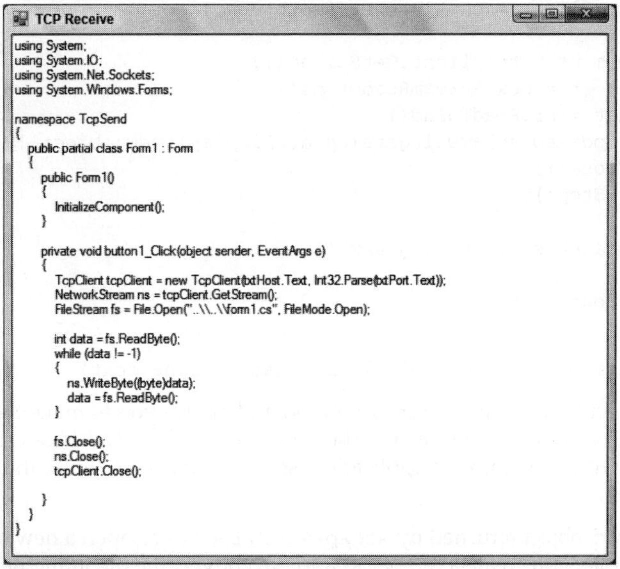

```
TCP Receive

using System;
using System.IO;
using System.Net.Sockets;
using System.Windows.Forms;

namespace TcpSend
{
    public partial class Form1 : Form
    {
        public Form1()
        {
            InitializeComponent();
        }

        private void button1_Click(object sender, EventArgs e)
        {
            TcpClient tcpClient = new TcpClient(txtHost.Text, Int32.Parse(txtPort.Text));
            NetworkStream ns = tcpClient.GetStream();
            FileStream fs = File.Open("..\\..\\form1.cs", FileMode.Open);

            int data = fs.ReadByte();
            while (data != -1)
            {
                ns.WriteByte((byte)data);
                data = fs.ReadByte();
            }

            fs.Close();
            ns.Close();
            tcpClient.Close();
        }
    }
}
```

Figure 41-12

The form consists of a single `TextBox` control, named `txtDisplay`. The `TcpReceive` application uses a `TcpListener` to wait for the incoming connection. To prevent freezing the application interface, you use a background thread to wait for and then read from the connection. Thus, you need to include the `System.Threading` namespace as well these other namespaces:

```
using System;
using System.IO;
using System.Net;
using System.Net.Sockets;
using System.Threading;
using System.Windows.Forms;
```

Inside the form's constructor, you spin up a background thread:

```
public Form1()
{
    InitializeComponent();
    Thread thread = new Thread(new ThreadStart(Listen));
    thread.Start();
}
```

The remaining important code is this:

```
public void Listen()
{
    IPAddress localAddr = IPAddress.Parse("127.0.0.1");
    Int32 port = 2112;
    TcpListener tcpListener = new TcpListener(localAddr, port);
    tcpListener.Start();

    TcpClient tcpClient = tcpListener.AcceptTcpClient();

    NetworkStream ns = tcpClient.GetStream();
    StreamReader sr = new StreamReader(ns);
    string result = sr.ReadToEnd();
    Invoke(new UpdateDisplayDelegate(UpdateDisplay),new object[] {result} );
    tcpClient.Close();
    tcpListener.Stop();
}
public void UpdateDisplay(string text)
{
    txtDisplay.Text= text;
}

protected delegate void UpdateDisplayDelegate(string text);
```

The thread begins execution in the `Listen()` method and allows you to make the blocking call to `AcceptTcpClient()` without halting the interface. Notice that the IP address (`127.0.0.1`) and the port number (`2112`) are hard-coded into the application, so you will need to enter the same port number from the client application.

You use the `TcpClient` object returned by `AcceptTcpClient()` to open a new stream for reading. As with the earlier example, you create a `StreamReader` to convert the incoming network data into a string. Before you close the client and stop the listener, you update the form's text box. You do not want to access the text box directly from your background thread, so you use the form's `Invoke()` method with a delegate and pass the result string as the first element in an array of `object` parameters. `Invoke()` ensures that your call is correctly marshaled into the thread that owns the control handles in the user interface.

TCP versus UDP

The other protocol covered in this section is UDP (User Datagram Protocol). UDP is a simple protocol with few features and little overhead. Developers often use UDP in applications where the speed and performance requirements outweigh the reliability needs, for example, video streaming. In contrast, TCP offers a number of features to confirm the delivery of data. TCP provides error correction and retransmission in the case of lost or corrupted packets. Last, but hardly least, TCP buffers incoming and outgoing data and also guarantees that a sequence of packets scrambled in transmission is reassembled before delivery to the application. Even with the extra overhead, TCP is the most widely used protocol across the Internet because of its high reliability.

The UDP Class

As you might expect, the `UdpClient` class features a smaller and simpler interface than `TcpClient`. This reflects the relatively simpler nature of the protocol. Although both TCP and UDP classes use a socket underneath the covers, the `UdpClient` class does not contain a method to return a network stream for reading and writing. Instead, the member function `Send()` accepts an array of bytes as a parameter, and the `Receive()` function returns an array of bytes. Also, because UDP is a connectionless protocol, you can wait to specify the endpoint for the communication as a parameter to the `Send()` and `Receive()`

methods, instead of specifying it earlier in a constructor or `Connect()` method. You can also change the endpoint on each subsequent send or receive.

The following code fragment uses the `UdpClient` class to send a message to an echo service. A server with an echo service running accepts TCP or UDP connections on port 7. The echo service simply echoes any data sent to the server back to the client. This service is useful for diagnostics and testing, although many system administrators disable echo services for security reasons:

```
using System;
using System.Text;
using System.Net;
using System.Net.Sockets;
namespace Wrox.ProCSharp.InternetAccess.UdpExample
{

    class Class1
    {
        [STAThread]
        static void Main(string[] args)
        {
            UdpClient udpClient = new UdpClient();
            string sendMsg = "Hello Echo Server";
            byte [] sendBytes = Encoding.ASCII.GetBytes(sendMsg);
            udpClient.Send(sendBytes, sendBytes.Length, "SomeEchoServer.net", 7);
            IPEndPoint endPoint = new IPEndPoint(0,0);
            byte [] rcvBytes = udpClient.Receive(ref endPoint);
            string rcvMessage = Encoding.ASCII.GetString(rcvBytes,
                                                         0,
                                                         rcvBytes.Length);
            // should print out "Hello Echo Server"
            Console.WriteLine(rcvMessage);
        }
    }
}
```

You make heavy use of the `Encoding.ASCII` class to translate strings into arrays of `byte` and vice versa. Also note that you pass an `IPEndPoint` by reference into the `Receive()` method. Because UDP is not a connection-oriented protocol, each call to `Receive()` might pick up data from a different endpoint, so `Receive()` populates this parameter with the IP address and port of the sending host.

Both `UdpClient` and `TcpClient` offer a layer of abstraction over the lowest of the low-level classes: the `Socket`.

The Socket Class

The `Socket` class offers the highest level of control in network programming. One of the easiest ways to demonstrate the class is to rewrite the `TcpReceive` application with the `Socket` class. The updated `Listen()` method is listed in this example:

```
public void Listen()
{
    Socket listener = new Socket(AddressFamily.InterNetwork,
                                 SocketType.Stream,
                                 ProtocolType.Tcp);
    listener.Bind(new IPEndPoint(IPAddress.Any, 2112));
    listener.Listen(0);
    Socket socket = listener.Accept();
```

(continued)

(continued)

```
        Stream netStream = new NetworkStream(socket);
        StreamReader reader = new StreamReader(netStream);

        string result = reader.ReadToEnd();
        Invoke(new UpdateDisplayDelegate(UpdateDisplay),
                    new object[] {result} );
        socket.Close();
        listener.Close();
    }
```

The `Socket` class requires a few more lines of code to complete the same task. For starters, the constructor arguments need to specify an IP addressing scheme for a streaming socket with the TCP protocol. These arguments are just one of the many combinations available to the `Socket` class. The `TcpClient` class can configure these settings for you. You then bind the listener socket to a port and begin to listen for incoming connections. When an incoming request arrives, you can use the `Accept()` method to create a new socket to handle the connection. You ultimately attach a `StreamReader` instance to the socket to read the incoming data, in much the same fashion as before.

The `Socket` class also contains a number of methods for asynchronously accepting, connecting, sending, and receiving. You can use these methods with callback delegates in the same way you used the asynchronous page requests with the `WebRequest` class. If you really need to dig into the internals of the socket, the `GetSocketOption()` and `SetSocketOption()` methods are available. These methods allow you to see and configure options, including timeout, time-to-live, and other low-level options. Next, this chapter looks at another example of using sockets.

Building a Server Console Application

Looking further into the `Socket` class, this next example will create a console application that acts as a server for incoming socket requests. From there, a second example will be created in parallel (another console application), which sends a message to the server console application.

The first application you will build is the console application that acts as a server. This application will open a socket on a specific TCP port and listen for any incoming messages. The code for this console application is presented in its entirety here:

```
using System;
using System.Net;
using System.Net.Sockets;
using System.Text;
namespace SocketConsole
{
    class Program
    {
        static void Main()
        {
            Console.WriteLine("Starting: Creating Socket object");
            Socket listener = new Socket(AddressFamily.InterNetwork,
                                    SocketType.Stream,
                                    ProtocolType.Tcp);
            listener.Bind(new IPEndPoint(IPAddress.Any, 2112));
            listener.Listen(10);
            while (true)
            {
                Console.WriteLine("Waiting for connection on port 2112");
                Socket socket = listener.Accept();
                string receivedValue = string.Empty;
```

```
            while (true)
            {
                byte[] receivedBytes = new byte[1024];
                int numBytes = socket.Receive(receivedBytes);
                Console.WriteLine("Receiving ...");
                receivedValue += Encoding.ASCII.GetString(receivedBytes,
                                    0, numBytes);
                if (receivedValue.IndexOf("[FINAL]") > -1)
                {
                    break;
                }
            }
            Console.WriteLine("Received value: {0}", receivedValue);
            string replyValue = "Message successfully received.";
            byte[] replyMessage = Encoding.ASCII.GetBytes(replyValue);
            socket.Send(replyMessage);
            socket.Shutdown(SocketShutdown.Both);
            socket.Close();
        }
        listener.Close();
    }
  }
}
```

This example sets up a socket using the `Socket` class. The socket created uses the TCP protocol and is set up to receive incoming messages from any IP address using port 2112. Values that come in through the open socket are written to the console screen. This consuming application will continue to receive bytes until the `[FINAL]` string is received. This `[FINAL]` string signifies the end of the incoming message, and the message can then be interpreted.

After the end of the message is received from a client, a reply message is sent to the same client. From there, the socket is closed using the `Close()` method, and the console application will continue to stay up until a new message is received.

Building the Client Application

The next step is to build a client application that will send a message to the first console application. The client will be able to send any message that it wants to the server console application as long as it follows some rules that were established by this application. The first of these rules is that the server console application is listening only on a particular protocol. In the case of this server application, it is listening using the TCP protocol. The other rule is that the server application is listening only on a particular port — in this case, port 2112. The last rule is that in any message that is being sent, the last bits of the message need to end with the string `[FINAL]`.

The following client console application follows all of these rules:

```
using System;
using System.Net;
using System.Net.Sockets;
using System.Text;
namespace SocketConsoleClient
{
    class Program
    {
        static void Main()
        {
            byte[] receivedBytes = new byte[1024];
```

(continued)

(continued)

```
            IPHostEntry ipHost = Dns.Resolve("127.0.0.1");
            IPAddress ipAddress = ipHost.AddressList[0];
            IPEndPoint ipEndPoint = new IPEndPoint(ipAddress, 2112);
            Console.WriteLine("Starting: Creating Socket object");

            Socket sender = new Socket(AddressFamily.InterNetwork,
                                        SocketType.Stream,
                                        ProtocolType.Tcp);
            sender.Connect(ipEndPoint);
            Console.WriteLine("Successfully connected to {0}",
                    sender.RemoteEndPoint);
            string sendingMessage = "Hello World Socket Test";
            Console.WriteLine("Creating message: Hello World Socket Test");
            byte[] forwardMessage = Encoding.ASCII.GetBytes(sendingMessage
                + "[FINAL]");
            sender.Send(forwardMessage);
            int totalBytesReceived = sender.Receive(receivedBytes);
            Console.WriteLine("Message provided from server: {0}",
                            Encoding.ASCII.GetString(receivedBytes,
                            0, totalBytesReceived));
            sender.Shutdown(SocketShutdown.Both);
            sender.Close();
            Console.ReadLine();
        }
    }
}
```

In this example, an `IPEndPoint` object is created using the IP address of *localhost* as well as using port 2112 as required by the server console application. In this case, a socket is created and the `Connect()` method is called. After the socket is opened and connected to the server console application socket instance, a string of text is sent to the server application using the `Send()` method. Because the server application is going to return a message, the `Receive()` method is used to grab this message (placing it in a byte array). From there, the byte array is converted into a string and displayed in the console application before the socket is shut down.

Running this application will produce the results presented in Figure 41-13.

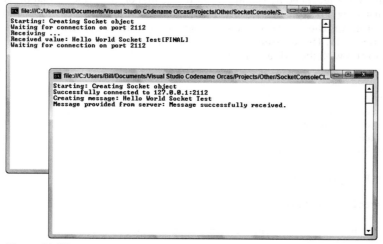

Figure 41-13

Reviewing the two console applications in the figure, you can see that the server application opens and awaits incoming messages. The incoming message is sent from the client application, and the string sent is then displayed by the server application. The server application waits for other messages to come in, even after the first message is received and displayed. You can see this for yourself by shutting down the client application and re-running the application. You will then see that the server application again displays the message received.

Summary

In this chapter, you reviewed the .NET Framework classes available in the System.Net namespace for communication across networks. You have seen some of the .NET base classes that deal with opening client connections on the network and Internet, and how to send requests to and receive responses from servers (the most obvious use of this being to receive HTML pages). By taking advantage of the WebBrowser control in .NET 3.5, you can easily make use of Internet Explorer from your desktop applications.

As a rule of thumb, when programming with classes in the System.Net namespace, you should always try to use the most generic class possible. For instance, using the TCPClient class instead of the Socket class isolates your code from many of the lower-level socket details. Moving one-step higher, the WebRequest class allows you to take advantage of the pluggable protocol architecture of the .NET Framework. Your code will be ready to take advantage of new application-level protocols as Microsoft and other third-party developers introduce new functionality.

Finally, you learned how to use the asynchronous capabilities in the networking classes, which give a Windows Forms application the professional touch of a responsive user interface.

Now you move on to learning about Windows Communication Foundation.

42

Windows Communication Foundation

Previous to .NET 3.0, several communication technologies were required in a single enterprise solution. For platform-independent communication, ASP.NET Web services were used. For more advanced Web services, technologies such as reliability, platform-independent security, and atomic transactions, Web Services Enhancements added a complexity layer to ASP.NET Web services. If the communication needed to be faster, and both the client and service were .NET applications, .NET Remoting was the technology of choice. .NET Enterprise Services with its automatic transaction support, by default, was using the DCOM protocol that was even faster than .NET Remoting. DCOM was also the only protocol to allow passing transactions. All of these technologies have different programming models that require many skills from the developer.

.NET Framework 3.0 introduced a new communication technology that includes all the features from the predecessors and combines them into one programming model: Windows Communication Foundation (WCF).

In particular, this chapter discusses the following topics:

- ❏ WCF overview
- ❏ A simple service and client
- ❏ Contracts
- ❏ Service implementation
- ❏ Binding
- ❏ Hosting
- ❏ Clients
- ❏ Duplex communication

WCF Overview

WCF combines the functionality from ASP.NET Web services, .NET Remoting, Message Queuing, and Enterprise Services. What you get from WCF is:

- **Hosting for components and services** — Just as you can use custom hosts with .NET Remoting and WSE, you can host a WCF service in the ASP.NET runtime, a Windows service, a COM+ process, or just a Windows Forms application for peer-to-peer computing.

- **Declarative behavior** — Instead of the requirement to derive from a base class (this requirement exists with .NET Remoting and Enterprise Services), attributes can be used to define the services. This is similar to Web services developed with ASP.NET.

- **Communication channels** — Although NET Remoting is very flexible with changing the communication channel, WCF is a good alternative because it offers the same flexibility. WCF offers multiple channels to communicate using HTTP, TCP, or an IPC channel. Custom channels using different transport protocols can be created as well.

- **Security infrastructure** — For implementing platform-independent Web services, a standardized security environment must be used. The proposed standards are implemented with WSE 3.0, and this continues with WCF.

- **Extensibility** — .NET Remoting has a rich extensibility story. It is not only possible to create custom channels, formatters, and proxies, but also to inject functionality inside the message flow on the client and on the server. WCF offers similar extensibilities; however, here, the extensions are created by using SOAP headers.

- **Support of previous technologies** — Instead of rewriting a distributed solution completely to use WCF, WCF can be integrated with existing technologies. WCF offers a channel that can communicate with serviced components using DCOM. Web services that have been developed with ASP.NET can be integrated with WCF as well.

The final goal is to send and receive messages from a client to a service either across processes or different systems, across a local network, or the Internet. This should be done if required in a platform-independent way and as fast as possible. On a distant view, the service offers an endpoint that is described by a contract, binding, and an address. The contract defines the operations offered by the service, binding gives information about the protocol and encoding, and the address is the location of the service. The client needs a compatible endpoint to access the service.

Figure 42-1 shows the components that participate with a WCF communication.

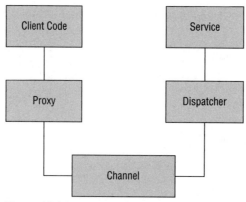

Figure 42-1

The client invokes a method on the proxy. The proxy offers methods as defined by the service, but converts the method call to a message and transfers the message to the channel. The channel has a client-side and a server-side part that communicate across a networking protocol. From the channel, the message is passed to the dispatcher, which converts the message to a method call that is invoked with the service.

WCF supports several communication protocols. For platform-independent communication, Web services standards are supported. For communication between .NET applications, faster communication protocols with less overhead can be used.

The following sections look at the functionality of core services used for platform-independent communication.

SOAP

For platform-independent communication, the SOAP protocol can be used and is directly supported from WCF. SOAP originally was shorthand for Simple Object Access Protocol, but since SOAP 1.2 this is no longer the case. SOAP no longer is an object access protocol, because, instead, messages are sent that can be defined by an XML schema.

A service receives a SOAP message from a client and returns a SOAP response message. A SOAP message consists of an envelope, which contains a header and a body:

```
<s:Envelope xmlns:a="http://www.w3.org/2005/08/addressing"
    xmlns:s="http://www.w3.org/2003/05/soap-envelope">
  <s:Header>
  </s:Header>
  <s:Body>
    <ReserveRoom xmlns="http://www.wrox.com/ProCSharp/2008">
      <roomReservation
xmlns:d4p1="http://schemas.datacontract.org/2004/07/Wrox.ProCSharp.WCF"
xmlns:i="http://www.w3.org/2001/XMLSchema-instance">
        <d4p1:RoomName>Hawelka</d4p1:RoomName>
        <d4p1:StartDate>2007-06-21T08:00:00</d4p1:StartDate>
        <d4p1:EndDate>2007-06-21T14:00:00</d4p1:EndDate>
        <d4p1:Contact>Georg Danzer</d4p1:Contact>
        <d4p1:Event>White Horses</d4p1:Event>
      </roomReservation>
    </ReserveRoom>
  </s:Body>
</s:Envelope>
```

The header is optional and can contain information about addressing, security, and transactions. The body contains the message data.

WSDL

A WSDL (Web Services Description Language) document describes the operations and messages of the service. WSDL defines metadata of the service that can be used to create a proxy for the client application.

The WSDL contains this information:

❑ **Types** for the messages that are described using an XML schema.

❑ **Messages** that are sent to and from the service. Parts of the messages are the types that are defined with an XML schema.

❑ **Port types** map to service contracts and list operations that are defined with the service contract. Operations contain messages; for example, an input and an output message as used with a request and response sequence.

❑ **Binding** information that contains the operations listed with the port types and that defines the SOAP variant used.

❑ **Service** information that maps port types to endpoint addresses.

With WCF, WSDL information is offered by MEX (Metadata Exchange) endpoints.

JSON

Instead of sending SOAP messages, accessing services from JavaScript can best be done using JSON (JavaScript Object Notation). .NET 3.5 includes a data contract serializer to create objects with the JSON notation.

JSON has less overhead than SOAP because it is not XML, but optimized for JavaScript clients. This makes it extremely useful from Ajax clients. Ajax is discussed in Chapter 39, "ASP.NET AJAX." JSON does not offer reliability, security, and transaction features that can be sent with the SOAP header, but these are features usually not needed by JavaScript clients.

Simple Service and Client

Before going into the details of WCF, let's start with a simple service. The service is used to reserve meeting rooms.

For a backing store of room reservations, a simple SQL Server database with the table `RoomReservations` is used. The table and its properties are shown in Figure 42-2. You can download the database together with the sample code of this chapter.

Figure 42-2

Create an empty solution with the name `RoomReservation` and add a new Component Library project with the name `RoomReservationData` to the solution. The first project that is implemented contains just the code to access the database. Because LINQ to SQL makes the database access code much easier, this .NET 3.5 technology is used here.

Chapter 27 gives you the details of LINQ to SQL.

Add a new item, LINQ to SQL Classes, and name it `RoomReservation.dbml`. With the LINQ to SQL designer, open the Server Explorer to drop the `RoomReservation` database table onto the designer as shown in Figure 42-3. This designer creates an entity class, `RoomReservation`, that contains properties for every column of the table and the class `RoomReservationDataContext`. `RoomReservationDataContext` connects to the database.

Figure 42-3

Change the Serialization Mode property of the LINQ to SQL designer from None to Unidirectional. This way, the generated class RoomReservation gets a data contract that allows the entity classes to serialize across WCF.

To read and write data from the database using LINQ to SQL, add the class RoomReservationData. The method ReserveRoom() writes a room reservation to the database. The method GetReservations() returns an array of room reservations from a specified date range.

```
using System;
using System.Linq;

namespace Wrox.ProCSharp.WCF.Data
{
    public class RoomReservationData
    {
        public void ReserveRoom(RoomReservation roomReservation)
        {
            using (RoomReservationDataContext data =
                new RoomReservationDataContext())
            {
                data.RoomReservations.Add(roomReservation);
                data.SubmitChanges();
            }
        }

        public RoomReservation[] GetReservations(DateTime fromDate,
                                                 DateTime toDate)
        {
            using (RoomReservationDataContext data =
                new RoomReservationDataContext())
            {
                return (from r in data.RoomReservations
                        where r.StartDate > fromDate && r.EndDate < toDate
                        select r).ToArray();
            }
        }
    }
}
```

Now start creating the service.

Service Contract

Add a new project of type WCF Service Library to the solution and name the project
RoomReservationService. Rename the generated files IService1.cs to IRoomService.cs and
Service1.cs to RoomReservationService.cs and change the namespace within the generated files
to Wrox.ProCSharp.WCF.Service. The assembly RoomReservationData needs to be referenced to
have the entity types and the RoomReservationData class available.

The operations offered by the service can be defined by an interface. The interface IRoomService
defines the methods ReserveRoom and GetRoomReservations. The service contract is defined with the
attribute [ServiceContract]. The operations defined by the service have the attribute
[OperationContract] applied.

```
using System;
using System.ServiceModel;
using Wrox.ProCSharp.WCF.Entities;

namespace Wrox.ProCSharp.WCF.Service
{
    [ServiceContract()]
    public interface IRoomService
    {
        [OperationContract]
        bool ReserveRoom(RoomReservation roomReservation);

        [OperationContract]
        RoomReservation[] GetRoomReservations(DateTime fromDate,
                                              DateTime toDate);
    }
}
```

Service Implementation

The service class RoomReservationService implements the interface IRoomService. The service is
implemented just by invoking the appropriate methods of the RoomReservationData class:

```
using System;
using System.ServiceModel;
using Wrox.ProCSharp.WCF.Data;
using Wrox.ProCSharp.WCF.Entities;

namespace Wrox.ProCSharp.WCF
{
    public class RoomReservationService : IRoomService
    {
        public bool ReserveRoom(RoomReservation roomReservation)
        {
            RoomReservationData data = new RoomReservationData();
            data.ReserveRoom(roomReservation);

            return true;
        }

        public RoomReservation[] GetRoomReservations(DateTime fromDate,
                                                     DateTime toDate)
```

```
        {
            RoomReservationData data = new RoomReservationData();
            return data.GetReservations(fromDate, toDate);
        }
    }
}
```

WCF Service Host and WCF Test Client

The WCF Service Library project template creates an application configuration file named `App.config` that you need to adapt to the new class and interface names. The `service` element references the service type `RoomReservationService` including the namespace; the contract interface needs to be defined with the `endpoint` element.

```xml
<?xml version="1.0" encoding="utf-8" ?>
<configuration>
  <system.serviceModel>
    <services>
      <service name="Wrox.ProCSharp.WCF.Services.RoomReservationService"
          behaviorConfiguration="RoomReservationsService.Service1Behavior">
        <host>
          <baseAddresses>
            <add baseAddress =
    "http://localhost:8731/Design_Time_Addresses/RoomReservationService/" />
          </baseAddresses>
        </host>
        <!-- Service Endpoints -->
        <endpoint address ="" binding="wsHttpBinding"
            contract="Wrox.ProCSharp.WCF.Services.IRoomService" />
        <!-- Metadata Endpoints -->
        <endpoint address="mex" binding="mexHttpBinding"
            contract="IMetadataExchange" />
      </service>
    </services>
    <behaviors>
      <serviceBehaviors>
        <behavior name="RoomReservationsService.Service1Behavior">
          <serviceMetadata httpGetEnabled="True"/>

          <serviceDebug includeExceptionDetailInFaults="False" />
        </behavior>
      </serviceBehaviors>
    </behaviors>
  </system.serviceModel>
</configuration>
```

The service address `http://localhost:8731/Design_Time_Addresses` *has an access control list (ACL) associated that allows the interactive user to create a listener port. By default, a non-administrative user is not allowed to open ports in listening mode. You can view the ACLs with the command-line utility* `netsh http show urlacl`, *and add new entries with* `netsh http add url=http://+8080/MyURI user=someUser`.

Starting this library from Visual Studio 2008 starts the WCF Service Host, which appears as an icon in the notification area of the taskbar. Clicking this icon opens the dialog (see Figure 42-4) of this application where you can see the status of the service. The project properties have the command-line arguments /client: "WcfTestClient.exe" defined. With this option, the WCF Service host starts the WCF Test Client (see Figure 42-5) that you can use to test the application. When you double-click an operation, input fields appear on the right side of the application that you can fill to send data to the service. When you click the XML tab, you can see the SOAP messages that have been sent and received.

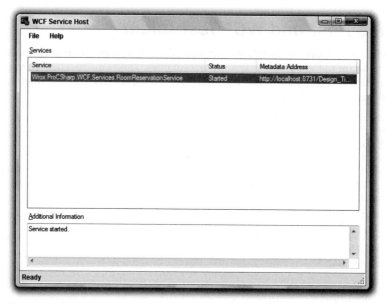

Figure 42-4

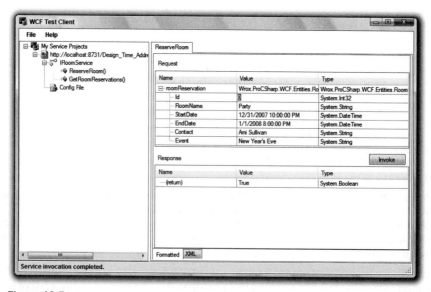

Figure 42-5

Custom Service Host

WCF allows services to run in any host. You can create a Windows Forms or WPF application for peer-to-peer services, you can create a Windows service, or host the service with Windows Activation Services (WAS). A console application is also good to demonstrate a simple host.

With the service host, you must reference the library RoomReservationService. The service is started by instantiating and opening an object of type ServiceHost. This class is defined in the namespace System.ServiceModel. The RoomReservationService class that implements the service is defined in the constructor. Invoking the Open() method starts the listener channel of the service — the service is ready to listen for requests. The Close() method stops the channel.

```
using System;
using System.ServiceModel;
using Wrox.ProCSharp.WCF.Services;

namespace Wrox.ProCSharp.WCF
{
    class Program
    {
        internal static ServiceHost myServiceHost = null;

        internal static void StartService()
        {
            myServiceHost = new ServiceHost(typeof(RoomReservationService));
            myServiceHost.Open();
        }

        internal static void StopService()
        {
            if (myServiceHost.State != CommunicationState.Closed)
                myServiceHost.Close();
        }

        static void Main()
        {
            StartService();

            Console.WriteLine("Server is running. Press return to exit");
            Console.ReadLine();

            StopService();
        }
    }
}
```

For the WCF configuration, you need to copy the application configuration file that was created with the service library to the host application. You can edit this configuration file with the WCF Service Configuration Editor (see Figure 42-6).

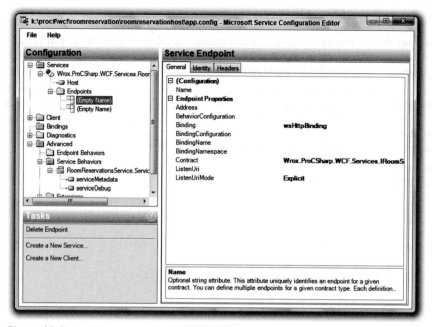

Figure 42-6

WCF Client

For the client, WCF is flexible again in what application type can be used. The client can be a simple console application as well. However, for reserving rooms, create a WPF application with controls, as shown in Figure 42-7.

Figure 42-7

Because the service offers a MEX endpoint with the binding `mexHttpBinding`, and metadata access is enabled with the behavior configuration, you can add a service reference from Visual Studio. When you add a service reference, the dialog shown in Figure 42-8 pops up. When you click the Discover button, you can find services within the same solution.

Enter the link to the service and set the service reference name to `RoomReservationService`. The service reference name defines the namespace of the generated proxy class.

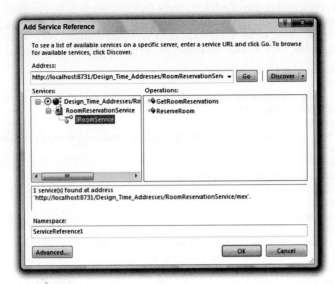

Figure 42-8

Adding a service reference adds references to the assemblies `System.Runtime.Serialization` and `System.ServiceModel` and a configuration file containing the binding information and the endpoint address to the service.

From the data contract the class `RoomReservation` is generated. This class contains all `[DataMember]` elements of the contract. The class `RoomServiceClient` is the proxy for the client that contains methods that are defined by the service contract. Using this client you can send a room reservation to the running service.

```
private void OnReserveRoom(object sender, RoutedEventArgs e)
{
    RoomReservation reservation = new RoomReservation()
    {
        RoomName = textRoom.Text,
        Event = textEvent.Text,
        Contact = textContact.Text,
        StartDate = DateTime.Parse(textStartTime.Text),
        EndDate = DateTime.Parse(textEndTime.Text)
    };

    RoomServiceClient client = new RoomServiceClient();
    client.ReserveRoom(reservation);
    client.Close();
}
```

By running both the service and the client, you can add room reservations to the database.

Diagnostics

When running a client and service application, it can be very helpful to know what's happening behind the scenes. For this, WCF makes use of a trace source that just needs to be configured. You can configure tracing using the Service Configuration Editor, selecting Diagnostics, and enabling Tracing and Message Logging. Setting the trace level of the trace sources to Verbose produces very detailed information. This configuration change adds trace sources and listeners to the application configuration file as shown here:

```
<system.diagnostics>
  <sources>
    <source name="System.ServiceModel" switchValue="Verbose,ActivityTracing"
      propagateActivity="true">
      <listeners>
        <add type="System.Diagnostics.DefaultTraceListener" name="Default">
          <filter type="" />
        </add>
        <add name="ServiceModelTraceListener">
          <filter type="" />
        </add>
      </listeners>
    </source>
    <source name="System.ServiceModel.MessageLogging"
        switchValue="Verbose,ActivityTracing">
      <listeners>
        <add type="System.Diagnostics.DefaultTraceListener" name="Default">
          <filter type="" />
        </add>
        <add name="ServiceModelMessageLoggingListener">
          <filter type="" />
        </add>
      </listeners>
    </source>
  </sources>
  <sharedListeners>
    <add initializeData="c:\logs\app_tracelog.svclog"
        type="System.Diagnostics.XmlWriterTraceListener, System,
        Version=2.0.0.0, Culture=neutral, PublicKeyToken=b77a5c561934e089"
        name="ServiceModelTraceListener" traceOutputOptions="Timestamp">
      <filter type="" />
    </add>
    <add initializeData="c:\logs\app_messages.svclog"
        type="System.Diagnostics.XmlWriterTraceListener, System,
        Version=2.0.0.0, Culture=neutral, PublicKeyToken=b77a5c561934e089"
        name="ServiceModelMessageLoggingListener"
        traceOutputOptions="Timestamp">
      <filter type="" />
    </add>
  </sharedListeners>
</system.diagnostics>
<system.serviceModel>
  <diagnostics>
    <messageLogging logEntireMessage="true" logMalformedMessages="true"
      logMessagesAtServiceLevel="true" logMessagesAtTransportLevel="true" />
  </diagnostics>
  <!-- ... -->
```

The implementation of the WCF classes uses the trace sources named System.ServiceModel *and* System.ServiceModel.MessageLogging *for writing trace messages. You can read more about tracing and configuring trace sources and listeners in Chapter 18, "Tracing and Events."*

When you start the application, the trace files soon get large with verbose trace settings. To analyze the information from the XML log file, the .NET SDK includes the Service Trace Viewer tool, svctraceviewer.exe. Figure 42-9 shows the view from this tool after selecting the trace and message log files. With the default configuration you can see several messages exchanged; many of them are related to security. Depending on your security needs, you can choose other configuration options.

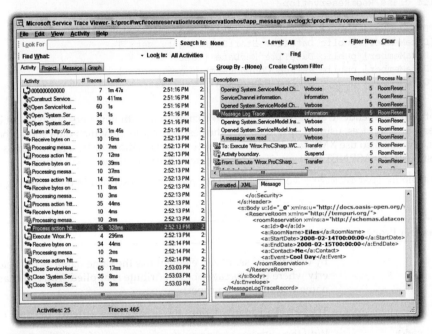

Figure 42-9

The following sections discuss the details and different options of WCF.

Contracts

A contract defines what functionality a service offers and what functionality can be used by the client. The contract can be completely independent of the implementation of the service.

The contracts defined by WCF can be grouped into three different contract types: data, service, and message. The contracts can be specified by using .NET attributes:

❑ **Data contract** — The data contract defines the data received by and returned from the service. The classes used for sending and receiving messages have data contract attributes associated.

❑ **Service contract** — The service contract is used to define the WSDL that describes the service. This contract is defined with interfaces or classes.

❑ **Message contract** — If complete control over the SOAP message is needed, a message contract can specify what data should go into the SOAP header, and what belongs in the SOAP body.

The following sections explore these contract types further.

Data Contract

With the data contract, CLR types are mapped to XML schemas. The data contract is different from other .NET serialization mechanisms: with runtime serialization, all fields are serialized (including private fields); with XML serialization only the public fields and properties are serialized. The data contract requires explicit marking of the fields that should be serialized with the [DataMember] attribute. This attribute can be used regardless of whether the field is private or public, or if it is applied to a property.

```
[DataContract(Namespace="http://www.thinktecture.com/SampleServices/2008"]
public class RoomReservation
{
    [DataMember] public string Room { get; set; }
    [DataMember] public DateTime StartDate { get; set; }
    [DataMember] public DateTime EndDate { get; set; }
    [DataMember] public string ContactName { get; set; }
    [DataMember] public string EventName { get; set; }
}
```

To be platform-independent, and give the option to change data with new versions without breaking older clients and services, using data contracts is the best way to define which data should be sent. However, you can also use XML serialization and runtime serialization. XML serialization is the mechanism used by ASP.NET Web services; .NET Remoting uses runtime serialization.

With the attribute [DataMember], you can specify the properties described in the following table.

DataMember Property	Description
Name	By default, the serialized element has the same name as the field or property where the [DataMember] attribute is applied. You can change the name with the Name property.
Order	The Order property defines the serialization order of the data members.
IsRequired	With the IsRequired property, you can specify that the element must be received with serialization. This property can be used for versioning.
	If you add members to an existing contract, the contract is not broken because, by default, the fields are optional (IsRequired=false). You can break an existing contract by setting IsRequired to true.
EmitDefaultValue	The property EmitDefaultValue defines whether the member should be serialized if it has the default value. If EmitDefaultValue is set to true, the member is not serialized if it has the default value for the type.

Versioning

When you create a new version of a data contract, pay attention to the kind of change and act accordingly if old and new clients and old and new services should be supported simultaneously.

When defining a contract, you should add XML namespace information with the Namespace property of the DataContractAttribute. This namespace should be changed if a new version of the data contract is created that breaks compatibility. If just optional members are added, the contract is not broken — this is a compatible change. Old clients can still send a message to the new service because the additional data is not needed. New clients can send messages to an old service because the old service just ignores the additional data.

Removing fields or adding required fields breaks the contract. Here, you should also change the XML namespace. The name of the namespace can include the year and the month, for example http:// thinktecture.com/SampleServices/2008/02. Every time a breaking change is done, the namespace is changed; for example, by changing the year and month to the actual value.

Service Contract

The service contract defines the operations the service can perform. The attribute [ServiceContract] is used with interfaces or classes to define a service contract. The methods that are offered by the service have the attribute [OperationContract] applied, as you can see with the interface IRoomService:

```
[ServiceContract]
public interface IRoomService
{
    [OperationContract]
    bool ReserveRoom(RoomReservation roomReservation);
}
```

The possible properties that you can set with the [ServiceContract] attribute are described in the following table.

ServiceContract Property	Description
ConfigurationName	This property defines the name of the service configuration in a configuration file.
CallbackContract	When the service is used for duplex messaging, the property CallbackContract defines the contract that is implemented in the client.
Name	The Name property defines the name for the <portType> element in the WSDL.
Namespace	The Namespace property defines the XML namespace for the <portType> element in the WSDL.
SessionMode	With the SessionMode property, you can define whether sessions are required for calling operations of this contract. The possible values Allowed, NotAllowed, and Required are defined with the SessionMode enumeration.
ProtectionLevel	The ProtectionLevel property defines whether the binding must support protecting the communication. Possible values defined by the ProtectionLevel enumeration are None, Sign, and EncryptAndSign.

With the [OperationContract], you can specify properties as shown in the following table.

OperationContract Property	Description
Action	WCF uses the Action of the SOAP request to map it to the appropriate method. The default value for the Action is a combination of the contract XML namespace, the name of the contract, and the name of the operation. If the message is a response message, Response is added to the Action string. You can override the Action value by specifying the Action property. If you assign the value "*", the service operation handles all messages.
ReplyAction	Whereas Action sets the Action name of the incoming SOAP request, ReplyAction sets the Action name of the reply message.
AsyncPattern	If the operation is implemented by using an asynchronous pattern, set the AsyncPattern property to true. The async pattern is discussed in Chapter 19.
IsInitiating IsTerminating	If the contract consists of a sequence of operations, the initiating operation should have the IsInitiating property assigned to it; the last operation of the sequence needs the IsTerminating property assigned. The initiating operation starts a new session; the server closes the session with the terminating operation.
IsOneWay	With the IsOneWay property set, the client does not wait for a reply message. Callers of a one-way operation have no direct way to detect a failure after sending the request message.
Name	The default name of the operation is the name of the method the operation contract is assigned to. You can change the name of the operation by applying the Name property.
ProtectionLevel	With the ProtectionLevel property, you define whether the message should be signed or encrypted and signed.

With the service contract, you can also define the requirements that the service has from the transport with the attribute [DeliveryRequirements]. The property RequireOrderedDelivery defines that the messages sent must arrive in the same order. With the property QueuedDeliveryRequirements, you can define that the message is sent in a disconnected mode, for example, by using Message Queuing (covered in Chapter 45).

Message Contract

A message contract is used if complete control over the SOAP message is needed. With the message contract, you can specify what part of the message should go into the SOAP header and what belongs in the SOAP body. The following example shows a message contract for the class ProcessPersonRequestMessage. The message contract is specified with the attribute [MessageContract]. The header and body of the SOAP message are specified with the attributes [MessageHeader] and [MessageBodyMember]. By specifying the Position property, you can define the element order within the body. You can also specify the protection level for header and body fields.

```
[MessageContract]
public class ProcessPersonRequestMessage
{
    [MessageHeader]
    public int employeeId;

    [MessageBodyMember(Position=0)]
    public Person person;
}
```

The class ProcessPersonRequestMessage is used with the service contract that is defined with the interface IProcessPerson:

```
[ServiceContract]
public interface IProcessPerson
{
    [OperationContract]
    public PersonResponseMessage ProcessPerson(
        ProcessPersonRequestMessage message);
}
```

Service Implementation

The implementation of the service can be marked with the attribute [ServiceBehavior], as shown with the class RoomReservationService:

```
[ServiceBehavior]
public class RoomReservationService : IRoomService
{
    public bool ReserveRoom(RoomReservation roomReservation)
    {
    // implementation
    }
}
```

The attribute [ServiceBehavior] is used to describe behavior as is offered by WCF services to intercept the code for required functionality, as shown in the following table.

ServiceBehavior Property	Description
TransactionAutoComplete OnSessionClose	When the current session is finished without error, the transaction is automatically committed. This is similar to the [AutoComplete] attribute that is discussed with Enterprise Services in Chapter 44.
TransactionIsolationLevel	To define the isolation level of the transaction within the service, the property TransactionIsolationLevel can be set to one value of the IsolationLevel enumeration. You can read information about transaction information levels in Chapter 22.
ReleaseServiceInstanceOn TransactionComplete	When the transaction is finished, the instance of the service is recycled.

ServiceBehavior Property	Description
AutomaticSessionShutdown	If the session should not be closed when the client closes the connection, you can set the property `AutomaticSessionShutdown` to `false`. By default, the session is closed.
InstanceContextMode	With the property `InstanceContextMode`, you can define whether stateful or stateless objects should be used. The default setting is `InstanceContextMode.PerCall` to create a new object with every method call. You can compare this with .NET Remoting well-known `SingleCall` objects. Other possible settings are `PerSession` and `Single`. With both of these settings, stateful objects are used. However, with `PerSession` a new object is created for every client. `Single` allows sharing the same object with multiple clients.
ConcurrencyMode	Because stateful objects can be used by multiple clients (or multiple threads of a single client), you must pay attention to concurrency issues with such object types. If the property `ConcurrencyMode` is set to `Multiple`, multiple threads can access the object, and you must deal with synchronization. If you set the option to `Single`, only one thread accesses the object at a time. Here, you don't have to do synchronization; however, scalability problems can occur with a higher number of clients. The value `Reentrant` means that only a thread coming back from a callout might access the object. For stateless objects, this setting has no meaning, because new objects are instantiated with every method call and thus no state is shared.
UseSynchronizationContext	With Windows Forms and WPF, members of controls can be invoked only from the creator thread. If the service is hosted in a Windows application, and the service methods invoke control members, set the `UseSynchronizationContext` to `true`. This way, the service runs in a thread defined by the `SynchronizationContext`.
IncludeExceptionDetail InFaults	With .NET, errors show up as exceptions. SOAP defines that a SOAP fault is returned to the client in case the server has a problem. For security reasons, it's not a good idea to return details of server-side exceptions to the client. Thus, by default, exceptions are converted to unknown faults. To return specific faults, throw an exception of type `FaultException`. For debugging purposes, it can be helpful to return the real exception information. This is the case when changing the setting of `IncludeExceptionDetailIn Faults` to `true`. Here a `FaultException<TDetail>` is thrown where the original exception contains the detail information.
MaxItemsInObjectGraph	With the property `MaxItemsInObjectGraph`, you can limit the number of objects that are serialized.
ValidateMustUnderstand	The property `ValidateMustUnderstand` set to `true` means that the SOAP headers must be understood (which is the default).

To demonstrate a service behavior, the interface IStateService defines a service contract with two operations to set and get state. With a stateful service contract, a session is needed. That's why the SessionMode property of the service contract is set to SessionMode.Required. The service contract also defines methods to initiate and close the session by applying the IsInitiating and IsTerminating properties to the operation contract:

```
[ServiceContract(SessionMode=SessionMode.Required)]
public interface IStateService
{
    [OperationContract(IsInitiating=true)]
    void Init(int i);

    [OperationContract]
    void SetState(int i);

    [OperationContract]
    int GetState();

    [OperationContract(IsTerminating=true)]
    void Close();
}
```

The service contract is implemented by the class StateService. The service implementation defines the InstanceContextMode.PerSession to keep state with the instance:

```
[ServiceBehavior(InstanceContextMode=InstanceContextMode.PerSession)]
public class StateService : IStateService
{
    int i = 0;

    public void Init(int i)
    {
        this.i = i;
    }

    public void SetState(int i)
    {
        this.i = i;
    }

    public int GetState()
    {
        return i;
    }

    public void Close()
    {
    }
}
```

Now the binding to the address and protocol must be defined. Here, the basicHttpBinding is assigned to the endpoint of the service:

```
<?xml version="1.0" encoding="utf-8" ?>
<configuration>
  <system.serviceModel>
```

(continued)

(continued)

```
        <services>
          <service behaviorConfiguration="StateServiceSample.Service1Behavior"
            name="Wrox.ProCSharp.WCF.StateService">
            <endpoint address="" binding="basicHttpBinding"
                bindingConfiguration=""
                contract="Wrox.ProCSharp.WCF.IStateService">
            </endpoint>
            <endpoint address="mex" binding="mexHttpBinding"
                contract="IMetadataExchange" />
            <host>
              <baseAddresses>
                <add baseAddress="http://localhost:8731/Design_Time_Addresses/
                              StateServiceSample/Service1/" />
              </baseAddresses>
            </host>
          </service>
        </services>
        <behaviors>
          <serviceBehaviors>
            <behavior name="StateServiceSample.Service1Behavior">
              <serviceMetadata httpGetEnabled="True"/>
              <serviceDebug includeExceptionDetailInFaults="False" />
            </behavior>
          </serviceBehaviors>
        </behaviors>
      </system.serviceModel>
    </configuration>
```

If you start the service host with the defined configuration, an exception of type `InvalidOperationException` is thrown. The error message with the exception gives this error message: "Contract requires Session, but Binding `'BasicHttpBinding'` doesn't support it or isn't configured properly to support it."

Not all bindings support all services. Because the service contract requires a session with the attribute `[ServiceContract(SessionMode=SessionMode.Required)]`, the host fails because the configured binding does not support sessions.

As soon as you change the configuration to a binding that supports sessions (for example, the `wsHttpBinding`), the server starts successfully:

```
        <endpoint address="" binding="wsHttpBinding"
            bindingConfiguration=""
            contract="Wrox.ProCSharp.WCF.IStateService">
        </endpoint>
```

Now a client application can be created. In the previous example, the client application was created by adding a service reference. Instead of adding a service reference, you can directly access the assembly containing the contract interface, and use the `ChannelFactory<TChannel>` class to instantiate the channel to connect to the service.

The constructor of the class `ChannelFactory<TChannel>` accepts the binding configuration and endpoint address. The binding must be compatible with the binding defined with the service host, and the address defined with the `EndpointAddress` class references the URI of the running service.

The CreateChannel() method creates a channel to connect to the service. Then, you can invoke methods of the service, and you can see that the service instance holds state until the Close() method is invoked that has the IsTerminating operation behavior assigned:

```
using System;
using System.ServiceModel;

namespace Wrox.ProCSharp.WCF
{
    class Program
    {
        static void Main()
        {
            WSHttpBinding binding = new WSHttpBinding();
            EndpointAddress address =
                    new EndpointAddress("http://localhost:8731/" +
                    !Design_Time_Addresses/StateServiceSample/Service1/");

            ChannelFactory<IStateService> factory =
                    new ChannelFactory<IStateService>(binding, address);

            IStateService channel = factory.CreateChannel();
            channel.Init(1);
            Console.WriteLine(channel.GetState());
            channel.SetState(2);
            Console.WriteLine(channel.GetState());
            channel.Close();

            factory.Close();
        }
    }
}
```

With the implementation of the service, you can apply the properties in the following table to the service methods, with the attribute [OperationBehavior].

OperationBehavior	Description
AutoDisposeParameters	By default, all disposable parameters are automatically disposed. If the parameters should not be disposed, you can set the property AutoDisposeParameters to false. Then the sender is responsible for disposing the parameters.
Impersonation	With the Impersonation property, the caller can be impersonated and the method runs with the identity of the caller.
ReleaseInstanceMode	The InstanceContextMode defines the lifetime of the object instance with the service behavior setting. With the operation behavior setting, you can override the setting based on the operation. The ReleaseInstanceMode defines an instance release mode with the enumeration ReleaseInstanceMode. The value None uses the instance context mode setting. With the values BeforeCall, AfterCall, and BeforeAndAfterCall you can define recycle times with the operation.

OperationBehavior	Description
TransactionScopeRequired	With the property `TransactionScopeRequired`, you can specify if a transaction is required with the operation. If a transaction is required, and the caller already flows a transaction, the same transaction is used. If the caller doesn't flow a transaction, a new transaction is created.
TransactionAutoComplete	The `TransactionAutoComplete` property specifies whether the transaction should complete automatically. If the `TransactionAutoComplete` property is set to `true`, the transaction is aborted if an exception is thrown. The transaction is committed if it is the root transaction and no exception is thrown.

Error Handling

By default, the detailed exception information that occurs in the service is not returned to the client application. The reason for this behavior is security. You wouldn't want to give detailed exception information to a third party using your service. Instead, the exception should be logged on the service (which you can do with tracing and event logging), and an error with useful information should be returned to the caller.

You can return SOAP faults by throwing a `FaultException`. Throwing a `FaultException` creates an untyped SOAP fault. The preferred way of returning errors is to generate a strongly typed SOAP fault.

The information that should be passed with a strongly typed SOAP fault is defined with a data contract as shown with the `StateFault` class:

```
[DataContract]
public class StateFault
{
    [DataMember]
    public int BadState { get; set; }
}
```

The type of the SOAP fault must be defined using the `FaultContractAttribute` with the operation contract:

```
[FaultContract(typeof(StateFault))]
[OperationContract]
void SetState(int i);
```

With the implementation, a `FaultException<TDetail>` is thrown. With the constructor you can assign a new `TDetail` object, which is a `StateFault` in the example. In addition, error information within a `FaultReason` can be assigned to the constructor. `FaultReason` supports error information in multiple languages.

```
public void SetState(int i)
{
    if (i == -1)
    {
        FaultReasonText[] text = new FaultReasonText[2];
        text[0] = new FaultReasonText("Sample Error",
```

```
                new CultureInfo("en"));
        text[1] = new FaultReasonText("Beispiel Fehler",
                new CultureInfo("de"));
        FaultReason reason = new FaultReason(text);

        throw new FaultException<StateFault>(
            new StateFault() { BadState = i }, reason);
    }
    else
    {
        this.i = i;
    }
}
```

With the client application, exceptions of type FaultException<StateFault> can be caught. The reason for the exception is defined by the Message property; the StateFault is accessed with the Detail property:

```
try
{
    channel.SetState(-1);
}
catch (FaultException<StateFault> ex)
{
    Console.WriteLine(ex.Message);
    StateFault detail = ex.Detail;
    Console.WriteLine(detail.BadState);
}
```

In addition to catching the strongly typed SOAP faults, the client application can also catch exceptions of the base class of FaultException<Detail>: FaultException and CommunicationException. By catching CommunicationException, you can also catch other exceptions related to the WCF communication.

Binding

A binding describes how a service wants to communicate. With binding, you can specify the following features:

- ❑ Transport protocol
- ❑ Security
- ❑ Encoding format
- ❑ Transaction flow
- ❑ Reliability
- ❑ Shape change
- ❑ Transport upgrade

A binding is composed of multiple binding elements that describe all binding requirements. You can create a custom binding or use one of the predefined bindings that are shown in the following table.

Standard Binding	Description
BasicHttpBinding	BasicHttpBinding is the binding for the broadest interoperability, the first-generation Web services. Transport protocols used are HTTP or HTTPS; security is available only from the transport protocol.
WSHttpBinding	WSHttpBinding is the binding for the next-generation Web services, platforms that implement SOAP extensions for security, reliability, and transactions. The transports used are HTTP or HTTPS; for security the WS-Security specification is implemented; transactions are supported, as has been described, with the WS-Coordination, WS-AtomicTransaction, and WS-BusinessActivity specifications; reliable messaging is supported with an implementation of WS-ReliableMessaging. WS-Profile also supports MTOM (Message Transmission Optimization Protocol) encoding for sending attachments. You can find specifications for the WS-* standards at http://www.oasis-open.org.
WS2007HttpBinding	WS2007HttpBinding derives from the base class WSHttpBinding and supports security, reliability, and transaction specifications defined by OASIS (Organization for the Advancement of Structured Information Standards). This class is new with .NET 3.0 SP1.
WSHttpContextBinding	WSHttpContextBinding derives from the base class WSHttpBinding and adds support for a context without using cookies. This binding adds a ContextBindingElement to exchange context information.
WebHttpBinding	This binding is used for services that are exposed through HTTP requests instead of SOAP requests. This is useful for scripting clients, for example, ASP.NET AJAX.
WSFederationHttpBinding	WSFederationHttpBinding is a secure and interoperable binding that supports sharing identities across multiple systems for authentication and authorization.
WSDualHttpBinding	The binding WSDualHttpBinding, in contrast to WSHttpBinding, supports duplex messaging.
NetTcpBinding	All standard bindings prefixed with the name Net use a binary encoding used for communication between .NET applications. This encoding is faster than the text encoding with WSxxx bindings. The binding NetTcpBinding uses the TCP/IP protocol.
NetTcpContextBinding	Similar to WSHttpContextBinding, NetTcpContextBinding adds a ContextBindingElement to exchange context with the SOAP header.

Standard Binding	Description
NetPeerTcpBinding	NetPeerTcpBinding provides a binding for peer-to-peer communication.
NetNamedPipeBinding	NetNamedPipeBinding is optimized for communication between different processes on the same system.
NetMsmqBinding	The binding NetMsmqBinding brings queued communication to WCF. Here, the messages are sent to the message queue.
MsmqIntegrationBinding	MsmqIntegrationBinding is the binding for existing applications that uses message queuing. In contrast, the binding NetMsmqBinding requires WCF applications both on the client and server.
CustomBinding	With a CustomBinding the transport protocol and security requirements can be completely customized.

Depending on the binding, different features are supported. The bindings starting with WS are platform-independent, supporting Web services specifications. Bindings that start with the name Net use binary formatting for high-performance communication between .NET applications. Other features are support of sessions, reliable sessions, transactions, and duplex communication; the following table lists the bindings supporting these features.

Feature	Binding
Sessions	WSHttpBinding, WSDualHttpBinding, WsFederationHttpBinding, NetTcpBinding, NetNamedPipeBinding
Reliable Sessions	WSHttpBinding, WSDualHttpBinding, WsFederationHttpBinding, NetTcpBinding
Transactions	WSHttpBinding, WSDualHttpBinding, WSFederationHttpBinding, NetTcpBinding, NetNamedPipeBinding, NetMsmqBinding, MsmqIntegrationBinding
Duplex Communication	WsDualHttpBinding, NetTcpBinding, NetNamedPipeBinding, NetPeerTcpBinding

Along with defining the binding, the service must define an endpoint. The endpoint is dependent on the contract, the address of the service, and the binding. In the following code sample, a ServiceHost object is instantiated, and the address http://localhost:8080/RoomReservation, a WsHttpBinding instance, and the contract are added to an endpoint of the service:

```
static ServiceHost host;

static void StartService()
{
    Uri baseAddress = new Uri("http://localhost:8080/RoomReservation");
    host = new ServiceHost(
```

(continued)

(continued)

```
                typeof(RoomReservationService));

        WSHttpBinding binding1 = new WSHttpBinding();
        host.AddServiceEndpoint(typeof(IRoomService), binding1, baseAddress);
        host.Open();
    }
```

In addition to defining the binding programmatically, you can define it with the application configuration file. The configuration for WCF is placed inside the element `<system.serviceModel>`. The `<service>` element defines the services offered. Similarly, as you've seen in the code, the service needs an endpoint, and the endpoint contains address, binding, and contract information. The default binding configuration of `wsHttpBinding` is modified with the `bindingConfiguration` XML attribute that references the binding configuration `wsHttpConfig1`. This is the binding configuration you can find inside the `<bindings>` section, which is used to change the `wsHttpBinding` configuration to enable `reliableSession`.

```xml
<?xml version="1.0" encoding="utf-8" ?>
<configuration>
  <system.serviceModel>
    <services>
      <service name="Wrox.ProCSharp.WCF.RoomReservationService">
        <endpoint address=" http://localhost:8080/RoomReservation"
            contract="Wrox.ProCSharp.WCF.IRoomService"
            binding="wsHttpBinding" bindingConfiguration="wsHttpBinding" />
      </service>
    </services>
    <bindings>
      <wsHttpBinding>
        <binding name="wsHttpBinding">
          <reliableSession enabled="true" />
        </binding>
      </wsHttpBinding>
    </bindings>
  </system.serviceModel>
</configuration>
```

Hosting

WCF is very flexible when choosing a host to run the service. The host can be a Windows service, a COM+ application, WAS (Windows Activation Services) or IIS, a Windows application, or just a simple console application. When creating a custom host with Windows Forms or WPF, you can easily create a peer-to-peer solution.

Custom Hosting

Let's start with a custom host. The sample code shows hosting of a service within a console application; however, in other custom host types such as Windows services or Windows applications you can program the service in the same way.

In the `Main()` method, a `ServiceHost` instance is created. After the `ServiceHost` instance is created, the application configuration file is read to define the bindings. You can also define the bindings programmatically, as shown earlier. Next, the `Open()` method of the `ServiceHost` class is invoked, so the service accepts client calls. With a console application, you need to be careful not to close the main thread until the service should be closed. Here, the user is asked to "press return" to exit the service. When the user does this, the `Close()` method is called to actually end the service:

```
using System;
using System.ServiceModel;

public class Program
{
    public static void Main()
    {
        using (ServiceHost serviceHost = new ServiceHost())
        {
            serviceHost.Open();

            Console.WriteLine("The service started. Press return to exit");
            Console.ReadLine();

            serviceHost.Close();
        }
    }
}
```

To abort the service host, you can invoke the `Abort()` method of the `ServiceHost` class. To get the current state of the service, the `State` property returns a value defined by the `CommunicationState` enumeration. Possible values are `Created`, `Opening`, `Opened`, `Closing`, `Closed`, and `Faulted`.

> **If you start the service from within a Windows Forms or WPF application and the service code invokes methods of Windows controls, you must be sure that only the control's creator thread is allowed to access the methods and properties of the control. With WCF, this behavior can be achieved easily by setting the `UseSynchronizatonContext` property of the attribute `[ServiceBehavior]`.**

WAS Hosting

With WAS (Windows Activation Services) hosting, you get the features from the WAS worker process such as automatic activation of the service, health monitoring, and process recycling.

To use WAS hosting, you just need to create a Web site and a `.svc` file with the `ServiceHost` declaration that includes the language and the name of the service class. The code shown here is using the class `Service1`. In addition, you must specify the file that contains the service class. This class is implemented in the same way as you saw earlier when defining a WCF service library.

```
<%@ServiceHost language="C#" Service="Service1"
        CodeBehind="Service1.svc.cs" %>
```

If you use a WCF service library that should be available from WAS hosting, you can create a `.svc` file that just contains a reference to the class:

```
<%@ ServiceHost
        Service="Wrox.ProCSharp.WCF.Services.RoomReservationService" %>
```

With Windows Vista and Windows Server 2008, WAS allows defining .NET TCP and Message Queue bindings. If you are using the previous edition, IIS 6 or IIS 5.1 that is available with Windows Server 2003 and Windows XP, activation from a `.svc` file can be done only with an HTTP binding.

You can also add a WCF service to Enterprise Service components. This is discussed in Chapter 44.

Clients

A client application needs a proxy to access a service. There are three ways to create a proxy for the client:

❑ **Visual Studio Add Service Reference** — This utility creates a proxy class from the metadata of the service.

❑ **ServiceModel Metadata Utility tool (Svcutil.exe)** — You can create a proxy class with the Svcutil utility. This utility reads metadata from the service to create the proxy class.

❑ **ChannelFactory class** — This class is used by the proxy generated from Svcutil; however, it can also be used to create a proxy programmatically.

Adding a service reference from Visual Studio requires accessing a WSDL document. The WSDL document is created by a MEX endpoint that needs to be configured with the service. With the following configuration, the endpoint with the relative address mex is using the mexHttpBinding and implements the contract IMetadataExchange. For accessing the metadata with an HTTP GET request, the behaviorConfiguration MexServiceBehavior is configured.

```xml
<?xml version="1.0" encoding="utf-8" ?>
<configuration>
  <system.serviceModel>
    <services>
      <service behaviorConfiguration=" MexServiceBehavior "
        name="Wrox.ProCSharp.WCF.Services.RoomReservationService">
        <endpoint address="Test" binding="wsHttpBinding"
            contract="Wrox.ProCSharp.WCF.Services.IRoomService" />
        <endpoint address="mex" binding="mexHttpBinding"
            contract="IMetadataExchange" />
        <host>
          <baseAddresses>
            <add baseAddress=
  "http://localhost:8731/Design_Time_Addresses/RoomReservationService/" />
          <baseAddresses>
        </host>
      </service>
    </services>
    <behaviors>
      <serviceBehaviors>
        <behavior name="MexServiceBehavior">
          <!-- To avoid disclosing metadata information,
          set the value below to false and remove the metadata endpoint above
          before deployment -->
          <serviceMetadata httpGetEnabled="True"/>
        </behavior>
      </serviceBehaviors>
    </behaviors>
  </system.serviceModel>
</configuration>
```

Similar to the Add service reference from Visual Studio, the Svcutil utility needs metadata to create the proxy class. The Svcutil utility can create a proxy from the MEX metadata endpoint, the metadata of the assembly, or WSDL and XSD documentation:

```
        {
            Console.WriteLine("message from the client: {0}", message);
            IMyMessageCallback callback =
                OperationContext.Current.
                    GetCallbackChannel<IMyMessageCallback>();

            callback.OnCallback("message from the server");

            new Thread(ThreadCallback).Start(callback);
        }

        private void ThreadCallback(object callback)
        {
            IMyMessageCallback messageCallback = callback as IMyMessageCallback;
            for (int i = 0; i < 10; i++)
            {
                messageCallback.OnCallback("message " + i.ToString());
                Thread.Sleep(1000);
            }
        }
    }
```

Hosting the service is the same as it was with the previous samples, so it is not shown here. However, for duplex communication, you must configure a binding that supports a duplex channel. One of the bindings supporting a duplex channel is wsDualHttpBinding, which is configured in the application configuration file:

```xml
<?xml version="1.0" encoding="utf-8" ?>
<configuration>
  <system.serviceModel>
    <services>
      <service name="Wrox.ProCSharp.WCF.MessageService">
        <endpoint contract="Wrox.ProCSharp.WCF.IMyMessage"
            binding="wsDualHttpBinding"/>
        <host>
          <baseAddresses>
            <add baseAddress="http://localhost:8731/Service1" />
          </baseAddresses>
        </host>
      </service>
    </services>
  </system.serviceModel>
</configuration>
```

With the client application, the callback contract must be implemented as shown here with the class ClientCallback that implements the interface IMyMessageCallback:

```
    class ClientCallback : IMyMessageCallback
    {
        public void OnCallback(string message)
        {
            Console.WriteLine("message from the server: {0}", message);
        }
    }
```

With a duplex channel, you cannot use the `ChannelFactory` to initiate the connection to the service as was done previously. To create a duplex channel, you can use the `DuplexChannelFactory` class. This class has a constructor with one more parameter in addition to the binding and address configuration. This parameter specifies an `InstanceContext` that wraps one instance of the `ClientCallback` class. When passing this instance to the factory, the service can invoke the object across the channel. The client just needs to keep the connection open. If the connection is closed, the service cannot send messages across it.

```
WSDualHttpBinding binding = new WSDualHttpBinding();
EndpointAddress address =
    new EndpointAddress("http://localhost:8731/Service1");

ClientCallback clientCallback = new ClientCallback();
InstanceContext context = new InstanceContext(clientCallback);

DuplexChannelFactory<IMyMessage> factory =
    new DuplexChannelFactory<IMyMessage>(context, binding, address);

IMyMessage messageChannel = factory.CreateChannel();

messageChannel.MessageToServer("From the client");
```

Duplex communication is achieved by starting the service host and the client application.

Summary

In this chapter, you learned how to use Windows Communication Foundation for communication between a client and a server. WCF is platform-independent like ASP.NET Web services, but it offers features similar to .NET Remoting, Enterprise Services, and Message Queuing.

WCF has a heavy focus on contracts to make it easier to isolate developing clients and services, and to support platform independence. It defines three different contract types: service contracts, data contracts, and message contracts. You can use several attributes to define the behavior of the service and its operations.

You have seen how to create clients from the metadata offered by the service, but also by using the .NET interface contract.

You have learned the features of different binding options. WCF offers not only bindings for platform independence but also bindings for fast communication between .NET applications.

You've seen how to create custom hosts and also make use of the WAS host.

You've seen how duplex communication is achieved by defining a callback interface, applying a service contract, and implementing a callback contract in the client application.

The next few chapters continue with WCF features. In Chapter 44, "Enterprise Services," you learn how to integrate Enterprise Services with WCF. Chapter 45, "Message Queuing," explains how disconnected Message Queuing features can be used with WCF bindings. And, in Chapter 43, you learn about Windows Workflow Foundation where WCF is used to communicate with Workflow instances.

43

Windows Workflow Foundation

This chapter presents an overview of the Windows Workflow Foundation (known as WF throughout the rest of this chapter), which provides a model to define and execute processes using a set of building blocks called *activities*. WF provides a Designer that, by default, is hosted within Visual Studio, and that allows you to drag and drop activities from the toolbox onto the design surface to create a workflow template.

This template can then be executed by creating a `WorkflowInstance` and then running that instance. The code that executes a workflow is known as the `WorkflowRuntime`, and this object can also host a number of services that the running workflows can access. At any time, there may be several workflow instances executing, and the runtime deals with scheduling these instances and saving and restoring state; it can also record the behavior of each workflow instance as it executes.

A workflow is constructed from a number of activities, and these activities are executed by the runtime. An activity might send an email, update a row in a database, or execute a transaction on a back-end system. There are a number of built-in activities that can be used for general-purpose work, and you can also create your own custom activities and plug these into the workflow as necessary. In this chapter you see the following:

❑   The different types of workflows that can be created

❑   A description of some of the built-in activities

❑   How to create custom activities

We begin with the canonical example that everyone uses when faced with a new technology — Hello World — and also describe what you need to get workflows running on your development machine.

Hello World

Visual Studio 2008 contains built-in support for creating workflows, and when you open the New Project dialog you will see a list of workflow project types as shown in Figure 43-1.

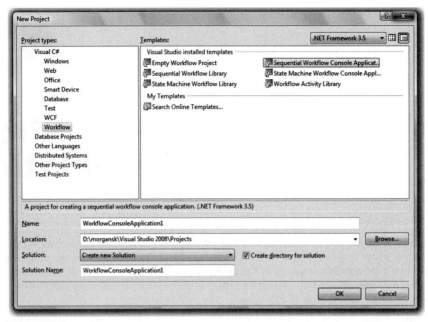

Figure 43-1

Select Sequential Workflow Console Application from the available templates (that will create a console application that hosts the workflow runtime) and a default workflow that you can then drag and drop activities onto.

Next, drag a `Code` activity from the toolbox onto the design surface so that you have a workflow that looks like that shown in Figure 43-2.

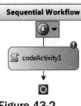

Figure 43-2

The exclamation mark glyph on the top right of the activity indicates that a mandatory property of that activity has not been defined — in this case it is the `ExecuteCode` property, which indicates the method that will be called when the activity executes. You learn how to mark your own properties as mandatory in the section on activity validation. If you double-click the code activity, a method will be created for you in the code-behind class, and here you can use `Console.WriteLine` to output the "Hello World" string as shown in the following code snippet:

```
private void codeActivity1_ExecuteCode(object sender, EventArgs e)
{
    Console.WriteLine("Hello World");
}
```

If you then build and run the program, you will see the output text on the console. When the program executes, an instance of the `WorkflowRuntime` is created, and then an instance of your workflow is constructed and executed. When the code activity executes, it calls the method defined and that outputs the string to the console. The section entitled "The Workflow Runtime" later in the chapter describes in detail how to host the runtime. The code for the preceding example is available in the `01 HelloWorkflowWorld` folder.

Activities

Everything in a workflow is an activity, including the workflow itself. The workflow is a specific type of activity that typically allows other activities to be defined within it — this is known as a composite activity, and you see other composite activities later in this chapter. An activity is just a class that ultimately derives from the `Activity` class.

The `Activity` class defines a number of overridable methods, and arguably the most important of these is the `Execute` method shown in the following snippet:

```
protected override ActivityExecutionStatus Execute
  ( ActivityExecutionContext executionContext )
{
    return ActivityExecutionStatus.Closed;
}
```

When the runtime schedules an activity for execution, the `Execute` method is ultimately called, and that is where you have the opportunity to write custom code to provide the behavior of the activity. In the simple example in the previous section, when the workflow runtime calls `Execute` on the `CodeActivity`, the implementation of this method on the code activity will execute the method defined in the code-behind class, and that displays the message on the console.

The `Execute` method is passed a context parameter of type `ActivityExecutionContext`. You will see more about this as the chapter progresses. The method has a return value of type `ActivityExecutionStatus`, and this is used by the runtime to determine whether the activity has completed successfully, is still processing, or is in one of several other potential states that can describe to the workflow runtime what state the activity is in. Returning `ActivityExecutionStatus.Closed` from this method indicates that the activity has completed its work and can be disposed of.

Numerous standard activities are provided with WF, and the following sections provide examples of some of these together with scenarios in which you might use these activities. The naming convention for activities is to append `Activity` to the name; so for example, the code activity shown in Figure 43-2 is defined by the `CodeActivity` class.

All of the standard activities are defined within the `System.Workflow.Activities` namespace, which in turn forms part of the `System.Workflow.Activities.dll` assembly. There are two other assemblies that make up WF — these are `System.Workflow.ComponentModel.dll` and `System.Workflow.Runtime.dll`.

IfElseActivity

As its name implies, this activity acts like an If-Else statement in C#.

When you drop an IfElseActivity onto the design surface, you will see an activity as displayed in Figure 43-3. The IfElseActivity is a composite activity in that it constructs two branches (which themselves are types of activity, in this case IfElseBranchActivity). Each branch is also a composite activity that derives from SequenceActivity — this class executes each activity in turn from top to bottom. The Designer adds the "Drop Activities Here" text to indicate where child activities can be added.

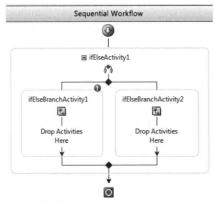

Figure 43-3

The first branch, as shown in Figure 43-3, includes a glyph indicating that the Condition property needs to be defined. A condition derives from ActivityCondition and is used to determine whether that branch should be executed.

When the IfElseActivity is executed, it evaluates the condition of the first branch, and if the condition evaluates to true the branch is executed. If the condition evaluates to false the IfElseActivity then tries the next branch, and so on until the last branch in the activity. It is worth noting that the IfElseActivity can have any number of branches, each with its own condition. The last branch needs no condition because it is in effect the else part of the If-Else statement. To add a new branch, you can display the context menu for the activity and select Add Branch from that menu — this is also available from the *Workflow* menu within Visual Studio. As you add branches, each will have a mandatory condition except for the last one.

Two standard condition types are defined in WF — the CodeCondition and the RuleConditionReference. The CodeCondition class executes a method on your code-behind class, which can return true or false as appropriate. To create a CodeCondition, display the property grid for the IfElseActivity and set the condition to Code Condition, then type in a name for the code to be executed, as shown in Figure 43-4.

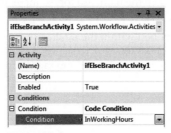

Figure 43-4

When you have typed the method name into the property grid, the Designer will construct a method on your code-behind class, as shown in the following snippet:

```
private void InWorkingHours(object sender, ConditionalEventArgs e)
{
    int hour = DateTime.Now.Hour;

    e.Result = ((hour >= 9) && (hour <= 17));
}
```

This code sets the `Result` property of the passed `ConditionalEventArgs` to `true` if the current hour is between 9 AM and 5 PM. Conditions can be defined in code as shown here, but another option is to define a condition based on a rule that is evaluated in a similar manner. The Workflow Designer contains a rule editor, which can be used to declare conditions and statements (much like the `If-Else` statement shown previously). These rules are evaluated at runtime based on the current state of the workflow.

ParallelActivity

This activity permits you to define a set of activities that execute in parallel — or rather in a pseudo-parallel manner. When the workflow runtime schedules an activity, it does so on a single thread. This thread executes the first activity, then the second, and so on until all activities have completed (or until an activity is waiting on some form of input). When the `ParallelActivity` executes, it iterates through each branch and schedules execution of each branch in turn. The workflow runtime maintains a queue of scheduled activities for each workflow instance, and typically executes these in a FIFO (first in, first out) manner.

Assuming that you have a `ParallelActivity`, as shown in Figure 43-5, this will schedule execution of `sequenceActivity1` and then `sequenceActivity2`. The `SequenceActivity` type works by scheduling execution of its first activity with the runtime, and when this activity completes, it then schedules the second activity. This schedule/wait for completion method is used to traverse through all child activities of the sequence, until all child activities have executed, at which time the sequence activity can complete.

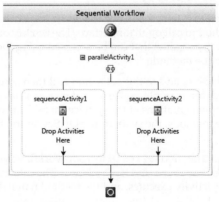

Figure 43-5

Given that the `SequenceActivity` schedules execution of one activity at a time, it means that the queue maintained by the `WorkflowRuntime` is continually updated with schedulable activities. Assuming that we have a parallel activity P1 that contains two sequences, S1 and S2, each with two code activities, C1 and C2, this would produce entries in the scheduler queue, as shown in the following table.

Workflow Queue	Initially There Are No Activities in the Queue
P1	Parallel is executed when the workflow runs.
S1, S2	Added to the queue when P1 executes.
S2, S1.C1	S1 executes and adds S1.C1 to the queue.
S1.C1, S2.C1	S2 executes and adds S2.C1 to the queue.
S2.C1, S1.C2	S1.C1 completes, so S1.C2 is queued.
S1.C2, S2.C2	S2.C1 completes, so S2.C2 is queued.
S2.C2	The last entry in the queue.

Here, the queue processes the first entry (the parallel activity P1), and this adds the sequence activities S1 and S2 to the workflow queue. As the sequence activity S1 executes, it pushes its first child activity (S1.C1) to the end of the queue, and when this activity is scheduled and completes, it then adds the second child activity to the queue.

As can be seen from the preceding example, execution of the `ParallelActivity` is not truly parallel — it effectively interleaves execution between the two sequential branches. From this, you could infer that it's best that an activity execute in a minimal amount of time because, given that there is only one thread servicing the scheduler queue for each workflow, a long-running activity could hamper the execution of other activities in the queue. That said, often, an activity needs to execute for an arbitrary amount of time, so there must be some way to mark an activity as "long-running" so that other activities get a chance to execute. You can do this by returning `ActivityExecutionStatus.Executing` from the `Execute` method, which lets the runtime know that you will call it back later when the activity has finished. An example of this type of activity is the `DelayActivity`.

CallExternalMethodActivity

A workflow will typically need to call methods outside of the workflow, and this activity allows you to define an interface and a method to call on that interface. The `WorkflowRuntime` maintains a list of services (keyed on a `System.Type` value) that can be accessed using the `ActivityExecutionContext` parameter passed to the `Execute` method.

You can define your own services to add to this collection and then access these services from within your own activities. You could, for example, construct a data access layer exposed as a service interface and then provide different implementations of this service for SQL Server and Oracle. Because the activities simply call interface methods, the swap from SQL Server to Oracle would be opaque to the activities.

When you add a `CallExternalMethodActivity` to your workflow, you then define the two mandatory properties of `InterfaceType` and `MethodName`. The interface type defines which runtime service will be used when the activity executes, and the method name defines which method of that interface will be called.

When this activity executes, it looks up the service with the defined interface by querying the execution context for that service type, and it then calls the appropriate method on that interface. You can also pass parameters to the method from within the workflow — this is discussed later in the section titled "Binding Parameters to Activities."

DelayActivity

Business processes often need to wait for a period of time before completing. Consider using a workflow for expense approval. Your workflow might send an email to your immediate manager asking him or her to approve your expense claim. The workflow then enters a waiting state, where it either waits for approval (or, horror of horrors, rejection), but it would also be nice to define a timeout so that if no response is returned within, say, one day, the expense claim is then routed to the next manager up the chain of command.

The `DelayActivity` can form part of this scenario (the other part is the `ListenActivity` defined later). Its job is to wait for a predefined time before continuing execution of the workflow. There are two ways to define the duration of the delay — you can either set the `TimeoutDuration` property of the delay to a string such as "1.00:00:00" (1 day, no hours, minutes, or seconds), or you can provide a method that is called when the activity is executed that sets the duration to a value from code. To do this, you need to define a value for the `InitializeTimeoutDuration` property of the delay activity. This creates a method in the code behind, as shown in the following snippet:

```
private void DefineTimeout(object sender, EventArgs e)
{
    DelayActivity delay = sender as DelayActivity;

    if (null != delay)
    {
        delay.TimeoutDuration = new TimeSpan(1, 0, 0, 0);
    }
}
```

Here, the `DefineTimeout` method casts the sender to a `DelayActivity` and then sets the `TimoutDuration` property in code to a `TimeSpan`. Even though the value is hard-coded here, it is more likely that you would construct this from some other data — maybe a parameter passed into the workflow or a value read from the configuration file. Workflow parameters are discussed in the section "Workflows" later in the chapter.

ListenActivity

A common programming construct is to wait for one of a set of possible events — one example of this is the `WaitAny` method of the `System.Threading.WaitHandle` class. The `ListenActivity` is the way to do this in a workflow, because it can define any number of branches, each with an event-based activity as that branch's first activity.

An event activity is one that implements the `IEventActivity` interface defined in the `System .Workflow.Activities` namespace. There are currently three such activities defined as standard in WF — `DelayActivity`, `HandleExternalEventActivity`, and the `WebServiceInputActivity`. Figure 43-6 shows a workflow that is waiting for either external input or a delay — this is an example of the expense approval workflow discussed earlier.

In the example, the `CallExternalMethodActivity` is used as the first activity in the workflow. This calls a method defined on a service interface that would prompt the manager for approval or rejection. Because this is an external service, this prompt could be an email, an IM message, or any other manner of notifying your manager that an expense claim needs to be processed. The workflow then executes the `ListenActivity`, which awaits input from this external service (either an approval or a rejection), and also waits on a delay.

When the listen executes, it effectively queues a wait on the first activity in each branch, and when one event is triggered, this cancels all other waiting events and then processes the rest of the branch where the event was raised. So, in the instance where the expense report is approved, the `Approved` event is raised and the `PayMe` activity is then scheduled. If, however, your manager rejects the claim, the `Rejected` event is raised, and in the example you then `Panic`.

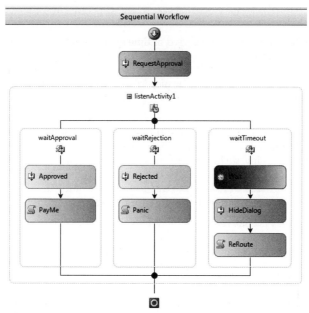

Figure 43-6

Last, if neither the Approved nor Rejected event is raised, the DelayActivity ultimately completes after its delay expires, and the expense report could then be routed to another manager — potentially looking up that person in Active Directory. In the example, a dialog is displayed to the user when the RequestApproval activity is executed, so if the delay executes, you also need to close the dialog, which is the purpose of the activity named HideDialog in Figure 43-6.

The code for this example is available in the 02 Listen directory. Some concepts used in that example have not been covered yet — such as how a workflow instance is identified and how events are raised back into the workflow runtime and ultimately delivered to the right workflow instance. These concepts are covered in the section titled "Workflows."

Activity Execution Model

So far, this chapter has discussed the execution of an activity only by the runtime calling the Execute method. However, an activity may go through a number of states while it executes — these are presented in Figure 43-7.

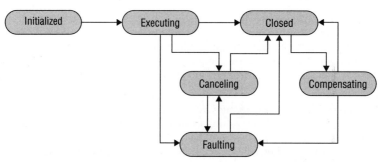

Figure 43-7

An activity is first initialized by the WorkflowRuntime when the runtime calls the activity's Initialize method. This method is passed an IServiceProvider instance, which maps to the services available within the runtime. These services are discussed in the "Workflow Services" section later in the chapter. Most activities do nothing in this method, but the method is there for you to do any setup necessary.

The runtime then calls the Execute method, and the activity can return any one of the values from the ActivityExecutionStatus enum. Typically, you will return Closed from your Execute method, which indicates that your activity has finished processing; however, if you return one of the other status values, the runtime will use this to determine what state your activity is in.

You can return Executing from this method to indicate to the runtime that you have extra work to do — a typical example of this is when you have a composite activity that needs to execute its children. In this case, your activity can schedule each child for execution and then wait for all children to complete before notifying the runtime that your activity has completed.

Custom Activities

So far, you have used activities that are defined within the System.Workflow.Activities namespace. In this section, you learn how to create custom activities and extend these activities to provide a good user experience at both design time and runtime.

To begin, you create a WriteLineActivity that can be used to output a line of text to the console. Although this is a trivial example, it will be expanded to show the full gamut of options available for custom activities using this example. When creating custom activities, you can simply construct a class within a workflow project; however, it is preferable to construct your custom activities inside a separate assembly, because the Visual Studio design time environment (and specifically workflow projects) will load activities from your assemblies and can lock the assembly that you are trying to update. For this reason, you should create a simple class library project to construct your custom activities within.

A simple activity such as the WriteLineActivity will be derived directly from the Activity base class. The following code shows a constructed activity class and defines a Message property that is displayed when the Execute method is called:

```
using System;
using System.ComponentModel;
using System.Workflow.ComponentModel;

namespace SimpleActivity
{
  /// <summary>
  /// A simple activity that displays a message to the console when it executes
  /// </summary>
  public class WriteLineActivity : Activity
  {
    /// <summary>
    /// Execute the activity - display the message on screen
    /// </summary>
    /// <param name="executionContext"></param>
    /// <returns></returns>
    protected override ActivityExecutionStatus Execute
      (ActivityExecutionContext executionContext)
```

(continued)

(continued)

```
    {
      Console.WriteLine(Message);

      return ActivityExecutionStatus.Closed;
    }

    /// <summary>
    /// Get/Set the message displayed to the user
    /// </summary>
    [Description("The message to display")]
    [Category("Parameters")]
    public string Message
    {
      get { return _message; }
      set { _message = value; }
    }

    /// <summary>
    /// Store the message displayed to the user
    /// </summary>
    private string _message;
  }
}
```

Within the `Execute` method, you can write the message to the console and then return a status of `Closed` to notify the runtime that the activity has completed.

You can also define attributes on the `Message` property so that a description and category are defined for that property. This is used in the property grid within Visual Studio, as shown in Figure 43-8.

The code for the activities created in this section is in the `03 CustomActivities` solution. If you compile that solution, you can then add the custom activities to the toolbox within Visual Studio by choosing the Choose Items menu item from the context menu on the toolbox and navigating to the folder where the assembly containing the activities resides. All activities within the assembly will be added to the toolbox.

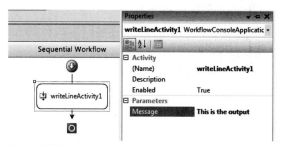

Figure 43-8

As it stands, the activity is perfectly usable; however, there are several areas that should be addressed to make this more user-friendly. As you saw with the `CodeActivity` earlier in the chapter, it has some mandatory properties that, when not defined, produce an error glyph on the design surface. To get the same behavior from your activity, you need to construct a class that derives from `ActivityValidator` and associate this class with your activity.

Activity Validation

When an activity is placed onto the design surface, the Workflow Designer looks for an attribute on that activity that defines a class that performs validation on that activity. To validate your activity, you need to check if the Message property has been set.

A custom validator is passed the activity instance, and from this you can then determine which mandatory properties (if any) have not been defined and add an error to the ValidationErrorCollection used by the Designer. This collection is then read by the Workflow Designer, and any errors found in the collection will cause a glyph to be added to the activity and optionally link each error to the property that needs attention.

```csharp
using System;
using System.Workflow.ComponentModel.Compiler;

namespace SimpleActivity
{
  public class WriteLineValidator : ActivityValidator
  {
    public override ValidationErrorCollection Validate
      (ValidationManager manager, object obj)
    {
      if (null == manager)
        throw new ArgumentNullException("manager");
      if (null == obj)
        throw new ArgumentNullException("obj");

      ValidationErrorCollection errors = base.Validate(manager, obj);

      // Coerce to a WriteLineActivity
      WriteLineActivity act = obj as WriteLineActivity;

      if (null != act)
      {
        if (null != act.Parent)
        {
          // Check the Message property
          if (string.IsNullOrEmpty(act.Message))
            errors.Add(ValidationError.GetNotSetValidationError("Message"));
        }
      }

      return errors;
    }
  }
}
```

The Validate method is called by the Designer when any part of the activity is updated and also when the activity is dropped onto the design surface. The Designer calls the Validate method and passes through the activity as the untyped obj parameter.

In this method, first validate the arguments passed in, and then call the base class Validate method to obtain a ValidationErrorCollection. Although this is not strictly necessary here, if you are deriving from an activity that has a number of properties that also need to be validated, calling the base class method will ensure that these are also checked.

Coerce the passed `obj` parameter into a `WriteLineActivity` instance, and check if the activity has a parent. This test is necessary because the `Validate` function is called during compilation of the activity (if the activity is within a workflow project or activity library), and, at this point, no parent activity has been defined. Without this check, you cannot actually build the assembly that contains the activity and the validator. This extra step is not needed if the project type is class library.

The last step is to check that the `Message` property has been set to a value other than an empty string. This uses a static method of the `ValidationError` class, which constructs an error that specifies that the property has not been defined.

To add validation support to your `WriteLineActivity`, the last step is to add the `ActivityValidation` attribute to the activity, as shown in the following snippet:

```
[ActivityValidator(typeof(WriteLineValidator))]
public class WriteLineActivity : Activity
{
    ...
}
```

If you compile the application and then drop a `WriteLineActivity` onto the workflow, you should see a validation error, as shown in Figure 43-9; clicking this error will take you to that property within the property grid.

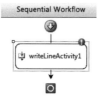

Figure 43-9

If you enter some text for the `Message` property, the validation error will be removed, and you can then compile and run the application.

Now that you have completed the activity validation, the next thing to do is to change the rendering behavior of the activity to add a fill color to that activity. To do this, you need to define both an `ActivityDesigner` class and an `ActivityDesignerTheme` class, as described in the next section.

Themes and Designers

The onscreen rendering of an activity is performed using an `ActivityDesigner` class, and this can also use an `ActivityDesignerTheme`.

The theme class is used to make simple changes to the rendering behavior of the activity within the Workflow Designer:

```
public class WriteLineTheme : ActivityDesignerTheme
{
    /// <summary>
    /// Construct the theme and set some defaults
    /// </summary>
    /// <param name="theme"></param>
    public WriteLineTheme(WorkflowTheme theme)
      : base(theme)
```

```
    {
        this.BackColorStart = Color.Yellow;
        this.BackColorEnd = Color.Orange;
        this.BackgroundStyle = LinearGradientMode.ForwardDiagonal;
    }
}
```

A theme is derived from `ActivityDesignerTheme`, which has a constructor that is passed a `WorkflowTheme` argument. Within the constructor, set the start and end colors for the activity, and then define a linear gradient brush, which is used when painting the background.

The `Designer` class is used to override the rendering behavior of the activity. In this case, no override is necessary, so the following code will suffice:

```
[ActivityDesignerTheme(typeof(WriteLineTheme))]
public class WriteLineDesigner : ActivityDesigner
{
}
```

Note that the theme has been associated with the Designer by using the `ActivityDesignerTheme` attribute.

The last step is to adorn the activity with the `Designer` attribute:

```
[ActivityValidator(typeof(WriteLineValidator))]
[Designer(typeof(WriteLineDesigner))]
public class WriteLineActivity : Activity
{
    ...
}
```

With this in place, the activity is rendered as shown in Figure 43-10.

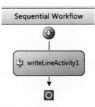

Figure 43-10

With the addition of the Designer and the theme, the activity now looks much more professional. A number of other properties are available on the theme — such as the pen used to render the border, the color of the border, and the border style.

By overriding the `OnPaint` method of the `ActivityDesigner` class, you can have complete control over the rendering of the activity. Be sure to exercise restraint here, because you could get carried away and create an activity that doesn't resemble any of the other activities in the toolbox.

One other useful override on the `ActivityDesigner` class is the `Verbs` property. This allows you to add menu items on the context menu for the activity. It is used by the Designer of the `ParallelActivity` to insert the Add Branch menu item into the activities context menu and also the Workflow menu. You can also alter the list of properties exposed for an activity by overriding the `PreFilterProperties` method of the Designer — this is how the method parameters for the `CallExternalMethodActivity` are surfaced into the property grid. If you need to do this type of extension to your Designer, you should run Lutz Roeder's Reflector (available from `http://www.aisto.com/roeder/dotnet`) and load the workflow assemblies into it to see how Microsoft has defined some of these extended properties.

This activity is nearly done, but now you need to define the icon used when rendering the activity and also the toolbox item to associate with the activity.

ActivityToolboxItem and Icons

To complete your custom activity, you need to add an icon. You can optionally create a class deriving from `ActivityToolboxItem` that is used when displaying the activity in the toolbox within Visual Studio.

To define an icon for an activity, create a 16 × 16 pixel image and include it into your project. When it has been included, set the build action for the image to be `Embedded Resource`. This will include the image in the manifest resources for the assembly. You can add a folder to your project called Resources, as shown in Figure 43-11.

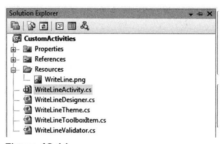

Figure 43-11

Once you have added the image file and set its build action to `Embedded Resource`, you can then attribute the activity as shown in the following snippet:

```
[ActivityValidator(typeof(WriteLineValidator))]
[Designer(typeof(WriteLineDesigner))]
[ToolboxBitmap(typeof(WriteLineActivity),"Resources.WriteLine.png")]
public class WriteLineActivity : Activity
{
    ...
}
```

The `ToolboxBitmap` attribute has a number of constructors defined, and the one being used here takes a type defined in the activity assembly and the name of the resource. When you add a resource to a folder, its name is constructed from the namespace of the assembly and the name of the folder that the image resides within — so the fully qualified name for the resource here is `CustomActivities.Resources .WriteLine.png`. The constructor used with the `ToolboxBitmap` attribute appends the namespace that the type parameter resides within to the string passed as the second argument, so this will resolve to the appropriate resource when loaded by Visual Studio.

The last class you need to create is derived from `ActivityToolboxItem`. This class is used when the activity is loaded into the Visual Studio toolbox. A typical use of this class is to change the displayed name of the activity on the toolbox — all of the built-in activities have their names changed to remove the word "Activity" from the type. In your class, you can do the same by setting the `DisplayName` property to "WriteLine."

```
[Serializable]
public class WriteLineToolboxItem : ActivityToolboxItem
{
    /// <summary>
    /// Set the display name to WriteLine - i.e. trim off
    /// the 'Activity' string
    /// </summary>
    /// <param name="t"></param>
    public WriteLineToolboxItem(Type t)
        : base(t)
    {
        base.DisplayName = "WriteLine";
    }

    /// <summary>
    /// Necessary for the Visual Studio design time environment
    /// </summary>
    /// <param name="info"></param>
    /// <param name="context"></param>
    private WriteLineToolboxItem(SerializationInfo info,
                                StreamingContext context)
    {
        this.Deserialize(info, context);
    }
}
```

The class is derived from `ActivityToolboxItem` and overrides the constructor to change the display name; it also provides a serialization constructor that is used by the toolbox when the item is loaded into the toolbox. Without this constructor, you will receive an error when you attempt to add the activity to the toolbox. Note that the class is also marked as `[Serializable]`.

The toolbox item is added to the activity by using the `ToolboxItem` attribute as shown:

```
[ActivityValidator(typeof(WriteLineValidator))]
[Designer(typeof(WriteLineDesigner))]
[ToolboxBitmap(typeof(WriteLineActivity),"Resources.WriteLine.png")]
[ToolboxItem(typeof(WriteLineToolboxItem))]
public class WriteLineActivity : Activity
{
    ...
}
```

With all of these changes in place, you can compile the assembly and then create a new workflow project. To add the activity to the toolbox, open a workflow and then display the context menu for the toolbox and click Choose Items.

You can then browse for the assembly containing your activity, and once you have added it to the toolbox, it will look something like Figure 43-12. The icon is somewhat less than perfect, but it's close enough.

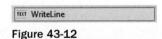

Figure 43-12

You revisit the `ActivityToolboxItem` in the next section on custom composite activities, because there are some extra facilities available with that class that are necessary only when adding composite activities to the design surface.

Custom Composite Activities

There are two main types of activity. Activities that derive from `Activity` can be thought of as callable functions from the workflow. Activities that derive from `CompositeActivity` (such as `ParallelActivity`, `IfElseActivity`, and the `ListenActivity`) are containers for other activities. Their design-time behavior is considerably different from simple activities in that they present an area on the Designer where child activities can be dropped.

In this section, you create an activity that you can call the `DaysOfWeekActivity`. This activity can be used to execute different parts of a workflow based on the current date. You might, for instance, need to execute a different path in the workflow for orders that arrive over the weekend than for those that arrive during the week. In this example, you learn about a number of advanced workflow topics, and by the end of this section, you should have a good understanding of how to extend the system with your own composite activities. The code for this example is also available in the `03 CustomActivities` solution.

To begin, you create a custom activity that has a property that will default to the current date/time. You will allow that property to be set to another value that could come from another activity in the workflow or a parameter that is passed to the workflow when it executes. This composite activity will contain a number of branches — these will be user defined. Each of these branches will contain an enumerated constant that defines which day(s) that branch will execute. The following example defines the activity and two branches:

```
DaysOfWeekActivity
   SequenceActivty: Monday, Tuesday, Wednesday, Thursday, Friday
      <other activites as appropriate>
   SequenceActivity: Saturday, Sunday
      <other activites as appropriate>
```

For this example, you need an enumeration that defines the days of the week — this will include the `[Flags]` attribute (so you can't use the built-in `DayOfWeek` enum defined within the `System` namespace, because this doesn't include the `[Flags]` attribute).

```
[Flags]
[Editor(typeof(FlagsEnumEditor), typeof(UITypeEditor))]
public enum WeekdayEnum : byte
{
    None = 0x00,
    Sunday = 0x01,
    Monday = 0x02,
    Tuesday = 0x04,
    Wednesday = 0x08,
    Thursday = 0x10,
    Friday = 0x20,
    Saturday = 0x40
}
```

Also included is a custom editor for this type, which will allow you to choose enum values based on check boxes. This code is available in the download.

With the enumerated type defined, you can take an initial stab at the activity itself. Custom composite activities are typically derived from the `CompositeActivity` class, because this defines among other things an `Activities` property, which is a collection of all subordinate activities.

```
public class DaysOfWeekActivity : CompositeActivity
{
    /// <summary>
    /// Get/Set the day of week property
    /// </summary>
    [Browsable(true)]
    [Category("Behavior")]
    [Description("Bind to a DateTime property, set a specific date time,
                  or leave blank for DateTime.Now")]
    [DefaultValue(typeof(DateTime),"")]
    public DateTime Date
    {
        get { return (DateTime)
                base.GetValue(DaysOfWeekActivity.DateProperty); }
        set { base.SetValue(DaysOfWeekActivity.DateProperty, value); }
    }

    /// <summary>
    /// Register the DayOfWeek property
    /// </summary>
    public static DependencyProperty DateProperty =
        DependencyProperty.Register("Date", typeof(DateTime),
            typeof(DaysOfWeekActivity));
}
```

The `Date` property provides the regular getter and setter, and we've also added a number of standard attributes so that it displays correctly within the property browser. The code, though, looks somewhat different from a normal .NET property, because the getter and setter are not using a standard field to store their values, but instead are using what's called a `DependencyProperty`.

The `Activity` class (and therefore this class, because it's ultimately derived from `Activity`) is derived from the `DependencyObject` class, and this defines a dictionary of values keyed on a `DependencyProperty`. This indirection of getting/setting property values is used by WF to support binding; that is, linking a property of one activity to a property of another. As an example, it is common to pass parameters around in code, sometimes by value, sometimes by reference. WF uses binding to link property values together — so in this example, you might have a `DateTime` property defined on the workflow, and this activity might need to be bound to that value at runtime. You see an example of binding later in the chapter.

If you build this activity, it won't do much; indeed it will not even allow child activities to be dropped into it, because you haven't defined a `Designer` class for the activity.

Adding a Designer

As you saw with the `WriteLineActivity` earlier in the chapter, each activity can have an associated `Designer` class, which is used to change the design-time behavior of that activity. You saw a blank `Designer` in the `WriteLineActivity`, but for the composite activity you need to override a couple of methods to add some special case processing:

```
public class DaysOfWeekDesigner : ParallelActivityDesigner
{
    public override bool CanInsertActivities
        (HitTestInfo insertLocation, ReadOnlyCollection<Activity> activities)
    {
        foreach (Activity act in activities)
```

(continued)

(continued)

```
        {
            if (!(act is SequenceActivity))
                return false;
        }

        return base.CanInsertActivities(insertLocation, activitiesToInsert);
    }

    protected override CompositeActivity OnCreateNewBranch()
    {
        return new SequenceActivity();
    }
}
```

This `Designer` derives from `ParallalActivityDesigner`, which provides you with good design-time behavior when adding child activities. You will need to override `CanInsertActivities` to return `false` if any of the dropped activities is not a `SequenceActivity`. If all activities are of the appropriate type, you can call the base class method, which makes some further checks on the activity types permitted within your custom activity.

You should also override the `OnCreateNewBranch` method that is called when the user chooses the Add Branch menu item. The `Designer` is associated with the activity by using the `[Designer]` attribute, as shown here:

```
[Designer(typeof(DaysOfWeekDesigner))]
public class DaysOfWeekActivity : CompositeActivity
{
}
```

The design-time behavior is nearly complete; however, you also need to add a class that is derived from `ActivityToolboxItem` to this activity, because that defines what happens when an instance of that activity is dragged from the toolbox. The default behavior is simply to construct a new activity; however, in the example you also want to create two default branches. The following code shows the toolbox item class in its entirety:

```
[Serializable]
public class DaysOfWeekToolboxItem : ActivityToolboxItem
{
    public DaysOfWeekToolboxItem(Type t)
        : base(t)
    {
        this.DisplayName = "DaysOfWeek";
    }

    private DaysOfWeekToolboxItem(SerializationInfo info,
                                    StreamingContext context)
    {
        this.Deserialize(info, context);
    }

    protected override IComponent[] CreateComponentsCore(IDesignerHost host)
    {
        CompositeActivity parent = new DaysOfWeekActivity();
        parent.Activities.Add(new SequenceActivity());
```

```
        parent.Activities.Add(new SequenceActivity());

        return new IComponent[] { parent };
    }
}
```

As shown in the code, the display name of the activity was changed, a serialization constructor was implemented, and the `CreateComponentsCore` method was overridden.

This method is called at the end of the drag-and-drop operation, and it is where you construct an instance of the `DaysOfWeekActivity`. In the code, you are also constructing two child sequence activities, because this gives the user of the activity a better design-time experience. Several of the built-in activities do this, too — when you drop an `IfElseActivity` onto the design surface, its toolbox item class adds two branches. A similar thing happens when you add a `ParallelActivity` to your workflow.

The serialization constructor and the `[Serializable]` attribute are necessary for all classes derived from `ActivityToolboxItem`.

The last thing to do is associate this toolbox item class with the activity:

```
[Designer(typeof(DaysOfWeekDesigner))]
[ToolboxItem(typeof(DaysOfWeekToolboxItem))]
public class DaysOfWeekActivity : CompositeActivity
{
}
```

With that in place, the UI of your activity is almost complete, as you can see in Figure 43-13.

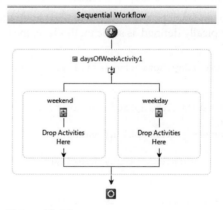

Figure 43-13

Now, you need to define a property on each of the sequence activities shown in Figure 43-13, so that the user can define which day(s) the branch will execute. There are two ways to do this in Windows Workflow: you can create a subclass of `SequenceActivity` and define it there, or you can use another feature of dependency properties called Attached Properties.

You will use the latter method, because this means that you don't have to subclass but instead can effectively extend the sequence activity without needing the source code of that activity.

Attached Properties

When registering dependency properties, you can call the `RegisterAttached` method to create an attached property. An attached property is one that is defined on one class but is displayed on another. So here, you define a property on the `DaysOfWeekActivity`, but that property is actually displayed in the UI as attached to a sequential activity.

The code in the following snippet shows a property called `Weekday` of type `WeekdayEnum`, which will be added to the sequence activities that reside within your composite activity:

```
public static DependencyProperty WeekdayProperty =
    DependencyProperty.RegisterAttached("Weekday",
        typeof(WeekdayEnum), typeof(DaysOfWeekActivity),
        new PropertyMetadata(DependencyPropertyOptions.Metadata));
```

The final line allows you to specify extra information about a property. In this instance, it is specifying that it is a `Metadata` property.

Metadata properties differ from normal properties in that they are effectively read only at runtime. You can think of a `Metadata` property as similar to a constant declaration within C#. You cannot alter constants while the program is executing, and you cannot change `Metadata` properties while a workflow is executing.

In this example, you wish to define the days that the activity will execute, so you could in the Designer set this field to "Saturday, Sunday". In the code emitted for the workflow, you would see a declaration as follows (I have reformatted the code to fit the confines of the page):

```
this.sequenceActivity1.SetValue
    (DaysOfWeekActivity.WeekdayProperty,
    ((WeekdayEnum)((WeekdayEnum.Sunday | WeekdayEnum.Saturday))));
```

In addition to defining the dependency property, you will need methods to get and set this value on an arbitrary activity. These are typically defined as static methods on the composite activity and are shown in the following code:

```
public static void SetWeekday(Activity activity, object value)
{
    if (null == activity)
        throw new ArgumentNullException("activity");
    if (null == value)
        throw new ArgumentNullException("value");

    activity.SetValue(DaysOfWeekActivity.WeekdayProperty, value);
}

public static object GetWeekday(Activity activity)
{
    if (null == activity)
        throw new ArgumentNullException("activity");

    return activity.GetValue(DaysOfWeekActivity.WeekdayProperty);
}
```

You need to make two other changes in order for this extra property to show up attached to a `SequenceActivity`. The first is to create an *extender provider*, which tells Visual Studio to include the extra property in the sequence activity. The second is to register this provider, which is done by overriding the `Initialize` method of the Activity Designer and adding the following code to it:

```
protected override void Initialize(Activity activity)
{
    base.Initialize(activity);

    IExtenderListService iels = base.GetService(typeof(IExtenderListService))
        as IExtenderListService;

    if (null != iels)
    {
        bool extenderExists = false;

        foreach (IExtenderProvider provider in iels.GetExtenderProviders())
        {
            if (provider.GetType() == typeof(WeekdayExtenderProvider))
            {
                extenderExists = true;
                break;
            }
        }
        if (!extenderExists)
        {
            IExtenderProviderService ieps =
                base.GetService(typeof(IExtenderProviderService))
                    as IExtenderProviderService;
            if (null != ieps)
                ieps.AddExtenderProvider(new WeekdayExtenderProvider());
        }
    }
}
```

The calls to GetService in the preceding code allow the custom Designer to query for services proffered by the host (in this case Visual Studio). You query Visual Studio for the IExtenderListService, which provides a way to enumerate all available extender providers, and if no instance of the WeekdayExtenderProvider service is found, then query for the IExtenderProviderService and add a new provider.

The code for the extender provider is shown here:

```
[ProvideProperty("Weekday", typeof(SequenceActivity))]
public class WeekdayExtenderProvider : IExtenderProvider
{
    bool IExtenderProvider.CanExtend(object extendee)
    {
        bool canExtend = false;

        if ((this != extendee) && (extendee is SequenceActivity))
        {
            Activity parent = ((Activity)extendee).Parent;

            if (null != parent)
                canExtend = parent is DaysOfWeekActivity;
        }

        return canExtend;
    }
```

(continued)

(continued)

```
    public WeekdayEnum GetWeekday(Activity activity)
    {
        WeekdayEnum weekday = WeekdayEnum.None;

        Activity parent = activity.Parent;

        if ((null != parent) && (parent is DaysOfWeekActivity))
            weekday = (WeekdayEnum)DaysOfWeekActivity.GetWeekday(activity);

        return weekday;
    }

    public void SetWeekday(Activity activity, WeekdayEnum weekday)
    {
        Activity parent = activity.Parent;

        if ((null != parent) && (parent is DaysOfWeekActivity))
            DaysOfWeekActivity.SetWeekday(activity, weekday);

    }
}
```

An extender provider is attributed with the properties that it provides, and for each of these properties it must provide a public Get<Property> and Set<Property> method. The names of these methods must match the name of the property with the appropriate *Get* or *Set* prefix.

With the preceding changes made to the Designer and the addition of the extender provider, when you click a sequence activity within the Designer, you will see the properties in Figure 43-14 within Visual Studio.

Figure 43-14

Extender providers are used for other features in .NET. One common one is to add tooltips to controls in a Windows Forms project — this registers an extender and adds a Tooltip property to each control on the form.

Workflows

Up to this point, the chapter has concentrated on activities but has not discussed workflows. A workflow is simply a list of activities, and indeed a workflow itself is just another type of activity. Using this model simplifies the runtime engine, because the engine just needs to know how to execute one type of object — that being anything derived from the Activity class.

Each workflow instance is uniquely identified by its `InstanceId` property — this is a `Guid` that can be assigned by the runtime, or this `Guid` can be provided to the runtime by your code. A common use of this is to correlate a running workflow instance with some other data maintained outside of the workflow, such as a row in a database. You can access the specific workflow instance by using the `GetWorkflow(Guid)` method of the `WorkflowRuntime` class.

Two types of workflows are available with WF — sequential and state machine.

Sequential Workflows

The root activity in a sequential workflow is the `SequentialWorkflowActivity`. This class is derived from `SequenceActivity`, which you have already seen, and it defines two events that you can attach handlers to as necessary. These are the `Initialized` and `Completed` events.

A sequential workflow starts executing the first child activity within it, and typically continues until all other activities have executed. There are a couple of instances when a workflow will not continue through all activities — one is if an exception is raised while executing the workflow, and the other is if a `TerminateActivity` exists within the workflow.

A workflow may not be executing at all times. For example, when a `DelayActivity` is encountered, the workflow will enter a wait state and can be removed from memory if a workflow persistence service is defined. Persistence of workflows is covered in "The Persistence Service" section later in this chapter.

State Machine Workflows

A state machine workflow is useful when you have a process that may be in one of several states, and transitions from one state to another can be made by passing data into the workflow.

One example is when a workflow is used for access control to a building. In this case, you may model a door class that can be closed or open, and a lock class that can be locked or unlocked. Initially when you boot up the system (or building!), you start at a known state — for sake of argument, assume that all doors are closed and locked, so the state of a given door is *closed locked*.

When an employee enters his or her building access code at the front door, an event is sent to the workflow, which includes details such as the code entered and possibly the user ID. You might then need to access a database to retrieve details such as whether that person is permitted to open the selected door at that time of day, and assuming that access is granted, the workflow would change from its initial state to the *closed unlocked* state.

From this state, there are two potential outcomes — the employee opens the door (you know this because the door also has an open/closed sensor), or the employee decides not to enter because he has left something in his car, and so after a delay you relock the door. The door could revert to its *closed locked* state or move to the *open unlocked* state.

From here, assume that the employee enters the building and then closes the door. Again, you would then like to transition from the *open unlocked* state to *closed unlocked*, and again, after a delay, would then transition to the *closed locked* state. You might also want to raise an alarm if the door was *open unlocked* for a long period.

Modeling this scenario within Windows Workflow is fairly simple. You need to define the states that the system can be in, and then define events that can transition the workflow from one state to the next. The following table describes the states of the system and provides details of the transitions that are possible from each known state and the inputs (either external or internal) that change the states.

State	Transitions
Closed Locked	This is the initial state of the system. In response to the user swiping her card (and a successful access check), the state changes to closed unlocked, and the door lock is electronically opened.
Closed Unlocked	One of two events can occur when the door is in this state: The user opens the door — you transition to the open unlocked state. A timer expires, and the door reverts to the closed locked state.
Open Unlocked	From this state, the workflow can only transition to closed unlocked.
Fire Alarm	This is the final state for the workflow and can be transitioned to from any of the other states.

One other feature you might want to add to the system is the capability to respond to a fire alarm. When the fire alarm goes off, you would want to unlock all of the doors so that anyone can exit the building, and the fire service can enter the building unimpeded. You might want to model this as the final state of the doors workflow, because from this state the full system would be reset once the fire alarm had been canceled.

The workflow in Figure 43-15 defines this state machine and shows the states that the workflow can be in. The lines denote the state transitions that are possible within the system.

The initial state of the workflow is modeled by the ClosedLocked activity. This consists of some initialization code (which locks the door) and then an event-based activity that awaits an external event — in this case, the employee entering his building access code. Each of the activities shown within the state shapes consist of sequential workflows, so we have defined a workflow for the initialization of the system (CLInitialize) and a workflow that responds to the external event raised when the employee enters her PIN (RequestEntry). If you look at the RequestEntry workflow, it is defined as shown in Figure 43-16.

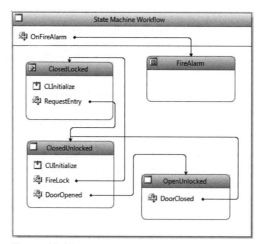

Figure 43-15

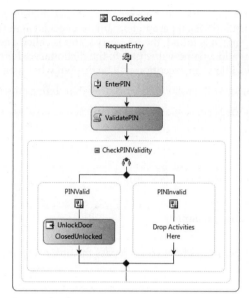

Figure 43-16

Each state consists of a number of subworkflows, each of which has an event-driven activity at the start and then any number of other activities that form the processing code within the state. In Figure 43-16, there is a HandleExternalEventActivity at the start that awaits the entry of the PIN. This is then checked, and if it is valid, the workflow transitions to the ClosedUnlocked state.

The ClosedUnlocked state consists of two workflows — one that responds to the door open event, which transitions the workflow to the OpenUnlocked state, and the other, which contains a delay activity that is used to change the state to ClosedLocked. A state-driven activity works in a similar manner to the ListenActivity shown earlier in the chapter — the state consists of a number of event-driven workflows, and on arrival of an event, just one of the workflows will execute.

To support the workflow, you need to be able to raise events in the system to affect the state changes. This is done by using an interface and an implementation of that interface; this pair of objects is termed an *external service*. The interface used for this state machine is described later in the chapter.

The code for the state machine example is available in the 04 StateMachine solution. This also includes a user interface in which you can enter a PIN and gain access to the building through one of two doors.

Passing Parameters to a Workflow

A typical workflow requires some data in order to execute. This could be an order ID for an order-processing workflow, a customer account ID for a payment-processing workflow, or any other items of data necessary.

The parameter-passing mechanism for workflows is somewhat different from that of standard .NET classes, in which you typically pass parameters in a method call. For a workflow, you pass parameters by storing those parameters in a dictionary of name-value pairs, and when you construct the workflow, you pass through this dictionary.

When WF schedules the workflow for execution, it uses these name-value pairs to set public properties on the workflow instance. Each parameter name is checked against the public properties of the workflow, and if a match is found, the property setter is called and the value of the parameter is passed to this setter. If you add a name-value pair to the dictionary where the name does not correspond to a property on the workflow, an exception will be thrown when you try to construct that workflow.

As an example, consider the following workflow that defines the `OrderID` property as an integer:

```
public class OrderProcessingWorkflow: SequentialWorkflowActivity
{
    public int OrderID
    {
        get { return _orderID; }
        set { _orderID = value; }
    }

    private int _orderID;
}
```

The following snippet shows how you can pass the order ID parameter into an instance of this workflow:

```
WorkflowRuntime runtime = new WorkflowRuntime ();

Dictionary<string,object> parms = new Dictionary<string,object>();
parms.Add("OrderID", 12345) ;

WorkflowInstance instance = runtime.CreateWorkflow(typeof(OrderProcessingWorkflow),
parms);

instance.Start();

... Other code
```

In the example code, you construct a `Dictionary<string, object>` that will contain the parameters you wish to pass to the workflow and then use this when the workflow is constructed. The preceding code includes the `WorkflowRuntime` and `WorkflowInstance` classes, which haven't been described yet but are discussed in the "Hosting Workflows" section later in the chapter.

Returning Results from a Workflow

Another common requirement of a workflow is to return output parameters, which might then be used to record data within a database or other persistent storage.

Because a workflow is executed by the workflow runtime, you can't just call a workflow using a standard method invocation — you need to create a workflow instance, start that instance, and then await the completion of that instance. When a workflow completes, the workflow runtime raises the `WorkflowCompleted` event. This is passed contextual information about the workflow that has just completed and contains the output data from that workflow.

So, to harvest the output parameters from a workflow, you need to attach an event handler to the `WorkflowCompleted` event, and the handler can then retrieve the output parameters from the workflow. The following code shows an example of how this can be done:

```
using(WorkflowRuntime workflowRuntime = new WorkflowRuntime())
{
    AutoResetEvent waitHandle = new AutoResetEvent(false);
    workflowRuntime.WorkflowCompleted +=
        delegate(object sender, WorkflowCompletedEventArgs e)
        {
            waitHandle.Set();
            foreach (KeyValuePair<string, object> parm in e.OutputParameters)
            {
                Console.WriteLine("{0} = {1}", parm.Key, parm.Value);
            }
        };

    WorkflowInstance instance =
        workflowRuntime.CreateWorkflow(typeof(Workflow1));
    instance.Start();

    waitHandle.WaitOne();
}
```

You have attached a delegate to the `WorkflowCompleted` event, and within this you iterate through the `OutputParameters` collection of the `WorkflowCompletedEventArgs` class passed to the delegate and display the output parameters on the console. This collection contains all public properties of the workflow. There is actually no notion of specific output parameters for a workflow.

Binding Parameters to Activities

Now that you know how to pass parameters into a workflow, you also need to know how to link these parameters to activities. This is done via a mechanism called binding. In the `DaysOfWeekActivity` defined earlier, there was a `Date` property that could be hard-coded or bound to another value within the workflow. A bindable property is displayed in the property grid within Visual Studio, as shown in Figure 43-17. The icon to the right of the property name indicates that this is a bindable property — in the image the `Date` property is bindable.

Figure 43-17

Double-clicking the bind icon will display the dialog shown in Figure 43-18. This dialog allows you to select an appropriate property to link to the `Date` property.

In Figure 43-18, we have selected the `OrderDate` property of the workflow (which is defined as a regular .NET property, as shown in an earlier code snippet). Any bindable property can be bound to either a property of the workflow that the activity is defined within or a property of any activity that resides in the workflow above the current activity. Note that the data type of the property being bound must match the data type of the property you are binding to — the dialog will not permit you to bind nonmatching types.

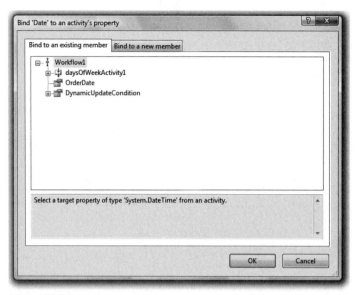

Figure 43-18

The code for the `Date` property is repeated here to show how binding works and is explained in the following paragraphs:

```
public DateTime Date
{
    get { return (DateTime)base.GetValue(DaysOfWeekActivity.DateProperty); }
    set { base.SetValue(DaysOfWeekActivity.DateProperty, value); }
}
```

When you bind a property in the workflow, an object of type `ActivityBind` is constructed behind the scenes, and it is this "value" that is stored within the dependency property. So, the property setter will be passed an object of type `ActivityBind`, and this is stored within the dictionary of properties on this activity. This `ActivityBind` object consists of data that describes the activity being bound to and the property of that activity that is to be used at runtime.

When reading the value of the property, the `GetValue` method of the `DependencyObject` is called, and this method checks the underlying property value to see if it is an `ActivityBind` object. If so, it then resolves the activity to which this binding is linked and then reads the real property value from that activity. If, however, the bound value is another type, it simply returns that object from the `GetValue` method.

The Workflow Runtime

In order to start a workflow, it is necessary to create an instance of the `WorkflowRuntime` class. This is typically done once within your application, and this object is usually defined as a static member of the application so that it can be accessed anywhere within the application.

When you start the runtime, it can then reload any workflow instances that were executing the last time the application was executed by reading these instances from the persistence store. This uses a service called the *persistence service*, which is defined in the following section.

The runtime contains six various `CreateWorkflow` methods that can be used to construct workflow instances. The runtime also contains methods for reloading a workflow instance and enumerating all running instances.

The runtime also has a number of events that are raised while workflows are executing — such as `WorkflowCreated` (raised when a new workflow instance is constructed), `WorkflowIdled` (raised when a workflow is awaiting input such as in the expense-processing example shown earlier), and `WorkflowCompleted` (raised when a workflow has finished).

Workflow Services

A workflow doesn't exist on its own. As described in the previous section, a workflow is executed within the `WorkflowRuntime`, and this runtime provides *services* to running workflows.

A service is any class that may be needed while executing the workflow. Some standard services are provided to your workflow by the runtime, and you can optionally construct your own services to be consumed by running workflows.

This section describes two of the standard services provided by the runtime. It then shows how you can create your own services and some instances of when this is necessary.

When an activity runs, it is passed some contextual information via the `ActivityExecutionStatus` parameter of the `Execute` method:

```
protected override ActivityExecutionStatus Execute
    (ActivityExecutionContext executionContext)
{
    ...
}
```

One of the methods available on this context parameter is the `GetService<T>` method. This can be used as shown in the following code to access a service attached to the workflow runtime:

```
protected override ActivityExecutionStatus Execute
    (ActivityExecutionContext executionContext)
{
    ICustomService myService = executionContext.GetService<ICustomService>();
    ... Do something with the service
}
```

The services hosted by the runtime are added to the runtime prior to calling the `StartRuntime` method. An exception is raised if you attempt to add a service to the runtime once it has been started.

Two methods are available for adding services to the runtime. You can construct the services in code and then add them to the runtime by calling the `AddService` method. Or, you can define services within the application configuration file, and these will be constructed for you and added to the runtime.

The following code snippet shows how to add services to the runtime in code — the services added are those described later in this section:

```
using(WorkflowRuntime workflowRuntime = new WorkflowRuntime())
{
    workflowRuntime.AddService(
        new SqlWorkflowPersistenceService(conn, true, new TimeSpan(1,0,0),
                                          new TimeSpan(0,10,0)));
    workflowRuntime.AddService(new SqlTrackingService(conn));
    ...
}
```

Here are constructed instances of the `SqlWorkflowPersistenceService`, which is used by the runtime to store workflow state, and an instance of the `SqlTrackingService`, which records the execution events of a workflow while it runs.

To create services using an application configuration file, you need to add a section handler for the workflow runtime and then add services to this section as shown here:

```xml
<?xml version="1.0" encoding="utf-8" ?>
<configuration>
  <configSections>
    <section name="WF"
      type="System.Workflow.Runtime.Configuration.WorkflowRuntimeSection,
      System.Workflow.Runtime, Version=3.0.00000.0, Culture=neutral,
      PublicKeyToken=31bf3856ad364e35" />
  </configSections>

  <WF Name="Hosting">
    <CommonParameters/>
      <Services>
        <add type="System.Workflow.Runtime.Hosting.SqlWorkflowPersistenceService,
                   System.Workflow.Runtime, Version=3.0.00000.0, Culture=neutral,
                   PublicKeyToken=31bf3856ad364e35"
          connectionString="Initial Catalog=WF;Data Source=.;
                            Integrated Security=SSPI;"
          UnloadOnIdle="true"
          LoadIntervalSeconds="2"/>
        <add type="System.Workflow.Runtime.Tracking.SqlTrackingService,
                   System.Workflow.Runtime, Version=3.0.00000.0, Culture=neutral,
                   PublicKeyToken=31bf3856ad364e35"
          connectionString="Initial Catalog=WF;Data Source=.;
                            Integrated Security=SSPI;"
          UseDefaultProfile="true"/>
      </Services>
  </WF>
</configuration>
```

Within the configuration file, you have added the WF section handler (the name is unimportant but must match the name given to the later configuration section) and then created the appropriate entries for this section. The `<Services>` element can contain an arbitrary list of entries that consist of a .NET type and then parameters that will be passed to that service when constructed by the runtime.

To read the configuration settings from the application configuration file, you call another constructor on the runtime, as shown here:

```csharp
using(WorkflowRuntime workflowRuntime = new WorkflowRuntime("WF"))
{
    . . .
}
```

This constructor will instantiate each service defined within the configuration file and add these to the services collection on the runtime.

The following sections describe some of the standard services available with WF.

The Persistence Service

When a workflow executes, it may reach a wait state. This can occur when a delay activity executes or when you are waiting for external input within a listen activity. At this point, the workflow is said to be *idle* and as such is a candidate for persistence.

Let's assume that you begin execution of 1,000 workflows on your server, and each of these instances becomes idle. At this point, it is unnecessary to maintain data for each of these instances in memory, so it would be ideal if you could unload a workflow and free up the resources in use. The persistence service is designed to accomplish this.

When a workflow becomes idle, the workflow runtime checks for the existence of a service that derives from the `WorkflowPersistenceService` class. If this service exists, it is passed the workflow instance, and the service can then capture the current state of the workflow and store it in a persistent storage medium. You could store the workflow state on disk in a file, or store this data within a database such as SQL Server.

The workflow libraries contain an implementation of the persistence service, which stores data within a SQL Server database — this is the `SqlWorkflowPersistenceService`. In order to use this service, you need to run two scripts against your SQL Server instance. One of these constructs the schema, and the other creates the stored procedures used by the persistence service. These scripts are, by default, located in the `C:\Windows\Microsoft.NET\Framework\v3.5\Windows Workflow Foundation\SQL\EN` directory.

The scripts to execute against the database are `SqlPersistenceProviderSchema.sql` and `SqlPersistenceProviderLogic.sql`. These need to be executed in order, with the schema file first and then the logic file. The schema for the SQL persistence service contains two tables: `InstanceState` and `CompletedScope`. These are essentially opaque tables, and they are not intended for use outside the SQL persistence service.

When a workflow idles, its state is serialized using binary serialization, and this data is then inserted into the `InstanceState` table. When a workflow is reactivated, the state is read from this row and used to reconstruct the workflow instance. The row is keyed on the workflow instance ID and is deleted from the database once the workflow has completed.

The SQL persistence service can be used by multiple runtimes at the same time — it implements a locking mechanism so that a workflow is accessible by only one instance of the workflow runtime at a time. When you have multiple servers all running workflows using the same persistence store, this locking behavior becomes invaluable.

To see what is added to the persistence store, construct a new workflow project and add an instance of the `SqlWorkflowPersistenceService` to the runtime. The following code shows an example using declarative code:

```
using(WorkflowRuntime workflowRuntime = new WorkflowRuntime())
{
    workflowRuntime.AddService(
        new SqlWorkflowPersistenceService(conn, true, new TimeSpan(1,0,0),
                                    new TimeSpan(0,10,0)));
    // Execute a workflow here...
}
```

If you then construct a workflow that contains a `DelayActivity` and set the delay to something like 10 seconds, you can then view the data stored within the `InstanceState` table. The `05 WorkflowPersistence` example contains the preceding code and executes a delay within a 20-second period.

The parameters passed to the constructor of the persistence service are shown in the following table.

Parameter	Description	Default
ConnectionString	The database connection string used by the persistence service.	None
UnloadOnIdle	Determines whether a workflow is unloaded when it idles. This should always be set to `true`; otherwise no persistence will occur.	False
InstanceOwnershipDuration	This defines the length of time that the workflow instance will be owned by the runtime that has loaded that workflow.	None
LoadingInterval	The interval used when polling the database for updated persistence records.	2 Minutes

These values can also be defined within the configuration file.

The Tracking Service

When a workflow executes it might be necessary to record which activities have run, and in the case of composite activities such as the `IfElseActivity` or the `ListenActivity`, which branch was executed. This data could be used as a form of audit trail for a workflow instance, which could then be viewed at a later date to prove which activities executed and what data was used within the workflow. The tracking service can be used for this type of recording and can be configured to log as little or as much information about a running workflow instance as is necessary.

As is common with WF, the tracking service is implemented as an abstract class called `TrackingService`, so it is easy to replace the standard tracking implementation with one of your own. There is one concrete implementation of the tracking service available within the workflow assemblies — this is the `SqlTrackingService`.

To record data about the state of a workflow, it is necessary to define a `TrackingProfile`. This defines which events should be recorded, so you could, for example, record just the start and end of a workflow and omit all other data about the running instance. More typically, you will record all events for the workflow and each activity in that workflow to provide a complete picture of the execution profile of the workflow.

When a workflow is scheduled by the runtime engine, the engine checks for the existence of a workflow tracking service. If one is found, it asks the service for a tracking profile for the workflow being executed, and then uses this to record workflow and activity data. You can, in addition, define user tracking data and store this within the tracking data store without needing to change the schema.

The tracking profile class is shown in Figure 43-19. The class includes collection properties for activity, user, and workflow *track points*. A track point is an object (such as `WorkflowTrackPoint`) that typically defines a *match location* and some extra data to record when this track point is hit. The match location defines where this track point is valid — so for example, you could define a `WorkflowTrackPoint`, which will record some data when the workflow is created, and another to record some data when the workflow is completed.

Figure 43-19

Once this data has been recorded, it may be necessary to display the execution path of a workflow, as in Figure 43-20. This shows the workflow that was executed, and each activity that ran includes a glyph to show that it executed. This data is read from the tracking store for that workflow instance.

To read the data stored by the `SqlTrackingService`, you could execute queries against the SQL database directly; however, Microsoft has provided the `SqlTrackingQuery` class defined within the `System.Workflow.Runtime.Tracking` namespace for this purpose. The following example code shows how to retrieve a list of all workflows tracked between two dates:

```
public IList<SqlTrackingWorkflowInstance> GetWorkflows
   (DateTime startDate, DateTime endDate, string connectionString)
{
   SqlTrackingQuery query = new SqlTrackingQuery (connectionString);

   SqlTrackingQueryOptions queryOptions = new SqlTrackingQueryOptions();
   query.StatusMinDateTime = startDate;
   query.StatusMaxDateTime = endDate;

   return (query.GetWorkflows (queryOptions));
}
```

This uses the `SqlTrackingQueryOptions` class, which defines the query parameters. You can define other properties of this class to further constrain the workflows retrieved.

In Figure 43-20 you can see that all activities have executed. This might not be the case if the workflow were still running or if there were some decisions made within the workflow so that different paths were taken during execution. The tracking data contains details such as which activities have executed, and this data can be correlated with the activities to produce the image in Figure 43-20. It is also possible to extract data from the workflow as it executes, which could be used to form an audit trail of the execution flow of the workflow.

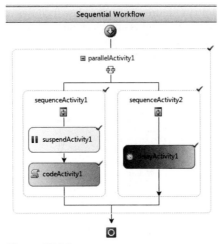

Figure 43-20

Custom Services

In addition to built-in services such as the persistence service and the tracking service, you can add your own objects to the services collection maintained by the `WorkflowRuntime`. These services are typically defined using an interface and an implementation, so that you can replace the service without recoding the workflow.

The state machine presented earlier in the chapter uses the following interface:

```
[ExternalDataExchange]
public interface IDoorService
{
    void LockDoor();
    void UnlockDoor();

    event EventHandler<ExternalDataEventArgs> RequestEntry;
    event EventHandler<ExternalDataEventArgs> OpenDoor;
    event EventHandler<ExternalDataEventArgs> CloseDoor;
    event EventHandler<ExternalDataEventArgs> FireAlarm;

    void OnRequestEntry(Guid id);
    void OnOpenDoor(Guid id);
    void OnCloseDoor(Guid id);
    void OnFireAlarm();
}
```

The interface consists of methods that are used by the workflow to call the service and events raised by the service that are consumed by the workflow. The use of the `ExternalDataExchange` attribute indicates to the workflow runtime that this interface is used for communication between a running workflow and the service implementation.

Within the state machine, there are a number of instances of the `CallExternalMethodActivity` that are used to call methods on this external interface. One example is when the door is locked or unlocked — the workflow needs to execute a method call to the `UnlockDoor` or `LockDoor` methods, and the service responds by sending a command to the door lock to unlock or lock the door.

When the service needs to communicate with the workflow, this is done by using an event, because the workflow runtime also contains a service called the `ExternalDataExchangeService`, which acts as a proxy for these events. This proxy is used when the event is raised, because the workflow may not be loaded in memory at the time the event is delivered. So the event is first routed to the external data exchange service, which checks to see if the workflow is loaded, and, if not, rehydrates it from the persistence store and then passes the event on into the workflow.

The code used to construct the `ExternalDataExchangeService` and to construct proxies for the events defined by the service is shown here:

```
WorkflowRuntime runtime = new WorkflowRuntime();
ExternalDataExchangeService edes = new ExternalDataExchangeService();

runtime.AddService(edes);
DoorService service = new DoorService();
edes.AddService(service);
```

This constructs an instance of the external data exchange service and adds it to the runtime. It then creates an instance of the `DoorService` (which itself implements `IDoorService`) and adds this to the external data exchange service.

The `ExternalDataExchangeService.Add` method constructs a proxy for each event defined by the custom service so that a persisted workflow can be loaded prior to delivery of the event. If you don't host your service within the external data exchange service, when you raise events there will be nothing listening to these events, so they will not be delivered to the correct workflow.

Events use the `ExternalDataEventArgs` class, because this includes the workflow instance ID that the event is to be delivered to. If there are other values that need to be passed from an external event to a workflow, you should derive a class from `ExternalDataEventArgs` and add these values as properties to that class.

Integration with Windows Communication Foundation

Two new activities are available with .NET 3.5 that support integration between workflows and WCF. These are the `SendActivity` and the `ReceiveActivity`. The `SendActivity` could more aptly be called the `CallActivity`, because what it does is issue a request to a WCF service and can optionally surface the results as parameters that can be bound to within the calling workflow.

Somewhat more interesting, however, is the new `ReceiveActivity`. This allows a workflow to become the implementation of a WCF service, so now the workflow is the service. The following example exposes a service using a workflow and also uses the new service test host tool to test the service without having to write a separate test harness.

From the New Project menu in Visual Studio 2008, choose the WCF node and then the Sequential Workflow Service Library entry as shown in Figure 43-21.

Figure 43-21

This will create a library that contains a workflow as shown in Figure 43-22, an application configuration file, and a service interface.

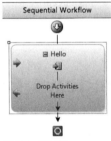

Figure 43-22

The workflow exposes the Hello operation of the contract and also defines properties for the arguments passed to this operation, and the return value of the operation. Then, all you need to do is to add code that provides the execution behavior of the service, and your service is complete.

To do this for the example, drag a `CodeActivity` onto the `ReceiveActivity` as shown in Figure 43-23, and then double-click that activity to supply the service implementation.

The code shown in the following snippet is all that there is to this service implementation:

```
public sealed partial class Workflow1: SequentialWorkflowActivity
{
    public Workflow1()
    {
        InitializeComponent();
    }
```

```
        public String returnValue = default(System.String);
        public String inputMessage = default(System.String);

        private void codeActivity1_ExecuteCode(object sender, EventArgs e)
        {
            this.returnValue = string.Format("You said {0}", inputMessage);
        }
    }
```

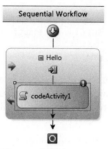

Figure 43-23

Because the service contract for the Hello operation includes both a parameter (`inputMessage`) and a return value, these have been exposed to the workflow as public fields. Within the code, we have set the `returnValue` to a string value, and this is what is returned from a call to the WCF service.

If you compile this service and hit F5, you will notice another new feature of Visual Studio 2008 — the WCF Test Client application, as shown in Figure 43-24.

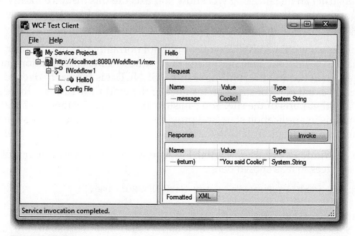

Figure 43-24

Here you can browse for the operations that the service exposes, and by double-clicking an operation, the right-hand side of the window is displayed, which lists the parameters used by that service and any return value(s) exposed.

To test the service, enter a value for the message property and click the Invoke button. This will then make a request over WCF to the service, which will construct and execute the workflow, call the code activity, which then runs the code-behind, and ultimately return to the WCF Test Client the result from the workflow.

If you wish to manually host workflows as services, you can use the new `WorkflowServiceHost` class defined within the `System.WorkflowServices` assembly. The following snippet shows a minimal host implementation:

```
using (WorkflowServiceHost host = new WorkflowServiceHost
                                    (typeof(YourWorkflow)))
{
  host.Open();
  Console.WriteLine ( "Press [Enter] to exit" );
  Console.ReadLine();
}
```

Here we have constructed an instance of `WorkflowServiceHost` and passed it the workflow that will be executed. This is similar to how you would use the `ServiceHost` class when hosting WCF services. It will read the configuration file to determine which endpoints the service will listen on and then await service requests.

The next section describes some other options you have for hosting workflows.

Hosting Workflows

The code to host the `WorkflowRuntime` in a process will vary based on the application itself.

For a Windows Forms application or a Windows Service, it is typical to construct the runtime at the start of the application and store this in a property of the main application class.

In response to some input in the application (such as the user clicking a button on the user interface), you might then construct an instance of a workflow and execute this instance locally. The workflow may well need to communicate with the user — so, for example, you might define an external service that prompts the user for confirmation before posting an order to a back-end server.

When hosting workflows within ASP.NET, you would not normally prompt the user with a message box but instead navigate to a different page on the site that requested the confirmation and then present a confirmation page. When hosting the runtime within ASP.NET, it is typical to override the `Application_Start` event and construct an instance of the workflow runtime there so that it is accessible within all other parts of the site. You can store the runtime instance in a static property, but it is more usual to store this in application state and provide an accessor method that will retrieve the workflow runtime from application state so that it can be used elsewhere in the application.

In either scenario — Windows Forms or ASP.NET — you will construct an instance of the workflow runtime and add services to it as shown here:

```
WorkflowRuntime workflowRuntime = new WorkflowRuntime();

workflowRuntime.AddService(
    new SqlWorkflowPersistenceService(conn, true, new TimeSpan(1,0,0),
                                    new TimeSpan(0,10,0)));
// Execute a workflow here...
```

To execute a workflow, you need to create an instance of that workflow using the `CreateInstance` method of the runtime. There are a number of overrides of this method that can be used to construct an instance of a code-based workflow or a workflow defined in XML.

Up to this point in the chapter, you have considered workflows as .NET classes — and indeed that is one representation of a workflow. You can, however, define a workflow using XML, and the runtime will construct an in-memory representation of the workflow and then execute it when you call the Start method of the WorkflowInstance.

Within Visual Studio, you can create an XML-based workflow by choosing the Sequential Workflow (with code separation) or the State Machine Workflow (with code separation) items from the Add New Item dialog. This will create an XML file with the extension .xoml and load it into the Designer.

When you add activities to the Designer, these activities are persisted into the XML, and the structure of elements defines the parent/child relationships between the activities. The following XML shows a simple sequential workflow that contains an IfElseAcvtivity and two code activities, one on each branch of the IfElseActivity:

```
<SequentialWorkflowActivity x:Class="DoorsWorkflow.Workflow1" x:Name="Workflow1"
  xmlns:x="http://schemas.microsoft.com/winfx/2006/xaml"
  xmlns="http://schemas.microsoft.com/winfx/2006/xaml/workflow">
  <IfElseActivity x:Name="ifElseActivity1">
    <IfElseBranchActivity x:Name="ifElseBranchActivity1">
      <IfElseBranchActivity.Condition>
        <CodeCondition Condition="Test" />
      </IfElseBranchActivity.Condition>
      <CodeActivity x:Name="codeActivity1" ExecuteCode="DoSomething" />
    </IfElseBranchActivity>
    <IfElseBranchActivity x:Name="ifElseBranchActivity2">
      <CodeActivity x:Name="codeActivity2" ExecuteCode="DoSomethingElse" />
    </IfElseBranchActivity>
  </IfElseActivity>
</SequentialWorkflowActivity>
```

The properties defined on the activities are persisted into the XML as attributes, and each activity is persisted as an element. As you can see from the XML, the structure defines the relationship between parent activities (such as the SequentialWorkflowActivity and the IfElseActivity) and the child activities.

Executing an XML-based workflow is no different from executing a code-based workflow — you simply use an override of the CreateWorkflow method that takes an XmlReader instance, and then start that instance by calling the Start method.

One benefit of using XML-based workflows over code-based workflows is that you can then easily store the workflow definition within a database. You can load up this XML at runtime and execute the workflow, and you can very easily make changes to the workflow definition without having to recompile any code.

Changing a workflow at runtime is also supported whether the workflow is defined in XML or code. You construct a WorkflowChanges object, which contains all of the new activities to be added to the workflow, and then call the ApplyWorkflowChanges method defined on the WorkflowInstance class to persist these changes. This is exceptionally useful, because business needs often change and, for example, you might want to apply changes to an insurance policy workflow so that you send an email to the customers a month prior to the renewal date to let them know their policy is due for renewal. Changes are made on an instance-by-instance basis, so if you had 100 policy workflows in the system, you would need to make these changes to each individual workflow.

The Workflow Designer

To complete this chapter, we've left the best until last. The Workflow Designer that you use to design workflows isn't tied to Visual Studio — you can rehost this Designer within your own application as necessary.

This means that you could deliver a system containing workflows and permit end users to customize the system without requiring them to have a copy of Visual Studio. Hosting the Designer is, however, fairly complex, and we could devote several chapters to this one topic, but we are out of space. A number of examples of rehosting are available on the Web — we recommend reading the MSDN article on hosting the Designer available at `http://msdn2.microsoft.com/en-us/library/aa480213.aspx` for more information.

The traditional way of allowing users to customize a system is by defining an interface and then allowing the customer to implement this interface to extend processing as required.

With Windows Workflow that extension becomes a whole lot more graphical, because you can present users with a blank workflow as a template and provide a toolbox that contains custom activities that are appropriate for your application. They can then author their workflows and add in your activities or custom activities they have written themselves.

Summary

Windows Workflow will produce a radical change in the way that applications are constructed. You can now surface complex parts of an application as activities, and permit users to alter the processing of the system simply by dragging and dropping activities into a workflow.

There is almost no application that you could not apply workflow to — from the simplest command-line tool to the most complex system containing many hundreds of modules. Although the new communication capabilities of WCF and the new UI capabilities of Windows Presentation Foundation are a great step forward for applications in general, the addition of Windows Workflow will produce a seismic change in the way that applications are developed and configured.

If you have time to invest in only one of the new facilities available with the .NET Framework 3.0, we suggest concentrating on Windows Workflow. We expect skills in workflow to be very highly sought after for years to come.

Now that this chapter is complete, the next chapter goes over enterprise services in detail.

Enterprise Services

Enterprise Services is the name of the Microsoft application server technology that offers services for distributed solutions. Enterprise Services is based on the COM+ technology that has already been in use for many years. However, instead of wrapping .NET objects as COM objects to use these services, .NET offers extensions for .NET components to take direct advantage of these services. With .NET you get easy access to COM+ services for .NET components.

Enterprise Services also has a great integration story with WCF. You can use a tool to automatically create a WCF service front-end to a serviced component, and you can invoke a WCF service from a COM+ client.

This chapter covers the following topics:

- ❏ When to use Enterprise Services
- ❏ What services you get with this technology
- ❏ How to create a serviced component to use Enterprise Services
- ❏ How to deploy COM+ applications
- ❏ How to use transactions with Enterprise Services
- ❏ How to create a WCF front-end to Enterprise Services
- ❏ How to use Enterprise Services from a WCF Client

This chapter is using the sample database Northwind, which you can download from the Microsoft downloads page: `www.microsoft.com/downloads`.

Overview

The complexity of Enterprise Services and the different configuration options (many of them are not needed if all the components of the solution are developed with .NET) can be more easily understood if you know the history of Enterprise Services. This chapter starts with that history. After that, you get an overview of the different services offered by the technology, so you know what features could be useful for your application.

The topics covered in this section are:

- ❏ History
- ❏ Where to use Enterprise Services
- ❏ Contexts
- ❏ Automatic transactions
- ❏ Distributed transactions
- ❏ Object pooling
- ❏ Role-based security
- ❏ Queued components
- ❏ Loosely coupled events

History

Enterprise Services can be traced back to Microsoft Transaction Server (MTS), which was released as an option pack for Windows NT 4.0. MTS extended COM by offering services such as transactions for COM objects. The services could be used by configuring metadata: the configuration of the component defined whether or not a transaction was required. With MTS it was no longer necessary to deal with transactions programmatically. However, MTS had a big disadvantage. COM was not designed to be extensible, so MTS made extensions by overwriting the COM component registry configuration to direct the instantiation of the component to MTS, and some special MTS API calls have been required to instantiate COM objects within MTS. This problem was solved with Windows 2000.

One of the most important features of Windows 2000 was the integration of MTS and COM in a new technology with the name COM+. In Windows 2000, COM+ base services are aware of the context that is needed by COM+ services (previously MTS services), so the special MTS API calls are no longer needed. With COM+ services some new service functionality is offered in addition to distributed transactions.

Windows 2000 includes COM+ 1.0. COM+ 1.5 is available since Windows XP and Windows Server 2003. COM+ 1.5 adds more features to increase scalability and availability, including application pooling and recycling, and configurable isolation levels.

.NET Enterprise Services allows you to use COM+ services from within .NET components. Support is offered for Windows 2000 and later. When .NET components are run within COM+ applications, no COM callable wrapper is used (see Chapter 24, "Interoperability"); the application runs as a .NET component instead. When you install the .NET runtime on an operating system, some runtime extensions are added to COM+ Services. If two .NET components are installed with Enterprise Services, and component A is using component B, COM marshaling is not used; instead, the .NET components can invoke each other directly.

Where to Use Enterprise Services

Business applications can be logically separated into presentation, business, and data service layers. The *presentation service layer* is responsible for user interaction. Here, the user can interact with the application to enter and view data. Technologies used with this layer are Windows Forms and ASP.NET Web Forms. The *business service layer* consists of business rules and data rules. The *data service layer* interacts with persistent storage. Here, you can use components that make use of ADO.NET. Enterprise Services fits both to the business service layer and to the data service layer.

Figure 44-1 shows two typical application scenarios. Enterprise Services can be used directly from a rich client using Windows Forms or WPF or from a Web application that is running ASP.NET.

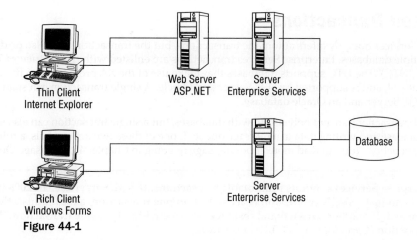

Figure 44-1

Enterprise Services is also a scalable technology. Using *component load balancing* makes it possible to distribute the load of the clients across different systems.

You can also use Enterprise Services on the client system, because this technology is included in Windows Vista and Windows XP.

Contexts

The base functionality behind the services offered by Enterprise Services is the context. The context makes it possible to intercept a method call, and some service functionality can be carried out before the expected method call is invoked. For example, a transactional or a synchronization scope can be created before the method implemented by the component is invoked.

With the contexts here, a COM component and a .NET component can participate in the same transaction. All this is done with the help of the base class ServicedComponent that itself derives from MarshalByRefObject to integrate .NET and COM+ contexts.

Automatic Transactions

The most commonly used feature of Enterprise Services is *automatic transactions*. With automatic transactions, it is not necessary to start and commit a transaction in the code; an attribute can be applied to a class instead. By using the [Transaction] attribute with the options Required, Supported, RequiresNew, and NotSupported, you can mark a class with the requirements it has for transactions. If you mark the class with the option Required, a transaction is created automatically when a method starts and is committed to or aborted when the root component of the transaction is finished.

Such a declarative way to program is of particular advantage when a complex object model is developed. Here, automatic transactions have a big advantage over programming transactions manually. Assume that you have a Person object with multiple Address and Document objects that are associated with the Person, and you want to store the Person object together with all associated objects in a single transaction. Doing transactions programmatically would mean passing a transaction object to all the related objects so that they can participate in the same transaction. Using transactions declaratively means there is no need to pass the transaction object, because this happens behind the scenes by using the context.

Distributed Transactions

Enterprise Services not only offers automatic transactions, but the transactions can also be distributed across multiple databases. Enterprise Services transactions are enlisted with the *Distributed Transaction Coordinator* (DTC). The DTC supports databases that make use of the XA protocol, which is a two-phase commit protocol, and is supported by SQL Server and Oracle. A single transaction can span writing data to both a SQL Server and an Oracle database.

Distributed transactions are not only useful with databases, but a single transaction can also span writing data to a database and writing data to a message queue. If one of these two actions fails, a rollback is done with the other action. You can read more about message queuing in Chapter 45, "Message Queuing."

> Enterprise Services supports promotable transactions. If SQL Server 2005 or 2008 is used and just a single connection is active within one transaction, a local transaction is created. If another transactional resource is active within the same transaction, the transaction is promoted to a DTC transaction.

Later in this chapter, you see how to create a component that requires transactions.

Object Pooling

Pooling is another feature offered by Enterprise Services. These services use a pool of threads to answer requests from clients. Object pooling can be used for objects with a long initialization time. With object pooling, objects are created in advance so that clients don't have to wait until the object is initialized.

Role-Based Security

Using *role-based security* allows you to define roles declaratively and define what methods or components can be used from what roles. The system administrator assigns users or user groups to these roles. In the program there is no need to deal with access control lists; instead, roles that are simple strings can be used.

Queued Components

Queued components is an abstraction layer to message queuing. Instead of sending messages to a message queue, the client can invoke methods with a recorder that offers the same methods as a .NET class configured in Enterprise Services. The recorder in turn creates messages that are transferred via a message queue to the server application.

Queued components and message queuing are useful if the client application is running in a disconnected environment (for example, on a laptop that does not always has a connection to the server), or if the request that is sent to the server should be cached before it is forwarded to a different server (for example, to a server of a partner company).

Loosely Coupled Events

Chapter 7, "Delegates and Events," explained the event model of .NET. Chapter 24, "Interoperability," describes how to use events in a COM environment. With both of these event mechanisms, the client and the server do have a tight connection. This is different with *loosely coupled events* (LCE). With LCE the COM+ facility is inserted between client and server (see Figure 44-2). The publisher registers the events it will offer with COM+ by defining an event class. Instead of sending the events directly to the client, the publisher sends events to the event class that is registered with the LCE service. The LCE service forwards the events to the subscriber, which is the client application that registered a subscription for the event.

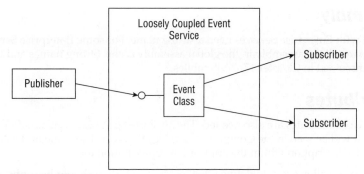

Figure 44-2

Creating a Simple COM+ Application

To create a .NET class that can be configured with Enterprise Services, you have to reference the assembly `System.EnterpriseServices` and add the namespace `System.EnterpriseServices` to the using declarations. The most important class to use is `ServicedComponent`.

The first example shows the basic requirements to create a serviced component. You start by creating a C# library application. All COM+ applications must be written as library applications regardless of whether they will run in their own process or in the process of the client. Name the library `SimpleServer`. Reference the assembly `System.EnterpriseServices` and add the declaration using `System.EnterpriseServices;` to the `assmblyinfo.cs` and `class1.cs` files.

The ServicedComponent Class

Every serviced component class must derive from the base class `ServicedComponent`. `ServicedComponent` itself derives from the class `ContextBoundObject`, so an instance is bound to a .NET Remoting context.

The class `ServicedComponent` has some protected methods that can be overridden, as shown in the following table.

Protected Method	Description
`Activate()` `Deactivate()`	The `Activate()` and `Deactivate()` methods are called if the object is configured to use object pooling. When the object is taken from the pool, the `Activate()` method is called. Before the object is returned to the pool, `Deactivate()` is called.
`CanBePooled()`	This is another method for object pooling. If the object is in an inconsistent state, you can return `false` in your overridden implementation of `CanBePooled()`. This way the object is not put back into the pool, but destroyed instead. A new object will be created for the pool.
`Construct()`	This method is called at instantiation time, where a construction string can be passed to the object. The construction string can be modified by the system administrator. Later in this chapter, you use the construction string to define the database connection string.

Sign the Assembly

Libraries configured with Enterprise Services need a strong name. For some Enterprise Services features it is also necessary to install the assembly in the global assembly cache. Strong names and the global assembly cache are discussed in Chapter 17, "Assemblies."

Assembly Attributes

Some Enterprise Services attributes are also needed. The attribute ApplicationName defines the name of the application as it will be seen in the Component Services Explorer. The value of the Description attribute shows up as a description within the application configuration tool.

ApplicationActivation allows you to define whether the application should be configured as a library application or a server application, using the options ActivationOption.Library or ActivationOption.Server. With a library application, the application is loaded inside the process of the client. In that case the client might be the ASP.NET runtime. With a server application, a process for the application is started. The name of the process is dllhost.exe. With the attribute ApplicationAccessControl, you can turn off security so that every user is allowed to use the component.

Rename the file Class1.cs to SimpleComponent.cs and add these attributes outside the namespace declaration:

```
[assembly: ApplicationName("Wrox EnterpriseDemo")]
[assembly: Description("Wrox Sample Application for Professional C#")]
[assembly: ApplicationActivation(ActivationOption.Server)]
[assembly: ApplicationAccessControl(false)]
```

The following table lists the most important assembly attributes that can be defined with Enterprise Services applications.

Attribute	Description
[ApplicationName]	The attribute [ApplicationName] defines the name for the COM+ application that shows up in the Component Services Explorer after the component is configured.
[ApplicationActivation]	The attribute [ApplicationActivation] defines if the application should run as a library within the client application or if a separate process should be started. The options to configure are defined with the enumeration ActivationOption. ActivationOption.Library defines to run the application inside the process of the client; ActivationOption.Server starts its own process, dllhost.exe.
[ApplicationAccessControl]	The attribute [ApplicationAccessControl] defines the security configuration of the application. Using a Boolean value you can enable or disable access control. With the Authentication property you can set privacy levels — whether the client should be authenticated with every method call or just with the connection, and whether the data sent should be encrypted.

Creating the Component

In the `SimpleComponent.cs` file, you can create your serviced component class. With serviced components, it is best to define interfaces that are used as the contract between the client and the component. This is not a strict requirement, but some of the Enterprise Services features (such as setting role-based security on a method or interface level) do require interfaces. Create the interface `IGreeting` with the method `Welcome()`. The attribute `[ComVisible]` is required for serviced component classes and interfaces that can be accessed from Enterprise Services features.

```
using System;
using System.EnterpriseServices;
using System.Runtime.InteropServices;

namespace Wrox.ProCSharp.EnterpriseServices
{
    [ComVisible(true)]
    public interface IGreeting
    {
        string Welcome(string name);
    }
}
```

The class `SimpleComponent` derives from the base class `ServicedComponent` and implements the interface `IGreeting`. The class `ServicedComponent` acts as a base class of all serviced component classes, and offers some methods for the activation and construction phases. Applying the attribute `[EventTrackingEnabled]` to this class makes it possible to monitor the objects with the Component Services Explorer. By default, monitoring is disabled because using this feature reduces performance. The `[Description]` attribute only specifies text that shows up in the Explorer:

```
[EventTrackingEnabled(true)]
[ComVisible(true)]
[Description("Simple Serviced Component Sample")]
public class SimpleComponent : ServicedComponent, IGreeting
{
    public SimpleComponent()
    {
    }
```

The method `Welcome()` returns only `"Hello, "` with the name that is passed to the argument. So that you can see some visible result in the Component Services Explorer while the component is running, `Thread.Sleep()` simulates some processing time:

```
    public string Welcome(string name)
    {
        // simulate some processing time
        System.Threading.Thread.Sleep(1000);
        return "Hello, " + name;
    }
}
```

Other than applying some attributes and deriving the class from `ServicedComponent`, there's nothing special to do with classes that should use Enterprises Services features. All that is left to do is build and deploy a client application.

In the first sample component, the attribute `[EventTrackingEnabled]` was set. Some more commonly used attributes that influence the configuration of serviced components are described in the following table.

Attribute Class	Description
[EventTrackingEnabled]	Setting the attribute [EventTrackingEnabled] allows monitoring the component with the Component Services Explorer. Setting this attribute to true has some additional overhead associated; that's why, by default, event tracking is turned off.
[JustInTimeActivation]	With this attribute, the component can be configured to not activate when the caller instantiates the class, but instead when the first method is invoked. Also, with this attribute the component can deactivate itself.
[ObjectPooling]	If the initialization time of a component is long compared to the time of a method call, an object pool can be configured with the attribute [ObjectPooling]. With this attribute, minimum and maximum values can be defined that influence the number of objects in the pool.
[Transaction]	The attribute [Transaction] defines transactional characteristics of the component. Here, the component defines whether a transaction is required, supported, or not supported.

Deployment

Assemblies with serviced components must be configured with COM+. This configuration can be done automatically or by registering the assembly manually.

Automatic Deployment

If a .NET client application that uses the serviced component is started, the COM+ application is configured automatically. This is true for all classes that are derived from the class ServicedComponent. Application and class attributes such as [EventTrackingEnabled] define the characteristics of the configuration.

Automatic deployment has an important drawback. For automatic deployment to work, the client application needs administrative rights. If the client application that invokes the serviced component is ASP.NET, the ASP.NET runtime usually doesn't have administrative rights. With this drawback, automatic deployment is useful only during development time. However, during development, automatic deployment is an extremely advantageous feature because it is not necessary to do manual deployment after every build.

Manual Deployment

You can deploy the assembly manually with the command-line utility .NET Services installation tool regsvcs.exe. Starting the command

```
regsvcs SimpleServer.dll
```

registers the assembly SimpleServer as a COM+ application and configures the included components according to their attributes; it also creates a type library that can be used by COM clients accessing the .NET component.

After you've configured the assembly, you can start the Component Services Explorer by selecting Administrative Tools ⇨ Component Services from the Windows menu on Windows XP or Windows Server 2003. On Windows Vista you have to start the MMC and add the Component Services snap-in to see the Component Services Explorer. In the left tree view of this application, you can select Component Services ⇨ Computers ⇨ My Computer ⇨ COM+ Applications to verify that the application was configured.

Creating an Installer Package

With the Component Services Explorer, you can create Windows installer packages for server or client systems. An installer package for the server includes the assemblies and configuration settings to install the application on a different server. If the serviced component is invoked from applications running on different systems, a proxy must be installed on the client system. The installer package for the client includes assemblies and configuration for proxies.

To create an installer package, you can start the Component Services Explorer, select the COM+ application, select the menu options Action ⇨ Export, and click the Next button in the first dialog. The dialog shown in Figure 44-3 opens. In this dialog, you can export either a Server application or an application proxy. With the option Server application you can also configure to export user identities with roles. This option should be selected only if the target system is in the same domain as the system where the package is created, because the configured user identities are put into the installer package. With the option application proxy, an installer package for the client system is created.

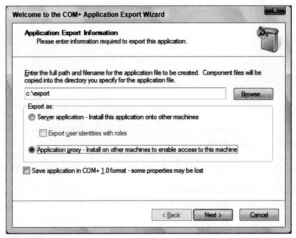

Figure 44-3

The option to create an application proxy is not available if the application is configured as a library application.

To install the proxy, you just have to start setup.exe from the installer package. Be aware that an application proxy cannot be installed on the same system where the application is installed. After installation of the application proxy, you can see an entry in Component Services Explorer that represents the application proxy. With the application proxy the only option that can be configured is the name of the server in the Activation tab, as discussed in the next section.

Component Services Explorer

After a successful configuration, you can see `Wrox EnterpriseDemo` as an application name in the tree view of the Component Services Explorer. This name was set by the attribute `[ApplicationName]`. Selecting Action ⇨ Properties opens the dialog box shown in Figure 44-4. Both the name and the description have been configured by using attributes. When you select the Activation tab, you can see that the application is configured as a server application because this has been defined with the `[ApplicationActivation]` attribute, and selecting the Security tab shows that the "Enforce access checks for this application" option is not selected because the attribute `[ApplicationAccessControl]` was set to `false`.

Figure 44-4

The following is a list of some more options that can be set with this application:

❑ **Security** — With the security configuration, you can enable or disable access checks. If security is enabled, you can set access checks to the application level, the component, the interface, and to the method level. It is also possible to encrypt messages that are sent across the network using packet privacy as an authentication level for calls. Of course, this also increases the overhead.

❑ **Identity** — With server applications, you can use the Identity tab to configure the user account that will be used for the process that hosts the application. By default, this is the interactive user. This setting is very useful while debugging the application but cannot be used on a production system if the application is running on a server, because there might not be anybody logged on. Before installing the application on the production system you should test the application by using a specific user for the application.

❑ **Activation** — The Activation tab allows you to configure the application either as a library or as a server application. Two new options with COM+ 1.5 are the option to run the application as a Windows Service and to use SOAP to access the application. Windows Services are discussed in Chapter 23, "Windows Services." Selecting the SOAP option uses .NET Remoting configured within Internet Information Server to access the component. Instead of using .NET Remoting, later in this chapter the component will be accessed using WCF. WCF is discussed in Chapter 42, "Windows Communication Foundation."

With an application proxy, the option "Remote server name" is the only option that can be configured. This option sets the name of the server. By default, the DCOM protocol is used as the network protocol. However, if SOAP is selected in the server configuration, the communication happens through .NET Remoting.

❑ **Queuing** — The Queuing configuration is required for service components that make use of message queuing.

❑ **Advanced** — On the Advanced tab, you can specify whether the application should be shut down after a certain period of client inactivity. You can also specify whether to lock a certain configuration so that no one can change it accidentally.

❑ **Dump** — If the application crashes, you can specify the directory where the dumps should be stored. This is useful for components developed with C++.

❑ **Pooling and Recycling** — Pooling and recycling is a new option with COM+ 1.5. With this option, you can configure whether the application should be restarted (recycled) depending on application lifetime, memory needs, number of calls, and so on.

With the Component Services Explorer, you can also view and configure the component itself. When opening child elements of the application, you can view the component `Wrox.ProCSharp.EnterpriseServices.SimpleComponent`. Selecting Action ⇨ Properties opens the dialog box shown in Figure 44-5.

Using this dialog box, you can configure these options:

❑ **Transactions** — On the Transactions tab, you can specify whether the component requires transactions. You use this feature in the next example.

❑ **Security** — If security is enabled for the application, with this configuration you can define what roles are allowed to use the component.

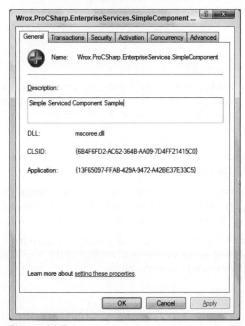

Figure 44-5

❑ **Activation** — The Activation configuration enables you to set object pooling and to assign a construction string.

❑ **Concurrency** — If the component is not thread-safe, concurrency can be set to Required or Requires New. This way the COM+ runtime allows only one thread at a time to access the component.

Client Application

After building the serviced component library, you can create a client application. This can be as simple as a C# console application. After you've created the project for the client, you have to reference both the assembly from the serviced component, SimpleServer, and the assembly System.EnterpriseServices. Then you can write the code to instantiate a new SimpleComponent instance and invoke the method Welcome(). In the following code, the Welcome() method is called 10 times. The using statement helps to release the resources allocated with the instance before the garbage collector takes action. With the using statement, the Dispose() method of the serviced component is called when the scope of the using statement ends.

```
using System;

namespace Wrox.ProCSharp.EnterpriseServices
{
    class Program
    {
        static void Main()
        {
            using (SimpleComponent obj = new SimpleComponent())
            {
                for (int i = 0; i < 10; i++)
                {
                    Console.WriteLine(obj.Welcome("Katie"));
                }
            }
        }
    }
}
```

If you start the client application before configuring the server, the server will be configured automatically. The automatic configuration of the server is done with the values that you've specified using attributes. For a test you can unregister the serviced component and start the client again. If the serviced component is configured during the start of the client application, the startup needs more time. Remember that this feature is useful only during development time. Administrative rights are also needed for automatic deployment. If you are starting the application from within Visual Studio, that means you should start Visual Studio with administrative rights.

While the application is running, you can monitor the serviced component with the Component Services Explorer. By selecting Components in the tree view and choosing View ⇨ Detail, you can view the number of instantiated objects if the attribute [EventTrackingEnabled] is set.

As you've seen, creating serviced components is just a matter of deriving the class from the base class ServicedComponent and setting some attributes to configure the application. Next, you see how transactions can be used with serviced components.

Transactions

Automatic transactions are the most frequently used feature of Enterprise Services. Using Enterprise Services, you can mark the components as requiring a transaction, and the transaction is then created from the COM+ runtime. All transaction-aware objects inside the component, such as ADO.NET connections, run inside the transaction.

You can read more about the concepts of transactions in Chapter 22, "Transactions."

Transaction Attributes

Serviced components can be marked with the [Transaction] attribute to define if and how transactions are required for the component.

Figure 44-6 shows multiple components with different transactional configurations. The client invokes component A. Because component A is configured with Transaction Required and no transaction existed previously, the new transaction, 1, is created. Component A invokes component B, which in turn invokes component C. Because component B is configured with Transaction Supported, and the configuration of component C is set to Transaction Required, all three components (A, B, and C) do use the same transaction context. If component B were configured with the transaction setting NotSupported, component C would get a new transaction. Component D is configured with the setting New Transaction Required, so a new transaction is created when it is called by component A.

The following table lists the different values that you can set with the TransactionOption enumeration:

TransactionOption Value	Description
Required	Setting the [Transaction] attribute to TransactionOption .Required means that the component runs inside a transaction. If a transaction has been created already, the component will run in the same transaction. If no transaction exists, a transaction will be created.
RequiresNew	TransactionOption.RequiresNew always results in a newly created transaction. The component never participates in the same transaction as the caller.
Supported	With TransactionOption.Supported, the component doesn't need transactions itself. However, the transaction will span the caller and the called component, if these components require transactions.
NotSupported	The option TransactionOption.NotSupported means that the component never runs in a transaction, regardless of whether the caller has a transaction.
Disabled	TransactionOption.Disabled means that a possible transaction of the current context is ignored.

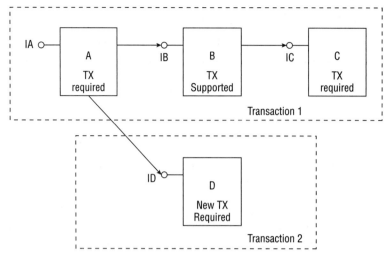

Figure 44-6

Transaction Results

A transaction can be influenced by setting the *consistent* and the *done* bit of the context. If the consistent bit is set to `true`, the component is happy with the outcome of the transaction. The transaction can be committed if all components participating with the transaction are similarly successful. If the consistent bit is set to `false`, the component is not happy with the outcome of the transaction, and the transaction will be aborted when the root object that started the transaction is finished. If the done bit is set, the object can be deactivated after the method call ends. A new instance will be created with the next method call.

The consistent and done bits can be set using four methods of the `ContextUtil` class with the results that you can see in the following table.

ContextUtil Method	Consistent Bit	Done Bit
SetComplete	true	true
SetAbort	false	true
EnableCommit	true	false
DisableCommit	false	false

With .NET it is also possible to set the consistent and done bit by applying the attribute `[AutoComplete]` to the method instead of calling the `ContextUtil` methods. With this attribute the method `ContextUtil.SetComplete()` will be called automatically if the method is successful. If the method fails and an exception is thrown, with `[AutoComplete]` the method `ContextUtil.SetAbort()` will be called.

Sample Application

This sample application simulates a simplified scenario that writes new orders to the Northwind sample database. As shown in Figure 44-7, multiple components are used with the COM+ application. The class `OrderControl` is called from the client application to create new orders. `OrderControl` uses the `OrderData` component. `OrderData` has the responsibility of creating a new entry in the `Order` table of the Northwind database. The `OrderData` component uses the `OrderLineData` component to write Order Detail entries to the database. Both `OrderData` and `OrderLineData` must participate in the same transaction.

Start by creating a C# Component library with the name `NorthwindComponent`. Sign the assembly with a keyfile, and define the Enterprise Services application attributes as shown in the following code:

```
[assembly: ApplicationName("Wrox.NorthwindDemo")]
[assembly: ApplicationActivation(ActivationOption.Server)]
[assembly: ApplicationAccessControl(false)]
```

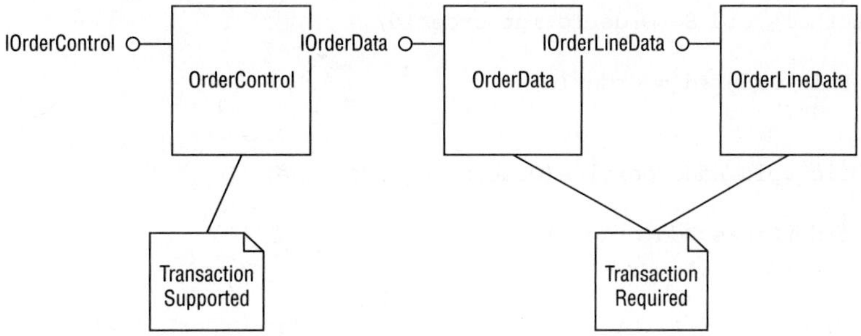

Figure 44-7

Entity Classes

Next add the entity classes `Order` and `OrderLine` that represent the columns in the Northwind database tables `Order` and `Order Details`. Entity classes are just data holders representing the data that is important for the application domain — in that case for doing orders. The class `Order` has a static method `Create()` that creates and returns a new instance of the class `Order`, and initializes this instance with the arguments passed to this method. Also, the class `Order` has some read-only properties `OrderId`, `CustomerId`, `OrderData`, `ShipAddress`, `ShipCity`, and `ShipCountry`. The value of the `OrderId` property is not known at creation time of the class `Order`, but because the `Order` table in the Northwind database has an auto-increment attribute, the value is just known after the order is written to the database. The method `SetOrderId()` is used to set the corresponding ID after the order has been written to the database. Because this method is called by a class inside the same assembly, the access level of this method is set to `internal`. The method `AddOrderLine()` adds order details to the order:

```
using System;
using System.Collections.Generic;

namespace Wrox.ProCSharp.EnterpriseServices
{
    [Serializable]
    public class Order
    {
        public static Order Create(string customerId, DateTime orderDate,
                     string shipAddress, string shipCity, string shipCountry)
        {
            return new Order()
            {
                CustomerId = customerId,
                OrderDate = orderDate,
                ShipAddress = shipAddress,
```

(continued)

(continued)

```
                    ShipCity = shipCity,
                    ShipCountry = shipCountry
                }
            }

            public Order()
            {
            }

            internal void SetOrderId(int orderId)
            {
                this.OrderId = orderId;
            }

            public void AddOrderLine(OrderLine orderLine)
            {
                orderLines.Add(orderLine);
            }

            private List<OrderLine> orderLines = new List<OrderLine>();

            public int OrderId { get; private set; }
            public string CustomerId { get; private set; }
            public DateTime OrderDate { get; private set; }
            public string ShipAddress { get; private set; }
            public string ShipCity { get; private set; }
            public string ShipCountry { get; private set; }

            public OrderLine[] OrderLines
            {
                get
                {
                    OrderLine[] ol = new OrderLine[orderLines.Count];
                    orderLines.CopyTo(ol);
                    return ol;
                }
            }
        }
    }
```

The second entity class is `OrderLine`. `OrderLine` has a static `Create()` method similar to the one of the `Order` class. Other than that, the class only has some properties for the fields `productId`, `unitPrice`, and `quantity`:

```
using System;

namespace Wrox.ProCSharp.EnterpriseServices
{
    [Serializable]
    public class OrderLine
    {
        public static OrderLine Create(int productId, float unitPrice,
                                       int quantity)
        {
            return new OrderLine()
```

```
        {
            ProductId = productId,
            UnitPrice = unitPrice,
            Quantity = quantity
        };
    }
    public OrderLine()
    {
    }

    public int ProductId { get; set; }
    public float UnitPrice { get; set; }
    public int Quantity { get; set; }
  }
}
```

The OrderControl Component

The class OrderControl represents a simple business services component. In this example, just one method, NewOrder(), is defined in the interface IOrderControl. The implementation of NewOrder() does nothing more than instantiate a new instance of the data services component OrderData and call the method Insert() to write an Order object to the database. In a more complex scenario, this method could be extended to write a log entry to a database or to invoke a queued component to send the Order object to a message queue:

```
using System;
using System.EnterpriseServices;
using System.Runtime.InteropServices;

namespace Wrox.ProCSharp.EnterpriseServices
{
    [ComVisible(true)]
    public interface IOrderControl
    {
        void NewOrder(Order order);
    }

    [Transaction(TransactionOption.Supported)]
    [EventTrackingEnabled(true)]
    [ComVisible(true)]
    public class OrderControl : ServicedComponent, IOrderControl
    {
        [AutoComplete()]
        public void NewOrder(Order order)
        {
            using (OrderData data = new OrderData())
            {
                data.Insert(order);
            }
        }
    }
}
```

The OrderData Component

The OrderData class is responsible for writing the values of Order objects to the database. The interface IOrderUpdate defines the Insert() method. You can extend this interface to also support an Update() method where an existing entry in the database is updated:

```
using System;
using System.Data.SqlClient;
using System.EnterpriseServices;
using System.Runtime.InteropServices;

namespace Wrox.ProCSharp.EnterpriseServices
{
    [ComVisible(true)]
    public interface IOrderUpdate
    {
        void Insert(Order order);
    }
```

The class OrderData has the attribute [Transaction] with the value TransactionOption.Required applied. This means that the component will run in a transaction in any case. Either a transaction is created by the caller and OrderData uses the same transaction, or a new transaction is created. Here a new transaction will be created because the calling component OrderControl doesn't have a transaction.

With serviced components, you can use only default constructors. However, you can use the Component Services Explorer to configure a construction string that is sent to a component (see Figure 44-8). Selecting the Activation tab of the component configuration enables you to change the construction string. The option "Enable object construction" is turned on when the attribute [ConstructionEnabled] is set, as it is with the class OrderData. The Default property of the [ConstructionEnabled] attribute defines the default connection string shown in the Activation settings after registration of the assembly. Setting this attribute also requires you to overload the method Construct() from the base class ServicedComponent. This method is called by the COM+ runtime at object instantiation, and the construction string is passed as an argument. The construction string is set to the variable connectionString, which is used later to connect to the database:

```
[Transaction(TransactionOption.Required)]
[EventTrackingEnabled(true)]
[ConstructionEnabled(true, Default="server=(local);" +
                        "database=northwind;trusted_connection=true")]
[ComVisible(true)]
public class OrderData : ServicedComponent, IOrderUpdate
{
    private string connectionString;

    protected override void Construct(string s)
    {
        connectionString = s;
    }
```

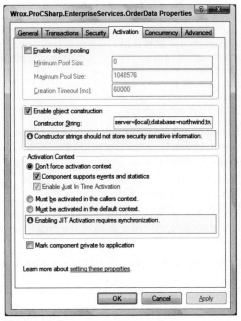

Figure 44-8

The method `Insert()` is at the heart of the component. Here, you use ADO.NET to write the `Order` object to the database. (ADO.NET is discussed in more detail in Chapter 26, "Data Access.") In this example, you create a `SqlConnection` object where the connection string that was set with the `Construct()` method is used to initialize the object.

The attribute `[AutoComplete()]` is applied to the method to use automatic transaction handling as discussed earlier:

```
[AutoComplete()]
public void Insert(Order order)
{
    SqlConnection connection = new SqlConnection(connectionString);
```

The method `connection.CreateCommand()` creates a `SqlCommand` object where the `CommandText` property is set to a SQL `INSERT` statement to add a new record to the `Orders` table. The method `ExecuteNonQuery()` executes the SQL statement:

```
try
{
    SqlCommand command = connection.CreateCommand();
    command.CommandText = "INSERT INTO Orders (CustomerId," +
        "OrderDate, ShipAddress, ShipCity, ShipCountry)" +
        "VALUES(@CustomerId, @OrderDate, @ShipAddress, @ShipCity, " +
        "@ShipCountry)";
    command.Parameters.AddWithValue("@CustomerId", order.CustomerId);
    command.Parameters.AddWithValue("@OrderDate", order.OrderDate);
    command.Parameters.AddWithValue("@ShipAddress",
                                        order.ShipAddress);
```

(continued)

(continued)

```
                command.Parameters.AddWithValue("@ShipCity", order.ShipCity);
                command.Parameters.AddWithValue("@ShipCountry",
                                                order.ShipCountry);

                connection.Open();

                command.ExecuteNonQuery();
```

Because `OrderId` is defined as an auto-increment value in the database, and this ID is needed for writing the Order Details to the database, `OrderId` is read by using `@@IDENTITY`. Then it is set to the `Order` object by calling the method `SetOrderId()`:

```
                command.CommandText = "SELECT @@IDENTITY AS 'Identity'";
                object identity = command.ExecuteScalar();
                order.SetOrderId(Convert.ToInt32(identity));
```

After the order is written to the database, all order lines of the order are written using the `OrderLineData` component:

```
                using (OrderLineData updateOrderLine = new OrderLineData())
                {
                    foreach (OrderLine orderLine in order.OrderLines)
                    {
                        updateOrderLine.Insert(order.OrderId, orderLine);
                    }
                }
```

Finally, regardless of whether the code in the `try` block was successful or an exception occurred, the connection is closed:

```
            finally
            {
                connection.Close();
            }
        }
    }
}
```

The OrderLineData Component

The `OrderLineData` component is implemented similarly to the `OrderData` component. You use the attribute `[ConstructionEnabled]` to define the database connection string:

```
using System;
using System.EnterpriseServices;
using System.Runtime.InteropServices;
using System.Data;
using System.Data.SqlClient;

namespace Wrox.ProCSharp.EnterpriseServices
{
    [ComVisible(true)]
    public interface IOrderLineUpdate
    {
        void Insert(int orderId, OrderLine orderDetail);
    }
```

```
[Transaction(TransactionOption.Required)]
[EventTrackingEnabled(true)]
[ConstructionEnabled(true, Default="server=(local);database=northwind;" +
    "trusted_connection=true")]
[ComVisible(true)]
public class OrderLineData : ServicedComponent, IOrderLineUpdate
{
    private string connectionString;

    protected override void Construct(string s)
    {
        connectionString = s;
    }
```

With the Insert() method of the OrderLineData class in this example, the [AutoComplete] attribute isn't used to demonstrate a different way to define the transaction outcome. It shows how to set the consistent and done bits with the ContextUtil class instead. The method SetComplete() is called at the end of the method, depending on whether inserting the data in the database was successful. If there is an error where an exception is thrown, the method SetAbort() sets the consistent bit to false instead, so that the transaction is undone along with all components participating in the transaction:

```
    public void Insert(int orderId, OrderLine orderDetail)
    {
        SqlConnection connection = new SqlConnection(connectionString);
        try
        {
            SqlCommand command = connection.CreateCommand();
            command.CommandText = "INSERT INTO [Order Details] (OrderId, " +
                "ProductId, UnitPrice, Quantity)" +
                "VALUES(@OrderId, @ProductId, @UnitPrice, @Quantity)";
            command.Parameters.AddWithValue("@OrderId", orderId);
            command.Parameters.AddWithValue("@ProductId",
                                        orderDetail.ProductId);
            command.Parameters.AddWithValue("@UnitPrice",
                                        orderDetail.UnitPrice);
            command.Parameters.AddWithValue("@Quantity",
                                        orderDetail.Quantity);

            connection.Open();

            command.ExecuteNonQuery();
        }
        catch (Exception)
        {
            ContextUtil.SetAbort();
            throw;
        }
        finally
        {
            connection.Close();
        }
        ContextUtil.SetComplete();
    }
}
}
```

Client Application

Having built the component, you can create a client application. For testing purposes, a console application serves the purpose. After referencing the assembly `NorthwindComponent` and the assembly `System.EnterpriseServices`, you can create a new order with the static method `Order.Create()`. `order.AddOrderLine()` adds an order line to the order. `OrderLine.Create()` accepts product IDs, the price, and quantity to create an order line. In a real application, it would be useful to add a `Product` class instead of using product IDs, but the purpose of this example is to demonstrate transactions in general.

Finally, the serviced component class `OrderControl` is created to invoke the method `NewOrder()`:

```
Order order = Order.Create("PICCO", DateTime.Today, "Georg Pipps",
                           "Salzburg", "Austria");
order.AddOrderLine(OrderLine.Create(16, 17.45F, 2));
order.AddOrderLine(OrderLine.Create(67, 14, 1));

using (OrderControl orderControl = new OrderControl())
{
    orderControl.NewOrder(order);
}
```

You can try to write products that don't exist to the `OrderLine` (using a product ID that is not listed in the table Products). In this case, the transaction will be aborted, and no data will be written to the database.

While a transaction is active, you can see the transaction in the Component Services Explorer by selecting Distributed Transaction Coordinator in the tree view (see Figure 44-9).

You might have to add a sleep time to the `Insert()` method of the `OrderData` class to see the live transaction; otherwise, the transaction might be completed too fast to display.

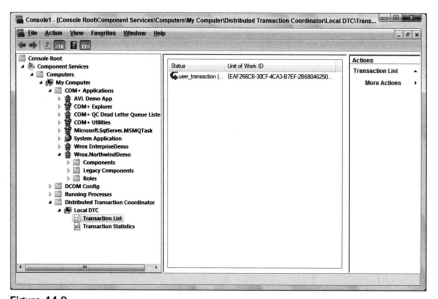

Figure 44-9

> If you are debugging the serviced component while it is running inside a transaction, be aware that the default transaction timeout is 60 seconds for serviced components. You can change the default for the complete system in the Component Services Explorer by clicking My Computer, selecting Action ⇨ Properties, and opening the Options tab. Instead of changing the value for the complete system, the transaction timeout can also be configured on a component-by-component level with the Transaction options of the component.

Integrating WCF and Enterprise Services

Windows Communication Foundation (WCF) is a new communication technology that is part of .NET Framework 3.0. WCF is covered in detail in Chapter 42, "Windows Communication Foundation." .NET Enterprise Services offers a great integration model with WCF.

WCF Service Façade

Adding a WCF façade to an Enterprise Services application allows using WCF clients to access the serviced components. Instead of using the DCOM protocol, with WCF you can have different protocols such as HTTP with SOAP or TCP with a binary formatting.

You can create a WCF façade from Visual Studio 2008 by selecting Tools ⇨ WCF SvcConfigEditor. With this tool started select File ⇨ Integrate ⇨ COM+ Application . . . . Select the COM+ Application Wrox.NorthwindDemo, the component `Wrox.ProCSharp.EnterpriseServices.OrderControl`, and the interface `IOrderControl` as shown in Figure 44-10.

Instead of using Visual Studio to create the WCF façade, you can use the command-line utility `comsvcconfig.exe`. *You can find this utility in the directory* `<Windows>\Microsoft.NET\ Framework\v3.0\Windows Communication Foundation`.

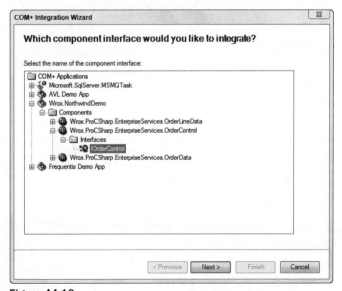

Figure 44-10

With the next dialog you can select all the methods from the interface `IOrderControl` that should be available to WCF clients. With the interface `IOrderControl` just one method, `NewOrder()`, is shown.

The next dialog shown in Figure 44-11 allows configuration of the hosting options. With the hosting option, you can specify in which process the WCF service should run. When you select the COM+ hosted option, the WCF façade runs within the `dllhost.exe` process of COM+. This option is possible only if the application is configured as a server application: `[ApplicationActivation(ActivationOption.Server)]`. The Web hosted it is specifies that the WCF channel is listens inside a process of the IIS or WAS (Windows Activation Services) worker process. WAS is new with Windows Vista and Windows Server 2008. Selecting "Web hosted in-process" means that the library of the Enterprise Services component runs within the IIS or WAS worker process. This configuration is possible only if the application is configured as a library application. `[ApplicationActivation(ActivationOption.Library)]`.

Selecting the "Add MEX endpoint" option adds a MEX (Metadata Exchange) endpoint to the WCF configuration file, so that the client programmer can access the metadata of the service using WS-Metadata Exchange.

MEX is explained in Chapter 42, "Windows Communication Foundation."

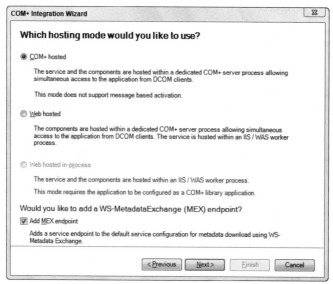

Figure 44-11

With the next dialog shown in Figure 44-12 you can specify the communication mode to access the WCF façade. Depending on your requirements, if the client is accessing the service across a firewall or platform-independent communication is required, HTTP is the best choice. TCP offers faster communication across machines for .NET clients, and Named Pipes is the fastest option if the client application is running on the same system as the service.

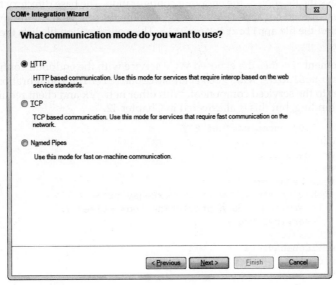

Figure 44-12

The next dialog requests information about the base address of the service that depends on the communication protocol selection, as shown in Figure 44-13.

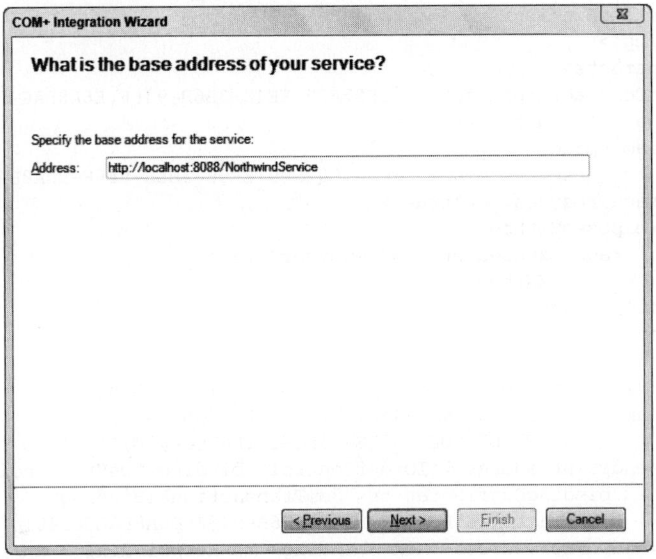

Figure 44-13

The last dialog shows the location of the endpoint configuration. The base directory for the configurations is `<Program Files>\ComPlus Applications` followed by the unique ID of the application. In this directory you can find the file `application.config`. This configuration file lists the behaviors and endpoints for WCF.

The `<service>` element specifies the exposed WCF service with the endpoint configuration. The binding is set to `wsHttpBinding` with a `comTransactionalBinding` configuration, so transactions can flow from the caller to the serviced component. With other network and client requirements, you can specify a different binding, but this is all covered in Chapter 42.

```xml
<?xml version="1.0" encoding="utf-8"?>
<configuration>
    <system.serviceModel>
        <behaviors>
            <serviceBehaviors>
                <behavior name="ComServiceMexBehavior">
                    <serviceMetadata httpGetEnabled="false" />
                    <serviceDebug />
                </behavior>
            </serviceBehaviors>
        </behaviors>
        <bindings>
            <netNamedPipeBinding>
                <binding name="comNonTransactionalBinding" />
                <binding name="comTransactionalBinding" transactionFlow="true" />
            </netNamedPipeBinding>
            <wsHttpBinding>
                <binding name="comNonTransactionalBinding" />
                <binding name="comTransactionalBinding" transactionFlow="true" />
            </wsHttpBinding>
        </bindings>
        <comContracts>
            <comContract contract="{E1B02E09-EE48-3B6B-946F-E6A8BAEC6340}"
                name="IOrderControl"
                namespace=
                    "http://tempuri.org/E1B02E09-EE48-3B6B-946F-E6A8BAEC6340"
                requiresSession="true">
                <exposedMethods>
                    <add exposedMethod="NewOrder" />
                </exposedMethods>
            </comContract>
        </comContracts>
        <services>
            <service behaviorConfiguration="ComServiceMexBehavior"
                name="{BC198295-74F7-4441-8EC1-04A174C6BA45},
                    {D30F79D7-6DE7-33DE-B3FC-C21F6B02A48D}">
                <endpoint address="IOrderControl" binding="wsHttpBinding"
                    bindingConfiguration="comTransactionalBinding"
                    contract="{E1B02E09-EE48-3B6B-946F-E6A8BAEC6340}" />
                <endpoint address="mex" binding="mexHttpBinding"
                    contract="IMetadataExchange" />
                <host>
                    <baseAddresses>
```

```
            <add baseAddress=
                "http://localhost:8088/NorthwindService" />
            </baseAddresses>
          </host>
        </service>
      </services>
    </system.serviceModel>
  </configuration>
```

Before you can start the server application you need to change the security to allow the user that runs the application to register ports for listening. Otherwise a normal user is not allowed to register a listener port. On Windows Vista you can do this with the `netsh` command as shown. The option `http` changes the ACL for the HTTP protocol. The port number and the name of the service are defined with the URL, and the user option specifies the name of the user that starts the listener service.

```
netsh http urlacl url=http://+:8088/NorthwindService user=username
```

Client Application

Create a new console application named `WCFClientApp`. Because the service offers a MEX endpoint, you can add a service reference from Visual Studio by selecting Project ⇨ Add Service Reference . . . (see Figure 44-14).

If the service is COM+ hosted, you have to start the application before you can access the MEX data. If the service is hosted inside WAS, the application is started automatically.

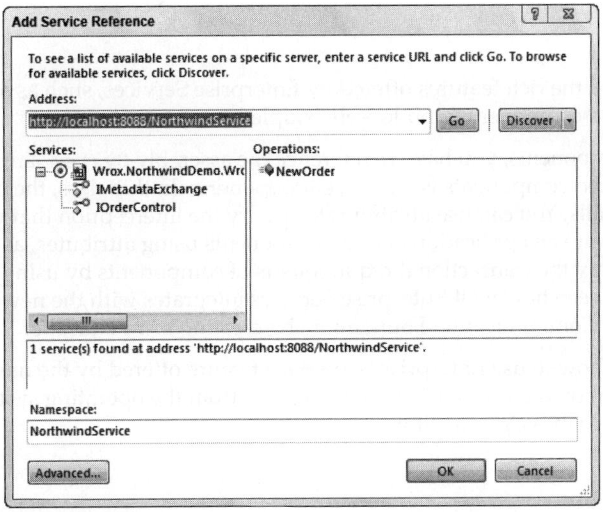

Figure 44-14

With the service reference a proxy class is created, the assemblies `System.ServiceModel` and `System.Runtime.Serialization` are referenced, and an application configuration file referencing the service is added to the client application.

Now, you can use the generated entity classes and the proxy class `OrderControlClient` to send an order request to the serviced component:

```
static void Main()
{
    Order order = new Order();
    order.customerId = "PICCO";
    order.orderDate = DateTime.Today;
    order.shipAddress = "Georg Pipps";
    order.shipCity = "Salzburg";
    order.shipCountry = "Austria";
    OrderLine line1 = new OrderLine();
    line1.productId = 16;
    line1.unitPrice = 17.45F;
    line1.quantity = 2;
    OrderLine line2 = new OrderLine();
    line2.productId = 67;
    line2.unitPrice = 14;
    line2.quantity = 1;
    OrderLine[] orderLines = { line1, line2 };
    order.orderLines = orderLines;

    OrderControlClient occ = new OrderControlClient();
    occ.NewOrder(order);
}
```

Summary

This chapter discussed the rich features offered by Enterprise Services, such as automatic transactions, object pooling, queued components, and loosely coupled events.

To create serviced components, you have to reference the assembly `System.EnterpriseServices`. The base class of all serviced components is `ServicedComponent`. In this class, the context makes it possible to intercept method calls. You can use attributes to specify the interception that will be used. You also learned how to configure an application and its components using attributes, as well as how to manage transactions and specify the transactional requirements of components by using the `[Transaction]` attribute. You've also seen how well Enterprise Services integrates with the new communication technology Windows Communication Foundation, by creating a WCF façade.

This chapter showed how to use Enterprise Services, a feature offered by the operating system. The next chapter gives information on how to use another feature from the operating system that is used for communication as well: message queuing.

45

Message Queuing

`System.Messaging` is a namespace that includes classes for reading and writing messages with the Message Queuing facility of the Windows operating system. Messaging can be used in a disconnected scenario where the client and server needn't be running at the same time.

This chapter looks at the following topics:

❑ An overview of Message Queuing

❑ Message Queuing architecture

❑ Message queue administrative tools

❑ Programming Message Queuing

❑ Course order sample application

❑ Message Queuing with WCF

Overview

Before diving into programming Message Queuing, this section discusses the basic concepts of messaging and compares it to synchronous and asynchronous programming. With synchronous programming, when a method is invoked, the caller has to wait until the method is completed. With asynchronous programming, the calling thread starts the method that runs concurrently. Asynchronous programming can be done with delegates, class libraries that already support asynchronous methods (for example, Web service proxies, `System.Net`, and `System.IO` classes), or by using custom threads (see Chapter 19, "Threading and Synchronization"). With both synchronous and asynchronous programming, the client and the server must be running at the same time.

Although Message Queuing operates asynchronously, because the client (sender) does not wait for the server (receiver) to read the data sent to it, there is a crucial difference between Message Queuing and asynchronous programming: Message Queuing can be done in a disconnected environment. At the time data is sent, the receiver can be offline. Later, when the receiver goes online, it receives the data without intervention from the sending application.

You can compare connected and disconnected programming with talking to someone on the phone and sending an email. When talking to someone on the phone, both participants must be connected at the same time; the communication is synchronous. With an email, the sender isn't sure when the email will be dealt with. People using this technology are working in a disconnected mode. Of course the email may never be dealt with — it may be ignored. That's in the nature of disconnected communication. To avoid this problem, it is possible to ask for a reply to confirm that the email has been read. If the answer doesn't arrive within a time limit, you may be required to deal with this "exception." This is also possible with Message Queuing.

In some ways, Message Queuing is email for application-to-application communication, instead of person-to-person communication. However, this gives you a lot of features that are not available with mailing services, such as guaranteed delivery, transactions, confirmations, express mode using memory, and so on. As you see in the next section, Message Queuing has a lot of features useful for communication between applications.

With Message Queuing, you can send, receive, and route messages in a connected or disconnected environment. Figure 45-1 shows a very simple way of using messages. The sender sends messages to the message queue, and the receiver receives messages from the queue.

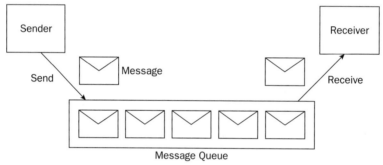

Figure 45-1

When to Use Message Queuing

One case in which Message Queuing is useful is when the client application is often disconnected from the network (for example, when a salesperson is visiting a customer onsite). The salesperson can enter order data directly at the customer's site. The application sends a message for each order to the message queue that is located on the client's system (see Figure 45-2). As soon as the salesperson is back in the office, the order is automatically transferred from the message queue of the client system to the message queue of the target system, where the message is processed.

In addition to using a laptop, the salesperson could use a Pocket Windows device where Message Queuing is available.

Message Queuing can also be useful in a connected environment. Imagine an e-commerce site (see Figure 45-3) where the server is fully loaded with order transactions at certain times, for example, early evening and weekends, but the load is low at nighttime. A solution would be to buy a faster server or to add additional servers to the system so that the peaks can be handled. But there's a cheaper solution: flatten the peak loads by moving transactions from the times with higher loads to the times with lower loads. In this scheme, orders are sent to the message queue, and the receiving side reads the orders at the rates that are useful for the database system. The load of the system is now flattened over time so that the server dealing with the transactions can be less expensive than an upgrade of the database server(s).

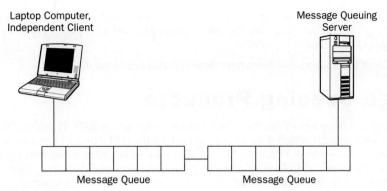

Figure 45-2

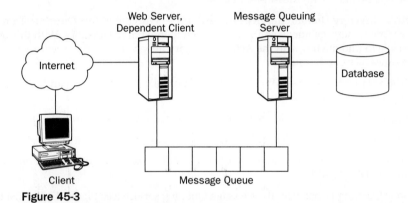

Figure 45-3

Message Queuing Features

Message Queuing is part of the Windows operating system. The main features of this service are:

❑ Messages can be sent in a disconnected environment. It is not necessary for the sending and receiving applications to run at the same time.

❑ With express mode, messages can be sent very quickly. Express-mode messages are just stored in memory.

❑ For a recoverable mechanism, messages can be sent using guaranteed delivery. Recoverable messages are stored within files. They are delivered even in cases when the server reboots.

❑ Message queues can be secured with access-control lists to define which users can send or receive messages from a queue. Messages can also be encrypted to avoid network sniffers reading them. Messages can be sent with priorities so that high-priority items are handled faster.

❑ Message Queuing 3.0 supports sending multicast messages.

❑ Message Queuing 4.0 supports poison messages. A poison message is one that isn't getting resolved. You can define a *poison queue* where unresolved messages are moved. For example, if the job after reading the message from the normal queue was to insert it into the database, but the message did not get into the database and thus this job failed, it would get sent to the poison queue. It is someone's job to handle the poison queue — and that person should deal with the message in a way that resolves it.

Because Message Queuing is part of the operating system, you cannot install Message Queuing 4.0 on a Windows XP or Windows Server 2003 system. Message Queuing 4.0 is part of Windows Server 2008 and Windows Vista.

The remainder of this chapter discusses how these features can be used.

Message Queuing Products

Message Queuing 4.0 is part of Windows Vista and Windows Server 2008. Windows 2000 was delivered with Message Queuing 2.0, which didn't have support for the HTTP protocol and multicast messages. Message Queuing 3.0 is part of Windows XP and Windows Server 2003. When you use the link "Turn Windows Features on or off" in Configuring Programs and Features of Windows Vista, there is a separate section for Message Queuing options. With this section, you can select these components:

❑ **Microsoft Message Queue (MSMQ) Server Core** — The Core subcomponent is required for base functionality with Message Queuing.

❑ **Active Directory Domain Services Integration** — With the Active Directory Domain Services Integration, message queue names are written to the Active Directory. With this option, it is possible to find queues with the Active Directory integration, and to secure queues with Windows users and groups.

❑ **MSMQ HTTP Support** — MSMQ HTTP Support allows you to send and receive messages using the HTTP protocol.

❑ **Triggers** — With triggers, applications can be instantiated on the arrival of a new message.

❑ **Multicast Support** — With multicasting, a message can be sent to a group of servers.

❑ **MSMQ DCOM Proxy** — With the DCOM proxy, a system can connect to a remote server by using the DCOM API.

When Message Queuing is installed, the Message Queuing service (see Figure 45-4) must be started. This service reads and writes messages and communicates with other Message Queuing servers to route messages across the network.

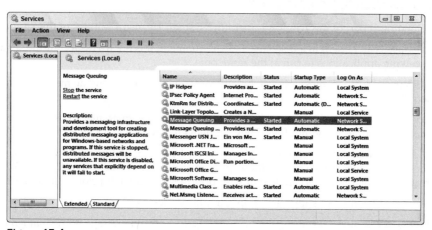

Figure 45-4

Message Queuing Architecture

With Message Queuing, messages are written to and read from a message queue. Messages and message queues have several attributes that must be further elaborated.

Messages

A message is sent to a message queue. The message includes a body containing the data that is sent and a label that is the title of the message. Any information can be put into the body of the message. With .NET, several formatters convert data to be put into the body. In addition to the label and the body, the message includes more information about the sender, timeout configuration, transaction ID, or priority.

Message queues have several types of messages:

❑ A *normal message* is sent by an application.

❑ An *acknowledgment message* reports the status of a normal message. Acknowledgment messages are sent to administration queues to report success or failure when sending normal messages.

❑ *Response messages* are sent by receiving applications when the original sender requires some special answer.

❑ A *report message* is generated by the Message Queuing system. Test messages and route-tracking messages belong to this category.

A message can have a priority that defines the order in which the messages will be read from the queue. The messages are sorted in the queue according to their priority, so the next message read in the queue is the one with the highest priority.

Messages have two delivery modes: *express* and *recoverable*. Express messages are delivered very quickly because memory is used only for the message store. Recoverable messages are stored in files at every step along the route until the message is delivered. This way, delivery of the message is assured, even with a computer reboot or network failure.

Transactional messages are a special version of recoverable messages. With transactional messaging, it is guaranteed that messages arrive only once and in the same order that they were sent. Priorities cannot be used with transactional messages.

Message Queue

A message queue is a message store. Messages that are stored on disk can be found in the `<windir>` `\system32\msmq\storage` directory.

Public or private queues are usually used for sending messages, but other queue types also exist:

❑ A *public queue* is published in the Active Directory. Information about these queues is replicated across Active Directory domains. You can use browse and search features to get information about these queues. A public queue can be accessed without knowing the name of the computer where it is placed. It is also possible to move such a queue from one system to another without the client knowing it. It's not possible to create public queues in a Workgroup environment because the Active Directory is needed. The Active Directory is discussed in Chapter 46, "Directory Services."

❑ *Private queues* are not published in the Active Directory. These queues can be accessed only when the full path name to the queue is known. Private queues can be used in a Workgroup environment.

❑ *Journal queues* are used to keep copies of messages after they have been received or sent. Enabling journaling for a public or private queue automatically creates a journal queue. With journal queues, two different queue types are possible: source journaling and target journaling. *Source journaling* is turned on with the properties of a message; the journal messages are stored with the source system. *Target journaling* is turned on with the properties of a queue; these messages are stored in the journal queue of the target system.

❑ *Dead-letter queues* store messages if a message doesn't arrive at the target system before a specific timeout is reached. Contrary to synchronous programming where errors are immediately detected, errors must be dealt with differently using Message Queuing. The dead-letter queue can be checked for messages that didn't arrive.

❑ *Administration queues* contain acknowledgments for messages sent. The sender can specify an administration queue from which it receives notification of whether the message was sent successfully.

❑ A *response queue* is used if more than a simple acknowledgment is needed as an answer from the receiving side. The receiving application can send response messages back to the original sender.

❑ A *report queue* is used for test messages. Report queues can be created by changing the type (or category) of a public or private queue to the predefined ID {55EE8F33-CCE9-11CF-B108-0020AFD61CE9}. Report queues are useful as a testing tool to track messages on their route.

❑ *System queues* are private and are used by the Message Queuing system. These queues are used for administrative messages, storing of notification messages, and to guarantee the correct order of transactional messages.

Message Queuing Administrative Tools

Before looking at how to deal with Message Queuing programmatically, this section looks at the administrative tools that are part of the Windows operating system to create and manage queues and messages. The tools shown here are not used only with Message Queuing. The Message Queuing features of these tools are available only if Message Queuing is installed.

Creating Message Queues

Message queues can be created with the Computer Management MMC snap-in. On a Windows Vista system, you can start the Computer Management MMC snap-in with the Start ➪ Control Panel ➪ Administrative Tools ➪ Computer Management menu. In the tree view pane, Message Queuing is located below the Services and Applications entry. By selecting Private Queues or Public Queues, new queues can be created from the Action menu (see Figure 45-5). Public queues are available only if Message Queuing is configured in Active Directory mode.

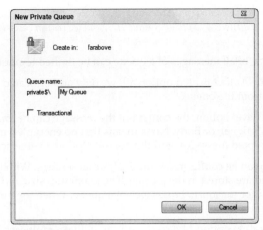

Figure 45-5

Message Queue Properties

After a queue is created, you can modify the queue's properties with the Computer Management snap-in by selecting the queue in the tree pane and selecting the Action ⇨ Properties menu (see Figure 45-6).

Figure 45-6

Several options can be configured:

❑ The label is the name of the queue that can be used to search for the queue.

❑ The type ID, which is, by default, set to {00000000-0000-0000-0000-000000000000} to map multiple queues to a single category or type. Report queues use a specific type ID, as discussed earlier. A type ID is a universal unique ID (UUID) or GUID.

Custom type identifiers can be created with the uuidgen.exe *or* guidgen.exe *utilities.* uuidgen.exe *is a command-line utility used to create unique IDs, and* guidgen.exe *is a graphical version to create UUIDs.*

❑ The maximum size of all messages of a queue can be limited to not fill up the disk.

❑ When checked, the Authenticated option allows only authenticated users to write and read messages to and from the queue.

❑ With the Privacy Level option, the content of the message can be encrypted. The possible values to set are None, Optional, or Body. None means that no encrypted messages are accepted, Body accepts only encrypted messages, and the default Optional value accepts both.

❑ Target journaling can be configured with the Journal settings. With this option, copies of the messages received are stored in the journal. The maximum size of disk space that is occupied can be configured for the journal messages of a queue. When the maximum size is reached, target journaling is ceased.

❑ With the configuration option *Multicast,* you can define a multicast IP address for the queue. The same multicast IP address can be used with different nodes in the network, so that a message sent to a single address is received with multiple queues.

Programming Message Queuing

Now that you understand the architecture of Message Queuing, you can look into the programming. In the next sections, you see how to create and control queues, and how to send and receive messages.

You also build a small course order application that consists of a sending and a receiving part.

Creating a Message Queue

You've already seen how to create message queues with the Computer Management utility. Message queues can be created programmatically with the Create() method of the MessageQueue class.

With the Create() method, the path of the new queue must be passed. The path consists of the host name where the queue is located and the name of the queue. In the example, the queue MyNewPublicQueue is created on the local host. To create a private queue, the path name must include Private$; for example, \Private$\MyNewPrivateQueue.

After the Create() method is invoked, properties of the queue can be changed. For example, using the Label property, the label of the queue is set to Demo Queue. The sample program writes the path of the queue and the format name to the console. The format name is automatically created with a UUID that can be used to access the queue without the name of the server:

```
using System;
using System.Messaging;

namespace Wrox.ProCSharp.Messaging
{
    class Program
    {
        static void Main()
        {
            using (MessageQueue queue =
                    MessageQueue.Create(@".\MyNewPublicQueue"))
```

```
        {
            queue.Label = "Demo Queue";
            Console.WriteLine("Queue created:");
            Console.WriteLine("Path: {0}", queue.Path);
            Console.WriteLine("FormatName: {0}", queue.FormatName);
        }
    }
  }
}
```

*Administrative privileges are required to create a queue. Usually, you cannot expect the user of
your application to have administrative privileges. That's why queues usually are created with
installation programs. Later in this chapter, you see how message queues can be created with the
MessageQueueInstaller class.*

Finding a Queue

The path name and the format name can be used to identify queues. To find queues, you must
differentiate between public and private queues. Public queues are published in the Active Directory. For
these queues, it is not necessary to know the system where they are located. Private queues can be found
only if the name of the system where the queue is located is known.

You can find public queues in the Active Directory domain by searching for the queue's label, category,
or format name. You can also get all queues on a machine. The class MessageQueue has static methods
to search for queues: GetPublicQueuesByLabel(), GetPublicQueuesByCategory(), and
GetPublicQueuesByMachine(). The method GetPublicQueues() returns an array of all public
queues in the domain:

```
using System;
using System.Messaging;

namespace Wrox.ProCSharp.Messaging
{
    class Program
    {
        static void Main()
        {
            foreach (MessageQueue queue in MessageQueue.GetPublicQueues())
            {
                Console.WriteLine(queue.Path);
            }
        }
    }
}
```

The method GetPublicQueues() is overloaded. One version allows passing an instance of the
MessageQueueCriteria class. With this class, you can search for queues created or modified before or
after a certain time, and you can also look for a category, label, or machine name.

Private queues can be searched with the static method GetPrivateQueuesByMachine(). This method
returns all private queues from a specific system.

Opening Known Queues

If the name of the queue is known, it is not necessary to search for it. Queues can be opened by using the
path or format name. They both can be set in the constructor of the MessageQueue class.

Path Name

The path specifies the machine name and the queue name to open the queue. This code example opens the queue `MyPublicQueue` on the local host. To be sure that the queue exists, you use the static method `MessageQueue.Exists()`:

```
using System;
using System.Messaging;

namespace Wrox.ProCSharp.Messaging
{
    class Program
    {
        static void Main()
        {
            if (MessageQueue.Exists(@".\MyPublicQueue"))
            {
                MessageQueue queue = new MessageQueue(@".\MyPublicQueue");
                //...
            }
            else
            {
                Console.WriteLine("Queue .\MyPublicQueue not existing");
            }
        }
    }
}
```

Depending on the queue type, different identifiers are required when queues are opened. The following table shows the syntax of the queue name for specific types.

Queue Type	Syntax
Public queue	MachineName\QueueName
Private queue	MachineName\Private$\QueueName
Journal queue	MachineName\QueueName\Journal$
Machine journal queue	MachineName\Journal$
Machine dead-letter queue	MachineName\DeadLetter$
Machine transactional dead-letter queue	MachineName\XactDeadLetter$

When you use the path name to open public queues, it is necessary to pass the machine name. If the machine name is not known, the format name can be used instead. The path name for private queues can be used only on the local system. The format name must be used to access private queues remotely.

Format Name

Instead of the path name, you can use the format name to open a queue. The format name is used for searching the queue in the Active Directory to get the host where the queue is located. In a disconnected environment where the queue cannot be reached at the time the message is sent, it is necessary to use the format name:

```
MessageQueue queue = new MessageQueue(
        @"FormatName:PUBLIC=09816AFF-3608-4c5d-B892-69754BA151FF");
```

The format name has some different uses. It can be used to open private queues and to specify a protocol that should be used:

❑   To access a private queue, the string that has to be passed to the constructor is `FormatName: PRIVATE=MachineGUID\QueueNumber`. The queue number for private queues is generated when the queue is created. You can see the queue numbers in the `<windows>\System32\msmq\ storage\lqs` directory.

❑   With `FormatName:DIRECT=Protocol:MachineAddress\QueueName`, you can specify the protocol that should be used to send the message. The HTTP protocol is supported since Message Queuing 3.0.

❑   `FormatName:DIRECT=OS:MachineName\QueueName` is another way to specify a queue using the format name. This way you don't have to specify the protocol but still can use the machine name with the format name.

Sending a Message

You can use the `Send` method of the `MessageQueue` class to send a message to the queue. The object passed as an argument of the `Send()` method is serialized to the associated queue. The `Send()` method is overloaded so that a label and a `MessageQueueTransaction` object can be passed. Transactional behavior of Message Queuing is discussed later.

The code example first checks if the queue exists. If it doesn't exist, a queue is created. Then the queue is opened and the message `Sample Message` is sent to the queue using the `Send()` method.

The path name specifies a dot (just like a period) for the server name, which is the local system. Path names to private queues work only locally.

```
using System;
using System.Messaging;

namespace Wrox.ProCSharp.Messaging
{
    class Program
    {
        static void Main()
        {
            try
            {
                if (!MessageQueue.Exists(@".\Private$\MyPrivateQueue"))
                {
                    MessageQueue.Create(@".\Private$\MyPrivateQueue");
                }
                MessageQueue queue =
                    new MessageQueue(@".\Private$\MyPrivateQueue");

                queue.Send("Sample Message", "Label");
            }
            catch (MessageQueueException ex)
            {
                Console.WriteLine(ex.Message);
            }
        }
    }
}
```

Figure 45-7 shows the Computer Management admin tool where you can see the message that arrived in the queue.

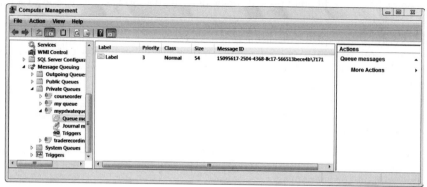

Figure 45-7

By opening the message and selecting the Body tab (see Figure 45-8) of the dialog, you can see that the message was formatted using XML. How the message is formatted is the function of the formatter that's associated with the message queue.

Figure 45-8

Message Formatter

The format in which messages are transferred to the queue depends on the formatter. The `MessageQueue` class has a `Formatter` property through which a formatter can be assigned. The default formatter, `XmlMessageFormatter`, will format the message in XML syntax as shown in the previous example.

A message formatter implements the interface `IMessageFormatter`. Three message formatters are available with the namespace `System.Messaging`:

- ❑ The `XmlMessageFormatter` is the default formatter. It serializes objects using XML. See Chapter 28, "Manipulating XML," for more on XML formatting.

- ❑ With the `BinaryMessageFormatter`, messages are serialized in a binary format. These messages are shorter than the messages formatted using XML.

- ❑ The `ActiveXMessageFormatter` is a binary formatter, so that messages can be read or written with COM objects. Using this formatter, it is possible to write a message to the queue with a .NET class and to read the message from the queue with a COM object or vice versa.

The sample message shown in Figure 45-8 with XML is formatted with the `BinaryMessageFormatter` in Figure 45-9.

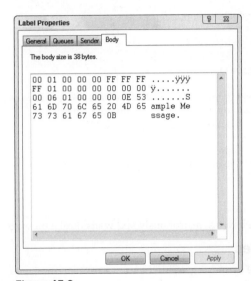

Figure 45-9

Sending Complex Messages

Instead of passing strings, it is possible to pass objects to the `Send()` method of the `MessageQueue` class. The type of the class must fulfill some specific requirements, but they depend on the formatter.

For the binary formatter, the class must be serializable with the `[Serializable]` attribute. With the .NET runtime serialization, all fields are serialized (this includes private fields). Custom serialization can be defined by implementing the interface `ISerializable`. You can read more about the .NET runtime serialization in Chapter 25, "Manipulating Files and the Registry."

XML serialization takes place with the XML formatter. With XML serialization, all public fields and properties are serialized. The XML serialization can be influenced by using attributes from the `System.Xml.Serialization` namespace. You can read more about XML serialization in Chapter 28, "Manipulating XML."

Receiving Messages

To read messages, again, the `MessageQueue` class can be used. With the `Receive()` method, a single message is read and removed from the queue. If messages are sent with different priorities, the message with the highest priority is read. Reading messages with the same priority may mean that the first message sent is not the first message read because the order of messages across the network is not guaranteed. For a guaranteed order, you should use transactional message queues.

In the following example, a message is read from the private queue `MyPrivateQueue`. Previously, a simple string was passed to the message. When you read a message using the `XmlMessageFormatter`, you have to pass the types of the objects that are read to the constructor of the formatter. In the example, the type `System.String` is passed to the argument array of the `XmlMessageFormatter` constructor. This constructor allows either a `String` array that contains the types as strings to be passed or a `Type` array.

The message is read with the `Receive()` method, and then the message body is written to the console:

```
using System;
using System.Messaging;

namespace Wrox.ProCSharp.Messaging
{
    class Program
    {
        static void Main()
        {
            MessageQueue queue = new MessageQueue(@".\Private$\MyPrivateQueue");
            queue.Formatter = new XmlMessageFormatter(
                new string[] {"System.String"});

            Message message = queue.Receive();
            Console.WriteLine(message.Body);
        }
    }
}
```

The `Receive()` message behaves synchronously and waits until a message is in the queue if there is none.

Enumerating Messages

Instead of reading message by message with the `Receive()` method, an enumerator can be used to walk through all messages. The `MessageQueue` class implements the interface `IEnumerable` and thus can be used with a `foreach` statement. Here, the messages are not removed from the queue, but you get just a peek at the messages to get their content:

```
MessageQueue queue = new MessageQueue(@".\Private$\MyPrivateQueue");
queue.Formatter = new XmlMessageFormatter(
    new string[] {"System.String"});

foreach (Message message in queue)
{
    Console.WriteLine(message.Body);
}
```

Instead of using the `IEnumerable` interface, the class `MessageEnumerator` can be used. `MessageEnumerator` implements the interface `IEnumerator`, but has some more features. With the `IEnumerable` interface, the messages are not removed from the queue. The method `RemoveCurrent()` of the `MessageEnumerator` removes the message from the current cursor position of the enumerator.

In the example, the `MessageQueue` method `GetMessageEnumerator()` is used to access the `MessageEnumerator`. The `MoveNext()` method takes a peek message by message with the `MessageEnumerator`. The `MoveNext()` method is overloaded to allow a time span as an argument. This is one of the big advantages when using this enumerator. Here, the thread can wait until a message arrives in the queue, but only for the specified time span. The `Current` property, which is defined by the `IEnumerator` interface, returns a reference to a message:

```
MessageQueue queue = new MessageQueue(@".\Private$\MyPrivateQueue");
queue.Formatter = new XmlMessageFormatter(
        new string[] {"System.String"});

using (MessageEnumerator messages = queue.GetMessageEnumerator())
{
    while (messages.MoveNext(TimeSpan.FromMinutes(30)))
    {
        Message message = messages.Current;
        Console.WriteLine(message.Body);
    }
}
```

Asynchronous Read

The Receive method of the MessageQueue class waits until a message from the queue can be read. To avoid blocking the thread, a timeout can be specified in an overloaded version of the Receive method. To read the message from the queue after the timeout, Receive() must be invoked again. Instead of polling for messages, the asynchronous method BeginReceive() can be called. Before starting the asynchronous read with BeginReceive(), the event ReceiveCompleted should be set. The ReceiveCompleted event requires a ReceiveCompletedEventHandler delegate that references the method that is invoked when a message arrives in the queue and can be read. In the example, the method MessageArrived is passed to the ReceivedCompletedEventHandler delegate:

```
MessageQueue queue = new MessageQueue(@".\Private$\MyPrivateQueue");
queue.Formatter = new XmlMessageFormatter(
        new string[] {"System.String"});

queue.ReceiveCompleted +=
    new ReceiveComletedEventHandler(MessageArrived);
queue.BeginReceive();
// thread does not wait
```

The handler method MessageArrived requires two parameters. The first parameter is the origin of the event, the MessageQueue. The second parameter is of type ReceiveCompletedEventArgs that contains the message and the asynchronous result. In the example, the method EndReceive() from the queue is invoked to get the result of the asynchronous method, the message:

```
public static void MessageArrived(object source,
        ReceiveCompletedEventArgs e)
{
    MessageQueue queue = (MessageQueue)source;
    Message message = queue.EndReceive(e.AsyncResult);
    Console.WriteLine(message.Body);
}
```

If the message should not be removed from the queue, the BeginPeek() and EndPeek() methods can be used with asynchronous I/O.

Course Order Application

To demonstrate the use of Message Queuing, in this section you create a sample solution to order courses. The sample solution is made up of three assemblies:

❑   A component library (CourseOrder) that includes entity classes for the messages that are sent and received in the queue

❑   A WPF application (CourseOrderSender) that sends messages to the message queue

❑   A WPF application (CourseOrderReceiver) that receives messages from the message queue

Course Order Class Library

Both the sending and the receiving application need the order information. For this reason, the entity classes are put into a separate assembly. The CourseOrder assembly includes three entity classes: CourseOrder, Course, and Customer. With the sample application, not all properties are implemented as they would be in a real application, but just enough properties to show the concept.

In the file Course.cs, the class Course is defined. This class has just one property for the title of the course:

```
namespace Wrox.ProCSharp.Messaging
{
    public class Course
    {
        public string Title { get; set; }
    }
}
```

The file Customer.cs includes the class Customer, which includes properties for the company and contact names:

```
namespace Wrox.ProCSharp.Messaging
{
    public class Customer
    {
        public string Company { get; set; }
        public string Contact { get; set; }
    }
}
```

The class CourseOrder in the file CourseOrder.cs maps a customer and a course inside an order and defines whether the order is high priority:

```
namespace Wrox.ProCSharp.Messaging
{
    public class CourseOrder
    {
        public Customer Customer { get; set; }
        public Course Course { get; set; }
    }
}
```

Course Order Message Sender

The second part of the solution is a Windows application called CourseOrderSender. With this application, course orders are sent to the message queue. The assemblies System.Messaging and CourseOrder must be referenced.

The user interface of this application is shown in Figure 45-10. The items of the combo box comboBoxCourses include several courses such as Advanced .NET Programming, Programming with LINQ, and Distributed Application Development using WCF.

When the Submit the Order button is clicked, the handler method buttonSubmit_Click() is invoked. With this method, a CourseOrder object is created and filled with the content from the TextBox and ComboBox controls. Then a MessageQueue instance is created to open a public queue with a format name. The format name is used to send the message, even if the queue cannot be reached currently. You can get the format name by using the Computer Management snap-in to read the ID of the message queue. With the `Send()` method, the `CourseOrder` object is passed to serialize it with the default `XmlMessageFormatter` and to write it to the queue:

```
private void buttonSubmit_Click(object sender, RoutedEventArgs e)
{
    try
    {
        CourseOrder order = new CourseOrder();
        order.Course = new Course()
        {
            Title = comboBoxCourses.SelectedItem.ToString()
        };
        order.Customer = new Customer()
        {
            Company = textCompany.Text,
            Contact = textContact.Text
        };

        using (MessageQueue queue = new MessageQueue(
                "FormatName:Public=D99CE5F3-4282-4a97-93EE-E9558B15EB13")
        {
            queue.Send(order, String.Format("Course Order {{0}}",
                order.Customer.Company);
        }
        MessageBox.Show("Course Order submitted", "Course Order",
            MessageBoxButton.OK, MessageBoxImage.Information);
    }
    catch (MessageQueueException ex)
    {
        MessageBox.Show(ex.Message, "Course Order Error",
            MessageBoxButton.OK, MessageBoxImage.Error);
    }
}
```

Figure 45-10

Sending Priority and Recoverable Messages

Messages can be prioritized by setting the `Priority` property of the `Message` class. If messages are specially configured, a `Message` object must be created where the body of the message is passed in the constructor.

In the example, the priority is set to `MessagePriority.High` if the `checkBoxPriority` check box is checked. `MessagePriority` is an enumeration that allows you to set values from `Lowest` (0) to `Highest` (7). The default value, `Normal`, has a priority value of 3.

To make the message recoverable, the property `Recoverable` is set to `true`:

```
private void buttonSubmit_Click(object sender, RoutedEventArgs e)
{
    try
    {
        CourseOrder order = new CourseOrder();
        order.Course = new Course()
        {
            Title = comboBoxCourses.SelectionBoxItem.ToString()
        };
        order.Customer = new Customer()
        {
            Company = textCompany.Text,
            Contact = textContact.Text
        };

        using (MessageQueue queue = new MessageQueue(
                "FormatName:Public=D99CE5F3-4282-4a97-93EE-E9558B15EB13"))
        using (Message message = new Message(order))
        {
            if (checkBoxPriority.IsChecked == true)
            {
                message.Priority = MessagePriority.High;
            }
            message.Recoverable = true;
            queue.Send(message,  String.Format("Course Order {{{0}}}",
                order.Customer.Company);
        }
        MessageBox.Show("Course Order submitted");
    }
    catch (MessageQueueException ex)
    {
        MessageBox.Show(ex.Message, "Course Order Error",
            MessageBoxButton.OK, MessageBoxImage.Error);
    }
}
```

By running the application, you can add course orders to the message queue (see Figure 45-11).

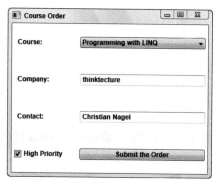

Figure 45-11

Course Order Message Receiver

The design view of the Course Order receiving application that reads messages from the queue is shown in Figure 45-12. This application displays labels of every order in the `listOrders` list box. When an order is selected, the content of the order is displayed with the controls on the right side of the application.

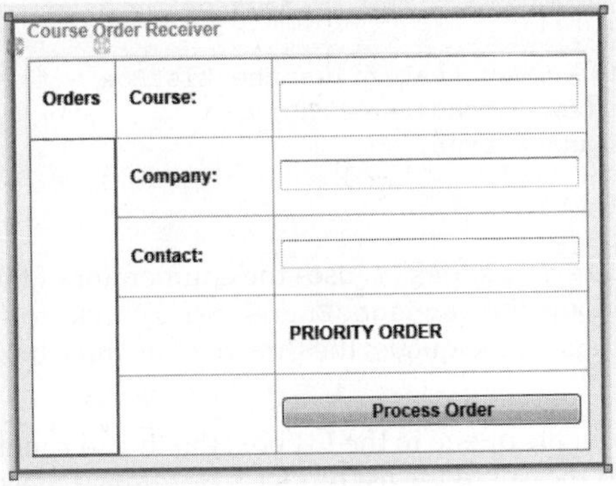

Figure 45-12

In the constructor of the `Window` class `CourseOrderReceiverWindow`, the `MessageQueue` object is created that references the same queue that was used with the sending application. For reading messages, the `XmlMessageFormatter` with the types that are read is associated with the queue using the `Formatter` property.

To display the available messages in the list, a new thread is created that peeks at messages in the background. The thread's main method is `PeekMessages`.

You can read more about threads in Chapter 19, "Threading and Synchronization."

```
using System;
using System.Messaging;
using System.Threading;
using System.Windows;
using System.Windows.Controls;
using System.Windows.Threading;

namespace Wrox.ProCSharp.Messaging
{
    public partial class CourseOrderReceiverWindow : Window
    {
        private MessageQueue orderQueue;

        public CourseOrderReceiverWindow()
        {
            InitializeComponent();

            string queueName =
                "FormatName:Public=D99CE5F3-4282-4a97-93EE-E9558B15EB13";

            orderQueue = new MessageQueue(queueName);
```

(continued)

(continued)

```
System.Type[] types = new Type[]
{
    typeof(CourseOrder),
    typeof(Customer),
    typeof(Course)
}
orderQueue.Formatter = new XmlMessageFormatter(types);

// start the thread that fills the ListBox with orders
Thread t1 = new Thread(PeekMessages);
t1.IsBackground = true;
t1.Start();
}
```

The thread's main method, PeekMessages(), uses the enumerator of the message queue to display all messages. Within the while loop, the messagesEnumerator checks to see if there is a new message in the queue. If there is no message in the queue, the thread waits three hours for the next message to arrive before it exits.

To display every message from the queue in the list box, the thread cannot directly write the text to the list box, but needs to forward the call to the list box's creator thread. Because Windows Forms controls are bound to a single thread, only the creator thread is allowed to access methods and properties. The Invoke() method forwards the request to the creator thread:

```
private delegate void MethodInvoker(LabelIdMapping labelIdMapping);

private void PeekMessages()
{
    using (MessageEnumerator messagesEnumerator =
        orderQueue.GetMessageEnumerator2())
    {
        while (messagesEnumerator.MoveNext(TimeSpan.FromHours(3)))
        {
            LabelIdMapping labelId = new LabelIdMapping()
            {
                Id = messagesEnumerator.Current.Id,
                Label = messagesEnumerator.Current.Label
            };
            Dispatcher.Invoke(DispatcherPriority.Normal,
                new MethodInvoker(AddListItem), labelId);
        }
    }
    MessageBox.Show("No orders in the last 3 hours. Exiting thread",
        "Course Order Receiver", MessageBoxButton.OK,
        MessageBoxImage.Information);
}

private void AddListItem(LabelIdMapping labelIdMapping)
{
    listOrders.Items.Add(labelIdMapping);
}
```

The `ListBox` control contains elements of the `LabelIdMapping` class. This class is used to display the labels of the messages in the list box, but to keep the ID of the message hidden. The ID of the message can be used to read the message at a later time:

```
private class LabelIdMapping
{
    private string Label { get; set; }
    private string Id { get; set; }

    public override string ToString()
    {
        return label;
    }
}
```

The `ListBox` control has the `SelectedIndexChanged` event associated with the method `listOrders_SelectionChanged()`. This method gets the `LabelIdMapping` object from the current selection, and uses the ID to peek at the message once more with the `PeekById()` method. Then the content of the message is displayed in the `TextBox` control. Because by default the priority of the message is not read, the property `MessageReadPropertyFilter` must be set to receive the `Priority`:

```
private void listOrders_SelectionChanged(object sender,
    RoutedEventArgs e)
{
    LabelIdMapping labelId = listOrders.SelectedItem as LabelIdMapping;
    if (labelId == null)
        return;

    orderQueue.MessageReadPropertyFilter.Priority = true;
    Message message = orderQueue.PeekById(labelId.Id);

    CourseOrder order = message.Body as CourseOrder;
    if (order != null)
    {
        textCourse.Text = order.Course.Title;
        textCompany.Text = order.Customer.Company;
        textContact.Text = order.Customer.Contact;
        buttonProcessOrder.IsEnabled = true;

        if (message.Priority > MessagePriority.Normal)
        {
            labelPriority.Visibility = Visibility.Visible;
        }
        else
        {
            labelPriority.Visibility = Visibility.Hidden;
        }
    }
    else
    {
        MessageBox.Show("The selected item is not a course order",
                "Course Order Receiver", MessageBoxButton.OK,
                MessageBoxImage.Warning);
    }
}
```

When the Process Order button is clicked, the handler method `OnProcessOrder()` is invoked. Here again, the currently selected message from the list box is referenced, and the message is removed from the queue by calling the method `ReceiveById()`:

```
private void buttonProcessOrder_Click(object sender, RoutedEventArgs e)
{
    LabelIdMapping labelId = listOrders.SelectedItem as LabelIdMapping;
    Message message = orderQueue.ReceiveById(labelId.Id);

    listOrders.Items.Remove(labelId);
    listOrders.SelectedIndex = -1;
    buttonProcessOrder.Enabled = false;
    textCompany.Text = string.Empty;
    textContact.Text = string.Empty;
    textCourse.Text = string.Empty;

    MessageBox.Show("Course order processed", "Course Order Receiver",
        MessageBoxButton.OK, MessageBoxImage.Information);
    }
  }
}
```

Figure 45-13 shows the running receiving application that lists three orders in the queue, and one order is currently selected.

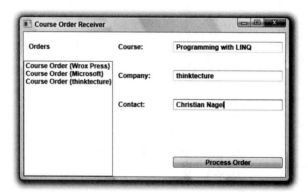

Figure 45-13

Receiving Results

With the current version of the sample application, the sending application never knows if the message is ever dealt with. To get results from the receiver, acknowledgment queues or response queues can be used.

Acknowledgment Queues

With an acknowledgment queue, the sending application can get information about the status of the message. With the acknowledgments, you can define if you would like to receive an answer, if everything went OK, or if something went wrong. For example, acknowledgments can be sent when the message reaches the destination queue or when the message is read, or if it didn't reach the destination queue or was not read before a timeout elapsed.

In the example, the `AdministrationQueue` of the `Message` class is set to the `CourseOrderAck` queue. This queue must be created similar to a normal queue. This queue is just used the other way around: the original sender receives acknowledgments. The `AcknowledgeType` property is set to `AcknowledgeTypes.FullReceive` to get an acknowledgment when the message is read:

```
Message message = new Message(order);

message.AdministrationQueue =
    new MessageQueue(@".\CourseOrderAck");
message.AcknowledgeType = AcknowledgeTypes.FullReceive;

queue.Send(message, String.Format("Course Order {{0}}",
    order.Customer.Company);

string id = message.Id;
```

The *correlation ID* is used to determine what acknowledgment message belongs to which message sent. Every message that is sent has an ID, and the acknowledgment message that is sent in response to that message holds the ID of the originating message as its correlation ID. The messages from the acknowledgment queue can be read using `MessageQueue.ReceiveByCorrelationId()` to receive the associated acknowledgment.

Instead of using acknowledgments, the dead-letter queue can be used for messages that didn't arrive at their destination. By setting the `UseDeadLetterQueue` property of the `Message` class to `true`, the message is copied to the dead-letter queue if it didn't arrive at the target queue before the timeout was reached.

Timeouts can be set with the `Message` properties `TimeToReachQueue` and `TimeToBeReceived`.

Response Queues

If more information than an acknowledgment is needed from the receiving application, a response queue can be used. A response queue is like a normal queue, but the original sender uses the queue as a receiver and the original receiver uses the response queue as a sender.

The sender must assign the response queue with the `ResponseQueue` property of the `Message` class. The sample code here shows how the receiver uses the response queue to return a response message. With the response message `responseMessage`, the property `CorrelationId` is set to the ID of the original message. This way the client application knows to which message the answer belongs. This is similar to acknowledgment queues. The response message is sent with the `Send()` method of the `MessageQueue` object that is returned from the `ResponseQueue` property:

```
public void ReceiveMessage(Message message)
{
    Message responseMessage = new Message("response");
    responseMessage.CorrelationId = message.Id;

    message.ReesponseQueue.Send(responseMessage);
}
```

Transactional Queues

With recoverable messages, it is not guaranteed that the messages will arrive in order and just once. Failures on the network can cause messages to arrive multiple times; this happens also if both the sender and receiver have multiple network protocols installed that are used by Message Queuing.

Transactional queues can be used when these guarantees are required:

❑ Messages arrive in the same order they have been sent.

❑ Messages arrive only once.

With transactional queues, a single transaction doesn't span the sending and receiving of messages. The nature of Message Queuing is that the time between send and receive can be quite long. In contrast, transactions should be short. With Message Queuing, the first transaction is used to send the message into the queue, the second transaction forwards the message on the network, and the third transaction is used to receive the messages.

The next example shows how to create a transactional message queue and how to send messages using a transaction.

A transactional message queue is created by passing `true` with the second parameter of the `MessageQueue.Create()` method.

If you would like to write multiple messages to a queue within a single transaction, you have to instantiate a `MessageQueueTransaction` object and invoke the `Begin()` method. When you are finished with sending all messages that belong to the transaction, the `Commit()` method of the `MessageQueueTransaction` object must be called. To cancel a transaction (and have no messages written to the queue), the `Abort()` method must be called, as you can see within the `catch` block:

```
using System;
using System.Messaging;

namespace Wrox.ProCSharp.Messaging
{
    class Program
    {
        static void Main()
        {
            if (!MessageQueue.Exists(@".\MyTransactionalQueue"))
            {
                MessageQueue.Create(@".\MyTransactionalQueue", true);
            }
            MessageQueue queue = new MessageQueue(@".\MyTransactionalQueue");
            MessageQueueTransaction transaction =
                    new MessageQueueTransaction();
            try
            {
                transaction.Begin();
                queue.Send("a", transaction);
                queue.Send("b", transaction);
                queue.Send("c", transaction);
                transaction.Commit();
            }
            catch
            {
                transaction.Abort();
            }
        }
    }
}
```

Message Queuing with WCF

Chapter 42 covered the architecture and core features of Windows Communication Foundation. With WCF, you can configure a Message Queuing binding that makes use of the Windows Message Queuing architecture. With this, WCF offers an abstraction layer to Message Queuing. Figure 45-14 explains the architecture in a simple picture. The client application invokes a method of a WCF proxy to send a message to the queue. The message is created by the proxy. For the client developer, there's no need to know that a message is sent to the queue. The client developer just invokes a method of the proxy. The proxy abstracts dealing with the classes from the System.Messaging namespace and sends a message to the queue. The MSMQ listener channel on the service side reads messages from the queue, converts them to method calls, and invokes the method calls with the service.

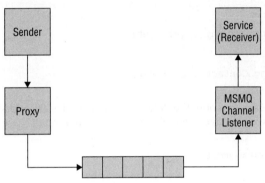

Figure 45-14

Next, the Course Ordering application gets converted to make use of Message Queuing from a WCF viewpoint. With this solution, the three projects done earlier are modified, and one more assembly is added that includes the contract of the WCF service:

❑ The component library (CourseOrder) includes entity classes for the messages that are sent across the wire. These entity classes are modified to fulfill the data contract for serialization with WCF.

❑ A new library is added (CourseOrderService) that defines the contract offered by the service.

❑ The WPF sender application (CourseOrderSender) is modified to not send messages but instead invoke methods of a WCF proxy.

❑ The WPF receiving application (CourseOrderReceiver) is modified to make use of the WCF service that implements the contract.

Entity Classes with a Data Contract

In the library CourseOrder, the classes Course, Customer, and CourseOrder are modified to apply the data contract with the attributes [DataContract] and [DataMember]. For using these attributes, you have to reference the assembly System.Runtime.Serialization and import the namespace System.Runtime.Serialization:

```
using System.Runtime.Serialization;

namespace Wrox.ProCSharp.Messaging
```

(continued)

(continued)

```
    {
        [DataContract]
        public class Course
        {
            [DataMember]
            public string Title { get; set; }
        }
    }
```

The `Customer` class requires the data contract attributes as well:

```
    [DataContract]
    public class Customer
    {
        [DataMember]
        public string Company { get; set; }

        [DataMember]
        public string Contact { get; set; }
    }
```

With the class `CourseOrder`, not only the data contract attributes are added, but an override of the `ToString()` method as well to have a default string representation of these objects:

```
    [DataContract]
    public class CourseOrder
    {
        [DataMember]
        public Customer Customer { get; set; }

        [DataMember]
        public Course Course { get; set; }

        public override string ToString()
        {
            return String.Format("Course Order {{{0}}}", Customer.Company);
        }
    }
```

WCF Service Contract

For offering the service with a WCF service contract, add a WCF service library with the name `CourseOrderServiceContract`. The contract is defined by the interface `ICourseOrderService`. This contract needs the attribute `[ServiceContract]`. If you want to restrict using this interface only with message queues, you can apply the `[DeliveryRequirements]` attribute and assign the property `QueuedDeliveryRequirements`. Possible values of the enumeration `QueuedDeliveryRequirementsMode` are `Required`, `Allowed`, and `NotAllowed`. The method `AddCourseOrder()` is offered by the service. Methods used by Message Queuing can only have input parameters. Because the sender and receiver can run independent of each other, the sender cannot expect an immediate result. With the attribute `[OperationContract]`, the `IsOneWay` property is set. The caller of this operation does not wait for an answer from the service:

```
    using System.ServiceModel;

    namespace Wrox.ProCSharp.Messaging
```

```
    {
        [ServiceContract]
        [DeliveryRequirements(
                QueuedDeliveryRequirements=QueuedDeliveryRequirementsMode.Required)]
        public interface ICourseOrderService
        {
            [OperationContract(IsOneWay = true)]
            void AddCourseOrder(CourseOrder courseOrder);
        }
    }
```

You can use acknowledgment and response queues to get answers to the client.

WCF Message Receiver Application

The WPF application CourseOrderReceiver is now modified to implement the WCF service and receive the messages. References to the assembly System.ServiceModel and the WCF contract assembly CourseOrderServiceContract are required.

The class CourseOrderService implements the interface ICourseOrderService. With the implementation, the event CourseOrderAdded is fired. The WPF application will register to this event to receive CourseOrder objects.

Because WPF controls are bound to a single thread, the property UseSynchronizationContext is set with the [ServiceBehavior] attribute. This is a feature of the WCF runtime to pass the method call invocation to the thread that is defined by the synchronization context of the WPF application:

```
using System.ServiceModel;

namespace Wrox.ProCSharp.Messaging
{
    public delegate void CourseOrderInfoHandler(CourseOrder courseOrder);

    [ServiceBehavior(UseSynchronizationContext=true)]
    public class CourseOrderService : ICourseOrderService
    {
        public static event CourseOrderInfoHandler CourseOrderAdded;

        public void AddCourseOrder(CourseOrder courseOrder)
        {
            if (CourseOrderAdded != null)
                CourseOrderAdded(courseOrder);
        }
    }
}
```

Chapter 19, "Threading and Synchronization," explains the synchronization context.

With the constructor of the class CourseReceiverWindow, a ServiceHost object is instantiated and opened to start the listener. The binding of the listener will be done in the application configuration file.

In the constructor, the event CourseOrderAdded of the CourseOrderService is subscribed. Because the only thing that happens here is adding the received CourseOrder object to a collection, a simple Lambda expression is used.

Lambda expressions are explained in Chapter 7, "Delegates and Events."

The collection class that is used here is `ObservableCollection<T>` from the namespace `System.Collections.ObjectModel`. This collection class implements the interface `INotifyCollectionChanged`, and thus the WPF controls bound to the collection are informed about dynamic changes to the list:

```
using System;
using System.Collections.ObjectModel;
using System.ServiceModel;
using System.Windows;

namespace Wrox.ProCSharp.Messaging
{
    public partial class CourseOrderReceiverWindow : Window
    {
        private ObservableCollection<CourseOrder> courseOrders =
            new ObservableCollection<CourseOrder>();

        public CourseOrderReceiverWindow()
        {
            InitializeComponent();

            CourseOrderService.CourseOrderAdded +=
                courseOrder => courseOrders.Add(courseOrder);

            ServiceHost host = new ServiceHost(typeof(CourseOrderService));
            try
            {
                host.Open();
            }
            catch (Exception ex)
            {
                Console.WriteLine(ex.Message);
            }

            this.DataContext = courseOrders;
        }
}
```

The WPF elements in the XAML code now make use of data binding. The `ListBox` is bound to the data context, and the single-item controls are bound to properties of the current item of the data context:

```
<ListBox Grid.Row="1" x:Name="listOrders" ItemsSource="{Binding}"
    IsSynchronizedWithCurrentItem="true" />

<!-- ... -->

<TextBox x:Name="textCourse" Grid.Row="0" Grid.Column="1"
    Text="{Binding Path=Course.Title}" />
<TextBox x:Name="textCompany" Grid.Row="1" Grid.Column="1"
    Text="{Binding Path=Customer.Company}" />
<TextBox x:Name="textContact" Grid.Row="2" Grid.Column="1"
    Text="{Binding Path=Customer.Contact}" />
```

The application configuration file defines the `netMsmqBinding`. For reliable messaging, transactional queues are required. To receive and send messages to non-transactional queues, the `exactlyOnce` property must be set to `false`.

netMsmqBinding *is the binding to be used if both the receiver and the sender application are WCF applications. If one of these applications is using the* System.Messaging *API to send or receive messages, or is an older COM application, you can use the* msmqIntegrationBinding.

```xml
<?xml version="1.0" encoding="utf-8" ?>
<configuration>
  <system.serviceModel>
    <bindings>
      <netMsmqBinding>
        <binding name="NonTransactionalQueueBinding" exactlyOnce="false">
          <security mode="None" />
        </binding>
      </netMsmqBinding>
    </bindings>
    <services>
      <service name="Wrox.ProCSharp.Messaging.CourseOrderService">
        <endpoint address="net.msmq://localhost/private/courseorder"
          binding="netMsmqBinding"
          bindingConfiguration="NonTransactionalQueueBinding"
          name="OrderQueueEP"
          contract="Wrox.ProCSharp.Messaging.ICourseOrderService" />
      </service>
    </services>
  </system.serviceModel>
</configuration>
```

The Click event handler of the buttonProcessOrder button removes the selected course order from the collection class:

```
private void buttonProcessOrder_Click(object sender, RoutedEventArgs e)
{
    CourseOrder courseOrder = listOrders.SelectedItem as CourseOrder;
    courseOrders.Remove(courseOrder);
    listOrders.SelectedIndex = -1;
    buttonProcessOrder.IsEnabled = false;

    MessageBox.Show("Course order processed", "Course Order Receiver",
        MessageBoxButton.OK, MessageBoxImage.Information);

}
```

WCF Message Sender Application

The sending application is modified to make use of a WCF proxy class. For the contract of the service, the assembly CourseOrderServiceContract is referenced, and the assembly System.ServiceModel is required for use of the WCF classes.

In the Click event handler of the buttonSubmit control, the ChannelFactory class returns a proxy. The proxy sends a message to the queue by invoking the method AddCourseOrder():

```
private void buttonSubmit_Click(object sender, RoutedEventArgs e)
{
    try
    {
        CourseOrder order = new CourseOrder();
        order.Course = new Course()
        {
```

(continued)

(continued)

```
                    Title = comboCourses.SelectionBoxItem.ToString()
            };
            order.Customer = new Customer()
            {
                Company = textCompany.Text,
                Contact = textContact.Text
            };

            ChannelFactory<ICourseOrderService> factory =
                    new ChannelFactory<ICourseOrderService>("queueEndpoint");
            ICourseOrderService proxy = factory.CreateChannel();
            proxy.AddCourseOrder(order);
            factory.Close();

            MessageBox.Show("Course order submitted", "Course Order",
                    MessageBoxButton.OK, MessageBoxImage.Information);
        }
        catch (Exception ex)
        {
            MessageBox.Show(ex.Message, "Course Order Error",
                    MessageBoxButton.OK, MessageBoxImage.Error);
        }
    }
}
```

The application configuration file defines the client part of the WCF connection. Again, the netMsmqBinding is used:

```xml
<?xml version="1.0" encoding="utf-8" ?>
<configuration>
    <system.serviceModel>
        <bindings>
            <netMsmqBinding>
                <binding name="nonTransactionalQueueBinding"
                        exactlyOnce="false">
                    <security mode="None" />
                </binding>
            </netMsmqBinding>
        </bindings>
        <client>
            <endpoint address="net.msmq://localhost/private/courseorder"
                    binding="netMsmqBinding"
                    bindingConfiguration="nonTransactionalQueueBinding"
                    contract="Wrox.ProCSharp.Messaging.ICourseOrderService"
                    name="queueEndpoint" />
        </client>
    </system.serviceModel>
</configuration>
```

When you start the application now, it works in a similar way as before. There is no longer a need to use classes of the System.Messaging namespace to send and receive messages. Instead, you write the application in a similar way as using TCP or HTTP channels with WCF.

However, to create message queues and to purge messages, you still need the MessageQueue class. WCF is only an abstraction to send and receive messages.

If you need to have a `System.Messaging` *application to communicate with a WCF application, you can do this by using the* `msmqIntegrationBinding` *instead of the* `netMsmqBinding`. *This binding uses the message format that is used with COM and* `System.Messaging`.

Message Queue Installation

Message queues can be created with the `MessageQueue.Create()` method. However, the user running an application usually doesn't have the administrative privileges that are required to create message queues.

Usually, message queues are created with an installation program. For installation programs, the class `MessageQueueInstaller` can be used. If an installer class is part of an application, the command-line utility `installutil.exe` (or a Windows Installation Package) invokes the `Install()` method of the installer.

Visual Studio has a special support for using the `MessageQueueInstaller` with Windows Forms applications. If a `MessageQueue` component is dropped from the toolbox onto the form, the smart tag of the component allows you to add an installer with the menu entry Add Installer. The `MessageQueueInstaller` object can be configured with the properties editor to define transactional queues, journal queues, the type of the formatter, the base priority, and so on.

Installers are discussed in Chapter 16, "Deployment."

Summary

In this chapter, you've seen how Message Queuing can be used. Message Queuing is an important technology that offers not only asynchronous, but also disconnected communication. The sender and receiver can be running at different times, which makes Message Queuing an option for smart clients and also useful to distribute the load on the server over time.

The most important classes with Message Queuing are `Message` and `MessageQueue`. The `MessageQueue` class allows sending, receiving, and peeking at messages, and the `Message` class defines the content that is sent.

WCF offers an abstraction to message queuing. You can use the concepts offered by WCF to send messages by calling methods of a proxy and to receive messages by implementing a service.

The next chapter dives into Directory Services, how and when to use these hierarchical data stores, and different ways to connect to this service.

46

Directory Services

Microsoft's Active Directory is a *directory service* that provides a central, hierarchical store for user information, network resources, services, and so on. The information in this directory service can be extended to also store custom data that is of interest for the enterprise. For example, Microsoft Exchange Server and Microsoft Dynamics use Active Directory intensively to store public folders and other items.

Before the release of Active Directory, Exchange Server used its own private store for its objects. It was necessary for a system administrator to configure two user IDs for a single person: a user account in the Windows NT domain to enable a logon and a user in Exchange Directory. This was necessary because of the additional information required by users (such as email addresses, phone numbers, and so on), and the user information for the NT domain was not extensible to add the required information. Now, the system administrator has to configure just a single user for a person in Active Directory; the information for a user object can be extended so that it fits the requirements of Exchange Server. You can also extend this information. For example, you can extend user information in Active Directory with a skills list. Then it would easily be possible to track down a C# developer by searching for the required C# skill.

This chapter shows how you can use the .NET Framework to access and manipulate the data in a directory service using classes from the System.DirectoryServices, System.DirectoryServices.AccountManagement, and System.DirectoryServices.Protocols namespaces.

> This chapter uses Windows Server 2008 with Active Directory configured. You can also use Windows 2003 Server or other directory services.

This chapter covers the following:

- ❑ The architecture of Active Directory, including features and basic concepts
- ❑ Some of the tools available for administration of Active Directory and their benefit to programming
- ❑ How to read and modify data in Active Directory
- ❑ Searching for objects in Active Directory
- ❑ Account management
- ❑ Accessing a DSML Web service to search for objects

After discussing the architecture and how to program Active Directory, you create a Windows application in which you can specify properties and a filter to search for user objects. Similar to other chapters, you can also download the code for the examples in this chapter from the Wrox Web site at www.wrox.com.

The Architecture of Active Directory

Before starting to program Active Directory, you need to know how it works, what it is used for, and what data can be stored there.

Features

The features of Active Directory can be summarized as follows:

❑ The data in Active Directory is grouped *hierarchically*. Objects can be stored inside other container objects. Instead of having a single, large list of users, you can group users inside organizational units. An organizational unit can contain other organizational units, so you can build a tree.

❑ Active Directory uses a *multimaster replication*. With Active Directory, every *domain controller* (DC) is a master. With multiple masters, updates can be applied to any DC. This model is much more scalable than a single-master model because updates can be made to different servers concurrently. The disadvantage of this model is more complex replication, which is discussed later in this chapter.

❑ The *replication topology* is flexible, to support replications across slow links in WANs. How often data should be replicated is configurable by the domain administrators.

❑ Active Directory supports *open standards*. The *Lightweight Directory Access Protocol* (LDAP) is an Internet standard that can be used to access many different directory services, including the data in Active Directory. With LDAP, a programming interface, LDAP API, is also defined. The LDAP API can be used to access Active Directory with the C language. Another standard used within Active Directory is *Kerberos*, which is used for authentication. The Windows Server Kerberos service can also be used to authenticate UNIX clients.

❑ *Active Directory Service Interface* (ADSI) defines COM interfaces to access directory services. ADSI makes it possible to access all features of Active Directory. Classes from the namespace System.DirectoryServices wrap ADSI COM objects to make directory services accessible from .NET applications.

❑ *Directory Service Markup Language* (DSML) is another standard to access directory services. DSML is a platform-independent approach and is supported by the OASIS group.

❑ With Active Directory, a fine-grained security is available. Every object stored in Active Directory can have an associated access-control list that defines who can do what with that object.

The objects in the directory are *strongly typed*, which means that the type of an object is exactly defined; no attributes that are not specified may be added to an object. In the *schema*, the object types as well as the parts of an object (attributes) are defined. Attributes can be mandatory or optional.

Active Directory Concepts

Before programming Active Directory, you need to know some basic terms and definitions.

Objects

Active Directory stores objects. An object refers to something concrete such as a user, a printer, or a network share. Objects have mandatory and optional attributes that describe them. Some examples of the attributes of a `user` object are the first name, last name, email address, phone number, and so on.

Figure 46-1 shows a container object called `Wrox Press` that contains some other objects: two user objects, a contact object, a printer object, and a user group object.

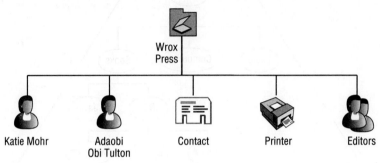

| Katie Mohr | Adaobi
Obi Tulton | Contact | Printer | Editors |

Figure 46-1

Schema

Every object is an instance of a class defined in the *schema*. The schema *defines the types* and is itself stored in objects in Active Directory. You must differentiate between `classSchema` and `attributeSchema`: `classSchema` defines the types of objects and details what mandatory and optional attributes an object has. `attributeSchema` defines what an attribute looks like and the allowed syntax for a specific attribute.

You can define custom types and attributes and add these to the schema. Be aware, however, that a new schema type cannot be removed from Active Directory. You can mark it as inactive so that new objects cannot be created, but there can be existing objects of that type, so it is not possible to remove classes or attributes defined in the schema.

The user group Administrator doesn't have enough rights to create new schema entries; the group Enterprise Admins is needed for that.

Configuration

In addition to objects and class definitions stored as objects, the configuration of Active Directory itself is stored in Active Directory. It stores the information about all sites, such as the replication interval, which is set up by the system administrator. Because the configuration itself is stored in Active Directory, you can access the configuration information like all other objects in Active Directory.

The Active Directory Domain

A domain is a security boundary of a Windows network. In the Active Directory domain, the objects are stored in a hierarchical order. Active Directory itself is made up of one or more domains. Figure 46-2 shows the hierarchical order of objects in a domain; the domain is represented by a triangle. Container objects such as `Users`, `Computers`, and `Books` can store other objects. Each oval in the picture represents an object, with the lines between the objects representing parent-child relationships. For example, `Books` is the parent of `.NET` and `Java`, and `Pro C#`, `Beg C#`, and `ASP.NET` are child objects of the `.NET` object.

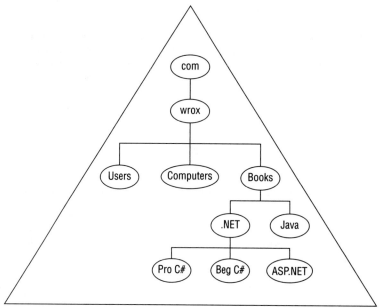

Figure 46-2

Domain Controller

A single domain can have multiple domain controllers, each of which stores all of the objects in the domain. There is no master server, and all DCs are treated equally; you have a multimaster model. The objects are replicated across the servers inside the domain.

Site

A *site* is a location in the network that holds at least one DC. If you have multiple locations in the enterprise, which are connected with slow network links, you can use multiple sites for a single domain. For backup or scalability reasons, each site can have one or more DCs running. Replication between servers in a site can happen at shorter intervals due to the faster network connection. Replication is configured to occur at larger time intervals between servers across sites, depending on the speed of the network. Of course, replication intervals can be configured by the domain administrator.

Domain Tree

Multiple domains can be connected by trust relationships. These domains share a *common schema*, a *common configuration*, and a *global catalog* (more on global catalogs shortly). A common schema and a common configuration imply that this data is replicated across domains. Domain trees share the same class and attribute schema. The objects themselves are not replicated across domains.

Domains connected in such a way form a domain tree. Domains in a domain tree have a contiguous, hierarchical namespace. This means that the domain name of the child domain is the name of that child domain appended to the name of the parent domain. Between domains, trusts using the Kerberos protocol are established.

For example, you have the root domain wrox.com, which is the *parent domain* of the child domains india.wrox.com and uk.wrox.com. A trust is set up between the parent and the child domains, so that accounts from one domain can be authenticated by another domain.

Forest

Multiple domain trees that are connected by using a common schema, a common configuration, and a global catalog without a contiguous namespace are called a *forest*. A forest is a set of domain trees; it can be used if the company has a subcompany for which a different domain name should be used. Here is one example: `wrox.com` should be relatively independent of the domain `wiley.com`, but it should be possible to have a common management, and be possible for users from `wrox.com` to access resources from the `wiley.com` domain and vice versa. With a forest, you can have trusts between multiple domain trees.

Global Catalog

A search for an object can span multiple domains. If you look for a specific `user` object with some attributes, you must search every domain. Starting with `wrox.com`, the search continues to `uk.wrox.com` and `india.wrox.com`; across slow links such a search could take a while.

To make searches faster, all objects are copied to the *global catalog* (GC). The GC is replicated in every domain of a forest. There is at least one server in every domain holding a GC. For performance and scalability reasons, you can have more than one GC server in a domain. Using a GC, a search through all the objects can happen on a single server.

The GC is a *read-only cache* of all the objects that can be used only for searches; the domain controllers must be used to do updates.

Not all attributes of an object are stored in the GC. You can define whether an attribute should be stored with an object. The decision whether to store an attribute in the GC depends on how the attribute is used. If the attribute is frequently used in searches, putting it into the GC makes the search faster. A picture of a user isn't useful in the GC because you would never search for a picture. Conversely, a phone number would be a useful addition to the store. You can also define that an attribute should be indexed so that a query for it is faster.

Replication

As a programmer, you are unlikely ever to configure replication, but because it affects the data you store in Active Directory, you need to know how it works. Active Directory uses a *multimaster* server architecture. Updates happen to every domain controller in the domain. The *replication latency* defines how long it takes until an update starts:

- ❑ The configurable *change notification* happens, by default, every 5 minutes inside a site if some attributes change. The DC where a change occurred informs one server after the other with 30-second intervals, so the fourth DC can get the change notification after 7 minutes. The default change notification across sites is set to 180 minutes. Intra- and intersite replication can each be configured to other values.

- ❑ If no changes have occurred, the *scheduled replication* occurs every 60 minutes inside a site. This is to ensure that a change notification wasn't missed.

- ❑ For security-sensitive information, such as account lockout, *immediate notification* can occur.

With a replication, only the changes are copied to the DCs. With every change of an attribute, a version number (update sequence number or USN) and a time stamp are recorded. These are used to help resolve conflicts if updates happened to the same attribute on different servers.

Here's an example. The mobile phone attribute of the user John Doe has the USN number 47. This value is already replicated to all DCs. One system administrator changes the phone number. The change occurs on the server DC1; the new USN of this attribute on the server DC1 is now 48, whereas the other DCs still have the USN 47. For someone still reading the attribute, the old value can be read until the replication to all domain controllers has occurred.

The rare case can happen that another administrator changes the phone number attribute, and a different DC is selected because this administrator received a faster response from the server DC2. The USN of this attribute on the server DC2 is also changed to 48.

At the notification intervals, notification happens because the USN for the attribute changed, and the last time replication occurred was with a USN value of 47. The replication mechanism now detects that the servers DC1 and DC2 both have a USN of 48 for the phone number attribute. Which server is the winner is not really important, but one server must definitely win. To resolve this conflict, the time stamp of the change is used. Because the change happened later on DC2, the value stored in the DC2 domain controller is replicated.

> When reading objects, you must be aware that the data is not necessarily current. The currency of the data depends on replication latencies. When updating objects, another user can still read some old values after the update. It's also possible that different updates can happen at the same time.

Characteristics of Active Directory Data

Active Directory doesn't replace a relational database or the registry, so what kind of data would you store in it?

❑ With Active Directory you get *hierarchical data*. You can have containers that store further containers and objects, too. Containers themselves are objects as well.

❑ The data should be used for *read-mostly*. Because of replication occurring at certain time intervals, you cannot be sure that you will read up-to-date data. You must be aware that in applications, the information you read is possibly not the current up-to-date information.

❑ Data should be of *global interest* to the enterprise, because adding a new data type to the schema replicates it to all the servers in the enterprise. For data types of interest to only a small number of users, the domain enterprise administrator normally wouldn't install new schema types.

❑ The data stored should be of *reasonable size* because of replication issues. It is fine to store data with a size of 100K in the directory, if the data changes only once a week. However, if the data changes every hour, data of this size is too large. Always think about replicating the data to different servers: where the data gets transferred to and at what intervals. If you have larger data, it's possible to put a link into Active Directory and store the data itself in a different place.

To summarize, the data you store in Active Directory should be hierarchically organized, of reasonable size, and of importance to the enterprise.

Schema

Active Directory objects are strongly typed. The schema defines the types of the objects, mandatory and optional attributes, and the syntax and constraints of these attributes. As mentioned earlier, in the schema, it is necessary to differentiate between class-schema and attribute-schema objects. A class is a collection of attributes. With the classes, single inheritance is supported. As you can see in Figure 46-3, the user class derives from the organizationalPerson class, organizationalPerson is a subclass of person, and the base class is top. The classSchema that defines a class describes the attributes with the systemMayContain attribute.

Figure 46-3 shows only a few of all the systemMayContain values. Using the ADSI Edit tool, you can easily see all the values; you look at this tool in the next section. In the root class top you can see that every object can have common name (cn), displayName, objectGUID, whenChanged, and whenCreated attributes. The person class derives from top. A person object also has a userPassword and a telephoneNumber. organizationalPerson is derived from person. In addition to the attributes of person, it has a manager, department, and company, and a user has extra attributes needed to log on to a system.

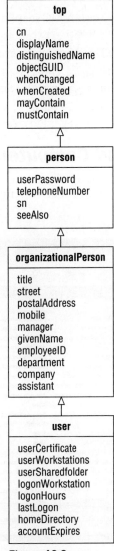

Figure 46-3

Administration Tools for Active Directory

Looking into some of the Active Directory administration tools can help to give you an idea of Active Directory, what data is in there, and what can be done programmatically.

The system administrator has many tools to enter new data, update data, and configure Active Directory:

❑ The *Active Directory Users and Computers* MMC snap-in is used to enter new users and update user data.

❑ The *Active Directory Sites and Services* MMC snap-in is used to configure sites in a domain and for replication between these sites.

❑ The *Active Directory Domains and Trusts* MMC snap-in can be used to build up a trust relationship between domains in a tree.

❑ *ADSI Edit* is the editor for Active Directory, where every object can be viewed and edited.

To run these tools on Windows Vista or Windows XP, you need to install Windows Server 2003 Admin Pack. ADSI Edit is available with the Windows Server 2003 Support tools.

The following sections get into the functionality of the tools Active Directory Users and Computers and ADSI Edit because these tools are important in regard to creating applications using Active Directory.

Active Directory Users and Computers

The Active Directory Users and Computers snap-in is the tool that system administrators use to manage users. Select Start ➪ Programs ➪ Administrative Tools ➪ Active Directory Users and Computers to start this program (see Figure 46-4).

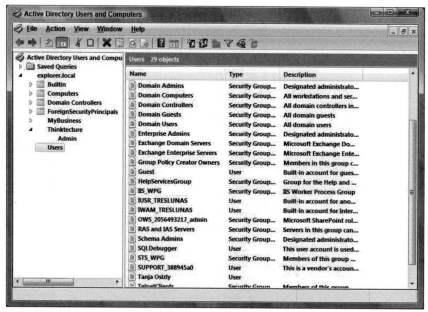

Figure 46-4

With this tool you can add new users, groups, contacts, organizational units, printers, shared folders, or computers, and modify existing ones. Figure 46-5 shows the attributes that can be entered for a `user` object: office, phone numbers, email addresses, Web pages, organization information, addresses, groups, and so on.

Figure 46-5

Active Directory Users and Computers can also be used in big enterprises with millions of objects. It's not necessary to look through a list with a thousand objects, because you can select a custom filter to display only some of the objects. You can also perform an LDAP query to search for the objects in the enterprise. You explore these possibilities later in this chapter.

ADSI Edit

ADSI Edit is the editor of Active Directory. This tool is not installed automatically; on the Windows Server 2003 CD, you can find a directory named Support Tools. When the support tools are installed, you can access ADSI Edit by invoking the program `adsiedit.msc`.

ADSI Edit offers greater control than the Active Directory Users and Computers tool (see Figure 46-6); with ADSI Edit, everything can be configured, and you can also look at the schema and the configuration. This tool is not very intuitive to use, however, and it is very easy to enter wrong data.

By opening the properties window of an object, you can view and change every attribute of an object in Active Directory. With this tool, you can see mandatory and optional attributes, with their types and values (see Figure 46-7).

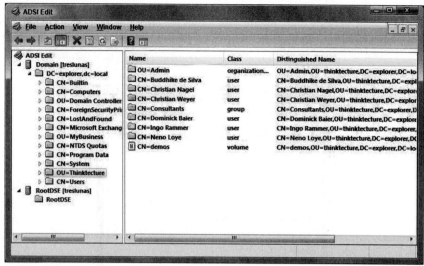

Figure 46-6

Figure 46-7

Programming Active Directory

To develop programs for Active Directory, you can use the classes from either the
`System.DirectoryServices` or the `System.DirectoryServices.Protocols` namespaces.
In the namespace `System.DirectoryServices`, you can find classes that wrap *Active Directory
Service Interfaces* (ADSI) COM objects to access Active Directory.

ADSI is a programmatic interface to directory services. It defines some COM interfaces that are
implemented by ADSI providers. This means that the client can use different directory services with the

same programmatic interfaces. The .NET Framework classes in the `System.DirectoryServices` namespace make use of ADSI.

Figure 46-8 shows some ADSI Providers (LDAP, IIS, and NDS) that implement COM interfaces such as `IADs` and `IUnknown`. The assembly `System.DirectoryServices` makes use of the ADSI providers.

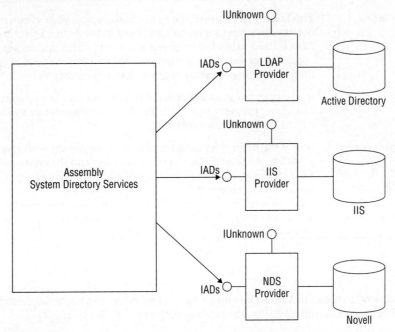

Figure 46-8

Classes from the namespace `System.DirectoryServices.Protocols` make use of Directory Services Markup Language (DSML) Services for Windows. With DSML, standardized Web service interfaces are defined by the OASIS group (`www.oasis-open.org/committees/dsml`).

To use the classes from the `System.DirectoryServices` namespace, you need to reference the `System.DirectoryServices` assembly. With the classes in this assembly, you can query objects, view and update properties, search for objects, and move objects to other container objects. In the code segments that follow later in this section, you use a simple C# console application that demonstrates the functionality of the classes in the `System.DirectoryServices` namespace.

This section covers the following:

❑ Classes in the `System.DirectoryServices` namespace

❑ The process of connecting to Active Directory (binding)

❑ Getting directory entries, creating new objects, and updating existing entries

❑ Searching Active Directory

Classes in System.DirectoryServices

The following table shows the major classes in the System.DirectoryServices namespace.

Class	Description
DirectoryEntry	This is the main class of the System.DirectoryServices namespace. An object of this class represents an object in the Active Directory store. This class is used to bind to an object and to view and update properties. The properties of the object are represented in a PropertyCollection. Every item in the PropertyCollection has a PropertyValueCollection.
DirectoryEntries	DirectoryEntries is a collection of DirectoryEntry objects. The Children property of a DirectoryEntry object returns a list of objects in a DirectoryEntries collection.
DirectorySearcher	This is the main class used for searching for objects with specific attributes. To define the search, the SortOption class and the enumerations SearchScope, SortDirection, and ReferralChasingOption can be used. The search results in a SearchResult or a SearchResultCollection. You also get ResultPropertyCollection and ResultPropertyValueCollection objects.

Binding

To get the values of an object in Active Directory, you need to connect to the Active Directory service. This connecting process is called *binding*. The binding path can look like this:

```
LDAP://dc01.thinktecture.com/OU=Development, DC=thinktecture, DC=Com
```

With the binding process, you can specify these items:

- ❏ The *protocol*; this specifies the provider to be used.
- ❏ The *server name* of the domain controller.
- ❏ The *port number* of the server process.
- ❏ The *distinguished name* of the object; this identifies the object you want to access.
- ❏ The *username and password*, if the user who is allowed to access Active Directory is different from the current logged-on user.
- ❏ An *authentication* type, if encryption is needed.

The following subsections discuss these options in more detail.

Protocol

The first part of a binding path specifies the ADSI provider. The provider is implemented as a COM server; for identification, a progID can be found in the registry directly under HKEY_CLASSES_ROOT. The providers that are available with Windows Vista are listed in the following table.

Provider	Description
LDAP	LDAP Server, such as the Exchange directory and Windows 2000 Server or Windows Server 2003 Active Directory Server.
GC	GC is used to access the global catalog in Active Directory. It can be used for fast queries.
IIS	With the ADSI provider for IIS, it's possible to create new Web sites and to administer them in the IIS catalog.
NDS	This progID is used to communicate with Novell Directory Services.
NWCOMPAT	With NWCOMPAT, you can access old Novell directories, such as Novell Netware 3.x.

Server Name

The *server name* follows the protocol in the binding path. The server name is optional if you are logged on to an Active Directory domain. Without a server name, *serverless binding* occurs; this means that Windows Server 2008 tries to get the "best" domain controller in the domain that's associated with the user doing the bind. If there is no server inside a site, the first domain controller that can be found will be used.

A serverless binding might look like this: LDAP://OU=Sales, DC=Thinktecture, DC=Local.

Port Number

After the server name, you can specify the *port number* of the server process by using the syntax :xxx. The default port number for the LDAP server is port 389: LDAP://dc01.sentinel.net:389. The Exchange server uses the same port number as the LDAP server. If the Exchange server is installed on the same system — for example, as a domain controller of Active Directory — a different port can be configured.

Distinguished Name

The fourth part that you can specify in the path is the *distinguished name* (DN). The distinguished name is a unique name that identifies the object you want to access. With Active Directory, you can use LDAP syntax that is based on X.500 to specify the name of the object.

This is an example of a distinguished name:

```
CN=Christian Nagel, OU=Consultants, DC=thinktecture, DC=local
```

This distinguished name specifies the common name (CN) of Christian Nagel in the organizational unit (OU) called Consultants in the domain component (DC) called thinktecture of the domain thinktecture.local. The part specified to the right is the root object of the domain. The name must follow the hierarchy in the object tree.

You can find the LDAP specification for the string representation of distinguished names in RFC 2253 at www.ietf.org/rfc/rfc2253.txt.

Relative Distinguished Name

A *relative distinguished name* (RDN) is used to reference objects within a container object. With an RDN, the specification of OU and DC is not needed because a common name is enough. CN=Christian Nagel is the relative distinguished name inside the organizational unit. A relative distinguished name can be used if you already have a reference to a container object and if you want to access child objects.

Default Naming Context

If a distinguished name is not specified in the path, the binding process will be made to the default naming context. You can read the default naming context with the help of rootDSE. LDAP 3.0 defines rootDSE as the root of a directory tree on a directory server. For example:

```
LDAP://rootDSE
```

or

```
LDAP://servername/rootDSE
```

By enumerating all properties of the rootDSE, you can get the information about the defaultNamingContext that will be used when no name is specified. schemaNamingContext and configurationNamingContext specify the required names to be used to access the schema and the configuration in the Active Directory store.

The following code is used to get all properties of rootDSE:

```
try
{
    using (DirectoryEntry de = new DirectoryEntry())
    {
        de.Path = "LDAP://treslunas/rootDSE";
        de.Username = @"explorer\christian";
        de.Password = "password";

        PropertyCollection props = de.Properties;
        foreach (string prop in props.PropertyNames)
        {
            PropertyValueCollection values = props[prop];
            foreach (string val in values)
            {
                Console.Write("{0}: ", prop);
                Console.WriteLine(val);
            }
        }
    }
}
catch (COMException ex)
{
    Console.WriteLine(ex.Message);
}
```

This program shows the default naming context (defaultNamingContext DC=explorer, DC=local), the context that can be used to access the schema (CN=Schema, CN=Configuration, DC=explorer, DC=local), and the naming context of the configuration (CN=Configuration, DC=explorer, DC=local), as you can see here:

```
currentTime: 20071012063000.0Z
subschemaSubentry: CN=Aggregate,CN=Schema,CN=Configuration,DC=explorer,DC=local
dsServiceName: CN=NTDS Settings,CN=TRESLUNAS,CN=Servers,
CN=Default-First-Site-Name,CN=Sites,CN=Configuration,DC=explorer,DC=local
namingContexts: DC=explorer,DC=local
namingContexts: CN=Configuration,DC=explorer,DC=local
namingContexts: CN=Schema,CN=Configuration,DC=explorer,DC=local
namingContexts: DC=DomainDnsZones,DC=explorer,DC=local
namingContexts: DC=ForestDnsZones,DC=explorer,DC=local
```

```
defaultNamingContext: DC=explorer,DC=local
schemaNamingContext: CN=Schema,CN=Configuration,DC=explorer,DC=local
configurationNamingContext: CN=Configuration,DC=explorer,DC=local
rootDomainNamingContext: DC=explorer,DC=local
supportedControl: 1.2.840.113556.1.4.319
supportedControl: 1.2.840.113556.1.4.801
```

Object Identifier

Every object has a *globally unique identifier* (GUID). A GUID is a unique 128-bit number as you may already know from COM development. You can bind to an object using the GUID. This way, you always get to the same object, regardless of whether the object was moved to a different container. The GUID is generated at object creation and always remains the same.

You can get to a GUID string representation with `DirectoryEntry.NativeGuid`. This string representation can then be used to bind to the object.

This example shows the path name for a serverless binding to bind to a specific object represented by a GUID:

```
LDAP://<GUID=14abbd652aae1a47abc60782dcfc78ea>
```

Username

If a different user from the one of the current process must be used for accessing the directory (maybe this user doesn't have the required permissions to access Active Directory), explicit *user credentials* must be specified for the binding process. Active Directory has multiple ways to specify the username.

Downlevel Logon

With a downlevel logon, the username can be specified with the pre-Windows 2000 domain name:

```
domain\username
```

Distinguished Name

The user can also be specified by a distinguished name of a `user` object, for example:

```
CN=Administrator, CN=Users, DC=thinktecture, DC=local
```

User Principal Name

The *user principal name* (UPN) of an object is defined with the `userPrincipalName` attribute. The system administrator specifies this with the logon information in the Account tab of the User properties with the Active Directory Users and Computers tool. Note that this is not the email address of the user.

This information also uniquely identifies a user and can be used for a logon:

```
Nagel@thinktecture.local
```

Authentication

For secure encrypted authentication, the *authentication* type can also be specified. The authentication can be set with the `AuthenticationType` property of the `DirectoryEntry` class. The value that can be assigned is one of the `AuthenticationTypes` enumeration values. Because the enumeration is marked with the `[Flags]` attribute, multiple values can be specified. Some of the possible values are where the data sent is encrypted; `ReadonlyServer`, where you specify that you need only read access; and `Secure` for secure authentication.

Binding with the DirectoryEntry Class

The `System.DirectoryServices.DirectoryEntry` class can be used to specify all the binding information. You can use the default constructor and define the binding information with the properties `Path`, `Username`, `Password`, and `AuthenticationType`, or pass all the information in the constructor:

```
DirectoryEntry de = new DirectoryEntry();
de.Path = "LDAP://platinum/DC=thinktecture, DC=local";
de.Username = "nagel@thinktecture.local";
de.Password = "password";

// use the current user credentials
DirectoryEntry de2 = new DirectoryEntry(
                     "LDAP://DC=thinktecture, DC=local");
```

Even if the construction of the `DirectoryEntry` object is successful, this doesn't mean that the binding was a success. Binding will happen the first time a property is read to avoid unnecessary network traffic. At the first access of the object, you can see if the object exists and if the specified user credentials are correct.

Getting Directory Entries

Now that you know how to specify the binding attributes to an object in Active Directory, you can move on to read the attributes of an object. In the following example, you read the properties of user objects.

The `DirectoryEntry` class has some properties to get information about the object: the `Name`, `Guid`, and `SchemaClassName` properties. The first time a property of the `DirectoryEntry` object is accessed, the binding occurs, and the cache of the underlying ADSI object is filled. (This is discussed in more detail shortly.) Additional properties are read from the cache, and communication with the server isn't necessary for data from the same object.

In the following example, the `user` object with the common name `Christian Nagel` in the organizational unit `thinktecture` is accessed:

```
using (DirectoryEntry de = new DirectoryEntry())
{
    de.Path = "LDAP://treslunas/CN=Christian Nagel, " +
              "OU=thinktecture, DC=explorer, DC=local";

    Console.WriteLine("Name: {0}", de.Name);
    Console.WriteLine("GUID: {0}", de.Guid);
    Console.WriteLine("Type: {0}", de.SchemaClassName);
    Console.WriteLine();

    //...
}
```

To have this code running on your machine, you must change the path to the object to access including the server name.

An Active Directory object holds much more information, with the information available depending on the type of the object; the `Properties` property returns a `PropertyCollection`. Each property is a collection itself, because a single property can have multiple values; for example, the user object can have multiple phone numbers. In this case, you go through the values with an inner `foreach` loop. The collection returned from `properties[name]` is an `object` array. The attribute values can be strings, numbers, or other types. Here, just the `ToString()` method is used to display the values:

```
Console.WriteLine("Properties: ");
PropertyCollection properties = de.Properties;
```

```
foreach (string name in properties.PropertyNames)
{
    foreach (object o in properties[name])
    {
        Console.WriteLine("{0}: {1}", name, o.ToString());
    }
}
```

In the resulting output, you can see all attributes of the specified user object. Some properties such as otherTelephone have multiple values. With this property, many phone numbers can be defined. Some of the property values just display the type of the object, System.__ComObject; for example, lastLogoff, lastLogon, and nTSecurityDescriptor. To get the values of these attributes, you must use the ADSI COM interfaces directly from the classes in the System.DirectoryServices namespace.

```
Name: CN=Christian Nagel
GUID: 7705eb3c-d5aa-40a4-97f9-2649c7693f39
Type: user

Properties:
objectClass: top
objectClass: person
objectClass: organizationalPerson
objectClass: user
cn: Christian Nagel
sn: Nagel
description: Author
givenName: Christian
distinguishedName: CN=Christian Nagel,OU=thinktecture,DC=explorer,DC=local
instanceType: 4
whenCreated: 22.08.2004 13:31:10
whenChanged: 24.05.2005 12:26:05
displayName: Christian Nagel
uSNCreated: System.__ComObject
uSNChanged: System.__ComObject
company: Thinktecture
extensionName: 5717D53E-DD6D-4d1e-8A1F-C7BE620F65AA:L
wWWHomePage: http://www.christiannagel.com
name: Christian Nagel
objectGUID: System.Byte[]
userAccountControl: 514
badPwdCount: 0
```

Access a Property Directly by Name

With DirectoryEntry.Properties, you can access all properties. If a property name is known, you can access the values directly:

```
foreach (string homePage in de.Properties["wWWHomePage"])
    Console.WriteLine("Home page: " + homePage);
```

Object Collections

Objects are stored hierarchically in Active Directory. Container objects contain children. You can enumerate these child objects with the Children property of the class DirectoryEntry. In the other direction, you can get the container of an object with the Parent property.

A `user` object doesn't have children, so you use an organizational unit in the following example. Non-container objects return an empty collection with the `Children` property. Get all `user` objects from the organizational unit `thinktecture` in the domain `explorer.local`. The `Children` property returns a `DirectoryEntries` collection that collects `DirectoryEntry` objects. You iterate through all `DirectoryEntry` objects to display the name of the child objects:

```
using (DirectoryEntry de = new DirectoryEntry())
{
    de.Path = "LDAP://treslunas/OU=thinktecture, " +
              "DC=explorer, DC=local";

    Console.WriteLine("Children of {0}", de.Name);
    foreach (DirectoryEntry obj in de.Children)
    {
        Console.WriteLine(obj.Name);
    }
}
```

When you run the program, the common names of the objects are displayed:

```
Children of OU=thinktecture
OU=Admin
CN=Buddhike de Silva
CN=Christian Nagel
CN=Christian Weyer
CN=Consultants
CN=demos
CN=Dominick Baier
CN=Ingo Rammer
CN=Neno Loye
```

In this example, you see all the objects in the organizational unit: `users`, `contacts`, `printers`, `shares`, and others. If you want to display only some object types, you can use the `SchemaFilter` property of the `DirectoryEntries` class. The `SchemaFilter` property returns a `SchemaNameCollection`. With this `SchemaNameCollection`, you can use the `Add()` method to define the object types you want to see. Here, you are just interested in seeing the `user` objects, so `user` is added to this collection:

```
using (DirectoryEntry de = new DirectoryEntry())
{
    de.Path = "LDAP://treslunas/OU=thinktecture, " +
              "DC=explorer, DC=local";

    Console.WriteLine("Children of {0}", de.Name);
    de.Children.SchemaFilter.Add("user");
    foreach (DirectoryEntry obj in de.Children)
    {
        Console.WriteLine(obj.Name);
    }
}
```

As a result, you see only the `user` objects in the organizational unit:

```
Children of OU=thinktecture
CN=Buddhike de Silva
CN=Christian Nagel
CN=Christian Weyer
CN=Dominick Baier
CN=Ingo Rammer
CN=Neno Loye
```

Cache

To reduce the network transfers, ADSI uses a cache for the object properties. As mentioned earlier, the server isn't accessed when a `DirectoryEntry` object is created; instead, with the first reading of a value from the directory store, all the properties are written into the cache so that a round trip to the server isn't necessary when the next property is accessed.

Writing any changes to objects changes only the cached object; setting properties doesn't generate network traffic. You must use `DirectoryEntry.CommitChanges()` to flush the cache and to transfer any changed data to the server. To get the newly written data from the directory store, you can use `DirectoryEntry.RefreshCache()` to read the properties. Of course, if you change some properties without calling `CommitChanges()` and do a `RefreshCache()`, all your changes will be lost, because you read the values from the directory service again using `RefreshCache()`.

It is possible to turn off this property cache by setting the `DirectoryEntry.UsePropertyCache` property to `false`. However, unless you are debugging your code, it's better not to turn off the cache because of the extra round trips to the server that will be generated.

Creating New Objects

When you want to create new Active Directory objects — such as users, computers, printers, contacts, and so on — you can do this programmatically with the `DirectoryEntries` class.

To add new objects to the directory, first you have to bind to a container object, such as an organizational unit, where new objects can be inserted — you cannot use objects that are not able to contain other objects. The following example uses the container object with the distinguished name `CN=Users`, `DC=thinktecture, DC=local`:

```
DirectoryEntry de = new DirectoryEntry();
de.Path = "LDAP://treslunas/CN=Users, DC=explorer, DC=local";
```

You can get to the `DirectoryEntries` object with the `Children` property of a `DirectoryEntry`:

```
DirectoryEntries users = de.Children;
```

The class `DirectoryEntries` offers methods to add, remove, and find objects in the collection. Here, a new `user` object is created. With the `Add()` method, the name of the object and a type name are required. You can get to the type names directly using ADSI Edit.

```
DirectoryEntry user = users.Add("CN=John Doe", "user");
```

The object now has the default property values. To assign specific property values, you can add properties with the `Add()` method of the `Properties` property. Of course, all of the properties must exist in the schema for the `user` object. If a specified property doesn't exist, you'll get a `COMException`: `"The specified directory service attribute or value doesn't exist"`:

```
user.Properties["company"].Add("Some Company");
user.Properties["department"].Add("Sales");
user.Properties["employeeID"].Add("4711");
user.Properties["samAccountName"].Add("JDoe");
user.Properties["userPrincipalName"].Add("JDoe@explorer.local");
user.Properties["givenName"].Add("John");
user.Properties["sn"].Add("Doe");
user.Properties["userPassword"].Add("someSecret");
```

Finally, to write the data to Active Directory, you must flush the cache:

```
user.CommitChanges();
```

Updating Directory Entries

Objects in the Active Directory service can be updated as easily as they can be read. After reading the object, you can change the values. To remove all values of a single property, you can call the method `PropertyValueCollection.Clear()`. You can add new values to a property with `Add()`. `Remove()` and `RemoveAt()` remove specific values from a property collection.

You can change a value simply by setting it to the specified value. The following example uses an indexer for `PropertyValueCollection` to set the mobile phone number to a new value. With the indexer a value can be changed only if it exists. Therefore, you should always check with `DirectoryEntry.Properties.Contains()` to see if the attribute is available:

```
using (DirectoryEntry de = new DirectoryEntry())
{
    de.Path = "LDAP://treslunas/CN=Christian Nagel, " +
              "OU=thinktecture, DC=explorer, DC=local";

    if (de.Properties.Contains("mobile"))
    {
        de.Properties["mobile"][0] = "+43(664)3434343434";
    }
    else
    {
        de.Properties["mobile"].Add("+43(664)3434343434");
    }

    de.CommitChanges();
}
```

The `else` part in this example uses the method `PropertyValueCollection.Add()` to add a new property for the mobile phone number, if it doesn't exist already. If you use the `Add()` method with already existing properties, the resulting effect would depend on the type of the property (single-value or multivalue property). Using the `Add()` method with a single-value property that already exists results in a COMException: `"A constraint violation occurred."` Using `Add()` with a multivalue property, however, succeeds, and an additional value is added to the property.

The `mobile` property for a `user` object is defined as a single-value property, so additional mobile phone numbers cannot be added. However, a user can have more than one mobile phone number. For multiple mobile phone numbers, the `otherMobile` property is available. `otherMobile` is a multivalue property that allows setting multiple phone numbers, and so calling `Add()` multiple times is allowed. Note that multivalue properties are checked for uniqueness. If the second phone number is added to the same `user` object again, you get a COMException: `"The specified directory service attribute or value already exists."`

> Remember to call `DirectoryEntry.CommitChanges()` **after creating or updating new directory objects. Otherwise, only the cache gets updated, and the changes are not sent to the directory service.**

Accessing Native ADSI Objects

Often, it is much easier to call methods of predefined ADSI interfaces instead of searching for the names of object properties. Some ADSI objects also support methods that cannot be used directly from the `DirectoryEntry` class. One example of a practical use is the `IADsServiceOperations` interface, which has methods to start and stop Windows services. (For more details on Windows services see Chapter 23, "Windows Services.")

The classes of the `System.DirectoryServices` namespace use the underlying ADSI COM objects as mentioned earlier. The `DirectoryEntry` class supports calling methods of the underlying objects directly by using the `Invoke()` method.

The first parameter of `Invoke()` requires the method name that should be called in the ADSI object; the `params` keyword of the second parameter allows a flexible number of additional arguments that can be passed to the ADSI method:

```
public object Invoke(string methodName, params object[] args);
```

You can find the methods that can be called with the `Invoke()` method in the ADSI documentation. Every object in the domain supports the methods of the `IADs` interface. The `user` object that you created previously also supports the methods of the `IADsUser` interface.

In the following example, the method `IADsUser.SetPassword()` changes the password of the previously created `user` object:

```
using (DirectoryEntry de = new DirectoryEntry())
{
    de.Path = "LDAP://treslunas/CN=John Doe, " +
              "CN=Users, DC=explorer, DC=local";

    de.Invoke("SetPassword", "anotherSecret");
    de.CommitChanges();
}
```

It is also possible to use the underlying ADSI object directly instead of using `Invoke()`. To use these objects, choose Project ⇨ Add Reference to add a reference to the Active DS Type Library (see Figure 46-9). This creates a wrapper class where you can access these objects in the namespace `ActiveDs`.

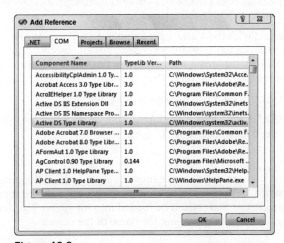

Figure 46-9

The native object can be accessed with the `NativeObject` property of the `DirectoryEntry` class. In the following example, the object `de` is a user object, so it can be cast to `ActiveDs.IADsUser`. `SetPassword()` is a method documented in the `IADsUser` interface, so you can call it directly instead of using the `Invoke()` method. By setting the `AccountDisabled` property of `IADsUser` to `false`, you can enable the account. As in the previous examples, the changes are written to the directory service by calling `CommitChanges()` with the `DirectoryEntry` object:

```
ActiveDs.IADsUser user = (ActiveDs.IADsUser)de.NativeObject;
user.SetPassword("someSecret");
user.AccountDisabled = false;
de.CommitChanges();
```

.NET 3.5 reduces the need to invoke the native objects behind the .NET class `DirectoryEntry`. .NET 3.5 gives you new classes to manage users in the namespace `System.DirectoryServices.AccountManagement`. The classes from this namespace are explained later in this chapter.

Searching in Active Directory

Because Active Directory is a data store optimized for *read-mostly* access, you will generally search for values. To search in Active Directory, the .NET Framework provides the `DirectorySearcher` class.

You can use `DirectorySearcher` only with the LDAP provider; it doesn't work with the other providers such as NDS or IIS.

In the constructor of the `DirectorySearcher` class, you can define four important parts for the search. You can also use a default constructor and define the search options with properties.

SearchRoot

The search root specifies where the search should start. The default of `SearchRoot` is the root of the domain you are currently using. `SearchRoot` is specified with the `Path` of a `DirectoryEntry` object.

Filter

The filter defines the values where you want to get hits. The filter is a string that must be enclosed in parentheses.

Relational operators such as `<=`, `=`, and `>=` are allowed in expressions. `(objectClass=contact)` searches all objects of type `contact`; `(lastName>=Nagel)` searches all objects alphabetically where the `lastName` property is equal to or larger than `Nagel`.

Expressions can be combined with the `&` and `|` prefix operators. For example, `(&(objectClass=user)(description=Auth*))` searches all objects of type `user` where the property description starts with the string `Auth`. Because the `&` and `|` operators are at the beginning of the expressions, it is possible to combine more than two expressions with a single prefix operator.

The default filter is `(objectClass=*)` so all objects are valid.

The filter syntax is defined in RFC 2254, "The String Representation of LDAP Search Filters." You can find this RFC at `www.ietf.org/rfc/rfc2254.txt`.

PropertiesToLoad

With `PropertiesToLoad`, you can define a `StringCollection` of all the properties in which you are interested. Objects can have a lot of properties, most of which will not be important for your search request. You define the properties that should be loaded into the cache. The default properties that are returned if nothing is specified are the path and the name of the object.

SearchScope

SearchScope is an enumeration that defines how deep the search should extend:

- ❑ SearchScope.Base searches only the attributes in the object where the search started, so at most one object is found.

- ❑ With SearchScope.OneLevel, the search continues in the child collection of the base object. The base object itself is not searched for a hit.

- ❑ SearchScope.Subtree defines that the search should go down the complete tree.

The default value of the SearchScope property is SearchScope.Subtree.

Search Limits

A search for specific objects in a directory service can span multiple domains. To limit the search to the number of objects or the time taken, you have some additional properties to define, as shown in the following table.

Property	Description
ClientTimeout	The maximum time the client waits for the server to return a result. If the server does not respond, no records are returned.
PageSize	With a *paged search*, the server returns a number of objects defined with the PageSize instead of the complete result. This reduces the time for the client to get a first answer and the memory needed. The server sends a cookie to the client, which is sent back to the server with the next search request so that the search can continue at the point where it finished.
ServerPageTimeLimit	For paged searches, this value defines the time a search should continue to return a number of objects that are defined with the PageSize value. If the time is reached before the PageSize value, the objects that were found up to that point are returned to the client. The default value is –1, which means infinite.
SizeLimit	Defines the maximum number of objects that should be returned by the search. If you set the limit to a value larger than defined by the server (which is 1000), the server limit is used.
ServerTimeLimit	Defines the maximum time the server will search for objects. When this time is reached, all objects that are found up to this point are returned to the client. The default is 120 seconds, and you cannot set the search to a higher value.
ReferralChasing	A search can cross multiple domains. If the root that's specified with SearchRoot is a parent domain or no root was specified, the search can continue to child domains. With this property, you can specify if the search should continue on different servers. ReferralChasingOption.None means that the search does not continue on other servers. The value ReferralChasingOption.Subordinate specifies that the search should go on to child domains. When the search starts at DC=Wrox, DC=com the server can return a result set and the referral to DC=France, DC=Wrox, DC=COM. The client can continue the search in the subdomain.

Property	Description
	ReferralChasingOption.External means that the server can refer the client to an independent server that is not in the subdomain. This is the default option.
	With ReferralChasingOption.All, both external and subordinate referrals are returned.
Tombstone	If the property Tombstone is set to true, all deleted objects that match the search are returned, too.
VirtualListView	If large results are expected with the search, the property VirtualListView can be used to define a subset that should be returned from the search. The subset is defined with the class DirectoryVirtual ListView.

In the search example, all user objects with a property description value of Author are searched in the organizational unit thinktecture.

First, bind to the organizational unit thinktecture. This is where the search should start. Create a DirectorySearcher object where the SearchRoot is set. The filter is defined as (&(objectClass=user)(description=Auth*)), so that the search spans all objects of type user with a description of Auth followed by something else. The scope of the search should be a subtree so that child organizational units within thinktecture are searched, too:

```
using (DirectoryEntry de =
    new DirectoryEntry("LDAP://OU=thinktecture, DC=explorer, DC=local"))
using (DirectorySearcher searcher = new DirectorySearcher())
{
    searcher.SearchRoot = de;
    searcher.Filter = "(&(objectClass=user)(description=Auth*))";
    searcher.SearchScope = SearchScope.Subtree;
```

The properties that should be in the result of the search are name, description, givenName, and wWWHomePage:

```
    searcher.PropertiesToLoad.Add("name");
    searcher.PropertiesToLoad.Add("description");
    searcher.PropertiesToLoad.Add("givenName");
    searcher.PropertiesToLoad.Add("wWWHomePage");
```

You are ready to do the search. However, the result should also be sorted. DirectorySearcher has a Sort property, where you can set a SortOption. The first argument in the constructor of the SortOption class defines the property that will be used for a sort; the second argument defines the direction of the sort. The SortDirection enumeration has Ascending and Descending values.

To start the search, you can use the FindOne() method to find the first object, or FindAll(). FindOne() returns a simple SearchResult, whereas FindAll() returns a SearchResultCollection. Here, all authors should be returned, so FindAll() is used:

```
    searcher.Sort = new SortOption("givenName", SortDirection.Ascending);

    SearchResultCollection results = searcher.FindAll();
```

With a `foreach` loop, every `SearchResult` in the `SearchResultCollection` is accessed. A `SearchResult` represents a single object in the search cache. The `Properties` property returns a `ResultPropertyCollection`, where you access all properties and values with the property name and the indexer:

```
SearchResultCollection results = searcher.FindAll();

foreach (SearchResult result in results)
{
    ResultPropertyCollection props = result.Properties;
    foreach (string propName in props.PropertyNames)
    {
        Console.Write("{0}: ", propName);
        Console.WriteLine(props[propName][0]);
    }
    Console.WriteLine();
}
```

It is also possible to get the complete object after a search: `SearchResult` has a `GetDirectoryEntry()` method that returns the corresponding `DirectoryEntry` of the found object.

The resulting output shows the beginning of the list of all `thinktecture` associates with the properties that have been chosen:

```
name: Christian Nagel
wwwhomepage: http://www.christiannagel.com
description: Author
givenname: Christian
adspath: LDAP://treslunas/CN=Christian Nagel,OU=thinktecture,DC=explorer,DC=local

name: Christian Weyer
description: Author
givenname: Christian
adspath: LDAP://treslunas/CN=Christian Weyer,OU=thinktecture,DC=explorer,DC=local

name: Ingo Rammer
wwwhomepage: http://www.thinktecture.com
description: Author
givenname: Ingo
adspath: LDAP://treslunas/CN=Ingo Rammer,OU=thinktecture,DC=explorer,DC=local
```

Searching for User Objects

In this section, you build a Windows Forms application called `UserSearch`. This application is flexible insofar as a specific domain controller, username, and password to access Active Directory can be entered; otherwise, the user of the running process is used. In this application, you access the schema of the Active Directory service to get the properties of a `user` object. The user can enter a filter string to search all `user` objects of a domain. It's also possible to set the properties of the `user` objects that should be displayed.

User Interface

The user interface shows numbered steps to indicate how to use the application (see Figure 46-10):

1. In the first step, `Username`, `Password`, and the `Domain Controller` can be entered. All this information is optional. If no domain controller is entered, the connection works with serverless binding. If the username is missing, the security context of the current user is taken.

2. A button allows all the property names of the `user` object to be loaded dynamically in the `listBoxProperties` list box.

3. After the property names are loaded, the properties to be displayed can be selected. The `SelectionMode` of the list box is set to `MultiSimple`.

4. The filter to limit the search can be entered. The default value set in this dialog box searches for all `user` objects: `(objectClass=user)`.

5. Now the search can start.

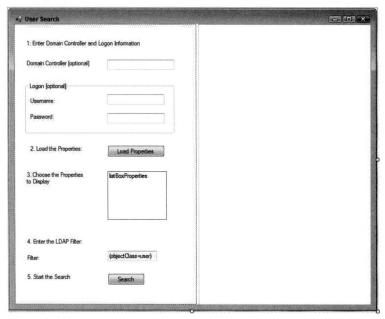

Figure 46-10

Get the Schema Naming Context

This application has only two handler methods: one method for the button to load the properties and one to start the search in the domain. First, you read the properties of the `user` class dynamically from the schema to display it in the user interface.

In the handler `buttonLoadProperties_Click()` method, `SetLogonInformation()` reads the username, password, and host name from the dialog box and stores them in members of the class. Next, the method `SetNamingContext()` sets the LDAP name of the schema and the LDAP name of the default context. This schema LDAP name is used in the call to set the properties in the list box: `SetUserProperties()`.

```
private void OnLoadProperties(object sender, System.EventArgs e)
{
    try
    {
        SetLogonInformation();
```

```
            SetNamingContext();

            SetUserProperties(schemaNamingContext);
        }
        catch (Exception ex)
        {
            MessageBox.Show("Check your inputs! " + ex.Message);
        }
    }
    protected void SetLogonInformation()
    {
        username = (textBoxUsername.Text == "" ? null : textBoxUsername.Text);
        password = (textBoxPassword.Text == "" ? null : textBoxPassword.Text);
        hostname = textBoxHostname.Text;

        if (hostname != "")
        {
            hostname += "/";
        }
    }
```

In the helper method `SetNamingContext()`, you are using the root of the directory tree to get the properties of the server. You are interested in the value of only two properties: `schemaNamingContext` and `defaultNamingContext`.

```
    protected void SetNamingContext()
    {
        using (DirectoryEntry de = new DirectoryEntry())
        {
            string path = "LDAP://" + hostname + "rootDSE";
            de.Username = username;
            de.Password = password;
            de.Path = path;
            schemaNamingContext =
                    de.Properties["schemaNamingContext"][0].ToString();
            defaultNamingContext =
                    de.Properties["defaultNamingContext"][0].ToString();
        }
    }
```

Get the Property Names of the User Class

You have the LDAP name to access the schema. You can use this to access the directory and read the properties. You are interested in not only the properties of the `user` class, but also those of the base classes of `user`: `Organizational-Person`, `Person`, and `Top`. In this program, the names of the base classes are hard-coded. You could also read the base class dynamically with the `subClassOf` attribute.

`GetSchemaProperties()` returns `IEnumerable<string>` with all property names of the specific object type. All the property names are added to the list box:

```
    protected void SetUserProperties(string schemaNamingContext)
    {
        var properties =
            from p in
                GetSchemaProperties(schemaNamingContext, "User").Concat(
                    GetSchemaProperties(schemaNamingContext,
```

(continued)

(continued)

```
                    "Organizational-Person")).Concat(
              GetSchemaProperties(schemaNamingContext, "Person")).Concat(
              GetSchemaProperties(schemaNamingContext, "Top"))
         orderby p
         select p;

    listBoxProperties.Items.Clear();
    foreach (string s in properties)
    {
        listBoxProperties.Items.Add(s);
    }
}
```

In `GetSchemaProperties()`, you are accessing the Active Directory service again. This time, `rootDSE` is not used but rather the LDAP name to the schema that you discovered earlier. The property `systemMayContain` holds a collection of all attributes that are allowed in the class `objectType`:

```
protected IEnumerable<string> GetSchemaProperties(string schemaNamingContext,
                                                   string objectType)
{
    IEnumerable<string> data;
    using (DirectoryEntry de = new DirectoryEntry())
    {
        de.Username = username;
        de.Password = password;

        de.Path = String.Format("LDAP://{0}CN={1},{2}", hostname, objectType,
                          schemaNamingContext);

        PropertyValueCollection values = de.Properties["systemMayContain"];
        data = from s in values.Cast<string>()
               orderby s
               select s;
    }
    return data;
}
```

Step 2 in the application is completed. The `ListBox` control has all the property names of the user objects.

Search for User Objects

The handler for the search button calls only the helper method `FillResult()`:

```
private void OnSearch(object sender, System.EventArgs e)
{
    try
    {
        FillResult();
    }
    catch (Exception ex)
    {
        MessageBox.Show(String.Format("Check your input: {0}", ex.Message));
    }
}
```

In `FillResult()`, you do a normal search in the complete Active Directory Domain as you saw earlier. `SearchScope` is set to `Subtree`, the `Filter` to the string you get from a `TextBox` object, and the properties that should be loaded into the cache are set by the values the user selected in the list box. The `PropertiesToLoad` property of the `DirectorySearcher` is of type `StringCollection` where the properties that should be loaded can be added using the `AddRange()` method that requires a string array. The properties that should be loaded are read from the `ListBox` `listBoxProperties` with the property `SelectedItems`. After setting the properties of the `DirectorySearcher` object, the properties are searched by calling the `SearchAll()` method. The result of the search inside the `SearchResultCollection` is used to generate summary information that is written to the text box `textBoxResults`:

```
protected void FillResult()
{
    using (DirectoryEntry root = new DirectoryEntry())
    {
        root.Username = username;
        root.Password = password;
        root.Path = String.Format("LDAP://{0}{1}", hostname,
                                    defaultNamingContext);

        using (DirectorySearcher searcher = new DirectorySearcher())
        {
            searcher.SearchRoot = root;
            searcher.SearchScope = SearchScope.Subtree;
            searcher.Filter = textBoxFilter.Text;
            searcher.PropertiesToLoad.AddRange(
                    listBoxProperties.SelectedItems.Cast<string>().ToArray());

            SearchResultCollection results = searcher.FindAll();
            StringBuilder summary = new StringBuilder();
            foreach (SearchResult result in results)
            {
                foreach (string propName in result.Properties.PropertyNames)
                {
                    foreach (string s in result.Properties[propName])
                    {
                        summary.AppendFormat(" {0}: {1}\r\n", propName, s);
                    }
                }
                summary.Append("\r\n");
            }
            textBoxResults.Text = summary.ToString();
        }
    }
}
```

Starting the application gives you a list of all objects where the filter is valid (see Figure 46-11).

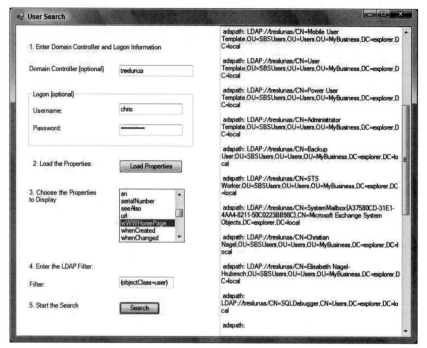

Figure 46-11

Account Management

Previous to .NET 3.5, it was difficult to create and modify user and group accounts. One way to do that was by using the classes from the `System.DirectoryServices` namespace, or by using the strongly typed native COM interfaces. New with .NET 3.5 is the assembly `System.DirectoryServices.AccountManagement` that offers an abstraction to the `System.DirectoryServices` classes by offering specific methods and properties to search, modify, create, and update users and groups.

The classes and their functionality are explained in the following table.

Class	Description
PrincipalContext	With the `PrincipalContext`, you configure the context of the account management. Here you can define if an Active Directory Domain, the accounts from the local system, or an application directory should be used. You set this by setting the `ContextType` enumeration to one of the values `Domain`, `Machine`, or `ApplicationDirectory`. Depending on the context type, you can also define the name of the domain and specify a username and password that are used for access.

Class	Description
Principal	Principal is the base class of all principals. With the static method FindByIdentity(), you can get a Principal identity object. With a principal object, you have access to various properties such as name, description, distinguished name, and also the object type from the schema. In case you need more control about the principal than is available from the properties and methods of this class, the method GetUnderlyingType() returns the underlying DirectoryEntry object.
AuthenticablePrincipal	AuthenticablePrincipal derives from Principal and is the base class for all principals that can be authenticated. There are several static methods to find principals, such as by logon or lockout times, by incorrect password attempts, or by password set time. Using instance methods, you can change the password and unlock an account.
UserPrincipal ComputerPrincipal	UserPrincipal and ComputerPrincipal derive from the base class AuthenticablePrincipal and thus have all properties and methods the base class has. UserPrincipal is the object that maps to a user account, and ComputerPrincipal maps to a computer account. With UserPrincipal, you have many properties to get and set information about the user, for example, EmployeeId, EmailAddress, GivenName, VoiceTelephoneNumber.
GroupPrincipal	Groups cannot authenticate; that's why GroupPrincipal derives directly from the Principal class. With GroupPrincipal, you can get members of the group with the Members property and the GetMembers() method.
PrincipalCollection	The PrincipalCollection contains a group of Principal objects; for example, the Members property from the GroupPrincipal class returns a PrincipalCollection object.
PrincipalSearcher	PrincipalSearcher is an abstraction of the DirectorySearcher class with special use for account management. With PrincipalSearcher, there's no need to know about the LDAP query syntax because this is created automatically.
PrincipalSearchResult<T>	Search methods from the PrincipalSearcher and Principal classes return a PrincipalSearchResult<T>.

The following sections look at some scenarios in which you can use the classes from the System.DirectoryServices.AccountManagement namespace.

Display User Information

The static property `Current` of the `UserPrincipal` class returns a `UserPrincipal` object with information about the currently logged-on user:

```
using (UserPrincipal user = UserPrincipal.Current)
{
    Console.WriteLine("Context Server: {0}",
            user.Context.ConnectedServer);
    Console.WriteLine(user.Description);
    Console.WriteLine(user.DisplayName);
    Console.WriteLine(user.EmailAddress);
    Console.WriteLine(user.GivenName);
    Console.WriteLine("{0:d}", user.LastLogon);
    Console.WriteLine(user.ScriptPath);
}
```

Running the application displays information about the user:

```
Context Server: treslunas.explorer.local
Power User
Christian Nagel
Christian.Nagel@thinktecture.com
Christian
2007/10/14
SBS_LOGIN_SCRIPT.bat
```

Create a User

You can use the `UserPrincipal` class to create a new user. First a `PrincipalContext` is required to define where the user should be created. With the `PrincipalContext`, you set the `ContextType` to an enumeration value of `Domain`, `Machine`, or `ApplicationDirectory` depending on whether the directory service, the local accounts of the machine, or an application directory should be used. If the current user does not have access to add accounts to Active Directory, you can also set a user and password with the `PrincipalContext` that is used to access the server.

Next, you can create an instance of `UserPrincipal` passing the principal context, and setting all required properties. Here, the `GivenName` and `EmailAddress` properties are set. Finally, you must invoke the `Save()` method of the `UserPrincipal` to write the new user to the store:

```
using (PrincipalContext context =
        new PrincipalContext(ContextType.Domain, "explorer"))
using (UserPrincipal user = new UserPrincipal(context, "Tom",
        "P@ssw0rd", true)
        {
            GivenName = "Tom",
            EmailAddress = "test@test.com"
        })
{
    user.Save();
}
```

Reset a Password

To reset a password from an existing user, you can use the `SetPassword()` method from a `UserPrincipal` object:

```
using (PrincipalContext context =
        new PrincipalContext(ContextType.Domain, "explorer"))
using (UserPrincipal user = UserPrincipal.FindByIdentity(
        context, IdentityType.Name, "Tom"))
{
    user.SetPassword("Pa$$w0rd");
    user.Save();
}
```

The user running this code needs to have the privilege to reset a password. To change the password from an old one to a new one, you can use the method ChangePassword().

Create a Group

A new group can be created in a similar way to creating a new user. Here, just the class GroupPrincipal is used instead of the class UserPrincipal. As in creating a new user, the properties are set, and the Save() method is invoked:

```
using (PrincipalContext ctx =
        new PrincipalContext(ContextType.Domain, "explorer"))
using (GroupPrincipal group = new GroupPrincipal(ctx)
        {
            Description = "Sample group",
            DisplayName = "Wrox Authors",
            Name = "WroxAuthors"
        })
{
    group.Save();
}
```

Add a User to a Group

To add a user to a group, you can use a GroupPrincipal and add a UserPrincipal to the Members property of the group. To get an existing user and group, you can use the static method FindByIdentity():

```
using (PrincipalContext context =
        new PrincipalContext(ContextType.Domain))
using (GroupPrincipal group = GroupPrincipal.FindByIdentity(
        context, IdentityType.Name, "WroxAuthors"))
using (UserPrincipal user = UserPrincipal.FindByIdentity(
        context, IdentityType.Name, "Verena Oslzly"))
{
    group.Members.Add(user);
    group.Save();
}
```

Finding Users

Static methods of the UserPrincipal object allow finding users based on some predefined criteria. The sample here shows finding users who didn't change their passwords within the last 30 days by using the method FindPasswordSetTime(). This method returns a

PrincipalSearchResult<UserPrincipal> collection that is iterated to display the user name, the last logon time, and the time when the password was reset:

```
using (PrincipalContext context =
       new PrincipalContext(ContextType.Domain, "explorer"))
using (PrincipalSearchResult<UserPrincipal> users =
       UserPrincipal.FindByPasswordSetTime(context,
       DateTime.Today - TimeSpan.FromDays(30), MatchType.LessThan))
{
    foreach (var user in users)
    {
        Console.WriteLine("{0}, last logon: {1}, " +
               "last password change: {2}", user.Name, user.LastLogon,
               user.LastPasswordSet);
    }
}
```

Other methods offered by the UserPrincipal class to find users are FindByBadPasswordAttempt(), FindByExpirationTime(), FindByLockoutTime(), and FindByLogonTime().

You can get more flexibility in finding users by using the PrincipalSearcher class. This class is an abstraction of the DirectorySearcher class and uses this class behind the scenes. With the PrincipalSearcher class, you can assign any Principal object to the QueryFilter property. In the example here, a UserPrincipal object with the properties Surname and Enabled is set to the QueryFilter. This way, all user objects starting with the surname Nag and which are enabled are returned with the PrincipalSearchResult collection. The PrincipalSearcher class creates an LDAP query string to do the search.

```
PrincipalContext context = new PrincipalContext(ContextType.Domain);

UserPrincipal userFilter = new UserPrincipal(context);
userFilter.Surname = "Nag*";
userFilter.Enabled = true;

using (PrincipalSearcher searcher = new PrincipalSearcher())
{
    searcher.QueryFilter = userFilter;
    PrincipalSearchResult<Principal> searchResult =
        searcher.FindAll();
    foreach (var user in searchResult)
    {
        Console.WriteLine(user.Name);
    }
}
```

DSML

With the namespace System.DirectoryServices.Protocols, you can access Active Directory through DSML (Directory Services Markup Language). DSML is a standard defined by the OASIS group (www.oasis-open.org) that allows you to access directory services through a Web service.

To make Active Directory available through DSML, you must have at least Windows Server 2003 R2 or you must install DSML Services for Windows. You can download DSML Services for Windows from the Microsoft Web site: www.microsoft.com/windowsserver2003/downloads/featurepacks/default.mspx.

Figure 46-12 shows a configuration scenario with DSML. A system that offers DSML services accesses Active Directory via LDAP. On the client system, the DSML classes from the namespace System. DirectoryServices.Protocols are used to make SOAP requests to the DSML service.

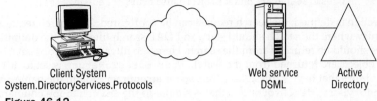

Client System
System.DirectoryServices.Protocols

Web service
DSML

Active
Directory

Figure 46-12

Classes in System.DirectoryServices.Protocols

The following table shows the major classes in the System.DirectoryServices.Protocols namespace.

Class	Description
DirectoryConnection	DirectoryConnection is the base class of all the connection classes that can be used to define the connection to the directory service. The classes that derive from DirectoryConnection are LdapConnection (for using the LDAP protocol), DsmlSoapConnection, and DsmlSoapHttpConnection.With the method SendRequest, a message is sent to the directory service.
DirectoryRequest	A request that can be sent to the directory service is defined by a class that derives from the base class DirectoryRequest. Depending on the request type, classes such as SearchRequest, AddRequest, DeleteRequest, and ModifyRequest can be used to send a request.
DirectoryResponse	The result that is returned with a SendRequest is of a type that derives from the base class DirectoryResponse. Examples for derived classes are SearchResponse, AddResponse, DeleteResponse, and ModifyResponse.

Searching for Active Directory Objects with DSML

This section looks at an example of how a search for directory services objects can be performed. As you can see in the code that follows, first a DsmlSoapHttpConnection object is instantiated that defines the connection to the DSML service. The connection is defined with the class DsmlDirectoryIdentifier that contains an Uri object. Optionally, the user credentials can be set with the connection:

```
Uri uri = new Uri("http://dsmlserver/dsml");
DsmlDirectoryIdentifier identifier = new DsmlDirectoryIdentifier(uri);

NetworkCredential credentials = new NetworkCredential();
credentials.UserName = "cnagel";
credentials.Password = "password";
```

(continued)

(continued)

```
credentials.Domain = "explorer";

DsmlSoapHttpConnection dsmlConnection =
        new DsmlSoapHttpConnection(identifier, credentials);
```

After the connection is defined, the search request can be configured. The search request consists of the directory entry where the search should start, an LDAP search filter, and the definition of what property values should be returned from the search. Here, the filter is set to (objectClass=user), so that all user objects are returned from the search. attributesToReturn is set to null, and you can read all attributes that have values. SearchScope is an enumeration in the namespace System.DirectoryServices.Protocols that is similar to the SearchScope enumeration in the namespace System.DirectoryServices used to define how deep the search should go. Here, the SearchScope is set to Subtree to walk through the complete Active Directory tree.

The search filter can be defined with an LDAP string or by using an XML document contained in the XmlDocument class:

```
string distinguishedName = null;
string ldapFilter = "(objectClass=user)";
string[] attributesToReturn = null;// return all attributes

SearchRequest searchRequest = new SearchRequest(distinguishedName,
        ldapFilter, SearchScope.Subtree, attributesToReturn);
```

After the search is defined with the SearchRequest object, the search is sent to the Web service by calling the method SendRequest. SendRequest is a method of the DsmlSoapHttpConnection class. SendRequest returns a SearchResponse object where the returned objects can be read.

Instead of invoking the synchronous SendRequest method, the DsmlSoapHttpConnection class also offers the asynchronous methods BeginSendRequest and EndSendRequest that conform to the asynchronous .NET pattern.

The asynchronous pattern is explained in Chapter 19, "Threading and Synchronization."

```
SearchResponse searchResponse =
        (SearchResponse)dsmlConnection.SendRequest(searchRequest);
```

The returned Active Directory objects can be read within the SearchResponse. SearchResponse .Entries contains a collection of all entries that are wrapped with the type SearchResultEntry. The SearchResultEntry class has the Attributes property that contains all attributes. Each attribute can be read with help of the DirectoryAttribute class.

In the code example, the distinguished name of each object is written to the console. Next, the attribute values for the organizational unit (OU) are accessed, and the name of the organizational unit is written to the console. After this, all values of the DirectoryAttribute objects are written to the console:

```
Console.WriteLine("\r\nSearch matched {0} entries:",
        searchResponse.Entries.Count);
foreach (SearchResultEntry entry in searchResponse.Entries)
{
    Console.WriteLine(entry.DistinguishedName);

    // retrieve a specific attribute
    DirectoryAttribute attribute = entry.Attributes["ou"];
    Console.WriteLine("{0} = {1}", attribute.Name, attribute[0]);

    // retrieve all attributes
```

```
        foreach (DirectoryAttribute attr in entry.Attributes.Values)
        {
            Console.Write("{0}=", attr.Name);

            // retrieve all values for the attribute
            // the type of the value can be one of string, byte[] or Uri
            foreach (object value in attr)
            {
                Console.Write("{0} ", value);
            }
            Console.WriteLine();
        }
    }
```

Adding, modifying, and deleting objects can be done similarly to searching objects. Depending on the action you want to perform, you can use the corresponding classes.

Summary

This chapter discussed the architecture of Active Directory: the important concepts of domains, trees, and forests. You can access information in the complete enterprise. When writing applications that access Active Directory services, you must be aware that the data you read might not be up to date because of the replication latency.

The classes in the `System.DirectoryServices` namespaces give you easy ways to access Active Directory services by wrapping to the ADSI providers. The `DirectoryEntry` class makes it possible to read and write objects directly in the data store.

With the `DirectorySearcher` class, you can perform complex searches and define filters, timeouts, properties to load, and a scope. By using the global catalog, you can speed up the search for objects in the complete enterprise, because it stores a read-only version of all objects in the forest.

DSML is another API that allows accessing the Active Directory through a Web service interface.

Classes in `System.DirectoryServices.AccountManagement` offer an abstraction to make it easier to create and modify user, group, and computer accounts.

The next chapter gives you another view on networking with peer-to-peer communication.

47

Peer-to-Peer Networking

Peer-to-peer networking, often referred to as P2P, is perhaps one of the most useful and yet misunderstood technologies to emerge in recent years. When people think of P2P they usually think of one thing: sharing music files, often illegally. This is because file-sharing applications such as BitTorrent have risen in popularity at a staggering rate, and these applications use P2P technology to work.

However, though P2P is used in file-sharing applications, that isn't to say that it doesn't have other applications. Indeed, as you see in this chapter, P2P can be used for a vast array of applications, and is becoming more and more important in the interconnected world in which we live. You learn about this in the first part of this chapter, when you look at an overview of P2P technologies.

Microsoft has not been oblivious to the emergence of P2P, and has been developing its own tools and technologies to use it. You can use the Microsoft Windows Peer-to-Peer Networking platform as a communication framework for P2P applications. This platform includes the important components Peer Name Resolution Protocol (PNRP) and People Near Me (PNM). Also, version 3.5 of the .NET Framework includes a new namespace, `System.Net.PeerToPeer`, and several new types and features that you can use to build P2P applications yourself with a minimum of effort.

In this chapter you look at:

❑ An overview of P2P

❑ The Microsoft Windows Peer-to-Peer Networking platform, including PNRP and PNM

❑ How to build P2P applications with the .NET Framework

❑ An example P2P application built using the .NET Framework

Peer-to-Peer Networking Overview

Peer-to-peer networking is an alternative approach to network communication. In order to understand how P2P differs from the "standard" approach to network communication it is necessary to take a step backward and look at client-server communications. Client-server communications are ubiquitous in networked applications today.

Client-Server Architecture

Traditionally, you interact with applications over a network (including the Internet) using a client-server architecture. Web sites are a great example of this. When you look at a Web site you send a request over the Internet to a Web server, which then returns the information that you require. If you want to download a file, you do so directly from the Web server.

Similarly, desktop applications that include local or wide area network connectivity will typically connect to a single server, for example, a database server or a server that hosts other services.

This simple form of client-server architecture is illustrated in Figure 47-1.

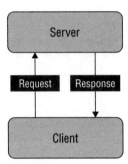

Figure 47-1

There is nothing inherently wrong with the client-server architecture, and indeed in many cases it will be exactly what you want. However, there is a scalability problem. Figure 47-2 shows how the client-server architecture scales with additional clients.

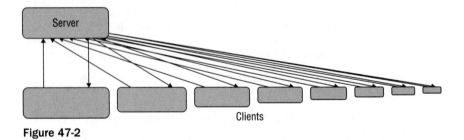

Figure 47-2

With every client that is added an increased load is placed on the server, which must communicate with each client. To return to the Web site example, this is how Web sites collapse. When there is too much traffic the server simply becomes unresponsive.

There are of course scaling options that you can implement to mitigate this situation. You can scale up by increasing the power and resources available to the server, or you can scale out by adding additional servers. Scaling up is of course limited by the technology available and the cost of better hardware. Scaling out is potentially more flexible, but requires an additional infrastructure layer to ensure that clients either communicate with individual servers or that clients can maintain session state independent of the server with which they are communicating. Plenty of solutions are available for this, such as Web or server farm products.

P2P Architecture

The peer-to-peer approach is completely different from either the scaling up or scaling out approach. With P2P, instead of focusing on and attempting to streamline the communication between the server and its clients, you instead look at ways in which clients can communicate with each other.

Say, for example, that the Web site that clients are communicating with is wrox.com. In our imaginary scenario, Wrox has announced that a new version of this book is to be released on the wrox.com web site and will be free to download to anyone who wants it, but that it will be removed after one day. Before the book is available on the Web site you might imagine that an awful lot of people will be looking at the Web site and refreshing their browsers, waiting for the file to appear. Once the file is available, everyone will try to download it at the same time, and more than likely the wrox.com Web server will collapse under the strain.

You could use P2P technology to prevent this Web server collapse from occurring. Instead of sending the file directly from the server to all the clients, you send the file to just a few clients. A few of the remaining clients then download the file from the clients that already have it, a few more clients download it from those second-level clients, and so on. In fact, this process is made even faster by splitting the file into chunks and dividing these chunks between clients, some of whom download it directly from the server, and some of whom download chunks from other clients. This is how file-sharing technologies such as BitTorrent work, and is illustrated in Figure 47-3.

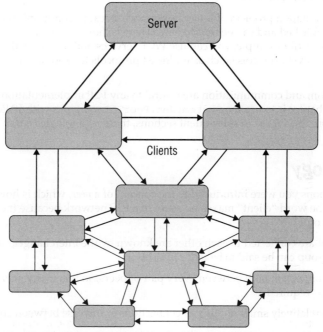

Figure 47-3

P2P Architectural Challenges

There are still problems to solve in the file-sharing architecture discussed here. For a start, how do clients detect that other clients exist, and how do they locate chunks of the file that other clients might have? Also, how can you ensure optimal communication between clients that may be separated by entire continents?

Every client participating in a P2P network application must be able to perform the following operations to overcome these problems:

- ❏ It must be able to *discover* other clients.
- ❏ It must be able to *connect* to other clients.
- ❏ It must be able to *communicate* with other clients.

The discovery problem has two obvious solutions. You can either keep a list of the clients on the server so clients can obtain this list and contact other clients (known as *peers*), or you can use an infrastructure (for example PNRP, covered in the next section) that enables clients to find each other directly. Most file-sharing systems use the "list on a server" solution, by using servers know as trackers. Also, in file-sharing systems any client may act as a server as shown in Figure 47-3, by declaring that it has a file available and registering it with a tracker. In fact, a pure P2P network needs no servers at all, just peers.

The connection problem is a more subtle one, and concerns the overall structure of the networks used by a P2P application. If you have one group of clients, all of which can communicate with one another, the topology of the connections between these clients can become extremely complex. You can often improve performance by having more than one group of clients, each of which consists of connections between clients in that group, but not to clients in other groups. If you can make these groups locale-based you will get an additional performance boost, because clients can communicate with each other with fewer hops between networked computers.

Communication is perhaps a problem of lesser importance, because communication protocols such as TCP/IP are well established and can be reused here. There is, however, scope for improvement in both high-level technologies (for example, you can use WCF services and therefore all the functionality that WCF offers) and low-level protocols (such as multicast protocols to send data to multiple endpoints simultaneously).

Discovery, connection, and communication are central to any P2P implementation. The implementation you look at in this chapter is to use the `System.Net.PeerToPeer` types with PNM for discovery and PNRP for connection. As you see in subsequent sections, these technologies cover all three of these operations.

P2P Terminology

In the previous sections you were introduced to the concept of a *peer*, which is how clients are referred to in a P2P network. The word "client" makes no sense in a P2P network because there is not necessarily a server to be a client of.

Groups of peers that are connected to each other are known by the interchangeable terms *meshes, clouds,* or *graphs*. A given group can be said to be *well-connected* if:

- ❏ There is a connection path between every pair of peers, so that every peer can connect to any other peer as required.
- ❏ There are a relatively small number of connections to traverse between any pair of peers.
- ❏ Removing a peer will not prevent other peers from connecting to each other.

Note that this does not mean that every peer must be able to connect to every other peer. In fact, if you analyze a network mathematically you will find that peers need to connect only to a relatively small number of other peers in order for these conditions to be met.

Another P2P concept to be aware of is that of *flooding*. Flooding is the way in which a single piece of data may be propagated through a network to all peers, or of querying other nodes in a network to locate a specific piece of data. In unstructured P2P networks this is a fairly random process of contacting nearest neighbor peers, which in turn contact their nearest neighbors, and so on until every peer in the network is contacted. It is also possible to create structured P2P networks such that there are well-defined pathways for queries and data flow among peers.

P2P Solutions

Once you have an infrastructure for P2P you can start to develop not just improved versions of client-server applications, but entirely new applications. P2P is particularly suited to the following classes of applications:

❑   Content distribution applications, including the file-sharing applications discussed earlier.

❑   Collaboration applications, such as desktop sharing and shared whiteboard applications.

❑   Multi-user communication applications that allow users to communicate and exchange data directly rather than through a server.

❑   Distributed processing applications, as an alternative to supercomputing applications that process enormous amounts of data.

❑   Web 2.0 applications that combine some or all of the above in dynamic next-generation Web applications.

Microsoft Windows Peer-to-Peer Networking

The Microsoft Windows Peer-to-Peer Networking platform is Microsoft's implementation of P2P technology. It is part of Windows XP SP2 and Windows Vista, and is also available as an add-on for Windows XP SP1. It includes two technologies that you can use when creating .NET P2P applications:

❑   The Peer Name Resolution Protocol (PNRP), which is used to publish and resolve peer addresses

❑   The People Near Me server, which is used to locate local peers (currently Vista only)

In this section you learn about both of these.

Peer Name Resolution Protocol (PNRP)

You can of course use any protocol at your disposal to implement a P2P application, but if you are working in a Microsoft Windows environment (and, let's face it, if you're reading this book you probably are) it makes sense to at least consider PNRP. There have been two versions of PNRP released to date. PNRP version 1 was included in Windows XP SP2, Windows XP Professional x64 Edition, and Windows XP SP1 with the Advanced Networking Pack for Windows XP. PNRP version 2 was released with Windows Vista, and was made available to Windows XP SP2 users through a separate download (see KB920342 at `support.microsoft.com/kb/920342`). Version 1 and version 2 of PNRP are not compatible, and this chapter covers only version 2.

In itself, PNRP doesn't give you everything you need to create a P2P application. Rather, it is one of the underlying technologies that you use to resolve peer addresses. PNRP enables a client to register an endpoint (known as a *peer name*) that is automatically circulated among peers in a cloud. This peer name is encapsulated in a *PNRP ID*. A peer that discovers the PNRP ID is able to use PNRP to resolve it to the actual peer name, and can then communicate directly with it.

For example, you might define a peer name that represents a WCF service endpoint. You could use PNRP to register this peer name in a cloud as a PNRP ID. A peer running a suitable client application that uses a discovery mechanism that can identify peer names for the service you are exposing might then discover this PNRP ID. Once discovered, the peer would use PNRP to locate the endpoint of the WCF service and then use that service.

> *An important point is that PNRP makes no assumptions about what a peer name actually represents. It is up to peers to decide how to use them once discovered. The information a peer receives from PNRP when resolving a PNRP ID includes the IPv6 (and usually also the IPv4) address of the publisher of the ID, along with a port number and optionally a small amount of additional data. Unless the peer knows what the peer name means it is unlikely to be able to do anything useful with this information.*

PNRP IDs

PNRP IDs are 256-bit identifiers. The low-order 128 bits are used to uniquely identify a particular peer, and the high-order 128 bits identify a peer name. The high-order 128 bits are a hashed combination of a hashed public key from the publishing peer and a string of up to 149 characters that identifies the peer name. The hashed public key (known as the *authority*) combined with this string (the *classifier*) are together referred to as the P2P ID. It is also possible to use a value of 0 instead of a hashed public key, in which case the peer name is said to be *unsecured* (as opposed to *secured* peer names, which use a public key).

The structure of a PNRP ID is illustrated in Figure 47-4.

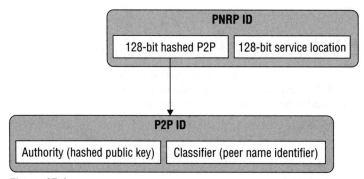

Figure 47-4

The PNRP service on a peer is responsible for maintaining a list of PNRP IDs, including the ones that it publishes as well as a cached list of those it has obtained by PNRP service instances elsewhere in the cloud. When a peer attempts to resolve a PNRP ID, the PNRP service either uses a cached copy of the endpoint to resolve the peer that published the PNRP or it asks its neighbors if they can resolve it. Eventually a connection to the publishing peer is made and the PNRP service can resolve the PNRP ID.

Note that all of this happens without you having to intervene in any way. All you have to do is ensure that peers know what to do with peer names once they have resolved them using their local PNRP service.

Peers can use PNRP to locate PNRP IDs that match a particular P2P ID. You can use this to implement a very basic form of discovery for unsecured peer names. This is because if several peers expose an unsecured peer name that uses the same classifier, the P2P ID will be the same. Of course, because any peer can use an unsecured peer name you have no guarantee that the endpoint you connect to will be the sort of endpoint you expect, so this is only really a viable solution for discovery over a local network.

PNRP Clouds

In the preceding discussion you learned how PNRP registers and resolves peer names in clouds. A cloud is maintained by a *seed server*, which can be any server running the PNRP service that maintains a record of at least one peer. Two types of cloud are available to the PNRP service:

❑ **Link local** — These clouds consist of the computers attached to a local network. A PC may be connected to more than one link local cloud if it has multiple network adapters.

❑ **Global** — This cloud consists of computers connected to the Internet by default, although it is also possible to define a private global cloud. The difference is that Microsoft maintains the seed server for the global Internet cloud, whereas if you define a private global cloud you must use your own. If you use your own seed server you must ensure that all peers connect to it by configuring policy settings.

In past releases of PNRP there was a third type of cloud, site local. This is no longer used and you won't look at it in this chapter.

You can discover what clouds you are connected to with the following command:

```
netsh p2p pnrp cloud show list
```

A typical result is shown in Figure 47-5.

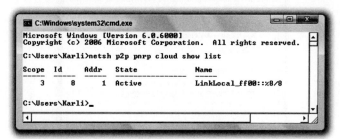

Figure 47-5

Figure 47-5 shows that a single cloud is available, and that it is a link local cloud. You can tell this from both the name and the `Scope` value, which is 3 for link local clouds and 1 for global clouds. In order to connect to a global cloud you must have a global IPv6 address. The computer used to generate Figure 47-5 does not have one, which is why only a local cloud is available.

Clouds may be in one of the following states:

❑ **Active** — If the state of a cloud is active, you can use it to publish and resolve peer names.

❑ **Alone** — If the peer you are querying the cloud from is not connected to any other peers, it will have a state of alone.

❑ **No Net** — If the peer is not connected to a network, the cloud state may change from active to no net.

❑ **Synchronizing** — Clouds will be in the synchronizing state when the peer is connecting to them. This state will change to another state extremely quickly because this connection does not take long, so you will probably never see a cloud in this state.

❑ **Virtual** — The PNRP service connects to clouds only as required by peer name registration and resolution. If a cloud connection has been inactive for more than 15 minutes it may enter the virtual state.

If you experience network connectivity problems you should check your firewall in case it is preventing local network traffic over the UDP ports 3540 or 1900. UDP port 3540 is used by PNRP, and UDP port 1900 is used by the Simple Service Discovery Protocol (SSDP), which in turn is used by the PNRP service (as well as UPnP devices).

People Near Me

PNRP, as you saw in the previous section, is used to locate peers. This is obviously important as an enabling technology when you consider the discovery/connection/communication process of a P2P application, but in itself is not a complete implementation of any of these stages. The People Near Me service is an implementation of the discovery stage, and enables you to locate peers that are signed into the Window People Near Me service in your local area (that is, in a link local cloud that you are connected to).

You may have come across this service because it is built into Vista, and is used in the Windows Meeting Space application, which you can use for sharing applications among peers. You can configure this service through the Start menu with the dialog shown in Figure 47-6.

Figure 47-6

Once signed in the service is available to any application that is built to use the PNM service.

At the time of writing, PNM is available only on the Windows Vista family of operating systems. However, it is possible that future service packs or additional downloads may make it available on Windows XP.

Building P2P Applications

Now that you have learned what P2P networking is and what technologies are available to .NET developers to implement P2P applications, it is time to look at how you can build them. From the previous discussion you know that you will be using PNRP to publish, distribute, and resolve peer names, so the first thing you look at here is how to achieve that using .NET. Next you look at how to use PNM as a framework for a P2P application. This can be advantageous because you do not have to implement your own discovery mechanisms.

To examine these subjects you need to learn about the classes in the following namespaces:

❑   `System.Net.PeerToPeer`

❑   `System.Net.PeerToPeer.Collaboration`

To use these classes you must have a reference to the `System.Net.dll` assembly.

System.Net.PeerToPeer

The classes in the `System.Net.PeerToPeer` namespace encapsulate the API for PNRP and enable you to interact with the PNRP service. You will use these classes for two main tasks:

❑   Registering peer names

❑   Resolving peer names

In the following sections, all the types referred to come from the `System.Net.PeerToPeer` namespace unless otherwise specified.

Registering Peer Names

To register a peer name you must carry out the following steps:

1.   Create a secured or unsecured peer name with a specified classifier.

2.   Configure a registration for the peer name, specifying some or none of the following optional information:

❑   A TCP port number

❑   The cloud or clouds to register the peer name with (if unspecified, PNRP will register the peer name in all available clouds)

❑   A comment of up to 39 characters

❑   Up to 4096 bytes of additional data

❑   Whether to generate endpoints for the peer name automatically (the default behavior, where endpoints will be generated from the IP address or addresses of the peer and, if specified, the port number)

❑   A collection of endpoints

3.   Use the peer name registration to register the peer name with the local PNRP service.

After Step 3 the peer name will be available to all peers in the selected cloud (or clouds). Peer registration continues until it is explicitly stopped, or until the process that registered the peer name is terminated.

To create a peer name you use the `PeerName` class. You create an instance of this class from a string representation of a P2P ID in the form `authority.classifier` or from a classifier string and a `PeerNameType`. You can use `PeerNameType.Secured` or `PeerNameType.Unsecured`. For example:

```
PeerName pn = new PeerName("Peer classifier", PeerNameType.Secured);
```

Because an unsecured peer name uses an authority value of 0, the following lines of code are equivalent:

```
PeerName pn = new PeerName("Peer classifier", PeerNameType.Unsecured);

PeerName pn = new PeerName("0.Peer classifier");
```

Once you have a `PeerName` instance you can use it along with a port number to initialize a `PeerNameRegistration` object:

```
PeerNameRegistration pnr = new PeerNameRegistration(pn, 8080);
```

Alternatively, you can set the `PeerName` and (optionally) the `Port` properties on a `PeerNameRegistration` object created using its default parameter. You can also specify a `Cloud` instance as a third parameter of the `PeerNameRegistration` constructor, or through the `Cloud` property. You can obtain a `Cloud` instance from the cloud name or by using one of the following static members of `Cloud`:

❑ `Cloud.Global` — This static property obtains a reference to the global cloud. This may be a private global cloud depending on peer policy configuration.

❑ `Cloud.AllLinkLocal` — This static field gets a cloud that contains all the link local clouds available to the peer.

❑ `Cloud.Available` — This static field gets a cloud that contains all the clouds that are available to the peer, which includes link local clouds and (if available) the global cloud.

Once created, you can set the `Comment` and `Data` properties if you want to. Be aware of the limitations of these properties, though. You will receive a `PeerToPeerException` if you try to set `Comment` to a string of greater than 39 Unicode characters or an `ArgumentOutOfRangeException` if you try to set `Data` to a `byte[]` of greater than 4096 bytes. You can also add endpoints by using the `EndPointCollection` property. This property is a `System.Net.IPEndPointCollection` collection of `System.Net.IPEndPoint` objects. If you use the `EndPointCollection` property you might also want to set the `UseAutoEndPointSelection` property to `false` to prevent automatic generation of endpoints.

When you are ready to register the peer name you can call the `PeerNameRegistration.Start()` method. To remove a peer name registration from the PNRP service you use the `PeerNameRegistration.Stop()` method.

The following code registers a secured peer name with a comment:

```
PeerName pn = new PeerName("Peer classifier", PeerNameType.Unsecured);
PeerNameRegistration pnr = new PeerNameRegistration(pn, 8080);
pnr.Comment = "Get pizza here";
pnr.Start();
```

Resolving Peer Names

To resolve a peer name you must carry out the following steps:

1. Generate a peer name from a known P2P ID or a P2P ID obtained through a discovery technique.

2. Use a resolver to resolve the peer name and obtain a collection of peer name records. You can limit the resolver to a particular cloud and/or a maximum number of results to return.

3. For any peer name records that you obtain, obtain peer name, endpoint, comment, and additional data information as required.

This process starts with a `PeerName` object just like peer name registration. The difference here is that you use a peer name that is registered by one or more remote peers. The simplest way to get a list of active peers in your link local cloud is for each peer to register an unsecured peer name with the same classifier and to use the same peer name in the resolving phase. However, this is not a recommended strategy for global clouds because unsecured peer names are easily spoofed.

To resolve peer names you use the `PeerNameResolver` class. Once you have an instance of this class you can choose to resolve peer names synchronously by using the `Resolve()` method, or asynchronously using the `ResolveAsync()` method.

You can call the `Resolve()` method with a single `PeerName` parameter, but you can also pass an optional `Cloud` instance to resolve in, an `int` maximum number of peers to return, or both. This method returns a `PeerNameRecordCollection` instance, which is a collection of `PeerNameRecord` objects. For example, the following code resolves an unsecured peer name in all link local clouds and returns a maximum of 5 results:

```
PeerName pn = new PeerName("0.Peer classifier");
PeerNameResolver pnres = new PeerNameResolver();
PeerNameRecordCollection pnrc = pnres.Resolve(pn, Cloud.AllLinkLocal, 5);
```

The `ResolveAsync()` method uses a standard asynchronous method call pattern. You pass a unique `userState` object to the method, and listen for `ResolveProgressChanged` events for peers being found and the `ResolveCompleted` event when the method terminates. You can cancel a pending asynchronous request with the `ResolveAsyncCancel()` method.

Event handlers for the `ResolveProgressChanged` event use the `ResolveProgressChangedEventArgs` event arguments parameter, which derives from the standard `System.ComponentModel.ProgressChangedEventArgs` class. You can use the `PeerNameRecord` property of the event argument object you receive in the event handler to get a reference to the peer name record that was found.

Similarly, the `ResolveCompleted` event requires an event handler that uses a parameter of type `ResolveCompletedEventArgs`, which derives from `AsyncCompletedEventArgs`. This type includes a `PeerNameRecordCollection` parameter you can use to obtain a complete list of the peer name records that were found.

The following code shows an implementation of event handlers for these events:

```
private pnres_ResolveProgressChanged(object sender,
    ResolveProgressChangedEventArgs e)
{
    // Use e.ProgressPercentage (inherited from base event args)
    // Process PeerNameRecord from e.PeerNameRecord
}

private pnres_ResolveCompleted(object sender,
    ResolveCompletedEventArgs e)
{
    // Test for e.IsCancelled and e.Error (inherited from base event args)
    // Process PeerNameRecordCollection from e.PeerNameRecordCollection
}
```

Once you have one or more `PeerNameRecord` objects you can proceed to process them. This `PeerNameRecord` class exposes `Comment` and `Data` properties to examine the comment and data set in the peer name registration (if any), a `PeerName` property to get the `PeerName` object for the peer name record, and, most importantly, an `EndPointCollection` property. As with `PeerNameRegistration`, this property is a `System.Net.IPEndPointCollection` collection of `System.Net.IPEndPoint` objects. You can use these objects to connect to end points exposed by the peer in any way you want.

Code Access Security in System.Net.PeerToPeer

The `System.Net.PeerToPeer` namespace also includes the following two classes that you can use with CAS (see Chapter 20):

❑ `PnrpPermission`, which inherits from `CodeAccessPermission`

❑ `PnrpPermissionAttribute`, which inherits from `CodeAccessSecurityAttribute`

You can use these classes to provide permissions functionality for PNRP access in the usual CAS way.

Sample Application

The downloadable code for this chapter includes a sample P2P application (P2PSample) that uses the concepts and namespace introduced in this section. It is a WPF application that uses a WCF service for a peer endpoint.

The application is configured with an application configuration file, in which you can specify the name of the peer and a port to listen on as follows:

```xml
<?xml version="1.0" encoding="utf-8" ?>
<configuration>
  <appSettings>
    <add key="username" value="Karli" />
    <add key="port" value="8731" />
  </appSettings>
</configuration>
```

Once you have built the application you can test it either by copying it to other computers in your local network and running all instances, or by running multiple instances on one computer. If you choose the latter option you must remember to change the port used for each instance by changing individual config files (copy the contents of the `Debug` directory on your local computer and edit each config file in turn). Things will be clearer in both ways of testing this application if you also change the username for each instance.

Once the peer applications are running, you can use the Refresh button to obtain a list of peers asynchronously. When you have located a peer you can send a default message by clicking the Message button for the peer.

Figure 47-7 shows this application in action with three instances running on one machine. In the figure, one peer has just messaged another and this has resulted in a dialog box.

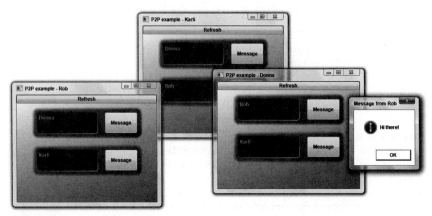

Figure 47-7

Most of the work in this application takes place in the `Window_Loaded()` event handler for the `Window1` window. This method starts by loading configuration information and setting the window title with the username:

```csharp
private void Window_Loaded(object sender, RoutedEventArgs e)
{
    // Get configuration from app.config
    string port = ConfigurationManager.AppSettings["port"];
```

```
string username = ConfigurationManager.AppSettings["username"];
string machineName = Environment.MachineName;
string serviceUrl = null;

// Set window title
this.Title = string.Format("P2P example - {0}", username);
```

Next the peer host address is used along with the configured port to determine the endpoint on which to host the WCF service. The service will use `NetTcpBinding` binding, so the URL of the endpoint uses the `net.tcp` protocol:

```
// Get service url using IPv4 address and port from config file
foreach (IPAddress address in Dns.GetHostAddresses(Dns.GetHostName()))
{
    if (address.AddressFamily ==
        System.Net.Sockets.AddressFamily.InterNetwork)
    {
        serviceUrl = string.Format("net.tcp://{0}:{1}/P2PService",
            address, port);
        break;
    }
}
```

The endpoint URL is validated, and then the WCF service is registered and started:

```
// Check for null address
if (serviceUrl == null)
{
    // Display error and shutdown
    MessageBox.Show(this, "Unable to determine WCF endpoint.",
        "Networking Error", MessageBoxButton.OK, MessageBoxImage.Stop);
    Application.Current.Shutdown();
}

// Register and start WCF service.
localService = new P2PService(this, username);
host = new ServiceHost(localService, new Uri(serviceUrl));
NetTcpBinding binding = new NetTcpBinding();
binding.Security.Mode = SecurityMode.None;
host.AddServiceEndpoint(typeof(IP2PService), binding, serviceUrl);
try
{
    host.Open();
}
catch (AddressAlreadyInUseException)
{
    // Display error and shutdown
    MessageBox.Show(this, "Cannot start listening, port in use.",
        "WCF Error", MessageBoxButton.OK, MessageBoxImage.Stop);
    Application.Current.Shutdown();
}
```

A singleton instance of the service class is used to enable easy communication between the host app and the service (for sending and receiving messages). Also, note that security is disabled in the binding configuration for simplicity.

Next, the `System.Net.PeerToPeer` namespace classes are used to register a peer name:

```
    // Create peer name
    peerName = new PeerName("P2P Sample", PeerNameType.Unsecured);

    // Prepare peer name registration in link local clouds
    peerNameRegistration = new PeerNameRegistration(peerName, int.Parse(port));
    peerNameRegistration.Cloud = Cloud.AllLinkLocal;

    // Start registration
    peerNameRegistration.Start();
}
```

When the Refresh button is clicked the `RefreshButton_Click()` event handler uses `PeerNameResolver.ResolveAsync()` to get peers asynchronously:

```
private void RefreshButton_Click(object sender, RoutedEventArgs e)
{
    // Create resolver and add event handlers
    PeerNameResolver resolver = new PeerNameResolver();
    resolver.ResolveProgressChanged +=
        new EventHandler<ResolveProgressChangedEventArgs>(
            resolver_ResolveProgressChanged);
    resolver.ResolveCompleted +=
        new EventHandler<ResolveCompletedEventArgs>(
            resolver_ResolveCompleted);

    // Prepare for new peers
    PeerList.Items.Clear();
    RefreshButton.IsEnabled = false;

    // Resolve unsecured peers asynchronously
    resolver.ResolveAsync(new PeerName("0.P2P Sample"), 1);
}
```

The remainder of the code is responsible for displaying and communicating with peers, and you can explore it at your leisure.

Exposing WCF endpoints through P2P clouds is a great way of locating services within an enterprise, as well as being an excellent way to communicate between peers as in this example.

System.Net.PeerToPeer.Collaboration

The classes in the `System.Net.PeerToPeer.Collaboration` namespace provide a framework you can use to create applications that use the People Near Me service and the P2P collaboration API. As mentioned earlier, this is possible only if you are using Windows Vista at the moment.

You can use the classes in this namespace to interact with peers and applications in a number of ways, including:

❑ Signing in and signing out

❑ Discovering peers

❑ Managing contacts and detecting peer presence

You can also use the classes in this namespace to invite other users to join an application, and to exchange data between users and applications. However, in order to do this you need to create your own PNM-capable applications, which is beyond the scope of this chapter.

In the following sections, all the types referred to come from the `System.Net.PeerToPeer.Collaboration` namespace unless otherwise specified.

Signing In and Signing Out

One of the most important classes in the `System.Net.PeerToPeer.Collaboration` namespace is the `PeerCollaboration` class. This is a static class that exposes numerous static methods that you can use for various purposes, as you will see in this and subsequent sections. You can use two of the methods it exposes, `SignIn()` and `SignOut()`, to (unsurprisingly) sign in and sign out of the People Near Me service. Both of these methods take a single parameter of type `PeerScope`, which can be one of the following values:

❑ `PeerScope.None` — If you use this value, `SignIn()` and `SignOut()` will have no effect.

❑ `PeerScope.NearMe` — This will sign you in to or out of the link local clouds.

❑ `PeerScope.Internet` — This will sign you in to or out of the global cloud (which may be necessary to connect to a contact who is not currently on your local subnet).

❑ `PeerScope.All` — This will sign you in to or out of all available clouds.

If necessary, calling `SignIn()` will cause the People Near Me configuration dialog to be displayed.

When a peer is signed in you can use the `PeerCollaboration.LocalPresenceInfo` property to a value of type `PeerPresenceInfo`. This enables standard IM functionality, such as setting your status to away. You can set the `PeerPresenceInfo.DescriptiveText` property to a Unicode string of up to 255 characters, and the `PeerPresenceInfo.PresenceStatus` property to a value from the `PeerPresenceStatus` enumeration. The values that you can use for this enumeration are as follows:

❑ `PeerPresenceStatus.Away` — The peer is away.

❑ `PeerPresenceStatus.BeRightBack` — The peer is away, but will be back soon.

❑ `PeerPresenceStatus.Busy` — The peer is busy.

❑ `PeerPresenceStatus.Idle` — The peer isn't active.

❑ `PeerPresenceStatus.Offline` — The peer is offline.

❑ `PeerPresenceStatus.Online` — The peer is online and available.

❑ `PeerPresenceStatus.OnThePhone` — The peer is busy with a phone call.

❑ `PeerPresenceStatus.OutToLunch` — The peer is away, but will be back after lunch.

Discovering Peers

You can obtain a list of peers near you if you are logged in to the link local cloud. You do this by using the `PeerCollaboration.GetPeersNearMe()` method. This returns a `PeerNearMeCollection` object containing `PeerNearMe` objects.

You can use the `Nickname` property of `PeerNearMe` to obtain the name of a peer, `IsOnline` to determine whether the peer is online, and (for lower-level operations) the `PeerEndpoints` property to determine endpoints related to the peer. `PeerEndPoints` is also necessary if you want to find out the online status of a `PeerNearMe`. You can pass an endpoint to the `GetPresenceInfo()` method to obtain a `PeerPresenceInfo` object, as described in the previous section.

Managing Contacts and Detecting Peer Presence

Contacts are a way in which you can remember peers. You can add a peer discovered through the People Near Me service and from then onward you can connect to them whenever you are both online. You can connect to a contact through link local or global clouds (assuming you have IPv6 connectivity to the Internet).

You can add a contact from a peer that you have discovered, by calling the `PeerNearMe` `.AddToContactManager()` method. When you call this method you can choose to associate a display name, nickname, and email address with the contact. Typically, though, you will manage contacts by using the `ContactManager` class.

However you manipulate contacts, you will be dealing with `PeerContact` objects. `PeerContact`, like `PeerNearMe`, inherits from the abstract `Peer` base class. `PeerContact` has more properties and methods than `PeerNearMe`. `PeerContact` includes `DisplayName` and `EmailAddress` properties that further describe a PNM peer, for example. Another difference between these two types is that `PeerContact` has a more explicit relationship with the `System.Net.PeerToPeer.PeerName` class. You can get a `PeerName` from a `PeerContact` through the `PeerContact.PeerName` property. Once you have done this you can proceed to use techniques you looked at earlier to communicate with any endpoints the `PeerName` exposes.

Information about the local peer is also accessible through the `ContactManager` class, through the static `ContactManager.LocalContact` property. This gets you a `PeerContact` property with details of the local peer.

You can add `PeerNearMe` objects to the local list of contacts by using either the `ContactManager` `.CreateContact()` or `CreateContactAsync()` method, or `PeerName` objects by using the `GetContact()` method. You can remove contacts represented by a `PeerNearMe` or `PeerName` object with the `DeleteContact()` method.

Finally, there are events that you can handle to respond to changes to contacts. For example, you can use the `PresenceChanged` event to respond to changes of presence for any of the contacts known by the `ContactManager`.

Sample Application

There is a second sample application in the downloadable code for this chapter that illustrates the use of classes in the `System.Net.PeerToPeer.Collaboration` namespace. This application is similar to the other sample, but much simpler. You will need two computers that can both sign in to the PNM server in order to see this application in action, because it enumerates and displays PNM peers from the local subnet.

When you run the application with at least one peer available for discovery the display will be similar to Figure 47-8.

Figure 47-8

The code is structured in the same way as the previous example, so if you've read through that code you should be familiar with this code. This time there is not much work to do in the `Window_Loaded()` event handler except sign in, because there is no WCF service to initialize or peer name registration to achieve:

```
private void Window_Loaded(object sender, RoutedEventArgs e)
{
    // Sign in to PNM
    PeerCollaboration.SignIn(PeerScope.NearMe);
```

To make things look a little nicer, though, `ContactManager.LocalContact.Nickname` is used to format the window title:

```
    // Get local peer name to display
    this.Title = string.Format("PNMSample - {0}",
        ContactManager.LocalContact.Nickname);
}
```

In `Window_Closing()` the local peer is automatically signed out of PNM:

```
private void Window_Closing(object sender,
    System.ComponentModel.CancelEventArgs e)
{
    // Sign out of PNM
    PeerCollaboration.SignOut(PeerScope.NearMe);
}
```

Most of the work is done in the `RefreshButton_Click()` event handler. This uses the `PeerCollaboration.GetPeersNearMe()` method to obtain a list of peers, and add those peers to the display using the `PeerEntry` class defined in the project, or a failure message if none are found.

```
private void RefreshButton_Click(object sender, RoutedEventArgs e)
{
    // Get local peers
    PeerNearMeCollection peersNearMe = PeerCollaboration.GetPeersNearMe();

    // Prepare for new peers
    PeerList.Items.Clear();

    // Examine peers
    foreach (PeerNearMe peerNearMe in peersNearMe)
    {
        PeerList.Items.Add(
            new PeerEntry
            {
                PeerNearMe = peerNearMe,
                PresenceStatus = peerNearMe.GetPresenceInfo(
                    peerNearMe.PeerEndPoints[0]).PresenceStatus,
                DisplayString = peerNearMe.Nickname
            });
    }

    // Add failure message if necessary
    if (PeerList.Items.Count == 0)
    {
        PeerList.Items.Add(
            new PeerEntry
            {
                DisplayString = "No peers found."
            });
    }
}
```

As you can see from this example, interacting with the PNM service is made very simple by the classes you have learned about.

Summary

This chapter demonstrated how to implement peer-to-peer (P2P) functionality in your applications by using the new P2P classes in .NET 3.5.

You have looked at the types of solutions that P2P makes possible and how these solutions are structured, how to use PNRP and PNM, and how to use the types in the `System.Net.PeerToPeer` and `System.Net.PeerToPeer.Collaboration` namespace. You also saw the extremely useful technique of exposing WCF services as P2P endpoints.

If you are interested in developing P2P applications it is well worth investigating PNM further. It is also worth looking at the peer channel, by which WCF services can broadcast communications among multiple clients simultaneously.

In the next chapter you look at syndication, and you see how you can expose data in RSS and Atom feeds.

48
Syndication

Do you have some structured data to offer, data that changes from time to time? With many web sites, RSS or Atom symbols allow you to subscribe with feed readers. Really Simple Syndication (RSS) is an XML format that allows syndicate information. RSS became very popular with blogs. This XML information makes it easy to subscribe to using RSS readers.

Nowadays, RSS is not only used with blogs but with many different data sources, such as online news magazines. Any data that changes from time to time is offered by RSS or by its successor protocol Atom. Internet Explorer 7 and Outlook 2007 offer RSS and Atom readers that are integrated into the product.

.NET 3.5 extends Windows Communication Foundation (WCF) with syndication features. Syndication classes are defined within the namespace `System.ServiceModel.Syndication`. This namespace provides classes that can be used to both read and write RSS and Atom feeds.

This chapter shows you how to create syndication readers, as well as how data can be offered. This chapter offers the following:

- ❑ An overview of `System.ServiceModel.Syndication`
- ❑ Information about Syndication Reader
- ❑ Information about Syndication Feeds

Overview of System.Servicemodel. Syndication

`System.ServiceModel.Syndication` is a new namespace with .NET 3.5 that allows you to offer data in the RSS or Atom format.

With the release of RSS version 2.0, RSS is now the shorthand notation for Really Simple Syndication. In earlier versions, it had the name RDF Site Summary and Rich Site Summary. RDF is the abbreviation for Resource Description Framework. The first version was created by Netscape to describe content of its portal site. It became successful when the *New York Times* began offering its readers subscriptions to RSS news feeds in 2002. Figure 48-1 shows the RSS logo. If a site shows this logo, then an RSS feed is offered.

Figure 48-1

Atom was designed to be the successor for RSS and is a proposed standard with RFC 4287: www.ietf.org/rfc/rfc4287.txt. The major difference between RSS and Atom is in the content that can be defined with an item. With RSS, the description element can contain simple text or HTML content in which the reading application does not care about this content. Atom requires that you define a specific type for the content with a type attribute, and it also allows you to have XML content with defined namespaces.

The following table lists classes from .NET 3.5 that allow you to create a syndication feed. These classes are independent of the syndication type, RSS or Atom.

Class	Description
SyndicationFeed	SyndicationFeed represents the top-level element of a feed. With Atom, the top-level element is <feed>; RSS defines <rss> as the top-level element.
	With the static method Load(), a feed can be read using an XmlReader.
	Properties of this class such as Authors, Categories, Contributors, Copyright, Description, ImageUrl, Links, Title, and Items allow you to define child elements.
SyndicationPerson	SyndicationPerson represents a person with Name, Email, and Uri that can be assigned to the Authors and Contributors collection.
SyndicationItem	A feed consists of multiple items. Some of the properties of an item are Authors, Contributors, Copyright, and Content.
SyndicationLink	SyndicationLink represents a link within a feed or an item. This class defines the properties Title and Uri.
SyndicationCategory	A feed can group items into categories. The keyword of a category can be set to the Name and Label properties of SyndicationCategory.
SyndicationContent	SyndicationContent is an abstract base class that describes the content of an item. Content can be of type HTML, plain text, XHTML, XML, or a URL, described with the concrete classes TextSyndicationContent, UrlSyndicationContent, and XmlSyndicationContent.
SyndicationElement-Extension	With an extension element, you can add additional content. The SyndicationElementExtension can be used to add information to a feed, a category, a person, a link, and an item.

To format a feed to the RSS and Atom formats, you can use classes from the following table.

Class	Description
`Atom10FeedFormatter` `Rss20FeedFormatter`	`Atom10FeedFormatter` and `Rss20FeedFormatter` derive from the abstract base class `SyndicationFeedFormatter`. `Atom10FeedFormatter` serializes a `SyndicationFeed` to the Atom 1.0 format, the `Rss20FeedFormatter` to the RSS 2.0 format.
`Atom10ItemFormatter` `Rss20ItemFormatter`	`Atom10ItemFormatter` and `Rss20ItemFormatter` derive from the abstract base class `SyndicationItemFormatter`. `Atom10ItemFormatter` serializes a `SyndicationItem` to the Atom 1.0 format, the `Rss20ItemFormatter` to the RSS 2.0 format.

Syndication Reader

Our first example is a Syndication Reader application with a user interface developed with WPF. The user interface of the WPF application is shown in Figure 48-2.

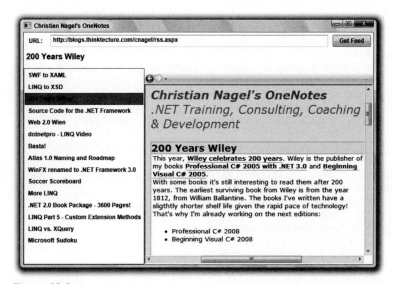

Figure 48-2

To use the Syndication API, the assembly `System.ServiceModel.Web` is referenced with the application. The `OnGetFeed()` event handler method is set to the `Click` event of the button showing the Get Feed text. The code needed to read the application is really simple. First, the XML content from the RSS feed is read into the `XmlReader` class from the `System.Xml` namespace. `Rss20FeedFormatter` accepts an `XmlReader` with the `ReadFrom()` method. For data-binding, the `Feed` property that returns a `SyndicationFeed` is assigned to the `DataContext` of the `Window`, and the `Feed.Items` property that returns `IEnumerable<SyndicationItem>` is assigned to the `DataContext` of a `DockPanel` container.

```
private void OnGetFeed(object sender, RoutedEventArgs e)
{
    XmlReader reader = XmlReader.Create(textUrl.Text);
    Rss20FeedFormatter formatter = new Rss20FeedFormatter();
    formatter.ReadFrom(reader);
    reader.Close();
    this.DataContext = formatter.Feed;
    this.feedContent.DataContext = formatter.Feed.Items;
}
```

The XAML code that defines the user interface is shown next. The `Title` property of the `Window` class is bound to the `Title.Text` property of the `SyndicationFeed` to display the title of the feed.

In the XAML code, a `DockPanel` named `heading`, which contains a `Label` bound to `Title.Text` and a `Label` bound to `Description.Text`, is defined. Because these labels are contained within the `DockPanel` named `feedContent`, and `feedContent` is bound to the `Feed.Items` property, these labels give title and description information about the current selected item.

A list of items is displayed in a `ListBox` that uses an `ItemTemplate` to bind a label to the `Title`.

The `DockPanel` named content contains a `Frame` element that binds the `Source` property to the first link of an item. With that setting, the `Frame` control uses the web browser control to display the content from the link, as shown in Figure 48-2.

```xml
<Window x:Class="RSSReader.Window1"
    xmlns="http://schemas.microsoft.com/winfx/2006/xaml/presentation"
    xmlns:x="http://schemas.microsoft.com/winfx/2006/xaml"
    Title="{Binding Path=Title.Text}" Height="300" Width="345">
    <Window.Resources>
        <Style x:Key="listTitleStyle" TargetType="{x:Type ListBox}">
            <Setter Property="ItemTemplate">
                <Setter.Value>
                    <DataTemplate>
                        <Label Content="{Binding Title.Text}" />
                    </DataTemplate>
                </Setter.Value>
            </Setter>
        </Style>
    </Window.Resources>
    <DockPanel x:Name="feedContent">
        <Grid DockPanel.Dock="Top">
            <Grid.ColumnDefinitions>
                <ColumnDefinition Width="50" />
                <ColumnDefinition Width="*" />
                <ColumnDefinition Width="90" />
            </Grid.ColumnDefinitions>
            <Label Grid.Column="0" Margin="5">URL:</Label>
            <TextBox Grid.Column="1" x:Name="textUrl" MinWidth="150"
                Margin="5">http://blogs.thinktecture.com/cnagel/rss.aspx
            </TextBox>
            <Button Grid.Column="2" Margin="5" MinWidth="80"
                Click="OnGetFeed">Get Feed</Button>
        </Grid>
        <DockPanel DockPanel.Dock="Top" x:Name="heading">
            <Label DockPanel.Dock="Top" Content="{Binding Path=Title.Text}"
                FontSize="16" />
```

```
        <Label DockPanel.Dock="Top"
              Content="{Binding Path=Description.Text}" />
      </DockPanel>
      <ListBox DockPanel.Dock="Left" ItemsSource="{Binding}"
            Style="{StaticResource listTitleStyle}"
            IsSynchronizedWithCurrentItem="True" />
      <DockPanel x:Name="content" >
        <Label DockPanel.Dock="Top"
              Content="{Binding Path=Description.Text}"></Label>
        <Frame Source="{Binding Path=Links[0].Uri}">
        </Frame>
      </DockPanel>
    </DockPanel>
  </Window>
```

Offering Syndication Feeds

Reading syndication feeds is one scenario in which the Syndication API can be used. Another is to offer a syndication feed to RSS and Atom clients.

For this, Visual Studio 2008 offers the Syndication Service Library template, which you can use to start with. This template defines a reference to the System.ServiceModel.Web library, and adds an application configuration file to define a WCF endpoint.

To offer data for the syndication feed, the LINQ provider LINQ to SQL is helpful. In the sample application, the Formula 1 database is used, which you can download from the Wrox web site at www.wrox.com with the sample applications for the book. The "LINQ to SQL Classes" item with the name Formula1 is added to the project. Here, the tables Racers, RaceResults, Races, and Circuits are mapped to entity classes Racer, RaceResult, Race, and Circuit, as shown in Figure 48-3.

LINQ to SQL is discussed in Chapter 27.

The project template creates a file IService1.cs that contains the contract of the WCF service. The interface contains the CreateFeed() method, which returns a SyndicationFeedFormatter. Because SyndicationFeedFormatter is an abstract class, and the real types returned are either Atom10FeedFormatter or Rss20FeedFormatter, these types are listed with the ServiceKnownTypeAttribute, so that the type is known for serialization.

The attribute WebGet defines that the operation can be called from a simple HTTP GET request that can be used to request syndication feeds. WebMessageBodyStyle.Bare defines that the result (the XML from the syndication feed) is sent as it is without adding an XML wrapper element around it.

```
using System.ServiceModel;
using System.ServiceModel.Syndication;
using System.ServiceModel.Web;
namespace Wrox.ProCSharp.Syndication
{
    [ServiceContract]
    [ServiceKnownType(typeof(Atom10FeedFormatter))]
    [ServiceKnownType(typeof(Rss20FeedFormatter))]
    public interface IFormula1Feed
    {
        [OperationContract]
        [WebGet(UriTemplate = "*", BodyStyle = WebMessageBodyStyle.Bare)]
        SyndicationFeedFormatter CreateFeed();
    }
}
```

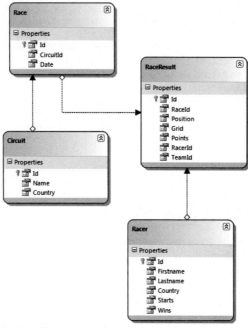

Figure 48-3

The implementation of the service is done in the class `Formula1Feed`. Here, a `SyndicationFeed` item is created, and various properties of this class such as `Generator`, `Language`, `Title`, `Categories`, and `Authors` are assigned. The `Items` property is filled from a LINQ to SQL query that requests the winners of Formula 1 races of the year 2007. With the `select` clause of this query, a `SyndicationItem` is created for every winner. With the `SyndicationItem`, the `Title` property is assigned to plain text containing the country of the race. The `Content` property is filled with the help of LINQ to XML. `XElement` classes are used to create XHTML code that can be interpreted by the browser. This content shows the date of the race, the country, and the name of the winner.

Depending on the query string to request the syndication, the `SyndicationFeed` is formatted with the `Atom10FeedFormatter` or the `Rss20FeedFormatter`.

```
using System;
using System.Linq;
using System.ServiceModel.Syndication;
using System.ServiceModel.Web;
using System.Xml.Linq;
namespace Wrox.ProCSharp.Syndication
{
    public class Formula1Feed : IFormula1Feed
    {
        public SyndicationFeedFormatter CreateFeed()
        {
            // Create a new Syndication Feed.
            SyndicationFeed feed = new SyndicationFeed();
            feed.Generator = "Pro C# 2008 Sample Feed Generator";
            feed.Language = "en-us";
            feed.LastUpdatedTime = new DateTimeOffset(DateTime.Now);
```

```
        feed.Title = SyndicationContent.CreatePlaintextContent(
            "Formula1 results");
        feed.Categories.Add(new SyndicationCategory("Formula1"));
        feed.Authors.Add(new SyndicationPerson("web@christiannagel.com",
            "Christian Nagel", "http://www.christiannagel.com"));
        feed.Description = SyndicationContent.CreatePlaintextContent(
            "Sample Formula 1");
        Formula1DataContext data = new Formula1DataContext();
        feed.Items = from racer in data.Racers
                     from raceResult in racer.RaceResults
                     where raceResult.Race.Date >
                           new DateTime(2007, 1, 1) &&
                           raceResult.Position == 1
                     orderby raceResult.Race.Date
                     select new SyndicationItem()
                     {
                         Title =
                             SyndicationContent.CreatePlaintextContent(
                             String.Format("G.P. {0}",
                             raceResult.Race.Circuit.Country)),
                         Content = SyndicationContent.CreateXhtmlContent(
                         new XElement("p",
                            new XElement("h3", String.Format("{0}, {1}",
                                raceResult.Race.Circuit.Country,
                                raceResult.Race.Date.
                                    ToShortDateString())),
                            new XElement("b", String.Format(
                                "Winner: {0} {1}",
                                racer.Firstname,
                                racer.Lastname))).ToString())
                     };
        // Return ATOM or RSS based on query string
        // rss ->
        // http://localhost:8731/Design_Time_Addresses/SyndicationService/Feed1/
        // atom ->
        // http://localhost:8731/Design_Time_Addresses/SyndicationService/
        //      Feed1/?format=atom
        string query =
            WebOperationContext.Current.IncomingRequest.UriTemplateMatch.
                QueryParameters["format"];
        SyndicationFeedFormatter formatter = null;
        if (query == "atom")
        {
            formatter = new Atom10FeedFormatter(feed);
        }
        else
        {
            formatter = new Rss20FeedFormatter(feed);
        }
        return formatter;
    }
  }
}
```

When you start the service from within Visual Studio 2008, the WCF Service Host starts up to host the service, and you can see the feed result formatted in Internet Explorer, as shown in Figure 48-4.

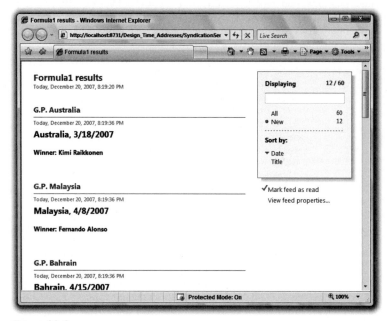

Figure 48-4

With the default request to the service, the RSS feed is returned. An extract of the RSS feed with the `rss` root element follows. With RSS, the `Title` property is translated to the `title` element, and the `Description` property goes to the `description` element. The `Authors` property of the `SyndicationFeed` that contains `SyndicationPerson` just uses the e-mail address to create the `managingEditor` element. To add more information to the feed, the formatter also places some Atom elements in the RSS feed. Placing Atom elements in an RSS feed is a common practice that provides information that is not defined by RSS.

```xml
<?xml version="1.0" encoding="utf-8"?>
<rss version="2.0" xmlns:atom="http://www.w3.org/2005/Atom"
  xmlns:cf="http://www.microsoft.com/schemas/rss/core/2005"
  xmlns:a10="http://www.w3.org/2005/Atom">
  <channel
      xmlns:cfi="http://www.microsoft.com/schemas/rss/core/2005/internal"
      cfi:lastdownloaderror="None">
    <title cf:type="text">Formula1 results</title>
    <description cf:type="text">Sample Formula 1</description>
    <language>en-us</language>
    <managingEditor>web@christiannagel.com</managingEditor>
    <atom:author>
      <atom:email>web@christiannagel.com</atom:email>
    </atom:author>
    <lastBuildDate>Tue, 04 Dec 2007 21:07:48 GMT</lastBuildDate>
    <atom:updated>2007-12-04T21:07:48Z</atom:updated>
    <category>Formula1</category>
```

```
<generator>Pro C# 2008 Sample Feed Generator</generator>
<item>
  <title xmlns:cf="http://www.microsoft.com/schemas/rss/core/2005"
        cf:type="text">G.P. Australia</title>
  <description xmlns:cf="http://www.microsoft.com/schemas/rss/core/2005"
        cf:type="html">&lt;p&gt;&lt;h3&gt;Australia, 18.03.2007&lt;/h3&gt;
        &lt;b&gt;Winner: Kimi Raikkonen&lt;/b&gt;&lt;/p&gt;
  </description>
  <cfi:id>47</cfi:id><cfi:read>true</cfi:read>
  <cfi:downloadurl>
        http://localhost:8731/Design_Time_Addresses/SyndicationService/Feed1/
  </cfi:downloadurl>
  <cfi:lastdownloadtime>2007-12-04T21:05:16.486Z</cfi:lastdownloadtime>
</item>
<item>
  <!-- ... -->
</channel>
</rss>
```

An Atom formatted feed is returned with the query `?format=atom` with the result shown. The root element now is the `feed` element; the `Description` property turns into a `subtitle` element; and the values for the `Author` property are now shown completely differently from the RSS feed shown earlier. Atom allows the content to be unencoded. You can easily find the XHTML elements.

```
<feed xml:lang="en-us" xmlns="http://www.w3.org/2005/Atom">
  <title type="text">Formula1 results</title>
  <subtitle type="text">Sample Formula 1</subtitle>
  <id>uuid:c19284e7-aa40-4bc2-9be8-f1960b0f747e;id=1</id>
  <updated>2007-12-05T00:46:35+01:00</updated>
  <category term="Formula1"/>
  <author>
    <name>Christian Nagel</name>
    <uri>http://www.christiannagel.com</uri>
    <email>web@christiannagel.com</email>
  </author>
  <generator>Pro C# 2008 Sample Feed Generator</generator>
  <entry>
    <id>uuid:c19284e7-aa40-4bc2-9be8-f1960b0f747e;id=2</id>
    <title type="text">G.P. Australia</title>
    <updated>2007-12-04T23:46:43Z</updated>
    <content type="xhtml">
      <p><h3>Australia, 18.03.2007</h3><b>Winner: Kimi Raikkonen</b></p>
    </content>
  </entry>
  <entry>
    <id>uuid:c19284e7-aa40-4bc2-9be8-f1960b0f747e;id=3</id>
    <title type="text">G.P. Malaysia</title>
    <updated>2007-12-04T23:46:43Z</updated>
    <content type="xhtml">
      <p><h3>Malaysia, 08.04.2007</h3><b>Winner: Fernando Alonso</b></p>
    </content>
  </entry>
  <!-- ... -->
</feed>
```

Summary

In this chapter, you have seen how the classes from the `System.ServiceModel.Syndication` namespace, which is new in .NET 3.5, can be used to create an application that receives a feed, as well as an application that offers a feed. The syndication API supports RSS 2.0 and Atom 1.0. As these standards emerge, new formatters will be available. You have seen that the SyndicationXXX classes are independent of the format that is generated. The concrete implementation of the abstract class `SyndicationFeedFormatter` defines what properties are used and how they are translated to the specific format.

This chapter concludes the communication part of the book. You've read about communication technologies to directly use sockets, and abstraction layers that are offered. Windows Communication Foundation is a technology that has been discussed in several chapters. With message queuing (Chapter 45), WCF offers a disconnected communication model. In Chapter 44, "Enterprise Services," you have seen WCF integration with existing COM+ applications.

Throughout this book, you've seen the language features of C#, including the features that are new with C# 3.0, such as extension methods and LINQ queries. C# 3.0 features have been used throughout the book, where you've read about core .NET Framework features, data access to databases and XML, user interfaces with Windows Forms, Windows Presentation Foundation, ASP.NET, and Microsoft Office.

There's still more to read. The appendices cover ADO.NET Entities, a mapping technology to map objects to relational databases, applications for Windows Vista and Windows Server 2008, and a language comparison of C#, Visual Basic, and C++/CLI.

Part VII

Appendices

Appendix A: ADO.NET Entity Framework

Appendix B: C#, Visual Basic, and C++/CLI

Appendix C: Windows Vista and Windows Server 2008

ADO.NET Entity Framework

The ADO.NET Entity Framework is an object-relational mapping framework that is based on .NET 3.5. Chapter 27 demonstrated object-relational mapping with LINQ to SQL. LINQ to SQL offers simple mapping features for associations and inheritance. The ADO.NET Entity Framework gives you many more options for associations and inheritance. Another difference between LINQ to SQL and the ADO.NET Entity Framework is that the ADO.NET Entity Framework is a provider-based model that allows other database vendors to plug into it.

This appendix covers the following:

- ❑ The ADO.NET Entity Framework
- ❑ Entity Framework layers
- ❑ Entities
- ❑ Object contexts
- ❑ Relationships
- ❑ Object queries
- ❑ Updates
- ❑ LINQ to Entities

This appendix is based on the Beta 3 version of this framework, which is due to be released some months after the .NET 3.5 product, so some class or method names may be different than what you read here.

This appendix uses the Books, Formula1, and Northwind databases. You can download the Northwind database from msdn.microsoft.com; *the Books and Formula1 databases are included with the download of the code samples.*

Overview of the ADO.NET Entity Framework

The ADO.NET Entity Framework provides a mapping from the relational database schema to objects. Relational databases and object-oriented languages define associations differently. For example, the Microsoft sample database Northwind contains the `Customers` and `Orders` tables. To access all the Orders rows for a customer, you need to do a SQL join statement. With object-oriented languages, it is more common to define a `Customer` and an `Order` class and access the orders of a customer by using an `Orders` property from the `Customer` class.

For object-relational mapping since .NET 1.0, it was possible to use the `DataSet` class and typed datasets. Datasets are very similar to the structure of a database containing `DataTable`, `DataRow`, `DataColumn`, and `DataRelation` classes. The ADO.NET Entity Framework gives support to directly define entity classes that are completely independent of a database structure and map them to tables and associations of the database. Using objects with the application, the application is shielded from changes in the database.

The ADO.NET Entity Framework makes use of Entity SQL to define entity-based queries to the store. LINQ to Entities makes it possible to use the LINQ syntax to query data.

An object context keeps knowledge about entities that are changed, to have information when the entities should be written back to the store.

The namespaces that contain classes from the ADO.NET Entity Framework are listed in the following table.

Namespace	Description
`System.Data`	This is a main namespace for ADO.NET. With the ADO.NET Entity Framework, this namespace contains exception classes related to entities — for example `MappingException` and `QueryException`.
`System.Data.Common`	This namespace contains classes shared by .NET data providers. The class `DbProviderServices` is an abstract base class that must be implemented by an ADO.NET Entity Framework provider.
`System.Data.Common.CommandTrees`	This namespace contains classes to build an expression tree.
`System.Data.Entity.Design`	This namespace contains classed used by the designer to create Entity Data Model (EDM) files.
`System.Data.EntityClient`	This namespace specifies classes for the .NET Framework Data Provider to access the Entity Framework. `EntityConnection`, `EntityCommand`, and `EntityDataReader` can be used to access the Entity Framework.
`System.Data.Objects`	This namespace contains classes to query and update databases. The class `ObjectContext` encapsulates the connection to the database and serves as a gateway for create, read, update, and delete methods. The class `ObjectQuery` represents a query against the store. `CompiledQuery` is a cached query.
`System.Data.Objects.DataClasses`	This namespace contains classes and interfaces required for entities.

Entity Framework Layers

The ADO.NET Entity Framework offers several layers to map database tables to objects. You can start with a database schema and use a Visual Studio item template to create the complete mapping. You can also start designing entity classes with the designer and map it to the database where the tables and associations between the tables can have a very different structure.

The layers that need to be defined are as follows:

❑ *Logical* — This layer defines the relational data.

❑ *Conceptual* — This layer defines the .NET classes.

❑ *Mapping* — This layer defines the mapping from .NET classes to relational tables and associations.

Let's start with a simple database schema, as shown in Figure A-1 with the tables Books and Authors, and an association table BookAuthors that maps the authors to books.

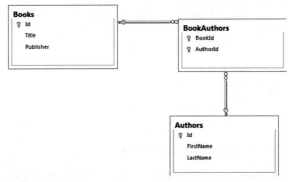

Figure A-1

Logical

The logical layer is defined by the Store Schema Definition Language (SSDL) and describes the structure of the database tables and their relations.

The following code uses SSDL to describe the three tables: Books, Authors, and BookAuthors. The EntityContainer element describes all the tables with EntitySet elements, and associations with AssociationSet elements. The parts of a table are defined with the EntityType element. With EntityType Books you can see the columns Id, Title, and Publisher defined by the Property element. The Property element contains XML attributes to define the data type. The Key element defines the key of the table.

```
<Schema Namespace="BookEntities.Store" Alias="Self"
    ProviderManifestToken="09.00.3054"
    xmlns="http://schemas.microsoft.com/ado/2006/04/edm/ssdl">
  <EntityContainer Name="dbo">
    <EntitySet Name="Authors" EntityType="Wrox.ProCSharp.Entities.Store.Authors" />
    <EntitySet Name="BookAuthors"
        EntityType=" Wrox.ProCSharp.Entities.Store.BookAuthors" />
    <EntitySet Name="Books" EntityType=" Wrox.ProCSharp.Entities.Store.Books" />
    <AssociationSet Name="FK_BookAuthors_Authors"
```

(continued)

(continued)

```
            Association=" Wrox.ProCSharp.Entities.Store.FK_BookAuthors_Authors">
        <End Role="Authors" EntitySet="Authors" />
        <End Role="BookAuthors" EntitySet="BookAuthors" />
      </AssociationSet>
      <AssociationSet Name="FK_BookAuthors_Books"
            Association="BookDemoEntities.Store.FK_BookAuthors_Books">
        <End Role="Books" EntitySet="Books" />
        <End Role="BookAuthors" EntitySet="BookAuthors" />
      </AssociationSet>
    </EntityContainer>
    <EntityType Name="Authors">
      <Key><PropertyRef Name="Id" /></Key>
      <Property Name="Id" Type="int" Nullable="false" StoreGeneratedPattern="Identity" />
      <Property Name="FirstName" Type="nvarchar" Nullable="false" MaxLength="50" />
      <Property Name="LastName" Type="nvarchar" Nullable="false" MaxLength="50" />
    </EntityType>
    <EntityType Name="BookAuthors">
      <Key><PropertyRef Name="BookId" /><PropertyRef Name="AuthorId" /></Key>
      <Property Name="BookId" Type="int" Nullable="false" />
      <Property Name="AuthorId" Type="int" Nullable="false" />
    </EntityType>
    <EntityType Name="Books">
      <Key><PropertyRef Name="Id" /></Key>
      <Property Name="Id" Type="int" Nullable="false" StoreGeneratedPattern="Identity" />
      <Property Name="Title" Type="nvarchar" Nullable="false" MaxLength="50" />
      <Property Name="Publisher" Type="nvarchar" Nullable="false" MaxLength="50" />
    </EntityType>
    <Association Name="FK_BookAuthors_Authors">
      <End Role="Authors"
          Type=" Wrox.ProCSharp.Entities.Store.Authors" Multiplicity="1" />
      <End Role="BookAuthors"
          Type=" Wrox.ProCSharp.Entities.Store.BookAuthors"
          Multiplicity="*" />
      <ReferentialConstraint>
        <Principal Role="Authors"><PropertyRef Name="Id" /></Principal>
        <Dependent Role="BookAuthors"><PropertyRef Name="AuthorId" /></Dependent>
      </ReferentialConstraint>
    </Association>
    <Association Name="FK_BookAuthors_Books">
      <End Role="Books" Type=" Wrox.ProCSharp.Entities.Store.Books" Multiplicity="1" />
      <End Role="BookAuthors" Type=" Wrox.ProCSharp.Entities.Store.BookAuthors"
          Multiplicity="*" />
      <ReferentialConstraint>
        <Principal Role="Books"><PropertyRef Name="Id" /></Principal>
        <Dependent Role="BookAuthors"><PropertyRef Name="BookId" /></Dependent>
      </ReferentialConstraint>
    </Association>
  </Schema>
```

Conceptual

The conceptual layer defines .NET classes. This layer is created with the Conceptual Schema Definition Language (CSDL).

Figure A-2 shows the entities `Author` and `Book` defined with the ADO.NET Entity Data Model Designer.

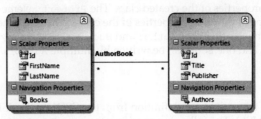

Figure A-2

The following is the CSDL content to define the entity types `Book` and `Author`. This was created from the Books database.

```
<Schema Namespace="BookEntities" Alias="Self"
    xmlns="http://schemas.microsoft.com/ado/2006/04/edm">
  <EntityContainer Name="BookEntities">
    <EntitySet Name="Authors" EntityType="Wrox.ProCSharp.Entities.Author" />
    <EntitySet Name="Books" EntityType="Wrox.ProCSharp.Entities.Book" />
    <AssociationSet Name="BookAuthors"
        Association=" Wrox.ProCSharp.Entities.BookAuthors">
      <End Role="Authors" EntitySet="Authors" />
      <End Role="Books" EntitySet="Books" />
    </AssociationSet>
  </EntityContainer>
  <EntityType Name="Author">
    <Key>
      <PropertyRef Name="Id" />
    </Key>
    <Property Name="Id" Type="Int32" Nullable="false" />
    <Property Name="FirstName" Type="String" Nullable="false" MaxLength="50" />
    <Property Name="LastName" Type="String" Nullable="false" MaxLength="50" />
    <NavigationProperty Name="Books" Relationship="BookDemoEntities
      .BookAuthors" FromRole="Authors" ToRole="Books" />
  </EntityType>

  <EntityType Name="Book">
    <Key>
      <PropertyRef Name="Id" />
    </Key>
    <Property Name="Id" Type="Int32" Nullable="false" />
    <Property Name="Title" Type="String" Nullable="false" MaxLength="50" />
    <Property Name="Publisher" Type="String" Nullable="false" MaxLength="50" />
    <NavigationProperty Name="Authors"
        Relationship=" Wrox.ProCSharp.Entities.BookAuthors" FromRole="Books"
        ToRole="Authors" />
  </EntityType>

  <Association Name="BookAuthors">
```

(continued)

(continued)

```
                <End Type=" Wrox.ProCSharp.Entities.Author" Role="Authors" Multiplicity="*" />
                <End Type=" Wrox.ProCSharp.Entities.Book" Role="Books" Multiplicity="*" />
            </Association>
        </Schema>
```

The entity is defined by an `EntityType` element that contains `Key`, `Property`, and `NavigationProperty` elements to describe the properties of the created class. The `Property` element contains attributes to describe the name and type of the .NET properties of the classes that are generated by the designer. The `Association` element connects the types `Author` and `Book`. `Multiplicity="*"` means that one `Author` can write multiple `Books`, and one `Book` can be written by multiple `Authors`.

Mapping

The mapping layer maps the entity type definition from the CSDL to the SSDL by using the Mapping Specification Language (MSL). The following specification includes a `Mapping` element that contains the `EntityTypeMapping` element to reference the `Book` type of the CSDL and defines the `MappingFragment` to reference the `Authors` table from the SSDL. The `ScalarProperty` maps the property of the .NET class with the `Name` attribute to the column of the database table with the `ColumnName` attribute.

```
<Mapping Space="C-S" xmlns="urn:schemas-microsoft-com:windows:storage:mapping:CS">
    <EntityContainerMapping StorageEntityContainer="dbo"
        CdmEntityContainer="BookEntities">
      <EntitySetMapping Name="Authors">
        <EntityTypeMapping TypeName="IsTypeOf(Wrox.ProCSharp.Entities.Author)">
          <MappingFragment StoreEntitySet="Authors">
            <ScalarProperty Name="LastName" ColumnName="LastName" />
            <ScalarProperty Name="FirstName" ColumnName="FirstName" />
            <ScalarProperty Name="Id" ColumnName="Id" />
          </MappingFragment>
        </EntityTypeMapping>
      </EntitySetMapping>
      <EntitySetMapping Name="Books">
        <EntityTypeMapping TypeName="IsTypeOf(Wrox.ProCSharp.Entities.Book)">
          <MappingFragment StoreEntitySet="Books">
            <ScalarProperty Name="Publisher" ColumnName="Publisher" />
            <ScalarProperty Name="Title" ColumnName="Title" />
            <ScalarProperty Name="Id" ColumnName="Id" />
          </MappingFragment>
        </EntityTypeMapping>
      </EntitySetMapping>
      <AssociationSetMapping Name="AuthorBook"
          TypeName=" Wrox.ProCSharp.Entities.AuthorBook"
          StoreEntitySet="BookAuthors" >
        <EndProperty Name="Book">
          <ScalarProperty Name="Id" ColumnName="BookId" />
        </EndProperty>
        <EndProperty Name="Author">
          <ScalarProperty Name="Id" ColumnName="AuthorId" />
        </EndProperty>
      </AssociationSetMapping>
    </EntityContainerMapping>
  </Mapping>
```

Entities

Entity classes that are created with the designer and are created by CSDL typically derive from the base class `EntityObject`, as shown with the `Book` class in the code that follows.

This class derives from the base class `EntityObject` and defines properties that fire change information in the set accessor. The created class `Book` is a partial class that can be extended in a new source file defining the same class in the same namespace. Methods that are called within the set accessor such as `OnTitleChanging()` and `OnTitleChanged()` are partial as well, so it is possible to implement these methods in the custom extension of the class. The `Authors` property uses the `RelationshipManager` class to return the `Books` for an author.

```
[EdmEntityTypeAttribute(NamespaceName="Wrox.ProCSharp.Entities", Name="Book")]
[DataContractAttribute()]
[Serializable()]
public partial class Book : global::System.Data.Objects.DataClasses.EntityObject
{
    public static Book CreateBook(int ID, string title, string publisher)
    {
        Book book = new Book();
        book.Id = ID;
        book.Title = title;
        book.Publisher = publisher;
        return book;
    }
    [EdmScalarPropertyAttribute(EntityKeyProperty=true, IsNullable=false)]
    [DataMemberAttribute()]
    public int Id
    {
        get
        {
            return this._Id;
        }
        set
        {
            this.OnIdChanging(value);
            this.ReportPropertyChanging("Id");
            this._Id = StructuralObject.SetValidValue(value);
            this.ReportPropertyChanged("Id");
            this.OnIdChanged();
        }
    }
    private int _Id;
    partial void OnIdChanging(int value);
    partial void OnIdChanged();
    [EdmScalarPropertyAttribute(IsNullable=false)]
    [DataMemberAttribute()]
    public string Title
    {
        get
        {
            return this._Title;
        }
        set
```

(continued)

(continued)

```
        {
            this.OnTitleChanging(value);
            this.ReportPropertyChanging("Title");
            this._Title = StructuralObject.SetValidValue(value, false, 50);
            this.ReportPropertyChanged("Title");
            this.OnTitleChanged();
        }
    }
    private string _Title;
    partial void OnTitleChanging(string value);
    partial void OnTitleChanged();
    [EdmScalarPropertyAttribute(IsNullable=false)]
    [DataMemberAttribute()]
    public string Publisher
    {
        get
        {
            return this._Publisher;
        }
        set
        {
            this.OnPublisherChanging(value);
            this.ReportPropertyChanging("Publisher");
            this._Publisher = StructuralObject.SetValidValue(value, false, 50);
            this.ReportPropertyChanged("Publisher");
            this.OnPublisherChanged();
        }
    }
    private string _Publisher;
    partial void OnPublisherChanging(string value);
    partial void OnPublisherChanged();
    [EdmRelationshipNavigationPropertyAttribute("BookDemoEntities", "AuthorBook",
        "Author")]
    [XmlIgnoreAttribute()]
    [SoapIgnoreAttribute()]
    [BrowsableAttribute(false)]
    public EntityCollection<Author> Authors
    {
        get
        {
            return ((IEntityWithRelationships)(this)).RelationshipManager.
                GetRelatedCollection<Author>("WroxProCSharp.Entities.AuthorBook",
                "Author");
        }
    }
}
```

The classes and interfaces important in regard to entity classes are explained in the following table. With the exception of INotifyPropertyChanging and INotifyPropertyChanged, the types are defined in the namespace System.Data.Objects.DataClasses.

Class or Interface	Description
StructuralObject	StructuralObject is the base class of the classes EntityObject and ComplexObject. This class implements the interfaces INotifyPropertyChanging and INotifyPropertyChanged.
INotifyPropertyChanging INotifyPropertyChanged	These interfaces define the PropertyChanging and PropertyChanged events to allow subscribing to information when the state of the object changes. Different from the other classes and interfaces here, these interfaces are defined in the namespace System.ComponentModel.
EntityObject	This class derives from StructuralObject and implements the interfaces IEntityWithKey, IEntityWithChangeTracker, and IEntityWithRelationships. EntityObject is a commonly used base class for objects mapped to database tables that contain a key and relationships to other objects.
ComplexObject	This class can be used as a base class for entity objects that do not have a key. It derives from StructuralObject but does not implement other interfaces as the EntityObject class does.
IEntityWithKey	This interface defines an EntityKey property that allows fast access to the object.
IEntityWithChangeTracker	This interface defines the method SetChangeTracker() where a change tracker that implements the interface IChangeTracker can be assigned to get information about state change from the object.
IEntityWithRelationships	This interface defines the read-only property RelationshipManager, which returns a RelationshipManager object that can be used to navigate between objects.

For an entity class, it's not necessary to derive from the base classes EntityObject or ComplexObject. Instead, an entity class can implement the required interfaces.

The Book entity class can easily be accessed by using the object context class BookEntities. The Books property returns a collection of Book objects that can be iterated:

```
BookEntities data = new BookEntities();

foreach (var book in data.Books)
{
    Console.WriteLine("{0}, {1}", book.Title, book.Publisher);
}
```

Running the program, books queried from the database are shown at the console:

```
Professional C# 2008, Wrox Press
Beginning Visual C# 2008, Wrox Press
Working with Animation in Silverlight 1.0, Wrox Press
Professional WPF Programming, Wrox Press
```

Object Context

To retrieve data from the database, the `ObjectContext` class is needed. This class defines the mapping from the entity objects to the database. With ADO.NET, you can compare this class to the data adapter that fills a `DataSet`.

The `BookEntities` class created by the designer derives from the base class `ObjectContext`. This class adds constructors to pass a connection string. With the default constructor, the connection string is read from the configuration file. It is also possible to pass an already opened connection to the constructor in the form of an `EntityConnection` instance. If you pass a connection to the constructor that is not opened, the object context opens and closes the connection; if you pass an opened connection you also need to close it.

The created class defines `Books` and `Authors` properties, which return an `ObjectQuery`, and methods to add authors and books — `AddToAuthors()` and `AddToBooks()`.

```
public partial class BookEntities : ObjectContext
{
    public BookEntities() :
            base("name=BookEntities", "BookEntities") { }
    public BookEntities(string connectionString) :
            base(connectionString, "BookEntities") { }
    public BookEntities(EntityConnection connection) :
            base(connection, "BookEntities") { }
    [BrowsableAttribute(false)]
    public ObjectQuery<Author> Authors
    {
        get
        {
            if ((this._Authors == null))
            {
                this._Authors = base.CreateQuery<Author>("[Authors]");
            }
            return this._Authors;
        }
    }
    private ObjectQuery<Author> _Authors;
    [BrowsableAttribute(false)]
    public ObjectQuery<Book> Books
    {
        get
        {
            if ((this._Books == null))
            {
                this._Books = base.CreateQuery<Book>("[Books]");
            }
            return this._Books;
        }
    }
    private ObjectQuery<Book> _Books;
    public void AddToAuthors(Author author)
    {
        base.AddObject("Authors", author);
    }
```

```
        public void AddToBooks(Book book)
        {
            base.AddObject("Books", book);
        }
    }
```

In case you pass a connection string to the constructor of the BookEntities class, the connection string of type EntityConnection defines the keyword Metadata, which requires three things: a delimited list of mapping files, Provider for the invariant provider name to access the data source, and Provider connection string to assign the provider-dependent connection string.

```
EntityConnection conn = new EntityConnection(
        "Metadata=./BookModel.csdl|./BookModel.ssdl|./BookModel.msl;" +
        "Provider=System.Data.SqlClient;" +
        "Provider connection string=\"Data Source=(local);" +
        "Initial Catalog=EntitiesDemo;Integrated Security=True\"");
```

The ObjectContext class provides several services to the caller:

❑ It keeps track of entity objects that are already retrieved. If the object is queried again, it is taken from the object context.

❑ It keeps state information about the entities. You can get information about added, modified, and deleted objects.

❑ You can update the entities from the object context to write the changes to the underlying store.

Methods and properties of the ObjectContext class are listed in the following table.

ObjectContext Methods and Properties	Description
Connection	Returns a DbConnection object that is associated with the object context.
MetadataWorkspace	Returns a MetadataWorkspace object that can be used to read the metadata and mapping information.
QueryTimeout	With this property you can get and set the timeout value for the queries of the object context.
ObjectStateManager	This property returns an ObjectStateManager. The ObjectStateManager keeps track of entity objects retrieved and object changes in the object context.
CreateQuery()	This method returns an ObjectQuery to get data from the store. The Books and Authors properties shown earlier use this method to return an ObjectQuery.
GetObjectByKey() TryGetObjectByKey()	These methods return the object by the key either from the object state manager or the underlying store. GetObjectByKey() throws an exception of type ObjectNotFoundException if the key does not exist. TryGetObjectByKey() returns false.
AddObject()	This method adds a new entity object to the object context. This method is invoked by the AddToAuthors() and AddToBooks() methods.

ObjectContext Methods and Properties	Description
DeleteObject()	This method deletes an object from the object context.
Detach()	This method detaches an entity object from the object context, so it is no longer tracked if changes occur.
Attach() AttachTo()	The Attach() method attaches a detached object to the store. Attaching objects back to the object context requires that the entity object implements the interface IEntityWithKey. The AttachTo() method does not have the requirement for a key with the object, but it requires the entity set name where the entity object needs to be attached.
ApplyPropertyChanges()	If an object was detached from the object context, then the detached object is modified, and afterwards the changes should be applied to the object within the object context, you can invoke the ApplyPropertyChanges() method to apply the changes. This is useful in a scenario where a detached object was returned from a Web service, changed from a client, and passed to the Web service in a modified way.
Refresh()	The data in the store can change while entity objects are stored inside the object context. To make a refresh from the store, the Refresh() method can be used. With this method you can pass a RefreshMode enumeration value. If the values for the objects are not the same between the store and the object context, passing the value ClientWins changes the data in the store. The value StoreWins changes the data in the object context.
SaveChanges()	Adding, modifying, and deleting objects from the object context does not change the object from the underlying store. Use the SaveChanges() method to persist the changes to the store.
AcceptAllChanges()	This method changes the state of the objects in the context to unmodified. SaveChanges() invokes this method implicitly.

Relationships

The entity types Book and Author are related to each other. A book is written by one or more authors, and an author can write one or more books. Relationships are based on the count of types they relate and the multiplicity. The first version of the ADO.NET Entity Framework supports a Table per Type (TPT) and Table per Hierarchy (TPH). Multiplicity can be one-to-one, one-to-many, or many-to-many.

Table per Hierarchy

With TPH, there's one table in the database that corresponds to a hierarchy of entity classes. The database table Payments (see Figure A-3) contains columns for a hierarchy of entity types. Some of the columns are common to all entities in the hierarchy, such as Id and Amount. The CreditCard column is only used by a credit card payment.

Figure A-3

The entity classes that all map to the same `Payments` table are shown in Figure A-4. `Payment` is an abstract base class to contain properties common for all types in the hierarchy. Concrete classes that derive from `Payment` are `CreditCardPayment`, `CashPayment`, and `ChequePayment`. `CreditCardPayment` has a `CreditCard` property in addition to the properties of the base class; `ChequePayment` has a `BankName` property.

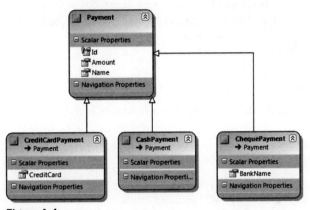

Figure A-4

The selection of the type of the concrete class is done based on a `Condition` element as you can see with the MSL file. Here, the type is selected based on the value of the `Type` column. Other options to select the type are also possible; for example, you can verify if a column is not null.

```
<Mapping Space="C-S"
  xmlns="urn:schemas-microsoft-com:windows:storage:mapping:CS">
  <EntityContainerMapping StorageEntityContainer="dbo"
      CdmEntityContainer="EntitiesDemoEntities">
    <EntitySetMapping Name="Payments">
      <EntityTypeMapping TypeName="IsTypeOf(Wrox.ProCSharp.Entities.Payment)">
        <MappingFragment StoreEntitySet="Payments">
          <ScalarProperty Name="Id" ColumnName="Id" />
          <ScalarProperty Name="Amount" ColumnName="Amount" />
          <ScalarProperty Name="Name" ColumnName="Name" />
        </MappingFragment>
      </EntityTypeMapping>
      <EntityTypeMapping
        TypeName="IsTypeOf(Wrox.ProCSharp.Entities.CashPayment)">
        <MappingFragment StoreEntitySet="Payments">
          <ScalarProperty Name="Id" ColumnName="Id" />
```

(continued)

(continued)

```
                    <Condition ColumnName="Type" Value="CASH" />
            </MappingFragment>
        </EntityTypeMapping>
        <EntityTypeMapping
            TypeName="IsTypeOf(Wrox.ProCSharp.Entities.CreditCardPayment)">
            <MappingFragment StoreEntitySet="Payments">
            <ScalarProperty Name="Id" ColumnName="Id" />
            <ScalarProperty Name="CreditCard" ColumnName="CreditCard" />
                    <Condition ColumnName="Type" Value="CREDIT" />
            </MappingFragment>
        </EntityTypeMapping>
        <EntityTypeMapping
            TypeName="IsTypeOf(Wrox.ProCSharp.Entities.ChequePayment)">
            <MappingFragment StoreEntitySet="Payments">
            <ScalarProperty Name="Id" ColumnName="Id" />
            <ScalarProperty Name="BankName" ColumnName="BankName" />
                    <Condition ColumnName="Type" Value="CHEQUE" />
            </MappingFragment>
        </EntityTypeMapping>
        </EntitySetMapping>
      </EntityContainerMapping>
    </Mapping>
```

Now it's possible to iterate the data from the `Payments` table, and different types are returned based on the mapping:

```
PaymentEntities data = new PaymentEntities();
foreach (var p in data.Payments)
{
    Console.WriteLine("{0}, {1} - {2:C}", p.GetType().Name,
        p.Name, p.Amount);
}
```

Running the application returns two `CashPayment` and one `CreditCardPayment` object from the database:

```
CreditCardPayment, Gustav - $22.00
CashPayment, Donald - $0.50
CashPayment, Dagobert - $80,000.00
```

Table per Type

With TPT, one table maps to one type. The Northwind database has a schema with the tables `Customers`, `Orders`, and `Order Details` (see Figure A-5). The `Orders` table maps to the `Customers` table with the foreign key `CustomerId`; the `Order Details` table maps to the `Orders` table with the foreign key `OrderID`.

Figure A-6 shows the entity types `Customer`, `Order`, and `OrderDetail`. `Customer` and `Order` have a zero or one-to-many relationship; `Order` to `OrderDetail` has a one-to-many relationship. There is a zero or one-to-many relationship with `Customer` and `Order` because the `CustomerID` with the `Order` table is defined as `Nullable` in the database schema.

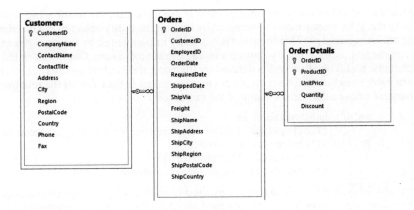

Figure A-5

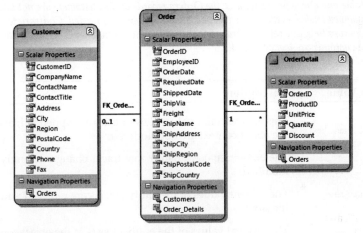

Figure A-6

You access the customers and their orders with two iterations shown here. First the `Customer` objects are accessed, and the value of the `CompanyName` property is written to the console. Then all orders are accessed by using the `Orders` property of the `Customer` class. Because the related orders are not loaded to the object context by default, the `Load()` method of the `EntityCollection<Order>` object is returned from the `Orders` property.

```
NorthwindEntities data = new NorthwindEntities();
foreach (Customer customer in data.Customers)
{
    Console.WriteLine("{0}", customer.CompanyName);
    if (!customer.Orders.IsLoaded)
        customer.Orders.Load();
    foreach (Order order in customer.Orders)
    {
        Console.WriteLine("{0} {1:d}", order.OrderID, order.OrderDate);
    }
}
```

Behind the scenes, the `RelationshipManager` class is used to access the relationship. The `RelationShipManager` instance can be accessed by casting the entity object to the interface `IEntityWithRelationships`. This interface is explicitly implemented by the class `EntityObject`. The `RelationshipManager` property returns a `RelationshipManager` that is associated with the entity object at one end. The other end is defined by invoking the method `GetRelatedCollection()`. The first parameter `NorthwindModel.FK_Orders_Customers` is the name of the relationship: the second parameter `Orders` defines the name of the target role.

```
RelationshipManager rm =
        ((IEntityWithRelationships)customer).RelationshipManager;
EntityCollection<Order> orders =
        rm.GetRelatedCollection<Order>(
        "NorthwindModel.FK_Orders_Customers", "Orders");
```

Relationships are delayed loaded. The `Load()` method of the `EntityCollection` class gets the data from the store. One overload of the `Load()` method accepts a `MergeOption` enumeration. The possible values are explained in the following table.

> By default, relationships are delayed loaded. For example, if you define a relation with the Customers and Orders table and query for customers, the Orders records of the customers are not loaded. The term used here is delayed loaded as the orders can be loaded afterwards as needed. Contrary to delay loading you have the option to eager fetch records. Eager fetching means that as you access a customer record, orders for the customer are loaded as well.

MergeOption Value	Description
AppendOnly	This is the default value. New entities are appended; existing entities in the object context are not modified.
NoTracking	The `ObjectStateManager` that tracks changes to entity objects is not modified.
OverwriteChanges	The current values of the entity objects are replaced with the values from the store.
PreserveChanges	The original values of the entity objects in the object context are replaced with the values from the store.

Object Query

Querying objects is one of the services offered by the ADO.NET Entity Framework. Queries can be done using LINQ to Entities, Entity SQL, and Query Builder methods that create Entity SQL. LINQ to Entities is covered in the last section of this appendix; let's get into the other two options first.

The following sections of this book make use of a Formula 1 database where you can see the entities created from the designer in Figure A-7.

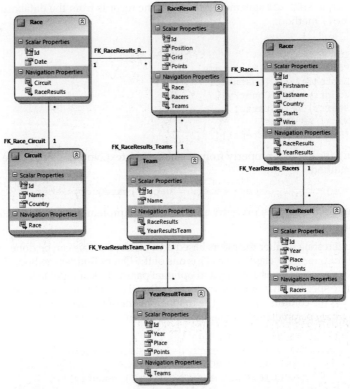

Figure A-7

Queries can be defined with the `ObjectQuery<T>` class. Let's start with a simple query to access all `Racer` entities. With this example, the connection is already opened, passing it to the object context `Formula1Entities`. This way it is possible to retrieve the generated SQL statement of the `ObjectQuery<Racer>` class with the `ToTraceString()` method. This method requires an open connection.

```
ConnectionStringSettings connSettings =
        ConfigurationManager.ConnectionStrings["Formula1Entities"];
EntityConnection connection =
        new EntityConnection(connSettings.ConnectionString);
connection.Open();
using (Formula1Entities data = new Formula1Entities(connection))
{
        ObjectQuery<Racer> racers = data.Racers;
        Console.WriteLine(racers.CommandText);
        Console.WriteLine(racers.ToTraceString());
        connection.Close();
}
```

The Entity SQL statement that is returned from the `CommandText` property is shown here:

```
[Racers]
```

And this is the generated SELECT statement to retrieve the records from the database that is shown by the ToTraceString() method:

```
SELECT
[Extent1].[Id] AS [Id],
[Extent1].[Firstname] AS [Firstname],
[Extent1].[Lastname] AS [Lastname],
[Extent1].[Country] AS [Country],
[Extent1].[Starts] AS [Starts],
[Extent1].[Wins] AS [Wins]
FROM [dbo].[Racers] AS [Extent1]
```

Instead of accessing the Racers property from the object context, you can also create a query with the CreateQuery() method:

```
ObjectQuery<Racer> racers = data.CreateQuery<Racer>("[Racers]");
```

This is similar to using the Racers property and, in fact, the implementation of the Racers property creates a query this way.

Now it would be interesting to filter the racers based on a condition. This can be done by using the Where() method of the ObjectQuery<T> class. Where() is one of the Query Builder methods that create Entity SQL. This method requires a predicate as a string, and optional parameters of type ObjectParameter. The predicate shown here specifies that only the racers from Brazil are returned. it specifies the item of the result, and Country is the column Country. The first parameter of the ObjectParameter constructor references the @Country parameter of the predicate, but doesn't list the @ sign.

```
string country = "Brazil";
ObjectQuery<Racer> racers = data.Racers.Where(
    "it.Country = @Country",
    new ObjectParameter("Country", country));
```

The magic behind it can be seen immediately by accessing the CommandText property of the query. With Entity SQL, SELECT VALUE it declares it to access the columns.

```
SELECT VALUE it
FROM (
[Racers]
) AS it
WHERE
it.Country = @Country
```

The method ToTraceString() shows the generated SQL statement:

```
SELECT
[Extent1].[Id] AS [Id],
[Extent1].[Firstname] AS [Firstname],
[Extent1].[Lastname] AS [Lastname],
[Extent1].[Country] AS [Country],
[Extent1].[Starts] AS [Starts],
[Extent1].[Wins] AS [Wins]
FROM [dbo].[Racers] AS [Extent1]
WHERE [Extent1].[Country] = @Country
```

Of course you can also specify the complete Entity SQL:

```
string country = "Brazil";
ObjectQuery<Racer> racers = data.CreateQuery<Racer>(
    "SELECT VALUE it FROM ([Racers]) AS it WHERE it.Country = @Country",
    new ObjectParameter("Country", country));
```

The class `ObjectQuery<T>` offers several Query Builder methods as explained in the following table. Many of these methods are very similar to the LINQ extension methods that you learned about in Chapter 11, "Language Integrated Query."

ObjectQuery<T> Query Builder Methods	Description
Where()	This method allows you to filter the results based on a condition.
Distinct()	This method creates a query with unique results.
Except()	This method returns the result without the items that meet the condition with the except filter.
GroupBy()	This method creates a new query to group entities based on a specified criteria.
Include()	With relations you've seen earlier that related items are delay loaded, it was required to invoke the Load() method of the EntityCollection<T> class to get related entities into the object context. Instead of using the Load() method, you can specify a query with the Include() method to eager fetch related entities.
OfType()	This method specifies to return only those entities of a specific type. This is very helpful with TPH relations.
OrderBy()	This method is for defining the sort order of the entities.
Select() SelectValue()	These methods return a projection of the results. Select() returns the result items in the form of a DbDataRecord; SelectValue() returns the values as scalars or complex types as defined by the generic parameter TResultType.
Skip() Top()	These methods are useful for paging. Skip a number of items with the Skip() method and take a specified number as defined by the Top() method.
Intersect() Union() UnionAll()	These methods are used to combine two queries. Intersect() returns a query containing only the results that are available in both of the queries. Union() combines the queries and returns the complete result without duplicates. UnionAll() also includes duplicates.

Let's get into one example on how to use these Query Builder methods. Here, the racers are filtered with the `Where()` method to return only racers from the USA; the `OrderBy()` method specifies descending sort order first based on the number of wins, next the number of starts. Finally, only the first three racers are in the result using the `Top()` method.

```
using (Formula1Entities data = new Formula1Entities())
{
    string country = "USA";
    ObjectQuery<Racer> racers = data.Racers.Where("it.Country = @Country",
        new ObjectParameter("Country", country))
        .OrderBy("it.Wins DESC, it.Starts DESC")
        .Top("3");
```

(continued)

(continued)

```
            foreach (var racer in racers)
            {
                Console.WriteLine("{0} {1}, wins: {2}, starts: {3}",
                        racer.Firstname, racer.Lastname, racer.Wins, racer.Starts);
            }
        }
```

This is the result from this query:

```
Mario Andretti, wins: 12, starts: 128
Dan Gurney, wins: 4, starts: 87
Phil Hill, wins: 3, starts: 48
```

Updates

Reading, searching, and filtering data from the store are just one part of the work that usually needs to be done with data-intensive applications. Writing changed data back to the store is the other part you need to know.

The sections that follow cover these topics:

❑   Object tracking

❑   Change information

❑   Attaching and detaching entities

❑   Storing entity changes

Object Tracking

To allow data read from the store to be modified and saved, the entities must be tracked after they are loaded. This also requires that the object context be aware if an entity has already been loaded from the store. If multiple queries are accessing the same records, the object context needs to return already loaded entities.

The ObjectStateManager is used by the object context to keep track of entities that are loaded into the context.

The following sample demonstrates that indeed if two different queries are done that return the same record from the database, the state manager is aware of that and does not create a new entity. Instead, the same entity is returned. The ObjectStateManager instance that is associated with the object context can be accessed with the ObjectStateManager property. The ObjectStateManager class defines an event named ObjectStateManagerChanged that is invoked every time a new object is added or removed from the object context. Here, the method ObjectStateManager_ ObjectStateManagerChanged is assigned to the event to get information about changes.

Two different queries are used to return an entity object. The first query gets the first racer from the country Austria with the last name Lauda. The second query asks for the racers from Austria, sorts the racers by the number of races won, and gets the first result. As a matter of fact, that's the same racer. To verify that the same entity object is returned, the method Object.ReferenceEquals() is used to verify if the two object references indeed reference the same instance.

```
static void Tracking()
{
    using (Formula1Entities data = new Formula1Entities())
    {
        data.ObjectStateManager.ObjectStateManagerChanged +=
            ObjectStateManager_ObjectStateManagerChanged;
        Racer niki1 = data.Racers.Where(
            "it.Country='Austria' && it.Lastname='Lauda'").First();
        Racer niki2 = data.Racers.Where("it.Country='Austria'").
            OrderBy("it.Wins DESC").First();
        if (Object.ReferenceEquals(niki1, niki2))
        {
            Console.WriteLine("the same object");
        }
    }
}
static void ObjectStateManager_ObjectStateManagerChanged(object sender,
        CollectionChangeEventArgs e)
{
    Console.WriteLine("Object State change - action: {0}", e.Action);
    Racer r = e.Element as Racer;
    if (r != null)
        Console.WriteLine("Racer {0}", r.Lastname);
}
```

Running the application you can see that the event of the ObjectStateManagerChanged of the ObjectStateManager occurs only once, and the references niki1 and niki2 are indeed the same:

```
Object state change - action: Add
Racer Lauda
The same object
```

Change Information

The object context is also aware of changes with the entities. The following sample adds and modifies a racer from the object context and gets information about the change. First, a new racer is added with the AddToRacers() method of the Formula1Entities class. This designer-generated method invokes the AddObject() method of the base class ObjectContext. This method adds a new entity with the EntityState.Added information. Next, a racer with the Lastname Alonso is queried. With this entity class, the Starts property is incremented and thus the entity is marked with the information EntityState.Modified. Behind the scenes, the ObjectStateManager is informed about a state change in the object based on the interface implementations INotifyPropertyChanged. This interface is implemented in the entity base class StructuralObject. The ObjectStateManager is attached to the PropertyChanged event, and this event is fired with every property change.

To get all added or modified entity objects, you can invoke the GetObjectStateEntries() method of the ObjectStateManager and pass an EntityState enumeration value as it is done here. This method returns a collection of ObjectStateEntry objects that keep information about the entities. The helper method DisplayState iterates through this collection to give detail information.

You can also get state information about a single entity passing the EntityKey to the GetObjectStateEntry() method. The EntityKey property is available with entity objects implementing the interface IEntityWithKey, which is the case with the base class EntityObject. The ObjectStateEntry object returned offers the method GetModifiedProperties() where you can read all property values that have been changed, and also access the original and the current information about the properties with the OriginalValues and CurrentValues indexers.

```
static void ChangeInformation()
{
    using (Formula1Entities data = new Formula1Entities())
    {
        Racer sebastien = new Racer()
        {
            Firstname = "Sébastien",
            Lastname = "Bourdais",
            Country = "France",
            Starts = 0
        };
        data.AddToRacers(sebastien);
        Racer fernando = data.Racers.Where("it.Lastname='Alonso'").First();
        fernando.Starts++;
        DisplayState(EntityState.Added.ToString(),
                data.ObjectStateManager.GetObjectStateEntries(
                    EntityState.Added));
        DisplayState(EntityState.Modified.ToString(),
                data.ObjectStateManager.GetObjectStateEntries(
                    EntityState.Modified));
        ObjectStateEntry stateOfFernando =
                data.ObjectStateManager.GetObjectStateEntry(fernando.EntityKey);
        Console.WriteLine("state of Fernando: {0}",
                stateOfFernando.State.ToString());
        foreach (string modifiedProp in
            stateOfFernando.GetModifiedProperties())
        {
            Console.WriteLine("modified: {0}", modifiedProp);
            Console.WriteLine("original: {0}",
                    stateOfFernando.OriginalValues[modifiedProp]);
            Console.WriteLine("current: {0}",
                    stateOfFernando.CurrentValues[modifiedProp]);
        }
    }
}
static void DisplayState(string state, IEnumerable<ObjectStateEntry> entries)
{
    foreach (var entry in entries)
    {
        Racer r = entry.Entity as Racer;
        if (r != null)
        {
            Console.WriteLine("{0}: {1}", state, r.Lastname);
        }
    }
}
```

When you run the application, the added and modified racers are displayed, and the properties changed with their original and current values are shown.

```
Added: Bourdais
Modified: Alonso
state of Fernando: Modified
modified: Starts
original: 95
current: 96
```

Attaching and Detaching Entities

Returning entity data to the caller it might be important to detach the objects from the object context. This is necessary, for example, if an entity object is returned from a Web service. Here, if the entity object is changed on the client, the object context is not aware of the change.

With the sample code, the `Detach()` method of the `ObjectContext` detaches the entity named `fernando` and thus the object context is not aware of any change done on this entity. If a changed entity object is passed from the client application to the service, it can be attached again. Just attaching it to the object context might not be enough because this doesn't give the information that the object was modified. Instead, the original object must be available inside the object context. The original object can be accessed from the store by using the key with the method `GetObjectByKey()`. If the entity object is already inside the object context, the existing one is used; otherwise it is fetched newly from the database. Invoking the method `ApplyPropertyChanges()` passes the modified entity object to the object context, and if there are changes, the changes are done within the existing entity with the same key inside the object context, and the `EntityState` is set to `Modified`. Remember that the method `ApplyPropertyChanges()` requires the object to exist within the object context; otherwise the new entity object is added with `EntityState Added`.

```
using (Formula1Entities data = new Formula1Entities())
{
    data.ObjectStateManager.ObjectStateManagerChanged +=
        ObjectStateManager_ObjectStateManagerChanged;
    ObjectResult<Racer> racers = data.Racers.Where("it.Lastname='Alonso'");
    Racer fernando = racers.First();
    EntityKey key = fernando.EntityKey;
    data.Detach(fernando);
    // Racer is now detached and can be changed independent of the
    // object context
    fernando.Starts++;
    Racer originalObject = (Racer)data.GetObjectByKey(key);
    data.ApplyPropertyChanges(key.EntitySetName, fernando);
}
```

Storing Entity Changes

Based on all the change information with the help of the `ObjectStateManager`, the added, deleted, and modified entity objects can be written to the store with the `SaveChanges()` method of the `ObjectContext` class. To verify changes within the object context, you can assign a handler method to the `SavingChanges` event of the `ObjectContext` class. This event is fired before the data is written to the store, so you can add some verification logic to see if the changes should be really done. `SaveChanges()` returns the number of entity objects that have been written.

What happens if the records in the database that are represented by the entity classes have been changed after reading the record? The answer depends on the `ConcurrencyMode` property that is set with the model. With every property of an entity object, you can configure the `ConcurrencyMode` to `Fixed` or `None`. The value `Fixed` means that the property is validated at write time to determine if the value was not changed in the meantime. `None` — which is the default — ignores any change. If some properties are configured to the `Fixed` mode, and data changed between reading and writing the entity objects, an `OptimisticConcurrencyException` occurs. You can deal with this exception by invoking the `Refresh()` method to read the actual information from the database into the object context. This method accepts two refresh modes configured by a `RefreshMode` enumeration value: `ClientWins` or `StoreWins`. `StoreWins` means that the actual information is taken from the database and set to the current values of the entity objects. `ClientWins` means that the database information is set to the original values of the entity objects, and thus the database values will be overwritten with the next `SaveChanges`. The second parameter of the `Refresh()` method is either a collection of entity objects or a single entity object. You can decide the refresh behavior on entity by entity.

```
static void ChangeInformation()
{
    //...
        int changes = 0;
        try
        {
            changes = data.SaveChanges();
        }
        catch (OptimisticConcurrencyException ex)
        {
            data.Refresh(RefreshMode.ClientWins, ex.StateEntries);
            changes = data.SaveChanges();
        }
        Console.WriteLine("{0} entities changed", changes);
```

LINQ to Entities

In several chapters of this book you've seen LINQ to Query objects, databases, and XML. Of course, LINQ is also available to query entities.

With LINQ to Entities, the source for the LINQ query is `ObjectQuery<T>`. Because `ObjectQuery<T>` implements the interface `IQueryable`, the extension methods selected for the query are defined with the class `Queryable` from the namespace `System.Linq`. The extension methods defined with this class have a parameter `Expression<T>`; that's why the compiler writes an expression tree to the assembly. You can read more about expression trees in Chapter 11, "Language Integrated Query." The expression tree is then resolved from the `ObjectQuery<T>` class to the SQL query.

You can use a simple LINQ query as shown here to return the racers that won more than 40 races:

```
using (Formula1Entities data = new Formula1Entities())
{
    var racers = from r in data.Racers
                 where r.Wins > 40
                 orderby r.Wins descending
                 select r;
    foreach (Racer r in racers)
    {
        Console.WriteLine("{0} {1}", r.Firstname, r.Lastname);
    }
}
```

This is the result of accessing the Formula 1 database:

```
Michael Schumacher
Alain Prost
Ayrton Senna
```

You can also define a LINQ query to access relations as shown here. Variable `r` references racers, variable `rr` references all race results. The filter is defined with the `where` clause to retrieve only racers from

Switzerland who had a race position on the podium. To get the podium finishes, the result is grouped, and the podium count calculated. Sorting is done based on the podium finishes.

```
using (Formula1Entities data = new Formula1Entities())
{
    var query = from r in data.Racers
                from rr in r.RaceResults
                where rr.Position <= 3 && rr.Position >= 1 &&
                        r.Country == "Switzerland"
                group r by r.Id into g
                let podium = g.Count()
                orderby podium descending
                select new { Racer = g.FirstOrDefault(), Podiums = podium };
    foreach (var r in query)
    {
        Console.WriteLine("{0} {1} {2}", r.Racer.Firstname,
            r.Racer.Lastname,r.Podiums);
    }
}
```

The names of three racers from Switzerland are returned when you run the application:

```
Clay Regazzoni 28
Jo Siffert 6
Rudi Fischer 2
```

Summary

In this chapter, you've seen the features of the ADO.NET Entity Framework. Unlike LINQ to SQL, which is covered in Chapter 27, this framework offers a provider-based mapping, and other database vendors can implement their own providers.

The ADO.NET Entity Framework is based on mapping that is defined by CSDL, MSL, and SSDL — XML information to describe the entities, the mapping, and the database schema. Using this mapping technique, you can create different relation types to map entity classes to database tables.

You've seen how the object context keeps knowledge about entities retrieved and updated, and how the changes can be written to the store.

LINQ to Entities is just a facet of the ADO.NET Entity Framework that allows you to use the new query syntax to access entities.

B

C#, Visual Basic, and C++/CLI

C# is *the* programming language designed for .NET. More than 50 languages exist for writing .NET applications — for example, Eiffel, Smalltalk, COBOL, Haskell, Pizza, Pascal, Delphi, Oberon, Prolog, and Ruby. Microsoft alone delivers the languages C#, Visual Basic, C++/CLI, J#, and JScript.NET.

Every language has advantages and disadvantages; some things can be done easily with one language but are complicated with another one. The classes from the .NET Framework are always the same, but the syntax of the language abstracts various features from the Framework. For example, the C# `using` statement makes it easy to use the objects implementing the `IDisposable` interface. Other languages need more code for the same functionality.

The most commonly used .NET languages from Microsoft are C# and Visual Basic. C# was newly designed for .NET with ideas from C++, Java, Pascal, and other languages. Visual Basic has its roots in Visual Basic 6 and was extended with object-oriented features for .NET.

C++/CLI is an extension to C++ that is an ECMA standard (ECMA 372). The big advantage of C++/CLI is the ability to mix native code with managed code. You can extend existing native C++ applications and add .NET functionality, and you can add .NET classes to native libraries so that they can be used from other .NET languages such as C#. It is also possible to write completely managed applications with C++/CLI.

This chapter shows you how to convert .NET applications from one language to another. If you see sample code with Visual Basic or C++/CLI, you can easily map this to C#, and the other way around.

The following topics are covered in this chapter:

❑ Namespaces

❑ Defining types

❑ Methods

❑ Arrays

❑ Control statements

❑ Loops

❑ Exception handling

❑ Inheritance

❑ Resource management

❑ Delegates

❑ Events

❑ Generics

❑ LINQ Queries

❑ C++/CLI mixing native and managed code

For this chapter, I assume that you know C# and have read the first few chapters of this book. It is not necessary to know Visual Basic and C++/CLI.

Namespaces

.NET types are organized into namespaces. The syntax for defining and using namespaces is quite different between the three languages.

To import namespaces, C# uses the using keyword. C++/CLI is fully based on the C++ syntax with the using namespace statement. Visual Basic defines the Imports keyword to import namespaces.

With C#, you can define an alias to classes or other namespaces. With C++/CLI and Visual Basic namespace, an alias can reference other namespaces, but not classes. C++ requires the namespace keyword to define an alias — the same keyword is used to define a namespace. Visual Basic uses the Imports keyword again.

For defining namespaces, all three languages use the namespace keyword, but there's still a difference. With C++/CLI, you can't define hierarchical namespaces with one namespace statement; instead the namespaces must be nested. There's one important difference with the project settings: defining a namespace in the project settings of C# defines a default namespace that shows up in the code of all new items that you add to the project. With Visual Basic project settings, you define the root namespace that is used by all items in the project. Namespaces declared in the source code define only the sub-namespace inside the root namespace.

```
// C#
using System;
using System.Collections.Generic;
using Assm = Wrox.ProCSharp.Assemblies;
namespace Wrox.ProCSharp.Languages
{
}
// C++/CLI
using namespace System;
using namespace System::Collections::Generic;
namespace Assm = Wrox.ProCSharp.Assemblies;
namespace Wrox
{
    namespace ProCSharp
```

```
        {
            namespace Languages
            {
            }
        }
    }
    '' Visual Basic
    Imports System
    Imports System.Collections.Generic
    Imports Assm = Wrox.ProCSharp.Assemblies
    Namespace Wrox.ProCSharp.Languages
    End Namespace
```

Defining Types

.NET differentiates between reference types and value types. With C#, reference types are defined with classes, and value types with structs. In addition to reference and value types, this section also shows you how to define an interface (a reference type) and an enumeration (a value type).

Reference Types

To declare a reference type, C# and Visual Basic use the class keyword. In C++/CLI, a class and a struct are nearly the same; you don't have the separation between a reference type and a value type as you do with C# and Visual Basic. C++/CLI has a ref keyword to define a managed class. You can create a reference type by defining ref class or ref struct.

Both with C# and C++/CLI the class is surrounded by curly brackets. With C++/CLI don't forget the semicolon at the end of the class declaration. Visual Basic uses the End Class statement at the end of the class.

```
// C#
public class MyClass
{
}
// C++/CLI
public ref class MyClass
{
};
public ref struct MyClass2
{
};
' Visual Basic
Public Class MyClass
End Class
```

When using a reference type, a variable needs to be declared, and the object must be allocated on the managed heap. When declaring a handle to a reference type, C++/CLI defines the handle operator ^, which is somewhat similar to the C++ pointer *. The gcnew operator allocates the memory on the managed heap. With C++/CLI, it is also possible to declare a variable locally, but for reference types, the object is still allocated on the managed heap. With Visual Basic, the variable declaration starts with the statement Dim followed by the name of the variable. With new and the object type, memory is allocated on the managed heap.

```
// C#
MyClass obj = new MyClass();
// C++/CLI
MyClass^ obj = gcnew MyClass();
MyClass obj2;
' Visual Basic
Dim obj as New MyClass()
```

If a reference type does not reference memory, all three languages use different keywords: C# defines the null literal, C++/CLI defines nullptr (NULL is valid only for native objects), and Visual Basic defines Nothing.

Predefined reference types are listed in the following table. C++/CLI does not define the object and string type as is done with the other languages. Of course, you can use the classes defined by the Framework.

.NET Type	C#	C++/CLI	Visual Basic
System.Object	object	Not defined	Object
System.String	string	Not defined	String

Value Types

To declare a value type, C# uses the struct keyword; C++/CLI, the keyword value; and Visual Basic, Structure.

```
// C#
public struct MyStruct
{
}
// C++/CLI
public value class MyStruct
{
};
' Visual Basic
Public Structure MyStruct
End Structure
```

With C++/CLI, you can allocate a value type on the stack, on the native heap by using the new operator, and on the managed heap by using the gcnew operator. C# and Visual Basic do not have these options, but these options become important when native and managed code is mixed with C++/CLI.

```
// C#
MyStruct ms;
// C++/CLI
MyStruct ms1;
MyStruct* pms2 = new MyStruct();
MyStruct^ hms3 = gcnew MyStruct();
' Visual Basic
Dim ms as MyStruct
```

Predefined value types for the different languages are listed in the following table. In C++/CLI, the char type has a size of just 1 byte for an ASCII character. In C#, char has a size of 2 bytes for Unicode characters; that's a `wchar_t` in C++/CLI. The ANSI standard for C++ just defines `short <= int <= long`. With 32-bit machines, `int` and `long` both have a size of 32 bits. To define a 64-bit variable in C++, you need `long long`.

.NET Type	C#	C++/CLI	Visual Basic	Size
Char	char	wchar_t	Char	2 bytes
Boolean	bool	bool	Boolean	1 byte, contains true or false
Int16	short	short	Short	2 bytes
UInt16	ushort	unsigned short	UShort	2 bytes with no sign
Int32	int	int	Integer	4 bytes
UInt32	uint	unsigned int	UInteger	4 bytes with no sign
Int64	long	long long	Long	8 bytes
UInt64	ulong	unsigned long long	ULong	8 bytes with no sign

Type Inference

C# 3.0 allows you to define a local variable without an explicit data type declaration with the `var` keyword. The type is inferred from the initial value that is assigned. Visual Basic offers the same feature using the `Dim` keyword as long as *Option infer* is turned on. This can be done with the compiler setting / optioninfer+ or by using the project configuration page with Visual Studio.

```
// C#
var x = 3;
' Visual Basic
Dim x = 3
```

Interfaces

Defining interfaces is very similar for all three languages. All languages use the keyword `interface`:

```
// C#
public interface IDisplay
{
    void Display();
}
// C++/CLI
public interface class IDisplay
{
    void Display();
};
' Visual Basic
Public Interface IDisplay
    Sub Display
End Interface
```

Implementing interfaces is different. C# and C++/CLI use a colon after the class name followed by the interface name. The methods defined with the interface are implemented. With C++/CLI, the methods must be declared `virtual`. Visual Basic uses the `Implements` keyword to implement an interface, and the methods that are defined by the interface also need the `Implements` keyword attached.

```
// C#
public class Person : IDisplay
{
    public void Display()
    {
    }
}
// C# explicit interface implementation
public class Person : IDisplay
{
    void IDisplay.Display()
    {
    }
}
// C++/CLI
public ref class Person : IDisplay
{
public:
    virtual void Display();
};
' Visual Basic
Public Class Person
    Implements IDisplay
    Public Sub Display Implements IDisplay.Display
    End Sub
End Class
```

Enumerations

Enumerations are defined similarly in all three languages with the enum keyword (only Visual Basic uses a new line instead of a comma to separate the elements):

```
// C#
public enum Color
{
    Red, Green, Blue
}
// C++/CLI
public enum class Color
{
    Red, Green, Blue
};
' Visual Basic
Public Enum Color
    Red
    Green
    Blue
End Enum
```

Methods

Methods are always declared within a class. The syntax from C++/CLI is very similar to C# except that the access modifier is not part of the method declaration but is written before that. The access modifier must end with a colon. With Visual Basic, the `Sub` keyword is used to define a method.

```
// C#
public class MyClass
{
    public void Foo()
    {
    }
}
// C++/CLI
public ref class MyClass
{
public:
    void Foo()
    {
    }
};
' Visual Basic
Public Class MyClass
    Public Sub Foo
    End Sub
End Class
```

Method Parameters and Return Types

With C# and C++/CLI, parameters that are passed to methods are defined inside a bracket. The type of the parameter is declared before the variable name. If a value is returned from a method, the method is defined with the type to return instead of `void`.

Visual Basic uses `Sub` statements to declare a method without returning a value, and the `Function` statement with a method that does have a return type. The return type is followed after the method name and the brackets. Visual Basic also has a different order with variable declaration and type in the parameter. The type follows the variable, which is the reverse direction from C# and C++/CLI.

```
// C#
public class MyClass
{
    public int Foo(int i)
    {
        return 2 * i;
    }
}
// C++/CLI
public ref class MyClass
{
public:
    int Foo(int i)
    {
        return 2 * i;
    }
};
```

(continued)

(continued)

```
' Visual Basic
Public Class MyClass
    Public Sub Foo1(ByVal i as Integer)
    End Sub
    Public Function Foo(ByVal i As Integer) As Integer
        Return 2 * i
    End Sub
End Class
```

Parameter Modifiers

By default, value types are passed by value, and reference types are passed by reference. If a value type that is passed as a parameter should be changed within a calling method, with C# you can use the parameter modifier `ref`.

C++/CLI defines a managed reference operator `%`. This operator is similar to the C++ reference operator `&` except that `%` can be used with managed types and the garbage collector can keep track of these objects in case they are moved within the managed heap.

With Visual Basic, the keyword `ByRef` is used for passing parameters by reference:

```
// C#
public class ParameterPassing
{
    public void ChangeVal(ref int i)
    {
        i = 3;
    }
}
// C++/CLI
public ref class ParameterPassing
{
public:
    int ChangeVal(int% i)
    {
        i = 3;
    }
};
' Visual Basic
Public Class ParameterPassing
    Public Sub ChangeVal(ByRef i as Integer)
        i = 3
    End Sub
End Class
```

When invoking a method with reference parameters, only the C# language requires you to apply a parameter modifier. C++/CLI and Visual Basic don't differentiate calling a method with or without the parameter modifier. C# has the advantage here because you can immediately see in the calling method the parameter values can be changed.

Because of the caller syntax, which is not differentiated, Visual Basic does not allow you to overload methods just by changing the modifier. The C++/CLI compiler allows you to overload the method just by changing the modifier, but you cannot compile the caller because the resolved method is ambiguous. With C# it is possible to overload and use methods with just the parameter modifier, but it's not a good programming practice.

```
// C#
     ParameterPassing obj = new ParameterPassing();
     int a = 1;
     obj.ChangeVal(ref a);
     Console.WriteLine(a);       // writes 3
// C++/CLI
     ParameterPassing obj;
     int a = 1;
     obj.ChangeVal(a);
     Console.WriteLine(a);       // writes 3
' Visual Basic
     Dim obj as new ParameterPassing()
     Dim i as Integer = 1
     obj.ChangeVal(i)
     Console.WriteLine(i)        // writes 3
```

C# also defines the out *keyword when a parameter is just returned from a method. This option is not available from C++/CLI and Visual Basic. As long as the caller and callee are in the same application domain, there's really no difference between* out *and* ref *behind the scenes, and you can use a method declared with the C#* out *parameter modifier from Visual Basic and C++/CLI in the same way as* ref *parameter modifiers. If the method is used across application domains or processes, the attribute* [out] *can be used with Visual Basic and C++/CLI.*

Constructors

With both C# and C++/CLI, the constructor has the same name as the class. Visual Basic uses a procedure named New. The this and Me keywords are used to access a member of this instance. When invoking another constructor within a constructor, a member initializion is required with C#. With C++/CLI and Visual Basic, it is possible to invoke the constructor as a method.

```
// C#
public class Person
{
    public Person()
        : this("unknown", "unknown")
    { } public Person(string firstName, string lastName)
    {
        this.firstName = firstName;
        this.lastName = lastName;
    }
    private string firstName;
    private string lastName;
}
// C++/CLI
public ref class Person
{
public:
    Person()
    {
        Person("unknown", "unknown");
    }
    Person(String^ firstName, String^ lastName)
```

(continued)

(continued)

```cpp
        {
            this->firstName = firstName;
            this->lastName = lastName;
        }
    private:
        String^ firstName;
        String^ lastName;
    };
' Visual Basic
Public Class Person
    Public Sub New()
        Me.New("unknown", "unknown")
    End Sub
    Public Sub New(ByVal firstName As String, ByVal lastName As String)
        Me.MyFirstName = firstName
        Me.MyLastName = lastName
    End Sub
    Private MyFirstName As String
    Private MyLastName As String
End Class
```

Properties

To define a property, C# just requires a get and set accessor within a property block. With the set accessor, the variable value is automatically created by the C# compiler. C# 3.0 also has a new shorthand notation where an implementation is not needed if just a simple variable is returned or set by the get and set accessors. The syntax is different both with C++/CLI and Visual Basic. Both of these languages have a `property` keyword, and it is necessary to define a variable `value` with the set accessor. C++/CLI also requires a return type with the get accessor and a parameter type with the set accessor.

C++/CLI also has a short version of writing a property. Using the `property` keyword, you just have to define the type and the name of the property; the get and set accessors are created automatically by the compiler. If there's nothing else needed than setting and returning a variable, the short version is good enough. If the implementation of the accessors requires more — for example, checking the value or doing a refresh — you must write the full syntax for properties. The designers of C# 3.0 learned from C++/CLI to offer a short notation as well.

```csharp
// C#
public class Person
{
    private string firstName;
    public string FirstName
    {
        get { return firstName; }
        set { firstName = value; }
    }
    public string LastName { get; set; }
}
// C++/CLI
public ref class Person
{
private:
    String^ firstName;
public:
    property String^ FirstName
```

```
        {
            String^ get()
            {
                return firstName;
            }
            void set(String^ value)
            {
                firstName = value;
            }
        }
        property String^ LastName;
    };
    ' Visual Basic
    Public Class Person
        Private myFirstname As String
        Public Property FirstName()
            Get
                Return myFirstName
            End Get
            Set(ByVal value)
                myFirstName = value
            End Set
        End Property
        Private myLastName As String
        Public Property LastName()
            Get
                Return myLastName
            End Get
            Set(ByVal value)
                myLastName = value
            End Set
        End Property
    End Class
```

With C# and C++/CLI, read-only properties just have a get accessor. With Visual Basic, you must also specify the ReadOnly modifier. Write-only properties must be defined with the WriteOnly modifier and a set accessor.

```
    ' Visual Basic
    Public ReadOnly Property Name()
        Get
            Return myFirstName & " " & myLastName
        End Get
    End Property
```

Object Initializers

With C# 3.0 and Visual Basic, properties can be initialized using an object initializer. The properties can be initialized using curly brackets similar to an array initializer. The syntax from C# and Visual Basic is very similar; Visual Basic just uses the With keyword.

```
    // C#
    Person p = new Person() { FirstName = "Tom", LastName = "Turbo" };
    ' Visual Basic
    Dim p As New Person With { .FirstName = "Tom", .LastName = "Turbo" }
```

Extension Methods

Extension methods are the foundation of LINQ. With both C# and Visual Basic, it is possible to create extension methods. However, the syntax is different. C# marks an extension method with the this keyword in the first parameter, Visual Basic marks an extension method with the attribute <Extension>.

```
// C#
public static class StringExtension
{
    public static void Foo(this string s)
    {
        Console.WriteLine("Foo {0}", s);
    }
}
' Visual Basic
Public Module StringExtension
    <Extension()> _
    Public Sub Foo(ByVal s As String)
        Console.WriteLine("Foo {0}", s)
    End Sub
End Module
```

Static Members

A static field is instantiated only once for all objects of the type. C# and C++/CLI both use the static keyword; Visual Basic offers the same functionality with the Shared keyword.

To use static members, you use the name of the class followed by the . operator and the name of the static member. C++/CLI uses the :: operator for accessing static members.

```
// C#
public class Singleton
{
    private static SomeData data = null;
    public static SomeData GetData()
    {
        if (data == null)
        {
            data = new SomeData();
        }
        return data;
    }
}
// use:
SomeData d = Singleton.GetData();
// C++/CLI
public ref class Singleton
{
private:
    static SomeData^ hData;
public:
    static SomeData^ GetData()
    {
        if (hData == nullptr)
```

```
        {
            hData = gcnew SomeData();
        }
        return hData;
    }
};
// use:
SomeData^ d = Singleton::GetData();
' Visual Basic
Public Class Singleton
    Private Shared data As SomeData
    Public Shared Function GetData() As SomeData
        If data is Nothing Then
            data = new SomeData()
        End If
        Return data
    End Function
End Class
' Use:
Dim d as SomeData = Singleton.GetData()
```

Arrays

Arrays are discussed in Chapter 5, "Arrays." The `Array` class is always behind the scenes of .NET arrays; declaring an array, the compiler creates a class that derives from the `Array` base class. When C# was designed, the designers of the C# language took the bracket syntax for arrays from C++ and extended it with array initializers.

```
// C#
int[] arr1 = new int[3] {1, 2, 3};
int[] arr2 = {1, 2, 3};
```

If you use brackets with C++/CLI, you create a native C++ array but not an array that is based on the `Array` class. To create .NET arrays, C++/CLI introduced the `array` keyword. This keyword uses a generic-like syntax with angle brackets. Within the angle brackets, the type of the elements is defined. C++/CLI supports array initializers with the same syntax as C#.

```
// C++/CLI
array<int>^ arr1 = gcnew array<int>(3) {1, 2, 3};
array<int>^ arr2 = {1, 2, 3};
```

Visual Basic uses braces for arrays. It requires the last element number instead of the number of elements with the array declaration. With every .NET language, arrays begin with element number 0. This is also the same for Visual Basic. To make that clearer, Visual Basic 9 introduced the `0 To number` expression with the array declaration. It always starts with 0; `0 To` just makes this more readable.

Visual Basic also supports array initializers if the array is initialized with the `New` operator:

```
' Visual Basic
Dim arr1(0 To 2) As Integer()
Dim arr2 As Integer() = New Integer(0 To 2) {1, 2, 3};
```

Control Statements

Control statements define what code should run. C# defines the `if` and `switch` statements, and the conditional operator.

if Statement

The C# `if` statement is the same as the C++/CLI version. Visual Basic uses `If-Then/Else/End If` instead of curly brackets.

```
// C# and C++/CLI
if (a == 3)
{
    // do this
}
else
{
    // do that
}
' Visual Basic
If a = 3 Then
  ' do this
Else
  ' do that
End If
```

Conditional Operator

C# and C++/CLI support the conditional operator, a lightweight version of the `if` statement. In C++/CLI, this operator is known as a *ternary* operator. The first argument has a Boolean result. If the result is true, the first expression is evaluated; otherwise, the second one is. Visual Basic has the `IIf` function in the Visual Basic Runtime Library, which offers the same functionality.

```
// C#
string s = a > 3 ? "one" : "two";
// C++/CLI
String^ s = a > 3 ? "one" : "two";
' Visual Basic
Dim s As String = IIf(a > 3, "one", "two")
```

switch Statement

The `switch` statement looks very similar in C# and C++/CLI, but there are important differences. C# supports strings with the case selection. This is not possible with C++. With C++ you have to use `if-else` instead. C++/CLI does support an implicit fall-through from one case to the next. With C#, the compiler complains if there's not a `break` or a `goto` statement. C# has only implicit fall-through if there's not a statement for the case.

Visual Basic has a `Select/Case` statement instead of `switch/case`. A break is not only not needed but also not possible. An implicit fall-through from one case to the next is not possible, even if there's not a single statement following `Case`; instead, `Case` can be combined with `And`, `Or`, and `To` — for example, `3 To 5`.

```csharp
// C#
string GetColor(Suit s)
{
    string color;
    switch (s)
    {
        case Suit.Heart:
        case Suit.Diamond:
            color = "Red";
            break;
        case Suit.Spade:
        case Suit.Club:
            color = "Black";
            break;
        default:
            color = "Unknown";
            break;
    }
    return color;
}
```

```cpp
// C++/CLI
String^ GetColor(Suit s)
{
    String^ color;
    switch (s)
    {
        case Suit::Heart:
        case Suit::Diamond:
            color = "Red";
            break;
        case Suit::Spade:
        case Suit::Club:
            color = "Black";
            break;
        default:
            color = "Unknown";
            break;
    }
    return color;
}
```

```vb
' Visual Basic
Function GetColor(ByVal s As Suit) As String
    Dim color As String = Nothing
    Select Case s
        Case Suit.Heart And Suit.Diamond
            color = "Red"
        Case Suit.Spade And Suit.Club
            color = "Black"
        Case Else
            color = "Unknown"
    End Select

    Return color
End Function
```

Loops

With loops, code is executed repeatedly until a condition is met. Loops with C# are discussed in Chapter 2, "C# Basics," including: `for`, `while`, `do...while`, and `foreach`. C# and C++/CLI are very similar with the looping statements; Visual Basic defines different statements.

for Statement

The `for` statement is similar with C# and C++/CLI. With Visual Basic, you can't initialize a variable inside the `For/To` statement; you must initialize the variable beforehand. `For/To` doesn't require a `Step` to follow — `Step 1` is the default. Just in case you don't want to increment by 1, the `Step` keyword is required with `For/To`.

```
// C#
for (int i = 0; i < 100; i++)
{
    Console.WriteLine(i);
}
// C++/CLI
for (int i = 0; i < 100; i++)
{
    Console::WriteLine(i);
}
' Visual Basic
Dim count as Integer
For count = 0 To 99 Step 1
    Console.WriteLine(count)
Next
```

while and do . . . while Statements

The `while` and `do...while` statements are the same in C# and C++/CLI. Visual Basic has very similar constructs with `Do While/Loop` and `Do/Loop While`.

```
// C#
int i = 0;
while (i < 3)
{
    Console.WriteLine(i++);
}
i = 0;
do
{
    Console.WriteLine(i++);
} while (i < 3);
// C++/CLI
int i = 0;
while (i < 3)
{
    Console::WriteLine(i++);
}
i = 0;
do
{
    Console::WriteLine(i++);
} while (i < 3);
```

```
' Visual Basic
Dim num as Integer = 0
Do While (num < 3)
    Console.WriteLine(num)
    num += 1
Loop
num = 0
Do
    Console.WriteLine(num)
    num += 1
Loop While (num < 3)
```

foreach Statement

The foreach statement makes use of the interface IEnumerable. foreach doesn't exist with ANSI C++ but is an extension of ANSI C++/CLI. Unlike the C# foreach, in C++/CLI there's a blank space between for and each.

```
// C#
int[] arr = {1, 2, 3};
foreach (int i in arr)
{
    Console.WriteLine(i);
}
// C++/CLI
array<int>^ arr = {1, 2, 3};
for each (int i in arr)
{
    Console::WriteLine(i);
}
' Visual Basic
Dim arr() As Integer = New Integer() {1, 2, 3}
Dim num As Integer
For Each num as Integer In arr
Console.WriteLine(num)
Next
```

While foreach *makes it easy to iterate through a collection, C# supports creating enumerations by using the* yield *statement. With Visual Basic and C++/CLI, the* yield *statement is not available. Instead, with these languages it is necessary to implement the interfaces* IEnumerable *and* IEnumerator *manually. The* yield *statement is explained in Chapter 5, "Arrays."*

Exception Handling

Exception handling is discussed in Chapter 14, "Errors and Exceptions." This is extremely similar among all three languages. All these languages use try/catch/finally for handling exceptions, and the throw keyword to create an exception:

```
// C#
public void Method(Object o)
{
    if (o == null)
        throw new ArgumentException("Error");
}
```

(continued)

1697

(continued)

```csharp
public void Foo()
{
    try
    {
        Method(null);
    }
    catch (ArgumentException ex)
    { }
    catch (Exception ex)
    { }
    finally
    { }
}
// C++/CLI
public:
    void Method(Object^ o)
    {
        if (o == nullptr)
            throw gcnew ArgumentException("Error");
    }
    void Foo()
    {
        try
        {
            Method(nullptr);
        }
        catch (ArgumentException^ ex)
        { }
        catch (Exception^ ex)
        { }
        finally
        { }
    }
' Visual Basic
Public Sub Method(ByVal o As Object)
    If o = Nothing Then
        Throw New ArgumentException("Error")
End Sub
Public Sub Foo()
    Try
        Method(Nothing)
    Catch ex As ArgumentException
        '
    Catch ex As Exception
        '
    Finally
        '
    End Try
End Sub
```

Inheritance

.NET languages offer many keywords to define polymorphic behavior, to override or hide methods, access modifiers to allow or not allow member access. For C#, this functionality is discussed in Chapter 4, "Inheritance." The functionality of C#, C++/CLI and Visual Basic is very similar, but the keywords are different.

Access Modifiers

The access modifiers of C++/CLI and Visual Basic are very similar to C#, with some notable differences. Visual Basic uses the `Friend` access modifier instead of `internal` for accessing the types in the same assembly. C++/CLI has one more access modifier: `protected private`. `internal protected` allows accessing the members from within the same assembly, and also from other assemblies if the type is derived from the base type. C# and Visual Basic don't have a way to allow only derived types within the same assembly. This is possible with `protected private` from C++/CLI. Here `private` means that outside the assembly there's no access, but from inside the assembly protected access is possible. The order — whether you write `protected private` or `private protected` — does not matter. The access modifier allowing more is always located within the assembly, and the access modifier allowing less is always outside of the assembly.

C#	C++/CLI	Visual Basic
public	public	Public
protected	protected	Protected
private	private	Private
internal	internal	Friend
internal protected	internal protected	Protected Friend
not possible	protected private	not possible

Keywords

Keywords important for inheritance are mapped in the following table.

C#	C++/CLI	Visual Basic	Functionality
:	:	Implements	Implement an interface
:	:	Inherits	Inherits from a base class
virtual	virtual	Overridable	Declare a method to support polymorphism
overrides	override	Overrides	Override a virtual method
new	new	Shadows	Hide a method from a base class
abstract	abstract	MustInherit	Abstract class

C#	C++/CLI	Visual Basic	Functionality
sealed	sealed	NotInheritable	Sealed class
abstract	abstract	MustOverride	Abstract method
sealed	sealed	NotOverridable	Sealed method
this	this	Me	Reference the current object
base	Classname::	MyBase	Reference the base class

The order in which you place the keywords is important in the languages. In the code sample, an abstract base class Base with one abstract method and one implemented method that is virtual are defined. The class Base is derived from the class Derived, where the abstract method is implemented, and the virtual method is overridden:

```
// C#
public abstract class Base
{
    public virtual void Foo()
    {
    }
    public abstract void Bar();
}
public class Derived : Base
{
    public override void Foo()
    {
        base.Foo();
    }
    public override void Bar()
    {
    }
}
// C++/CLI
public ref class Base abstract
{
public:
    virtual void Foo()
    {
    }
    virtual void Bar() abstract;
};
public ref class Derived : public Base
{
public:
    virtual void Foo() override
    {
        Base::Foo();
    }
    virtual void Bar() override
```

```
        {
        }
};
' Visual Basic
Public MustInherit Class Base
    Public Overridable Sub Foo()
    End Sub
    Public MustOverride Sub Bar()
End Class
Public class Derived
    Inherits Base
    Public Overrides Sub Foo()
        MyBase.Foo()
    End Sub
    Public Overrides Sub Bar()
    End Sub
End Class
```

Resource Management

Working with resources is covered in Chapter 12, "Memory Management and Pointers," both implementing the IDisposable interface and implementing a finalizer. How this looks in C++/CLI and Visual Basic is covered in this section.

IDisposable Interface Implementation

For freeing resources, the interface IDisposable defines the Dispose() method. Using C# and Visual Basic, you have to implement the interface IDisposable. With C++/CLI the interface IDisposable is implemented as well, but this is done by the compiler if you just write a destructor.

```
// C#
public class Resource : IDisposable
{
    public void Dispose()
    {
        // release resource
    }
}
// C++/CLI
public ref class Resource
{
public:
    ~Resource()
    {
        // release resource
    }
};
' Visual Basic
Public Class Resource
    Implements IDisposable
    Public Sub Dispose() Implements IDisposable.Dispose
        ' release resource
    End Sub
End Class
```

With C++/CLI, the Dispose() *method is invoked by using the* delete *statement.*

Using Statement

The C# using statement implements an acquire/use/release pattern to release a resource as soon as it is no longer used, even in the case of an exception. The compiler creates a try/finally statement and invokes the Dispose method inside the finally. Version 9 of Visual Basic supports the using statement just as C# does. C++/CLI has an even more elegant approach to this problem. If a reference type is declared locally, the compiler creates a try/finally statement to invoke the Dispose() method at the end of the block.

```
// C#
using (Resource r = new Resource())
{
    r.Foo();
}
// C++/CLI
{
    Resource r;
    r.Foo();
}
' Visual Basic
Using r As New Resource
    r.Foo()
End Using
```

Override Finalize

If a class contains native resources that must be freed, the class must override the Finalize() method from the Object class. With C#, this is done by writing a destructor. C++/CLI has a special syntax with the ! prefix to define a finalizer. Within a finalizer, you cannot dispose contained objects that have a finalizer as well because the order of finalization is not guaranteed. That's why the Dispose pattern defines an additional Dispose() method with a Boolean parameter. With C++/CLI, it is not necessary to implement this pattern in the code because this is done by the compiler. The C++/CLI destructor implements both Dispose() methods. With Visual Basic, both Dispose() and the finalizer must be implemented manually. However, most Visual Basic classes do not use native resources directly, just with the help of other classes. With Visual Basic, usually it is not necessary to override the Finalize() method, but an implementation of the Dispose() method is often required.

Writing a destructor with C# overrides the Finalize() *method of the base class. A C++/CLI destructor implements the* IDisposable *interface.*

```
// C#
public class Resource : IDisposable
{
    ~Resource // override Finalize
    {
        Dispose(false);
    }
    protected virtual void Dispose(bool disposing)
    {
        if (disposing) // dispose embedded members
        {
        }
```

```
        // release resources of this class
        GC.SuppressFinalize(this);
    }
    public void Dispose()
    {
        Dispose(true);
    }
}
// C++/CLI
public ref class Resource
{
public:
    ~Resource() // implement IDisposable
    {
        this->!Resource();
    }
    !Resource()   // override Finalize
    {
        // release resource
    }
};
' Visual Basic
Public Class Resource
    Implements IDisposable
    Public Sub Dispose() Implements IDisposable.Dispose
        Dispose(True)
        GC.SuppressFinalize(Me)
    End Sub
    Protected Overridable Sub Dispose(ByVal disposing)
        If disposing Then
            ' Release embedded resources
        End If
        ' Release resources of this class
    End Sub
    Protected Overrides Sub Finalize()
        Try
            Dispose(False)
        Finally
            MyBase.Finalize()
        End Try
    End Sub
End Class
```

Delegates

Delegates — type-safe pointers to methods — are discussed in Chapter 7, "Delegates and Events." In all three languages, the keyword `delegate` can be used to define a delegate. The difference is with using the delegate.

The sample code shows a class `Demo` with a static method `Foo()` and an instance method `Bar()`. Both of these methods are invoked by delegate instances of type `DemoDelegate`. `DemoDelegate` is declared to invoke a method with `void` return type and an `int` parameter.

When using the delegate, C# supports delegate inference, where the compiler creates a delegate instance and passes the address of the method.

With C# and C++/CLI, two delegates can be combined into one by using the + operator:

```
// C#
public delegate void DemoDelegate(int x);
public class Demo
{
    public static void Foo(int x) { }
    public void Bar(int x) { }
}
Demo d = new Demo();
DemoDelegate d1 = Demo.Foo;
DemoDelegate d2 = d.Bar;
DemoDelegate d3 = d1 + d2;
d3(11);
```

Delegate inference is not possible with C++/CLI. With C++/CLI, you must create a new instance of the delegate type and pass the address of the method to the constructor:

```
// C++/CLI
public delegate void DemoDelegate(int x);
public ref class Demo
{
public:
    static void Foo(int x) { }
    void Bar(int x) { }
};
Demo^ d = gcnew Demo();
DemoDelegate^ d1 = gcnew DemoDelegate(&Demo::Foo);
DemoDelegate^ d2 = gcnew DemoDelegate(d, &Demo::Bar);
DemoDelegate^ d3 = d1 + d2;
d3(11);
```

Similarly to C++/CLI, Visual Basic does not support delegate inference. You have to create a new instance of the delegate type and pass the address of a method. Visual Basic has the AddressOf operator to pass the address of a method.

Visual Basic doesn't overload the + operator for delegates, so it is necessary to invoke the Combine() method from the Delegate class. The Delegate class is written inside brackets because Delegate is a Visual Basic keyword, and thus it is not possible to use a class with the same name. Putting brackets around Delegate ensures that the class is used instead of the Delegate keyword.

```
' Visual Basic
Public Delegate Sub DemoDelegate(ByVal x As Integer)
Public Class Demo
    Public Shared Sub Foo(ByVal x As Integer)
        '
    End Sub
    Public Sub Bar(ByVal x As Integer)
        '
    End Sub
End Class
Dim d As New Demo()
Dim d1 As New DemoDelegate(AddressOf Demo.Foo)
Dim d2 As New DemoDelegate(AddressOf d.Bar)
Dim d3 As DemoDelegate = [Delegate].Combine(d1, d2)
d3(11)
```

Events

With the `event` keyword, a subscription mechanism can be done that is based on delegates. Again, all languages define an `event` keyword for offering events from a class. The class `EventDemo` fires events with the name `DemoEvent` of type `DemoDelegate`.

In C#, the syntax for firing the event looks like a method call of the event. The event variable is `null` as long as nobody registered to the event, so a check for not `null` must be done before firing the event. The handler method is registered by using the `+=` operator and passing the address of the handler method with the help of delegate inference:

```
// C#
    public class EventDemo
    {
        public event DemoDelegate DemoEvent;
        public void FireEvent()
        {
            if (DemoEvent != null)
                DemoEvent(44);
        }
    }
    public class Subscriber
    {
        public void Handler(int x)
        {
            // handler implementation
        }
    }
//...
EventDemo evd = new EventDemo();
Subscriber subscr = new Subscriber();
evd.DemoEvent += subscr.Handler;
evd.FireEvent();
```

C++/CLI is very similar to C# except that when you fire the event, you do not first need to see that the event variable is not `null`. This is automatically done by the IL code created from the compiler.

Both C# and C++/CLI use the += operator to unregister from an event.

```
// C++/CLI
    public ref class EventDemo
    {
    public:
        event DemoDelegate^ DemoEvent;
        public void FireEvent()
        {
            DemoEvent(44);
        }
    }
    public class Subscriber
    {
    public:
        void Handler(int x)
```

(continued)

(continued)

```
        {
            // handler implementation
        }
    }
//...
EventDemo^ evd = gcnew EventDemo();
Subscriber^ subscr = gcnew Subscriber();
evd->DemoEvent += gcnew DemoDelegate(subscr, &Subscriber::Handler);
evd->FireEvent();
```

Visual Basic has a different syntax. The event is declared with the Event keyword, which is the same as in C# and C++/CLI. However, the event is raised with the RaiseEvent statement. The RaiseEvent statement checks if the event variable is initialized by a subscriber. To register a handler, the AddHandler statement has the same functionality as the += operator in C#. AddHandler requires two parameters: the first defines the event, the second the address of the handler. The RemoveHandler statement is used to unregister a handler from the event.

```
' Visual Basic
  Public Class EventDemo
      Public Event DemoEvent As DemoDelegate
      public Sub FireEvent()
          RaiseEvent DemoEvent(44);
      End Sub
  End Class
  Public Class Subscriber
      Public Sub Handler(ByVal x As Integer)
          ' handler implementation
      End Sub
  End Class
'...
Dim evd As New EventDemo()
Dim subscr As New Subscriber()
AddHandler evd.DemoEvent, AddressOf subscr.Handler
evd.FireEvent()
```

Visual Basic offers another syntax that is not available with the other languages: you can also use the Handles keyword with the method that subscribes to the event. The requirement for this is to define a variable with the WithEvents keyword:

```
Public Class Subscriber
    Public WithEvents evd As EventDemo
    Public Sub Handler(ByVal x As Integer) Handles evd.DemoEvent
        ' Handler implementation
    End Sub
    Public Sub Action()
        evd = New EventDemo()
        evd.FireEvent()
    End Sub
End Class
```

Generics

All three languages support the creation and use of generics. Generics are discussed in Chapter 9, "Generics."

To use generics, C# borrowed the syntax from C++ templates to define the generic type with angle brackets. C++/CLI uses the same syntax. In Visual Basic, the generic type is defined with the Of keyword in braces.

```
// C#
List<int> intList = new List<int>();
intList.Add(1);
intList.Add(2);
intList.Add(3);
// C++/CLI
List<int>^ intList = gcnew List<int>();
intList->Add(1);
intList->Add(2);
intList->Add(3);
' Visual Basic
Dim intList As List(Of Integer) = New List(Of Integer)()
intList.Add(1)
intList.Add(2)
intList.Add(3)
```

Because you use angle brackets with the class declaration, the compiler knows to create a generic type. Constraints are defined with the where clause.

```
public class MyGeneric<T>
    where T : IComparable<T>
{
    private List<T> list = new List<T>();
    public void Add(T item)
    {
        list.Add(item);
    }
    public void Sort()
    {
        list.Sort();
    }
}
```

Defining a generic type with C++/CLI is similar to defining a template with C++. Instead of the template keyword, with generics the generic keyword is used. The where clause is similar to that in C#; however, C++/CLI does not support a constructor constraint.

```
generic <typename T>
where T : IComparable<T>
ref class MyGeneric
{
private:
    List<T>^ list;
public:
    MyGeneric()
    {
        list = gcnew List<T>();
    }
```

(continued)

(continued)

```
    void Add(T item)
    {
        list->Add(item);
    }
    void Sort()
    {
        list->Sort();
    }
};
```

Visual Basic defines a generic class with the `Of` keyword. Constraints can be defined with `As`:

```
Public Class MyGeneric(Of T As IComparable(Of T))
    Private myList = New List(Of T)
    Public Sub Add(ByVal item As T)
        myList.Add(item)
    End Sub
    Public Sub Sort()
        myList.Sort()
    End Sub
End Class
```

LINQ Queries

Language-integrated queries are a feature of C# 3.0 and Visual Basic 9.0. The syntax is very similar between these two languages.

LINQ is discussed in Chapter 11, "Language Integrated Query."

```
// C#
var query = from r in racers
            where r.Country == "Brazil"
            orderby r.Wins descending
            select r;
' Visual Basic
Dim query = From r in racers _
            Where r.Country = "Brazil" _
            Order By r.Wins Descending _
            Select r
```

C++/CLI does not support LINQ queries.

C++/CLI Mixing Native and Managed Code

One of the big advantages of C++/CLI is the capability to mix native and managed code. You use native code from C# through a mechanism known as *platform invoke*, which is discussed in Chapter 24, "Interoperability." Using native code from C++/CLI is known as *It just works*.

In a managed class, you can use both native and managed code, as you can see here. The same is true for a native class. You can mix native and managed code as well within a method.

```
#pragma once
#include <iostream>     // include this header file for cout
using namespace std;    // the iostream header defines the namespace std
using namespace System;
public ref class Managed
```

```
    {
    public:
        void MixNativeAndManaged()
        {
            cout << "Native Code" << endl;
            Console::WriteLine("Managed Code");
        }
    };
```

In a managed class, you can also declare a field of a native type or a pointer to a native type. Doing the same the other way around is not possible to accomplish directly. You must take care that an instance of a managed type can be moved by the garbage collector when cleaning up memory.

To use managed classes as a member within native classes, C++/CLI defines the keyword gcroot, which is defined in the header file gcroot.h. gcroot wraps a GCHandle that keeps track of a CLR object from a native reference.

```
#pragma once
#include "gcroot.h"
using namespace System;
public ref class Managed
{
public:
    Managed() { }
    void Foo()
    {
        Console::WriteLine("Foo");
    }
};
public class Native
{
private:
    gcroot<Managed^> m_p;
public:
    Native()
    {
        m_p = gcnew Managed();
    }
    void Foo()
    {
        m_p->Foo();
    }
};
```

C# Specifics

Some C# syntax features were not covered in this appendix. C# defines the yield statement, which makes it easy to create enumerators. This statement is not available with C++/CLI and Visual Basic; with these languages an enumerator must be implemented manually. Also, C# defines a special syntax for nullable types, whereas with the other languages you have to use the generic struct Nullable<T> instead.

C# allows for unsafe code blocks where you can use pointers and pointer arithmetic. This feature can be extremely helpful for invoking methods from native libraries. Visual Basic does not have this capability; this is a real advantage of C#. C++/CLI does not need the unsafe keyword to define unsafe code blocks. It's very natural with C++/CLI to mix native and managed code.

Summary

In this chapter, you've learned how to map the syntax from C# to Visual Basic and C++/CLI. C++/CLI defines extensions to C++ for writing .NET applications and draws on C# for the syntax extensions. Although C# and C++/CLI have the same roots, there are many important differences. Visual Basic does not use curly brackets, but is chattier instead.

With the syntax mapping, you've seen how to map the C# syntax to C++/CLI and Visual Basic; how the other two languages look, with defining types, methods, and properties; what keywords are used for OO features; how resource management is done; and how delegates, events and generics are implemented with the three languages.

While it is possible to map most of the syntax, the languages are still different in their functionality.

Windows Vista and Windows
Server 2008

C

This appendix gives you the information you need to know about developing applications for Windows Vista and Windows Server 2008, and how you can use new Windows features from .NET applications. This chapter does not cover features useful for a Windows Vista user or a Windows Server 2008 administrator, but features important for developers.

If your applications are not targeting Windows Vista alone, you should be aware that while WPF, WCF, WF, and LINQ are also available for Windows XP, this is not the case with the topics covered here. If you're still targeting Windows XP, you still should be aware of issues running your applications on Windows Vista and what you should pay attention to. In that case, you should have a special focus on user account control and directory changes.

The topics covered in this appendix are:

❑ Vista Bridge

❑ User account control

❑ Directory structure

❑ New controls and dialogs

❑ Search

Vista Bridge

With the release of .NET 3.5, many new Windows API calls available with Windows Vista and Windows Server 2008 are not available from the .NET Framework. However, the Windows SDK contains a sample with the name Vista Bridge that wraps native API calls to make them available from a .NET library. You can use this library within your Windows Forms or WPF applications.

After installing the Windows SDK, you can find the Vista Bridge sample in the `.zip` file `<program files>\Microsoft SDKs\Windows\v6.0\Samples\CrossTechnologySamples.zip`. Extract the `.zip` file to get three projects: `VistaBridgeLibrary`, `VistaBridgeControls`, and `VistaBridgeDemoApp`. The `VistaBridgeLibrary` project contains several classes and controls.

User Account Control

As a developer, *user account control* (UAC) is one of the features you can see immediately with Windows Vista and Windows Server 2008. Although Windows guidelines have always mentioned this issue, many applications still need to run with the administrator account. For example, a normal user is not allowed to write data to the program files directory; administrative privileges are required. Because many applications don't run without administrative privileges (although from the functionality that is offered by the program this wouldn't be required, the developer just didn't follow the guidelines), many users log in to the system with an Administrator account. In doing so, you can unintentionally install Trojan horse programs.

Windows Vista avoids this problem because the Administrator, by default, doesn't have administrative privileges. The process has two security tokens associated with it, one with normal user privileges and one with admin privileges (in the case where the login is done to the Administrator account). With applications that require administrative privileges, the user can elevate the application to run with Administrator rights. This is either done from the context menu "Run as Administrator," or an application can be configured to always require administrator privileges in the Compatibility properties of the application, as shown in Figure C-1. This setting adds application compatibility flags to the registry at `HKCU\Software\Microsoft\Windows NT\CurrentVersion\AppCompatFlags\Layers` with a value for `RUNASADMIN`.

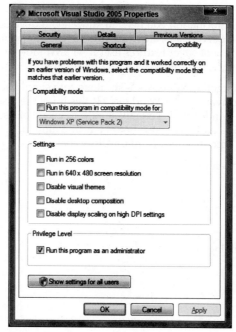

Figure C-1

Applications Requiring Admin Privileges

For applications that require administrative privileges, you can also add an application manifest. Visual Studio 2008 has a new item template to add an application manifest to an application. Such a manifest can either be done by adding a manifest file to an existing application or by embedding a Win32 resource file within the assembly. After adding a manifest file to a Visual Studio project, the manifest file is added to the resources of the project, as you can see with the project properties, selecting the Application tab, in the Resources category. Having the entry here embeds the manifest as a Win32 resource to the assembly. An application manifest is an XML file similar to the application configuration file. While the application configuration file has the file extension `.config`, the manifest ends with `.manifest`. The name of the file must be set to the name of the application, including the `exe` file extension followed by `.manifest`. Visual Studio renames and copies the `app.manifest` file just as it does with an application configuration file. The manifest file contains XML data as shown here. The root element is `<assembly>`, which contains the child element `<trustInfo>`. The administrator requirement is defined with the `level` attribute of the `<requestedExecutionLevel>` element.

```xml
<?xml version="1.0" encoding="UTF-8"?>
<asmv1:assembly manifestVersion="1.0" xmlns="urn:schemas-microsoft-com:asm.v1"
    xmlns:asmv1="urn:schemas-microsoft-com:asm.v1"
    xmlns:asmv2="urn:schemas-microsoft-com:asmv2"
    xmlns:xsi="http://www.w3.org/2001/XMLSchema-instance">
  <assemblyIdentity version="1.0.0.0" name="MyApplication.app" />
  <trustInfo xmlns="urn:schemas-microsoft-com:asm.v2">
    <security>
      <requestedPrivileges xmlns="urn:schemas-microsoft-com:asm.v3">
        <requestedExecutionLevel level="requireAdministrator"
            uiAccess="false"/>
      </requestedPrivileges>
    </security>
  </trustInfo>
</asmv1:assembly>
```

When starting the application this way, you get an elevation prompt where the user is asked if he or she trusts the application to run with administrative privileges.

With the `requestedExecutionLevel` setting, you can specify the values `requireAdministrator`, `highestAvailable`, and `asInvoker`. The value `highestAvailable` means that the application gets the privileges the user has — but only after getting the consent from the user. The value `requireAdministrator` requires Administrator privileges. If the user is not logged on to the system as Administrator, a login dialog appears where the user can log in as Administrator for the application. The value `asInvoker` means that the application is running with the security token of the user.

The `uiAccess` attribute specifies if the application requires input to a higher-privilege-level window on the desktop. For example, an onscreen keyboard needs to drive input to other windows on the desktop, so the setting should be set to `true` for the application's displaying the onscreen keyboard. Non–UI-accessibility applications should set this attribute to `false`.

> *Another way to get admin privileges to an application is to write a Windows service. Because UAC applies to interactive processes only, a Windows service can get admin privileges. You can also write an unprivileged Windows application to communicate with the privileged Windows service by using WCF or another communication technology.*

> *Windows services are covered in Chapter 23, "Windows Services." WCF is covered in Chapter 42, "Windows Communication Foundation."*

Shield Icon

If an application or a task from an application requires administrative privileges, the user is informed by an easily recognizable shield icon. The shield icon is attached to the controls that require elevation. The user expects to see an elevation prompt when clicking on an item with a shield. Figures C-2 and C-3 show the shield in use. The Task Manager requires elevation to see processes from all users. With User Accounts, changing the account type and giving other users access to the computer requires elevation.

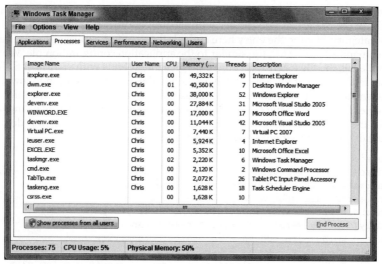

Figure C-2

Figure C-3

You can create shield icons in your application by using the new command link control that is shown later in this appendix.

When the user clicks a control with a shield icon, an elevation prompt is shown. Elevation prompts are different, depending on the type of application that is elevated:

❑ Windows needs your permission to continue. This elevation prompt is shown for applications that are delivered with Windows.

❑ A program needs your permission to continue. This elevation prompt is shown with applications that contain a certificate to provide information about the publisher.

❑ An unidentified program wants access to your computer. This elevation prompt is shown with applications that don't contain a certificate.

Directory Structure

The directory structure of Windows has changed in Windows Vista. There's no longer a directory `c:\Documents and Settings\<username>`. It has been replaced by the new folder `c:\Users\<username>`. Windows XP defines the subdirectory `My Documents` for storing user-specific data. Windows Vista defines `c:\Users\<username>\Documents`.

If you follow just the simple rule not to use hard-coded path values with the program, it doesn't matter where the real folders are located. The folders differ with different Windows languages anyway. For special folders, use the `Environment` class and the `SpecialFolder` enumeration:

```
string folder = Environment.GetFolderPath(
        Environment.SpecialFolder.Personal);
```

Some of the folders defined by the `SpecialFolder` enumeration are described in the following table.

Content	SpecialFolder Enumeration	Windows Vista default directory
User-specific documents	`Personal`	`c:\Users\<User>\Documents`
User-specific data for roaming users	`ApplicationData`	`c:\Users\<User>\AppData\Roaming`
User-specific data that is local to a system	`LocalApplicationData`	`c:\Users\<User>\AppData\Local`
Program files	`ProgramFiles`	`c:\Program Files`
Program files that are shared among different programs	`CommonProgramFiles`	`c:\Program Files\Common Files`
Application data common to all users	`CommonApplicationData`	`c:\ProgramData`

At logoff, the content of roaming directories is copied to the server, so if the user logs on to a different system, the same content is copied and is thus available on all systems accessed by the user.

With the special folders, you must be careful that a normal user doesn't have write access to the program files directory. You can write user-specific data from the application to `LocalApplicationData`, or with roaming users to `ApplicationData`. Data that should be shared among different users can be written to `CommonApplicationData`.

Because many applications write content to the program files directory, they won't run on Windows Vista without administrative privileges. Windows Vista has a solution for dealing with these programs — redirecting the folder to a virtual store that the applications can read from and write to without generating errors. This technique is called *file virtualization*.

Let's verify this by writing a simple program that writes a file to the subdirectory WroxSampleApp in the Program Files folder. Using Environment.GetFolderPath() with the SpecialFolder enumeration value ProgramFiles returns the Program Files folder; this folder is different depending on the Windows language used. The Program Files folder is combined with the directory WroxSampleApp, and in this directory the file samplefile.txt is written.

```
string programFiles = Environment.GetFolderPath(
        Environment.SpecialFolder.ProgramFiles);
string appDir = Path.Combine(programFiles,
        "WroxSampleApp");
if (!Directory.Exists(appDir))
{
    Directory.CreateDirectory(appDir);
}
string demoFile = Path.Combine(appDir,
        "samplefile.txt");
File.WriteAllText(demoFile, "test content");
```

When running the application without elevation, the file is not written to the directory c:\Program Files\WroxSampleApp. Instead, you can find the file in c:\Users\<username>\AppData\Local\ Virtual Store\Program Files\WroxSampleApp.

As you can see, the data is stored in a user-specific directory and is not shared between different users on the same system. If this is a requirement, you have to start the application in elevated mode. When you run the application from an elevated Visual Studio process, the file is written to the Program Files folder instead of the virtual store, as an application started from an elevated process is elevated as well.

For reading files, a different mechanism is needed. Because an installation program is allowed to write content to the Program Files folder, it is valid for a program to read data from the Program Files folder. As soon as the program writes to this folder without being elevated, the redirection occurs. When it reads the written content again, the redirection is done with the read as well.

Virtualization is not only done with folders but also with registry entries. If the application writes to the registry key Software in the HKEY_LOCAL_MACHINE hive, it is redirected to the HKEY_CURRENT_USER hive. Instead of writing to HKLM_Software\{Manufacturer}, it writes to HKCU\Software\Classes\VirtualStore\ MACHINE\SOFTWARE\{Manufacturer}.

File and registry virtualization is available only for 32-bit applications. This feature is not available for 64-bit applications on Windows Vista.

> *Don't use file and registry virtualization as a feature of your application. It is better to fix the application than to write to the Program Files folder and the HKLM registry hive without elevated user privileges. Redirection is only a temporary means to fix broken applications.*

New Controls and Dialogs

Windows Vista delivers several new controls. The command link control is an extension to the Button control and is used in combination with several other controls. The task dialog is a next-generation MessageBox, and for opening and saving files new dialogs are available as well.

Command Link

Command link controls are an extension to the Windows `Button` control. Command links contain an optional icon and note text. This control is often used in task dialogs and wizards. Figure C-4 shows two command link controls that give much more information than `Button` controls with OK and Cancel content.

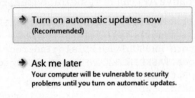

Figure C-4

With .NET applications, you can create command link controls by using the Vista Bridge sample library. If you add the project `VistaBridgeLibrary` to your solution, you can add `CommandLinkWinForms` controls from the toolbox to your Windows Forms application. The class `CommandLinkWinForms` derives from the `System.Windows.Forms.Button` class. A command link is an extension to the native Windows `Button` and defines additional Windows messages and a new style to configure the `Button`. The wrapper class `CommandLinkWinForms` sends the Windows messages `BCM_SETNOTE` and `BCM_SETSHIELD` and sets the style `BS_COMMANDLINK`. The public methods and properties offered in addition to the members of the `Button` class are `NoteText` and `ShieldIcon`.

The following code segment creates a new command link control that sets the `NoteText` and `ShieldIcon`. Figure C-5 shows the configured command link during runtime.

```
this.commandLinkDemo = new
    Microsoft.SDK.Samples.VistaBridge.Library.
    CommandLinkWinForms();
this.commandLinkDemo.NoteText =
    "The application deletes important files on " +
    "your system";
this.commandLinkDemo.ShieldIcon = true;
this.commandLinkDemo.Size = new System.Drawing.Size(
    275, 68);
this.commandLinkDemo.Text = "Give access to this " +
    "computer";
this.commandLinkDemo.UseVisualStyleBackColor = true;
this.Controls.Add(commandLinkDemo);
```

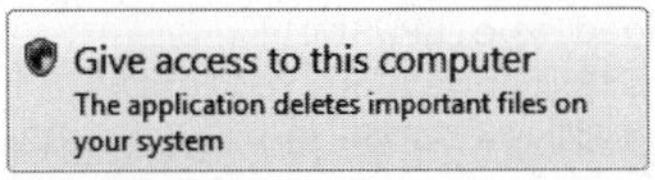

Figure C-5

Task Dialog

The task dialog is a next-generation dialog that replaces the old message box. The task dialog is part of the new common controls. The Windows API defines the functions `TaskDialog` and `TaskDialogIndirect` to create task dialogs. `TaskDialog` allows you to create simple dialogs; `TaskDialogIndirect` is used to create more complex dialogs that contain command link controls and expanded content.

With the Vista Bridge library, the native API call to `TaskDialogIndirect()` is wrapped with `PInvoke`:

```
[DllImport(ExternDll.ComCtl32, CharSet = CharSet.Auto,
    SetLastError = true)]
internal static extern HRESULT TaskDialogIndirect(
    [In] NativeMethods.TASKDIALOGCONFIG pTaskConfig,
    [Out] out int pnButton,
    [Out] out int pnRadioButton,
    [Out] out bool pVerificationFlagChecked);
```

The first parameter of `TaskDialogIndirect()` is defined as a `TASKDIALOGCONFIG` class that maps to the same structure of the native API call:

```
[StructLayout(LayoutKind.Sequential, CharSet = CharSet.Auto, Pack = 4)]
internal class TASKDIALOGCONFIG
{
    internal uint cbSize;
    internal IntPtr hwndParent;
    internal IntPtr hInstance;
    internal TASKDIALOG_FLAGS dwFlags;
    internal TASKDIALOG_COMMON_BUTTON_FLAGS dwCommonButtons;
    [MarshalAs(UnmanagedType.LPWStr)]
    internal string pszWindowTitle;
    internal TASKDIALOGCONFIG_ICON_UNION MainIcon;
    [MarshalAs(UnmanagedType.LPWStr)]
    internal string pszMainInstruction;
    [MarshalAs(UnmanagedType.LPWStr)]
    internal string pszContent;
    internal uint cButtons;
    internal IntPtr pButtons;
            // Ptr to TASKDIALOG_BUTTON structs
    internal int nDefaultButton;
    internal uint cRadioButtons;
    internal IntPtr pRadioButtons;
            // Ptr to TASKDIALOG_BUTTON structs
    internal int nDefaultRadioButton;
    [MarshalAs(UnmanagedType.LPWStr)]
    internal string pszVerificationText;
    [MarshalAs(UnmanagedType.LPWStr)]
    internal string pszExpandedInformation;
    [MarshalAs(UnmanagedType.LPWStr)]
    internal string pszExpandedControlText;
    [MarshalAs(UnmanagedType.LPWStr)]
    internal string pszCollapsedControlText;
    internal TASKDIALOGCONFIG_ICON_UNION FooterIcon;
    [MarshalAs(UnmanagedType.LPWStr)]
```

```
internal string pszFooter;
internal PFTASKDIALOGCALLBACK pfCallback;
internal IntPtr lpCallbackData;
internal uint cxWidth;
}
```

The public class from Vista Bridge used to show task dialogs is `TaskDialog`. To display a simple dialog, only the static method `Show()` must be invoked. The simple dialog is shown in Figure C-6.

```
TaskDialog.Show("Simple Task Dialog");
```

Figure C-6

For more features of the `TaskDialog` class, you can set the `Caption`, `Content`, `StandardButtons`, and `MainIcon` properties. You can see the result in Figure C-7.

```
TaskDialog dlg1 = new TaskDialog();
dlg1.Caption = "Title";
dlg1.Content = "Some Information";
dlg1.StandardButtons =
    TaskDialogStandardButtons.OkCancel;
dlg1.MainIcon = TaskDialogStandardIcon.Information;
dlg1.Show();
```

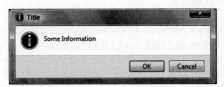

Figure C-7

With the task dialog, you can set the shield icon that was first shown with command links. Also, you can expand it by setting the `ExpansionMode` property. With the enumeration `TaskDialogExpandedInformationLocation`, you can specify that either the content or the footer should be expanded. Figure C-8 shows the task dialog in collapsed mode; Figure C-9 shows it in expanded mode.

```
TaskDialog dlg2 = new TaskDialog();
dlg2.Caption = "Title";
dlg2.Content = "Some Information";
dlg2.StandardButtons = TaskDialogStandardButtons.YesNo;
dlg2.MainIcon = TaskDialogStandardIcon.Shield;
dlg2.ExpandedText = "Additional Text";
dlg2.ExpandedControlText = "More information";
dlg2.CollapsedControlText = "Less information";
```

(continued)

(continued)

```
dlg2.ExpansionMode =
        TaskDialogExpandedInformationLocation.
        ExpandContent;
dlg2.FooterText = "Footer Information";
dlg2.FooterIcon = TaskDialogStandardIcon.Information;
dlg2.Show();
```

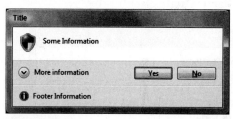

Figure C-8

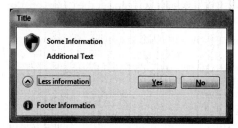

Figure C-9

A task dialog can also contain other controls. In the following code snippet, a task dialog is created that contains two radio buttons, a command link, and a marquee control. You've already seen command links in the previous section, and indeed command links are used very frequently within task dialogs. Figure C-10 shows the task dialog with the controls in the content area. Of course, you can also combine the expansion mode with controls.

```
TaskDialogRadioButton radio1 =
        new TaskDialogRadioButton();
radio1.Name = "radio1";
radio1.Text = "One";
TaskDialogRadioButton radio2 =
        new TaskDialogRadioButton();
radio2.Name = "radio2";
radio2.Text = "Two";
TaskDialogCommandLink commandLink =
        new TaskDialogCommandLink();
commandLink.Name = "link1";
commandLink.ShowElevationIcon = true;
commandLink.Text = "Information";
commandLink.Instruction = "Sample Command Link";
TaskDialogMarquee marquee = new TaskDialogMarquee();
marquee.Name = "marquee";
marquee.State = TaskDialogProgressBarState.Normal;
TaskDialog dlg3 = new TaskDialog();
dlg3.Caption = "Title";
```

```
dlg3.Instruction = "Sample Task Dialog";
dlg3.Controls.Add(radio1);
dlg3.Controls.Add(radio2);
dlg3.Controls.Add(commandLink);
dlg3.Controls.Add(marquee);
dlg3.Show();
```

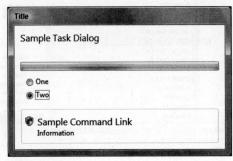

Figure C-10

File Dialogs

Dialogs to open and save files have changed. Figure C-11 shows the traditional file open dialog that is wrapped both from the Windows Forms class `System.Windows.Forms.OpenFileDialog` and the wrapper class for WPF in the assembly PresentationFramework: `Microsoft.Win32.OpenFileDialog`.

The new Windows Vista dialog is shown in Figure C-12. This dialog has Navigation, Details, and Preview panes that can be configured from the Organize ⇨ Layout menu. This dialog also contains search functionality and is completely customizable. In the Vista Bridge library, this dialog is wrapped from the `CommonOpenFileDialog` class.

```
CommonOpenFileDialog dlg = new CommonOpenFileDialog();
dlg.ShowDialog();
```

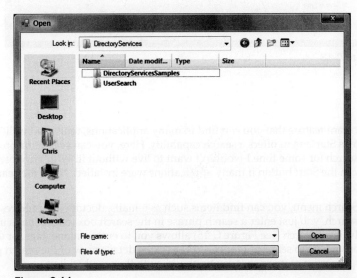

Figure C-11

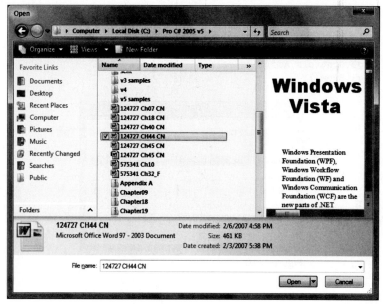

Figure C-12

The new Windows Vista dialog for saving files is customizable as well. By default, it defines a collapsed (see Figure C-13) and an expanded mode (see Figure C-14). This dialog is wrapped in the class `CommonSaveDialog`.

Figure C-13

Search

Search is an important feature that you can find in many applications, tools, and utilities with Windows Vista. The Windows Start menu offers a search capability. Here, you can search for programs to start. After using this search for some time I wouldn't want to live without it. With Windows XP it was hard to find programs from the Start button if many applications were installed. Now, the search function makes it really easy.

By selecting the Search menu, you can find items such as e-mails, documents, pictures, music, and more. With the simple search, you just enter a search phrase in the search box to find items in indexed locations. The advanced search (see Figure C-15) allows you to enter a name, tags, or an author, and to define the locations where to search. Figure C-16 shows the details view of the search page where you can select all the properties of items that can be shown with the searched items.

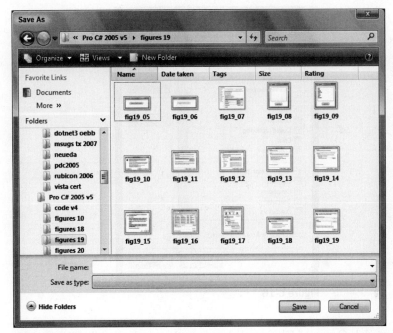

Figure C-14

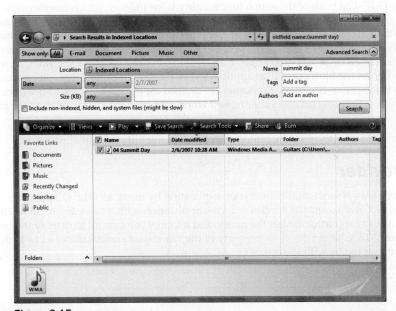

Figure C-15

Figure C-16

The Windows Vista File Open and File Save dialogs have the search capability integrated as well. The search function can be integrated into your applications, and your applications can take full advantage of the Windows search functionality. To understand the architecture of the Windows search capability, examine Figure C-17. The heart of the search functionality is the indexer, which examines content and writes it to the content index. For each store (file system, MAPI), a protocol handler is responsible for getting data to the indexer. Protocol handlers implement the interface `Ifilter`, which is used by the indexer to analyze content for indexing. The property system describes the properties that can be searched. Properties are described by property schemas. If an application has a custom file format, it can implement a property handler for the file format. If an application has custom properties that can be searched, it can add properties to the property system. Properties are defined for the generic files, Office documents, pictures, and videos. Property handlers are invoked when content is indexed to analyze the properties of the content.

Let's make use of the query system by building search functionality into an application.

OLE DB Provider

You can integrate search functionality into your application by using an OLE DB provider to search for items in the index. Create a simple Windows Forms application with a `TextBox` to allow the user to input a query, a `Button` control to start the query, and a `ListView` control to display the result, as shown in Figure C-18. Change the `View` property of the `ListView` control to `Details` to display all the information the user enters with the query.

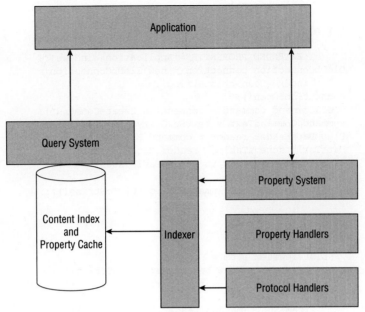

Figure C-17

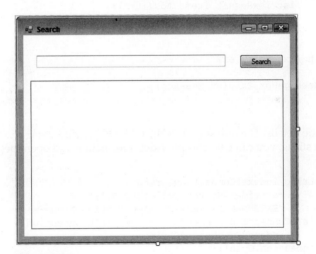

Figure C-18

Import the namespace `System.Data.OleDb` and add the following code to the `Click` event of the Search button.

```
private void buttonSearch_Click(object sender, EventArgs e)
{
    try
    {
        listViewResult.Clear();
```

(continued)

(continued)

```
            string indexerConnectionString =
                    "provider=Search.CollatorDSO.1;" +
                    "EXTENDED PROPERTIES='Application=Windows'";
            OleDbConnection connection = new OleDbConnection(
                    indexerConnectionString);
            connection.Open();
            OleDbCommand command = connection.CreateCommand();
            command.CommandText = textBoxQuery.Text;
            OleDbDataReader reader = command.ExecuteReader();
            DataTable schemaTable = reader.GetSchemaTable();
            foreach (DataRow row in schemaTable.Rows)
            {
                listViewResult.Columns.Add(row[0].ToString());
            }

            while (reader.Read())
            {
                ListViewItem item =
                        new ListViewItem(reader[0].ToString());
                for (int i = 1; i < reader.FieldCount; i++)
                {
                    item.SubItems.Add(reader[i].ToString());
                }
                listViewResult.Items.Add(item);
            }
            connection.Close();
        }
        catch (Exception ex)
        {
            MessageBox.Show(ex.Message);
        }
    }
```

Let's get into the code details. The indexer offers the OLE DB provider `Search.CollatorDSO`. With the OLE DB connection string, you can pass this provider information and open the connection to the indexer.

```
            string indexerConnectionString =
                    "provider=Search.CollatorDSO.1;" +
                    "EXTENDED PROPERTIES='Application=Windows'";
            OleDbConnection connection = new OleDbConnection(
                    indexerConnectionString);
            connection.Open();
```

The query that is used with the indexer is read from the `TextBox` control `textBoxQuery`. Because during compile time it is not known which properties will be selected by the user, the columns in the `ListView` control must be added dynamically. The method `GetSchemaTable()` of the `OleDbDataReader` returns the dynamically created schema information that relates to the query. Every row describes an item in the SELECT statement, and the first column inside this item gives the name of the item. By iterating through every row of the returned schema, a new column is added to the `ListView` control, and the heading of this column is set to the item name.

```
            OleDbCommand command = connection.CreateCommand();
            command.CommandText = textBoxQuery.Text;
            OleDbDataReader reader = command.ExecuteReader();
```

```
DataTable schemaTable = reader.GetSchemaTable();
foreach (DataRow row in schemaTable.Rows)
{
    listViewResult.Columns.Add(row[0].ToString());
}
```

Next, every row from the `OleDbDataReader` is read. The first column creates a new `ListViewItem`, and every further column in the result set adds a subitem that is shown with the detail information of the list view.

```
while (reader.Read())
{
    ListViewItem item =
            new ListViewItem(reader[0].ToString());
    for (int i = 1; i < reader.FieldCount; i++)
    {
        item.SubItems.Add(reader[i].ToString());
    }
    listViewResult.Items.Add(item);
}
```

Now, you can start the application, enter a query and get the result, as shown in Figure C-19.

```
SELECT System.ItemName, System.ItemTitle, System.Size FROM SYSTEMINDEX
    WHERE System.Size > 1024
```

In the `SELECT` statement of the query, you specify the properties that should be returned. `System.ItemName`, `System.ItemTitle`, and `System.Size` are predefined properties. You can find other predefined properties in the MSDN and TechNet documentation for the Windows Desktop Search 3.0 properties. Some of the generic file properties are `System.Author`, `System.Category`, `System.Company`, `System.DateCreated`, `System.DateModified`, `System.FileName`, `System.ItemName`, `System.ItemUrl`, and `System.Keywords`. For audio files, digital photos, graphics files, media files, Office documents, music files, and Outlook calendar items, additional properties are defined — for example, `System.Photo.Orientation`, `System.Photo.DateTaken`, `System.Music.Artist`, `System.Music.BeatsPerMinute`, `System.Music.Mood`, `System.Calendar.Location`, `System.Calendar.Duration`, and `System.Calendar.Location`.

With the `WHERE` clause, you can define predicates such as literal value comparisons <, >, =, and `LIKE`; full-text searches such as `CONTAINS` and `FREETEXT`; and also the search depth predicates `SCOPE` and `DIRECTORY`.

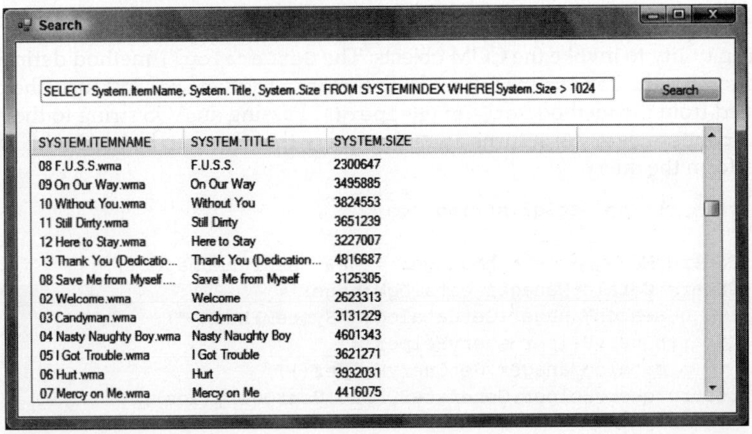

Figure C-19

Advanced Query Syntax

You wouldn't want to let a user search by specifying a SELECT statement such as the ones used in the previous example. You can create a user interface to ask for specific items and build the SELECT statement programmatically. Another way to let users do their own searching is by using Advanced Query Syntax (AQS).

The Advanced Query Syntax enables you to specify search terms and restrict a search based on properties. For example, the query Wrox date:past week searches all the items that contain the string Wrox that changed in the last week. Wrox date:past week kind:documents restricts the search further by accepting documents only.

The following are examples of how you can restrict a search:

❑ You can restrict the search by defining the store. For example, store:outlook gets items just from Outlook. store:file gets items from the file system.

❑ With the search functionality, you can specify what kind of items should be in the result — for example, kind:text, kind:tasks, kind:contacts, kind:emails, and kind:folders.

❑ Boolean operators can be used to restrict the search. For example, the OR operator used in Wrox OR Wiley. date:>11/25/07 gets items dated after November 11, 2007. For items between two dates, you can use 11/25/06..11/27/07.

❑ You can use some item properties to search for items — for example, webpage:www.wrox.com, birthday:2/14/65, firstname:Christian.

You don't have to manually translate the AQS to the SELECT query; there's a COM object that does it for you. In the Windows SDK Lib directory, you can find the file SearchAPI.tlb. This is a type library that describes the COM object used to do the AQS translation. By using COM Interop, you can use a COM object from .NET.

Create a .NET callable wrapper by using the tlbimp utility to import the type library SearchAPI.tlb:

```
tlbimp c:\Program Files\Microsoft SDKs\Windows\v6.0\Lib\SearchAPI.tlb
    /out:Interop.SearchAPI.dll
```

COM Interop is described in Chapter 24, "Interoperability."

Referencing the generated interop assembly from the Windows Forms project created previously allows you to use the SearchAPI from the .NET application. Because the type library importer defined the namespace Interop.SearchAPI with the generated assembly, import this namespace from the application and add the GetSql() method to the Windows Forms class.

The classes CSearchManager, CsearchCatalogManager, and CSearchQueryHelper are generated from the tlbimp utility to invoke the COM objects. The GetCatalog() method defines the catalog that is queried and returns the catalogManager. With the catalogManager instance, the query helper object is returned from the method GetQueryHelper(). Passing an AQS string to the method GenerateSQLFromUserQuery() returns a SELECT query that then can be used with the OLE DB provider to perform the query.

```csharp
private string GetSql(string aqs)
{
    CSearchManager searchManager = new CSearchManager();
    CSearchCatalogManager catalogManager =
        searchManager.GetCatalog(""SystemIndex"");
    CSearchQueryHelper queryHelper =
        catalogManager.GetQueryHelper();
    return queryHelper.GenerateSQLFromUserQuery(aqs);
}
```

Now, you just have to change the implementation from the `Click` handler of the `Button` control. With the implementation the AQS needs to be converted to the SELECT query, which is done by the `GetSql()` method.

```
private void buttonSearch_Click(object sender, EventArgs e)
{
    try
    {
        listViewResult.Clear();
        string indexerConnectionString =
                "provider=Search.CollatorDSO.1;" +
                "EXTENDED PROPERTIES='Application=Windows'";
        OleDbConnection connection =
                new OleDbConnection(indexerConnectionString);
        connection.Open();
        OleDbCommand command = connection.CreateCommand();
        command.CommandText = GetSql(textBoxQuery.Text);
        OleDbDataReader reader = command.ExecuteReader();
        //...
```

You can start the application and pass an AQS query, as shown in Figure C-20.

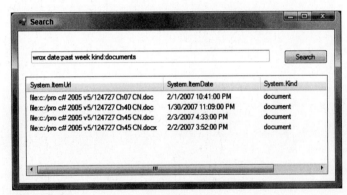

Figure C-20

Summary

In this chapter, you've seen various features available only in Windows Vista and Windows Server 2008 and important for development of applications.

Microsoft has defined guidelines for many years that state that non-administrative applications should not require administrative privileges. Because many applications have failed to comply with that requirement, the operating system is now strict about UAC. The user must explicitly elevate admin rights to applications. You've seen how this, and folder and registry virtualization, affect applications.

This chapter covered several new dialogs available only with Windows Vista for better user interaction. These include new File Open and File Save dialogs, the new task dialog that replaces the message box, and the command link extension to the `Button` control.

You've also seen the Windows query system with the new Advanced Query Syntax and extendable property system to integrate search into your applications.

Some more features that are available only with Windows Vista and Windows Server 2008 are covered in other chapters:

- ❑ Chapter 18, "Tracing and Events" discusses the new event logging facility, Event Tracing for Windows (ETW).

- ❑ Chapter 20, "Security" gives information about Cryptography Next Generation (CNG), the new Crypto API.

- ❑ Chapter 22, "Transactions" gives information about file-based and registry-based transactions.

- ❑ Chapter 42, "Windows Communication Foundation" uses Windows Activation Services (WAS) to host a WCF service.

Index

Index

Symbols and Numerics

A

casts
QueryInterface( ) method and, 752
user-defined. *See* user-defined casts
catalogs, global (Active Directory), 1591
catch blocks
defined, 379–380
examples, 382–386
multiple, 382–385
catching exceptions, 379–381, 385
catching user-defined exceptions, 390–391
CCW (COM callable wrapper), 771
certificates, distributing code with, 631–637
ChangeState( ) method (threading), 545–547
ChannelFactory class, 1482–1483
character types
basics, 39
in C#, 37
Unicode characters and, 641
characters
grouping with regular expressions, 220
in regular expressions, 217–218
CheckBox control (Windows Forms), 1028
checked/unchecked operator, 145
**CheckedListBox control (Windows Forms),
1029–1031**
child domains (Active Directory), 1590, 1609
child elements, properties as (XAML), 1152
ChildrenAsTriggers property, 1370, 1371
classes. *See also* derived classes
3-D (WPF), 1237–1238
abstract, 106–107
account management (Active Directory),
1616–1617
adapter, 1262–1264
calculator add-in, 1264
casts between base and derived, 169–170
class hierarchy (Windows Forms), 1023
class library using sockets, 719–722
class members, pointers to, 346–347
Class View window, VS 2008, 424
collections, 250
commands classes, 1224
converting casts between, 168–169
Course Order application, 1570
for creating syndication feeds,
1644–1645
data members, 77
database, 681–683

database-specific (ADO.NET), 847–849
defining Ajax Library, 1376
dictionaries, 284–285
entity, 681–683, 1579–1580, 1661–1663
event logging, 519–520
exception, 378–379
for file system management, 791–792
function members, 77–78
generic, creating, 226–230
generic, features, 231–235
generic library, 178
host adapter (add-ins), 1265–1266
inheritance and, 102
to integrate Windows Forms and WPF, 1245
Internet protocols, lower level, 1444
for IP addresses, 1441–1443
LINQ to SQL (example), 898–899
members, 76
Microsoft.SqlServer.Server namespace,
987–988
.NET, and file/folder management,
792–794
.NET base classes, 28
.NET data access, 846–847
.NET Framework, 17–18
.NET Registry, 830–833
partial, 95–96
performance monitoring, 528
principal, 583–585
sealed, 107
shape (WPF), 1162
shared in System.Data namespace, 847
static, 96–97
stream-related, 809
vs. structs, 76, 102
System.Data.Common namespace, 847
System.DirectoryServices namespace,
1597, 1598
System.DirectoryServices.Protocols
namespace, 1597, 1621
System.Net.Sockets namespace, 3
System.Windows.Forms namespace, 1076
System.Xml.Serialization, 957
System.Xml.XPath namespace, 936–942
timer, 568
for tracing, 510–511. *See also* tracing
TriggerAction, 1236
UpdatePanel control, 1371

custom resource managers, 703–709
customizing Office applications. *See Visual
    Studio Tools for Office (VSTO)*

D

data
accessing (.NET), xliv
classes, defined, 420
columns, 867–868
constraints, 874–876
contracts (WCF), 1467–1468, 1579–1580
Data Model Designer (ADO.NET Entity
    Framework), 1659
display controls (ASP.NET), 1287–1288
displaying. *See DataGridView control*
members (classes), 77
passing to threads, 540–541
querying (XQuery), 1008–1010
readers, 863–865
relational, and XML data type, 1003
relationships, 873–874
rows, 868–871
service layer, 1528
sets, populating, 883–884
templates and WPF binding, 1214–1217
triggers and data integrity, 1002
XML, and tables, 1003–1005
**data access (Visual Studio .NET),
    1080–1092**
data, selecting, 1084
data source, updating, 1084
database connections, creating,
    1080–1084
pop-up menu for rows example.
    See pop-up menu for rows
data access with ADO.NET. *See also* ADO.NET
commands. *See commands, ADO.NET*
data adapters, updating with, 885–887
data reader, 863–865
data sets, populating, 883–884
database connections. *See database
    connections*
DataSet class. *See DataSet class*
overview, 845
persisting DataSet changes, 884–888
XML output, writing, 887–889
XML schema definitions (XSD), 877–883

data adapters
populating DataSet class with, 883–884
updating with, 885–887
data binding
ADO.NET, 1295–1307
DataBindings property, 1076
DataGridView control, 1061
defined, 1075
objects, 1076–1080
simple, 1075–1076
data binding and ADO.NET
basics, 1295, 1302–1303
event-booking application. *See event-booking
    application*
templates, data display with, 1303–1304
templates, using, 1305–1307
data binding and WPF
binding modes, 1200
data templates, 1214–1217
list binding, 1208–1211
list items, adding dynamically, 1213–1214
object data provider, 1206–1207
overview, 1199–1200
simple object binding, 1203–1206
strings for list binding, 1212–1213
validation. *See validation, binding*
with XAML, 1200–1203
to XML, 1217–1219
data sources
Data source controls (ASP.NET), 1287
overview, 1063
updating, 1084
data tables
basics, 866–867
data columns, 867–868
data rows, 868–871
deleting rows, 887
inserting rows, 885–886
schema generation, 871–873
updating existing rows, 887
data types. *See also* XML data type
blittable, 755, 990
COM and .NET related, 756
immutable, 205
nonblittable, 756
reference for memory management,
    331–333
registry entries, 830

S

V